AMERICAN STORIES

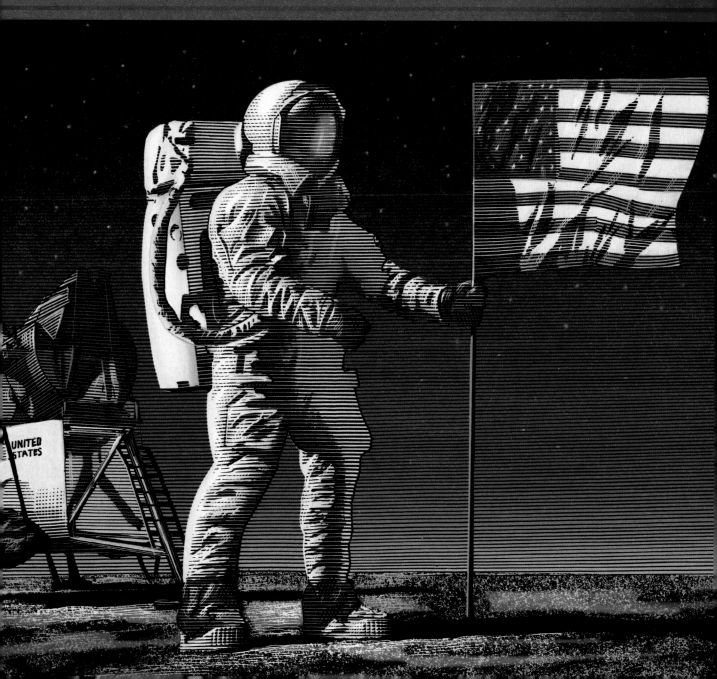

The Space Race

The space race was a competition that started in 1957 between the United States and the Soviet Union to see which nation could make the greatest advances in space travel and technology. In 1961, President John F. Kennedy set a lofty goal: to send American astronauts to the moon.

His dream was realized on July 16, 1969, by the Apollo 11 mission. Astronauts Buzz Aldrin and Neil Armstrong landed a small lunar module on the moon's surface and Armstrong took the first steps. It was an important moment for humankind, for the United States, and for technology—a moment that continues to shape history.

For more information about the space race and the lunar landing, read Lesson 1.2 in Chapter 27 and Lesson 1.3 in Chapter 28.

Acknowledgments

Grateful acknowledgment is given to the authors, artists, photographers, museums, publishers, and agents for permission to reprint copyrighted material. Every effort has been made to secure the appropriate permission. If any omissions have been made or if corrections are required, please contact the Publisher.

Credits

Wrap Cover: Mark Summers/National Geographic Learning

Acknowledgments and credits continue on page R89.

"National Geographic", "National Geographic Society" and the Yellow Border Design are registered trademarks of the National Geographic Society ® Marcas Registradas

For product information and technology assistance, contact us at Customer & Sales Support, 888-915-3276

For permission to use material from this text or product, submit all requests online at **www.cengage.com/permissions**

Further permissions questions can be emailed to **permissionrequest@cengage.com**

National Geographic Learning | Cengage
1 N. State Street, Suite 900
Chicago, IL 60602

Cengage is a leading provider of customized learning solutions with office locations around the globe, including Singapore, the United Kingdom, Australia, Mexico, Brazil, and Japan. Locate your local office at **www.cengage.com/global.**

Visit National Geographic Learning online at **NGL.Cengage.com/school**

Visit our corporate website at **www.cengage.com**

ISBN: 978-133-711-135-5

Printed in the United States of America.
Print Number: 04   Print Year: 2022

Senior Consultants

Fredrik Hiebert

Fred Hiebert is National Geographic's Archaeologist-in-Residence. He has led archaeological expeditions at ancient Silk Roads sites across Asia. Hiebert was curator of National Geographic's exhibition "Afghanistan: Hidden Treasures from the National Museum, Kabul," and its most recent exhibition, "The Greeks: Agamemnon to Alexander the Great."

Peggy Altoff

Peggy Altoff's career includes teaching middle school and high school students, supervising teachers, and serving as adjunct university faculty. Altoff served as a state social studies specialist in Maryland and as a K–12 coordinator in Colorado Springs. She is a past president of the National Council for the Social Studies (NCSS) and served on the task force for the 2012 NCSS National Curriculum Standards.

Fritz Fischer

Fritz Fischer is a professor and Director of History Education at the University of Northern Colorado, where he teaches U.S. History and Social Studies Education courses. Fischer is also Chair Emeritus of the Board of Trustees of the National Council for History Education (NCHE), the largest national membership organization focusing on history education at the K–12 level.

Program Consultants

Terence Clark
Director, Shíshálh Archaeological
Research Project
University of Saskatchewan

William Parkinson
Associate Curator of Anthropology,
Field Museum of Natural History
National Geographic Explorer

Ken Garrett
National Geographic
Photographer

Robert Reid
Travel Writer
National Geographic
Digital Nomad

Kathryn Keane
Vice President, National
Geographic Exhibitions

Andrés Ruzo
Geothermal Scientist
National Geographic Explorer

National Geographic Teacher Reviewers

National Geographic works with teachers at all grade levels from across the country.
The following teachers reviewed chapters in *U.S. History: American Stories*.

Wesley Brown
Ravenscroft School
Raleigh, North Carolina

Karen Davis
St. Joseph School
Conway, Arkansas

Tama Nunnelley
Guntersville
Middle School
Guntersville, Alabama

Natalie Wojinski
West Contra Costa USD
Richmond, California

Crystal Culp
McCracken
Regional School
Paducah, Kentucky

Jessica Lura
Bullis Charter School
Los Altos, California

Ann Viegut
John Muir Middle School
Wausau, Wisconsin

National Geographic Society

The National Geographic Society contributed significantly to National Geographic *U.S. History: American Stories*. Our collaboration with each of the following has been a pleasure and a privilege: National Geographic Maps, National Geographic Education and Children's Media, and National Geographic Missions programs. We thank the Society for its guidance and support.

National Geographic Exploration

National Geographic supports the work of a host of anthropologists, archaeologists, adventurers, biologists, educators, writers, and photographers across the world. The individuals below each contributed substantially to *U.S. History: American Stories*.

Jason De León

Anthropologist

National Geographic Explorer

Ken Garrett

National Geographic Photographer

Caroline Gerdes

Writer

National Geographic Explorer

Barrington Irving, Jr.

Aviator

National Geographic Explorer

John Kelly

Archaeologist

National Geographic Explorer

William Kelso

Archaeologist

National Geographic Explorer

Robert Reid

Travel Writer

National Geographic Digital Nomad

Pardis Sabeti

Computational Geneticist

National Geographic Explorer

Joel Sartore

National Geographic Photographer

Donald Slater

Educator

National Geographic Explorer

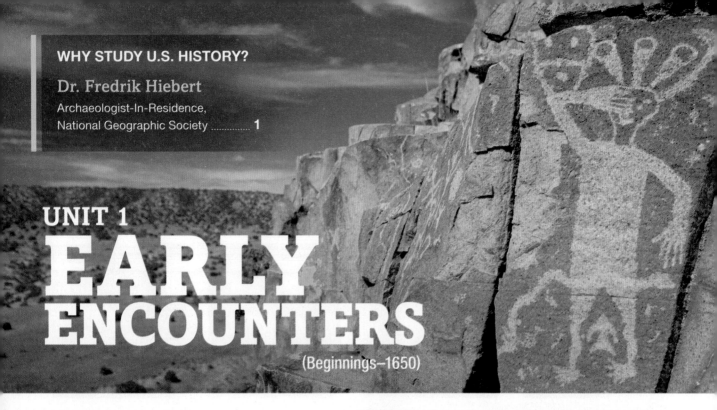

UNIT 1
EARLY ENCOUNTERS
(Beginnings–1650)

UNIT 2
ENGLISH SETTLEMENT
(1585–1763)

UNIT 3
A NEW NATION
(1763–1791)

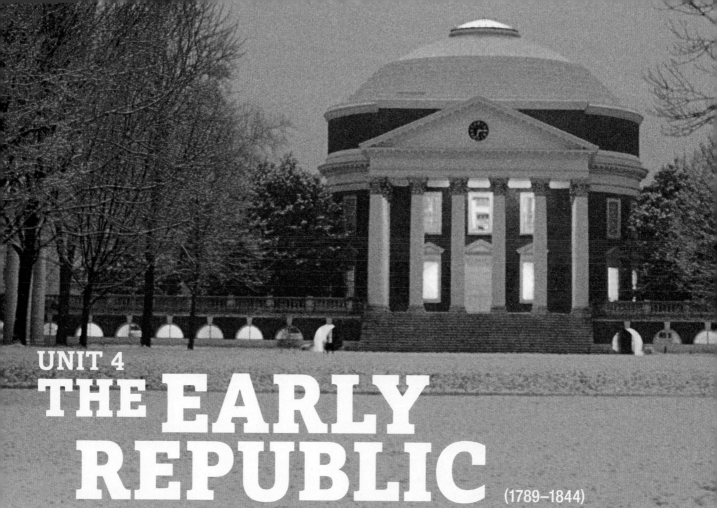

UNIT 4
THE EARLY REPUBLIC
(1789–1844)

UNIT 5
PUSHING NATIONAL BOUNDARIES
(1821–1860)

UNIT 6
CIVIL WAR AND RECONSTRUCTION
(1846–1877)

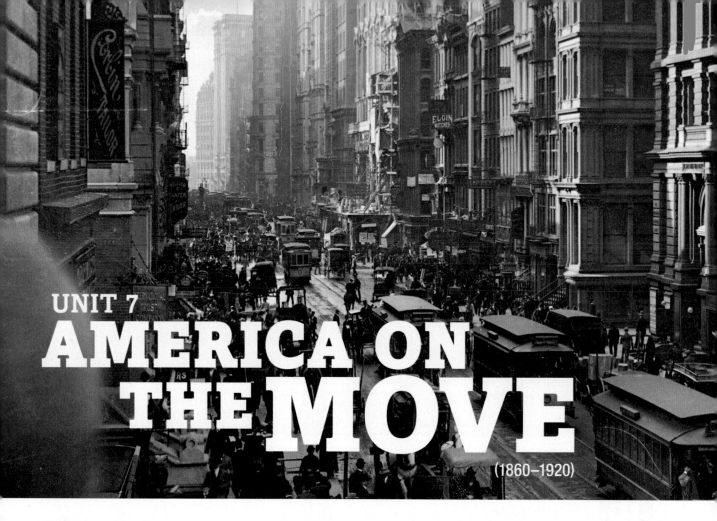

UNIT 7
AMERICA ON THE MOVE
(1860–1920)

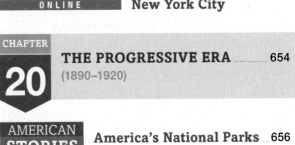

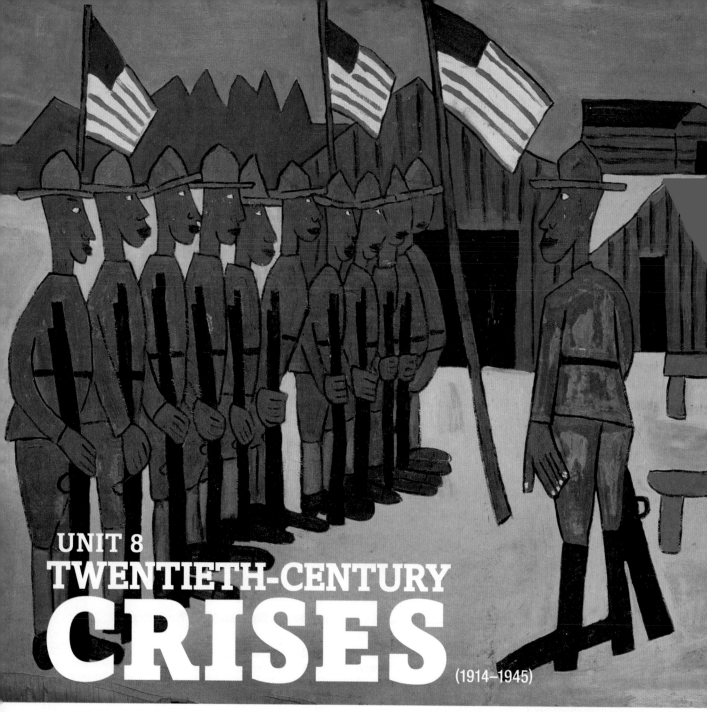

UNIT 8
TWENTIETH-CENTURY
CRISES
(1914–1945)

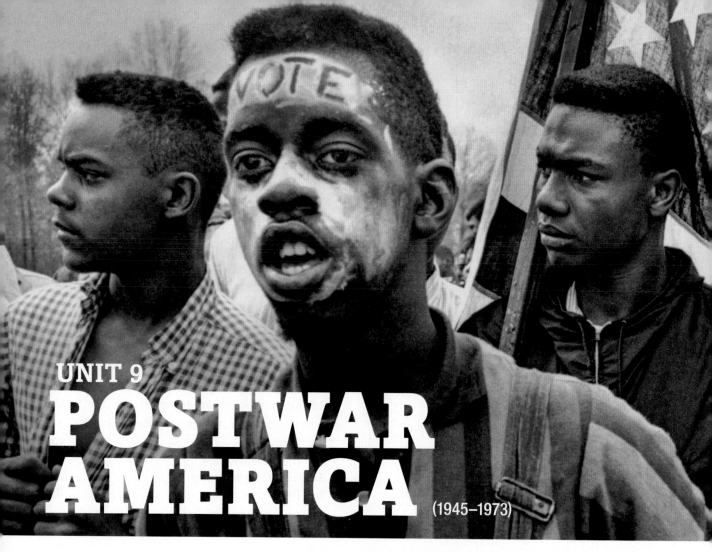

UNIT 9
POSTWAR AMERICA
(1945–1973)

UNIT 10
AMERICA IN A CHANGING WORLD

(1969–Present)

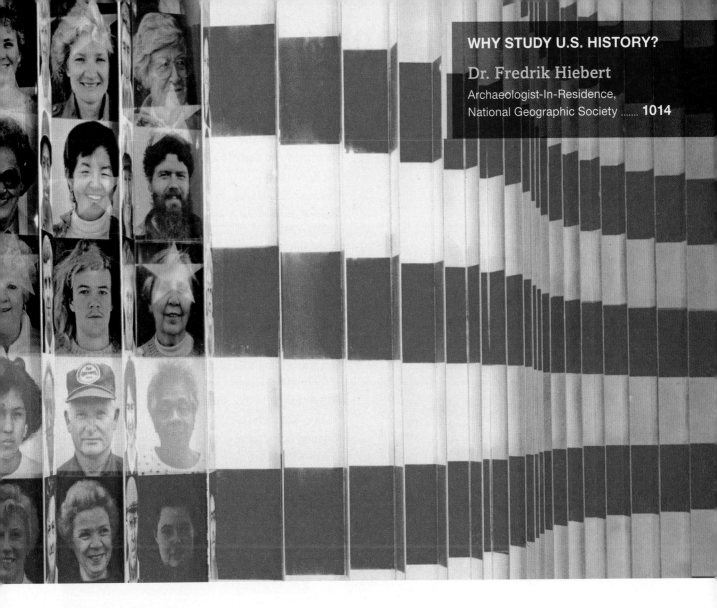

National Geographic Features

Maps

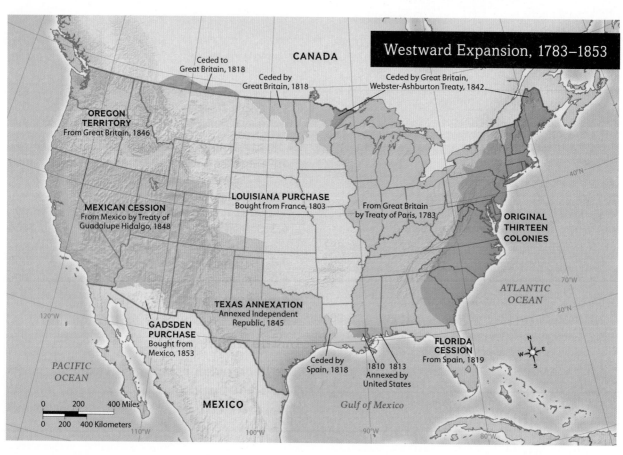

Westward Expansion, 1783–1853

CANADA

Ceded to Great Britain, 1818

Ceded by Great Britain, 1818

Ceded by Great Britain, Webster-Ashburton Treaty, 1842

OREGON TERRITORY
From Great Britain, 1846

MEXICAN CESSION
From Mexico by Treaty of Guadalupe Hidalgo, 1848

LOUISIANA PURCHASE
Bought from France, 1803

From Great Britain by Treaty of Paris, 1783

ORIGINAL THIRTEEN COLONIES

ATLANTIC OCEAN

40°N

70°W

30°N

TEXAS ANNEXATION
Annexed Independent Republic, 1845

GADSDEN PURCHASE
Bought from Mexico, 1853

120°W

PACIFIC OCEAN

Ceded by Spain, 1818

1810 1813
Annexed by United States

FLORIDA CESSION
From Spain, 1819

N
W—E
S

0 200 400 Miles
0 200 400 Kilometers

MEXICO

Gulf of Mexico

110°W 100°W 90°W 80°W

National Geographic Explorer Barrington Irving, Jr.

National Geographic Explorers

Curating History

Valley Forge National Historical Park, Pennsylvania

Document-Based Questions

American Stories

American Stories Online

The Mississippi River

Why Study U.S. History?

I'm Fred Hiebert, National Geographic's Archaeologist-in-Residence. Like you, I live in the United States. But my work takes me all over the world, and that gives me a chance to view the United States from a global perspective. I think a lot about what it means to be an American.

The history of the United States is a chronicle of different regions that today are pulled together on a cultural basis. In the early years, our identity as a nation was defined on a military or political basis— and we're still struggling with those differences.

As we look back on U.S. history, we'll consider the role of justice and American values in giving people an opportunity to make a life for themselves and to move between these regions. One of our freedoms is the ability to move across the country and experience different ideas about what it means to be American.

📓 HISTORY NOTEBOOK

Find "Why Study U.S. History?" in your History Notebook. The questions and activities will help you begin to find meaning in what you're reading. Use the notebook to record your ideas and questions as you read.

What makes the history of the United States special?

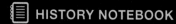

PERSONAL **FREEDOM**

 THE PROMISE OF **JUSTICE FOR ALL**

 AN **OPEN SOCIETY**

U.S. history is a microcosm of world history; think of it as a mini-world history. It includes the history of our natural resources and how they've been conserved— or not. It involves the defense of our nation and the United States' role in the world. U.S. history examines our collective identity as American citizens or people who call this country home. And on a personal level, U.S. history explores how our identity has been shaped by critical events from the past and the key women and men who brought them about.

Has anyone ever said to you, "Who *are* you?" What did that person mean by asking that? How did you respond? And how does that question relate to U.S. history?

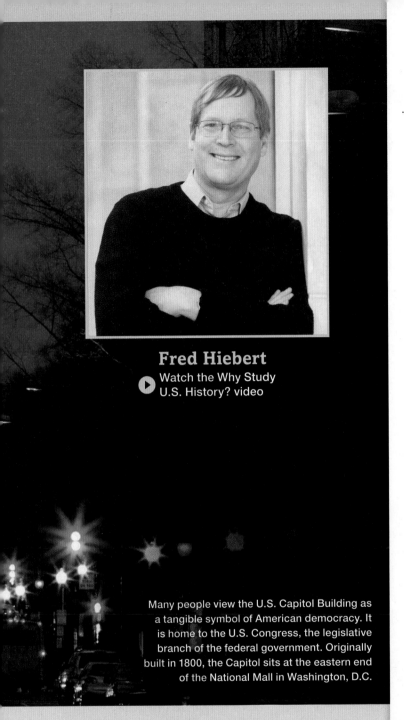

Fred Hiebert

▶ Watch the Why Study
U.S. History? video

Many people view the U.S. Capitol Building as a tangible symbol of American democracy. It is home to the U.S. Congress, the legislative branch of the federal government. Originally built in 1800, the Capitol sits at the eastern end of the National Mall in Washington, D.C.

The fact is your life today is the result of events and ideas that make up the history of the United States. We study history to learn how we became who we are at this place and at this time, which helps us actually answer that question for ourselves.

History really can tell you something about yourself and your identity.

Think about ways in which you are unique: What factors affect your personal identity, your home, your family, your community, your country? How can you shape who you are and who you want to be?

National Geographic Framework for U.S. History

The **Framework for U.S. History** can help you use your text to explore these questions—and to start a dialogue with your classmates about the history and culture of the United States. Your *American Stories* textbook divides history into these general categories:

UNITS 1 AND 2
Core Populations

The United States is made up of indigenous peoples as well as people from other lands, other traditions, and other cultures, including north Asian, Scandinavian, Spanish, English, French, and African.

UNITS 3, 4, AND 5
Primary Development of the American Republic

The early American republic unifies as a new nation and begins to develop a national identity. Americans act on a spirit of boundless possibility as they push westward and stretch national borders.

UNITS 6 AND 7
Second Stage of National Development

The young country endures deep political and philosophical divisions that result in the Civil War. Postwar changes lead to new freedoms for formerly enslaved people and make Americans more mobile than ever before. The building of the Panama Canal brings economic excitement, but optimism is overshadowed by political uncertainty in Europe and the ways conflict and war might affect the United States.

UNITS 8, 9, AND 10
Modern America Emerges

On the world's stage, the United States faces international conflict. At home, social changes divide and unite, reshaping American culture. How our country's leaders deal with these issues impacts what the nation will become.

To explore what it means to be an American

U.S. history is full of stories. Some of those stories may seem a little slow-moving, but others couldn't be more exciting. You live in the United States, and whether you are a citizen or not, those stories belong to you and to all of us—and you have your own story to tell. Use Fred Hiebert's personal story below as a model for capturing your own story about life in this country.

FRED'S AMERICAN STORY

My great-great-grandparents were invited to homestead in the Great Plains region of Kansas and raise a new strain of wheat that is planted in the fall and harvested in the spring. This type of wheat revolutionized farming in this country.

Both my mom's and dad's families came from the same Kansas community. Their way of life was disrupted by the Great Depression of 1929, a financial low point in American history during which many farmers found themselves greatly in debt.

Fred's grandmother, Helen Hiebert, is shown here on her father's farm about 1912, bringing lunch to harvesters.

This postage stamp—shown here on its first day of issue in 1974—celebrates the centennial of the introduction of winter wheat to the Great Plains, where it became an important commercial crop. Winter wheat usually produces higher crop yields than other types of wheat. This intersection between the lives of individual Americans like Fred Hiebert's grandparents and the development of the United States into a major economic force still happens today in large and small ways across the country.

My parents' families lived in the Dust Bowl, the area within the Great Plains of the Midwest where extended drought and soil erosion sometimes made farming impossible. That forced my dad's family to move to Nebraska and later to California.

My mom's family stayed in Kansas, and my parents met at a local college before World War II. During the war, my dad got interested in health care and, like his brothers and sisters, went to college. Eventually they settled in cities from Bakersfield, California, to Chicago, Illinois. I was born in Washington, D.C., while my dad was interning in a hospital, and I grew up in Michigan.

For the last 18 years, my hometown has been in Haverford Township, Pennsylvania, close to Philadelphia. I'm connected by train service to New York City and Washington, D.C., where my office at the National Geographic Society is located. Today, from my suburban hometown I am linked to the world through internet, telephone, and a close airport, making me a "global citizen."

As You Read

We all have our own stories about life in the United States. The important thing is to share our experiences and be good listeners, showing respect and tolerance for the storytellers.

In your History Notebook, write a paragraph on what the term *identity* means to you. Think about how the events you read about might connect to your own life and how these events helped shape the community and country you live in today. And finally, think about how you might answer this question:

What does it mean to be an American?

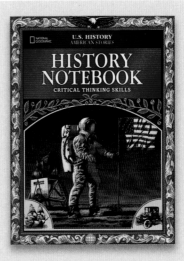

THE STORY OF A CONTINENT

BY DR. WILLIAM PARKINSON

National Geographic Explorer
Associate Curator of Anthropology
Field Museum of Natural History

CRITICAL VIEWING This artist's rendering shows the Laurentide Ice Sheet, which, at times, covered large parts of North America during the Pleistocene epoch. Present-day glaciers, particularly in Canada, are remnants of this ice sheet. What does the image reveal about this glacial period?

EARTH'S TIME LINE —— 100 Million Years

Earth Forms	First Life Appears on Earth
4.5 Billion Years Ago	3.8 Billion Years Ago

Close your eyes for a minute. Try to imagine the United States without any of the familiar trappings of 21st-century life—no smartphones, hoverboards, or tablets. No iTunes, YouTube, or video games.

Imagine moving from place to place without paved roads to follow—in fact, with no roads at all, and no wheeled vehicles or even horses to carry you. Instead of strip malls, fast-food chains, and electric streetlights, there are lush, dark forests, pristine rivers and streams, and abundant plant and animal life as far as your eye can see.

Take a deep breath—you're in for an adventure. Travel back to the earliest history of North America, from the beginnings of civilization and even further back to a time when mammoths and mastodons, saber-toothed cats, and giant ground sloths roamed the lands of North America. It was a time when your own species, *Homo sapiens*, evolved and spread throughout the world.

This is the moment in a play just before the main curtain rises on North America—a continent with a story much longer than you may think.

GEOLOGY AND LANDSCAPE

North America is geologically dramatic. It features towering mountains, vast deserts, sandy beaches, and rolling hills. But the landscape that Europeans like Christopher Columbus encountered when they arrived in the "New World" just a few hundred years ago was profoundly different from the world that the earliest humans experienced when they first came to North America.

Let's go way back in time. The first modern humans arrived in North America at the end of a period geologists refer to as the **Pleistocene epoch** (PLEIS-toh-seen EH-puhk). The Pleistocene lasted over 2 million years. During this period, the climate and ecology of North America was completely different from the climate and ecology of today. It included supersized animals and plants that no longer exist. During the Pleistocene epoch, modern humans across the world honed their skills in hunting, created early artwork, developed fire, and began to use language.

Many people think the climate during the Pleistocene was always cold. In fact, there were dramatic fluctuations in temperature over relatively short periods of time. At some points, the climate during the Pleistocene was about the same as it is today. During **glacial periods**, or **ice ages**, when glaciers expanded across Earth's surface, the global average annual temperature was significantly colder.

There were more than 20 cycles of glacial periods during the Pleistocene epoch. The movement of ice and water during these cycles changed the landscape and shorelines of the continents drastically, especially around the edges of the Arctic Circle and in present-day Europe, Asia, and North America.

◄ 2.6 MILLION YEARS AGO

TODAY ►

PLEISTOCENE EPOCH ⊢——⊣ 100 Thousand Years
2.6 Million to 11,700 Years Ago

People Arrive in North America 18–12,000 Years Ago

Modern Humans Evolve 75,000 Years Ago

↑
HOLOCENE EPOCH
11,700 Years Ago to Today

North America Splits from Pangea
200 Million Years Ago

TODAY ►

BRIDGING THE CONTINENTS

In Europe, Asia, and Africa, modern humans evolved between 75,000 and 35,000 years ago—long before they arrived in North America. By the end of the Pleistocene, about 12,000 years ago, the only surviving hominid species was modern humans.

Scientists love debates, and one of the biggest debates in archaeology centers around the arrival of the earliest modern humans in North America. We know that when the Pleistocene ended, there were modern human societies living throughout the continent. The debate revolves around pinpointing when during the Pleistocene the first people migrated to the Americas and whether they came by boat or walked. Could people have *walked* from Europe and Asia to the Americas? Yes! But the continents are separated by oceans!

Remember during the Pleistocene, there were glacial periods when ice sheets covered the continents. The oceans contained less water, and the coastlines of the continents were much larger. After the last major glacial period, about 20,000 years ago, the two ice sheets that covered northern North America began to melt. North America was temporarily connected to Asia by a large stretch of land between modern-day Alaska and Siberia that scientists call the **Bering Land Bridge**. About 11,000 to 12,000 years ago, the land bridge disappeared as the ice melted, the oceans filled with the water, and the coastlines receded.

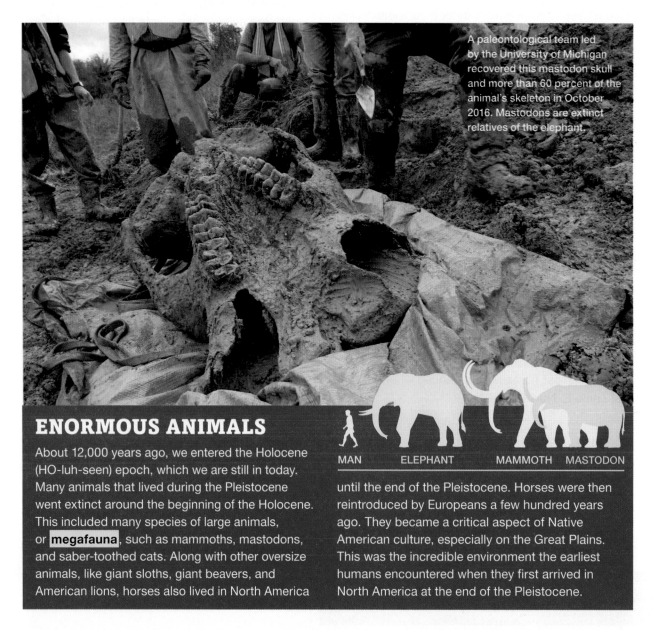

A paleontological team led by the University of Michigan recovered this mastodon skull and more than 60 percent of the animal's skeleton in October 2016. Mastodons are extinct relatives of the elephant.

MAN   ELEPHANT   MAMMOTH   MASTODON

ENORMOUS ANIMALS

About 12,000 years ago, we entered the Holocene (HO-luh-seen) epoch, which we are still in today. Many animals that lived during the Pleistocene went extinct around the beginning of the Holocene. This included many species of large animals, or **megafauna**, such as mammoths, mastodons, and saber-toothed cats. Along with other oversize animals, like giant sloths, giant beavers, and American lions, horses also lived in North America until the end of the Pleistocene. Horses were then reintroduced by Europeans a few hundred years ago. They became a critical aspect of Native American culture, especially on the Great Plains. This was the incredible environment the earliest humans encountered when they first arrived in North America at the end of the Pleistocene.

THE GREAT DEBATE

Until recently, scientists believed that the earliest people— **hunter-gatherers** —arrived in the Americas just before the land bridge disappeared. They specialized in hunting large herd animals that migrated back and forth across the continent. Archaeologists call them the Clovis Culture, based on a kind of stone tool—a Clovis point—that people made at that time.

But there is growing evidence that other groups may have reached the Americas before the Clovis Culture. Sites in Chile and Pennsylvania suggest that there was a pre-Clovis occupation of North America, and some scientists even speculate that people may have arrived by boats earlier in the Pleistocene, perhaps from Europe rather than Asia.

By the end of the Pleistocene, the climate began to stabilize, and modern humans spread throughout the Americas. They were specialized, mobile hunters and gatherers like their contemporaries elsewhere in the world, and they used the same technology—Clovis points—to hunt. These points have been found throughout North America, and similar ones have appeared as far south as Venezuela. People began to settle in different regions of the North American continent. These regions can be distinguished according to the specialized stone tools that were made and used in the Holocene.

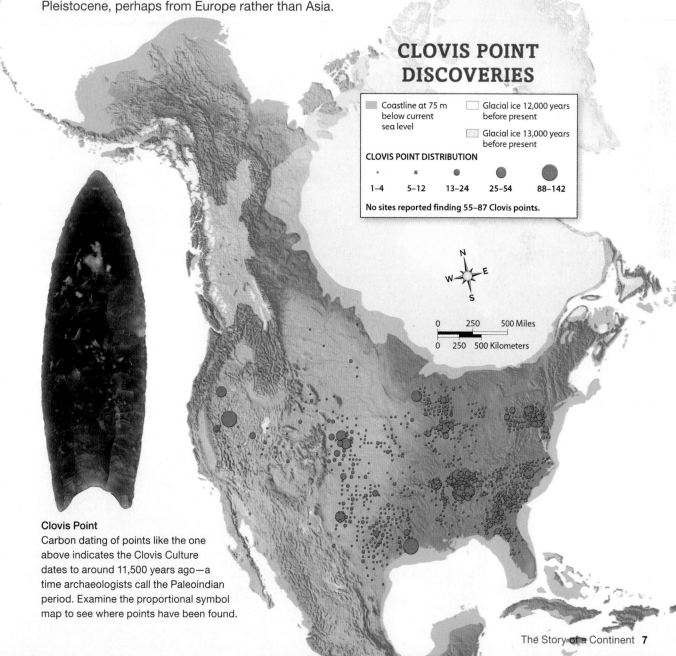

CLOVIS POINT DISCOVERIES

- Coastline at 75 m below current sea level
- Glacial ice 12,000 years before present
- Glacial ice 13,000 years before present

CLOVIS POINT DISTRIBUTION

| 1–4 | 5–12 | 13–24 | 25–54 | 88–142 |

No sites reported finding 55–87 Clovis points.

| 0 | 250 | 500 Miles |
| 0 | 250 | 500 Kilometers |

Clovis Point
Carbon dating of points like the one above indicates the Clovis Culture dates to around 11,500 years ago—a time archaeologists call the Paleoindian period. Examine the proportional symbol map to see where points have been found.

CORN EVOLVES

Corn's wild ancestor is a grass called *teosinte*, which doesn't look much like corn but has a very similar genetic makeup. After corn was introduced to North America 6,000 to 10,000 years ago, it spread from Mexico into the American Southwest and across the continent. Early farmers learned to grow types of corn with qualities they valued, such as resistance to pests and the ability to grow in different types of soil. That led to a great diversity of species.

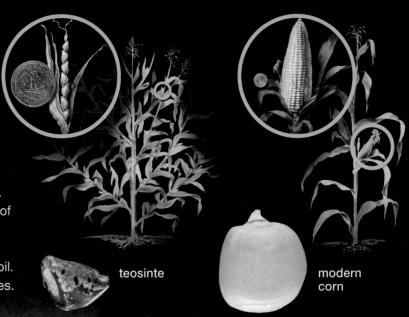

teosinte

modern corn

Greater Southwest c. 1000 B.C.
Corn cobs and kernels found in Bat Cave in New Mexico were carbon-dated to around 1000 B.C. and had characteristics similar to older corn remnants found in Mexico.

East Coast c. 100 B.C.
Corn was probably first grown in the area that is now the eastern United States around 100 B.C., but people in this region had been domesticating other crops, like beans, gourds, and sunflowers, for thousands of years. Once introduced, maize quickly spread across agricultural communities.

Mexico c. 5000 B.C.
Samples from archaeological sites in Oaxaca and Tehuacán, Mexico, are believed to represent the earliest examples of farmed corn on the North American continent, including teosinte and later, more domesticated varieties.

THE SPREAD OF CORN

Analyze the map above. What do you observe about the movement of corn across the North American continent?

THE AGRICULTURAL REVOLUTION

For several thousand years during the Holocene, people continued to live in small groups and move frequently throughout the year. Everything changed when some groups of mobile hunters and gatherers started to experiment with planting their own crops. This transition from relying on gathering wild plants and hunting animals to planting crops and raising animals is called the **Agricultural Revolution**.

The practice of bringing plants and animals under human control is called **domestication**. Almost all the foods we eat today are domesticated instead of wild. This means that they have been modified from their wild forms and are to some extent reliant upon humans for their existence. Corn, for example, is the domesticated form of a plant called *teosinte* (TAY-oh-SIN-tay), and cows are the domestic form of a wild herd animal called an *aurochs* (OR-auks). Domestication had a dramatic impact on society. Once people settled down and became reliant upon domestic plants and animals, human life transformed.

This c. 1250 cedar mask was discovered in Fulton, Illinois, and provides evidence of Mississippian cultures outside of Cahokia.

Out of all the plants domesticated in North America thousands of years ago, the real game changer was corn. The hunters and gatherers who began experimenting with the domestication of corn had no idea of the impact their little experiment would have on the world in the years to come. Corn is now grown almost everywhere in the world and tied to almost everything Americans eat. It's even used to make toothpaste and gasoline. But the biggest impact corn had in North America was its unparalleled ability to feed large populations.

SETTLING DOWN

It took a while for corn to be adopted and widely used in North America. In eastern North America, for example, it wasn't a major part of the human diet until about 1,000 years ago. Growing crops like corn and remaining in one location allowed social groups to grow larger and develop more complex political systems. In some places, these groups built massive cities and had extensive trade networks that moved goods across the continent.

One of these cities was located in present-day Illinois along the Mississippi River near the modern town of St. Louis, Missouri. Founded around A.D. 800, Cahokia would come to be the capital of a large community called a **chiefdom**. By A.D. 1250, Cahokia was a thriving community. This large city controlled a massive geographic area at the confluence of three rivers (the Missouri, Illinois, and Mississippi), and at its height may have had a population of about 15,000 people. It is considered the most sophisticated prehistoric native civilization north of Mexico.

The fertile soil of Cahokia was easy to farm and well suited to growing corn. As a result, people farmed more and hunted less. And archaeological evidence unearthed from the site indicates the people of Cahokia ate well.

Although Cahokia and other similar sites in the southeastern United States were heavily dependent upon domestic crops like corn, communities in other parts of North America were not. They continued to hunt and gather wild resources as a major part of their diet.

A CULTURAL MOSAIC

Before the 1500s, the Americas, Europe, and Africa had been isolated from one another. But as Europeans began looking beyond their shores for riches and resources, Africa's mighty empires wanted to show their strength. Both continents were on a collision course with the Americas, but the Europeans got there first.

When the Europeans arrived in the "New World," they experienced a mosaic of diverse cultures and landscapes. From the hierarchical chiefdoms of Florida to the more mobile, less hierarchical groups of the Great Basin, the cultures of North America made up a patchwork quilt of societies with distinct languages, economic practices, political systems, and traditions as varied as the landscape.

This bird-shaped tobacco pipe was found in Canada in the Pacific Northwest region of North America.

Groups such as the Chumash, who settled along the California coastline, fished from canoe-like boats made of rushes.

Chumash fishing hook, carved from a shell

As you read in Why Study U.S. History, everyone has a personal American story to tell, and those stories often reflect the diversity of our cultural mosaic. That diversity is one of the best things about life in the United States. It's not always easy to build consensus or get everyone "on the same page," but that's what's exciting. With so many opinions and perspectives and our dogged American drive, we have the potential to develop amazingly creative solutions to 21st-century issues.

Believed to be 1,000 years old, the Pilling Figurines from the Fremont group in Utah were named for the rancher who discovered them in 1950.

So raise the curtain on this incredibly rich and varied landscape, well equipped to sustain and nurture the promise of a unique new country and a vibrant people. The action and the drama are just about to begin.

NORTHWEST

PLATEAU

BASIN

CALIFORNIA

SOUTHWEST

Like other groups in the Southwest, the Hohokam of southern Arizona frequently painted birds on items, such as the pot from which this shard came.

THINK ABOUT IT

What does the fact that these diverse cultures all expressed themselves through art suggest about early humans?

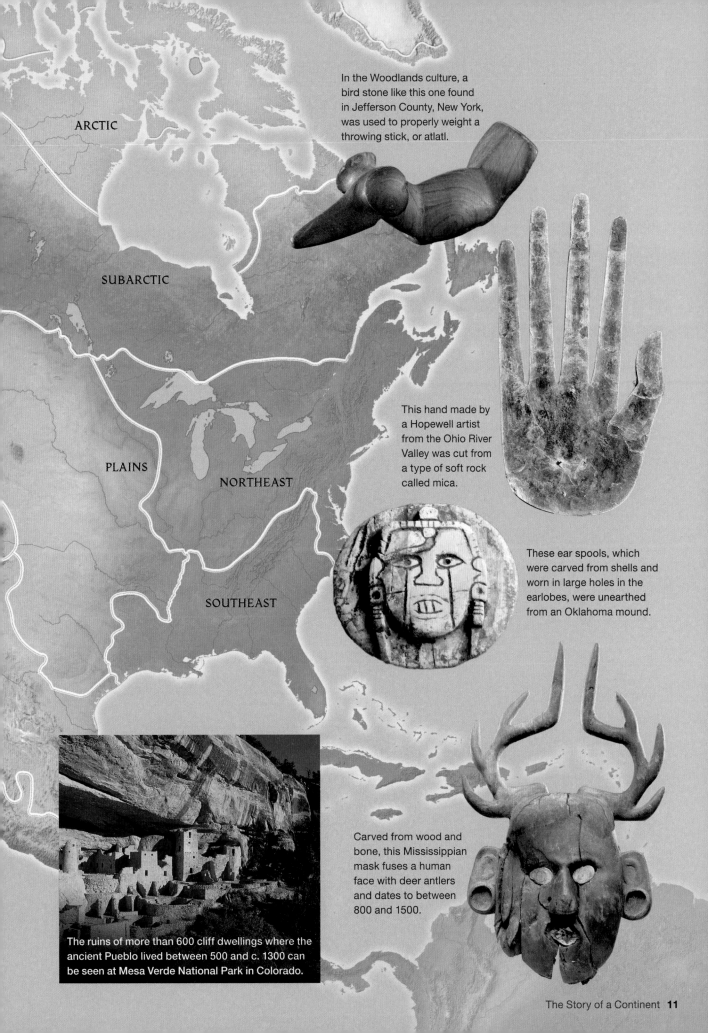

ARCTIC

SUBARCTIC

In the Woodlands culture, a bird stone like this one found in Jefferson County, New York, was used to properly weight a throwing stick, or atlatl.

PLAINS

NORTHEAST

This hand made by a Hopewell artist from the Ohio River Valley was cut from a type of soft rock called mica.

SOUTHEAST

These ear spools, which were carved from shells and worn in large holes in the earlobes, were unearthed from an Oklahoma mound.

The ruins of more than 600 cliff dwellings where the ancient Pueblo lived between 500 and c. 1300 can be seen at Mesa Verde National Park in Colorado.

Carved from wood and bone, this Mississippian mask fuses a human face with deer antlers and dates to between 800 and 1500.

EARLY ENCOUNTERS

CRITICAL VIEWING A Pueblo artist created this petroglyph, or rock carving, as many as 700 years ago. The petroglyph shown in this photo, by National Geographic photographer Ralph Lee Hopkins, is found in the desert of present-day New Mexico. Although the meaning of this and most Pueblo petroglyphs is no longer known, some may tell a story or celebrate an event. What story or event might this figure and the items surrounding it convey?

THE
AMERICAS

1325
The Aztec found Tenochtitlán and build a great civilization.
(Aztec mosaic of a serpent, possibly used in religious ceremonies)

A.D. 250
The Maya Classic Period begins.
(Maya temple in Tikal, Guatemala)

1200
More than 20,000 people live in the Mississippian city of Cahokia.

1200

c. 1000 B.C.
The ancient Pueblo begin to farm in the southwestern region of North America.

A.D. 1

c. 500 AFRICA
Ghana becomes the first great trading state in West Africa.

1000 B.C.

THE
WORLD

1200 AFRICA
The empire of Mali, built on trade and gold, arises in West Africa.
(terra cotta horse and rider created in Mali around the early 1300s)

A.D. 476 EUROPE
The Western Roman Empire falls, and the period known as the Middle Ages soon begins in Western Europe.

HISTORICAL THINKING: DETERMINE CHRONOLOGY

What activities were undertaken throughout much of the world beginning in the 1400s?

1450
The Inca build Machu Picchu in the Andes Mountains. *(golden Inca artifact)*

1519
Hernán Cortés leads the invasion of Mexico and conquers the Aztec.

1492
Columbus makes the first of several voyages to the Americas.

1626
The Dutch buy Manhattan Island from Native Americans and found New Amsterdam (present-day New York City) on the site. *(fine art image of the New Amsterdam settlement)*

1400

1800

1405 ASIA
Zheng He begins the first of seven voyages from China, exploring Asia and Africa.

1650 AFRICA
More than 40 trading posts on Africa's west coast send slaves to the New World.

1300 EUROPE
The Renaissance begins in Europe. *(Renaissance artist Leonardo da Vinci's painting, the Mona Lisa)*

THREE WORLDS
BEFORE 1500

ESSENTIAL QUESTION
How were early civilizations in the Americas, Africa, and Europe both similar and different?

 AMERICAN STORIES **Land of Plenty**

SECTION 1 **Societies of the Americas**

KEY VOCABULARY

civilization	irrigation	physical geography
domesticate	kayak	potlatch
geographic perspective	matrilineal	slash-and-burn agriculture
human geography	migrate	tepee
Iroquois League		tundra

SECTION 2 **Societies of Europe**

KEY VOCABULARY

caravel	manor system	Protestant
feudalism	navigation	serf
hierarchy	printing press	vassal
humanism	profit	

SECTION 3 **Societies of West Africa**

KEY VOCABULARY

caravan	oasis	steppe
convert	pilgrimage	trans-Saharan

AMERICAN GALLERY
ONLINE   **Cahokia: A Native American City**

READING STRATEGY

COMPARE AND CONTRAST
To compare and contrast, note similarities and differences between two or more people, places, events, or things. As you read, use a graphic organizer like this one to compare and contrast the societies discussed.

Americas	Europe	Africa
empires		

"All things
are bound together. All things
connect."
—Seattle, Duwamish leader

CRITICAL VIEWING Rivers, brooks,
and waterfalls flow through the rugged
landscape of Vermont's Green Mountain
National Forest. The 400,000-acre forest
also holds archaeological evidence of the
Native American "Original Vermonters"
dating back 10,000 years. What natural
resources can you identify in the photo
that Native American populations might
have used to survive?

LAND OF
PLENTY

CRITICAL VIEWING Deer run through Tuolumne Meadows in California's Yosemite National Park. What details in this photo represent North America as a "land of plenty"?

BY DR. TERENCE CLARK
Director, Shíshálh Archaeological Research Project,
University of Saskatchewan

What does *plenty* mean to you? For the first people who lived in North America, the concept of plenty revolved around food. Hunting, gathering, and growing food took up a lot of their time. Lucky for them, they lived in a Land of Plenty.

As you have just read, North America is one of the most geographically varied places in the world. It has towering mountain ranges, wide, grassy plains, rocky coasts, and gentle valleys. Networks of powerful rivers support rich soil. Countless species thrive in every part of the continent. For thousands of years, North America's varied environments have provided people, both ancient and modern, with lush natural resources. Whether bison on the Great Plains, berries from a rain forest, elk in the Rocky Mountains, or fish along the coasts, the first residents had plenty to eat.

In addition, Native Americans across the continent developed ways to produce even more food. In the southwestern deserts, they raised crops like corn, beans, and squash. In the eastern woodlands, they devised a slash-and-burn method to create land on which to farm. Native Americans knew a great deal about the world around them, and they understood the delicate balance of taking from nature in moderation and with respect.

How might the concept of plenty have defined people who lived in North America in the past?

CULTURES OF THE NORTHWEST COAST

Let's take a look at one region in particular—the Pacific Northwest—that demonstrates the powerful relationship between Native Americans and the natural world. The Pacific Northwest is a geographic and cultural area that stretches from what is now northern California to present-day Alaska. It includes coastal areas, inland forests, and several mountain ranges. It is also where the massive Columbia River flows through the Cascade Mountains and into the Pacific Ocean.

One unique feature of the Pacific Northwest is its temperate rain forests, which are characterized by heavy rainfall—as much as 14 feet per year—and by moderate temperatures. These rain forests are also home to some of the biggest trees in the world, including Sitka spruce, giant sequoia, and Douglas fir. These trees can grow to more than 250 feet tall and live for hundreds of years.

The first people who lived in the Pacific Northwest developed distinctive cultures, including the Kwakiutl (kwah-kee-YOO-tuhl), the Tlingit (KLING-kit), the Haida (HIGH-dah), the Chinook (SHIH-nuhk), and many others.

Because they lived among giant trees, these cultures mastered skills in woodworking. They built huge cedar plank houses, some large enough for hundreds of people. They also carved sturdy and seaworthy boats out of enormous tree trunks.

Northwest Coast people used woodworking in other ways, too. Intricately carved and painted totem poles towered over villages. Totems demonstrated village or family identities and indicated families' positions in the tribal social structure. They incorporated colorful representations of Pacific Northwest wildlife, including bears, ravens, whales, and eagles, as well as human figures and supernatural spirits. Totems functioned as collective histories, and the stories they told have been passed down among the generations.

Woodcarving also played a role in Northwest Coast ceremonies. Several ceremonies marked important times of the year or life events, and others reinforced social ties. Shamans, or people who were believed to be able to help others communicate with the spirit world, guided the carving of masks used during some ceremonies.

The Columbia River rises in British Columbia, Canada, and empties into the Pacific Ocean in Astoria, Oregon, not far from the coastline shown here.

OCEANS, FORESTS, AND RIVERS

Unlike groups in many other areas of North America, the coastal people of the Pacific Northwest did not farm to obtain food. Instead, they relied on the plentiful natural resources available to them. The many rivers that flow into the Pacific Ocean nourished the land and provided a welcome habitat for hundreds of species of plants and animals.

Perhaps the most important of these was the salmon. Since the earliest days of North America, five species of salmon born in rivers and lakes have traveled downstream to live their adult lives in the ocean. They only return to fresh water to spawn, or reproduce, and die. These spawning events, when millions of fish return to the streams and lakes where they were born, are some of the greatest migrations on Earth.

For early Northwest Coast people, abundant and predictable salmon migrations, or runs, provided the backbone of their traditional economies. The spring salmon runs in April and May were, and continue to be, incredibly important in providing food for Northwest Coast people. After a long winter of subsisting on dried foods—including smoked and dried salmon—spring was a time of plenty as fresh foods returned to the menu. Historically, the coming of the salmon often saved tribes from starvation as their winter supplies dwindled.

In addition to salmon, Northwest Coast people harvested a variety of shellfish, including clams, cockles, mussels, and oysters. They also hunted many land animals and birds, gathered a wide variety of plants and berries, and even hunted whales in some areas.

Northwest Coast totem poles are truly distinctive, with bright colors, detailed carving, and graphic patterns. What animals can you see on this totem?

A UNIQUE WORLDVIEW

Northwest Coast people saw themselves as an important part of their environment. Respect for the natural world was at the core of their worldview. They believed the plants and animals around them were as important as their human neighbors. How does this compare with the view people today have about the relationship between humans and nature?

Northwest Coast cultures also believed that many animals possessed human-like abilities. Some could even change into human form and take on traits such as anger if they were not treated with respect. If someone didn't hunt or fish in a respectful way, the animal might tell its kin to refuse to be caught in the future. All this added up to one clear point: survival required living in balance with animals and plants and respecting the natural world. Living a balanced life would ensure that food would be available year after year. Not doing so would bring dire consequences to the tribe.

Northwest Coast people adapted to and were shaped by their environments. In what ways does your environment shape who you are?

KING OF THE SALMON

Northwest Coast cultures performed special ceremonies to honor nature and to show respect for the plants and animals that kept them alive. One of the most important of these was the First Salmon ceremony. After a grueling winter of cold rain, with little access to fresh foods, spring brought new hope and abundance. People anxiously awaited the arrival of the salmon to usher in a season of plenty.

The first salmon to return to the river was called the King of the Salmon. People believed that as the leader, the King of the Salmon had the power to encourage other salmon to come and be caught or to scare away the other fish. If he was not treated with respect, the entire salmon run could be affected. To welcome the King of the Salmon, shamans conducted the First Salmon ceremony. Whole communities gathered to pay respect.

Although the First Salmon ceremony varied among different groups, three steps (described at right) characterize this ritual, which is still performed today. Once the ceremony is complete, the salmon fishing season is declared officially open and everyone can begin catching fish for food.

Students at the Lummi Nation School in Bellingham, Washington, prepare to bring in the First Salmon at their annual celebration of this traditional ceremony.

1. **Catching and welcoming the salmon**
   The chief selects a fisherman to catch the King of the Salmon. Once caught, tribal members carry it to the chief on a bed made of cedar.

2. **Cleaning, cooking, and eating the fish**
   Cooks delicately remove the meat from the fish. The head, entrails, and bones are set aside. Then community members eat the fish.

3. **Returning the remains to the water**
   Tribal members place the remains, which are considered sacred, in a cedar basket with its head facing upstream, pointing the way home. Then the salmon is released back into the water, where it is believed it will become whole again to continue its journey.

A master of ceremony named La-mos lifts the King of the Salmon to the sky as part of the Lummi Nation's First Salmon ceremony in May 2010.

This Tlingit wood rattle carved in the shape of a salmon is an excellent example of Northwest Coast art. It has bold shapes and colors and takes the form of wildlife native to the region.

CULTURAL REVIVAL

When European settlers arrived in the region in the early 1800s, two different worldviews came into contact with one another. In many cases, this contact led to changes among native traditions and practices.

Missionaries introduced Christianity and pressured native people to change their traditions. Europeans frowned on native beliefs that elevated the natural world to the level of humans, so they halted some ceremonies and declared others illegal. Along with ceremonies and religious beliefs, Europeans also replaced native foods with Western ones. Over time, Northwest Coast people began to shift away from traditional practices and focused on trade with the newcomers. By the late 1800s, the First Salmon ceremony began to die out.

During the 20th century, large commercial fisheries depleted salmon stocks all along the Pacific Coast. Development, overfishing, and pollution endangered the rivers and streams where the salmon migrated to spawn. According to the Native American worldview, this lack of respect for nature led to negative consequences, which included much smaller salmon runs than had been historically known.

In the 1970s, the Lummi people of Puget Sound, near Seattle, Washington, decided to bring back the First Salmon ceremony. They had never lost their belief in the importance of the plants and animals around them. And they felt the ceremony could help the salmon and the Lummi people.

In addition to reviving the First Salmon ceremony, the Lummi have also reclaimed salmon spawning habitats. They have restored streams to their natural state, ensuring the vital environment that salmon need to reproduce. The Lummi's efforts are paying off. Growing numbers of salmon are returning to their territory, and the Lummi are able to teach their children about the importance of respecting nature.

THINK ABOUT IT

The Lummi revived a ceremony to reinforce their connection to the natural world. What kinds of ceremonies or celebrations do you participate in that reinforce beliefs in your family and community?

A CEREMONIAL BLESSING

After the King of the Salmon is caught, cleaned, and cooked, it is ready to be eaten—after a blessing.

Among the Kwakiutl, this blessing is recited to honor the First Salmon. It has likely been handed down from generation to generation of Kwakiutl and is delivered before the salmon can be enjoyed. From this primary source, what can you conclude about how the Kwakiutl viewed their relationship with the King of the Salmon?

PRIMARY SOURCE

We have come to meet alive, Swimmer.
Do not feel wrong about what I have done to you,
friend Swimmer, for that is the reason why you come
that I may spear you, that I may eat you,
Supernatural One, you, Long-Life-Giver,
you, Swimmer.
Now protect us, (me) and my wife, that we may keep
well, that nothing may be difficult for us.

Source: from *The Religion of the Kwakiutl Indians*, by Frank Boas, New York: Columbia University Press, 1930, p. 207

Early American Civilizations

The Americas were never a blank slate, waiting for someone to "discover" them. People began arriving in the region about 20,000 years ago. Over time, they developed cultures that would influence all of the Americas and the world.

MAIN IDEA Civilizations emerged and thrived in Mesoamerica and South America for thousands of years.

MESOAMERICA

Long before 1492, great **civilizations**, or complex societies, arose in the Americas. The earliest of these civilizations began in **Mesoamerica**, which stretches from southern Mexico into part of Central America. Mesoamerica's landscape consists of two main areas: highlands and lowlands. The highlands lie between the mountains of the Sierra Madre (see-AIR-uh MAH-dray), a mountain system in Mexico. The lowlands are found along the coast of the Gulf of Mexico and in the jungles of the Yucatán (yoo-kuh-TAN) Peninsula. Both areas provided fertile land for agriculture.

The fertile land allowed several civilizations to develop in Mesoamerica. The **Olmec**, **Maya**, and **Aztec** thrived at different times from around 1200 B.C. to about A.D. 1520. The oldest civilization, the Olmec society, settled along present-day Mexico's Gulf Coast. The Maya, who were influenced by Olmec culture, mainly lived in parts of the countries we now call Mexico, Guatemala, and Belize. The Aztec were the last of the major Mesoamerican civilizations, establishing their empire in central and southern Mexico.

SOUTH AMERICA

To the south of Mesoamerica lies South America, a continent twice the size of the United States. South America contains coastal plains, dry forests and deserts, and vast river basins covered by dense rain forests and grasslands. The Andes Mountains rise along the continent over a distance of about 5,500 miles, extending from the northwestern coast all the way down to the southern tip. The mountains divide the Pacific coast from the continent's interior and separated the early civilizations in lands that are now the countries of Peru, Bolivia, Argentina, and Chile.

The **Moche** (MOH-chay) and the **Inca** were two of the most important early civilizations. The Moche lived on the arid northern coast of present-day Peru between about A.D. 100 and 800. They developed a complex **irrigation** system that channeled water to their crops. The rise of the Inca started in the 12th century. They established a capital city in Cusco (KOOS-koh), Peru, and later built the complex and mysterious city of Machu Picchu (MAH-choo PEE-choo) high in the Andes Mountains.

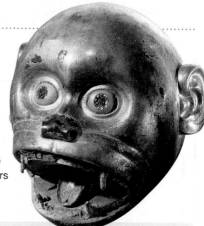

Moche Metalworking
The Moche were known for their vibrant murals, fine pottery, and advanced metalwork. Gold monkey-head beads, like this one, were often buried with members of the Moche nobility.

HISTORICAL THINKING

1. **READING CHECK** Which three civilizations developed in Mesoamerica?

2. **COMPARE AND CONTRAST** How were the highlands and lowlands of Mesoamerica similar?

3. **INTERPRET MAPS** How do you think the Andes Mountains benefited both the Moche and the Inca?

Early American Civilizations, 1200 B.C.–A.D. 1535

Gulf of Mexico
Chichén Itzá
Tenochtitlán
AZTEC
MESOAMERICA
La Venta
YUCATÁN PENINSULA
OLMEC
MAYA
CENTRAL AMERICA
ATLANTIC OCEAN
20°N
Caribbean Sea
N
W
E
S
0 250 500 Miles
0 250 500 Kilometers
• Cities and centers
Equator 0°
AMAZON
Amazon R.
BASIN
SOUTH AMERICA
Sipán
MOCHE
ANDES
Ucayali R.
Machu Picchu
Cusco
Lake Titicaca
INCA
20°S
100°W
80°W
PACIFIC OCEAN

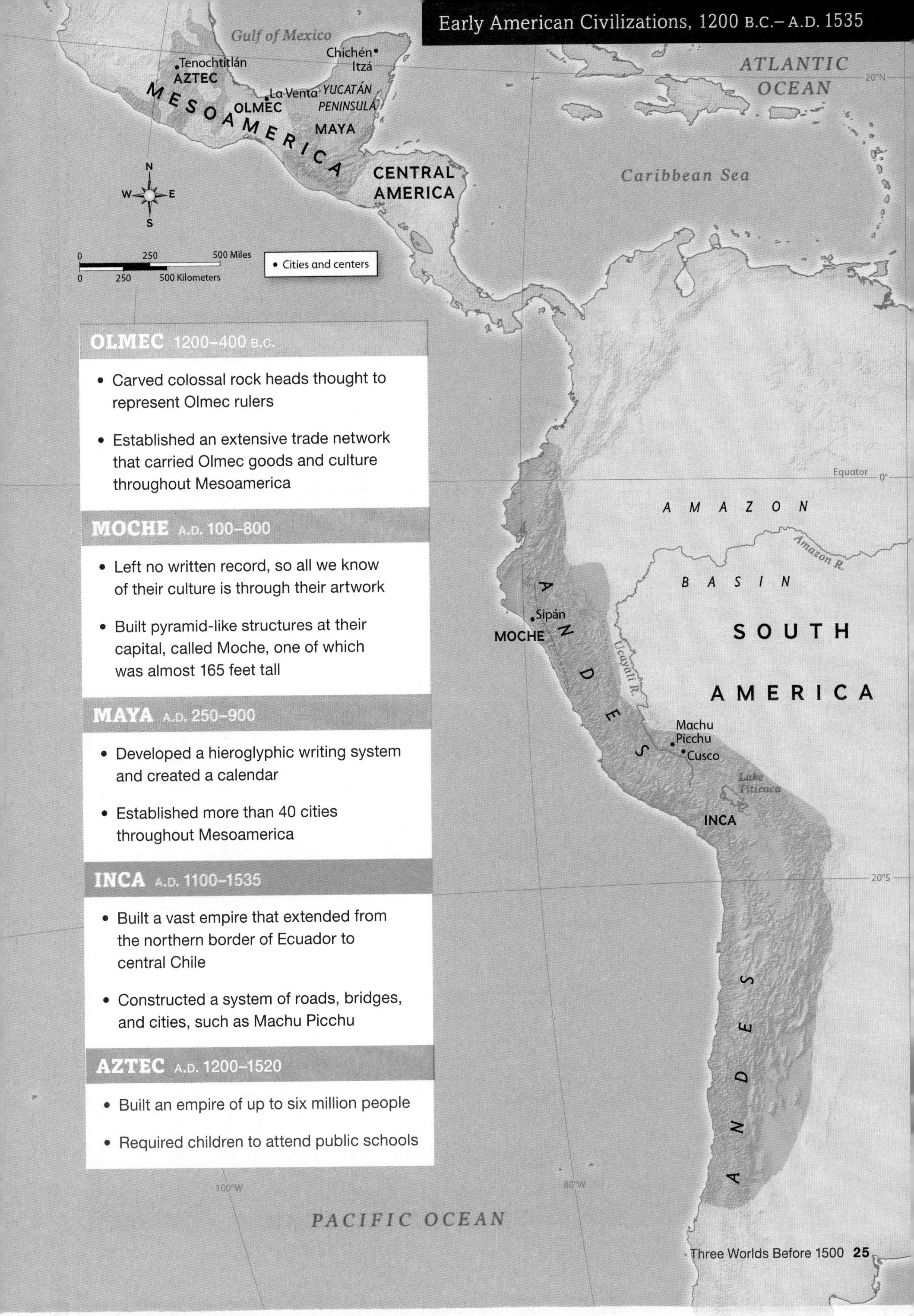

OLMEC 1200–400 B.C.

- Carved colossal rock heads thought to represent Olmec rulers
- Established an extensive trade network that carried Olmec goods and culture throughout Mesoamerica

MOCHE A.D. 100–800

- Left no written record, so all we know of their culture is through their artwork
- Built pyramid-like structures at their capital, called Moche, one of which was almost 165 feet tall

MAYA A.D. 250–900

- Developed a hieroglyphic writing system and created a calendar
- Established more than 40 cities throughout Mesoamerica

INCA A.D. 1100–1535

- Built a vast empire that extended from the northern border of Ecuador to central Chile
- Constructed a system of roads, bridges, and cities, such as Machu Picchu

AZTEC A.D. 1200–1520

- Built an empire of up to six million people
- Required children to attend public schools

1.2 Western American Cultures

How do you get food if you can't grow it—or buy it? You work with what you've got. Like the Mesoamericans and South Americans, people in the north adapted to their environments.

MAIN IDEA A variety of environments, characterized by climate and landforms, influenced the development of western North American cultures.

THE FAR NORTH AND PACIFIC COAST

South America and Mesoamerica weren't the only places where civilizations developed in the Western Hemisphere. In the extreme northwest of North America, several Native American groups flourished in particularly harsh climates. The Aleut (a-lee-OOT) lived on the cold, nearly treeless islands off the coast of what is now Alaska. The Inuit (IH-noo-wit) lived on the flat, frozen Arctic **tundra** of present-day Alaska and northwestern Canada. Since the weather did not favor growing crops, the groups fished and hunted sea mammals for food. They used **kayaks**, light boats made of wood and seal or walrus hides.

Farther to the south, a number of tribes lived in the evergreen forests that swept down the coast from present-day British Columbia to Oregon. Groups such as the Kwakiutl (kwah-kee-YOO-tuhl) and Haida (HI-duh) hunted and fished, and the ocean provided plenty of food. The abundance of trees made wood the preferred material for houses, boats, and household goods. The Kwakiutl also hosted **potlatches**, feasts where families gave gifts to guests to show social rank and wealth.

Even farther down the coast, in what is now California, the Pomo lived as hunter-gatherers. The Pomo didn't need to farm because the

A kiva, like the one shown here, was a round, semi-subterranean structure that the ancient Pueblo used for ceremonies, meetings, and as living spaces. These kivas are part of Pueblo Bonito, an ancient Pueblo settlement in Chaco Canyon in New Mexico.

streams were full of fish, and plenty of edible wild plants, nuts, and berries grew on the land. The Pomo had a unique religion. Worshippers dressed as animal spirits and other beings to sing, dance, and distribute gifts.

THE DESERTS AND PLAINS

Like the people of the North and the West, Native Americans living in the Southwest and Great Plains had to adapt to special climates and conditions. In the arid American Southwest, the **ancient Pueblo** (PWAY-bloh) and the **Hohokam** (ho-ho-KOM) thrived during the time of the Maya. In fact, Mesoamerican culture heavily influenced these groups. Not only did the Hohokam trade with Mesoamericans, they also **domesticated**, or grew, similar crops for food. They irrigated their crops in the dry climate. The Hohokam grew cotton, squash, beans, and maize, or corn, by digging canals from their fields to nearby rivers. Having extra food allowed the population to grow.

Early North American Civilizations, c. 1400

Around A.D. 1000, both the Hohokam and the ancient Pueblo built large adobe (uh-DOH-bee) homes made of sun-dried clay and straw bricks. These dwellings were similar to apartment buildings with multiple floors. For example, Pueblo Bonito, pictured to the left, once had as many as five floors and at least 600 rooms.

The ancient Pueblo were once referred to as the Anasazi, a name given them by the Navajo. In the 1990s, descendants of the ancient Pueblo protested the use of the term, pointing out that it means "enemy ancestor." Today many historians use the term "ancient Pueblo."

Northeast of the Hohokam, the Great Plains tribes experienced a very different way of life. Vast grasslands stretched from the Mississippi River to the Rocky Mountains. Native Americans who lived in the eastern part of the Great Plains, such as the Mandan and Pawnee, lived the settled lives of farmers, building villages of earthen lodges. In the western grasslands, the Blackfoot and other

tribes like them **migrated**, or moved from place to place, hunting herds of bison (also commonly called buffalo) and other game for food and clothing. **Tepees**, or tents made of bison hides, served as their portable homes.

At this time, tribes herded bison on foot. They steered the animals over cliffs or into corrals where men could kill them with arrows. Nonetheless, Plains Indian tribes considered the bison sacred. They used every part of the animal: meat for food, skin and fur for clothes and tepees, and bones for tools and crafts.

HISTORICAL THINKING

1. **READING CHECK** How did the tribes of northern and western North America adapt to their environments?

2. **COMPARE AND CONTRAST** How did lifestyles differ among Great Plains tribes?

3. **DRAW CONCLUSIONS** What can you conclude about similarities between the Maya culture and those of the ancient Pueblo and the Hohokam?

1.3 Eastern American Cultures

You climb to the top of the tower at Serpent Mound in southern Ohio and look down at the amazing sight below. It really does appear to be a gigantic, grass-covered snake slithering across the landscape with an egg or a jewel in its mouth. How did it get here? Who made it, and when?

MAIN IDEA Native Americans in eastern North America established stable agricultural societies and specialized burial and religious practices.

Ancient Mounds
Serpent Mound in Adams County, Ohio, resembles a writhing snake. The mound stretches more than 1,300 feet. It is estimated to be between 1,000 and 2,000 years old.

THE MOUND BUILDERS

Serpent Mound and other mounds like it began dotting the North American landscape around 1000 B.C. The people who created these structures are known as the **Mound Builders**. They lived in the river valleys of the Midwest and eastern United States. These earthen mounds came in different shapes and sizes and served a variety of purposes. Some housed the dead, and others served as temples.

The Adena and Hopewell were two cultures that built mounds. Both groups lived chiefly in the southern part of present-day Ohio, where Serpent Mound is located. They also settled in the region we now call Indiana, Kentucky, West Virginia, Michigan, Wisconsin, and Pennsylvania. Both groups were primarily hunter-gatherers, though the Hopewell farmed as well. Studies of the Hopewell Mound Group have determined that their mounds served as ancient burial sites.

A couple of hundred years after the Hopewell culture died out, the Mississippians emerged. Beginning in about A.D. 700, this group spread across North America from present-day Georgia to Minnesota. The Mississippians topped their mounds with grand temples or chiefs' residences. Cahokia (kuh-HO-kee-yuh), a grouping of mounds located in Illinois, served as the culture's capital. At the Cahokia Mounds site, Monks Mound stands nearly 100 feet high. Its base is larger than that of the Great Pyramid of Giza in Egypt.

Unlike the hunter-gatherer cultures of the Adena and Hopewell, the Mississippians were largely agricultural. For food, they planted crops such as corn, beans, and squash. Having a large and dependable harvest helped them feed a large population. Cahokia alone may have housed as many as 15,000 people.

PEOPLE OF THE WOODLANDS

Just as the Mississippians depended on farming for their livelihoods, so too did the tribes who lived after them in the woodlands of eastern and southeastern North America.

The mild climate of the Southeast made it an ideal place to grow crops. The Chickasaw and Choctaw of present-day Mississippi and Alabama grew corn, beans, and pumpkins. Women planted and harvested the crops. They also cooked, cared for the children, and made baskets, clothes, and other goods. Men cleared the land, constructed buildings, hunted, served as warriors, and engaged in trade. Both the Chickasaw and Choctaw societies were **matrilineal**, meaning they traced their family lines through their mothers.

Agriculture was so important to these groups that one of their religious ceremonies was a Green Corn festival. The festival was held each summer as the corn began to ripen. Over a series of days, people fasted, feasted, danced, played games, and prayed.

The region in which the Eastern Woodlands people lived was heavily wooded, which explains its name. The tribes of the Eastern Woodlands practiced a technique known as **slash-and-burn agriculture**. This method involved cutting down and burning trees to clear land, and it supported the groups' pattern of moving frequently. Their farms were not permanent.

Two groups, named for the languages they spoke, lived in the Eastern Woodlands: the Algonquian (al-GAHN-kwee-uhn) and the Iroquois (IHR-uh-kwoy). The Algonquian lived along the Atlantic coast. The Iroquois primarily lived in the central part of present-day New York State. In Algonquian groups, men were the heads of households, but Iroquois society was matrilineal, and women shared political power with men. Five Iroquois-speaking nations banded together to form the **Iroquois League**: the Mohawk, Oneida, Onondaga, Cayuga (kah-YOO-guh), and Seneca. This brought long-lasting peace among them. The Iroquois nations still exist to this day.

HISTORICAL THINKING

1. **READING CHECK** How did farming help maintain a large population in Cahokia?

2. **IDENTIFY PROBLEMS AND SOLUTIONS** How did the Eastern Woodlands people solve the problem of growing food in forests?

3. **MAKE INFERENCES** Why would the mild climate of the Southeast have made it an ideal place to grow crops?

The Birdman Tablet depicts a man with wings and was found on the east side of Monks Mound.

Mounds
on the Mississippi

"Cahokia has changed our ideas about ancient Native American culture." —John Kelly

Once one of the greatest cities in North America, Cahokia went largely unstudied for hundreds of years. Then in the 1950s, President Dwight Eisenhower initiated the interstate highway program with a provision for archaeological excavations along the new roads. What the archaeologists found at the East St. Louis, Illinois, mound center astounded them: over a thousand houses that had been built in an amazingly short span of time. What had drawn so many people to the site? Who were they? Archaeologist **John Kelly** has been working on the answers to these and other questions for about 40 years.

^
Highways run on either side of Cahokia's Monks Mound, the largest pyramid north of Mesoamerica. A temple may have once stood on the platform atop the mound. After climbing to the top, a priest would have had a magnificent view of Cahokia's vast floodplain, known as the American Bottom.

MAIN IDEA Archaeologist John Kelly's excavations of the Cahokia Mounds have provided insight into the city's culture and its rise and fall.

Kelly (center) works with students at the site of Cahokia's Mound 34. They are actually standing underneath the mound, which was removed. Artifacts suggest that a special society of hunters or warriors may have used the building that stood on top of the mound. Monks Mound rises in the background.

CITY OF MYSTERY

National Geographic Explorer John Kelly has his work cut out for him. We know very little about Cahokia. The people who lived there didn't have a written language. We don't even know what they called themselves or the city they lived in. Cahokia was the name of people who lived briefly on the site in the 1700s, long after the city had disappeared. Archaeologists have pieced together what evidence they've found to expand our understanding of Cahokia. But as Kelly admits, "People still aren't really sure what it was."

According to Kelly, one thing we do know is that people had been living in Cahokia for years. The area was easy to reach along the Missouri, Illinois, and Mississippi rivers, and the land was good for growing a variety of crops, including corn. But why did the population swell from about 7,000 to 15,000 people between 1000 and 1100? One surprising theory states that people arrived after an extremely bright star called a supernova appeared around this time.

For whatever reason, people arrived in Cahokia in large numbers to build a ritual city with houses, farmland, and great plazas for religious celebrations. Above all—literally—they built the mounds. Monks Mound was the tallest. Named for the French monks who once lived in its shadow, the mound rose 100 feet in the center of the city. Laborers toiled on it for about 25 years using only baskets and stone hoes.

RISE AND FALL

Over time, the Cahokians built at least 110 other mounds. Some of these were used as burial sites. Archaeologists working at one called Mound 72 unearthed the remains of a man surrounded by ornaments and weapons. They also discovered the bodies of men and young women buried with and near him. Some were likely human sacrifices.

Kelly has spent much of his time investigating a mound that wasn't used for burials: Mound 34. Actually, his research takes him underneath the mound. The Cahokians constructed a building on top of the mound's platform, but other buildings and a copper workshop stood beneath the mound. According to Kelly, the buildings may have been placed there and covered with earth to represent the view of the world as existing in three layers: the beneath world with Earth Mother, this world, and the upper world. As Kelly says, "We focus on the mounds, but the history's really about the building that was there before the mound!"

Around the end of the 1100s, a different kind of construction began in Cahokia. Walls were erected around the city, possibly as protection against attack. But by then, the population had already begun to dwindle and the city to decline. Some say climate change or disease may have led to the fall of Cahokia. Kelly says that a massive flood may have covered the city and caused the people to leave for a brief time. Over a century later, a long drought may have led to the eventual abandonment. What we do know is that, for some reason, by the late 1300s, the residents had left the city. Cahokia remains mysterious to the end.

HISTORICAL THINKING

1. **READING CHECK** What did the Cahokians build in their city?

2. **ANALYZE CAUSE AND EFFECT** Why did Cahokia decline?

1.5 National Museum of the American Indian Washington, D.C.

The National Museum of the American Indian (NMAI) is located in Washington, D.C., on the National Mall. The museum and its grounds were designed with the help of tribes and communities from across the hemisphere to share the sense and spirit of Native Americans with its many visitors. NMAI has a tremendous collection of Native American arts and artifacts—over 800,000 items representing more than 1,200 cultures throughout the Americas and over 12,000 years of history. Visitors experience everything from ancient tools and weapons to modern Native American art, cultural and religious artifacts, and everyday items. Which of the items below were used for everyday activities and which ones served a different purpose?

Tlingit Canoe Paddles

These Tlingit paddles date to the early 1900s. The Tlingit are indigenous people of the Pacific Northwest in North America, where fish are abundant. For the Tlingit, canoes and paddles are tools necessary for survival.

Odawa Moccasins

This pair of beaded Odawa (Ottawa) moccasins was purchased by a trader at Crown Point, Indiana, a fur trade depot. The moccasins feature folded-down silk cuffs decorated with small beads arranged in dashed lines, a pattern often found on this type of Odawa moccasins. Silk teardrops and diamond shapes also decorate the moccasins and are outlined with even smaller white glass beads.

What do you observe about the craftsmanship of these Odawa moccasins?

Chief of the Undersea Mask

This colorful carved wood mask is made of western red cedar. It represents the chief of the undersea kingdom. He is believed to live in a copper home under the ocean, guarded by sea monsters. Ceremonial masks like this one usually depict characters from family histories or from the supernatural. This mask was carved by a master carver from the New Vancouver Tribe in western Canada in the late 1800s or early 1900s.

The U-shaped designs that surround the face represent the scales of a fish or a sea creature. They may have been added to the mask later by a second artist.

"We seek to bring the Native voice into **every school, every library, every university,** indeed, every home."

—Kevin Gover (Pawnee)
Director, National Museum of the American Indian

The paddles are made of yellow cedar and ornately painted with a wolf design.

1.6 Native American Environments

MAIN IDEA Before European settlement, 500 Native American tribes inhabited North America. Geography helped to shape their diverse cultures.

PHYSICAL AND HUMAN GEOGRAPHY

When you examine how geography affected people and culture, you are taking a **geographic perspective**. That is, you are looking at culture through the lens of geography. You can examine two aspects of geography: physical geography and human geography.

Physical geography refers to the physical characteristics of a region. It includes the surface of the earth, soil, bodies of water, climate, and glaciers and ice sheets. It also includes plant and animal life.

Human geography examines how people and their cultures are affected by physical geography, and how human activities affect the environment. For example, geography has a great impact on how people make a living. People who live near the sea often make a living by fishing, and in regions with fertile soils, farming is usually an important economic activity.

Use physical geography and human geography to study these Native American tribes before the arrival of Christopher Columbus in the Americas. For each group, you will find an explanation of their physical geography and human geography.

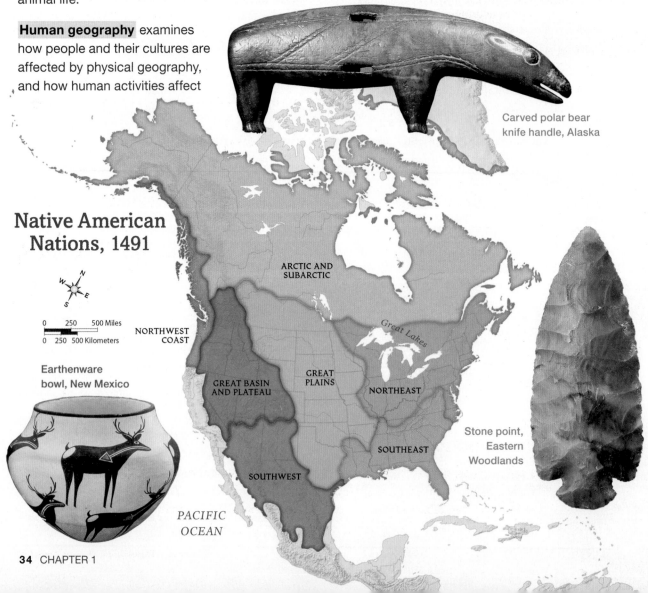

Carved polar bear knife handle, Alaska

Native American Nations, 1491

0 250 500 Miles
0 250 500 Kilometers

Earthenware bowl, New Mexico

ARCTIC AND SUBARCTIC

NORTHWEST COAST

Great Lakes

GREAT BASIN AND PLATEAU

GREAT PLAINS

NORTHEAST

SOUTHEAST

SOUTHWEST

Stone point, Eastern Woodlands

PACIFIC OCEAN

PHYSICAL GEOGRAPHY	HUMAN GEOGRAPHY

ARCTIC AND SUBARCTIC

The Inuit, Aleut, and other tribes of this region lived in one of the harshest environments on Earth—the land that we now call Alaska. It is a land of snow and ice, with little vegetation in the winter.

The people living in the far north creatively adapted to their harsh environment. They hunted for seals and whales and built igloos out of ice to protect themselves from the extreme cold.

NORTHWEST COAST

The tribes of the Northwest Coast lived in the region that is now the states of Washington and Oregon and the Canadian province of British Columbia. It is a rich environment with lush forests and rivers filled with fish.

The tribes of the Northwest included the Chinook and the Tlingit. They fished and hunted for bears and other large game. The abundance of the region allowed families to accumulate wealth. Families gained honor by giving away part of their wealth in a ceremony called the potlatch.

GREAT BASIN AND PLATEAU

This region, west of the Great Plains, features soaring mountains and plateaus with long stretches of grassland. The land supported large mammals, including antelope, moose, elk, mountain goat, and bison.

The Utes, Shoshone, and other tribes hunted for game and fished in the rivers for salmon and trout. Some Native Americans even created dances to mimic the movement of the grass in the wind.

SOUTHWEST

The Southwest, which includes today's Arizona and New Mexico, is a region of deserts with very little rainfall. The climate is harsh, with temperatures soaring to 110 degrees Fahrenheit or more in the summer. But the region also has rivers.

The rivers are critical to this region because of the lack of rainfall. The Pueblo tribes, who lived near the Rio Grande in what is now New Mexico, planted maize (corn) and other crops near the river.

GREAT PLAINS

The Great Plains stretch from present-day Iowa to Wyoming. The region is flat, with plains and tallgrass prairies. The most important resource was once the bison, or buffalo, which numbered at least 30 million in the 1400s.

The Great Plains had many tribes, including the Lakota, the Blackfoot, and the Mandan. These tribes had one thing in common—they used the bison for food, shelter, and clothing.

NORTHEAST

The Northeast region spans the present-day states from Virginia to Maine. This land has ample rainfall, many rivers and streams, and a wealth of natural resources, including wild game, fish, and fertile soil.

The Algonquian- and Iroquois-speaking people who lived in this region used the many rivers and streams as highways. They built canoes out of wood and birchbark to use for long-distance trading.

SOUTHEAST

The Southeast reaches from today's North Carolina to Florida and offers many natural gifts: a mild climate, plentiful rainfall, and fertile soil.

The Cherokee, the Choctaw, and other groups grew maize, beans, squash, and other crops in the fertile soil. Because of the mild climate, the land supported a large population and tribes thrived.

THINK LIKE A GEOGRAPHER

1. **IDENTIFY MAIN IDEAS AND DETAILS** How did different Native American groups adapt to the amount of rainfall they received?

2. **MAKE INFERENCES** What does the potlatch reveal about the attitudes toward wealth among Native Americans of the Northwest?

The Middle Ages

For hundreds of years, the Roman Empire united much of Europe. So when the western part of the empire fell in A.D. 476, its laws and social structures collapsed, too. With the empire no longer in control, "Now what?" could well have been the question on almost everyone's mind.

MAIN IDEA During the Middle Ages, Western Europe underwent many political, economic, and social changes.

A FEUDAL SOCIETY

Political, economic, and social problems led to the decline of the Western Roman Empire. As the empire weakened, Germanic tribes from Northern Europe invaded Western Europe and overthrew the emperor.

The end of the Western Roman Empire signaled the beginning of a period known as the **Middle Ages**, which lasted from about A.D. 500 to 1450. With no central government after the fall of Rome, Western Europe largely consisted of small kingdoms ruled by Germanic tribes, such as the Franks, Visigoths, and Vikings. Over time, the kingdoms grew and became very powerful.

To help the leaders of these kingdoms hold onto their land and protect their subjects, a political and social system called **feudalism** developed. Feudalism helped ensure the defense and security of kingdoms, which were constantly at war with one another. It achieved this security by maintaining a strict social **hierarchy**, or order.

Kings sat atop this structure. They gave pieces of their land to noblemen, known as lords. A lord, in turn, granted parts of this land to lesser noblemen called **vassals**. Vassals paid taxes on the land and pledged their military service to the lord.

Structure of Feudal Society

A *king* inherited his position, but none could rule without the support of the noblemen.

Church officials and noblemen often exercised more power than the king.

Knights guarded their lord's castle and fought for him according to a strict code of conduct.

Serfs worked the land. In exchange for protection, a serf provided loyalty, labor, and crops.

Many vassals themselves were soldiers in the army and served as knights, who were warriors on horseback. Peasants called **serfs** were at the bottom of the heap.

The **manor system** emerged as a result of feudalism. The system consisted of peasants bound to a lord's land, or manor. Landowners maintained a tight grip on both their land and their workers, while the peasant workers received a level of military protection they could not provide for themselves. Feudalism and the manor system remained in place throughout the Middle Ages, providing some stability to Western Europe.

WARS, TRADE, AND TOWNS

Still, feudalism was not the only source of stability. The Roman Catholic Church served as the strongest unifying force in medieval Europe. Late in the 11th century, the Church waged the **Crusades**, wars against the spread of **Islam**. That religion's followers, called **Muslims**, had seized control of the Holy Land—the city of Jerusalem and the surrounding area. They'd also begun to attack the Christian Byzantine Empire, once the eastern half of the Roman Empire.

The Crusades continued for two centuries, allowing Crusaders to acquire land in areas previously conquered by Muslims. The land acquisition led to the establishment of trade centers. Though the Crusaders were ultimately unsuccessful—they eventually lost any land they captured—their actions increased trade between Europe and the eastern Mediterranean region.

As trade increased in Europe, businesses and the economy grew. Towns grew, too, as people left their positions on the manors for better jobs.

Outbreaks of a devastating disease called the bubonic plague also created jobs. In the 14th century, the plague killed as many as one-third of all Europeans. Those laborers lucky enough to survive the illness found better work prospects as a result of the decline in population. Less competition led to greater opportunities for those who survived.

The plague, along with the movement to cities and towns, helped bring about the decline of feudalism and the end of the Middle Ages. Europe began to experience cultural changes that would mark the beginning of a new age of creativity.

HISTORICAL THINKING

1. **READING CHECK** How are the manor system and feudalism similar to each other?

2. **EVALUATE** In what way were the Crusaders both successful and unsuccessful?

3. **COMPARE AND CONTRAST** How did feudalism and the Church affect Europe similarly and differently?

▥ J. Paul Getty Museum, Los Angeles

Francesco Ubertini (1494–1557), known as Bacchiacca, was a Renaissance painter from Florence, Italy. This painting, *Portrait of a Woman with a Book of Music*, reflects the new styles and techniques employed by Renaissance artists. For example, look at the column and vase in this painting.

By painting them proportionally smaller, Bacchiacca has produced the impression that these items are placed well behind the woman. This technique, called perspective, gives the illusion of depth and distance and helped Bacchiacca create a work that looks three-dimensional.

2.2 Renaissance and Reformation

In the 1300s, a revolution began to brew in Europe. But this revolution didn't involve weapons and war. It involved ideas. People focused on the individual and believed every person had unlimited possibilities. These, indeed, were revolutionary ideas.

MAIN IDEA The Renaissance marked a time of curiosity, learning, experimentation, communication, and change.

REBIRTH OF ART AND LEARNING

Historians called the revolutionary movement that began at the end of the Middle Ages the **Renaissance**, which means "rebirth." The Renaissance originated in Italy and spread to other parts of Europe. The movement had its roots in the classical writings of ancient Greece and Rome and the philosophy of **humanism**. Humanists encouraged freedom of thought and the development of new ideas.

The Renaissance also saw the revival of elements of ancient Greek and Roman architecture, such as columns and arches. This revival enabled generations of artists and architects to achieve levels of artistic creation not seen in Europe for a thousand years. Painters such as Raphael and Michelangelo, and architects such as Brunelleschi, created works that still inspire awe in people today. **Leonardo da Vinci** is considered by many to be the ideal Renaissance figure. Leonardo not only painted artistic masterpieces, but he was also an inventor, sculptor, and architect. His studies of anatomy and other sciences proved to be ahead of their time.

The ideas of the Renaissance also had an effect on literature. In the mid-1400s, **Johann Gutenberg's** invention of the **printing press**, which used movable metal type to print pages, allowed for mass distribution of classical and humanist literary works. As the availability of printed materials increased, more people learned to read, and the philosophy of the Renaissance and humanist movement began to spread rapidly across Europe.

DIVISIONS IN THE CHURCH

Around the time of the Renaissance, the Catholic Church began to lose some of its power. Some members charged the Church with corruption and called for reform. This gradual progression toward change within the Church eventually led to the **Reformation**, a split from the Catholic Church that took place in the early 16th century. **Martin Luther**, a German pastor and university professor, led this movement. He believed biblical scripture was more important than the pope's authority. He also believed that Christians achieved God's favor through faith rather than by doing good works. Luther was eventually excommunicated, or expelled, from the Catholic Church for his teachings.

Followers of the Reformation became known as **Protestants**, and the Church split between the Protestants and Catholics. Over time, many different Protestant churches, called denominations, developed, each with its own set of beliefs within the framework of Christianity.

HISTORICAL THINKING

1. **READING CHECK** From which ancient cultures did the Renaissance receive inspiration?

2. **DESCRIBE** Why was the printing press such an important invention during the Renaissance?

3. **DRAW CONCLUSIONS** Why do you think the Catholic Church excommunicated Martin Luther?

2.3 Trade Expands

Just as the Renaissance spurred an expansion in people's thoughts and attitudes, it also inspired a spirit of adventure and curiosity about the world. Sea voyagers set out to explore new lands and, above all, to find new trading opportunities and markets.

MAIN IDEA New sea routes and developments in sailing technology allowed for an expansion of trade between European societies and the East.

EXPANDING TRADE WITH ASIA

In the mid-15th century, the Turks of the Ottoman Empire captured the city of Constantinople. Located on a peninsula between Europe and Asia, Constantinople joined the two continents. Capturing the city gave the Turks complete control of the land trade routes that connected the continents. This control allowed the Turks to charge Europeans high prices for Asian goods. Turkish merchants could then make a **profit**, or earn more money than they spent, on the goods.

To avoid trading with the Turks over land, Europeans explored new sea routes to Asia. At the end of the 15th century, Portuguese navigator **Vasco da Gama** sailed to India via one of these routes. He and his fleet traveled around the Cape of Good Hope at the southern tip of Africa. Portuguese navigator **Bartholomeu Dias** had first discovered this route about a decade earlier. Da Gama was able to return from his trip with Indian spices. This journey helped reestablish direct trade between Europe and the East.

PORTUGAL AND AFRICA

In the early 1400s, **Prince Henry the Navigator** established a school on the Atlantic coast in Sagres, Portugal. The school consisted of mathematicians, mapmakers, astronomers, instrument makers, and other instructors who taught students about sailing. Henry's goal was to train sailors about shipbuilding and **navigation**, or planning and following a route. He wanted to send his students on ocean explorations.

Students learned, among other lessons, how to build a special new ship called a **caravel**. The caravel was a light sailing ship that was both quick and able to sail windward, or into the wind. These characteristics made the ship a particularly good choice for the long voyages Henry had in mind.

Caravels made it possible for explorers to sail farther down the West African coast—and elsewhere. Even Christopher Columbus used two caravels during his historic voyage to the Americas in 1492. In the 1420s, Henry began funding caravel expeditions to Africa. Though Henry himself never joined these expeditions, he instructed his sailors to return with goods from Africa's western coast. During part of the Middle Ages, Portugal was under Islamic rule, and Muslim traders had long told stories about a "land of gold" near the African coast. A series of powerful African empires had inspired these stories. And the stories weren't that far from the truth.

HISTORICAL THINKING

1. **READING CHECK** What was the new sea route that Bartholomeu Dias first discovered and Vasco da Gama later followed to get to India?

2. **ANALYZE CAUSE AND EFFECT** Why did Europeans want to find new sea routes to Asia in the 15th century?

3. **EVALUATE** What might have been some of the advantages and disadvantages of taking a long voyage in a caravel?

CRITICAL VIEWING This sculpture in Lisbon, Portugal, called *Monument to the Discoveries,* celebrates the voyages of Portuguese explorers of the 15th and 16th centuries. Henry the Navigator stands at the top part of the monument, which is shaped like the front of a ship. Behind him are explorers, mapmakers, and others who played an important role in early exploration. Why is the monument's setting a fitting choice?

3.1 The Kingdom of Ghana

After Arab traders reached West Africa during the 700s, they talked of a land where even the horses were draped in gold cloth. This was the land of Ghana, and for centuries it was the wealthiest kingdom in West Africa.

MAIN IDEA West Africa's location made it a major trade center, leading to the rise of the kingdom of Ghana and the spread of Islam.

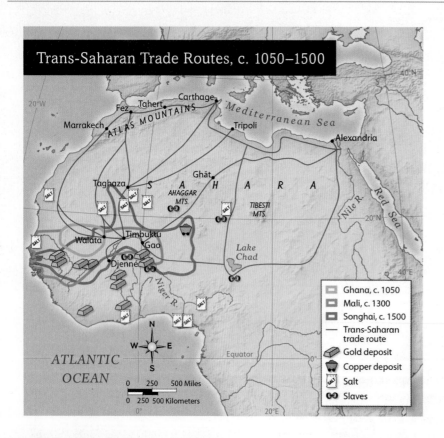

Trans-Saharan Trade Routes, c. 1050–1500

- Ghana, c. 1050
- Mali, c. 1300
- Songhai, c. 1500
- — Trans-Saharan trade route
- Gold deposit
- Copper deposit
- Salt
- Slaves

Travelers had to carry enough fresh water to last until the next **oasis**, one of those rare areas in the desert that contain freshwater sources.

People who traveled across the Sahara discovered that camels were well suited to the desert climate and could carry humans and goods long distances through the Sahara. Camels can survive traveling up to 100 miles without water, and they can carry heavy loads. Nomadic traders began to lead camel **caravans**, or groups of people traveling together. In their caravans, they carried goods on **trans-Saharan** trade routes between sub-Saharan Africa and northern Africa, which lay within reach of Europe and Southwest Asia. Market towns started to flourish where trading routes met.

Two kinds of goods dominated trans-Saharan trade: gold and salt. Gold was mined in the forests south of Ghana and was regularly used as a trade item. Salt, however, was not produced naturally in this area. People had to look north to the Sahara, which had an abundance of this valuable and essential nutrient. In fact, buildings in the Saharan trading town of Taghaza were constructed of salt blocks because that was the building material in largest supply.

GOLD AND SALT IN GHANA

To reach the golden land, the kingdom of Ghana in West Africa, traders had to cross the largest hot desert in the world, the **Sahara**. Covered in dunes, rippling sheets of sand, and rocky formations, the desert extends over an area a little smaller than the United States. South of the desert is a **steppe** region of West Africa called the Sahel. Steppes are flat grasslands with very few trees.

The Sahara could have easily isolated the lands south of it. Extreme heat and a lack of water made travel through the region difficult for humans.

A POWERFUL KINGDOM

Gold and salt traders met in West Africa, with gold flowing north and salt moving south. Near the midway point, the **kingdom of Ghana** grew and profited from the rising economy as the king collected taxes on the import and export of goods.

By the ninth century, Ghana was rich and powerful and able to conquer nearby lands with its strong army. The kingdom was structured according to a feudal system, with many princes ruling over various parts of the kingdom on behalf of the king.

In addition to goods, traders from North Africa carried their Islamic faith. Islam was the dominant religion of much of southwestern Asia at this time. Rising Muslim empires in North Africa made efforts to **convert**, or change, the people of West Africa to Islam and take over Ghana's trade, which weakened the power of the kingdom's rulers.

These efforts were so successful that in the mid-11th century, a historian named al-Bakri from al-Andalus (now Spain) described Ghana's capital as consisting of two towns. One was home to Muslim traders. The other was the palace of the king. By 1100, Ghana had declined as a result of droughts and unrest, providing an opportunity for a new Muslim empire to take control of the region.

HISTORICAL THINKING

1. **READING CHECK** How did Ghana's location help it become wealthy?

2. **INTERPRET MAPS** Identify two geographic features that the people of West Africa would have to travel through to trade with others.

3. **MAKE INFERENCES** Why did the movement of traders help spread the influence of Islam?

° **CRITICAL VIEWING** The Great Mosque in Djenné (jen-AY), Mali, is an architectural wonder. A mosque is a Muslim place of worship. What distinctive features does the photo show?

3.2 Mali and Songhai

In the 1300s, new legends spread to Europe about an impossibly wealthy king from West Africa who traveled with hundreds of camels and thousands of servants. This man, Mansa Musa, gave away so much gold that it led to a decline in the precious metal's value in parts of Africa.

MAIN IDEA Wealth from the kingdoms of Mali and Songhai spread along trans-Saharan trade routes to northern Africa and Europe.

MALI TAKES OVER GHANA

After Ghana's decline in the 1200s, the kingdom of **Mali** took control of the gold and salt trades in West Africa. Mali's first king was **Sundiata Keita** (sun-JAHT-ah KAY-tah). Sundiata led military forces to defeat the weakened kingdom of Ghana, uniting the conquered lands into a peaceful, prosperous empire stretching along the Niger River and up into the Sahara.

Though Sundiata ruled well, it was **Mansa Musa** who first introduced Mali to the world. Musa became king in the 1300s. As a Muslim, he decided to make a **pilgrimage**, or religious journey, to the holy city of Mecca in 1324. He took thousands of servants and dozens of camels. The caravan gave gold and other luxurious goods to people along the way. Europeans and Asians, upon hearing accounts of the generous king, became more motivated to trade with the wealthy empire.

Mansa Musa returned from Mecca a year later with new knowledge and ideas. He turned the city of Timbuktu into a center for culture and learning. He also encouraged his people to learn Arabic so they could study the holy book of Islam, the Qur'an.

SONGHAI

The **Songhai** people lived to the east of the Mali Empire. Their capital city, Gao, became such a wealthy, thriving city that the Mali Empire conquered it in 1325 and ruled over it for the next 50 years. When the Songhai finally retook their capital city, they began to build their own empire. In the process, Songhai assumed control of trans-Saharan trade. The Songhai ruler Askia Mohammed then continued to expand the kingdom and strengthen ties with other Muslims. He also reformed government, banking, and education. Later rulers fought each other for control, making the Songhai vulnerable to the ambitions of their envious neighbors. Songhai lost Timbuktu and its capital, Gao, when Morocco captured the two cities in 1591. The invasion by Morocco marked the end of the Songhai Empire.

As Ghana, Mali, and Songhai rose and fell, other West African cultures developed. The Hausa (HOW-suh) and Yoruba (YOR-uh-buh) practiced agriculture and crafts. While the Hausa and Yoruba were allied with each other, they never combined forces to engage in war for other territories. The kingdom of Benin (buh-NEEN) rose to power in the late 1400s, conquered many of its neighbors, and successfully engaged in trade with Europeans.

The Europeans, meanwhile, had set their sights on other lands by the late 1400s. Soon they would be exploring territory in the Americas.

HISTORICAL THINKING

1. **READING CHECK** How did the rise of Mali and Songhai affect trans-Saharan trade?

2. **ANALYZE CAUSE AND EFFECT** How did Mansa Musa's pilgrimage lead to changes in Timbuktu?

3. **COMPARE AND CONTRAST** How were the empires of Mali and Songhai similar?

3.3 Impressions of Mali

Travelers have long recorded their observations as they explore new places. Travel journals from the past reveal details about places as they were long ago and also give us insight into how people reacted to different cultures.

This painting is an illustration from an Arabic manuscript from the 1200s and shows a wealthy pilgrim on his hajj, or pilgrimage to Mecca in present-day Saudi Arabia. Moroccan traveler Ibn Battuta (IBH-uhn bah-TOO-tuh) began his travels by going on his hajj in 1325. This was one year after Mansa Musa made his hajj. Stopping in Cairo, Ibn Battuta heard about Mansa Musa. The two never met, but later Ibn Battuta visited Mali. There he met Mansa Musa's brother Mansa Suleyman and began recording his observations.

CRITICAL VIEWING What mood does the painting convey?

DOCUMENT ONE

Primary Source: Atlas
from the *Catalan Atlas, c. 1375*

Drawn by a European mapmaker, this detail from a medieval map shows West Africa and Mansa Musa, the man wearing a gold crown and holding a ball of gold. The map was made after Mansa Musa's pilgrimage to Mecca, which literally put West Africa on the map.

CONSTRUCTED RESPONSE What does this image suggest about the impression Mansa Musa made on people outside of Mali?

DOCUMENT TWO

Primary Source: Travel Memoir
from *Travels in Asia and Africa 1325–1354*, by Ibn Battuta

Ibn Battuta traveled throughout Africa, Europe, and Asia and wrote about his experiences. His writings help us understand the history and cultures of the places he visited. In this excerpt from his writing, he describes the entrance of the sultan, or ruler, of Mali, Mansa Suleyman.

CONSTRUCTED RESPONSE What impression do you think the sultan made on his audience?

On certain days the sultan holds audiences in the palace yard, where there is a platform under a tree, with three steps. . . . The sultan comes out of a door in a corner of the palace, carrying a bow in his hand and a quiver on his back. . . . His usual dress is a velvety red tunic, made of the European fabrics called "mutanfas." The sultan is preceded by his musicians, who carry gold and silver guimbris [two-stringed guitars], and behind him come three hundred armed slaves. He walks in a leisurely fashion. . . . As he takes his seat the drums, trumpets, and bugles are sounded.

DOCUMENT THREE

Primary Source: Travel Memoir
from *Travels in Asia and Africa 1325–1354*, by Ibn Battuta

As a Muslim, Ibn Battuta was interested to see how people in other regions practiced his religion. In this excerpt, he notes what he witnessed about the observance of Islam in Mali. He admired the commitment of the people there to the religion.

CONSTRUCTED RESPONSE What does this description tell you about the importance of Islam in Mali?

On Fridays, if a man does not go early to the mosque, he cannot find a corner to pray in, on account of the crowd. It is a custom of theirs to send each man his boy [to the mosque] with his prayer-mat; the boy spreads it out for his master in a place befitting him [and remains on it] until he comes to the mosque. . . . Yet another is their zeal for learning the Koran [Qur'an] by heart. They put their children in chains if they show any backwardness in memorizing it, and they are not set free until they have it by heart.

SYNTHESIZE & WRITE

1. **REVIEW** Review what you have learned about travel, trade, and religion in West Africa.

2. **RECALL** Think about your responses to the constructed response questions above. What details in the documents caused you to form these impressions?

3. **CONSTRUCT** Write a topic sentence that answers this question: What impressions did Mali make on those who traveled there?

4. **WRITE** Using evidence from this chapter and the documents, write a paragraph that supports your topic sentence.

VOCABULARY

Use each of the following vocabulary terms in a sentence that shows an understanding of the term's meaning and its connection to the information in this chapter.

1. civilization
    Once humans started growing their own food, cities and civilizations could grow.

2. migrate

3. matrilineal

4. slash-and-burn agriculture

5. feudalism

6. navigation

7. trans-Saharan

8. caravan

READING STRATEGY
COMPARE AND CONTRAST

If you haven't already, complete your table to list the characteristics of the three societies discussed in the chapter. List at least four characteristics of each. Then answer the question.

Americas	Europe	Africa
empires		

9. What conflicts might arise among these three societies based on what you've learned about them?

MAIN IDEAS

Answer the following questions. Support your answers with evidence from the chapter.

10. How did the land in Mesoamerica contribute to the rise of civilizations there? **LESSON 1.1**

11. What determined whether a group of people in North America took up farming or continued to live as hunter-gatherers? **LESSON 1.2**

12. What was the significance of the Green Corn festival in the lives of the people of southeastern North America? **LESSON 1.3**

13. Why did the Roman Catholic Church begin the Crusades? **LESSON 2.1**

14. How did the Renaissance influence religious thought and pave the way for the Reformation? **LESSON 2.2**

15. Why did Prince Henry the Navigator establish a school to train sailors? **LESSON 2.3**

16. What caused the eventual decline of the kingdom of Ghana? **LESSON 3.1**

17. How did Mansa Musa increase his trade business on his pilgrimage to Mecca? **LESSON 3.2**

18. Why are the writings of Ibn Battuta considered such an important source for understanding West Africa in the 1300s? **LESSON 3.3**

HISTORICAL THINKING

Answer the following questions. Support your answers with evidence from the chapter.

19. **SUMMARIZE** What purposes did mounds serve in the Adena, Hopewell, and Mississippian cultures?

20. **ANALYZE CAUSE AND EFFECT** Why did trading across continents become important to European merchants?

21. **MAKE INFERENCES** What do you think happened to the kingdom of Songhai as other kingdoms and empires arose in the region?

22. **DRAW CONCLUSIONS** In what way did the Crusades help weaken feudalism?

23. **FORM AND SUPPORT OPINIONS** Which South American, Mesoamerican, or North American civilization do you think was most advanced? Explain and support your answer.

INTERPRET MAPS

Look closely at this map of Vasco da Gama's voyage around Africa to reach India and return to Europe. Then answer the questions that follow.

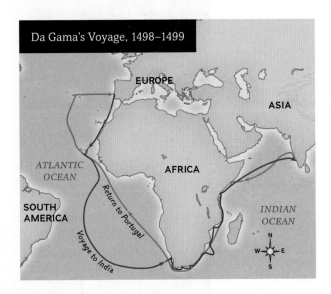

Da Gama's Voyage, 1498–1499

24. As you have read, overland trade routes were used for centuries to link Europe and Asia. Why did Vasco da Gama sail all the way around Africa to reach the same Asian trading centers?

25. Do you think Europeans who followed da Gama traded only with Indian merchants? What information on the map helped you answer the question?

ANALYZE SOURCES

Here is an account of an experience from Vasco da Gama's ship's log. The encounter he describes took place near the southern tip of Africa in 1498. Read the passage and answer the question.

> On the following day (November 10) fourteen or fifteen natives came to where our ships lay. The captain-major landed and showed them a variety of merchandise, with the view of finding out whether such things were to be found in their country. This merchandise included cinnamon, cloves, seed-pearls, gold, and many other things, but it was evident that they had no knowledge whatever of such articles, and they were consequently given round bells and tin rings.

26. Why do you think the captain-major wants to know if "such things were to be found in their country"?

CONNECT TO YOUR LIFE

27. **ARGUMENT** Think about the way trading across societies and continents affected the civilizations you have read about in this chapter. Today, nations still trade with one another. Does modern trade have the same cultural impact as it did 600 years ago or more? Write a paragraph stating your opinion, and offer reasons to support your opinion.

TIPS

- Look back on the chapter and list ways in which trading affected the cultures. Then think about how trade affects cultures today. What are the similarities and differences? Make notes and then review them to help you formulate your opinion.

- Include examples of similarities or differences to support your opinion. Use evidence from the text and two or three key terms from the chapter to make your point.

- Conclude your argument by restating your opinion and summarizing your reasoning.

CHAPTER **2**

EUROPEAN EXPLORATION OF
THE AMERICAS
1492–1650

ESSENTIAL QUESTION
What impact did European exploration have on the Americas?

 AMERICAN STORIES ONLINE **The Missions of New Mexico**

SECTION 1 **Spain Claims an Empire**
KEY VOCABULARY

conquistador	missionary	viceroy
mercantilism	smallpox	viceroyalty

SECTION 2 **Europe Fights Over North America**
KEY VOCABULARY

circumnavigate	Northwest Passage	privateer
galleon	persecute	watershed
heretic		

SECTION 3 **Spanish Rule in the Americas**
KEY VOCABULARY

Columbian Exchange	hacienda	mestizo	plantation
encomienda	immunity	mission	quinine

SECTION 4 **Slavery Begins in the Americas**
KEY VOCABULARY

African diaspora	institution	slavery
chattel slavery	Middle Passage	triangular trade

AMERICAN GALLERY ONLINE **The Inca Empire**

READING STRATEGY

DRAW CONCLUSIONS
Drawing conclusions between ideas and events in informational texts is important to building understanding. As you read this chapter, use a chart like this one to note specific details about how European exploration affected the Western Hemisphere.

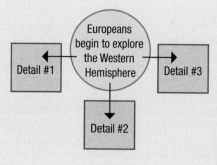

Europeans begin to explore the Western Hemisphere

Detail #1

Detail #2

Detail #3

"Set sail...
at 8 o'clock, and proceeded
with a strong breeze till sunset."
—Christopher Columbus

A reproduction of one of Columbus's ships sets
sail more than 500 years after that world-changing
voyage in 1492. Today, replicas of the *Niña* and the
Pinta make stops in ports along the East Coast, the
Great Lakes, and the Mississippi River as traveling
museums for visitors to enjoy.

1.1 The Age of Exploration

Imagine setting sail in a direction no one you know has ever gone. Would you be excited or scared? European explorers probably felt both as they set out without smartphones, GPS, or even accurate maps. Now, that's an adventure!

MAIN IDEA The search for a western route to Asia during the late 15th and early 16th centuries opened the Americas to European settlement.

The exact location where Christopher Columbus and his crew landed in October 1492 remains a mystery, but this sandy beach on the island of Samana Cay in the Bahamas might be one possibility. Scientists used Columbus's navigation log with computer modeling to determine his journey.

COLUMBUS SETS SAIL

In the 1440s, Portugal established trade on the West African coast. Seeing the success of the Portuguese, merchants from other countries also tried to participate. However, Pope Nicholas V gave Portugal sole possession of the African and Indian coasts in 1455.

King Ferdinand and **Queen Isabella** of Spain were determined to continue trading despite the pope's decree. They found a strong willed and obsessed navigator to search for a western route to Asia. **Christopher Columbus** gladly accepted the challenge for the Spanish monarchs. In October 1492, Columbus and his fleet of ships arrived in the Bahamas. As he traveled from island to island, he believed—incorrectly, of course—that he was exploring islands south of China. He encountered people called the **Taino** (TIE-noh) and received gold in return for his goods. Leaving a few men behind, Columbus set out for home in January 1493. When he returned a year later, he discovered that the Taino had killed all his crew after his men had abused and badly harmed them. The men's actions were the start of the mistreatment of Native Americans that would last for centuries.

Ferdinand and Isabella petitioned Pope Alexander VI to allow them to colonize the lands Columbus claimed for Spain. Spain's economy was based on **mercantilism**, a system in which countries kept the sole right to trade with their colonies. Under this system, more colonies equaled more wealth—and power.

In 1494, the **Treaty of Tordesillas** established a boundary—called the **Line of Demarcation**—that passed vertically through the Atlantic and present-day Brazil. The boundary gave Portugal a portion of South America to colonize, control of the sea routes around Africa, and control of the Atlantic slave trade. Spain received permission to colonize all of the land west of the line.

Both Portugal and Spain also sent **missionaries**, or people who travel to other places to spread their own religion, to these new lands. The two countries wanted to convert the people who lived there to Christianity.

EXPLORING NEW LANDS

As Europeans continued exploring lands in the Western Hemisphere, they realized that Columbus had not reached Asia. In 1499 and 1501, the Italian captain **Amerigo Vespucci** (uh-MEHR-ih-goh veh-SPOO-chee) made two voyages—one for Spain and one for Portugal. His explorations revealed that South America was a huge landmass, which he later named **Mundus Novus**, meaning "New World" in Latin. Of course, the land was only new to the Europeans; Native Americans had already been living there for centuries. Vespucci's explorations inspired a German cartographer to name the continents *America*, after Vespucci's given name, *Amerigo*.

In 1513, Vasco Núñez Balboa led explorers across the Isthmus of Panama, and they became the first Europeans to see the eastern rim of the Pacific Ocean. Balboa claimed everything he saw for Spain.

Six years later, Ferdinand Magellan departed Spain with five ships to sail around South America and on to Asia. But the Pacific Ocean was much wider than the navigator expected. By the time the ships reached the island of Guam, the sailors were near starvation. After inhabitants killed Magellan, another sailor, Sebastian del Cano, took command of the one remaining ship. He returned to Spain after a three-year voyage, completing the first navigation around the world.

The Controversy Over Columbus Day

Was Christopher Columbus a great explorer or a ruthless invader? The question is at the heart of the controversy over Columbus Day, an annual mid-October holiday that celebrates the explorer's "achievements."

Supporters of the holiday argue that Columbus opened two continents to trade and further settlement, forever changing the world. Opponents say the holiday glorifies a man who nearly destroyed the livelihood of the native peoples of the Americas. They argue instead for celebrating Indigenous Peoples Day to remember the native peoples lost through European colonization. Various city councils have replaced Columbus Day observances with celebrations of Indigenous Peoples Day. The state of South Dakota renamed the holiday Native Americans' Day.

HISTORICAL THINKING

1. **READING CHECK** Why did the Spanish want to find a western route to Asia?

2. **DRAW CONCLUSIONS** In what ways did the Treaty of Tordesillas support Spain's mercantilist economy?

3. **IDENTIFY MAIN IDEAS AND DETAILS** How did further exploration prove that Christopher Columbus had not landed in Asia?

1.2 Christopher Columbus 1451–1506

"By prevailing over all obstacles and distractions, one may unfailingly arrive at his chosen goal or destination." —Christopher Columbus

Of course, since Christopher Columbus's chosen goal was Asia, he didn't actually arrive at his destination. He got distracted by North America, which he confused with India. And Columbus didn't know that a group of Vikings led by Leif Eriksson got to North America more than 500 years before him. Still, in a very real sense, Columbus didn't fail at all. His discoveries and the impact they had were far greater than the route he set out to find.

EXPLORATION OBSESSION

Like many boys born in the coastal city of Genoa, Italy, in the 1400s, young Christopher Columbus sought his fortune on the sea. He first set sail in 1465, when he was just a teenager. About 10 years later, he was on a ship bound for the Mediterranean when the vessel was sunk by pirates. Luckily, Columbus was able to cling to a bit of wreckage from the ship and swim to shore.

Hero or villain? The debate over Columbus's legacy has raged, particularly over the last several decades. Whether he's seen as the discoverer of the New World or the destroyer of native peoples, the fact is that Columbus's voyages opened up the world. Our global society wouldn't exist without him.

With perhaps even greater luck, he ended up in Lisbon, Portugal, where the exploration craze was at its height. There, Columbus studied navigation, cartography (mapmaking), and astronomy, and became obsessed with finding a westward route to Asia. He also read accounts of the riches of the East and decided he would try to bring these precious items back to Europe.

Columbus planned his journey to Asia based on the misinformation that most Europeans of the time accepted as fact—including an underestimation of Earth's circumference. Based on what he thought he knew, Columbus calculated the distance from Portugal to Japan and determined that the seagoing vessels of the day could handle it. Plan in hand, he looked for a sponsor to fund his journey. He finally found his backers in King Ferdinand and Queen Isabella of Spain.

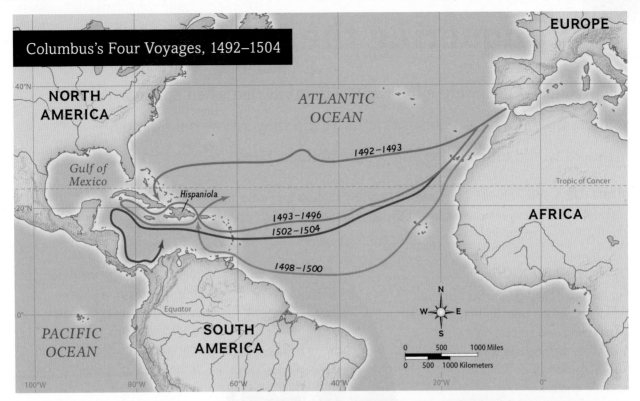

Columbus's Four Voyages, 1492–1504

EUROPE

NORTH AMERICA

ATLANTIC OCEAN

40°N

Gulf of Mexico

Tropic of Cancer

Hispaniola

1492–1493

1493–1496
1502–1504

AFRICA

20°N

1498–1500

Equator

0°

PACIFIC OCEAN

SOUTH AMERICA

N
W   E
S

0   500   1000 Miles
0   500   1000 Kilometers

100°W   80°W   60°W   40°W   20°W   0°

Portraits of Columbus

These three portraits of Columbus are very different because no one really knows what he looked like. But his contemporaries described him as a tall man with blond or red hair and beard and blue eyes.

VOYAGES TO THE "NEW WORLD"

On October 8, 1492, as Columbus neared the island he would call San Salvador, he declared "the air soft as that of Seville [a city in Spain] in April, and so fragrant that it was delicious to breathe it." It must have seemed a promising beginning, but his voyages did not turn out the way he hoped.

On the first voyage, he established a settlement on the island of Hispaniola. On the second voyage, he discovered the settlement had been destroyed. He left his two brothers in charge and then returned on his third voyage to find the colonists in revolt. The situation got so bad that a new governor was sent to the island, and Columbus was brought back to Spain in chains. Ferdinand and Isabella eventually pardoned him and even funded his fourth voyage. But he returned from this final trip empty-handed.

Columbus died a few years later, still believing he had found a route to Asia. No matter, though. While he hadn't discovered the riches he dreamed of, he had blazed a trail from Europe to what came to be known as the West Indies. He had opened up a "new world" to exploration and colonization and changed the course of history.

HISTORICAL THINKING

1. **READING CHECK** How did Columbus plan to sail to Asia?

2. **ANALYZE CAUSE AND EFFECT** What happened as a result of Columbus's voyages?

3. **MAKE INFERENCES** What qualities do you think Columbus must have possessed to plan and carry out his voyages?

Conquering the Aztec and Inca

The Aztec and Inca were more curious than worried when Spanish soldiers first arrived on horseback. Little did they know that Spanish invaders would enlist allies and topple both empires.

MAIN IDEA A variety of factors helped Spanish soldiers and adventurers conquer the Aztec and Inca empires in the 16th century.

INVADING MEXICO

For several decades, the Spanish had little interference from other Europeans in exploring and colonizing the Americas. **Conquistadors** (kon-KEE-stuh-dohrz), or Spanish soldiers and adventurers, conquered the native tribes of many Caribbean islands, claiming the lands for Spain. They then moved through present-day Mexico and Central America. By 1543, Spanish settlements extended south to Chile, north to present-day Florida, and west to California.

Hernán Cortés was one of the most successful conquistadors. In 1519, he launched an expedition into the vast Aztec Empire in Mexico. As Cortés and his small Spanish force moved toward the Aztec capital of Tenochtitlán (tay-nohch-teet-LAHN), they recruited allies from some Native American tribes that were dissatisfied with

Aztec rule. They seized the Aztec emperor **Moctezuma** (mahk-tuh-ZOO-muh), who believed the light-skinned, bearded Spaniards signaled the return of the Aztec god Quetzalcoatl (kwet-sul-kuh-WAH-tuhl). Some historians think this is one reason Cortés was able to capture Moctezuma.

Controlling Tenochtitlán proved more difficult. When the Spanish outlawed human sacrifice—an important part of Aztec religion—and demanded more gold, the Aztec rebelled. They forced the Spanish and their allies to retreat, killing many in the process. After Cortés regrouped, he returned in May 1521 with more Spanish troops and allies and laid siege to Tenochtitlán.

The Aztec fought bravely, even though they were already weakened by a deadly outbreak of a disease the Spanish carried, called **smallpox**. In the end, though, the Spanish destroyed the city of Tenochtitlán. Over time, the Spanish colonizers spread their culture throughout Mexico. In fact, the Spanish built Mexico City on the ruins of Tenochtitlán.

🏛 The Museum of Fine Arts, Houston

The Inca were spectacular artisans. This figure, fashioned from silver, copper, shell, and polished stone, dates from between 1200 and 1532. The Spanish melted most such figures to reuse the precious metals.

CONQVISTA DE MEXICO POR CORTES. C7

PIZARRO'S QUEST FOR GOLD

When the Spanish arrived in the Americas, the Inca already controlled a powerful empire stretching along the Andes Mountains in South America. Stories of Inca gold and silver interested the Spanish conquistador **Francisco Pizarro**. So in the 1530s, with around 180 men and a small number of horses, Pizarro set out from Panama to conquer the Inca.

In 1532, the Inca emperor **Atahualpa** invited Pizarro and his men to a meeting in the northern part of present-day Peru. At the meeting, Atahualpa and Pizarro exchanged gifts to show goodwill toward each other. Atahualpa was confident that the presence of his 6,000 warriors would discourage Pizarro from attacking. But the emperor was wrong.

Pizarro's men opened fire on the mostly unarmed Inca and took Atahualpa prisoner. Atahualpa offered Pizarro gold and silver, which Pizarro took. Then he had Atahualpa killed. By 1537, the Spanish had crushed Inca opposition.

Several factors helped the Spanish conquer the Aztec and the Inca. Smallpox and other European diseases killed or weakened many Aztec, Inca, and Native Americans. The Spanish were masterful at forming alliances with Native American groups, especially with tribes opposing the Aztec. Aztec and Inca weapons were no match for the guns and swift horses of the Spanish. Finally, the Spanish used violence and forced labor to control Native American populations and put down revolts.

HISTORICAL THINKING

1. **READING CHECK** What was the goal of the Spanish conquistadors?

2. **ANALYZE CAUSE AND EFFECT** What factors helped the Spanish defeat the Aztec and Inca?

3. **DRAW CONCLUSIONS** What might have led Aztec and Inca leaders to underestimate the Spanish invaders?

1.4 Conquistadors in the North

When conquistadors eager for riches, power, and fame heard news of Cortés's and Pizarro's triumphs, they may have thought to themselves, "How hard could it be?" As it turned out, it was pretty hard.

MAIN IDEA Conquistadors exploring North America in the 1540s were less successful than Cortés and Pizarro.

EXPLORERS REACH FLORIDA

In their search for wealth and new lands, the Spanish did not limit their American explorations to Mesoamerica and South America. Soon they set their sights northward. **Álvar Núñez** (NOO-nyez) **Cabeza de Vaca** was part of an expedition that sailed from Spain in 1527 aiming to claim North America for the king. After he and his fellow voyagers landed on the west coast of present-day Florida, they marched north through insect- and snake-infested swamps. They kidnapped a Native American chief, which triggered an attack from his people. They fled on hastily built rafts, quickly became lost in the Gulf of Mexico, and were captured by Native Americans after a hurricane washed them up on an island near the western shore of the Gulf.

After befriending and living with their captors for several years, de Vaca and three others escaped. They traveled west, passing through southwestern deserts all the way to the Gulf of California. Finally, they encountered other Spaniards near the Pacific coast of Mexico in 1536. De Vaca later commented that on that day the men were "dumbfounded at the sight of me, strangely dressed and in the company of Indians." In his tales, de Vaca mentioned the possibility of riches to the north, which inspired more explorers to try their luck. He returned to Spain the next year and became a governor and judge, standing up for better treatment of Native Americans.

In 1539, **Hernando de Soto**, the governor of Cuba, launched a three-year expedition through the southeast part of North America. His expedition also landed on the west coast of Florida and then trekked northward on foot. The group traveled through the Southeast to the Tennessee River Valley and then turned south toward the Gulf of Mexico, destroying Native American communities, stealing from them, and enslaving or killing people who resisted them. De Soto caught a fever and died in 1542, and the survivors of the expedition returned to Spain.

THE SEARCH FOR GOLDEN CITIES

As the Spanish explored and conquered new lands in the Americas, they set up a system to rule these faraway places. **Viceroys** were colonial leaders who were appointed by the king. Viceroys governed **viceroyalties**, or territories in the Americas "owned" by Spain.

In 1540, the viceroy of one of these territories, **New Spain,** ordered **Francisco Vásquez de Coronado** to lead an expedition of 336 Spaniards and nearly 1,000 Native Americans through the American Southwest. The expedition was to search for the golden cities described in Native American legends.

Conquistador Spur
This sparkling spur is similar to those worn by Spanish explorers on their boots to control their horses. It is an early version of the types of spurs some American cowboys wear today.

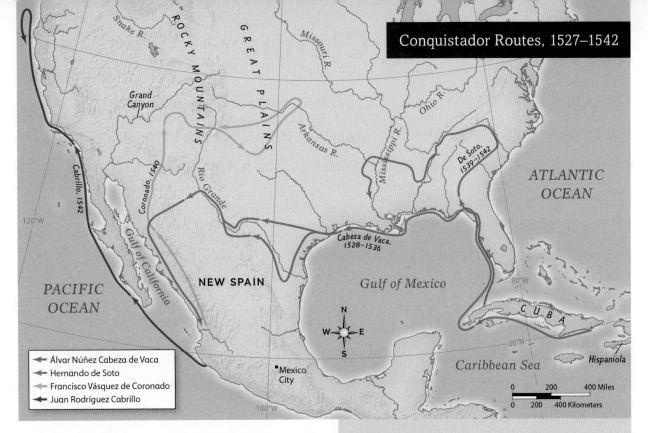

Conquistador Routes, 1527–1542

Álvar Núñez Cabeza de Vaca
Hernando de Soto
Francisco Vásquez de Coronado
Juan Rodríguez Cabrillo

Traveling through the Southwest and the Great Plains, Coronado and his men saw and experienced many things not known to the Spanish before. They encountered the Hopi, Native Americans who lived in the Southwest. They also saw giant herds of buffalo, and some of the party stood on the rim of the Grand Canyon. But they found no gold. They returned to Mexico empty-handed.

Two years later, **Juan Rodríguez Cabrillo** (kuh-BREE-yoh) led a voyage of exploration north from Mexico along the California coast in search of a northern water route from the Pacific to the Atlantic Ocean. His expedition may have traveled as far as the Pacific Northwest before turning back south, but he never returned home. He died from injuries received in a battle with Native Americans, and his crew brought his ships back to Mexico.

None of these conquistadors found cities of gold or riches. Despite these failures, Europeans' interest in claiming land in the Americas continued. As you will learn, these interests would lead to international tensions and even war.

Cities of Gold

De Soto, de Vaca, Coronado, and Cabrillo explored a great deal of southern North America. De Soto hunted the southeastern forests of North America for Cofitachiqui (koh-FEE-tah-CHEE-kee), a rich Native American city. De Vaca and his shipmates searched the Southwest looking for a kingdom called Cíbola (SEE-bow-lah). Coronado also searched for Cíbola in lands farther north on the southern Great Plains. Cabrillo hoped to find wealthy civilizations as he sailed along the California coast. In the end, none of these explorers found what they were looking for because the rumored cities of gold had never existed.

HISTORICAL THINKING

1. **READING CHECK** Why weren't Spanish explorations successful in North America?

2. **ANALYZE CAUSE AND EFFECT** What social impact did conquistadors have on native populations of the American Southwest and Southeast?

3. **INTERPRET MAPS** Look at the routes of the conquistadors on the map. What is one common feature of each of these expeditions?

Competing Claims

You're probably used to friendly competitions in your classroom or among friends. For European countries in the 1500s, however, intense competition for land and resources in North America led to some not-so-friendly conflicts.

MAIN IDEA Struggles arose in Europe when other countries challenged the claims Spain and Portugal had made in the Americas.

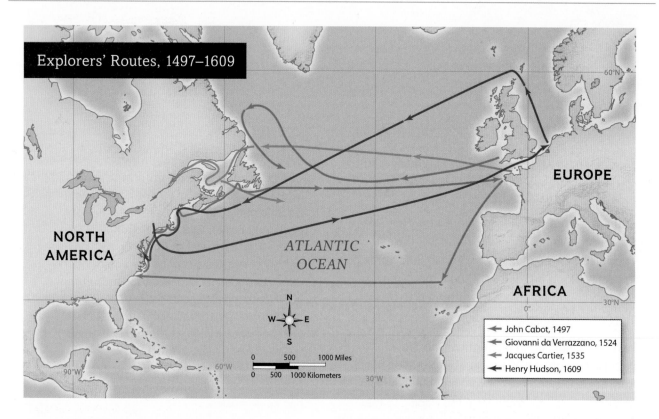

Explorers' Routes, 1497–1609

← John Cabot, 1497
← Giovanni da Verrazzano, 1524
← Jacques Cartier, 1535
← Henry Hudson, 1609

THE NORTHWEST PASSAGE

European kings and queens hoped to find a water route to Asia through the Western Hemisphere. Several monarchs sent explorers to find such a route, or a **Northwest Passage**. In 1497, King Henry VII of England commissioned the Italian navigator **John Cabot**. Cabot left the harbor at Bristol, England, and sailed to Newfoundland, in present-day Canada, where he claimed land for the king. France sent another Italian, **Giovanni da Verrazzano**, to the Americas in January 1524. His ship *La Dauphine* landed near Cape Fear, North Carolina, and continued north along the coast to Newfoundland.

Ten years later, French seafarer **Jacques Cartier** explored the coast of Canada and the St. Lawrence River three different times. His interactions with the Native Americans there led to the name *Canada*. The name is derived from the Huron-Iroquois word *kanata*, meaning "village or settlement."

After voyaging to the Americas twice for England, an explorer named **Henry Hudson** made his final trip in 1609—this time for the Dutch in the Netherlands. Hudson sailed along the Atlantic coast after failing to navigate the Arctic Ocean. Today, a river, a strait, and a bay carry his name.

Just as the conquistadors who searched for golden cities failed, none of these explorers found what they were looking for: a western route to Asia. However, the knowledge gained from these explorations did prove useful. It aided the countries when they later laid claim to land in North America.

TENSIONS GROW

While explorers searched for a Northwest Passage, religious and political unrest grew in Europe. The Spanish were already angry with the French and English for claiming lands in the New World. Tensions increased when France and England challenged Catholicism, the dominant faith in Spain.

As you have read, the Reformation began in 1517 when a German monk named Martin Luther accused the Catholic Church of corruption. At the time, Catholic priests were selling indulgences, which forgave sins in exchange for money. In response, Luther put together a document called the 95 Theses, which pointed out the Church's hypocritical and greedy practices. Luther's teachings divided European Christians, as some common people and rulers alike adopted his Protestant beliefs. Some of Luther's followers formed the branch of Protestantism that now bears his name: Lutheranism. The Catholic Church officially excluded him from Church rituals and membership. In addition, the Catholic Church **persecuted**, or punished, all followers of Protestantism.

One Protestant group, the French Huguenots, looked to the Americas for refuge. They tried settling in Brazil and South Carolina before founding a colony near St. Augustine, Florida, around 1564. This enraged Spain's **King Philip II**, but not only because he was Catholic. The Huguenots had chosen South Carolina with the intention of attacking Spanish ships carrying silver. It was not enough that they were **heretics**, or people who held beliefs different from teachings of the Catholic Church. Philip perceived them as a menace. The king sent General Pedro Menéndez de Avilés to remove the Huguenot colony. After a brief encounter at sea, Menéndez captured the French settlement at Fort Caroline. Most of the men who refused to return to Catholicism were killed.

🏛 The Cleveland Museum of Art, Cleveland

Looking at this gold, enamel, and citrine cameo, it may be hard to believe that King Philip II was actually in financial trouble during his reign. When he took the throne in 1556, he assumed the kingdom's debt. The debt only grew as Philip waged war after war and built a lavish palace. Eventually, Philip's spending would be a factor in the fall of the Spanish Empire.

King Philip II of Spain

HISTORICAL THINKING

1. **READING CHECK** What was Spain's response to the claims of other European countries in North America?

2. **INTERPRET MAPS** Based on the sea routes shown on the map, which countries were likely competing over land claims in the Western Hemisphere?

3. **DRAW CONCLUSIONS** How did the Protestant Reformation influence European relations in the Americas?

2.2 Defeat of the Spanish Armada

Fans of any sport love a major upset. In much the same way, when England's small but mighty fleet of ships defeated Spain in 1588, the world took notice.

MAIN IDEA Because of England's strong naval fleet, an English victory at sea challenged Spanish dominance in Europe and the Americas.

MONARCHS AND SEA DOGS

Spain had a head start on settling North America, but England started to catch up, largely because of **Queen Elizabeth I**. The Protestant queen ascended to the English throne in 1558. She saw Spain as a threat to England's independence. Her brother-in-law, Philip II of Spain, like many Catholics, wished to see Elizabeth unseated from the throne. He supported Mary, Queen of Scots, Elizabeth's Catholic cousin and the heir to the English throne. But after being implicated in a plot to take Elizabeth's life, Mary was arrested, tried, and beheaded for conspiracy.

Both Philip and Elizabeth had powerful navies. Spain's fleet was made up of large, full-rigged sailing ships called **galleons**, mainly used to transport goods from the Americas. They were heavily armed, but their cannons weren't secured to the deck, which made these large weapons difficult to reload and discharge.

By contrast, English ships were nimble. They carried fewer goods and soldiers, but their mounted artillery was more quickly discharged. English ships were also fast, and their sailors, the **Sea Dogs**, appreciated this quality.

Perhaps the most famous of these sailors was Francis Drake. Drake and other Sea Dogs were **privateers**, or seafarers licensed by a monarch to attack enemy ships. Drake sailed the world stealing treasure from Spanish ports and ships. He and his crew were the first Englishmen to **circumnavigate**, or sail around, the globe.

ENGLISH VICTORY

Under the leadership of Elizabeth I, England challenged Spain's claims to the Western Hemisphere. England supported the Dutch revolt against Philip II. When part of the Netherlands declared its independence from Spain and became the United Provinces in 1585, Elizabeth sent aid there. In doing so, she was essentially declaring war on Spain.

King Philip sent his "invincible" navy to conquer England in May 1588. The **Spanish Armada** was a fleet of about 130 warships. Knowing their vessels

Queen Elizabeth I
In a society where women rarely held any political authority, Elizabeth ruled as a popular, strong, and capable monarch. During the 45 years of her reign, England prospered and became one of the most powerful nations in history. In this portrait, painted around 1588, the English fleet appears behind Elizabeth, likely an acknowledgment of England's increasing naval power.

were slower and had fewer and smaller cannons than the English, the Spanish captains hoped to take advantage of their own greater numbers. Their plan was to have their men board the enemy ships and defeat the English in hand-to-hand combat.

Stormy weather delayed the armada. This gave English admiral Charles Howard, commander of England's fleet, a chance to join up with Francis Drake's advance force. England's fleet had smaller ships and fewer soldiers, but its superior speed and artillery demolished the Spanish. Many thousands of Spanish men were killed, while England lost several hundred. With only 60 ships remaining, the Spanish returned home in shame.

The defeat of the Spanish Armada was a blow to Spain's position as the dominant world power in both Europe and the New World. Through its victory, England ensured its own continued independence from foreign domination while preserving the Netherlands' United Provinces.

Spain's power weakened further as Sea Dogs continued to harass Spanish vessels and ports. At the same time, Protestant sects in Europe and later in the New World would continue to challenge the supremacy of Spain and the pope on colonization and commerce. Spain found itself on the defensive.

HISTORICAL THINKING

1. **READING CHECK** What political changes did England's defeat of the Spanish Armada bring to Europe?

2. **COMPARE AND CONTRAST** What were the different advantages and disadvantages of the Spanish and English ships?

3. **DRAW CONCLUSIONS** How did the Spanish captains' strategy to combat the English fleet lead to their own defeat?

CRITICAL VIEWING French artist Philippe-Jacques de Loutherbourg painted *Defeat of the Spanish Armada, 8 August 1588* in 1796. How does the artist use color to show the drama of the battle?

2.3 French and Dutch Colonies

If you visit a coffee shop in Burlington, Vermont, you might see a menu that has both French and English descriptions. Walk around New York City and you'll see Dutch names for streets. Different languages and names are the remnants of European exploration in the 17th century.

MAIN IDEA The French and Dutch claimed North American lands as rich sources of trade and wealth, but they had trouble establishing colonies.

OUTPOSTS IN NEW FRANCE

In 1608, explorer and cartographer **Samuel de Champlain** established a fur-trading base at a point along the St. Lawrence River that became the first permanent French settlement in North America. For two decades, Champlain explored the **watershed** lands, or the area drained by rivers, surrounding his post. As he explored, he strengthened trading ties with the Huron, the Algonquian, and the Montagnai. Champlain also allied with these Native Americans against the Iroquois. Champlain's new trading partners brought him valuable furs, which he then shipped to Europe to be sold. Hearing of Champlain's success, other French traders joined him. This system resulted in an international fur trade so robust the country claimed the region, naming it **New France**.

Population growth in New France was slow. Twenty years after Champlain began his business, the post, which was later named Quebec (kuh-BEK), was home to only about 100 people. By comparison, Jamestown, Virginia, grew from 105 people at its founding in 1607 to 1,240 people in 1622.

In an effort to encourage French people to settle in New France, Champlain's company expanded its charter to include lands from Florida to the Arctic. The company sent Jesuit priests to Native American villages in the hope of learning their languages and converting them to Christianity in accordance with France's Catholic beliefs. However, the French government's refusal to allow Protestants, the most likely immigrants, to settle in the Americas kept the outposts' populations small.

Another factor limiting population growth in New France was its social structure. France was still a feudal society, and settlers brought this system to the Western Hemisphere. Large manors belonged to wealthy settlers. All others worked as tenant farmers. Peasants living in France saw little chance to improve their status in the Americas, where they still could not own and work their own land.

CONFLICT IN NEW NETHERLAND

As you have read, Henry Hudson was searching for a passage to Asia through North America when he discovered the river that would bear his name in what is today New York State. On behalf of the Dutch, Hudson sailed up the river, trading European knives and beads for furs from the Native Americans. The pelts brought a good price in Holland, the Dutch homeland, which is also known as the Netherlands. Traders responded by setting up a post near Albany, New York. In 1614, the Dutch built **Fort Nassau** in that same area. Like the French, the Dutch cooperated with local tribes to establish a thriving fur trade, and the colony of **New Netherland** was established.

The Dutch purchased the island of Manhattan from Native Americans in 1626. They developed the community of New Amsterdam, named for the capital of the Netherlands, but there was a misunderstanding. The Native Americans believed they had sold rights to share the land and could continue using it themselves. The Dutch believed they had purchased exclusive rights to the land. By 1640, the Dutch and the Native Americans were at war over the misunderstanding.

Manhattan, New York

Long before skyscrapers towered above its shores, members of the Lenape tribe lived on this island at the mouth of the Hudson River. They called it Mannahatta, "the island of many hills." Compare and contrast the two views of Manhattan shown below. The photo on top is a computer model that suggests what the island might have looked like when Henry Hudson arrived in 1609. The photo at the bottom shows Manhattan 400 years later, in 2009. Manhattan is a borough of New York City, which is the largest city by population in the United States.

The conflict over Manhattan represented a larger issue. Native American tribes, such as the Abenaki and Powhatan, had been living in eastern North America for centuries before Europeans arrived. English settlements in New England and near Chesapeake Bay were agricultural societies, while the French, Dutch, and Swedes focused on trade. Conflicts over land arose between Europeans and Native Americans in these areas. Different European groups sometimes involved Native American trading partners in their arguments over trading opportunities. Some disputes ended in violence. Additionally, many Native Americans succumbed to European diseases, resulting in a decrease in their populations.

HISTORICAL THINKING

1. **READING CHECK** How did explorers influence international trade during the 17th century?

2. **FORM AND SUPPORT OPINIONS** In your opinion, what could the French have done differently to attract settlers and grow the population of New France? Support your opinion with evidence from the text.

3. **INTERPRET VISUALS** What physical features might have made Mannahatta an attractive place for the Dutch to build a community?

3.1 Spanish Colonial Rule

Imagine invaders from far away taking over your town. They would know little about your culture and would likely try to change it. When the Spanish claimed territory in the Americas, they forced a number of social and economic changes, many of which were far from positive.

MAIN IDEA Spanish colonial social and agricultural practices in the Americas had a dramatic effect on Native American cultures.

A SOCIAL PYRAMID

As you have read, to control such a huge and distant territory in the Americas, the king of Spain divided it into two viceroyalties. Viceroys governed New Spain and Peru from their capitals, Mexico City and Lima, respectively.

Society in Spanish colonies was hierarchical, or organized like a pyramid. Spanish-born people and their American-born children, called Creoles, were the smallest but most powerful group. **Mestizos** (mes-TEE-zohs), people of mixed Spanish and Native American ancestry, occupied the middle part of society. Native Americans and enslaved Africans were the least powerful but most numerous group.

The Spanish government gave the wealthiest Spanish colonists **haciendas** (hah-see-EHN-dah), or tracts of land to farm. On Caribbean islands, most haciendas were sugarcane **plantations**, or large farms. Sugarcane was an important crop from which colonists made sugar and molasses, which they traded with Europe.

With the hacienda came an **encomienda** (en-coe-mee-AYN-dah), a grant to owners of a certain number of Native American laborers. In return for their labor, the Native Americans received protection from enemies, but never any payment. Native Americans had little power within this social and labor system. Additionally, so many Native Americans died from working in hot and dangerous conditions that the Spanish began to import enslaved Africans to replace them.

IMPACT OF THE CHURCH

The Catholic Church played a major role in Spanish colonization by establishing hundreds of **missions**, or religious settlements, in the Americas. Priests and missionaries wanted to convert Native Americans to Christianity and they also taught skills such as masonry and carpentry.

Some priests brutally punished those who would not adopt Spanish culture. **Bartolomé de Las Casas**, a Spanish priest himself, wrote about the abuses of Native Americans that he'd witnessed. He convinced the Spanish king to pass laws to protect Native Americans from mistreatment, but landowners forced the reversal of those laws.

In 1680, a Pueblo leader named **Popé** led a revolt in present-day New Mexico and drove the Spanish from the area. Popé freed the region of Spanish influence, but Spain restored its control after his death in 1692. By 1700, Spain controlled much of the Americas and remained a powerful presence and a major social influence into the 1800s.

HISTORICAL THINKING

1. **READING CHECK** Who were the mestizos and where did they fit in Spanish colonial society?

2. **COMPARE AND CONTRAST** How did the encomienda and mission systems compare?

3. **ANALYZE CAUSE AND EFFECT** How did the Spanish mission system affect Native American societies?

Carmel Mission, California

Founded in 1771, Carmel Mission served as the center of the Catholic mission system in California until 1834. Its founder, Father Junipero Serra, dedicated his life to building seven more missions in California. Today, visitors to the mission can tour an exhibit of his living quarters.

Genetics, Disease, and Native Americans

"The impact that science has on the world around us is something I'm enthralled with." —Pardis Sabeti

Meet National Geographic Explorer **Pardis Sabeti**. She is a research scientist, a musician, a teacher, and a volleyball player. She also doesn't sleep much. When Sabeti is not teaching a class at Harvard University, you might find her analyzing data in her lab, playing bass with her band, collecting virus samples in West Africa, or using mathematics to understand the latest epidemic.

∧
Pardis Sabeti, shown here in her Harvard University lab, loves to engage with her students and collaborate with colleagues all over the world to prevent major outbreaks of deadly diseases.

MAIN IDEA Modern scientific research can help explain how diseases from Europe impacted Native Americans in North America.

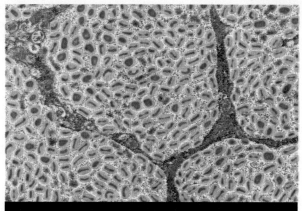
Doctors dread seeing the smallpox virus, shown here, in patients. Smallpox is highly contagious and could cause a major human catastrophe if uncontrolled.

REFUGEE TO RESEARCH SCIENTIST

When Pardis Sabeti was two years old, she and her family escaped Iran just before its 1979 revolution and settled in Florida. In school, Sabeti learned that she loved math. That's right: math. She followed her interests into medical school, where she fell in love with research and data analysis. That's right: research and data analysis.

While in graduate school, Sabeti developed a pathbreaking algorithm, or a procedure for solving a problem or analyzing data using a computer. She used this algorithm to analyze a specific gene, or the part of a cell that controls growth, appearance, and traits. She knew she'd made a great discovery. She recalls, "I realized I'd found a trait that had to be the result of natural selection—a trait that likely helped the population I was looking at cope with malaria better than others. It was an amazing feeling because at that moment I knew something about how people evolved that nobody else knew."

Today, Sabeti specializes in the study of infectious diseases, or diseases that spread from person to person. She uses mathematical and computer science tools to analyze the different ways diseases change over time and how they influence changes in human biology. Sabeti works in her lab at Harvard University and in countries impacted by diseases such as malaria and Lassa fever.

UNDERSTANDING DISEASE

Sabeti's research has an urgency, and it's risky. Recently, she led a research team during an outbreak of Ebola in Sierra Leone, a country in West Africa. She and her colleagues determined that the Ebola virus actually spread through human-to-human contact, not from contact with bats or other animals. This knowledge helped health professionals stop, or at least slow down, the epidemic and save many lives.

Her research also reveals how infectious diseases have been some of the most important factors in human history. According to Sabeti, more soldiers have died of infections or from exposure to new climates—and therefore new diseases—than from battle itself. Disease also played an enormous role when Europeans and Native Americans came into contact with each other. Europeans brought diseases to North America, including tuberculosis and smallpox. Europeans likely had inherited immunity, or a genetic protection, against these diseases. But Native Americans had not yet been exposed to them. Smallpox, especially, ravaged Native American populations. This disease also became a weapon of war when European colonizers realized the effect that blankets infected with smallpox could have on native populations.

If you ask Sabeti what she most enjoys about her work, she'd likely respond with more than one answer. She's inspired by colleagues in Africa researching the treatment and prevention of Lassa fever. She thrives on working with her students in classes and in the lab. And she's thrilled to be utilizing her skills in math, research, and data analysis to help develop new treatments for devastating diseases like malaria, a disease that kills more than 1 million people every year.

HISTORICAL THINKING

1. **READING CHECK** What kind of research does Pardis Sabeti do?

2. **SUMMARIZE** In what ways have infectious diseases shaped human history?

3. **MAKE INFERENCES** In what ways might understanding how diseases change over time help doctors prevent future epidemics?

3.3 The Columbian Exchange

One of the best parts about traveling to different places is encountering new and unusual foods, plants, and animals. Beginning in the 1500s, European explorers and colonists encountered and introduced hundreds of new and amazing things.

MAIN IDEA The Columbian Exchange was a significant biological event that changed societies and environments around the world.

TWO WORLDS CONNECT

Millions of years ago, the landmasses of North and South America were connected to Eurasia and Africa. Over time, they drifted far apart and an ocean filled the gap between them. The two hemispheres developed in isolation from each other, resulting in distinct plants and animals evolving in each half of the world. Farmers in the two hemispheres developed and planted different crops and raised different livestock.

The European encounter with the Americas coincided with improved methods of sea travel and the desire to explore and conquer new lands. The combined impact was enormous. Places and people that were once isolated from one another became part of a global exchange network. The contact and trade between these far-flung lands helped some people—and harmed others.

When Europeans crossed the Atlantic in 1492, they carried more than just their ideas—they also brought plants and animals. As they prepared to sail home, they packed new plants and animals they found in the Americas to introduce to the people of Europe. This period of biological mixing between the New World of the Americas and the Old World of Europe, Africa, and Asia is known as the **Columbian Exchange** —named after Christopher Columbus. This momentous swap of biological matter had major economic and social effects in the Americas, both good and bad.

Some of the species the Europeans introduced to the Americas caused significant environmental changes. For example, the Spanish transported livestock, including cattle, horses, sheep, and goats, to the Americas. These animals' roaming and grazing habits altered native landscapes. Europeans also slashed and burned forests to clear lands for farming.

Additionally, Europeans introduced deadly new diseases to the Western Hemisphere. Because they had already encountered diseases such as smallpox, Europeans had developed an **immunity**, or a natural protection, to those diseases. They could even carry the diseases without showing symptoms or appearing sick.

Native Americans had not been exposed to European diseases, so they did not have immunity to them. Epidemics of smallpox, influenza, measles, and other diseases spread quickly after Europeans arrived in the Americas. Between 1519 and 1565, the native population of Central America fell from about 25 million to 2.5 million due to disease alone. Within three centuries of Columbus's landing, about 90 percent of the Native American population had died of disease.

CHANGES FOR THE BETTER

Not all of the consequences of the Columbian Exchange were so negative, however. The great transatlantic swap introduced positive things to both sides. Europeans imported pigs, chickens, and other domesticated animals and brought horses with them, which Native Americans incorporated into their cultures. Europeans also introduced new crops to the Americas. Wheat, barley, rye, rice, and cotton were some of the plants introduced to the Western Hemisphere.

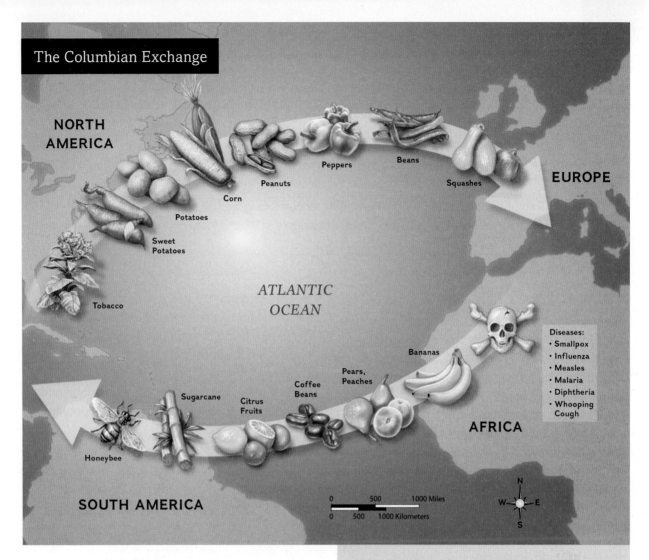

The Columbian Exchange

NORTH AMERICA

Corn
Peanuts
Peppers
Beans
Squashes

EUROPE

Potatoes
Sweet Potatoes
Tobacco

ATLANTIC OCEAN

Diseases:
• Smallpox
• Influenza
• Measles
• Malaria
• Diphtheria
• Whooping Cough

Bananas
Pears, Peaches
Coffee Beans
Citrus Fruits
Sugarcane
Honeybee

AFRICA

SOUTH AMERICA

0   500   1000 Miles
0   500   1000 Kilometers

Other crops included bananas, coffee beans, and sugarcane, all of which grew especially well in Central and South America.

The Western Hemisphere also contributed an important medicine called **quinine** to Europe, Africa, and Asia. Europeans learned about quinine, which comes from the bark of a tree in South America, in the 1600s. For about 300 years, it served as the only effective remedy for malaria, which is carried by mosquitoes. Quinine's use as a treatment for malaria benefited millions of people, but it allowed Europeans to later colonize malaria-ridden areas of the world.

The Columbian Exchange affected the lives of people throughout the world. Some changes were positive, such as improved nutrition because of a greater variety of foods. However, the effect of the Columbian Exchange on native populations in the Americas was disastrous.

More Options, New Troubles

The exchange of crops and animals increased agricultural options and enriched diets on the continents of Europe, North America, Africa, and South America. Some elements of the exchange, such as tobacco and a host of European diseases, were not as positive.

HISTORICAL THINKING

1. **READING CHECK** Why was the Columbian Exchange such an important phenomenon in world history?

2. **INTERPRET MAPS** Based on what you notice on the map, what foods do you enjoy today that originated in the Americas?

3. **DRAW CONCLUSIONS** Which hemisphere benefited most from the Columbian Exchange and why?

4.1 A New Kind of Slavery

Hundreds of newly enslaved people chained together so they can barely move sounds horrifying, because it was. In the 1600s, Europeans seeking wealth in the Americas turned to an ancient and brutal practice: slavery.

MAIN IDEA Demand for labor in Europe and the Americas drove the development of a new kind of slavery, beginning with the capture of people in West Africa.

A NEW FORM OF SLAVERY

Slavery is a social system in which human beings take complete control of others. It has existed throughout human history. In ancient societies around the world, prisoners of war were a main source of slaves. People also bonded themselves into slavery to pay off debts. Such slaves rarely stayed in bondage all their lives. They could usually buy or work for their freedom, and many of them had certain legal rights. Their children almost never became slaves themselves.

However, during European colonization of the Americas, a new kind of slavery developed. Under **chattel slavery**, people were classified as goods with virtually no human rights. Their bondage—and that of their children—was permanent.

Chattel slavery originated in the mid-1400s when the Portuguese started to trade with West African kingdoms for slaves

to work on sugar plantations. Kingdoms such as Dahomey and Ashanti became powerful centers of slave trade commerce, partly by capturing people in raids on inland villages. Raiders marched captives in chains to the coast and locked them in holding pens. The slave traders exchanged goods for the newly enslaved people and shipped them across the Atlantic.

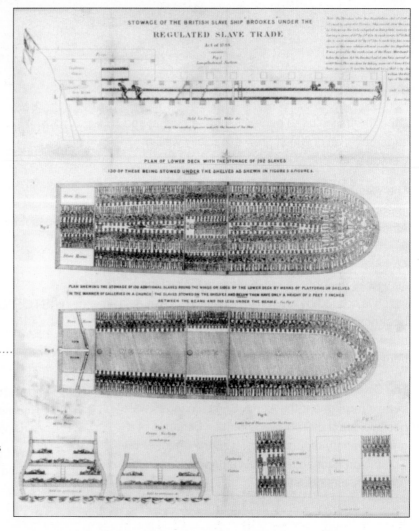

Slave Ship Diagram
The slave trade involved a lot of money and investment on the part of slave traders, merchants, and ship captains. This slave ship diagram shows the precise planning that went into transporting humans across the Atlantic Ocean.

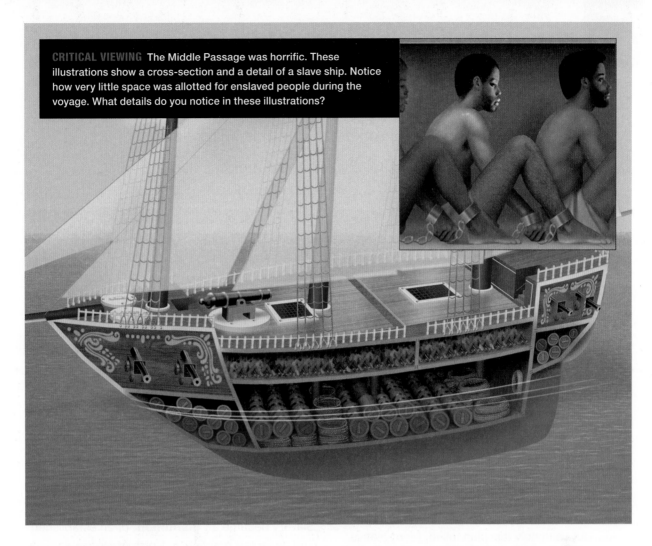

CRITICAL VIEWING The Middle Passage was horrific. These illustrations show a cross-section and a detail of a slave ship. Notice how very little space was allotted for enslaved people during the voyage. What details do you notice in these illustrations?

THE TRIANGULAR TRADE

As you read earlier in this chapter, the Columbian Exchange transformed the Americas and Europe through a massive transfer of plants, animals, and diseases. Another exchange also transformed the Americas, only this one included humans as goods. This exchange formed part of the **triangular trade**, a three-part system of trade that connected Europe, Africa, and the Americas during the 17th and 18th centuries.

In the first leg of the triangular trade route, traders from Europe brought goods to West Africa to exchange for captured and enslaved Africans. The second and most infamous leg was the **Middle Passage**. Slave traders forced enslaved Africans onto ships where they were confined in sickening, often fatal conditions. The 5,000-mile voyage took from three weeks to three months. Approximately 10 to 15 percent of the people held captive on slave ships died of disease or despair before reaching the Americas.

Once the ships reached port, the captured Africans were sold again or traded for goods. On the third leg of the voyage, ships loaded with products from the Americas returned to Europe, and the pattern repeated.

The triangular trade lasted until the slave trade was abolished in the early 1800s. Meanwhile, the people who were captured, transported, and sold were unlikely ever to taste freedom again.

HISTORICAL THINKING

1. **READING CHECK** How was chattel slavery different from most forms of slavery practiced in ancient societies?

2. **SUMMARIZE** What was the triangular trade?

3. **INTEGRATE VISUALS** How would you describe the Middle Passage? Use details from the illustrations and the text in your description.

4.2 The Growth of Slavery

In 2015, author Ta-Nehisi Coates described enslaved Africans as "people turned to fuel for the American machine." The slave labor system that Europeans established in the Americas had an enormous human cost.

MAIN IDEA European access to African slave labor paved the way for the growth of slave labor in the Americas and the expansion of the slave trade.

SLAVERY IN THE AMERICAS

The encomienda and hacienda systems established in Spain's American colonies encouraged the growth of sugar plantations in the West Indies and set the stage for the growth of slavery in North America. These plantations supplied the European market with sugar, and they required a considerable workforce in order to grow and process enough sugarcane to make a profit.

At first, the Spanish forced the islands' Native American populations to work in the sugarcane fields, but ultimately this plan failed. Many Native Americans died of European diseases, while others escaped their bondage.

The inability to force Native Americans into slavery led Spain to turn to Africa as a source of captive labor. At first, the Spanish bought Africans who had been enslaved on the Portuguese plantations. Soon, however, they began buying enslaved Africans directly from West Africa. By the end of the 1500s, 75,000 enslaved Africans were working on Spanish plantations in the Caribbean. The North American slave trade expanded from there.

FAR FROM HOME

Europeans began to buy and ship so many people to the Americas that West African slave hunters had to travel farther into the continent in order to capture and enslave more people to meet the demand. The forced march to the coast was even longer and more brutal, and many people died before they even boarded a ship. Because the slave raiders captured the youngest and most productive members of inland societies, the transatlantic slave trade devastated entire cultures and economies in Africa.

Altogether, the slave trade between Africa and the Americas lasted for about 400 years. From the 16th to the 19th century, traders shipped between 7 and 10 million people to the Western Hemisphere. The removal of so many Africans from their homeland to the Americas is known as the **African diaspora**.

Slavery became an **institution**, or an established and accepted practice, in North America, particularly in the Southern Colonies and then in the new nation, the United States. The international slave trade ended in 1807, and the United States abolished slavery completely in 1865. There is no doubt that slavery as an institution shaped the social, economic, and cultural development of the United States and that it still casts its shadow today.

HISTORICAL THINKING

1. **READING CHECK** How did the slave trade change as demand for African slaves grew?

2. **MAKE INFERENCES** In what ways did the African diaspora change the population of the African continent?

3. **DRAW CONCLUSIONS** How did Portuguese slave trading off the western coast of Africa help contribute to the development of slavery in the Americas?

The Jamaica Train

When sugar refining first began, enslaved workers used four vats of decreasing size called the Jamaica Train. One of the most dangerous jobs on a sugar plantation was boiling the sugarcane water in vats like the ones shown here. When enough liquid had evaporated from one vat, the water was ladled into the next, smaller, vat. The process occurred two more times with more batches following. Enslaved workers had to move quickly so that all the vats were always full.

Indoor Sugar Refining

This painting by William Clark captures work in a large sugar plantation after technology improved the sugar refining process. Moving this process indoors better regulated the heat. Using brick ovens reduced the number of fires needed to boil the sugarcane, but these advances did not make the work much easier for enslaved workers. They still faced scalding, heat exhaustion, and grueling physical labor.

In 1843, Norbert Rillieux invented an evaporating machine. Additional inventions, such as steam power and a process that lowered the boiling point of liquid, continued to improve the sugar refining process.

EUROPEAN EXPLORATION OF THE AMERICAS

2 REVIEW

VOCABULARY

Use vocabulary words to complete the sentences.

1. In the 1500s, Spain's economy was based on _____.

2. King Philip II considered Protestants to be _____ because they held beliefs different from those of the Catholic Church.

3. Francis Drake and his crew were the first Englishmen to _____ the globe.

4. Francisco Pizarro was a _____ who conquered the Inca in the 1530s.

5. Spain divided the lands it claimed in the Americas into two _____.

6. The Catholic Church _____ followers of Protestantism in the 16th century.

7. _____ were large tracts of land granted to wealthy Spanish colonists.

8. Native Americans did not have _____ against diseases carried by Europeans.

READING STRATEGY
DRAW CONCLUSIONS

If you haven't already, complete your chart to analyze how European exploration affected the Western Hemisphere. List three details, and then answer the question.

9. What were the ways in which Europeans transformed the Western Hemisphere?

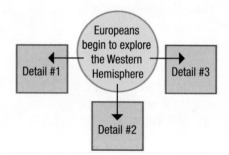

MAIN IDEAS

Answer the following questions. Support your answers with evidence from the chapter.

10. Why were European countries seeking a western route to Asia? **LESSON 1.1**

11. What strategies did the Spanish use to topple the Aztec and the Inca? **LESSON 1.3**

12. What challenges did the conquistadors encounter in North America? **LESSON 1.4**

13. Why did the French Huguenots feel they needed to escape Europe? **LESSON 2.1**

14. Why did King Philip II want Mary, Queen of Scots, to rule England instead of Queen Elizabeth I? **LESSON 2.2**

15. How did the feudal system hinder the growth of New France? **LESSON 2.3**

16. What effect did Spanish rule have on Native American cultures? **LESSON 3.1**

17. What were some of the effects of the Columbian Exchange? **LESSON 3.3**

18. In what ways did the slave trade change cultures and economies in Africa? **LESSON 4.1**

19. Why did the Spanish and Portuguese choose to use slave labor in their New World colonies? **LESSON 4.2**

Answer the following questions. Support your answers with evidence from the chapter.

20. **DRAW CONCLUSIONS** How did competition for land and resources in the Americas lead to conflicts in Europe?

21. **MAKE GENERALIZATIONS** How did the use of slave labor by Europeans in the Americas differ from its use in ancient societies?

22. **MAKE INFERENCES** Why did Bartolomé de Las Casas set himself apart from other Spaniards?

23. **COMPARE AND CONTRAST** What was similar about the colonization of New France and New Netherland? What was different?

24. **FORM AND SUPPORT OPINIONS** What do you think was the most important social or economic effect of the Columbian Exchange? Support your opinion with evidence.

This bar graph shows numbers of enslaved Africans who got on (embarked) and got off (disembarked) slave ships from West Africa between 1500 and 1807. Study the graph and answer the questions below.

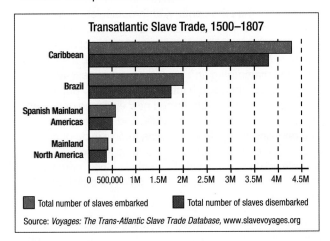

Transatlantic Slave Trade, 1500–1807

■ Total number of slaves embarked   ■ Total number of slaves disembarked

Source: *Voyages: The Trans-Atlantic Slave Trade Database*, www.slavevoyages.org

25. Which region in the Americas imported the most enslaved Africans between 1500 and 1807?

26. What do the two bars for each region show, and what evidence about the Middle Passage do they provide?

In 1524, Giovanni da Verrazzano wrote a letter to King Francis I of France. He described an encounter with Native Americans that he'd witnessed. Read the passage and answer the question.

We sent one of our young sailors swimming ashore to take the people some trinkets, such as little bells, mirrors, and other trifles, and when he came within four fathoms of them, he threw them the goods and tried to turn back, but he was so tossed about by the waves that he was carried up onto the beach half dead. Seeing this, the native people immediately ran up; they took him by the head, the legs, and arms and carried him some distance away. Whereupon the youth, realizing he was being carried away like this, was seized with terror, and began to utter loud cries.

27. Based on the excerpt, do you think the young sailor misread the intentions of the Native Americans? Explain your answer.

28. **EXPLANATORY** In his letter, Verrazzano describes a crew member's first interaction with a new culture. Connect your knowledge about cultural encounters in the 1500s to a time in your life when you experienced something new for the first time. Write a paragraph connecting the two events.

TIPS

- After you decide on a story of your own to share, use a Venn diagram to organize similarities and differences between your story and Verrazzano's story.

- Use text evidence to compare or contrast the crew member's behavior with actions in your own story.

- After you have finished writing, reread your paragraph to make sure the essay does not slip into informal language, especially when telling your own story.

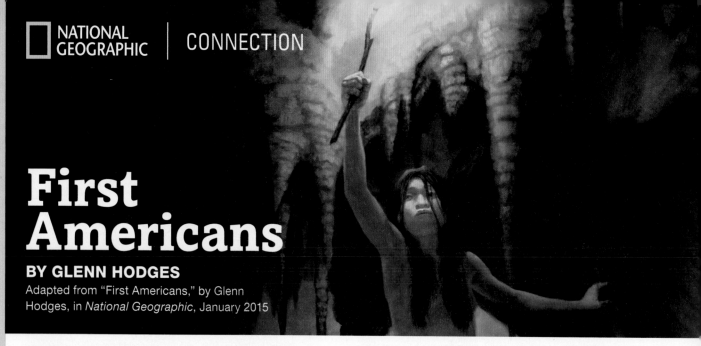

First Americans

BY GLENN HODGES

Adapted from "First Americans," by Glenn Hodges, in *National Geographic*, January 2015

The story begins with an unlucky teenage girl who fell to her death in a cave in Mexico's Yucatán about 12,000 to 13,000 years ago. But her prehistoric bad luck is modern science's good fortune. The skeleton, called Naia (NY-ah), turned out to be one of the oldest ever found in the Americas, and it provides evidence of North America's first inhabitants.

In 2007, a team of Mexican divers led by Alberto Nava made a startling find: an immense submerged cavern they named Hoyo Negro, the "black hole." At the bottom of the abyss, their lights revealed a bed of prehistoric bones, including a nearly complete human skeleton. It was intact enough to provide a foundation for a facial reconstruction. Geneticists were even able to extract a sample of DNA.

Together, these clues may help explain a mystery about the peopling of the Americas. If Native Americans are descendants of Asian trailblazers who migrated into the Americas toward the end of the last Ice Age, why don't they look like their ancient ancestors?

By all appearances, the earliest Americans were a rough bunch. If you look at the skeletal remains of Paleo-Americans, more than half the men have injuries caused by violence. Their wounds do not appear to have been the result of hunting accidents or warfare. Instead, it appears that these men fought violently among themselves. Female skeletons do not reveal the same kinds of injuries. Additionally, female skeletons are much smaller than male skeletons, and they show signs of malnourishment.

Jim Chatters, archaeologist and co-leader of the Hoyo Negro research team that found Naia, theorizes that the earliest Americans were bold pioneers whose behaviors and physical traits changed as they became more settled. This change over time, he explains, is why the earliest Americans' facial features look so different from those of later Native Americans.

According to this hypothesis, men fought for dominance in the group. They also ate better, grew larger, and lived longer than the women did. The men who were able to establish their dominance in the group were the ones who were able to pass on their genes. As a result, their strong traits and features were selected over the softer and more domestic features evident in later, more settled populations.

Chatters's hypothesis is speculative, but his team's findings are not. Naia has the facial features typical of the earliest Americans as well as the genetic signatures common to modern Native Americans. This means that the two groups do not look different because later groups from Asia replaced the earliest populations. Instead, they look different because the first Americans changed after they got here.

For most of the 20th century, anthropologists pointed to spearpoints found near Clovis, New Mexico, and dated to 13,000 years ago as the oldest evidence of ancient hunters. They concluded that the first Americans had followed mammoths and other prey out of Asia, across Beringia, and then south into North America. But in 1997, archaeologists confirmed new evidence of human occupation in Monte Verde, Chile, and the story of the peopling of the Americas was thrown wide open. How did they get there? Given that the Monte Verde people made it all the way to southern Chile more than 14,000 years ago, it would be surprising if they hadn't journeyed by boat.

The story of how and when humans began to inhabit the Americas continues to develop. What is clear is that the Americas hosted diverse communities of people long before the Clovis culture began to spread across North America. We may never know the whole story, but each new discovery gets us closer to a more complete one.

For more from National Geographic, check out "Scurvy Struck Columbus's Crew" online.

UNIT INQUIRY: Establish an Empire

In this unit, you learned about three worlds before 1500 and about the European exploration of the Americas. Based on your reading, what happened when people from Europe, Africa, and the Americas encountered each other on African and American soils? Which societies fared better than others, particularly when Europeans began to establish empires in North, Central, and South America? Why did Europeans establish empires? Which empires were more successful and why?

ASSIGNMENT

Design an empire you think would be successful today. Consider factors such as geography, government, the economy, social structure, and culture. Be prepared to present your plan for an empire to the class.

Gather Evidence As you design your empire, gather evidence from this unit about the factors that made European empires successful and what factors eventually led to their fall. Make a list of both sets of factors. Then develop a plan about how you would use similar or different strategies in your empire. Use a graphic organizer like this one to help organize your thoughts.

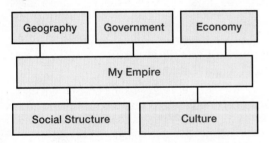

Produce Use your notes to produce detailed descriptions of each component of your empire. Write a short paragraph describing your empire's geography, government, economy, social structure, and culture. To support your ideas, make sure to use evidence from the chapters in this unit.

Present Choose a creative way to present your empire to the class. Consider one of these options:

- Write an introduction to a travel guide that describes your empire. Use a narrative style that gives your audience a "tour" of your empire.

- Draw a map of your empire to accompany the descriptions you provide. Include a legend, geographic features, and other details that help give a visual summary of your empire.

- Create a multimedia presentation using photos, drawings, text, and maps to illustrate your empire and its various components.

NATIONAL GEOGRAPHIC | LEARNING FRAMEWORK ACTIVITIES

Create a Map

SKILLS Observation, Collaboration

KNOWLEDGE Our Living Planet

Team up with a partner to create a map of the continents discussed in this unit. Include as many civilizations, landforms, bodies of water, and labels on your map as possible. Draw arrows to represent migration routes, or how groups of people began to move from place to place. You might also consider using arrows to show these civilizations' trade routes and drawing icons to represent products that were traded along those routes. When you have finished your map, compare it to other teams' maps. Offer your own observations, and ask your classmates to make observations about your map.

Think Like an Archaeologist

ATTITUDE Curiosity

KNOWLEDGE Our Human Story

Civilizations leave behind clues about what they were like and how people lived. Archaeologists all over the world follow very strict procedures when they excavate a site to ensure that no information is lost. They also have to make sure that in digging, they don't destroy or ruin artifacts, structures, or art. In groups of four, imagine that you are in charge of a dig site in the location of one of the civilizations covered in this unit. Make a list of items you might find on your site and describe what challenges you think your crew might face on the dig. Then share your imagined dig experience with the class.

ENGLISH SETTLEMENT

CRITICAL VIEWING In this 1941 painting by Newell Wyeth, the Pilgrims watch the *Mayflower* depart on its return voyage to England in April, 1621. What mood does the artist convey by showing the Pilgrims as they watch their ship return to England?

ENGLISH SETTLEMENT

COLONIAL AMERICA

1607
English settlers found Jamestown in Virginia. *(sealing wax stamp owned by Jamestown resident)*

1620
Pilgrims sign the Mayflower Compact, establishing a self-governing colony at Plymouth, Massachusetts.

1585
Roanoke, the first English colony, is established. *(engraving showing the English arriving in Virginia in 1585)*

1600

1676
Nathaniel Bacon leads a rebellion against the governor of Virginia and demands war against the Native Americans.

1500

c. 1620 AFRICA
The West African kingdom of Dahomey, which would become rich in part through the Atlantic slave trade, is founded.

1644 ASIA
The Manchus overthrow the Ming and found the Qing dynasty in China. *(lion statue before palace of Ming and Qing emperors)*

THE WORLD

1735
John Peter Zenger is tried for printing articles criticizing the English governor of New York. *(block of movable type used in 1700s America)*

HISTORICAL THINKING: DETERMINE CHRONOLOGY

What two events, nearly 70 years apart, indicate the American and British concern with the power of government?

1763
After the French and Indian War ends, the Proclamation of 1763 is issued.

1692
The Salem witch trials are held in Massachusetts.

1754
The French and Indian War between Great Britain and France is fought on American soil. *(pipe tomahawk, a blend of Native American and European cultures)*

1800

1700

1688 EUROPE
Britain's Glorious Revolution begins and results in greatly increased power for Parliament.

c. 1750 EUROPE
The Industrial Revolution begins in Great Britain. *(spinning jenny, which helped industrialize Britain's textile production)*

1722 ASIA
Chinese emperor Kangxi dies after reigning for 61 years.

CHAPTER 3

THE THIRTEEN COLONIES

1585–1732

ESSENTIAL QUESTION
How did early settlers cope with challenges as they established the first 13 colonies?

AMERICAN STORIES The Lost Colony of Roanoke

SECTION 1 **Early Colonies Have Mixed Success**

KEY VOCABULARY

charter	joint-stock company
indentured servant	traitor

SECTION 2 **New England Colonies**

KEY VOCABULARY

banish	King Philip's War	self-governance
dissenter	levy	separatist
Fundamental Orders of Connecticut	Mayflower Compact	

SECTION 3 **Middle and Southern Colonies**

KEY VOCABULARY

alliance	natural resource	raw material
confederacy	neutrality	royal colony
doctrine	proprietor	tributary
economic activity		

AMERICAN GALLERY
ONLINE A Portrait of the Pilgrims

READING STRATEGY

MAKE INFERENCES
When you make inferences, you use what you already know to figure out the meaning of the text. Use a chart like this one to make inferences about the challenges settlers faced as they established the first 13 colonies.

I READ	I KNOW	AND SO
The settlers lived under difficult conditions.	Many settlers died of diseases.	

"As a **city upon a hill,** the eyes of all people are upon us."

—John Winthrop

CRITICAL VIEWING Founded in 1947, Plimoth Plantation, a living museum in Plymouth, Massachusetts, provides an experience of what life was like for the Pilgrims and the Native Americans after the Pilgrims' arrival in 1620. From details in the photo, what materials can you identify that Pilgrims used to build houses and objects that were once part of daily life?

Dasamonquepeuc

Roanoac

CRITICAL VIEWING Which groups are represented in this historical map of Roanoke Island, and how did you identify them?

torasck

THE LOST COLONY OF
ROANOKE

Have you ever read about an unsolved mystery that really haunts you? Something unexplainable has happened, and you just can't get it out of your mind. The "Lost Colony" of Roanoke is an unsolved mystery that has haunted Americans since the late 1500s, when a group of 118 English colonists disappeared from the shore of North Carolina sometime between 1587 and 1590.

Watercolor by John White
of the Roanoke Colony

TRYING TO COLONIZE

In 1584, nearly 100 years after Christopher Columbus had landed in North America, Queen Elizabeth of England grew tired of watching the Spanish grow rich off the "New World." Eager for the wealth and fame that the colonies might bring, and for the opportunity to expand English control, she granted nobleman Walter Raleigh permission to set up a colony in North America. Raleigh sent more than 100 colonists to Roanoke Island, part of the island chain now known as the Outer Banks of North Carolina.

The colony lasted less than a year. The colonists had no farming or fishing skills and had to rely on trade with Native Americans named the Roanoac to feed themselves. Foolishly, they soured relations with the tribe by treating them with suspicion and ordering the killing of a Roanoac chief. When the explorer Sir Francis Drake arrived with his fleet in June 1586, the colonists were sorely in need of food and supplies and desperate to leave. They gladly accepted Drake's offer to bring them back to England.

SOMETIMES, EVIDENCE GROWS ON TREES

Scientists who study tree rings have offered an intriguing clue about the fate of the lost colony. Trees grow a new outer layer of wood each year during the growing season—that's why you can tell the age of a tree by counting its rings. In years with good growing conditions, a wider ring forms. Narrow rings indicate poor years for growth. Long-lived trees, such as the bald cypress trees in some North Carolina rivers, can help researchers determine what growing conditions were like centuries ago.

By studying local trees, scientists have determined that Roanoke Island experienced one of its worst droughts in centuries during the years 1587–1589. Which explanation for the colony's disappearance do you think this evidence supports?

Lost Colony
Drought:
1587–1589

Jamestown
Drought:
1606–1612

Nearby Jamestown's drought can be seen in the tree rings, too.

FOUND AND LOST

Soon, Raleigh decided to try again, this time with a different type of colony. Unlike the all-male group that made the first attempt, these colonists would be a mixed group of men, women, and some children—families aspiring to be planters in the new colony. The governor would be John White, who had been a member of the earlier, failed expedition and had some knowledge of the local geography and tribes. Among the settlers were White's pregnant daughter Eleanor and her husband Ananias Dare.

The colonists reached Roanoke Island in July 1587. Because of the first colony's experiences, they were wary of the Roanoac, but they began a friendly relationship with a different local tribe, the Croatoan. On August 18, 1587, Virginia Dare was born, the first English baby born in North America.

The settlers soon realized they would need more supplies to get through the coming winter. In August, John White returned to England with the ships that had brought the colonists, intending to ask Raleigh for the much-needed goods. But because of England's war with Spain, White was unable to return to Roanoke for three years.

When John White came ashore on an eerily silent Roanoke Island in August 1590, not a single human—colonist or Native American—was present. White found the word *CROATOAN* carved into a post in the former settlement's gate, and a nearby tree bore the letters *CRO*. According to his journal, White concluded that the settlers were "safe . . . at Croatoan, where . . . the Savages of the Island [are] our friends." But he would never learn whether his assumption was correct.

The next day, a strong storm blew up, forcing White's ships away from the Outer Banks. Under an onslaught of continuing bad weather, the small fleet had no choice but to retreat to England. White never succeeded in mounting another expedition to Roanoke or finding the missing colonists.

LOST COLONY FOUND?

Like John White in 1590, researchers today wonder about what happened to the missing colonists. Were the colonists indeed with the Croatoan, just a few miles away from White as he searched the ruined settlement? Did baby Virginia Dare grow up in America? Many plausible explanations exist. The colonists may have moved in with the Croatoan and eventually become part of the tribe. It is also possible they were killed by a hostile native group or by soldiers from a passing Spanish ship.

In recent years, two teams of researchers have found new evidence about the colony's possible fate. In 2012, one group took a closer look at a map of the region drawn by John White. Underneath a paper patch on the map, they found a star-shaped symbol indicating a spot about 50 miles inland from Roanoke. Archaeologists digging at the spot, which they named Site X, uncovered pottery in a style that was also used by the Roanoke colonists.

Meanwhile, researchers digging at Cape Creek on Hatteras Island, where the Croatoan lived, have also discovered a number of objects that may have come from the Roanoke colony.

Many believe the finds at Cape Creek and Site X indicate that the Roanoke colonists left the island to live with different native tribes. Definite proof of the colonists' fate, however, remains tantalizingly out of reach. Charles Ewen, an archaeologist at East Carolina University, sums up the situation. "We still don't know what happened," he reflects, "and we are waiting to be persuaded."

THINK ABOUT IT

How does the story of Roanoke remind you of fictional mystery stories you have read or watched?

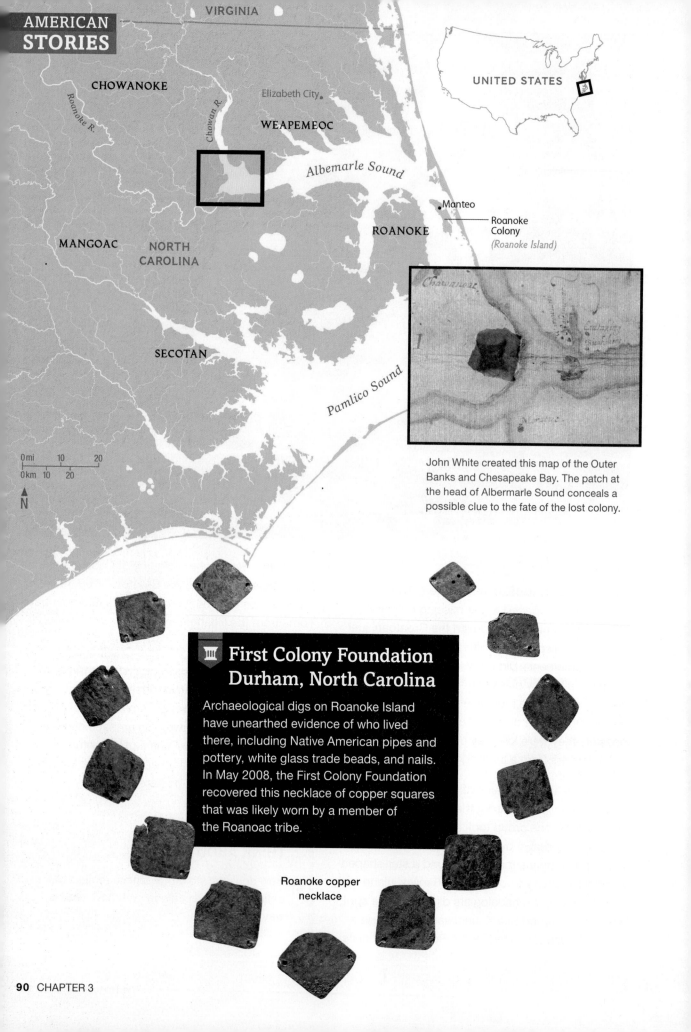

VIRGINIA

CHOWANOKE

Roanoke R.

Chowan R.

Elizabeth City.

WEAPEMEOC

Albemarle Sound

UNITED STATES

.Manteo

Roanoke
Colony
(Roanoke Island)

ROANOKE

MANGOAC

NORTH
CAROLINA

SECOTAN

Pamlico Sound

0 mi   10   20
0 km 10   20

N

John White created this map of the Outer
Banks and Chesapeake Bay. The patch at
the head of Albermarle Sound conceals a
possible clue to the fate of the lost colony.

First Colony Foundation
Durham, North Carolina

Archaeological digs on Roanoke Island
have unearthed evidence of who lived
there, including Native American pipes and
pottery, white glass trade beads, and nails.
In May 2008, the First Colony Foundation
recovered this necklace of copper squares
that was likely worn by a member of
the Roanoac tribe.

Roanoke copper
necklace

THE ARTWORK OF JOHN WHITE

John White was an accomplished artist and cartographer. In 1585, he voyaged from England to the Outer Banks. During his year-long stay at Roanoke, he created more than 70 watercolor drawings of indigenous people, plants, and animals to give the English a sense of the environment in the "New World."

John White's watercolor of the Native American town of Pomeiooc

MANTEO AND WANCHESE

Manteo and Wanchese were two of the first Native Americans to have extensive contact with the English. Manteo was a Croatoan chief, and Wanchese was from the Roanoac tribe. Both men encountered a scouting party that Walter Raleigh sent before the first Roanoke colony, and both returned with the group to England.

Wanchese came to dislike the English and felt like a prisoner in England. Manteo, on the other hand, became friendly with the English and remained loyal to them for years. Both Manteo and Wanchese came to Roanoke with the first colony. Wanchese rejoined his people, but Manteo stayed with the English as an interpreter and guide. When the first colony failed, Manteo returned to England with the former settlers. Later, he accompanied White's group of colonists, once again serving as an interpreter and helping to smooth relations with the Croatoans. In August 1587, before White left for England, Manteo was baptized and officially converted to Christianity.

John White's watercolor of a Native American chief

1.1 | Colonizing Virginia

Imagine settling in an entirely new place, far across an ocean from your home. How would you prepare for this adventure? The founders of Jamestown, Virginia, found out the hard way just what it was like.

MAIN IDEA Virginia's first colonists struggled with starvation, wars, and disease before finally finding success in their new home.

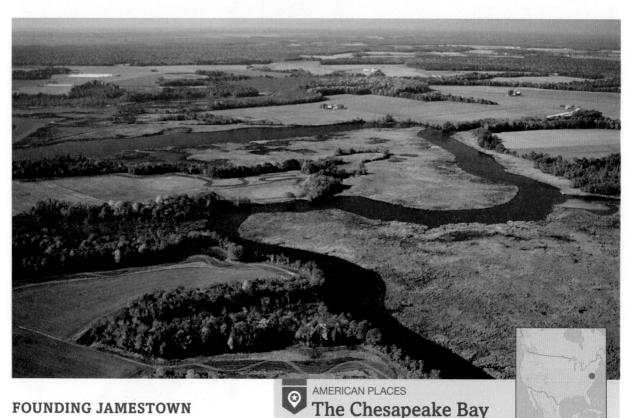

AMERICAN PLACES
The Chesapeake Bay

The Chesapeake Bay is a large inlet that extends through the present-day states of Virginia and Maryland. It is a rich ecosystem, with more than 150 rivers and streams flowing into it. The area around the bay provided rich farmland to colonists who established farms and plantations there.

FOUNDING JAMESTOWN

In the early 1600s, England began establishing colonies in America. As with Spain and its colonies, England pursued the economic policy of mercantilism, giving it a trade monopoly with its colonies. The colonies provided raw materials to England, where workers made them into goods. Finished goods were then shipped back to the colonies and sold or traded, helping England increase its wealth.

At the same time, merchants and investors developed a new type of business, called a **joint-stock company**. Wealthy individuals invested in a venture, or business project. Their funds paid for the endeavor, and the individuals shared ownership in the venture. This business raised money for exploring trade routes and establishing markets in new locations. In late 1606, a joint-stock company called the **Virginia Company** funded the first English settlement at **Jamestown** in the colony of Virginia. King James I had provided a **charter**, or written grant detailing rights and privileges, to the company to settle the colonies. After a difficult winter voyage across the Atlantic Ocean, more than 100 settlers arrived in the **Chesapeake Bay** and established a fort along the James River.

The settlers were ill-equipped to establish a colony. They had little experience with farming, hunting, or fishing and were more interested in searching for gold. Soon they were starving. To make matters worse, Jamestown was located in a low-lying area— perfect for mosquitoes that carried malaria, a disease that killed many settlers.

Colonial officer John Smith established a mutually beneficial trade relationship with the Powhatan, a Native American tribe. The Powhatan grew corn that the settlers could use, and the English had goods that the Powhatan wanted, such as weapons. In 1608, Smith became president of the colony and put the settlers to work planting crops, fishing, and building houses. The state of the colony improved.

Then in September 1609, Smith was injured and returned to England. That same year, the Virginia Company angered Chief Powhatan, who then cut off trade with the settlers. Winter came, and the settlers began to starve again. Any colonist who left the fort risked being attacked. Only 60 colonists survived the winter. In 1614, Chief Powhatan's daughter, Pocahontas, married colonist John Rolfe. The marriage helped usher in peace between the two groups.

SUCCESS AT LAST

In about 1612, Rolfe started to grow a new variety of tobacco in Virginia. He used seeds he had acquired in the West Indies. Rolfe's new tobacco was less bitter than the variety that had been grown in the colony, and by the following year, he began shipping it to England, where it became very popular. Tobacco farmers tried to produce enough to meet rising demand, and tobacco became a driving economic force in the colonies.

In 1619, the Virginia Company tried to persuade English citizens to move to Virginia to build this labor force. Some citizens were freeholders who

Pocahontas
Artists have portrayed Pocahontas in various ways, almost always based on information rather than actually seeing her. The top left painting as Lady Rebecca Rolfe in England (1616) is the only known portrait of her from life. Other artists have imagined her as the Powhatan princess who captivated John Rolfe (top right, painting dated 1945), and shortly after her marriage to Rolfe in 1614 (painting dated c. 1852).

paid their own transportation and received land in exchange. Others were **indentured servants**, who gave up several years of freedom to have their travel fees paid by the company or another person. Indentured servants were bound for a certain length of time to work to pay off their traveling expenses.

Also in 1619, the Virginia Company established an assembly of elected delegates in Virginia, called the **House of Burgesses**. It became the first representative assembly in the American colonies, and it gave the colonists more local control.

HISTORICAL THINKING

1. **READING CHECK** What was the purpose for establishing an English settlement in Virginia?

2. **FORM AND SUPPORT OPINIONS** How important do you think John Smith was to the settlers? Use evidence from the reading to support your opinion.

3. **MAKE INFERENCES** Why did John Rolfe's marriage to Pocahontas bring about peace between the Powhatan and the colonists?

1.2 Voorhees Archaearium Jamestown, Virginia

Located near the site of the original Jamestown Settlement, America's first permanent English colony, the Voorhees Archaearium captures the story of Virginia in the 1600s. Artifacts from the arrival of English colonists to Jamestown in 1607 and the earliest cultural encounters and events are housed in this archaeology museum. Visitors can explore the cultures of the Native Americans, Europeans, and Africans who intersected in 17th-century Virginia, and trace Jamestown's beginnings in England. They can even climb aboard replicas of the three ships, moored nearby, that crossed the Atlantic, bringing the earliest colonists from England to Virginia. What can you infer about the lives of the colonists based on the artifacts below?

Lead Toy Horse

A collection of tiny toy horses like this one was found in a trash heap along with food remains, broken pottery, and shattered glassware from the James Fort. Long ago, this horse may have carried a toy rider in its saddle and had wheels so a child could push or pull it around.

Gaming Dice

Excavations have revealed more than 60 gaming dice at the James Fort. Many of the dice are made of animal bone, but some are made of ivory or lead. It's possible that the lead dice may have been made by a soldier who also made lead shot (fired by weapons) at the fort. Like modern dice, the opposing sides of the Jamestown dice add up to seven. Soldiers passed the long hours at the remote fort playing dice games.

Brass Thimble

This 16th-century thimble was made in Nuremberg, Germany, and is one of 11 brass thimbles found at the James Fort. Several tailors joined the Jamestown colonists in 1607 and 1608, and their ability to sew and repair cloth was important to the frontier settlement. Other tailoring tools have also been found, including needles, irons, and pins.

Ear Picker

Believe it or not, a Jamestown colonist once used this silver sea creature to scrape teeth, clean dirt from fingernails, and scoop out earwax. Gold and silver grooming tools were often worn like jewelry in Europe during the late 1500s and early 1600s. The first settlers at Jamestown included a surgeon and a barber who could perform basic medical care like removing infected teeth—and excessive earwax.

Tailors sometimes used earwax to make their thread stronger if they had no beeswax!

Why might the English have felt it was safer to drink wine than water in the early 1600s?

Monogrammed Wine Bottles

Discovered by Jamestown archaeologists, these wide glass bottles were made in England between 1680 and 1700 and found upright on the dirt floor of a rectangular cellar. One of the intact bottles is marked with the initials *FN*, which reveals it once belonged to someone of wealth and status. During the 17th century, high-ranking gentlemen liked to order wine bottles from England stamped with their personal seal.

Uncovering
Where America Began

"The American dream was born on the banks of the James River." —William Kelso

The experts said the Jamestown fort had washed away without a trace, but **William Kelso** didn't believe them. He saw something in a glassed-in cross-section of dirt exhibited at the Jamestown ranger station that suggested something might still lie below the surface. So, in 1994, Kelso set out alone with his shovel and hit pay dirt almost immediately: earth stained dark by logs that had decayed long ago. Thus began his quest for Jamestown's buried truths.

^
Kelso stands next to a portion of the Jamestown fort that he and his team reconstructed. The archaeologist has worked for more than 20 years in Jamestown in part because, as he says, "This is America's site. It belongs to the people."

MAIN IDEA Archaeologist William Kelso has uncovered evidence at Jamestown that is changing how people view the settlement.

This map shows the triangular Jamestown fort and the houses that stood within it. Chief Powhatan sits at the top right of the map, while ships full of settlers arrive on the island along the James River.

EARLY DISCOVERIES

National Geographic Explorer William Kelso's search began in 1994. In anticipation of the 400th anniversary of Jamestown's founding, the Association for the Preservation of Virginia Antiquities had announced plans to investigate the island. Kelso volunteered for the job.

About all he had to go on were some historical accounts and documents, including a roughly drawn Spanish map from 1608 showing the triangular Jamestown fort. But he also knew that the only aboveground ruins that had survived in Jamestown were parts of a church tower. Kelso reasoned that the settlers would have built the fort near the church, so he began there. Fragments of early 1600s ceramics and the dark-stained dirt told him that he was on the right track.

THE TRUTH ABOUT JAMESTOWN

In time, Kelso identified evidence of all but one corner of the fort's structure as well as thousands of artifacts. He and his team—at this point, Kelso wasn't working alone anymore—began reconstructing the fort, using the materials and tools available to the Jamestown settlers. During this process, he discovered just how tough the settlers had been. Kelso says, "They were cutting down trees, digging holes, building forts, building buildings, digging ditches." The skeletons that Kelso has excavated also reveal how hard the settlers' lives were. Many died during the starving time of the early years and in the wars with Native Americans. Others couldn't adapt to the new environment. Lifespans were short.

One misconception about Jamestown is that it was a failure, but the settlers got many things right. Historians have often faulted them for establishing their colony in what was basically a marsh. But they needed to find a place where they could defend themselves against the Spanish. Locating their settlement on an island worked—the Spanish never attacked. Above all, they developed a new form of government. Around 1619, the settlers organized a representative assembly that met at the church. According to Kelso, "That's when liberty got out of the bag, and nobody could stuff it back in."

These findings have told us a lot about the site, and Kelso hopes to uncover more. But now the sea level around Jamestown Island is rising. Soon, important evidence may disappear. And Kelso believes the site is worth preserving. For, as he says, "This is where America began. This is where the English settlers first became American."

HISTORICAL THINKING

1. **READING CHECK** What did Kelso learn about the Jamestown settlers from his excavations?

2. **ANALYZE CAUSE AND EFFECT** Why did the settlers choose Jamestown as the site for their colony?

3. **DRAW CONCLUSIONS** What action on the settlers' part was key to the development of American constitutional democracy?

1.4 Conflicts with Native Americans

When something that belongs to you is taken away, it can be difficult to keep the peace. Native Americans in the 1600s faced this challenge when colonists began to take over their ancestral lands.

MAIN IDEA Wars between Native Americans and Virginian colonists raged on and off for decades as each group laid claim to the land.

WARS WITH THE POWHATAN

For about eight years after John Rolfe and Pocahontas were married, the Jamestown colonists and the Powhatan lived in peace. During that time, the Powhatan helped the colonists plant corn, catch fish, and capture wild fowl. But as thousands of new colonists arrived to work for the Virginia Company, the Powhatan saw their land and culture taken away. In 1622, one Powhatan leader staged a rebellion against the English and their European and Christian customs. Colonists killed him, and the Powhatan responded by launching an attack on the colony, killing hundreds of settlers.

This attack set off a 10-year war. When peace finally came, it lasted for more than a decade. But even during the peaceful years, the colonists' desire for land continued to provoke the Powhatan. As the demand for tobacco as a cash crop increased, colonists, claiming the English king owned the colony and its land, simply grabbed land they deemed to be unoccupied. Although no one lived on the land, the Powhatan hunted, fished, and farmed on it. Two years later, the Powhatan attacked the colony again, triggering yet another war. In 1646, the Powhatan surrendered. Their leader was captured and later killed.

The two groups signed a treaty that required the Powhatan to live on lands north of the York River. They also had to make a yearly payment to the colonists of 20 beaver skins. The Powhatan had lost their power in Jamestown.

BACON'S REBELLION

As years passed, conflicts between Native Americans and colonists increased. In the 1660s, the governor of Virginia, William Berkeley, urged colonists to interact peacefully and maintain trading to avoid a costly war. However, by 1670, tensions surfaced among colonists who owned land and those who did not. Landless freemen resented their lack of property and wanted a stronger voice in Virginia's government.

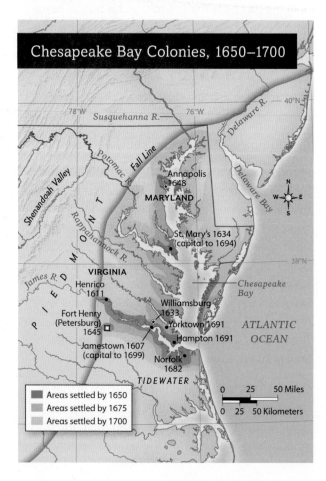

Chesapeake Bay Colonies, 1650–1700

Areas settled by 1650
Areas settled by 1675
Areas settled by 1700

Many of them had the right to purchase land, but low tobacco prices and high land prices made it difficult for them to find land they could afford to buy. They also claimed that the Powhatan controlled too much land, even though this land had been granted to the Native Americans by the 1646 treaty.

A young councilman and wealthy planter named Nathaniel Bacon, who was actually Berkeley's cousin by marriage, challenged Berkeley's leadership. He argued that the governor held too much power and that the colonists should be more involved with the government. He also wanted to claim more land from the Powhatan. Bacon and a group of landless followers attacked Native Americans in 1676 in an attempted revolution later called **Bacon's Rebellion**.

Berkeley accused Bacon of being a traitor, or someone disloyal to his or her own people or cause, because he believed Bacon had challenged the power of the governor and his fellow wealthy planters. Bacon had growing public support, however. Bowing to this pressure, Berkeley agreed to be lenient with Bacon if he turned himself in and went to England to be tried before King Charles II. But the House of Burgesses did not approve of Berkeley's leniency. They forced Bacon to apologize to Berkeley. The power struggle between Bacon and Berkeley continued for several months. Bacon and his army even burned Jamestown to the ground in September 1676.

The rebellion ended a month later when Bacon died unexpectedly. Berkeley ordered Bacon's fellow leaders to be executed. Angered by these events, King Charles II demanded that Berkeley return to England. Some historians have interpreted Bacon's Rebellion as a fight against the authority of the local government, while others have described it as a power struggle between a powerful governor and a wealthy colonist. However, the Native Americans who were driven from their lands were ultimately the ones who lost the most.

CRITICAL VIEWING Bacon's followers included men from all walks of life. In his painting of the burning of Jamestown in 1676, Howard Pyle shows Bacon in the center but not ahead of everyone else. What can you infer from Bacon's placement about the spirit of the rebellion?

HISTORICAL THINKING

1. **READING CHECK** How did the treaty of 1646 lead to Bacon's Rebellion?

2. **INTERPRET MAPS** How does the map reflect Native American concerns about land?

3. **MAKE INFERENCES** Why did Nathaniel Bacon have public support for his rebellion?

2.1 Pilgrims and Puritans

"Are we there yet?" You've probably asked this question during a long car ride. Imagine sailing across an ocean in a cramped wooden ship. Colonists who braved the long voyage from England to North America may have thought they'd never arrive.

MAIN IDEA The New England colonies became a new home for groups who wished to create societies centered on their religious principles.

THE PILGRIMS FIND A HOME

During the early 1600s, European settlers continued to arrive in the American colonies, despite ongoing conflicts between Native Americans and colonists. At this time in England, religious **dissenters**, or people who disagreed with the beliefs of the Church of England, could be imprisoned or fined. Dissenters yearned for religious freedom so intensely that they left their homes, sailed across the ocean, and settled in the colonies. They became **separatists**, or people who created their own congregations outside of the Church of England.

The **Pilgrims** were one such group. They did not believe in the reforms instituted by the Church of England and saw complete separation as their only spiritual option. In September 1620, a group of Pilgrims boarded the *Mayflower* in England, bound for the northern part of Virginia. The ship strayed off course and landed on Cape Cod. Once they realized they would not land in Virginia, the Pilgrims established and signed the **Mayflower Compact**. This agreement laid out a plan for governing a new colony.

From Cape Cod, the Pilgrims moved to the area around what is now Plymouth, Massachusetts. During their first winter, half of the Pilgrims died from illness or exposure to the cold. The following spring, Native Americans who lived nearby, including Squanto, a member of the Pawtuxet, helped the Pilgrims grow their own food. They identified which crops grew best and when to plant them. They also showed the Pilgrims how to use herring, a local fish, to fertilize the crops. As experienced local planters, Native Americans also shared their knowledge of how to plant corn, beans, and squash together for the best results. The two groups celebrated the Pilgrims' first harvest in a three-day celebration considered the first Thanksgiving.

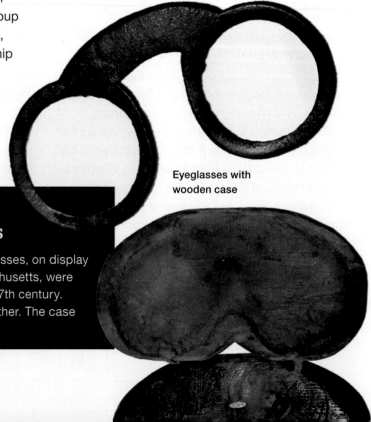

Eyeglasses with wooden case

🏛 Pilgrim Hall Museum
Plymouth, Massachusetts

Even Pilgrims wore spectacles. These eyeglasses, on display at Pilgrim Hall Museum in Plymouth, Massachusetts, were probably made in England sometime in the 17th century. They are made of glass, horn, wood, and leather. The case is carved from pinewood.

A CITY UPON A HILL

Like the Pilgrims, the **Puritans** believed that the Church of England needed additional reform. Unlike the Pilgrims, however, the Puritans wanted to reform the church from within.

Beginning in 1630, the Puritans began their migration from England to Massachusetts Bay. They arrived as part of the Massachusetts Bay Company, believing God wanted them to create a moral community. As Puritan leader John Winthrop said, the colony would be "as a City upon a Hill, the Eyes of all people are upon us."

The Puritans' system of self-governance was called the New England Way. The church was the center of the community, and all citizens were required to attend. Puritans believed that a congregation, bound by a sacred oath, held all authority and could punish members who disagreed with church doctrine. People who tried to leave a congregation could lose their property. The Puritans were dissenters who did not allow dissent within their own communities.

Not all Puritans agreed with the New England Way. In 1636, clergyman Thomas Hooker and a group of Puritans left Massachusetts to found a new colony in Connecticut. Three years later, in a sermon, Hooker provided inspiration for the **Fundamental Orders of Connecticut**. This document established a General Assembly of representatives from many towns. Unlike in Massachusetts, church membership was not a condition for voting.

In 1631, religious dissenter and Pilgrim minister **Roger Williams** arrived in Massachusetts Bay Colony. He attacked laws requiring church attendance and tax support of Puritan churches and was **banished**, or sent away from the colony. In 1636, he bought land from the Narragansett and founded the colony of Rhode Island. He based this new colony on the idea that church and state affairs should be kept separate.

In 1637, Massachusetts Bay Colony leaders banished another dissenter. **Anne Hutchinson** had angered orthodox Puritans by teaching that people had to respond directly to God, not the church, for their actions. Hutchinson also believed that ministers were unnecessary. She founded a settlement in the colony of Rhode Island.

Built in England in 1956, the *Mayflower II* is a full-scale replica of the vessel that brought the Pilgrims from England to North America in 1620. Upon completion, it sailed from England to New England following the Pilgrims' route. It remains a working sailing ship, moored at Plymouth, Massachusetts.

HISTORICAL THINKING

1. **READING CHECK** What was the Mayflower Compact and why was it important?

2. **MAKE INFERENCES** Why did the Puritans link citizenship to church membership?

3. **MAKE GENERALIZATIONS** Why did some groups leave the Massachusetts Bay Colony to establish new colonies?

> "[Squanto] was a special instrument sent of God for [the Pilgrims'] good beyond their expectation."
>
> —from the journal of William Bradford, governor of Plymouth Colony

The Pilgrims certainly couldn't have expected that a fluent English-speaking Native American would happen on the scene and choose to act as their interpreter and guide. So Squanto, also known as Tisquantum, must have seemed like a gift indeed. He taught the Pilgrims how to grow maize and where to catch fish, and generally showed them the ropes so they could survive in Plymouth. Squanto even died in the Pilgrims' service. What we don't know for sure is exactly what came before.

EARLY LIFE

Part folk hero, part myth, much of what we know—or think we know—about Squanto comes from often conflicting eyewitness accounts. According to some sources, he was kidnapped from his Massachusetts home in 1605 by Englishman George Weymouth and taken to England. While there, he was apparently treated well and taught English—the idea being that he would serve as an interpreter for those settling the colonies. John Smith, one of the founders of Jamestown Colony, is said to have returned him to America for that purpose around 1615.

Remarkably, Squanto was kidnapped a second time, an event on which most authorities agree. One of Smith's men,

Wooden sculpture of Squanto

🏛 **Pilgrim Hall Museum**
Plymouth, Massachusetts

The nation's oldest continuously operating public museum, Pilgrim Hall, tells the founding story of America: the Pilgrims' arrival, struggles, and first Thanksgiving in Plymouth. This 19th-century sculpture of Squanto forms part of the museum's collection. It shows what one artist thinks the Native American guide might have looked like.

Squanto was known for his role as the Pilgrims' guide. But stories have also circulated about trouble he caused. For example, fearful of losing his position of power, Squanto tried to pit the Pilgrims against the Native Americans. He spread rumors that Massasoit was joining forces with other tribes in a plan to attack the Pilgrims.

When Squanto's plot was uncovered, Massasoit demanded that Squanto be turned over for punishment. Certain that the Wampanoag chief would execute Squanto, William Bradford refused. With more colonial ships arriving in the area, Bradford knew that he and the new settlers would need Squanto more than ever.

Before long, Squanto became an indispensable member of the colony. He taught the settlers how to plant local crops and served as their ambassador on trading expeditions. He even helped negotiate a peace treaty between the Pilgrims and the Wampanoag chief, Massasoit. In the fall of 1621, the Wampanoag, the Pilgrims, and Squanto celebrated the peace and Plymouth's successful harvest with the first Thanksgiving.

Squanto's time in Plymouth turned out to be brief. While guiding William Bradford on an expedition around Cape Cod, the Native American contracted a fever and died. According to some sources, Squanto said to Bradford on his deathbed, "Pray for me, Governor, that I might go to the Englishmen's God in heaven." Apparently, the Pilgrims had had a powerful influence on Squanto. He could have no idea that his own influence and aid had helped secure the survival of the colonists.

Thomas Hunt, took Squanto and several other Native Americans to Spain where the Englishman hoped to sell them into slavery. Fortunately, Squanto managed to get away. Some say Spanish priests rescued him. Most accounts, though, have him escaping to England and befriending merchants in London. This period, then, may have been when Squanto learned English. In 1619, he sailed with the merchants to New England to help them establish trade with the Native Americans.

LIFE AMONG THE PILGRIMS

Squanto returned to his homeland only to find that most of his people—the Pawtuxet—had been wiped out by disease. For a time, he lived with the Wampanoag (WAHMP-uh-noh-ag). Then, in early 1621, a Native American named Samoset brought Squanto to Plymouth Colony. Samoset had been the first Native American to greet the Pilgrims. But, with his limited understanding of English, he couldn't really speak to them. Squanto, he knew, had a far better command of the language.

HISTORICAL THINKING

1. **READING CHECK** How did Squanto help the Pilgrims in Plymouth?

2. **FORM AND SUPPORT OPINIONS** Do you think the treaty with the Wampanoag could have been created without Squanto? Why or why not?

3. **DRAW CONCLUSIONS** Based on his dying words, what did Squanto learn from the Pilgrims?

2.3 Foundations of Democracy

Democracy is founded on a number of principles, one of which is equality. Throughout history, legal documents have outlined rights and created rules for governing communities fairly. Some of these writings inspired the authors of the Declaration of Independence and the Constitution.

In colonial New England, the Puritans established a style of governing that revolved around town hall meetings. These meetings were some of the first experiments in American democracy. Certain requirements limited who could vote in the meetings, however. In most cases, only male, property-owning church members had a vote. Today, all citizens can participate fully in town hall meetings, regardless of gender, race, or wealth.

CRITICAL VIEWING Old Town Hall, located in Canterbury, New Hampshire, was built in 1736. It continues to function as a meeting and polling place. Below, a Canterbury citizen leaves Old Town Hall after voting in a primary during the 2012 election. What details from the photo indicate that the citizens of Canterbury value their town hall?

DOCUMENT ONE

Primary Source: Legal Document
from the Magna Carta, 1215

The Magna Carta, or "Great Charter," served as a peace treaty between King John of England and his barons, who rebelled against the heavy taxes the king **levied** on them, or required that they pay. The original document contained 63 clauses detailing laws that everyone was expected to follow. Principles in the Magna Carta were later embodied in the 1689 English Bill of Rights, such as the right to a trial by jury and protection from excessive fines and cruel punishment.

CONSTRUCTED RESPONSE Why is it significant that the Magna Carta includes the phrase "lawful judgment of his equals"?

No free man shall be seized or imprisoned, or stripped of his rights or possessions, or outlawed or exiled, or deprived of his standing in any other way, nor will we proceed with force against him, or send others to do so, except by the lawful judgment of his equals or by the law of the land.

DOCUMENT TWO

Primary Source: Legal Document
from the Mayflower Compact, 1620

Just prior to settling Plymouth, Massachusetts, the settlers-to-be signed the Mayflower Compact on board their ship. The agreement established **self-governance**, or control of the colony based on the democratic principle of common consent.

CONSTRUCTED RESPONSE What reasons do the Mayflower Compact signers give for working together as a "civil body politic"?

Having undertaken . . . a voyage to plant the first colony in the northern parts of Virginia, do . . . solemnly and mutually in the presence of God and one another, covenant [promise], and combine ourselves together into a civil body politic, for our better ordering and preservation, and furtherance of the ends aforesaid; and . . . to enact, constitute, and frame such just and equal laws . . . as shall be thought most meet and convenient for the general good of the colony.

DOCUMENT THREE

Primary Source: Legal Document
from the Fundamental Orders of Connecticut, 1639

The founders of Connecticut drafted a plan of government called the Fundamental Orders of Connecticut. The document created an assembly of elected representatives from each town in the colony. The ideas captured in this document were later reflected in the U.S. Constitution.

CONSTRUCTED RESPONSE Why do you think it was important to the colony founders that the representatives lived in the towns they represented?

It is Ordered . . . and decreed, that there shall be yearly two General Assemblies or Courts. The first shall be called the Court of Election, wherein shall be yearly chosen from time to time, so many Magistrates and other public Officers as shall be found requisite [necessary] . . . which choice shall be made by all that are admitted freemen and have taken the Oath of Fidelity [loyalty], and do cohabit within this Jurisdiction . . . of the Town wherein they live.

SYNTHESIZE & WRITE

1. **REVIEW** Review what you have learned about the Magna Carta, the Mayflower Compact, and the Fundamental Orders of Connecticut.

2. **RECALL** On your own paper, write the main ideas about government expressed in the Magna Carta, the Mayflower Compact, and the Fundamental Orders of Connecticut.

3. **CONSTRUCT** Construct a topic sentence that answers this question: How is the Magna Carta, written in 1215, similar to the Mayflower Compact and the Fundamental Orders of Connecticut?

4. **WRITE** Using evidence from this chapter and the documents, write a paragraph that supports your topic sentence in Step 3.

2.4 War and Witch Trials

The continued takeover of Native American lands by colonists caused conflicts in the 1670s. Conflicts also arose among colonists, and in one New England town, accusations of witchcraft and wickedness flew.

MAIN IDEA In the late 1600s, wars with Native Americans raged in the New England colonies and witch trials nearly tore the town of Salem apart.

KING PHILIP'S WAR

In 1671, because of increasing tensions with Native Americans, the Plymouth government forced the Wampanoag to surrender their guns. Four years later, a chain of events led to a bloody war.

A Native American named John Sassamon was a convert to Christianity and an interpreter for English colonists. Soon after he warned of an impending attack by a Wampanoag leader named **Metacom**, he was found dead. With little or no evidence, authorities tried and hanged three Wampanoag for his murder.

In response, Metacom and his troops attacked 52 towns throughout New England, destroying 12 of them completely. By the next summer, Metacom's troops were suffering from disease, hunger, and a shortage of weapons, so the campaign came to an end.

English settlers had given Metacom the nickname "King Philip"—no one remembers why—and these attacks became known as **King Philip's War**. Around 600 colonists and thousands of Native Americans died in the war, including Metacom.

ACCUSATIONS IN SALEM

In February 1692, authorities in the village of Salem, Massachusetts, accused three women of witchcraft. Presumably, the charges stemmed from the strange behavior of some village girls. But it didn't take long for people to believe that witches existed and were living in Salem.

Authorities began to arrest people accused by fellow villagers. Nearly 200 women and men were accused and brought to trial for witchcraft.

"Evidence" consisted largely of accusations and little more. Twenty of the accused were put to death, most by hanging.

Historians think the issue underlying the trials may have been women's ownership of property. In Puritan society, women were rarely allowed to own property. When a man died, his son or sons usually inherited his property. If he had no male children, his wife or daughter could inherit.

Many Salem residents accused of witchcraft were women who had inherited property. Their status as property owners went against the societal norm and threatened to challenge traditional gender roles. The threat posed by women as property owners may have driven many witchcraft accusations.

Governor William Phips and Increase Mather, an influential minister, initially supported the trials but then realized things had gone too far. By May 1693, Phips had pardoned all of those still imprisoned. Additionally, courts dismissed charges and returned not-guilty verdicts in the remaining cases. The strange episode of the Salem witch trials was over.

HISTORICAL THINKING

1. **READING CHECK** Why did Metacom attack New England towns?

2. **ANALYZE CAUSE AND EFFECT** What effect did King Philip's War have on Native Americans in the region?

3. **MAKE INFERENCES** Why were landowning women targets of witchcraft accusations?

The Wonders of the Invisible World.

OBSERVATIONS

As well *Historical* as *Theological*, upon the NATURE, the NUMBER, and the OPERATIONS of the

DEVILS.

Accompany'd with,

I. Some Accounts of the Grievous Molestations, by DÆ-MONS and WITCHCRAFTS, which have lately annoy'd the Countrey; and the Trials of some eminent *Malefactors* Executed upon occasion thereof: with several Remarkable *Curiosities* therein occurring.

II. Some Counsils, Directing a due Improvement of the terrible things, lately done, by the Unusual & Amazing Range of EVIL SPIRITS, in Our Neighbourhood: & the methods to prevent the *Wrongs* which those *Evil Angels* may intend against all sorts of people among us; especially in Accusations of the Innocent.

III. Some Conjectures upon the great EVENTS, likely to befall, the WORLD in General, and NEW-ENGLAND in Particular; as also upon the Advances of the TIME, when we shall see BETTER DAYES.

IV. A short Narrative of a late Outrage committed by a knot of WITCHES in *Swedeland*, very much Resembling, and so far Explaining, *That* under which our parts of *America* have laboured!

V. THE DEVIL DISCOVERED: In a Brief Discourse upon those TEMPTATIONS, which are the more Ordinary *Devices* of the Wicked One.

By **Cotton Mather**.

Boston Printed by *Benj. Harris* for *Sam. Phillips.* 1693.

CRITICAL VIEWING The fiery New England preacher named Cotton Mather wrote a book on the Salem witch trials. At left is a page from his book. In the 1890s, 200 years after the Salem witch trials, illustrator Joseph E. Baker reimagined the events reported to have taken place in Salem. What are the different ways witches are portrayed in Mather's writing and these drawings?

3.1 The Middle Colonies

Have you ever traveled to a new place and discovered a culture different from that of your hometown? A colonist traveling south from New England to the Middle Colonies would meet people from European countries who were forging a unique colonial identity.

MAIN IDEA The Middle Colonies included a diverse mix of cultures and religions as people from different countries began to settle in the region.

NEW NETHERLAND TO NEW YORK

Situated in the mid-Atlantic region of North America, the **Middle Colonies** included New York, New Jersey, Pennsylvania, and Delaware. Settlers from countries such as England, France, the Netherlands, Germany, Sweden, and Portugal came to the colonies for different reasons. Some were fleeing religious wars in their home countries. Others were conducting trade.

The first Dutch settlers arrived about 1614 and began trading with Native Americans. In 1624, Cornelius Jacobsen May, working on behalf of the Dutch West India Company, founded New Netherland to provide a base for trade in the Hudson River region. The first settlers of New Netherland worked for the company.

For about 15 years, colonists maintained good relations with Native Americans. However, disputes over land ownership grew. In particular, Native Americans objected to the Dutch settling on lands without a clear agreement that they could do so. Eventually, wars broke out.

In 1664, King Charles II of England gave his brother James, the duke of York, permission to force the Dutch out. The overwhelming English presence in the area made doing so easy and ensured the English complete control of eastern North America. James took over the colony and renamed it New York, and the English made peace with Native Americans living there.

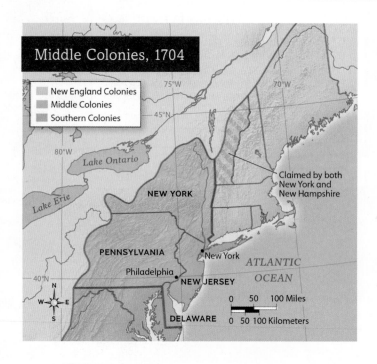

Middle Colonies, 1704

- New England Colonies
- Middle Colonies
- Southern Colonies

PENN'S WOODS

After assuming control of New York, James granted land between the Delaware and lower Hudson rivers to Lord John Berkeley and Sir George Carteret, who named the area New Jersey. New Jersey eventually split into West Jersey and East Jersey.

In 1681, Charles II granted a charter for a colony to an Englishman named **William Penn**. Penn wanted to establish a safe home for his fellow **Quakers**—members of the Religious Society of Friends, a Christian movement devoted to peaceful principles. Quakers emphasized education and equality and rejected formal worship and ministry. Because they were perceived by others as

CRITICAL VIEWING In 1682, William Penn met with leaders of the Lenni Lenape under an elm tree on the Delaware River in present-day Philadelphia. There they signed a treaty promising cooperation. In this frieze, or sculpted panel, from the U.S. Capitol Rotunda, Penn is in the center, gesturing toward the activity around the chest. What details in this frieze reveal the reactions of the participants to the treaty signing?

anti-authority and even dangerous, thousands of Quakers were persecuted in England and even in the American colonies. Penn named his colony Sylvania, which means "woods." Charles II renamed it Pennsylvania, after Penn's father.

Penn set out to create a colony based on the Quaker **doctrine**—a principle or policy accepted by a group—that all are equal in the eyes of God. By applying this doctrine, he made Pennsylvania into an extremely diverse society, partly by encouraging religious minorities to settle there. Quaker doctrine also emphasized tolerance for others. In Pennsylvania, all colonists, no matter their religion, could worship in their own way.

Penn encouraged diversity in other ways, too. He kept peace with Native Americans, such as the Lenni Lenape. He purchased land from them, which he then sold to a variety of buyers—people from other colonies, different countries in Europe, and the West Indies. The Swedes, Finns, and Dutch who already inhabited the area became English subjects under Penn.

European settlers who lived in the "Lower Counties" in the southern part of the colony did not like living under Penn's government and at times clashed with Pennsylvania's authority. Penn tried unsuccessfully to unite the English and the Europeans, but in 1704, after two decades of difficulties, he allowed Delaware to form its own assembly. Elsewhere, and following Penn's death, conflicts between Native Americans and colonists continued.

HISTORICAL THINKING

1. **READING CHECK** What factors contributed to the diversity of the Middle Colonies?

2. **ANALYZE CAUSE AND EFFECT** What caused William Penn to allow Delaware to form its own assembly?

3. **INTERPRET MAPS** Locate Delaware on the map. Why does it make sense that Penn might have difficulty uniting people who settled there with the settlers who lived in the rest of Pennsylvania?

3.2 Forming Alliances

Have you ever heard the phrase "strength in numbers"? In the 1600s, as Native Americans and Europeans battled with each other in the Middle Colonies, they discovered that it's sometimes better to be part of a larger group than to stand alone.

MAIN IDEA The Iroquois Confederacy consisted of five tribes that worked together to defeat other Native American tribes and the French.

CLASHES AMONG CULTURES

As white colonists continued moving into New England and the Middle Colonies, two groups of Native Americans began to feel increasingly threatened by their presence.

One group that banded together was the Algonquian (al-GAHN-kwee-uhn). It consisted of the tribes who lived along the Atlantic coast and spoke similar languages. The Pequot tribe resided in New England. The Lenape inhabited the region that became the Middle Colonies. The Algonquian were hunters and gatherers. While they also fished and planted crops, they moved each season to follow the supply of food and lived in temporary camps while away from their villages.

Historically, the Algonquian were the enemies of another united group of tribes, the Iroquois (IHR-uh-kwoy). The Iroquois lived in what is currently central New York State. The French gave these Native Americans the name *Iroquois*, but they called themselves the Haudenosaunee (hah-duh-NAH-suh-nee), or "People of the Longhouse," for the style of home that they built and lived in with their families.

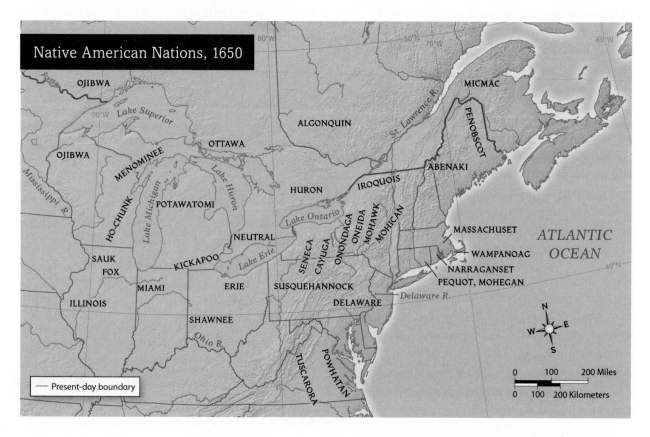

Native American Nations, 1650

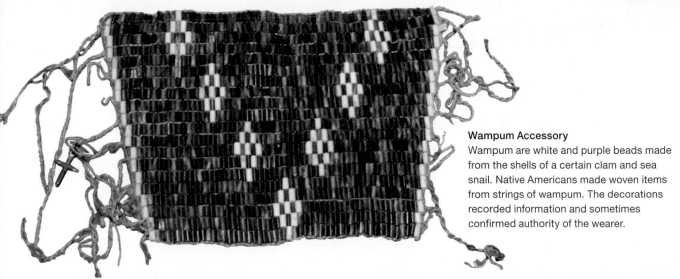

Wampum Accessory
Wampum are white and purple beads made from the shells of a certain clam and sea snail. Native Americans made woven items from strings of wampum. The decorations recorded information and sometimes confirmed authority of the wearer.

The arrival of colonists from Europe added another source of tension to the region. Yet another wave of settlers was now occupying disputed tribal territories, disrupting hunting grounds, communities, and sacred sites.

UNITED WE STAND

Even before Europeans began colonizing and claiming land in North America, conflicts among groups of Native Americans led some of them to form **alliances**, or agreements, with one another. One of the most important alliances was the **Iroquois Confederacy**. A **confederacy** is an agreement among several groups to protect and support one another in battle or other endeavors. In about 1600, the Iroquois Confederacy joined together five tribes: the Mohawk, Onondaga, Oneida, Cayuga, and Seneca, ending the fighting that had once raged among them. The addition of the Tuscarora about 120 years later would change the confederacy's name to the Six Nations.

By banding together, Native Americans hoped to protect their lands and culture and prevent further strife, but they also formed alliances with the French and British. These alliances shifted over time. Sometimes Native Americans even pitted the French, British, and colonists from other countries against one another.

The Iroquois—the Mohawk, in particular—often traded furs with Dutch and British settlers in exchange for firearms. In this way, the trading partners came to rely on each other, and they supported each other in battle. Likewise, the Lenape and the Huron, both enemies of the Iroquois, allied with the French.

Battles between the French and Iroquois over control of the fur trade continued. Due to high demand for their fur, beavers became scarce in the East by the mid-1600s. As a result, the Iroquois Confederacy moved west to gain greater access to beavers in the region, warring with competing tribes along the way. The Iroquois also attacked New France in the North, hoping to end French fur trading in the Ohio Valley and beyond.

In 1689, the Iroquois attacked the settlement of Lachine, near Montreal, in present-day Canada. The attack was in response to a raid two years earlier in which the French had destroyed Iroquois corn. The Iroquois killed about 250 settlers and burned the settlement. More back-and-forth retaliation followed until both sides grew weary of conflict. The weakened Iroquois made peace and, in 1701, signed a treaty of **neutrality**, in which they agreed not to take sides in future wars. But the conflict over land and furs was to grow even more.

HISTORICAL THINKING

1. **READING CHECK** How did forming alliances help the members of the Iroquois Confederacy?

2. **MAKE INFERENCES** In what ways did the demand for beaver fur affect alliances among Native Americans and Europeans?

3. **INTERPRET MAPS** How does the map help you understand why some Native Americans living near the Great Lakes might have been easy targets for the Iroquois Confederacy?

3.3 The Southern Colonies

Have you ever made a plan that didn't work out as you expected? Leaders developed detailed plans for the Southern Colonies. But as more colonists arrived, some of the plans worked better than others.

> **MAIN IDEA** The Southern Colonies provided economic opportunities and social challenges for the colonists who settled in them.

COLONIAL EXPANSION AND COMMERCE

As you have read, in 1607 Jamestown became the first colonial settlement. In 1699, Williamsburg became the new capital of the Virginia colony. Over time, Europeans established settlements in many parts of the South. Maryland, Virginia, North Carolina, South Carolina, and Georgia together formed the **Southern Colonies**.

In 1632, King Charles I of England granted a charter to George Calvert, who held the title Lord Baltimore, to establish a new colony called Maryland, made up of the northern part of Virginia. Most of its settlers were small landowners and renters. Upon Calvert's untimely death, his son became Lord Baltimore and Maryland's **proprietor**—the person responsible for the colony. Maryland's location on the Chesapeake Bay provided easy access to trade, and the region's rich, fertile soil was ideal for growing tobacco. Wealthy plantation owners and merchants built docks on **tributaries**, or small rivers that flow into larger bodies of water, of the Chesapeake Bay. There, they could more easily load ships with tobacco for export and receive ships from around the world loaded with goods.

By 1670, Carolina had become a colony. By 1691, it had split into two colonies: North Carolina, already settled by small planters from Virginia, and South Carolina. Many of South Carolina's settlers came from Barbados in the West Indies. They established large plantations where they grew tobacco, rice, cotton, sugarcane, and other crops. They purchased enslaved Africans to work these plantations. By 1729, both Carolinas had become **royal colonies**, or colonies with a governor and council appointed by the king.

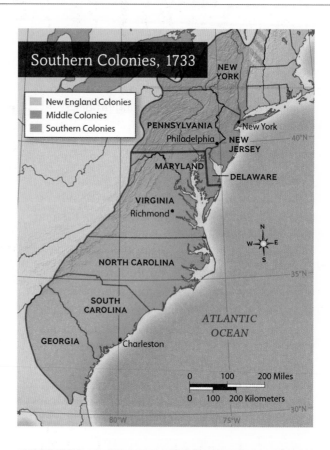

Southern Colonies, 1733

- New England Colonies
- Middle Colonies
- Southern Colonies

GEORGIA: A GRAND EXPERIMENT FAILS

Most of Britain's American colonies were founded for profit or religious freedom. But Georgia, the last mainland British colony in North America, began with a different idea. **James Oglethorpe** and Viscount John Percival envisioned a colony in which debtors and the very poor could make a new start.

King George II wasn't interested in helping the poor, but he understood that Georgia could be a military buffer between Spanish Florida and South Carolina. He granted the charter, placing control of the colony in the hands of trustees who could neither receive financial gain from Georgia nor own

CRITICAL VIEWING Tobacco was one of the major crops in the Southern Colonies. Today, the work of planting, harvesting, and preparing tobacco for market is much the same as it was during the colonial period. In the top photo, a man in Tennessee harvests the whole tobacco plant by chopping it at its base. In the bottom photo, bundles of tobacco hang to cure, or dry and preserve. Based on details you notice in both photos, what kinds of challenges do you think tobacco farmers encounter?

land within it. As governor, Oglethorpe required that all colonists follow three rules based on his own beliefs: no slaves, no liquor, and limited land ownership for each settler. His lofty vision did not last long.

Settlers began arriving in 1733. Many of them found the colony's strict policies unreasonable, so Georgia's population grew slowly. Its role as military buffer between the Spanish and British colonies soon became a source of conflict. The Spanish, suspecting the British of smuggling slaves and goods into Spanish provinces, began searching British ships. Then, in 1740, Oglethorpe attacked Florida, in an attempt to drive the Spanish out. The Spanish, in turn, invaded Georgia in 1742. After a number of other conflicts, both sides gave up, and calm was restored to the buffer zone.

The trustees recognized that Georgia would not thrive under Oglethorpe's strict rules. By 1750, laws allowed liquor and slavery, and there were no limits on land ownership. In 1752, control of Georgia returned to Great Britain. The grand experiment had failed.

HISTORICAL THINKING

1. **READING CHECK** In what ways was Georgia different from the other Southern Colonies?

2. **MAKE INFERENCES** Why might James Oglethorpe have insisted on limiting the amount of land a settler could have?

3. **INTERPRET MAPS** Find the city of Charleston on the map. What advantages do you think this city enjoyed due to its geographic location?

3.4 Economic Activities in the Thirteen Colonies

MAIN IDEA Colonists used the abundant resources around them to develop thriving economies in three colonial regions.

SHAPING THE COLONIAL ECONOMY

When European settlers came to North America, they took advantage of the region's **natural resources**. Natural resources are divided into two categories: living and nonliving. The earth provides living resources, such as plants, trees, and animals, that help feed, shelter, and clothe humans. The earth also provides nonliving resources, such as minerals, water, and soil. Both living and nonliving natural resources provide **raw materials**, or substances used to make products.

People use natural resources to engage in **economic activities**, or the production, distribution, and consumption of goods and services. When you go to the store to buy groceries, you are engaging in an economic activity.

How are natural resources, raw materials, and economic activities related? Consider this example. Colonists in New England chopped down trees in the region's thick forests for timber, or wood used for building. Timber became one of New England's most important raw materials. Shipbuilding became one of its most important economic activities.

The natural resources and raw materials available in different regions shaped how the colonies developed. Some natural resources, raw materials, and economic activities were unique to one region, but others were common among all three.

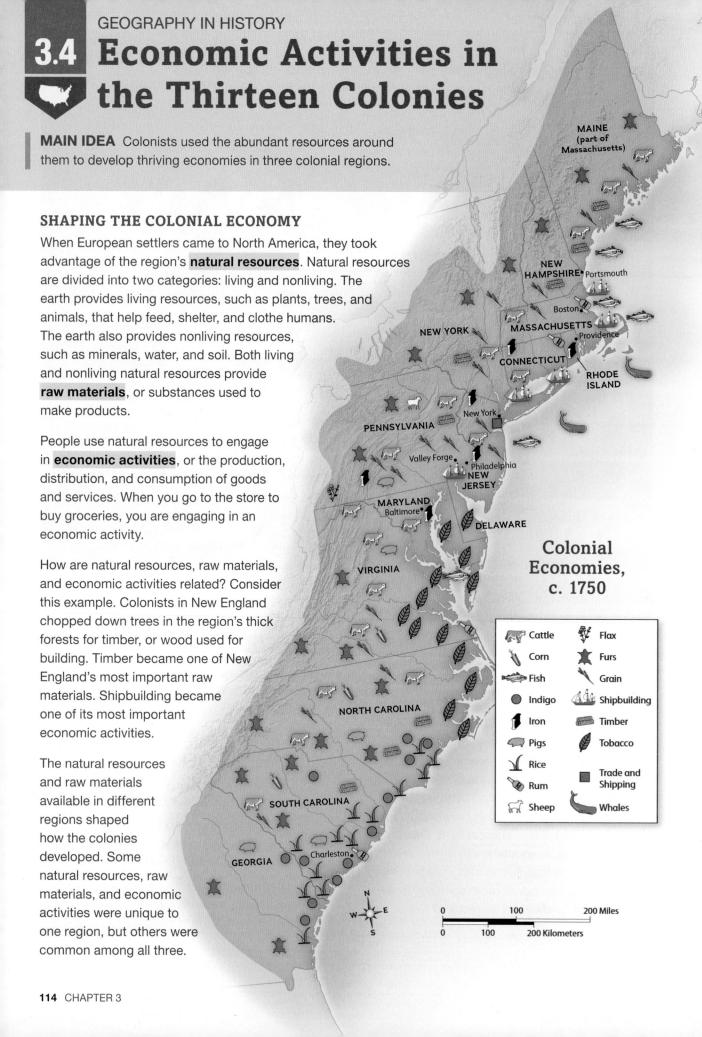

Colonial Economies, c. 1750

Legend:
- Cattle
- Corn
- Fish
- Indigo
- Iron
- Pigs
- Rice
- Rum
- Sheep
- Flax
- Furs
- Grain
- Shipbuilding
- Timber
- Tobacco
- Trade and Shipping
- Whales

COLONIAL TRADE

NORTH
AMERICA

The American colonies exported raw materials and agricultural products such as timber and tobacco to Europe. In exchange, they imported manufactured goods from Europe.

EUROPE

RAW MATERIALS AND AGRICULTURAL PRODUCTS →

← MANUFACTURED GOODS

AMERICAN
COLONIES

	CLIMATE	PHYSICAL FEATURES	RAW MATERIALS	ECONOMIC ACTIVITIES
NEW ENGLAND COLONIES				
MASSACHUSETTS	mild, short summers; long, cold winters	mountains, forests, rivers, poor soil	fish, whales, timber, cattle, wheat	farming, fishing, shipbuilding, rum production
CONNECTICUT	mild, short summers; long, cold winters	mountains, rivers, and poor, rocky soil	cattle, iron	shipbuilding, rum production
MIDDLE COLONIES				
NEW YORK	humid summers; cold, snowy winters	mountains, plains, hills, rivers	furs, timber, cattle, wheat	trade and shipping, shipbuilding, farming
PENNSYLVANIA	mild summers; mild winters	mountains, plains, fertile soil, rivers	flax, wheat, sheep, cattle, pigs	farming, shipbuilding
SOUTHERN COLONIES				
VIRGINIA	warm, humid; plentiful rainfall	rich soil, rivers, coastal lowlands	furs, cattle, pigs, wheat, corn, tobacco, fish	farming, fishing, rum production
NORTH CAROLINA	warm, humid; plentiful rainfall	deep forests, rivers, grasslands	indigo, tobacco, furs, timber, pigs, cattle, rice, corn	farming

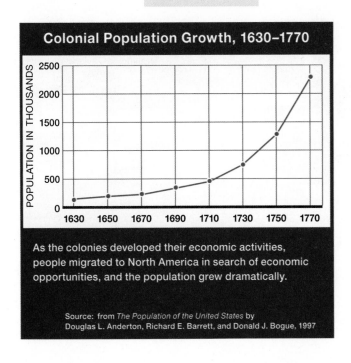

Colonial Population Growth, 1630–1770

As the colonies developed their economic activities, people migrated to North America in search of economic opportunities, and the population grew dramatically.

Source: from *The Population of the United States* by Douglas L. Anderton, Richard E. Barrett, and Donald J. Bogue, 1997

THINK LIKE A GEOGRAPHER

1. **IDENTIFY MAIN IDEAS AND DETAILS** For each colonial region, identify an example of a natural resource that helped the region develop a specific economic activity.

2. **INTERPRET CHARTS** In what ways are the raw materials and economic activities of the New England Colonies and the Southern Colonies alike and different?

3. **ANALYZE ENVIRONMENTAL CONCEPTS** In what ways did the quality and quantity of natural resources impact population growth in the 13 colonies?

3.5 Werowocomoco, the Powhatan Capital

In 1607, Europe had long-established capital cities such as London, Paris, and Madrid. When the Jamestown colonists first met the Native American chief they called Powhatan, they visited him in an equally sophisticated capital.

MAIN IDEA In the 1600s, Werowocomoco was the capital of the Powhatan tribes. Today researchers are exploring its site to learn about the tribes and their interactions with English colonists.

SEAT OF POWER FOR A CHIEFDOM

It was in Werowocomoco (wayr-wuh-KAH-muh-koh) that John Smith first met Powhatan's daughter Pocahontas, who eventually married colonist John Rolfe. Smith would later tell a dramatic tale of being rescued by Pocahontas from certain execution at the hands of Chief Powhatan's warriors. Historians suspect the true story of the meeting was a little less exciting, but it nevertheless was a key moment in the relationship between the colonists and the Powhatan people.

The village of Werowocomoco must have presented a real contrast to the Jamestown Colony in 1607. While Jamestown had been built on swampy ground, Werowocomoco was built on bluffs above the Pamunkey River, which the Europeans later renamed the York River, in present-day Virginia.

The village had many geographical advantages. River bluffs and nearby creeks served as natural defenses against attackers. Nearby waterways were a source of drinking water and fish. The surrounding

Archaeologists and members of Virginia's Native American tribes spend long hours carefully excavating the Werowocomoco dig site adjacent to the York River.

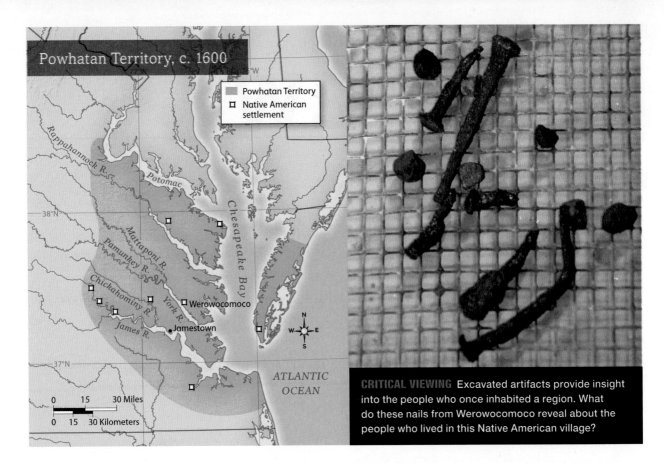

Powhatan Territory, c. 1600

Powhatan Territory
☐ Native American settlement

Rappahannock R.
Potomac
Chesapeake Bay
Mattaponi R.
Pamunkey R.
Chickahominy R.
York R.
Werowocomoco
James R.
Jamestown
38°N
37°N
ATLANTIC OCEAN

0   15   30 Miles
0   15   30 Kilometers

CRITICAL VIEWING Excavated artifacts provide insight into the people who once inhabited a region. What do these nails from Werowocomoco reveal about the people who lived in this Native American village?

land was suitable for farming, and nearby forests provided wood for building and fires.

Archaeological evidence suggests that Virginia Indians had lived on the Werowocomoco site since around 8000 B.C. By the early 1600s, the village was the seat of power for Chief Powhatan. He ruled over a group of more than 30 Algonquian-speaking tribes spread out over more than 8,000 square miles around Chesapeake Bay.

EXPLORING WEROWOCOMOCO TODAY

Today, Werowocomoco's wealth lies in the knowledge it reveals about Powhatan society. In 1609, Chief Powhatan abandoned the village, and in time the location of Werowocomoco was forgotten. Then in 2003, researchers announced they had used evidence from historical maps and documents to pinpoint the village's location. Since then, archaeologists have been actively excavating the site.

Finding Werowocomoco has allowed researchers to learn not only about how Powhatan society evolved but also about the meeting of the English and Native American cultures that took place between 1607 and 1609. Archaeologists found a number of English artifacts that closely

resembled lists of trade goods John Smith kept in his Jamestown journals. These included several copper-alloy items such as a pot, fragments of a spoon, and small beads. In order to enhance his importance among local tribes, Chief Powhatan had tried to maintain an exclusive trade in objects such as these with the English.

Within a few years, the English and the Powhatan would be at war. Werowocomoco preserves evidence that for brief but significant moments before the conflict, the two sides engaged in mutual bonds of trade and cultural exchange.

HISTORICAL THINKING

1. **READING CHECK** What types of items did the Powhatan and the Jamestown settlers trade with each other?

2. **MAKE CONNECTIONS** Think about what you learned about Jamestown in this chapter. In what ways did geography affect the relationship between Jamestown and Werowocomoco?

3. **MAKE GENERALIZATIONS** What purposes do exploring and preserving sites like Werowocomoco serve?

3 REVIEW

VOCABULARY

Use vocabulary words to complete the sentences.

1. _____ had to work for a set number of years to pay off their passages to the colonies.

2. Governor Berkeley accused Nathaniel Bacon of being a _____ .

3. The Virginia Company was known as a _____ because its shareholders also owned stock in the company.

4. When Lord Baltimore died, his son became the _____ of the Maryland colony.

5. The company had received a _____ from King James I to establish a colony in Virginia.

6. Governed by the crown through an appointed governor and council, Carolina was a _____ .

7. In the early 1600s, a _____ who disagreed with the beliefs of the Church could be punished.

READING STRATEGY
MAKE INFERENCES

If you haven't already, complete your chart of inferences about the challenges of establishing the first 13 colonies. List at least four inferences. Then answer the question.

8. What kind of physical dangers did settlers face in the colonies?

I READ	I KNOW	AND SO
The settlers lived under difficult conditions.	Many settlers died of diseases.	

MAIN IDEAS

9. How did John Smith help keep the settlers from starving at Jamestown? **LESSON 1.1**

10. What caused the conflict between colonists at Jamestown and the Powhatan? **LESSON 1.4**

11. Why did Nathaniel Bacon stage a rebellion? **LESSON 1.4**

12. How were the Pilgrims' and Puritans' involvement with the Church of England different? **LESSON 2.1**

13. What was the reason for massive arrests in Salem in 1692? **LESSON 2.4**

14. How did England benefit from taking control of New Netherland? **LESSON 3.1**

15. How did William Penn's Quaker beliefs help influence the diverse makeup of Pennsylvania? **LESSON 3.1**

16. Why did the Iroquois attack New France? **LESSON 3.2**

17. How did Maryland's access to the Chesapeake Bay benefit the colony? **LESSON 3.3**

Answer the following questions. Support your answers with evidence from the chapter.

18. **EVALUATE** In what ways was control of land central to struggles between Native Americans and European colonists?

19. **SYNTHESIZE** Why did the American colonies represent a safe haven for religious groups willing to move to a new place in the 17th and 18th centuries?

20. **COMPARE AND CONTRAST** How were the settlers in the New England colonies different from and similar to settlers in the Middle Colonies?

21. **FORM AND SUPPORT OPINIONS** Why do you think some Puritans in Salem might have felt threatened by women owning property? Use information from the chapter to support your opinion.

22. **DISTINGUISH FACT AND OPINION** Was the idea that Georgia could help debtors and the very poor overcome their difficulties a fact or an opinion? Explain why you think so.

INTERPRET MAPS

Look closely at the map of the Pilgrims' intended route and where they actually sailed. Then answer the questions that follow.

23. What was the Pilgrims' planned destination?

24. Between what latitudes did the Pilgrims go off their planned course, and where did they land?

Pilgrims' Route, 1620

ANALYZE SOURCES

Transcriptions of court records from the 1692 Salem witch trials include testimony from the accused. In the following transcription, Reverend Increase Mather relays information about his conversation with prisoner Mary Bridges. Read the passage and answer the question.

> Goodwife Bridges said that she had confessed against herself things which were all utterly false; and that she was brought to her confession by being told that she certainly was a witch, and so made to believe it,—though she had no other grounds so to believe.

25. What does Mather's statement reveal about the likely cause of many people's confessions?

CONNECT TO YOUR LIFE

26. **INFORMATIVE** Think about how and why people left their homelands to settle in the 13 colonies. Then think of a present-day group of people who have moved to a new place. Write a paragraph that connects the two groups.

TIPS

• Before you start writing, organize your ideas in a two-column chart. On the left, list your two groups. On the right, list the reasons why each group decided to move.

• Include textual evidence and one or two vocabulary terms from the chapter.

• Conclude the paragraph with your observations about the reasons why colonists came to America and why the group you selected decided to move to a new place.

COLONIAL DEVELOPMENT
1651–1763

ESSENTIAL QUESTION
How did a developing American identity unite the colonies?

AMERICAN STORIES ONLINE Colliding Cultures: The Fur Trade

SECTION 1 **New England: Commerce and Religion**

KEY VOCABULARY

apprentice	provisions	smuggle
common school	religious freedom	subsistence farming
Navigation Acts		

SECTION 2 **The Southern Colonies**

KEY VOCABULARY

artisan	cash crop	overseer	Stono Rebellion
backcountry	indigo	Piedmont	

SECTION 3 **The Middle Colonies**

KEY VOCABULARY

arable	Conestoga wagon	diversity	tolerance
commodity	conformity	gristmill	

SECTION 4 **Roots of American Democracy**

KEY VOCABULARY

burgeon	libel	Parliament
Enlightenment	midwife	salutary neglect
Great Awakening	natural rights	salvation

SECTION 5 **The French and Indian War**

KEY VOCABULARY

trading post   treaty

AMERICAN GALLERY ONLINE Colonial Graveyards

READING STRATEGY

Colonial Development

IDENTIFY MAIN IDEAS AND DETAILS
To identify a main idea and details, state the most important idea and find facts that support it. Use a diagram like this one to find a main idea and details about the development of the colonies as you read the chapter.

Main Idea:
Detail:
Detail:
Detail:

"The ground is very fruitful,
and produceth plentiful crops with great speed."
—Nathaniel Shrigley, author and British Army officer

CRITICAL VIEWING The Piedmont in Virginia and North Carolina, shown here, is a land of rolling hills and rich farmland. How does the photo illustrate the description in the quotation above?

Sperm whales, like the one shown here, have huge heads and a full set of teeth along the inside of their long jaws. Colonial whalers frequently hunted this type of whale, venturing far out to sea to search for them. The oil of these whales burned more brightly than other whale oils and made finer candles, which became important export items.

1.1 Harvesting Land and Sea

In 17th-century New England, you basically had two choices: toil day and night as a farmer, or toil day and night as a sailor. Neither option left much time for anything else.

MAIN IDEA New England's colonial economy was based on agriculture, commerce, and small-scale manufacturing.

FARMING HILLY, ROCKY LAND

Most New England colonists were farmers. Their farms were small and were frequently located on hilly and forested land with rocky soil. The long, cold winters made for a short growing season.

Farmers relied on their large families to clear the fields, plant and harvest the crops, and care for the farm animals. This all added up to something called **subsistence farming**. This means the farmers produced about enough food to provide for their family with only a little, if any, left over to sell or trade. In other words, they were barely scraping by. Without much in savings or extra food, a poor year of farming could ruin a family.

Because farming was so tough, the size and quality of a family's farmland mattered. Colonists were at the mercy of their town's powerful Puritan founders, who led the church and the town. The founders decided the location and amount of land a family received. One man might be given 50 acres with grazing fields attached, another only 3 acres with grazing fields a mile away. It wasn't fair, and these differences in land ownership created distinct social classes within the town.

Harpoon
Whalers used harpoons to stun and capture their prey. Sailors launched whaleboats from the ship, surrounded the whale, and threw their weapons. Once the whale was fully pierced by harpoons, which were attached to ropes, the sailors towed the huge animal back to the ship.

FISHING, WHALING, AND TRADE

The Atlantic Ocean provided greater economic opportunities than agriculture. Colonial fishers could engage in international trade, selling their catch to London merchants in exchange for goods such as shoes, textiles, and metal products. Whaling provided the colonists with many commercial products, including whale oils and waxes, meat, fat, bones, and leather. Colonists sold and exported the whale meat and blubber, or fat. People used the blubber to light oil lamps, make candles, and soften leather.

Fishing and whaling led to the growth of a shipbuilding industry. New England's plentiful forests supplied the shipyards with timber—and employment. Building a single ship could employ 200 workers. Shipbuilders also kept sawmills, rope makers, and iron foundries busy. By the end of the 1700s, New England built one-third of all British ships and almost all of its own merchants' and fishers' ships. This economic activity made New England a natural center of colonial trade.

HISTORICAL THINKING

1. **READING CHECK** What four economic activities were important in New England?

2. **DRAW CONCLUSIONS** What conclusion can you draw about the relationship between a family's farm and its social class?

3. **ANALYZE CAUSE AND EFFECT** In what ways were the goods provided by the Atlantic Ocean essential to the livelihood, economy, and culture of the New England colonists?

1.2 Colonial Trade

It was good to be a trader in New England. The region's shipyards turned out many ships that carried goods along the North American coast and across the Atlantic. If colonial trade were a race, the merchants of New England were winning.

MAIN IDEA New England merchants expanded the colonial economy through Atlantic trade.

TRADE IN THE ATLANTIC

As its fishing and whaling industries continued to thrive, New England found itself at the center of America's trade. New England merchants traded with other colonies. They also engaged in direct trade with Europe. Soon the New England merchants became the chief traders along the coast from Newfoundland to Georgia.

The merchants also conducted business through the triangular trade. As you have learned, the triangular trade routes crossed the Atlantic and connected North America, Europe, and Africa. New England merchants sent goods such as rum and cotton to Europe. The merchants received imported goods including wine, fruit, and salt from islands off the coast of North Africa. Molasses, rum, sugar, and dyes came from the Caribbean. Food and drink weren't the only goods New England merchants traded. As you know, the merchants also acquired enslaved people from Africa in exchange for rum and other goods.

The growth of trade across the Atlantic created great demand for sailors and other workers. Shipbuilders and sailmakers crafted vessels.

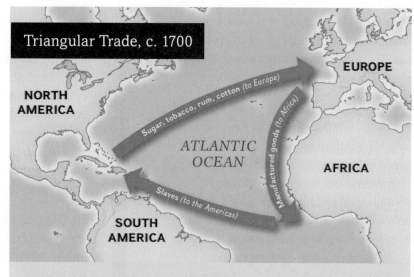

Colonial Trade Routes and Goods

The colonial economy depended on ships trading goods between North America, Europe, and Africa. So did the economies of most European countries. France, England, the Netherlands, Portugal, and Spain were willing to fight for a share of the wealth the trade routes generated. Many ships on the triangular trade routes sailed only between North America and Africa or Europe and Africa. Some ships bound for New England also stopped in Brazil or the Caribbean, where some of the enslaved Africans onboard were sold.

Suppliers stocked ships with **provisions**, which consisted of the food, water, and other supplies needed for the voyages. Dockworkers loaded and unloaded goods that laborers transported in carts. As a result of the thriving trade, port cities sprang up in New York, Philadelphia, and Charleston after 1750. Colonial trade was no longer dominated entirely by the merchants of Boston and other port cities in Massachusetts and Rhode Island.

Blackbeard the Pirate

Smuggling was not the only illegal activity on the high seas. Pirates prowled the Atlantic looking for ships and cargo to steal. One such pirate was called Blackbeard.

According to some, the English pirate's real name was Edward Teach. He tried to make his appearance frightening by putting pieces of burning rope under his hat, as shown in the illustration. For two years, he and his pirates terrorized merchant ships in the Atlantic and the Caribbean. In 1718, Blackbeard met his end at the hands of Lieutenant Robert Maynard of the Royal Navy. Maynard chopped off the pirate's head and threw his body overboard.

ENGLAND'S CUT OF THE PROFITS

When New England began to earn huge profits from trade, the English decided to begin taking their cut. To ensure their share of the profits, the English passed a series of laws called the **Navigation Acts** in 1651. The acts required that goods brought to England or its colonies in Asia, Africa, or America be carried on English ships or ships made in the colonies. Furthermore, the acts identified a list of colonial products that could only be sold to England or its colonies. These products included tobacco, sugar, cotton, and dyes.

The acts also made sure that England controlled—and taxed—all trade to and from the colonies. So, for instance, all European goods bound for the colonies had to go to England first. There, English dockworkers would unload, inspect, and reload the goods back onto English or colonial-made ships. These ships then carried the goods to colonial ports where the English charged additional taxes on the imports. Worst of all for the colonists, the English taxed all colonial goods that were not going to be shipped to England.

Not surprisingly, the colonists resented the additional charges to products going in both directions. Some colonists turned to trading goods illegally, or **smuggling**. The colonists proved hard to control as they resisted attempts to enforce the acts.

While New England colonists protested their treatment at the hands of the English government, many in their own society had far more cause for complaint. But enslaved African Americans and some Protestant groups were powerless to change their situation.

HISTORICAL THINKING

1. **READING CHECK** What different types of trade did New England merchants carry out?

2. **ANALYZE CAUSE AND EFFECT** Why did Parliament pass the Navigation Acts?

3. **INTERPRET MAPS** How do the items sent from North America differ from those exported from Europe?

1.3 Society and Religion

In New England, some African Americans performed tasks that were not available in other colonies—small consolation for their far-from-equal treatment.

> **MAIN IDEA** New England was different from other colonial regions in terms of its use of enslaved labor and its religious views.

ENSLAVED LABOR IN NEW ENGLAND

Enslaved African Americans accounted for only 2 to 3 percent of New England's population. But this wasn't really due to colonial opposition to enslavement. Some of the wealthiest New England merchants made their money in the slave trade. The low percentage was due to geography and economics. New England farms were generally small. Most colonial farmers had no need for large numbers of enslaved workers, and they couldn't afford them, anyway.

The enslaved African Americans who came to New England worked as household servants, farmhands, artisans, and laborers. In the Southern Colonies, slaveholders generally wanted to purchase enslaved people who could work in the fields immediately, but slaveholders in New England were often more willing to purchase young people who could be trained for specific household or business duties.

Enslaved people generally lived in their masters' houses and worked by their sides. They practiced carpentry, printing, baking, and making cloth, shoes, and clothing, among other trades. In seaport towns, enslaved African Americans sometimes worked alongside free African Americans in the shipyards and on the docks as fishers, whalers, and shipbuilders.

Some African Americans were born free, but most free African Americans spent part of their lives in enslavement. Some achieved freedom by fulfilling the terms of a work contract. Some escaped. Others were freed by their master for faithful service or as part of their master's will. Although both enslaved and free African Americans in New England enjoyed some legal rights, they were not treated equally. For example, a 1703 Massachusetts law stated that African Americans could not be outdoors after 9:00 P.M. unless they were on business for their masters.

THE DECLINE OF PURITANISM

Some religious groups were treated unfairly, although not to the extent suffered by African Americans. The Puritans saw other Protestant groups, such as the Quakers and Baptists, as a threat to the harmony of their society. Therefore, Puritan leaders allowed only the male members of the Puritan church to vote and hold most public offices. Puritans clashed with other Protestant sects that disagreed with their teachings. They punished citizens who did not share their beliefs and even hanged several Quaker missionaries. They also objected to a newly emerging merchant class and its focus on commercial values and worried that the younger generation was only concerned with making money.

Beginning in 1650, membership in the Puritan church had begun to decline, especially among men. Quakers who had been deported from Massachusetts kept coming back. King Charles II of England sent a letter forbidding the execution of Quakers. Quaker communities and Baptist congregations began to flourish throughout New England.

The crown gave the Puritans two options: they could either obey the terms of the colonial charter of Massachusetts Bay or they could have the charter revoked. And the charter guaranteed **religious freedom**, or the right to practice the religion of one's choosing, for all.

But the Puritan leaders believed themselves to be the highest authority in Massachusetts and did not feel that they answered to the king. Charles II disagreed. In 1684, the king canceled the colonial charter of Massachusetts Bay. Charles died in 1685, but that didn't do the Puritans any good. Charles's successor, James II, tried to strengthen English control even more. He combined Massachusetts with other northern colonies to form the **Dominion of New England**.

Eventually, the Dominion included Massachusetts Bay, Plymouth, New Hampshire, Maine, Rhode Island, Connecticut, New York, and New Jersey. Both the decision to create the Dominion and to appoint its new governor were extremely unpopular with the colonists. They felt stripped of the rights and freedoms they had enjoyed under their own colonial charters.

In 1691, Massachusetts received a new charter to replace the one King Charles had canceled. It guaranteed religious freedom for all Protestants, further undermining Puritan influence. It also opened up the right to vote to any man owning property, regardless of his religion. The number of property owners was much greater than the number of churchgoers. As a result, the charter led to a large increase in the number of voters in New England.

As Puritanism declined, education in New England was on the rise. Acquiring knowledge was becoming a new priority in the colony.

🏛 New Britain Museum of American Art
New Britain, Connecticut

In *Gentleman with Attendant,* painted between 1785–88, artist Ralph Earl characterizes the enslaved African Americans of New England as serving their masters more directly. This is in contrast to slavery in the Southern Colonies, where enslaved people worked in fields far from the owners, under the supervision of hired bosses.

HISTORICAL THINKING

1. **READING CHECK** Why was the percentage of enslaved African Americans low in New England?

2. **IDENTIFY MAIN IDEAS AND DETAILS** What types of tasks did most enslaved and free African Americans in New England perform?

3. **ANALYZE CAUSE AND EFFECT** What impact did the 1691 Massachusetts charter have on Puritanism?

1.4 Education and Literacy

Why do you read? Probably for fun or to learn new things. Colonial children mostly learned to read so they could understand the Bible.

MAIN IDEA Education and literacy were important to New England colonists and had a major impact on the region's economic and social development.

AMERICAN PLACES
Harvard University, Cambridge, Massachusetts

Harvard began as a private college founded along the Charles River in 1636 to educate ministers of the church. It is called "Harvard" after John Harvard, from England, who left a gift of 779 English pounds and 400 books to the college. Increase Mather and John Sassamon, whom you have already read about, were both students there. Mather later served as the college's president from 1692 to 1701. The student housing shown here opened in 1931.

A NEW ENGLAND EDUCATION

New Englanders believed people needed to be able to read so they could learn about God. They set up schools that focused on the Bible, religious study, and texts that taught moral behavior. In the 1640s, the Massachusetts legislature established **common schools**, the colonial name for elementary schools, and secondary schools called Latin grammar schools. Connecticut and other colonies followed with similar legislation. Eventually, more people in New England were able to read than in any other colony.

Early education also involved teaching children skills that would help them thrive in their community. For many colonial boys, this meant becoming an **apprentice**. An apprentice lived with a master craftsman for a set number of years in order to learn a trade, such as butchering, baking, or carpentry. Girls, on the other hand, often stayed with their mothers to learn cooking, sewing, and other skills necessary to manage a household.

Communities established colleges for older students. The Puritans founded Harvard College in Massachusetts in 1636 and Yale College in Connecticut in 1701. Harvard and Yale joined William and Mary College in Virginia to make up the only three colleges in the colonies. All three have grown into modern universities that offer a wide range of subjects and the chance to earn many different degrees. Most of the graduates of colonial colleges became members of the clergy. None, however, were women. Colonial colleges only admitted men.

NEWSPAPERS AND BOOKS

The rising rate of literacy throughout the colonies created a big demand for newspapers and books. Starting in 1704, newspapers popped up in Boston, Philadelphia, New York, and Charleston. These early newspapers focused on European

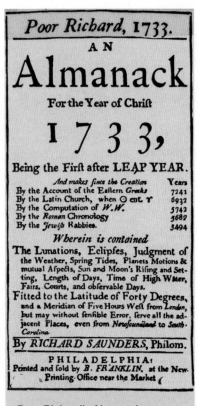

Poor Richard's Almanack
Ben Franklin created the almanac under the name Richard Saunders, but he credited himself as the volume's printer.

events and politics. They helped colonists feel less separated from faraway Europe and more connected to England.

The general reading tastes of colonial people ranged across many subjects, but readers especially enjoyed topics unique to the American experience. In New England, books about being captured by Native Americans attracted interest. One of the most popular of these was by **Mary Rowlandson**. In her account, she describes being taken prisoner with her three children during King Philip's War. The Native Americans who had captured her then released her for 20 pounds' ransom. After her husband, a Puritan minister, died, Rowlandson moved to Boston and wrote the story for which she is famous.

Another favorite genre, the almanac, stuffed many types of useful information together in one volume. *Poor Richard's Almanack*, published by **Benjamin Franklin**, proved a best seller. It mixed calendars, information about the weather and planting, medical advice, and witty proverbs, such as "Fish and visitors stink after three days." Also around this time, writers began to compose the first histories of their lives in the colonies. Meanwhile, to the south, life was very different—particularly for African slaves.

HISTORICAL THINKING

1. **READING CHECK** What types of schools did colonial New Englanders establish?

2. **DRAW CONCLUSIONS** What role did religion play in the importance of education in New England?

3. **MAKE GENERALIZATIONS** Why would a newspaper's emphasis on European events and politics be helpful to colonial merchants?

Slater studies gravestones like this one from 1729. Its imagery is softened by daisy wheels, spiritually protective symbols.

Graveyards,
Buildings, and American Identity

"Archaeology is an adventure. Even graveyards and buildings have exciting tales to tell." —Donald Slater

When **Donald Slater** was growing up in Massachusetts, his parents drove him to a swim club during the summer. On the way, they passed an old graveyard that always caught his eye. It stood abandoned and disordered, with gravestones tilted every which way—some nearly falling over. "I knew there was a story there," Slater remembers thinking. Years later, he became an archaeologist and decided to uncover the stories at such sites himself.

^
Donald Slater enjoys providing students with hands-on archaeological experience. Here, Slater (far left), his colleagues, and students work at a dig at the Rebecca Nurse Homestead to learn about Nurse, who was believed to be a witch and hanged in 1692.

THE GRAVE WHISPERER

National Geographic Explorer Donald Slater studies graveyards from the 1600s and 1700s. Luckily for him, he lives in New England where there are lots of graveyards from these periods. One of his favorites is the Old Burying Ground, established in 1634 in Ipswich, Massachusetts. It contains the region's oldest documented gravestones, including those of the wife and child of John Winthrop, Jr., the town's chief founder.

As Slater examines a graveyard, he pays particular attention to the iconography of the gravestones—the stone's carved design. Although the details are hotly debated among scholars, Slater believes that changes in the designs point to evolving religious ideas in the New England Colonies. A death's head, showing a stylized skull with wings or crossed bones, appeared on most early gravestones. As the 18th century progressed, however, death's heads were replaced by winged cherub, or angel, heads.

Slater believes a religious movement that began in the 1720s caused the graveyard iconography to soften. The movement—called the Great Awakening—which you'll learn more about later in this chapter, emphasized the idea that people could ascend to heaven by demonstrating their faith in God. Earlier Puritan beliefs held that people's place after death—heaven or hell—was predestined, or determined, by God at birth.

Around the same time, the epitaphs, or inscriptions, carved on the gravestones also became more hopeful. Instead of focusing on mortality, later epitaphs celebrate the deceased's reward in heaven for a life well lived. Some provide a brief narrative of the person's life. According to Slater, one such epitaph reveals that the man buried was born a slave but died free.

OUR AMERICAN IDENTITY

Like gravestones, colonial architectural styles also evolved over time. Some of these changes reflect cultural change—and the increasing American identity of the colonies. In the early 1600s, builders

Slater reads a gravestone at the South Parish Burial Ground in Andover, Massachusetts. Established in 1709, the cemetery is Andover's oldest museum.

in New England based their structures on English architecture. But instead of brick, the colonists most often used wood and other rustic building materials, which resulted in a uniquely American style. Builders adapted structures to conditions in the colony. For example, they constructed summer kitchens at the rear of a house to avoid heating up the entire home, applying construction techniques they used in England.

Much of New England is a treasure trove of colonial sites and artifacts. But what if you don't live there? Slater suggests you visit your local historical society to learn about early American sites in your community, including those of Native Americans, or ask your neighborhood librarian for information. All these sources can help you discover your American identity. And Slater believes this is important. For, as he says, "There is no better way to preserve our cultural heritage than to educate today's youth on the subject, because it is they who will be making tomorrow's decisions that will determine whether sites are protected or destroyed."

HISTORICAL THINKING

1. **READING CHECK** What does Slater study when he investigates colonial graveyards?

2. **ANALYZE CAUSE AND EFFECT** According to Slater, why might a cherub head have replaced the death's head on later graves?

3. **MAKE INFERENCES** What do you think the architectural developments by the early 1700s suggest about New England colonists?

2.1 Slavery Expands

A person journeying from New England to the Southern Colonies would be amazed by its large plantations—quite a contrast to New England's small farms. And the warm climate would probably make the traveler shed his or her jacket. What a difference geography makes!

MAIN IDEA The Southern Colonies developed a system of plantation agriculture that relied on increasing numbers of enslaved Africans.

PLANTATION CROPS

The geography of New England was very different from that of the Southern Colonies. The fertile land and milder climate of the Southern Colonies—Maryland, Virginia, the Carolinas, and Georgia—made it possible to grow **cash crops**, crops grown for sale rather than for use by the farmers themselves. The main cash crops were tobacco, rice, and **indigo**, a plant whose leaves provide a source of blue dye for cloth. Tobacco thrived in the hot and humid growing season of Virginia and coastal Maryland. Rice was well suited to the swampy lowlands and tidal areas of coastal rivers in the Carolinas. However, the colonists had no experience in rice cultivation. They depended on enslaved Africans, who had been taken from rice-growing regions in West Africa, to farm the rice and ensure successful yields.

Plantations sprang up along the rivers so planters could use the water for their rice fields. Ships sailed up tributaries from the Chesapeake Bay and docked at the plantations. Because of the ease of transporting goods directly from their farms, southern colonists had little need for port cities.

One exception was the busy seaport of **Charles Town** (now called Charleston). As Carolina planters developed cash crops, Charles Town grew as a port. Many plantation owners lived there part of the year to escape the isolation of their plantations. Although Charles Town became the fourth-largest colonial city, after Boston, Philadelphia, and New York, it never grew larger because English and New England shippers controlled its trade. Without a strong merchant community, the city failed to attract large numbers of new workers.

NEW SLAVE TRADING

Planters in the Southern Colonies originally hired white indentured servants to work for several years in exchange for a plot of land. But in 1698, England gave all English merchants permission to participate in slave trading. As a result, planters who lived in the **Chesapeake**, the settled land around the Chesapeake Bay, turned to enslaved Africans to farm their land. In 1660, only 900 Africans resided in the Chesapeake, some of whom had arrived as servants and lived free. By 1720, one-fifth of the population of that area were Africans. By 1770, that number ranged from one-third to one-half. African populations in Virginia and the Carolinas also increased dramatically during this period. By 1750, African Americans accounted for over 40 percent of Virginia's total population and more than half of South Carolina's. More than 90 percent of the total African-American population was enslaved.

HISTORICAL THINKING

1. **READING CHECK** Why were tobacco and rice good cash crops for Virginia, Maryland, and the Carolinas?

2. **ANALYZE VISUALS** After which step in the rice process are the grains of rice collected?

3. **IDENTIFY MAIN IDEAS AND DETAILS** What factors led to the expansion of slave labor in the Southern Colonies?

RICE PRODUCTION

Rice production required many steps and many people to grow enough grain to make a profit. Below are some of the steps of this labor-intensive process.

1 Flooding

Farmworkers built flood gates and dug ditches. They planted, then opened the floodgates to fill the rice fields with water. After the seeds sprouted, the fields were drained so the women could weed. Then the fields were reflooded.

2 Harvesting

Workers harvested, or reaped, the ripened rice plants with a cutting tool called a scythe (SIGHTH).

3 Threshing

On colonial plantations, threshing meant beating the plants with a stick called a flail until the grains fell from the plants.

4 Winnowing

Winnowing was the process of tossing the rice grains in a basket to separate them from their tissue-like outer coating, or chaff.

In 1915, when these photographs were taken, slavery had been abolished, but workers still used tools similar to ones that had been used more than 200 years ago.

5 Pounding

The winnowed rice was poured into a hollowed-out log and pounded with a staff called a mortar. This removed the tough outer husk from the grain.

2.2 From Plantations to the Backcountry

There's a saying that "the rich get richer," and it seemed to be true on the large plantations. More land and slaves meant more cash crops—and more money.

MAIN IDEA Life in the coastal areas of the Southern Colonies differed greatly from life further inland, and revolved extensively around slavery.

WEALTH AND CLASS

Over time, wealthy planters in Maryland, Virginia, and the Carolinas bought more and more land and slaves. The expanding plantations produced increasing amounts of tobacco, rice, and indigo. The owners reaped the profits.

Not all farmers became wealthy, but the owners of the largest plantations became so wealthy and powerful that distinct classes formed among southern farmers. With their luxurious homes and leisurely lifestyle, rich landowners lived like nobles in Europe.

An army of slaves made this way of life possible. The work the slaves performed depended on where they lived. In South Carolina, each enslaved person received certain jobs to complete each day—a field to hoe, a fence to build. In the Chesapeake, most enslaved people worked on the plantation for a specific number of hours or until the **overseer**, or supervisor, told them to stop. As a result, many slaves worked long into the night.

While some plantation owners treated enslaved people fairly well, others did not. But the terrible workload took its toll on all the laborers. As work increased and the hours grew even longer, death rates among enslaved people surged dramatically.

THE BACKCOUNTRY

A different kind of culture arose as some settlers in the Southern Colonies sought their fortune in the backcountry. The **backcountry** stretched along the Appalachian Mountains from Pennsylvania south through the Shenandoah Valley to the Carolinas. This region included the rich soil, rolling hills, and deep forests of the **Piedmont**, a relatively flat area between the mountains and the coastal plain.

In the early 1700s, European settlers such as the Scots-Irish, immigrants from the northern part of Ireland, came to the colonies. They began settling in the backcountry and establishing farms outside the first English settlements, carving their farmland out of the forests.

Backcountry farmers learned to be self-sufficient. They used one of the most plentiful natural resources of this region—timber—to build simple log cabins. They hunted and raised enough crops and livestock to feed their families. Women in the backcountry worked in the home, the fields, and the wild. Many of them carried guns. Also, unlike many people in the Southern Colonies, most of the immigrants living in the backcountry didn't rely on slaves.

HISTORICAL THINKING

1. **READING CHECK** What was the social structure like in the Chesapeake in the 1700s?

2. **COMPARE AND CONTRAST** How did work patterns differ for slaves in South Carolina and the Chesapeake?

3. **ANALYZE CAUSE AND EFFECT** How did the environment of the backcountry affect how the people settling there made a living?

Shenandoah Valley

In the 1700s, Scots-Irish settlers who had come to Pennsylvania began moving into the Shenandoah Valley in present-day West Virginia and Virginia. The rich soil of the valley made it a dream for farming, and at the time, the Scots-Irish had little competition from other Europeans. They did, however, compete for the land with Native Americans who had long called the region home.

2.3 Life Under Slavery

After days of hard work, enslaved Africans gathered together—sometimes secretly—on Sundays. They cooked African foods and played music based on African rhythms. As much as they could, they hung on to pieces of their past.

MAIN IDEA Plantation slaves kept their African culture and traditions alive, even though their living and working conditions were often very difficult.

LIVING CONDITIONS

As you've read, most plantation slaves—both men and women—spent long hours planting, weeding, and harvesting tobacco, rice, and indigo. Overseers sometimes used whips and other harsh instruments and measures to force workers to work harder or more productively. Some owners also recruited slaves, called drivers, to push their fellow workers to pick up the pace.

Work in the slaveowner's household was sometimes less brutal. Both men and women cooked and did gardening chores. Women often took care of the children as well. Some

men became **artisans**, or skilled workers who crafted things by hand. Some women served as nurses and weavers.

Marriage between slaves was illegal in the colonies. An enslaved couple had to obtain their master's permission to live together as husband and wife. Slave marriages were torn apart when

Slave Housing

Only nine of the 27 slave houses that once stood at Boone Hall Plantation near Charleston, South Carolina, still remain. The houses together make up what is called a "slave street." The nine houses, five of which appear in this photograph, were home to the servants at the plantation house. Each house was divided into two rooms and had either a dirt or a wooden floor. Dirt floors were common in the houses provided for slaves.

one of the pair was sold to a different slaveowner. In those cases, slaves often walked long distances at night to visit and hold the family together.

Slaves often built their own houses, which were typically one-room cabins. Many planters provided only basic foods for their enslaved workers, such as corn and a little pork. Enslaved people often planted gardens with vegetables like yams and squash to enhance their diet. They also raised hogs and chickens and hunted and fished for extra food.

People from different parts of West Africa often found themselves thrown together on large plantations. To speak to each other, they blended African languages with English. By this means, such African words as *yam* and *tote* were introduced into the English language.

Africans influenced colonial culture, as well as that of early national America, in many other ways. Their music, with its rhythmic beat, had a huge impact on jazz and blues. They made clay pottery, baskets, and musical instruments with African designs. They also popularized new foods, including okra, melons, and bananas. In Boston, a slave taught his owner the practice of vaccination, which he had learned in Africa. As a result of the slave's help, the city's people were protected from a smallpox outbreak.

ACTS OF REBELLION

Enslaved people did what they could to cope with their situation, but many actively rebelled against their treatment. They resisted the slave owner's power by staging slowdowns, faking illness, and secretly destroying crops and tools. Others ran away. Some enslaved people became violent, killing the slave owners or setting fire to fields and homes.

In 1739, a group of more than 50 enslaved people revolted near the Stono River in South Carolina. Their leader was a literate slave named Jemmy (also known as Cato) whose master had taught him to read and write. When armed planters defeated the rebels in battle, some of the slaves headed to St. Augustine, Florida, where the Spanish government had promised them freedom. But the South Carolina militia pursued them, putting to death everyone suspected of being involved. Although similar rebellions had already taken place in the Middle Colonies, the **Stono Rebellion** sent fear throughout the American colonies.

The South Carolina legislature enacted a harsh slave code in 1740 in an effort to prevent future revolts. The new code made all enslaved people and their children permanent slaves. In addition, the code prohibited enslaved people from learning to read and write. In spite of these new laws, some slaves did learn to read and write. And they used this knowledge to tell their stories and let the world know what was happening to them.

Banjo
Africans on plantations played instruments made of a gourd cut in half with a goatskin stretched over it, a stick, and three strings. The banjo shown here was made in Baltimore, Maryland, in 1845. In this banjo, the gourd has been replaced with a circular wooden frame and the stick with a flat piece of wood. In other modern versions, the frame is sometimes made of metal.

HISTORICAL THINKING

1. **READING CHECK** What measures did owners use to force slaves to work harder?

2. **IDENTIFY MAIN IDEAS AND DETAILS** What are some of the ways in which enslaved people asserted their humanity and kept their traditions alive?

3. **ANALYZE CAUSE AND EFFECT** What were the long-term negative consequences of the Stono Rebellion on enslaved people?

2.4 Slave Narratives

After gaining their freedom, some former slaves wrote about their experiences and the cruelty they'd endured. They wanted to open up people's eyes to the true nature of slavery.

Engraving of Olaudah Equiano from his book, *The Interesting Narrative of the Life of Olaudah Equiano*

Olaudah Equiano (oh-LOW-duh ehk-wee-AHN-oh) was born in Benin, an empire in Africa that you have learned about previously. Equiano was sold into slavery at the age of 11. About 10 years later, he bought his freedom from his last owner, a Quaker from Philadelphia. He made his way to England, where he lectured on the evils of slavery.

In 1789, in London, Equiano published his autobiography, an excerpt from which appears on the next page. He had the image shown here created for the book. Copies sold quickly, and the popularity of *The Interesting Narrative of the Life of Olaudah Equiano* contributed to a law being passed in England in 1807 that made slavery illegal in England and its colonies. By then, as you will learn, America was no longer a British colony.

CRITICAL VIEWING Why do you think Equiano wanted to have his portrait show him holding a book?

DOCUMENT ONE

Primary Source: Autobiography
from *The Interesting Narrative of the Life of Olaudah Equiano*, 1789

In this excerpt from his autobiography, Equiano describes the brutal conditions aboard the slave ship during the passage from Africa to the Americas—the notorious Middle Passage.

CONSTRUCTED RESPONSE What details help you understand the horror the slaves endured in the Middle Passage?

I was soon put down under the decks, and there I received such a salutation [greeting] in my nostrils as I had never experienced in my life: so that, with the loathsomeness of the stench [smell], and crying together, I became so sick and low that I was not able to eat, nor had I the least desire to taste any thing.

. . . Many a time we were near suffocation from the want [lack] of fresh air, which we were often without for whole days together. This, and the stench of the necessary tubs, carried off [killed] many.

DOCUMENT TWO

Primary Source: Autobiography
from *A Narrative of the Most Remarkable Particulars in the Life of James Albert Ukawsaw Gronniosaw, An African Prince, as Related by Himself*, 1772

James Albert Ukawsaw Gronniosaw was sold into slavery at age 15. Upset with his family, Gronniosaw had believed the promise of a slave merchant and voluntarily left his home in Africa. He realized his mistake too late.

CONSTRUCTED RESPONSE How does the merchant make the idea of going with him sound like a fascinating adventure rather than the entry into a nightmare?

About this time there came a merchant from the Gold Coast. . . . He told me that if I would go with him I should see houses with wings to them walk upon the water, and should also see the white folks; and that he had many sons of my age, which should be my companions; and he added to all this that he would bring me safe back again soon. I was highly pleased with the account of this strange place, and was very desirous of going.

DOCUMENT THREE

Primary Source: Autobiography
from *A Narrative of the Life and Adventures of Venture, a Native of Africa: But Resident Above Sixty Years in the United States of America*, 1798

Venture Smith was born in West Africa, captured as a young child by an enemy army, and then sold as a slave in Rhode Island. He published his autobiography in 1798. The excerpt details how he obtained freedom for his family.

CONSTRUCTED RESPONSE What can you infer about the personal qualities that enabled Venture Smith to accomplish all that he describes?

Being thirty-six years old, I left Col. Smith once for all . . . [having] paid an enormous sum for my freedom. . . . When I had [raised enough money to purchase] my two sons, I had then left more than one hundred pounds. . . . The rest of my money I laid out in land, in addition to a farm which I owned before, and a dwelling house thereon . . . [In] my forty-fourth year, I purchased my wife Meg . . . Being about forty-six years old, I bought my oldest child Hannah . . . I had already redeemed from slavery, myself, my wife and three children.

SYNTHESIZE & WRITE

1. **REVIEW** Review what you have learned about the slave trade and slavery in colonial America.

2. **RECALL** On your own paper, write the main ideas expressed in each document.

3. **CONSTRUCT** Construct a topic sentence that answers this question: How did formerly enslaved persons endure and overcome slavery?

4. **WRITE** Using evidence from this chapter and the documents, write an informative paragraph that supports your topic sentence in Step 3.

3.1 Agricultural Production

The basics of farming haven't changed. Farmers today need fertile soil and a good climate to grow abundant crops, just like their counterparts in the colonies. Good climates in the Middle Colonies attracted immigrant farmers from Britain and other parts of Europe.

MAIN IDEA The fertile land of the Middle Colonies allowed farmers to raise cash crops and livestock for sale and export, resulting in a booming economy.

FARMLAND AND FREEDOM

Just like the settlers of New England and the Southern Colonies, immigrants who came to the Middle Colonies of New York, New Jersey, Pennsylvania, and Delaware found ways to support themselves in their new environment. There were navigable rivers and harbors, and rich farmland rolled across the region. The area's weather was warmer than New England's but avoided the sticky heat farther south. Settlers soon discovered that grains such as wheat, corn, rye, and barley thrived in the climate. As a result, the region earned the nickname "breadbasket of the colonies."

Immigrants from all over Europe heard about the **arable**, or fertile, land and decided to move to the Middle Colonies. Attracted by cheap land, limited government control, and religious tolerance, more than 100,000 Germans immigrated to the area between 1683 and 1783.

The majority of Germans headed for the backcountry of Pennsylvania. They brought with them new farming techniques, such as providing shelter for their animals in the winter. Some farmers used indentured servants and enslaved people to tend their fields. As the settlers grew wealthier, they sold more of their harvest as cash crops and raised livestock for sale and export.

The residents of the breadbasket enjoyed more prosperous lives than farmers in New England. Unfortunately, there was a cost—though not directly to the settlers. Their growing farms continued to edge out the Native Americans who lived on the land.

GRIST FOR THE MILL

Many Middle Colony farmers grew grains, and wheat was the most popular grain in colonial America. The plant made a finer flour than corn, which in turn produced softer bread. Colonists enjoyed wheat bread with their meals, but making the flour required grinding. Grinding the grain by hand took a long time and resulted in flour that was rough in texture. Farmers found they could save time and energy by taking their wheat to a **gristmill**, a building that housed machinery for grinding grain.

Since human and animal labor was in short supply in the Middle Colonies, many colonists built their gristmills near a river and harnessed the power of water to operate the gristmill. At that time, water mills were the latest technology. The water spun a wheel outside that turned grinding stones within the gristmill.

Workers called millers ran the gristmills and generally took a portion of the flour they ground as payment. They also took other goods in exchange. Some millers opened stores to sell the surplus flour, grain, or other goods. These stores became the centers of communities. Neighbors would gather there to exchange goods and catch up on news. As demand grew, some millers bought larger mills or moved their mill to a spot on the river with a faster current.

But not all of the immigrants who came to the Middle Colonies became farmers or millers. Some settled in the cities hoping to find greater opportunities in the fast-growing coastal towns.

How a Gristmill Works

With the exception of a few metal parts and the stone grinding blocks, most colonial gristmills were made of wood. Some had foundations of stone. A channel called a millrace was dug from a stream or river to direct fast-running water to the waterwheel. Water falling from the millrace turned the wheel. The moving waterwheel then turned gears inside the building, which rotated the top grinding block. This block could be raised and lowered to vary its closeness to the bottom block, depending upon the size of the grain being ground between the stones. As the top block turned, it pressed and rolled the grains, cracking away the hard outer layers and grinding all the parts into soft flour.

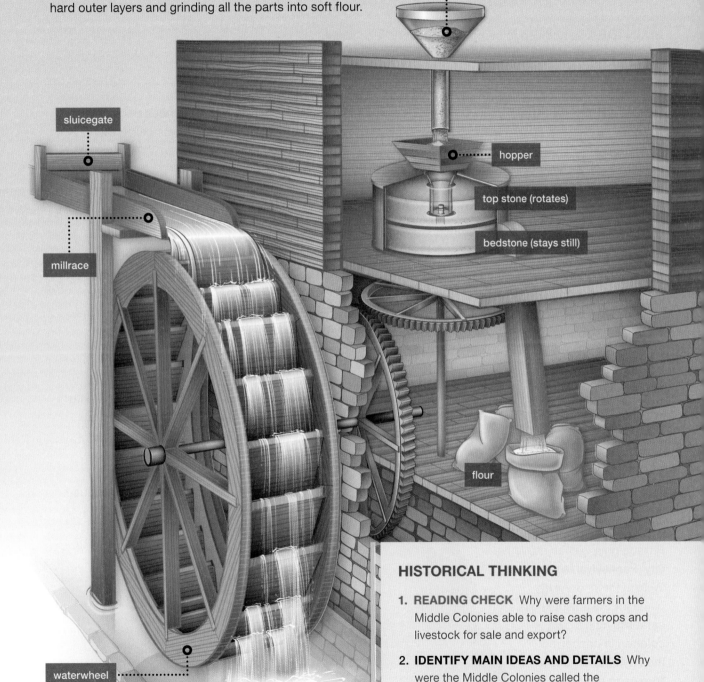

grain

sluicegate

hopper

top stone (rotates)

bedstone (stays still)

millrace

flour

waterwheel

HISTORICAL THINKING

1. **READING CHECK** Why were farmers in the Middle Colonies able to raise cash crops and livestock for sale and export?

2. **IDENTIFY MAIN IDEAS AND DETAILS** Why were the Middle Colonies called the "breadbasket of the colonies"?

3. **ANALYZE VISUALS** Use the diagram to explain how the flour got into the sacks.

3.2 A Diverse Society

What would you look for if you were searching for a new homeland? You might look for a place that was prosperous and productive and tolerant of differences. For many immigrants, the Middle Colonies seemed like such a place.

MAIN IDEA In addition to being economically successful, the Middle Colonies were culturally diverse.

GROWTH OF CITIES

A stream of settlers, hungry for new opportunities, moved to cities along the Atlantic coast, especially the ports of New York City and Philadelphia. As the colonies produced more and more goods, trade from these ports also grew, and people could find a variety of work in the cities.

Founded in 1681, Philadelphia was the fastest-growing city in the colonies. It started out as a village on the Delaware River and grew to more than 2,000 people in 1700. By 1760, the population had rocketed to roughly 23,000 people, outstripping New York and Boston. The city thrived on crops and trade. Philadelphia's merchants forged relationships with farmers who needed to sell their wheat, livestock, and lumber and with dealers who wanted to market these **commodities**, or goods, in the West Indies and elsewhere.

Philadelphia was an attractive city. Pennsylvania's founder, William Penn, drew up plans for Philadelphia while establishing his own colony. He conceived the city as a large "green country town," with wide streets in a grid pattern, public parks, ample lots, and brick houses.

One of Philadelphia's most famous brick buildings is Independence Hall, which was called the Pennsylvania State House when it was first established in 1753.

Meanwhile, New York City was also expanding. The English acquired the city in 1664 as part of their takeover of the Dutch colony New Netherland. The brick houses with low-sloping tile roofs that lined the city's cobblestoned streets looked exactly like those in Dutch towns. As the city expanded, the English made their mark by building houses of brick and wood in their own style.

After the English took over the city, New York merchants maintained ties with the Netherlands and its colony, the Dutch West Indies. They continued to ship grain, flour, dried fish, timber, and other goods to Amsterdam. Because of these ties, New York City's population more than doubled between 1720 and 1760.

American Products
Cities in the colonies wouldn't have grown without the work of artisans like Cornelius Kierstede of New York. He made this silver teapot around 1720. He shaped the spout into the form of a bird and engraved the purchaser's initials into the side.

Philadelphia Rowhouses

The houses of Society Hill date to around 1690. Rowhouses like these helped support the growing number of people living near the busy docks where goods were traded.

VARIETY OF IMMIGRANTS

When the English took possession of New Netherland, it was already home to the Dutch, Swedes, Finns, Norwegians, French Protestants, Jews, and other settlers. This **diversity**, or wide variety of people, was partly due to the Dutch, who had opened immigration to many different groups. It made the population of the Middle Colonies unique among the regions of America.

After the English takeover, most new immigrants came from England and Germany. German artisans created the Pennsylvania long rifle for hunting. They also designed the **Conestoga wagon**, which was capable of carrying up to four tons of cargo. Other German artisans were ironworkers and makers of glass, furniture, and kitchenware.

The farmland and cities drew immigrants to the Middle Colonies. But immigrants also came to enjoy something that was much less concrete but, perhaps, even more important: religious freedom.

HISTORICAL THINKING

1. **READING CHECK** What ideas or events caused the populations of Philadelphia and New York City to change over time?

2. **COMPARE AND CONTRAST** What caused the population of the Middle Colonies to differ from that of New England and the Southern Colonies?

3. **IDENTIFY MAIN IDEAS AND DETAILS** How did German immigrants contribute to the success of the Middle Colonies?

3.3 Cultures of the Middle Colonies

You probably know this from your own experience with your classmates: Things just go better if you try to get along. For the most part, that's what people in the Middle Colonies discovered, too.

MAIN IDEA While the Middle Colonies made an honest attempt to tolerate different religions, tensions still existed between different races.

RELIGIOUS TOLERANCE

With people from all walks of life pouring into the Middle Colonies, neighbors needed to show religious **tolerance**, or acceptance of others, in order to establish community. This open-mindedness was part of the legacy of the Dutch. In the Netherlands, Jews practiced their religion freely and became citizens. The Dutch also welcomed many Protestant groups not recognized by the church, including Puritans, Quakers, and Lutherans. In fact, the Pilgrims who settled at Plymouth, Massachusetts, had originally gone to live in the city of Leiden in the Netherlands because of the religious tolerance they found there. The Dutch carried their practice of tolerance across the sea to New Netherland, where it continued after the English took over.

Less than 100 miles away, William Penn founded Pennsylvania as a free colony—not just for Quakers, but for other religions as well. He promised equal rights and opportunities. As a result, the colony attracted many different Protestant faiths, including the Amish. This group emphasized personal faith and a simple life. They also valued humility and submission.

Quakers believed all people were equal in the eyes of God. They saw religion as a personal matter, and they did not demand **conformity**, or obedience, to a strict set of beliefs. Quakers were also the first group in America to ban slaveholding.

TENSIONS BETWEEN RACES

But most people in the Middle Colonies didn't share the Quakers' view. When the English acquired New Netherland in 1664, an estimated 20 percent of the population was African. The Dutch West India Company provided "half freedom" to older enslaved Africans. This meant that the company released the older slaves, but not their children, from slavery. Other slaves worked for wages to buy their freedom. As a result, by 1664, one-fifth of all Africans were free. But tolerance for diversity did not extend to these Africans and African Americans, whether they were free or slaves.

Most African Americans in the Middle Colonies lived in New York City. By 1711, about 40 percent of white households there had at least one slave. Many enslaved people were skilled workers and lived and worked next to free and indentured whites.

Enslaved African Americans whose owners had run out of tasks for them often sought work on their own, looking for paid work throughout New York. However, the sight of so many African Americans on the streets of New York made white people fearful. A law was put into effect requiring that all hiring of slaves be done at one place, the slave market. This put still more restrictions on the lives of the African Americans, and in turn, white people began to worry about a slave rebellion.

These fears became reality on the night of April 6, 1712, when about 20 enslaved people set fire to a building, attacking the white men who came to put it out. Nine white people were killed, and terror spread up and down the Atlantic coast.

As in the case of later slave revolts and conspiracies, the revenge taken on the African-American community far outweighed any

🏛 Museum of Fine Arts, Boston

Like many Protestant groups, Quakers did not have a paid clergy. Instead, they believed every individual should decide how to worship. People sat silently at Quaker meetings, thinking and praying, until they felt that God moved them to speak. They wore plain clothes and spoke plainly, even to nobility. This painting by an unknown artist from the late 1700s or early 1800s captures the feeling of a Quaker meeting.

violence the rebels had committed. In the wake of the New York revolt, 13 enslaved African Americans were hanged, 3 were burned at the stake, 1 was tortured, and another starved to death in chains.

Some white colonists, however, questioned the morality of slavery. Wasn't it a violation of the Bible's golden rule, which says to act toward others as you want others to act toward you? A person who enslaves another certainly would not like to be enslaved in return. Other whites opposed slavery simply because they feared slave rebellions. Despite these considerations, slavery became a part of early American culture and would remain so for more than 150 years.

HISTORICAL THINKING

1. **READING CHECK** How did the Dutch colonists show tolerance for religious diversity in New Netherland?

2. **MAKE INFERENCES** Why do you think Quakers accepted other religions and races?

3. **EVALUATE** The text claims that "the revenge taken on the African-American community far outweighed any violence the rebels had committed." What evidence supports this?

4.1 Colonial Men and Women

As a girl, can you imagine rights reserved only for boys? As a boy, can you imagine being denied rights because of your family's lack of wealth? That's the way it was in the colonies.

MAIN IDEA Rights and wealth were not evenly distributed across religions, social classes, races, and genders in colonial American society.

RIGHTS AND WEALTH

Between 1720 and 1763, the diverse American population experienced changes in many aspects of their lives. In science, doctors made strides in understanding how diseases spread. People reexamined traditions and laws. The changes spread throughout the colonies.

However, other ideas were resistant to change. Voting was restricted to white men—and to a select group. Only landowning men could vote. But there were exceptions. Men who were Catholic or Jewish were denied the vote based on religion. Servants, slaves, and men without property were also barred. Men with a small amount of land or personal property had to pay to vote.

Although land was plentiful and industry booming, wealth in the colonies was not evenly distributed. This was especially visible in the cities. Fabulously wealthy merchants built mansions and bought coaches with income from trade with other nations or colonies. Less fortunate city dwellers worked for low wages or lacked employment altogether. For instance, seamen and artisans who relied on trade could be out of a job if the demand for goods decreased. In addition, the **burgeoning**, or quickly growing, towns lacked sanitation, putting many people at risk from the spread of disease.

ROLE OF WOMEN

Life was tough for both colonial men and women, but the women had even fewer choices. In rural areas, white wives cooked, cleaned, sewed, reared children, and helped with farm tasks. Many also made candles, soap, and other items to sell or exchange for goods. Most African-American women were enslaved. They worked in the fields, cooked, cleaned, and tended to the slaveholder's family. Only the wives of plantation owners led an easy life. They supervised the household slaves and servants and oversaw meal preparation.

In cities, women cared for their children and the household. Wealthier wives employed servants, and some depended on slaves. Some worked alongside their husbands in shops and businesses. Other women served as **midwives**, helping deliver babies. Poor women often made money by mending, washing, and ironing clothes or providing domestic services. Few women worked outside the home.

Women had few legal rights throughout most of the colonial period. They could not vote. They lost the right to manage their property and earn a living once they married. Many women relied on the church for their social life. Soon, all colonists would be asked to pay more attention to their spiritual lives as well.

HISTORICAL THINKING

1. **READING CHECK** What requirements did a person have to meet to be eligible to vote in colonial America?

2. **IDENTIFY MAIN IDEAS AND DETAILS** What details support the idea that wealth was not evenly distributed in colonial American cities?

3. **ANALYZE VISUALS** Which household task may have posed the biggest problem for colonial women? Use the information in the visual to explain your answer.

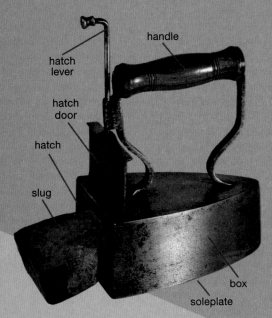

handle

hatch
lever

hatch
door

hatch

slug

box

soleplate

BOX IRON

Easy-care fabrics did not exist in colonial times, so ironing was an essential part of laundry, which was hard work at every stage. The box iron had a hatch in the back where the woman inserted a hot metal piece called a slug. One slug sat on the fire until the one in the iron cooled. Then the woman switched them.

The first electric iron was introduced in 1882.

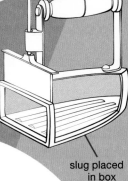

slug heated in the fire

slug placed in box

ALL IN A DAY'S WORK

In the days before electricity and grocery stores, colonial women—and, later, the women of early national America—labored to maintain their homes and families. There was cream to churn into butter, and there were fires to stoke and clothes to iron, along with all the other aspects of making sure the family was fed and warm.

BUTTER CHURN

For a colonial woman, making butter began with milking a cow. The milk sat in a container until the cream rose to the top. Then the woman skimmed off the cream and put it into a butter churn. She moved the dasher up and down and in circles, churning the cream. After what could be minutes or hours, butter formed, along with buttermilk. The final step was to strain the butter to separate the two.

The first U.S. butter factory opened in 1856.

dasher

splasher top

cream

plunger disc

BED WARMER

Heat from the fireplace of a colonial home did not spread from room to room. If the house couldn't be heated, however, the beds could. A colonial woman filled the pan of a bed warmer with glowing coals and took it from room to room. She moved the pan around under the covers to distribute the heat evenly. Then she went along to the next bed.

The first electric blanket was introduced in 1912.

holes to vent

hot coals, rocks, or brick

4.2 Great Awakening and Enlightenment

Have you ever listened to someone who made you think about a familiar topic in a new way? Something like that happened to colonists in the early 1700s and reawakened their dedication to religion.

MAIN IDEA The Enlightenment, emphasizing reason, and the Great Awakening, a religious renewal, helped shape colonial thought.

THE GREAT AWAKENING

You probably remember that many of the first colonists came to America to seek religious freedom. But once they'd achieved it, they began to focus on the material concerns of everyday life. People concentrated on their work and their homes. As a result, by the early 1700s, people's passion for religion had begun to die down. Some even stopped going to church regularly.

Many Protestant ministers feared that colonists were losing sight of the importance of God. In an effort to inspire people to recommit to their spiritual beliefs, these ministers gave stirring—and sometimes frightening—sermons during a series of religious revivals known as the **Great Awakening**.

One of the most effective of these ministers was **Jonathan Edwards** of Massachusetts. In 1734, he began preaching sermons on **salvation**, or the deliverance from sin. In his most famous sermon, "Sinners in the Hands of an Angry God," Edwards compared his listeners to spiders. God, he said, held them by a string over the fires of hell. If they failed to seek salvation, he warned, God would simply let go of the string.

Another minister, **George Whitefield**, came from Britain to preach salvation to the colonists. With his theatrical gestures and thundering words, he appealed to people's emotions and brought them to tears. Some even fainted.

The revivals of the Great Awakening changed how people viewed religion and morality. People began to believe they did not need church officials to

A Ray of Hope

Jonathan Edwards delivered "Sinners in the Hands of an Angry God" in 1741 to a congregation in Connecticut. Unlike George Whitefield, Edwards spoke in a quiet voice and used few gestures, but his message caused near-hysteria in his listeners. In this excerpt from the sermon, after threatening his audience with damnation, Edwards offers them a chance to be saved. How do you think Edwards's listeners responded to his words of hope?

PRIMARY SOURCE

And now you have an extraordinary opportunity, a day wherein Christ has thrown the door of mercy wide open, and stands in the door calling and crying with a loud voice to poor sinners. How awful is it to be left behind at such a day! To see so many rejoicing and singing for joy of heart, while you have cause to mourn for sorrow of heart. How can you rest one moment in such a condition? Therefore let every one that is out of Christ [that has not accepted Christ], now awake and fly from the wrath [fury] to come.

–from "Sinners in the Hands of an Angry God," by Jonathan Edwards, 1741

Church of England minister George Whitefield appealed to many races and classes with his promise of a more equal, or egalitarian, relationship between believers and their God. Here, artist John Collet portrays a meeting during one of Whitefield's seven visits to the colonies. The painting dates to the mid-1700s.

connect with God. Even more dangerously, they began to challenge authority and think themselves equal to those in power.

THE ENLIGHTENMENT

The Great Awakening was not the only movement that helped pave the way for revolutionary fervor. The intellectual movement known as the **Enlightenment** spread from Great Britain to the colonies in the 1700s. Enlightenment thinkers believed that the "light" of human reason would shatter the "darkness" of ignorance, superstition, and unfair authority. In part, they were influenced by the **Scientific Revolution**, which began in Europe around the mid-1550s and used logical thinking to answer scientific questions. The Enlightenment encouraged people to use logic and ask questions instead of just accepting what religious and political figures told them.

The ideas of **John Locke**, a 17th-century English philosopher, greatly influenced Enlightenment thought. Locke asserted that humans were born free and equal with **natural rights**, or rights such as life or liberty that a person is born with. He also claimed that a leader could rule only with the consent of the people. If a ruler failed to protect the people's rights, Locke believed they had the right to overthrow him.

These ideas would prove hugely influential in the colonies. American Enlightenment leaders included Benjamin Franklin, who devoted his life to public service and science. In time, Franklin and many other American founders would start to demand their own rights and freedoms.

HISTORICAL THINKING

1. **READING CHECK** What was the Great Awakening?

2. **IDENTIFY MAIN IDEAS AND DETAILS** What were some of John Locke's beliefs?

3. **DRAW CONCLUSIONS** What did the Enlightenment and the Great Awakening contribute to colonial views about equality and government?

4.3 Rights in England and the Colonies

The colonists considered themselves English and felt they were entitled to the same rights that the citizens of England enjoyed. And for a while, the English government let them think that.

MAIN IDEA Political changes in England that balanced the power between Parliament and the king helped set the American colonies on the path to democracy.

ENGLISH PARLIAMENT

Of course, the English themselves hadn't always enjoyed many rights. As you have learned, the Magna Carta, or Great Charter, began to change all that. The Magna Carta put protections in place to keep the English people from losing their freedom or property unless the law of the land ruled against them.

This important document helped give rise to **Parliament**, the legislative body of England, and later, Great Britain. Parliament consisted of two houses: the House of Lords, made up of nobles and high church officials, and the House of Commons, whose members were elected by male landowners.

Parliament's power grew in the late 1600s after clashing with King James II, who was a Catholic. Fearing James would make England a Catholic country under authoritarian rule, parliamentary leaders exiled him to France. They then invited his Protestant daughter, Mary, and her husband, William, to take the throne.

The Magna Carta and the Colonies

This stained glass in the Mansion House in London, England, home to the city's Lord Mayor, depicts the signing of the Magna Carta. The document established that the king was not above the law. Henry III, John's successor, reissued slightly revised Magna Cartas in 1216, 1217, and 1225. The 1225 version became English law in 1297. Hundreds of years later, the English colonists believed that they, too, possessed the rights guaranteed in the Magna Carta. During the American Revolution, colonists drew on principles in the Magna Carta for their Declaration of Independence and rebellion against the tyranny of King George III.

James II was often in conflict with the Parliament in England and with the colonies. He revoked colonial charters from New Jersey to Maine and established the Dominion of New England. What details in this painting convey the king's high status?

COLONIAL ASSEMBLIES

The American colonies modeled their governments after Parliament by forming elected assemblies similar to the House of Commons. The colonial assemblies consisted of representatives elected by property owners. The assemblies could collect money through taxes and decide how to spend it.

Unlike the English legislature, however, elected officials in the assemblies lived in the area they represented. The colonists believed that representatives who lived among the people who elected them would better understand local interests and needs.

As colonists came to enjoy making decisions and managing some of their own affairs, they began to resent English authority. The colonists had no representatives in Parliament and sometimes felt they were treated unfairly—especially when Parliament passed laws the colonists didn't like.

For the most part, though, the English government was busy fighting foreign wars and dealing with disagreements within the country itself. So the government adopted a policy of **salutary neglect** toward the colonies. Under this policy, the English government did not strictly enforce its colonial policies. As a result, the colonies grew happily accustomed to living in relative isolation from British authority and largely governing themselves. They were generally content with British rule. But that state of affairs was about to change.

At the same time, Parliament permanently limited the English monarch's power. It established Parliament's control of taxation, and its right to pass laws, and it also secured the independence of the courts. Parliament's consent was necessary for raising an army in peacetime and in the case of any foreign invasions. The bloodless overthrow of James II and the transferring of power to Parliament was called the Glorious Revolution. Parliament created the **English Bill of Rights of 1689** (more formally known as "An Act Declaring the Rights and Liberties of the Subject and Settling the Succession of the Crown") to officially protect the rights of English citizens and Parliament.

Many believed the balancing of powers would prevent a single individual or social group from becoming too dominant. Power shared by the king, the nobles, and the common people was thought to be the way to avoid more destructive forms of government that could threaten the liberty of some portion of the population.

HISTORICAL THINKING

1. **READING CHECK** How did Parliament influence the growth of representative government in the colonies?

2. **SUMMARIZE** How did the Magna Carta pave the way for the English Bill of Rights?

3. **IDENTIFY MAIN IDEAS AND DETAILS** What rights did Parliament establish in the English Bill of Rights?

4.4 John Peter Zenger and Free Speech

Today, we expect talk show hosts to joke about politicians and criticize our government. We take for granted that people in the media are free to say what they want. That was not always the case in the colonies.

MAIN IDEA The trial of John Peter Zenger helped pave the way for freedom of the press.

LIBEL OR FREE SPEECH?

Under Great Britain's policy of salutary neglect, the colonists became used to determining what they could and couldn't do. In 1733 by British law, it was illegal to criticize the government in print. But **John Peter Zenger**, the publisher of the *New-York Weekly Journal,* did it anyway. In his newspaper, he printed a series of articles about the British colonial governor of New York, William Cosby. A few years before, Cosby had removed a judge who had ruled against him and then tried to rig, or tamper with the outcome of, an election.

Another person, a lawyer named James Alexander, wrote the articles, but his name didn't appear in the paper. Unable to determine the author, Cosby went after Zenger. Police arrested Zenger for **libel**, the publishing of lies, in November 1734. He remained in jail until his trial in August 1735.

Governor Cosby expected the trial to be an open and shut case. Any criticism of the government, true or not, was considered libel. The paper had definitely criticized the governor—there was no question about that—so as far as Cosby was concerned, the jury had to find Zenger guilty.

Andrew Hamilton, John Peter Zenger's lawyer, reasoned convincingly on Zenger's behalf. In this illustration from 1877, Hamilton makes his case before the judge.

High Court Upholds Students' Peaceful Protest

Continued From Page 1, Col. 4

demonstrate and would embroil the Supreme Court in public school affairs.

Justice Abe Fortas emphasized in the Court's opinion that school children's free speech rights are limited to conduct that does not disrupt discipline or interfere with the rights of others.

He also said that their rights included only political expression, and that the Federal courts would not become involved in disputes over the permissible length of students' hair

and more acid in recent years, spoke extemporaneously for about 20 minutes this morning.

At one point he used mocking tones to quote from an old opinion with which he disagreed, and he finished by stating that "I want it thoroughly known that I disclaim any sentence, any word, any part of what the Court does today."

Justice Black will observe his 83d birthday next Thursday.

The events leading to today's decision go back to December, 1965, when antiwar groups in Des Moines began to plan the armband protest. The Board of Education voted to prohibit the

The suit, sponsored by the American Civil Liberties Union, was brought in the names of three of the suspended students: John F. Tinker, then 15; his sister Mary Beth, then 13, and Christopher Eckhardt, 16.

The father of the Tinker children is a Methodist minister employed by the American Friends Service Committee. Young Eckhardt's mother is an officer in the Women's International League for Peace and Freedom.

The United States District Court in Des Moines refused to enjoin the school officials from forbidding the armband

ZENGER CLEARED

Although he was confident of the outcome, Cosby didn't want to take any chances. He packed the jury with his own supporters. However, Zenger's wife Anna found out and revealed Cosby's misdeed in the *New-York Weekly Journal*, which she had continued to publish while her husband was in jail. The judge replaced Cosby's jury with a jury of colonists, but Zenger's problems continued. The judge dismissed Zenger's lawyers when they challenged the judge's authority. Meanwhile, Zenger's friends brought Andrew Hamilton, a famous Philadelphia lawyer, to take over the case.

Hamilton took a novel approach. He admitted that Zenger had printed articles criticizing Cosby. Hamilton argued, however, that the jury should consider the fact that the criticisms were true. Should Zenger be jailed for doing his job correctly as a newspaper publisher by printing the truth? Hamilton went on to argue that freedom of the press was especially important in the colonies because it acted as a check against the abuses of colonial governors. In his closing, Hamilton urged

the jury to grant "that, to which Nature and the Laws of our Country have given us a Right, . . . both of exposing and opposing arbitrary Power . . . by speaking and writing Truth."

After a short time, the jury returned to the court with a verdict of not guilty, and Zenger was released. The victory paved the way to gaining freedom of the press. It also unified the colonists in their pursuit of their rights. But the colonists still considered themselves British citizens. Soon, they'd unite and join forces with Britain in war.

HISTORICAL THINKING

1. **READING CHECK** Why was John Peter Zenger charged with libel?

2. **IDENTIFY MAIN IDEAS AND DETAILS** Why did William Cosby assume that John Peter Zenger would be found guilty?

3. **SYNTHESIZE** How was the outcome of *Tinker* v. *Des Moines* similar to the outcome of Zenger's trial?

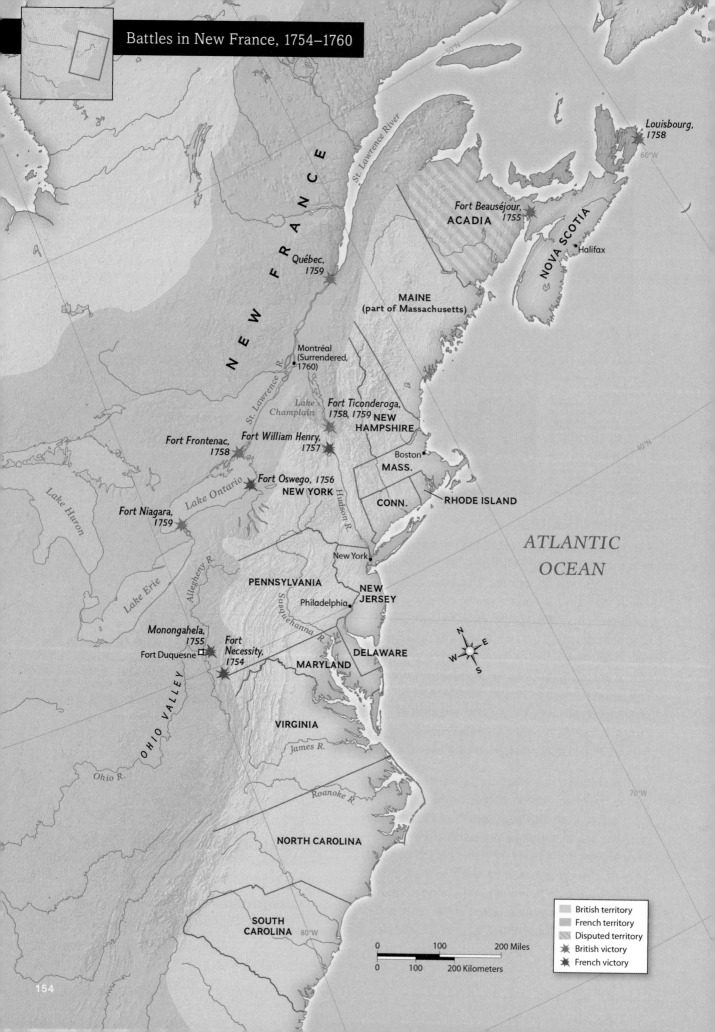

Battles in New France, 1754–1760

Louisbourg, 1758

Fort Beauséjour, 1755
ACADIA

NOVA SCOTIA

Halifax

NEW FRANCE

St. Lawrence River

Québec, 1759

MAINE
(part of Massachusetts)

Montréal
(Surrendered, 1760)

St. Lawrence R.

Lake Champlain

Fort Ticonderoga, 1758, 1759
NEW HAMPSHIRE

Fort Frontenac, 1758

Fort William Henry, 1757

Boston
MASS.

Fort Oswego, 1756
NEW YORK

Lake Ontario

CONN.

RHODE ISLAND

Fort Niagara, 1759

Lake Huron

Lake Erie

Hudson R.

New York

PENNSYLVANIA

NEW JERSEY

Allegheny R.

Susquehanna R.

Philadelphia

ATLANTIC OCEAN

DELAWARE

Monongahela, 1755

Fort Duquesne

Fort Necessity, 1754

MARYLAND

N
W   E
S

OHIO VALLEY

VIRGINIA

James R.

Ohio R.

Roanoke R.

NORTH CAROLINA

SOUTH CAROLINA

80°W

50°N

60°W

40°N

70°W

0   100   200 Miles

0   100   200 Kilometers

British territory
French territory
Disputed territory
★ British victory
✴ French victory

154

5.1 War Begins

Finders keepers. That's what the French might have said when they claimed prime real estate in the Ohio Valley for themselves. But the British and the American colonists begged to differ.

MAIN IDEA Competition for land and furs involved France and Great Britain in many years of war in North America, starting with the French and Indian War.

SEEDS OF CONFLICT

When French fur traders first came to North America in the 1600s, they set up a few forts and **trading posts** in the St. Lawrence Valley. As you may recall, the French traded with the Huron and Algonquian there for almost 100 years. But after French trappers killed many of the animals in the area and fur supplies dwindled, they resettled in the Ohio Valley. This land was also claimed by Great Britain. So in the 1740s, the British joined forces with the Iroquois and pushed the French traders out of the valley.

The fertile land of the Ohio Valley appealed to colonial settlers. In 1749, they were eager to buy land shares from the Ohio Company of Virginia, which promoted the westward settlement of colonists from Virginia. But the French hadn't given up their claim to the land. They built a number of forts there, including Fort LeBoeuf (luh-BUHF) in northwest Pennsylvania. Then in 1752, the French destroyed Pickawillany, a colonial trading post. In an effort to settle the dispute over the Ohio Valley peacefully, the British governor of Virginia sent a young colonial army leader named **George Washington** to Fort LeBoeuf to ask the French to leave. Not surprisingly, they refused.

COLONIAL INVOLVEMENT

In 1754, the British decided to take more forceful measures and sent the newly promoted Colonel Washington and a small number of troops to capture Fort Duquesne (doo-KAYN) in present-day Pittsburgh. When he arrived, Washington quickly realized he was outnumbered. Scrambling to defend his troops, he built a wooden barrier, or stockade, which he fittingly named Fort Necessity. But the situation was hopeless. French and Native American troops surrounded the fort and attacked, causing heavy losses for Washington's troops. Defeated, Washington surrendered and abandoned the fort.

Many consider this battle the beginning of the **French and Indian War**. For Britain and France, this war would become part of a larger one, called the Seven Years' War, that officially began in 1756. It pitted these two great powers in a struggle over land in Europe.

The colonists, meanwhile, were concerned with land in North America. Seven colonies sent delegates to a congress in Albany, New York, to discuss uniting the colonies to fight the French for that land. The delegates adopted Benjamin Franklin's **Albany Plan of Union**, which proposed granting a central government the power to tax, pass laws, and oversee military defense for the colonies. When the delegates returned home with the proposal, none of the colonies approved it. But the colonists were united in their determination to fight for land they considered theirs. And they soon persuaded the British to help them.

HISTORICAL THINKING

1. **READING CHECK** How did the fur trade cause conflict between the French and the British?

2. **INTERPRET MAPS** Around what bodies of water were many of the battles fought?

3. **IDENTIFY MAIN IDEAS AND DETAILS** What was the purpose of the Albany Plan of Union?

5.2 Quebec and the British Victory

The stakes were high in the French and Indian War. Ultimately, the outcome of the war would determine which countries controlled North America.

MAIN IDEA The British and French fought for control of North America in the French and Indian War, with extensive losses on both sides.

EARLY BRITISH LOSSES

In response to the colonists' request for help, the British jumped into the fight. In 1755, they sent British general Edward Braddock and two regiments to North America to destroy French forts. George Washington accompanied Braddock as he marched with his more than 2,000 soldiers through the Virginia backcountry on a mission to capture Fort Duquesne. Braddock was confident that his highly trained soldiers would quickly defeat the enemy.

He was wrong. The British soldiers were totally unprepared for fighting on the frontier. Their wagons were too big for the paths, and they offended many of the Native American scouts they'd recruited to lead the way, causing most of them to abandon the soldiers. The army's slow progress gave the French plenty of notice of their clumsy arrival.

As a result, the French and Native American troops were lying in wait for them. In the **Battle of the Monongahela**, fought just east of present-day Pittsburgh, they hid behind trees and ambushed Braddock's army as it marched by. Used to fighting on battlegrounds where both sides formed neat rows,

the British soldiers were caught completely off guard. Washington suggested they break ranks and fight from behind trees like the French, but Braddock refused. Within a few hours, nearly two-thirds of the British forces lay dead or wounded. Braddock himself soon died of his wounds. Washington, his uniform ripped by bullets, helped lead the retreat.

Losses continued to plague the British in the early years of the war. In New York, the French seized Fort William Henry, Fort Oswego, and 2,000 British soldiers at Lake George. The British defeats emboldened Native American tribes allied with the French to attack British settlements in the backcountry, where they killed and captured hundreds of settlers. Things looked bleak for the British and colonial forces.

Native American club
Braddock and his men likely faced Native Americans holding weapons like this one, made of wood and brass. The maker of the weapon carved the ball on the end from wood. Two-and-a-half feet, or nearly one yard, long, these clubs could be devastating weapons.

FRENCH DEFEATS

The tide turned after British statesman **Sir William Pitt** poured money and men into the war. In July 1758, the British captured Louisbourg in Nova Scotia (NOH-vuh SKOH-shuh). Alarmed, the French pulled their troops from the Ohio Valley so they could protect Quebec and Montreal. The retreat allowed the British to take control of the west. Cut off from French supplies and weakened by smallpox, Native Americans ended their war in the backcountry.

Even with extra troops, the French could not save Quebec. The British captured the city in 1759 during the **Battle of Quebec**. Encouraged by these victories, the Iroquois joined forces with Britain. In 1760, the British captured Montreal, ending French control of Canada.

The defeat of the French in Canada marked the end of the war with France in North America. A treaty would be signed, but the war had a lasting impact on everyone who had taken part in it. For one thing, thousands of colonists had joined the British army. They found that, at best, the British soldiers and officers looked down on them, and at worst, the British dealt out severe punishments to soldiers for small offenses. Colonial soldiers didn't feel they'd been treated like allies. The war would also cause great suffering to Native Americans. Soon settlers would invade even more of their homeland.

HISTORICAL THINKING

1. **READING CHECK** How did Braddock's defeat at Fort Duquesne show that the British were not ready to fight a frontier war?

2. **IDENTIFY MAIN IDEAS AND DETAILS** What turned the tide of the French and Indian War?

3. **DETERMINE CHRONOLOGY** What happened after Braddock and Washington marched to capture Fort Duquesne?

5.3 Impact of the War

The colonists celebrated Britain's victory in the French and Indian War. New York City even raised a statue of King George III. Would the colonists' love of the king endure? We'll see.

> **MAIN IDEA** Victory in the French and Indian War expanded British territory but led to conflict with Native Americans in the Ohio Valley.

THE TREATY OF PARIS

In 1763, diplomats from Britain and France met in Paris to negotiate a **treaty**, or peace agreement. The resulting **Treaty of Paris** officially ended the French and Indian War.

According to its terms, France lost all of its territory—and thus all of its power—in North America. As Britain's ally, Spain acquired New Orleans and the Louisiana Territory west of the Mississippi. The British gained Canada from France and Florida from Spain in exchange for Cuba and the Philippines. Britain now controlled all of the land in North America east of the Mississippi River.

The colonists also reaped some rewards from the treaty. They received the right to fish in the North Atlantic off the coast of Canada. The colonists also assumed they were now free to settle the Ohio Valley.

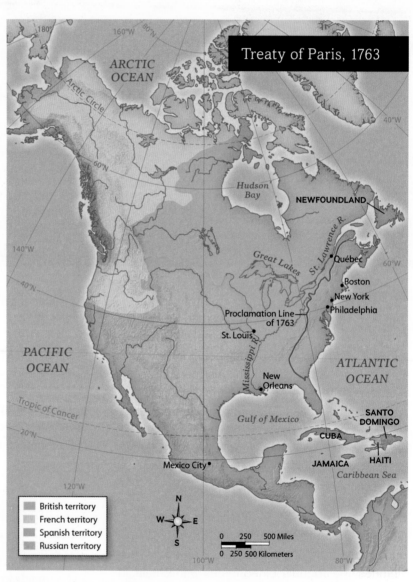

Treaty of Paris, 1763

British territory
French territory
Spanish territory
Russian territory

PONTIAC'S REBELLION

Not everyone in North America was happy when the French and Indian War ended. The war had been a disaster for Native Americans. While the French had presented them with gifts each year, the British ended this custom and then raised prices on trade goods. Worse yet, the British government limited what—and how much—Native Americans could trade. Additionally, white settlers streamed into the Ohio Valley after the war, in clear violation of existing treaties.

The British trade policies and land-grabbing drove large numbers of Delaware, Shawnee, Iroquois, and other Native Americans to take up arms.

When I go to see the English commander and say to him that some of our comrades are dead, instead of bewailing their death, as our French brothers do, he laughs at me and at you. If I ask for anything for our sick, he refuses with the reply that he has no use for us. From all this you can well see that they are seeking our ruin. Therefore, my brothers, we must all swear their destruction and wait no longer.

—Chief Pontiac in a speech to a council of Native Americans near Detroit, May 1763

Ottawa leader **Pontiac** urged Native Americans in the region to band together and rise up against the British. Many listened.

Pontiac had fought alongside the French in the French and Indian War. In 1763, he led Native Americans in launching what came to be called **Pontiac's Rebellion**. His forces defeated 13 British outposts. However, the British successfully defended their most important forts, including Fort Pitt, sometimes by ruthless means.

When Pontiac launched his rebellion, he needed help to replenish ammunition supplies and strengthen the Native Americans' ranks throughout the Great Lakes region and western Pennsylvania. He counted on the French to come to his aid. But they never did. Then, when British commanders met with Native American leaders at Fort Pitt, they are said to have given them smallpox-infested blankets and handkerchiefs as gifts, hoping to spread disease among many of the tribes.

Fighting continued for two more years. Sick of war, the king issued a proclamation that colonists could not settle west of a line drawn along the crest of the Appalachian Mountains from Maine to Georgia. This angered colonists, who wondered what they had been fighting for. They also resented the continued presence of British troops in their homeland. The soldiers and their somewhat coarse behavior served as a daily reminder of the mother colony. In time, colonists began to regard British authority more critically.

HISTORICAL THINKING

1. **READING CHECK** How did the Treaty of Paris affect power in North America?

2. **INTERPRET MAPS** Which countries gained the most territory after 1763?

3. **SYNTHESIZE** How did the outcome of the war impact Native Americans?

COLONIAL DEVELOPMENT
REVIEW

VOCABULARY

Use each of the following vocabulary words in a sentence that shows an understanding of the term's meaning.

1. subsistence farming
   If a family practices subsistence farming, they usually harvest just enough food to survive and sometimes will have a little left over to sell.

2. provisions

3. religious freedom

4. apprentice

5. cash crop

6. backcountry

7. gristmill

8. diversity

9. libel

10. trading post

READING STRATEGY
IDENTIFY MAIN IDEAS AND DETAILS

If you haven't done so already, complete your chart to identify details about the development of the colonies. Then answer the question.

Colonial Development

Main Idea:
Detail:
Detail:
Detail:

11. Why did the use of enslaved African labor grow over time in the Southern Colonies?

MAIN IDEAS

Answer the following questions. Support your answers with evidence from the chapter.

12. Why was fishing important to the economy of New England? **LESSON 1.1**

13. How did triangular trade contribute to the expansion of slavery? **LESSON 1.2**

14. Why did Charles Town remain smaller than the largest northern cities? **LESSON 2.1**

15. What was the Stono Rebellion? **LESSON 2.3**

16. How did gristmills affect the economy of the Middle Colonies? **LESSON 3.1**

17. What were indicators of racial tension in New York City in the early 1700s? **LESSON 3.3**

18. In what ways did women add to the colonial economy? **LESSON 4.1**

19. How did ministers like Jonathan Edwards and George Whitefield contribute to the Great Awakening? **LESSON 4.2**

20. What led to the creation of the Albany Plan of Union? **LESSON 5.1**

21. Why did Pontiac rebel? **LESSON 5.3**

HISTORICAL THINKING

Answer the following questions. Support your answers with evidence from the chapter.

22. **MAKE INFERENCES** How did the Navigation Acts lead to an increase in smuggling?

23. **ANALYZE CAUSE AND EFFECT** How did the beliefs of the Puritans lead to the growth of education in the colonies?

24. **COMPARE AND CONTRAST** How was society in the backcountry different from society in the Chesapeake and South Carolina?

25. **SYNTHESIZE** How did the Great Awakening and the Enlightenment contribute to revolutionary thought?

26. **FORM AND SUPPORT OPINIONS** Were the Native Americans better off dealing with French fur traders or the British settlers? Support your opinion with evidence from the chapter.

27. **DRAW CONCLUSIONS** How did the British victory in the French and Indian War change the distribution of power in North America?

Look closely at the map of the African-American population in the British colonies around 1760. Then answer the questions that follow.

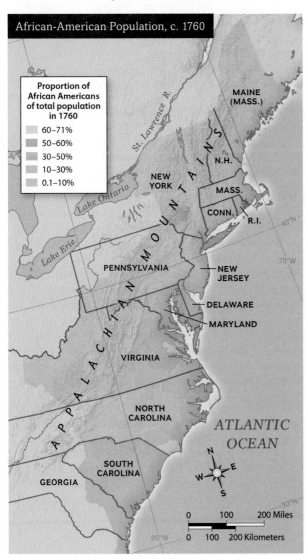

African-American Population, c. 1760

Proportion of African Americans of total population in 1760

- 60–71%
- 50–60%
- 30–50%
- 10–30%
- 0.1–10%

28. Which two areas had the highest proportion of African Americans in their population?

29. How did the African-American population in South Carolina differ from that in Virginia?

In 1704, French and Native American forces attacked Deerfield, Massachusetts, killing 50 people and taking 112 captives. Stephen Williams, an 11-year-old captive, kept a journal while a prisoner. Here he describes the attack. Read the excerpt and answer the question.

> The French and Indians came and surprised our fort and took it. And after they had broken into our house and took us prisoners, they barbarously murdered a brother and sister of mine as they did several of our neighbors. They rifled our house and then marched away with us that were captives, and set our house and barn afire as they did the greatest part of the town.

30. How does this source help to develop an understanding of the attack?

31. **NARRATIVE** Think about the tasks and adjustments of someone who moves and starts at a new school. What work is involved in physically moving? What does a person do to get to know new neighbors, teachers, and friends? Write a paragraph in which you make connections between this experience and that of the colonists.

TIPS

- List the challenges that the colonists faced coming to British America. Then make a list of the challenges involved in moving.

- Use two or three vocabulary terms from the chapter in your narrative.

- Conclude the narrative with a comment that ties the colonists' experiences to that of a modern student's move.

Before New York

BY PETER MILLER

Adapted from "Before New York," by Peter Miller, in *National Geographic*, September 2009

Of all the visitors to New York City in recent years, one of the most surprising was a beaver named José. No one knows exactly where he came from. He just showed up one wintry morning in 2007 on a riverbank in the Bronx Zoo, where he built a lodge.

During the early 17th century, when the city was the Dutch village of New Amsterdam, beavers were widely hunted for their pelts, which were fashionable in Europe. The fur trade grew into such a profitable business that a pair of beavers earned a place on the city's official seal, where they remain today.

Because of the high demand for their pelts, the real animals vanished. According to Eric Sanderson, an ecologist at the Wildlife Conservation Society (WCS) headquartered at the Bronx Zoo, "There hasn't been a beaver in New York City in more than 200 years." That's why he was skeptical when a colleague told him he'd seen evidence of a beaver during a walk along the river. But it was true. Sanderson and his colleague found José's lodge, and a couple of weeks later, they ran into José himself.

The beaver's return to the Big Apple was hailed as a victory by those who have spent more than three decades restoring the health of the Bronx River, once a dumping ground for abandoned cars and trash. José was named in honor of José E. Serrano, the congressman from the Bronx who'd secured more than $15 million in federal funds to support the river cleanup.

For almost a decade, Sanderson has led a project at WCS to imagine and digitally recreate what the island of Manhattan might have looked like before the city took root. The Mannahatta Project, as it's called (after the Lenape name for "island of many hills"), is an effort to turn back the clock to 1609, just before Henry Hudson and his crew sailed into New York Harbor and spotted the island.

Long before its hills were bulldozed and its wetlands paved over, Manhattan was a wilderness of chestnut, oak, and hickory trees. It was full of salt marshes and grasslands with turkey, elk, and black bear—and "as pleasant a land as one can tread upon," Hudson reported. Sandy beaches ran along stretches of both coasts on the narrow, 13-mile-long island where the Lenape feasted on clams and oysters. More than 66 miles of streams flowed through Manhattan.

"You might find it difficult to imagine today, but 400 years ago there was a red maple swamp right here in Times Square," Sanderson mentioned while waiting to cross Seventh Avenue. "Just over there was a beaver pond," he said, as a bus rumbled by.

"The landscape in Manhattan is so transformed, it makes you wonder what was here before," Sanderson remarked. As a landscape ecologist, his goal is to figure out how wild places work. So he and his colleagues built a landscape from the bottom up. They began by listing the various ecosystems they could safely assume existed on the island, such as old-growth forests, wetlands, or plains. In all, they identified 55 different ecological communities. Then they filled in the wildlife, discovering a dense network of relationships among species, habitats, and ecosystems. In the end, they identified 1,300 species and at least 8,000 relationships linking them to one another and their habitats.

Sanderson hopes his project will stimulate a new curiosity about what existed on Manhattan before Hudson arrived. "I'd like every New Yorker to know that they live in a place that had this fabulous ecology," he said. "New York isn't just a place of fabulous art, music, culture, and communications. It's also a place of amazing natural potential—even if you have to look a little harder here."

For more from National Geographic, check out "America, Found and Lost" online.

UNIT INQUIRY: Envision an Ideal Community

In this unit, you learned about the visions different groups had about what newly founded communities should be. Some groups built communities based on shared religious beliefs. Other groups focused on profiting from the rich natural resources the new continent offered. Based on your understanding of the text, what factors are involved in envisioning a new community? How might some groups' visions conflict with others?

ASSIGNMENT

Envision an ideal community. All new colonies began with people who imagined a new way of living or a new world. Consider factors such as what the "goal" of your community is, what sort of rules would govern your community, and how the community would thrive. Be prepared to present your community to the class.

Gather Evidence As you envision your community, gather evidence from this unit about the various factors that founders of new communities had to consider. Make a list of categories and subcategories that you consider the most important. Review the unit to gather evidence that supports your vision. Use a graphic organizer like this one to help organize your thoughts.

Ideal Community

Produce Use your notes to produce a detailed vision of your new community. Write a short paragraph on each component, using evidence from this unit to support your ideas.

Present Choose a creative way to present your ideal community to the class. Consider one of these options:

- Create a commercial to persuade people to move to your new community. Include details that describe where it is, who would prosper there, what the "goal" of the community would be, and what people who move there might expect.

- Organize teams and hold a classroom discussion on establishing a new community. Explore questions such as who would hold power, who might be included (or excluded), and how the community would support its residents.

- Design a flag or symbol for your new community. Describe how the elements you include on your flag represent your community and why these factors would be important to people who might choose to settle there.

NATIONAL GEOGRAPHIC | LEARNING FRAMEWORK ACTIVITIES

Prepare a Leadership Memo

ATTITUDE Responsibility

SKILLS Observation, Problem-Solving

Effective leaders possess solid diplomatic, communication, and problem-solving skills. Choose a leader that you read about in this unit and, using evidence from the reading, prepare a memo from that leader's point of view. In your memo, outline what you as that leader accomplished—or wish you had—by approaching problems in your community or colony with diplomacy. Offer examples of specific events or problems that your leader participated in or encountered. Then present your leadership memo to the class.

Create a Trade Network

SKILL Collaboration

KNOWLEDGE Our Human Story

Work with a team of classmates to create a trade network. Decide what products or resources you would trade with other groups and what products or resources you would like to acquire. Collaborate with your classmates on setting prices and quantities for products and resources to be traded. Then determine how your network will exchange goods. Illustrate your trade network on a classroom whiteboard. When all groups have added their networks to the board, discuss the ways in which the networks are similar to and different from each other.

A NEW NATION

THE UNITED STATES

1776

The Declaration of Independence, which announces the formation of the United States of America and its independence from Britain, is adopted on July 4. *(the original Declaration of Independence)*

1775
After a shot is fired in Lexington, Massachusetts, the American Revolution begins.

1773
Colonists board three ships in Boston Harbor and throw 342 boxes of tea overboard to protest the Tea Act. The protest comes to be known as the Boston Tea Party.

1765
The Stamp Act is imposed, requiring American colonists to pay a tax on nearly every piece of paper they use. *(colonial teapot protesting the Stamp Act)*

1770

1760

1765 ASIA
China invades Burma and begins a war with that country.

THE WORLD

1763 AMERICAS
France is defeated in the French and Indian War and surrenders most of its North American colonies to Britain and Spain.

1770 OCEANIA
British captain James Cook explores the east coast of Australia and claims the region for Great Britain. *(replica of James Cook's ship, the Endeavour)*

HISTORICAL THINKING: DETERMINE CHRONOLOGY

What world events occurred at the same time as events leading to the formation of the United States?

1789
George Washington becomes the first president of the United States. *(Statue on the steps of New York's Federal Hall celebrates the site of Washington's inauguration.)*

1787–1788
Delegates at the Constitutional Convention draft, sign, and ratify the U.S. Constitution, which becomes the supreme law of the land.

1791
The Bill of Rights, guaranteeing individual rights, is added to the U.S. Constitution.

1790

1783
The United States defeats Britain, and the American Revolution ends when representatives from both sides sign the Treaty of Paris.

1791 AMERICAS
In the French colony of Saint-Domingue on the Caribbean island of Hispaniola, slaves rebel against French authority.

1800

1780

1779 AFRICA
Luanda, a city on Africa's Atlantic coast, becomes the leading port in the African slave trade.

1789 EUROPE
Inspired by Enlightenment thinkers, the French people attack the Bastille, a prison in Paris, and start a revolution. (Storming of the Bastille *by Jean-Pierre Houël*)

CHAPTER

5

THE ROAD TO
REVOLUTION
1763–1776

ESSENTIAL QUESTION
Why did the colonists decide to break from Britain?

 AMERICAN STORIES Our American Identity

SECTION 1 **British Control**

KEY VOCABULARY

boycott	militia	repeal	Stamp Act
Currency Act	Proclamation of 1763	revenue	Sugar Act
duty	Quartering Act	Sons of Liberty	tyranny
grievance			

SECTION 2 **Rebellion in the Colonies**

KEY VOCABULARY

Boston Massacre	committee of correspondence	Townshend Acts
Boston Tea Party	Tea Act	writ of assistance

SECTION 3 **Lexington and Concord**

KEY VOCABULARY

First Continental Congress	Loyalist	Patriot
Intolerable Acts	minutemen	

SECTION 4 **Declaring Independence**

KEY VOCABULARY

artillery	earthwork	Second Continental Congress
Continental Army	geology	terrain
Declaration of Independence	Hessian	unalienable right
drumlin		

AMERICAN GALLERY
ONLINE Colonial Boston

READING STRATEGY

ANALYZE CAUSE AND EFFECT
When you analyze cause and effect, you note the consequences of an event, an action, or a condition. As you read the chapter, use a graphic organizer like this one to identify the causes of the colonies' separation from Britain.

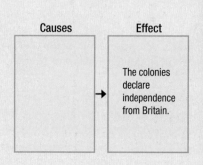

Causes

Effect

The colonies declare independence from Britain.

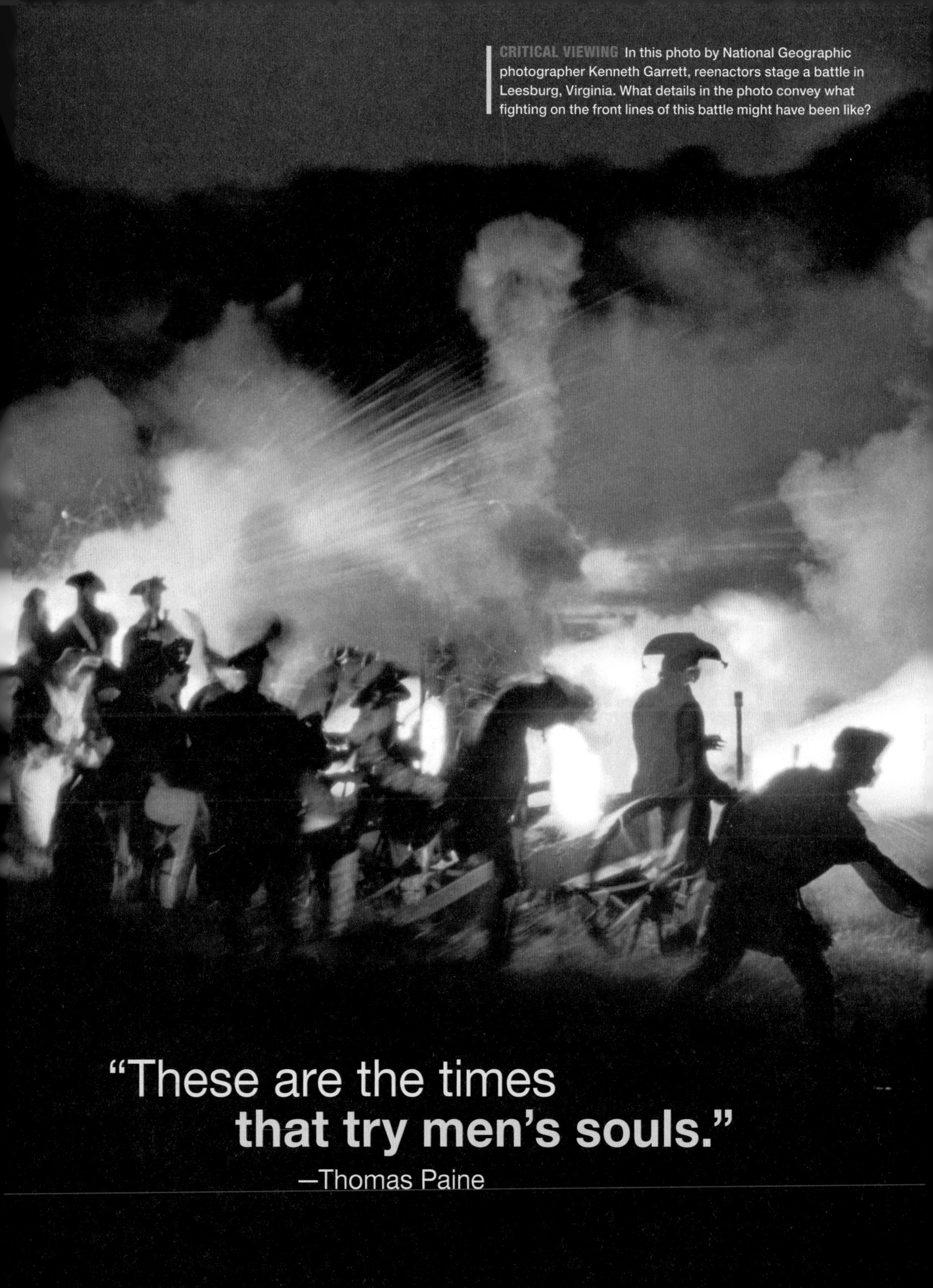

CRITICAL VIEWING In this photo by National Geographic photographer Kenneth Garrett, reenactors stage a battle in Leesburg, Virginia. What details in the photo convey what fighting on the front lines of this battle might have been like?

"These are the times **that try men's souls.**"

—Thomas Paine

OUR
AMERICAN
IDENTITY

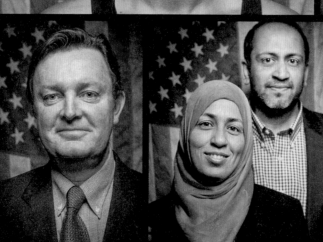

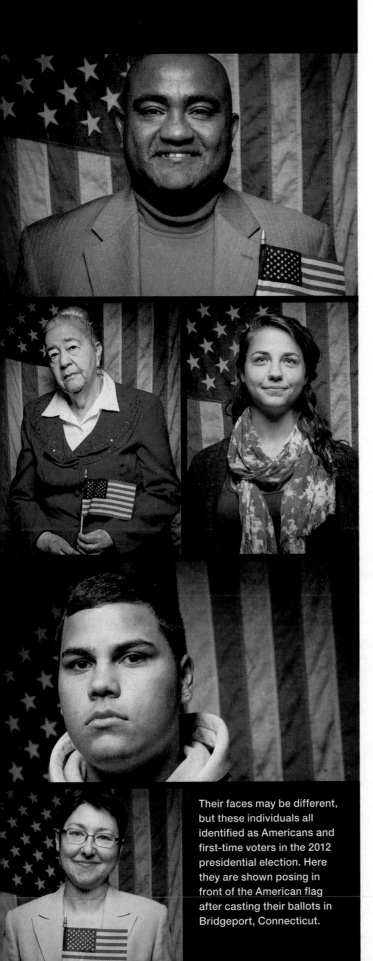

Their faces may be different, but these individuals all identified as Americans and first-time voters in the 2012 presidential election. Here they are shown posing in front of the American flag after casting their ballots in Bridgeport, Connecticut.

The American flag is one of the most recognizable national symbols. For many of us, seeing it at just the right moment or in just the right setting sends shivers down our spines, raises goosebumps on our arms, or brings tears to our eyes.

Why does a simple piece of cloth have the power to provoke such a physical reaction in so many people? The answer may be simple: identity. For many, being an American is part of our identity, and the flag may be a symbol of that part of us. It reminds us that being part of a country influences who we are as individuals.

The Stars and Stripes solemnly drapes the caskets of fallen heroes returning from battle, sheltering them with the gratitude of their country as they are laid to rest. The flag waves proudly at sporting events, representative of the strength and perseverance the United States was built upon and the country's passion for sports and competition. Clothing that bears the flag is often worn to make a statement—to identify the wearer. It says: I'm a firefighter. I'm a soldier. I'm a Girl Scout. I'm an astronaut. I'm a veteran. I'm an athlete. I'm a relief worker. I live in the United States. I represent the United States. I support the United States.

Where did this important icon come from, and what does its story tell us about the establishment of national identity?

On July 4, 1776, representatives of the 13 American colonies approved the Declaration of Independence, formally announcing their break with Britain. Soon after the Declaration was drafted, the Continental Congress passed an act establishing an official flag for the new nation: "Resolved, that the flag of the United States be thirteen stripes, alternate red and white; that the union be thirteen stars, white in a blue field, representing a new constellation." This description doesn't fit the look of the flag as we know it today, but it describes the first of many versions of the flag—the earliest official national symbol and the emblem of independence from Great Britain.

Fast forward to September 13, 1814. The War of 1812 rages on, with British and American troops battling fiercely at Fort McHenry in Baltimore, Maryland. At this point in history, the American flag featured 15 stars and 15 stripes. Fort McHenry served both as the military stronghold that stood between the harbor and the city and as the United States' last hope to prevent a major British military victory. As British rockets and bombs flew from ships, letting loose a deadly deluge of shrapnel and fire over the fort, American gunners responded with their own fire, pushing the British back. The fighting continued all night as a young Washington lawyer named Francis Scott Key watched from a boat in the harbor. While the fiery battle carried on, Key wondered which country would emerge victorious and whose flag he would see flying above the fort in the morning.

It was the American Stars and Stripes—a huge flag measuring 30 feet by 42 feet, made out of red, white, and blue wool by a Baltimore seamstress. The sight of the flag flying proudly over Fort McHenry that morning was so moving it inspired Key to draft the original version of the poem that would become our national anthem: "The Star-Spangled Banner."

CRITICAL VIEWING Think about a time you attended an event or game that began with "The Star-Spangled Banner," and consider this photograph of the stadium. What might a person from another country infer about American identity from these traditions?

THE STAR-SPANGLED BANNER

O say can you see, by the dawn's early light,
What so proudly we hail'd at the twilight's last gleaming,
Whose broad stripes and bright stars through the perilous fight
O'er the ramparts we watch'd were so gallantly streaming?
And the rocket's red glare, the bombs bursting in air,
Gave proof through the night that our flag was still there,
O say does that star-spangled banner yet wave
O'er the land of the free and the home of the brave?

Inspired by the sight of the American flag after a U.S. victory over the British during the War of 1812, Francis Scott Key wrote the 1814 lyrics that were set, ironically, to the tune of a popular British song and became "The Star-Spangled Banner." This song is still the go-to musical expression of patriotism in the United States.

After the United States entered World War I, patriotic music was often played at professional baseball games. In game one of the 1918 World Series, the Cubs and Red Sox players faced the American flag while the band played "The Star-Spangled Banner" with the crowd singing along. This sparked the tradition of playing the song at U.S. sporting events, even though it wouldn't be declared the national anthem by Congress until 1931.

This three-cent stamp honoring Francis Scott Key was issued August 9, 1948. It features Key's portrait and home, the American flags of 1814 and 1948, and Fort McHenry.

For the next 100 years, American military families cared for and proudly displayed the famous Fort McHenry flag. During the Civil War, they hid the flag to keep it safe. Until 1880, small pieces of the flag were even cut and given to war veterans and others—something considered disrespectful and unpatriotic by today's standards. The flag finally landed safely in the Smithsonian National Museum in 1912, 98 years after it flew over Fort McHenry. It remains part of the Smithsonian collection today.

The look of the American flag has evolved along with the nation. Stars and stripes have been added and relocated as the country has expanded, endured the horrors of civil and global wars, and acquired new territories. But the impact and symbolic value of the flag has remained steadfast to many Americans. Many of us view the American flag as a symbol of our identity as U.S. citizens, but it's not the only symbol of national identity, nor does a person have to attach to *any* symbol in order to establish his or her identity. Maybe your identity as an American is revealed in a different way. Or maybe a different symbol of national identity has more meaning to you. A person. A logo. A slogan. A poem. When it comes to what defines your unique identity, you have many rich and wonderful choices.

THINK ABOUT IT

What type of symbol represents your identity as an American? Why?

THE PLEDGE OF ALLEGIANCE

I pledge allegiance to the flag of the United States of America, and to the republic for which it stands, one nation under God, indivisible, with liberty and justice for all.

If you go to school in the United States, you've probably recited the Pledge of Allegiance many times. Written in 1892 by Francis Bellamy, a Baptist minister from New York, the pledge was intended as a salute to the American flag, to be read in unison by schoolchildren. Over time, its words have been changed and debated—especially the phrase "under God," which some people feel violates the constitutional separation of church and state. What do you think?

Young U.S. citizenship candidates take the oath of citizenship with their parents during a naturalization ceremony in Los Angeles, California.

A SYMBOL OF A NATION

You'd expect to see the American flag on American soil, but the Stars and Stripes can be seen in many interesting and meaningful places across the world—and out of this world!

Why might people visiting faraway destinations want others to know about their nation's flag? Maybe it's the item they feel identifies them most clearly as Americans. Think about what symbol of national identity you might use when visiting another country.

1 Marchers carry American and Cuban flags at a 2015 rally focused on human rights abuses by the Castro regime. The United States restored diplomatic ties with Cuba in late 2014 after 53 years of distrust.

2 The famous sculpture at the Marine Corps Memorial in Arlington, Virginia, depicts U.S. Marines raising the flag on the island of Iwo Jima, Japan, after a major victory during World War II. The sculpture is based on a photo of the actual flag-raising captured by photographer Joe Rosenthal in February 1945.

3 This customized version of the flag was used at a peaceful protest at the Washington Monument in 1969.

4 Astronaut Buzz Aldrin posed for this 1969 photograph beside the American flag he and Neil Armstrong planted on the moon.

PRESERVING THE STAR-SPANGLED BANNER

The enormous flag raised over Baltimore's Fort McHenry to announce the American victory over the British during the War of 1812 has seen better days. Time, use, and questionable storage have rendered it dirty and fragile, and the flag itself—this important relic of American history—is now at risk of falling apart.

Beginning in 1998, great efforts have been made to preserve this 1814 flag, the inspiration for Francis Scott Key's composition of "The Star-Spangled Banner." The flag has been safely housed in the National Museum of American History since the early 1900s. It is now stored with attention to preservation, at a 10-degree angle in a low-oxygen, low-light chamber. Experts routinely examine the flag's delicate fibers with microscopes, looking for signs of decay or damage.

As you read about the events leading up to the American Revolution in this chapter, consider why having a flag to represent an emerging American identity would have been important to the colonists.

CRITICAL VIEWING What details from these photographs reveal how this museum balances preserving the flag with displaying it for public view?

1 For more than 30 years, the Star-Spangled Banner hung in the central Flag Hall at the museum. But in 1998, the flag entered a 10-year-long restoration process.

2 To repair the flag, the conservation team had to first remove its soiled linen backing. This meant clipping about 1.7 million stitches that had held the backing in place since 1914 and using tweezers to lift each one away.

3 The team used dry sponges to gently remove dirt from the side of the flag that had been covered by the linen. The dirt itself was analyzed to learn more about the flag's history.

4 Much of the restoration of the flag was done in a special lab that allowed museum visitors to watch the process through a glass wall. A movable bridge called a gantry allowed conservation team members to hang above the flag as they restored it.

1.1 Limits on Freedom

As far as the British were concerned, 1763 was a great year. They had won the French and Indian War—a major victory. Business in the colonies was booming, which put money into the British economy. What could possibly go wrong?

MAIN IDEA After the French and Indian War, the British government enacted laws that restricted some of the colonies' freedoms.

PROBLEMS ARISE

At the end of the French and Indian War, the British colonists in North America had plenty of reasons to be optimistic about their future as British subjects. The colonies' **militias**, or groups of local men who organized to protect their town or colony, had proven themselves to be able fighters alongside British soldiers. After decades of economic growth, the colonies were prosperous. Still, some of the colonists felt a growing dissatisfaction.

The British colonies were the only European settlements in North America where ordinary people could vote for their local legislatures. This freedom to govern, however, was limited by **King George III** and the British Parliament. King George believed the role of a colony was to support the mother country. He was determined to maintain control of Britain's North American colonies.

Concerned about the high cost of the French and Indian War, the king was eager to limit contact between the Native Americans and the colonists in order to keep the peace. As you have read, the king issued a law requiring colonists to stay east of a line drawn on a map along the crest of the Appalachian Mountains. This law was called the **Proclamation of 1763**.

Settlers in the western areas objected to the proclamation. They felt the king was restricting their freedom to expand colonial territories westward. In fact, people continued to settle west of the line decreed by the proclamation. The British government, weighed down by debt from the French and Indian War, could not afford to send soldiers to enforce the law.

SOLDIERS IN THE COLONIES

Soon, colonists along the eastern coast also found themselves frustrated by laws they found oppressive. After the war, many British soldiers were moved into port cities such as New York and Boston to help enforce laws. In 1765, the British Parliament passed the **Quartering Act**. The Quartering Act required colonists to provide

CRITICAL VIEWING This hand-colored engraving (right) shows British soldiers housed in an American home during the 1770s. What do the details in this image help you infer about the colonists' reactions to the Quartering Act?

The Proclamation of 1763

This historical map shows the land assigned to the colonists and Native Americans by the Proclamation of 1763. The colonists resented the proclamation, and many continued to push west of the Appalachians into land long inhabited by Native Americans. This migration weakened an agreement called the Covenant Chain. A covenant is an agreement or promise between two parties.

The Covenant Chain was a complicated system of alliances established between the nations of the Iroquois League and the northernmost colonies. The chain originated around 1677 and lasted for a century. It helped European settlers and some Native American groups maintain mostly peaceful relationships, but that friendship was tested as new settlers began to claim Native American lands.

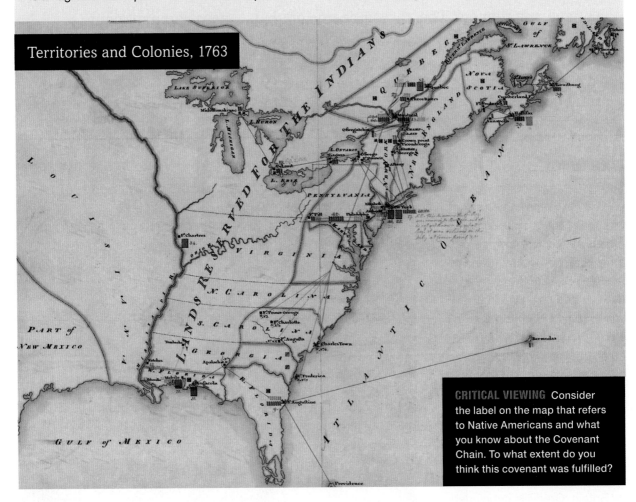

Territories and Colonies, 1763

CRITICAL VIEWING Consider the label on the map that refers to Native Americans and what you know about the Covenant Chain. To what extent do you think this covenant was fulfilled?

housing for British soldiers. If a city did not have barracks to house the soldiers, the men were housed in local inns, homes, and stables, or vacant houses or barns.

While the Quartering Act did not allow the British troops to kick people out of their homes, local governments and residents still resented being forced to house the soldiers. The New York colonial assembly refused to enforce the Quartering Act. In all the colonies, the presence of British troops provoked tension and hostility between soldiers and the civilians who had begun to identify less with the British and more as Americans.

HISTORICAL THINKING

1. **READING CHECK** What were the goals of the Proclamation of 1763 and the Quartering Act?

2. **COMPARE AND CONTRAST** In what ways were the complaints of eastern and western colonists similar and different?

3. **DETERMINE WORD MEANING** What does *prosperous* mean in the sentence, "After decades of economic growth, the colonists were prosperous"?

1.2 Taxation Without Representation

If you borrow money from a friend to buy an amazing pair of sneakers, eventually you'll have to pay off your debt. But how can you do that if you don't have any money? The answer seems obvious—earn some money. But it wasn't that simple for King George and Parliament.

MAIN IDEA British attempts to impose taxes and exert greater control over the colonies caused growing anger and resentment among colonists.

WAR DEBT

The French and Indian War had been an expensive undertaking for the British government. Maintaining and supplying an army in distant colonies had left King George with a hefty debt. In addition, Britain was still keeping 10,000 soldiers in North America to protect the colonies. The British government needed **revenue**, or income, to pay off its debts and expenses.

King George appointed a new prime minister, George Grenville, who agreed that the colonies should be strictly controlled by Britain. Grenville concluded that the colonies should pay for the war debt and the continuing maintenance of the troops in North America. After all, he reasoned, the colonies had benefited the most from the French and Indian War. To raise the money, Grenville sought ways to tax the colonies directly, rather than allowing colonial assemblies to pass taxes. What followed was a series of acts that would have big consequences.

King George III

King George III (1738–1820) ruled Britain for 59 years. "Born and educated in this country," he said, "I glory in the name of Britain." But the war with America was hard on George. He became seriously ill around 1788 and continued to decline until 1811, when his son, George IV, became the acting king and eventually took the throne. A 2005 study of a hair sample from George III suggested that the king may have become ill and died from arsenic poisoning.

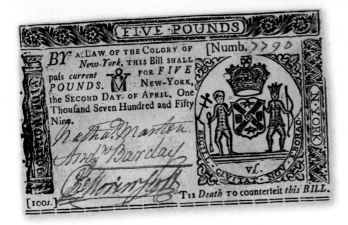

Colonial Currency
Colonial currency came in different shapes, and its designs were very detailed, as the five-pound note (left) issued in New York in 1759 shows. The Pennsylvania 15-shilling note below was produced by Benjamin Franklin and issued on January 1, 1756. It featured multiple anti-counterfeiting processes invented by Franklin, including the blue thread that ran through the note.

ACTS OF PARLIAMENT

The **Sugar Act** of 1764 was among the first of the new taxes. This law was designed to raise revenue as well as to reinforce British control over the colonies. The Sugar Act actually lowered the **duty**, or tax, on the imported molasses used to produce rum in the colonies. The goal of the Sugar Act was to encourage merchants to pay the lower duty instead of smuggling molasses into the colonies to avoid paying the tax, as they had been doing before. This would then increase revenue to the British government.

The **Currency Act**, also passed in 1764, aimed to more tightly control the colonial economy. Previously, different colonies had issued their own paper money. The Currency Act declared that only British currency could be used in the colonies. As colonists discarded the now-useless colonial paper money, the resulting shortage of British currency in the colonies created a number of economic difficulties.

Not surprisingly, the colonists voiced several **grievances**, or objections, to Britain's attempts to tax and control them. They had come to resent the policy of mercantilism—trade designed to bring wealth primarily to the mother country—which was now strengthened by the Sugar Act and Currency Act. The colonists were further frustrated when a new prime minister tightened the Navigation Acts, which controlled colonial trade and shipping, to benefit Britain.

Some accused the British of **tyranny**, or unjust rule by an absolute ruler. They used the slogan "no taxation without representation." Colonists argued that Parliament did not have the right to impose direct taxes on them because they did not have representatives in Parliament who could vote on taxes.

HISTORICAL THINKING

1. **READING CHECK** In what ways did the British government try to raise revenue and control the colonies at the same time?

2. **MAKE INFERENCES** How did the Sugar Act and Currency Act reinforce Britain's policy of mercantilism?

3. **ANALYZE CAUSE AND EFFECT** What impact did these acts likely have on the ways colonists did business?

1.3 The Stamp Act

In 1765, the easiest way to become unpopular with your neighbors was to be appointed by the king to collect his latest tax.

MAIN IDEA An attempt to impose a new type of tax sparked open protests and violent action, which forced the British government to repeal the tax.

A NEW KIND OF TAX

Passed by Parliament in 1765, the **Stamp Act** provoked an even greater storm of protest. Unlike previous laws, the Stamp Act did nothing to further Britain's mercantilist aims. Instead, it was designed purely to raise revenue to pay for the soldiers stationed in the colonies.

The Stamp Act required that all printed materials have a special government stamp. Items subject to the law included newspapers, playing cards, court documents, and sales receipts for land. So, for example, a person selling or buying a piece of land would also pay a British official to stamp the sales document. Colonists could only pay officials for the stamp with gold or silver coins—both of which were rare in the colonies. British courts enforced the Stamp Act by taking away any land or property involved in sales conducted without the stamps.

To the colonists, the Stamp Act was a shocking example of taxation without representation. Philadelphia merchant John Reynell said, "The point in dispute is a very important one, if the Americans are to be taxed by a Parliament where they are not nor can be Represented, they are no longer Englishmen but Slaves."

PROTESTING BRITISH GOODS

Colonial reactions to the Stamp Act were increasingly angry. **Patrick Henry** was a young politician and newly elected to Virginia's House of Burgesses. He persuaded the assembly to pass a series of resolutions that defended the colonists' right to tax themselves rather than to be taxed by Parliament. The resolutions declared that "the General Assembly of this colony . . . have the sole right . . . to lay taxes and impositions upon its inhabitants." When newspapers spread word of

Stamp Act Resistance
The hated Stamp Act was scheduled to take effect on November 1, 1765. Philadelphia newspaper printer William Bradford designed the October 31 "tombstone edition" of the *Pennsylvania Journal* with this skull and crossbones "stamp" to represent the death of the newspaper due to the Stamp Act. Bradford then ignored the act and continued publishing his paper.

Virginia's action, other colonies responded. Rhode Island instructed officials to ignore the stamp tax. Several other colonies passed resolutions similar to Virginia's resolution.

Colonists in cities such as Boston and Philadelphia soon realized they had more in common with each other than with Britain, and they began to organize. In Boston, a group rioted against the Stamp Act.

Museum of Fine Arts, Boston

Paul Revere was a father, husband, silversmith, and member of the Sons of Liberty. He left his mark on America by crafting many treasures relating to the American Revolution. Some of Revere's finest work is housed in Boston's Museum of Fine Arts.

The Sons of Liberty Bowl featured the engraved names of 92 members of the Massachusetts House of Representatives. In 1767, they refused to retract a letter sent throughout the colonies protesting the Townshend Acts, which taxed paper, tea, glass, and other goods imported from Britain. This act of peaceful protest by the "Glorious Ninety-Two" was a major step leading to the American Revolution.

In the same year that Paul Revere crafted the Sons of Liberty Bowl, artist John Singleton Copley (KOP-lee) honored the silversmith by painting his portrait. Copley's decision to represent Revere as an artisan at work embodies the concept of Americans as builders and crafters throughout history.

Sons of Liberty Bowl Commissioned by the Sons of Liberty and made by Paul Revere, this silver bowl joins the Declaration of Independence and the Constitution as the nation's three most precious historical treasures.

Paul Revere In 1768, Copley painted Paul Revere engraving a teapot. It is his only finished portrait of an artisan at work.

They damaged the home of Andrew Oliver, the official in charge of stamping documents, and destroyed the governor's house. Oliver promptly resigned. Protestors in other colonies also acted to prevent the distribution of stamps. By the end of 1765, the stamp distributors in all the colonies except Georgia had resigned.

Some of the men who led the angry crowds called themselves the **Sons of Liberty**. They were mostly merchants, shopkeepers, and craftsmen. The Sons of Liberty also organized a **boycott**, a form of protest that involves refusing to purchase goods or services. Merchants in New York City, Boston, and Philadelphia agreed to stop importing goods from Britain.

In 1766, the protestors succeeded. Parliament **repealed**, or canceled, the Stamp Act. The colonists had taken their first major step toward independence from Britain and creating a new American identity.

HISTORICAL THINKING

1. **READING CHECK** How did the Stamp Act raise revenue for the British government?

2. **MAKE INFERENCES** Why did the Stamp Act provoke such a strong response?

3. **ANALYZE CAUSE AND EFFECT** What events led up to the repeal of the Stamp Act?

1.4 Benjamin Franklin 1706–1790

"To succeed, jump as quickly at opportunities as you do at conclusions."—Benjamin Franklin

Benjamin Franklin seized just about every opportunity that came his way. When he was 17, he ran away from his home in Boston to seek a fresh start in a new city. He eventually ended up in Philadelphia. There, the multitalented Franklin worked as a printer, an inventor, and a scientist. His experiments on the nature of electricity, conducted with his famous kite, brought him international fame. But it is as a statesman that he is best known—and honored.

A REPRESENTATIVE IN ENGLAND

When the Stamp Act was passed in 1765, Franklin was in England, serving as a colonial representative. He'd been in the country off and on since 1757 and, by all accounts, enjoyed his stay there. Franklin liked to dine in fine restaurants and go to the theater—comforts that the more rustic colonies lacked. He opposed the Stamp Act but didn't think it could be stopped. Franklin had even ordered British stamps to be used in his Philadelphia printing firm.

The colonists' response to the passage of the act took him completely by surprise. Franklin learned that mobs of Americans were joining together to prevent the act's enforcement. He also discovered that his acceptance of the despised Stamp Act

The National Portrait Gallery Washington, D.C.

French artist Joseph Siffred Duplessis painted two very similar portraits of Benjamin Franklin, but only this one hangs in the National Portrait Gallery. For the most part, only the color and style of Franklin's coat differ in the two paintings. In both, as one person noted, the subject's "large forehead suggests strength of mind" and his expression conveys "the smile of an unshakeable serenity."

Our American Identity

You may have seen the "Join, or Die" cartoon before, but did you know that Franklin was the artist? The pieces of the snake are meant to roughly represent the 13 colonies. "N.E." stands for the New England colonies of New Hampshire, Massachusetts, Rhode Island, and Connecticut.

Franklin's cartoon found its most popular meaning later, when the colonists' futures were at risk. For many, the choice to support the colonies in North America involved abandoning their identity as Europeans and, instead, identifying themselves as Americans at a time when no one knew what that might mean. The stakes were high, but the eloquent words of people like Franklin carried the day.

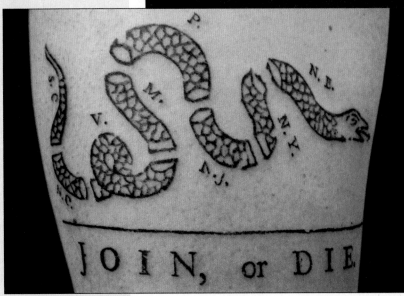

JOIN, or DIE

had begun to tarnish his reputation. Stirred to action, Franklin spoke eloquently to Parliament, condemning the act and explaining the colonists' position. His speech was instrumental in the act's repeal. The experience made Franklin feel what he called his "Americanness" as never before. He also began to question his loyalty to Britain and its treatment of the colonies.

A SUPPORTER OF INDEPENDENCE

Over the next few years, Franklin tried to smooth over the differences between Britain and the colonies and help each side understand the other. To achieve that goal, he worked closely with Thomas Hutchinson, the governor of Massachusetts. Hutchinson was supposed to defend the rights of the colonists, but he really acted on behalf of King George. Secretly, he was working to limit the colonists' rights. When Franklin uncovered letters that detailed Hutchinson's intentions, he sent them to America. The letters fueled the colonists' anger with British rule.

The letters' release also led the British government to condemn Franklin, who shortly thereafter returned to America. His experiences in England had convinced him that the colonies should break away from Britain. At the outset of the French and

Indian War in 1754, Franklin had created a political cartoon called "Join, or Die" to urge the colonies to unite and fight with Great Britain against the French. Now the cartoon came to symbolize colonial unity against the British.

As colonial protests mounted against Britain and the king, Franklin became a strong voice for independence and democracy. He would help draft the Declaration of Independence and was among the first to sign it, saying as he did so, "We must indeed all hang together, or most assuredly we shall all hang separately."

HISTORICAL THINKING

1. **READING CHECK** What official role did Franklin have while he lived in England?

2. **ANALYZE CAUSE AND EFFECT** What realization led to Franklin's dissatisfaction with British rule?

3. **MAKE INFERENCES** Franklin said he was feeling his "Americanness" as never before. How might Franklin have described the American identity at that time in history?

2.1 Colonial Protests Grow

You're a young Boston colonist in 1768. "Sorry, son. There's no tea today," your mother says at breakfast. "We're boycotting British imports again." How would you feel about doing without your favorite food or drink to make a point?

MAIN IDEA Britain's attempt to raise revenue and control the colonies through the Townshend Acts led to protests and violence.

THE TOWNSHEND ACTS

Colonists celebrated the Stamp Act's repeal. However, the British government insisted that it had not lost any authority over the colonies. But with the Stamp Act repealed, Britain had to figure out other ways of gaining revenue.

In 1767, Parliament passed the **Townshend Acts**, named after Charles Townshend, a British royal treasurer. The acts placed duties on tea, glass, paper, lead, and paint—all goods that the colonies were required to purchase only from Britain. The revenue from the Townshend Acts would be used by the British to pay the salaries of colonial governors and judges. Previously, these officials had been paid by the colonial assemblies. By paying officials directly, the British government would establish greater control over the day-to-day running of the colonies.

The Townshend Acts also required colonial courts to provide **writs of assistance**, or search warrants, so officials could search houses and businesses for smuggled goods. Writs of assistance had existed for several years, and colonists had protested them. To the colonists, the writs allowed the British to search without cause and to justify random searches, and the Townshend Acts only expanded their use.

THE COLONISTS REACT

Colonists once again protested and accused the British government of tyranny. The protestors were strongly influenced by the 17th century British philosopher **John Locke**, who wrote that a leader could rule only with the consent of the people.

Daughters of Liberty

In the 1770s, colonial women contributed significantly to the anti-British movement. They even spun yarn to reduce colonial dependence on British textiles, prompting Samuel Adams to declare, "With the ladies on our side, we can make every Tory tremble."

This image of a colonial woman holding a flintlock musket appeared on a broadside, a single-sided newspaper, around 1779. A symbol of strength and patriotism, she wears a man's hat, holds her weapon and powder horn, and is pictured in front of a British fort.

He stated that government exists to uphold natural rights, or rights such as life or liberty that a person is born with. Any government that failed in this task should be overthrown. The colonists strongly identified with Locke's way of thinking.

Samuel Adams was a follower of Locke's philosophy, a member of the Massachusetts Assembly, and a leader of the Sons of Liberty. In 1768, Adams cowrote a letter with lawyer James Otis to the other colonial assemblies. The letter objected to the new duties and proposed a boycott of British goods. The British governor of Massachusetts threatened to dismiss the assembly if it did not take back the letter. Defiantly, the assembly refused, and it was disbanded.

Samuel Adams and the Sons of Liberty vigorously continued to support actions against the Townshend Acts. Colonists in Boston signed an agreement to boycott British imports, and merchants in New York soon followed. Women also used their purchasing power to protest the Townshend Acts. A group called **Daughters of Liberty** boycotted imported tea and clothing. To replace imported cloth, they wove their own fabric, known as homespun, from American yarn and wool.

The Great Awakening of the 1730s and 1740s also helped push the colonists toward rebellion and independence. During that revival movement, believers challenged the authority of their church leaders. They learned to use their own judgment in matters of religion. The habit of thinking independently spread throughout the colonies. By the 1770s, the ideas of the Great Awakening had helped create a revolutionary fervor among the colonists, which led them to challenge Britain's authority.

Tar and Feathers
Sometimes angry protestors used tar and feathers to punish people who supported British taxes. Victims would be dragged to a public place. Then they would be coated with hot, sticky tar and covered in feathers, as shown in this 1774 political cartoon. Tarring and feathering was often portrayed in a humorous way, but it was in fact horribly painful.

HISTORICAL THINKING

1. **READING CHECK** How were the Townshend Acts intended to accomplish Britain's goals in the colonies?

2. **ANALYZE CAUSE AND EFFECT** In what ways did Locke's philosophy influence the colonists in their protest against British actions?

3. **MAKE PREDICTIONS** What might result from the boycotts against the Townshend Acts?

2.2 The Boston Massacre

If you place a flame too close to a powder keg full of explosive gunpowder, it will blow up spectacularly. In 1770, Boston was like a powder keg, and a hot flame was quickly approaching.

> **MAIN IDEA** Tensions between the British troops and the colonists in Boston reached a breaking point when some soldiers fired on an angry crowd of citizens.

TENSIONS RISE

In response to growing protests and increasing unrest among colonists, British authorities brought additional troops to Boston. Some of the soldiers camped out on Boston Common, an open area that was intended for all Bostonians to use.

This arrangement made for a tense situation. Frequent fights broke out between soldiers and civilians. To annoy the British soldiers, children followed them in the streets, taunting them and calling them names such as "redcoats" and "lobsterbacks" because of the bright red uniforms they wore.

In addition, the British soldiers were poorly paid. To make extra money, they took jobs as workers during their off-duty hours. This took jobs away from some Bostonians, who were angry at losing work to soldiers they already despised.

On March 5, 1770, a boy began yelling insults at a British soldier standing guard at a government building. The soldier hit the boy with his gun. A rowdy crowd gathered around the commotion, and Captain Thomas Preston led a group of seven additional soldiers out to diffuse the situation. The crowd grew larger, throwing snowballs, ice, and sticks at the soldiers. Then someone hit a soldier with a club, knocking his gun out of his hands.

TENSIONS EXPLODE

Suddenly Preston's men were firing at the crowd. Five townspeople were killed and six were injured. This event soon became known as the **Boston Massacre**. To the colonists, the killings would come to symbolize all that they hated about British rule.

The first man shot and killed was **Crispus Attucks**, an African American and former slave who worked as a sailor and rope maker in Boston. Attucks is considered to be the first person to die in the quest for American independence.

After the shooting, the soldiers were arrested and put on trial for murder. At the trial, they were represented by lawyer **John Adams**, a cousin of Samuel Adams. This surprised some people because John Adams was a well-known Patriot, or supporter of colonial self-rule, in addition to being a respected lawyer. But he was also a firm believer in the right to a fair trial for everyone, no matter how unpopular they were.

Adams claimed that the soldiers had fired in self-defense. He made his case so eloquently that Captain Preston and all but two of the soldiers were found not guilty. Many people, including John Adams, thought this trial would be the end of his legal career. Yet in the end, Bostonians came to respect Adams for making the unpopular but ethical choice. He went on to have a distinguished career in politics, including serving as the first vice president and second president of the United States.

HISTORICAL THINKING

1. **READING CHECK** What events led up to the Boston Massacre?

2. **MAKE INFERENCES** What was the general feeling in Boston in 1770?

3. **ANALYZE VISUALS** What similarities and differences can you identify in the two depictions of the Boston Massacre at right?

The Bloody Massacre

American Patriot Paul Revere wasn't the first person to use a tragic incident to sway people's opinions, but he did it particularly effectively in the engraved print on the left. Titled *The Bloody Massacre in King Street*, the print shows a line of British soldiers firing into an unarmed crowd when, in fact, violence erupted on both sides. If you look closely at the white building on the right—the Customs House—you can also see that Revere changed its name to "Butcher's Hall." You may also notice that Crispus Attucks isn't represented in the print.

In fact, Attucks wouldn't be portrayed as a person of color until artist William L. Champney depicted him at the event in his 1855 drawing *Boston Massacre*. The antislavery movement was at its height, so the artist placed Attucks squarely in the center of the action. He also shows the colonists taking a more active role in the fight—probably a more accurate depiction of the incident.

A GLOBAL PERSPECTIVE We may be an ocean apart, but the people of the United States and France are similar in many ways. When a protest march was cancelled in Paris's Place de la Republique in 2015 due to concerns about terrorism, protestors placed thousands of pairs of shoes in the square as a silent yet effective expression of their protest and presence. How does this public protest compare to the Boston Tea Party?

2.3 The Boston Tea Party

Sit-ins, marches, posters, and chants are the tools of peaceful protest. They help people express displeasure or opposition without violence. The colonists were angry with the British, but sometimes they found ways to make their feelings known without lifting a weapon.

MAIN IDEA When Parliament imposed new laws to regulate tea, colonists responded by throwing a cargo of British tea into Boston Harbor.

NEW LAW, OLD TAX

At about the same time as the Boston Massacre, the British government decided to repeal most of the Townshend Acts. The taxes on all the items listed in the act were lifted, except for the tax on tea. There were fewer protests, and for two years, the relationship between Britain and the colonies was generally calm.

But in 1772, Patriots in Rhode Island burned a British ship that had been searching local boats for smugglers. When news of the attack reached England, Parliament once again began passing laws to gain greater control over the colonies. In Massachusetts, Samuel Adams responded by forming a **committee of correspondence**. This group made a list of British offenses against the colonies' rights and published it in Massachusetts. Other colonies joined in the movement by forming their own committees.

The committees soon had a new complaint. In 1773, Parliament passed the **Tea Act**, allowing the British East India Company to sell tea directly in the colonies. This lowered the price of tea, but it also took money away from colonial tea merchants. The prime minister also refused to repeal the Townshend Acts' tax on tea.

Despite the fact that cheaper tea would now be available, the new law fanned the flames of colonial resentment toward Britain. Colonial tea merchants were close to going out of business, and Parliament was still taxing the colonists without representation.

TEA OVERBOARD!

At first, the colonists protested by making it difficult for the British East India Company to deliver shipments of tea. Workers in major cities refused to unload shipments of tea from ships in port. In New York and Philadelphia, the ships' captains were told to return to England.

On the night of December 16, 1773, members of the Sons of Liberty disguised themselves as Native Americans and boarded three ships loaded with tea in Boston Harbor. Without harming the ships' other cargo, they dumped the tea into the icy water while thousands of people on shore watched the events of the **Boston Tea Party** unfold.

The Boston Tea Party was not the only act of colonial defiance that involved tea. On October 14, 1774, in Annapolis, Maryland, a ship with a cargo of tea was set on fire. King George was furious. Soon Parliament would enact new laws to punish the colonists for their actions, and the stage would be set for further conflicts.

HISTORICAL THINKING

1. **READING CHECK** In what ways did the colonists protest the Tea Act?

2. **FORM AND SUPPORT OPINIONS** Was the Boston Tea Party an effective form of protest? Support your opinion with evidence from the text.

3. **MAKE GENERALIZATIONS** How did the Tea Act reflect the attitude of the British government toward the colonies?

2.4 Museum of the American Revolution, Philadelphia

The Museum of the American Revolution is located in the heart of historic Philadelphia. Visitors find themselves across the street from Carpenter's Hall, the first meeting place of the Continental Congress, and a short walk to the home of founding father Benjamin Franklin. The museum's rich collection of artifacts includes many personal belongings of George Washington, early American weapons, artwork, documents, and thousands of other items that date to the American Revolution. These items help tell the earliest stories of American independence from Britain. How would each of the artifacts shown have been used during the war?

American War Drum

This drum dates to 1740, well before the American Revolution had begun. It is believed to be the second-oldest dated American drum that exists. The drum is inscribed with the name of its maker, Robert Crosman, from Taunton, Massachusetts.

Considered a piece of standard equipment for New Englanders, drums and small, shrill flutes called fifes served as signal instruments for the infantry. They provided musical "commands" to soldiers in the battlefield and around camp. Fife and drum music also distracted soldiers from the drudgery of long marches.

What role did fife and drum music play in the American Revolution?

The stamp or brand on this musket is unique. It reads "U. States," which was a label required by the Congress to show that this gun was American-made, not European.

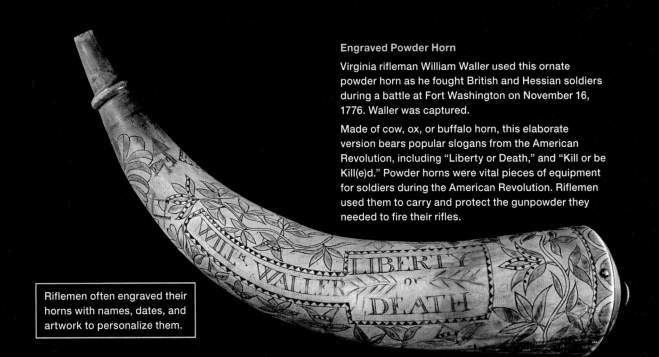

Engraved Powder Horn

Virginia rifleman William Waller used this ornate powder horn as he fought British and Hessian soldiers during a battle at Fort Washington on November 16, 1776. Waller was captured.

Made of cow, ox, or buffalo horn, this elaborate version bears popular slogans from the American Revolution, including "Liberty or Death," and "Kill or be Kill(e)d." Powder horns were vital pieces of equipment for soldiers during the American Revolution. Riflemen used them to carry and protect the gunpowder they needed to fire their rifles.

Riflemen often engraved their horns with names, dates, and artwork to personalize them.

"The need for wider, **deeper understanding of the Revolution,** and respect for those who championed the cause at the time, has never been greater than now."

—David McCullough
Pulitzer Prize-winning author

The design on the musket's flintlock was modeled after the Continental three-dollar bill.

American Military Musket

Made around 1775, this musket is pretty rare. By 1777, weapons imported from France and other countries had replaced American-made firearms from the early days of the American Revolution. This particular musket features a flintlock mechanism. The flintlock creates a spark that lights the gunpowder stored in the barrel of the gun. What challenges might the use of this weapon have posed to soldiers?

3.1 Preparing to Fight

King George had reached his limit. He believed the colonies were out of control and had to be reined in. Maybe the king didn't understand that the colonists had reached their limits, too. Could there be a war on the horizon?

MAIN IDEA Britain enacted a series of laws to punish Boston and force the colonies into obedience, but the colonies united to resist the laws.

INTOLERABLE LAWS

Parliament decided to punish the Bostonians. It passed a series of laws called the Coercive Acts. In the colonies, these laws quickly became known as the **Intolerable Acts**.

The Intolerable Acts prevented Massachusetts from governing itself. The Massachusetts Assembly would no longer be made up of representatives elected by the people of the colony. Instead, it was to be replaced by a ruling council of officials appointed by the king. The Quartering Act was strengthened. Now, if no barracks were available, troops could take over private homes. In addition, the port of Boston would be closed until the residents could pay for the tea they had destroyed.

The British government expected the new laws to isolate Boston and convince the other colonies to be obedient. Instead, towns near Boston sent much-needed supplies to the city and took in Bostonians looking for work. Other colonies called for a meeting to decide on a united response to the Intolerable Acts. According to the Virginia House of Burgesses, "an attack made on one of our sister colonies . . . is an attack made on all British America."

Patrick Henry
Patrick Henry was known for crafting speeches on the spot with no notes. In one of his most famous speeches, given on March 23, 1775, Henry ended with the now-famous phrase, "Give me liberty or give me death!"

AMERICAN PLACES

Carpenters' Hall Philadelphia

Books were hard to find in the 1700s, so in 1731, Benjamin Franklin established the Library Company of Philadelphia, America's first lending library. For the first time, the public had access to a collection of books that could be borrowed and shared. In September 1773, the library moved to Carpenters' Hall (left).

Members of both Continental Congresses used the library, making it the first unofficial Library of Congress. Officers of the British Army were also permitted to borrow books, provided that they returned them in good condition.

SEEDS OF WAR

The meeting of the colonies—called the **First Continental Congress**—took place in Philadelphia on September 5, 1774. Every colony except Georgia sent delegates. The 56 representatives included Patrick Henry, Samuel and John Adams, and George Washington. The main purpose of the First Continental Congress was to discuss ways to have the Intolerable Acts repealed.

The delegates wanted to assert the rights of the 13 British colonies in North America. One of the resolutions they passed stated that the Intolerable Acts were "gross infractions of those rights to which we are justly entitled by the laws of nature, the British constitution, and the charter of this province." However, the First Continental Congress was not ready to declare independence. In the end, the delegates simply voted to end all trade with Britain and Ireland—still a significant step.

Several delegates believed it was also time to start training for a possible fight with Britain. One of the other resolutions stated that everyone qualified to fight should learn "the art of war as soon as possible." Some delegates may have believed that if there was any fighting, it would be over quickly. But others, like Patrick Henry, expected all-out war.

HISTORICAL THINKING

1. **READING CHECK** How did the colonies react to the Intolerable Acts?

2. **MAKE INFERENCES** What might learning "the art of war" have meant to colonists?

3. **ANALYZE CAUSE AND EFFECT** What were the Intolerable Acts, and how did they backfire on the British government?

3.2 The Midnight Ride of Paul Revere

If you wanted to spread important news, you'd probably text it or put it out on social media for everyone to see. In 1775, spreading information wasn't that simple. "Social media" meant a man on a horse racing from town to town.

MAIN IDEA The British wanted to take control of military supplies in the colonies, but Paul Revere and others warned colonists of the coming attack.

STORED ARMS

After the First Continental Congress, militia units across the colonies began to step up their training and stockpile supplies. Remember, militias were not professional soldiers; they were groups of local men who organized to protect their town or colony. Companies of handpicked, specially trained militia members called **minutemen** were also assembled. The minutemen were known for their ability to be ready to fight with practically no warning—in a "minute."

Revere's Lantern
This iron and glass piece of American history was identified as one of the two lanterns used to signal that the British were coming by sea. It's an important artifact. Without it, the minutemen might not have been prepared for the arrival of the British troops, and Paul Revere's late-night ride might have been in vain.

General Thomas Gage, the British governor of Massachusetts, was ordered by the British government to take forceful action against the militias. In April 1775, he learned that the Massachusetts militia was storing military supplies in the town of Concord. He decided to take the supplies and also to arrest Samuel Adams and **John Hancock**. Both men were staying in Lexington, on the road from Boston to Concord. Like Adams, Hancock was a leading figure in the protests against British laws and a member of the First Continental Congress.

ONE IF BY LAND, TWO IF BY SEA

Gage's plans were leaked, however. Paul Revere, a silversmith who had taken part in the Boston Tea Party, formed a plan to warn the Massachusetts militias. He arranged to signal the Sons of Liberty in Charlestown when the British soldiers left for Concord. He would use lanterns in the Old North Church steeple, which was visible from Charlestown. If the British troops left Boston by land, there would be one lantern in the steeple. If they left by water, there would be two lanterns.

On the night of April 18, 1775, Revere learned that British soldiers were preparing to cross the bay. He had a friend hang two lanterns in the steeple, and he rowed to Charlestown in a small boat. There, the Sons of Liberty had a horse waiting for him, and he set off on his famous ride, stopping at houses and villages to warn the local militias that the British troops were coming.

AMERICAN PLACES
Old North Church Boston

The Old North Church, shown here behind a statue of Paul Revere, is an important part of Revere's famous late-night ride. Founded in 1722, it is Boston's oldest surviving church.

On the night of April 18, 1775, the church caretaker and a close friend of Revere's squeezed behind a pipe organ and entered a small door in the church tower. They then climbed eight more stories of winding stairs into the steeple and lit two lanterns to signal Paul Revere.

Paul Revere was not the only rider that night. When he stopped in Lexington to tell Adams and Hancock that the troops were on their way, he was joined by William Dawes. A third rider, Dr. Samuel Prescott, caught up with Revere and Dawes farther down the road.

Soon, a patrol of British soldiers stopped the riders. Dawes and Prescott escaped, but Revere was held and questioned by the soldiers. Prescott was able to complete the ride and alert the militia in Concord. When the British troops arrived, the minutemen were ready.

HISTORICAL THINKING

1. **READING CHECK** How did Paul Revere and others alert the Massachusetts militia about the approaching British soldiers?

2. **INTERPRET VISUALS** How do the photo and caption above help you understand the events described in the text?

3. **FORM AND SUPPORT OPINIONS** Is Paul Revere an important figure in American history? Why or why not?

3.3 Shot Heard Round the World

In 1837, American poet Ralph Waldo Emerson referred to a bullet fired in Lexington, Massachusetts, as "the shot heard round the world" in his poem "Concord Hymn." Nobody knows who fired that shot, but it started a revolution that changed the world.

MAIN IDEA The American Revolution began when Massachusetts militia fought the British forces in the towns of Lexington and Concord.

THE REVOLUTION BEGINS

As the British Army marched toward Concord, they heard church bells and saw lights in windows. The colonists were awake and aware. Soon after sunrise on April 19, the troops reached Lexington. There, they met about 70 armed militiamen, nearly half of the town's adult males. But the Lexington militia was inexperienced and faced a much larger British force.

The scene was chaos as both the British commander and the militia leader called orders to their troops. The British officer, Major John Pitcairn, wanted to disarm the Americans, not engage in battle. But as the British advanced, a shot rang out. Then there were several more. Pitcairn tried to stop his troops, but the shooting continued for 20 minutes, leaving eight Lexington men dead and 10 wounded. Only one British soldier was wounded and none were killed.

The British reached Concord at about eight o'clock in the morning. Using previously hidden military supplies, the Americans inflicted more casualties than the British did this time. The British soldiers attempted an orderly retreat back to Boston. But hundreds of militiamen fired at them from behind trees, walls, rocks, and buildings and forced many British soldiers to panic. The British countered by sending advance parties to set fire to homes and kill residents along the way back to Boston.

The fighting at **Lexington and Concord** is considered the first battle of the American Revolution. By the end of the day, British losses totaled 73 dead and 200 wounded or missing. The Americans counted 49 killed and at least 39 wounded or missing.

CHOOSING SIDES

As tensions between Britain and the colonies turned into open violence, colonists took sides in the conflict. Those who called themselves **Patriots** supported the right of the colonies to rule themselves. At first, not all Patriots wanted to separate from Britain. Over time, however, those on the Patriot side became convinced that independence was necessary.

The **Loyalists**, colonists who supported Britain, increasingly found themselves an uncomfortable minority. As time went on, it became dangerous to sympathize with the British cause. Some Loyalists were beaten or saw their homes burned by fellow colonists. In 1775, a Loyalist who spoke openly about his opinions was ordered to leave Maryland by the Maryland Provincial Convention.

HISTORICAL THINKING

1. **READING CHECK** What were the results of the fighting at Lexington and Concord?

2. **ANALYZE CAUSE AND EFFECT** Why did the battles of Lexington and Concord increase tensions between Patriots and Loyalists?

3. **IDENTIFY MAIN IDEAS AND DETAILS** What details support the idea that the Patriots won the battles?

LOYALISTS CALLED THE **PATRIOTS**

Whig! **Rebel!** **Yankee!**

PATRIOTS CALLED THE **LOYALISTS**

King's Man! **Royalist!** **Tory!**

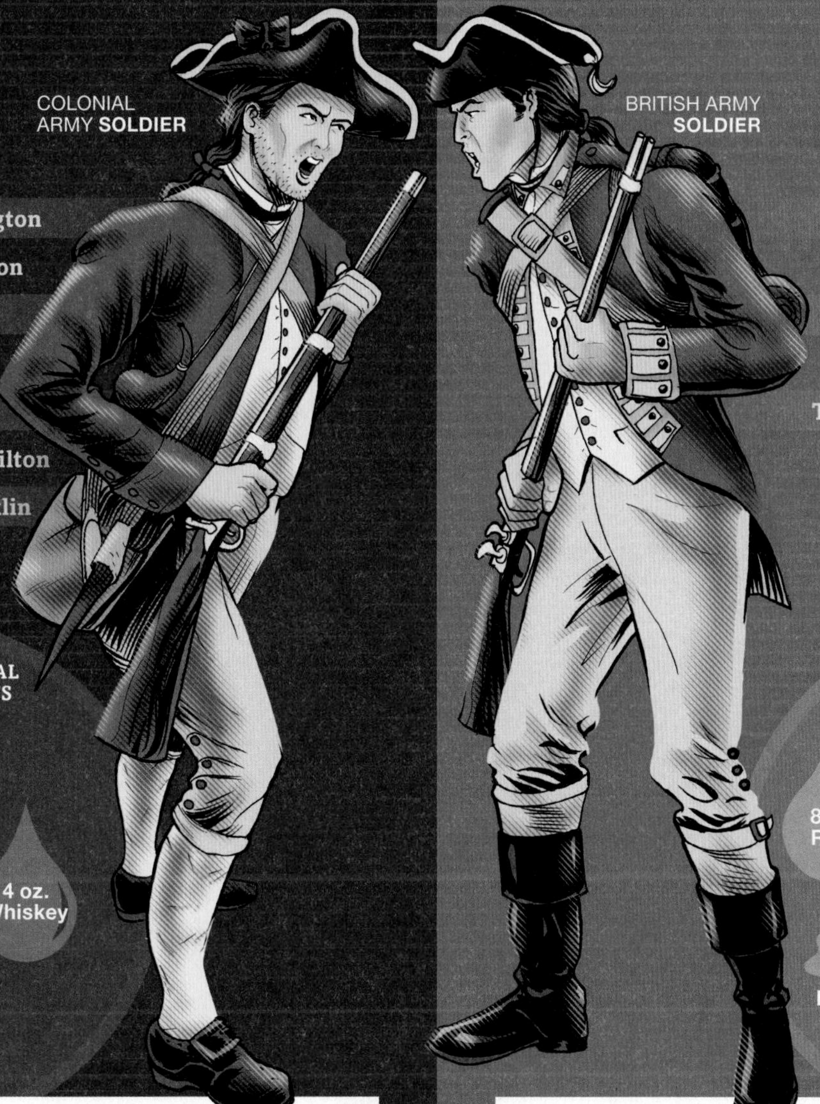

COLONIAL ARMY SOLDIER
BRITISH ARMY SOLDIER

FAMOUS **PATRIOTS**

- George Washington
- Thomas Jefferson
- James Madison
- Patrick Henry
- John Adams
- Alexander Hamilton
- Benjamin Franklin

FAMOUS **LOYALISTS**

- John Howe
- Mary Dowd
- Myles Cooper
- William Franklin
- Thomas Hutchinson

DAILY COLONIAL ARMY RATIONS

- **1 1/2 lb. Bread** or Flour
- **4 oz. Whiskey**
- **1 lb. Beef** or 3/4 lb. Pork

DAILY BRITISH ARMY RATIONS

- **8 oz. Rum**
- **1 1/2 lb. Bread** or Flour
- **1/4 pint Canned Peas** and 1 oz. Rice
- **1 oz. Butter**
- **1 lb. Beef** or 1/2 lb. Pork

COLONISTS VS BRITISH

ALLIES

France · Spain · United Netherlands

ALLIES

Many Native American Tribes · Hessian Troops

2.5 Million American Colonists

20% Supported Britain

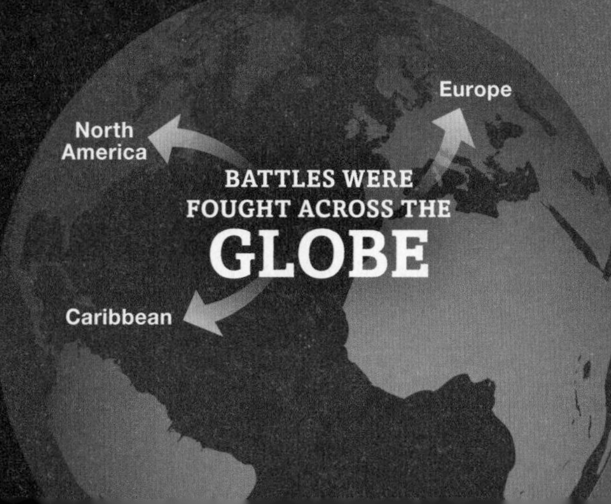

North America
Europe
Caribbean
BATTLES WERE FOUGHT ACROSS THE
GLOBE

11 Million People in Great Britain

2.5 Million Colonists in America

SOURCE: Civil War Trust Online

3.4 North Bridge
Concord, Massachusetts

North Bridge is more than just a quaint path over the Concord River in Massachusetts. Located in **Minute Man National Historical Park**, it's a solemn place—American hallowed ground. It is also the site where some of the first shots of the American Revolution were fired on April 19, 1775. The original "battle bridge" that existed when the war broke out has long since been replaced, but the symbolism of this historical landscape remains. Based on what you see here, how might the geography of this place have impacted colonial and British soldiers?

CRITICAL VIEWING The 1875 bronze Minute Man statue (right background) was made from melted Civil War cannons for the 100th anniversary of the battle in this location. It symbolizes the colonial farmers who replaced their plows with muskets to defend their land and liberty. What does this tell you about how the colonial soldiers differed from British soldiers?

4.1 Colonial Army Forms

You nervously count and recount your bullets as you and your fellow militiamen stand at the top of the hill. Below, a line of red-coated British soldiers marches toward you, pausing only to fire in unison. This is it. This is war.

MAIN IDEA Colonial leaders remained reluctant to fully declare independence, but battles between the British and colonial militias continued to break out.

CRITICAL VIEWING Originally built by the French in 1755, Fort Ticonderoga was constructed to guard a strategic strip of land that connected New France and the American colonies. What do you observe about the fort's location that may have been significant during the American Revolution?

VICTORY AT FORT TICONDEROGA

The next battle in the growing conflict took place on May 10, 1775. At dawn that morning, **Ethan Allen**, a Patriot and colonial leader from Vermont, and **Benedict Arnold**, from Connecticut, led a troop of militia in an attack on Fort Ticonderoga in northeastern New York. In a classic example of "timing is everything," the militia known as the Green Mountain Boys surprised the sleeping British soldiers and captured the fort without firing a shot.

The victory at Fort Ticonderoga gave the colonial forces an important advantage. The Green Mountain Boys captured the fort's **artillery**, or large guns that could fire a long distance. In all, they claimed 59 cannons and 19 other pieces of heavy artillery for the colonies. It was an epic gain.

On the same day that Ethan Allen took Fort Ticonderoga, the **Second Continental Congress** met in Philadelphia. Many of the delegates had also been part of the First Continental Congress. New delegates included Thomas Jefferson of Virginia and Benjamin Franklin of Pennsylvania.

The Congress recognized the need to prepare for war and wanted to make sure the army would be under its control. So it appointed **George Washington** as the commander in chief of the colonial forces, which would now be called the **Continental Army**. Despite this warlike decision, however, many of the delegates were still opposed to declaring independence.

BATTLE OF BUNKER HILL

Before Washington could even take command of the troops, another battle broke out. The militia around Boston learned that the British were planning to seize the hills overlooking the city. On June 16, a troop of militiamen occupied Bunker Hill and Breed's Hill to prevent the British from taking the high ground.

The next morning, the British troops attacked. The militia fighters were greatly outnumbered. They were also short of ammunition, so they had to make every shot count. Colonel William Prescott, their commander, is said to have told his men, "Don't fire until you can see the whites of their eyes."

An American Traitor

Benedict Arnold was an early hero in the American Revolution who went on to become one of the most infamous traitors in American history. After helping capture Fort Ticonderoga in 1775, Arnold continued his support of the American war efforts but felt his work went unrecognized. In 1779, he secretly negotiated with the British to turn over an American post in exchange for a commanding position in the British army and a cash reward. Arnold's plot was discovered by the Americans, but he escaped to British territory.

The militia did have one key advantage: the British troops had to charge uphill to reach them. The redcoats tried storming Breed's Hill three times. The first two attempts failed, resulting in a huge loss of lives. On the third try, the Patriots were overrun by the redcoats. Britain won the battle, but at an enormous cost. Today, the encounter is known as the Battle of Bunker Hill, even though most of the fighting took place on Breed's Hill.

HISTORICAL THINKING

1. **READING CHECK** What happened at the battles of Fort Ticonderoga and Bunker Hill?

2. **ANALYZE CAUSE AND EFFECT** Why did the Second Continental Congress decide to prepare for war?

3. **FORM AND SUPPORT OPINIONS** Do you think peace between Britain and the colonies could have been possible in 1775? Why or why not?

4.2 How Geology Shapes the Battlefield

MAIN IDEA Geologic forces shape the landscape, impacting the outcome of many battles.

By Andrés Ruzo, **National Geographic Explorer**

Mill Pond

Bunker

Tricky Terrain
Seemingly open stretches of land were obstacle courses for the British. Tall grasses hid rocks and holes. Fences and stone walls also slowed them down.

Glasgow

British troops

Patriot troops

British advance

Patriot advance

British ship

TAKE THE HIGH GROUND

Taking advantage of a battlefield can mean the difference between victory and defeat, and there is a geologic story behind every great battle. An area's **geology**—the local geologic features such as rocks, landforms, and the processes that created and shaped them—can define a battlefield. Over millions, even billions of years, colliding tectonic plates and volcanic activity give rise to great landforms like mountain ranges. Erosion from weathering, moving glaciers, and other destructive forces break down these landforms. The eroded material is transported and re-deposited, customizing each region with its distinctive **terrain**, the physical features of the land.

Throughout history, successful commanders were the ones who understood how to use the local terrain to their advantage. The names of American Revolution battle sites like Brooklyn Heights (New York), Bunker Hill (Massachusetts), and Kings Mountain (South Carolina) are clues to the importance of battlefield geology. Hills, cliffs, bluffs, and other elevated landforms played a key role in the war. Elevation gave soldiers a strategic military advantage. Think about running uphill with a heavy rifle straight into enemy gunfire. Now consider the benefits of firing down on your enemies from a well-fortified position as they advance up difficult terrain. It's no wonder military commanders try to "take the high ground."

BUNKER HILL

Study the map of Bunker Hill. This landscape tells a geologic story. Over 20,000 years ago, a massive melting glacier slowly began to reveal the landscape that would one day become Boston. Geologically, Bunker Hill and Breed's Hill are called **drumlins**, smooth-sloped hills made of glacial sediments. In 1775, the Americans took the high ground and fortified these drumlins by building 6-foot **earthworks**, human-made land modifications, out of the silty glacial soils. This put the Americans in an ideal defensive position overlooking the battlefields.

But taking the high ground doesn't always ensure victory. At Bunker Hill, the Americans held their ground until they ran out of ammunition. As you

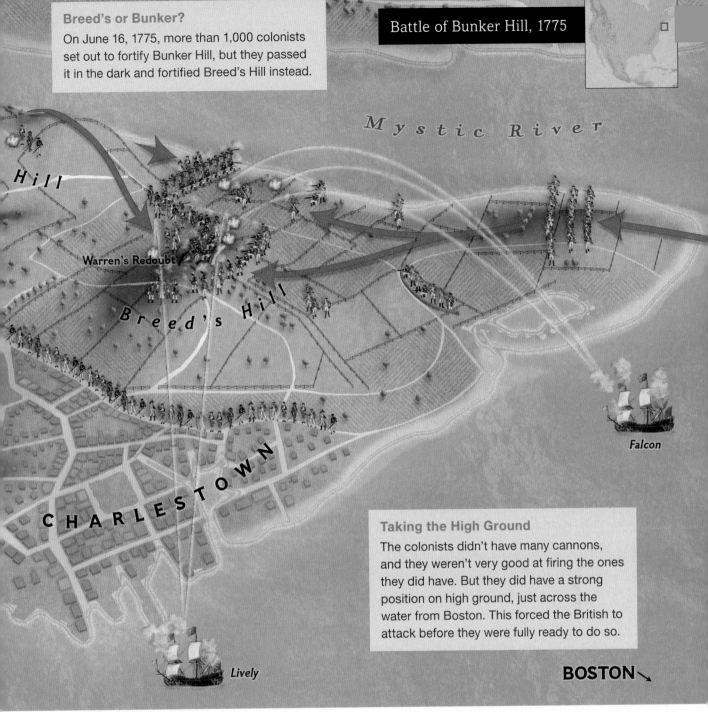

Breed's or Bunker?
On June 16, 1775, more than 1,000 colonists set out to fortify Bunker Hill, but they passed it in the dark and fortified Breed's Hill instead.

M y s t i c   R i v e r

H i l l

Warren's Redoubt

B r e e d's   H i l l

Falcon

C H A R L E S T O W N

Taking the High Ground
The colonists didn't have many cannons, and they weren't very good at firing the ones they did have. But they did have a strong position on high ground, just across the water from Boston. This forced the British to attack before they were fully ready to do so.

Lively

BOSTON ↘

have read, the British won the battle, but at a terrible cost. Over 1,000 British soldiers were killed or wounded, compared to over 400 Americans. This showed that the Patriots could hold their own against a better-trained, better-equipped, and far larger British force. Clearly local terrain played a role in how the battle unfolded.

War commanders probably don't think much about the geologic story that shaped their battlefields, but that doesn't mean the geology isn't significant.

THINK LIKE A GEOLOGIST

1. **IDENTIFY MAIN IDEAS AND DETAILS** If you were a commander defending your city, where would you set up troops? Why?

2. **DESCRIBE** What advantages or disadvantages would your local terrain present in battle?

3. **INTERPRET MAPS** Aside from hills, which geologic features do you think affected the battle?

4.3 Breaking with Britain

Congress has always had a difficult job, making decisions that will impact a large number of people. In 1775, the Second Continental Congress faced a hard choice: pursue peace or prepare for war.

MAIN IDEA The Second Continental Congress made one last attempt to make peace with Britain, but fighting continued and public opinion moved toward declaring independence.

PEACE REJECTED

During the summer of 1775, the Continental Congress made moves toward both peace and war. In an attempt to restore peace with Britain, delegates sent the king a petition. They asked him to resolve the conflict between the colonies and Parliament. Instead, he proclaimed that the colonies were in "an open and avowed rebellion."

At the same time, Congress sent an army north to invade Canada and take on the British forces there. This proved to be a poor decision. The Canada campaign was long, bloody, and unsuccessful. British troops successfully pushed the colonial army back into New York.

In December 1775, Parliament decided to punish the colonies by cutting off all trade. Then in January 1776, King George signed a treaty with Germany that allowed him to hire more than 20,000 German soldiers and send them to the colonies. These soldiers for hire were known as **Hessians**, and they had a reputation as fierce fighters. For many Americans, these actions proved that the British government intended to crush the colonies both militarily and economically, at any cost.

TIME TO PART

Meanwhile, the colonial army was meeting with greater success in Boston. George Washington had arrived there during the summer of 1775, determined to drive the British from the city. The following winter, he sent troops to drag the heavy guns from Fort Ticonderoga and install them on high ground overlooking Boston. In the spring of 1776, under the threat of the looming artillery, the British withdrew from the city. They sailed north to Canada in preparation for an eventual invasion of New York City. More than a thousand Loyalists left with the British because they feared they would not be safe from angry Patriots if they stayed in Boston.

Alarmed by the colonists' show of force in Boston, the British government sent a massive force to put down the revolt. Nearly 400 ships set sail from England carrying 32,000 troops, including at least 12,000 Hessians. The soldiers would join the British troops already gathering in Canada for an attack on New York City. The warships would attack seaports and disrupt colonial shipping.

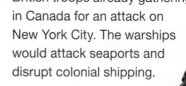

Hessian miter cap

 National Museum of American History Washington, D.C.

This hat, called a miter cap, was worn by a Hessian infantry soldier from the Fusilier Regiment, which served under the British Army during the American Revolution. The cap has a cloth body covered with a brass cap plate and is stamped with a Hessian lion.

Printing *Common Sense*

Colonial printers working on printing presses similar to the one shown here created publications one page at a time. They carefully folded paper onto set and inked letters and then used a lever to press the images and words onto the page.

Thousands of copies of *Common Sense* were printed, sold, and read aloud in meeting rooms and inns throughout the colonies. Because it was originally anonymous, many initially attributed *Common Sense* to Ben Franklin. As you have read, before he was a scientist and revolutionary, Ben Franklin was a printer and publisher in Philadelphia. He even owned his own printing press, so it is not a surprise that some would think he published *Common Sense*.

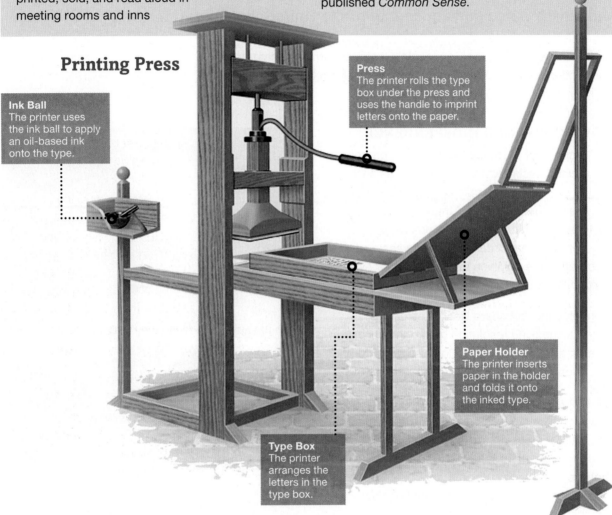

Printing Press

Ink Ball
The printer uses the ink ball to apply an oil-based ink onto the type.

Press
The printer rolls the type box under the press and uses the handle to imprint letters onto the paper.

Paper Holder
The printer inserts paper in the holder and folds it onto the inked type.

Type Box
The printer arranges the letters in the type box.

In January 1776, **Thomas Paine** published a pamphlet called *Common Sense* to argue the case for independence. In the pamphlet, Paine made several practical arguments for independence. He claimed that France and Spain would only aid the colonies if they broke with Britain. He also pointed out that European countries would continue to purchase American exports if the colonies declared independence. "'Tis time to part," he urged his readers. As the eventful year unfolded, more and more Americans agreed with him.

HISTORICAL THINKING

1. **READING CHECK** Which events in 1775 and 1776 led the colonies toward independence?

2. **ANALYZE CAUSE AND EFFECT** Why did the British government respond with overwhelming force to events in North America, and what was the colonial response?

3. **IDENTIFY MAIN IDEAS AND DETAILS** What was Thomas Paine's principal argument in favor of independence?

4.4 Drafting the Declaration

Every Fourth of July, the air fills with the sound of marching bands and the night sky with fireworks—all to celebrate a piece of paper? It's not just any piece of paper. It's the document that launched a new country and gave a name and an identity to the United States of America.

MAIN IDEA In 1776, the Continental Congress formally declared the independence of the United States of America from Great Britain.

MOVING TOWARD INDEPENDENCE

By the spring of 1776, the Continental Congress was making decisions for the colonies as a whole, serving in effect as the colonial government. In this role, the Congress declared that American ports would accept ships from any country—except, however, for Great Britain. The Congress also encouraged the colonies to establish their own independent governments.

Then, on June 7, Richard Henry Lee of Virginia placed a shocking resolution before the delegates. It stated that "these United Colonies are, and of right ought to be, free and independent States."

Not all the delegates were in favor of Lee's resolution to separate completely from Britain. Still, the Congress appointed a committee to draft an official statement to declare independence. **Thomas Jefferson** of Virginia, a brilliant scholar and persuasive writer, would be the principal author.

John Adams and Benjamin Franklin were also on the committee to create the document. Franklin had lived in England for several years, serving as a representative from several colonies to the British government. Adams suggested that Jefferson should write the first draft. Franklin gave Jefferson advice and helped revise the document.

On July 2, 1776, the Continental Congress voted to approve independence from Britain. Two days later, the Congress adopted Jefferson's document, the **Declaration of Independence**.

Thomas Jefferson
In addition to drafting the Declaration of Independence, Jefferson served his country for more than 50 years as a historian, public official, president, and founder of the University of Virginia. His famous words captured the voice and identity of a new America like no one else's could.

SELF-EVIDENT TRUTHS

Many of the ideas expressed in the Declaration of Independence can be traced to John Locke. The first part states, "We hold these truths to be self-evident, that all men are created equal, that they are endowed by their Creator with certain unalienable Rights, that among these are Life, Liberty, and the Pursuit of Happiness." An **unalienable right** is one that cannot be taken away.

National Archives Washington, D.C.

Visitors to Washington, D.C., can stop by the Rotunda of the National Archives Building to see the original Declaration of Independence, safely encased in bulletproof glass and under the watchful eye of armed guards. You can read the Declaration in its entirety in the Citizenship Handbook.

Yet the unalienable rights of two large groups were not discussed in the Declaration. In his first draft, Jefferson had listed slavery as one of the king's offenses. After an intense debate, this section was removed. The Declaration was silent on the rights of women, too, even though John Adams's wife, Abigail, had pleaded with him in a letter to "remember the ladies and be more generous and favorable to them than your ancestors."

The second part of the Declaration listed the offenses of the king against the colonies. These included refusing to approve laws passed by the colonial assemblies, placing a standing army in the colonies, and imposing taxes without colonial consent. For these reasons and more, the Continental Congress declared the 13 colonies "free and independent states," the United States of America.

HISTORICAL THINKING

1. **READING CHECK** What are the principal parts of the Declaration of Independence?

2. **ANALYZE LANGUAGE USE** What is an "unalienable right," and how did the inclusion of these words in the Declaration point to a new philosophy of governing?

3. **MAKE CONNECTIONS** What laws did Jefferson refer to when he listed the complaints against the British king?

4.5 Declarations of Freedom

Beginning in the late-1600s, political thinkers put forth new ideas about natural rights and human equality in books, articles, essays, and pamphlets. These writings set the stage for a revolution that created a nation and transformed the world.

This painting by John Trumbull, titled *Declaration of Independence,* depicts the moment on June 28, 1776, when the first draft of the document was presented to the Second Continental Congress in the Pennsylvania State House. In the painting, Thomas Jefferson, thought to be the main author of the document, places the document in front of John Hancock, who was the president of the Congress, surrounded by members of the committee who helped create the draft.

CRITICAL VIEWING What do you notice about the people who are gathered for the presentation of the first draft of the Declaration of Independence?

🏛 U.S. Capitol Rotunda, Washington, D.C.

Declaration of Independence, John Trumbull, 1817

This is the first of four Revolutionary-era scenes that the U.S. Congress commissioned from John Trumbull. The artist had created a smaller version of this painting to document the events of the American Revolution, and he enlarged the painting for the Rotunda between August 1817 and September 1818. It was installed in the Rotunda in 1826, along with three other Trumbull paintings.

DOCUMENT ONE

Primary Source: Legal Document
from the Declaration of Independence, 1776

The Declaration of Independence begins with a clear statement of its writers' beliefs. The goal of the Declaration was to unify the colonies as one new nation in opposition to Great Britain.

CONSTRUCTED RESPONSE In what ways is this vision of governing different from how the British monarchy governed?

We hold these truths to be self-evident, that all men are created equal, that they are endowed by their Creator with certain unalienable Rights, that among these are Life, Liberty and the pursuit of Happiness. That to secure these rights, Governments are instituted among Men, deriving their just powers from the consent of the governed, That whenever any Form of Government becomes destructive of these ends, it is the Right of the People to alter or to abolish it, and to institute new Government.

DOCUMENT TWO

Primary Source: Legal Document
from the Declaration of Independence, 1776

The second part of the Declaration contains a long list of offenses by the king against the colonies. In total, Jefferson included 27 grievances that referred to the Quartering Act, the Intolerable Acts, and several other British attempts to impose their will on the colonies.

CONSTRUCTED RESPONSE Why do you think the writers included such a complete list of grievances against the king?

To prove this, let Facts be submitted to a candid world.

He has refused his Assent to Laws, the most wholesome and necessary for the public good.

He has dissolved Representative Houses repeatedly, for opposing with manly firmness his invasions on the rights of the people.

He has kept among us, in times of peace, Standing Armies without the Consent of our legislatures.

DOCUMENT THREE

Primary Source: Essay
from *Two Treatises on Government,* by John Locke, 1689

Nearly a century before the American Revolution, John Locke outlined his theories of government in two treatises, or essays. In the second treatise, he explained his thoughts on liberty and the consent of people to be governed. Thomas Jefferson drew heavily on Locke's political theories when creating the Declaration.

CONSTRUCTED RESPONSE In what ways did Locke's ideas directly influence the actions of the colonies and the writing of the Declaration of Independence?

Men being . . . by nature, all free, equal, and independent, no one can be put out of this estate, and subjected to the political power of another, without his own consent. The only way . . . any one divests himself of his natural liberty, and puts on the bonds of civil society, is by agreeing with other men to join and unite into a community, for their comfortable, safe and peaceable living one amongst another.

Read the full Declaration of Independence in the Citizenship Handbook.

SYNTHESIZE & WRITE

1. **REVIEW** Review what you have learned about the events leading up to the Declaration of Independence.

2. **RECALL** On your own paper, write the main ideas about government expressed in the Declaration of Independence and Locke's *Second Treatise on Government.*

3. **CONSTRUCT** Construct a topic sentence that answers this question: How did beliefs about the nature of government and human freedom lead to the colonies' break with Britain?

4. **WRITE** Using evidence from this chapter and the documents, write an informative paragraph that supports your topic sentence in Step 3.

5 REVIEW

VOCABULARY

Use each of the following vocabulary words in a sentence that shows an understanding of the term's meaning.

1. **revenue**
   Because the British government needed money after the French and Indian War, it imposed taxes to raise revenue.

2. unalienable right

3. militia

4. tyranny

5. boycott

6. committee of correspondence

7. repeal

8. artillery

READING STRATEGY
ANALYZE CAUSE AND EFFECT

If you haven't already, complete your chart to analyze the causes that led up to the colonies' break with Britain. List at least four key causes. Then answer the question.

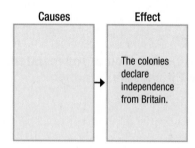

Causes	Effect
	The colonies declare independence from Britain.

9. What changes in the way Britain treated the American colonies caused the colonies to revolt?

MAIN IDEAS

Answer the following questions. Support your answers with evidence from the chapter.

10. What changes did the British government make in the colonies after the French and Indian War? **LESSON 1.1**

11. Why did the colonists protest the Sugar Act and Currency Act as forms of "taxation without representation"? **LESSON 1.2**

12. How did the colonists bring about the repeal of the Stamp Act? **LESSON 1.3**

13. Why did the colonists consider the Townshend Acts to be oppressive? **LESSON 2.1**

14. Why did the Tea Act result in such violent opposition? **LESSON 2.3**

15. In what ways did the Intolerable Acts build on earlier British laws? **LESSON 3.1**

16. What was the result of the battles at Lexington and Concord for the British and the colonists? **LESSON 3.3**

17. How did the Second Continental Congress pursue both peace and war? **LESSON 4.1**

18. What were the main goals of the two parts of the Declaration of Independence? **LESSON 4.4**

HISTORICAL THINKING

Answer the following questions. Support your answers with evidence from the chapter.

19. **SYNTHESIZE** How did the events of the French and Indian War help lead to the American Revolution?

20. **MAKE INFERENCES** Why did the Patriots find the ideas of John Locke appealing?

21. **ANALYZE CAUSE AND EFFECT** How did the passage of the Townshend Acts lead to the Boston Tea Party?

22. EVALUATE Were boycotts an effective form of protest against British taxes and laws? Explain.

23. FORM AND SUPPORT OPINIONS Which of the British laws and taxes placed the greatest burden on the colonies? Support your opinion with evidence from the chapter.

INTERPRET MAPS

Look closely at the map of eastern North America in 1763. Then answer the questions that follow.

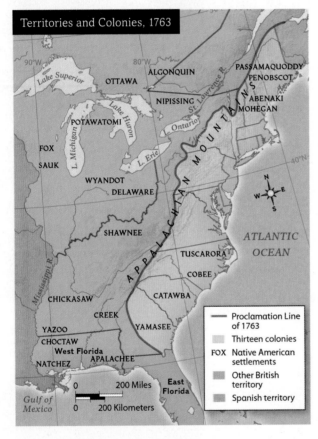

Territories and Colonies, 1763

24. What groups were impacted the most by the Proclamation of 1763?

25. How did the geography of the Proclamation Line make it hard for the British to enforce it?

26. Compare this historical map to a present-day map of the eastern part of the United States. What similarities do you observe? What differences? How might those similarities and differences be explained?

ANALYZE SOURCES

In *Common Sense*, published in January 1776, Thomas Paine included a variety of arguments in favor of independence. In addition to the reasons you have already read, he stated the one below. Read the passage and answer the question.

> As to government matters, it is not in the power of Britain to do this continent justice: The business of it will soon be too weighty, and intricate, to be managed with any tolerable degree of convenience, by a power, so distant from us, and so very ignorant of us; for if they cannot conquer us, they cannot govern us.

27. What argument does Paine make about the British government in this passage?

CONNECT TO YOUR LIFE

28. NARRATIVE Think about the events that led up to the Declaration of Independence and why the colonists felt they had to separate from Great Britain. Make a connection between that time in history and a recent protest that you have read about, heard about, or seen. Write a paragraph connecting the two events.

TIPS

• Make a time line of the principal events leading up to the colonists' action or decision. Then make a time line showing what led up to the present-day protest you have chosen.

• Use textual evidence and two or three vocabulary terms from the chapter in your narrative.

• Conclude the narrative with a comment that ties the colonists' actions to those of people today.

CHAPTER

6

THE AMERICAN
REVOLUTION
1775–1783

ESSENTIAL QUESTION
What factors helped America win the war?

 AMERICAN STORIES Bitter Winter at Valley Forge

SECTION 1 **Early War Years**
KEY VOCABULARY

Articles of Confederation	mercenary
counterattack	reinforcements
defensive war	republic
fortification	

SECTION 2 **The War Expands**
KEY VOCABULARY

bayonet	desert	financier
blockade	espionage	skirmish

SECTION 3 **The Path to Victory**
KEY VOCABULARY

expertise	provisions
guerrilla	republicanism
pacifist	Treaty of Paris of 1783

AMERICAN GALLERY
ONLINE Colonial Vernacular Architecture

READING STRATEGY

FORM AND SUPPORT OPINIONS
You often form opinions while reading. As you read the chapter, decide what factor was most important in achieving an American victory in the Revolution. Use a graphic like this one to write your opinion and record your reasons for supporting it.

Opinion:

Supporting statement:

Supporting statement:

Supporting statement:

Supporting statement:

"It is a common observation here that **our cause is the cause of all mankind.**"

—Benjamin Franklin

BITTER WINTER AT VALLEY FORGE

Valley Forge is now a National Historical Park in Pennsylvania. These re-created soldier cabins in the park give visitors a sense of what the living conditions were like for the Continental Army in the winter of 1777–78.

COLD, HUNGRY, AND SICK

Think of the images you have seen of U.S. Army units marching on parade. The soldiers are strong, healthy, and clothed in matching uniforms. They move with assurance and discipline, each soldier knowing his or her place in the formation. It's a sight that inspires confidence in the armed forces.

In the winter of 1777, the sight of George Washington's troops straggling into Valley Forge would have inspired anything but confidence. Instead, some viewers felt pity and shock. The army had been defeated twice by the British, and now the soldiers were going into winter quarters to rest and regroup. The city of Philadelphia, 20 miles away, was in British hands.

The soldiers were in desperate need of relief. They were exhausted, underfed, diseased, and freezing. Albigence Waldo, an army doctor, described their plight in his journal: "There comes a Soldier, his bare feet are seen thro' his worn out Shoes." Joseph Plumb Martin, an army private, later recalled his fellow soldiers walking barefoot "till they might be tracked by their blood upon the rough frozen ground." At one point during the long winter, 7,000 soldiers were too sick to be on duty.

NO RELIEF IN SIGHT

George Washington was well aware of his men's suffering. In a letter to Congress, he wrote, "I am now convinced, beyond a doubt that unless some great and capital change suddenly takes place . . . this Army must inevitably be reduced to one or other of these three things. Starve, dissolve, or disperse in order to obtain subsistence [food] in the best manner they can."

Congress, however, did not send Washington the relief he needed in the form of either supplies or money. Instead, some members pressured him to send his starving army against the British troops in Philadelphia. Some, including John Adams, had lost confidence in General Washington and wanted to replace him. Another Patriot, Alexander Hamilton, demonstrated his faith in Washington by joining the general's staff in 1777, a position he would hold until 1781.

Of even greater concern was the trust of Washington's officers and men. In all, 1,000 soldiers deserted during that harsh winter, and several hundred officers resigned. Most, however, remained loyal to their general and their cause. Joseph Plumb Martin wrote, "We had engaged in the defense of our injured country and were . . . determined to persevere."

Boots weren't exactly weatherproof in the 1700s. Valley Forge soldiers lucky enough to have footwear wore boots like these. Others simply wrapped their feet in rags, which provided little protection from the hard ground and cold snow.

Valley Forge

After British forces took control of Philadelphia, George Washington and his troops fled 20 miles northwest to take refuge at Valley Forge. This location was close enough to put pressure on the British but far enough away to make an enemy attack unlikely.

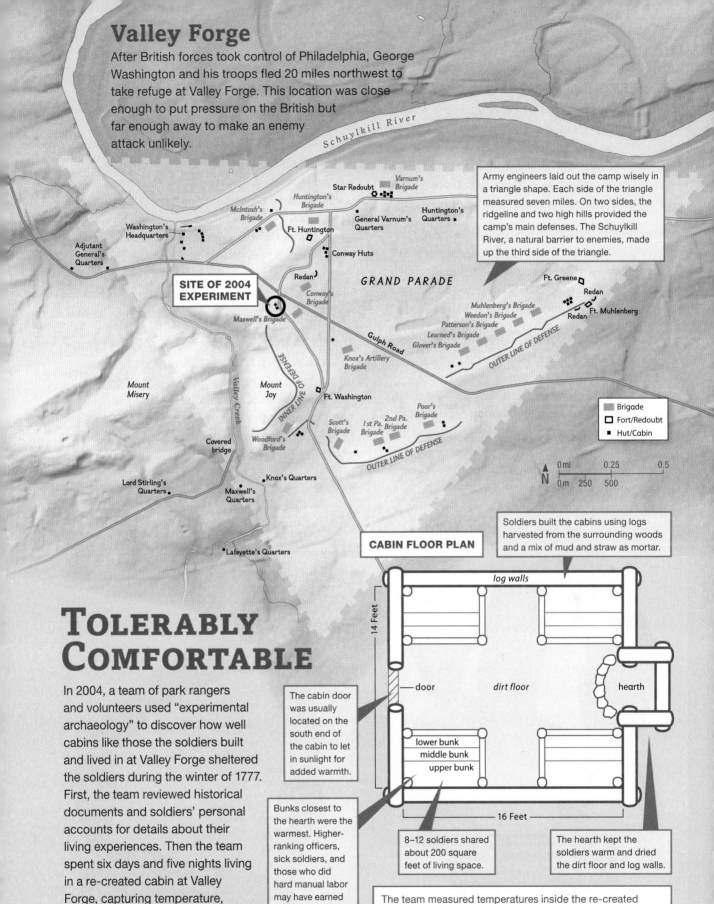

Schuylkill River

Army engineers laid out the camp wisely in a triangle shape. Each side of the triangle measured seven miles. On two sides, the ridgeline and two high hills provided the camp's main defenses. The Schuylkill River, a natural barrier to enemies, made up the third side of the triangle.

Varnum's Brigade

Star Redoubt

Huntington's Brigade

McIntosh's Brigade

Huntington's Quarters

General Varnum's Quarters

Washington's Headquarters

Ft. Huntington

Adjutant General's Quarters

Conway Huts

Redan

GRAND PARADE

Ft. Greene

Redan

SITE OF 2004 EXPERIMENT

Conway's Brigade

Muhlenberg's Brigade
Weedon's Brigade
Patterson's Brigade
Learned's Brigade
Glover's Brigade

Redan

Ft. Muhlenberg

Maxwell's Brigade

Gulph Road

OUTER LINE OF DEFENSE

Knox's Artillery Brigade

Mount Misery

Valley Creek

Mount Joy

INNER LINE OF DEFENSE

Ft. Washington

Poor's Brigade

Covered bridge

Scott's Brigade

Woodford's Brigade

1st Pa. Brigade

2nd Pa. Brigade

OUTER LINE OF DEFENSE

Lord Stirling's Quarters

Maxwell's Quarters

Knox's Quarters

Lafayette's Quarters

	Brigade
☐	Fort/Redoubt
■	Hut/Cabin

0 mi　　0.25　　0.5

N

0 m　250　500

TOLERABLY COMFORTABLE

In 2004, a team of park rangers and volunteers used "experimental archaeology" to discover how well cabins like those the soldiers built and lived in at Valley Forge sheltered the soldiers during the winter of 1777. First, the team reviewed historical documents and soldiers' personal accounts for details about their living experiences. Then the team spent six days and five nights living in a re-created cabin at Valley Forge, capturing temperature, humidity, and weather data. While conditions weren't cozy, the study led the team to conclude the soldiers' cabins were well-built and relatively comfortable.

SOURCE: National Park Service

CABIN FLOOR PLAN

Soldiers built the cabins using logs harvested from the surrounding woods and a mix of mud and straw as mortar.

log walls

14 Feet

door　　*dirt floor*　　hearth

The cabin door was usually located on the south end of the cabin to let in sunlight for added warmth.

lower bunk
middle bunk
upper bunk

16 Feet

Bunks closest to the hearth were the warmest. Higher-ranking officers, sick soldiers, and those who did hard manual labor may have earned warmer bunks.

8–12 soldiers shared about 200 square feet of living space.

The hearth kept the soldiers warm and dried the dirt floor and log walls.

The team measured temperatures inside the re-created cabin up to 50° F warmer than outdoor conditions during the day, and up to 35° F warmer at night. They concluded that the well-designed structures likely made the soldiers feel like it was **"April inside while it was January outside."**

GATHERING STRENGTH AND TRAINING

The painful irony was that the Continental Army was starving in a land of plenty. The area around Valley Forge was fertile farmland. However, the Americans were competing with the British for the region's resources, and the British were very effective at buying—or taking—what they wanted.

Once the soldiers were fed, they would also need training to fight the well-equipped, professional British Army. The soldiers came from state militias that were each organized differently. They did not know how to work together as an effective force.

Fortunately, Washington had two men at Valley Forge who could address these problems. He put General Nathanael Greene in charge of supplies. Greene organized groups of soldiers to go foraging, or seeking food, in the countryside. Greene found ways to help the army get food and horses, and he set up a system of supply sites and roads for moving the goods. By springtime, the troops were properly fed and supplied.

At Ben Franklin's suggestion, Friedrich von Steuben (FREE-drihk von STOO-buhn), formerly an officer in the Prussian Army, came to Valley Forge to train Washington's troops. Von Steuben was an expert in the military tactics used by modern armies. A colorful figure, he barked out commands in German, drilling the soldiers for hours each day. Private Martin recalled, "I was kept constantly, when off other duty, engaged in learning the Baron de Steuben's new Prussian exercise." The Americans emerged from von Steuben's special brand of boot camp ready to fight like professionals.

The Continental Army marched out of Valley Forge on June 19, 1778. The tattered, starving, desperate group had been transformed into a confident, disciplined army. A week later, Washington's soldiers fought the British Army at the Battle of Monmouth. There was no turning back on the path to independence.

THINK ABOUT IT

How would you feel if you were a soldier in the Continental Army and you felt you lacked the support of Congress?

Soldiers strapped these iron and leather ice creepers to their ragged shoes or boots to cross the ice and snow.

LIFE GOES ON

While the soldiers starved, struggled, and battled illness at Valley Forge, life went on as usual in Philadelphia. This is evident in these two wildly different personal accounts of the same time period. Read and compare these primary sources.

PRIMARY SOURCE

You can have no idea of the life of continued amusement I live in. I can scarce have a moment to myself. I have stole this while everybody is retired to dress for dinner . . . and most elegantly am I dressed for a ball this evening at Smith's where we have one every Thursday.

—from a letter by Rebecca Franks, 1778

PRIMARY SOURCE

I lay two nights and one day, and had not a morsel of any thing to eat all the time, save half of a small pumpkin, which I cooked by placing it upon a rock, the skin side uppermost, and making a fire upon it; by the time it was heat through I devoured it with as keen an appetite as I should a pie made of it at some other time.

—from *Memoir of a Revolutionary Soldier*, by Joseph Plumb Martin, 1830

Despite the grim living conditions—or perhaps because of them—the men at Valley Forge found ways to have fun when they were not drilling or scouting for food. Sometimes, soldiers would play "base," a very early form of baseball. George Washington himself once joined a group of men playing cricket, a British sport that also involves a type of bat and ball. Some officers put on plays in a stone building on the Valley Forge site. The men were not allowed to play cards or gamble, but many ignored this rule to pass the time with a friendly card game or two. After all, the winter nights at Valley Forge were long, dull, and uncomfortable.

Soldiers also played games of dice by shaking ivory dice in this leather cup and rolling them out.

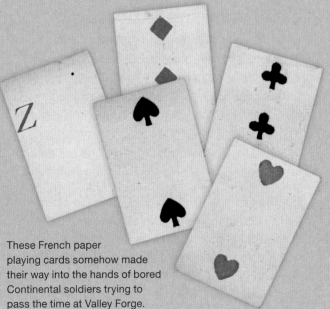

These French paper playing cards somehow made their way into the hands of bored Continental soldiers trying to pass the time at Valley Forge.

1.1 War in the Middle States

Have you ever been surprised when a team that seems to have no chance at all actually wins the big game? The Continental Army was that kind of team.

> **MAIN IDEA** Despite its disadvantages, the Continental Army managed to win important battles early on in the American Revolution.

CREATING AN ARMY

In 1775, Great Britain had one of the most powerful armies in the world. Its soldiers were well-trained, experienced professionals, and about 42,000 of them came to fight in the colonies. Great Britain was prepared to meet the troops' needs for arms and other supplies. As you have read, the British also hired Hessian soldiers to join them in the colonies—about 30,000 men. These **mercenaries**, or soldiers who are paid to fight for a country other than their own, further swelled the number of British forces.

On September 9, 1776, the Continental Congress voted to rename the colonies the "United States of America," but the new nation did not have a strong central government. Congress did not have the power to provide funding for arms, other supplies, or soldiers' pay.

This situation didn't change until the next year, when the Continental Congress drafted and adopted the **Articles of Confederation** in 1777. Under the Articles of Confederation, the 13 states mostly governed themselves as small **republics**. A republic is a form of government in which the people elect representatives to speak for them and enact laws based on the people's needs. James Madison helped organize the state government of Virginia. The Articles granted Congress the authority to call on states to help fund the war.

Compared with the British Army, the young Continental Army was ill prepared and disorganized. The Patriots had other problems as well. George Washington faced a huge challenge in turning a collection of local militias into a disciplined, united fighting force. He also had trouble recruiting more troops. Few eligible men had formal military training, and many were unwilling to leave their farms or jobs. Also, not everyone was eager for independence. Families and communities found themselves split between Loyalists and Patriots.

Both free and enslaved African Americans were in a unique situation when it came to deciding where their loyalties lay. The British promised freedom to many enslaved people if they promised to fight on the British side. Other African Americans, both free and unfree, were motivated to try to secure freedom for all and served in the war with the Patriots.

In 1776, only around 20,000 men had joined the Continental Army, but despite this and its numerous other problems, the Continental Army did have some advantages over the British. Most importantly, its soldiers were fighting a **defensive war**, or a war to protect one's own land, on familiar ground, while the British Army was far from home. And Americans were fighting for their homes and way of life.

EARLY VICTORIES AND DEFEATS

Even though the Revolution started in New England, it quickly spread to the Middle States of New York, New Jersey, Pennsylvania, and Delaware. In July 1776, British troops landed on New York's Staten Island and pushed American troops back to Manhattan Island and then New Jersey. The Continental Army soon had to escape across the Delaware River into Pennsylvania.

But the Continental Army had a change of luck by the end of the year. When they crossed the icy Delaware River on Christmas Day, Washington and his troops surprised and defeated the Hessian defenders in Trenton, New Jersey. The Hessian commander had received orders to build defenses

GREAT NEWS FROM NEW-YORK.

Each December, the Old Barracks Museum in Trenton, New Jersey, hosts a reenactment of the battle that showed the determination of American troops as they marched in blinding snow. The leaflet shown here provides an account of the battle—which lasted only 35 minutes—and the American victory. It took the news 11 days to reach Salem, Massachusetts, and appear in print on January 6.

around Trenton, but he had ignored them. On the night before the battle, he got a message informing him that the Continental Army was on its way. He ignored this as well, and the result was a major defeat for the British. After this American victory, called the **Battle of Trenton**, British general **William Howe** withdrew most of his army back to New York. In the words of one British officer, the Americans had "become a formidable [fearsome] enemy." This victory resulted in a wave of support and enthusiasm for the American cause, which encouraged recruitment—and greater victories.

HISTORICAL THINKING

1. **READING CHECK** What advantages and disadvantages did the Continental Army have at the start of the American Revolution?

2. **FORM AND SUPPORT OPINIONS** How do you think questions over national identity might have affected military recruitment? Explain why.

3. **ANALYZE CAUSE AND EFFECT** How did the Articles of Confederation impact the American Revolution?

1.2 The Struggle for New York

One of the worst things you can do is underestimate an opponent.
The Americans looked like a ragtag bunch, but they had advantages the
more disciplined British failed to see, and this oversight cost them.

MAIN IDEA Due to poor planning, the British expectation that they would
dominate the Hudson River Valley proved to be incorrect.

HUDSON RIVER VALLEY

Even though Washington's troops were victorious in New Jersey, the British still controlled New York City. From there, they planned to capture the Hudson River Valley. They hoped to divide New England from the rest of the states and bring a swift conclusion to the colonial rebellion.

General Howe, a lieutenant general of British forces in North America, planned to seize the Hudson River Valley using three armies. In 1777, he sent a regiment under the command of British general **John Burgoyne** from Boston to Canada. Burgoyne's troops were to move by boat down Lake Champlain. Howe's own troops would move north to meet them. Another force, led by British lieutenant colonel Barry St. Leger, would move east from western New York along the Mohawk River to link up with the other two armies in Albany, New York.

On their way south from Lake Champlain, Burgoyne's troops took Fort Ticonderoga, but they quickly ran into problems. Burgoyne had overloaded his troops with baggage, including cartloads of his own clothing. American forces chopped down trees and rolled boulders into the path of the British troops, making a march of 23 miles take 24 days. Then, near Saratoga, New York, the Americans surrounded Burgoyne's troops. When Burgoyne called

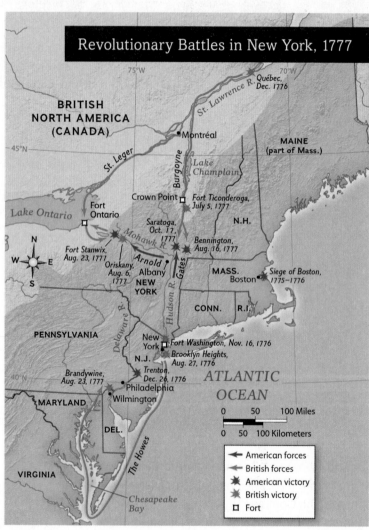

Revolutionary Battles in New York, 1777

for **reinforcements**, or more soldiers and supplies, from New York, he found that Howe had changed his plans. Instead of joining Burgoyne's troops, Howe had decided to head for Philadelphia. His route there was roundabout. He sailed around Delaware and up Chesapeake Bay to Pennsylvania. Washington tried and failed to block Howe's advance through Pennsylvania. The British

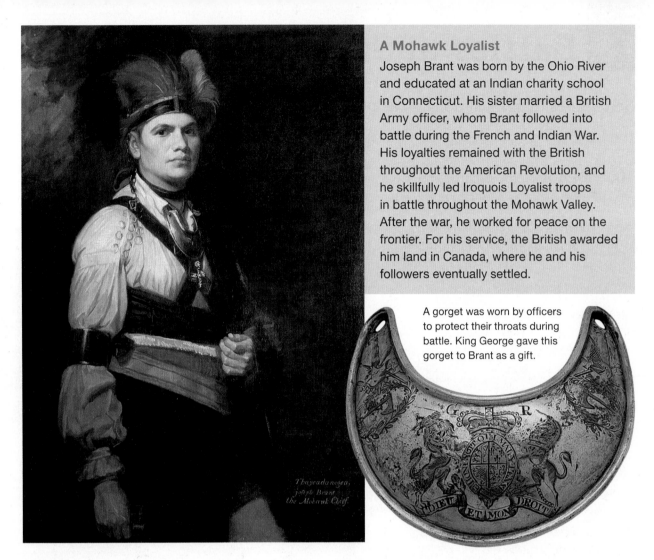

Thayeadanegea, Joseph Brant, the Mohawk Chief.

A gorget was worn by officers to protect their throats during battle. King George gave this gorget to Brant as a gift.

occupied and successfully defended Philadelphia and nearby Germantown against another attack by Washington's troops in October 1777.

ALONG THE MOHAWK RIVER

Meanwhile, St. Leger continued to push toward Albany. After crossing Lake Ontario, he led his army along the Mohawk River. And he was not alone. Iroquois warriors from the region supported St. Leger's troops.

The Six Nations of the Iroquois had formed their alliance around 1720. They signed a treaty with Britain in 1768 to establish a boundary between Native American and European lands. Then, in 1775, as the American Revolution approached, the Six Nations agreed to remain neutral. However, after war broke out, both the Americans and the British pressured the nations in the alliance to choose sides. Eventually the Six Nations decided to split their loyalties. The Mohawk sided with the British.

Mohawk chief **Joseph Brant** commanded his troops as they fought alongside St. Leger in the Mohawk River Valley. But they encountered American resistance at Fort Stanwix in 1777. When they heard that officer Benedict Arnold was approaching from the east with more American troops—and Native American allies—St. Leger and his Iroquois allies retreated. Their flight and Howe's change of plans meant that no one would be coming to help Burgoyne once he got to Albany.

HISTORICAL THINKING

1. **READING CHECK** What errors did Burgoyne make as he headed to the Hudson River Valley?

2. **INTERPRET MAPS** Along what river did most of the American victories occur in 1777?

3. **FORM AND SUPPORT OPINIONS** Do you think Burgoyne and Howe were ready for battle in America? Why or why not?

1.3 Battles of Saratoga

Sometimes things just don't go as planned. Unexpected events can derail even the best strategy—events like being hopelessly outnumbered, for example.

MAIN IDEA American planning and coordination, along with British miscalculation, led to Patriot victories at Saratoga and a turning point in the American Revolution.

AMERICAN PLACES
Saratoga Battlefield, New York

In order to hold off British forces, American troops under General Horatio Gates built two fortified walls along Bemis Heights, overlooking the Hudson River and the road beside it. They lined up 22 cannons along the walls, which helped them successfully defend their line. Today, the battlefield where these important American victories were won is open to all as part of the Saratoga National Historical Park.

A TURNING POINT

As you have read, General Burgoyne found himself in a tricky situation as he moved south—without backup—toward Albany after his victory at Fort Ticonderoga. He expected to be joined by British troops moving north from New York, but that support never came.

Here's what happened: In September 1777, 12,000 members of the Continental Army under General Horatio Gates surrounded Burgoyne and his 5,800 men at Saratoga, New York. The Americans were well prepared for this clash. Gates and Polish military engineer Tadeusz Kościuszko (tah-DAY-oosh kos-CHOOS-ko) had overseen a plan to build up American **fortifications**, or structures built to protect a place from attack.

They had brought in reinforcements from other states as well, including the Light Horse Volunteers commanded by Colonel John Langdon. One of Langdon's men was Wentworth Cheswell, an African-American government official from Massachusetts. Though the British Army had been more welcoming of African-American volunteers, soldiers such as Cheswell had started to support the Patriot cause in larger numbers.

On September 19, 1777, the British and Continental armies clashed at what would later be known as the First Battle of Saratoga, also called the Battle of Freeman's Farm. Burgoyne failed to cross Gates's lines. The British struck at the Americans again on October 7, but General Benedict Arnold staged a strong American **counterattack**, or attack in response, in what would be known as the Second Battle of Saratoga. At this point, 20,000 American troops surrounded Burgoyne's men. Burgoyne had requested that General Howe send reinforcements, but, as you may recall, Howe and his troops were on their way to Philadelphia. Greatly outnumbered, Burgoyne surrendered at Saratoga on October 17.

An African-American Hero of the Revolution

Wentworth Cheswell is most often remembered today as one of the early African-American heroes of the American Revolution. As the town messenger of Newmarket, New Hampshire, Cheswell once had to ride all night to warn his community of an impending British invasion. He also served in the Continental Army with John Langdon's Light Horse Volunteers.

But this was just one facet of a man whose career in politics lasted nearly 50 years. His ancestry was part European, part African American. Formally educated in Byfield, Massachusetts, the 22-year-old Cheswell was elected in 1768 to his first political office—town constable of Newmarket. Over the course of his impressive career, he held other prominent posts, including justice of the peace for Rockingham County, New Hampshire.

Wentworth Cheswell

A NEW ALLY

The **Battles of Saratoga** proved to be an important turning point in the American Revolution. As with the Battle of Trenton, the victories boosted Americans' morale and gave them hope that they could defeat a larger, well-established army.

Success at Saratoga also earned the Americans a valuable asset: an alliance with France. France was already supporting the United States with economic and military assistance, and these victories convinced the French government that the Americans could win the war. No longer feeling outmatched, the Americans now had military help from a wealthy nation, and they had experienced significant victories themselves.

HISTORICAL THINKING

1. **READING CHECK** Why were the battles of Saratoga important for the Continental Army?

2. **ANALYZE CAUSE AND EFFECT** How did an error in strategy affect the outcome of the Battles of Saratoga?

3. **IDENTIFY PROBLEMS AND SOLUTIONS** What problems did the Continental Army face at Saratoga, and what steps did it take to solve them?

2.1 Seeking Help from Europe

It's hard to face a tough challenge alone. This is especially true in times of war. During the Revolution, America looked for help from other countries.

MAIN IDEA Assistance from European powers and from heroes of various backgrounds helped Americans overcome some of their disadvantages in the American Revolution.

POWERFUL FRIENDS

The alliance between France and the United States did not happen immediately. Taking advantage of the Continental Army's momentum, the Continental Congress sent Benjamin Franklin and John Adams to Europe. Congress hoped to persuade France to become an official ally of the United States. The French considered Britain to be their main enemy and wanted to avenge their loss in the French and Indian War. These considerations helped Franklin and Adams convince France to sign the Treaty of Alliance in February 1778 and provide the United States with financial assistance.

France and Spain were allies, and they both had lost significant lands in North America at the end of the French and Indian War. In addition to money and supplies, France provided the Americans with troops. Both nations helped the Americans by drawing Britain's military and naval attention in different directions. The French navy engaged the British in the West Indies, pulling resources away from the North American mainland. Spanish military leader Bernardo de Gálvez forced the British to send troops to the Mississippi Valley to defend forts formerly held by the Spanish. Then Gálvez helped defeat the British in Florida and claimed that territory for Spain.

HEROES FROM HOME AND ABROAD

France and Spain also played pivotal roles in affecting the course of the war. You've learned that Tadeusz Kościuszko from Poland helped win the Battles of Saratoga. You've also read about the contributions of Prussia's **Baron Friedrich von Steuben** at Valley Forge. From von Steuben, the inexperienced American soldiers rapidly learned skills such as marching, making quick decisions in combat, and using weapons, including the **bayonet** (BAY-uh-net), a sharp blade attached to a musket.

The **Marquis de Lafayette** (mar-KEE duh lah-fy-EHT), a French nobleman, had already offered his assistance to the American war effort and had become a general in the Continental Army. He took a break from the fighting and returned to France to help Franklin and Adams get funding and support from the king. With that goal accomplished, Lafayette came back to America and took part in many battles, including the one that would end the war.

Although the Continental Army did not actively welcome African Americans, those who sympathized with the Patriot cause found ways to help. An enslaved man named **James Armistead** was allowed by his owner to spy for Lafayette. Gaining the trust of British officers, Armistead gathered information that helped the Americans win key battles.

Even with France and Spain helping to pay for some of the costs of the war, the United States faced major economic challenges during the conflict. Before the war, Britain and the West Indies had been markets for American goods and sources of goods for the American markets. Now British ships **blockaded** American ports by refusing to let vessels enter or leave these harbors. Towns and farms were destroyed as battles raged near or around them. And war is expensive. American troops had to be fed, and they needed uniforms, dependable weapons, and a steady supply of ammunition. Battle wounds and

In this 1853 painting by Andre Jolly, Benjamin Franklin is shown as the center of attention among French royalty at the home of Princess Elizabeth. Diane de Polignac, placing a laurel wreath on Franklin's head, ran the household. Elizabeth stands behind her brother, King Louis XVI, who is seated at the right. To his right is his wife, Marie-Antoinette, the queen.

outbreaks of disease led to an increasing need for medical supplies. And, of course, the soldiers expected to be paid.

Unfortunately, Congress did not have the power to collect taxes to help fund the war. Instead, Congress decided to make up for the shortfall by printing more money, even though it had no real wealth to back it up. In 1782, John Adams obtained a loan from Dutch bankers but also looked to American citizens for additional help.

Many Americans contributed what they could to the cause. For example, American Jewish **financier** Haym Salomon lent funds to help pay the costs of the revolution. A financier raises and provides funds for a business or undertaking. Salomon's generous gesture was never repaid, however, and he died in 1785 without a penny to his name. Financial problems were not the only challenges Americans faced, however. The war was still far from over.

HISTORICAL THINKING

1. **READING CHECK** How did France and Spain help the Americans?

2. **MAKE INFERENCES** Why did other nations offer to help the Americans?

3. **DRAW CONCLUSIONS** How did Britain wage war against the Americans off the battlefield?

2.2 Hardship and Challenges

Even the most satisfying success can be short-lived, especially in wartime. You're up one day and down the next. Challenging as it may be, you just have to hang in there.

> **MAIN IDEA** The Continental Army faced hardship and challenges at Valley Forge and on the frontier.

VALLEY FORGE

As you have read, the victory at Saratoga boosted American morale, but there was much more work to be done. The focus of the war shifted to Pennsylvania, where General Howe now occupied Philadelphia. You probably remember that the Continental Army set up camp at **Valley Forge**, northwest of the city, in the dead of the winter of 1777. George Washington set up camp alongside his men high atop a series of hills. Washington vowed to "share in the hardship" and "partake of [take part in] every inconvenience" his soldiers

CRITICAL VIEWING William T. Trego based this 1883 painting on a line from literature: "Sad and dreary was the march to Valley Forge." What details in the painting convey the soldiers' weariness?

experienced. While Washington certainly suffered, he lived with his aides in a stone house at Valley Forge. His men lived in the small wooden huts they'd built themselves and used straw they gathered for bedding.

Meanwhile, General **Henry Clinton** had become the new commander of British forces in North America. In contrast to the Americans, Clinton and his men settled into quarters in Philadelphia, where they lived in relative comfort. Loyalist families gave them places to stay, and Clinton and his officers enjoyed parties and good food.

As you've read, the soldiers in the Continental Army suffered greatly from the cold and a lack of food, and some chose to **desert**, or run away from the army. But despite the horrible conditions, most soldiers chose to stay. Loyal to General Washington and determined to keep up the fight, they spent the winter training under von Steuben.

As winter wore on, others arrived to help the American cause. Lafayette came to command a division at Valley Forge. In addition to sharing his men's hardships, the Frenchman provided uniforms and muskets to those who needed them.

Spring's arrival brought not only better weather but also great news. Word of the alliance between America and France reached the camp. To celebrate, Washington had his men line up and shoot their guns in the air. They were poised and ready to do battle at Monmouth.

WAR ON THE FRONTIER

Pennsylvania wasn't the only place where war raged. From New York to Georgia, **skirmishes**, or small, short battles, took place along the rural western boundary of the frontier. Small divisions of the British Army guarded forts in this region, supported by Native American volunteers. Remember that at the outset of the American Revolution, many Native Americans supported the British. They feared that if the Americans won, they would take over more Native American land.

British general Henry Hamilton and his Native American allies planned to invade the frontier. But American frontiersman George Rogers Clark heard of these plans and led a small force in a surprise attack on one of the British bases, Fort Vincennes (vihn-SEHNZ). Hamilton surrendered, and the joint British–Native American offensive was halted.

Despite Clark's victory at Vincennes, American settlers found themselves constantly battling Iroquois forces. The fighting caused homelessness and food shortages in many communities.

HISTORICAL THINKING

1. **READING CHECK** What did George Washington's men have to do when they first arrived at Valley Forge?

2. **COMPARE AND CONTRAST** How did the experiences of the British and Continental armies in the winter of 1777–78 differ?

3. **IDENTIFY MAIN IDEAS AND DETAILS** How and why did Native Americans participate in the American Revolution?

2.3 Women's Roles in the Revolution

If colonial women could time travel to the present day, many would probably be surprised to see American women working alongside men in most settings. But some would feel right at home.

MAIN IDEA Even though they could not officially serve in the army, women played many key roles in the American Revolution.

BEFORE THE REVOLUTION

Colonial women had long stood with men against the British. For instance, do you remember that before the American Revolution, the Daughters of Liberty helped organize a boycott of British goods? **Mercy Otis Warren** was an outspoken supporter of these boycotts. She became active in colonial politics through one of the committees of correspondence and went on to become a notable historian of the Revolutionary era.

John Adams's wife, **Abigail Adams**, also played a vital role from the earliest days of the Revolution. Along with Mercy Otis Warren and the governor's wife, Hannah Winthrop, Adams was appointed by the Massachusetts Colony General Court to question and report on local women suspected of being Loyalists. Both Adams and Warren were sharp thinkers and skilled writers who freely voiced their ideas about liberty, independence, women's rights, and a new government.

DURING THE REVOLUTION

As often happens in wartime, women took over many duties at home traditionally performed by men. Women ran farms, shops, and businesses. They also supported soldiers who passed through their communities, giving them housing and food. Some women took more direct action. They traveled with the troops, working as nurses, cooking men's meals, and washing their clothes.

You may be surprised to learn that some women excelled at **espionage**, or spying. This was due in great part to the fact that men tended to underestimate them. Many of these spies worked as maids or cooks for British officers and so had access to valuable information. Some women even took part in combat, disguising themselves as men or at times simply stepping into battle. They risked not only the dangers of combat but also jail if it were discovered that they were women.

In 1777, **Sybil Ludington** rode more than 40 miles in a single night to warn forces commanded by her father of a British attack in Connecticut. The British planned to destroy American supplies there. She also warned the people along the way.

When women did not have a defined role in the war, they were resourceful in finding ways to help—some of which could be very risky. Abigail Adams's appeal to her husband still did not bring equal rights to American women. But colonial women had shown their ability to participate in the building of a new nation.

HISTORICAL THINKING

1. **READING CHECK** How did women contribute to the success of the American Revolution?

2. **FORM AND SUPPORT OPINIONS** Which woman named in this lesson do you think contributed most to the American Revolution? Use evidence from the text to explain and support your opinion.

3. **DRAW CONCLUSIONS** In what way do Abigail Adams's comments to her husband reflect ideas in the Declaration of Independence?

Remember the Ladies

The four women featured on this page—Abigail Adams, Anna Smith Strong, Mary Ludwig Hays McCauly, and Phillis Wheatley—provide examples of women who were every bit as involved and took the same or greater risks in the American Revolution as the men.

Portrait of Abigail Adams by Benjamin Blyth, c. 1766

Abigail Adams wrote the following to her husband, John Adams, affirming that women were as much a force behind the war as men and deserved to be heard.

"In the new Code of Laws which I suppose it will be necessary for you to make I desire you would **Remember the Ladies** . . . we are determined to foment a Rebellion, and will not hold ourselves bound by any Laws in which we have no voice, or Representation."

—Abigail Adams in a letter to John Adams, March 31, 1776

Molly Pitcher at the Cannon's Mouth postcard, 1909

MOLLY PITCHER AT THE CANNON'S MOUTH.

Mary Ludwig Hays McCauly carried water to cool off the soldiers and the hot cannon her husband was firing during battles. This earned her the nickname Molly Pitcher. She also worked with her husband to fire the cannon. Other women served in combat during the war. One of them was Margaret Corbin, who is buried and honored with a monument at the United States Military Academy at West Point, New York. The woman in the postcard above represents not just Molly Pitcher but all the brave women who faced combat during the Revolution.

Phillis Wheatley proved the pen could also be a mighty weapon. She was born in Africa, enslaved as a young girl, and sold to a family of Boston Quakers who provided her with a good education. She became a poet who called for freedom for all, praised George Washington, and supported the American Revolution. She was the first African-American poet to have her work published.

Anna Smith Strong was a member of a spy ring on the coast of New York. She used a code based on how she hung out her laundry to let other members of the ring know when a messenger with information was arriving. A black petticoat on her clothesline meant the messenger was coming. The number of handkerchiefs scattered on the line indicated the cove in which he would land.

2.4 War at Sea

When you're used to walking on land, it can be hard to adjust to the tossing and swaying of a boat. Some people refer to this as "getting your sea legs." Sailors in the Continental Navy were about to get theirs.

MAIN IDEA The Continental Navy needed teamwork, determination, and strategy as it faced almost impossible odds against Britain's Royal Navy.

ATTACKS ON MERCHANT SHIPS

On land, Americans had the advantage of fighting on familiar terrain, or landforms and other physical features. And even though the British sent great numbers of troops to fight in North America, they were spread out across vast distances, so the Continental Army often faced smaller numbers of British troops at a time. In this way, it was able to hold its own.

The war at sea was a different story. Through the efforts of John Adams, the Continental Congress had established the Continental Navy in 1775, but the navy never had many ships. In contrast, Britain's Royal Navy was the largest and most powerful in the world, capable of causing great damage to the Americans' forces and economy. Even as the American Revolution began, British naval vessels had blockaded American harbors. Now they were attacking both American naval and merchant ships. The tiny Continental Navy could not hope to match its enemy's strength and resources.

Quickly building up and supporting a naval fleet was much more difficult than recruiting troops for land conflict. However, Benjamin Franklin's visit to France paid off. The French and Spanish navies helped swell the ranks of the Continental Navy.

Americans also turned to privateers—privately owned ships authorized to participate in warfare—to help protect their own shipping industry and damage Britain's. The Continental Congress granted privateers official permission to attack any British naval and merchant ships they encountered. During the war, as many as 2,000 vessels were put into use for privateering.

Privateer crews included a number of African-American sailors, both enslaved and free. Slave catchers rarely tried to capture runaway slaves who had stowed away on a ship. And the pay onboard was good, even though all privateer sailors worked in dangerous conditions. In fact, they were often captured and taken as prisoners of war.

Teenage African-American crewmember **James Forten** was taken aboard a British ship when it captured his vessel, the *Royal Louis*. The British captain assigned Forten to care for his young son, and the two became fast friends. As a result, the

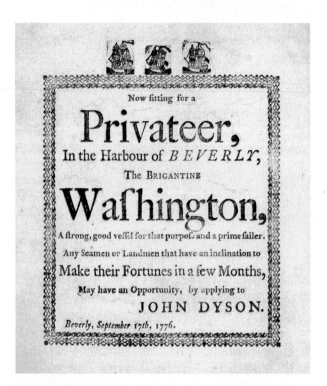

Calling All Able Sailors
This handbill advertised for experienced sailors to sail with the *Washington*, a vessel that went on to capture several enemy ships.

The Ordeal of John Paul Jones
Illustrator Anton Otto Fischer captures the drama on the *Bonhomme Richard* as
John Paul Jones (background, right) and his crew fight to keep sailors on the British ship
Serapis from boarding their ship. About 150 people were killed on each side in this battle.

captain's son asked his father to grant Forten his freedom instead of turning him over to a prison ship. The captain offered Forten a chance to return to Britain with them, but Forten refused. He believed in the principles of the American Revolution, especially the natural rights of freedom and the opportunity for democracy.

JOHN PAUL JONES

What the Continental Navy lacked in ships it made up for in determination, strategy, and sheer heroism. One American captain, **John Paul Jones**, had all three of these strengths. In September 1779, Jones was in command of a ship called the *Bonhomme Richard* when he encountered the British ship *Serapis*. The *Serapis* was escorting British merchant ships carrying military supplies. Jones attacked the *Serapis*, and the battle was on.

Disaster struck for the American ship when its main gun battery exploded. Soon after, the *Bonhomme Richard* caught fire and was damaged

beyond repair. Legend has it that with both ships fighting side by side, the British called on Jones to surrender. But he yelled back, "I have not yet begun to fight!" The battle raged on, and soon it fell to the British to surrender. Jones boarded and took control of the *Serapis*. In a war with few victories for the Continental Navy, Jones's success boosted American morale as the conflict moved into its final stage.

HISTORICAL THINKING

1. **READING CHECK** How was the Continental Navy able to hold its own against Britain's Royal Navy?

2. **ANALYZE CAUSE AND EFFECT** How were France and Spain affected by the war at sea?

3. **MAKE INFERENCES** What do you think James Forten hoped to gain by fighting to uphold the American principles of freedom?

3.1 War in the Southern Colonies

When you're losing a game, sometimes it helps to change your strategy. That's what the British decided to do. But would moving the war south help or hurt them?

MAIN IDEA At first, southern battles went badly for the Continental Army, but the Patriots soon found ways to torment the British.

EARLY LOSSES

The British deployed a new strategy in the Southern Colonies in 1778. They counted on Loyalist and African-American support in Georgia, the Carolinas, and Virginia. They used the islands of the British West Indies to gather and transport supplies and recruits for the British and their allies.

But French-held territory in the Caribbean provided aid to the Continental Army's southern campaign. The French Colonial Army recruited many soldiers for the American cause from its islands, such as Saint-Domingue (san dom-ANG), or present-day Haiti. Their numbers included enslaved men willing to fight against the British.

Enslaved African Americans in the Southern Colonies were also recruited to fight for the British. General Henry Clinton offered freedom to enslaved men who joined the British Army. As a result, African-American support for the British grew in the Southern Colonies.

CRITICAL VIEWING In 1780, Francis Marion lured a British force 26 miles into the heart of a South Carolina swamp. Will Anderson illustrated this episode in a mural he painted in 2001. Why do you think the British (on horseback) might have had a difficult time fighting on the Swamp Fox's terms?

In 1778, Clinton sent thousands of troops to Georgia. There they captured Savannah and Augusta, followed by Charleston, South Carolina. In an effort to combat the British onslaught, in July 1780, American general Horatio Gates arrived to build a new southern army. But Gates failed to prepare these troops properly for battle. **Lord Cornwallis**, the British commander, had learned of Gates's movements and attacked the Americans at Camden, South Carolina. The British scored an overwhelming victory that spelled disaster for the Continental Army and disgrace for Gates.

THE SWAMP FOX

While the Continental Army suffered major losses in the South, nontraditional military units strengthened the American cause. **Guerrilla** units, or independent military groups that used methods such as sneak attacks, thrived in the rural wetlands of the American Southeast. South Carolina officer **Francis Marion** and his small group of guerrillas harassed British troops through the swamps of Georgia and the Carolinas. Because he was so clever and good at dodging the British, Marion soon earned the nickname "the Swamp Fox."

Marion had once been a regular soldier fighting for the Patriots. But General Gates dismissed him before the disastrous Battle of Camden to focus on defending other territories. Marion soon discovered his genius for guerrilla warfare—conducting surprise attacks on the British, gathering intelligence about the enemy, and winning the loyalty of local people. Despite the many early American defeats in the Southern Colonies, guerilla leaders such as Marion caused enough trouble for the British to keep the United States competitive—and, eventually, on the path to victory.

HISTORICAL THINKING

1. **READING CHECK** What early wins did the British score in the Southern Colonies?

2. **IDENTIFY MAIN IDEAS AND DETAILS** What role did France play in the war in the Southern Colonies?

3. **DRAW CONCLUSIONS** What characteristics of a fox did Francis Marion demonstrate as a guerrilla leader?

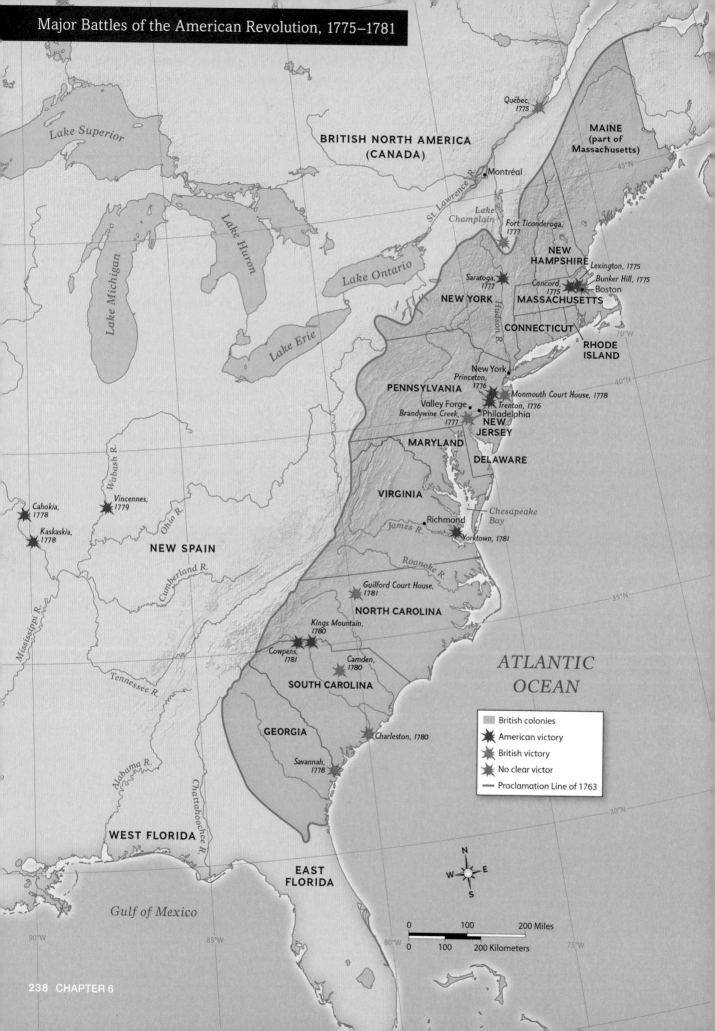

Major Battles of the American Revolution, 1775–1781

Lake Superior

BRITISH NORTH AMERICA (CANADA)

Québec, 1775

MAINE (part of Massachusetts)

Montréal

St. Lawrence

Lake Champlain

Fort Ticonderoga, 1777

Lake Michigan

Lake Huron

Lake Erie

Lake Ontario

NEW HAMPSHIRE

Lexington, 1775

Saratoga, 1777

Bunker Hill, 1775

Concord, 1775

Boston

NEW YORK

MASSACHUSETTS

Hudson R.

CONNECTICUT

RHODE ISLAND

New York

Princeton, 1776

PENNSYLVANIA

Monmouth Court House, 1778

Valley Forge

Trenton, 1776

Brandywine Creek, 1777

Philadelphia

NEW JERSEY

MARYLAND

DELAWARE

Wabash R.

Vincennes, 1779

VIRGINIA

Chesapeake Bay

Cahokia, 1778

Ohio R.

Richmond

Kaskaskia, 1778

James R.

Yorktown, 1781

NEW SPAIN

Cumberland R.

Roanoke R.

Guilford Court House, 1781

Mississippi R.

NORTH CAROLINA

Kings Mountain, 1780

Cowpens, 1781

Camden, 1780

Tennessee R.

SOUTH CAROLINA

ATLANTIC OCEAN

GEORGIA

Charleston, 1780

Savannah, 1778

Alabama R.

Chattahoochee R.

WEST FLORIDA

EAST FLORIDA

■	British colonies
✶	American victory
✶	British victory
✶	No clear victor
—	Proclamation Line of 1763

Gulf of Mexico

N W E S

0	100	200 Miles
0	100	200 Kilometers

3.2 The Tide Turns

Sometimes a new leader brings new energy and ideas to a situation and makes all the difference. That's just what happened when a new commander was brought in to lead the southern troops.

MAIN IDEA A change in leadership and a victory in the Carolinas helped change the course of the war in the Southern Colonies.

A NEW GENERAL

The tide of the war in the Southern Colonies began to turn in 1780. That's when General **Nathanael Greene** replaced Horatio Gates as commander of the Continental Army's southern troops. As a Quaker, Greene should have been a **pacifist**, or a person who stood against war and violence. So when Greene expressed his desire to organize troops against the British, the Quakers expelled him. After serving with Washington and leading troops in New York, New Jersey, and Pennsylvania, Greene was sent to the Southern Colonies to try to change the direction of the war for the Americans.

Greene's strategy involved increasing the Continental Army's mobility and agility. Spread out over the Southern Colonies, the large British Army had trouble moving quickly and changing plans. Greene used smaller forces to draw British troops away from strategic locations. He also benefited from a growing southern dislike of the British, whose troops and supporters had destroyed local houses and farms, executed prisoners of war, and made false promises of protection. Greene impressed southern colonists, including Loyalists, by protecting their property and enforcing order. Growing numbers in the Southern Colonies joined Greene's army or guerrilla forces.

PATRIOTS AND LOYALISTS CLASH

While the Americans changed their strategy, the British did not. British strategy in the Southern Colonies depended heavily on Loyalist support. The British relied on pitting American Loyalists and Patriots against each other, with little British troop involvement. That strategy failed at the **Battle of Kings Mountain**.

In the fall of 1780, Lord Cornwallis headed north from South Carolina, believing the time had come for British forces to conquer all the Southern Colonies. His troops met with heavy resistance. At Kings Mountain, near the border between the Carolinas, 2,000 Patriots, fighting independently from the Continental Army, clashed with an enemy force made up almost entirely of other Americans. These frontier Patriots dealt a resounding defeat to 1,100 Loyalist soldiers fighting under Major Patrick Ferguson, the only British Army member at the battle. Patriot fighters put to death some Loyalists who surrendered, perhaps as revenge for recent British executions of American prisoners.

The Battle of Kings Mountain was the first of many victories for the Patriots in the Southern Colonies. Loyalists sustained big losses at Cowpens in South Carolina, and Cornwallis and his troops suffered casualties at Guildford Court House in North Carolina. As a result, Cornwallis headed back toward Virginia. Because of the importance of the Battle of Kings Mountain, Thomas Jefferson called it "the turn of the tide of success."

HISTORICAL THINKING

1. **READING CHECK** How did Nathanael Greene's leadership affect the war in the Southern Colonies?

2. **INTERPRET MAPS** Why might frontiersmen have fought the Battle of Kings Mountain?

3. **SUMMARIZE** Why did Cornwallis's plan to control the Southern Colonies by enlisting the aid of Loyalists fail?

3.3 The War Ends

How often does winning against impossible odds happen in real life?
When that first shot was fired in Lexington, no one could have predicted
that 13 small colonies would defeat one of the world's greatest armies.

MAIN IDEA The British defeat at the Battle of Yorktown
brought an end to the American Revolution.

A PIVOTAL YEAR

As you've read, British hopes for victory in the South began to fade after their defeat at Kings Mountain. In 1781, American general Nathanael Greene moved south to regain South Carolina and Georgia, where the British still had 8,000 men spread thinly throughout the large region. Greene's 1,500 Continental soldiers and the guerilla units helping them were able to defeat small groups one by one. Americans were able to take back most of the area. Meanwhile, in Virginia, Lord Cornwallis replaced

Benedict Arnold as commander of the British forces in the area. In Yorktown, with an army of almost 8,000 men, Cornwallis camped on a peninsula facing the York River. His aim was to protect the harbor for the use of the British fleet. Cornwallis requested more troops from New York, but the British were slow in sending them.

🏛 U.S. Capitol Rotunda, Washington, D.C.

John Trumbull's painting *Surrender of Lord Cornwallis* depicts the British surrender in Yorktown. In the painting, American troops (on the right) and French troops (on the left) are all on horseback. Cornwallis's soldiers appear in the center of the painting. Why do you think the British soldiers are all on foot?

Setting up camp on the peninsula would prove to be a fatal mistake for Lord Cornwallis and his soldiers.

THE WORLD TURNED UPSIDE DOWN

American and French troops surrounded Cornwallis's camp by land and by sea. French naval officer admiral Comte de Grasse (duh-GRAHS) commanded a French fleet on the York River. He approached the British camp from the water. Meanwhile, a combined army of French soldiers, commanded by Comte de Rochambeau (ROH-sham-BOH), and Americans, led by General George Washington, marched south from New York, approaching the camp by land. In a show of military **expertise**, or skill, these three commanders led their 17,000 troops against Cornwallis, trapping him on the peninsula. Cornwallis had no choice but to surrender.

Charles O'Hara, second in command to Cornwallis, tried to surrender his general's sword to Rochambeau, but the French leader steered him to Washington instead. The British military band played a song called "The World Turned Upside Down," a fitting comment on the victory. The **Battle of Yorktown** was the last major battle of the war. In 1782, more than six years after the first shots were fired, the British Parliament officially voted to end the war.

The impact of this victory was staggering. Once only the dream of a group of visionaries seeking freedom from unreasonable laws and taxes, the young country had come through the fire of war to take its place as a full-fledged nation. In the decades and centuries that followed, the United States of America—established with the promise of equality for all—would rise to become one of the most powerful and influential nations on Earth. In time, people in many countries around the world would draw inspiration from America's example and fight for their own freedom and independence.

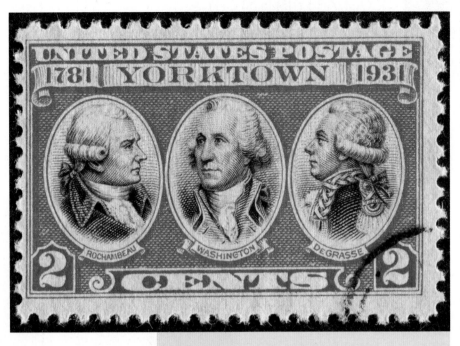

Remembering the Victors

This stamp commemorates the 150th anniversary of the victory at Yorktown. We all know George Washington, who is shown in the middle, but what about the other two leaders who helped the Americans win at Yorktown?

Comte de Rochambeau (on the left), was born in Vendôme, France. Commissioned into the French army at age 17, he was a veteran of 14 military sieges in Europe. King Louis XVI sent him to lead the French force in America in 1780.

Comte de Grasse (on the right), was born in Le Bar, France, and started working on ships when he was only about 12 years old. At 18, he joined the French navy. DeGrasse was fighting the British in the West Indies when General Washington asked for his help in Virginia against Cornwallis. The rest is history.

HISTORICAL THINKING

1. **READING CHECK** What factors led to the American victory at Yorktown?

2. **DRAW CONCLUSIONS** What statement was Rochambeau making when he made O'Hara surrender the British general's sword to Washington?

3. **ANALYZE CAUSE AND EFFECT** What happened as a result of the American victory in both the long- and short-term?

3.4 An Ally in the American Victory

MAIN IDEA The physical and human characteristics, as well as the "site" and "situation," of locations have helped shape events in history.

In 1776, no one in the world believed the American colonists could defeat the mighty British Army. Yet throughout history, geography has affected how events have unfolded, and this was certainly the case during the American Revolution. The Continental Army had several types of geographic advantages: terrain, population distribution, distance, and climate. For example, the Continental Army spent the winter of 1777–78 at Valley Forge in Pennsylvania. The climate there was cold—and the cold shaped events. As you know, the soldiers suffered greatly from a lack of sufficient clothing and shelter. Yet the bad weather prevented the British from attacking them.

The Catskill Mountains in New York State are covered with thick forests that provided cover for the Continental Army and challenges for the British as they approached.

Study these examples of the geographic advantages that favored the Continental Army. Consider the information provided about each site—the physical characteristics of the example given. Then consider the situation or the location of each site in relation to other places.

TERRAIN

SITE The terrain of upstate New York is mountainous and heavily forested, with many rivers and streams.

SITUATION The Americans were familiar with the terrain, which gave them an enormous advantage. For example, in 1777, British troops marched from Canada toward New York to attack the Continental Army. Americans cut down trees and wrecked bridges, slowing down British troops. This gave the Americans time to gather more than 11,000 troops at Saratoga, where they defeated the British.

European Claims in North America, 1776

unexplored

BRITISH CLAIM

SPANISH CLAIM

AMERICAN COLONIES

40,000 people
population of Philadelphia in 1776

POPULATION DISTRIBUTION

SITE The area of the colonies was large, but the population was relatively small—about 2.5 million people. Cities were also small, as most people lived on farms, so the population was widely scattered.

SITUATION The population was so widely distributed that the British couldn't simply attack one or two cities to defeat the Americans. In addition, the Continental Army could hide from British troops in unpopulated territory.

97 miles
from New York City to Philadelphia

370 miles
from New York City to Fort Pitt

COLONIAL POPULATION, 1776

Philadelphia, PA	40,000
New York, NY	25,000
Boston, MA	15,000
Charleston, SC	12,000
Newport, RI	11,000

Source: *The Economist*

1,580 miles
from northern border of Maine to southern border of Georgia

DISTANCE

SITE The colonies stretched more than 1,500 miles from north to south and more than 350 miles from east to west.

SITUATION The 13 colonies were located more than 3,000 miles from Great Britain. The distance created enormous problems for the British. They had to transport soldiers, supplies, and munitions by sailing ships. When the troops reached North America, they took weeks to march from one field of combat to another.

3,460 miles
from London, England, to New York City

CLIMATE

SITE The British were not used to the cold winters of the northern states. The heat and humidity of the southern states were unfamiliar to the British, too.

SITUATION The Americans used their knowledge of the climate during the war. In the winter of 1775, Washington wanted artillery transported from New York to Boston. Colonel Henry Knox used 42 sleds pulled by oxen to transport the artillery over snow and ice. The Americans used the weapons to drive the British out of Boston.

763 miles
from New York City to Charleston

Map labels: MASSACHUSETTS (District of Maine), Portsmouth, NEW HAMPSHIRE, Saratoga, Boston, MASSACHUSETTS, Providence, NEW YORK, RHODE ISLAND, CONNECTICUT, New York, NEW JERSEY, PENNSYLVANIA, Valley Forge, Philadelphia, Fort Pitt, Baltimore, MARYLAND, DELAWARE, Proclamation Line of 1763, Indian Reserve, VIRGINIA, NORTH CAROLINA, SOUTH CAROLINA, Charles Town (Charleston), GEORGIA, West Florida, East Florida

THINK LIKE A GEOGRAPHER

1. **IDENTIFY MAIN IDEAS AND DETAILS** Why did distance pose problems for British troops during the American Revolution?

2. **ANALYZE CAUSE AND EFFECT** How did the Americans use geography to gain an advantage over the British?

3. **FORM AND SUPPORT OPINIONS** Of the four geographic factors, which one do you think had the greatest impact on the war? Explain your reasons.

3.5 Legacy of the War

With the war finally over, the young country assessed its costs and looked toward the future. The citizens of the United States had some hard decisions to make. What direction would the new country take?

MAIN IDEA Once a formal treaty was negotiated and signed, the United States began to forge its new identity as an independent nation.

NEGOTIATING THE PEACE

The American Revolution was over. It would soon inspire other nations, including France and the French colony of Haiti, to revolt and demand democracy. But war always comes at a high price. Thousands of soldiers—both American and British—lost their lives in combat, and even more died of disease. Now it was time to heal and begin building the nation. First, though, the United States and Great Britain had to make peace. The two countries did so in the **Treaty of Paris of 1783**.

Benjamin Franklin, John Jay, and John Adams negotiated skillfully for the United States. The treaty they produced included two extremely important **provisions**, or legal conditions, that aided the country. The British agreed both to recognize the independence of the United States of America and to approve the new American boundaries. The new country was bounded on the west by the Mississippi River, on the north by Canada, and on the south by Florida. The United States would have plenty of growing room.

Florida, from which Britain had created **East Florida** and **West Florida**, went back to Spain in a separate agreement. The British also made a separate agreement with France over parts of the West Indies and Canada.

A NEW IDENTITY

Not all Americans were happy with the outcome of the war. Many Loyalists and Native Americans, furious that their British allies had signed away their lands, moved to Canada. Some former slaves freed by the British also made their way to Canada, but others were returned to slavery. The majority of Americans, though, stayed right where they were

and began rebuilding. Britain's economic control and taxation had spurred the Revolution. Freedom of trade took firm hold, laying the groundwork for growing commerce and industry.

Liberty and equality were central to the new national identity as well. In 1781, an enslaved woman named Mum Betts sued and won her freedom in court. Taking the name **Elizabeth Freeman**, she inspired Massachusetts to become the first state to abolish slavery. In Delaware, **Richard Allen** bought his freedom and later founded one of the first independent black churches in Philadelphia.

The most difficult task facing the United States was establishing a plan for government. Citizens favored **republicanism**, a system with no king or queen, where the people choose representatives to make their laws. They also stressed civic republicanism, or responsibility for the common good. Americans hoped to blend civic republicanism and ideals of classical liberal principles, including private property and individual and religious freedoms, to create their new government.

HISTORICAL THINKING

1. **READING CHECK** How did the Treaty of Paris of 1783 secure the future of the United States?

2. **DESCRIBE** How did the U.S. government plan reflect the ideals of civic republicanism, classical liberal principles, and English parliamentary traditions?

3. **FORM AND SUPPORT OPINIONS** Do you think African Americans were better off after the revolution? Explain why or why not.

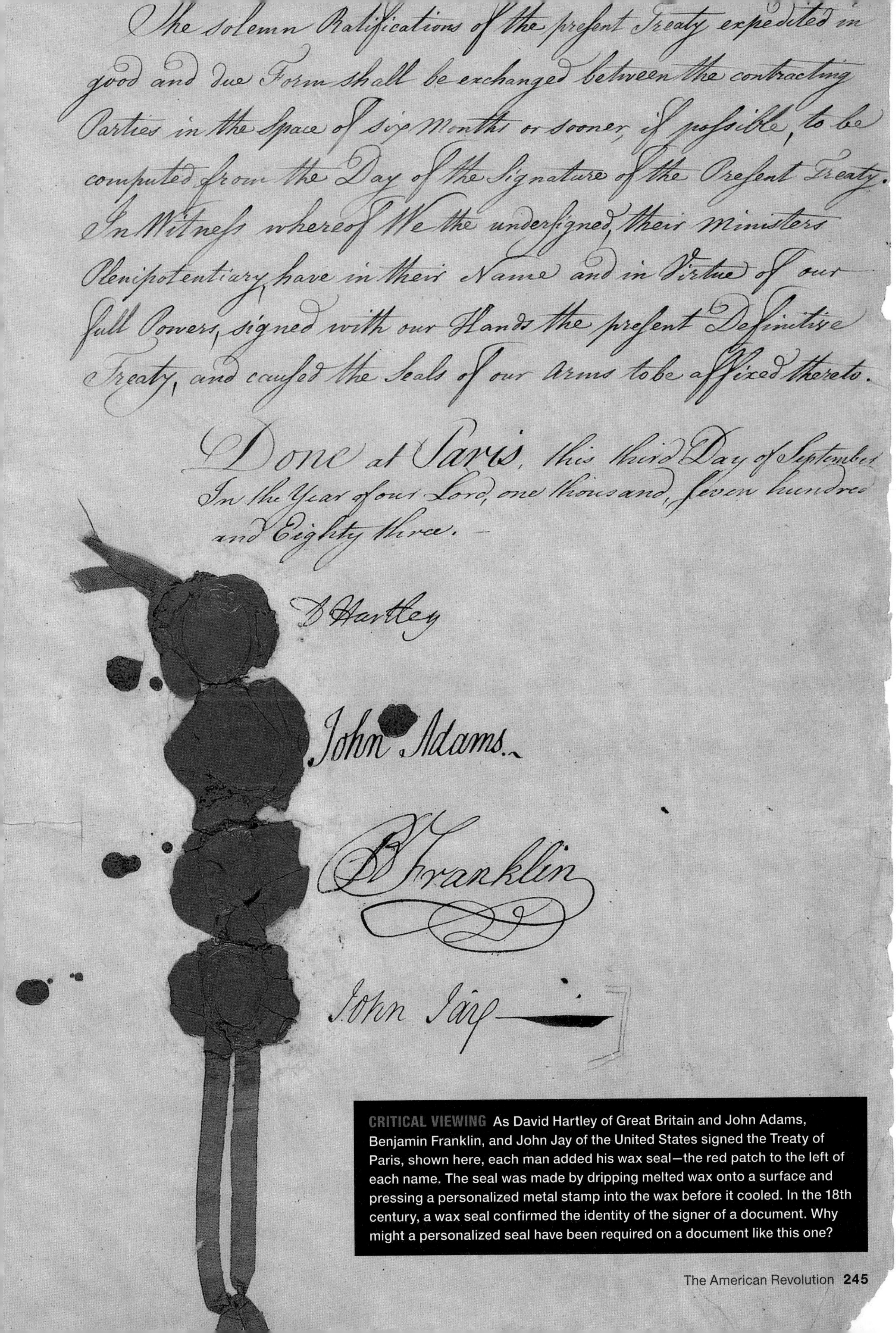

The solemn Ratifications of the present Treaty expedited in good and due Form shall be exchanged between the contracting Parties in the Space of six Months or sooner, if possible, to be computed from the Day of the Signature of the Present Treaty. In Witness whereof We the undersigned their Ministers Plenipotentiary have in their Name and in Virtue of our full Powers, signed with our Hands the present Definitive Treaty, and caused the Seals of our Arms to be affixed thereto.

Done at Paris, this third Day of September In the Year of our Lord, one thousand, seven hundred and Eighty three. —

D Hartley

John Adams.

B Franklin

John Jay

CRITICAL VIEWING As David Hartley of Great Britain and John Adams, Benjamin Franklin, and John Jay of the United States signed the Treaty of Paris, shown here, each man added his wax seal—the red patch to the left of each name. The seal was made by dripping melted wax onto a surface and pressing a personalized metal stamp into the wax before it cooled. In the 18th century, a wax seal confirmed the identity of the signer of a document. Why might a personalized seal have been required on a document like this one?

THE AMERICAN REVOLUTION

REVIEW

VOCABULARY

Match the following vocabulary terms with their definitions.

1. mercenary
2. blockade
3. skirmish
4. desert
5. pacifist
6. provision
7. republicanism
8. espionage

a. legal condition or requirement
b. the act of spying to gather information
c. to leave military service illegally
d. a soldier who is paid to fight for a country other than his or her own
e. a small, short battle
f. a form of government in which the people elect representatives
g. to use ships or other means to keep ships and commerce from entering a port
h. a person who stands against war and violence

READING STRATEGY
FORM AND SUPPORT OPINIONS

If you haven't already, complete your chart listing your opinion and supporting statements regarding the factor that most helped secure an American victory in the Revolution. Then answer the following question.

9. What factor was key to the U.S. victory in the American Revolution? Include your supporting statements in your answer.

Opinion:

Supporting statement:

Supporting statement:

Supporting statement:

Supporting statement:

MAIN IDEAS

Answer the following questions. Support your answers with evidence from the chapter.

10. What disadvantages did the Americans face at the beginning of the war? **LESSON 1.1**

11. How did the alliances and treaties made by Native Americans affect their relationships with both the Patriots and the British? **LESSON 1.2**

12. How did other nations come to the aid of the Americans? **LESSON 2.1**

13. Compare the experiences of the American and British armies in the winter of 1777–78. **LESSON 2.2**

14. Why did Abigail Adams ask her husband to "Remember the Ladies"? **LESSON 2.3**

15. What strategy did the Americans use to face the powerful British Navy? **LESSON 2.4**

16. How did Nathanael Greene and Francis Marion help change the course of the war in the Southern Colonies? **LESSON 3.2**

17. How did the Americans earn a victory at Yorktown? **LESSON 3.3**

18. How did American calls for independence inspire other nations, such as France and the French colony of Haiti? **LESSON 3.5**

Answer the following questions. Support your answers with evidence from the chapter.

19. **ANALYZE CAUSE AND EFFECT** Besides the death toll, what was a negative effect of the war?

20. **SYNTHESIZE** How did American women and men work together in the war?

21. **DRAW CONCLUSIONS** What groups of people did not benefit from the Revolution?

22. **FORM AND SUPPORT OPINIONS** What British mistake led most directly to their defeat?

INTERPRET MAPS

Look closely at the map of the Battle of Yorktown. Then answer the questions that follow.

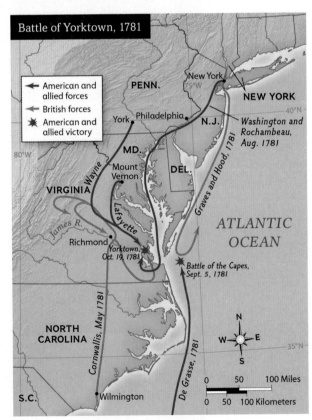

Battle of Yorktown, 1781

23. According to the map, what happened in the Battle of the Capes?

24. How does the map illustrate cooperation between the Americans and the French?

ANALYZE SOURCES

Timothy Pickering, Jr., was an officer in the Continental Army. In 1778, when he read that his father, a Loyalist, was dying, Pickering wrote him a letter. Read the excerpt from the letter and answer the question.

When I look back on past time, I regret our difference of sentiment in great as well as (sometimes) in little politics; as it was a deduction [subtraction] from the happiness otherwise to have been enjoyed. Yet you had always too much regard to freedom in thinking & the rights of conscience, to lay upon me any injunctions [commands] which could interfere with my own opinion of what was [my] duty. Often have I thanked my Maker for the greatest blessing of my life—your example & instructions in all the duties I owe to God, and my neighbor. They have not been lost upon me.

—*Letter from Timothy Pickering, Jr., to Timothy Pickering, Sr., February 23, 1778*

25. What emotions does Pickering express toward his father?

CONNECT TO YOUR LIFE

26. **EXPOSITORY** Think about the different people you read about in the chapter. How did individuals, both Americans and others, show heroism in the American Revolution? Write a paragraph about two individuals mentioned in the chapter, explaining why they should be considered heroes.

TIPS

• Review the chapter and choose two individuals whom you consider heroes. Write a topic sentence about their heroism during the American Revolution.

• Support your choices with evidence from the chapter.

• Conclude your paragraph with a summary of the individuals' heroism.

FROM CONFEDERATION TO
CONSTITUTION
1776–1791

ESSENTIAL QUESTION

How did ideas about the role of state and national government evolve?

READING STRATEGY

DETERMINE CHRONOLOGY

When you analyze chronology, you determine how ideas and events unfold over time. As you read the chapter, use an organizer like this one to record how ideas about state and national government developed in the United States.

1 → 2 → 3 → 4

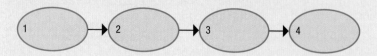

"The people are the only legitimate fountain of power."
—James Madison

CRITICAL VIEWING The National Mall in Washington, D.C., is a park that extends about two miles from the Capitol Building to the Lincoln Memorial, with the Washington Monument in between. Americans gather there to celebrate and to express various aspects of our democracy as embodied in the Constitution. How does the crowd gathered for President Barack Obama's first inauguration represent our unity as a nation?

1.1 State and National Governments

The last thing revolutionaries who have broken free from oppressive rulers want is the same way of governing. American revolutionaries wanted a new style of government—and one with limited power.

> **MAIN IDEA** The Articles of Confederation limited the power of the new national government, while state governments retained much of their independence.

CREATING ORDER

Part of the legacy of the American struggle for independence included the establishment of a government based on republicanism, or the idea that government's power comes from its citizens and their representatives. Even as the war raged, each state moved forward and set up its own government.

Elected representatives from each state met and drafted a **constitution**, or a plan for government. Many state constitutions included lists of rights to which every citizen was entitled, such as the freedom to practice any religion. Once the constitutions were drafted and revised, the state representatives **ratified**, or approved, them.

Many states decided to organize their governments with governors and two-house legislatures elected by the people. Organizing legislatures into two parts, instead of one, ensured that lawmakers would have to share power and limited the power of governors. Some states, such as Pennsylvania, opted for no governor at all.

State constitutions were a new concept at the time. Most western European countries did not grant such power to elected legislatures. The process of writing and ratifying state constitutions served as a model for the new national government to introduce future political institutions and ideas. One of the new ideas that emerged was a constitution that would govern all American states.

ARTICLES

OF

CONFEDERATION

AND

PERPETUAL UNION

BETWEEN THE

STATES

OF

NEW-HAMPSHIRE, MASSACHUSETTS-BAY, RHODE-ISLAND AND PROVIDENCE PLANTATIONS, CONNECTICUT, NEW-YORK, NEW-JERSEY, PENNSYLVANIA, DELAWARE, MARYLAND, VIRGINIA, NORTH-CAROLINA, SOUTH-CAROLINA AND GEORGIA.

The Articles of Confederation went through six drafts between 1775 and 1777 before Congress finally approved it and then submitted it to the 13 states for ratification.

A NATIONAL PLAN

After the states ratified their constitutions, they decided to band together to defeat the British. Representatives from many of the states started meeting regularly to draft a plan for unification called the Articles of Confederation.

The Articles of Confederation gave Congress the ability to make decisions about the military. They also outlined a national plan of **sovereign**, or self-governing, states. The **federal**, or national, government would have little power of its own, nor would it include a president or a federal court system. It would simply serve as an administrator to help unify the states. This limited federal government reflected the ideals first put forth in the Declaration of Independence, which stated that a government should derive its powers "from the consent of the governed."

The Articles of Confederation assigned foreign affairs and relations with Native Americans, the ability to declare war and peace, and the postal

Maryland State House, Annapolis

Did you know that the nation's capital wasn't always Washington, D.C.? The Maryland State House is the only state capitol building that has also served as the nation's capital. It is located in Annapolis, Maryland, a city often referred to as the "Athens of America" because of its rich cultural and political history and coastal location.

Between November 1783 and August 1784, the Continental Congress met at the Maryland State House. In the Old Senate Chamber, the Congress accepted Washington's resignation as commander in chief of the Continental Army. It also ratified the Treaty of Paris. Both events signaled the end of the American Revolution.

service to Congress. The national government could produce money but not levy taxes. If it needed money, it had to ask the states for funds. Congress needed to approve any legislation that would affect the country.

Americans liked these ideas because they addressed liberties denied to them under British rule. They also laid the foundation for **constitutionalism**, an approach to government that strictly defines and limits its powers. In March 1781, all 13 states finally ratified the Articles of Confederation, which would serve as the first constitution of the United States for eight years.

HISTORICAL THINKING

1. **READING CHECK** What responsibilities did the national government have under the Articles of Confederation?

2. **ANALYZE CAUSE AND EFFECT** How did the development of state constitutions influence the national plan for government?

3. **IDENTIFY MAIN IDEAS AND DETAILS** How were the ideals put forth in the Declaration of Independence reflected in the new American government?

1.2 Ordinances of 1785 and 1787

When large groups of people get together but have few rules to follow, things can get wild fast. As settlers moved into territory northwest of the Ohio River, the new United States struggled to maintain law and order beyond its official boundaries.

MAIN IDEA The ordinances of 1785 and 1787 allowed the federal government to better regulate westward expansion and distribute land to new settlers.

GO WEST!

You have read that the Treaty of Paris of 1783 granted the United States most of the territory from the Atlantic Ocean to the Mississippi River. This land extended north to the St. Lawrence River and the Great Lakes and south to the Spanish colony of Florida. Under the Articles of Confederation, the national government controlled all this territory.

Fertile soil attracted white settlers to the land beyond the Appalachian (a-puh-LATCH-uhn) Mountains. Settlers had begun arriving there in 1775, when frontier adventurers such as

Northwest Territory, 1787

Boundaries indefinite

Northwest Territory
— Present-day state boundary

BRITISH NORTH AMERICA (CANADA)

L. Superior

L. Michigan

L. Huron

L. Erie

Mississippi R.

SPANISH LOUISIANA

PENN.

Ohio R.

VIRGINIA

KENTUCKY

Cumberland Gap

NORTH CAROLINA

TENNESSEE

0   100   200 Miles
0   100   200 Kilometers

Daniel Boone and some companions created a route through the Appalachian Mountains from Virginia to Kentucky. The new route, called the **Wilderness Road**, enabled large numbers of people to move west. The "western lands," as they were called, included present-day Ohio, Indiana, Illinois, Michigan, Wisconsin, and part of Minnesota.

THE NORTHWEST TERRITORY

Territorial expansion and its consequences created a new set of problems for the federal government. Congress recognized the need to provide safety and order within the new settlements, and it also wanted to establish a strong governmental presence in the western lands. Operating under the Articles of Confederation, Congress passed a series of **ordinances**, or laws, for settling the western lands. These ordinances established an orderly system for transferring federally owned land into private holdings, townships, and states. The first ordinance, passed in 1784, divided the territory into a small number of self-governing districts that could later become states.

The second ordinance was the **Ordinance of 1785**. It called for surveying and organizing districts into townships. The townships would be further divided into lots that the government would sell at a minimum of $1 per acre. Each township also had to set aside land for a school.

Finally, the **Northwest Ordinance of 1787** renamed the land the **Northwest Territory**. The ordinance provided for ownership of land by individuals and for the creation of new states out of this territory. Because it applied a portion of funds

AMERICAN PLACES
Cumberland Gap, Appalachian Mountains

Many Americans who moved west to settle in the Northwest Territory traveled through the Cumberland Gap. It was the only place where settlers could reasonably cross the Appalachian Mountains from Virginia into Kentucky. As the map to the left shows, the Cumberland Gap is located where the states of Virginia, Kentucky, and Tennessee meet.

from the sale of lands toward building schools, it established the first system of public education and reinforced the Founders' belief that the success of a republican government relies on an educated people. The ordinance prohibited slavery in the Northwest Territory. It guaranteed the rights of the people who settled there and stated that "the utmost good faith shall always be observed" toward Native Americans. The ordinances of 1785 and 1787 created a plan for westward expansion. They also caused some unforeseen problems for the new nation. One of these problems would be growing conflict with Native Americans in the Northwest Territory.

HISTORICAL THINKING

1. **READING CHECK** What problems did territorial expansion create for the new nation?

2. **DETERMINE CHRONOLOGY** How did the Articles of Confederation and each of the land ordinances build on one another to pave the way for settlement?

3. **INTERPRET MAPS** Based on what you see on the map, what major waterways were newly available to settlers in the Northwest Territory?

1.3 Controversies About the Articles

Have you ever thought of a brilliant solution to a problem that only led to more problems? In the 1780s, the Articles of Confederation were exactly that: a solution that led to more problems.

MAIN IDEA The Articles of Confederation limited the federal government's effectiveness and led to economic problems and challenges to its authority.

THE PRICE OF WAR

The Articles of Confederation provided a governing structure during the Revolution but quickly proved inadequate for the needs of the new nation. The Articles created 13 sovereign states instead of one unified nation. So when the national government faced growing economic problems, it did not have an effective system in place to solve them.

One economic problem was the amount of debt that remained after the Revolution. By 1790, the U.S. government owed around $50 million to American merchants and farmers and also to the French government. The shortfall in funds also meant soldiers could not be paid, which led to angry protests.

Because of the limitations of the Articles, Congress could not impose taxes or regulate trade. Individual states refused to contribute enough money to help the national government pay these debts. Rewriting the Articles so that Congress could levy taxes was nearly impossible because the representatives of all 13 states had to approve such a measure. Few, if any, states were likely to offer their support, so the debts went unpaid.

Before the war, many Americans relied on receiving **credit**, or the privilege of purchasing something and paying the cost back over time. British companies wanted to encourage the colonists to buy their goods, and giving credit made that possible. As British subjects, farmers could repay their debts with goods, such as livestock and crops. After the war, British manufacturers demanded that all debts be repaid with money instead of goods. At the same time, state governments started to impose heavy taxes upon their citizens. Few farmers had cash on

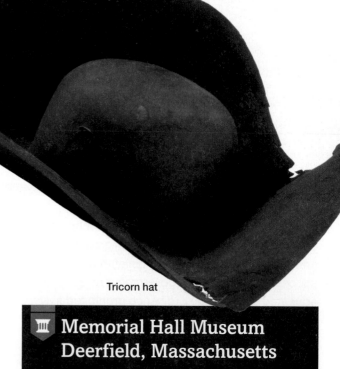

Tricorn hat

🏛 Memorial Hall Museum Deerfield, Massachusetts

Tricorn hats like this one, dated 1775, were popular in Europe and America in the 1700s. Notice how the tricorn hat appears in the illustration on the opposite page, flying off the head of the man attacking the official. Other men in the scene are wearing tricorn hats as well.

hand, and many Americans, especially farmers, faced financial ruin. When farmers failed to repay their debts, they often faced prosecution and the loss of their farms.

In some states, those who owed money demanded new laws that would allow them to settle their debts and pay taxes with goods. Citizens also wanted fewer requirements for voting so that they would have better representation in state governments. When governments did not respond, citizens challenged their authority and legitimacy by rebelling.

SHAYS'S REBELLION

In the fall of 1786, Daniel Shays, a veteran of the American Revolution, led rifle-carrying farmers into various Massachusetts courthouses and demanded the end of debt hearings. The Massachusetts government frantically asked Congress for help to put down the armed rebellion. In turn, Congress requested that the states help by sending money and soldiers, but the states refused. Its inability to respond to the domestic crisis of citizen rebellion revealed how ineffective Congress was under the Articles of Confederation.

Citizens became angrier when the state of Massachusetts passed the Riot Act, which prohibited armed groups from gathering in public. To prove its point, the state government sent armed troops, who defeated Shays's men easily. Shays and his supporters risked losing their voting rights and even imprisonment. However, **Shays's Rebellion** inspired other people to stand up to the government. One effect of the uprising was that in the following year's election, voter participation increased dramatically. Citizens wanted input into how problems such as debt repayment could be resolved.

CRITICAL VIEWING A protestor attacks an official during Shays's Rebellion in an attempt to disrupt court proceedings in Springfield, Massachusetts. Protests over the repayment of debts occurred in many states but reached a higher level of intensity in Massachusetts. Confrontations between farmers and government officials also occurred in the Massachusetts towns of Northampton, Concord, and Worcester. What details in the illustration convey the drama of Shays's Rebellion?

HISTORICAL THINKING

1. **READING CHECK** How did the Articles of Confederation limit the effectiveness of the federal government?

2. **DETERMINE CHRONOLOGY** In what ways did the economics of the American Revolution lead to Shays's Rebellion?

3. **ANALYZE CAUSE AND EFFECT** What effect did Shays's Rebellion have on the election of 1787?

2.1 The Constitutional Convention

Would you like to travel for weeks by horse-drawn wagon along bumpy dirt roads in bad weather to help decide your country's fate? That's what 55 government representatives did to attend a meeting in the spring of 1787.

MAIN IDEA American leaders met at the Constitutional Convention to debate and decide how to reform the national government.

Legend
1 James Madison
2 George Mason
3 George Washington
4 Benjamin Franklin
5 Gouverneur Morris
6 Alexander Hamilton

CRITICAL VIEWING This mural is one of two large-scale scenes painted by Barry Faulkner in 1936. It hangs in the Rotunda for the Charters of Freedom in the National Archives. What do you think the artist meant to convey by the setting he created for James Madison's presentation of the U.S. Constitution to George Washington?

DELEGATES GATHER

By 1787, it was clear the Articles of Confederation were not very effective. The United States was growing geographically and economically, and the Articles were not able to address complications from that growth. Robert Morris of Pennsylvania and **Alexander Hamilton** of New York pointed to Shays's Rebellion and other crises as evidence in support of their message. Morris and Hamilton believed the country needed a stronger government in order to deal with its problems.

Leaders called for a meeting to discuss reform. The meeting, held in Philadelphia on May 25, 1787, was called the **Constitutional Convention**.

Every state sent **delegates**, or representatives, except Rhode Island. The tiny state did not trust the concept of a powerful federal government, which it feared would be the outcome of the Constitutional Convention. Rhode Island's decision not to send delegates irritated many, including the normally even-tempered George Washington.

Independence Hall Philadelphia

When Washington presided over the Constitutional Convention, he occupied this chair, called the Rising Sun chair. Note the intricate, carved detail of the sun that would appear behind the head of its occupant. John Folwell designed and carved the Rising Sun chair in 1779. Today, it is housed in the Assembly Room at Independence Hall.

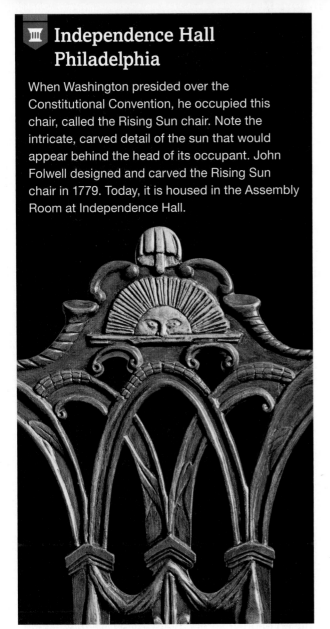

Those who gathered at the Convention to create the Constitution became known as the **Framers**. The Framers were wealthy, influential, and well educated. Many of the Framers had also been leaders during the Revolution, including Pennsylvania delegate Benjamin Franklin. The Framers elected George Washington from Virginia to lead the Convention.

Of the Framers at the Convention, James Madison, from Virginia, was the best prepared to craft a constitution for the new nation. His research and knowledge proved the most influential in shaping the ideas the delegates debated and ultimately included in the final document. Because of his active role, Madison is often called the "Father of the Constitution."

Some notable American leaders did not attend. Thomas Jefferson and John Adams were serving as ministers to France and Great Britain. Patrick Henry refused to attend because he fiercely opposed a strong central government.

GOALS AND CHALLENGES

The delegates debated for four months. Because of their experience, the Framers aimed to create a government that was neither too strong, like the British monarchy, nor too weak, as under the Articles of Confederation. The delegates wanted national, state, and local governments to share governing power, an idea called **federalism**. They also felt **dual sovereignty**, or giving state governments certain powers that the national government could not overrule, was important.

Delegates at the Convention agreed upon other main principles. One was republicanism. In a republican government, citizens elect officials to represent them, and these officials must act and govern according to the law. Another principle that guided the delegates was that elections and legislative votes would be decided by majority rule. Majority rule requires that the candidates or legislation receive at least one more than one-half of all votes, even when there are more than two choices. Majority rule means that support for a successful candidate or law must be strong.

Convention delegates supported the idea of federalism but debated how to divide state-federal power. They disagreed about how much power state and national governments should have and about how much authority they should grant the three branches of the federal government.

HISTORICAL THINKING

1. **READING CHECK** In what ways did James Madison contribute to the Constitutional Convention?

2. **DESCRIBE** What were the main issues of debate among delegates at the Constitutional Convention?

3. **FORM AND SUPPORT OPINIONS** Which principle under debate at the Convention do you think was most important to the new nation? Support your opinion with evidence from the text.

2.2 The Big Question: How to Divide Power

Imagine listening in on the debates at the Constitutional Convention. Delegates from more populous states want more representatives than smaller states. Other delegates want the same number of representatives for all states. How do they resolve this issue? They compromise.

MAIN IDEA Delegates at the Constitutional Convention decided how to divide power in the government and how to elect the president.

THE GREAT COMPROMISE

As you have read, the Constitutional Convention embraced the idea that the federal government should rely on three branches of government based on the principles of **separation of powers** and **checks and balances**. Each branch would have unique powers. None would have more power than any other, and each branch would be a check on the other two. The **legislative branch** would create and pass legislation, or make laws. The **executive branch** would lead the nation and enforce laws, and the **judicial branch** would interpret laws.

Most delegates agreed on a judicial branch headed by a **Supreme Court** and that one leader, a president, should head the executive branch. But they could not agree on how the legislative branch should work. Delegates Edmund Randolph and William Paterson proposed two different plans, the **Virginia Plan** and the **New Jersey Plan**, shown at right. Smaller states, such as Delaware, Maryland, and New Jersey, were uncomfortable with the Virginia Plan. Larger states didn't like the New Jersey Plan. Delegates voted for the Virginia Plan as the draft framework for the Constitution, but many remained dissatisfied.

Roger Sherman of Connecticut combined the best ideas from both plans to craft the **Great Compromise**. He proposed a legislative branch with two houses. Delegates voted in favor of Sherman's plan and established the legislative branch that exists today.

PRESIDENTIAL ELECTIONS

The delegates agreed on the executive role of the president of the United States, but not on how to select this leader. Some argued for a direct election—the candidate with the majority of votes would win. Others wanted Congress or the state legislatures to choose, fearing that the people might elect someone unqualified for the job.

The Convention delegates landed on another compromise: the **electoral college**. States would be granted a specific number of electors equal to their numbers of senators and representatives in Congress. States would then choose their electors, who would cast their votes for president based on their voters' preferences. Though voting rights would eventually expand over time, after the Revolution, voting was limited to white males.

HISTORICAL THINKING

1. **READING CHECK** What compromises did the Convention delegates reach when planning for the legislative and executive branches?

2. **DETERMINE CHRONOLOGY** What two proposals preceded the Great Compromise?

3. **FORM AND SUPPORT OPINIONS** Of the Virginia Plan and the New Jersey Plan, which do you think best reflected the spirit of the new nation? Support your opinion with evidence from the text.

TOTAL POPULATION OF THE UNITED STATES, 1790: 3,929,214

Population of Virginia
19%, 747,610

Population of New Jersey
4.7%, 184,139

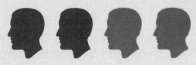 = one representative from New Jersey

SC

NH
ME
VT
GA
KY
RI
DE

PA

CT

NC

MD

NY   MA

 = one representative from Virginia

Edmund Randolph's
Virginia Plan

TWO HOUSES

| UPPER HOUSE | |
| LOWER HOUSE | |

The number of representatives from each state is **proportionate to the state's population.**

This plan made delegates from small states nervous.

William Paterson's
New Jersey Plan

ONE HOUSE

Each state has an equal number of representatives, **regardless of population.**

Delegates from larger states didn't like this plan.

ROGER SHERMAN'S
GREAT COMPROMISE

HOUSE OF REPRESENTATIVES

The number of representatives from each state is **proportionate to the state's population.**

SENATE

Each state has an equal number of representatives, **regardless of population.**

Source: United States Census Bureau

SEPARATION OF POWERS

THREE BRANCHES OF GOVERNMENT

| **LEGISLATIVE BRANCH** | **EXECUTIVE BRANCH** | **JUDICIAL BRANCH** |
| MAKES LAWS | ENFORCES LAWS | INTERPRETS LAWS |

2.3 Slavery and Trade

When people in power make decisions, the consequences are often immediate and long-lasting. That was the case during the Constitutional Convention when the Framers made decisions about slavery and trade.

MAIN IDEA Before the delegates approved the final draft of the Constitution, they had to compromise about slavery and settle issues about commerce.

SLAVERY AND REPRESENTATION

Even though the word *slavery* does not appear in the original body of the Constitution, slavery was a major topic at the Constitutional Convention. In fact, the delegates negotiated several compromises that firmly preserved the institution of slavery.

All delegates, whether from the North or the South, were especially concerned with how the practice of slavery affected state representation in Congress. Southern states depended more on enslaved labor than northern states. As a result, southern delegates wanted enslaved people to be counted as members of a state's population. Doing so would increase the number of delegates representing southern states in the House of Representatives. It would also increase the region's electoral votes. Northerners argued that enslaved people should not be counted because they were legally defined as property.

As part of the Great Compromise, the Convention delegates decided that five enslaved Americans would count as three free persons and approved inserting what is called the **Three-Fifths Compromise** into Article 1 of the Constitution. The Three-Fifths Compromise increased the power of white voters in the South at the expense of enslaved African Americans, who were each counted as less than a full person.

Article 1 also included a **slave importation clause** stating that Congress could not ban the importation of slaves for 20 years and that the tax on importing an enslaved person could not exceed $10 per person. Southern delegates also supported

Enslaved Population, 1790

Region	Total Population	Enslaved Population	Percentage of Population
New England	1,009,522	3,886	0.38%
Middle Atlantic	1,017,726	45,371	4.46%
South	1,866,387	645,023	34.56%
TOTAL	3,893,635	694,280	17.83%

Source: United States Census Bureau

the addition of the **fugitive slave clause** into Article 4 of the Constitution. This clause barred people who had escaped slavery in the South from living as free people in northern states.

Some delegates, especially those from northern states, wondered if the nation's ideals of freedom, liberty, and democracy could coexist alongside slavery. Benjamin Franklin wanted to abolish slavery from Pennsylvania altogether, but other representatives from northern free states approved the provisions. Most did not oppose slavery.

FREE AND OPEN TRADE

The southern representatives' other concern was the government's taxation of exports. The South's strong agricultural economy depended on the export of goods to other countries. Southerners believed that requiring foreign buyers to pay taxes on exported goods would hurt this trade. A weakened agricultural trade, in turn, would hurt the southern economy. The delegates agreed.

The Constitution placed few limits on the nation's commerce. One exception was the **commerce clause**, which gave Congress the power "to

Washington and Slavery
George Washington speaks with an overseer at his Mount Vernon farm in this 1851 painting by Junius Brutus Stearns. Twenty-five of the 55 delegates to the Convention owned slaves. Only Washington would grant some of his slaves freedom. His will specified that 123 of the 317 slaves at Mount Vernon be freed upon the death of his wife. Instead, Martha Washington freed them in 1800, before she died.

regulate commerce with foreign nations, and among the several states, and with the Indian tribes." Under the commerce clause, Native American tribes were considered sovereign governments and were not subject to the same regulations as states. The coinage clause required all states to use common coinage, or the same kind of money. Finally, according to the full-faith and credit clause, all states were required to respect the public acts, records, and judicial proceedings of all other states. Together, these three clauses gave Congress the authority to oversee interstate commerce and keep trade free and open among states. Delegates decided the country's economy would work under a **common market**, which meant that no tax could be charged on trade between states.

At last, the delegates had settled the most important issues for the new nation. Gouverneur Morris, a delegate from New York, perfected the wording of the proposed Constitution and organized it into seven articles, or main sections. On September 15, 1787, the delegates approved the final draft. They signed it two days later. As he observed the signing of the Constitution, Benjamin

Franklin commented that the sun on George Washington's chair at the Convention must be a rising sun. The United States was at the beginning, and not the end, of its time.

Thirty-nine of the 55 Convention delegates, or more than two-thirds, signed the document. Some delegates who approved of the final draft did not sign it because they were not in attendance. After it was signed, the Constitution was sent to the states for ratification and became the subject of yet more debate.

HISTORICAL THINKING

1. **READING CHECK** How did the Constitution reflect specific concerns of southern states?

2. **ANALYZE DATA** Why did southern delegates want to insert clauses about slavery into the Constitution? Use evidence from the population chart and the text to support your answer.

3. **MAKE GENERALIZATIONS** What advantages did the states experience under the common market?

3.1 Federalists and Antifederalists

Sometimes a fight between two people can spread until everyone takes a side. After the Constitutional Convention, citizens in the new nation faced this situation as two separate groups argued that their ideal vision was the right one.

MAIN IDEA Americans with opposite views about a strong central government engaged in intense debates over the ratification of the Constitution.

DIFFERENT POINTS OF VIEW

September 17, 1787, was a big day for the new United States. It was the day its Framers signed the Constitution. However, after it was signed, much more work was yet to come. Every state legislature had to ratify this new document. Given the spirited debates at the Constitutional Convention itself, it is not surprising that legislators and citizens quickly split into two factions. Those who supported the Constitution as it was written were known as **federalists**. Those who opposed all or parts of the Constitution were called **antifederalists**.

As you have read, federalism is a principle of governing in which a strong national government shares powers with the states. Federalists tended to live in big coastal cities and work in commerce. They hoped for more international trade and wanted to establish a strong and stable federal government. Some federalists were also frontier settlers, and they believed a strong central government could help defend them against attacks by Native Americans.

Antifederalists believed the Constitution did not provide strong enough barriers against the potential abuse of power by the federal government. They favored giving more power to state governments and believed only a government closest to the people could properly protect their liberties. Antifederalists tended to be from more rural areas, and they perceived the federal government as distant and separate from their interests. Antifederalists Patrick Henry and **George Mason**, a delegate from Virginia, gave impassioned speeches criticizing the Constitution.

Many newspapers supported the federalist cause. In New York, James Madison, Alexander Hamilton, and **John Jay**, who had been working behind the scenes in helping to craft the new government, published a series of essays in newspapers that argued in favor of the Constitution. In the spring of 1788, they published a book of the 85 essays called *The Federalist*. Despite these convincing essays, some key states, such as North Carolina, Virginia, and New York, resisted ratification at first.

RATIFYING THE CONSTITUTION

Each state held a convention to debate and vote on the Constitution. Delaware was the first to ratify, followed by Pennsylvania, New Jersey, Georgia, Connecticut, and Massachusetts. Except for Pennsylvania, all these states had small populations. Delegates to conventions in these states understood the advantages of joining a union in which their representation was equal to that of larger states. In Pennsylvania, federalists led by James Wilson moved quickly to secure ratification before antifederalists in the rural west could organize.

Many state constitutions already included a bill of rights, and the federalists argued that for this reason, another bill of rights was unnecessary. But in Virginia, antifederalists George Mason and Patrick Henry argued that adding a bill of rights to the Constitution was necessary to protect individuals and states and to prevent abuse of power by the federal government. Political writer Mercy Otis Warren also advocated for a bill of rights. In 1788, horrified by the violence she witnessed during Shays's Rebellion, she argued that the revolutionaries did not fight against Britain only to meet with more tyranny.

In 1939, Congress commissioned artist Howard Chandler Christy to paint *Signing of the Constitution* in honor of the 150-year anniversary of the Constitution. It is an enormous work, 20 by 30 feet in size, and it hangs in the House wing of the U.S. Capitol. In this painting, Christy depicts the events of September 17, 1787.

George Washington stands in front of his Rising Sun chair during the signing, which was held at Independence Hall. The 81-year-old Ben Franklin listens to something Alexander Hamilton is telling him, and Richard Spaight signs the document. How does this painting convey the importance of the event it depicts?

By July 1788, all but two states—North Carolina and Rhode Island—had voted for ratification. Rhode Island, again a holdout, refused to ratify the Constitution until a list of changes was included. The vote for ratification was so close that James Madison finally proposed to Congress that a set of 12 official **amendments**, or changes, be added to the Constitution to provide greater constitutional protection for individual liberties. The states ratified 10 of these amendments, and Congress added them to the Constitution. These amendments, which place specific restrictions on governmental power, became known as the **Bill of Rights**. Together, the Constitution and the Bill of Rights have provided the foundation for the U.S. government for more than 200 years.

HISTORICAL THINKING

1. **READING CHECK** What were the main arguments between the federalists and the antifederalists?

2. **COMPARE AND CONTRAST** What are some general characteristics of the people who identified as federalists and those who identified as antifederalists?

3. **DESCRIBE** Why did Congress add the Bill of Rights to the Constitution?

3.2 Constitutional Debates

Legislators and ordinary citizens had a lot to say both for and against ratifying the proposed Constitution. As people on both sides of the debate published their arguments, it became clear that some kind of compromise was necessary for this plan of government to survive.

Federalists and antifederalists circulated their opinions to appeal to and persuade their audiences. As you have read, Alexander Hamilton, John Jay, and James Madison published *The Federalist* in support of ratification of the Constitution as written. Writer

George Mason argued against the Constitution without certain guarantees. Writing under the pen name of "A Columbian Patriot," Mercy Otis Warren presented a strong antifederalist argument, which antifederalist newspapers used to challenge federalist ideas.

CRITICAL VIEWING John Singleton Copley painted this 1763 portrait of Mercy Otis Warren. Warren grew up in a wealthy and politically active family. Though she did not receive a formal education, she became a poet, a playwright, and a historian. Her social position allowed her a unique view of the events of the American Revolution. What details in her portrait convey her social status?

DOCUMENT ONE

Primary Source: Essay
from "Federalist No. 1," by Alexander Hamilton, 1788

Originally appearing as an anonymous series of 85 newspaper essays in favor of the Constitution, the authors' work was bound into the book *The Federalist* in 1788. These essays are considered among the most important examples of political philosophy in American history. This excerpt, from the first essay, was written by Hamilton.

CONSTRUCTED RESPONSE What was the author's opinion about a strong government versus the opinions of those who advocated for more rights for the people?

History will teach us that [dangerous ambition] has been found a much more certain road to the introduction of despotism [government with an absolute ruler] than the [firmness and efficiency of government], and that of those men who have overturned the liberties of republics, the greatest number have begun their career by paying . . . court to the people; commencing demagogues [absolute rulers], and ending tyrants.

DOCUMENT TWO

Primary Source: Essay
from "Objections to the Constitution of Government Formed by the Convention," by George Mason, 1787

During the Constitutional Convention in 1787, George Mason wrote an essay about why he refused to sign the Constitution. In his essay, which was published in the *Virginia Journal*, Mason predicted what would become of the union if individual rights weren't made clear. His ideas reflected principles in the Declaration of Independence.

CONSTRUCTED RESPONSE How does Mason's essay about government differ from ideas expressed in *The Federalist*?

This government will set out a moderate aristocracy [a class system based on birth or wealth]: it is at present impossible to foresee whether it will, in its operation, produce a monarchy, or a corrupt, tyrannical aristocracy; it will most probably vibrate some years between the two, and then terminate in the one or the other.

DOCUMENT THREE

Primary Source: Essay
from "Observations on the New Constitution," by Mercy Otis Warren, 1788

As a woman in the new United States, Mercy Otis Warren could not vote or take part in any conventions or lawmaking. That did not stop her from voicing a strong antifederalist viewpoint in the hopes of swaying those who had the power to ratify or reject the Constitution.

CONSTRUCTED RESPONSE What concerns about the Constitution did Warren express?

[The] Constitution, which, by the undefined meaning of some parts, and the ambiguities of expression in others, is dangerously adapted to the purposes of . . . tyranny. There is no security in the proffered [presented] system, either for the rights of conscience, or liberty of the press. There are no well-defined limits of the Judiciary Powers. The Executive and Legislative are so dangerously blended as to give just cause of alarm.

SYNTHESIZE & WRITE

1. **REVIEW** Review what you have learned about the arguments for and against the ratification of the Constitution.

2. **RECALL** On your own paper, write details about the arguments in favor of and opposed to the ratification of the Constitution, as revealed by the three excerpts.

3. **CONSTRUCT** Construct a topic sentence that answers this question: What were the main philosophies that supported the arguments for and against the ratification of the Constitution?

4. **WRITE** Using evidence from this chapter and the documents, write an informative paragraph that supports your topic sentence in Step 3.

3.3 The Bill of Rights

Americans enjoy many rights every day, from freely expressing opinions in public and in the press to protesting government actions. These and other fundamental rights are part of our identity as a nation, and we have the Framers of the Constitution to thank for them.

MAIN IDEA The Framers included a Bill of Rights in the Constitution to protect the fundamental rights and individual liberties of all citizens.

AMENDING THE CONSTITUTION

In 1787, the United States Constitution represented a bold new way of governing based on the consent of the governed. It also established a government that has survived for more than 200 years. Its survival has resulted from the control of power and interests through a system of checks and balances. Through Article 5, the Constitution provided a process by which it could adapt to the needs of a changing society. This process made possible a series of amendments protecting individual liberties from governmental abuses.

In order to amend, or change, the Constitution, Congress or two-thirds of the state legislatures must propose an amendment. Then three-fourths of the state legislatures must approve it. If they do, the amendment is ratified. This vigorous process helps protect citizens from unreasonable amendments.

Congress added the first 10 amendments, known as the Bill of Rights, to the Constitution in 1791. The amendments were intended to protect the freedoms of life, liberty, and the pursuit of happiness—all ideals that were put forth in the Declaration of Independence.

INDIVIDUAL FREEDOMS

The First Amendment protects fundamental individual freedoms: freedom of religion, freedom of speech and the press, and freedom of peaceful assembly and petitioning. In 1786,

THE BILL OF RIGHTS	
FIRST AMENDMENT	Freedoms of speech, religion, the press, and the right to peacefully assemble and to petition the government
SECOND AMENDMENT	The right to form a well-regulated militia and to keep and bear arms
THIRD AMENDMENT	Protection from being forced to quarter soldiers
FOURTH AMENDMENT	Protection against searches and seizures without a warrant based on reasonable grounds
FIFTH AMENDMENT	The right of an arrested individual to know what he or she is accused of; protection against being tried for the same crime twice; protection against unjustified deprivation of life, liberty, or property; the right to refuse to testify against oneself
SIXTH AMENDMENT	The right to a fair and speedy trial by jury; the right to a lawyer
SEVENTH AMENDMENT	The right to a jury trial in certain civil cases
EIGHTH AMENDMENT	Protection against excessive bail and cruel or unusual punishment
NINTH AMENDMENT	Protection against others taking away rights not mentioned in the Bill of Rights
TENTH AMENDMENT	The right of states and citizens to retain powers not given to the federal government

See the Citizenship Handbook for the full text of the United States Constitution.

CRITICAL VIEWING On August 28, 1963, 250,000 participants at the March on Washington for Jobs and Freedom gathered in front of the Lincoln Memorial in Washington, D.C., where they heard speeches on issues of racial equality and economic justice. The event concluded with Dr. Martin Luther King, Jr., delivering his "I Have a Dream" speech. What does this photo convey about the participants' confidence in enjoying the protection of the First Amendment?

Thomas Jefferson wrote a **statute**, or a law written by a legislative body, for the state of Virginia that served as a forerunner to the First Amendment. In the Statute for Religious Freedom, Jefferson strongly advocated for religious liberty and the separation of church and state. Some delegates objected to including this idea in the Constitution, believing that the Constitution should reflect the nation's Christian foundation. Other delegates, such as James Madison, contended that safeguarding people's "natural right" to worship freely, or not worship at all, was more important. Because of the First Amendment, Americans have the right to practice any religion or no religion without fear of discrimination or persecution.

Freedom of the press, another First Amendment right, was a new concept in the 1780s, when governments routinely blocked the publication of stories they disliked. Governments also forced newspapers to print articles that suited their own purposes. The First Amendment made both acts illegal, and today the American press can report and publish freely. The First through Eighth

Amendments focus on individual rights. The Ninth Amendment protects any personal freedoms not specified in the Bill of Rights. The Tenth Amendment allows citizens and states to keep any powers not mentioned in the Constitution.

Throughout our nation's history, we, the people, have added additional amendments to the Constitution to expand and clarify our rights. These amendments have been vital to the development of an American identity. They have established many of the essential freedoms Americans enjoy today.

HISTORICAL THINKING

1. **READING CHECK** Why was protecting the rights and freedoms listed in the Bill of Rights important to citizens of the new nation?

2. **MAKE GENERALIZATIONS** In what ways are natural rights protected in the Bill of Rights?

3. **EXPLAIN** What requirements are involved for proposed and ratified amendments, and why is this process in place?

VOCABULARY

Write a sentence for each group of words that explains the relationship between them.

1. federalist / antifederalist

2. commerce clause / common market

3. legislative branch / executive branch / judicial branch

4. Bill of Rights / amendment

5. separation of powers / checks and balances

6. constitution / constitutionalism

7. statute / ordinance

8. sovereign / dual sovereignty

9. delegates / Framers

READING STRATEGY
DETERMINE CHRONOLOGY

If you haven't done so already, complete your sequence chain to show how the roles of state and federal governments evolved in the early United States. Then answer the question.

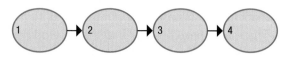

10. From 1776 to 1791, how did the role of the federal government develop in the United States?

MAIN IDEAS

Answer the following questions. Support your answers with evidence from the chapter.

11. In what ways did the Articles of Confederation limit the effectiveness of the national government? **LESSON 1.1**

12. What did the ordinances of 1785 and 1787 regulate? **LESSON 1.2**

13. What were Daniel Shays and his followers protesting? **LESSON 1.3**

14. What was the purpose of the Constitutional Convention of 1787? **LESSON 2.1**

15. What three principles did delegates at the Constitutional Convention want to include? **LESSON 2.1**

16. Why did the Framers insist on separation of powers in the Constitution? **LESSON 2.2**

17. How did the Great Compromise help both large and small states? **LESSON 2.2**

18. What was the Three-Fifths Compromise and who did it benefit? **LESSON 2.3**

19. How did James Madison, Alexander Hamilton, and John Jay present the arguments of the federalists? **LESSON 3.1**

20. Why was the Bill of Rights added to the Constitution? **LESSON 3.3**

HISTORICAL THINKING

Answer the following questions. Support your answers with evidence from the chapter.

21. **ANALYZE CAUSE AND EFFECT** What factors prompted leaders to work to replace the Articles of Confederation with a new constitution?

22. **IDENTIFY PROBLEMS AND SOLUTIONS** What problem did the establishment of the electoral college solve?

23. **SYNTHESIZE** How does the Bill of Rights represent the ideals that Americans fought for in the American Revolution?

24. **FORM AND SUPPORT OPINIONS** Do you think the Constitution reflects a fair balance between federalist and antifederalist arguments? Support your opinion with evidence from the chapter.

25. **EVALUATE** How did the Framers reconcile the ideals of freedom, liberty, and democracy with slavery?

26. **EXPLAIN** Why did James Wilson want a quick ratification of the Constitution?

This statue, called *Guardianship,* stands in front of the National Archives building in Washington, D.C., where the foundational documents of the United States are housed. The inscription at the base of the statue reads, "Eternal vigilance is the price of liberty." Study the statue and its inscription. Then answer the questions below.

ETERNAL VIGILANCE IS THE PRICE OF LIBERTY

27. Why might the inscription on this statue refer to "eternal vigilance," or keeping a careful watch over something, as the "price of liberty"?

28. *Guardianship* means taking care of something. In what ways were the Framers guardians of the new nation?

In 1788, as part of "Federalist No. 38," James Madison wrote the following opinion about the process of forming a government through history. Read the passage and answer the question.

It is a matter both of wonder and regret, that those who raise so many objections against the new Constitution should never call to mind the defects of that which is to be exchanged for it. It is not necessary that the former should be perfect; it is sufficient that the latter is more imperfect.

29. What is Madison saying to those who disagree with the new Constitution?

30. To what is Madison referring when he mentions "the defects of that which is to be exchanged for it"?

31. **NARRATIVE** Review the rights granted by the First Amendment. Think about a time when one of the rights played a role in your own life or that of someone you know. Write a paragraph connecting that right to your life as an American today.

TIPS

- Read through the text of the First Amendment. List the specific freedoms mentioned. Then choose a freedom that has had an impact on your life.

- Use textual evidence from the amendment in your paragraph. Cite the specific language used to describe the freedom, and then explain the impact that freedom has had on your life.

- Conclude the paragraph with a comment about what you think is most important about the First Amendment.

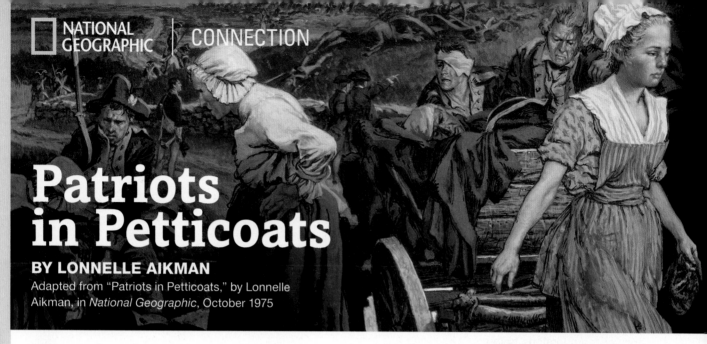

Patriots in Petticoats

BY LONNELLE AIKMAN

Adapted from "Patriots in Petticoats," by Lonnelle Aikman, in *National Geographic*, October 1975

Schooled in an untamed land of hardships, the women of colonial America were conditioned to independence. They grew their own food, sewed their own clothing, and made their own medicines. All this, while rearing children and running their families.

Given their willingness to endure, women in colonial America were more than ready to give up imported luxuries rather than submit to British taxation. Better, they said, to wear plain homespun dresses than to wear European imports. As for British tea, there were plenty of native substitutes—such as sage and currant—which they brewed and served as Liberty Tea. As the war began and spread, women of all classes, from frontier wives to managers of great plantations, participated fully in the conflict. Throughout the colonies, women replaced soldier-husbands in fields and shops and often spied on the enemy.

Abigail Adams, one of the first American women patriots, promoted activities from sewing uniforms to making bullets. She fed and sheltered soldiers and welcomed temporary refugees from neighboring towns. She also provided military and political intelligence to her husband by reporting on enemy troops and ships, as well as on Tories, inflation, and other American problems. John Adams appreciated Abigail's specific and accurate information, saying that she supplied him "with dearer and fuller Intelligence, than I can get from a whole Committee of Gentlemen."

Martha Washington traveled with General Washington throughout the war, which may astonish those who think of her as a sheltered elite. She was with him in New York City, Morristown, Valley Forge, and Middlebrook, and she helped him through two mutinies by his starving troops. Even after the guns were silent, Martha was with George while both waited impatiently for news of the final peace treaty in 1783.

If following the army was hard on the general's wife, it was more challenging for the ordinary women who trudged with the troops. Armies reluctantly allowed women to work alongside their husbands and other men of the corps, to carry water, to swab cannons, and to ease the wounded on the battlefield.

Some women fought side-by-side with men, including Margaret Cochran Corbin. When her husband John joined an artillery corps, Margaret went along. "Molly," as her comrades called her, helped the gunner's team swab out the bore and ram down the ammunition. When John was shot and killed, Margaret jumped into his battle station. Then she, too, went down, her shoulder torn by grapeshot. She never regained the use of her arm. Recognizing her courage under fire, Congress made her the first woman to receive a pension from the United States.

An equally brave woman posed as a man in order to fight. When Deborah Sampson was a child, poverty forced her widowed mother to give her up for indentured service. She emerged a strong woman, quite able to take on men's work. When the Revolution began, she made herself a man's suit, walked to a recruiting post in another town, and enlisted as Robert Shurtleff. She was wounded twice but managed to keep her secret until she went to Philadelphia as a general's orderly. There she came down with a "malignant fever" and was sent to a hospital, where a startled doctor discovered that she was a woman.

Martha Washington, Deborah Sampson, and Abigail Adams were women of strength who continue to capture the spotlight of history. Behind them stand all those others, the nameless Founding Mothers, without whom independence would have been impossible.

For more from National Geographic, check out "Two Revolutions" online.

UNIT INQUIRY: Prepare an Argument

In this unit, you learned about the factors that led to the American Revolution, the war itself, and the creation of the Constitution. Use what you learned from the text and do further research if necessary to determine why all colonists didn't support separating from Great Britain.

ASSIGNMENT

Prepare an argument for or against independence from Great Britain from the perspective of a Patriot and a Loyalist, respectively. Your arguments should offer examples of the benefits and drawbacks or risks involved in becoming independent from Great Britain. Be prepared to present both sides to your class.

Gather Evidence As you consider both sides of the argument, use what you learned in this unit to think of the reasons an American colonist would have either supported or opposed the separation from Great Britain. Make a list of these reasons, and try to incorporate them into your argument. Use a table like this one to help organize your evidence.

Patriot Reasons	Loyalist Reasons

Produce Use your notes to craft a solid argument for both sides of the issue—thinking like a Loyalist and like a Patriot. You may wish to write the arguments in paragraph form or bullet points on index cards and label them either "Patriot" or "Loyalist."

Present Choose a creative way to present both sides of this debate to the class. Consider one of these options:

- Use two different props, such as different hats, to transform yourself into a Patriot and a Loyalist. Wearing the Patriot hat, give a short speech expressing why it makes sense for the colonies to separate from Great Britain. Then put on the Loyalist hat and give a short speech expressing the other side of the debate. Alternate between Patriot and Loyalist hats to change your persona and add to each side of the argument.

- Organize your classmates into teams (Patriots and Loyalists). Familiarize each team with one side of the argument, and have a classroom debate about the benefits or dangers of separating from Great Britain.

NATIONAL GEOGRAPHIC | LEARNING FRAMEWORK ACTIVITIES

Research a Colonial American

ATTITUDE Curiosity

KNOWLEDGE Our Human Story

Choose one of the historical figures from this unit that you are still curious about, and do online research to learn more about him or her. Develop a biography for this individual in a traditional written format, or do something more visual, such as a poster or digital presentation. You could even give a costumed speech to your class as that individual. Be sure your biography—in whatever form it takes—includes common information such as birth and death dates, where the person lived, and the work he or she did. Also consider including information about how this person influenced colonial America, how the American Revolution or the Constitution might have been different without him or her, and the legacy this person left behind.

Build a Time Line

SKILLS Collaboration, Communication

KNOWLEDGE Our Human Story

Work with a partner or small group to capture the "story" of the formation of the United States in the form of a time line. First discuss how your time line will work. For example, decide if it will flow left to right or top to bottom, how it will be divided into intervals, and when the time line will start and end. Then refer to the chapters in this unit to determine which significant events will be included on your time line. Once you have gathered the information you need, work together to craft the physical time line. Consider the following questions: Will you use a symbol or color to represent types of events, such as battles? Will you use each side of the time line to represent different events or eras? What will make your time line clear and easy to read?

THE EARLY REPUBLIC

The Rotunda, University of Virginia
Charlottesville, Virginia

Thomas Jefferson designed the Rotunda, his greatest architectural work, when he was 70 years old. With its domed top and graceful columns, the Rotunda is modeled after a temple in ancient Rome. The Rotunda's interior contains a library, said to be one of the most beautiful rooms in America, as well as classrooms and lecture halls. Jefferson founded the University of Virginia and had that achievement—but not his term as president of the United States—commemorated on his gravestone.

CRITICAL VIEWING What words would you use to describe the Rotunda?

UNIT 4 — THE EARLY REPUBLIC

THE UNITED STATES

1797
John Adams, a Federalist, becomes president, while Thomas Jefferson, a Democratic-Republican, becomes vice president.

1803
Thomas Jefferson sends Meriwether Lewis and William Clark on an expedition to explore the western territory included in the Louisiana Purchase. *(coin featuring Sacagawea, Lewis and Clark's Native American interpreter)*

1789
George Washington takes office as president and sets up his government.

1780

1800

1789 EUROPE
France explodes into revolution against the royal ruling class.

1799 EUROPE
Napoleon Bonaparte seizes control of the French government. *(statue of Napoleon on horseback)*

THE WORLD

1812

The War of 1812 erupts between Britain and the United States over British violations of American rights at sea. *(American infantry drum used during the War of 1812)*

HISTORICAL THINKING: DETERMINE CHRONOLOGY

Which strong leaders came to power within ten years of each other?

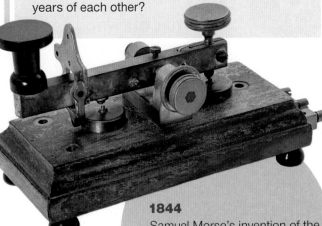

1844

Samuel Morse's invention of the telegraph allows messages to be sent between Washington, D.C., and Baltimore, Maryland. *(early telegraph developed by Samuel Morse)*

1813

As the textile industry expands during the Industrial Revolution, the first Lowell mill is built in Massachusetts.

1831

Nat Turner leads an armed rebellion in an effort to free the slaves.

1820

1840

1833 EUROPE

Britain abolishes slavery in the British Empire.

1836 AFRICA

The Boers, farmers of Dutch, French, and German descent, undertake their "Great Trek" through southern Africa.

1821 AMERICAS

Venezuela gains independence from Spain.

1839–1842 ASIA

The first Opium War is fought between China and Britain after the Chinese government tries to stop the trade of opium in its country. *(Chinese junk boat similar to those used by China during the Opium War)*

GROWING PAINS
IN THE NEW REPUBLIC
1789–1800

ESSENTIAL QUESTION
What challenges did Americans in the
new republic confront?

AMERICAN STORIES ONLINE   **George Washington's Mount Vernon**

SECTION 1 **Washington's Presidency**

KEY VOCABULARY

attorney general	national debt
Cabinet	precedent
Chief Justice	tariff
inauguration	

SECTION 2 **Politics in the 1790s**

KEY VOCABULARY

Alien and Sedition Acts	radical
cede	sedition
envoy	states' rights
French Revolution	strict interpretation
loose interpretation	Treaty of Greenville
power base	Whiskey Rebellion
	XYZ Affair

AMERICAN GALLERY ONLINE   **Federal Washington**

READING STRATEGY

**IDENTIFY PROBLEMS
AND SOLUTIONS**

By identifying problems and
solutions, you can better
understand why decision-
makers took the courses of
action they did. As you read
the chapter, use a graphic
organizer like this one to
identify and analyze each
problem the new nation faced
and how it was solved.

Issue: After the Revolution, the nation
and individual states had huge debts.

↓

Problem 1: Foreign governments were waiting to be paid.

Problem 2:

Problem 3:

↓

Solution:

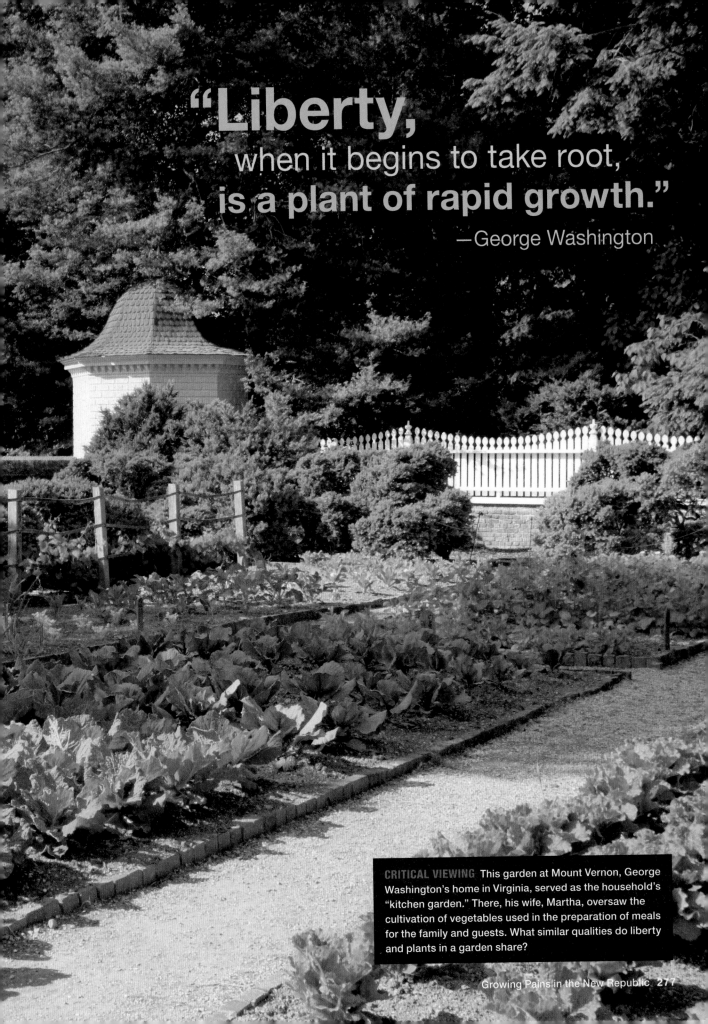

"Liberty,
when it begins to take root,
is a plant of rapid growth."

—George Washington

CRITICAL VIEWING This garden at Mount Vernon, George Washington's home in Virginia, served as the household's "kitchen garden." There, his wife, Martha, oversaw the cultivation of vegetables used in the preparation of meals for the family and guests. What similar qualities do liberty and plants in a garden share?

1.1 Setting Up the Government

Would you want to be president of the United States? You might be surprised to hear that George Washington did *not* want the job. He knew that being the first president of the new country wouldn't be easy. But his countrymen wanted Washington.

MAIN IDEA The Constitution established some guidelines, but for the first president, starting up the new government was a complex and difficult undertaking.

THE FIRST PRESIDENT

George Washington was the obvious choice to be the nation's first president—he was a dignified man of strong character. Better yet, he was a natural leader, which he had proved during the American Revolution. Success in the new republic was not at all assured, but Washington accepted the challenge. Even though he didn't want the job, Washington guided the new government through its early years.

As the newly written Constitution directed, the electoral college determined who would be president in this first election—not the people. Every one of the 69 electors voted for Washington. The reluctant candidate won hands down. John Adams, who was runner-up, became the vice president.

On April 23, 1789, thousands of cheering citizens in New York City, the country's temporary capital, welcomed Washington. He took the oath of office a week later and began his difficult task. Washington had to invent the role of president as he went along. "My station is new; and . . . [I] walk on untrodden ground," he wrote in a letter. Everything he did would set a **precedent**, or establish an example, for all future presidents.

🏛 The Clark Art Institute Williamstown, Massachusetts

Gilbert Stuart painted 104 portraits of George Washington, including the one shown here, which was painted some time between 1796 and 1803. John Jay, whom you may remember as an author of *The Federalist* papers, introduced Washington to the painter. Stuart began creating his likenesses of the president in 1795. Washington became extremely impatient sitting for his portrait, however. Even though Stuart was known as an entertaining conversationalist, Washington remained mostly silent during their sessions.

Washington particularly wanted to make it clear that he was *president* of the United States, not its *king*. He dressed plainly for his **inauguration**, the ceremony that marked the beginning of his presidency, in an American-made brown suit. And he refused to be called "His Excellency" or "Your Highness," as John Adams had suggested. After much debate, Washington decided that "Mr. President" would do just fine.

AN OCEAN OF DIFFICULTIES

Once in office, Washington got to work—and there was a lot to do. As he himself described it, the nation faced "an ocean of difficulties." The new government had to deal with problems within the country as well as conflicts in the Northwest Territory and wars across the Atlantic.

To tackle all these situations, both the president and Congress had certain responsibilities and powers, as spelled out in the Constitution. Essentially, Congress would make the laws, and the president would ensure they were carried out.

But not everything was covered in the Constitution. Here, too, Washington set precedents. For example, he took control of treaty negotiations, bypassing Congress, and established a policy of neutrality in foreign conflicts—insisting it was within the president's power to do so.

Fortunately, the framers of the Constitution did foresee the need for departments to assist the president. Congress had the power to create the departments, and the president decided who would head them. Together, the heads of the departments are called a **Cabinet**.

Washington picked men from a variety of geographical areas and with a mix of political views for his Cabinet. He strongly advocated political moderation and tried to keep himself, as president, above the bickering that went on between political factions. That way, he believed, he could do what was best for the country. Washington appointed a group of highly talented men to his Cabinet—and hoped they'd put aside their political differences, too.

The First Inaugural Address

Washington wasn't required to give a speech at his inauguration, but he decided to do so. Every president since has done the same. To mark the occasion, people attending the ceremony could purchase copper buttons, like the ones below, as souvenirs.

As he gave this First Inaugural Address, Washington was nervous. His hands and voice trembled, but his words were powerful: "The preservation of the sacred fire of liberty, and the destiny of the Republican model of government, are justly considered as deeply . . . staked on the experiment entrusted to the hands of the American people." In other words, the future of the country depended on the success of this new government.

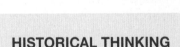

Washington inaugural souvenirs

HISTORICAL THINKING

1. **READING CHECK** Why did George Washington write that he was walking "on untrodden ground"?

2. **IDENTIFY PROBLEMS AND SOLUTIONS** How did Washington deal with treaty negotiations, since no process was spelled out in the Constitution?

3. **MAKE CONNECTIONS** How did Washington's presidency help establish an American identity?

AMERICAN PLACES

U.S. Treasury Building
Washington, D.C.

In the early years of the nation, the Department of the Treasury was housed in Philadelphia. When the capital moved to Washington, D.C., so did the Treasury. After two Treasury Buildings burned down, construction on a final structure began in 1836—and this time, its architects made it fireproof. A statue of Alexander Hamilton stands before the south entrance of the building, shown here.

THE TREASURY DEPARTMENT

1.2 Cabinet and Courts

Imagine trying to play a game of soccer or basketball without any teammates. It wouldn't work. George Washington didn't guide the new country alone, either. He gathered an A-list of team members to help him.

MAIN IDEA The first order of business for George Washington and Congress was to assemble a presidential Cabinet and create a court system.

ASSEMBLING A TEAM

In the summer of 1789, Congress created the Departments of State, Treasury, and War as part of the executive branch. Washington appointed the department heads, called secretaries, and they formed his Cabinet.

To oversee relations with other countries, Washington chose Thomas Jefferson as Secretary of State. As Secretary of War, former general Henry Knox would see to the country's defense. And to manage the government's money, Washington selected Alexander Hamilton as Secretary of the Treasury. Congress also created the office of the **attorney general**, whose primary role was to represent the United States before the Supreme Court. He would be a member of Washington's Cabinet, but unlike the others, he would not head an executive department. Edmund Randolph served as the first attorney general.

The president called his Cabinet secretaries together for regular meetings. However, you might be surprised to learn that Vice President John Adams was *not* invited to these meetings. The vice president soon realized the limitations of his position. "My country," he wrote, "has in its wisdom contrived [designed] for me the most insignificant office that ever the invention of man contrived or his imagination conceived."

THE HIGHEST COURT IN THE LAND

In addition to building the Cabinet, Washington and Congress created a court system. The Constitution established a Supreme Court as the nation's highest court. But it left the question of how many justices would sit on the Court to Congress and didn't specify what its powers would be. So, in 1789, Congress passed the Federal Judiciary Act. It called for the Supreme Court to have six justices—one **Chief Justice** and five associate justices. Today, eight associate justices sit on the court. The Chief Justice presides over the judicial branch of the U.S. government as well as over the Supreme Court itself. John Jay became the country's first Chief Justice.

The act created the world's first dual-court system, with responsibilities split between state and federal courts. Federal courts handled interstate and international cases, disputes regarding the U.S. Constitution, and civil and criminal cases relating to federal laws. State courts dealt with cases involving state laws and civil disputes within states. The act also created lower, or less powerful, federal courts.

The federal government established executive departments and a working system of courts, but more challenges lay in store. For one thing, there was the small matter of a very large war debt to be paid.

HISTORICAL THINKING

1. **READING CHECK** What departments made up Washington's Cabinet?

2. **DRAW CONCLUSIONS** What do the Cabinet departments suggest about what was important to the new government?

3. **MAKE INFERENCES** Why do you think the Federal Judiciary Act created both state and federal courts?

Hamilton's Economic Plan

Can you spare a cool $54 million? The American Revolution was a success, but that's how much the Patriots had to borrow to pull it off. Now it was time to pay back the debt. The question was how?

> **MAIN IDEA** The United States had to develop an economic strategy for the new nation, but conflicting political points of view made planning difficult.

THE PRICE OF WAR

In addition to America's whopping **national debt**, individual states collectively owed another $25 million. Foreign governments and Americans who had helped finance the war were waiting to be repaid. Secretary of the Treasury Alexander Hamilton wanted the U.S. government to demonstrate it could be trusted to take care of its financial responsibilities. Doing so would improve America's credit and encourage new business.

An ardent federalist, Hamilton suggested that the federal government assume, or take over, the war debts of each state. This strategy would give the government more power to run the country's financial affairs. Under Hamilton's plan, sales of federal lands in the West would finance the repayment of European loans. More money would come from increased **tariffs**, or taxes on imports and exports. Tariffs would also encourage Americans to buy American goods, which would help protect industries from foreign competition.

Hamilton suggested the government pay off the rest of its debts by levying, or charging, certain taxes and by issuing new bonds, or investments promising interest on money

loaned. Investors would buy these bonds because the interest would produce big profits over the long run. Finally, to stabilize the nation's finances, Hamilton proposed a common currency and a National Bank. This bank would collect taxes, hold government funds, and promote business and industry by issuing loans. Hamilton envisioned the United States as a strong industrial nation.

The engraving of Alexander Hamilton, shown here, appears on the ten-dollar bill. Very narrow lines are used to create the engravings on U.S. money, making them so detailed that it is virtually impossible to copy exactly, or counterfeit, paper money.

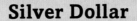

Silver Dollar

During the American Revolution, individual states and the Continental Congress printed their own paper money. Those notes lost value very quickly and were worth almost nothing by the end of the war. Later, when the Constitution gave Congress the sole power to issue national currency, Alexander Hamilton recommended the nation adopt a silver dollar coin. He also suggested using fractional coins to represent smaller parts of a dollar. The Coinage Act of 1792 established the United States Mint—a facility for manufacturing coins—and regulated the coinage of the United States.

The act established the dollar, half-dollar, quarter-dollar, "disme," "half-disme," cent, and half-cent as the denominations of coins. The word *disme* became what we know as "dime." A "half-disme" is now a nickel.

The first dollar coin, called the "Flowing Hair Dollar," from 1794, showed Liberty as a woman on one side (top) and an eagle surrounded by a wreath on the other (bottom). In 1790, you could have used this coin to buy a bag or two of groceries. Ten of the coins could buy you a cow.

CRITICS WEIGH IN

Thomas Jefferson, on the other hand, envisioned an agricultural nation. He and other antifederalists opposed the strong central government and National Bank that Hamilton envisioned. A National Bank, they feared, would favor the interests of business over agriculture—specifically, the interests of the industrial North over those of the agricultural South. And southern states had even more reasons to oppose Hamilton's plan. Most had already paid their war debts. Hamilton ultimately won the South's favor by promising to relocate the nation's capital to Virginia, in an area that would eventually become Washington, D.C., the current capital of the United States.

Jefferson also opposed a National Bank because he believed it would give the federal government unlimited powers and go against the Constitution. But since the Constitution didn't expressly forbid the creation of a National Bank, Hamilton claimed the federal government had every right to establish one. Congress agreed. In 1791, it passed a bill creating a National Bank for a term of 20 years, and President Washington, who also supported Hamilton's views, signed it into law. In December of 1791, the Bank of the United States opened its doors in Philadelphia. Branches soon were established in major cities such as Boston, New York, Charleston, and Baltimore.

Both Jefferson and Hamilton were dedicated to the success of the new administration and the country. However, each man often advised Washington to ignore the counsel of the other. This made them personal adversaries, or opponents. In a letter to Washington written in 1792, Jefferson claimed that Hamilton's allies in Congress were a "corrupt squadron [military unit]," whose "ultimate object . . . is to prepare the way for a change, from the present republican form of government, to that of a monarchy, of which the English constitution is the model." The very nasty and public feud that developed between Jefferson and Hamilton greatly distressed Washington.

HISTORICAL THINKING

1. **READING CHECK** Why did Hamilton think it was crucial for the United States to repay its debts to European nations right away?

2. **COMPARE AND CONTRAST** Describe Jefferson's and Hamilton's different visions for the new nation.

3. **IDENTIFY PROBLEMS AND SOLUTIONS** How did Hamilton propose to pay off the national debt?

1.4 Broadway, New York City

New York's theater district revolves around a street you've probably heard of—Broadway. Some 40 theaters make up this famous district, including the Majestic, the Gershwin, and the Richard Rodgers Theatre, where ***Hamilton: An American Musical*** (shown below) made its Broadway debut in 2015. Since the early 1900s, small theaters have nestled between large ones under the glow of colorful signs advertising the latest productions. Countless actors have launched their careers in Broadway shows like ***Cats***, ***The Phantom of the Opera***, ***Mamma Mia!***, and ***The Lion King***, because if you've made it to Broadway, you've made it big. How is theater a part of American culture?

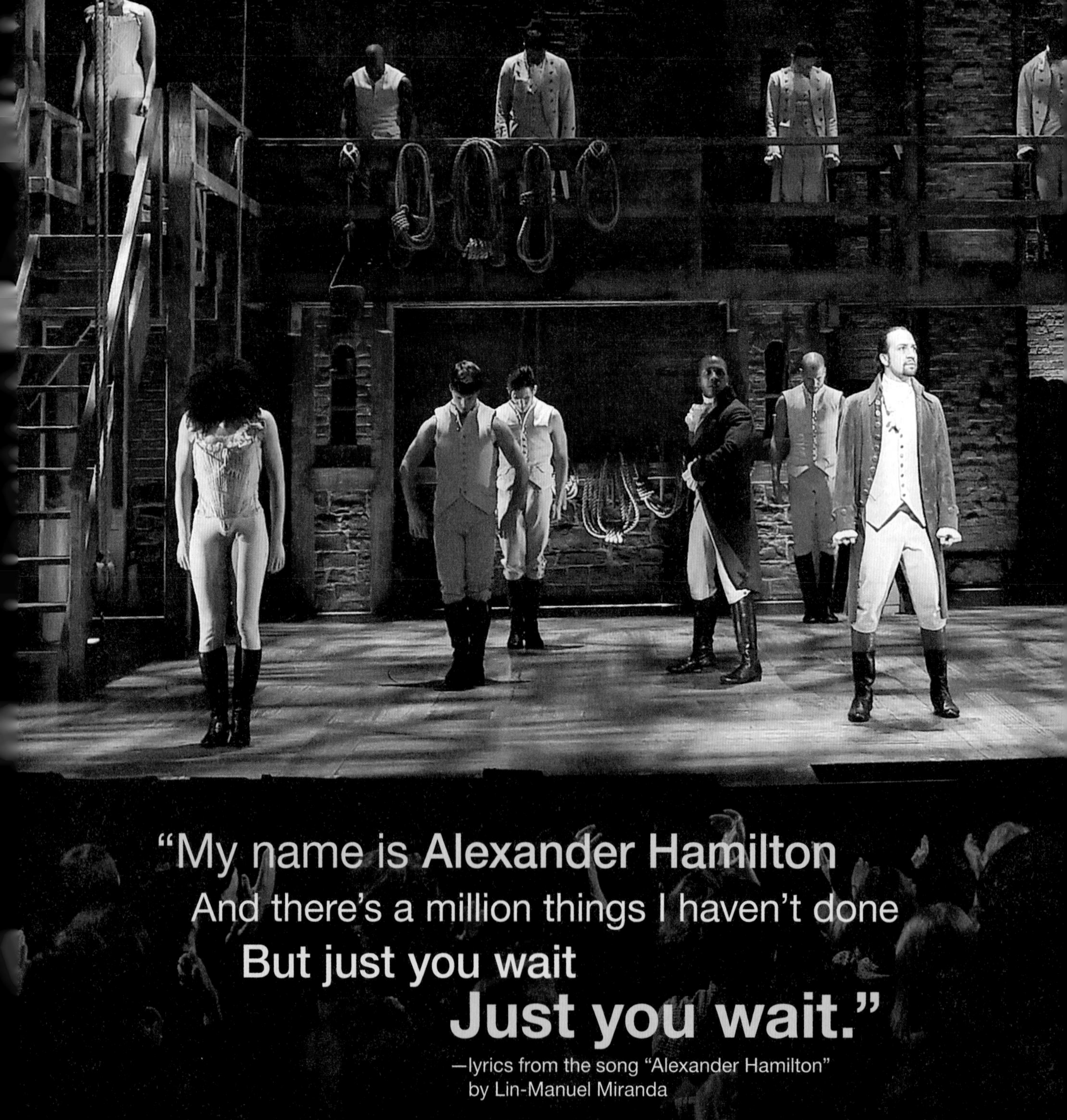

"My name is Alexander Hamilton
And there's a million things I haven't done
But just you wait
Just you wait."

—lyrics from the song "Alexander Hamilton" by Lin-Manuel Miranda

CRITICAL VIEWING Tony Award-winning *Hamilton* is likely the most unique Broadway production in decades. The hip-hop musical tells the story of Founding Father Alexander Hamilton, who authored several of the Federalist Papers. Actor Lin-Manuel Miranda (center) played Hamilton on Broadway to sold-out crowds and critical acclaim. Based on the photo, how do you think *Hamilton* connects a modern audience to American history?

2.1 Political Parties Form

You've probably seen the ads. "Vote for me! Don't vote for" — whomever. The candidates are usually from different political parties. You can thank (or blame) Hamilton and Jefferson for laying the groundwork for such parties.

MAIN IDEA Leaders formed political parties to promote their ideas, forming the basis of the modern American political system.

TAKING SIDES

During the 1790s, many congressional representatives sided with either Hamilton, who fought for a strong central government, or Jefferson, who feared the power such a government could wield. Eventually, the two sides formed two political parties—the **Federalist Party** and the **Democratic-Republican Party**. The Federalists backed Hamilton. The Democratic-Republicans sided more with Jefferson.

The Constitution made no provision for political parties, but it did not prohibit them. Still, the idea of divided political parties shocked the older leaders of the Revolutionary era. Washington warned against their "baneful [harmful] effects." If they were to play any role at all, he said, they needed to be kept in check. But the process was now in motion. Political parties had established themselves as a powerful force, and sides had been taken.

FACING OFF

On one side stood the Federalist Party, whose **power base**, or area of biggest influence, was in New England and the Middle Atlantic states. John Adams, Washington's vice president, joined the Federalists. They favored commercial development, a National Bank, the development of infrastructure to build canals, roads, and schools through land grants, and high tariffs to spur manufacturing. They also believed in a **loose interpretation** of the Constitution—one that gave broad powers to Congress and the president. Federalists were more likely than their opponents to be critical of slavery and so gained the allegiance of free African Americans in both the North and the South. Because their power base

lay in the Northeast, many Federalists didn't back the idea of western expansion and sometimes supported the rights of Native Americans.

On the other side was the Democratic-Republican Party, whose power base was in the South and the West. The party included many former antifederalists. Like Jefferson, the Democratic-Republicans believed in a **strict interpretation** of the Constitution—one that strictly followed the document and honored the rights of states over federal power. They opposed too much federal support for manufacturing and commerce. With its southern backing, the party rejected efforts to abolish slavery. Because it favored westward expansion and had little sympathy for the rights of Native Americans, the party also had the support of westerners on the frontier. The fundamental tension created by the development of a two-party system continues to influence American politics today.

In addition to these internal divisions within the government, the United States had to confront more fundamental challenges to its authority and legitimacy. Trouble was brewing in the Northwest Territory and abroad.

HISTORICAL THINKING

1. **READING CHECK** What regions of the United States supported each party, and why?

2. **IDENTIFY PROBLEMS AND SOLUTIONS** What problems might either a loose or strict interpretation of the Constitution create or solve?

3. **EVALUATE** What are the advantages and disadvantages of political parties?

Two-Party System

Although the parties have changed and shifted over the years, the United States still has two major political parties: the Democrats and the Republicans. A two-party system is relatively unique in the world. Some countries have only one party, while others have many. The symbols of each U.S. party are shown below: a donkey for the Democrats and an elephant for the Republicans. Neither modern party aligns closely with the political ideas of the Federalists or the Democratic-Republicans. However, like the parties in the 1790s, the parties today have regional characteristics. The Republicans tend to be stronger in the South and the West, and the Democrats stronger on the coasts, the Northeast, and the upper Midwest.

The campaign buttons shown are from the second half of the 20th century. Remember, though, that supporters purchased buttons honoring George Washington at his inauguration. In the 1840 election, people wore campaign buttons sewn on clothing. Pins were added around 1860, along with the first photograph to appear on a campaign button—a picture of Abraham Lincoln.

2.2 Competition for Territory and the French Revolution

George Washington had dealt with many challenging situations, but as president, he probably got more than he bargained for. As political conflict grew among U.S. citizens, conflicts over western lands heated to the boiling point.

MAIN IDEA As the young republic pushed west, conflicts both at home and abroad caused a host of challenges for the United States.

CONFLICTS IN THE WEST

The problem area was the Northwest Territory, located north of the Ohio River, between the western boundary of Pennsylvania and the Mississippi River. As you may remember, the Treaty of Paris of 1783 had established new boundaries for the United States and tried to settle claims on this land. But in the 1790s, the land seemed to be up for grabs once again. Spain, Britain, the United States, and Native American groups all claimed parts of the vast expanse for their own.

The United States mostly fought with Native Americans over rights to this land. Americans wanted to settle the land, not only for its rich soil but also for its minerals, such as copper, iron, and silver. Native Americans had lived in this region for thousands of years and attacked settlers who moved onto the land. In response, Washington sent in two military expeditions, but the Miami of Ohio, led by Chief Little Turtle, defeated them both. Then, in 1794, federal troops defeated the Miami at the Battle of Fallen Timbers. The British, who had usually helped the Miami, refused to protect them this time. They were tired of war. Without British support, the Miami and other Native Americans in the region signed the **Treaty of Greenville**, which **ceded**, or gave up, their lands in present-day Ohio and Indiana to the United States.

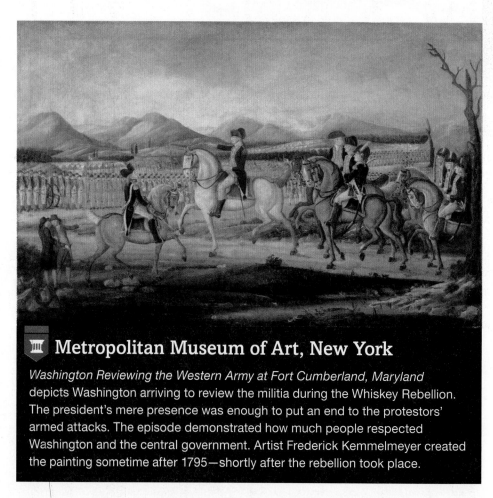

🏛 Metropolitan Museum of Art, New York

Washington Reviewing the Western Army at Fort Cumberland, Maryland depicts Washington arriving to review the militia during the Whiskey Rebellion. The president's mere presence was enough to put an end to the protestors' armed attacks. The episode demonstrated how much people respected Washington and the central government. Artist Frederick Kemmelmeyer created the painting sometime after 1795—shortly after the rebellion took place.

Meanwhile, another conflict brewed in western Pennsylvania. Farmers had been protesting a whiskey tax, claiming it was unfair. Secretary of the Treasury Alexander Hamilton had proposed the tax, which was passed by Congress in 1791 to raise money to pay down the national debt. The angry farmers who made, consumed, sold, and traded whiskey, tarred and feathered tax collectors and threatened armed attacks in what is known as the **Whiskey Rebellion**. President Washington sent nearly 13,000 soldiers into the region to demonstrate the power of the federal government. The rebels soon stood down.

THE FRENCH REVOLUTION

Across the Atlantic, the people in France were involved in a rebellion of their own. They sought to put an end to upper-class privilege and demanded equality for the lower classes. Many in the United States, and particularly the Democratic-Republicans, supported the **French Revolution**. But then in 1793, **radicals**, or people who support complete social or political change, executed the French king, Louis XVI. France then declared war on Spain, Britain, and other neighboring nations. In this international conflict, the Federalists sided with Britain, thereby increasing the division between the two American parties. So even though France had supported the American Revolution, Washington declared in 1793 that the United States would remain neutral, not taking sides with anyone.

But Britain made neutrality difficult. Its Royal Navy captured American citizens and forced them to work on British ships. They also blocked trade in the British West Indies and seized American ships. To make peace, Washington sent Chief Justice John Jay to England to work out a deal. Jay's Treaty required the British to pay for the American ships they had damaged, but it failed to reopen trade in the West Indies.

Meanwhile, **Thomas Pinckney**, an American statesman, traveled to Spain and negotiated Pinckney's Treaty in 1796 to maintain friendly relations between the United States and Spain. The treaty opened the Mississippi River to free navigation, allowed Americans to use the Spanish port of New Orleans, and settled a conflict regarding the Spanish colony of West Florida.

Guillotine
One of the most striking images of the French Revolution is the guillotine (GEE-yuh-teen), the machine used to execute thousands, including Louis XVI. The guillotine had a blade that plunged down grooves in two upright posts to slice through the victim's neck, beheading him or her in one stroke.

HISTORICAL THINKING

1. **READING CHECK** Why did farmers in western Pennsylvania stage the Whiskey Rebellion?

2. **IDENTIFY PROBLEMS AND SOLUTIONS** Describe the conflicts between American settlers and Native Americans in the Northwest Territory and how they were resolved.

3. **MAKE INFERENCES** Why do you think the United States wanted to remain neutral during the French Revolution?

2.3 Washington's Farewell Address

At the end of his first presidential term, George Washington wrote a goodbye letter to the American people. Then he ended up running for a second term. The letter—Washington's Farewell Address—was finally published in 1796, and it is an important American document.

When his eighth year as president was drawing to a close, Washington shared the letter with John Jay and Alexander Hamilton. The three men spent four months revising the letter, ensuring that Washington's ideas were crystal clear. Washington handwrote a clean copy of the finished letter—32 pages long—and addressed it to "Friends & Fellow-Citizens." It was published in the Philadelphia newspaper, *American Daily Advertiser,* on September 19, 1796. It was then printed in other newspapers throughout the country. Following his service as president of the United States, Washington moved back to Mount Vernon (shown in the photo), his home and plantation in Virginia. Washington grew up at Mount Vernon and had always dreamed of returning to his home life there. He lived at Mount Vernon until his death in 1799 and is buried there.

Mount Vernon, George Washington's home

DOCUMENT ONE

**Primary Source: Historical document
from Washington's Farewell Address, 1796**

In this excerpt from his address, Washington tells Americans that they form one united nation. United, he tells them, they are stronger and more secure than they could ever be as separate individuals.

CONSTRUCTED RESPONSE Why does Washington urge people to be proud to be called Americans?

The unity of government . . . is a main pillar in the edifice [structure] of your real independence, . . . of your tranquility at home, your peace abroad; of your safety; of your prosperity; of that very liberty which you so highly prize. The name of American, which belongs to you in your national capacity, must always exalt the just pride of patriotism.

DOCUMENT TWO

**Primary Source: Historical document
from Washington's Farewell Address, 1796**

Washington felt that political parties could pit one group of people against another, posing a threat to national unity. Here, he discusses the dangers of rival political parties.

CONSTRUCTED RESPONSE According to Washington, how might rival political parties affect a community?

In contemplating the causes which may disturb our Union, it occurs as matter of serious concern that any ground should have been furnished for characterizing parties by geographical discriminations [differences], . . . whence [by which] designing men may endeavor to excite a belief that there is a real difference of local interests and views.

DOCUMENT THREE

**Primary Source: Historical document
from Washington's Farewell Address, 1796**

In 1796, France was at war with many other European countries, including Britain. As you've read, some Americans supported the French cause, while others supported Britain. In this excerpt, Washington warns against forming permanent alliances and argues for neutrality in all overseas affairs. He believes such alliances would open the country to foreign influence and unnecessary wars.

CONSTRUCTED RESPONSE What did Washington's speech suggest about the policy the United States should follow with other nations?

Nothing is more essential than that permanent, inveterate antipathies [harsh opposition] against particular nations, and passionate attachments for others, should be excluded and that, in place of them, just and amicable [friendly] feelings towards all should be cultivated. Excessive partiality for one foreign nation and excessive dislike of another cause those whom they actuate [fire up] to see danger only on one side, and serve to veil [cover up] . . . the influence on the other. The great rule of conduct for us in regard to foreign nations is in extending our commercial relations, to have with them as little political connection as possible.

SYNTHESIZE & WRITE

1. **REVIEW** Review what you have learned about Washington's Farewell Address.

2. **RECALL** On your own paper, write the main idea that Washington expressed in each excerpt from his farewell address.

3. **CONSTRUCT** Construct a topic sentence that answers this question: What factors did Washington fear could disrupt the unity and peace of the United States?

4. **WRITE** Using evidence from this chapter and the documents, write an informative paragraph that supports your topic sentence in Step 3.

2.4 The Parties in Conflict

Politicians making negative remarks about each other. Citizens deeply divided over the candidates. A modern-day election? Nope. This happened in 1796, when political parties first competed in an election.

> **MAIN IDEA** Political clashes tested U.S. relationships abroad and the constitutionality of laws passed at home.

ADAMS VS. JEFFERSON

The Federalists and Democratic-Republicans waged a bitter campaign in 1796. John Adams ran on the Federalist side, and Thomas Jefferson represented the Democratic-Republicans. After attacks on both sides, Adams won with 71 electoral votes. He was the first president to govern from Washington, D.C. Jefferson came in second with 68 electoral votes and became vice president. It was not a happy arrangement.

Problems abroad claimed their attention. France began seizing American ships in an effort to prevent U.S. trade with Britain. In response, Adams sent three **envoys**, or ambassadors, to France to settle the problem. The envoys met with French agents known to the American public simply as X, Y, and Z. When the French agents made unreasonable demands and even insisted on being paid a bribe to begin negotiations, the shocked envoys turned them down and returned home.

The **XYZ Affair**, as the negotiations came to be called, further soured American relations with France. It also hurt the reputation of the Democratic-Republicans, who had supported the French Revolution. When Adams made reports of the affair public, most Americans felt their honor had been attacked, and war fever swept the country. Congress expanded the army, established the navy, and authorized naval vessels to attack French ships that threatened American merchant ships. Congress stopped all trade with France and ended the U.S. alliance with the country.

THE ALIEN AND SEDITION ACTS

Americans cheered Adams's response to the French threat. Riding on a wave of popularity, the Federalists passed the **Alien and Sedition Acts**. The Alien Act allowed the president to expel, for any reason, new immigrants, or aliens, living in the United States—most of whom were Democratic-Republicans. The Sedition Act targeted U.S. citizens, including journalists, who criticized the government. **Sedition** is the act of provoking rebellion.

Democratic-Republicans were quick to respond. For example, in the Kentucky Resolutions, Jefferson condemned the excess of the Alien and Sedition Acts, claiming they violated citizens' freedom of speech and freedom of the press. Adams's opponents fought the acts using a theory called **states' rights**, which declares that individual states have rights the federal government cannot violate. By 1802, the acts had expired, but they had undermined Adams's popularity. In the presidential election of 1800, Jefferson defeated him. The election marked the first peaceful transfer of power from one party to another.

HISTORICAL THINKING

1. **READING CHECK** How did Jefferson become Adams's vice president in 1796?

2. **ANALYZE CAUSE AND EFFECT** Why did the XYZ Affair increase Adams's popularity?

3. **SYNTHESIZE** How did the Sedition Acts contradict the rights guaranteed under the First Amendment?

A GLOBAL PERSPECTIVE When Congress passed the Sedition Act in 1798, the legislation threatened citizens' freedom of speech and press. Fortunately, Americans can protest against laws they deem unfair and work to overturn them. This is not the case today in North Korea, where any criticism of the government and its leaders results in imprisonment— or worse. The government uses a strong military to enforce its rigid laws. In the 2007 photo shown here, North Korean soldiers take part in a celebration of the 75th anniversary of the founding of the Korean People's Army. What impression do you think the soldiers conveyed to the people of North Korea and the world?

VOCABULARY

Complete each of the sentences below with one of the vocabulary words or terms from this chapter.

1. The department heads in Washington's _____ did not always agree.

2. Placing a _____ on imported goods helped make American goods more competitive.

3. U.S. journalists who criticized the government could be accused of _____ .

4. Federalists preferred a _____ of the Constitution rather than a rigid one.

5. Antifederalists tended to favor _____ rather than a strong central government.

6. The first presidential _____ took place in New York City.

READING STRATEGY
IDENTIFY PROBLEMS AND SOLUTIONS

Complete your chart to identify the problems the new nation faced. List at least three key problems. Then answer the question below.

Issue: After the Revolution, the nation and individual states had huge debts.

↓

Problem 1: Foreign governments were waiting to be paid.

Problem 2:

Problem 3:

↓

Solution:

7. How did Alexander Hamilton solve the problem of the nation's debt?

MAIN IDEAS

Answer the following questions. Support your answers with evidence from the chapter.

8. Why was George Washington the obvious choice to be the first president? **LESSON 1.1**

9. What three departments did Congress first create to be part of the executive branch? **LESSON 1.2**

10. What did the Federal Judiciary Act call for? **LESSON 1.2**

11. How did Hamilton's economic plan reflect his federalist philosophy? **LESSON 1.3**

12. Why did the South tend to support the Democratic-Republican Party? **LESSON 2.1**

13. Why did Washington warn against divided political parties? **LESSON 2.1**

14. Why did Native Americans in the Northwest Territory sign the Treaty of Greenville? **LESSON 2.2**

15. Why did Congress stop all U.S. trade with France? **LESSON 2.4**

16. What freedoms did the Sedition Act target? **LESSON 2.4**

HISTORICAL THINKING

Answer the following questions. Support your answers with evidence from the chapter.

17. **SYNTHESIZE** How did the choice of George Washington as the country's first president help to shape American identity?

18. **EVALUATE** Why would Washington want to avoid any suggestion that the office of president of the United States was similar to that of a king?

19. **MAKE CONNECTIONS** Identify a controversial issue mentioned in this chapter that is still causing disagreement today.

20. **DRAW CONCLUSIONS** Why did George Washington think it was important to leave some parting words to the American people in his farewell address?

21. **MAKE INFERENCES** Why might Adams have wanted to pass the Alien Act?

22. **IDENTIFY PROBLEMS AND SOLUTIONS** What new problem did the XYZ Affair cause, and what measures did Congress put in place to solve it?

INTERPRET MAPS

Study this map, which shows the results of the 1796 presidential election between John Adams and Thomas Jefferson. Note that the numbers represent the number of electoral college votes for each state. Remember that the electoral college consists of electors representing each state who vote to elect a president and vice president. The boxed numbers represent the number of electors in that state who voted differently from the others in the state. Then answer the questions that follow.

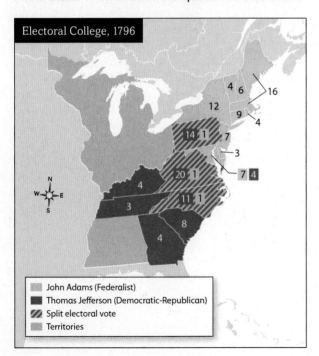

Electoral College, 1796

John Adams (Federalist)
Thomas Jefferson (Democratic-Republican)
Split electoral vote
Territories

23. Which state had the most electoral votes?

24. What generalization can you make regarding the geographic distribution of results?

ANALYZE SOURCES

In this excerpt from a letter written on February 28, 1796, by Thomas Jefferson to John Adams, Jefferson explains why he thinks Americans are especially suited to a democratic form of government. Read the passage and answer the question.

> Never was a finer canvas presented to work on than our countrymen. All of them engaged in agriculture or the pursuits of honest industry, independent in their circumstances, enlightened as to their rights, and firm in their habits of order and obedience to the laws. This I hope will be the age of experiments in government, and that their basis will be founded on principles of honesty, not of mere force.

25. How does Jefferson characterize the American people?

CONNECT TO YOUR LIFE

26. **EXPLANATORY** Think about the election of 1796, the first to involve political parties. Make a connection between that presidential election and a recent one. Write a paragraph explaining how the two elections are similar and different.

TIPS

- Take notes on the two elections. You may wish to use a Venn diagram or other graphic organizer to help organize your ideas.

- State your main idea clearly and support it with relevant facts, details, and examples.

- Use at least two vocabulary terms from the chapter.

- Provide a concluding statement about how the elections are similar and different.

THE JEFFERSON YEARS

1800–1816

ESSENTIAL QUESTION

In what ways did Thomas Jefferson's policies change the country?

AMERICAN STORIES Early Explorers Lewis and Clark

SECTION 1 Jeffersonian Democracy

KEY VOCABULARY

incumbent	unconstitutional
judicial review	writ
Judiciary Act of 1801	

SECTION 2 Westward Expansion

KEY VOCABULARY

Louisiana Purchase	yellow fever

SECTION 3 The War of 1812 Approaches

KEY VOCABULARY

customs	prophet
embargo	War Hawks
Embargo Act of 1807	War of 1812
impressment	

AMERICAN GALLERY
ONLINE New Orleans: A French, Spanish, and American City

READING STRATEGY

ANALYZE CAUSE AND EFFECT
When you analyze cause and effect, you note the consequences of an event, an action, or a condition. As you read this chapter, use a graphic organizer like this one to identify the causes that led to a second war with Britain in 1812.

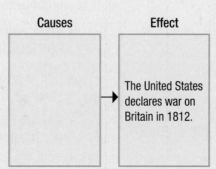

Causes

Effect

The United States declares war on Britain in 1812.

"I hold it that **a little rebellion now and then** is a good thing."

—Thomas Jefferson

CRITICAL VIEWING The Jefferson Memorial, which faces the White House in Washington, D.C., was completed in 1943. Its columns and dome were inspired by ancient Greek and Roman buildings. What other details of the memorial help convey a sense of awe and grandeur?

EARLY EXPLORERS

LEWIS AND CLARK

Captain
Meriwether Lewis

Second Lieutenant
William Clark

In 1803, Thomas Jefferson

sent Meriwether Lewis and William Clark to find a water route to the Pacific and explore the uncharted West. Jefferson believed woolly mammoths, erupting volcanoes, and a mountain of pure salt awaited them. What they found was no less mind-boggling: some 300 species unknown to science, nearly 50 Indian tribes, and the Rocky Mountains.

Lewis was Jefferson's private secretary, an army officer, and an enthusiastic amateur scientist. Clark was a friend of Lewis and also an army officer. On May 14, 1804, the two men set off from a camp near St. Louis, Missouri, accompanied by a group of about 40 men that they dubbed the Corps (KOR) of Discovery. Most of the explorers were soldiers, and one was Clark's African-American slave—a man named York. Packed into three boats along with their supplies, the men headed upstream on the Missouri River toward the regions that now have familiar names such as Kansas, North Dakota, and Idaho. In 1804, this area was called the Louisiana Territory. As far as Jefferson was concerned, it was the great unknown.

National Geographic photographer Sam Abell captured this image of the merging of the Yellowstone River (left) with the Missouri River (right) at one of the locations visited by Lewis and Clark during their expedition.

TO FORT MANDAN AND BEYOND

One of Jefferson's goals for the expedition was to establish friendly relationships with the Indian tribes living in the West. Lewis and Clark had mixed success with this effort. Some tribes welcomed the explorers' gifts and offers of alliance, while others were either uninterested or hostile. The Mandan, living in present-day North Dakota, were among the more welcoming groups. The Corps arrived at the villages of the Mandan and Hidatsa in October 1804. After being warmly received, Lewis and Clark decided to build their winter quarters nearby.

While building their camp, the explorers met Sacagawea (SAK-uh-juh-WE-uh), who would become an important member of the Corps of Discovery. She was a young woman of the Shoshone tribe, which lived just east of the Rocky Mountains. She had been kidnapped from her people as a small child and was now married to a French-Canadian trader named Toussaint Charbonneau. Knowing they would meet the Shoshone later in their travels, Lewis and Clark hired Sacagawea and Charbonneau as interpreters.

In April 1805, the Corps of Discovery broke camp and resumed its journey west. At the same time, they sent a boat back to Thomas Jefferson in Washington, D.C., loaded with 108 botanical specimens, 68 mineral specimens, and a map of the United States drawn by William Clark.

QUITE A SHOPPING LIST

Knowing they would be gone for a long time, Lewis and Clark stocked up on gear for the trip. Below are just a few items from the Corps of Discovery's supply list. Lewis spent $2,324 on supplies for the years-long expedition. That's the equivalent of around $40,000 in 2016 dollars.

Camping Equipment:
- 150 yards of cloth for making tents and sheets
- 25 hatchets
- 10.5 pounds of fishing hooks
- 12 pounds of soap
- 193 pounds of "portable soup"

Medicine:
- 50 dozen of "Rush's Thunderclapper" pills
- syringes
- tourniquets
- 3,500 doses of sweat inducer

Gifts for Native American Tribes:
- 12 dozen pocket mirrors
- 4,600 sewing needles
- 8 brass kettles
- 20 pounds of beads
- 288 brass thimbles

Meriwether Lewis also brought his spyglass on the expedition.

TIME LINE OF EVENTS

May 14, 1804 The Corps of Discovery leaves its camp near St. Louis and begins the journey west.

Early September 1804 The Corps enters the Great Plains. Lewis and Clark begin sighting unfamiliar animal species.

October 24, 1804 The Corps arrives at the villages of the Mandan and Hidatsa tribes near present-day Bismarck, North Dakota.

November 11, 1804 Lewis and Clark hire Sacagawea and Toussaint Charbonneau as interpreters for the rest of the journey.

1804

CRITICAL VIEWING National Geographic photographer Sam Abell captures the White Cliffs of the Missouri River. The Corps of Discovery compared these unique sandstone formations to the ruins of an ancient city. "As we passed on," Lewis wrote in his journal, "it seemed as if those scenes of visionary enchantment would never have an end." Why might the Corps have likened this geologic formation to ancient ruins?

FROM THE ROCKIES TO THE PACIFIC

Throughout the summer, the Corps made progress toward the Rocky Mountains, nervously watching as the imposing, snow-capped peaks grew taller and taller as they approached. When they reached the region we now call northern Montana, Lewis scouted ahead of the expedition, and came across "the grandest sight I ever beheld"—the Great Falls of the Missouri, along with four additional waterfalls immediately upriver. The expedition had no choice but to portage, or carry their canoes over land, for 18.5 miles in order to get around the falls. Extreme summer heat, dangerous storms, prickly pear cacti, and brush made the portage more challenging and time-consuming than anticipated, and the journey took nearly a month.

In August, the Corps reached a Shoshone village just east of the mountains. Here, they hoped to buy horses to help them cross the mountains. The next thing that happened could be described as one of history's most stunning coincidences. The Shoshone villagers recognized Sacagawea. To everyone's shock and delight, she learned that the chief of this group was her long-lost brother.

December 24, 1804 The Corps finishes building Fort Mandan near the Indian villages.

April 7, 1805 The Corps leaves Fort Mandan to resume its westward travel.

May 16, 1805 One of the expedition's boats almost flips over. Sacagawea saves many journals and important papers from going overboard.

August 17, 1805 The Corps reaches the Shoshone camp on the eastern edge of the Rockies. There, Sacagawea realizes the chief is her long-lost brother.

1805

THE CORPS OF DISCOVERY BY THE NUMBERS

PREVIOUSLY UNKNOWN PLANTS DESCRIBED	PREVIOUSLY UNKNOWN ANIMALS DESCRIBED	INDIAN TRIBES ENCOUNTERED	CORPS MEMBER CASUALTIES
178	122	48	ONE BY NATURAL CAUSES, PROBABLY APPENDICITIS

THE JOURNEY SPANNED OVER **8,000 MILES** AND WENT ON FOR . . .

. . . 863 DAYS.

JOYFUL ARRIVAL

At the end of August, the expedition set out to cross the Rockies with the 29 horses they had purchased. The crossing was brutal. At one point, the men lost the trail in the midst of a blinding snowstorm. By the time they stumbled out of the mountains, the men and Sacagawea were exhausted, almost frozen, and near starvation. Happily for the Corps, the Nez Perce Indians, who lived on the west side of the Rockies, were welcoming and willing to share their food.

Soon, the explorers were on the last leg of their westward journey, making their way down the swift-flowing Columbia River toward the Pacific Ocean. On November 7, Clark wrote in his journal, "Ocian in view! O! The joy!" In fact, the Corps had just reached the place where the Columbia widened before meeting the Pacific. The men were still 20 miles from the coast. Three weeks later, after battling fierce storms, the expedition finally reached the shore of the Pacific.

With winter approaching, the Corps built a settlement they named Fort Clatsop, after the Indians living nearby. Lewis and Clark hoped to avoid recrossing the Rockies on the return trip east. American and British trading ships often stopped near the mouth of the Columbia, and the plan was to take passage on one of these ships. However, the expedition never spotted a single ship during a long, dreary winter that had only 12 days without rain.

TIME LINE OF EVENTS CONTINUED

September 11, 1805 The Corps begins climbing up into the Bitterroots, a range of the Rocky Mountains.

September 23, 1805 The expedition completes the mountain crossing and meets the Nez Perce Indians.

October 16, 1805 They reach the Columbia River.

November 24, 1805 The Corps reaches the Pacific Ocean and decides to build Fort Clatsop on the south side of the Columbia.

1806

HOMEWARD BOUND

When spring finally arrived, the expedition was more than ready to leave Fort Clatsop. The trip back to St. Louis was difficult and filled with dangers. The Corps failed in its first attempt to cross the Rockies and had to try a second time. Before leaving the mountains, the expedition split into two to explore more territory, and both groups had hostile encounters with Native American groups. Lewis experienced a dramatic event when he was shot in the leg. The shot, however, was likely by accident from someone in his group. Luckily, it did not result in an injury that was life-threatening. Soon afterward the two halves of the expedition were reunited.

On September 23, the Corps of Discovery came ashore in St. Louis, nearly two and a half years after their departure. The entire city turned out to celebrate the return of the heroes who had been given up for dead. Unlike many earlier explorers, Lewis and Clark did not set off in search of gold or other monetary rewards. Instead, they were returning with a far richer treasure—knowledge about the people, places, plants, and animals in the lands far west of the Mississippi.

THINK ABOUT IT

Use the time line to help you describe the most significant challenges and successes of the Lewis and Clark expedition.

Lewis's silver pocket compass

SACAGAWEA

Kidnapped at the age of 12 by the Hidatsa, Sacagawea, a Shoshone, was taken from the Rocky Mountains to the Hidatsa-Mandan villages in North Dakota. That's where she met the Corps of Discovery in November 1804. Sacagawea's knowledge of languages and the land proved to be very valuable to the Corps as it moved west, passing through the territories of many Native American tribes, some of which had never seen white men before. When tribes saw Sacagawea and her baby traveling with the Corps, they knew the Corps was a friendly group disinterested in war. This statue of Sacagawea stands in a park in Portland, Oregon.

March 23, 1806
The expedition leaves Fort Clatsop to head home.

June 30, 1806 They pause at Traveler's Rest in the Bitterroot Mountains. Lewis and Clark decide to split up and divide the Corps into two groups to cover more ground.

August 12, 1806
The Corps reunites. From here, the swift-flowing Missouri River allows for rapid travel eastward.

September 23, 1806
The Corps of Discovery arrives at St. Louis and receives a hero's welcome.

1807

AMERICAN
STORIES

LEWIS
AND CLARK'S
JOURNALS

Among the treasures to emerge
from the Corps of Discovery
were the journals of Lewis and
Clark. In them, the men described
in detail the geography of the West
as well as the people, plants, and
animals they encountered. They also
narrated a thrilling tale of exploration
and adventure. Some have described
the journals as "our national poem."

**How do you think Americans living
in the eastern United States got their
information about the West before
Lewis and Clark?**

While it's uncertain exactly how Lewis and Clark assembled their field journals, it's likely that the men first made quick notes in portable notebooks they carried with them, including simple maps and sketches. When they returned to camp, they probably combined their notes and rewrote them into the more clear and detailed pages you see here.

1.1 Jefferson's Vision for America

John Adams and Thomas Jefferson didn't actually come to blows during the election of 1800, but they probably came close. They certainly exchanged insults. But when the dust settled, Jefferson was the winner.

MAIN IDEA After the election of Thomas Jefferson, the nation steered a course to a more limited and less expensive government.

BREAKING THE TIE

The election of 1800 was filled with tension and political divisions, and the fact that the frontrunners were the **incumbent**, or current, president and vice president added to it. President Adams, the Federalist, had spent the past four years building a strong government. Vice President Thomas Jefferson, the Democratic-Republican, believed Adams had favored businessmen from the North. To persuade the nation to elect him, Jefferson promised a limited government and lower taxes.

Jefferson favored Aaron Burr as his candidate for vice president. But remember that, at that time, potential running mates ran on their own. So for Burr to become Jefferson's vice president, Jefferson needed to receive the most votes, and Burr needed to come in second.

As it turned out, Jefferson and Burr received an equal number of votes for president. The tie had to be broken by the Federalist-dominated House of Representatives.

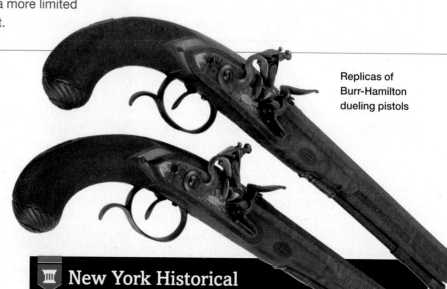

Replicas of Burr-Hamilton dueling pistols

🏛 New York Historical Society, New York

In the early 1800s, men engaged in pistol fights called duels to defend their honor. Although dueling was illegal in most states, it was an accepted practice.

On the morning of July 11, 1804, Vice President Aaron Burr and Alexander Hamilton dueled in a field in Weehawken, New Jersey. Burr had challenged Hamilton to the duel; Hamilton had provided the pistols. The men's rivalry had been building for a decade. In 1791, Burr defeated Hamilton's father-in-law in an election. In 1800, Burr publicly shamed Hamilton by publishing a private essay Hamilton had written criticizing his fellow Federalist, President John Adams. The final straw for Burr was when he read a newspaper article that quoted some of Hamilton's negative opinions of him.

Before that fateful morning, Hamilton had written in letters that he had no intention of killing Burr. The aim of Hamilton's first shot is disputed. Some say he pointed his pistol up in the air; others say he fired at Burr and missed. But Burr didn't miss. He shot Hamilton in the stomach, and Hamilton died the next day. Not only did the showdown end Hamilton's life, it also ended the vice president's political career. Burr was charged with Hamilton's death but received no punishment for the crime.

The World's Best Hope

Jefferson tried to unite Americans in his 1801 Inaugural Address and soothe their fears about what had happened in France during the French Revolution. In that country, radical elements in a republican government had seized control and terrorized the French people. In this excerpt from his address, Jefferson explains why he doesn't believe such a thing could happen in the United States. Why does Jefferson believe the United States has the strongest government on earth?

I know, indeed, that some honest men fear that a republican government can not be strong, that this Government is not strong enough, but would the honest patriot . . . abandon a government which has so far kept us free and firm on the theoretic and visionary [imaginary] fear that this Government, the world's best hope, may . . . want [lack] energy to preserve itself? I trust not. I believe this, on the contrary, the strongest Government on earth. I believe it the only one where every man . . . would meet invasions of the public order [would defend the country] as his own personal concern.

—from Thomas Jefferson's First Inaugural Address, March 4, 1801

The House spent six days casting votes 36 separate times. At first, most Federalists supported Burr, but Burr's bitter enemy Alexander Hamilton rallied support for Jefferson. On February 17, 1801, the House cast the final votes. Jefferson became the nation's third president, and Burr became his vice president.

SOOTHING FEARS

Jefferson's inauguration took place the following month, the first to be held in the new capital city of Washington, D.C. The new president was aware of the division in the country following the election. Many Federalists feared what they considered Jefferson's radical views. They saw what had happened during the French Revolution, when extreme revolutionaries took control and executed thousands of people. In his inaugural address, Jefferson tried to soothe their fears by saying, "We are all Republicans; we are all Federalists."

Jefferson's call for unity set the tone for his years in office. He clearly laid out his plan for governing to the people—and followed it. He lowered taxes and reduced the size of the federal judiciary. In addition, Jefferson continued to support the power of the states and championed low government spending. But he did not dismantle all Federalist institutions. He left the military and Hamilton's National Bank mostly intact.

A popular president, Jefferson easily won re-election in 1804. In his second term, Jefferson continued to combine Democratic-Republican beliefs with wise politics, shrinking the federal government, military, and national debt. Further, Jefferson's personal humility, or humbleness, went hand-in-hand with his philosophy of small government. Instead of hosting showy and expensive events, he insisted on meeting personally with members of Congress and foreign leaders for dinner and conversation. A seat at that table would have been a sought-after invitation for most. These dinners showcased not only Jefferson's taste for fine food but also his many talents.

HISTORICAL THINKING

1. **READING CHECK** What was Thomas Jefferson's political philosophy, and how was it reflected in his policies as president?

2. **MAKE INFERENCES** Based on what you have learned about the ideological differences between Jefferson and Hamilton, what can you infer about Hamilton's support of Jefferson in the 1800 election?

3. **DISTINGUISH FACT AND OPINION** What facts and opinions does Jefferson use to reduce the country's fears and unite Americans?

"I like the dreams of the future better than the history of the past." —Thomas Jefferson

A gifted writer, architect, scientist—you name it—Thomas Jefferson had the chops to carry out his dreams. He proposed a plan that laid the basis of our school system, restocked the Library of Congress with his own books, and penned America's creed. At a dinner at the White House in 1962, President John F. Kennedy remarked to a group of dignitaries that they represented the greatest talent ever assembled there, "with the possible exception of when Thomas Jefferson dined alone."

MONTICELLO

Because Jefferson was born into one of Virginia's foremost families, he received an education that allowed his natural abilities to flourish. As a young man, he studied law and, in time, developed a successful practice. While trying and winning most of the cases that came his way, the young lawyer met Martha Wayles Skelton, who would become his wife. A few years before they married, Jefferson began to design and build Monticello, which would be their home—aside from his years in the White House—for the rest of their lives.

New York Historical Society New York City

American artist Rembrandt Peale painted this portrait in 1805 after Jefferson won reelection in a landslide victory. Jefferson posed for the portrait in the White House, wearing a cape with a fur-lined collar, perhaps to lend an air of informality to the painting.

Jefferson built Monticello on land in Charlottesville, Virginia, that he inherited from his father. The home became his architectural masterpiece, which he constantly reimagined and reworked over more than 40 years. The exterior of the house, with its columns and dome, was inspired by ancient Greek and Roman temples. The interior, with its 40-plus

Monticello, Charlottesville, Virginia

When Jefferson rebuilt the front of Monticello, he had the eight-sided dome, shown here, constructed. A radical design feature at the time, the dome was the first in America to be installed on top of a private residence.

rooms, held some of Jefferson's own inventions, including a "turning-machine" for holding and rotating the clothes in his closet.

The extensive gardens at Monticello also contained his inventions and improvements, such as a sundial and a plow that could easily lift and turn the soil cut by the machine. Jefferson was a dedicated gardener. He cultivated seeds he'd obtained from Europe and Mexico and even some from Lewis and Clark's westward expedition. Jefferson's gardens were a botanic laboratory where he used the scientific method to determine which seeds and plants grew best in its soil and climate.

MAN OF CONTRADICTIONS

Unfortunately, Jefferson's building projects at Monticello and his lavish lifestyle—he loved to entertain—caused him to fall deeply in debt. This may seem odd for a man who once said, "Never spend your money before you have it," but then, Jefferson was full of contradictions. In the Declaration of Independence, he wrote that "all men are created equal," yet he owned more than 100 slaves. And while George Washington granted freedom to many of his slaves in his will, Jefferson only freed a handful of his. He staunchly supported states' rights, but as president, greatly expanded the power of the national government. In many ways, he embodied the social and political contradictions of America itself.

Jefferson died at Monticello on July 4, 1826—50 years to the day after the signing of the Declaration of Independence. By a strange coincidence, his old friend and rival, John Adams, died on the same day. The pair had often locked horns politically but had always maintained a strong mutual respect. When Adams died, his last words were, "Thomas Jefferson survives." He didn't know that his friend had passed away just a few hours before.

HISTORICAL THINKING

1. **READING CHECK** What were some of Jefferson's talents and accomplishments?

2. **EVALUATE** Why do you think it might have been difficult for Jefferson to live up to his principles?

3. **MAKE INFERENCES** Why do you think Adams might have been thinking of Jefferson in his last moments?

The Supreme Court

After winning the presidency, Thomas Jefferson might have thought that he and his opponents would be able to put aside their differences and work together. He didn't know John Adams would take one more parting shot.

MAIN IDEA The introduction of judicial review brought greater power to the Supreme Court and greater balance among the three branches of government.

MARSHALL'S COURT

John Adams and the Federalists lost the presidential and congressional elections in 1800, but they made the most of their remaining time in office. Just before the Democratic-Republicans took over, Congress passed the **Judiciary Act of 1801**. The act reduced the number of justices on the Supreme Court from six to five, which would deny Jefferson the chance to appoint a new justice when the next justice died or resigned. This power is important because the position of a Supreme Court justice is a lifetime appointment. The act also allowed Adams to appoint many new, Federalist lower-court judges before he stepped down. Adams worked late into the night of his last day signing commissions for these judges, who became known as "midnight judges."

Adams also chose a new Chief Justice of the United States, **John Marshall**—a Federalist. One of Marshall's earliest and most important cases was *Marbury* v. *Madison*. The case pitted one of Adams's midnight judges, William Marbury, against Jefferson's secretary of state, James Madison.

MARBURY V. MADISON

The case arose because Adams had signed Marbury's commission but left office before it was delivered. Adams believed that his signature alone made the commission valid. Jefferson disagreed and ordered Madison to block the commission. Marbury sued, saying that the Judiciary Act of 1789 required the Supreme Court to force Madison to give him his commission.

It seemed like a straightforward case. The Court had to decide three questions. First, was Marbury entitled to have the commission delivered to him? The Court said yes. Second, was it within the law

to have the courts issue a **writ**, or legal document, commanding Madison to deliver the commission? Again, the Court agreed. Third, was it legal for the Supreme Court to issue this writ? Here, the Court surprised everyone. Marshall answered with a resounding "No!" and decided against Marbury.

Even though the Judiciary Act of 1789 stated that the Supreme Court could issue such writs, Marshall argued that the U.S. Constitution did not give such power to the Court. The Court declared that part of the act to be **unconstitutional**, or against the Constitution. No law had ever been declared unconstitutional before. With his ruling, Marshall established **judicial review**, the power to invalidate any law the Court deems unconstitutional. *Marbury* v. *Madison* established the judiciary's role in the protection of the freedoms and individual rights detailed in the Bill of Rights. The case also strengthened the balance among the three branches of government, promoting the principle of checks and balances. Jefferson, however, would soon test the limits of the power of the branches and the Constitution.

HISTORICAL THINKING

1. **READING CHECK** How was Marbury appointed as a judge?

2. **ANALYZE CAUSE AND EFFECT** What unintended consequence did John Adams's plan to appoint midnight judges bring about?

3. **EVALUATE** What was surprising about Marshall's decision that the Supreme Court did not have the power to issue Marbury's writ?

The Supreme Court, Washington, D.C.

Surprisingly, the Supreme Court was not provided with its own building until 1935. Until that time, members of the Court met in several places, including the Capitol Building. Finally, Chief Justice William Howard Taft—who had also served as president—persuaded Congress to construct a permanent home for the Court. When work got underway, the architect built it in the style of an ancient Roman temple, similar to the style of nearby congressional buildings. The result was as Taft wished: "a building of dignity and importance suitable for use as the home of the Supreme Court of the United States."

2.1 The Louisiana Purchase

We all know our nation spans the continent from "sea to shining sea," but in the early 1800s, the western border of the United States was the Mississippi River. Thomas Jefferson took steps to change that.

MAIN IDEA Thomas Jefferson negotiated a deal with France to purchase the Louisiana Territory and doubled the size of the United States.

PORT OF NEW ORLEANS

While the Supreme Court dealt with the midnight judges, Jefferson set his sights on expansion. The population in the region between the Appalachian Mountains and the Mississippi River had grown steadily. Now farmers were settling the area and shipping their crops down the tributaries of the Mississippi to New Orleans. From there, ships carried cargo to ports all over the world. Jefferson wanted to acquire New Orleans. Only France stood in his way.

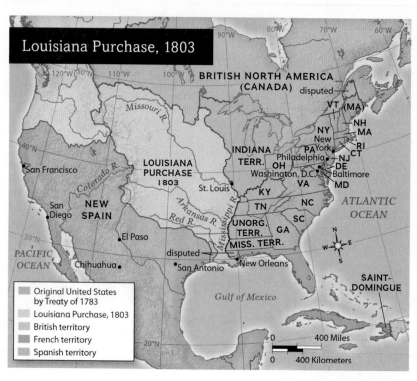

In 1799, **Napoleon Bonaparte** overthrew the revolutionary government in France and took power. In 1800, he signed a secret treaty requiring Spain to return Louisiana to France. The Spanish government had decided that, with only 50,000 settlers in all of Louisiana, the area was too expensive to maintain and produced too little profit. But Jefferson feared that once France owned Louisiana, it would interfere with American shipping in New Orleans. Fortunately for Jefferson, France now felt as burdened with Louisiana as Spain had and was very willing to sell the territory to another nation. Soon, peaceful negotiations began between Napoleon and the United States.

NAPOLEON'S OFFER

Jefferson began by sending James Monroe to France in 1803 to help negotiate the purchase of territory at the mouth of the Mississippi, including

New Orleans. However, negotiations began to stall on the French side. Napoleon was having trouble in another part of the Americas—the Caribbean colony of Saint-Domingue, now known as Haiti, on the island of Hispaniola. In 1791, **Toussaint L'Ouverture** (TOO-sahnt LOH-ver-toor) had led a successful revolution to free slaves in the French colony. L'Ouverture governed the island until 1802, when Napoleon decided he wanted the colony back. But his actions resulted in an all-out war.

Napoleon had had enough of the Americas. His forces had been reduced by **yellow fever**, an often-fatal disease carried by mosquitoes in tropical climates, and he surrendered to Haitian independence. Without Saint-Domingue, Napoleon felt that Louisiana had little value. As a result, the

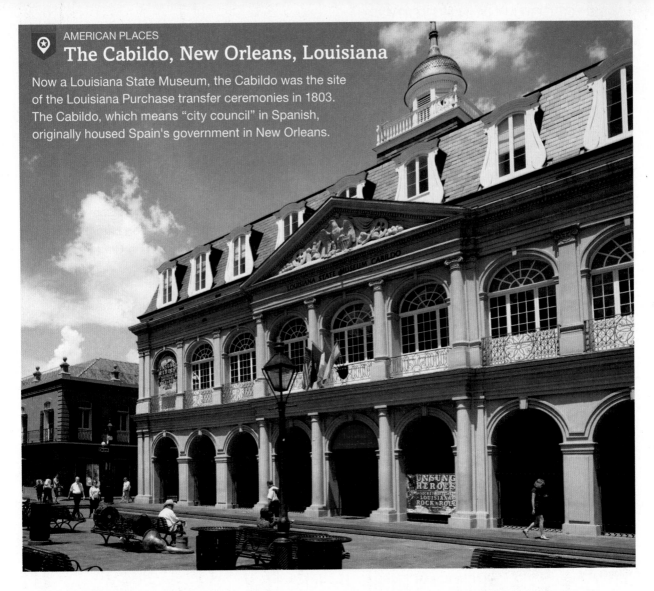

Now a Louisiana State Museum, the Cabildo was the site of the Louisiana Purchase transfer ceremonies in 1803. The Cabildo, which means "city council" in Spanish, originally housed Spain's government in New Orleans.

French leader decided to give up all his territory in continental North America. Instead of selling only New Orleans to the United States, Napoleon suggested selling the entire Louisiana Territory—all 828,000 square miles of it—for $15 million. In October 1803, the U.S. Senate ratified the treaty that established the **Louisiana Purchase**. France officially transferred the land to the United States, doubling the size of the nation.

Jefferson had some misgivings about the deal. He debated the constitutionality of the purchase, saying, "The General Government has no powers but such as the Constitution gives it. . . . It has not given it power of holding foreign territory, and still less of incorporating it into the Union. An amendment of the Constitution seems necessary for this." But Jefferson ended up putting his concerns aside. The land, he believed, would provide space for generations of American farmers and allow people in the region to trade freely on the Mississippi. Soon after the treaty with France was finalized, Jefferson funded an expedition to take a good look at the land and natural resources the country had bought. He could hardly wait to hear what the explorers learned about the plants, animals, and people in the region.

HISTORICAL THINKING

1. **READING CHECK** Why did Jefferson want to purchase Louisiana from France?

2. **ANALYZE CAUSE AND EFFECT** What happened as a result of war in Saint-Domingue?

3. **INTERPRET MAPS** What major river did the United States acquire the rights to in the Louisiana Purchase?

2.2 The Discoveries of Lewis and Clark

MAIN IDEA Lewis and Clark's expedition cleared up some of the geographic unknowns of the new, expansive lands that President Jefferson bought from France.

A SCIENTIFIC EXPEDITION

As you have read, Meriwether Lewis and William Clark's Corps of Discovery traveled almost 8,000 miles from St. Louis, Missouri, to the Pacific Ocean, then back to St. Louis. Few accurate maps of the West existed at that time, and there were many geographic unknowns about the region. Lewis and Clark's recorded observations changed Americans' understanding of the physical landscapes of the West.

Their journey also resulted in the discovery of plants and animals never seen before by European-Americans. Lewis and Clark recorded more than 120 new animal species, including mule deer and coyote. They described 178 new species of plants, like the big leaf maple, the Oregon crabapple, and the ponderosa pine.

Follow the journey of Lewis and Clark on the map below. Then read about three geographic unknowns in the West and the new geographic knowledge the explorers gained through their travels and observations.

Lewis and Clark's Expedition Route, 1804–1806

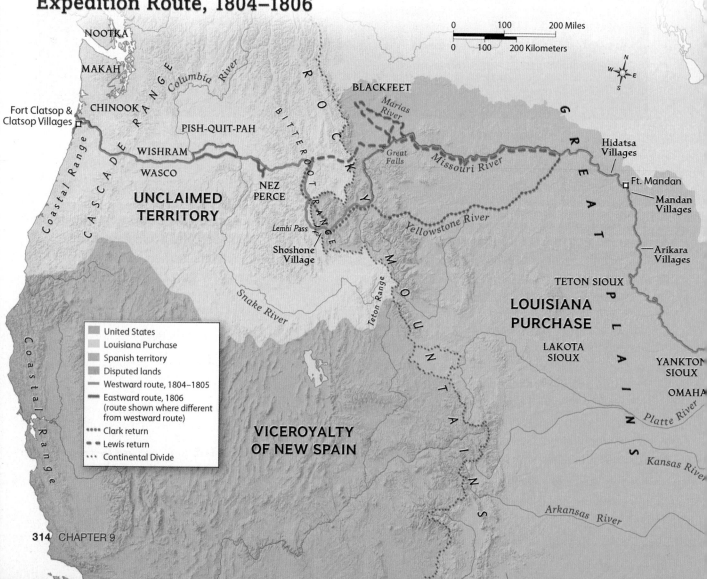

Legend:
- United States
- Louisiana Purchase
- Spanish territory
- Disputed lands
- Westward route, 1804–1805
- Eastward route, 1806 (route shown where different from westward route)
- •••• Clark return
- – • – Lewis return
- ···· Continental Divide

GEOGRAPHIC UNKNOWN	GEOGRAPHIC KNOWLEDGE

THE MISSOURI RIVER AND THE MARIAS RIVER

In June 1805, Lewis and Clark were sailing up the Missouri River in present-day Montana when they came to another river. One river flowed from the north, and the other flowed from the south. Which one was the main stem of the Missouri River? Which one should they continue to follow?

Most members of Lewis and Clark's expedition wanted to follow the river that flowed from the north. Lewis and Clark were not so sure. They split up, with Clark scouting the river to the south and Lewis scouting the river to the north. They returned from their quick explorations and agreed—the south branch was the Missouri River and the one they should continue to follow upstream. Lewis named the river to the north the Marias River, after his cousin Maria.

THE NORTHWEST PASSAGE

Jefferson had hoped Lewis and Clark would find a Northwest Passage, a water route that would connect the Missouri River to the Pacific Ocean and the riches of Asia. The country that found such a route first would control it. When the explorers arrived at the origin of the Missouri River in August 1805, they expected to have a short portage to the Columbia River, which would carry them to the Pacific.

Lewis reached Lemhi Pass, a two-mile span bridging the gap between the ranges of the Rockies near the border of present-day Montana and Idaho. There, Lewis discovered "immence ranges of high mountains still to the West of us with their tops partially covered with snow." There would not be a short portage to the Columbia River. Instead, the expedition had to cross the rugged Bitterroot Mountains, which took them until October. The hopes for a Northwest Passage had died.

BISON

When Lewis and Clark embarked on their expedition, they knew about bison. However, they had no idea how large the herds were or how vital these animals were to the Native Americans of the Great Plains. They also didn't know where the bison roamed.

As Lewis and Clark traveled west, they found enormous herds of bison and, like the Native Americans, they came to depend on the bison for the animals' nutritious meat. The explorers found no bison west of the Rocky Mountains, but when they took different routes east through the Rockies, the bison reappeared.

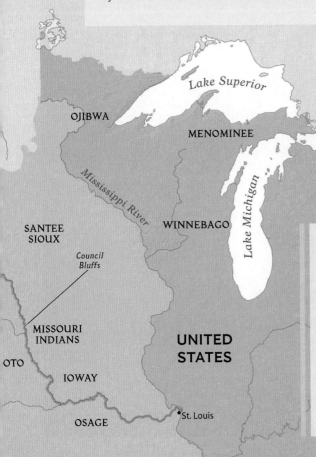

OJIBWA

Lake Superior

MENOMINEE

Lake Michigan

Lake Huron

Lake Ontario

Mississippi River

SANTEE SIOUX

Council Bluffs

WINNEBAGO

MISSOURI INDIANS

OTO

IOWAY

UNITED STATES

St. Louis

OSAGE

THINK LIKE A GEOGRAPHER

1. **IDENTIFY MAIN IDEAS AND DETAILS** How did Lewis and Clark determine that the Northwest Passage did not exist?

2. **ANALYZE ENVIRONMENTAL CONCEPTS** How might settlement in the lands obtained through the Louisiana Purchase affect the biological diversity of the plants and animals Lewis and Clark discovered?

3. **DRAW CONCLUSIONS** How did Lewis and Clark's perceptions of the West change as a result of their expedition?

Sharing the World

"Try to say yes when you travel. You'll open yourself up to so many new experiences." —Robert Reid

You might say **Robert Reid** has a pretty great job. As National Geographic's Digital Nomad, he investigates the whys and hows of how we experience the world, sharing his adventures with a global audience via social media, blog posts, and the occasional informal travel video.

Reid has traveled from coast to coast in the United States and extensively abroad, from Vietnam to England to Australia. He's been to Canadian Mountie boot camp, counted mustaches in Siberia, and poked around Atlantic City, New Jersey. He's even parachuted from a World War II-era plane in the middle of Russia. He gets around. Reid uses his own hobbies and interests to build trip itineraries, research articles, and provide a framework for the video storytelling he is famous for. (Look him up!)

^
The East African country of Kenya is only one of the amazing destinations Robert Reid has visited during his career as a travel writer.

MAIN IDEA Digital Nomad Robert Reid explains how travel enriches our lives.

ROAD TRIPPING

In spite of his extensive international travel experience, Reid admits if he could only visit one country for the rest of his life, it would be the United States. "It's so diverse," he explains, highlighting some of his favorite American places. "I love the Great Plains. Mountains are great, but they get in the way of a good view." He's also fond of New York City because of its cultural icons and famous places. Oregon, Reid's home state, is another favorite location. "Oregon is the most underrated state in the country. It has everything. Coastlines. Waterfalls. You name it. It's also where Lewis and Clark ended their great American road trip."

When he travels, Robert Reid gets to know the locals—in this case, a Rosie the Riveter reenactor he met in Ronks, Pennsylvania.

Reid identifies with Lewis and Clark in many ways. "I think the ultimate road trip of all time belongs to those guys," he says. "Their journey was just so American. Americans take road trips to understand their country, and that's what Lewis and Clark were doing." Reid points out the ability of the explorers to travel 8,000 miles—and survive—more than 200 years ago is downright incredible, but explainable. "They didn't overpack. We know that, because they left us lists of exactly what they brought. They knew how important it was to rely on the knowledge of the locals, so they used native guides who knew the language, the terrain, and the culture. And nearly everyone survived the expedition. That's incredible!"

TIPS FROM A TRAVELER

Most importantly to Reid as a travel writer, Lewis and Clark documented their journey. Extensively. So what suggestions does this travel guru have to offer the average tourist today? First, take photographs—lots of them—because they'll help you remember your trip. Secondly, write about who and what you encounter on your journey. Visit a place from different angles and talk to locals who can offer unique perspectives. For example, says Reid, "Go to Wyoming and find a geologist who is walking every square inch of the state to make maps. That person knows the land better than anyone and knows how to better appreciate things most people miss."

Everywhere he visits, Reid talks to people who live there and tries to see the place from their perspective, not from that of an outsider. "When you travel, do and see the things the locals like to do and see—and make sure you do that with the locals," he advises. Sound advice from someone who knows how to travel.

Check out the Reid on the Road videos online in this history program.

HISTORICAL THINKING

1. **FORM AND SUPPORT OPINIONS** Reid believes it's vital to interact with local residents when you travel. Why does he recommend this? Do you agree? Use evidence in the text to support your answer.

2. **COMPARE AND CONTRAST** What does Robert Reid have in common with Lewis and Clark? How are they different?

This busy port In Seattle demonstrates the strength of the U.S. economy today, with ships carrying imports and exports into and out of the harbor. In the early 1800s, the embargo Jefferson enforced against foreign imports really only hurt the United States. Once America became a strong economic power by the 20th century, the embargoes it placed on other countries, such as Cuba and Iran, were far more effective.

3.1 Neutrality or War?

When people get into a fight, do you join in or walk away? Thomas Jefferson probably wanted to focus on Lewis and Clark's discoveries in the Louisiana Territory. Unfortunately, the war brewing abroad kept demanding his attention.

MAIN IDEA Jefferson's plan to remain neutral during a war between Britain and France backfired.

JEFFERSON'S FOREIGN POLICY

In his 1801 Inaugural Address, Jefferson had explained his foreign policy. The United States, he said, was "separated by nature and a wide ocean from the exterminating havoc [deadly chaos] of one quarter of the globe." The last part referred to Europe. Among his "essential principles of government" were "peace, commerce, and honest friendship with all nations, entangling alliances with none." In other words, he wished the United States to remain neutral. Easier said than done.

After Napoleon gave up on expansion in North America, he turned to Europe and began a war with Britain in 1803. At first, American merchants profited from U.S. neutrality and sold provisions and weapons to both countries. Yet soon the British and French navies tried to block American ships from supplying their enemy. In addition, Britain authorized its navy to capture American ships and force the sailors to serve the British Navy—an act called **impressment**.

CUTTING OFF TRADE

Although many Americans called for war, the United States remained neutral. But trade with Britain and France became more difficult after Napoleon threatened to seize any ship that engaged in trade with Britain. In response, Jefferson urged Congress to pass the Non-Importation Act, which banned British imports. He also closed U.S. ports and waters to British ships. The British answered by continuing impressment, firing on U.S. coastal towns, and entering the Chesapeake Bay.

In response, Congress passed the **Embargo Act of 1807**. An **embargo** is a law that restricts commerce with one or more nations. The act was supposed to stop all foreign imports from arriving in American harbors, but smugglers still got through. Congress allowed the president to use militia against these illegal traders.

While these steps stopped the smuggling, the embargo had disastrous effects on the U.S. economy. The Treasury's chief source of income— **customs**, or taxes placed on imported and exported goods—dwindled. The embargo particularly affected New England farmers, whose crops were no longer being exported abroad, and New England merchants, who depended on European trade for much of their business. After New Englanders demanded an end to the embargo, Congress passed laws in 1809 that reopened trade with all nations except Britain and France.

Despite the impact of the embargo, Jefferson remained popular. His endorsement of fellow Democratic-Republican James Madison in the 1808 presidential election resulted in a landslide victory against the Federalists. The election proved that Americans still supported the policies of Jefferson's Democratic-Republicans. As it turned out, these policies would soon be tested at home.

HISTORICAL THINKING

1. **READING CHECK** What was Jefferson's foreign policy?

2. **ANALYZE CAUSE AND EFFECT** How did the Embargo Act of 1807 affect Americans?

3. **SUMMARIZE** What foreign actions tested Jefferson's policy of neutrality?

3.2 Native Americans Unite

Thomas Jefferson kept the United States out of war. But in the years shortly after he left office, the threat of war continued to grow. Conflict was in the air, and not only in Europe.

MAIN IDEA Native Americans across North America united to fight against the American government and its increasing expansion into their traditional lands.

TECUMSEH'S IDEA

While the United States was trying to maintain neutrality in the war in Europe, trouble was developing at home. American expansion into the Northwest Territory had increased conflict with Native American nations. Shawnee chief **Tecumseh** (tuh-KUM-suh), in particular, began to speak out against the destruction of native cultures and economies. He also criticized Native American leaders who sold their land to the United States.

A Gift from the British

This ceremonial tomahawk and pipe was a gift to Tecumseh from British colonel Henry Proctor. The two men fought together on the frontier and in Canada, but they fell out over Proctor's reluctance to attack American troops in Ohio. Proctor hoped to win back Tecumseh's respect and friendship by offering him this weapon, which was most likely made in France.

To present a united front against the United States, Tecumseh visited Native American tribes, including the Miami, the Delaware, and the Potawatomi, and spoke to them about forming a confederation, or alliance. In 1809, while Tecumseh traveled the country, the U.S. government negotiated the Treaty of Fort Wayne with several other tribes. According to the terms of the treaty, the Native American leaders who signed the agreement sold 2.9 million acres of their land to the government for a fraction of a penny per acre. This type of "deal" was just what Tecumseh had been trying to prevent. The treaty was the last straw and inspired many more Native American groups to join Tecumseh's cause.

Pipe tomahawk, c. 1810–1812

THE BATTLE OF TIPPECANOE

Meanwhile around 1808, Tecumseh had established **Prophetstown** on the Tippecanoe (tih-pee-kuh-NOO) River in the Indiana Territory. Prophetstown was a community devoted to Native American unity and opposition to U.S. expansion. Tecumseh's brother, Tenskwatawa (tens-qwah-TAH-wah), lived there, and people called him "the Prophet." A **prophet** is someone who is believed to deliver messages that come from God or some other divine source. Tecumseh's brother had become a religious leader in Prophetstown, and many of its inhabitants looked to him to foretell the future. The Prophet promoted a return to traditional ways of life and insisted that Native Americans reject all aspects of European culture.

In 1811, the governor of the Indiana Territory, William Henry Harrison, led about 1,000 men to attack the community and put an end to Tecumseh's confederacy. Tecumseh was away, trying to recruit Native Americans in the South to his cause. Acting against his brother's orders, the Prophet led an attack of his own on Harrison's camp early one morning but was soon forced to retreat. The next day, Harrison's forces found Prophetstown deserted and burned it to the ground. The skirmish came to be known as the **Battle of Tippecanoe**.

The battle infuriated many Americans. Rumors swirled that British forces in Canada had encouraged Tecumseh's confederacy and attacks by Native Americans. Some Americans who favored war, called **War Hawks**, even believed that the British had already formed an alliance with Native Americans against the United States. Many leaders felt, too, that the new nation had to demonstrate its viability, or skill, on the international stage. The War Hawks' anger boiled over in the Capitol, resulting in a call to arms. The shadow of war was falling on the country.

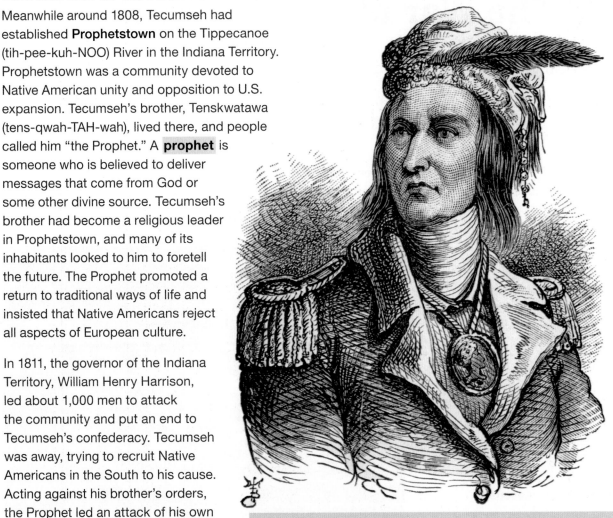

Tecumseh's Eloquence

Tecumseh traveled throughout the United States and Canada, persuading other tribes to join his confederacy. In one speech, he told the Osage that they "belong to one family" and were all "children of the Great Spirit." His goal of confederation, he explained, was "to assist each other to bear our burdens." Tecumseh insisted, "We walk in the same path. . . . We must be united; we must smoke the same pipe; we must fight each others' battles."

HISTORICAL THINKING

1. **READING CHECK** What was Tecumseh's plan, and how did he hope to accomplish it?

2. **ANALYZE CAUSE AND EFFECT** What main factors led Tecumseh to formulate his plan?

3. **EVALUATE** In what ways was Tecumseh's plan a good one, and in what ways was it likely to fail?

3.3 The War of 1812

Americans value their independence. That's what the American Revolution had been about, after all. Turns out, many Americans would be willing to fight for it a second time.

MAIN IDEA The War of 1812 unified the people of the United States and set the stage for expansion and economic prosperity.

A NATION AT ODDS

In June 1812, the War Hawks got their way. Congress declared war against Britain—again. However, despite the widespread belief that the British and Native Americans were working together, Americans had mixed feelings about the **War of 1812**. As you know, the war with Britain was especially unpopular with New England farmers and merchants for economic reasons.

Politicians also wondered how President James Madison planned to pay for the war. The National Bank's charter had expired, leaving only the less stable state banks to provide war loans. Also, you may remember that the United States had ended trade with Britain and France while those two countries were at war. The government had lost a great deal of income from tariffs as a result.

Francis Scott Key watched the American flag continue to fly above Fort McHenry, shown here, through bombardment by British warships.

THROUGH THE PERILOUS FIGHT

At first, busy fighting Napoleon, Britain all but ignored the war with the United States. However, Britain had to act when American forces attacked its fort near Detroit, Michigan. The British repelled the attack and even forced the U.S. militia to surrender Detroit. Things were beginning badly for the Americans.

In September 1813, American troops won their first victory when **Oliver Hazard Perry** and his fleet of ships defeated British troops on Lake Erie.

Soon after, William Henry Harrison's forces retook Detroit and defeated British forces at the Battle of the Thames (tehmz). Shawnee chief Tecumseh died on that battlefield fighting for the British.

By the summer of 1814, Britain's war against Napoleon in Europe was drawing to a close, so the country sent more troops to North America. British forces captured Washington, D.C., and burned down the Capitol and White House. Less than a month later, the British also attacked **Fort McHenry** and Baltimore, Maryland, but failed to take the city. The American flag flying amid the battle's flaming rockets and bombs inspired **Francis Scott Key** to memorialize the scene in his poem "The Star-Spangled Banner." The poem was later set to music and became the national anthem of the United States. (You can read more about Key's famous lyrics and our flag earlier in this text in the American Story, "Our American Identity.")

By the end of 1814, neither Britain nor the United States saw much hope for victory. Delegates from both countries met in Ghent, a city in present-day Belgium, where they signed the Treaty of Ghent and formally ended the war. News of the treaty did not come soon enough to stop one last British naval and ground attack on New Orleans, however. **Andrew Jackson**, a military leader from Tennessee, and his troops countered the attack and killed, captured, or wounded more than 2,000 British soldiers. Jackson lost only 13 soldiers.

The terms of the treaty restored things to the way they were before the war. All territory captured during the war was returned to its original owner, and all prisoners of war were freed.

Although the treaty did not declare a winner, many Americans felt they'd scored a diplomatic victory. The war confirmed U.S. sovereignty and boosted Americans' self-confidence and patriotism. It also encouraged yet more expansion and a new economic prosperity.

🏛 The White House
Washington, D.C.

This painting by Tom Freeman, called *Burning of the White House, 1814*, shows the structure in flames after British soldiers torched it during the War of 1812. Before their arrival, Madison's wife, Dolley, had a full-length portrait of George Washington removed and taken from the building for safekeeping.

CRITICAL VIEWING What emotions is the painting probably meant to inspire?

HISTORICAL THINKING

1. **READING CHECK** Why were Americans divided over fighting the War of 1812?

2. **ANALYZE CAUSE AND EFFECT** What happened because news of the Treaty of Ghent didn't arrive immediately?

3. **FORM AND SUPPORT OPINIONS** Do you think Americans were justified in their belief that they had won the war? Explain why or why not.

VOCABULARY

Use each of the following vocabulary words in a sentence that shows an understanding of the term's meaning.

1. **judicial review**
   After judicial review, the Supreme Court decided that the new law was invalid.

2. Louisiana Purchase

3. incumbent

4. unconstitutional

5. impressment

6. customs

7. embargo

READING STRATEGY
ANALYZE CAUSE AND EFFECT

If you haven't already done so, complete your chart to analyze causes that led President Madison to declare war on Britain in 1812. List at least four causes. Then answer the question.

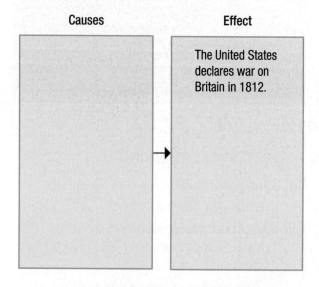

Causes	Effect
	The United States declares war on Britain in 1812.

8. How did Britain's war with France influence the outbreak of the War of 1812?

MAIN IDEAS

Answer the following questions. Support your answers with evidence from the chapter.

9. How was the 1800 election decided? **LESSON 1.1**

10. What were the effects of the Judiciary Act of 1801? **LESSON 1.3**

11. Why did William Marbury think *Marbury* v. *Madison* was a good case? **LESSON 1.3**

12. In what way did the Louisiana Purchase contradict Jefferson's philosophy of government? **LESSON 2.1**

13. What were some difficulties the United States encountered while remaining neutral during the war between Britain and France? **LESSON 3.1**

14. What geographic factor made Tecumseh's plan for union difficult? **LESSON 3.2**

15. What role did the War Hawks play in the War of 1812? **LESSON 3.2**

16. How would you summarize Britain's military situation during the War of 1812? **LESSON 3.3Z**

17. How was the Treaty of Ghent different from traditional treaties? **LESSON 3.3**

HISTORICAL THINKING

Answer the following questions. Support your answers with evidence from the chapter.

18. **COMPARE AND CONTRAST** How were Jefferson's beliefs similar to and different from those of the Federalists?

19. **ANALYZE CAUSE AND EFFECT** What was the most important lasting effect of the Judiciary Act of 1801?

20. **FORM AND SUPPORT OPINIONS** Do you think the Louisiana Purchase was constitutional? Explain why or why not.

21. **EVALUATE** What were the purpose, challenges, and economic incentives of the Lewis and Clark expedition?

22. **SYNTHESIZE** Why did the War of 1812 increase American patriotism?

23. **IDENTIFY** What experiences contributed to Napolean's loss of interest in the Americas?

INTERPRET MAPS

Look closely at the map below. Then answer the questions that follow.

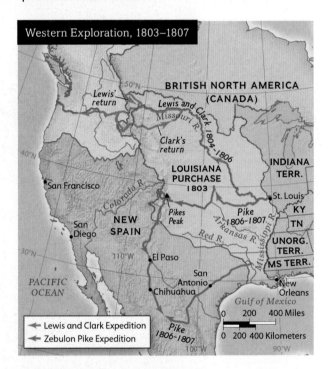

Western Exploration, 1803–1807

24. Based on the boundaries of the Louisiana Territory, which European nations might have come into conflict with the United States over territorial boundaries?

25. What two explorations does the map show, and which of these went into territory owned by another nation?

ANALYZE SOURCES

In an 1811 letter to Secretary of War William Eustis, William Henry Harrison, governor of the Indiana Territory, described Tecumseh's work in building a confederation to keep U.S. settlers and soldiers off Native American lands. Read the excerpt and answer the questions.

> The implicit [absolute] obedience and respect which the followers of Tecumseh pay to him, is really astonishing, and . . . bespeaks him [suggests that he is] one of those uncommon geniuses which spring up occasionally to produce revolutions. . . . If it were not for the vicinity of the United States, he would, perhaps, be the founder of an empire that would rival in glory that of Mexico or Peru. . . . I hope, however, . . . that that part of the fabric [unity among the tribes] which he considered complete, will be demolished, and even its foundations rooted up.

26. According to Harrison, how do other Native Americans regard Tecumseh?

27. What seems to be Harrison's opinion of Tecumseh?

CONNECT TO YOUR LIFE

28. **NARRATIVE** Choose an important U.S. figure from 1800 to 1816, such as Thomas Jefferson or John Marshall. Make a connection between that historical figure and a well-known person today. Write a paragraph in which you imagine what would happen if the two met.

TIPS

• List the historical figure's qualities and accomplishments. Then make a similar list for the present-day person you have chosen.

• Use textual evidence and vocabulary words from the chapter in your narrative.

• Include dialogue to convey the figures' personalities and philosophies.

• Conclude with a description of the connection that ties the two figures together.

EXPANSION AND GROWTH
1800–1844

ESSENTIAL QUESTION
How did new industries and inventions transform the United States economically, socially, and geographically?

 The Mighty Mississippi

SECTION 1 **America's First Industrial Revolution**

KEY VOCABULARY

factory system	market revolution	strike
Industrial Revolution	reaper	telegraph
interchangeable parts	steamboat	textile

SECTION 2 **Plantations and Slavery Spread**

KEY VOCABULARY

antebellum	interstate slave trade	spirituals
cotton gin	passive resistance	

SECTION 3 **Nationalism and Sectionalism**

KEY VOCABULARY

abolition	monopoly	sectionalism
American System	Monroe Doctrine	subsidy
implied power	nationalism	unorganized territory
Missouri Compromise	republican motherhood	

 **The American Railroads**

READING STRATEGY

DRAW CONCLUSIONS
When you draw conclusions, you support them with evidence from the text. As you read the chapter, use a graphic organizer like this one to draw conclusions about the expansion and growth of the United States during the 1800s.

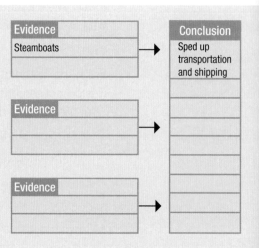

Evidence		Conclusion
Steamboats	→	Sped up transportation and shipping
Evidence	→	
Evidence	→	

"Railroad iron is a magician's wand,

in its power to evoke the sleeping
energies of land and water."

—Ralph Waldo Emerson

The railroad is one of the iconic symbols of U.S.
expansion. During the early 19th century, Americans
built railroads, canals, and roads that made traveling
and trading with distant places easier and more
efficient. The growing transportation network
unified the country physically and culturally.

1.1 From Farm to Factory

On a farm or in a factory—where would you rather work? In the first half of the 1800s, new inventions sparked the growth of factories. Many people left farm life behind, and this shift changed American culture in many ways.

MAIN IDEA Industrialization in the early 19th century transformed the ways in which Americans lived and worked.

CHANGES IN THE ECONOMY

In the early 1800s, different regions of the United States became more interdependent and connected. One factor that made this possible was the **market revolution**, or the transition from a pre-industrial economy to a market-oriented, capitalist economy. In part, this economic transition was prompted by the **Industrial Revolution**, or the widespread production by machinery, that had been underway in Europe since the mid-1700s.

The beginning of the Industrial Revolution in the United States is often dated to 1793, when **Samuel Slater** opened his first cloth factory in Rhode Island. Industrialization in the Northeast transformed social structures and had important consequences for the nation's economy and international position.

Newly introduced machines produced goods more rapidly and efficiently than people could make by hand, one at a time. A **factory system**, or a method of production in which large crews of people perform work in one location, developed. Mechanized production in factories and mills replaced skilled craftspeople. Factory managers recruited men and women from rural areas, many of whom embraced the idea of factory work.

New locations and types of work profoundly affected how people lived and worked. They also transformed the family economy. Furthermore, instead of working together on farms or in shops, men and women began to work in separate spheres. This shift was especially true for the emerging middle class.

THE MILL GIRLS

The United States entered the Industrial Revolution through the **textile** industry, which produced cloth and clothing from cotton and other raw materials. Initially, individual workers wove thread into large pieces of cloth on hand-operated looms. In 1785, an Englishman named Edmund Cartwright introduced the first power loom. Power looms required multiple workers, but by 1813, improvements had eliminated the general need for all but one person. This single-operator model became the basis for a faster, more efficient power loom developed by **Francis Cabot Lowell** at his textile mill in Massachusetts.

A mill town named in Lowell's honor was founded in 1823. Mill owners hired young girls and women because they would work for less pay than men. These female textile workers, some as young as 10 years old, were called the "Lowell girls." The Lowell girls lived in boarding houses and worked in the mills instead of attending school. Their letters home revealed that many enjoyed the independence factory work provided. These young women also published a monthly magazine of poetry and fiction, called the *Lowell Offering*.

Eventually, the Lowell workers' low wages and long hours in dangerous conditions soon became intolerable, so the young women banded together to protest. In the 1830s, the Lowell workers organized several **strikes**, or work stoppages, to protest cuts in wages. Their activism led to the formation of the Lowell Female Labor Reform Association, the first organization of working women in the United States.

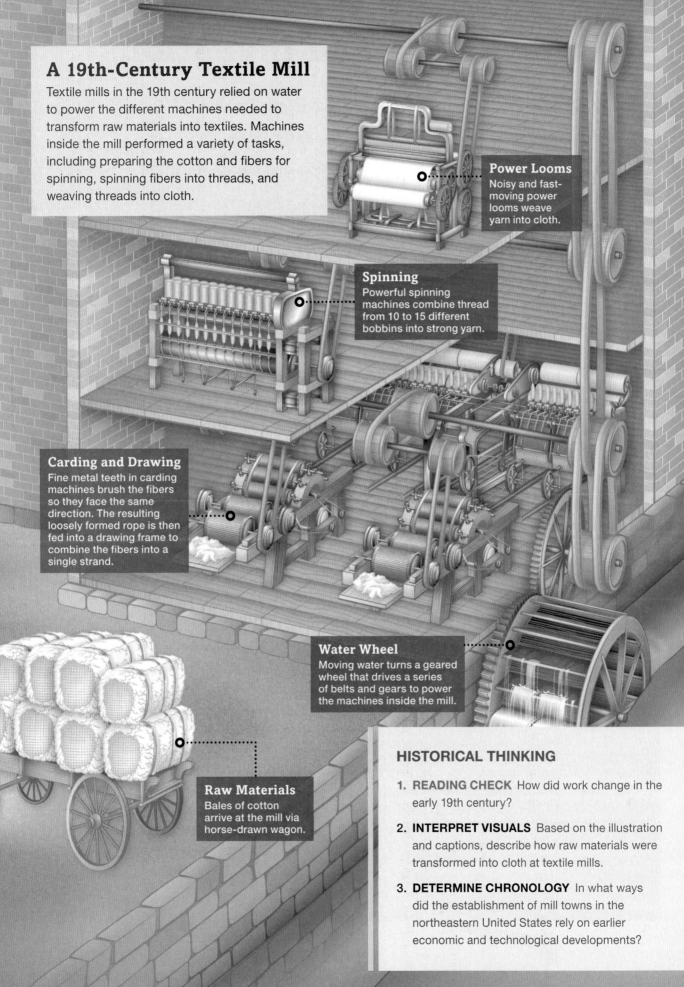

A 19th-Century Textile Mill

Textile mills in the 19th century relied on water to power the different machines needed to transform raw materials into textiles. Machines inside the mill performed a variety of tasks, including preparing the cotton and fibers for spinning, spinning fibers into threads, and weaving threads into cloth.

Power Looms
Noisy and fast-moving power looms weave yarn into cloth.

Spinning
Powerful spinning machines combine thread from 10 to 15 different bobbins into strong yarn.

Carding and Drawing
Fine metal teeth in carding machines brush the fibers so they face the same direction. The resulting loosely formed rope is then fed into a drawing frame to combine the fibers into a single strand.

Water Wheel
Moving water turns a geared wheel that drives a series of belts and gears to power the machines inside the mill.

Raw Materials
Bales of cotton arrive at the mill via horse-drawn wagon.

HISTORICAL THINKING

1. **READING CHECK** How did work change in the early 19th century?

2. **INTERPRET VISUALS** Based on the illustration and captions, describe how raw materials were transformed into cloth at textile mills.

3. **DETERMINE CHRONOLOGY** In what ways did the establishment of mill towns in the northeastern United States rely on earlier economic and technological developments?

1.2 Innovations and Inventions

In your lifetime, new ideas and technology have transformed communication in dramatic ways. During the early 1800s, new technologies started speeding up transportation and communication.

MAIN IDEA New inventions made American workers more productive, created new industries, and contributed to the nation's economic growth.

NEW MANUFACTURING METHODS

As industries began to flourish in the United States, innovative thinkers were making manufacturing more efficient and profitable. Eli Whitney, John Deere, Robert Fulton, and Samuel Morse were just a few of the many Americans who introduced new technologies in the early 19th century.

Eli Whitney, one of the most influential of these inventors, was born in 1765 in Massachusetts. From an early age, he showed a natural talent for mechanics and was able to skillfully improve useful items. In 1797, war between the United States and France seemed likely, and the nation's military needed more weapons. Whitney came up with an ambitious plan to supply the federal government

with 10,000 rifles in just two years' time. The challenge was this: Every weapon already in use was unique. Any repair required making a new custom part for that specific gun. So Whitney made his rifles using **interchangeable parts**. Each of his guns had the exact same parts.

Whitney completed the government's order in eight years, but his method of using interchangeable parts set the machine age in motion. The use of interchangeable parts soon spread to the production of nearly all goods. Having all parts ready to use meant that goods could be produced quickly and at a lower cost. This efficiency helped shape the identity of the United States as a nation of problem-solving, ingenuity, and progress.

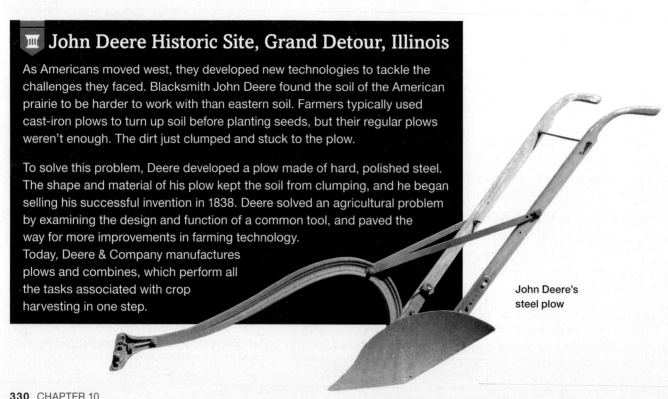

🏛 John Deere Historic Site, Grand Detour, Illinois

As Americans moved west, they developed new technologies to tackle the challenges they faced. Blacksmith John Deere found the soil of the American prairie to be harder to work with than eastern soil. Farmers typically used cast-iron plows to turn up soil before planting seeds, but their regular plows weren't enough. The dirt just clumped and stuck to the plow.

To solve this problem, Deere developed a plow made of hard, polished steel. The shape and material of his plow kept the soil from clumping, and he began selling his successful invention in 1838. Deere solved an agricultural problem by examining the design and function of a common tool, and paved the way for more improvements in farming technology. Today, Deere & Company manufactures plows and combines, which perform all the tasks associated with crop harvesting in one step.

John Deere's steel plow

CRITICAL VIEWING Today's combine harvesters definitely look different from Deere's original plow. These machines accomplish all the harvesting tasks: they thresh, separate, clean, and collect the grain. What effect do you think these machines have on farm life and food production?

STEAMBOATS AND TELEGRAPHS

New technologies also changed shipping, communication, and agriculture. Robert Fulton's **steamboats**, or boats outfitted with steam boiler engines to power their paddle wheels, revolutionized river travel and made shipping quicker. By 1811, Fulton had designed a steamboat powerful and sturdy enough for the strong currents of the Mississippi River. Soon, an upstream journey on the Mississippi and Ohio rivers from New Orleans to Louisville, Kentucky was shortened from several months to just 14 days. But even the swiftest ship could not carry a message across miles in a matter of minutes.

Samuel F. B. Morse's **telegraph** sent messages over electrical wires using a series of long and short pulses known as Morse code. An operator in one location tapped out a message on a device called a key. The message moved through wires to a machine that printed it out as dots and dashes punched onto a strip of paper. Another operator then transcribed the code into words. The first telegraph message was transmitted on May 24, 1844. Soon, telegraph wires stretched throughout the nation, and operators could interpret the code in real time. Widespread use of the telegraph for personal, business, and government communication continued for more than 100 years.

Innovations changed life on the farm as well. Cyrus Hall McCormick's horse-drawn mechanical **reaper** quickly cut, or reaped, stalks of wheat from the field and gathered them up for processing. Farmers who used this new machine no longer had to harvest wheat by hand. The reaper helped increase wheat production throughout the Great Plains. It changed not only American farming but also many of the world's farming methods. McCormick's reaper was so successful that he opened a factory in Chicago to produce his machines, advancing both rural farming technology and urban manufacturing techniques.

HISTORICAL THINKING

1. **READING CHECK** What was significant about manufacturing with interchangeable parts?

2. **DRAW CONCLUSIONS** How did McCormick's mechanical reaper contribute to agricultural and urban growth?

3. **MAKE CONNECTIONS** McCormick's reaper connected both rural and urban innovation. How might another invention described in the text connect the country and the city?

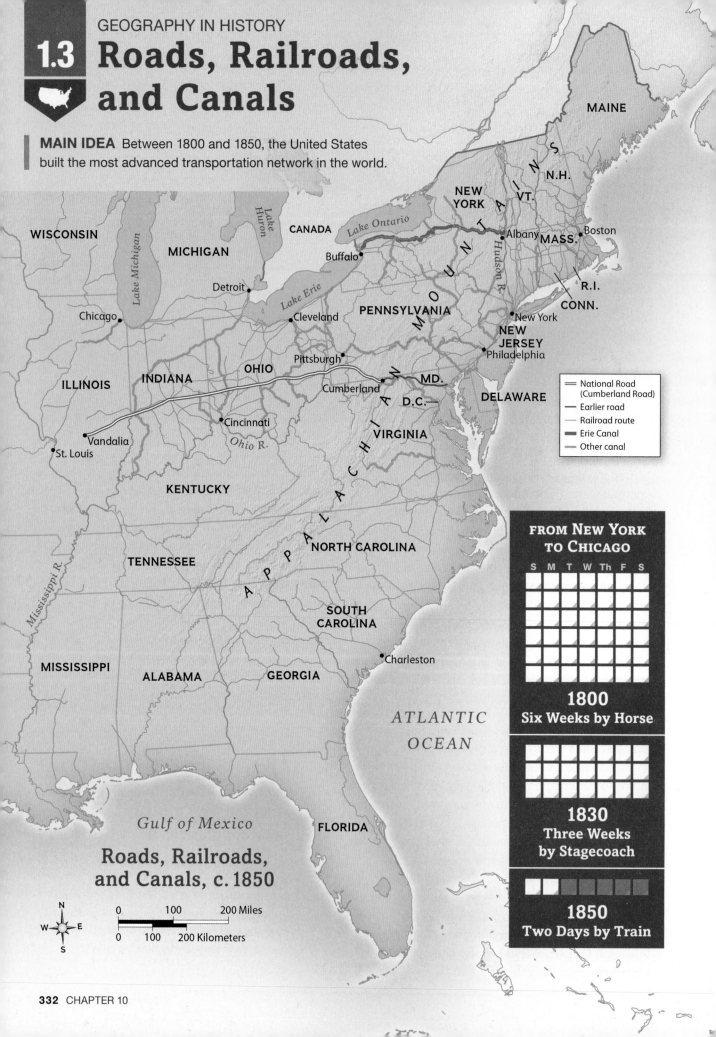

1.3 Roads, Railroads, and Canals

MAIN IDEA Between 1800 and 1850, the United States built the most advanced transportation network in the world.

MAINE

WISCONSIN

Lake Huron

MICHIGAN

CANADA

Lake Ontario

NEW YORK

VT.

N.H.

Albany

MASS.

Boston

Buffalo

Detroit

Lake Erie

Chicago

Cleveland

PENNSYLVANIA

Hudson R.

New York

R.I.

CONN.

NEW JERSEY

Philadelphia

ILLINOIS

INDIANA

OHIO

Pittsburgh

Cumberland

MD.

D.C.

DELAWARE

Cincinnati

Vandalia

Ohio R.

St. Louis

VIRGINIA

KENTUCKY

APPALACHIAN

MOUNTAINS

Mississippi R.

TENNESSEE

NORTH CAROLINA

SOUTH CAROLINA

MISSISSIPPI

ALABAMA

GEORGIA

Charleston

ATLANTIC OCEAN

Gulf of Mexico

FLORIDA

Legend:
- National Road (Cumberland Road)
- Earlier road
- Railroad route
- Erie Canal
- Other canal

Roads, Railroads, and Canals, c. 1850

N W E S

0   100   200 Miles

0   100   200 Kilometers

FROM NEW YORK TO CHICAGO

S M T W Th F S

1800
Six Weeks by Horse

1830
Three Weeks by Stagecoach

1850
Two Days by Train

OVERCOMING OBSTACLES

In the early 1800s, Americans moving west and south soon realized they needed more efficient ways to move people and goods across the country. But they faced several geographic challenges. One of these was distance. Today, you can fly from New York City to Miami, Florida, in a few hours. However, in 1800, that trip took three uncomfortable weeks by horse-drawn stagecoach. Travelers called stagecoaches "shake guts" because they shook so much as they rumbled over roads filled with holes and tree stumps.

The Appalachian Mountains represented another geographic challenge. This mountain range stretches north to south for more than 1,500 miles from Canada to Alabama and is up to 300 miles wide. Often steep and densely wooded, the Appalachians formed a physical barrier between the interior regions of the United States and thriving eastern ports such as New York City, Boston, Charleston, and Philadelphia. Americans innovated new solutions and overcame geographic challenges to build an enormous transportation network that produced major economic benefits.

TRANSPORTATION INNOVATION	ECONOMIC BENEFITS
THE NATIONAL ROAD	
During the early years of the United States, the roads were terrible. But in 1811, the federal government built the National Road, also known as the Cumberland Road. The road stretched west from Cumberland, Maryland, to Vandalia, Illinois. A good stretch of it had pavement, making for a much smoother ride. The states charged travelers tolls for their carriages and wagons—and even for their cattle!	The National Road moved mail, goods, and settlers between the East and the growing states of the Northwest Territory, including Ohio, Indiana, and Illinois. The federal government, states, and private companies soon built more roads connecting the East, the South, and the West. Trade expanded between the nation's interior and its bustling port cities, from Boston south to Charleston.
THE B&O RAILROAD	
During the 1820s, merchants in Baltimore, Maryland, struggled to compete with the merchants of New York City, who had the benefit of the Erie Canal to move goods. In 1826, a group of enterprising businessmen founded the Baltimore & Ohio (B&O) Railroad. They needed a steam-operated railroad to connect Baltimore to the growing cities of the interior, such as Cincinnati, Ohio, and St. Louis, Missouri. A steam locomotive called the Tom Thumb ran on the earliest line and proved that steam-powered cars could handle the steep, winding route.	The B&O proved an enormous success. Trains transported coal from the mines of western Virginia and Pennsylvania to the factories and furnaces of the East. The success of the B&O encouraged companies to build other railroads linking states and territories of the East, South, and West. By the 1850s, railroads were carrying all kinds of products. They transported Chesapeake Bay oysters, Florida oranges, and Georgia peaches to the restaurants of New York City. By 1860, the United States had 30,500 miles of track, about as much as the rest of the world.
THE ERIE CANAL	
Americans built a system of constructed waterways called canals that allowed boats and ships to travel inland to move goods. The largest of them, the Erie Canal, connected the Hudson River to the Great Lakes. It cut through 363 miles of land in upstate New York and linked New York City to growing cities such as Buffalo, Cleveland, Detroit, and Chicago.	Building the Erie Canal took eight years. But after it was completed, farmers in Ohio, Illinois, Indiana, and other states in the Midwest could ship their grain much more cheaply and quickly to the East. Before the canal, farmers had to pay $100 per wagon to ship their grain. By using the canal, their cost was only $10 per shipment. Instead of 20 days, the journey took just eight.

THINK LIKE A GEOGRAPHER

1. **IDENTIFY MAIN IDEAS AND DETAILS**
   What were some geographic challenges the young United States faced?

2. **INTERPRET MAPS** Study the map. How did the road, railroad, and canal systems work together as one transportation network?

1.4 The Mississippi River

The mighty Mississippi is the largest river in North America and one of the largest in the world. It lies entirely within the United States and flows south from Minnesota, collecting water from the Ohio and Missouri rivers and spilling from Louisiana into the Gulf of Mexico. As one of the world's busiest commercial waterways, the river is the lifeblood of a highly industrialized country. It snakes through some of the nation's most fertile farmland and moves most of our agricultural exports. The unique role the Mississippi has played in American history and literature has woven it deeply into the fabric of the country's folklore. As American author Mark Twain once said, "The Mississippi River will always have its own way; no engineering skill can persuade it to do otherwise." How might a geologic feature like a river serve as a "character" in a book?

CRITICAL VIEWING Steamboats have been chugging down the Mississippi River since the early 1800s, transforming how people and goods moved across the United States. Examine the front of the first steamboat (left) and the rear of the second steamboat (right). What can you infer about how these boats move through the water?

One of the world's wealthiest and most influential innovators, Henry Ford grew up on a farm and never lost his ties to rural life. He became a collector of objects from ordinary people and examples of industrial progress and opened a museum in 1929 to share them with the public. The Henry Ford Museum's mission is to provide unique educational exper based on authentic objects, stories, ar represent America's ingenuity, resourc and innovation. Its impressive collectic American artifacts includes many item the cotton industry. How do the artifac reflect the cotton production process?

One bale of cotton can make 1,217 men's T-shirts or 313,600 $100 bills.

Cotton Blossom

Cotton grows on shrubs in 17 states acrc the southern half of the country. Cotton plants first produce blossoms, which change from white to pink and fall off aft a few days. In their place grow small gree pods called bolls. Cotton seeds and their attached hairs develop within the bolls, which swell and grow. When the boll is ri it bursts into the white, fluffy balls show here. The seed hair has turned into the fibers used to make cloth and thread.

Once the cotton gin cotton easier to pro cotton became the crop in the America

Cotton Gin

Invented by Eli Whitney in 1793, the cotton gin machine revolutionized the process of cleaning seeds out of cotton. Whitney was visiting a friend in the South when he heard about how farmers struggled to efficiently process their cotton crops. He quickly solved their problem with a device that pulled the cotton through a set of wire teeth mounted on a spinning cylinder. The cotton fibers could fit through narrow slots in the machine, but the seeds couldn't.

Spinning Wheel

Spinning fibers into yarn that was then woven into cloth was an important task in many households in the 1600s and 1700s. Young or unmarried women often became experts at this tedious and physically tiring task. This large spinning wheel would have required its spinner to alternate between spinning fibers into yarn and winding the yarn onto the spindle.

Fluffy raw wool or cotton fibers were spun into fine yarn used to make clothing.

> "Ford's perspective on history was informed by a strong belief in **the power of learning by doing.**"
>
> —Marc Greuther, Chief Curator,
> The Henry Ford Museum

Why would advertising thread have been so common during the 1800s?

J&P. COATS'
FOR HAND AND MACHINE
BEST SIX CORD THREAD

Cotton Thread Trade Cards

Without cotton, there is no thread, and without thread, there is no clothing! The cotton industry remained strong throughout American history, as demonstrated by these trade cards for "spool cotton" or thread, which date to the late 1800s. Advertisers appealed to customers with colorful ads promoting consumer goods such as thread.

2.2 Growth of the Cotton Industry

Today, economies all over the world are connected to each other in visible and sometimes not-so-visible ways. The same was true for two seemingly very different parts of the United States—the South and the North—in the 19th century.

MAIN IDEA A new invention enabled southern plantation owners to grow more crops and increase profits.

THE COTTON BOOM

The South differed from the North in several ways. For example, the South relied more on an agrarian economy, while the North was rapidly becoming a major industrial center. But one invention brought the two regions closer together.

In 1793, Eli Whitney visited a southern plantation and observed that the system used to remove seeds from picked cotton was slow and labor intensive. To solve this problem, he designed the **cotton gin**, which, as you have read, is a machine fitted with teeth to grab the seeds and separate them from cotton tufts. The cotton gin increased the productivity of enslaved laborers,

and cotton became the main cash crop on many southern farms that had previously grown tobacco. Most southern farmers embraced cotton because years of tobacco cultivation had depleted the soil of the nutrients needed for growing healthy tobacco plants.

Because of more efficient cotton production in the early 19th century, cotton quickly became a central part of the U.S. economy. Both the South and the North relied on this crop. Slave labor produced the cotton and raw materials that enabled northern manufacturers, financiers, and other business interests to thrive. This, in turn, spurred a new consumer culture in individual families connected to the slave-based economy.

CRITICAL VIEWING *Plantation Economy*, by William Aiken Walker, c. 1881, depicts enslaved people working in a southern cotton field. What does the painting convey about the process of cotton production?

SLAVERY EXPANDS

Even with the advent of the cotton gin, growing and picking cotton was labor intensive, and the production of cotton relied on the labor system created to support it: slavery. The "peculiar institution" of slavery shaped the South's political, social, economic, and cultural development.

Southern plantation owners who wanted to maximize their profits from cotton production tried to do so by acquiring more land. As you have read, in the early 19th century, the federal government intentionally seized Native American lands. So when some southern landowners and farmers did the same in order to expand their farmlands, they did so with the blessing of the federal government. This land grab forced tribes to leave the Southeast and move to relocation areas in the West. Many Native Americans were permanently displaced from their homes.

Southern plantation owners also tried to maximize profits by increasing their enslaved workforces. In January 1807, Congress passed a new law that would "prohibit the importation of slaves into any port or place within the jurisdiction of the United States … from any foreign kingdom, place, or country." However, the slave importation clause that had been inserted into the Constitution 20 years prior prevented this new law from taking effect until January 1808. Once enacted, the ban caused the **interstate slave trade**, or the slave trade *within* the United States, to increase. Slave owners urged enslaved women to have more children. They then sold some slaves at slave auctions to make a profit and bought others to staff their plantations with specially skilled enslaved workers. Slave auctions separated families. Enslaved communities responded to forced separations by broadening kinship bonds, which meant considering non-blood-related fellow slaves as family members.

HISTORICAL THINKING

1. **READING CHECK** What impact did the cotton gin have on cotton production?

2. **DRAW CONCLUSIONS** How did the interstate slave trade affect enslaved communities?

3. **EVALUATE** In what ways did the institution of slavery shape the economic development of both the South and the North?

2.3 Slavery and Resistance

When one group of people oppresses another, the oppressed group eventually revolts. During the 19th century, enslaved communities and individuals alike rose up.

MAIN IDEA People trapped in the institution of slavery created a culture of survival, resistance, and, ultimately, rebellion.

Shackles

Tax badge

THE SOCIETAL IMPACT OF SLAVERY

The institution of slavery affected all parts of southern society: wealthy or poor, slave or free, white or black. Plantation owners greatly advanced their wealth through slavery. Even though the majority of southern white farmers workers did not own slaves, they supported the practice of slavery. In the **antebellum**, or prewar, South, the poorest whites held higher status than any African Americans.

During the early 19th century, more than 100,000 free African Americans lived in the South, and they most certainly did not support slavery. Though they were free, they could not vote, own property, or receive an education. Legally, their status was constantly in question. Traveling was dangerous because they ran the risk of being accused of being runaway slaves and losing their freedom. In order to prove their free status, free African Americans had to go to court for Certificates of Freedom. Even then, some were kidnapped and sold into slavery.

The greatest impact of slavery, of course, was on enslaved people themselves. Slaves were considered chattel, or property, of their owners and were denied rights, freedom, and sometimes even their lives. Slave owners held a particularly ominous form of power over slaves with the constant possibility of family separation. Just the threat of sale allowed slave owners to exercise enormous control over their slaves. Enslaved parents routinely saw their children sold away from them. Spouses and siblings were separated, and they knew that future contact would be nearly impossible.

🏛 Chicago History Museum, Chicago

The system of slavery relied on preventing escapes. Slave owners placed shackles like these on enslaved people's wrists or ankles. The cuffs were held closed by a screw. In Charleston, South Carolina, enslaved workers who were hired out by their owners had to wear tax badges engraved with tax registration numbers and job categories.

SURVIVAL AND RESISTANCE

Despite the horrific conditions under which they lived, enslaved people resisted the circumstances they faced every day. Many slave owners imposed their own religious beliefs on slaves because they suggested that a belief in Christianity would make slavery an acceptable situation. But enslaved people interpreted scripture for themselves, in ways that encouraged a quest for freedom. They also composed songs called spirituals based on scripture and biblical figures such as Moses, who led the Israelites out of slavery in Egypt.

In addition to their own religious practices, enslaved people developed a distinct African-American culture. They retained and adapted traditional customs including music, food, and dancing, as well as varied family structures. They created rich communities bound together by common experiences and shared traditions. In this way, enslaved people asserted their humanity, which could not be taken away by slave owners.

Passive resistance, or the nonviolent refusal to obey authority and laws, was another way enslaved people resisted slavery. Forms of passive resistance included breaking tools, working slowly, pretending to be ill, and learning to read.

Sometimes, though, resistance meant armed rebellion. Inspired by a slave uprising in Haiti, in 1800, a slave named Gabriel Prosser, who bore the last name of his cruel owner, Thomas Prosser, planned a revolt in Virginia. In 1822, a freed slave named Denmark Vesey used scripture to inspire others to take over arsenals and burn down buildings in Charleston, South Carolina. Most revolts, including these, were put down quickly before whites were killed, and they resulted in the deaths of the enslaved people who had planned the rebellions.

Enslaved people of all ages worked long hours in the fields, houses, and workshops of their owners. This family was photographed in a Georgia cotton field in 1860.

But in 1831, Nat Turner led a small group of fellow slaves in a violent rebellion in which more than 50 people were killed in one night. Turner and his men were captured and hanged. Southerners reacted to Turner's rebellion—as they had to others—with violence. Some took matters into their own hands and murdered hundreds of innocent slaves.

Like Gabriel Prosser and Denmark Vesey, Turner was a literate man who led an open, violent revolt against slave-owning whites. Southern authorities reacted to Turner's revolt forcefully and by instituting severe restrictions, including a ban on teaching slaves to read and write.

HISTORICAL THINKING

1. **READING CHECK** In what ways did enslaved people resist slavery?

2. **DRAW CONCLUSIONS** Why did free African Americans need Certificates of Freedom?

3. **MAKE CONNECTIONS** Why was literacy for slaves a threat to slave owners?

3.1 A Young Nation Expands

Being part of a strong family or a successful organization makes members proud to belong to that group. The same kind of pride developed in the early 1800s among Americans witnessing the massive changes in transportation and commerce in the United States.

| **MAIN IDEA** Americans developed a strong national identity during the administrations of presidents James Madison and James Monroe.

TRANSPORTATION AND COMMERCE

The market revolution changed how people worked, traveled, and did business. Eventually, it also encouraged a new philosophy of **nationalism**. Nationalism is the concept of loyalty and devotion to one's nation.

Congressmen **Henry Clay** and **John C. Calhoun** argued for tariffs, or taxes on imported goods, to promote American manufacturing and stimulate commerce. In 1816, Calhoun was instrumental in establishing the Second Bank of the United States. Clay and Calhoun also supported government **subsidies**, or government funds for improvements or support of commerce. Land subsidies, or land granted to private companies by the federal government, became an important part of building roads and railroads. Clay, Calhoun, and others engaged in heated debates with other legislators who favored a more limited federal government role in financing a national infrastructure. Ultimately, tariffs on import goods, the establishment of the National Bank, and government subsidies became known as the **American System**.

Under the American System, improvements in road systems, trains, and waterways united the country geographically and culturally. In 1817, construction began on the **Erie Canal**, which stretched from Buffalo near Lake Erie in western New York to Albany. The Hudson River connected Albany to New York City. When the canal was completed eight years later, farmers could ship their crops within the state and to international destinations through the port at New York City. The canal also encouraged the development of more industrial sites because improved transportation made it easier to move goods to markets.

The **Illinois and Michigan Canal,** completed in 1848, connected Lake Michigan to the Illinois and Mississippi rivers near the city of Chicago. After the construction of these canals, crops and manufactured goods could be shipped all the way from New York City to New Orleans on a water route. The canals also made it easier for people to move their families and belongings west.

NEW BOUNDARIES, NEW DECISIONS

At the same time, the nation was growing in size. General Andrew Jackson became a hero with his successful military campaigns in the War of 1812, including victory in the Battle of New Orleans. His reputation grew when he subdued Native Americans in the Southeast and wrested Florida from Spanish control. Under the terms of the Transcontinental Treaty of 1819, the United States formally received Florida from Spain and gave Spain sovereignty over Texas.

The years that followed the War of 1812 were fairly peaceful and smooth. Territorial conflicts with other nations were temporarily settled, and the economy was growing. The administration of **James Monroe**, who was elected president of the United States in 1816, is remembered as the **Era of Good Feelings**. When Monroe ran for re-election in 1820, the Federalist Party didn't even offer a candidate to oppose him. By 1820, the Federalist Party was no longer a national force.

The Erie Canal, Then and Now
Cranes powered by horses lifted buckets of rock from the canal bed,
swung them around, and dumped the rocks at the top of the canal
bank. George Catlin's 1825 lithograph, *Process of Excavation, Lockport,*
illustrates the ingenuity of this process. The original canal had 83 locks.
The photograph at right is a present-day aerial view of the Erie Canal and
two of the 35 modern locks positioned on the canal.

During this period, important Supreme Court
rulings strengthened the federal government's
power. In 1819, the Court affirmed the
constitutionality of the Second Bank of the United
States in the *McCulloch* v. *Maryland* decision.
According to the Necessary and Proper Clause in
the Constitution, Congress has **implied powers**,
or powers not explicitly stated in the Constitution.
In short, because a National Bank had previously
been established, Congress could establish the
Second Bank of the United States. Additionally,
the state of Maryland did not have the power to tax
that national bank.

In 1824, the case of *Gibbons* v. *Ogden* expanded
federal control over interstate commerce, or
business affairs between states. Aaron Ogden,
who owned steamboats that traveled on the
Hudson River, sued Thomas Gibbons for running
steamboat operations in the same waters.
Gibbons argued that Congress alone had the
power to regulate interstate commerce, and that

New York had been wrong to grant Ogden the sole
right to running his steamboats in the waterway in
the first place. The Court ruled in favor of Gibbons
to prevent the formation of a **monopoly**, or
complete control of an industry by one company.
More importantly, the decision solidified the
federal government's power to regulate interstate
commerce by eliminating the individual states' sole
control over it.

HISTORICAL THINKING

1. **READING CHECK** Why did nationalism grow
   stronger during the administrations of Madison
   and Monroe?

2. **DRAW CONCLUSIONS** What parts of the
   American System are still in effect today?

3. **SUMMARIZE** Why is Monroe's presidency
   remembered as the Era of Good Feelings?

3.2 Increasing Regional Tensions

When people find it impossible to agree, they may need to work out a compromise to resolve the issue. In the early 1800s, Americans wanted to maintain a balance of power between free states and slave states, so they came up with a compromise.

MAIN IDEA As the United States expanded its territory and its power, it negotiated how each new state would deal with the issue of slavery.

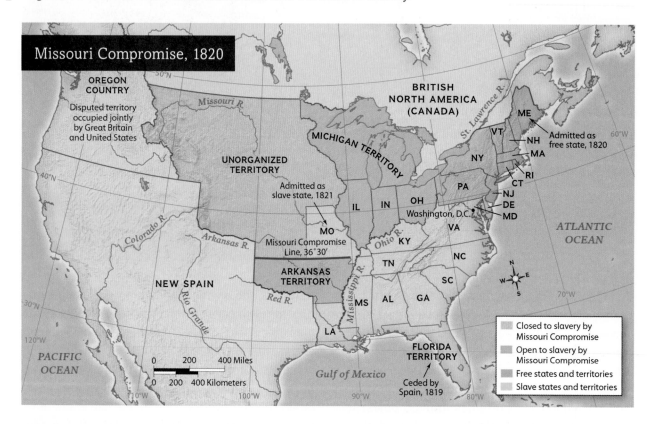

Missouri Compromise, 1820

OREGON COUNTRY
Disputed territory occupied jointly by Great Britain and United States

BRITISH NORTH AMERICA (CANADA)

UNORGANIZED TERRITORY

MICHIGAN TERRITORY

Admitted as slave state, 1821

MO
Missouri Compromise Line, 36°30'

NEW SPAIN

ARKANSAS TERRITORY

ME — Admitted as free state, 1820

Washington, D.C.

ATLANTIC OCEAN

PACIFIC OCEAN

0   200   400 Miles
0   200   400 Kilometers

FLORIDA TERRITORY
Ceded by Spain, 1819

Gulf of Mexico

Closed to slavery by Missouri Compromise
Open to slavery by Missouri Compromise
Free states and territories
Slave states and territories

THE MISSOURI COMPROMISE

Nationalism grew during the years of Madison's and Monroe's presidencies, and so did **sectionalism**. Sectionalism is the identification with and loyalty to a particular part of the country, such as the North or the South. The rise of sectionalism was driven by two main factors: the different economies of these regions and the practice of slavery. For the most part, the North was an industrial region, with mills and wage laborers, while the South was an agricultural region, producing cotton through slave labor.

The federal government wanted to admit the Missouri Territory as the 23rd state. The trick was how to do so without upsetting the balance of 11 slave states and 11 free states. Americans worried that admitting Missouri would create an imbalance in power between slave and free states. In 1819, the Senate proposed the **Missouri Compromise**. In it, the people of the state of Missouri could own slaves. Missouri would be admitted to the Union at the same time as Maine, a free state, which maintained the balance between the number of slave states and free states. The compromise prohibited slavery in all the lands acquired in the Louisiana Purchase north of the 36° 30' N latitude line. These lands were considered **unorganized territory**, or lands governed by the federal government but not belonging to any state. As a result of the compromise, any states formed from this unorganized territory would be free states. Even so, the compromise stated that enslaved people who escaped to free states could be captured and returned to their owners.

THE MONROE DOCTRINE

In December 1823, President Monroe delivered a speech in which he introduced a new approach to foreign policy. In it he stated, "The American continents, by the free and independent conditions which they have assumed and maintained, are henceforth not to be considered as subjects for future colonization by any European power." Monroe also promised that the United States would not fight in any European wars. In simple terms, the president said, "You stay out of our hemisphere, and we'll stay out of yours." His ideas became known as the **Monroe Doctrine**. Monroe warned European nations against interfering in the Western Hemisphere. Doing so would be considered an act of aggression that would result in military action from the United States. Monroe's declaration was bold because the United States had no actual authority over Central America or South America.

Part of the inspiration for the Monroe Doctrine stemmed from colonies in Central and South America rebelling against European rule. Monroe was concerned about European countries having so much presence and authority in Central and South America. He feared that European countries might try to re-assert their colonial power. He also had concerns over Russia's presence in what is now Alaska. Russia had issued a statement in 1821 that non-Russians could not enter its territory. Monroe did not want Russia to try to expand its North American territory.

Though Russia and Spain denounced the Monroe Doctrine, they tolerated it. Wars among European countries had wearied them, and they had little desire to expand their involvement in the Americas.

The Monroe Doctrine Desk

While serving as a minister to France under President George Washington, James Monroe purchased this mahogany desk in Paris. When he moved into the White House in 1817, he brought this desk with him and likely wrote the Monroe Doctrine while sitting at it. About 100 years after his presidency, Monroe's great-great-grandson discovered letters from Washington, Madison, Franklin, and Jefferson to Monroe, hidden in the desk's secret compartment.

HISTORICAL THINKING

1. **READING CHECK** What was Monroe's concern about Central and South America?

2. **IDENTIFY PROBLEMS AND SOLUTIONS** How did the Missouri Compromise attempt to solve a problem and cause a potential problem at the same time?

3. **INTERPRET MAPS** Based on details you notice on the map, what territories were open to slavery and what territories were closed to slavery?

3.3 The Monroe Doctrine

In the early 19th century, the United States began to position itself as a world power. One part of that new role for the young country, according to President James Monroe, was protecting countries in Central and South America from future interference from European monarchies. The Monroe Doctrine, as his 1823 statement came to be known, would shape U.S. foreign policy for more than a century.

On December 2, 1823, President Monroe delivered his seventh annual message to Congress, or what we know today as a State of the Union address. Monroe touched on many topics, but most significantly, he introduced a new policy toward Europe and the Western Hemisphere.

CRITICAL VIEWING In this 1912 painting by Clyde DeLand, titled *Birth of the Monroe Doctrine*, President Monroe is outlining his new policy to his cabinet in preparation for his address. Notice the map and the globe. What do you think their significance is?

Legend

1 John Quincy Adams

2 William Harris Crawford

3 William Wirt

4 James Monroe

5 John Caldwell Calhoun

6 Daniel D. Tompkins

7 John McLean

DOCUMENT ONE

Primary Source: Speech
from War Message to Congress,
by James Madison, June 1, 1812

The U.S. Navy was young compared to Great Britain's. While navigating Atlantic waters, American sailors had to deal with frequent interference from Great Britain. President Madison delivered this speech as a warning that further activity would initiate an open conflict.

CONSTRUCTED RESPONSE How does Madison's summary of British actions make a case for retaliation?

British cruisers have been in the practice also of violating the rights and the peace of our coasts. They hover over and harass our entering and departing commerce. When called on, nevertheless, by the United States to punish the greater offenses committed by her [Britain's] own vessels, her government has bestowed on their commanders additional marks of honor and confidence.

DOCUMENT TWO

Primary Source: Speech
from Seventh Annual Message to Congress,
by James Monroe, December 2, 1823

In this speech, President Monroe declared that from that point on, European monarchies were not allowed to interfere in Central and South America. At the same time, he promised that the United States would stay out of European affairs.

CONSTRUCTED RESPONSE How does Monroe's speech communicate a strategy for both peacetime and military action, if provoked?

In the wars of the European powers in matters relating to themselves we have never taken any part, nor does it comport with our policy to do so. It is only when our rights are invaded or seriously menaced that we resent injuries or make preparation for our defense. With the movements in this hemisphere we are of necessity more immediately connected, and by causes which must be obvious to all enlightened and impartial [unbiased] observers.

DOCUMENT THREE

Primary Source: Essay
from "The Monroe Doctrine and Spanish America,"
by Juan Bautista Alberdi, c. 1850

Juan Bautista Alberdi, a political thinker from Argentina, expressed concern that Monroe's new policy would threaten the political and economic independence of the countries it promised to protect.

CONSTRUCTED RESPONSE How does Alberdi's opinion of the Monroe Doctrine differ from Monroe's description of his new policy?

The doctrine attributed to Monroe is a contradiction, the daughter of egoism [self-centeredness]. Even though the United States owes everything to Europe, it wants to isolate America from Europe, from any influence that does not emanate [originate] from the United States, which will make the United States the only custom house [official port] for the civilization of transatlantic origin.

SYNTHESIZE & WRITE

1. **REVIEW** Review what you have learned about the position of the United States as a rising world power in the early 1800s.

2. **RECALL** On your own paper, write down the main ideas expressed in the excerpts from Madison's and Monroe's speeches and Alberdi's essay.

3. **CONSTRUCT** Construct a topic sentence that supports or opposes this statement: In the early 1800s, the United States established itself as a world power through a policy of protection and European nonintervention in the Americas.

4. **WRITE** Write a paragraph that presents an argument for or against the statement in Step 3 using evidence from the documents.

3.4 Women in the Early Republic

To people living in the 21st century, the saying "a woman's place is in the home" is not only dated, it's inaccurate. However, in the early years of the republic, home was considered the ideal sphere for a woman's power and influence.

MAIN IDEA Increased access to education and the rise of women's organizations expanded women's roles in the early republic.

REPUBLICAN MOTHERHOOD

In the years after the Revolution, a strong nationalist spirit took hold as the young United States began to grow and prosper. Citizens embraced their new, republican government. As you have read, in the context of the early republic, the word *republican* did not refer to a political party, but to the new form of representative rule. Citizens also embraced the ideal of civic republicanism, or promoting the common good in order to protect liberty. According to the ideal of republicanism, good government and virtuous citizens worked toward the public good instead of private interests.

What did that mean for women in the early republic? Many had fully participated in the American Revolution, just as their husbands and sons had done. But after the war, women returned to their roles as wives and mothers. No matter their race or class, women were not allowed to vote or even, in many cases, to own their

own property or hold public office. However, they participated in the republic by teaching republican ideals to their children—especially to their sons, who would grow up to be voters, property owners, and maybe even public officials or statesmen. Historians refer to this set of societal expectations for mothers as **republican motherhood**.

Mother as Teacher
The early 19th-century woman had a lot to live up to. Literature, art, and social expectations defined roles for women in narrow ways. Paintings such as this one cast women in a nearly angelic light and featured them as doting mothers.

Catharine Beecher

In a family portrait taken around 1860, Catharine Beecher is seated second from the left. Beecher championed free public education for all and a rigorous education for women. However, her support of women's education did not extend to other rights for women. She opposed granting women the right to vote. She believed that women should limit their efforts to home and school and that a woman's greatest roles were those of wife and mother. Even so, she never married or had children, and she supported herself throughout her life as an educator, writer, and lecturer.

THE IMPORTANCE OF EDUCATION

In the early 1800s, the ideal woman was pure, religiously devout, and a good housekeeper and mother. She also willingly deferred to all her husband's wishes. Such a role did not require women to be well educated, and few learned more than language arts and basic arithmetic—subjects that aided them in running an efficient home. But without adequate education, how could mothers be expected to teach their children, especially their sons, the basics of civic life and service in a republic?

This question had been brewing since the American Revolution, when Abigail Adams argued that in order to support male education, women should be educated as well: "If we mean to have heroes, statesmen, and philosophers, we should have learned [educated] women."

A few years later, **Judith Sargent Murray,** an American essayist and playwright in the early republic, was known for commenting on public issues, especially women's rights. She wrote that women were not intellectually inferior to men, as some believed. She argued that daughters could not reach their full potential if they were simply trained to be wives, housekeepers, and mothers. In order to teach their children republican values, mothers needed to learn science and higher math, which were traditionally taught only to men.

In 1822, **Catharine Beecher** founded the Hartford Female Seminary, a school for women in Connecticut. Students learned algebra, Latin, logic, and philosophy, among other subjects. The curriculum emphasized physical education and training in home economics. Many women who attended became teachers themselves.

As more girls and women received formal educations, women began to establish organizations that focused on helping others. Many of the organizations had a specific focus, such as helping orphans, people with physical handicaps, or war widows. Members soon began to see the positive effects of their work. Women's organizations grew and expanded, and their leaders became important agents for social change. Some of these women's organizations also laid the groundwork for budding political and social movements, such as securing the vote for women and the **abolition** of, or putting an end to, slavery.

HISTORICAL THINKING

1. **READING CHECK** How does the concept of republican motherhood align with the ideals women were expected to live up to in the early republic?

2. **DRAW CONCLUSIONS** What conclusions can you draw about the work that 19th-century women's organizations did?

3. **MAKE CONNECTIONS** How might a more comprehensive education and the expectation of rearing good citizens lead women to seek broader civic roles for themselves?

VOCABULARY

Use vocabulary words to complete the sentences.

1. Eli Whitney's invention of the _____ made the production of cotton more efficient.

2. *Gibbons* v. *Ogden* declared that a single company could not have a _____ on an industry.

3. _____ made manufacturing more structured and uniform, producing pieces that could fit in any component of its kind.

4. Young girls were recruited to work in mills in the _____ industry.

5. The _____ brought crews of people to one main site where work was done with machinery.

6. Congress used _____ in establishing the Second Bank of the United States.

7. _____ grew as the United States acquired more land, improved its financial system, and encouraged patriotic ideals.

8. The division between the North and the South was an example of _____.

READING STRATEGY
DRAW CONCLUSIONS

If you haven't already, complete your chart with evidence from the text to support conclusions. List at least three key conclusions. Then answer the question.

9. What is one conclusion you can draw about the growth and changes in the United States between 1800 and 1844, and what evidence helped you to draw that conclusion?

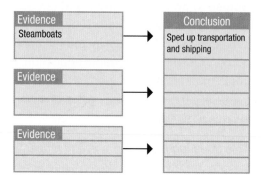

MAIN IDEAS

Answer the following questions. Support your answers with evidence from the chapter.

10. What type of work did the factory system replace? **LESSON 1.1**

11. How did Eli Whitney plan to deliver the most rifles ever produced by one factory? **LESSON 1.2**

12. Why did plantation owners want to use enslaved labor? **LESSON 2.2**

13. How did religion play a role in motivating the leaders of slave rebellions? **LESSON 2.3**

14. How did a strong economy benefit the spread of nationalism during the Era of Good Feelings? **LESSON 3.1**

15. What conditions gave rise to sectionalism in the United States? **LESSON 3.2**

16. What did President Monroe hope to achieve through his message to European powers in the Monroe Doctrine? **LESSON 3.3**

17. How did education help to change women's roles in society? **LESSON 3.4**

Answer the following questions. Support your answers with evidence from the chapter.

18. **MAKE GENERALIZATIONS** How did technological advancements change agriculture in the early 19th century?

19. **SEQUENCE EVENTS** What were the major events of the Industrial Revolution in the United States? Create a time line to illustrate your answer.

20. **DESCRIBE** What were enslaved people's daily lives like in the antebellum South?

21. **EVALUATE** How did the country become more connected in the first half of the 19th century?

22. **FORM AND SUPPORT OPINIONS** Which territorial expansions were of the most value to the United States? Support your opinion with evidence from the chapter.

INTERPRET MAPS

Cotton spindles are part of cotton spinning machinery. Larger mills had more spindles. Study the map and then answer the questions below.

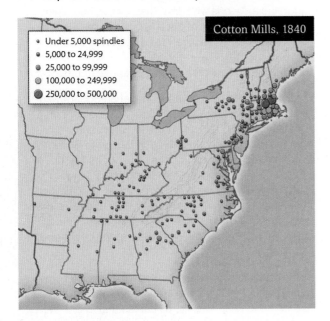

Cotton Mills, 1840

- Under 5,000 spindles
- 5,000 to 24,999
- 25,000 to 99,999
- 100,000 to 249,999
- 250,000 to 500,000

23. Which northern and southern states had the largest mills?

24. According to the map, where might ships carrying raw cotton be headed?

ANALYZE SOURCES

After visiting a plantation in Georgia in 1793, Eli Whitney designed a new machine to remove seeds from cotton. He wrote a letter to his father about his invention. Read the excerpt and then answer the question below.

> I tried some experiments. In about ten Days I made a little model, for which I was offered . . . a Hundred Guineas [about $450]. I concluded [decided] to . . . turn my attention to perfecting the Machine. I made one . . . which required the labor of one man to turn it and with which one man will clean ten times as much cotton as he can in any other way before known and also cleanse it much better than in the usual mode. This machine may be turned by water or with a horse, with the greatest ease, and one man and a horse will do more than fifty men with the old machine. It makes the labor fifty times less.

25. What benefits did Whitney point to when describing his new invention?

CONNECT TO YOUR LIFE

26. **NARRATIVE** Review the inventions and innovations in this chapter and consider how they changed people's lives. Then think of a new technology that has affected your life. Write a paragraph connecting your experience with the experience of someone in the early to mid-1800s whose life was similarly affected.

TIPS

- Make a list of important engineering or technological advances in the early to mid-1800s.

- Use two or three vocabulary terms from the chapter in your narrative.

- Reflect on new machines, products, or building projects during your lifetime.

- Conclude by stating how you think new technology changes people's lives.

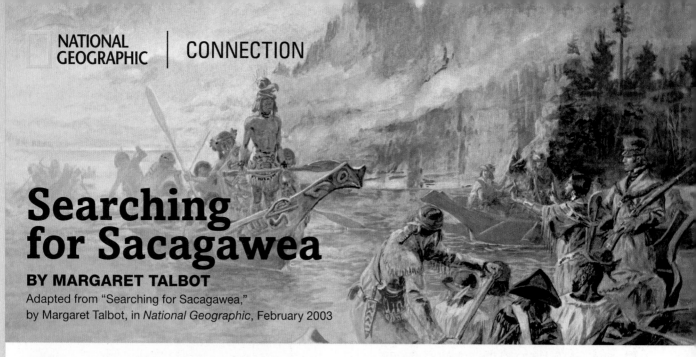

Searching for Sacagawea

BY MARGARET TALBOT

Adapted from "Searching for Sacagawea,"
by Margaret Talbot, in *National Geographic*, February 2003

The glimpses we are allowed of Sacagawea in Lewis and Clark's expedition journals tell us more about her than about almost any other Native American woman of her time. But the very sketchiness of our knowledge has permitted novelists, feminists, and Native American tribes to project what they wish upon Sacagawea. Many see her as a metaphor more than a human being. But who was Sacagawea, really?

From the age of about 13, Sacagawea had lived with the Hidatsa near the confluence of the Missouri and Knife rivers. Lewis and Clark first met Sacagawea when she was about 17 and pregnant with her first child. In November 1804, the Corps of Discovery, as the expedition was known, had arrived among the Mandan and Hidatsa on the upper Missouri River, in what is now North Dakota.

One warm afternoon in 2002, I spent some time there trying to reimagine Sacagawea's world. With me was Amy Mossett, a Mandan-Hidatsa from New Town, North Dakota, and an expert on Sacagawea. On a bluff above the Knife River, Mossett and I look out over shallow, bowl-shaped indentations in the ground where her ancestors' earth lodges once stood. "This is where I feel closest to Sacagawea," says Mossett.

The Corps of Discovery set out from its winter quarters on April 7, 1805. Less than two months after giving birth, Sacagawea gathered up her infant son and embarked with her husband, a French-Canadian fur trader, on a roughly 5,000-mile, 16-month journey. Contrary to her romanticized image, Sacagawea was not the expedition's "girl-guide." Most of the territory they passed through was as unfamiliar to her as it was to Lewis and Clark.

One of Sacagawea's greatest contributions was her mere presence, which seems to have disarmed potentially hostile tribes along the way. The journals record one of those fortunate coincidences.

Sacagawea, who spoke Hidatsa and Shoshone but neither English nor French, was to translate a Shoshone chief's words into Hidatsa for her husband, who was to translate into French for a member of the corps, who would translate into English for the captains. They were just about to begin this unwieldy relay when Sacagawea suddenly recognized the Shoshone chief. He was, of all people, her long-lost brother.

After the 21 months in which Sacagawea's story intersects with that of the expedition, she disappears almost entirely from our view. The best evidence we have suggests that she died in her mid-20s shortly after giving birth to a daughter. For many years, most white Americans wrote about Sacagawea as the archetypal "good Indian"—one who, like Pocahontas, had aided white men. But in recent decades, and especially for Native Americans, Sacagawea has become a different sort of symbol. She is a reminder of the extent to which the Lewis and Clark story is also a Native American story.

Disputes remain about where and when Sacagawea died and even how to spell and pronounce her name. For the 400 or so remaining Lemhi Shoshone who live on a reservation in Idaho, the connection to Sacagawea is one thread on which to hang their hopes for federal tribal recognition and a return of ancestral lands. The Wind River Shoshone in Wyoming insist "Sacajawea" (their spelling) died on their reservation, though most historians dispute this. But the Shoshone's cultural claim on Sacagawea anchors them in the Lewis and Clark story.

Some historians wonder why Sacagawea didn't stay behind with the Shoshone and her brother. Perhaps she had come to feel more like a Hidatsa than a Shoshone. Or perhaps she had been seized with curiosity about what came next and where the journey would take her.

For more from National Geographic, check out "Lost Missouri" online.

UNIT INQUIRY: Define Good Citizenship

In this unit, you learned about the political, economic, and geographic growth of the United States in the years of the early republic. Based on your understanding of the text, in what ways was good citizenship central to the success of the early republic? What role did citizenship play in how Americans defined themselves and others? Which groups of Americans were excluded from full citizenship, and why?

ASSIGNMENT

Create your own definition for good citizenship. Your definition should include several elements, including a statement of what constitutes good citizenship, why citizenship mattered in the early republic, and why citizenship still matters today. Be prepared to present your definition of citizenship to the class and explain your reasoning.

Gather Evidence As you develop your definition of good citizenship, gather evidence from this unit about the different ways in which concepts of citizenship shaped communities and a young nation. Think about the active roles citizens played in the early republic. Also consider the rights and responsibilities American citizens had—or did not have—and why. Use a graphic organizer like this one to help organize your thoughts.

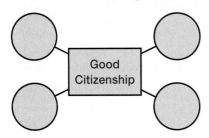

Produce Use your notes to produce descriptions of the elements that make up your definition of good citizenship. Write a short paragraph on each element using evidence from this unit to support your ideas.

Present Choose a creative way to present your definition of good citizenship to the class. Consider one of these options:

- Interview citizens in your community about what they think good citizenship entails. Ask them what they do to be good citizens and what rights and responsibilities are the most important to them. Present your interviews to the class.

- Create a good citizenship award. Work with a small team to design the award. Identify a person in your school who you think deserves this honor. Hold an award ceremony and appoint a class member to describe the ways in which your award recipient exemplifies good citizenship.

- Design a collaborative wall mural that illustrates the rights and responsibilities of good citizenship using words and drawings.

NATIONAL GEOGRAPHIC | LEARNING FRAMEWORK ACTIVITIES

Propose a New Invention

ATTITUDES Responsibility, Empowerment

SKILL Problem-Solving

Part of being a good citizen is taking care of the people and environment around you. The men and women who innovated new technologies in the early republic were all trying to solve some sort of problem or make a process more efficient. Using evidence from the reading, develop a proposal for a new invention. Define the problem that you are solving and how your invention would benefit your community or even the world. Consider including illustrations of your invention. Present your proposal to the class as if you were presenting to a panel of financial backers.

Write a Campaign Speech

SKILLS Collaboration, Communication

KNOWLEDGE Our Human Story

Political campaigns have been a part of American democracy since it began. Effective campaigns and their candidates have to deliver a clear message to potential voters if they want to win elections. Work with a small team of classmates to write a campaign speech about an important issue during the early republic. Use evidence from the reading to define your issue, craft your message, and select the candidate who would best deliver the speech. Present your team's speech and be prepared to listen to other teams' speeches.

To tell your American story

You've been reading about the founding of the country and the establishment of the American republic. Think about the individuals and families who established their homes in the United States. What does the idea of a "hometown" mean to you? And what can you learn when you investigate your own hometown?

Fred Hiebert
▶ Watch the Why Study U.S. History? video

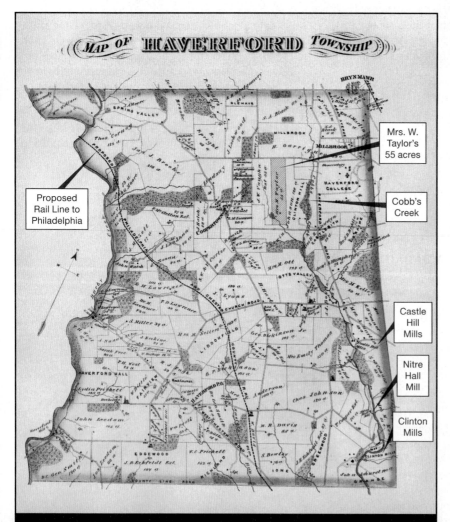

Proposed Rail Line to Philadelphia

Mrs. W. Taylor's 55 acres

Cobb's Creek

Castle Hill Mills

Nitre Hall Mill

Clinton Mills

This map of Haverford Township, published in 1875, reveals the kind of ground-level details those who lived there would have recognized—homes and farms belonging to prominent citizens, numerous creeks and ponds created for early mills, and the proposed Philadelphia–Chester County rail line.

If you look around my hometown (suburban Philadelphia), it's an area of houses and parks. But there are all sorts of clues to our history—strange names that don't seem to make sense. Like an old building called Nitre Hall on Karakung Drive, or a nearby street on a hillside called Lakeview Avenue (though there is no lake in sight).

So here's what I learned by going to my local library and historical society: This area west of Philadelphia has great agricultural land, watered by streams and creeks, and was acquired from Governor William Penn in 1680 for agricultural development. The largest stream in our part of Delaware County is Cobb's Creek, but the original name given by the Lenape Native Americans was *Karakung* (the place of wild geese). This name is still preserved as a road name.

Electric trolleys similar to this one were introduced in Haverford around the turn of the century. The electric railway transformed settled farmland into a thriving suburb accessible by a growing middle class.

By the early 1800s, the creeks were dammed, and the water flow was used to power mills of all sorts. A gunpowder mill operated from 1810 to 1840, using nitre (saltpeter), charcoal, and sulfur (all brought in), mixed here using the power of the waterwheels. Nitre Hall is actually the original house where the powder master (who mixed the dangerous powder together) lived. At that time, Nitre Hall Powder Mill was the second-largest black powder mill in the United States.

By 1840, the mills were converted to use water power to spin cotton and wool. During the Civil War, cloth for Union soldiers' uniforms was produced here. Following the Civil War and the increased dependence on steam power, the water mills disappeared. The last mill was a sawmill that closed in the mid-20th century.

It was pretty quiet here until—boom!—at the beginning of the 20th century, with the development of electric railways. In 1907, a tramline was built to the region from Philadelphia, and the area opened to provide housing for workers employed in Philadelphia. To increase visitors and make the suburbs more attractive, a large amusement park was built nearby with an artificial lake for boating. Lakeview Avenue was built near Nitre Hall. After three years of bad weather, however, the amusement park was an economic bust and the lake dried up.

Today, Nitre Hall is a local museum located on Karakung Drive, and the name Lakeview Avenue is all that's left of the lake. But together they tell the story of my neighborhood's place in the history of the United States.

What's your American story?

You can begin to recognize the connections between the events of our past and your life today. Look around your neighborhood and find an interesting street name or building name—you can discover your hometown's place in U.S. history, too.

 Use your History Notebook to comment on what you've read. And check out the "Documenting My America" project online to start telling your own American story.

PUSHING NATIONAL BOUNDARIES

CRITICAL VIEWING This painting by Thomas Cole, called *Scene from "The Last of the Mohicans,"* illustrates an event from a novel by American writer James Fenimore Cooper. But Cole, a landscape artist of the Hudson River School, also used the painting to depict the untamed American wilderness, which was soon to be conquered and settled. What challenges might a landscape like the one in this painting have posed to settlers?

1828
Andrew Jackson, a southerner, is elected president. *(Jackson presidential campaign poster)*

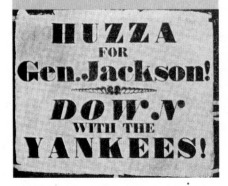

1836
Texans declare independence from Mexico. *(illustration of the Battle of the Alamo, a fort in San Antonio, Texas, where Texans fought Mexican troops)*

1838–1839
The journey of about 17,000 Cherokee forced to leave their homeland becomes known as the Trail of Tears.

1837
A panic over the state of the economy results in a severe depression.

THE UNITED STATES

1840

1830

1820

1821 AMERICAS
Mexico gains its independence from Spain.

1838 AFRICA
Zulus clash with Boers in what is known today as South Africa. *(Zulu shield and weapons)*

1839 AMERICAS
Antonio López de Santa Anna regains control of Mexico and rules as a dictator.

THE WORLD

HISTORICAL THINKING: DETERMINE CHRONOLOGY

What was happening in Europe at the same time American women were calling for their rights?

VOTES FOR WOMEN

1848

A convention calling for women's rights is held in Seneca Falls, New York. *(sash worn by women's rights activists)*

1855

Poet Walt Whitman publishes *Leaves of Grass*, a collection of poems about ordinary Americans. *(brass plate with reversed letters used to print the cover of Whitman's collection)*

1849

After gold is found in California's Sacramento Valley, thousands of people rush to the site.

1860

Shoemakers go on strike in Massachusetts, demanding higher wages.

1860

1850

1848 EUROPE

After a revolution in Germany fails, some Germans come to the United States.

1856 ASIA

The Second Opium War begins in China.

1845 EUROPE

The Great Irish Potato Famine kills more than one million people and forces many others to emigrate to the United States.

1847 AFRICA

Freed U.S. slaves and free African Americans establish the republic of Liberia in West Africa. *(The Liberian flag strongly resembles that of the United States.)*

THE AGE OF JACKSON

1824–1840

ESSENTIAL QUESTION

How did Andrew Jackson's policies impact different groups of people in America?

READING STRATEGY

COMPARE AND CONTRAST

When you compare and contrast two or more things, you note their similarities and differences. Use a Venn diagram like this one to help you compare and contrast the policies of Andrew Jackson and his opponents, such as John Quincy Adams.

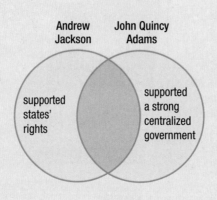

Andrew Jackson   John Quincy Adams

supported states' rights

supported a strong centralized government

"I was born for a storm, and a calm does not suit me."

—Andrew Jackson

CRITICAL VIEWING This statue of Andrew Jackson, created by sculptor Clark Mills, stands in a square across the street from the White House in Washington, D.C. The bronze statue—the first one made in the United States—celebrates Jackson's 1815 victory against the British at the Battle of New Orleans during the War of 1812. Mills obtained the bronze by melting down old weapons provided by the government. The statue was dedicated in 1853, on the 38th anniversary of the battle and 8 years after Jackson's death. What impression of Jackson does the statue convey?

1.1 Expanding Democracy

You back the candidate who's got your back. It's human nature. He or she supports your causes and promises to fix all the things you think are broken. Of course, these promises aren't always kept.

MAIN IDEA Regional differences fueled a battle over the presidency in the 1820s between John Quincy Adams and Andrew Jackson.

THE TIGHT ELECTION OF 1824

The presidential election of 1824 pitted **John Quincy Adams**, the current secretary of state and son of John Adams, against Andrew Jackson, who, as you may remember, fought in the War of 1812. The two candidates embodied the regional differences that divided the country. Adams represented the businessmen of the East. He wanted to build canals and roads to improve the nation's transportation system, and he promoted science and education. Jackson, representing the farmers of the West, supported states' rights. Adams and Jackson were the main candidates in 1824, but other candidates ran as well, including William Crawford, the secretary of the treasury, and Henry Clay, the speaker of the House of Representatives.

Andrew Jackson received the most popular votes in the election by a large margin. He also won the most electoral votes. However, he failed to win more than half of the total electoral votes, which then, as now, is required for victory. As a result, according to the 12th Amendment to the Constitution, the responsibility of choosing a winner among the top three candidates—Jackson, Adams, and Crawford—fell to the House of Representatives. By one vote, the House chose Adams to lead the country.

Adams took office in March 1825 and appointed Henry Clay as the secretary of state shortly thereafter. The appointment outraged Jackson. He believed that Adams and Clay had made a deal in which Clay persuaded other members of the House to vote for Adams in exchange for the prestigious, or highly respected, cabinet position. Jackson called the deal a "corrupt bargain" and

claimed the men stole the election from him. As president, Adams didn't gather much backing for his proposed canals and roads, in part because Jackson's supporters in Congress blocked them.

READY FOR A REMATCH

Meanwhile, Jackson had his eyes on the 1828 presidential election. Both Adams and Jackson were Democratic-Republicans, but the party had become deeply split. According to Jackson, on one side stood Adams and the rich easterners whose interests Adams favored. Jackson himself claimed to champion hardworking people whom he called the "common man." Eventually, two new parties arose. Adams and his followers formed the **National Republicans.** Jackson and his camp were known as **Democrats**.

During the 1828 campaign, both parties used speeches, parades, slogans, or sayings, and songs to build excitement for their candidate—an approach that changed the way politicians ran for office. Supporters on both sides also took part in mudslinging, or using insults to attack an opponent. In spite of all the name-calling, Jackson easily beat Adams in the election.

Voting rights, or laws that dictate which Americans have the right to vote, had been extended so more people could vote. You may recall that previously, only white men who owned property and paid taxes could vote. By contrast, in 1828, most white men in many states could vote whether they owned property or not. As a result, about 782,000 more "common men" participated in the 1828 election than in the previous one. Most Americans viewed Jackson's win as a victory over the privileged. **Jacksonian democracy** was the

Iraq

Afghanistan

Pakistan

political movement that celebrated the common man—farmers, craftsmen, laborers, and middle-class businessmen—and defended the will of the people. But women, African Americans, and Native Americans still could not vote or hold office. Nevertheless, Jackson's election in 1828 reflected the steady expansion of white male suffrage, symbolized the shift of political power to the West, and opened a new era of political democracy in the United States. President Jackson was a symbol of his age. People now believed they were represented by one of their own in the White House.

HISTORICAL THINKING

1. **READING CHECK** How was the presidential election of 1824 decided?

2. **COMPARE AND CONTRAST** How was Jacksonian democracy different from what had existed before?

3. **DRAW CONCLUSIONS** Why was Jacksonian democracy such an important development?

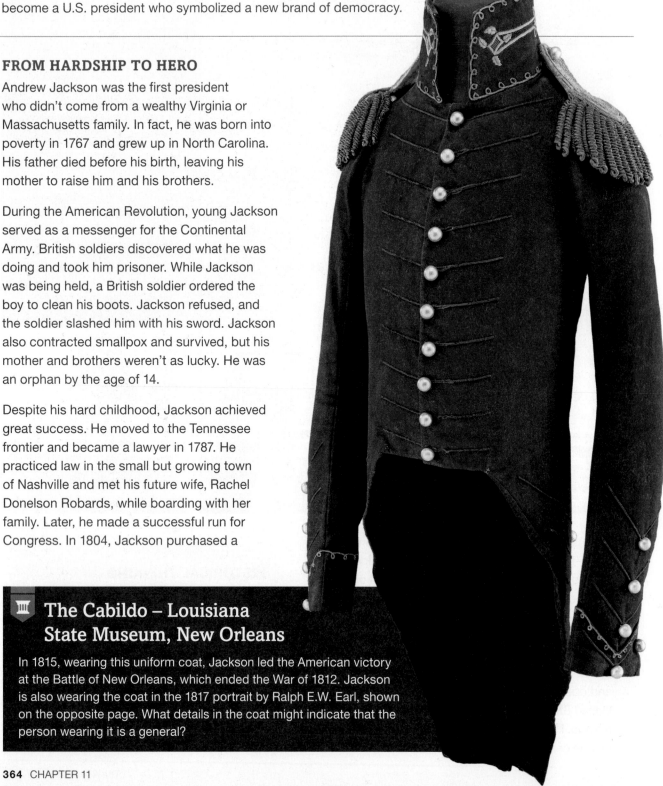

1.2 President of the People?

When you're considered an outsider and achieve something big, people expect great things of you. That was the position Andrew Jackson was in when he won the presidency, and now all eyes were on him.

MAIN IDEA Andrew Jackson rose from humble beginnings to become a U.S. president who symbolized a new brand of democracy.

FROM HARDSHIP TO HERO

Andrew Jackson was the first president who didn't come from a wealthy Virginia or Massachusetts family. In fact, he was born into poverty in 1767 and grew up in North Carolina. His father died before his birth, leaving his mother to raise him and his brothers.

During the American Revolution, young Jackson served as a messenger for the Continental Army. British soldiers discovered what he was doing and took him prisoner. While Jackson was being held, a British soldier ordered the boy to clean his boots. Jackson refused, and the soldier slashed him with his sword. Jackson also contracted smallpox and survived, but his mother and brothers weren't as lucky. He was an orphan by the age of 14.

Despite his hard childhood, Jackson achieved great success. He moved to the Tennessee frontier and became a lawyer in 1787. He practiced law in the small but growing town of Nashville and met his future wife, Rachel Donelson Robards, while boarding with her family. Later, he made a successful run for Congress. In 1804, Jackson purchased a

The Cabildo – Louisiana State Museum, New Orleans

In 1815, wearing this uniform coat, Jackson led the American victory at the Battle of New Orleans, which ended the War of 1812. Jackson is also wearing the coat in the 1817 portrait by Ralph E.W. Earl, shown on the opposite page. What details in the coat might indicate that the person wearing it is a general?

425-acre farm, later known as the Hermitage, where he built a plantation and used enslaved people to labor in his fields.

When the War of 1812 broke out between the United States and Great Britain, Jackson served as a general in command of soldiers from Tennessee. After crushing the British at the Battle of New Orleans, Jackson became a national hero.

A CLEAN SWEEP

Jackson's success was crowned by his election as president of the United States in 1828. About 30,000 people witnessed his inauguration in March 1829. But he endured the ceremony with a heavy heart. During the campaign, some of the mudslinging had been directed at his wife's reputation. When she died of a heart attack three months before her husband's inauguration, Jackson believed the personal attacks had caused her death.

Once he took office, however, Jackson assumed the presidency with enthusiasm and began carrying out the government reforms he'd promised to make during his campaign. First, Jackson replaced many of Adams's government officials with his own supporters. These appointees included newspaper editors who had been loyal to Jackson during the presidential campaign.

Critics claimed that what he'd done was corrupt. They believed Jackson was using the appointments to assume greater control of the federal government. But Jackson defended his actions by pointing out that completely removing officials from time to time prevents any one party from maintaining a stranglehold on government. The practice of rewarding political backers with government jobs became known as the **spoils system**, and it continues today. The term comes from the saying, "to the victors belong the spoils [goods or benefits] of the enemy." In this case, the "spoils" were the political positions Jackson had given to his supporters.

Controversy over appointments was just one of the problems Jackson faced early in his presidency. Soon he would find himself in a battle over taxes and states' rights that threatened to tear apart the Union.

Portrait of General Andrew Jackson, 1817

Mathew Brady photo of Jackson, 1845

HISTORICAL THINKING

1. **READING CHECK** What challenges did Andrew Jackson face growing up?

2. **COMPARE AND CONTRAST** How did Jackson differ from all preceding presidents?

3. **FORM AND SUPPORT OPINIONS** Do you think Jackson was right to initiate the use of the spoils system to appoint government officials? Support your opinion.

1.3 Debating States' Rights

When you get together with friends for a movie, you probably disagree sometimes about which one to see. Will it be sci-fi, a romantic comedy, or a thriller? But the real question is: Do you compromise or split up and see different films?

MAIN IDEA Conflicts over tariffs caused tensions—and triggered threats—in different parts of the country.

TROUBLE OVER TAXES

In the early years of Andrew Jackson's presidency, regions of the country were having trouble compromising. In particular, the Northeast and the South disagreed over tariffs, which are taxes a foreign country charges on its imported goods. The Northeast welcomed tariffs. Many northeasterners worked in manufacturing. Tariffs made foreign goods more expensive than those produced in the Northeast, and so increased sales of local goods. But people in the South didn't like tariffs. The South had an **agrarian**, or agricultural, economy. Southerners were mostly farmers who had to buy manufactured goods from other countries. Tariffs increased the cost of these goods.

So southerners were angry when Congress passed a bill in the last months of John Quincy Adams's presidency that greatly increased tariffs. The bill raised the price of foreign products sold in the United States. It also contained a clause that raised taxes on U.S. raw materials sold abroad. The clause hurt the South because it depended on the overseas sale of such raw materials as cotton and tobacco. Taxes made these items more expensive and, as a result, less attractive to foreign buyers.

The Tariff of 1828, as the bill was called, was a win-win for the federal government and the Northeast. Tariffs were the government's main source of revenue, or income. The fees caused foreign countries to charge more for their goods and helped protect northeastern industries. As you may recall, Adams represented the interests of the Northeast. In fact, the Adams-packed Congress passed the bill to appeal to northeastern voters.

Not surprisingly, southerners were outraged. They called the bill the **Tariff of Abominations**. An abomination is something that stirs feelings of disgust or hatred, which is exactly how southerners felt. But the bill backfired on Adams. The South helped vote him out of office partly in reaction to the tariff hike.

STATE VERSUS FEDERAL POWER

Political leaders in South Carolina hated the bill so much, they began to talk about the state's withdrawal from the Union. To prevent the country from breaking apart, South Carolina senator John C. Calhoun applied the **doctrine of nullification**, also called the states' rights doctrine. According to this doctrine, a state could nullify, or reject, a federal law it considered unconstitutional. By promoting the idea that a state could override a federal law, the doctrine opened up the debate over states' rights versus the authority of the federal government.

The issue placed Jackson in a tough position. He supported states' rights, and he had picked Calhoun to be his vice president. But he disagreed with Calhoun's notion that states should be able to prevent the federal government from acting on behalf of the nation as a whole.

Soon, other politicians joined in. Most famously, two senators took part in the **Webster-Hayne debate** in 1830. **Daniel Webster** from Massachusetts argued against nullification, claiming that it threatened the Union and freedom.

In this painting by George P.A. Healy, *Webster's Reply to Hayne*, Daniel Webster stands and delivers his speech in the Senate. Hayne sits to Webster's right with his hands held in front of him.

In a passionate plea, he called for "Liberty and Union, now and forever, one and inseparable!" Robert Y. Hayne from South Carolina made the case for nullification. He claimed that a state had the right to nullify a federal law, and he criticized those who, as he said, "are constantly stealing power from the States and adding strength to the Federal Government."

To ease the situation, Jackson and Congress agreed to reduce the tariff in 1832, but South Carolina's representatives still thought it was too high. They rejected the tariff in 1828 and 1832. The state's representatives even threatened **secession**, or withdrawal from the country, if the federal government tried to force it to pay the tariffs. Jackson responded by warning the representatives that he would consider secession an act of **treason**, or disloyalty to one's country. And Congress authorized Jackson to use force to collect tariffs.

The crisis finally ended in 1833 when Congress passed yet another bill that gradually reduced

tariffs. However, tensions between the North and the South did not go away. On the contrary, tensions would continue to escalate throughout the first half of the 1800s.

But, meanwhile, another crisis was brewing. Americans' demand for more land in the West was driving Native American populations from their homes. Jackson answered with a new set of policies toward Native Americans.

HISTORICAL THINKING

1. **READING CHECK** How did the doctrine of nullification help assert states' rights?

2. **ANALYZE CAUSE AND EFFECT** How did the Tariff of 1828 affect the agrarian economy in the South?

3. **FORM AND SUPPORT OPINIONS** Do you think states should have the right to nullify a federal law? Explain your answer.

2.1 Expanding into Native American Lands

Native Americans had lived in North America for centuries, enduring natural disasters, wars, and disease. Soon they would be forced to try to survive Andrew Jackson's Native American policies.

MAIN IDEA Native Americans lost land to white settlers as Andrew Jackson and the U.S. government forced their westward relocation.

TREATIES AND BATTLES

Andrew Jackson had a long history with Native Americans. After the War of 1812, he battled the Creek in Georgia and negotiated a treaty with them on behalf of the federal government. According to the terms of the treaty, the Creek gave up 22 million acres of land (an area larger than the state of South Carolina) to the government, which then sold pieces of the land to settlers.

More battles and treaties followed with the Creek, Cherokee, Choctaw, and Chickasaw, who held large areas of land throughout the South. Little by little, many of these groups were forced onto lands less suited to farming, as white settlers moved into what had once been Native American territory.

When Jackson became president, he offered Native Americans in the South two choices: either **assimilate**, or adopt, European ways of life and accept the authority of the states in which they lived, or move west of the Mississippi River. More than any other southeastern tribe, the Cherokee assimilated, taking up many aspects of white culture and customs. They dressed in western-style clothing and built plantations and ranches similar to those of white settlers.

One Cherokee named **Sequoya** (sih-KWOY-uh) developed a writing system and began publishing a newspaper. As a result, literacy quickly spread among the Cherokee. They even wrote a constitution, using the U.S. Constitution as a model, and established the **Cherokee Nation**. Despite these efforts, the Cherokee were under constant pressure to leave the region. The pressure came to a head in 1828, when Americans discovered gold on Cherokee lands in Georgia. Now both settlers and miners were eager to grab the land. That's when southern states passed laws allowing them to take over Native American lands.

THE INDIAN REMOVAL ACT

Jackson supported these laws and, in 1830, approved another law that took Native American relocation a step further. The law was the **Indian Removal Act**, which ended the U.S. government's earlier policy of respecting the rights of Native Americans to remain on land they'd lived on for generations. Under this policy, they were forced to move to an area of land that included present-day Oklahoma and parts of Kansas and Nebraska. The area came to be known as **Indian Territory**.

The act required the government to peacefully negotiate treaties with Native Americans and not force them off their land. But the U.S. government and Jackson often ignored this requirement. Jackson considered Native Americans conquered subjects of the United States. As such, he believed the government could decide where they would live.

Not all Americans supported the removal act. Many opposed it because of their dislike of Jackson. Others protested the cruelty of sending Native Americans into an unknown wilderness. Religious groups, such as the Quakers, opposed the act on moral grounds, claiming it wasn't just or right. Many Native Americans gave in and left their homes. But not all would go without a fight.

National Museum of the American Indian, Washington, D.C.

While the Cherokee assimilated European styles, they also held onto their own culture, as the traditional artifacts shown here demonstrate. The man's coat is made from the hide of deer, which the Cherokee hunted. Like all Cherokee baskets, the one shown here was woven by a woman and was used to store all sorts of household goods. The Cherokee would have filled the wooden water drum with a quantity of water to get a deep, echoing sound.

Man's coat, c. 1820

Water drum and drumstick, c. 1890

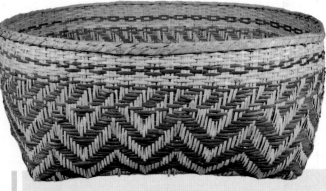

Basket of woven and dyed rivercane, c. 1900

HISTORICAL THINKING

1. **READING CHECK** What was Jackson's attitude toward Native Americans?

2. **MAKE INFERENCES** What do you think the Cherokee hoped to gain by establishing their own constitution?

3. **COMPARE AND CONTRAST** How were the stated policies toward Native Americans different from what actually occurred?

2.2 Native American Resistance

Sometimes you have to fight for your rights, even when it seems like a losing battle. But the fight is that much harder when the other side doesn't play fair.

MAIN IDEA Some Native Americans took up arms to resist their forced relocation by the U.S. government.

A TRAP IS SET

The **Seminole** were among the Native Americans who refused to leave their homes. They lived near the Everglades, a large wetlands region in southern Florida. After the Seminole rejected a removal treaty, President Jackson and the federal government declared war on them in 1835. But it didn't turn out to be an easy fight.

Seminole villages lay deep within the dangerous swampland of the Everglades, providing plenty of places where the Native Americans could hide and giving them a clear geographic advantage. When American soldiers came on the attack, Seminole leader **Osceola** (ahs-ee-OH-luh) and his warriors took them by surprise. They ambushed the soldiers, killing them with their tomahawks and

Threatened by Oil
Some Native Americans continue to protest their treatment today. In this photo, a Native American member of the Cowboy and Indian Alliance joined other Native Americans and non-native protestors in front of the Capitol in Washington, D.C., in April 2014. The thousands who gathered objected to the building of an oil pipeline through their land in the Great Plains region, saying it threatened water and other natural resources.

THE BLACK HAWK WAR

Native Americans in other parts of the country also resisted removal. At first, tribes north of the Ohio River in Illinois, including the Shawnee, Ottawa, Potawatomi, Sauk, and Fox, signed a treaty agreeing to relocate west of the Mississippi River. Once they had moved, however, the Sauk and Fox struggled to grow enough food for their people. They faced starvation. Then, in 1832, they rebelled. A Sauk leader named **Black Hawk** led his people and the Fox back to their lands in Illinois, where they meant to stay.

The U.S. military and Illinois militia had other ideas. To intimidate the Sauk and Fox, troops built large forts in the area. They also recruited members of other Native American tribes to fight Black Hawk and his followers. A young man named **Abraham Lincoln** served as a captain during this campaign. The Black Hawk War dragged on for a few months, but the Sauk and Fox were eventually overpowered. The war was brief but bloody, particularly for the Sauk and Fox. As many as 600 Native Americans died in the fighting, while only about 70 American soldiers perished.

In August 1832, Black Hawk surrendered, and the military imprisoned him for a time in a Virginia fort. He told his captors that he was not sorry for what he'd done. He was defending his land and his people from what he called "cheating men." When the American people read Black Hawk's words, many sympathized with him. Still, the Black Hawk War did not put an end to the government's efforts to drive Native Americans from their lands. Many more would be forced to leave—and at great cost.

Black Hawk

Black Hawk visited Washington, D.C., in 1837 to witness the sale of the last of Sauk land to the United States. During that visit, artist Charles Bird King painted Black Hawk's portrait. Homer Henderson painted this copy in the late 1800s from a print of the original. In the painting, the Native American leader wears a medallion, depicting an unknown man, which he probably received as a treaty gift from U.S. officials.

muskets. The Seminole also burned the homes and crops of American settlers, hoping to drive them from the region.

At the end of 1837, the government arranged to meet with Osceola at a so-called peace conference. The two sides had declared a **truce**, an agreement to stop fighting, while their leaders met to talk. But the meeting was actually a trap. As soon as Osceola arrived, American soldiers took him prisoner. He died three months later in captivity.

Fighting continued off and on for five more years before the Seminole finally surrendered. Some of the Seminole migrated to Indian Territory, but they never entirely left the Everglades. Their descendants continue to live there today.

HISTORICAL THINKING

1. **READING CHECK** How did Native Americans fight back against attempts to remove them?

2. **COMPARE AND CONTRAST** How were the reactions of Osceola and Black Hawk similar when they were forced to move westward?

3. **MAKE INFERENCES** Who were the "cheating men" Black Hawk referred to, and why did he characterize them in that way?

2.3 The Trail of Tears

When people believe a policy is unfair or unconstitutional, they can take it to the highest court in the land. You would think that everyone would have to abide by a Supreme Court ruling, right?

MAIN IDEA In defiance of a ruling from the Supreme Court, Andrew Jackson forced the Cherokee to relocate to Indian Territory.

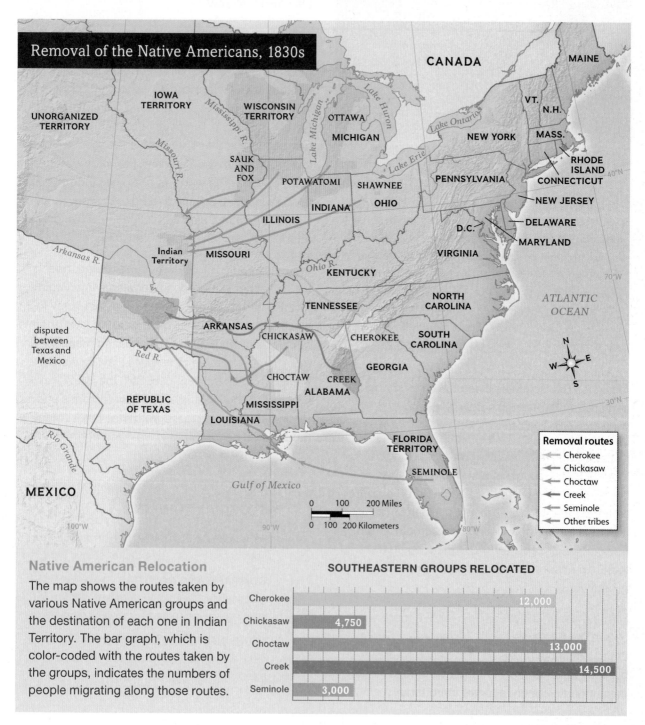

Removal of the Native Americans, 1830s

Removal routes
- Cherokee
- Chickasaw
- Choctaw
- Creek
- Seminole
- Other tribes

Native American Relocation

The map shows the routes taken by various Native American groups and the destination of each one in Indian Territory. The bar graph, which is color-coded with the routes taken by the groups, indicates the numbers of people migrating along those routes.

SOUTHEASTERN GROUPS RELOCATED

Group	Number
Cherokee	12,000
Chickasaw	4,750
Choctaw	13,000
Creek	14,500
Seminole	3,000

ONE LAST STAND

In an 1823 decision, *Johnson* v. *M'Intosh*, the Supreme Court had offered some protection for Native American lands. So, in 1832, the Cherokee turned to the Supreme Court to seek legal means to stay on their land. The Court ruled in their favor, determining that the Indian Removal Act was unconstitutional and that it violated previous treaties with the Cherokee. But the state of Georgia and President Andrew Jackson opposed the Supreme Court's decision. They wanted the Cherokee to go.

A small group of Cherokee signed the treaty, deciding that doing so was their only hope. They soon left for Indian Territory. But most of the Cherokee—about 17,000 people—opposed the treaty and remained on their land. **John Ross**, the principal chief of the Cherokee, led the resistance and tried to negotiate a better treaty. However, Jackson wasn't willing to enter into negotiations. In 1838, he sent General **Winfield Scott** and 7,000 federal troops into Cherokee lands in Georgia and Alabama. The soldiers forced people from their homes and placed them in camps. White settlers then looted and destroyed the Cherokee villages, leaving the Native Americans with only the few possessions they had taken to the camps.

A GRUELING MARCH

After the Cherokee had been confined in the camps for months, American soldiers forced them on a march to Indian Territory. The terrible journey lasted about four months, during the fall and winter of 1838 and 1839. The Cherokee weren't given adequate food, shelter, or clothing as they struggled in the rain and snow. Some soldiers even stole the few supplies that had been provided for the Native Americans.

Trail of Tears Sculpture
This sculpture from the Trail of Tears exhibit at the Cherokee Heritage Center in Tahlequah, Oklahoma, represents a Cherokee couple on the forced march. The exhibit includes a gallery that focuses on how the Cherokee started over after their relocation.

As a result, about 4,000 people died from cold, illness, and starvation on the march. One survivor remembered, "Children cry and many men cry, and all look sad like when friends die, but they say nothing." A witness to the forced migration reported that even old women "were traveling with heavy burdens attached to the back—on the sometimes frozen ground, and sometimes muddy streets, with no covering for the feet." Because of the suffering the Cherokee endured, the journey became known as the **Trail of Tears**.

To add to their burden, the soldiers made the Cherokee pay settlers for passing through their farms and boatmen for transporting them across rivers. By the time the Cherokee reached Indian Territory, they had little money left. They faced other challenges as well. Native Americans already living in the territory resented the newcomers. Not long after the Cherokee resettled, the Osage fought them over land. In addition, many Cherokee sought revenge against those of their tribe who had signed the treaty agreeing to move.

The Cherokee felt they had given up a part of their identity when they left their homeland. They had lost a spiritual connection to their ancestors, and they believed they had been betrayed by the U.S. government. Jackson's policies carried undertones of racial and political superiority and had a devastating impact on Native Americans.

HISTORICAL THINKING

1. **READING CHECK** What happened when some of the Cherokee resisted moving west?

2. **DESCRIBE** What challenges endured by Native Americans on the forced march to Indian Territory caused the journey to be known as the Trail of Tears?

3. **INTERPRET MAPS** Which southeastern Native American tribe traveled the farthest?

3.1 Economic Crises

In the 1830s, people were moving west. New railroads and canals carried people and goods from state to state. These were good times for the country. Most people thought they'd never end.

MAIN IDEA Andrew Jackson helped destroy the Second Bank of the United States, which had a severe impact on the economy.

THE BANK WAR

Andrew Jackson's domestic policies devastated the lives of Native Americans, but for many white Americans, life was good. The U.S. economy prospered during Jackson's presidency. Much of this prosperity was due to the country's powerful National Bank, the Second Bank of the United States, which played a big role in regulating the economy. Founded in 1816 after the first National Bank's charter, or permit to do business, had expired, the Second Bank was a huge federal bank that held power over smaller banks. It controlled the nation's money supply and, by doing so, kept down **inflation**. Inflation is a decrease in the value of money that causes an increase in the price of goods and services. The Second Bank also provided loans to many people who wanted to buy property or launch businesses.

Jackson hated the Second Bank. For one thing, he didn't trust paper currency or any form of money other than gold or silver. For another, Jackson claimed that the bank, led by its president

Bank Notes

The $5,000 bank note (top) is a copy of one that Nicholas Biddle might have issued to customers taking out a loan. As you can see, the Second Bank used the name "Bank of the United States" on its paper currency.

The 6-cent note (below) is actually a political cartoon commenting on the extent to which money had lost its value after 1837. The bank that supposedly issued the note is the "Humbug Glory Bank"—*humbug* means "false or deceiving." And the images at the top of the note may symbolize Andrew Jackson. The donkey represents the Democratic Party to which Jackson belonged, and the hickory leaf may be a reference to his nickname: "Old Hickory."

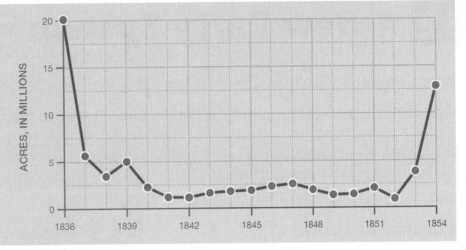

Land Sales, 1836–1854

The graph shows the impact of the Panic of 1837 on land sales after the government required people to buy land with only gold and silver.

Source: United States Census Bureau

ACRES, IN MILLIONS

20

15

10

5

0

1836   1839   1842   1845   1848   1851   1854

Nicholas Biddle, held a monopoly over all other banks. He thought its policies favored the wealthy over working people. Jackson may also have disliked the bank because it often made loans to members of Congress, possibly giving Biddle influence over the legislators.

The bank became a central issue during the 1832 election. The bank's charter was due to expire in 1836. Jackson's opponent in the 1832 election, National Republican Henry Clay, sponsored a bill to renew the bank's charter early. The bill passed in Congress, but Jackson **vetoed**, or rejected it—and beat Clay in the election.

When Jackson won the presidency in 1832, he believed his victory proved that the people supported his position on the bank. So in the four years that remained of its charter, Jackson waged an all-out war to destroy the bank. He had his treasury secretary withdraw government funds and deposit them in state banks. Jackson's opponents called these state banks his "pet banks." Biddle retaliated by withholding bank loans from customers, but his actions only turned more people against the bank. In time, Jackson got his way, and the Second Bank went out of business.

THE PANIC OF 1837

After the Second Bank closed, people flocked to Jackson's pet banks. These banks made it easier to take out loans. But this easy money led to inflation. During the last years of Jackson's presidency, he required that people use gold or silver to buy land rather than paper money as a way to fight the inflation.

Because the economy still seemed to be in good shape, Jackson's vice president, **Martin Van Buren**, easily won the presidential election in 1836. But within a few weeks of his inauguration, it became clear that the state banks were in trouble. Fear about the condition of the economy spread throughout the country. This widespread fear, or panic, became known as the **Panic of 1837**.

Panicked people ran to the banks to exchange their money for gold and silver, but the banks quickly ran out of the precious metals. When many of the banks closed, businesses collapsed and people lost their jobs and land. Soon, the country sank into a deep economic **depression**, or a period of slow economic activity. States no longer had enough money to finish public projects for developing infrastructure, such as building canals and roads. It wasn't the first depression the nation faced, and it wouldn't be the last. The country's economic problems did not improve during Van Buren's presidency, and he did little to try to resolve them. Van Buren's inaction made him unpopular with the people and set the stage for a change in government and politics.

HISTORICAL THINKING

1. **READING CHECK** Why did Jackson veto the bill to renew the National Bank's charter?

2. **ANALYZE CAUSE AND EFFECT** How did the Panic of 1837 affect the country economically and politically?

3. **INTERPRET GRAPHS** How would you describe land sales between 1836 and 1842?

3.2 A New Party System

When something isn't working, you probably want to change it—out with the old, in with the new. It often works that way in politics, too.

MAIN IDEA A new political party formed to oppose Jackson, and its candidate won the 1840 presidential election.

A CHANGE OF PARTIES

The old way of doing things definitely wasn't working in the United States in the late 1830s. While the economy slumped, the depression dragged on. Most of the factories in the East had let their workers go and closed down. Many of the unemployed in the cities went hungry and lived on the streets.

President Martin Van Buren didn't believe that government should interfere with the economy. But Jackson's old opponent, Senator Henry Clay, disagreed. He and Senator Daniel Webster claimed the government should step in and help fix the economic situation. Clay wanted the government to impose tariffs that would raise the price of imports and encourage Americans to buy domestically produced goods. He believed the federal government should fund infrastructure development by building a network of roads, canals, and railroads. Clay also called for the establishment of a new national bank. His economic program was called the American System.

In 1834, senators Clay and Webster had formed a new political party, which they called the **Whig Party** after a British political group that had criticized the monarchy. Clay, Webster, and other opponents of Andrew Jackson chose the name because they believed Jackson had exceeded his powers as president. In fact, they often referred to him as "King Andrew." Unlike the Democrats, who supported an agrarian society, the Whigs promoted business and the expansion of industry.

Harrison Campaign Flag
Throughout the 1840 presidential campaign, the Whigs made much of William Henry Harrison's war experience 28 years earlier at the Battle of Tippecanoe, where he won a victory over the Shawnee. The party created this banner, combining a picture of Harrison with the American flag and a label underscoring his heroism at Tippecanoe.

THE HERO OF TIPPECANOE

GEN. WM. H. HARRISON

THE ELECTION OF 1840

As the 1840 presidential election approached, the Whigs believed they had a good chance of winning it. Many Americans blamed the country's economic woes on Van Buren and seemed ready for a change. The Whigs nominated William Henry Harrison of Ohio as their candidate for president and **John Tyler** of Virginia as his running mate.

Harrison was a national figure because he had led U.S. Army troops against the Shawnee at the Battle of Tippecanoe in 1811. He'd also been a hero during the War of 1812. Making the most of Harrison's war experience, the Whigs came up with the catchy slogan "Tippecanoe and Tyler too."

Because Harrison lived on a farm, he also gained the reputation as a "common man" of the frontier. As a matter of fact, he came from a wealthy family. But that didn't stop the Whigs from including pictures of a rustic log cabin in banners and Harrison's campaign pamphlets. They also held parades, sang songs, and had their candidate go out on the campaign trail himself. Harrison was the first presidential candidate to do so.

Harrison narrowly defeated Van Buren in the 1840 election, but just 32 days after taking office, he died. He had delivered a long inaugural address—the longest on record—without wearing a hat or overcoat on a cold March day and came down with pneumonia.

Tyler took Harrison's place after his death but received little support from his party. Tyler's views were actually more in line with those of the Democrats. The Whigs had chosen him to attract southern voters. In time, they expelled him from the party and took to calling him "His Accidency." In spite of their differences, Tyler worked well with the mostly Whig Congress. During his single term in office, Tyler focused on strengthening the country by expanding and opening up the West.

There is something unique and unusual about each of the presidents you have read about in this lesson.

Martin Van Buren

Eighth president

- First president to be born a U.S. citizen rather than a British subject
- Nicknamed "Old Kinderhook" for his hometown, Kinderhook, New York. The expression "OK" (or *okay*) came into use during his presidency.

William Henry Harrison

Ninth president

- President for only 32 days
- First president to die in office
- Attended medical school to become a doctor, but he could not afford the tuition after his father died. He dropped out and joined the military.

John Tyler

Became tenth president when William Henry Harrison died in office

- Only former U.S. president to side with the Confederacy in the Civil War
- Father of 14 children who lived into adulthood

HISTORICAL THINKING

1. **READING CHECK** Why were the Whigs in a good position to win the 1840 election?

2. **COMPARE AND CONTRAST** How did the agrarians' and the industrialists' views on the economy differ?

3. **MAKE INFERENCES** Why did the Whigs use pictures of a log cabin in Harrison's campaign?

REVIEW

VOCABULARY

Use each of the following vocabulary words in a sentence that shows an understanding of the term's meaning.

1. agrarian

   The economy of the South was mostly agrarian, or based on farming.

2. voting rights

3. depression

4. inflation

5. spoils system

6. doctrine of nullification

7. assimilate

8. truce

READING STRATEGY
COMPARE AND CONTRAST

If you haven't done so already, complete your diagram to compare and contrast the policies of Andrew Jackson and John Quincy Adams. List at least two policies to compare and contrast. Then answer the question.

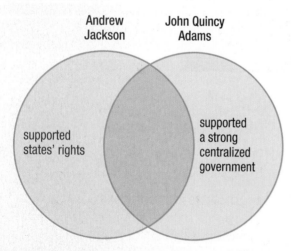

Andrew Jackson | John Quincy Adams

supported states' rights

supported a strong centralized government

9. What were some of the main policy differences between Jackson and Adams?

MAIN IDEAS

Answer the following questions. Support your answers with evidence from the chapter.

10. Why did Andrew Jackson think he had been robbed of the presidential election in 1824? **LESSON 1.1**

11. How does the spoils system work? **LESSON 1.2**

12. Why did Daniel Webster believe nullification would threaten the Union and freedom? **LESSON 1.3**

13. What two options did President Jackson offer Native Americans in the South? **LESSON 2.1**

14. What policy did the Indian Removal Act set in place? **LESSON 2.1**

15. How did the U.S. government trick Osceola? **LESSON 2.2**

16. What did John Ross hope to achieve by resisting the move west? **LESSON 2.3**

17. How did Andrew Jackson bring about the end of the Second Bank of the United States? **LESSON 3.1**

18. How did his opponents react to Andrew Jackson's transfer of funds out of the Second Bank? **LESSON 3.1**

19. What economic factors formed part of Henry Clay's American System? **LESSON 3.2**

HISTORICAL THINKING

Answer the following questions. Support your answers with evidence from the chapter.

20. **SYNTHESIZE** How did Andrew Jackson change the country?

21. **ANALYZE CAUSE AND EFFECT** How did Andrew Jackson's use of the spoils system lead to charges of corruption against him?

22. **COMPARE AND CONTRAST** In what ways were the rebellions of Black Hawk and the Cherokee similar and different?

23. **MAKE CONNECTIONS** John C. Calhoun applied the states' rights doctrine to prevent the country from breaking apart. When was states' rights first invoked, and what was it used to fight?

24. **DISTINGUISH FACT AND OPINION** Both Andrew Jackson and William Henry Harrison were said to represent the "common man." Did this label represent a fact or an opinion?

25. **FORM AND SUPPORT OPINIONS** Considering the legacy of Jackson's policies, do you think he lived up to his reputation as a hero for common people? Explain your answer.

INTERPRET MAPS

Study the map of the electoral college results for Andrew Jackson and John Quincy Adams in the 1828 presidential election. Then answer the questions that follow.

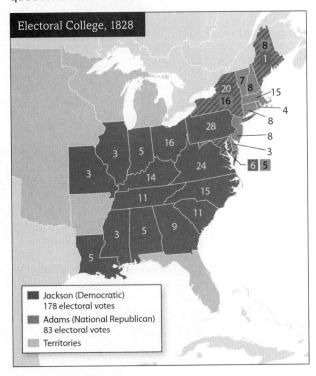

Electoral College, 1828

Jackson (Democratic)
178 electoral votes

Adams (National Republican)
83 electoral votes

Territories

26. Based on the map, what can you conclude about Jackson's victory?

27. Where did Adams gain votes and why?

ANALYZE SOURCES

In 1835, some Cherokee representatives signed, and Congress ratified, the Treaty of New Echota, in which the Cherokee sold all their lands east of the Mississippi River to the United States. The next year, Cherokee leader John Ross wrote a letter to Congress in response.

> Neither myself nor any other member of the regular delegation to Washington, can . . . ever recognize that paper as a Treaty, by assenting to its terms, or the mode of its execution. They are entirely inconsistent with the views of the Cherokee people. Three times have the Cherokee people formally and openly rejected conditions substantially [largely] the same as these. The Cherokee people, in two protests . . . spoke for themselves against the Treaty, even previous to its rejection by those whom they had selected to speak for them.

28. What does this excerpt tell you about Ross's opinion of the Treaty of New Echota?

CONNECT TO YOUR LIFE

29. **EXPLANATORY** This chapter describes many disputes among different groups of people. Think about disagreements you have had with others in your own life. How were they resolved? Make a connection between what you have learned about problem solving and how this information can be applied to resolve a dispute. Then write a paragraph in which you help two opposing groups overcome their dispute.

TIPS

- Fill in a problem-and-solution chart, listing the problem between the groups at the top, the steps for fixing the problem in the middle, and the plan's conclusion at the bottom.

- Include evidence and one or two vocabulary terms from the chapter.

- Conclude with a comment tying your suggested resolution of the argument to your own life.

CHAPTER 12

MANIFEST DESTINY
1821–1853

ESSENTIAL QUESTION
Why were Americans inspired to move west?

AMERICAN STORIES The Golden City

AMERICAN GALLERY ONLINE   The Westward Trails

READING STRATEGY

IDENTIFY MAIN IDEAS AND DETAILS
When you identify main ideas and details, you determine the most important idea in the text. Finding key details in the text helps you determine the main ideas they support. As you read the chapter, use an organizer like this one to record main ideas and details about the westward movement of Americans.

Main Idea:

Detail:

Detail:

Detail:

"We are the nation of **human progress."**

—John L. O'Sullivan

CRITICAL VIEWING Three bodies of water surround San Francisco: the Pacific Ocean, the Golden Gate Strait, and the San Francisco Bay. How might the geography of this city influence its population?

THE GOLDEN CITY

San Francisco is a vibrant, modern city known for its unique coastal skyline, diverse neighborhoods, sweeping bridges, and notorious fog. It's the Golden City in the Golden State— a city "built on gold" during the 1848 California gold rush.

This nugget sparked the gold rush after workers found it near Sutter's Mill in 1848.

It all started on January 24, 1848. James Marshall set out to inspect the progress his workers had made on a sawmill they were building for John Sutter on the American River near Coloma, California. Overnight, Marshall had left a trickle of water flowing through the mill to wash away some loose dirt and gravel. To his great surprise, some bright flakes of gold were left behind that morning. Shocked, Marshall showed the gold to his crew, swearing them to secrecy. He needed some time to process what had just happened before he took action. He also figured he'd better finish building Sutter's Mill.

But an exciting secret like that is impossible to keep. The word spread quickly, and over the next few years, hundreds of thousands of people streamed into California hoping to get rich. By 1856, around $465 million worth of gold had been mined in California.

A MINER'S LIFE

The Americans who moved from the East to California in 1849 in search of gold were nicknamed the "forty-niners." Most of them came with the plan to work hard for a short time, find enough gold to get rich, and return home wealthy.

In reality, mining was then, and still is, brutally hard work and very dangerous. During the gold rush, supplies were extremely expensive because the items were in such high demand. One miner reported that pork cost $1.25, beans $1, sugar $.75, and coffee $.50. That sounds pretty reasonable until you realize that a dollar in 1850 was worth about $30 today. Most miners only found enough gold to cover their expenses.

The dangerous and difficult nature of the work caught many new miners by surprise. One of them, William Swain, described his life in a letter to his brother back in New York: "George, I tell you this mining among the mountains is a dog's life."

CHALLENGES FOR IMMIGRANTS

William Swain was joined in his quest for gold by thousands of immigrants from Mexico, Chile, Peru, Germany, France, Turkey, China, and other countries. In China, people dreaming of California riches sometimes called the United States "the gold mountain." By 1848, the first Chinese miners began arriving in San Francisco, leaving behind China's high taxes and farming challenges. The arrival of so many different groups to California shaped the diversity of this exciting new place.

As the number of immigrants grew and as the U.S. economy weakened, the attitude of Americans toward the immigrants became increasingly resentful and discriminatory. In 1850, California's government placed a $20 tax on each immigrant miner—a tax American miners did not have to pay.

Miners pause for a photo while sluicing, or separating gold from dirt by using water. Early gold rush photographs provide insight into the diversity of many mining operations. What can you observe about this team of sluicers?

The Chinese endured other tough penalties. In 1852, the government imposed another tax on Chinese miners. When California governor John Bigler suggested the wave of Chinese immigrants should be stopped, a Chinese man responded in the *Daily Alta California*: "The effect of your late message has been thus far to prejudice the public mind against my people, to enable those who wait [for] the opportunity to hunt them down, and rob them of the rewards of their toil."

Many of the Chinese men who came to California were literate and eager for new possibilities, but the state's increasingly hostile social climate made mining unwise—and unsafe—for them to continue. Forced out of mining, they found other work, building railroads and operating laundries and stores. Despite ongoing discrimination, thousands of Chinese immigrants stayed in California, seeking refuge in the San Francisco neighborhood known as Chinatown, and contributing greatly to the state's economy and culture.

Gold Rush Mine Locations

- Historic gold mine location

Sacramento R.

Marysville

Lake Tahoe

Sacramento

UTAH TERRITORY

Stockton

San Francisco · Oakland

San Joaquin R.

San Jose

CALIFORNIA

NEW MEXICO TERRITORY

Tulare Lake

San Luis Obispo

Santa Barbara

Los Angeles

Colorado R.

PACIFIC OCEAN

San Diego

AMERICAN PLACES
Chinatown, San Francisco

Busy, colorful, and thriving, San Francisco's Chinatown is a testament to Chinese immigrants. United through heritage, culture, language, and economics, and living in a new and sometimes unwelcoming country, generations of Chinese immigrants established and still maintain a proud Chinese-American community.

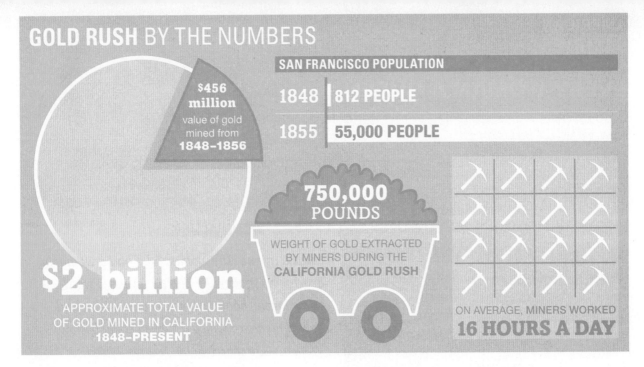

GOLD RUSH BY THE NUMBERS

$456 million value of gold mined from **1848–1856**

$2 billion APPROXIMATE TOTAL VALUE OF GOLD MINED IN CALIFORNIA 1848–PRESENT

SAN FRANCISCO POPULATION

1848 | 812 PEOPLE

1855 | 55,000 PEOPLE

750,000 POUNDS WEIGHT OF GOLD EXTRACTED BY MINERS DURING THE CALIFORNIA GOLD RUSH

ON AVERAGE, MINERS WORKED **16 HOURS A DAY**

NATIVE AMERICAN STRUGGLES

While many immigrants faced prejudice and opposition, the harshest treatment was reserved for the people who had been living in California all along. White miners used Native Americans for cheap labor and made them targets of violence. William Swain was upset by abuse against Native Americans that he witnessed, writing, "Such incidents have fallen under my notice that would make humanity weep and men disown their race." Historians estimate that around 150,000 Native Americans were living in California in 1848, but by 1870, fewer than 30,000 remained. Among the causes for the decline were starvation, violence, and diseases introduced by the miners.

A CITY ARISES

As the Native American population declined, populations of forty-niners and immigrants in northern California cities increased. In March of 1848, the *California Star* newspaper listed the city of San Francisco's population of non–Native Americans as 575 men, 177 women, 60 children— a total of 812 people. Within two years, the city's population had skyrocketed to more than 20,000.

San Francisco's natural wealth lay in its geography, a sheltered port on the Pacific Ocean. Immigrants and forty-niners arriving by ship passed through San Francisco, and many decided to stay. Clever businesspeople established shops, hotels, restaurants, and banks to accommodate the miners' needs, forming the base for what would evolve into a thriving local economy.

The money and people flooding into California also sped up the time it took for it to be granted statehood. In 1848, the federal government purchased the land that included California from Mexico as part of the treaty that ended the Mexican-American War. Just two short years later, California was admitted as the 31st state in the Union.

By the end of the 1850s, the gold rush had ended, but it had lasting effects. Like San Francisco, many cities that got their start during the gold rush still exist. And entrepreneurs who set up shop to sell goods to the miners established brands that are still familiar. In 1852, the bankers Henry Wells and William Fargo opened an office in San Francisco. Wells Fargo Bank remains one of America's top banking institutions. In the same year, Domingo Ghirardelli opened a sweet shop in San Francisco, launching the famous brand of chocolate many people enjoy today.

The California gold rush only lasted a few years, but it helped form a state and change a nation. California would play an increasingly significant role in the national economy.

THINK ABOUT IT

How did the California gold rush affect the economy and population of the United States?

EVERY WOMAN A QUEEN

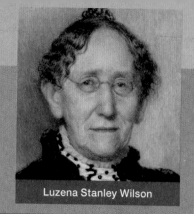

Luzena Stanley Wilson

Luzena Stanley Wilson was one of the few women to travel to California during the gold rush. She, her husband, and their two young sons left their cabin in Missouri to head west in the spring of 1849. It wasn't long before Wilson got her first inkling that she could make money in California. A man offered to buy a biscuit from her, saying he would pay "$10 for bread made by a woman."

The Wilsons settled in Sacramento and opened a hotel where Luzena did the cooking. Again she found that many miners would pay a premium for a meal made by an experienced female cook. The Wilsons went on to own several successful hotels in different California cities. After Luzena's husband left the family in 1872, she moved to San Francisco and made a living buying and selling real estate. She died in that city in 1902, at the age of 83.

PRIMARY SOURCE

I was a queen. Any woman who had a womanly heart, who spoke a kindly, sympathetic word to the lonely, homesick men, was a queen, and lacked no honor which a subject could bestow. Women were scarce in those days. I lived six months in Sacramento and saw only two.

—from *Luzena Stanley Wilson '49er, Her Memoirs as Taken Down by Her Daughter in 1881,* by Correnah Wilson Wright, 1937

BODIE, CALIFORNIA: GHOST TOWN

Shortly after the initial gold rush, Bodie, California, became a thriving mining town and home to nearly 10,000 people. Now it's a ghost town, an abandoned place that has fallen into ruin after a natural disaster, war, or economic depression. An 1875 mine cave-in led to the discovery of gold in Bodie, which went from a town of a few dozen people to a bustling boomtown. Today it sits in a state of arrested decay, visited by tourists, tumbleweeds, and maybe an occasional ghost.

LONG TOM

Many independent miners used a device called a long tom to separate gold from the California dirt. The largest part of the long tom was a shallow wooden trough about 15 feet long. This had to be placed near a water source, because a steady stream of water needed to flow through it.

A miner would put gold-bearing dirt at the top of the trough. The water washed the dirt through a screen that removed larger rocks. Next, the water flowed into a shallow box with wooden riffles sticking up from the bottom. The gold flakes caught on the riffles while the water and the rest of the dirt flowed out of the box. Shoveling dirt into a long tom all day was back-breaking work.

CRITICAL VIEWING Museum volunteers, or docents, demonstrate the art of using a long tom in the American River in Coloma, California. Based on details you notice in the photo, how did long tom operators use forces of gravity and motion to separate gold from dirt?

HOW THE LONG TOM WORKS

WATER IN

DIRT AND GRAVEL IN
Miners pour pay dirt into the top of the long tom. Water washes over the dirt.

GOLD SEPARATES
Flowing water helps separate gold from rocks and dirt particles.

SCREEN

RIFFLE BOX

RIFFLES CATCH GOLD
Heavy gold flakes get caught in the riffles. Light dirt and sand wash away.

WATER OUT

SETTLING POND

1.1 The Pull of the West

If you had trouble finding work and heard about opportunities in a completely different part of the country, you just might pack up and move. That's exactly what settlers from the eastern half of the United States did in the 19th century. They packed up and moved west.

> **MAIN IDEA** A tough economy and the promise of a rich and exciting future led Americans to look for opportunities in the West.

OPENING THE WEST

The boundaries of the nation shifted dramatically in the early 19th century, and the westward migration of easterners profoundly changed American culture. The West inspired ideals of **individualism**, or a self-reliant independence, and rugged frontier life that dramatically influenced our national self-image and sense of the American past.

In the early 19th century, Americans began to explore, move to, and live in the West. In 1806, Zebulon Pike led an expedition to discover the headwaters of the Arkansas River and was one of the first white men to explore the wilderness of Colorado. Many of these adventurous individuals were fur trappers and explorers, called **mountain men**. They spent most of their time in the wilderness trapping small animals for furs. Every summer from about 1825 to 1840, trappers met with fur traders at temporary markets called **rendezvous** (RAHN-deh-voo) to sell and buy goods and supplies. Trade opportunities like this were one of the economic incentives that drew people to the West.

Several mountain men became legendary. Kit Carson, a successful fur trapper in California, would later use his skills to guide U.S. Army officers in a war with Mexico. Another legend was **Jedediah Smith**. Smith had read of Lewis and Clark's expeditions and decided to explore the West for himself. He would eventually explore more of the unknown territory of the West than any other single person. In 1826, Smith crossed the Mojave (moh-HAH-vee) Desert into southern California. The next year, he hiked through California's high

A Seasoned Mountain Man

Jim Beckwourth's adventures took him from the Everglades of Florida to northern Mexico, southern Canada, and the Pacific coast. While exploring the West, he lived with a Crow tribe for several years. He was also a prospector and a U.S. Army scout, and he learned to overcome many challenges of the frontier.

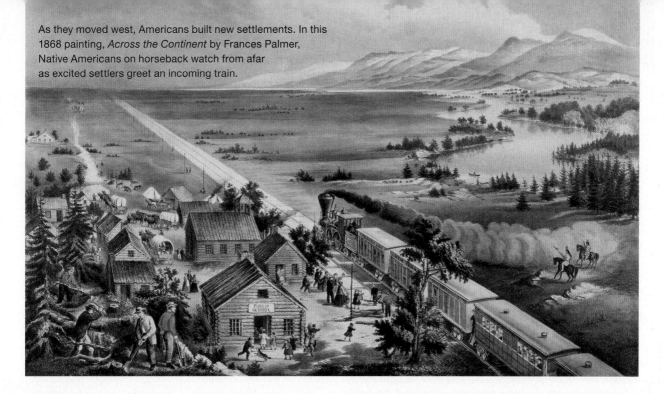

As they moved west, Americans built new settlements. In this 1868 painting, *Across the Continent* by Frances Palmer, Native Americans on horseback watch from afar as excited settlers greet an incoming train.

mountains, the Sierra Nevada, and became the first white American to travel overland from the East to California and back. Another mountain man who explored the Sierra Nevada was **Jim Beckwourth**. He had been born into slavery but was set free when he was 25. In 1850, he discovered a mountain pass through the Sierra Nevada for settlers to follow as they traveled to northern California. Today, that pass is still called Beckwourth Pass.

The mountain men's explorations opened lands that had previously seemed inaccessible. After the Panic of 1837, many Americans faced economic difficulties. Newly explored lands in the West started to look attractive to unhappy easterners, new immigrants, independent women, and others who were seeking a new start.

MANIFEST DESTINY

In 1845, magazine editor John O'Sullivan wrote an editorial urging the United States to **annex**, or add, Texas as a state. He also wrote that Americans had a "**manifest destiny** to overspread and possess the whole of the continent." The word *manifest* means "obvious," and *destiny* refers to the unavoidable events of the future. The phrase, and the purpose underlying manifest destiny, reflected several cultural assumptions, including the certainty that the United States would— indeed, should—one day stretch from the Atlantic Ocean to the Pacific Ocean. Those who embraced

this concept were driven by more than just the promise of new opportunities. O'Sullivan's editorial described a belief that God intended for white Protestant Americans to take over the continent. Such an idea blatantly ignored the fact that there were already people living on these lands.

For several decades, the federal government pursued the territorial acquisition of western lands. The Oregon Territory promised timber, furs, and rich fisheries. California offered fertile farmland and abundant mineral resources, and both California and Oregon provided ports on the Pacific Ocean for seaboard merchants to ship and receive goods. Texas held deposits of minerals and metals, such as silver. The desire for riches and the belief in manifest destiny inspired settlers and politicians to move westward.

HISTORICAL THINKING

1. **READING CHECK** How did the concept of manifest destiny encourage Americans to move west?

2. **IDENTIFY MAIN IDEAS AND DETAILS** What natural resources served as economic incentives for people moving west?

3. **EVALUATE** Why might lands in the West have seemed inaccessible to many Americans?

1.2 Manifest Destiny

John O'Sullivan might have thought he was onto something when he coined the phrase "manifest destiny." However, he could not have predicted the impact that Americans' movement west would have on the nation's identity.

For the 19th-century Americans already considering moving westward, the idea of manifest destiny—that they had not only the right but also the responsibility to help expand the nation—was quite appealing. Settlers by the hundreds began crossing the Mississippi River and heading west.

John Gast's 1872 painting *American Progress* depicts the "spirit of America" as a goddess-like woman bathed in light and floating westward. She is leading **pioneers**, or people moving to a new and unfamiliar land, as they leave their settled lives and communities behind. The spirit carries a schoolbook, and she strings telegraph wire as she moves across the open land. Notice Gast's use of light and dark in this painting and how Native Americans and wildlife seem to react to the people headed their way.

CRITICAL VIEWING What do you notice about the direction the painting's subjects are facing? How does that reflect the concept of manifest destiny?

🏛 **Autry Museum of the American West, Los Angeles**

Gast painted *American Progress* just a few years after the end of the Civil War. In some ways, the painting's themes of modernization and new frontiers reflect a cultural desire to begin anew.

DOCUMENT ONE

Primary Source: Essay
from "The Great Nation of Futurity,"
by John L. O'Sullivan, 1839

The concept of manifest destiny originated in John L. O'Sullivan's essay about what he perceived as the great future for the United States.

CONSTRUCTED RESPONSE On what authorities does O'Sullivan rest his ideas about the "onward march" of the United States?

The expansive future is our arena. We are entering on its untrodden space, with the truths of God in our minds, beneficent objects in our hearts, and with a clear conscience unsullied by the past. We are the nation of human progress, and who will, what can, set limits to our onward march? Providence is with us, and no earthly power can. We point to the everlasting truth on the first page of our national declaration. In its magnificent domain of space and time, the nation of many nations is destined to manifest to mankind the excellence of divine principles.

DOCUMENT TWO

Primary Source: Artifact
Wheel from a covered wagon, wood and iron, c. 1830

The wheels on the covered wagons that carried the pioneers, like the wagon depicted in *American Progress* at left, were about four feet across. An iron band encircled the outside of the wheel, and iron strengthened the opening for the axle.

CONSTRUCTED RESPONSE What characteristics of the wheel can you see that make it suited to carrying a one-ton load more than 1,000 miles?

DOCUMENT THREE

Primary Source: Diary
from "The Letters and Journals of Narcissa Whitman,"
by Narcissa Whitman, 1836

Some of the first white settlers in the West were missionaries. Narcissa Whitman and her husband Marcus traveled to Oregon Country, hoping to spread Christianity among the Native Americans. Her diaries and letters home capture the experience of traveling the Oregon Trail and living in the Northwest. This excerpt is from July 27, 1836.

CONSTRUCTED RESPONSE How does Whitman describe the hardships of travel to the West?

We are still in a dangerous country; but our company is large enough for safety. Our cattle endure the journey remarkably well. They supply us with sufficient milk for our tea and coffee, which is indeed a luxury. Do not think I regret coming. No, far from it; I would not go back for a world. I am contented and happy, notwithstanding I sometimes get very hungry and weary. Have six week's steady journey before us. Feel sometimes as if it were a long time to be traveling. Long for rest, but must not murmur. Feel to pity the poor Indian women, who are continually traveling in this manner during their lives, and know no other comfort.

SYNTHESIZE & WRITE

1. **REVIEW** Review what you have learned about the cultural, geographic, and political context in which the idea of manifest destiny emerged.

2. **RECALL** On your own paper, write the main ideas about manifest destiny inspired by Gast's painting, the writings of O'Sullivan and Whitman, and the wagon wheel.

3. **CONSTRUCT** Construct a topic sentence that answers this question: In what ways did Americans incorporate the idea of manifest destiny into their decisions about moving west?

4. **WRITE** Using evidence from this chapter and the documents and artifact, write an informative paragraph that supports your topic sentence in Step 3.

1.3 Trails to the West

Think of times when you've had several choices in front of you. In the mid-19th century, westward-bound Americans had to decide which road—or, more accurately, which trail—they would take.

MAIN IDEA Between 1841 and 1866, as many as a half million Americans followed trails to new lives in the West.

TRAVELING BY TRAIL

The story of one of the most important trails to the West begins in 1821, the year that Mexico won its independence from Spain. Under Spanish rule, trade with the United States had been heavily restricted. Mexico was eager to support individual land ownership and trade with the United States. Settlements at Santa Fe and Taos in the New Mexico territory, then part of Mexico, were ideally located for Mexican trade with the westernmost territories.

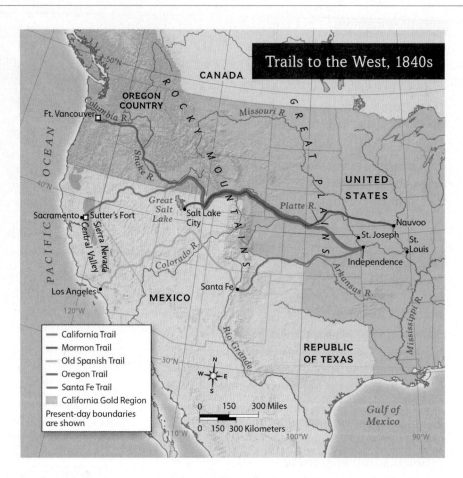

In 1822, a trader named William Becknell opened a new route that covered a distance of more than 900 miles from Independence, Missouri, to Santa Fe. Soon other traders began using this route, which became known as the **Santa Fe Trail**. They hauled their goods in caravans of covered wagons, similar to Conestoga wagons. Near the trail's western end, traders used a branch of the trail called the Cimarron Cutoff so they could avoid crossing the rugged Sangre de Cristo (SAHN-gray day KREE-stoh) Mountains.

From Santa Fe, traders traveled to the Pacific coast along the **Old Spanish Trail**, through territory controlled by Mexico. They brought Mexican woolen goods across the trail to trade for horses in California. Extending across high mountains and the scorching Mojave Desert, it was the most dangerous and difficult of the trails.

In the midst of building a new nation, Mexico struggled to govern its settlements along the American border, where traders and settlers from both countries lived. Cultural clashes over such issues as slavery—which had been outlawed in Mexico—were common.

The Santa Fe Trail represented only one of several important routes to the West. Independence was also the starting point for two other important trails. The **Oregon Trail** led to the Oregon Country in the Northwest. This region included the present-day states of Oregon, Washington, and Idaho as well as parts of Montana and the Canadian province of British Columbia.

In 1846, the United States and Great Britain signed a treaty setting the boundary between their territories in the Oregon Country. The treaty settled disputed land claims between the two nations, and the resulting stability encouraged even more American settlers to move to the **Oregon Territory**, the American portion of what had been Oregon Country. Between 1840 and 1860, from 300,000 to 400,000 Americans traveled the Oregon Trail. By 1860, about 52,000 people had settled in the new state of Oregon. Many settled in the fertile valley of the Willamette River located at the end of the trail.

THE MORMON TRAIL

Some trails were forged by people seeking new economic opportunities. But others were inspired by the religious faiths of the travelers. One of those was the **Mormon Trail**. In 1830, Joseph Smith founded the Mormon religion, the Church of Jesus Christ of Latter-day Saints, in New York. Smith and his followers moved west, establishing a community in Nauvoo, Illinois. There, because of the economic and political power they had achieved, they suffered harassment from their non-Mormon neighbors. When a mob killed Smith, the Mormons' new leader, **Brigham Young**, decided to move even farther west so that he and his fellow Mormons could practice their religion freely.

In 1846, Young led an **exodus**, or mass departure, of Mormons. They traveled westward until they reached the Missouri River near present-day Omaha, Nebraska. After wintering there, they continued west, sometimes following the Oregon Trail. When they neared the **Continental Divide**,

The National Museum of American History, Washington, D.C.

This sunstone carved from limestone is one of 30 that adorned the grand temple of the Church of Jesus Christ of Latter-day Saints, completed in 1846 in Nauvoo, Illinois, by architect William Weeks. Images of the sun, moon, and stars are important to Mormon symbolism and may pertain to the Old Testament story of Joseph. Joseph Smith said that a sun with a face like this had come to him in a vision.

the high point in the Rocky Mountains that divides the watersheds of the Atlantic and Pacific oceans, they headed southward into territory still owned by Mexico. After an arduous trek over the Rockies, they reached the Great Salt Lake. There, in present-day Utah, Young declared that they had reached their destination, and they established the community of Salt Lake City.

HISTORICAL THINKING

1. **READING CHECK** Where did the Santa Fe, Oregon, and Mormon trails begin and end?

2. **ANALYZE CAUSE AND EFFECT** Why did the Mormons move west from Illinois?

3. **INTERPRET MAPS** What major physical features did all or most of the trails shown on the map share?

1.4 Pioneers and Native Americans

Most people don't enjoy doing chores, even with the help of modern conveniences. Imagine how hard it was for families traveling along the Oregon Trail in the 1840s to prepare meals or wash clothes while also coping with illness and injuries in unfamiliar territory.

MAIN IDEA Pioneers who moved west endured hardships, and their encounters with Native Americans had profound effects on both cultures.

A DIFFICULT JOURNEY

Pioneers heading west usually traveled in groups of covered wagons called **wagon trains**. No matter the destination, the journey was grueling and took several months. Wagon trains crossed rivers and mountains as well as arid lands where water and vegetation were scarce. The long days demanded difficult chores and wearying travel.

Pioneers dealt with severe weather, including sandstorms, snowstorms, and floods. They also fought diseases such as cholera and typhoid. Because of the long distances between outposts, or settlements, running out of food, water, and supplies was a constant worry.

Pioneer women performed tasks such as cooking and cleaning. They also worked alongside men—tending to livestock, gathering supplies, and repairing tools and wagons. Everyone pitched in, no matter who they were or what job needed to be done.

Life on the frontier wagon trains changed conventional gender roles. Excerpts from men's and women's diaries and letters capture both the hope and excitement of seeing new lands, the day-to-day tasks they had to do, and the great losses and hardships endured on the trail. The journal entries below, of a man and a girl, describe very different pioneer experiences.

PRIMARY SOURCES

Today we met a large company, homeward bound. Some of our company purchased two milk cows from them. They say we never can get through, because there is no grass ahead, and the cholera is getting worse. Their wagons are crowded with sick men. Now our hearts began to fail us again and when we reflect that we have hardly made an introduction to our journey, the task becomes harder and we almost get weary of life.

—from "Journal of John Wood," by John Wood, 1852

One pleasant evening some Indian boys wanted to display their skill with bow and arrow. When we gave them a biscuit they would set it up, step off some distance and pierce it with an arrow. Father got a pan of biscuits and he would measure off a distance, set up one and tell them to shoot at it. The one who struck it first got it for his own. They had considerable sport over the biscuits.

—from *One Woman's West*, by Martha Gay Masterson, 1892

Like other mid-19th century painters, Albert Bierstadt depicted the splendor and beauty of the American landscape. He painted this work, *Oregon Trail*, around 1850. What details in this painting convey the challenges and adventures of life on the frontier?

CULTURAL ENCOUNTERS

Westward trails passed through lands inhabited by various Native American tribes. On the Great Plains, pioneers encountered the **Lakota**, and in the Oregon Territory they met the **Nez Perce**. Traders who traveled the Santa Fe Trail to the New Mexico territory interacted with southwestern tribes such as the **Zuni**.

The Lakota, Nez Perce, and Zuni had distinctive customs. Traditionally, the Lakota lived in tepees and hunted bison. The Nez Perce tended to settle along streams that provided a steady supply of food. Up to 30 families could live in one of their roomy lodges. The Zuni lived in adobe houses or dwellings built into cliffs.

Encountering Native Americans was a new experience for pioneers and for the people hearing about such encounters back home. In addition, works of fiction about westward journeys often exaggerated accounts of Native American attacks on pioneers. In reality, attacks were rare. Of the nearly 400,000 people who traveled the Oregon Trail in the mid-19th century, about 400 were killed in attacks by Native Americans. Most encounters were friendly, and Native Americans and settlers engaged in trade and sometimes helped each other.

Even so, as new settlers intruded on Native American land, conflicts did arise. In one instance, a cow wandered away from one of the pioneers traveling on the Oregon Trail, and was killed by a Native American. U.S. Army soldiers intervened by talking to the Native American chief. At first everyone behaved reasonably, but misunderstandings and a nervous soldier shooting his gun led to a battle near Fort Laramie, a U.S. military post in present-day Wyoming. By the time it ended, the Native American chief and 29 American soldiers had been killed in what is referred to as the Grattan Massacre of 1854.

HISTORICAL THINKING

1. **READING CHECK** In general, what were interactions between pioneers and Native Americans like?

2. **IDENTIFY MAIN IDEAS AND DETAILS** What kinds of challenges did pioneers heading west in wagon trains face?

3. **EVALUATE** What do we learn about family life on the frontier from the letters and diaries of travelers moving west?

2.1 The Tejanos

When Mexico took control of the territory that later became Texas, the Mexican government was concerned about how few people lived there. The solution? Offer free land and hope people would move there.

MAIN IDEA After achieving independence from Spain, Mexico encouraged American settlement in the territory of Texas.

SPANISH TERRITORY

In the early 1800s, some westward-bound Americans ended up in Spanish territory. What we know today as the state of Texas used to be the Spanish territory called **Tejas** (TAY-hahs). In 1598, Spanish conquistador Juan de Oñate (oh-NYAH-tay) and his soldiers reached the Rio Grande. De Oñate claimed all the land around the river for Spain, leading to 200 years of Spanish rule.

Tejas lay north of the Nueces (noo-AY-suhs) River and extended into present-day Louisiana. Spain established missions throughout the area, starting with San Francisco de los Tejas. Catholic priests and missionaries moved to these missions in order to convert the Coahuiltecan (koh-uh-WEEL-tek-un) and the Caddo (KAH-doh) people. **Presidios**, or military settlements, surrounded most missions. Other Spanish settlers built farms close to the presidios.

Tejas shared a border with the United States. As a result, Spain worried about the influence its northern neighbor might have on the territory. Settlers of Spanish or Mexican descent, called **Tejanos** (tay-HAH-nohs), were forbidden to trade with other countries. Even so, many Americans entered the territory

illegally to do business with Tejanos. Spanish authorities pursued and arrested Americans who did so. Meanwhile, many Native Americans attacked Spanish settlements because they were resentful that Spain limited their chances to trade with the United States and suspicious of the actions of Spanish missionaries. Spain tried to maintain peace with Native Americans in Tejas because it wanted to remain in control of the region. But the Spanish were unable to bring about stability there.

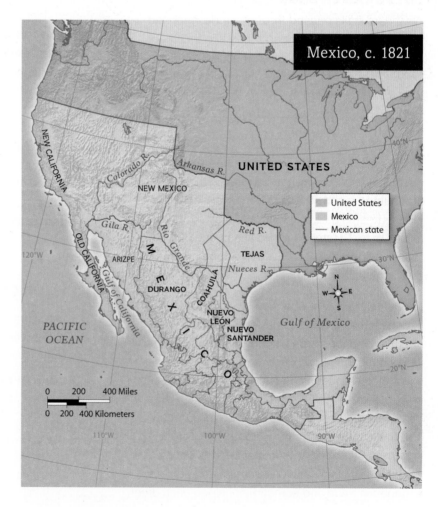

Mexico, c. 1821

UNITED STATES

United States
Mexico
Mexican state

NEW CALIFORNIA
OLD CALIFORNIA
Colorado R.
Arkansas R.
NEW MEXICO
Gila R.
Rio Grande
Red R.
ARIZPE
TEJAS
Nueces R.
DURANGO
COAHUILA
NUEVO LEÓN
NUEVO SANTANDER
Gulf of California
Gulf of Mexico
PACIFIC OCEAN

0 200 400 Miles
0 200 400 Kilometers

A bronze statue of a Tejano sitting astride his horse is part of the striking Tejano Monument, located on the grounds of the Texas state capitol in Austin. The monument honors the contributions of Tejanos and their roles in shaping Tejas—and eventually Texas.

LAND GRANTS AND SETTLERS

After an 11-year war, Mexico won its independence from Spain. As a result, in 1821, the Tejanos found themselves part of Mexico and no longer under Spanish rule. The new nation of Mexico included the lands that make up present-day Texas, New Mexico, Arizona, California, Nevada, and Utah, as well as parts of Colorado and Wyoming.

Few people lived in Tejas, and the Mexican government feared conflicts between Tejano settlements and Native Americans. Hoping that a larger population of settlers would stabilize the territory, Mexico encouraged American immigration and settlement and, unlike Spain, welcomed trade with Americans.

The Mexican government also gave land grants to American farmers and merchants. One American merchant received permission to form a colony even before Mexican independence. In 1820,

Moses Austin persuaded the Spanish governor to allow him to bring a few hundred families to settle in Tejas. He died a year later, before he could carry out his plan, but his son, **Stephen F. Austin**, inherited the land grant. Austin moved 300 American families into southeastern Tejas, establishing the territory's first legal American settlement. A rush of other American immigrants soon followed.

HISTORICAL THINKING

1. **READING CHECK** What influence did Mexican independence have on Americans' presence in Tejas?

2. **IDENTIFY MAIN IDEAS AND DETAILS** What did Mexico hope to accomplish through the land grants?

3. **INTERPRET MAPS** Based on details you notice on the map, describe the borders and territory of Mexico in 1821.

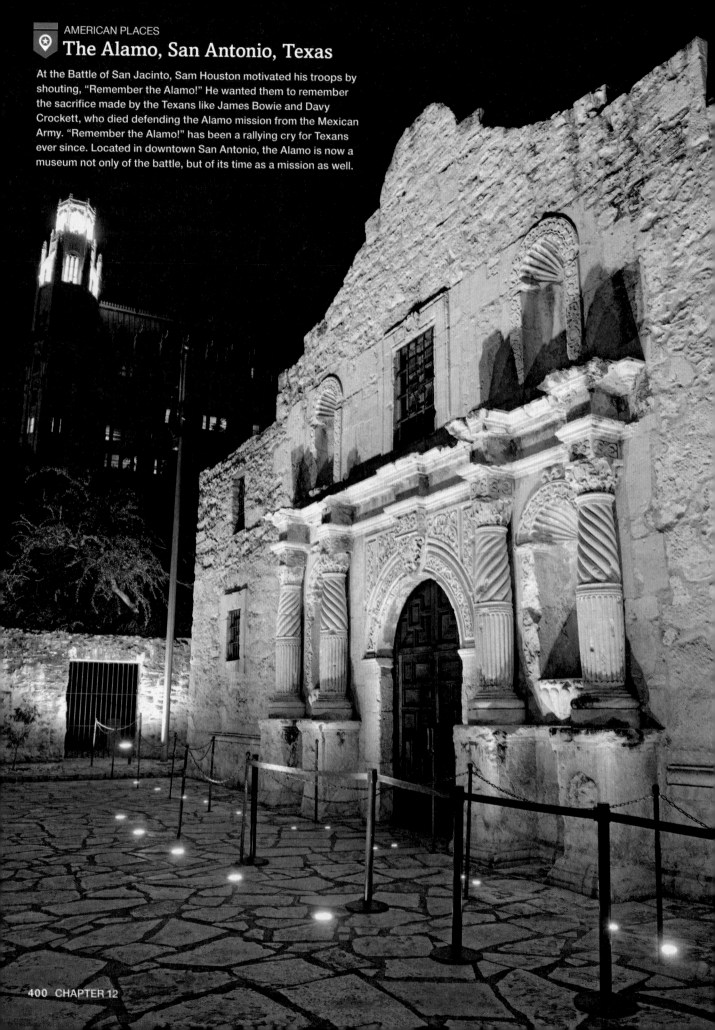

The Alamo, San Antonio, Texas

At the Battle of San Jacinto, Sam Houston motivated his troops by shouting, "Remember the Alamo!" He wanted them to remember the sacrifice made by the Texans like James Bowie and Davy Crockett, who died defending the Alamo mission from the Mexican Army. "Remember the Alamo!" has been a rallying cry for Texans ever since. Located in downtown San Antonio, the Alamo is now a museum not only of the battle, but of its time as a mission as well.

2.2 Settlement and Rebellion

Inviting new friends to your home for a party can sometimes lead to unexpected surprises. Mexico thought that inviting Americans to move to Texas would boost the population. It didn't anticipate what would happen next.

MAIN IDEA Cultural differences and disagreements with the Mexican government led Texans to declare independence from Mexico.

GROWING NUMBER OF SETTLERS

With the opportunity to own a great deal of land in exchange for a small fee, thousands of Americans arrived in Tejas—or Texas, as they called the territory—to take advantage of Mexico's settlement policies. Here, women were able to inherit land grants, and many owned and ran huge, profitable ranches. Women worked alongside men in the day-to-day operations of raising and selling livestock.

Texas quickly became a mix of cultures. Most American settlers were English-speaking Protestants, and the vast majority of Mexicans were Spanish-speaking Catholics. American settlers continued the practice of slavery in Texas, even though Mexico had outlawed slavery in 1829.

Though it had invited American settlement, the Mexican government grew concerned as the population of Texas became more American and less Mexican. By 1830, about 21,000 Americans lived there, including about 1,000 enslaved African Americans. On April 6, 1830, Mexico banned all further American settlement in Texas. Many European countries had already outlawed slavery, and the Mexican government hoped that a stronger European presence would encourage an end to the practice of slavery in the territory.

Texans—Americans and Tejanos alike— who disliked these changes called for more representation within the Mexican government. Revolts in 1832 and 1833 sent the message: Texans wanted Texas statehood within Mexico. General **Antonio López de Santa Anna**, who had recently become the president of Mexico, rejected this demand. Texans rebelled and the Texas War for Independence began.

TEXAS WAR FOR INDEPENDENCE

The war started in October 1835 with the Battle of Gonzales, a victory for Texas. More battles followed, and Santa Anna soon led an army from Mexico City to put down the rebellion. He reached San Antonio by mid-February 1836, where he encountered roughly 180 Texans guarding the **Alamo,** a mission building. For 13 days, 1,800 Mexican soldiers held the Alamo and its defenders under siege , which meant no one could leave or enter the building to bring food, supplies, or reinforcements. On March 2, Texans declared themselves a separate nation, the Republic of Texas. On March 6, the Mexican Army breached the Alamo's walls and killed almost everyone inside, including frontiersmen James Bowie, designer of the Bowie knife, and Davy Crockett, a U.S. congressman.

In response, on April 21, **Sam Houston**, the Texan Army's commander, attacked the Mexican Army near the San Jacinto River. He won the **Battle of San Jacinto** (sahn hah-SEEN-toh) and captured Santa Anna. Santa Anna agreed to withdraw and surrender. Texas had achieved independence.

HISTORICAL THINKING

1. **READING CHECK** Why did Texans want independence from Mexico?

2. **ANALYZE CAUSE AND EFFECT** How did the Texans' defeat at the Alamo affect the final outcome of the Texas War for Independence?

3. **DESCRIBE** What opportunities did Tejas offer women who settled and lived there?

2.3 Independence and Annexation

A "political football" is an issue that political opponents fight over. In 1836, the issue of annexing Texas became a political football in the United States, and it would be kicked back and forth for nearly a decade.

MAIN IDEA The annexation of the Republic of Texas as the 28th state caused tension between northern and southern states.

THE LONE STAR REPUBLIC

After the Texas War for Independence, Texas became an independent nation, the Republic of Texas. Texans elected Sam Houston as their first president. The flag of Texas, with a single star, earned the nation the nickname of **Lone Star Republic**. As proud as they were of their victory, Texans knew they were vulnerable to further attacks from Mexico. They also lacked an established economy. Most Texans favored annexation by the United States.

The United States initially rejected this plan, however. In 1836 and 1837, President Andrew Jackson and his successor Martin Van Buren turned down Texas lawmakers' proposals. For

one thing, they argued, annexing Texas would hurt American relations with Mexico and perhaps even lead to war. They also knew the American people were divided on the question, primarily because of the issue of slavery.

Before independence, Texas clashed with Mexico over slavery, which was prohibited by Mexican law. The ongoing use of enslaved labor in the Republic of Texas also became a concern for northern states in the United States. Admitting Texas as a state would upset the balance between states that had outlawed slavery and states where slavery was still practiced. Presidents Jackson and Van Buren argued that annexation was not in the best interest of the country.

1829 Texas State Flag
The flag of the Republic of Texas, which also became the state flag of Texas, is the only state flag that once flew as the flag of an independent country.

A GLOBAL PERSPECTIVE In recent decades, some Texans have supported a movement for Texas to leave the United States and become an independent republic again. Proponents of this effort believe that the state gives too much power and money to the federal government. Some have compared these views with those advocated by "Brexit," the British movement that voted to leave the European Union (EU) in June 2016. The Texan movement earned a similar nickname, "Texit," a combination of the words *Texas* and *exit*. In this photo, campaigners for and against Brexit pass out flyers in London. What historical precedent might supporters of Texit cite as evidence that Texas should leave the United States?

ANNEXATION OF TEXAS

Texas remained independent for almost 10 years. Then, in 1844, annexation gained a supporter in the White House—**James K. Polk**. Polk had been the Speaker of the House and the governor of Tennessee, but he was not a superstar politician. When the Democrats nominated him for president in 1844, he was an unknown candidate who had little chance of winning. But despite running as an unknown against Henry Clay, the prominent Whig candidate, Polk won the presidency, barely, with 49.5 percent of the popular vote and an electoral college **margin**, or amount by which something is won or lost, of 170–105.

As president, Polk managed to turn his political ambitions into policy. He supported the ideas of manifest destiny and favored the annexation of

Texas. He also believed that the United States should take complete control of the Oregon Territory, up to the latitude of 54° 40'. One of Polk's campaign slogans was "Fifty-four forty or fight!" Polk brought an enthusiasm to his presidency for expanding the country. Under his leadership, Texas became the 28th state.

HISTORICAL THINKING

1. **READING CHECK** What were the arguments against the annexation of Texas as a state?

2. **IDENTIFY MAIN IDEAS AND DETAILS** How was Polk's argument for annexation informed by the concept of manifest destiny?

3. **EVALUATE** What made James K. Polk an attractive but unlikely candidate for president?

2.4 Samuel "Sam" Houston 1793–1863

Antonio López de Santa Anna 1794–1876

"Santa Anna, living, can be of incalculable [great] benefit to Texas."—Sam Houston

Houston became known as the "George Washington of Texas." The city of Houston was named after him.

Santa Anna called himself the "Napoleon of the West" but left behind a legacy of chaos in 19th-century Mexico.

Not everyone agreed with Sam Houston about the value of Antonio López de Santa Anna's life. When the Texans won the Battle of San Jacinto, many of Houston's soldiers called for the Mexican leader's execution. After all, Santa Anna hadn't shown any mercy to the Texans at the Alamo. But Houston wanted independence for Texas—not revenge.

CONTRASTING PERSONALITIES

Houston and Santa Anna fought on opposite sides during the Texas War for Independence, but they had a number of things in common. Both pursued careers in the military and in politics. And, in the 1800s, both men were legends and dominant figures in the lands they loved—Houston in Texas and Santa Anna in Mexico.

But that's where the resemblance ended. Houston consistently demonstrated his loyalty and duty to the United States. He fought heroically in the War of 1812 under Andrew Jackson, whom Houston considered his mentor. It was Jackson

who encouraged Houston to enter politics. While living in Tennessee, Houston was first elected to Congress and later became governor of the state.

Santa Anna, on the other hand, often placed self-interest above duty, switching sides based on what was in it for him. He entered the Spanish army at 16 and fought with Spain when the war for Mexican independence broke out. (Mexico was a Spanish colony at that time.) But in 1821, Santa Anna shifted his loyalty and led the Mexican rebels to independence. As a reward, he was appointed governor of the Mexican state of Veracruz.

In 1833, the Mexican people elected Santa Anna president, but he soon lost interest in the office and left the real governing to his vice president. However, when the vice president began reforming the church, state, and army, Santa Anna was furious because the reforms threatened his interests. In response, he used military force to remove his vice president.

CLASHING ARMIES

Resuming authority, Santa Anna introduced a less democratic form of government in Mexico and in Texas. The Texans became dissatisfied with their lack of freedom and, in 1835, began a revolution. They called on Houston, who had relocated to Texas, to lead the rebel force.

From the outset, the Texans were outnumbered. They suffered terrible defeats at the Alamo and in the Texas town of Goliad, where about 350 rebels were taken prisoner and executed. The Texans finally seized their chance in 1836 when Santa Anna and a small number of his soldiers arrived at San Jacinto. Houston organized a surprise attack and quickly overpowered the Mexican Army.

For a time after his embarrassing defeat, Santa Anna fell from favor in Mexico. He returned to power eventually, but as you'll see, American troops would once again bring about his downfall.

As for Houston, he became the first president of the Republic of Texas and served as senator after Texas achieved statehood. He'd just been elected its governor when a number of southern states voted to separate from the United States. When Houston refused to allow Texas to join the southern states, he was removed from office.

HISTORICAL THINKING

1. **READING CHECK** In which two areas did both Houston and Santa Anna pursue careers?

2. **COMPARE AND CONTRAST** How did Houston's treatment of the enemy in the Texas War for Independence differ from the way in which Santa Anna treated his prisoners?

3. **EVALUATE** In what way did Santa Anna's character and judgment affect Texas and Mexico?

2.5 San Jacinto Museum of History La Porte, Texas

A museum with a unique location, the San Jacinto is housed in the base of the San Jacinto Monument. It was established as a steward of history to honor those who fought in the Texas War for Independence from Mexico and showcase the history of Texas and the Spanish Southwest. Visitors can view art and artifacts from the Spanish conquest, Spanish colonial life, the Mexican Revolution, the colonization of Mexican Texas, early Texas statehood, and the Civil War. What can you infer about the relationship between Mexico and Texas by examining the artifacts below?

Mexican Badge

This heavy brass badge, likely worn by a soldier in the Mexican Army, features the Mexican military insignia, an eagle perched on a cactus plant. The streamer beneath the eagle's talons reads: "LIBERTAD MEXICANA" (Mexican freedom).

Soldiers sharpened the curve on the top of the blade, called a clip point, to inflict a more serious wound as the knife was pulled out.

Texas Army Bowie Knife

Alamo hero and knife-fighter Jim Bowie knew what he wanted in a knife. He worked with blacksmiths to create knives like this one that had curved blades and cross-guards to protect hands. It was a handy weapon, useful for hunting, digging, or cutting down trees, as well as in hand-to-hand combat.

Santa Anna's Knee Buckle

In the late 1700s, many men wore knee buckles to secure their short pants, or breeches, at the knee. This buckle has 22 square diamonds, a handsome design, and an impressive history. Santa Anna gave this buckle to Sam Houston after Houston defeated him in the Battle of San Jacinto. Historians agree Santa Anna was a strong leader with a dynamic personality, but he also lacked principles and loved military glory, which often led Mexico down the wrong path.

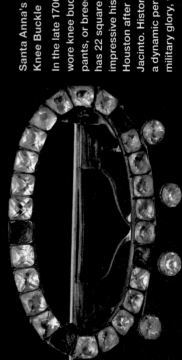

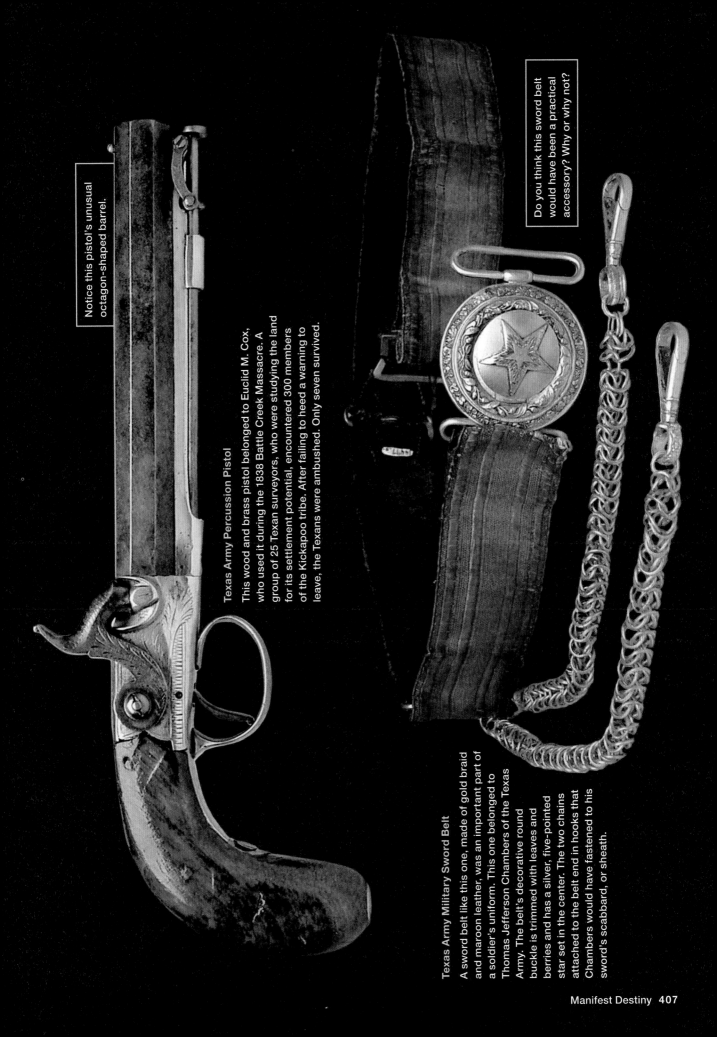

Notice this pistol's unusual octagon-shaped barrel.

Do you think this sword belt would have been a practical accessory? Why or why not?

Texas Army Percussion Pistol

This wood and brass pistol belonged to Euclid M. Cox, who used it during the 1838 Battle Creek Massacre. A group of 25 Texan surveyors, who were studying the land for its settlement potential, encountered 300 members of the Kickapoo tribe. After failing to heed a warning to leave, the Texans were ambushed. Only seven survived.

Texas Army Military Sword Belt

A sword belt like this one, made of gold braid and maroon leather, was an important part of a soldier's uniform. This one belonged to Thomas Jefferson Chambers of the Texas Army. The belt's decorative round buckle is trimmed with leaves and berries and has a silver, five-pointed star set in the center. The two chains attached to the belt end in hooks that Chambers would have fastened to his sword's scabbard, or sheath.

3.1 Tensions with Mexico

When you heat water in a teakettle, pressure builds until the water reaches the boiling point. In the 1840s, tensions between the United States and Mexico reached their boiling point: war.

MAIN IDEA The annexation of Texas upset the balance of slave and free states and led to the Mexican-American War.

POLK'S MISSION

James K. Polk was a firm believer in the concept of manifest destiny. When he became president in 1844, he focused on territorial expansion, including the annexation of Texas and the acquisition of California and Oregon. Southerners favored Polk because of his plans to annex Texas. Since slavery had long been practiced there, Texas would join the Union as a slave state. This infuriated northerners because it meant that slave states would outnumber free states. The threat of an unequal number of slave and free states had already reared its head in 1820, with Missouri's request to become a state. The political firestorm that ensued led to a solution in the Missouri Compromise. That solution proved to be temporary, as Congress voted to annex Texas as a new slave state in 1845.

AMERICAN PLACES
Big Bend National Park, Texas

Big Bend National Park is a protected area of canyons and waterfalls at the southernmost bend of the Rio Grande. The river forms the border between Mexico and the United States for about 1,000 miles. At the beginning of the Mexican-American War in 1846, the border, and therefore access to this important river, was disputed.

CROSSING THE NUECES RIVER

Relations between the United States and Mexico had been tense since the creation of the Republic of Texas. Mexican president Antonio López de Santa Anna had signed the Treaties of Velasco, giving Texas its independence, but the Mexican government never formally acknowledged the treaties as legal. Santa Anna had signed the treaties while he was a prisoner of the Texan Army, they argued, and therefore Texas was still a part of Mexico. Given this history, it's not surprising that Texas's annexation further worsened relations between the United States and Mexico.

At the time, Texas extended only as far south as the Nueces River. President Polk insisted that Texas's southern border should be the Rio Grande, much farther south than the Nueces. In July 1845, Polk sent American troops, led by General **Zachary Taylor**, to secure the area between the Rio Grande and the Nueces River. Polk also sent John Slidell, a **diplomat**, or person sent to represent a country, to Mexico City with an offer. Texas would extend to the Rio Grande, and the United States would buy California for $25 million. The Mexican government refused to negotiate.

Hearing about the snub, Polk told Taylor to advance on the Rio Grande. A skirmish between American and Mexican troops near the river gave Polk the excuse he needed to call for war. In an address to Congress, he declared that Mexico "has invaded our territory and shed American blood upon American soil." Even the Whigs, who had wanted to avoid conflict with Mexico, gave in. The **Mexican-American War** started on May 13, 1846.

Although Congress voted overwhelmingly in favor of the war, many Americans opposed Polk's tactics. Notable New Englanders, including John Quincy Adams and James Russell Lowell, claimed the war was a scheme to expand slavery. Henry David Thoreau even landed in jail when he refused to pay taxes to support the war. Abraham Lincoln, then a young congressman from Illinois, agreed with the New Englanders. He demanded an answer from Polk about "the particular spot of soil on which the blood of our citizens was so shed." Despite the protests, the United States remained at war with Mexico for more than a year.

⬛ Dallas Historical Society
Dallas, Texas

Zachary Taylor is memorialized as the king of diamonds on this 19th-century playing card. He is wearing a bicorn hat and elaborate epaulettes, or shoulder ornaments—both of which were typical of American and European military officers beginning in the 1790s.

HISTORICAL THINKING

1. **READING CHECK** What did President Polk want from Mexico, and how did the president of Mexico respond?

2. **IDENTIFY MAIN IDEAS AND DETAILS** What were the causes of the Mexican-American War?

3. **EVALUATE** How did President Polk use emotion to persuade Congress to vote for war with Mexico?

3.2 The United States at War

California's state flag features an unusual combination of items: a grizzly bear, a lone red star, and the words "California Republic." The history of this unique flag stems from an event that took place in the 1840s.

MAIN IDEA The United States took control of New Mexico and California after forcing Mexico to surrender at the end of the Mexican-American War.

TERRITORIAL SETTLEMENTS

Despite some Americans' opposition to the Mexican-American War, the United States had the upper hand from the start. On August 18, 1846, General **Stephen Kearny** and his troops marched into Santa Fe, the capital of the New Mexico Territory. They had expected to face strong opposition from Mexican troops and militia, but they found the city unguarded. For unknown reasons, Santa Fe's Mexican governor, Manuel Armijo (ahr-MEE-hoh), had decided not to fight. The United States claimed the New Mexico Territory without a single soldier firing a weapon.

Meanwhile, dramatic events unfolded in California. On June 14, 1846, American settlers took over the town of Sonoma and declared their independence from Mexico. They declared that their land was now the Republic of California. Because of their flag—which featured a grizzly bear—their **insurrection**, or rebellion, would become

known as the **Bear Flag Revolt**. American explorer and survey expedition leader **John C. Frémont** headed to Sonoma, where he gave his support to the settlers.

The Republic of California, with Frémont as its elected leader, had a very short life, however. The insurrection had been carried out by a group of settlers who were not connected with, or acting under orders from, the U.S. government. Within days, American forces took control of the area and claimed California for the United States. In August 1846, the U.S. Army also captured the city of Los Angeles, and by November, the conquest was complete.

By 1847, the United States controlled all of California and New Mexico. American military leaders then turned toward Mexico itself. The Mexican Army was busy in the California and New Mexico territories, leaving strategic Mexican cities vulnerable to attack.

State of California Flag
The present-day state flag of California is much like the one used by the California battalion that supported the U.S. Army in taking control of California. It includes the same elements as the Bear Flag of that battalion. The grizzly bear symbolizes strength, the star stands for independence, and the red color represents courage.

CRITICAL VIEWING In this 1847 color print, artist Christian Mayr depicts one of the more dramatic events of the Mexican-American War: General Scott's entrance into Mexico City. Based on what you see in the print, how does the artist represent people's reception of Scott and his troops?

INVADING MEXICO

Zachary Taylor, the leader of the troops that had crossed the Nueces River to spark the war, had enjoyed some success near the Rio Grande. Taylor now entered Mexico, pursuing retreating Mexican troops. He fought Santa Anna at Buena Vista in 1847. Though the battle seemed to be an even fight, Santa Anna withdrew his troops, and Taylor now controlled northern Mexico.

Because Taylor was reluctant to mount a large-scale invasion of Mexico, Polk changed the American strategy. He ordered General **Winfield Scott** to take his troops to Mexico by sea. Scott and his men landed at Veracruz, which they captured after a three-week siege. They then fought their way toward the capital, Mexico City.

After another fierce battle on the outskirts of the city, American troops entered the capital. In September 1847, Scott gained control of Mexico City and raised the flag of the United States.

Mexico had surrendered and the war was over, but politicians were divided about what to do with the conquered territory. Some wanted the United States to claim all of the territory conquered in the war, while others wanted to claim only the disputed territories. Some politicians argued that the United States should claim no territory at all. Any treaty between the United States and Mexico would have to settle this debate.

HISTORICAL THINKING

1. **READING CHECK** What was the Bear Flag Revolt?

2. **EXPLAIN** How did the battles over New Mexico and California territories give the U.S. Army an advantage?

3. **DRAW CONCLUSIONS** Why did some politicians argue that the United States should not claim any territory in Mexico?

3.3 Consequences of the War

Restless Americans dreaming of new opportunities set westward expansion in motion. Then the United States seized vast new western territories in a war with Mexico. Some Americans' dream of manifest destiny seemed to be coming true.

MAIN IDEA After a series of treaties, land purchases, and international agreements, the United States stretched from the Atlantic to the Pacific.

OCEAN TO OCEAN

With the fall of Mexico City, the United States had won the Mexican-American War. The war officially ended in February 1848, when the United States and Mexico signed the **Treaty of Guadalupe Hidalgo**. The treaty set the Rio Grande as the border between Texas and Mexico and, in exchange for $15 million, Mexico gave up its northernmost territories. These territories included present-day California, Nevada, and Utah, as well as parts of Arizona, New Mexico, Colorado, and Wyoming. Upon the signing of the treaty, tens of thousands of people who had previously considered themselves Mexicans became Americans overnight.

The United States now stretched from the Atlantic Ocean to the Pacific Ocean. But the victory over Mexico aggravated an already looming problem.

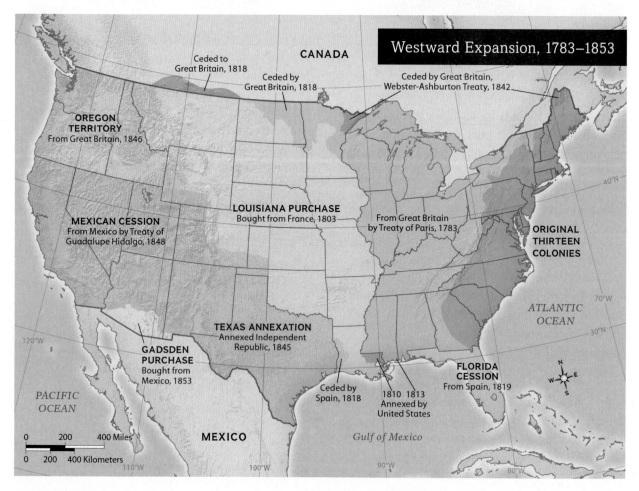

Westward Expansion, 1783–1853

The addition of so much land only worsened conflicts over slavery. The new territories were not part of the Missouri Compromise. What would happen when they gained enough population to become states? Would these states be free states or slave states?

While the Mexican-American War was still in progress, Representative David Wilmot of Pennsylvania introduced a plan called the **Wilmot Proviso**. A **proviso** is a condition attached to a legal document or legislation. The Wilmot Proviso was originally attached to a bill meant to pay for a portion of the Mexican-American War. It called for slavery to be barred from any territory gained from the Mexican-American War. President Polk and other pro-slavery southerners opposed this plan and offered an alternate proposal: to extend the Missouri Compromise line westward. Slavery would be allowed in territories south of the line and prohibited in territories north of it. The Wilmot Proviso passed several times in the House of Representatives but not in the Senate. Without passage of this proviso into law, the subject of slavery in new states remained a major concern.

NEW BORDERS, NORTH AND SOUTH

At the same time the United States was adding land in the West, it began to clash with Great Britain over land in the Northwest: the Oregon Territory. Fortunately, diplomacy, not war, ended this conflict. Lawmakers from the United States and Britain agreed to a compromise, setting the northern border of the United States at the 49th **parallel**, or line of latitude, located 49° N of the equator.

Another puzzle piece of American territory fell into place in 1853, when Mexico sold the United States a sliver of land located along the southern edges of present-day Arizona and New Mexico. This $10 million deal, called the **Gadsden Purchase**, granted the United States land it needed to

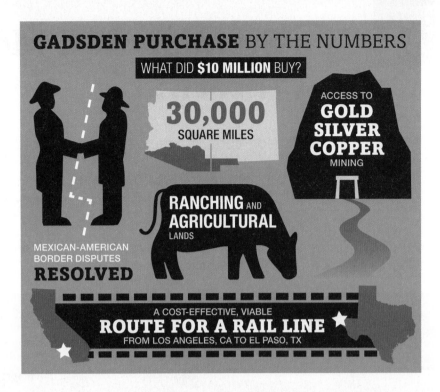

GADSDEN PURCHASE BY THE NUMBERS

WHAT DID **$10 MILLION** BUY?

30,000 SQUARE MILES

ACCESS TO **GOLD SILVER COPPER** MINING

RANCHING AND **AGRICULTURAL** LANDS

MEXICAN-AMERICAN BORDER DISPUTES **RESOLVED**

A COST-EFFECTIVE, VIABLE **ROUTE FOR A RAIL LINE** FROM LOS ANGELES, CA TO EL PASO, TX

complete a southern transcontinental railroad. It also completed the borders of the **contiguous**, or connected, United States.

The Mexican-American War led to a monumental increase in the size of the United States and an important addition to American culture and identity. For generations, Mexican Americans have contributed to and shaped the United States, and their culture has particularly deep roots in the region that once belonged to Spain and Mexico. Place names throughout the Southwest reflect their Hispanic heritage, and Mexican cultural traditions shape life and identity in many southwestern communities. Spanish and Mexican people and their descendants also played a large role in California's story as it moved toward statehood.

HISTORICAL THINKING

1. **READING CHECK** What events finalized the borders of the western United States?

2. **IDENTIFY MAIN IDEAS AND DETAILS** Why did each acquisition of new territory renew conflicts over slavery?

3. **INTERPRET MAPS** Locate present-day state borders on the map. How many states or parts of states were added to U.S. territory between 1803 and 1853?

4.1 The Spanish and Mexicans in California

Maps tell us about geography, but they also tell us about history. Just look at a map of California, and you'll see names such as Los Angeles, Palo Alto, and Sierra Nevada—evidence of a past rooted in Spanish culture.

MAIN IDEA Long before the United States acquired California, Spanish and Mexican settlers were founding missions and settlements there.

This statue of Junípero Serra, sculpted by Arthur Putnam in 1918, is located in the cemetery garden at Mission San Francisco. Serra founded Mission San Francisco, also known as Mission Dolores, in 1776.

SPANISH MISSIONS IN CALIFORNIA

As you have read, Spanish conquistadors first explored and claimed the area that is now California in the 16th century. The Spanish were slow to settle in California. The colonial government considered California too far north from its base in Mexico for the region to be a priority. In the 1700s, however, British and Russian fur traders expanded westward into the region to take advantage of the land's natural resources. As a defensive measure, Spain sent an expedition to establish communities in southern California in 1769.

One member of the expedition was **Father Junípero Serra** (hoo-NEE-peh-roh SEH-rah), a Catholic priest from Spain. Serra founded the first mission in California at San Diego. His relationship to the Native Americans he sought to convert to Christianity is still the subject of controversy. Some historians see him as a courageous and generous man who worked hard to improve Native American lives. Others point to his participation in the mistreatment and enslavement of Native Americans.

Over time, the Spanish established 21 missions in California. The names of these missions echo the cities that eventually grew up around them, such as San Francisco, Santa Clara, and San Luis Obispo.

The mission system itself was complicated. Mission residents established farms on the nearby lands and tried to convert Native Americans to Christianity. Spanish treatment of Native Americans was often cruel. Many settlers exploited and enslaved Native Americans they encountered near their farms. They pushed thousands of Native Americans off their land and forced hundreds of others to live and work at the missions.

MEXICAN RULE OF CALIFORNIA

When Mexico gained independence from Spain in 1821, California was one of the new nation's northernmost territories. Because of its enormous size and its great distance from Mexico City, California was difficult for Mexico to rule. As in Texas, the local Mexican government was often ineffective and corrupt.

In 1824, Mexico passed an act that granted land to settlers in the form of large estates. These land grants became new estates, called **ranchos**, which consisted of sprawling tracts of land covering thousands of acres. The ranchos formed the basis of the economy of the Mexican settlements in the region. The rancheros, or owners, raised huge herds of cattle and traded hides and the processed fat of the cattle for manufactured goods along the Pacific coast.

The economy expanded as American traders, trappers, farmers, and businesspeople moved into the territory in the decades after Mexican independence. Some received land grants for ranchos or other parcels of land.

One of these new settlers was a Swiss immigrant named **John Sutter**, who received several land grants from the Mexican government to start a colony. In 1843, he built what became known as Sutter's Fort, a huge, high-walled adobe structure at the future site of Sacramento. Sutter kept herds of cattle like other California rancheros, but he also helped diversify the region's economy and agriculture by raising grapes and wheat.

By 1848, Americans who had moved to California accounted for more than half of its non-Native American population. They faced a government they felt did not represent them, and as a result, the Americans entertained the idea of independence from Mexico.

They got their wish with the signing of the Treaty of Guadalupe Hidalgo in 1848. The United States acquired California just in time for an amazing discovery at a sawmill that John Sutter was building in the foothills of the Sierra Nevada.

HISTORICAL THINKING

1. **READING CHECK** Why did the Spanish establish communities in California?

2. **COMPARE AND CONTRAST** How were the histories of Texas and California alike under the rule of Spain and Mexico?

3. **IDENTIFY MAIN IDEAS AND DETAILS** How did the California economy change as American settlers received land grants?

4.2 The Gold Rush

A fever of sorts broke out in the late 1840s. Victims from all around the world quit their jobs, left their families, and set off on long, dangerous journeys. The "illness" they suffered from? Gold fever.

MAIN IDEA The discovery of gold in California in 1848 led to a boom in population and wealth.

EUREKA!

By the late 1840s, Sutter's Fort had become a thriving farm community. Various new projects were underway, including the construction of a sawmill upstream on the American River. You might recall from the American Story in this chapter that this was where workers spotted a few flecks of gold on January 24, 1848. Sutter swore the workers to secrecy, but the word soon got out. The next few years would be chaos for Sutter. His men immediately stopped working, abandoned the colony, and went hunting for gold instead.

At first, **prospectors**, or people in search of valuable resources in the earth, found a wealth of gold deposits that were easy to access. They struck gold by digging into hills or mountainsides, or by panning in rivers or streams. Panning involves using a shallow pan to scoop up gravel from the bed of a stream, dipping the pan in the stream to collect some water, and swishing the water around to wash away dirt, clay, and silt. Heavier materials, including particles of gold, remain in the pan.

When prospectors struck gold, they yelled "Eureka!" *Eureka* is an ancient Greek word that means "I have found it." During the California gold rush, shouts of "Eureka!" expressed the thrill and excitement accompanying the discovery of riches. The word was so closely associated with the gold rush that it would become the California state motto.

News of the gold discovery spread to the East Coast and then around the world. Thousands of people bitten by the "gold bug" began heading west to strike it rich.

CRITICAL VIEWING In 1858, George W. Northrup posed as a prospector for a photo to send home to his family in Minnesota. He is holding a pickaxe, a hoe, a pan, and two pistols. Note that he also has a bag labeled "gold" on his lap. What image do you think Northrup was trying to convey by posing in this way?

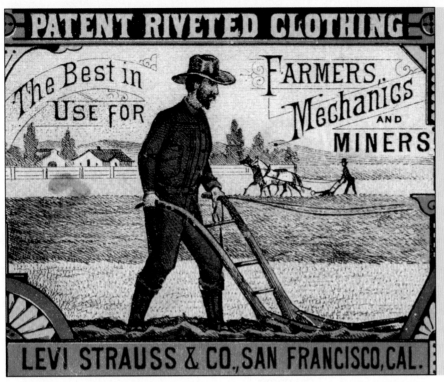

Levi Strauss's Blue Jeans

One merchant who became rich during the gold rush was **Levi Strauss**. A Jewish German immigrant, he arrived in San Francisco in 1850. His goal was to manufacture tents and wagon covers for miners. But after noticing a demand for durable work pants, he began producing trousers made from the tent canvas he had purchased.

People loved the pants. Strauss sold enough to open a factory and started to produce the pants using a denim cloth known as *gênes* in French. Levi Strauss invented blue jeans and founded a company and a unique American brand.

THE FORTY-NINERS

By the following year, around 80,000 new gold-seekers had moved to California. They earned the nickname **forty-niners** because they arrived in 1849. The forty-niners came from all over the United States and the world. Consequently, the mining towns that sprang up to house and feed the forty-niners included diverse mixes of nationalities and cultures. Because slavery was not commonly practiced in California, many free African Americans decided to try their luck in the gold fields. Thousands of immigrants also arrived from China.

Most of the fortune-seekers were single men who hoped to find riches quickly and move on. Others headed to California with plans to settle there permanently. Whether they struck gold or not, many ended up staying. The boom in population created opportunities for all kinds of settlers. With a bit of creativity and business knowledge, people could make a fortune providing goods and services to the miners and other new residents of California.

However, the gold rush did not have a positive impact on everyone. Many people who had long lived in California found their livelihoods destroyed. **Californios**, or residents of Spanish or Mexican descent, had thrived on California's abundant farmland and prosperous ranchos. Newcomers to the area did not respect Californios' customs or legal rights, and in some cases they seized Californios' property. In addition, thousands of Native Americans died at the hands of gold miners or from the diseases that they and other settlers brought into the region.

California's population increased quite rapidly because of the gold rush. Before 1848, about 1,000 non-native people lived there. By the end of 1849, that number reached nearly 100,000. Even though most of the easily found gold deposits had been depleted by then, more fortune-seekers arrived each day. With that fast-growing population came a need for the laws and government that statehood could provide.

HISTORICAL THINKING

1. **READING CHECK** How did the California gold rush start?

2. **ANALYZE CAUSE AND EFFECT** In what ways did the discovery of gold and the migration of the forty-niners affect Californios and others who had long lived in California?

3. **SUMMARIZE** How did the population of California change, and why?

4.3 The Mining Frontier

It's 1849 and you've journeyed to California to hunt for gold. You dreamed of adventure and riches, but the living and working conditions are miserable. Worst of all, you haven't found a speck of gold!

MAIN IDEA A population boom and growing lawlessness caused by the gold rush led to the demand for California statehood.

LIFE IN A MINING CAMP

When 100,000 people crowd into the same region within a short period of time, there are bound to be problems. Few of the single men who rushed west to search for gold were interested in building stable communities. A region that had been mostly rural was suddenly covered with **boomtowns**, or mining camps that grew into crowded towns overnight. These boomtowns had neither strong leadership nor government of any kind. Law enforcement could not keep up with the boomtowns of the gold rush. Thieves and swindlers often got richer than gold miners. Bored miners living far from home spent their free time gambling and fighting with each other.

As you have read, many westward moving pioneers arrived in wagon trains on overland trails. But others decided to travel by ship. Starting on the East Coast, they sailed southward around Cape Horn at the southernmost tip of South America, and then back north to California. Overland trips took from four to six months, and the Cape Horn route took about six months.

Immigrants arrived from many countries, including Chile, Mexico, and China. San Francisco's location made it particularly accessible for people crossing the Pacific Ocean. Immigrants from China were the most numerous. Many settled in California permanently, even though they had not planned on doing so initially.

As a result, these newly established communities included people who spoke different languages, had different customs, and practiced different religions. Sometimes, cultural differences led to misunderstandings or even violence. Among white Americans, prejudices against Native Americans, African Americans, and Chinese immigrants often boiled over into fights. When gold discoveries slowed down, competition for the dwindling gold became more intense. Tensions increased, and so did crime.

Women who moved to boomtowns were far outnumbered by men and faced many challenges. In addition to the hard labor typical of living in a frontier region, they also handled domestic duties for their households. To make extra money, some even took on housekeeping tasks for single men living around them. Many women discovered a liberating independence in California because they could make a good living there. In this frontier region, few laws existed to prohibit women from owning property or businesses. Women opened profitable boarding houses, taverns, and other businesses that catered to the populations of the mining camps. Others tried their luck at mining, and a few even struck gold.

STATEHOOD FOR CALIFORNIA

Many American territories waited years before achieving statehood, but not California. With its population booming and lawlessness plaguing its mining camps, California needed a strong government right away. Since it now easily met the population requirements, many people felt that it was time for California to become a state.

In 1849, territory leaders met at a convention in Monterey to draft a constitution and to make a plan to petition the federal government for statehood. California's first constitution prohibited

San Francisco, 1848

The California gold rush transformed the small mission of San Francisco into a thriving, vibrant city. Between 1848 and 1849, its population rose from 1,000 to 25,000. By 1860, the city had more than 50,000 people. The top illustration shows the city before the gold rush. The bottom lithograph, by the French illustrator Auguste-Victor Deroy, captures the city as he saw it in 1860. How do these two illustrations show how the landscape of San Francisco changed as more people arrived?

San Francisco, 1860

slavery. However, it did not grant civil rights to all of the state's nonwhite or female populations. Like the nation's other states at this time, California's constitution granted only white men the highest level of legal rights and protections.

In September 1850, less than two years after Sutter's workers glimpsed those first specks of gold in a Sierra mountain stream, California became the 31st state. Not surprisingly, its admission as a free state heightened the crisis over slavery that was already threatening to tear the country apart.

HISTORICAL THINKING

1. **READING CHECK** How did the gold rush lead to California's application for statehood?

2. **IDENTIFY MAIN IDEAS AND DETAILS** What opportunities were women able to pursue during the gold rush, and why?

3. **EVALUATE** Did the leaders at the 1849 California constitutional convention support ideas of freedom and equality? Support your response with evidence from the text.

VOCABULARY

Use each of the following vocabulary words in a sentence that shows an understanding of the term's meaning.

1. exodus
   The hurricane warning prompted an exodus of thousands of people from their coastal communities.

2. presidio
3. prospector
4. annex
5. proviso

6. rancho
7. insurrection
8. siege

READING STRATEGY
IDENTIFY MAIN IDEAS AND DETAILS

If you haven't done so already, complete your chart to identify details about Americans' westward movement. Then answer the question.

Main Idea:
Detail:
Detail:
Detail:

9. What factors drove Americans west between 1821 and 1853?

MAIN IDEAS

Answer the following questions. Support your answers with evidence from the chapter.

10. How did the concept of manifest destiny contribute to American expansion? **LESSON 1.1**

11. What groups traveled on the Santa Fe, Oregon, and Mormon Trails? **LESSON 1.3**

12. Why did the Mexican government encourage American settlement in Texas? **LESSON 2.1**

13. Describe the events and outcome of the Battle of the Alamo. **LESSON 2.2**

14. What was James K. Polk's stance on the concept of manifest destiny? **LESSON 2.3**

15. What was the significance of American troops crossing the Nueces River in 1845? **LESSON 3.1**

16. Who participated in the Bear Flag Revolt, and why? **LESSON 3.2**

17. What were the consequences of the Mexican-American War? **LESSON 3.3**

18. Who were the forty-niners? **LESSON 4.2**

19. What did California's first constitution say about slavery? **LESSON 4.3**

HISTORICAL THINKING

Answer the following questions. Support your answers with evidence from the chapter.

20. **IDENTIFY PROBLEMS AND SOLUTIONS** Why did the expansion of the United States create new problems regarding slavery?

21. **MAKE GENERALIZATIONS** How did the ideals of individualism and rugged frontier life shape American identity during the 1800s?

22. **DRAW CONCLUSIONS** Why did the Mexican government regret encouraging American settlement in Texas?

23. **DESCRIBE** In what ways had the borders of the United States changed by the 1850s?

24. **EVALUATE** How did the gold rush provide new opportunities for women, immigrants, and free African Americans?

Look closely at the map of the Mexican-American War. Then answer the questions that follow.

25. What was the final battle of the war, and when did it take place?

26. Based on the map, what type of war were the Mexicans fighting? Explain the reasons for your response.

27. Using the map scale, about what was the greatest distance from the United States that any battle was fought?

28. Which military expedition followed the Gila River? Why might it have done so?

Mexican-American War, 1846–1848

ANALYZE SOURCES

William Gilpin was an explorer, an author, and the first governor of the Colorado Territory. He wrote reports for the government, including "The Untransacted Destiny of the American People" for a U.S. Senate committee in 1846. Read the following excerpt from his report.

29. How were Gilpin's claims similar to President Polk's goals for the United States?

30. What does Gilpin mean when he says that the destiny of Americans is to "subdue the continent?"

> Two centuries have rolled over our race upon this continent. From nothing we have become 20,000,000. From nothing we are grown to be . . . the first among nations existing or in history. So much is our destiny—so far, up to this time— transacted, accomplished, certain, and not to be disputed. The untransacted [unfinished] destiny of the American people is to subdue the continent—to rush over this vast field to the Pacific Ocean.

CONNECT TO YOUR LIFE

31. ARGUMENT Think about the way the West represented a new frontier for Americans in the 1800s. Also think about the motivations of pioneers who moved west. Then consider what kinds of frontiers inspire the same kind of exploration today. Identify one present-day frontier that you would like to explore and write a paragraph that presents an argument for exploring the new frontier. In your argument, take into account new technologies and skills that you might need to explore the frontier.

TIPS

- Look back at the chapter and list ways in which expansion affected the United States during the 1800s. Then think about how present-day frontiers inspire exploration today. Make notes and then review them to help you craft your argument.

- Support your argument with examples of similarities and differences. Use evidence from the text and two or three key terms from the chapter to make your claims.

- Conclude your paragraph by restating your argument and summarizing your reasoning.

THE CHANGING AMERICAN

IDENTITY

1830–1860

ESSENTIAL QUESTION
How did immigration and reform influence American identity?

AMERICAN STORIES The Underground Railroad

SECTION 1 **The Immigrant Experience**

KEY VOCABULARY

assimilate	famine	prejudice
blight	immigrate	push-pull factor
domestic service	Know-Nothing party	steerage
emigrate	nativist	

SECTION 2 **Reforming American Society**

KEY VOCABULARY

asylum	revival meeting
common school movement	Second Great Awakening
craft union	temperance movement
evangelize	transcendentalism
labor union	

SECTION 3 **Abolition and Women's Rights**

KEY VOCABULARY

abolitionist	suffrage
emancipation	Underground Railroad
Seneca Falls Convention	

AMERICAN GALLERY
ONLINE **Women's Rights**

READING STRATEGY

SYNTHESIZE
When you synthesize, you combine related ideas into a single idea, a synthesis. As you read the chapter, use a chart like this one to synthesize ideas about the ways American identity changed between 1830 and 1860.

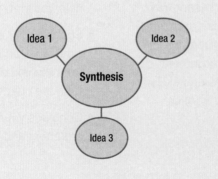

"I went to the woods because I wished to **live deliberately.**"
—Henry David Thoreau

The calm waters of Walden Pond, a lake located in Concord, Massachusetts, reflect the light of sunset. For two years in the 1840s, Henry David Thoreau lived in a cabin at Walden Pond. He wanted to live simply, in nature. His book *Walden,* published in 1854, is based on his years at Walden Pond.

"I think slavery is the next thing to hell."
—Harriet Tubman

CRITICAL VIEWING African-American artist Jacob Lawrence captured the spirit of the Underground Railroad in his moody, nighttime painting called *Forward Together*. Harriet Tubman is believed to be the figure wearing the red cloak on the right. How many other people can you find in the painting?

THE UNDERGROUND
RAILROAD

"When I found I had crossed that line, I looked at my hands to see if I was the same person. There was such a glory over everything; the sun came like gold through trees, and over the fields, and I felt like I was in Heaven."

—Harriet Tubman

CRITICAL VIEWING Based on details in this photograph, what would you infer about photographic practices in the late 1800s?

If you didn't know better,

you might think the Underground Railroad was similar to a city subway. In reality, this amazing railroad never had a single mile of track. In the years before the Civil War, the Underground Railroad was a path to freedom for enslaved African Americans, and its most famous conductor was Harriet Tubman.

Tubman was born into slavery with a different name—Araminta Ross—around 1822 in Dorchester County, Maryland. Minty, as she was called, was first put to work at five years old. By the time she was seven years old, she was cleaning her master's house and taking care of the family's baby. Throughout her childhood and youth, Minty was forced to do difficult jobs, both indoors and out in the fields. She was poorly fed and often beaten by her masters. However, hard work and cruel punishments never crushed Minty's independent nature.

In 1844, Minty married John Tubman, a free black man living in Maryland. Despite her marriage to a free man, she remained enslaved. That meant she could be sold to another owner far from her husband, possibly in the South where conditions for slaves were even worse.

In 1849, Minty learned that she might be sold, so she resolved to flee to Pennsylvania, the free state north of Maryland. As part of her escape, she changed her name to Harriet Tubman. Harriet was her mother's name; Tubman, of course, was her husband's. John Tubman chose to stay in Dorchester County, so Harriet was left to make the risky journey to freedom on her own.

One of the people who helped Tubman escape was a Quaker woman. As you have read, Quakers believed that all people, regardless of skin color, were created equal and that slavery was wrong. This unnamed woman sheltered Tubman for a night and helped her enter the Underground Railroad.

A DIFFERENT KIND OF RAILROAD

The Underground Railroad had no trains, nor was it a single path to freedom. Instead, it was a network of ways that enslaved people could escape to the northern states or Canada. An Underground Railroad "station" was a home or other building in which escaped slaves could take shelter and hide. "Conductors" risked their lives to guide groups of fugitive slaves on the perilous trek from the South and help them navigate the railroad's hidden network.

Because the Underground Railroad operated in deep secrecy, nobody knows exactly how many enslaved people it brought to freedom. One estimate is that around 100,000 people made their way to freedom and safety via the Underground Railroad between 1810 and 1860. Although there were some white supporters of the Underground Railroad, such as the Quakers, free African Americans in the North played the most active role in operating the Underground Railroad. And one of them was Harriet Tubman.

SINGING TO FREEDOM

Escaping slaves needed a secret way to communicate with each other and their conductors. Often they passed messages through songs with a religious theme, called spirituals. Singing while they worked was a tradition among enslaved people, so owners did not suspect an escape was underway when they heard them singing. Harriet Tubman told her biographer that she used the spirituals "Go Down Moses" and "Bound for the Promised Land" to signal to groups of fugitives when they should take cover and when it was safe to come out. "Wade in the Water" was another spiritual used by conductors to communicate with their groups. It was an instruction to jump into a river or stream to shake off possible pursuers.

PRIMARY SOURCE

Wade in the Water. God's gonna trouble the water.
Who are those children all dressed in Red?
God's gonna trouble the water.
Must be the ones that Moses led.
God's gonna trouble the water.

Who are those children all dressed in White?
God's gonna trouble the water.
Must be the ones of the Israelites.
God's gonna trouble the water.

Who are those children all dressed in Blue?
God's gonna trouble the water.
Must be the ones that made it through.
God's gonna trouble the water.

Chorus: *Wade in the Water, wade in the water children.*

THE CODE OF THE RAILROAD

The Underground Railroad used code words to conceal its operations from slave catchers. Several of the code words had their origins in the Bible. Moses—Harriet Tubman's code name—was especially appropriate, because she had a deep faith.

GOSPEL TRAIN the Underground Railroad	**HEAVEN** Canada, freedom
STATION home or other building where slaves could take shelter and hide	**BUNDLES OF WOOD** a group of fugitives that was expected at a station
STATION MASTER person who owned a station and told fugitives how to get to the next station	**STOCKHOLDER** person who donated money, food, or clothing to help the escaping slaves
AGENT person who planned the courses of escapes and contacted the helpers	**LOAD OF POTATOES** fugitives hidden under fruits or vegetables in a farm wagon
MOSES Harriet Tubman (in the Bible, prophet who helped the Israelites escape slavery in Egypt)	**RIVER JORDAN** the Ohio River (a river in Southwest Asia, mentioned in the Bible)

"I was the conductor of the Underground Railroad for eight years, and I can say what most conductors can't say — I never ran my train off the track and I never lost a passenger."

—Harriet Tubman

CRITICAL VIEWING After the Civil War, Harriet Tubman returned to the home she had purchased in Auburn, New York, and began the next phase of her work: caring for elderly African Americans. This photo from c. 1885 shows Tubman (far left) with friends, family members, and some of the aged people she cared for in Auburn. Based on this image and information you have read about Tubman, what conclusions can you draw about the nature of her work and the tasks that motivated and interested her?

CONDUCTOR AND HERO

Once she successfully made her own escape, Tubman decided her family and other slaves should also be free. For her, the best way to do that was to become a conductor herself.

Being a conductor required courage, intelligence, and nerves of steel. Slave catchers were always on the lookout for fugitives. Hired by slave owners to capture escaped slaves, the slave catchers, or bounty hunters as they were sometimes called, were not afraid to use force.

Quick thinking and tough, Tubman was up to the task. According to her own recollections, Tubman made around 19 trips back into Maryland and rescued up to 300 slaves, including her own parents. She gave directions to at least 70 more slaves so they could make their own escapes. Harriet Tubman was one of the most important faces of the Underground Railroad.

When the Civil War broke out, Tubman found other ways to help African Americans and support the Union Army. She worked as a nurse, aiding sick and wounded Union soldiers and escaped slaves. She also acted as spy, passing unnoticed in southern territory disguised as a slave. In 1863, she helped lead Union soldiers and African-American scouts in a raid on the Combahee River in South Carolina. The raid freed over 750 slaves.

After the Civil War, Tubman moved to Auburn, New York, but she did not retire from her mission to help others. She raised money to support schools for freed slaves in the South, participated in antislavery meetings, and campaigned for women's right to vote. She also established a home for elderly and disabled African Americans.

On March 10, 1913, Harriet Tubman died of pneumonia. She was buried in Fort Hill Cemetery in Auburn, New York, with full military honors.

THINK ABOUT IT

Do you think "Underground Railroad" is an appropriate name for the network to aid fugitive slaves? Why or why not? What might such a network be named today?

QUILTED CODES?

Some historians theorize quilts similar to these may have been used to communicate with enslaved people waiting to escape, or with those on the path to freedom. For example, a pattern like the Wagon Wheel could have been hung by seamstresses on plantations. A pattern like the Log Cabin could have been a welcome sight for weary travelers.

The patterns on this quilt may have been used as "maps" for escapees.

The **WAGON WHEEL** design may have told escapees to pack for traveling. It also could have meant escapees would be hiding in a wagon with a secret compartment.

Similar to the Wagon Wheel, the **TUMBLING BLOCKS** pattern might have announced a conductor was in the area, so it was time to pack for the journey.

The **BOW TIE** design could have meant escapees should wear disguises when they journeyed on the Underground Railroad.

The **BEAR PAW** pattern advised passengers to take a hidden path made by bear tracks, which would lead to water and food.

Like the Bow Tie pattern, the **BRITCHES**, or pants, pattern may have told escapees to dress like free people.

The **CROSSROADS** block represented the city of Cleveland, Ohio, one of the main corridors of the Underground Railroad.

The simple design of the **LOG CABIN** may have indicated that a home was a safe house, or a place where escapees could rest.

The floral pattern of the **ROSE WREATH** might have been an announcement that someone had died along the journey to freedom.

HARRIET TUBMAN ON THE $20 BILL?

In 2016, Treasury Secretary Jacob Lew announced his plan to replace President Andrew Jackson with Harriet Tubman on the $20 bill in 2020. However, a new administration entered the White House in 2017. Its leaders suggested they might block the plan or place Tubman on a $2 bill.

The Lure of America

Imagine sleeping in a small bed in a cramped room on a ship bound for New York City. The sea is rough. You try to ignore how sick you feel. Instead, you think about the new life you will make in America.

MAIN IDEA In the mid-1800s, millions of people from around the world left their homelands and moved to the United States.

PUSH AND PULL

When groups of people decide to move to a new country, they consider two types of reasons for the move. Some reasons push, or encourage people to **emigrate**, or leave their home countries. Other reasons pull, or encourage people to **immigrate**, or move to another country. Together, these reasons are known as **push-pull factors**.

Throughout history, crop failures, overpopulation, religious persecution, and wars have pushed people from their homelands. Immigrants usually chose to move to countries with plenty of land to farm, a better economy, and freedoms that appealed to them. For example, the Pilgrims' disagreements with the Church of England pushed them to leave England. Available land, the chance to earn a living, and the opportunity to practice their religion freely pulled them to North America. In every century that has followed, the promise of a better life has pulled immigrants to the United States from around the world.

Between 1840 and 1870, more than 7.5 million immigrants came to the United States. That's more people than the total U.S. population in 1810. Wars in Europe acted as a push factor on the people there. At the same time, the United States continued to exert pull factors on people experiencing hardship across the oceans.

LOOKING FOR OPPORTUNITIES

As you have read, in 1848, word spread in newspapers around the world that miners had discovered gold in California. Many Chinese men emigrated from China, in hopes of finding work in the American West.

Chinese men weren't the only people to immigrate to the United States or its territories to build new lives. Immigrants from northern Europe—including Britain, Ireland, Germany, and Scandinavia—also traveled across the ocean alone or with their families. Their journeys were often difficult. Many immigrants could only afford to travel in **steerage**, a small, confined space between the main decks of the ship. Steerage class was

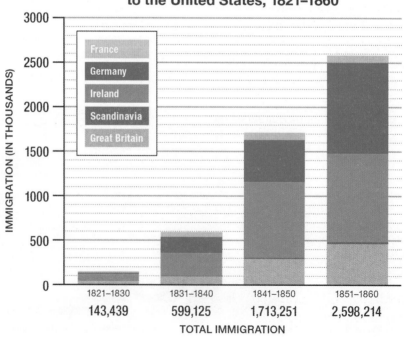

European Immigration to the United States, 1821–1860

IMMIGRATION (IN THOUSANDS)

Legend: France, Germany, Ireland, Scandinavia, Great Britain

TOTAL IMMIGRATION	
1821–1830	143,439
1831–1840	599,125
1841–1850	1,713,251
1851–1860	2,598,214

Source: Department of Homeland Security

CRITICAL VIEWING An Irish man in Dublin, Ireland, scours a poster advertising voyages to New York City in this lithograph by T.H. Maguire titled *Outward Bound*, c. 1840–1860. What details do you notice that indicate why he might be interested in leaving Ireland?

an inexpensive way to travel. However, it was crowded and dark, with almost no comforts. Steerage passengers had to bring mattresses, cooking pots, and even their own food for the voyage. Travelers in steerage class also dealt with rats, lice, and fleas during the journey. Seasickness and other illnesses made the area smelly, unpleasant, and unsanitary. Disease could spread rapidly, which was a problem because any illness put immigrants at risk for rejection when they reached the United States.

As new industries expanded in the northeastern United States, immigrants became an important source of labor. They arrived ready to take whatever work they could find in order to survive. The many job opportunities and the established immigrant population of large American cities encouraged many newcomers to stay in the city of their arrival. In fact, New York City had a large immigration center, called Castle Garden, which accepted new immigrants into the country. Immigrants joined with others from their home countries, and they established neighborhoods where people shared similar customs and traditions and spoke the same language. These neighborhoods grew and became vibrant parts of American culture.

The United States welcomed immigrants throughout the 19th and 20th centuries. Some immigrants decided to uproot their families because they hoped for new opportunities. Others wanted to escape a bleak future, or simply to feed their families.

HISTORICAL THINKING

1. **READING CHECK** Name two push-pull factors that drove mass immigration in the mid-1800s.

2. **ANALYZE GRAPHS** According to the graph, when did the largest number of Irish immigrants move to the United States?

3. **SYNTHESIZE** How do push factors and pull factors work together?

1.2 From Different Countries

You can probably think of a time when you were assigned a tough or boring task you didn't want to do. For some immigrants, only the hardest, lowest-paid work was available when they arrived in their new country.

MAIN IDEA Many immigrants came to the United States to escape food shortages and political conflicts in their home countries.

ESCAPING DISEASE AND POVERTY

Between the 1830s and 1860s, Irish immigrants represented the largest number of newcomers to the United States. Most were poor farmers who had no opportunities to improve their lives in their homeland. For centuries, Britain had claimed sovereignty over Ireland, and many of the Irish were dissatisfied with the oppression of British rule. To make matters worse, the country was experiencing widespread starvation due to the Great Irish Famine. A **famine** is an extreme shortage of food. From 1845 to 1852, a plant disease called **blight** killed the country's entire potato crop. The famine was made worse by the system of farming imposed by the British, because British landlords took what little food the Irish were able to farm. Approximately 1 million people died before the famine was over. For these reasons, or push factors, Irish immigrants came to the United States in record numbers.

Opportunities for jobs and new beginnings were pull factors for many Irish immigrants. American

CRITICAL VIEWING In 1850, British artist Frederick Goodall painted *An Irish Eviction.* He drew upon his experience of traveling in Ireland during the famine. Landlords eager to rid their lands of destitute laborers and farmers evicted hundreds of thousands of families. What details in Goodall's painting capture the despair of evicted tenants during the famine?

business owners recruited Irish immigrants because they would work for lower wages than many American workers. While skilled workers such as carpenters or bakers could earn adequate wages, most Irish men were unskilled. They found jobs building railroads, digging canals, and loading cargo onto ships. The work was difficult, dangerous, and paid the lowest wages. For Irish women, unskilled labor meant **domestic service**, or housework in another person's home. Maids and kitchen servants received about a dollar a day in 1870, which was better pay than most factories offered. Plus, domestic service often included food and housing.

Immigrants brought their possessions in large trunks. This handmade wooden trunk with rope handles belonged to a Swedish immigrant.

British immigrants didn't flee from famine, but they did hope to escape from the rigid British class system. Just as in Irish society, few opportunities existed for British farmers to avoid living in poverty. From their perspective, owning inexpensive and fertile American land was a chance at a whole new, and likely better, life.

When they arrived in the United States, most British and Irish immigrants wanted to **assimilate**, or become part of, their new country. But they also held on to their culture and traditions. In the neighborhoods where they lived close to each other, they formed groups and clubs and attended community dances, meals, and church services together. Preserving and maintaining many of their customs and traditions offered a relief from the strain of assimilation.

MOVING TO THE MIDWEST

Poverty and hunger were not the only push factors. Civil unrest, or open conflict within a society, also encouraged people to leave. For example, in the middle of the 19th century, areas in Germany experienced a series of revolutions. As a result, many Germans fled to the United States.

German immigrants differed in some ways from other groups of immigrants. One difference was that Germans held diverse religious beliefs. Most German immigrants were Protestant, many others were Catholic or Jewish. Also, unlike those who came to escape poverty and famine, many German immigrants were not poor and did not

have to travel in steerage. They could afford to continue traveling after they arrived in the country, oftentimes choosing to settle in the farmland between the present-day states of Nebraska and Minnesota. So many of them settled in this region, in fact, that the area became known as the "German Belt."

Especially after the 1860s, immigrants from Sweden, Norway, and Denmark joined the Germans in the upper Midwest. The population of Sweden was growing, farmland was scarce, and the same potato blight that hit Ireland struck Sweden around 1868. Some Swedes and other Scandinavian immigrants sought land in the United States. Others came for the growing number of well-paid factory jobs in midwestern cities such as Chicago and Minneapolis. Immigration increased the population and enriched the culture of the United States, but not all Americans welcomed the newcomers.

HISTORICAL THINKING

1. **READING CHECK** What factors prompted people to emigrate from their home countries?

2. **SYNTHESIZE** What pull factor drew so many different groups to the United States between 1830 and 1860?

3. **MAKE GENERALIZATIONS** What kinds of choices could wealthier immigrants make once they arrived in the United States?

1.3 Central Park
⊙ New York City

On July 21, 1853, the New York State Legislature set aside more than 750 acres of land in the middle of Manhattan Island to establish America's first major landscaped park. Sensibly called "the Central Park," it was designed by architects and social reformers who believed that great parks would benefit public health and contribute to a "civil society." Central Park sparked the urban park movement, one of the most significant developments in 19th-century America. After several decades of disrepair and neglect, the park was restored during the late 1900s and early 2000s, and it has never been more beautiful, safe, and clean. It proudly represents the American ideals of great public spaces, health and wellness, and the preservation of nature within an urban setting. Which different physical features do you observe in the photo of Central Park?

1.4 Opposition to Immigration

Some people feel afraid when they face something new or unfamiliar. Their fear may make them lash out toward others. In the mid-1800s, some Americans reacted negatively to the arrival of new immigrants.

MAIN IDEA Some native-born Americans tried to restrict immigrants' rights because they feared change and worried about the financial impact of immigration.

FEAR AND JUDGMENT

The numbers of immigrants coming to the United States alarmed some native-born Americans, or Americans who were born in the United States. They feared that the influence of new languages, different religious practices, and new cultural traditions might change the culture of the United States. Their fears inspired many **prejudices**, or broad judgments about groups of people that are not based on reason or fact.

Because many immigrants accepted jobs for very little pay, some native-born Americans believed their own wages would be reduced as a result. Newspaper articles reporting the failed rebellions in Germany gave some Americans the impression that immigrants would try to inspire revolution in the United States. They also worried that local governments would increase taxes and strain public services in order to care for so many poor immigrants. As one American writer put it, "They increase our taxes, eat our bread, and encumber [clog] our streets."

Some elected officials proposed passing **nativist** laws, or laws that favored native-born Americans over immigrants, often focusing on religion. Most native-born Americans were Protestant. Some Protestants formed prejudices against Catholic immigrants entering the country—especially the Irish. Protestants feared that Catholics held an allegiance to a foreign power because the leader of their church, the Pope, reigned over the Catholic Church from Italy. At times, violence erupted between Protestants and Catholics. Anti-Catholic mobs burned a convent, or a dwelling for nuns, near Boston in 1834. Prejudice against Catholics also influenced immigration laws.

EXCLUDING IMMIGRANTS

During the 1840s, nativists organized groups to oppose immigration. One of these groups called itself the American Party. Its leaders told new members to say "I know nothing" if anyone asked what the party did, so people began calling the American Party the **Know-Nothing party**. The party proposed laws that prevented immigrants, especially Irish Catholics, from voting and holding public office. They also wanted to require immigrants to live in the country for 21 years before they could become citizens.

Membership in the party continued to grow. In 1855, 43 members of Congress belonged to the Know-Nothing party. But Congress refused to pass most of the party's proposed legislation, and party members' involvement in violence and corruption in various states made the party increasingly unpopular. By 1860, differing views on slavery broke up the party, but that was not the end of nativist ideas in the United States.

HISTORICAL THINKING

1. **READING CHECK** What issues increased American prejudice toward immigrants in the mid-1800s?

2. **ANALYZE VISUALS** In which different ways do these two political cartoons portray immigrants, native-born Americans, and the political process?

3. **EVALUATE** What role did religion play in nativist prejudices?

CRITICAL VIEWING

These two cartoons from the 1850s reflect nativist attitudes toward immigrants. The first cartoon, published in a Know-Nothing newspaper, portrays an Irish and a German immigrant running away from a voting site with the ballot box, which they have stolen in the midst of a brawl. They are "clothed" in barrels that held whiskey and beer.

The second cartoon, from *Harper's Weekly*, shows a voter being pulled in two directions. On the left, a nativist politician attempts to persuade the voter. On the right, an Irish politician tries to do the same. What different characterizations of immigrant voters are shown in these cartoons?

2.1 The Second Great Awakening

Being part of a large gathering can be exciting and inspiring. In the mid-1800s, some religious events were so popular that they drew huge crowds, much like a music festival or sporting event does today.

MAIN IDEA In the early 19th century, new ideas about religion inspired people to reform problems in society.

A RETURN TO THE CHURCH

As you've read, the Enlightenment was a period in American history when political philosophers applied reason and logic to religion and society. New concepts about equality and government sparked the American Revolution. At the same time, scientific knowledge was expanding. The rush of new ideas caused many people to become skeptical of the power churches seemed to hold. Influenced by the Enlightenment, some people established new religions, such as Unitarianism, that combined the practical ideas of the Enlightenment with the teachings of the Bible.

In the 1790s, some Christians reexamined their religious practices. Many began to believe they should have a direct and emotional relationship with God. This movement is called the **Second Great Awakening**. To revive, or reawaken, religious enthusiasm, many Methodists and Baptists, among other denominations, organized **revival meetings**, or informal religious events held outdoors or in tents. Revivals became very popular because they drew people out of church buildings and into nature. Some preachers drew thousands of spectators. Audience members cried, shook, or rolled on the ground as preachers delivered sermons. Often, preachers **evangelized**, or spread the Christian gospel by delivering dramatic sermons and sharing personal experiences.

Many new believers joined Methodist and Baptist congregations as a result of the revivals. At these events, people felt a sense of freedom in worshiping with their friends and neighbors outside the formal organization of the church.

REFORMING SOCIAL PROBLEMS

One of the most prominent figures of the Second Great Awakening was a former lawyer and religious skeptic, or person who questions something others believe to be true, named **Charles Grandison Finney**. Finney became a fervent, or eager, Christian and preacher after his law studies led him to read and examine the Bible. He used his experience in arguing court cases to persuade others to adopt his beliefs.

Finney was as passionate about social reform as he was about his faith. He believed a just society had the responsibility to improve the lives of all its members. He delivered lively sermons calling for the end of slavery, the improvement of education for all citizens, and women's rights. Many other revivalist preachers shared Finney's views. As a result, religious groups actively promoted social reform causes.

The **temperance movement** was one part of this social reform effort. The word *temperance* means "moderation" or "self-restraint." This movement's proponents crusaded against the overuse of alcohol, which had become an integral part of daily life. On balance, 19th-century Americans consumed a lot of alcohol. In 1830, the average American drank seven gallons of alcohol per year—three times the average amount consumed today. Farmers earned extra money by making whiskey with leftover crops, local economies relied on alcohol sales, and drinking during working hours was commonplace. However, both public drunkenness and alcoholism had become significant social problems.

Temperance reformers approached the issue from different angles. Some wanted to curb the use of alcohol because they feared drunkenness was a threat to social order and economic prosperity. Others, motivated by the fervor of the Second Great Awakening, saw drinking as a sin. Some reformers wanted to protect women and children from neglect and mistreatment resulting from their husbands' and fathers' abuse of alcohol. Finally, medical professionals wanted Americans to limit their alcohol use for health reasons.

The reformers also looked beyond alcohol-related issues. They called attention to poor living conditions in overcrowded cities and advocated for working children's rights in factories and mills. Many, including California pioneer Annie Bidwell, also promoted free public education and voting rights for women.

HISTORICAL THINKING

1. **READING CHECK** What was the Second Great Awakening?

2. **DESCRIBE** How did Charles Grandison Finney play a significant role in society?

3. **COMPARE AND CONTRAST** What were the different ways in which reformers approached alcohol consumption in the 19th century?

2.2 Educating and Advocating

When you see a situation that seems unjust, you want to do something about it. Likewise, positive changes in society have often started with one brave person raising his or her voice.

MAIN IDEA Reform movements in the 1830s and 1840s led to improvements in the treatment of mental illness, the prison system, and public education.

EDUCATION FOR ALL

If you were female, African American, or an immigrant, it was hard to get a good education in the United States during the early 19th century. To address the lack of education for girls and women, a number of women established schools for them, including Emma Willard, who founded the Troy Female Seminary in 1821, and Mary Lyon, who founded Mount Holyoke Female Seminary in 1837. Schools and colleges for girls and women were a step forward, but women's literacy rates were still half those of men. Further, most young people who attended school, whether male or female, came from wealthy families. Many lower-income, working-class, and immigrant children could not afford formal education. They chose work over school to help support their families.

African-American children faced other obstacles in education as well. Laws barred enslaved African Americans from studying at all, and free African Americans could only attend certain

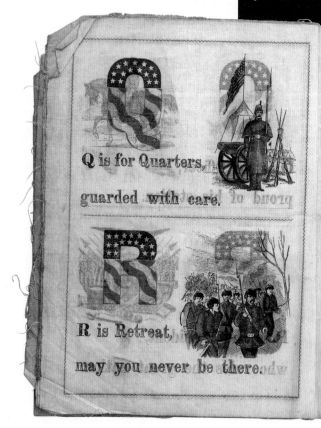

CRITICAL VIEWING Primers were small books used in schools to teach beginning reading and arithmetic. This primer was printed on cloth and sewn together by a Boston printer around 1860. What do you notice about the illustrations used in this primer?

Q is for Quarters, guarded with care.

S is a Sailor, who respected will be.

R is Retreat, may you never be there.

T is a Traitor, that was hung on a tree.

schools. **Prudence Crandall,** an educator from Connecticut, took a bold step to address racism in education. When she opened the Canterbury School for young African-American girls in 1831, her small Connecticut town became the center of controversy. Crandall was arrested several times for unlicensed instruction, the school's water well was poisoned, and townspeople threw eggs and stones at her students. Crandall's school closed in 1834 after a violent mob broke windows and ransacked the classrooms. Clearly, racism against African Americans was not confined to the South.

Individuals and groups worked to correct these injustices and to reform the education system as a whole. The clear solution was to offer every American child a public education. Religious and women's groups campaigned for a public investment in education, or free public schools that would be funded by the collection of property taxes and managed by the local government. This education reform was known as the **common school movement**.

In 1837, **Horace Mann** put the ideas of the common school movement into action. Mann wanted the public education system to be rooted in good citizenship and moral education that would prepare students for society and the workforce. His crusade helped establish a public education system in Massachusetts for students of all social classes, genders, races, ethnicities, and faiths. Soon, other states followed. The Northeast took the lead in establishing free public schools, but the South lagged behind the rest of the nation for several decades.

REFORMING INSTITUTIONS

In the early 1800s, people knew little about what caused mental illnesses or how to treat them. A mental illness is a long-term disorder, such as depression or addiction, that alters one's personality or way of thinking. Those who suffered from such ailments were often feared and misunderstood. Many mentally ill patients ended up living in prisons or poorhouses.

A shocking visit to a prison inspired **Louis Dwight**, a minister from Massachusetts, to help the mentally ill. While visiting inmates, Dwight recognized the need to remove people with mental illnesses from prisons and place them in hospitals called **asylums**. Because of Dwight's efforts, Massachusetts General Hospital opened the state's first asylum at Worchester in 1833.

Dorothea Dix, a teacher from Maine, joined Dwight's cause in 1841 after witnessing mentally ill women shivering in an unheated jail cell. The authorities tried to convince her that, because they were mentally ill, the women could not feel the cold. After that visit, Dix toured hundreds of prisons, jails, and poorhouses. She persuaded state legislators to develop tax-supported systems of care. Her influence helped open more asylums.

At the same time, Dwight, Dix, and others called for improvements in the treatment of prisoners. They believed it was better to rehabilitate inmates, or restore them to health, instead of putting them in solitary confinement, where they were locked up with no human contact. Reformers cited tragedies from the past to make their case.

For instance, in 1821, wardens of Auburn Prison in New York had placed 80 prisoners into solitary confinement for long periods of time. Some prisoners were confined for their entire sentence, which caused many to become mentally ill. In the weeks following their release, many prisoners committed suicide. Soon after, Auburn Prison eliminated solitary confinement for prisoners. The Auburn Prison's change in policies supported the reformers' insistence that solitary confinement damaged prisoners. Reformers went on to fight for prison libraries and literacy classes, programs that can still be found in prisons today.

HISTORICAL THINKING

1. **READING CHECK** How did the common school movement address inequalities in education?

2. **MAKE CONNECTIONS** What connections do you see between the school system Horace Mann helped establish and today's schools?

3. **DRAW CONCLUSIONS** How did American reformers help mentally ill and imprisoned people in the 19th century?

2.3 Fighting for Better Pay

The phrase "strength in numbers" applies to many situations. During the 1830s and 1840s, American workers in many different industries realized that groups were stronger than individuals.

MAIN IDEA During the mid-1800s, American workers banded together and demanded better, safer labor conditions.

LONG DAYS, HARD WORK

By the early 19th century, factory work had become widespread. Working conditions in most factories, however, were far from ideal.

Most factory workers toiled 10 to 14 hours per day, 6 days a week, no matter if they were elderly or 10 years old. They operated large and dangerous machines without safety gear. Many machine operators were maimed or killed on the job. If workers were injured during their shifts, they received no payment or paid time off to recover, and they often lost their jobs.

At the same time, the costs of living, such as rent and groceries, continually rose. Workers wanted better wages. They also wanted their employers to be held responsible for accidents on the job. Individually, workers knew they had little power to change their working conditions. In the 1820s, workers began to organize **labor unions**, or groups that advocate for workers rights and protections. Together, unionized workers had a much more powerful voice in demanding better pay and safer work environments.

A mill worker poses for a photograph around 1850. Many children worked in the textile mills, including this young girl. Her job may have been to straighten strands of cotton as they moved into the loom.

Leather Shoes
These leather baby shoes were produced by a Massachusetts shoe factory during the mid-19th century.

Craftsmen such as carpenters and shoemakers also formed organizations called **craft unions**. Craft unions differed from labor unions because most craftsmen did not work in factories, and they had learned a specialized skill. However, their objectives were the same: better wages and working conditions.

Labor and craft unions made progress in improving workplace conditions. But then in 1836, an economic depression hit the nation. Within a year, many factory workers and craftsmen were unemployed. Those fortunate enough to have jobs saw their wages cut by almost half. Displaced and underpaid workers were willing to take on whatever work they could find, and factory and shop owners knew it. As the economy struggled, the power of labor and craft unions decreased.

A WIN FOR WORKERS

When the economy improved in the early 1840s, unions reorganized. **Sarah Bagley**, a millworker in Lowell, Massachusetts, led the way for women's labor unions. She and her female coworkers worked up to 14 hours a day for lower wages than their male counterparts. In 1844, they joined together and established the **Lowell Female Labor Reform Association (LFLRA)**.

Bagley gave speeches denouncing her employer for not acknowledging the issues the mill workers faced daily. After she stopped working at the mill, she published stories about her experiences. Some politicians disliked her honesty and her critical view of mill owners. But her efforts improved the lives of women in the workforce.

Under the leadership of Bagley, the LFLRA appealed to the Massachusetts legislature to enact laws for shorter workdays. The legislature refused to confront mill owners, who agreed to shorten the workday to 13 hours only after public opinion pressured them into doing so in 1847. The LFLRA continued to advocate for shorter workdays. In 1853, mill owners cut the workday to 11 hours.

The actions of the LFLRA inspired other unions in the Northeast. In 1860, a shoe manufacturer in Massachusetts refused the shoemaker unions' request for wage increases. The shoemakers fought back by organizing a strike, or work stoppage. The workers walked out of the factory in protest. Their bold action encouraged similar strikes across New England. Ultimately, 20,000 shoemakers in 25 towns participated. As a result, most of the employers met the unions' demands. The successful strike emboldened the unions, which grew in strength and numbers and soon began to organize on a national level. Even so, Massachusetts did not pass a 10-hour workday law until 1874.

HISTORICAL THINKING

1. **READING CHECK** Why did factory workers and craftsmen form unions?

2. **SYNTHESIZE** Describe how and why the power of labor unions diminished in the 1830s.

3. **MAKE GENERALIZATIONS** What was work life like for 19th-century laborers?

2.4 Creative Expression

In every civilization, writers and artists ask important questions and help shape and define culture and identity. In the 19th century, American literature and art exploded with creativity.

MAIN IDEA Nineteenth-century American writers and artists helped define what it means to be an American.

AMERICAN AUTHORS ON THE RISE

As reformers advocated for solutions to social problems, writers in the 19th century set out to shape the American identity. Some used the events of American history as their setting. Others reflected social and intellectual movements.

Washington Irving's 1820 story "Rip Van Winkle" was a comment on the dramatic change the American Revolution had brought about. **Henry Wadsworth Longfellow's** poem "Paul Revere's Ride" created an American legend by fictionalizing and bringing to life one of the most exciting events of the Revolution. **James Fenimore Cooper** wrote the first American novel in 1823. *The Pioneers* described life for ordinary Americans on the New York frontier in the late 1700s, before the nation began its westward expansion.

Some 19th-century authors wrote about conflict and individualism. **Nathaniel Hawthorne** wrote during the mid-1800s, but his novel, *The Scarlet Letter,* focused on love and guilt among the Puritans of Massachusetts in the 1640s. **Herman Melville's** *Moby Dick* told the story of Captain Ahab pursuing the great white whale. The novel was Melville's allegory for Americans' reckless westward expansion and obsession with wealth.

One especially rich source of inspiration for some 19th-century writers was **transcendentalism**, an intellectual and social movement of the mid-1800s led by **Ralph Waldo Emerson**. The movement's goal was to transcend, or rise above, the expectations society placed on people. Transcendentalists thought that people should be self-reliant and connected to the natural world. Emerson's book *Nature* reflected these values.

Walt Whitman first published *Leaves of Grass* in 1855. One of the best-known poems in the collection is "Song of Myself," Whitman's celebration of individualism.

PRIMARY SOURCE

I CELEBRATE myself, and sing myself,
And what I assume you shall assume,
For every atom belonging to me as good
* belongs to you.*

. . .

I too am not a bit tamed, I too am
* untranslatable,*
I sound my barbaric yawp over the roofs of
* the world.*

—from "Song of Myself," by Walt Whitman, 1855

One of Emerson's students, **Henry David Thoreau,** lived alone in a simple cabin by Walden Pond for 26 months to write his memoir, *Walden*. **Louisa May Alcott**, the daughter of Bronson Alcott, a transcendentalist, grew up in the company of Emerson and Thoreau. Alcott wrote about family relationships and growing up as a female in the 19th century—the focus of her most successful work, *Little Women*.

Walt Whitman and **Emily Dickinson** forged new paths in poetry by breaking traditional rules. Poetry of the period was flowery and romantic, but Whitman and Dickinson wrote honestly and directly. In his most important work, *Leaves of Grass*, Whitman used free verse, or poetry that doesn't rhyme or depend upon a strict meter. Emily Dickinson also wrote poems that ignored established rules about rhyme and rhythm. She shared them with so few people that even her family members were not aware of all her poems until after her death.

Transcendentalists supported women's rights, abolition, and other social reforms. Organized religion, restrictive laws and social institutions, and industrialization inhibited individuals from fully expressing themselves. Certain authors gave a voice to those who were sometimes overlooked. Whitman, for example, wrote openly about love as well as same-sex relationships. His work also celebrated laborers, immigrants, and people who were all part of the growing diversity of the nation.

PAINTING AMERICAN BEAUTY

Nineteenth-century visual artists also shaped American identity through landscape paintings that celebrated the diverse beauty of the United States. **Thomas Cole** was one of the early leaders of an art movement known as the **Hudson River School**. In the 1820s, Cole hiked in New York's Catskill Mountains and painted magnificent scenes of the Hudson River Valley. Hudson River School painters became known for their landscapes, which often highlighted people's relationship with nature.

Asher B. Durand and **Frederic Edwin Church**, friends of Cole, were two artists to emerge from the Hudson River School. Cole inspired Durand to switch from painting portraits to painting landscapes. Church painted natural phenomena such as waterfalls, volcanoes, icebergs, and rainbows. A German immigrant and artist named **Albert Bierstadt** painted panoramic scenes of the Rocky Mountains, the Grand Canyon, and the Yosemite Valley using Hudson River School styles.

🏛 Crystal Bridges Museum of American Art, Bentonville, Arkansas

In 1848, Asher B. Durand completed *Kindred Spirits,* which he painted as a tribute to the friendship of painter Thomas Cole and poet William Cullen Bryant. The two artists are overlooking Fawns Leap and the Kaaterskill Falls—two sites in the Catskill Mountains of New York that cannot actually be viewed at the same time. Throughout their artistic lives, all three men—Durand, Cole, and Bryant—used the beauty of nature as their inspiration.

CRITICAL VIEWING Why might Durand have created a scene that brought two separate sites together?

HISTORICAL THINKING

1. **READING CHECK** What historical events influenced American literature and art in the 19th century?

2. **DESCRIBE** In what ways did common themes in artistic expression reveal the ideals and aspirations of the new nation?

3. **SYNTHESIZE** How did writers, visual artists, and transcendental thinkers shape American identity in the 19th century?

3.1 The Abolition Movement

Reformers in the 19th century didn't have cell phones or social media to spread the word. Instead, they wrote letters and newspaper articles, gave speeches, and even sent secret messages to communicate their ideas.

MAIN IDEA Brave individuals spoke out about the injustices of slavery in an attempt to end the institution in the United States.

SPEAKING OUT AGAINST SLAVERY

Many reformers who spoke out about social issues were also **abolitionists**, or people who wanted to end slavery. However, some Americans did not agree with abolitionists. Southerners and northerners alike considered abolitionists and their ideas too radical—as well as dangerous, un-Christian, and even unpatriotic.

In 1831, an abolitionist named **William Lloyd Garrison** published the first issue of his newspaper, *The Liberator.* His paper called for the immediate **emancipation**, or freedom, for all enslaved people. **Wendell Phillips**, a wealthy attorney, soon allied with Garrison. He wrote for *The Liberator* and contributed financially to the movement.

In 1839, former President John Quincy Adams argued that the ideals of the Declaration of Independence applied to all people. He called for a constitutional amendment to make every child born in the United States after July 4, 1842, free. He also proposed that no new state could enter the Union if it allowed slavery, but neither idea became law.

Two sisters, **Sarah Grimké** and **Angelina Grimké**, witnessed the cruelty of slavery firsthand while growing up on their parents' plantation in South Carolina. When the sisters took up the abolitionist cause, as some southerners did, their family disowned them. These determined women joined the Quakers and traveled the country giving speeches in support of abolition. In 1863, Angelina

The Iron Collar
One of the most horrifying tools slave owners subjected enslaved people to was the iron collar. They used this device to punish slaves, especially for attempts to escape. The prongs made it impossible to lie down to rest or sleep. They also caught on bushes and underbrush, making it hard to run. Abolitionists pointed to this kind of cruelty in demanding an end to slavery.

Grimké married fellow abolitionist **Theodore Weld**, a trainer and recruiter for the American Anti-Slavery Society.

STANDING UP FOR FREEDOM

Both free and enslaved African Americans actively challenged the existence of slavery. **David Walker** was a free African-American man who wrote for *Freedom's Journal*, an abolitionist newspaper. As the owner of a secondhand clothing store in Boston in the 1820s, Walker printed antislavery pamphlets and sewed them into the pockets of clothing he sold to sailors. Walker hoped the pamphlets would reach people in many ports, especially those in the South. One of his pamphlets, entitled *An Appeal to the Coloured Citizens of the World,* became one of the most radical antislavery documents of the movement, and southern states reacted by prohibiting the circulation of abolitionist literature.

Another African-American abolitionist was **Charles Remond**, who was born to a wealthy, free African-American family in Salem, Massachusetts. He worked as an agent of the Massachusetts Anti-Slavery Society, and he traveled and spoke with Garrison, Phillips, and others.

Robert Purvis was the son of a wealthy cotton broker and a free African-American woman. When he was nine years old, his family moved from South Carolina to Philadelphia. As an adult, Purvis became very active in abolition and in the **Underground Railroad**. In fact, he and his wife, **Harriet Forten**, housed escapees in their home, also known as the Purvis "safe house."

At the beginning of the chapter, you read about the courageous work of **Harriet Tubman**. Other African-American women played significant roles in the abolitionist movement as well. **Harriet Jacobs**, born into slavery, escaped to New York in 1842. She published *Incidents in the Life of a Slave Girl* in 1861, considered one of the most extensive slave narratives written by a woman.

Sojourner Truth was also a powerful abolitionist voice. Like Tubman and Jacobs, Truth was born into slavery. When she told a white neighbor that her owner broke his promise to release her, the neighbor paid the owner $20 for her and then set her free. She changed her enslaved name, Isabella, to Sojourner Truth. She captivated people with her simple, clear message: that all people deserved the same rights as white men.

HISTORICAL THINKING

1. **READING CHECK** How did abolitionists work to end slavery?

2. **DRAW CONCLUSIONS** Why did most Americans consider abolitionists' ideas radical?

3. **ANALYZE VISUALS** What details do you notice in the photo, and how might those—and the photo itself—have impacted people who saw it in the mid-1800s?

3.2 Voices Against Slavery

Abolitionists relied on shocking testimonials and appeals to good conscience in their fight to end slavery. They dared to write and publish newspaper articles to condemn the injustices of slavery. Others marshalled their strength to stand on a stage and share the indignities they had witnessed or personally endured.

In the first issue of the *The Liberator*, William Lloyd Garrison called slavery "America's all-conquering sin." He wrote, "I do not wish to think, or to speak, or write, with moderation. . . . I will not equivocate . . . I will not excuse . . . I will not retreat a single inch . . . AND I WILL BE HEARD!" Garrison also helped to found the American Anti-Slavery Society, members of which appear at a convention in New York in this 1850 photo. He would ally with women and men, African American and white, and wealthy and poor in his decades-long fight against slavery.

CRITICAL VIEWING What do you notice about the individuals gathered for a photo at this convention?

Primary Source: Speech
from "Address to the Slaves of the United States,"
by William Lloyd Garrison, 1843

When William Lloyd Garrison published this speech in *The Liberator*, slavery had long been the basis for the southern economy. Garrison's passion for the abolitionist cause is evident in the way he addresses enslaved people directly.

CONSTRUCTED RESPONSE How does Garrison describe enslaved people, and what specific actions does he encourage them to take?

We advise you to seize every opportunity to escape from your masters, and, fixing your eyes on the North Star, travel on until you reach a land of liberty. You are not the property of your masters. God never made one human being to be owned by another. Your right to be free, at any moment, is undeniable; and it is your duty, whenever you can, peaceably to escape from the plantations on which you are confined, and assert your manhood.

DOCUMENT TWO

Primary Source: Speech
from "On the Injustice of Slavery," by Sojourner Truth, 1856

Sojourner Truth dictated her life story to Olive Gilbert for her book *Narrative of Sojourner Truth, a Northern Slave,* published in 1850. In the following address to the Friends of Human Progress, Truth shares her grief over the loss of her children. Her story provided clear evidence of the ongoing mistreatment of vast numbers of people who were unable to care for their children or even keep them from being sold.

CONSTRUCTED RESPONSE How does Truth's account reflect the lack of basic freedom enslaved people endured?

I want to know what has become of the love I ought to have for my children? I did have love for them, but what has become of it? I cannot tell you. I have had two husbands, but I never possessed one of my own. I have had five children and never could take one of them up and say, "My child" or "My children," unless it was when no one could see me.

DOCUMENT THREE

Primary Source: Speech
from "What the Black Man Wants,"
by Frederick Douglass, 1865

Frederick Douglass, sitting next to the table in the photo on the left, was an escaped slave who taught himself to read and write. Douglass became one of the most powerful and outspoken opponents of slavery, and proponents, or supporters, of women's rights. He delivered this speech to the Massachusetts Anti-Slavery Society in 1865.

CONSTRUCTED RESPONSE Why does Douglass reject the pity and sympathy of other abolitionists?

I understand the anti-slavery societies of this country to be based on two principles–first, the freedom of the blacks of this country; and, second, the elevation of them. Let me not be misunderstood here. I am not asking for sympathy at the hands of abolitionists, sympathy at the hands of any. What I ask . . . is not benevolence, not pity, not sympathy, but simply justice.

SYNTHESIZE & WRITE

1. **REVIEW** Review what you have learned about 19th-century abolitionists, their ideas and motivations, and their movement.

2. **RECALL** On your own paper, write the main ideas expressed by Garrison, Truth, and Douglass.

3. **CONSTRUCT** Construct a topic sentence that answers this question: In what ways did abolitionists appeal to their fellow citizens' morality in order to gather support to abolish slavery?

4. **WRITE** Using evidence from this chapter and the documents, write an informative paragraph that supports your topic sentence in Step 3.

Women's Rights and Seneca Falls

Like activists in modern civil rights movements, 19th-century activists in the women's rights movement felt an urgent sense of purpose. And when it came to establishing basic rights for women, failure was impossible.

MAIN IDEA In 1848, supporters of women's rights laid the groundwork for a movement that would change the lives of American women.

LEADERS FOR WOMEN'S RIGHTS

Throughout the early 1800s, women played active roles in social reform and abolition movements. Yet women continued to occupy a secondary place to men in society. When women earned wages outside of the home, their pay was much lower than the wages men received for doing the same job. Married women could not own or purchase property or enter into contracts. Single women had all the property rights a man had but were taxed on that property by a government in which they had no voice. Furthermore, because educational and career opportunities were so limited for women, marriage was often the only possible path to a financially stable life for most women.

The fight for women's rights had its roots in the abolition movement. Female abolitionists gained public speaking and organization experience, and some began to ask why women were not granted the same rights as men. **Elizabeth Cady Stanton** and **Lucretia Mott** were early leaders in the women's rights movement, and both were abolitionists.

Elizabeth Cady came from a wealthy family and received an excellent education at Troy Female Seminary. She married abolitionist Henry Brewster Stanton, became an abolitionist herself, and met many other abolitionists, including Lucretia Mott. Mott was a Quaker from Massachusetts who housed escapees traveling on the Underground Railroad.

In 1848, Mott and Stanton organized the **Seneca Falls Convention** in central New York. There, they issued a "Declaration of Sentiments and Resolutions." The Declaration of Sentiments

Susan B. Anthony shows a document to Elizabeth Cady Stanton, seated, in 1900. In 1902, Anthony wrote to Stanton: "It is fifty-one years since we first met, and we have been busy through every one of them, stirring up the world to recognize the rights of women."

framed the injustices faced by women in familiar language. As you know, the Declaration of Independence introduced the idea that all men are created equal. The Declaration of Sentiments inserted "and women" into that fundamental idea to reinforce the assertion that "all men and women are created equal." In this spirit, Stanton went a

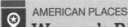
Women's Rights National Historical Park
Seneca Falls, New York

The Women's Rights National Historical Park honors women who produced the Declaration of Sentiments. The statues featured here are the centerpiece of the park's visitors' center lobby. Notice Frederick Douglass standing with the women. Like many women's rights activists, he supported both abolition and women's rights.

a friendship and a political partnership that lasted more than 50 years. They traveled together, delivered speeches to lawmakers, planned campaigns, and published *The Revolution*, a newspaper devoted to women's rights.

During the 1850s and 1860s, issues regarding women's rights became less pressing because of the impending Civil War. However, after the war was over, women's rights activists picked up the cause again. In 1869, Anthony and Stanton founded the **National Woman Suffrage Association**, the first national women's rights organization. Anthony believed that the best way to bring attention to women's suffrage was to violate the law—by voting. When she tried to vote in the 1872 election, she was arrested and fined. Anthony never paid the fine and never went to jail.

step further and included women's **suffrage**, or the right to vote, in the Declaration of Sentiments. She knew opponents of women's suffrage would claim the demand was outrageous, and that it might hinder the acceptance of other ideas about women's rights. But because Stanton believed the right to vote was essential, she and Mott listed it as the first grievance in the Declaration of Sentiments.

CONTINUING THE WORK

In 1851, Sojourner Truth, who had attended Seneca Falls, delivered a powerful speech at the Women's Rights Convention in Ohio. She asked, "Ain't I a woman?" and drew attention to race in the fight for women's rights. Truth was a passionate supporter of equality for men and women of all races. That same year, Elizabeth Cady Stanton met **Susan B. Anthony**. Coming from a Quaker family, Anthony supported both temperance and abolition. The two women began

The campaign for women's rights began in the early 1800s and continued through the rest of the 19th century and into the 20th. Some leaders worked until the day they died. Mott, Stanton, Truth, Anthony, and many other women's rights activists dedicated their lives to securing political and social equality for women.

HISTORICAL THINKING

1. **READING CHECK** What was the Seneca Falls Convention, and why was it significant?

2. **MAKE CONNECTIONS** In what ways were the movements for abolition and women's rights intertwined?

3. **SYNTHESIZE** How did women's rights activists link women's rights to the Founding Fathers' positions on equality and natural rights?

VOCABULARY

Use each of the following vocabulary terms in a sentence that shows an understanding of the term's meaning.

1. nativist
   Members of Congress passed nativist laws to limit the rights of immigrants.

2. blight

3. steerage

4. evangelize

5. labor union

6. revival meeting

7. temperance movement

8. suffrage

9. emancipation

READING STRATEGY
SYNTHESIZE

If you haven't already done so, complete the graphic organizer for this chapter. List at least three ideas and their synthesis. Then answer the question.

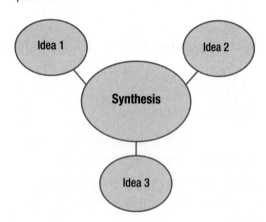

10. In what ways did the American identity change between 1830 and 1860?

MAIN IDEAS

Answer the following questions. Support your answers with evidence from the chapter.

11. Why did many immigrants choose to stay in the city of their arrival? **LESSON 1.1**

12. How did political problems in Europe affect immigration to the United States in the early 1800s? **LESSON 1.2**

13. How did the Know-Nothing party try to limit the freedoms of immigrants to the United States? **LESSON 1.4**

14. What role did religion have in changing the American identity? **LESSON 2.1**

15. What work did Dorothea Dix and Louis Dwight do? **LESSON 2.2**

16. What did the members of the Lowell Female Labor Reform Association seek to change? **LESSON 2.3**

17. From what sources did mid-19th century writers and artists draw their inspiration? **LESSON 2.4**

18. In what ways did abolitionists use print sources to build a case for the abolition of slavery? **LESSON 3.1**

19. Why was Susan B. Anthony arrested in 1872? **LESSON 3.3**

HISTORICAL THINKING

Answer the following questions. Support your answers with evidence from the chapter.

20. **SUMMARIZE** What were the goals of the 19th-century reform movements?

21. **IDENTIFY PROBLEMS AND SOLUTIONS** What problem did Horace Mann seek to solve?

22. **EVALUATE** How did Americans' understanding of the concept of freedom change during the 19th century?

23. **MAKE GENERALIZATIONS** Why did Elizabeth Cady Stanton and Lucretia Mott organize a convention at Seneca Falls?

24. **FORM AND SUPPORT OPINIONS** Which reform effort improved society the most during the 19th century? Support your opinion with evidence from the chapter.

INTERPRET MAPS

The map shows Underground Railroad routes from southern slave states to northern free states. The width of a path on the map corresponds to the number of people following it. Look closely at the map and then answer the questions that follow.

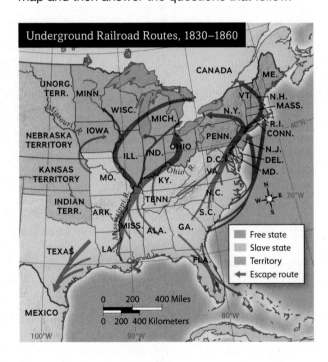

Underground Railroad Routes, 1830–1860

25. What routes indicate that the Underground Railroad was an international network?

26. In what ways did Underground Railroad routes rely on major rivers? Support your answer with details from the map.

ANALYZE SOURCES

Margaret Fuller's *Woman in the Nineteenth Century,* published in 1845, is a transcendentalist argument for women participating fully in society. Fuller points out that women constitute half of humanity. She goes on to argue that women's development contributes to the growth of men, too. Fuller makes the case that men are better off when women are able to lead fulfilling lives.

> Not a few believe, and men themselves have expressed the opinion that . . . the idea of Man, however imperfectly brought out, has been far more so [expressed] than that of Woman . . . that she, the other half of the same thought, the other chamber of the heart of life, needs now take her turn in the full pulsation, and that improvement in the daughters will best aid in the reformation of the sons of this age.

27. Why do you think Fuller describes women as "the other half of the same thought?"

CONNECT TO YOUR LIFE

28. **EXPLANATORY** Think about a 19th-century reform movement and a cause you support today. What common threads can you trace between then and now? Write a paragraph in which you describe how the cause you support can trace its roots to reform movements of the past.

TIPS

- Consider the mix of reforms happening at this time, and list the facts and details that best align with the cause you support.

- Explain your reasons for supporting your cause, and connect them with the reasons of early reformers.

- Use two or three vocabulary terms from the chapter in your paragraph.

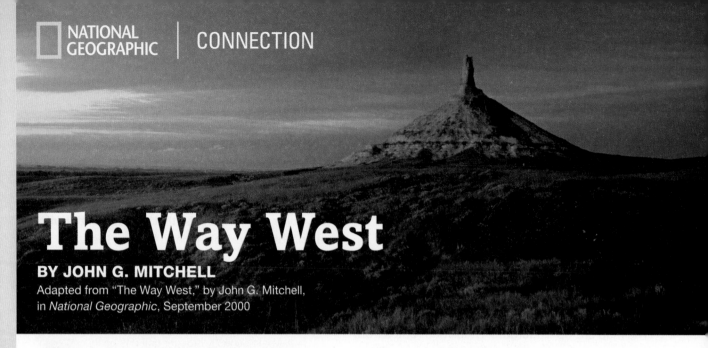

The Way West

BY JOHN G. MITCHELL

Adapted from "The Way West," by John G. Mitchell, in *National Geographic*, September 2000

The naysayers said it couldn't be done. No one had ever rounded up a party of tenderfoot pioneers, pointed their noses toward sundown, and, without benefit of compass or reliable map, dared them to bet their boots, wagons, and lives against the fearsome 2,000 miles between them and California. But at the far edge of Missouri, where the United States of America had come to a full stop, moving west was on people's minds. They *had* to try it. So in the spring of 1841, a handful of brave souls started out. No matter that they'd have to abandon their wagons on the arid plains and slaughter their livestock to survive in the mountains. All those who stayed the course—34 of them—got to California. It had never been done that way. But they did it.

In 1848, the year Mexico ceded California to the United States and gold was discovered at Sutter's Mill, California could claim a population of 14,000 Anglos and Hispanics. By the end of 1849, emigration by land and sea had pushed the population past 100,000. This number was sufficient for folks to start demanding that the territory be admitted to the Union, which it was on September 9, 1850. In the span of just one generation, even after most of the gold lodes had played out, nearly a quarter million emigrants came into the promised land the old-fashioned way, on foot and by wagon on the California Trail.

By some accounts, the few surviving ruts of that trail reflect one of the greatest human migrations in recorded history. Between the migration's peak years, 1849 to 1852, travelers described the scene as having the appearance of an army on the move. The journey started at the Missouri River, where feeder trails that originated from Independence, Westport Landing, St. Joseph, Council Bluffs, and other frontier towns converged near Fort Kearny on the River Platte. From the Platte's north fork, the trail picked up the Sweetwater River, crossed the Great Divide at South Pass, then dodged one mountain range after another on its way to Fort Hall, a fur post on the Snake River.

A bit beyond Fort Hall, the main trail split and the right fork—the homestretch of the Oregon Trail—continued down the Snake toward Oregon. The left fork turned southwest toward California. In the 1850s, some Oregonians liked to claim that at another place where the trails diverged, a pile of gold-bearing quartz showed the path to California, while a signpost with a written legend guided the traveler toward Oregon. Those who couldn't read, the slur alleged, went to California.

By one estimate, 20,000 people died on the California Trail between 1841 and 1859—an average of 10 graves for every mile. Most died from accidents, disease, contaminated water, inadequate food, or exhaustion from the constant toil. Contrary to what dime novelists would have had the world believe, trouble with Native Americans figured little with the mortality rate on the overland trails. Until 1849, fewer than 50 westward migrant deaths were attributed to Native American attack, and many of those occurred along the pathways to Oregon. However, as the numbers of overlanders increased, so did the fatal encounters. By 1860, pioneer casualties probably totaled close to 400. Even more Native Americans were killed by pioneers.

In the longer view of the great migration, gold was only one of many incentives that lured the wagonfolk west. More lasting was the human hunger for fertile land. But why would a family pack up and set out on a four-month journey when cheap and arable land was still available in the frontier states of the Mississippi Valley?

Perhaps there were as many motives as there were travelers to act on them. A politician might have attributed it all to manifest destiny and the course of empire. But that could not begin to explain the American people's westering tilt, and only the Pacific Ocean would prove big enough to stop it.

For more from *National Geographic*, check out "People of the Horse" online.

UNIT INQUIRY: Organize a Reform Campaign

In this unit, you learned about the ways in which the United States changed in the first part of the 19th century. New national boundaries enlarged the country, and immigrants from around the world enriched the population. Based on your understanding of the text, in what ways did these and other new developments lead to injustices or intensify social problems? What issues did reformers focus on?

ASSIGNMENT

Organize a reform campaign. Identify an injustice or social problem that you learned about in this unit. Then organize a reform campaign. Your plan should include specific actions the campaign could take and communication strategies to broadcast your campaign. Be prepared to present your campaign to the class and explain how it would address the issue you select.

Gather Evidence As you organize your reform campaign, gather evidence from this unit about the different challenges that Americans faced during this time period. Think about the ways in which some developments benefited one group over another. Also consider what principles motivated people to organize reform movements. Use a graphic organizer like this one to help organize your thoughts.

REFORM CAMPAIGN	
ACTIONS	COMMUNICATION

Produce Use your notes to produce descriptions of the specific actions your reform campaign will take and the different audiences it will try to reach. Write a short paragraph on each action and audience using evidence from this unit to support your ideas.

Present Choose a creative way to present your reform campaign to the class. Consider one of these options:

- Create slogans for your campaign that identify the injustice or social problem you are addressing. Carefully consider the campaign message you want to be the most prominent and memorable. Write your slogans on posters, banners, cards, or other forms of visual signage.

- Host a debate that engages different sides of the injustice or social problem your campaign aims to reform. Prepare research memos and talking points for both sides.

- Present your campaign in the character of a reformer from this unit. Research your reformer and consider dressing up as that person.

NATIONAL GEOGRAPHIC | LEARNING FRAMEWORK ACTIVITIES

Research a Mining Boomtown

ATTITUDES Empowerment, Curiosity

KNOWLEDGE Our Human Story

The mining boomtowns of the West were exciting places. In some ways, their remote locations and lack of formal structure allowed different groups a measure of freedom they did not enjoy in 19th-century society. Research the history of a western mining boomtown of your choice. Create a time line that includes major events during the heyday of the town, profiles of important figures and the different groups of people who sought opportunities there, and documents and artwork about the town. Present your research to the class.

Encounter Nature

SKILLS Observation, Collaboration

KNOWLEDGE Our Living Planet

Nineteenth-century artists celebrated the beauty and wonder of the American landscape through visual arts and creative writing. Select a nature site near you to explore. It could be a local park, a beach, a nature trail, or some other site. Explore the nature site you select with a group of classmates. While you are there, take notes on what you observe, including plant life, animals, and birds and the physical features of the site. Gather your notes and present your observations about your site to the class.

CIVIL WAR AND RECONSTRUCTION

CRITICAL VIEWING Modern-day Civil War reenactors fire a cannon in this photograph of a battle scene. Fighting during the Civil War was fierce and bloody, often resulting in staggering numbers of casualties among both northern and southern soldiers. Improved technologies, including more high-powered cannons, contributed to the high death toll. What details in the photo help convey what fighting in a Civil War battle must have been like?

CIVIL WAR AND
RECONSTRUCTION

THE UNITED STATES

1860
Abraham Lincoln is elected president. Soon after, South Carolina secedes from the Union. (*hat worn by Lincoln when he was assassinated in 1865*)

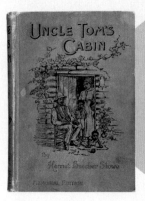

1852
Harriet Beecher Stowe's novel, *Uncle Tom's Cabin*, is published and stirs the debate over slavery. (*cover from 1897 edition of the book*)

1850
Congress passes the Compromise of 1850, which seeks to maintain a balance between slave and free states.

1861
The Civil War begins after the South attacks Fort Sumter, a garrison under federal control.

1846
Because he lives in a free state, Dred Scott sues for his freedom from slavery after his owner dies.

1850

1840

1860

1848 EUROPE
Nationalism incites unrest and revolution across Europe.

1861 EUROPE
The serfs in Russia are freed.

THE WORLD

1857 ASIA
Indian soldiers, called *sepoys*, revolt against British rule in India. (*illustration of sepoys*)

HISTORICAL THINKING: DETERMINE CHRONOLOGY

How long after Russia freed its serfs did the United States grant African-American men the right to vote?

1870
The 15th Amendment grants voting rights to African-American men. (*1884 glass ballot jar set in a slotted wooden box*)

1865
On April 9, the Civil War ends when southern general Robert E. Lee surrenders to northern general Ulysses S. Grant. On April 15, Lincoln is assassinated. (*Lee signed a letter of surrender at this table.*)

1867
The Reconstruction Acts of 1867 are passed, requiring southern states to satisfy several conditions before they can reenter the Union.

1863
The Union wins the Battle of Gettysburg, but both sides suffer thousands of casualties.

1877
Newly inaugurated president Rutherford B. Hayes puts an end to Reconstruction.

1870

1880

1864 AMERICAS
Napoleon III crowns Archduke Maximilian emperor of Mexico.

1876 AFRICA
The European scramble for African territory begins.

1867 ASIA
The Tokugawa shogunate is overthrown, and Meiji rule brings a period of modernization in Japan. (*Japanese print of a steam engine in a Tokyo station*)

A BROKEN NATION
1846–1861

ESSENTIAL QUESTION
How did slavery divide the country?

AMERICAN STORIES ONLINE · The Pony Express

SECTION 1 **Growing Tensions Between North and South**

KEY VOCABULARY
federal marshal   racism   segregation

SECTION 2 **Slavery Dominates Politics**

KEY VOCABULARY
Dred Scott decision   popular sovereignty   Republican Party

SECTION 3 **Lincoln's Election and Southern Secession**

KEY VOCABULARY
Confederacy   garrison   Unionist
Crittenden Plan   secede

AMERICAN GALLERY ONLINE   Abraham Lincoln

READING STRATEGY

IDENTIFY MAIN IDEAS AND DETAILS
When you identify a text's main idea and details, you state the most important idea about a topic and determine which facts support that idea. As you read the chapter, use a graphic organizer like this one to identify main ideas and details relating to the issue of slavery.

Main Idea: Tensions grew between slave states and free states.

| Detail | Detail |

CRITICAL VIEWING This monumental statue of a seated Abraham Lincoln is situated within the Lincoln Memorial in Washington, D.C. The memorial was completed in 1922, and the statue, designed by sculptor Daniel Chester French, took four years to carve. At 19 feet tall and 19 feet wide, the imposing statue creates a sense of awe and power. What characteristics does Lincoln's face convey?

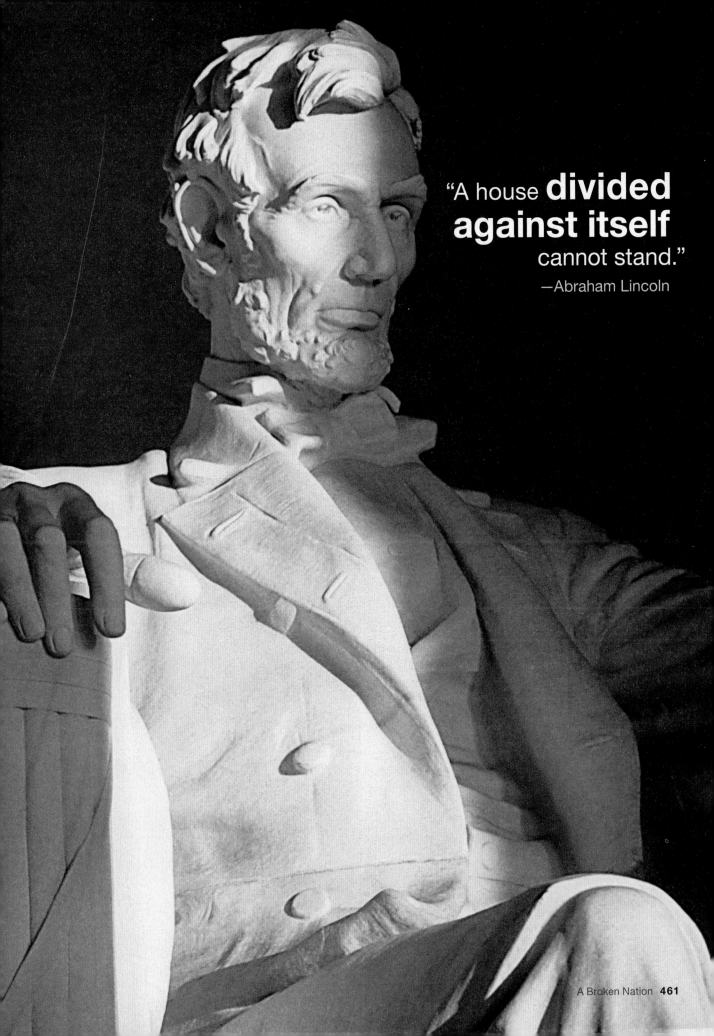

"A house **divided against itself** cannot stand."

—Abraham Lincoln

1.1 Controversy Over Territories

Sometimes friends disagree, and sometimes these disagreements can get out of hand. The United States had gained new territory, but the North and the South couldn't agree on how to use it.

MAIN IDEA Disputes over slavery in new territories and states led to growing tensions between the North and the South.

THE COMPROMISE OF 1850

As the middle of the 19th century approached, slavery had become too divisive, or a cause of conflict, for political leaders to ignore any longer. One of the major issues they debated was whether slaveholding should be allowed in new territories and any new states carved from them.

The Missouri Compromise had temporarily settled the issue in 1820. However, the nation once again split over the debate about the expansion of slavery into newly created western territories and states, especially after the Mexican-American War and the discovery of gold in California. In the run-up to the presidential election of 1848, people hotly argued over the future of the new western territories. Disappointed in the position taken by their parties' presidential candidates, antislavery Whigs and a few antislavery Democrats joined together to create the **Free-Soil Party,** which was dedicated to keeping slavery out of the new territories and states.

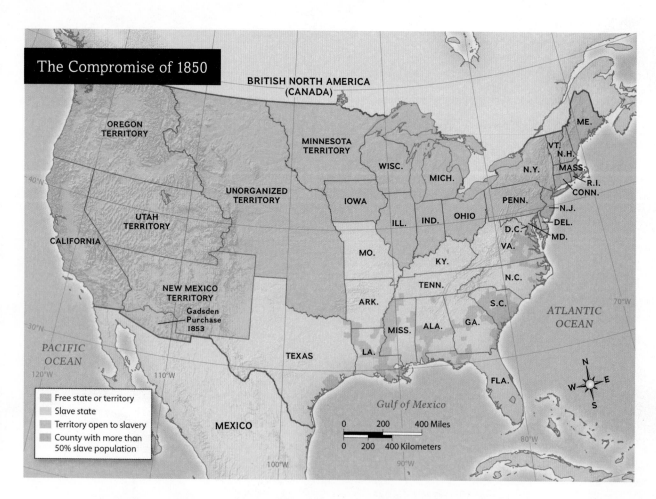

The Compromise of 1850

Legend:
- Free state or territory
- Slave state
- Territory open to slavery
- County with more than 50% slave population

In 1849, a national crisis erupted when California applied for statehood as a free state. For most of the period after the Missouri Compromise, the United States had been evenly split between free states and slave states. Statehood for California would upset this balance and give free states a majority in the U.S. Senate. They already enjoyed a majority in the U.S. House of Representatives. Fearing loss of political power and the possibility that slavery might be outlawed, the slave states threatened to withdraw from the Union.

Remember Henry Clay, the main force behind the Missouri Compromise? In January 1850, he presented a plan for a new compromise. It called for California to be admitted as a free state and for the issue of slavery to be left open in the other territories won from Mexico. Clay and two other famous legislators, John C. Calhoun and Daniel Webster, led a passionate debate over the plan, which lasted for eight months.

Finally, in September, the **Compromise of 1850** became law, preventing the Union from splitting apart. Statehood for California that same year would also give rise to the **Pony Express** in 1860. This mail service, delivered by horseback riders, established communication between the East and the West and so helped keep California connected to the rest of the country.

THE FUGITIVE SLAVE ACT

One of the most controversial parts of the Compromise of 1850 was the **Fugitive Slave Act**. The act strengthened an earlier Fugitive Slave Act passed by Congress in 1793 by enforcing greater penalties on runaways and those who aided them. Under this harsh new act, **federal marshals**, or law enforcers who worked for the U.S. government, could force ordinary citizens to help them capture runaway slaves. In addition, anyone who helped a slave escape faced penalties, as did any marshal who failed to enforce the law. Further, the law denied accused fugitives the right to a trial by jury.

The law provoked bitter anger in the northern states. Many people defied it, and some states passed new laws that protected runaway slaves. Armed groups confronted slave catchers and freed slaves from jails. Nevertheless, slavery continued to expand in the South.

Webster-Calhoun Debate

After Henry Clay proposed his plan, John Calhoun's speech was read in the Senate. Calhoun was too ill to stand and deliver it himself. Three days later, Daniel Webster responded to Calhoun, speaking for more than three hours. In the following excerpts from their speeches, Calhoun speaks for the South, while Webster pleads for saving the Union.

PRIMARY SOURCES

The equilibrium [balance] between [the North and the South] . . . has been destroyed. One section has the exclusive power of controlling the government, which leaves the other without any adequate means of protecting itself against its encroachment and oppression.

—John C. Calhoun, 1850

I wish to speak today, not as a Massachusetts man, nor as a Northern man, but as an American. It is not to be denied that we . . . are surrounded by very considerable dangers to our institutions of government. I speak today for the preservation of the Union. Hear me for my cause.

—Daniel Webster, 1850

HISTORICAL THINKING

1. **READING CHECK** Why did California's application for statehood upset some people?

2. **COMPARE AND CONTRAST** What conflicting views on state and federal authority are revealed in Webster's and Calhoun's speeches?

3. **INTERPRET MAPS** According to the Compromise of 1850, in which territories would settlers be allowed to decide whether slavery would be legal or illegal?

1.2 Slavery and Racism

Enslaved people in the South thought running away from their plantations would change their lives for the better. But would freedom in the North live up to its promise?

MAIN IDEA Racism and slavery were defining forces in the lives of African Americans in both the South and the North.

AFRICAN AMERICANS IN THE SOUTH

While some Americans began to harbor misgivings over slavery, the slave trade continued to thrive in the South. Enslaved people from Africa were no longer imported. But since the children of enslaved people in the United States also became slaves, the slave population grew steadily in the South. By 1860, there were nearly four million enslaved African Americans in the region.

Racism, or the belief that one race is superior to others, was the foundation upon which slavery was built. Many slave owners justified slavery by claiming that African Americans were better off under the care of plantation owners than they would be by caring for themselves. But, as you know, many slaves endured lives of unspeakable cruelty. Laws such as the Fugitive Slave Acts made sure their lives could never improve by sharply curbing their freedom and economic opportunities.

Racist attitudes also affected the lives of the more than 250,000 free African Americans in the South. Local laws prevented them from traveling or assembling in large groups. Free African Americans were also discouraged from

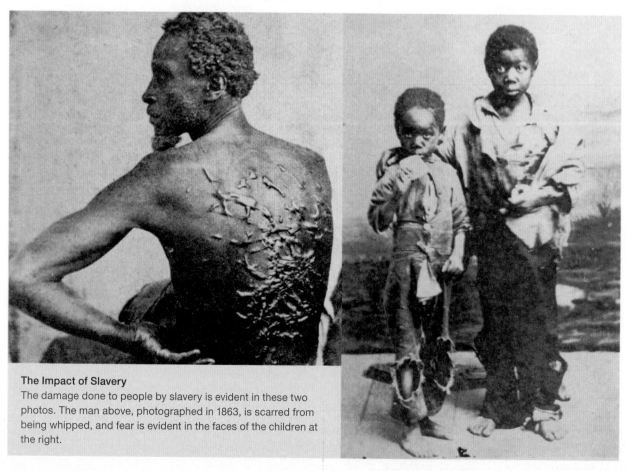

The Impact of Slavery
The damage done to people by slavery is evident in these two photos. The man above, photographed in 1863, is scarred from being whipped, and fear is evident in the faces of the children at the right.

A writer named **Harriet Beecher Stowe** channeled her anger over slavery into a novel called *Uncle Tom's Cabin.* This 1852 painting called *An American Slave Market,* by an artist known only as Taylor, depicts a scene in the novel in which a slave trader purchases a child.

Published in 1852, *Uncle Tom's Cabin* sold 300,000 copies in that year alone and was also turned into popular plays. It dramatically changed the national debate over slavery and racism.

organizing churches, schools, and fraternal orders, or social organizations, like the Masons.

Slavery was central to the economy and culture of the agrarian South. Concerned about the health of the South's economy, southern leaders not only fought for slavery but they also battled against tariffs. They argued that high tariffs favored the industrial North and hurt the South by forcing plantation owners to pay higher prices for manufactured goods.

Some wealthy plantation owners even tried to convince the U.S. government to acquire Cuba from Spain as a slave state. Their proposal was presented in the 1854 Ostend Manifesto and included the provision that the island be taken by force if necessary. The manifesto fell through, but it became a rallying cry for northern abolitionists, who saw the move as an attempt to extend slavery.

AFRICAN AMERICANS IN THE NORTH

Though some enslaved people dreamed of escaping to the North, those who succeeded found themselves facing many of the challenges they thought they had left behind. Many northerners held the same racist beliefs that were common among southerners. They did not want to live near, work with, or have their children go to school with African Americans. They cared little about ending slavery and looked upon free African Americans with scorn. Even as they worked to try to end the institution of slavery, some abolitionists held racist attitudes toward African Americans.

Discrimination took several forms. Some states passed laws restricting the rights of African Americans to vote, own property, and move about freely. **Segregation**, or the separation of people based on race, was common in northern cities, and African Americans often were forbidden from entering white churches, schools, and many other buildings. They were often blocked from employment for skilled jobs. Free African Americans even feared for their lives. Daily threats included attacks by white mobs and the possibility of being captured and sent back to a life of slavery.

HISTORICAL THINKING

1. **READING CHECK** What was the relationship between racism and slavery?

2. **IDENTIFY MAIN IDEAS AND DETAILS** What forms of discrimination did African Americans face in the North?

3. **COMPARE AND CONTRAST** How were the situations of free African Americans in the North and the South similar?

2.1 A Country in Crisis

In 1820 and again in 1850, compromises had held the United States together. But how many times can you compromise before someone finally cries, "enough already"?

MAIN IDEA The Kansas-Nebraska Act deepened the conflict over slavery and led to the eruption of violence in these territories.

THE KANSAS-NEBRASKA ACT

The discovery of gold in California in 1848 had increased interest in building a railroad to the Pacific coast. **Stephen A. Douglas**, a senator from Illinois, lobbied for the railroad to run through his state. Douglas, who was a great supporter of national expansion, proposed a route stretching from the Illinois city of Chicago west to San Francisco, California.

However, there were problems with this route. Before a railroad could cross the territory west of Minnesota, Iowa, and Missouri, the territory would have to be organized into new states. But the Missouri Compromise had banned slavery in this area. The prospect of new free states infuriated, or enraged, southerners and once again threatened the country's unity.

Douglas introduced a bill that dealt with these issues. It called for the territory to be split into two smaller territories called Kansas and Nebraska, which could then become states. It also called for the repeal of the Missouri Compromise, which would end the long-standing ban on slavery in the North.

The bill, however, did not dictate whether slavery would actually be permitted in the new states. It left that decision to the people. This approach is called **popular sovereignty** (SAHV-run-tee) and allows residents to decide an issue by voting. Douglas had developed this idea, but many northerners, especially in New England, disagreed with it. Despite the strong opposition to popular sovereignty, Douglas managed to push the bill through Congress. It was signed into law in May 1854 as the **Kansas-Nebraska Act**.

Three Compromise Acts, 1820–1854

Free states	Slave states
Territories closed to slavery	Territories open to slavery
Non-U.S. areas	

The Missouri Compromise, 1820–1821

The Compromise of 1850

The Kansas-Nebraska Act of 1854

"BLEEDING KANSAS"

Douglas predicted that the Kansas-Nebraska Act would "impart peace to the country [and] stability to the Union." Instead, Kansas became a battleground in the slavery conflict. Antislavery "Free-Soilers," or members of the Free-Soil Party in the North, organized like-minded groups of people to settle in the new territory and vote against slavery there. Free-Soilers hoped that by populating Kansas with people who felt as they did, they could ensure that the territory would become a free state.

But southerners were just as determined to make Kansas a slave state. When elections were held, thousands of slavery supporters from Missouri crossed the border to vote illegally. These "border ruffians," as they were called, were actually not needed because many southerners and slavery supporters already lived in Kansas. Proslavery forces gained control of the legislature in 1855 and passed a series of harsh laws against those who opposed slavery. Antislavery settlers then created their own government within the state and worked through the summer and fall of 1855 to write their own constitution. Over the winter, the Free-Soilers elected a legislature and governor. Groups sympathetic to their cause in the Northeast sent them rifles, while southerners sent a 300-man expedition to support the proslavery settlers.

The situation soon turned violent. In May 1856, a large group of slavery supporters raided the town of Lawrence, Kansas, a free-soil stronghold. They burned down a hotel, destroyed a newspaper office, and threw printing presses into the river. In revenge, a militant, or extremist, abolitionist named **John Brown** led four of his sons and several other men to a proslavery settlement at Pottawatomie (pot-uh-WAH-tuh-mee) Creek. There, they pulled five men out of their houses and brutally murdered them. Federal troops pursued Brown, but he managed to escape. Brown fled north where he was protected by other abolitionists. Because of the violence in Lawrence, Pottawatomie Creek, and other places, Americans

John Brown
With his furrowed brow and glaring eyes, John Brown's intensity clearly comes across in this 1859 print.

began calling the territory "Bleeding Kansas." Eventually, order was restored in Kansas, but the political struggle over slavery continued.

The violence even reached Washington, D.C. Preston Brooks, a representative from South Carolina, had been angered by an antislavery speech given by Massachusetts senator Charles Sumner. When Brooks entered the Senate chamber, he severely beat Sumner with a cane. Soon, the split in the country over slavery would involve the Supreme Court.

HISTORICAL THINKING

1. **READING CHECK** What approach did the Kansas-Nebraska Act take toward the issue of slavery in the Kansas and Nebraska territories?

2. **ANALYZE CAUSE AND EFFECT** What violent incident occurred as a result of a senator's speech opposing slavery?

3. **INTERPRET MAPS** How did U.S. territories represented in the Compromise of 1850 map change after the Kansas-Nebraska Act was passed?

2.2 The Dred Scott Decision

When things are going badly, we like to think that, at least,

they can't get any worse. Until, of course, they do.

MAIN IDEA The Dred Scott case and John Brown's attack on Harpers Ferry further divided the North and the South over the issue of slavery.

THE REPUBLICAN PARTY

The Kansas-Nebraska Act caused the political differences in the United States to erupt. The repeal of the Missouri Compromise and the opening of new territories to slavery angered many northerners and deepened North-South divisions in the Whig and Democratic parties. Many northerners began to feel that none of the existing political parties reflected their growing concerns over slavery.

In reaction, antislavery leaders founded a new party in 1854 dedicated to fighting the expansion of slavery. The **Republican Party**, as it was named, found a following among former Whigs, Free-Soilers, Democrats, and Know-Nothings.

Dred Scott was about 60 years old when this photo was taken during his Supreme Court case. His former master's sons purchased and freed Scott after the decision, but he died nine months later.

When the 1856 presidential election approached, the Republicans picked John C. Frémont, who was well-known for his explorations of the West, as their candidate. The Democrats chose **James Buchanan** to represent their party. Buchanan secured the presidency, but Frémont made a strong showing, winning 11 northern states. From the outset, the Republicans proved they were a force to be reckoned with.

DRED SCOTT AND JOHN BROWN

In March of 1857, two days after Buchanan took office, the U.S. Supreme Court issued a decision in *Dred Scott* v. *Sandford*, which had begun in 1846. The case involved a slave named Dred Scott. He had sued for his freedom on the grounds that his master had taken him to live in the free state of Illinois and in the Wisconsin Territory, where slavery was also prohibited.

The Court ruled that Scott should remain a slave, and the **Dred Scott decision** sent shockwaves through the nation. In his explanation of the ruling, Chief Justice **Roger Taney** asserted that "members of the negro African race" were not actually citizens of the United States. Therefore, Scott did not have the right to bring a lawsuit to a federal court. Taney further declared that since slaves were the personal property of slaveholders, Congress had never had the authority to restrict slavery in the territories. This rendered the Missouri Compromise of 1820 unconstitutional. The strongly proslavery decision sparked outrage in the North and raised fears that southerners might try to extend slavery to the whole country. The chasm between North and South grew even wider.

Two years later, yet another dramatic event in the struggle over slavery took center stage. John Brown, the abolitionist responsible for the Pottawatomie Creek massacre in Kansas, led an attack on the town of **Harpers Ferry**, in the part of Virginia that later became West Virginia. He and his armed band of 21 men captured a federal arsenal and a rifle-manufacturing plant and took dozens of hostages. Brown hoped to trigger a

Harpers Ferry National Historical Park, West Virginia

Harpers Ferry is located where the Shenandoah and Potomac rivers meet, as shown in this aerial image taken by National Geographic photographer Ken Garrett. The scene of John Brown's 1859 raid on the armory, the town later became the site of one of the first integrated schools—attended by both former slaves and whites—in the nation.

slave revolt and create an "army of emancipation" that would free slaves across the South. He was wounded and captured, however, and ten of his men were killed. After a short trial, he was hanged just six weeks after the attack. To the dismay of southerners, many northerners refused to condemn Brown. Instead, they viewed him as a hero and a martyr, or a person willing to die for his or her beliefs, to the cause of abolition. The raid at Harpers Ferry increased southerners' fear of slave rebellions and further heightened the tension between the North and the South. As a result, slavery was about to bring the country to the breaking point.

HISTORICAL THINKING

1. **READING CHECK** Why did Dred Scott believe he should be freed from slavery?

2. **IDENTIFY MAIN IDEAS AND DETAILS** What political ideas led to the formation of the Republican Party?

3. **DISTINGUISH FACT FROM OPINION** Is Roger Taney's assertion that "members of the negro African race" were not actually citizens of the United States a fact or opinion? Explain your answer.

2.3 Lincoln and Douglas

Republican Abraham Lincoln and Democrat Stephen Douglas opposed each other in two political races. In 1858, they fought for the U.S. Senate seat in Illinois, which Douglas won. In 1860, they ran against each other for president, with Lincoln the victor. Although both men disliked slavery, they had different views on the issue.

Lincoln and Douglas engaged in a series of debates during their race for the Illinois Senate seat. Their fourth debate was held on September 18, 1858, in Charleston, Illinois. There, Douglas attacked Lincoln by saying that his opponent favored racial equality, an unpopular position at the time, even in the North. The painting below shows Lincoln speaking to the crowd gathered for the outdoor event. Douglas sits to Lincoln's right, waiting his turn to speak.

CRITICAL VIEWING How does the artist portray the debate?

Abraham Lincoln and Stephen A. Douglas Debating at Charleston by Robert Marshall Root, 1918

DOCUMENT ONE

Primary Source: Speech
from Abraham Lincoln's speech at the Republican Convention in Springfield, Illinois, on June 16, 1858

This speech is known as the "House Divided" speech. Lincoln used a Bible metaphor, comparing the nation to a house, to express his view of the impact that conflicting laws about slavery were having on the country as a whole.

CONSTRUCTED RESPONSE What does Lincoln think will happen to the Union if the division continues?

> "A house divided against itself cannot stand." I believe this government cannot endure, permanently, half slave and half free. I do not expect the Union to be dissolved; I do not expect the house to fall; but I do expect it will cease to be divided. It will become all one thing, or all the other.

DOCUMENT TWO

Primary Source: Speech
from Stephen Douglas's speech at the Lincoln-Douglas debate in Freeport, Illinois, on August 27, 1858

In a debate held in Freeport, Illinois, Douglas addressed a question that Lincoln had put to him: Could the people of a territory keep slavery out? Douglas believed they could and, in this excerpt, he explains how.

CONSTRUCTED RESPONSE Describe how Douglas uses cause and effect to explain how people can keep slavery out of a territory.

> The people have the lawful means to introduce it [slavery] or exclude it as they please, for the reason that slavery cannot exist a day or an hour anywhere, unless it is supported by local police regulations. Those police regulations can only be established by the local legislature, and if the people are opposed to slavery they will elect representatives to that body who will by unfriendly legislation effectually prevent the introduction of it into their midst.

DOCUMENT THREE

Primary Source: Political Cartoon
from *Harper's Weekly*, 1860

This political cartoon suggests that the issue of slavery is tearing the United States apart. Seen here are the four candidates in the 1860 presidential election. From left to right are Abraham Lincoln, Stephen Douglas, John C. Breckinridge, and John Bell.

CONSTRUCTED RESPONSE What details in the cartoon suggest that slavery is tearing the United States apart?

SYNTHESIZE & WRITE

1. **REVIEW** Review what you have learned about Abraham Lincoln and Stephen Douglas and their debates.

2. **RECALL** On your own paper, write the main idea expressed in each document.

3. **CONSTRUCT** Construct a topic sentence that answers this question: What differing positions did Lincoln and Douglas take on the issue of slavery?

4. **WRITE** Using evidence from this chapter and the documents, write an informative paragraph that supports your topic sentence in Step 3.

3.1 The Election of 1860

Say you belong to a club and two groups within it often disagree.
Should they try to work things out? Or should one group break away
and form a new club? Maybe it depends on whether they're into politics.

MAIN IDEA The growing divide between the North and the South had
a strong impact on the 1860 presidential election.

POLITICAL PARTIES BREAK APART

"Bleeding Kansas," the Dred Scott decision,
John Brown's raid at Harpers Ferry: each of these
developments had left the United States more
divided over slavery. The Democratic Party found
it harder to hold itself together as tensions grew
between its powerful southern faction, or group,
and its smaller northern faction. When the
two factions could not agree on a candidate
for the 1860 presidential election, the party
split in two. Northern Democrats nominated
Stephen Douglas of Illinois, and southern
Democrats nominated **John Breckinridge**
of Kentucky.

Around this same time, a group of former
Whigs and Know-Nothings founded the
conservative **Constitutional Union Party**.
It appealed to people who believed that
preserving the Union and protecting the

Constitution outweighed concerns about slavery.
For the election, **Unionists**, as members of the
Constitutional Union Party were called, sought a
compromise candidate who could appeal to both
northerners and southerners. They chose John
Bell, a highly regarded former U.S. senator
from Tennessee.

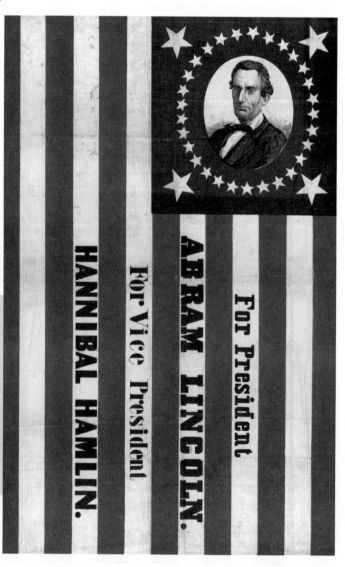

Lincoln Campaign Banner

Lincoln's running mate in the 1860 election
was Hannibal Hamlin, a senator from
Maine. In this cotton flag, Lincoln's first
name is spelled "Abram," possibly to
enable his name to appear larger. "Abram"
is also the original spelling of the biblical
Abraham. The portrait of Lincoln may have
been printed sideways so the flag could be
hung vertically.

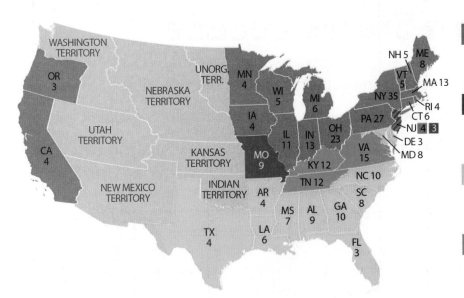

1860 Presidential Election

Lincoln, Republican
Electoral Vote: 180 votes, 59.4%
Popular Vote: 1,866,452 votes, 39.8%

Douglas, Northern Democrat
Electoral Vote: 12 votes, 3.9%
Popular Vote: 1,380,202 votes, 29.5%

Breckinridge, Southern Democrat
Electoral Vote: 72 votes, 23.8%
Popular Vote: 847,953 votes, 18.1%

Bell, Constitutional Unionist
Electoral Vote: 39 votes, 12.9%
Popular Vote: 590,901 votes, 12.6%

THE NOMINATION OF LINCOLN

In May 1860, Republicans gathered in Chicago, Illinois, for their national convention. Party strategists identified four states that would be key to winning the upcoming election: Illinois, Indiana, New Jersey, and Pennsylvania. The first three bordered southern states and were more moderate in their views about slavery than states farther north. The party decided to place its presidential hopes on a moderate from Illinois: Abraham Lincoln.

Born in a one-room log cabin, Lincoln grew up on frontier farms in Kentucky and Indiana. His mother died when he was just nine. Because the family was poor, they moved from place to place, struggling to survive. Young Lincoln developed a love of reading but had to work, so he received very little formal schooling. When Lincoln was 21, he moved with his family to Illinois. There, he taught himself law, built a thriving legal practice, and launched a successful political career. He served four terms in the Illinois state assembly and one term in the U.S. House of Representatives. He failed twice in bids for the U.S. Senate, but that didn't stop him from running for president in 1860.

In the presidential campaign, Lincoln did not try to win over southern voters, and Breckinridge spent little effort on the North. Southerners refused to consider Lincoln because they believed he was too antislavery, while northerners rejected Breckinridge's proslavery views. Bell focused his attention on like-minded Unionists in the states between the North and the South. Douglas, however, campaigned in both the North and the South, defending the Union and warning against voting along sectional lines. Because Bell and Douglas didn't propose enacting laws one way or the other on slavery, they were considered the moderate candidates.

When voters cast their ballots on election day, Lincoln won almost 40 percent of the popular vote, and he captured the electoral votes in every northern state except New Jersey, which he split with Douglas. Not surprisingly, he didn't win any electoral votes in the South. For the most part, voters cast their ballots along regional lines. The election proved they were tired of compromising. And for many southerners, the election also drew a line in the sand that they were not afraid to cross.

HISTORICAL THINKING

1. **READING CHECK** Why were there two Democratic candidates in the 1860 election?

2. **MAKE INFERENCES** Why might Abraham Lincoln's background have appealed to voters?

3. **INTERPRET MAPS** Why did winning just the northern states guarantee that Lincoln would secure the majority of electoral votes?

3.2 Southern States Secede

A crack in a mirror often starts out small, hardly visible. But over time, rough handling causes the crack to deepen and run the length of the glass. Pretty soon, the smallest added pressure will make it snap and break in two.

MAIN IDEA The election of Abraham Lincoln as president in 1860 led southern states to secede from the Union.

1860 campaign buttons feature Lincoln (left) and his running mate, Hamlin (right).

THE SOUTH DEBATES INDEPENDENCE

The South had reached its breaking point. Abraham Lincoln's victory in the 1860 election shocked and angered most southerners. They were suddenly faced with a northern president who had not won a single southern state. In fact, his name had not even appeared on the ballot in most of them. After all, Lincoln represented a party founded by people who wanted to keep slavery out of new territories and states.

Although Lincoln had not called for the abolition of slavery many proslavery southerners felt certain this was his goal. You've already read one excerpt from Lincoln's "House Divided" speech, delivered in 1858. In that speech he also said, "Either the opponents of slavery will arrest the further spread of it, . . . or its advocates [supporters] will push it forward, till it shall become alike lawful in all the States." In the South, many assumed this meant that Lincoln wished to abolish slavery throughout the United States.

On the day after the election, South Carolina's legislature gathered to debate the possibility of **seceding**, or formally withdrawing from the Union and becoming independent. Secession was not a new idea. Slave states had threatened to leave the Union on numerous occasions. In fact, South Carolina had come very close to doing so during the nullification crisis of the 1830s.

Supporters of secession justified it in terms of states' rights. The right that southern leaders most wanted to protect was their perceived right to own slaves. They argued that under the Constitution, the states retained certain rights, including the right to secede. Just as each state had once decided to join the Union, each state could decide to withdraw from it.

VOTES FOR SECESSION

On December 20, 1860, South Carolina became the first state in the nation to secede from the Union. The state's secession came in response to the presidential election of Abraham Lincoln the month before, even though he was not to take office until March 1861. South Carolina decided that Lincoln's presidential win as a Republican—a party that supported the Free-Soil platform, not the end of slavery in territories where it already existed—signaled that it could not continue as part of the United States.

South Carolina was joined by 10 other states in the coming months. In March 1861, the **Confederate States of America**, or the **Confederacy**, united and quickly formed a temporary government in Montgomery, Alabama, and adopted a new constitution. It was much like the U.S. Constitution, but it protected slavery and states' rights.

Jefferson Davis, a Mississippi senator who had spoken out against secession just weeks earlier, was chosen to be the temporary president of the Confederacy. In his inaugural address, Davis placed the blame for the secessions on the Union,

Abraham Lincoln
This 1860 photo by Alexander Hesler reveals Lincoln's lined face and rugged features.

arguing that protecting slavery had been the "well-known intent" of the Founders. Meanwhile, the issue of secession was proving to be divisive in the more northern part of the South. Many people opposed secession, calling it treason. They believed secession would be disastrous for the South. Others thought it would be best to wait before making a decision. For the time being, Virginia, Tennessee, North Carolina, and Arkansas remained in the Union. They still held out hope that the differences between the North and the South could be resolved.

HISTORICAL THINKING

1. **READING CHECK** Why did Lincoln's election drive southern states to secede from the Union?

2. **MAKE INFERENCES** Why do you think the Confederacy adopted a constitution that was very similar to the U.S. Constitution?

3. **DRAW CONCLUSIONS** What fundamental challenge to the Constitution did secession and the doctrine of nullification pose?

3.3 Efforts at Compromise

Who among your friends is the peacemaker? There's usually one who brings those in conflict together and tries to find common ground and iron out differences. Sometimes these efforts pay off. Sometimes they don't.

MAIN IDEA Leaders in the North and the South tried to resolve the secession crisis, but their attempts to reach a compromise failed.

THE CRITTENDEN PLAN

After South Carolina seceded from the Union, John J. Crittenden, a senator from Kentucky, tried to step in as peacemaker. In 1861, he offered a proposal that came to be known as the **Crittenden Plan**. Under the terms of this compromise plan, the federal government would have no power to abolish slavery in the states where it already existed. Further, the Missouri Compromise line would be reestablished and extended all the way to the Pacific Ocean. Slavery would be prohibited in territories north of the line, but in territories south of it, local residents would decide whether to allow slavery.

The proposal found many supporters in both the North and the South, and President James Buchanan pushed for its speedy approval in Congress. President-elect Abraham Lincoln and many Republicans, however, strongly objected to extending slavery in any new territories. After much debate, the Crittenden Plan was defeated in Congress, and the secession crisis continued.

LINCOLN BECOMES PRESIDENT

As his inauguration approached, Lincoln put together his government. For his Cabinet, he purposely chose men who represented competing factions within the Republican Party. Some of them could barely stand one another.

Surprisingly, four of the top positions went to men who had competed with Lincoln for the Republican nomination. He would later defend these appointments by saying, "We needed the strongest men of the party in the Cabinet. These were the very strongest men. Then I had no right to deprive the country of their services." Some have called the men he assembled "a team of rivals."

Lincoln took office on March 4, 1861, as the 16th president of the United States. In his inaugural address, Lincoln spoke sternly and directly about the crisis facing the country. He said his first task was to reunite the nation. Secession was illegal, he declared; no state could simply decide on its own to leave the Union. The Union was therefore

A Perpetual Union

At the beginning of his inaugural address, Lincoln stated that he was going to get directly to the point and talk about the matter of greatest concern to the country at that moment: the threat of southern secession. He assured the South that he did not support freeing its slaves. But he also emphasized that there was no constitutional basis for withdrawing from the Union.

PRIMARY SOURCE

I hold that, in contemplation of universal law and of the Constitution, the Union of these States is perpetual [everlasting]. Perpetuity [This permanence] is implied, if not expressed, in the fundamental law of all national governments. It is safe to assert that no government proper ever had a provision in its organic law [system of laws] for its own termination [end]. . . . The Union will endure forever.

—from Abraham Lincoln's First Inaugural Address, March 4, 1861

Lincoln with His Cabinet and Generals
In this engraving from 1866, Lincoln meets with his Cabinet and military leaders to discuss their response to the South's secession. Lincoln did not want war with the South, but he wanted to be prepared for it if it couldn't be avoided.

still intact, and he vowed to use his powers as president to protect places and property belonging to the federal government. He assured the South, however, that he did not intend to interfere with slavery where it already existed, and there would be no invasion or use of force by the government. "We are not enemies, but friends," Lincoln said. "Though passion may have strained, it must not break our bonds of affection."

Lincoln's words had little effect. The day after his address, a message arrived in Washington from **Fort Sumter**, which lay at the entrance to the harbor in Charleston, South Carolina. The fort was under threat from Confederate forces, and its **garrison**, or defense force, of about 85 federal soldiers would soon run out of food. After South Carolina seceded, the U.S. government

took control of the fort. But in January 1861, local militias prevented a ship from bringing supplies and additional troops to Fort Sumter. President Lincoln wanted to avoid conflict with the South, but a civil war looked more and more likely.

HISTORICAL THINKING

1. **READING CHECK** What compromise did the Crittenden Plan propose?

2. **IDENTIFY MAIN IDEAS AND DETAILS** Who did Lincoln choose to be in his Cabinet, and why did he appoint these individuals?

3. **DRAW CONCLUSIONS** Why did Confederate forces threaten Fort Sumter?

REVIEW

VOCABULARY

Use each of the following terms in a sentence that shows an understanding of the term's meaning.

1. secede
   Southern states seceded, breaking away from the United States.

2. federal marshal

3. racism

4. segregation

5. popular sovereignty

6. Dred Scott decision

7. garrison

8. Confederacy

READING STRATEGY
IDENTIFY MAIN IDEAS AND DETAILS

If you haven't done so already, complete your chart to identify the main ideas and details relating to the issue of slavery. List at least four main ideas and their supporting details. Then answer the question.

Main Idea: Tensions grew between slave states and free states.

Detail	Detail

9. What impact did Lincoln's "House Divided" speech have on the South and slavery?

MAIN IDEAS

Answer the following questions. Support your answers with evidence from the chapter.

10. How did the Compromise of 1850 help save the Union? **LESSON 1.1**

11. How did segregation affect free African Americans living in northern states? **LESSON 1.2**

12. Why did the Kansas Territory become known as "Bleeding Kansas"? **LESSON 2.1**

13. How did the Supreme Court decision in the Dred Scott case widen the divide between the North and the South? **LESSON 2.2**

14. Why did Jefferson Davis blame the Union for the secession? **LESSON 3.2**

15. Why did the election of Abraham Lincoln cause southern states to secede from the Union? **LESSON 3.2**

16. Under the terms of the Crittenden Plan, how would the issue of slavery be handled south of the Missouri Compromise line? **LESSON 3.3**

HISTORICAL THINKING

17. **SYNTHESIZE** Why didn't the compromises made in the first half of the 19th century last?

18. **DRAW CONCLUSIONS** How did John Brown's raid at Harpers Ferry increase tensions between the North and the South?

19. **MAKE CONNECTIONS** How did slavery as a political, economic, and social institution divide the country and lead to civil war?

20. **IDENTIFY MAIN IDEAS AND DETAILS** Why did the Supreme Court rule that Dred Scott should remain a slave?

21. **FORM AND SUPPORT OPINIONS** Based on the slavery-related developments of the 1850s, was it inevitable that southern states would eventually decide to separate from the Union? Support your opinion with evidence from the chapter.

22. **MAKE INFERENCES** What do you think might have been the strengths and weaknesses of having a "team of rivals" in Lincoln's Cabinet?

INTERPRET MAPS

The map below shows the percentage of enslaved people throughout the United States in 1860. The darkest green shading indicates areas in which more than 50 percent of the residents were enslaved. The lightest green shading indicates areas with no slaves. Look closely at the map and then answer the questions.

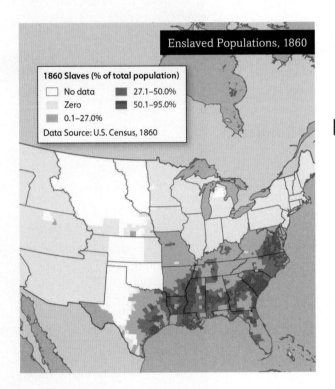

Enslaved Populations, 1860

1860 Slaves (% of total population)

☐ No data   ▨ 27.1–50.0%
☐ Zero   ▨ 50.1–95.0%
▨ 0.1–27.0%
Data Source: U.S. Census, 1860

23. What does this map reveal about the general geographic distribution of slavery across the South?

24. In which sections of the country were there zero populations of enslaved people?

ANALYZE SOURCES

In Harriet Beecher Stowe's novel *Uncle Tom's Cabin,* Eliza is an enslaved woman whose child has been sold to another plantation owner. Rather than see her son turned over to a new slaveholder, Eliza flees with her son in the early spring across the Ohio River to the free state of Ohio. The river is still partly frozen, and she crosses it by jumping from one block of ice to another. Read the following excerpt from the novel and then answer the question.

> Eliza made her desperate retreat across the river just in the dusk of twilight. The gray mist of evening, rising slowly from the river, enveloped her as she disappeared up the bank, and the swollen current and floundering [shifting] masses of ice presented a hopeless barrier between her and her pursuer.

25. What details in the excerpt help build suspense?

CONNECT TO YOUR LIFE

26. **INFORMATIVE** Think about what you have learned about slavery and how deeply it divided the United States. What issues divide the country today? Choose one issue and write a paragraph summarizing it and discussing its impact on the country.

TIPS

- Introduce the topic with a clear main idea statement.

- Develop the topic with relevant facts and concrete details. Be sure to present both sides of the issue.

- Compare the impact of the issue you have chosen to the impact of slavery.

- Provide a concluding statement that follows from and supports the information that you have presented.

CHAPTER 15

BEGINNINGS OF WAR
1861–1862

ESSENTIAL QUESTION

How did the early years of the Civil War affect people on both sides of the conflict?

AMERICAN STORIES Voices from the Civil War

SECTION 1 **War Erupts**

KEY VOCABULARY

border state   evacuate   mobilize

cavalry   infantry

SECTION 2 **Life in the Army**

KEY VOCABULARY

civilian   mortality   trench warfare

ironclad ship   philanthropist

SECTION 3 **A War Without End**

KEY VOCABULARY

Anaconda Plan   gunboat   pontoon

AMERICAN GALLERY ONLINE   The Daily Lives of Civil War Soldiers

READING STRATEGY

SUMMARIZE

When you summarize, you restate text in your own words and shorten it, including only the most important main ideas and details. As you read this chapter, use concept clusters like this one to help you summarize important information in the text. In the large oval, list a main idea. In the smaller ovals, note key supporting details. Then use your notes to write your summary.

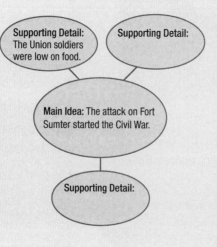

Supporting Detail: The Union soldiers were low on food.

Supporting Detail:

Main Idea: The attack on Fort Sumter started the Civil War.

Supporting Detail:

"War is the remedy our enemies have chosen . . .
let us give them all they want."
—General William Tecumseh Sherman

National Geographic photographer Ken Garrett took this photo of the Antietam National Battlefield in Sharpsburg, Maryland. The Battle of Antietam took place on September 17, 1862, and is still considered the bloodiest day in U.S. military history. Garrett shot the photo from the air to capture an area on the battlefield known as Sunken Road, or Bloody Lane, where some of the fiercest fighting took place. The statue standing near the Union lines commemorates a division of Pennsylvania soldiers who fought at Antietam.

VOICES FROM THE CIVIL WAR

CRITICAL VIEWING Some families camped with their soldiers during the Civil War. What does this photo reveal about the life of this 31st Pennsylvania Infantry soldier and his family?

In the 1860s, an event transformed the lives of all Americans. The Civil War between the northern and southern states would leave no person untouched. In the 1800s, people had limited options for describing their experiences. They used letters and journals, charcoal and paints, and photographs as their voices and means of expression. After the war, they wrote memoirs and recollections to preserve their stories and process their experiences.

You're about to read about the daily lives and hardships of the soldiers, the suffering of civilians in a battle zone, the agony of a family divided, and other struggles of a people divided by war. Through these primary sources, you will gain a firsthand understanding of what it was like to live through the Civil War, one American voice at a time.

JOHN D. BILLINGS

First, [the hardtack biscuits] may have been so hard that they could not be bitten; it then required a very strong blow of the fist to break them.

The second condition was when they were mouldy [moldy] or wet.

The third condition was when from storage they had become infested with maggots and weevils. These weevils were, in my experience, more abundant than the maggots. They were a little slim, brown bug an eighth of an inch in length, having the ability to completely riddle [poke holes in] the hardtack.

But hardtack was not so bad an article of food, even when traversed by insects. Eaten in the dark, no one could tell the difference between it and hardtack that was untenanted. It was no uncommon occurrence for a man to find the surface of his pot of coffee swimming with weevils, after breaking up hardtack in it . . . but they were easily skimmed off and left no distinctive flavour behind.

—from *Hardtack and Coffee,* by John D. Billings, 1888

HARDTACK

In the humorous excerpt from his postwar memoir (left), Union Army soldier John D. Billings describes the challenges of hardtack biscuits, one of the most common camp foods. Hardtack (shown here) is a hard cracker made of flour and water. It was a problematic food, but as you can see, some soldiers actually developed a fondness for it.

Soldiers from both the North and the South learned to live with minimal comfort when they were on the march or in camp. At night, they crowded into small tents, sometimes packed together so tightly, if one soldier wanted to roll over, he had to get his tent mates to roll over, too.

The food tasted awful and was sometimes inedible. When soldiers received "fresh" meat, it had often already gone bad. Preserved meat was so filled with salt that it had to be soaked in water for hours before a soldier even attempted to eat it. In southern camps, these poor rations were likely to run out, especially in the war's later years when many farms in the South had been destroyed.

A SOLDIER'S GEAR

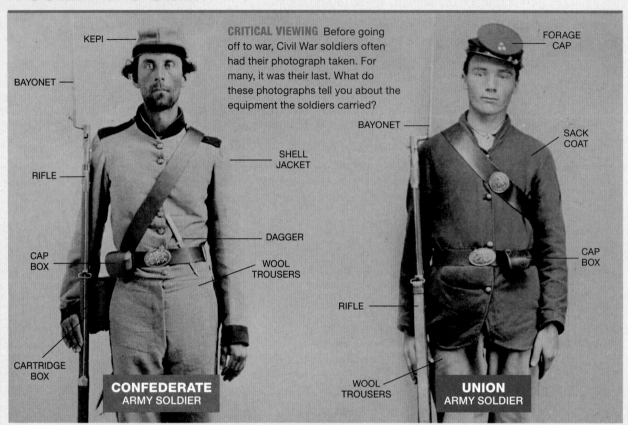

CRITICAL VIEWING Before going off to war, Civil War soldiers often had their photograph taken. For many, it was their last. What do these photographs tell you about the equipment the soldiers carried?

Confederate soldier labels: KEPI, BAYONET, RIFLE, CAP BOX, CARTRIDGE BOX, SHELL JACKET, DAGGER, WOOL TROUSERS

CONFEDERATE ARMY SOLDIER

Union soldier labels: FORAGE CAP, BAYONET, SACK COAT, CAP BOX, RIFLE, WOOL TROUSERS

UNION ARMY SOLDIER

GEORGE ALLEN

A woolen blanket and a piece of shelter tent twisted together, and thrown over our shoulders; haversack [knapsack] loaded with a dozen hard tack and a small piece of "salt horse," little bag of coffee and sugar, . . . all sorts of hats or caps; little to eat, but plenty of ammunition.

—from *Forty-Six Months with the Fourth R.I. Volunteers*, by Corp. George H. Allen, 1887

A SOLDIER'S GEAR

When a Union soldier like George Allen from Rhode Island joined the army, he was, of course, equipped with a rifle. He also received other gear, like a knapsack, a wool blanket, a cartridge box on a shoulder strap, a canteen, a bag for carrying food, and eating utensils. All together, he might find himself carrying 40 to 50 pounds of weapons and gear. But as time went on, most soldiers threw away the items they found to be unnecessary to make marching and moving easier. Corporal Allen's description of the simplicity of his gear after a year of fighting gives a sense of how practicality outweighed comfort.

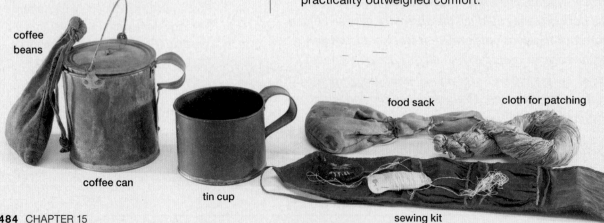

coffee beans

coffee can

tin cup

food sack

cloth for patching

sewing kit

THE CIVILIANS OF VICKSBURG

As the fighting raged through the border states and the South, civilians often found themselves on the front lines of the war. The people of Vicksburg, Mississippi, experienced life in a battle zone between 1861 and 1863.

Vicksburg sits on a high bluff overlooking the Mississippi River. At the start of the war, the Confederacy controlled Vicksburg, and therefore it controlled the river traffic that passed by the city. The Union Army made multiple attempts to take Vicksburg, and eventually put the city under siege, blocking the paths into town so that no food or ammunition could be brought in. Day and night, Union soldiers rained shells down onto Vicksburg from the opposite side of the Mississippi River. Abandoning their ruined houses, residents dug caves into the hillside beneath the town. As the weeks dragged on, food ran short. People were forced to eat mules, horses, dogs, and rats.

The siege ended on July 4, 1863, when the military commander of the Vicksburg troops surrendered. A chaplain for the southern troops commented, "We surrendered to famine, not to [the northern army]." One woman kept a diary of the civilians' daily life during the siege of Vicksburg. She described the cave she was living in as "suffocating" and like "a living tomb." Read more from her diary in the excerpt below.

April 28, 1863—I never understood before the full force of those questions—what shall we eat? what shall we drink? and wherewithal shall we be clothed?

May 28—The regular siege has continued. We are utterly cut off from the world, surrounded by a circle of fire. The fiery shower of shells goes on day and night. People do nothing but eat what they can get, sleep when they can, and dodge shells. There are three intervals when the shelling stops, either for the guns to cool or for the gunners' meals, I suppose— about eight in the morning, the same in the evening, and at noon. In that time we have to both prepare and eat ours. Clothing cannot be washed or anything else done. I think all the dogs and cats must be killed or starved; we don't see any more pitiful animals prowling around.

—from "A Woman's Diary of the Siege of Vicksburg," published in *The Century Illustrated Monthly Magazine,* 1885

CRITICAL VIEWING The Shirley family, who owned the house shown in this 1863 photograph, were forced to live in a manmade cave, like the ones dug into the ground in the photo, to avoid the cannon fire flying past their home. What does this photo reveal about the impact of the Civil War on the civilian population of cities like Vicksburg?

FAMILIES DIVIDED

They may not look much alike, but David Keener Shriver (left) and Mark Shriver (right) were family members—cousins, in fact—fighting on opposite sides of the Civil War.

David joined up to fight with Company 1 of the Union Army's 190th Regiment of Pennsylvania Volunteers. His cousin Mark was a member of the Confederate Army's 1st Virginia Cavalry. Because the young soldiers' parents were siblings, it's likely loyalty to opposing armies was a source of division and tension in the family.

D.P. CONYNGHAM

I had a Sergeant Driscoll, a brave man, and one of the best shots in the Brigade. When charging at Malvern Hill, a company was posted in a clump of trees, who kept up a fierce fire on us, and actually charged out on our advance. Their officer seemed to be a daring, reckless boy, and I said to Driscoll, "if that officer is not taken down, many of us will fall before we pass that clump."

"Leave that to me," said Driscoll; so he raised his rifle, and the moment the officer exposed himself again bang went Driscoll, over went the officer, his company at once breaking away.

As we passed the place I said, "Driscoll, see if that officer is dead—he was a brave fellow."

I stood looking on. Driscoll turned [the young soldier] over on his back. He opened his eyes for a moment, and faintly murmured "Father," and closed them forever.

I will forever recollect the frantic grief of Driscoll; it was harrowing to witness. [The young soldier] was his son, who had gone South before the war.

—from *The Irish Brigade and Its Campaigns,* by Union Army Capt. D.P. Conyngham, 1867

TRAGIC ENCOUNTERS

Most Americans sided with their home state in the Civil War, but some found it harder to choose a side. Political or personal beliefs, loyalty to the federal government, and pressure from loved ones often made for conflicted soldiers and broken family bonds.

The most heartbreaking tales of the Civil War may be those of families first divided, then reunited as enemies in battle. The personal account of Captain D.P. Conyngham of the Union Army (left) describes a tragic scene he witnessed during the battle at Malvern Hill, Virginia, on July 1, 1862.

CRITICAL VIEWING During the Grand Review in May 1865, the great armies of Grant and Sherman received a hero's welcome in Washington, D.C. What challenges do you think Union soldiers faced after the cheers subsided and they returned to their lives?

LEANDER STILLWELL

I now had only two miles to go, and was soon at the dear old boyhood home. My folks were expecting me, so they were not taken by surprise. There was no "scene" when we met, . . . but we all had a feeling of profound contentment and satisfaction which was too deep to be expressed by mere words.

When I returned home I found that the farm work my father was then engaged in was cutting up and shocking corn. So, the morning after my arrival, September 29th, I doffed my uniform of first lieutenant, put on some of father's old clothes, armed myself with a corn knife, and proceeded to wage war on the standing corn. The feeling I had while engaged in this work was "sort of queer." It almost seemed, sometimes, as if I had been away only a day or two, and had just taken up the farm work where I had left off.

—from *The Story of a Common Soldier of Army Life in the Civil War* by Leander Stillwell, 1920

GOING HOME

For some soldiers, the return home after the Civil War was warm, yet surprisingly undramatic. In his personal account (left), Union soldier Leander Stillwell describes his return home to Illinois.

When the war ended in 1865, thousands of soldiers were mustered out (dismissed from service). But first, for many Union soldiers, there was the Grand Review in Washington, D.C. Over the course of two days in May, thousands of Union troops paraded through the streets of the capital to the applause of large crowds. Then, with the cheers still ringing in their ears, the men returned to their homes.

On the Confederate side, it was harder for soldiers to return home. The war had left southern cities and farms in ruins, and the recovery process would be long and difficult.

Personal accounts shed new light on history.

When you read the words of someone who lived through an event like the Civil War, you draw conclusions that are probably different from those you'd draw from a secondary source like a textbook.

Primary sources like those included in this American Story provide varied perspectives and points of view. They capture the voices of the Civil War and help tell the story of this country-changing event in American history.

THINK ABOUT IT

How useful and credible are primary sources like those included in this American Story in helping you understand soldiers' and civilians' lives during the Civil War?

1.1 Shots at Fort Sumter

Imagine a hot, dry landscape where rain hasn't fallen for months. It would take only a spark to send the whole area up in flames. The spark that ignited the Civil War was the attack on Fort Sumter.

MAIN IDEA Once the northern states declared war and most southern states had seceded, the country waited to see whether the states in between would remain in the Union.

THE SPARK THAT CAUSED THE FIRE

As you have read, President Abraham Lincoln declared that secession was illegal under the Constitution. Southerners, on the other hand, claimed secession as a states' right guaranteed by the document. They decided to secede because they perceived Lincoln's election as a threat to the lawful institution of slavery.

After they split from the Union, the newly formed Confederate states declared that everything owned by the U.S. government within their boundaries now belonged to the Confederacy. Fort Sumter in Charleston, South Carolina, was among the possessions they claimed.

Union major **Robert Anderson**, who was in charge of the fort, had watched the people of Charleston get swept up in secession fever, and he was worried. More than 5,000 Confederate soldiers surrounded Anderson and his men, and the Union soldiers were so low on provisions that they faced starvation. Lincoln sent a message to the southern leaders stating that he was going to send food, but not weapons, to the soldiers at Fort Sumter.

On April 11, 1861, before the Union's provisions arrived, Confederate leaders demanded that the Union troops **evacuate**, or leave, the fort. Otherwise, Confederate forces would take the stronghold by force. Lincoln and Anderson refused to agree to this demand, and the next day, Confederate forces began bombarding the fort from all sides. The shelling lasted for 34 hours. On April 14, with no more food or ammunition, Anderson surrendered.

War was unpopular among northerners, but the attack stirred the Union to action. Lincoln declared South Carolina to be in rebellion and called to form a militia. The Civil War had begun. Its purpose then was not to end slavery but to reunite the nation.

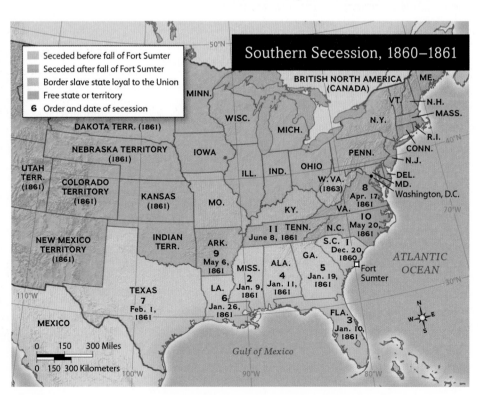

Southern Secession, 1860–1861

- Seceded before fall of Fort Sumter
- Seceded after fall of Fort Sumter
- Border slave state loyal to the Union
- Free state or territory
- **6** Order and date of secession

BRITISH NORTH AMERICA (CANADA)

DAKOTA TERR. (1861)

NEBRASKA TERRITORY (1861)

UTAH TERR. (1861)

COLORADO TERRITORY (1861)

KANSAS (1861)

NEW MEXICO TERRITORY (1861)

INDIAN TERR.

MEXICO

TEXAS 7 Feb. 1, 1861

ARK. 9 May 6, 1861

LA. 6 Jan. 26, 1861

MISS. 2 Jan. 9, 1861

ALA. 4 Jan. 11, 1861

GA. 5 Jan. 19, 1861

FLA. 3 Jan. 10, 1861

S.C. 1 Dec. 20, 1860

N.C. May 20, 1861

TENN. 11 June 8, 1861

KY.

VA. 10 Apr. 17, 1861

W. VA. (1863)

MO.

ILL. IND. OHIO

MINN. WISC. MICH.

IOWA

PENN.

N.Y.

CONN. N.J. DEL. MD. Washington, D.C.

ME. VT. N.H. MASS. R.I.

8

Fort Sumter

ATLANTIC OCEAN

Gulf of Mexico

0 150 300 Miles

0 150 300 Kilometers

AMERICAN PLACES
Fort Sumter

Fort Sumter was built after the War of 1812 with Britain had revealed the need for added defense along the U.S. coast. The five-sided island fort was designed to protect Charleston Harbor. No one was killed during the 1861 bombardment of the fort, but two Union soldiers accidentally died during a 100-gun salute.

THE GEOGRAPHY OF WAR

Within two days of Lincoln's call to arms, Virginia seceded. The Confederacy established its capital at Richmond, Virginia. Soon after, Arkansas, Tennessee, and North Carolina left the Union. However, four states bordering both the Union and the Confederacy—Maryland, Delaware, Missouri, and Kentucky—remained undecided. These states, called the **border states**, lay in the middle ground between the warring North and South and so were very important geographically.

Maryland, for example, bordered Washington, D.C., on three sides. If the state joined the Confederacy, the Union's capital would be completely surrounded by Confederate states. In an effort to keep Maryland in the Union, Lincoln threatened to jail any Confederate soldier who entered the state.

Missouri was also vital to the Union cause. With its large population, Missouri could supply the Union with many soldiers. The state also produced a great deal of food and protected the western side of the Union. In addition, its biggest city, St. Louis, was an important commercial and transportation center.

In Kentucky, both Confederate recruiters and pro-Union leaders tried to sway the state's citizens. But when Confederate forces invaded Kentucky in September 1861, the state asked the federal government for help. Lincoln sent troops to the state, the invaders were driven out, and Kentucky stayed in the Union.

The president gained more ground when 50 counties in northwest Virginia decided to form a new state. The people in those counties no longer wanted to be a part of pro-slavery Virginia and so, in 1863, West Virginia became part of the Union. Overall, Lincoln succeeded in keeping the border states in the Union. He would need all the forces he could gather to prepare for war and fight the long, tough battles ahead.

HISTORICAL THINKING

1. **READING CHECK** What happened after the Confederates attacked Fort Sumter?

2. **SUMMARIZE** Why was it important for the Union to keep the border states out of the Confederacy?

3. **IDENTIFY PROBLEMS AND SOLUTIONS** How did Lincoln deal with Confederate attempts to seize the border states?

An Early Confederate Victory

Sometimes you jump into something before you're really ready. Without enough time to make a plan or devise a strategy, you could find that you just have to "wing it." In a way, that's what happened to the Union and Confederate armies.

MAIN IDEA Confederate forces gained an early victory by winning the Battle of Bull Run.

Robert E. Lee

Born into a celebrated Virginia family, Robert E. Lee wanted to make a name for himself. He enrolled in the U.S. Military Academy at West Point in New York and was one of only six soldiers in his class who graduated with a clean record of behavior. After graduating, Lee met and married a descendant of Martha Washington, George Washington's wife. During the Mexican-American War, Lee impressed his commanding officer, General Winfield Scott, with his keen military mind. He became an officer in the Confederate Army after turning down Lincoln's offer to command the Union Army. His loyalty to his home state outweighed the president's request.

PREPARING FOR WAR

War had begun, but neither the Union nor the Confederacy was actually prepared for it. In April 1861, the Union forces included only 16,000 professional soldiers, while the Confederacy had fewer than 2,000. Both sides quickly took steps to **mobilize**, or organize and prepare troops for active service.

The North and the South enlisted troops at the local and state levels. A local leader would encourage men to join and serve under his command, or a group of men would get together and elect their commander. Many military units also formed along ethnic lines. Some northern regiments consisted only of European immigrants who communicated in their native language. Germans were the largest European immigrant group fighting for the Union. European immigrants also fought for the South, and a Texas regiment consisting of Mexicans called the Tejas soon joined the Confederate cause as well. Mobilization helped swell the ranks on both sides, but neither army was at full strength.

THE BATTLE OF BULL RUN

The armies were put to the test in July 1861. Hoping to bring a swift end to the war, Lincoln decided to send Union forces to seize Richmond. To carry out his plan, Lincoln first ordered General Irvin McDowell to attack the Confederate forces in Manassas, Virginia, a town less than 100 miles from Richmond. McDowell and his troops were in Washington, D.C., only 40 miles east of Manassas. But McDowell didn't believe his 35,000 volunteers were ready for battle, so he and his troops left

The first official Confederate flag is shown at the left. Often called the "Stars and Bars," it sometimes caused confusion on the battlefield because it looked so much like the U.S. flag. The flag below was first flown by a Virginia regiment. Soon other regiments began using it, but the Confederacy never officially adopted the flag.

Washington, D.C., more than a week later than planned. When the Confederate general stationed in Manassas, P.G.T. Beauregard, learned of the delay, he sent for help. Soon 11,000 more Confederate soldiers arrived to strengthen his forces.

The battle began on July 21, when Union forces crossed a small creek called Bull Run to attack the Confederates. As the Confederate soldiers charged, they unleashed a high-pitched battle cry that could be heard for miles. The earsplitting cry came to be known as the "rebel yell." Many Union soldiers wrote in letters and diaries about the terror the scream inspired.

During the battle, Confederate general Thomas Jackson and his forces filled a gap in the line of Confederate soldiers. He held the line so bravely that another general told his men to take heart from the sight of Jackson, "standing like a stone wall!" Jackson would be known by the nickname **Stonewall Jackson** for the rest of his life. Meanwhile, **J.E.B. Stuart**, the leader of the Virginia Confederate **cavalry**, or soldiers on horseback, watched Union movements on a hill overlooking the battlefield. At a critical point in the battle, Stuart's cavalry charged and scattered the

Union **infantry**, or foot soldiers. The charge forced the Union troops to retreat to Washington, D.C.

The Confederacy won the battle, but both sides suffered heavy casualties: about 3,000 soldiers for the North and more than 1,700 for the South. Another battle at Bull Run would take place more than a year later. Once again, the Confederates, under General **Robert E. Lee**, would win but with staggering casualties: nearly 15,000 for the Union and 9,000 for the Confederacy. These extremely high casualty rates continued to make the war unpopular in the North. Lincoln knew it would be a long and grueling war.

HISTORICAL THINKING

1. **READING CHECK** How did the North and the South prepare for the war?

2. **ANALYZE CAUSE AND EFFECT** How did the first Battle of Bull Run affect the course of the early part of the war?

3. **DRAW CONCLUSIONS** How did this battle reflect the beginnings of a broad pattern of leadership in the North and the South?

1.3 Confederate Memorial Hall
New Orleans, Louisiana

Confederate Memorial Hall opened its doors in New Orleans on January 8, 1891. The oldest museum in Louisiana, it celebrates southern heritage and history with a focus on Civil War artifacts from the Confederate Army. In fact, the museum houses one of the largest collections of Confederate memorabilia in the United States, including uniforms and boots, weapons, personal items, and photographs. What challenges and advantages might a museum face in choosing to showcase items from one side of a war rather than from both sides?

Binoculars and Case

These 1863 binoculars and leather case belonged to a Confederate soldier. Cavalry generals—generals who commanded soldiers on horseback—and officers carried binoculars as part of their gear. Confederate soldiers also commonly carried a canteen, blanket roll (similar to a sleeping bag), ammunition and a weapon, and very simple food.

New Yorker William Ketchum designed and patented this Civil War hand grenade.

How might binoculars like these have helped officers on the battlefield?

Ketchum Hand Grenade

Unexploded hand grenades make an interesting addition to any wartime museum exhibit—especially early ones from the Civil War. Confederate and Union soldiers tossed these three- and five-pound hand grenades like darts into enemy territory during battles. The weapons have been recovered from famous battle sites such as Vicksburg and Petersburg.

Tintype Portrait

A photographer captured this 1861 tintype portrait of Sergeant Joseph Corneille, a member of the 22nd Louisiana Infantry, in his full dress uniform. Tintypes were invented in the 1850s and involved the transfer of a photograph to a thin sheet of iron coated with enamel. These portraits were prized possessions. They were also expensive. People bought elaborate frames like the one shown here, so they could put their portraits on display. They also carried them in cases or envelopes so the tintypes would be protected.

Many Civil War soldiers in full uniform had a tintype created before they headed off to battle. Why do you think the soldiers wanted to have these portraits created?

Confederate Battle Flag

Many Confederate regiments designed and adopted their own personalized battle flags during the Civil War. The red and white Van Dorn battle flag shown below was used by the regiments under the command of Confederate general Earl Van Dorn in Louisiana, Missouri, Mississippi, and Arkansas between 1862 and 1863. The 13 white stars represent the 13 Confederate States of America.

2.1 Hardship and Weapons

Siblings fight over all kinds of things: household chores, toys, television programs. During the Civil War, however, some siblings argued over a much larger issue: whether to support the Union or the Confederacy.

MAIN IDEA Soldiers in the Civil War faced difficulties at home and in the field, including dealing with technological advances on the front lines.

A SOLDIER'S LIFE

The Civil War divided not only a nation but also families. Siblings, parents, and even spouses sometimes found themselves on different sides of the debate. It was not uncommon to hear of two brothers serving in opposing armies. No one was spared from these divisions, not even Abraham Lincoln. His brother-in-law, Ben Hardin Helm, was a Confederate general.

Whichever side the soldiers served on, life was difficult and dangerous. For every 30 days in the field, the average soldier engaged in battle one day and drilled, trained, and marched the remaining 29. Army leaders had difficulty keeping track of their units' needs, so supplies didn't always arrive when required. The soldiers were often cold and hungry as a result. Disease killed more men than fighting did.

And now army leaders had more soldiers under their command. After Bull Run, both the Confederate and Union leaders realized they needed larger armies. Farmers under the age of 30 made up about half of the men on both sides. Some older men joined the ranks as well, and boys as young as 12 served as drummers and buglers. About a quarter of the Union volunteers were young immigrants, mainly from Germany, Ireland, Canada, and England. Another group of people, African-American men, could have been drafted into fighting, but it would be several years before either army began to recruit them or even allow them to enlist.

A NEW KIND OF WAR

The Civil War battlefield was far more dangerous than it had been in previous American wars. Advances in technology made fighting more efficient and deadlier than ever. In earlier wars, soldiers carried muskets, which were not very accurate. The inside of a musket's barrel was polished smooth, causing the bullet's flight to be unpredictable. And a man fighting on the battlefield with a musket had to stand within 80 yards of his enemy in order to hit him. All that changed in the 1850s when a new kind of rifle replaced the musket. The grooves carved inside the barrel made the bullet spin as it hurtled toward its target. The spinning made the bullet fly in a straighter line and gave it a greater range—more than 1,000 yards.

Wooden Legs, Iron Arms
Approximately 70,000 soldiers lost limbs during the battles of the Civil War. The government offered veterans money to buy prosthetic, or artificial, arms, feet, and legs, like this one, to replace their missing limbs. Many options made of wood, iron, and leather were soon available. Few, however, were comfortable or functional. Most soldiers chose to use crutches and hooks instead.

CRITICAL VIEWING As this 1862 photograph of the Union Army reveals, Civil War soldiers used heavy guns and fought from trenches. What might have been some of the disadvantages of fighting and living in trenches such as these?

Some Union soldiers had another technological advantage in their hands: the repeating rifle. Instead of having to reload a gun after each shot, a soldier armed with a repeating rifle could fire several times before having to replenish his ammunition. These technological advances would continue to be improved and affect how future wars were fought.

With improvements to both rifles and larger cannons, soldiers increasingly resorted to **trench warfare** during the Civil War. Opposing armies dug lines of trenches, or ditches, roughly parallel to each other. The trenches gave soldiers both a vantage point from which to fire and a place to shelter from incoming rounds of ammunition. Advances in naval technology also brought changes to warfare at sea. Before, ordinary wooden ships were vulnerable to cannon and rifle fire. New **ironclad ships**, or ships plated with thick metal, could withstand this heavy artillery.

Unfortunately, the technology of medical treatment had not transformed as fast as the technology of war. Effective treatments for infections, such as antibiotics, had not yet been invented. **Mortality**, or the death rate, from wounds and disease was high. And the hundreds of thousands of sick and wounded required medical attention, which in turn created a shortage of people to care for them. Hard-working male doctors and nurses set up hospitals in makeshift buildings and did their best to treat the soldiers, but they struggled to keep up with the flood of patients. The acute need for more caregivers was soon answered, however. Large numbers of women volunteered to provide much-needed care as nurses and administrators.

HISTORICAL THINKING

1. **READING CHECK** What sort of struggles did Civil War soldiers face before they arrived on the battlefield?

2. **DETERMINE WORD MEANING** What context clues help you understand what *replenish* means?

3. **MAKE INFERENCES** What impact do you think technological advances had on the soldiers' mortality rate?

2.2 Women and the War

Think of a time when you stepped up and took on a role you'd never shouldered before. You might have felt uncomfortable about assuming the role, but—like women during the Civil War—you probably felt that you had to do it.

MAIN IDEA Women took an active role in the Civil War, both on the battlefield and at home.

WOMEN ON THE BATTLEFIELD

Just as they had in the American Revolution, women during the Civil War took on roles that brought them closer to the field of battle. Many women, in particular, became nurses. Before the war, society considered it inappropriate for women to care for injured and ill men. The Civil War quickly changed all that. Soon, most nurses were women, and at least one woman, **Mary Edwards Walker**, became a doctor.

In the North, Dorothea Dix and a **philanthropist** named **Clara Barton** led the nursing effort. A philanthropist is someone who actively promotes human welfare. Already known for her work on behalf of the mentally ill, Dix led volunteer nurses in a march on Washington in April 1861, demanding that women be allowed to help the Union forces. As a result, the Secretary of War gave Dix the responsibility of recruiting female nurses. Dix insisted that her volunteers be no younger than 30 years old. More than 2,000 women volunteered. For her part, Barton collected and delivered medical supplies, clothing, and food for Union soldiers throughout the war. She aided wounded Union soldiers and the Confederate prisoners they captured.

In the South, a young woman named **Sally Tompkins** led the effort to provide nursing care through her private hospital in Richmond, which she supported with her own personal fortune. The hospital treated more than 1,300 soldiers during the four years it was open, and it returned more men to the battlefield than any other hospital. In addition, more than 600 nuns from 12 different Catholic religious communities also served as nurses during the war and attended to both Union and Confederate soldiers.

The founder of the American Red Cross, Clara Barton was 29 years old when this photo was taken (1850). A former teacher, Barton was working as a clerk at the U.S. Patent Office in Washington, D.C., when the Civil War began. Determined to support the war effort, she set out to help the soldiers, some of whom were once her students. Soon, Barton was following the Union Army to the battlefields, where she tended to the wounded and dying.

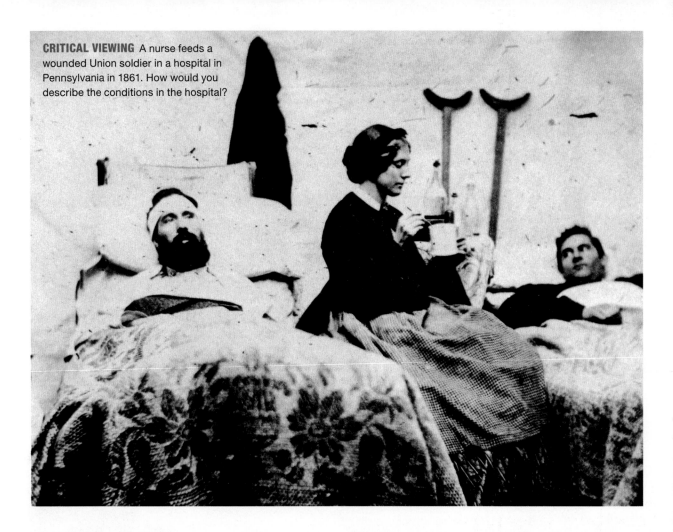

CRITICAL VIEWING A nurse feeds a wounded Union soldier in a hospital in Pennsylvania in 1861. How would you describe the conditions in the hospital?

WOMEN AT HOME

While some women helped on the battlefield, many more did their part at home. When war came, women all over the country took over the roles of their husbands, brothers, and sons in order to keep family farms and businesses running. On small farms, women and children took charge of raising animals and planting, tending, harvesting, and selling crops. On southern plantations, women directed the overseers and enslaved people. In the cities, women took jobs in factories and offices, replacing the men who had left to fight. Many women also volunteered to raise food and money, make clothing, and provide medical supplies for the troops and their communities.

Even for those women who stayed at home, the war sometimes came uncomfortably close. **Civilians**, or people not in the military, who lived near the battlefields had to deal with the sounds and dangers of battle. They could only watch as enemy combatants marched through their towns and raided their homes for supplies. To add to the stress, a family's only means of communicating with husbands and sons at war was through letters. Since troops were constantly on the move, delivering mail to them was difficult. If a soldier was killed or missing in action, the bad news arrived by letter. And since soldiers carried no official identification, many families were not informed at all. If a loved one's letters stopped coming, his family had to assume that he was not coming home.

HISTORICAL THINKING

1. **READING CHECK** How did Dorothea Dix open up the occupation of nursing to women?

2. **SUMMARIZE** What new roles did women play during the Civil War?

3. **ANALYZE CAUSE AND EFFECT** How did the war impact women, combatants, and civilians in different ways?

Photographer Ken Garrett makes a rare appearance in front of the lens at the Burnside Bridge near the Antietam battlefield in Maryland.

"When the photo reaches a wide audience and makes a difference in how we see the world, that is what makes it rewarding."

–Ken Garrett

Through the Lens—
Civil War Photography

For more than 40 years, National Geographic photographer Ken Garrett has documented images of past civilizations for *National Geographic* magazine. He has traveled to every continent, exploring and photographing ancient artifacts and ruins. But his passion for documenting the land and events associated with America's rich history keeps Garrett closer to home. He has found a wealth of subjects to photograph on the Civil War.

Garrett tells the stories of fallen Civil War soldiers through images of famous battlefields and reenactments. He hopes to help people learn from the past and use that knowledge to understand events today. His photographs of Civil War sites are a reminder of the blood shed on both sides of the conflict. The photos convey the emotions, confusion, and determination of the soldiers who fought on what Garrett refers to as "hallowed ground."

Lincoln Cemetery in Gettysburg, Pennsylvania, is the burial site of about 30 members of the U.S. Colored Troops. During the Civil War, African-American veterans were prohibited from being buried in the Soldiers' National Cemetery. In this photo taken by Garrett, reenactors pay tribute to African-American Civil War veterans during a Remembrance Day parade.

SIZING UP A SITE

When Garrett photographs a Civil War site, he likes to scout the area with a guide who can help him understand the events of the historic battle. The guide's insights help Garrett determine how to use his camera to capture the decisions made during the battle. He uses photography to show why one place was important to defend or what made another a superior place in which to hide, prepare, and attack.

Battery-powered lighting equipment helps Garrett capture the right photograph in the right light or season. "You should try to photograph a site during the season when the action took place," he adds. For example, by photographing Brandy Station, Virginia, during the summer, Garrett was able to provide insight into the heat and humidity both armies endured at this site of the largest cavalry battle in U.S. history.

Gettysburg is Garrett's favorite Civil War battlefield to photograph. "It is a very emotional place, where you really get an understanding of the horror of war. The thought that those boys walked out into that open field to be killed, sometimes by their own brothers, is a shocking realization." Gettysburg is also a popular site for reenactments. These re-creations put contemporary people in the shoes of people from 150 years earlier, bringing history to life and giving us valuable perspective on historic events.

A selection of Garrett's Gettysburg photographs as well as others from his Civil War collection are included in the following photo essay on the Civil War.

HISTORICAL THINKING

MAKE CONNECTIONS Why are Ken Garrett's Civil War photographs relevant today?

Union soldier reenactor, Fauquier County, Virginia

A Civil War Photo Essay

A story doesn't have to be made up of words. A photo essay—a collection of visuals organized to tell a story—can make as powerful a statement as any written words put down on a page.

To tell the story of the Civil War, National Geographic photographer Ken Garrett captures intricate details, sweeping landscapes, and the emotions of reenactors. His photos reveal important details about the uniforms, sites, and battlefields of the Civil War and provide us with insight into the thinking that led up to every battle, determined the fates of thousands of young soldiers, and ultimately transformed a country.

THINK ABOUT IT

How does this photo essay tell a Civil War story with very few words?

Union soldier reenactors, Crooked Run Valley, Virginia

Battle of Bull Run reenactment, Manassas, Virginia

Lincoln Cemetery, burial site for Gettysburg's African-American soldiers

Pickett's Charge reenactment, Gettysburg, Pennsylvania

Confederate cannon at Pickett's Charge site,
Gettysburg, Pennsylvania

Major Ulysses S. Grant statue, Vicksburg, Mississippi

Graves of unknown soldiers, Soldiers' National Cemetery, Gettysburg

Military earthworks, Petersburg National Battlefield, Virginia

3.1 Different Strategies

Everyone has strengths and weaknesses. You may be good at math and sports but not so great at science and card games. The trick is figuring out how to use what you've got to the best advantage.

MAIN IDEA Both the Union and the Confederacy had advantages and disadvantages, and each came up with strategies for winning the war.

STRENGTHS AND WEAKNESSES

During the Civil War, both the North and the South had strengths and weaknesses. The North had a much larger population than the South. And Union states were home to large cities, which were centers of business and industry. More than 100,000 factories were located in Union states—about five times the industrial capacity of the agrarian South.

The Union also boasted a stronger military infrastructure. It had a navy and many more ships than the South. West Point, the best military academy in the country to train leaders in the midst of war, was in the North. Many northern officers had trained there. However, the South also had talented graduates of West Point leading its soldiers. You may remember that Robert E. Lee graduated from the military academy, and so did Jefferson Davis, the Confederate president.

With its smaller numbers, the South fought the war largely on the defensive. Simply trying to defend itself seemed to be the best way to win the war, at least initially. As a result, most of the fighting took place in Confederate states. But this gave the Confederate forces a geographic advantage. They were fighting in areas they knew well, while the Union Army found itself on unfamiliar ground.

The South also used more offensive tactics to wear down the North. Confederate leaders encouraged private ship owners to intercept and capture northern merchant ships and their cargo in the Atlantic. And some southern generals planned to concentrate their forces and exert pressure on the northern capital of Washington, D.C., which bordered southern states.

MAKING A GAME PLAN

One of the renowned generals who led the Union, Winfield Scott, a hero of the Mexican-American War and the War of 1812, also had a plan. When the Civil War began, Scott was the commander-in-chief of the U.S. Army. In early 1861, he formulated a strategy he hoped would put an end to the war. His plan called for blocking Confederate ports along the Atlantic and Gulf coasts with Union warships. The North hoped to cripple the Confederate war effort and economy by preventing the delivery of weapons and halting cotton exports. Scott also proposed sending troops to gain control of the Mississippi River and capture major cities and river ports, creating divisions in the South.

Scott's massive blockade was risky. No blockade of this size had ever been tried before. There were more than 3,000 miles of coastline to block with fewer than 40 ships! Scott's idea was nicknamed the **Anaconda Plan** after a type of snake that strangles its prey. Within a week after the loss of Fort Sumter, Lincoln ordered the blockade to be carried out, and it was somewhat successful. However, many northern leaders ridiculed the plan. They wanted to take action and fight.

To counter the plan, the South tried to create a cotton shortage on the European market. The Confederacy hoped the shortage would force Great Britain and France, two major cotton consumers, to join the Confederate cause and help break up the Union blockade. The attempt backfired when both countries bought cotton from Egypt and India instead. Meanwhile, the Confederate Army engaged in terrible battles on the ground that would claim many lives and, eventually, give the South greater hope.

SCOTT'S GREAT SNAKE

The Anaconda Plan was meant to strangle the South by cutting off all trade among southern states and allowing the Union to take control of the Mississippi River. Scott believed his plan would put an early end to the war and limit the number of casualties.

Scott proposed sending a large naval force down the **Mississippi River** that would capture forts and towns along its banks.

Union ships patrolled the coastal border to prevent deliveries of weapons and supplies to southern states.

corn   oranges   cattle   sheep   coal

cotton   tobacco   hay   apples

peaches   horses   banking   sugar cane

Scott's plan was never fully implemented, but a naval blockade was maintained throughout the war. The blockade succeeded in cutting off the South's resources and probably did shorten the war. But not even Scott knew how the war would develop. He guessed it would go on for two years, not four.

HISTORICAL THINKING

1. **READING CHECK** What was General Scott's strategy for winning the war?

2. **COMPARE AND CONTRAST** What geographic advantages did the South have over the North?

3. **ANALYZE VISUALS** What resources did the Anaconda Plan attempt to prevent from being traded in the South?

3.2 Differences Between North and South

MAIN IDEA At the start of the Civil War, the Union and the Confederacy each had important geographic advantages.

GEOGRAPHIC ADVANTAGES

Geography is critically important in any war. Mountains and rivers can serve as natural defenses, helping an army to defend itself from invaders. Hills can provide a visual advantage for soldiers who are watching for enemy troops. Trees felled in a forest can slow down an army as it tries to pass through.

In the Civil War, the Union and the Confederacy had other types of geographic advantages. You've learned that the Union had a greater population spread across a wide geographic area, which helped boost the size of its army. It also had many industrial centers. As you know, too, the Confederacy had the advantage of fighting the war on familiar terrain. And the South grew abundant cotton, which could be sold to help cover Confederate war expenses.

Read the following text and examine the maps to see how four important geographical factors—population, railroads, industry, and agriculture—critically affected the Civil War.

RAIL TRANSPORTATION

As you can see on the large map, the Union had more than twice as many miles of railroad lines as the Confederacy. In the South, most railroads went from Mississippi, Alabama, and Georgia to Charleston, carrying cotton for exporting.

The Civil War was one of the first wars in which railroads played a critical role. The Union and the Confederacy both used railroads to ship equipment, weapons, and troops. Sometimes, officers even sent spies on trains to learn about the opponent's troop movements. However, the Confederacy began the war at a disadvantage. Their railroads were in bad shape, and repairs often had to wait. Many railroad workers had quit to fight the war.

INDUSTRY

Manufacturing, especially of iron and steel, was critically important to both the Union and the Confederacy during the Civil War. The large map shows the location of factories in the North and the South. As you've learned, the majority of the factories were in the North, but the Confederacy did have some in Virginia and other states. The largest Confederate iron works was in Richmond, Virginia. Confederate officers fought to protect their factories because they were so important to the South.

Because the Union did more manufacturing, it was able to produce more of the rifles, cannons, railroad tracks, locomotives, and other materials its army needed for war. That was a definite advantage.

POPULATION

In 1860, the North had a population of about 18.5 million people, of which about 3.8 million free men were of military age. In contrast, the South had about 5.5 million free persons and 3.5 million enslaved people. Only 1.1 million free men were of military age, and 80 percent of these went to war. This percentage reflects the South's dedication to the cause for independence, since Jefferson Davis and the Confederacy relied on the voluntary cooperation of state governments for troops.

Additionally, 19 of the largest cities in the United States were part of the Union. Because the South was an agricultural society with few industrial cities to attract large populations, the Confederacy had only two, New Orleans and Charleston.

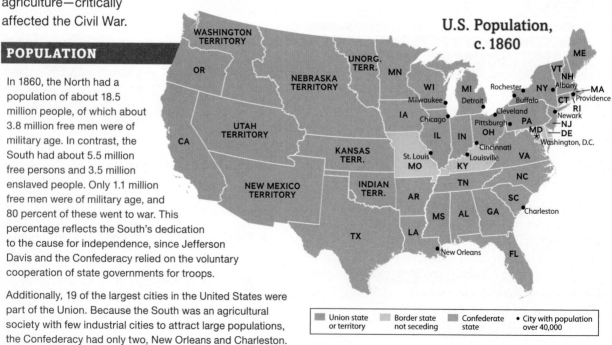

U.S. Population, c. 1860

■ Union state or territory	■ Border state not seceding	■ Confederate state	• City with population over 40,000

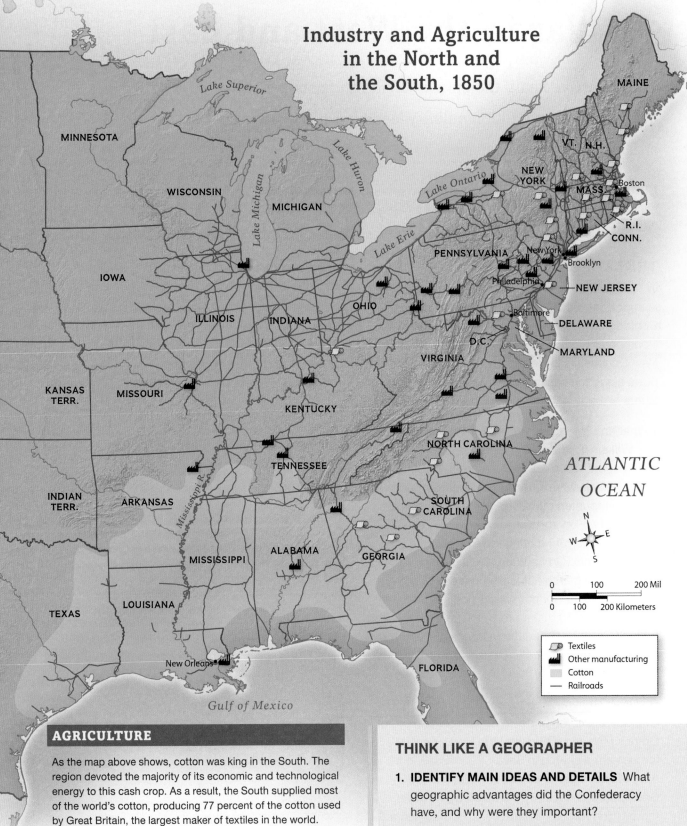

Industry and Agriculture in the North and the South, 1850

MINNESOTA

Lake Superior

WISCONSIN

MICHIGAN

Lake Michigan

Lake Huron

IOWA

ILLINOIS

INDIANA

Lake Ontario

Lake Erie

OHIO

NEW YORK

PENNSYLVANIA

MAINE

VT. N.H.

MASS. Boston

R.I.
CONN.

New York

Brooklyn

NEW JERSEY

Philadelphia

DELAWARE

Baltimore

D.C.

MARYLAND

KANSAS
TERR.

MISSOURI

KENTUCKY

VIRGINIA

INDIAN
TERR.

ARKANSAS

TENNESSEE

NORTH CAROLINA

ATLANTIC
OCEAN

Mississippi R.

SOUTH
CAROLINA

MISSISSIPPI

ALABAMA

GEORGIA

TEXAS

LOUISIANA

New Orleans

FLORIDA

Gulf of Mexico

0   100   200 Mil

0   100   200 Kilometers

Legend:
- Textiles
- Other manufacturing
- Cotton
- Railroads

AGRICULTURE

As the map above shows, cotton was king in the South. The region devoted the majority of its economic and technological energy to this cash crop. As a result, the South supplied most of the world's cotton, producing 77 percent of the cotton used by Great Britain, the largest maker of textiles in the world.

Cotton was critical to the Confederacy's ability to raise the huge amounts of money needed to fight a war. In addition to Great Britain, the South exported cotton to France and other European countries and used the profits to buy weapons and equipment and to fund the Confederate government. Even textile mills in the North bought cotton from the South. The Confederacy also borrowed against the promise of future cotton crops to pay for its war efforts.

THINK LIKE A GEOGRAPHER

1. **IDENTIFY MAIN IDEAS AND DETAILS** What geographic advantages did the Confederacy have, and why were they important?

2. **ANALYZE CAUSE AND EFFECT** How did the Union's superiority in rail transportation contribute to its victory in the war?

3. **FORM AND SUPPORT OPINIONS** In your opinion, what was the most important geographic factor in the outcome of the war?

3.3 War in the West and East

You may have heard the phrase "divide and conquer" from a parent or coach. Union military leaders used the same strategy to try to defeat the South.

MAIN IDEA The Union attacked strategic areas in the western and eastern parts of the Confederacy in the early years of the Civil War.

THE BATTLE OF SHILOH

In 1862, Union and Confederate forces clashed in important battles in the western part of the Confederacy. The region had some of the Confederacy's most important assets, including New Orleans, its largest city, and many major ports along the Mississippi River. The North set its sights on capturing the region.

To that end, two Union generals, **Ulysses S. Grant** and **William T. Sherman**, sailed troops on a fleet of 19 riverboats up the Tennessee River. Seven of the vessels were gunboats, small, fast ships carrying mounted guns. The fleet successfully captured two key forts in Tennessee, Fort Henry and Fort Donelson, forcing the Confederate Army to retreat. On February 25, the Union Army continued its march across Tennessee with the goal of reaching Corinth, Mississippi—a major rail center—where 20,000 more Union soldiers awaited them. If Grant captured the railroads at Corinth, the Union would control most of the western part of the Confederacy.

However, General Albert Sidney Johnston, the Confederate commander in the region, learned of Grant's plan and ambushed the Union general's forces near a church in Shiloh, Tennessee, on April 6. The larger Confederate forces drove Grant's troops back. By the next day, however, more Union forces had arrived, and Grant led a counterattack. The Confederates conceded defeat and withdrew to Corinth.

The two-day **Battle of Shiloh** was the bloodiest battle in the war to that point. The South lost more than 10,000 men, including General Johnston. Even though it won the battle, the Union Army actually lost more men: about 13,000 soldiers. Because of the high casualty count, some people called for Grant's removal, but Lincoln refused. He is said to have remarked, "I can't spare this man [Grant]; he fights!"

Ulysses S. Grant

After graduating from West Point, Ulysses S. Grant served with General Winfield Scott during the Mexican-American War, as had his Confederate opponent, Robert E. Lee. After the Civil War, Grant became president of the United States in 1868, when he was only 46 years old. His presidency was plagued by scandal, although Grant himself was an honest man.

CRITICAL VIEWING This illustration shows the *Monitor* (in the front) firing its guns at the *Virginia* (in the back) at Hampton Roads Harbor, Virginia. The *Virginia* began its life as a standard steam-powered vessel built in the North, when it was called the *Merrimack*. The Confederates salvaged the *Merrimack* from a navy yard in Norfolk and refitted it as an ironclad. How did the successful use of ironclad ships probably affect future warfare?

THE SEVEN DAYS' BATTLES

Meanwhile, the Union had undertaken another campaign in the eastern part of the Confederacy with the goal of capturing the Confederate capital of Richmond, Virginia. On March 9, 1862, the Confederate ironclad ship, the C.S.S. *Virginia*—also known as the *Merrimack*—faced off against the Union ironclad, the U.S.S. *Monitor*. It marked the first skirmish between ironclad warships. The battle took place in the harbor of Hampton Roads, Virginia, and ended in a standoff.

Lincoln urged General George B. McClellan to continue the advance toward Richmond. McClellan had replaced Winfield Scott as the leader of the Union Army and was a brilliant general. But McClellan's tendency to overestimate the enemy's strength and postpone troop movement often frustrated Lincoln. McClellan eventually set sail with about 120,000 troops to the coast of the Virginia Peninsula. The Union forces battled their way to within a few miles of Richmond. But, fearing that he might be outnumbered, McClellan pulled his men back.

On June 1, rebel forces led by the new commander of the Confederate Army, Robert E. Lee, took advantage of McClellan's caution and moved to protect Richmond. From June 25 to July 1, Lee and his forces went on the attack and fought an offensive war, called the **Seven Days' Battles**. Lee forced McClellan to retreat back down the Virginia Peninsula, but even as they were being pursued, the Union forces still managed to inflict heavy casualties on the Confederates.

Nonetheless, the victory of the Seven Days' Battles boosted southern morale, saved the Confederate capital, and made Lee a hero. But as Lee's star was rising, McClellan's was falling. McClellan's failures made Lincoln's opinion of him sink even lower.

HISTORICAL THINKING

1. **READING CHECK** What did the Union Army hope to accomplish in the western part of the Confederacy in 1862?

2. **SUMMARIZE** Describe the Union advance toward Richmond.

3. **ANALYZE CAUSE AND EFFECT** How did the Seven Days' Battles affect the combatants and the leaders of the war?

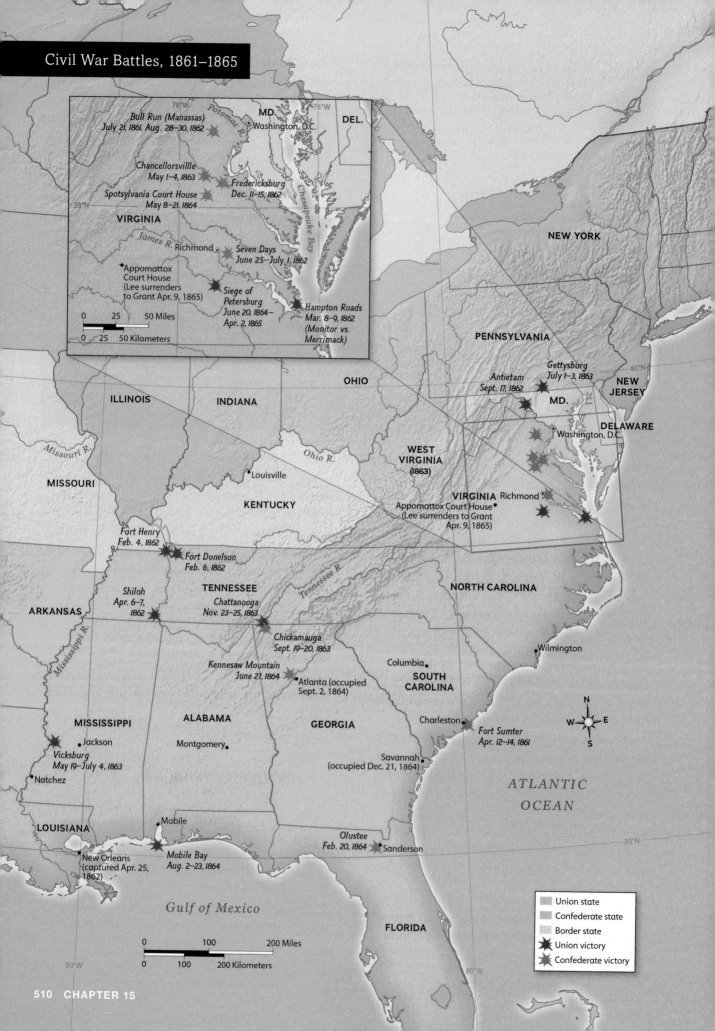

Civil War Battles, 1861–1865

Inset map (Virginia region):

78°W · 76°W

Potomac R.

MD.

DEL.

Bull Run (Manassas)
July 21, 1861, Aug. 28–30, 1862

Washington, D.C.

Chancellorsville
May 1–4, 1863

Fredericksburg
Dec. 11–15, 1862

Spotsylvania Court House
May 8–21, 1864

38°N

VIRGINIA

Chesapeake Bay

James R. · Richmond

Seven Days
June 25–July 1, 1862

Appomattox
Court House
(Lee surrenders
to Grant Apr. 9, 1865)

Siege of
Petersburg
June 20, 1864–
Apr. 2, 1865

Hampton Roads
Mar. 8–9, 1862
(Monitor vs.
Merrimack)

0 25 50 Miles

0 25 50 Kilometers

Main map:

NEW YORK

PENNSYLVANIA

OHIO

ILLINOIS

INDIANA

40°N

NEW
JERSEY

Gettysburg
July 1–3, 1863

Antietam
Sept. 17, 1862

MD.

DELAWARE

Washington, D.C.

Louisville

Missouri R.

Ohio R.

WEST
VIRGINIA
(1863)

MISSOURI

KENTUCKY

VIRGINIA   Richmond

Appomattox Court House
(Lee surrenders to Grant
Apr. 9, 1865)

Fort Henry
Feb. 4, 1862

Fort Donelson
Feb. 6, 1862

NORTH CAROLINA

ARKANSAS

Shiloh
Apr. 6–7,
1862

TENNESSEE

Chattanooga
Nov. 23–25, 1863

Tennessee R.

Mississippi R.

Chickamauga
Sept. 19–20, 1863

Wilmington

Kennesaw Mountain
June 27, 1864

Columbia

SOUTH
CAROLINA

MISSISSIPPI

Jackson

ALABAMA

Montgomery

GEORGIA

Atlanta (occupied
Sept. 2, 1864)

Charleston

Fort Sumter
Apr. 12–14, 1861

Vicksburg
May 19–July 4, 1863

Natchez

Savannah
(occupied Dec. 21, 1864)

ATLANTIC
OCEAN

N
W   E
S

LOUISIANA

Mobile

New Orleans
(captured Apr. 25,
1862)

Mobile Bay
Aug. 2–23, 1864

Olustee
Feb. 20, 1864

Sanderson

FLORIDA

30°N

Gulf of Mexico

0 100 200 Miles

0 100 200 Kilometers

90°W · 80°W

Legend:
- ☐ Union state
- ☐ Confederate state
- ☐ Border state
- ✷ Union victory
- ✷ Confederate victory

3.4 Bloody 1862

When a friend lets you down, you likely give him or her one more chance. But at a certain point, you get fed up. As Lincoln realized, you can give someone "just one more chance" only so many times.

> **MAIN IDEA** The bloody battles of Antietam and Fredericksburg exacted a high cost from both Union and Confederate forces.

THE BLOODIEST DAY

You've read about the first Battle of Bull Run in 1861. A second battle took place there in 1862. After driving General George McClellan and his troops back to Washington, D.C., General Robert E. Lee marched his men northward to battle again at Bull Run outside Manassas, Virginia. On the third day of fighting, the Confederates forced the Union soldiers to retreat. Afterward, Lee went on the offensive and marched his troops north into Maryland. He wanted to move the war into the Union states.

President Lincoln called McClellan back into action and ordered him to defend the Union capital. On his way to meet Lee, McClellan got lucky. By chance, a Union soldier found a packet of cigars in a field, dropped by a careless Confederate officer. Wrapped around the cigars were Lee's detailed plans for the assault on Maryland. McClellan learned that Lee's forces were in two groups several miles apart. If McClellan moved quickly, he could destroy Lee's army before the groups joined up. But McClellan acted too late. The Confederate Army met Union soldiers on the battlefield at Antietam (an-TEE-tuhm) Creek near Sharpsburg, Maryland, on September 17.

The casualties for both sides at the **Battle of Antietam** numbered at least 23,000 men. The day of the battle would later be called "America's Bloodiest Day." The Union considered it a victory because Lee's forces left Maryland. But Lincoln was frustrated with McClellan's errors. He said, "If General McClellan does not want to use the army, I would like to borrow it for a time." The president named Ambrose Burnside as the new commander.

THE BATTLE OF FREDERICKSBURG

For his first campaign, General Burnside decided to lead his troops back toward Richmond to try to capture the Confederate capital. To reach Richmond, Burnside marched to Falmouth, near Fredericksburg, Virginia, where he planned to cross the Rappahannock River. The Union troops arrived at Falmouth in December 1862, but Lee's army had got there first and destroyed all the bridges. Burnside ordered army engineers to build floating bridges using **pontoons**, or hollow metal cylinders, but Confederate soldiers shot at the Union engineers while they worked.

Meanwhile, Lee and the rest of his troops dug into the hills above Fredericksburg and readied their artillery. When Burnside finally crossed the Rappahannock River, his forces fought for three days in an unsuccessful effort to take the hills. The Battle of Fredericksburg ended when Burnside retreated across the river.

After so many defeats, northern civilians were becoming restless. They did not like the turn the war had taken, and neither did Lincoln.

HISTORICAL THINKING

1. **READING CHECK** How did McClellan discover Lee's plans at the Battle of Antietam?

2. **SUMMARIZE** How did these two battles reflect broader strategic patterns in the war?

3. **INTERPRET MAPS** Where were most of the Civil War battles fought, in the North or in the South? Explain why.

VOCABULARY

Use each of the following vocabulary words in a sentence that shows an understanding of the term's meaning.

1. cavalry

   The cavalry rode in on their horses to defend their fellow Union soldiers.

2. trench warfare

3. evacuate

4. gunboat

5. ironclad ship

6. mobilize

7. mortality

8. philanthropist

9. civilian

READING STRATEGY
SUMMARIZE

If you haven't done so already, complete your concept cluster of important information discussed in this chapter. Create at least four content clusters and summarize the information in each one. Then answer the question.

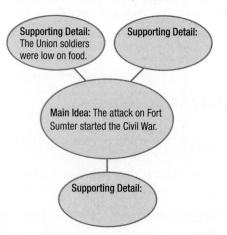

Supporting Detail: The Union soldiers were low on food.

Supporting Detail:

Main Idea: The attack on Fort Sumter started the Civil War.

Supporting Detail:

10. What was life like for a typical soldier in the Union or Confederate army?

MAIN IDEAS

Answer the following questions. Support your answers with evidence from the chapter.

11. How did the call for soldiers affect the states on the border between the North and the South? **LESSON 1.1**

12. Why did the first battle of the Civil War take place near Manassas, Virginia? **LESSON 1.2**

13. What new technological advances in weapons were introduced during the Civil War? **LESSON 2.1**

14. Who made up about half of the men who enlisted in the war on both sides? **LESSON 2.1**

15. What did Sally Tompkins contribute to the war effort? **LESSON 2.2**

16. Why did most of the fighting in the Civil War take place in the Confederate states? **LESSON 3.1**

17. Why did General Grant want to capture the railroads at Corinth, Mississippi? **LESSON 3.3**

18. What did Lee's troops do before Union troops arrived at Falmouth? **LESSON 3.4**

HISTORICAL THINKING

Answer the following questions. Support your answers with evidence from the chapter.

19. **MAKE INFERENCES** Why do you think Lincoln sent a message to southern leaders, stating that he would be sending only food, and not ammunition, to Fort Sumter?

20. **DRAW CONCLUSIONS** How did the attack on Fort Sumter make it clear that war was the necessary step to take toward reunification?

21. **COMPARE AND CONTRAST** What advantages did an ironclad ship have over a wooden ship?

22. **MAKE GENERALIZATIONS** Why was General McClellan unwilling to act quickly when leading the Union Army?

23. **SEQUENCE EVENTS** What were the major early battles of the Civil War? Create a time line of the battles in which you indicate their significance.

INTERPRET VISUALS

Look closely at the photograph of Union soldiers taken during the Civil War, and then answer the questions that follow.

24. What do the men in the photo appear to be doing?

25. What does the photo reveal about the lives of soldiers during the Civil War?

ANALYZE SOURCES

Clara Barton not only gathered supplies and clothing for the Union Army, but she also provided nursing care to wounded Union soldiers on many battlefields, including the Battle of Antietam. In this excerpt from one of her journals, Barton describes the danger she put herself in to help a soldier at Antietam. Read the excerpt and answer the question that follows.

> A man lying upon the ground asked for drink—I stooped to give it, and having raised him with my right hand, was holding the cup to his lips with my left, when I felt a sudden twitch of the loose sleeve of my dress—the poor fellow sprang from my hands and fell back quivering in the agonies of death—a ball [bullet] had passed between my body—and the right arm which supported him— cutting through the sleeve, and passing through his chest from shoulder to shoulder.

26. What happened as Barton was giving the soldier a drink?

CONNECT TO YOUR LIFE

27. **ARGUMENT** The Civil War was a terrible conflict, resulting in great loss of life. But, as you'll learn in the next chapter, the war had positive aspects as well, including helping to put an end to slavery. Think about conflicts in your life. Should they have been avoided, or did some good come out of them? Write a paragraph in which you make an argument for or against conflict.

TIPS

- Make a list of the positive and negative outcomes of conflicts you've experienced.

- Determine whether the positives outweighed the negatives, or vice versa.

- State your position on conflict in a topic sentence and support it with evidence from your own experience.

- Conclude your paragraph with a sentence summarizing your position.

TURNING POINTS OF
THE WAR
1863–1865

ESSENTIAL QUESTION
How did the United States transform during the Civil War?

 AMERICAN STORIES ONLINE The Secret Weapon of the South

SECTION 1 **The Emancipation Proclamation**

KEY VOCABULARY
Emancipation Proclamation   enlist   stalemate

SECTION 2 **Americans at War**

KEY VOCABULARY

bond	*habeas corpus*	ration
Conscription Act	Legal Tender Act	scapegoat
draft	quarantine	scurvy
exemption		

SECTION 3 **The Tide Turns**

KEY VOCABULARY

bluff	Gettysburg Address	total war
flotilla	morphine	veteran

SECTION 4 **The War's Aftermath**

KEY VOCABULARY

assassinate	Homestead Act	Reconstruction
casualty	jurisdiction	servitude

AMERICAN GALLERY ONLINE Battlefield Medicine

READING STRATEGY

ANALYZE LANGUAGE USE
When you analyze language use, you note how specific word choices shape the meaning or tone of a text. As you read the chapter, use a graphic organizer like this one to help you analyze how word choices help convey the realities of war.

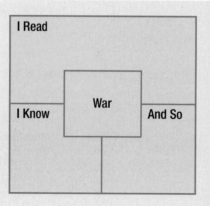

I Read

War

I Know   And So

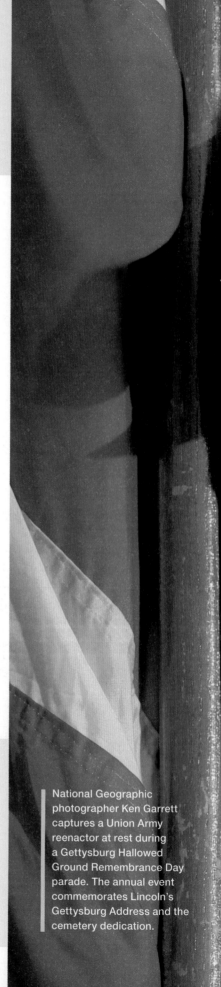

National Geographic photographer Ken Garrett captures a Union Army reenactor at rest during a Gettysburg Hallowed Ground Remembrance Day parade. The annual event commemorates Lincoln's Gettysburg Address and the cemetery dedication.

"It is well that war
is so terrible,
**or we would grow
too fond of it.**"
— General Robert E. Lee

Lincoln Issues the Emancipation Proclamation

In a game of tug-of-war, if both sides pull with equal force, neither wins. In the summer of 1862, the Union and Confederate armies were both tugging equally, and President Lincoln had to find a way to end the standoff.

MAIN IDEA In 1863, Abraham Lincoln issued the Emancipation Proclamation, which freed slaves in states under Confederate control.

GIVING PURPOSE TO THE WAR

Before September 17, 1862, the name "Antietam" referred only to a creek near Sharpsburg, Maryland. But by sunset that day, Antietam would become the name of one of the bloodiest battles ever fought on American soil. Despite battle after battle, the war had reached a **stalemate**, with neither side holding a clear path to a final victory. And still, the body count rose.

In both the North and the South, the loss of so many lives led many to question why Americans were fighting against one another. In the midst of all this suffering, President Lincoln sought to define a greater moral purpose for the war. He realized the Union could not defeat the Confederacy without first destroying slavery.

From the beginning of the war, President Lincoln had faced pressure from abolitionists to end slavery. Although personally opposed to the

CRITICAL VIEWING President Lincoln meets with General McClellan in the general's headquarters after the Battle of Antietam. What do you notice about the flags in the photo?

That on the first day of January, in the year of our Lord one thousand eight hundred and sixty-three, all persons held as slaves within any State or designated part of a State, the people whereof shall then be in rebellion against the United States, shall be then, thenceforward, and forever free.

—from the Emancipation Proclamation, issued by Abraham Lincoln, January 1, 1863

institution, Lincoln was initially reluctant to abolish it outright. Instead, he envisioned a gradual end to slavery, with slaveholders being paid for the loss of their property. Northern Democrats, whose support he needed, opposed abolition. Many of them were sympathetic to the South and to the cause of slavery, even as they remained loyal to the Union. They warned Lincoln against the social, economic, and political fallout of bringing an end to slavery, whether slowly or abruptly.

From a military standpoint, however, the institution of slavery gave the Confederacy an advantage over the Union. Slave labor kept the southern agrarian economy running, which meant more white southern men could join the Confederate Army. Although some members of Lincoln's party urged him to allow African-American men to fight on the side of the Union, the president remained hesitant to offend the border states by doing so. By the summer of 1862, Union troops had secured the slave-owning states of Missouri and Kentucky.

FOREVER FREE

The North had been fighting to preserve the Union, but a clearer moral purpose was emerging from the bloodshed. Five days after the Union victory at Antietam, Lincoln shifted the focus of the war. He issued a decree that emancipated, or freed, all Confederate slaves. Lincoln had purposely waited to submit a draft of the **Emancipation Proclamation** to his cabinet because he knew the timing had to be right for such a dramatic move. The five-page document declared that all slaves in

rebel states were "thenceforward, and forever free." It committed the government and armed forces of the United States to liberate enslaved people in rebel states. The final draft of the proclamation allowed the Union to accept freed slaves into its fighting forces. On January 1, 1863, Lincoln formally issued the Emancipation Proclamation.

At the time Lincoln wrote the proclamation, approximately 4 million enslaved people lived in the United States. However, the proclamation did not apply to slaves in the Union's slave-holding border states of Maryland, Missouri, Kentucky, Delaware, or West Virginia. Lincoln feared that emancipating slaves in all Union-controlled territories might cause border states to join the Confederacy. The Union couldn't afford that loss.

As you have read, the Declaration of Independence states that "all men are created equal." However, according to the Constitution, enslaved African Americans were not equal citizens with equal rights. By issuing the Emancipation Proclamation, Lincoln began the long process of addressing the vast discrepancies between the words of the Declaration of Independence and the realities experienced by African Americans, both enslaved and free.

Slaveholders in Confederate states did not consider themselves bound by U.S. law, and they refused to acknowledge the proclamation. In order to become free, enslaved people still had to escape to Union-controlled territory. About 500,000 African Americans emancipated themselves by escaping. Some young men who did so fled to Union camps and, after 1863, even joined the Union Army. However, many enslaved people in the South knew nothing about the Emancipation Proclamation until the war was over.

HISTORICAL THINKING

1. **READING CHECK** What were the goals of the Emancipation Proclamation?

2. **MAKE INFERENCES** To what extent did the Emancipation Proclamation extend the principles of the Declaration of Independence?

3. **ANALYZE CAUSE AND EFFECT** What factors affected President Lincoln's decision to issue the Emancipation Proclamation?

1.2 Frederick Douglass 1818–1895

"The white man's happiness cannot be purchased by the black man's misery."—Frederick Douglass

Frederick Douglass was deeply familiar with the miseries suffered by black men and women living in slavery. Born to an enslaved mother in 1818, he spent the early years of his childhood living on a plantation in Maryland. There, he endured cold and hunger, and he witnessed other slaves being whipped.

BALTIMORE AND BEYOND

When he was around eight years old, Douglass was sent to live in Baltimore with a shipbuilder named Hugh Auld. Auld's wife Sophia taught the young boy the alphabet. Auld quickly put a stop to the lessons because it was illegal to teach a slave to read. However, the child's passion for learning had been ignited, and he taught himself to read and write.

In 1832, Douglass was sent to work on a plantation, where he was regularly beaten and given little to eat. In his own words, he was "broken in body, soul, and spirit" as "the dark night of slavery closed in upon me." Eventually, he returned to Baltimore to work in the shipyards, where he made his escape in 1838 by fleeing to New York City. After his escape, he changed his name to reduce the risk of being found by slave catchers. Before, he had been called Frederick Augustus Washington Bailey. From this point on, he would call himself Frederick Douglass.

🏛 Art Institute of Chicago

This photograph by Samuel J. Miller shows Frederick Douglass in formal dress, staring forcefully at the viewer. Douglass, the most photographed American of the 19th century, insisted on posing this way. He wanted to reteach people how to see African Americans by replacing the stereotype of the oppressed slave with the portrait of a dignified, proud fellow citizen.

FIGHTER FOR FREEDOM

Douglass settled in New Bedford, Massachusetts, where he worked as a laborer and furthered his education by reading widely. In 1841, he made his first speech describing his life in slavery and calling for an end to the brutal practice. It was the beginning of a lifelong career in public speaking.

Douglass's speeches were so eloquent that some people suspected him of simply pretending to be a former slave. They reasoned that a man born in slavery could never have learned to speak with such brilliance. In many ways, Douglass remade how his fellow citizens viewed African Americans.

To tell his full story, Douglass wrote *Narrative of the Life of Frederick Douglass, an American Slave* in 1845. Publishing the autobiography was a special act of courage because it revealed details about his life that might enable slave catchers to find him. He traveled to Great Britain, where he promoted his book and gave lectures. There, he could speak out without fear of being captured. Over the course of his two-year tour, he gained many new friends and supporters, who helped him purchase his freedom.

Back in the United States, Douglass founded an abolitionist newspaper, wrote two more influential books, and continued to speak out. In 1852, he delivered one of his most famous speeches, "The Meaning of July Fourth for the Negro." In it, he asked why enslaved people should celebrate the country's freedom when they did not benefit from it themselves. "We need the storm, the whirlwind, the earthquake," he thundered. "[The] conscience of the nation must be roused."

When the Civil War broke out, Douglass helped recruit African-American soldiers, and he met with President Abraham Lincoln several times. After the war he held various government posts, including U.S. Marshall for the District of Columbia. He continued promoting civil rights for all Americans until his death in 1895.

CRITICAL VIEWING This painting, *Three Great Abolitionists: A. Lincoln, F. Douglass, J. Brown*, was created by William H. Johnson around 1945. Frederick Douglass stands in the middle, clasping hands with Abraham Lincoln on his left and John Brown on his right. Johnson depicted the three using a "primitive" style of painting, characterized by the work's bright colors and two-dimensional figures. Just behind John Brown, African Americans raise their hands in celebration of the abolitionists. What aspects of Civil War–era African-American life are depicted in the background of the painting?

HISTORICAL THINKING

1. **READING CHECK** Why was Douglass in danger of being enslaved again, even after he became well known?

2. **ANALYZE CAUSE AND EFFECT** How did a few lessons from Sophia Auld change the course of Douglass's life?

3. **DRAW CONCLUSIONS** Why do you think Douglass took the Fourth of July as a theme for a speech on slavery?

1.3 African-American Soldiers

Sometimes in war, people put goals ahead of prejudices. During the Civil War, the U.S. military accepted African-American soldiers into its ranks. Defeating the South had become more important than excluding fellow Americans from military service.

MAIN IDEA In 1863, African Americans began to join U.S. military units and proved to be valuable soldiers for the Union.

AFRICAN AMERICANS JOIN THE FIGHT

When the Civil War first began, many free African-American men rushed to **enlist** in, or join, the Union Army, but they were turned away. A 1792 law barred African Americans from joining the U.S. military. At first, members of Lincoln's administration resisted changing this prohibition. But the Emancipation Proclamation reversed the law with its provision that African-American men "will be received into the armed service of the United States," a critical development that affected the war's outcome.

By the end of the Civil War, African-American soldiers in the U.S. Army totaled nearly 180,000, or about 10 percent of total Union enlistments. Additionally, 19,000 African Americans served in the U.S. Navy. African-American troops faced the same danger and fought with as much commitment as white soldiers, but they were not treated equally.

The army assigned African-American soldiers to segregated units commanded by white officers. African-American soldiers received lower wages than most white soldiers until June 1864, when Congress granted equal pay to African-American military units.

Like all 19th-century American women, African-American women were barred from enlisting in the army. Still, some African-American women, including Harriet Tubman, served as nurses, spies, and scouts. As you have read, Tubman led people to freedom on the Underground Railroad. Tubman also worked as a nurse and scouted behind Confederate lines for the Union's 2nd South Carolina Volunteers. In 1863, she helped free 727 slaves at one time during the Combahee River Raid. That raid was the single largest liberation of slaves in American history.

THE 54TH MASSACHUSETTS REGIMENT

In February 1863, the governor of Massachusetts issued the first formal call for African-American soldiers to join the U.S. Army. He selected the **54th Massachusetts** infantry regiment under the command of Colonel **Robert Gould Shaw**, a white officer. In just two weeks, more than 1,000 African Americans enlisted. Charles and Lewis Douglass, two sons of Frederick Douglass, were among them.

On July 18, 1863, the 54th Massachusetts prepared to storm **Fort Wagner**, which guarded the Port of Charleston, South Carolina. At dusk, Shaw gathered 600 of his men on a narrow strip of sand just outside Fort Wagner's walls. He told them, "I want you to prove yourselves. The eyes of thousands will look on what you do tonight."

As night fell, Shaw led his men over the walls of the fort. They were met by 1,700 Confederate soldiers waiting inside the fort. The brutal hand-to-hand combat that followed took its toll: 281 of the 600 charging soldiers were killed, wounded, or captured. Shaw himself was shot in the chest and died instantly. The 54th lost the battle at Fort Wagner, but its valor, or courage, was beyond

Smithsonian National Gallery of Art, Washington, D.C.

In 1897, Augustus Saint-Gaudens unveiled his 14-year project of honoring the members of the 54th Massachusetts in a bronze relief called the Robert Gould Shaw Memorial. The sculpture depicts the regiment marching down Beacon Street in Boston, on its way to fight Confederate troops in South Carolina. The following year in Paris, Saint-Gaudens exhibited a second version of the memorial made of plaster and covered with bronze metallic paint. Today, the bronze-painted sculpture shown above is housed at the Smithsonian National Gallery of Art in Washington, D.C. The original sculpture is located at the Boston African American National Historic Site on Beacon Street, across the street from the Massachusetts State House. An inscription on the Boston memorial reads, "Together they gave to the nation and the world undying proof that Americans of African descent possess the pride, courage, and devotion of the patriot soldier."

question. For his bravery in the fight, **William H. Carney** became the first African American to receive the Congressional Medal of Honor.

For the next two years, the 54th Massachusetts took part in a number of sieges in South Carolina, Georgia, and Florida. The service and bravery of its members helped to win acceptance for other African-American regiments and solidified their importance in the war effort. Despite increased African-American enlistment, the need for more soldiers in both the North and the South grew.

HISTORICAL THINKING

1. **READING CHECK** Why did the Union wait until after the Emancipation Proclamation to enlist African Americans in the army?

2. **DRAW CONCLUSIONS** Why did the 54th Massachusetts gain great respect in the Union Army despite losing its first battle?

3. **ANALYZE LANGUAGE USE** What made the words Colonel Shaw used with his troops before the battle at Fort Wagner particularly effective?

2.1 Conflicts over the Draft

Imagine being told you have to fight in a war you may not even support. Then consider that your wealthy neighbor is told the same thing but can pay someone else to take his place. During the Civil War, many men realized they were getting a bad deal.

MAIN IDEA In reaction to forced military service during the Civil War, people in both the North and the South staged riots.

MILITARY SERVICE IN THE SOUTH

Waging a civil war required a steady supply of men volunteering to fight as soldiers. At first, men from both the North and the South rushed to sign up. However, as battles wore on, numbers of enthusiastic volunteers began to dwindle. The South was first to acknowledge this problem.

When war first broke out, 100,000 southern men volunteered to fight for the Confederacy. But as their yearlong enlistments were ending, many soldiers returned home to their families and farms. In 1862, the Confederate government, worried that its armies would be short of men as the Union was stepping up its attacks, instituted a **draft**, or a mandatory term of military service. The Confederacy required three years of service for all white men between the ages of 18 and 35.

The draft didn't apply to every man equally, however. Wealthy southerners could pay other men to serve in their places. They could also choose to pay a fee of $500—an amount out of reach for most men. Individuals who owned 20 slaves or more were excused from the draft and their voluntary enlistments altogether.

Military **exemptions**, or releases from the obligation to serve, widened the growing divide between rich and poor in the South. A non-slaveholding man named Jasper Collins remarked that exemptions made the Civil War a "rich man's war, and a poor man's fight." Some soldiers deserted, or left, their units. Desertion remained a major problem for the Confederacy throughout the war.

The gap between rich and poor spread beyond military service. Convinced that greedy merchants were hoarding flour and supplies, women rioted in Richmond, the Confederate capital. They smashed storefronts and stole bread and everything else they could grab, from bacon to boots. One young girl explained, "We are starving . . . each of us will take a loaf of bread. That is little enough for the government to give us after it has taken all our men."

DRAFTING SOLDIERS IN THE NORTH

The North also faced the need for new soldiers. Death, disease, and desertion continually reduced the size of the army, so the Union instituted its own draft in the form of a law called the **Conscription Act** in March 1863. Men between 20 and 45 years of age were liable to be drafted into the military, but, as in the South, they could pay to avoid service for $300—a fee only wealthy families could afford. These exemptions ignited draft riots in cities throughout the Northeast.

On July 13, the attempt to enforce the draft in New York City set off the most destructive civil disturbance in the city's history. Rioters torched government buildings. Police struggled for three days to control the riot. Eventually, Union troops had to rush from the battlefields in Pennsylvania to New York City to aid the police. Union soldiers fired into groups of fellow citizens who were rioting. About 300 people, more than half of them police officers and soldiers, were injured, and more than 100 people died, most of them rioters.

Some whites in New York blamed African Americans for the unrest surrounding the draft riots. In fact, African Americans became **scapegoats**, or individuals or groups blamed for the mistakes or faults of others. Some people claimed that African Americans were responsible for the war and that they were taking jobs away from white workers. Angry white rioters killed many African Americans and destroyed their homes. Such violence prompted many African Americans to flee New York City during the draft riots. They feared for their lives.

In an effort to control riots and curb criticism of the war, the Lincoln administration suspended the writ of *habeas corpus*, or the right of an arrested person to be brought before a judge before going to jail. More than 14,000 people were jailed after being accused of disloyalty to the Union. As a result of the riots, some New York men with families who had no other means of financial support received exemptions from the draft.

HISTORICAL THINKING

1. **READING CHECK** Why did both the North and the South enact military drafts?

2. **ANALYZE LANGUAGE USE** How did Jasper Collins describe the Civil War, and why?

3. **COMPARE AND CONTRAST** In what ways were the Confederate and Union drafts similar, and in what ways were they different?

CRITICAL VIEWING In this photo still from the 2016 film *Free State of Jones*, Newton Knight, center, and his fellow soldiers fight off Confederate troops trying to put down their rebellion. What do you notice about the men in the photo?

Open Rebellion in Mississippi

Newton Knight of Mississippi enlisted in the Confederate Army in July 1861. Angered by the law exempting white men who owned 20 or more slaves, Knight deserted his battalion in October 1862. Back home, he witnessed his fellow southerners suffer abuses at the hands of Confederate soldiers, and he decided to form an opposition group. Other deserting soldiers and escaped slaves joined him, and by late 1863, they had organized into the Jones County Scouts.

The Jones County Scouts eventually numbered more than 1,000. To symbolize their open rebellion, Knight and his men raised the American flag over the Jones County courthouse. They evaded capture by disappearing into the swamps, with local civilians supplying them with weapons, food, and information. Though Confederate officers eventually subdued the rebellion, the Jones County Scouts fought against the Confederacy until it fell.

2.2 Paying for War

Raising money to fight a war is difficult. In 1861, the federal government implemented several financial strategies to support the war effort. The Confederate government struggled with hard economic realities as it tried to do the same.

MAIN IDEA During the Civil War, both the North and the South had to devise new methods of funding their war efforts.

FINANCIAL STRATEGIES

War is incredibly expensive. Even though the Union and the Confederacy were both rich by any international standard, neither had ever supported a large army. Thousands of soldiers needed food, shelter, transportation, uniforms, weapons, ammunition, medical care, and a host of other supplies. As the costs increased, leaders on both sides discovered they had only a few choices: loans, new taxes, and the creation of paper money.

In the North, the federal government issued $2 billion worth of treasury **bonds**. Bonds are certificates offered for sale to the public with the promise that the government will pay the money back at a later date, usually with interest. In August 1861, Congress passed the first federal income tax in U.S. history. This law required citizens who earned more than $600 per year to pay a portion of their income to the government to fund the war.

In 1862, Congress passed the **Legal Tender Act**, an act that replaced currencies of individual banks with one national currency. Because the back of the money was colored green, the national notes were soon called "greenbacks." The Union issued $450 million in greenbacks during the war.

The sudden increase in money in the North had unexpected negative consequences. Greedy manufacturers took advantage of federal funds and urgent demand to produce poorly made and even defective goods. Uniforms sometimes fell apart in the first rain or had no buttons. Some shoemakers produced boots with soles made of cardboard. Not surprisingly, these boots didn't last on long marches. Some suppliers mixed sawdust in with the gunpowder that filled artillery shells. Dishonest businessmen profited from supplying Union troops with spoiled meat. A new word was invented to describe defective war material: *shoddy*.

PRINTING MONEY, SEIZING CROPS

As you have read, the North had a distinct industrial advantage over the agrarian South. It also had the support of the federal government. The South's lack of an industrial base and a strong government made it difficult for the Confederacy to raise funds to pay for war. It tried to borrow money from Britain and France, and it raised taxes to meet expenses. The Confederacy also printed money, but unlike in the North, this strategy resulted in severe inflation: prices for goods increased and the purchasing value of money decreased. The Confederate government also issued war bonds, but most southerners were too poor to buy them. Those wealthy enough to afford bonds soon discovered that inflation was rising faster than the rate of interest on their bonds.

In 1863, the Confederacy passed a law requiring all farmers to give 10 percent of all the crops they raised to the government for use in the war effort. In addition, Confederate citizens were subjected to impressment, a practice that allowed military officers to take anything they thought might be useful to the war effort, including slaves.

Thousands of African Americans were forced to leave their families to perform forced labor for the Confederate military. Many of them rebelled and escaped to the Union lines where they offered their

No matter when or where they are fought, civil wars have devastating consequences for ordinary people. Financial resources of nations are diverted away from supporting citizens in order to pay for war. Young men, and sometimes boys, are forced into military service. Day-to-day lives are disrupted, people are displaced from their homes and countries, and economies are damaged. These characteristics all apply to the civil war that took place after the African country of South Sudan achieved independence in 2011.

During that civil war, government spending on weapons took priority over other responsibilities, thousands of people were killed, and more than 1 million people fled the country. The military limited the movements of those who remained, which meant farmers could not plant crops, trade harvests, or tend livestock. The result was massive starvation and famine by 2016. How might the experience of South Sudanese like the young man shown below be similar to what families in the United States experienced during the Civil War?

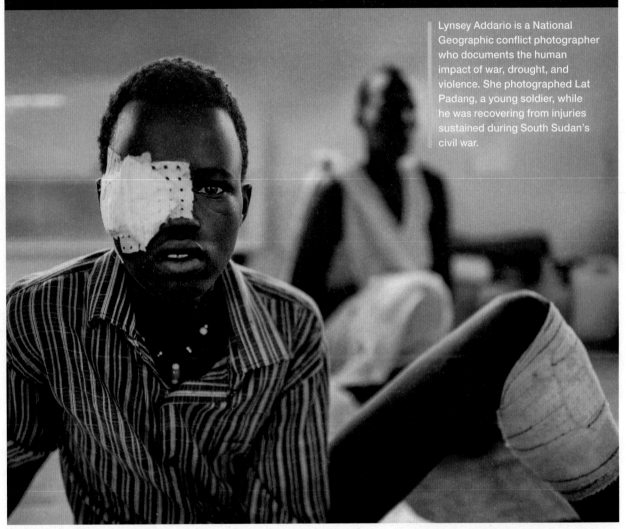

Lynsey Addario is a National Geographic conflict photographer who documents the human impact of war, drought, and violence. She photographed Lat Padang, a young soldier, while he was recovering from injuries sustained during South Sudan's civil war.

labor to the Union. Southern farms and plantations no longer had the labor necessary to grow food and cash crops.

Meanwhile, many southerners watched helplessly as armies stripped their farms of food and livestock. Some farmers grew cotton because it stored well and they thought it would fetch a high price after the war. As a result, the Confederacy devoted land and labor to growing cotton instead of growing food for its hungry citizens.

HISTORICAL THINKING

1. **READING CHECK** What methods did the North and the South use to raise money for the war?

2. **DESCRIBE** In what ways were civilians in the North and the South affected by the war?

3. **COMPARE AND CONTRAST** In terms of its economy and government, what advantages did the North have over the South?

2.3 Wartime Prison Camps

In war, there are always unintended consequences. During the Civil War, neither side was prepared to provide shelter and food for thousands of war prisoners. For those unfortunate enough to be captured, imprisonment could be worse than death.

MAIN IDEA Thousands of soldiers on both sides of the conflict died from exposure and disease in Civil War prison camps.

CRITICAL VIEWING On July 6, 1864, the first 400 Confederate prisoners arrived at the barracks of Camp Rathbun, soon to become the prison camp at Elmira, New York. The barracks could accommodate 6,000 soldiers, but housed more than 10,000 prisoners between 1864 and 1865. Based on details you notice in this photo of the Elmira prison camp, how would you describe the camp and the conditions for prisoners?

PRISONERS IN THE NORTH

In the early years of the Civil War, the Union and the Confederacy exchanged prisoners of war rather than maintaining prisons. Cooperation soon broke down between the two sides, however, and captured soldiers were confined in military prison camps on both sides.

Camp Douglas in Illinois received its first prisoners—approximately 5,500—in February 1862. It would house more than 26,000 Confederate prisoners by the end of the war. Many prisoners were already sick or wounded when they arrived at the camp, and many died while there due to lack of medical care. Poor sanitation, harsh weather conditions, and reduced **rations**, or supplied food, weakened the remaining prisoners. These circumstances left the prisoners susceptible to infectious diseases such as pneumonia and smallpox. Still others died from **scurvy**, a disease linked to malnutrition and a diet lacking in fruits and vegetables. The total death toll has been estimated to be as many as 6,129 men, the greatest mortality statistic of any Union prison.

Alton was another Illinois prison camp. Originally the first state penitentiary built in Illinois, it closed in 1860, but then reopened in 1862 to relieve overcrowding in other Union prisons. Soon Alton became overcrowded as well. When smallpox swept through the camp in 1862 and 1863, authorities built a hospital on an island in the Mississippi River to **quarantine** infected prisoners, or keep them away from those who had not yet contracted the disease.

Elmira prison camp in New York operated from July 6, 1864, until July 11, 1865. Even though it was set up for 6,000 men, more than 10,000 arrived. Because of overflow, some prisoners camped along the nearby Chemung River.

CAMPS IN THE SOUTH

The largest and most notorious Confederate military prison camp was **Andersonville**, located in Georgia. A creek that flowed through the 16-acre compound provided water for the prisoners, but it quickly became polluted with human waste, making it a perfect breeding ground for contagious diseases. The camp, built for 10,000 men, soon held 33,000 prisoners.

Situated on a 54-acre island in the James River near Richmond, Virginia, Belle Isle prison camp operated from 1862 to 1865, housing more than 30,000 men. In 1864, Surgeon De Witt Peters described the horrific conditions experienced by Union prisoners at Belle Isle.

PRIMARY SOURCE

Laboring under such diseases as chronic diarrhea, . . . scurvy, frost bites, general debility, caused by starvation, neglect, and exposure. Many of [the prisoners] had partially lost their reason. They were filthy in the extreme, covered in vermin. . . . nearly all were extremely emaciated [very thin]; so much so that they had to be cared for even like infants.

—from testimony to the U.S. Sanitary Commission, by De Witt Peters, 1864

Approximately 13,000 of the 45,000 Union prisoners eventually held at Andersonville died because of exposure, starvation, and brutality. Northerners were enraged when they heard about the conditions at the military prison. After the war, Andersonville's commander, Captain **Henry Wirz**, was executed for war crimes.

Overall, between 12 and 16 percent of southern and northern prisoners died in military prison camps during the war. The deplorable prison camp conditions, both in the North and in the South, led to prison reform efforts after the war to build safer, more sanitary, and more humane prisons in the United States.

HISTORICAL THINKING

1. **READING CHECK** What were the general conditions of most Civil War prison camps? Provide evidence to support your answer.

2. **ANALYZE LANGUAGE USE** What words did De Witt Peters use to describe Belle Isle prison camp, and why might he have chosen those words?

3. **ANALYZE CAUSE AND EFFECT** What effect did wartime deaths at prison camps have on the U.S. prison system after the war?

3.1 Battles of Vicksburg and Gettysburg

Sometimes you can recall the exact moment when things suddenly change and get either much better or much worse. For Civil War generals, two battles in particular dramatically shifted the war's direction.

> **MAIN IDEA** The battles of Vicksburg and Gettysburg were the key turning points in the Union's eventual victory in the Civil War.

SPLITTING THE CONFEDERACY

In the first months of 1863, the war was not going well for Union generals. In January, after a disastrous defeat at Fredericksburg, Lincoln replaced General **Ambrose Burnside** with General **Joseph Hooker** as commander of the Army of the Potomac. Then in May, Lee's army defeated Hooker's forces near **Chancellorsville**, Virginia. Hooker resigned after the loss and was replaced by General **George Meade**. Lee lost his own most capable commander when Stonewall Jackson was accidentally shot by one of his own soldiers. However, Lee's victory at Chancellorsville is widely considered his greatest of the entire war.

The battle that ensued further south, in Vicksburg, Mississippi, began to change the course of the war for the Union. By 1863, Vicksburg had been a Confederate stronghold for more than a year. Its position allowed the Confederacy to control a wide part of the region from **bluffs**, or cliffs, 200 feet above the Mississippi River. Capturing the city and silencing Confederate guns became a strategic necessity for the Union.

During the early spring of 1863, Union forces commanded by General Grant tried to find a way to take the city from their vantage point on the western bank of the river. But Confederate troops commanded by General **John C. Pemberton** turned them back. Then in early May, Admiral **David Porter**, under Grant's orders, ran a **flotilla**, or small fleet, of gunboats and barges past Confederate forces at Vicksburg under cover of night. Porter used these vessels to ferry Grant's troops across the river south of the city.

From there, Grant's troops marched northeastward before doubling back toward Vicksburg and cutting the city off from the east. In only three weeks, Grant's men marched 180 miles, won 5 battles, and captured 6,000 prisoners. Vicksburg was now surrounded and under siege. Food ran out and the residents began to starve. Pemberton surrendered on July 4, 1863. The Union victory at the **Battle of Vicksburg** gave the Union control of the Mississippi Valley and split the Confederacy in half. It also convinced President Lincoln of Grant's outstanding military ability.

THE TIDE TURNS AT GETTYSBURG

Despite his victory at Chancellorsville, Lee realized that the North's manpower advantage might be wearing down Confederate troops and that a victory on the attack would boost Confederate morale. He decided that his most effective move was to invade the North again. In late June 1863, Lee's troops advanced into Pennsylvania, where they met Meade's troops at the **Battle of Gettysburg**. At first, Lee succeeded in sending the Union troops into retreat. Then, on July 1, reinforcements arrived for both sides, bringing troop numbers to approximately 90,000 for the Union and about 75,000 for the Confederates. Union forces stopped retreating and stationed themselves on **Cemetery Hill**, where the high vantage point gave them a defensive edge.

Photography played a new and important role in the Civil War. This iconic photo, captured by Timothy O'Sullivan in July 1863, shows about 20 of the more than 3,100 fallen Union soldiers after the Battle of Gettysburg. What effect do you think this photo might have had on Americans who saw it in 1863?

On Friday, July 3, hoping to outflank Union forces on Cemetery Hill, Lee ordered Major General **George Pickett** and about 15,000 of his men to attack the Union troops on a plain just below the hill. Lee's strategy proved disastrous. The Union repelled Pickett's charge, killing or wounding more than half of Pickett's troops. The next day, Lee retreated, eventually crossing the Potomac River to Virginia. This retreat marked a turning point in the war. It put the Confederacy on the defensive and the Union in a favorable position for victory.

On November 19, 1863, President Lincoln delivered the **Gettysburg Address** at the battle site to commemorate the loss of so many men and to dedicate a military cemetery there. Throughout his speech, Lincoln referred to the Declaration of Independence directly and to its ideas. His address reinforced the Declaration's principles of equality and freedom for which the war was fought and for which so many died, and were still dying.

HISTORICAL THINKING

1. **READING CHECK** How did the battles of Vicksburg and Gettysburg affect the Civil War?

2. **IDENTIFY PROBLEMS AND SOLUTIONS** What challenges did Grant and his troops face, and how were they eventually able to capture the city of Vicksburg?

3. **EVALUATE** How did the Union's position on Cemetery Hill contribute to its victory at Gettysburg?

3.2 Sherman's March and Grant's Victory

Can you think of someone you know who, when challenged by what looks like impossible odds, simply refuses to give up? Historians attribute this kind of persistence to General Grant, especially in the last year of the Civil War.

MAIN IDEA Grant and his generals brought the full power of the Union Army down on the South in their campaign to capture the Confederate capital.

MARCHING THROUGH GEORGIA

In March 1864, President Lincoln named Ulysses S. Grant, the victor of Vicksburg, as commanding general of the Union Army. Grant immediately put a plan in place to wear down the Confederacy with a series of widespread and relentless attacks. Following a Union victory at Chattanooga, Tennessee, in 1864, Grant sent General William T. Sherman to deliver destruction to the heart of the Confederacy—Atlanta, Georgia, which Sherman captured in September 1864. This was an important feat because Atlanta was a railroad hub and the industrial center of the Confederacy.

The city was also a symbol of Confederate pride and strength. Its fall made even the most loyal southerners doubt that they could win the war. "Since Atlanta," South Carolinian Mary Chesnut wrote in her diary, "I have felt as if . . . we are going to be wiped off the earth."

From Atlanta, Sherman marched 62,000 Union troops through Georgia to Savannah, located on the Atlantic shore. His goal was to destroy southern property, crops, and other supplies. Early in 1865, Sherman and his men left Savannah, burning their way northward to Columbia, South Carolina. From there, they marched into North Carolina, battling Confederate troops before destroying the Fayetteville arsenal. In Bentonville, the Confederacy challenged Sherman for three days, but his troops gained the upper hand.

A **total war** is one in which all rules and laws of war are ignored and all resources are poured into defeating the enemy no matter what the cost. Sherman waged total war against the Confederacy, and his strategy was brutal and destructive. But it did what it was meant to do. It was a blow to southern morale and fighting

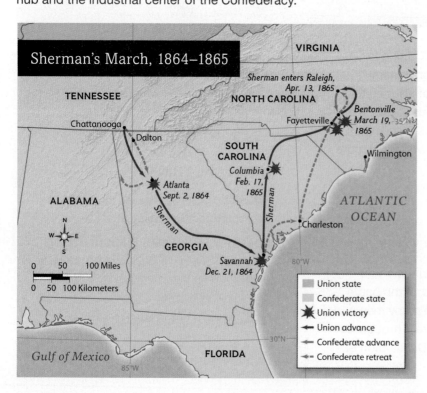

Sherman's March, 1864–1865

VIRGINIA

Sherman enters Raleigh, Apr. 13, 1865

TENNESSEE

NORTH CAROLINA

Chattanooga

Dalton

Fayetteville

Bentonville
March 19,
1865

SOUTH CAROLINA

Wilmington

Columbia
Feb. 17,
1865

Atlanta
Sept. 2, 1864

ALABAMA

ATLANTIC OCEAN

Charleston

GEORGIA

Savannah
Dec. 21, 1864

Gulf of Mexico

FLORIDA

0   50   100 Miles
0   50   100 Kilometers

- Union state
- Confederate state
- ✹ Union victory
- ← Union advance
- ← Confederate advance
- ←- Confederate retreat

AMERICAN PLACES

Savannah Historic District
Savannah, Georgia

The Savannah Historic District is a National Historic Landmark. James Oglethorpe founded the city in 1733 when Georgia was a British colony. Savannah's distinctive 18th- and 19th-century architecture is reflected in its numerous historic homes, gardens, and monuments. General Sherman used the Greene-Meldrim House, shown here, as a base of operations between 1864 and 1865. The house was built in 1853 in the Gothic Revival architectural style.

capacity. It led to a feeling in the North that the Union was winning the war and so helped with President Lincoln's reelection in November 1864.

Sherman and his troops spared the city of Savannah instead of burning it as they did Atlanta. Why? There are a number of theories, some more plausible than others. One is that Sherman found Savannah too beautiful to burn. Another is that he was lenient because city leaders surrendered before he could enter the city, agreeing they would not put up a fight if he spared life and property. Perhaps the strongest theory is that Savannah had a large port that could prove very useful to the Union.

GRANT FACES LEE

General Grant was pleased with Sherman's success in the South, and he became even more determined to capture Richmond, Virginia, the Confederate capital. The first large battle of Grant's campaign was the **Battle of the Wilderness**, fought in a heavily wooded area west of Fredericksburg and north of Richmond. The armies engaged in battle for two days with heavy casualties, especially on the Union side. Grant refused to retreat. Instead, he moved his army farther south. Lee followed him. On May 8, 1864, Grant attacked Lee's troops near **Spotsylvania**, beginning a battle that raged for 12 days. The Union's Army of the Potomac lost 18,000 men at the Battle of Spotsylvania; the Confederates lost

12,000. In less than three weeks, Grant had lost 33,000 men. On May 31, Lee and Grant collided again at **Cold Harbor**, where Grant's forces were defeated with heavy losses. The Union lost about 13,000 troops; the Confederates lost only 2,500 or fewer.

In 1865, Grant's forces broke through the last line of Richmond's defenses, and the city fell on April 3. Confederate troops and government officials fled Richmond, setting fire to parts of the city as they left to prevent Union troops from using it for shelter and supplies. The Union took control of what was left of the city. The Confederate capital was captured. President Lincoln traveled to Richmond a few days later to see the evidence of this significant Union victory for himself.

HISTORICAL THINKING

1. **READING CHECK** What was Grant's strategy in the South?

2. **ANALYZE LANGUAGE USE** Mary Chesnut used a figurative expression to describe how she felt about the fall of Atlanta. How did she articulate how she felt about the war? Use evidence from the text to support your answer.

3. **MAKE PREDICTIONS** What effect could you predict the Union capture of Richmond would have on the Civil War's outcome?

3.3 Lincoln's Vision

Politicians and public officials use speeches to express their views on public policy. During his political career, Abraham Lincoln delivered a number of speeches, several of which became some of the most formative speeches in U.S. history.

For nearly 100 years, historians believed that no photos existed of Lincoln delivering the Gettysburg Address. But in 1952, National Archives employee Josephine Cobb was examining a crowd shot taken by photographer Mathew Brady at Gettysburg on November 19, 1863. She had the photo enlarged and examined where she thought Lincoln might have been standing in that crowd. And right there, in the middle of the crowd, she identified the out-of-focus—but unmistakable image—of Abraham Lincoln delivering the Gettysburg Address. You can see this rare photo below.

Lincoln was not known as a speaker gifted with a captivating voice or dramatic delivery. Rather, the force of his speeches came from the words themselves. For example, the Gettysburg Address is just 272 words long, and it took only around three minutes for Lincoln to deliver it. But in this succinct address, Lincoln reminded Americans of the foundation on which the United States was built and on which it still rested. Quite intentionally, he framed his words around the principles of liberty and equality as set forth in the Declaration of Independence.

CRITICAL VIEWING Locate Abraham Lincoln in the photograph below. What do you notice about Lincoln's position in the crowd and how it differs from the ways in which the president is protected in public today?

Primary Source: Speech
The Gettysburg Address, by Abraham
Lincoln, November 19, 1863

As president, Lincoln used the opportunity of a battle site dedication to appeal to his fellow citizens to take up "unfinished work" of those who had died. He begins by situating his words in time by using the phrase "fourscore and seven" as a way of expressing the number 87. The word *score* means 20, so *fourscore* equals 80. By referring to 87 years ago, Lincoln asks his listeners to remember the American Revolution and the nation's founding principles of liberty and equality.

CONSTRUCTED RESPONSES
What did Lincoln mean by "testing whether that nation or any nation so conceived and so dedicated can long endure"?

What action did Lincoln propose as the best way to honor those who had died at Gettysburg?

Fourscore and seven years ago our fathers brought forth on this continent a new nation, conceived in liberty and dedicated to the proposition that all men are created equal.

Now we are engaged in a great civil war, testing whether that nation or any nation so conceived and so dedicated can long endure. We are met on a great battlefield of that war. We have come to dedicate a portion of that field as a final resting-place for those who here gave their lives that that nation might live. It is altogether fitting and proper that we should do this.

But in a larger sense, we cannot dedicate, we cannot consecrate, we cannot hallow this ground. The brave men, living and dead who struggled here have consecrated it far above our poor power to add or detract. The world will little note nor long remember what we say here, but it can never forget what they did here.

It is for us the living rather to be dedicated here to the unfinished work which they who fought here have thus far so nobly advanced. It is rather for us to be here dedicated to the great task remaining before us—that from these honored dead we take increased devotion to that cause for which they gave the last full measure of devotion—that we here highly resolve that these dead shall not have died in vain, that this nation under God shall have a new birth of freedom, and that government of the people, by the people, for the people shall not perish from the earth.

Primary Source: Speech
from Second Inaugural Address, by Abraham Lincoln,
March 4, 1865

When Lincoln delivered this speech in March 1865, the North was close to victory. Lincoln did not speak of happiness, nor did he gloat about the South's impending defeat. Instead, he spoke about his sadness over the loss of life during the war. Just over a month later, the president who had saved the Union would be assassinated.

CONSTRUCTED RESPONSE What was Lincoln referring to when he called on Americans "to bind up the nation's wounds"?

With malice toward none, with charity for all, with firmness in the right as God gives us to see the right, let us strive on to finish the work we are in, to bind up the nation's wounds, to care for him who shall have borne the battle and for his widow and his orphan, to do all which may achieve and cherish a just and lasting peace among ourselves and with all nations.

SYNTHESIZE & WRITE

1. **REVIEW** Review what you have learned about the events leading up to Lincoln's address at Gettysburg and his Second Inaugural Address.

2. **RECALL** On your own paper, write the main themes that emerge from the Gettysburg Address and this excerpt from Lincoln's Second Inaugural Address.

3. **CONSTRUCT** Construct a topic sentence that answers this question: What was President Lincoln's vision for the United States after the Civil War, and how did he try to persuade Americans to support that vision?

4. **WRITE** Using evidence from this chapter and the documents, write a persuasive paragraph that supports your topic sentence in Step 3.

3.4 Appomattox

Forgiving a sibling or a friend after a fight is hard to do. Generals Grant and Lee had a difficult task in front of them when they met to end the war. Grant wondered: Was it better to forgive former enemies, or punish them further?

MAIN IDEA The Civil War ended with the surrender of the Confederacy at a simple ceremony in Virginia.

SURRENDER AT LAST

By the beginning of 1865, war had nearly completely devastated the South. Sherman continued to march through the Carolinas, burning homes, barns, and crops. Knowing the end was near, Confederate president Jefferson Davis sent his vice president, **Alexander Stephens**, to meet with Lincoln on February 3, 1865. His goal was to negotiate peace and bring the war to an end. Not interested in negotiating, Lincoln demanded that the Confederacy surrender completely. Stephens refused, and the war continued.

Meanwhile, General Lee finally had to abandon his defense of Richmond after the Confederate government fled and Union troops marched in to take over the city. But Lee still had hopes of turning the situation around. He tried to move his forces south in order to join other Confederate forces in North Carolina. Lee's army never reached that goal. Union cavalry surrounded Lee and his troops near the Virginia town of **Appomattox Court House**, halting his progress. Following a brief battle, Lee agreed to surrender.

On April 9, 1865, Lee met Grant in the front room of Wilmer McLean's home in Appomattox Court House. Grant arrived in his muddy field uniform, while Lee wore his full dress uniform. Lee accepted Grant's terms of surrender. All Confederate officers and soldiers were pardoned. They could keep their private property, including their horses, which they would need for spring planting. Confederate officers were also allowed to keep their side arms. Grant made sure that Lee's

men, many of whom were starving, would receive Union rations. Grant told his officers: "The war is over. The Rebels are our countrymen again."

The Confederacy had fought with courage and endured almost unimaginable hardships. But courage was not enough to defeat the resources and manpower of the far more powerful industrial North. The Union prevailed.

COSTS OF THE WAR

In dollars and cents, the Union spent more than $3 billion on the war; the Confederacy spent about $1 billion. But these amounts of money for military expenditures barely compared to the massive loss of life. Roughly 620,000 men had died: 360,000 Union soldiers and 260,000 Confederate soldiers, the most American lives lost in any conflict to date.

Two out of every three deaths occurred not from battle, but from disease. The most common diseases in army camps were typhoid fever, smallpox, measles, diarrhea, pneumonia, malaria, and tuberculosis. Army surgeons relieved the pain of sick and wounded soldiers by prescribing millions of doses of a highly addictive medication called **morphine**. Morphine worked well to ease wounded soldiers' pain, but many Civil War **veterans**, or people who had served in the military, became addicted to it.

The war had direct economic consequences for American families. The loss of fathers or sons often meant the loss of family breadwinners. Countless wounded veterans were unable to work, and families fell into poverty. Many homes, farms,

CRITICAL VIEWING To commemorate the centennial anniversary of the end of the Civil War, the National Geographic Society commissioned Tom Lovell to paint *Surrender at Appomattox*. Lee, dressed in gray, signs the surrender terms while Grant and his officers look on. Their meeting was somber, but friendly. Upon signing, Lee is reported to have said, "This will have a very happy effect on my army." Based on details you notice in the painting, how did Grant treat Lee during the signing?

and businesses, particularly in the South, had been destroyed. Lives, careers, and communities had to be rebuilt.

Even after financial costs were recovered, the emotional toll of such intense loss persisted for generations. The war itself became the subject or backdrop for art and literature. In 1862, Louisa May Alcott served as a nurse in Washington, D.C., during the war. She was sent home when she contracted a serious disease called typhoid from the unsanitary conditions in the hospital. In 1863, Alcott published *Hospital Sketches*, a collection of stories crafted from her letters home about her hospital experiences. Thirty-two years later Stephen Crane published *The Red Badge of Courage*, a novel based on the life of Private Henry Fleming. Crane was not yet born when the war broke out, but his novel captured the horrific details of battlefield experiences nonetheless. That Crane's novel still resonated with American readers three decades after the war ended speaks to the profound effect the Civil War had on the country.

HISTORICAL THINKING

1. **READING CHECK** What were the terms of surrender that Grant delivered to Lee?

2. **ANALYZE LANGUAGE USE** What do you think Grant was saying about what it means to be an American when he stated, "The war is over. The Rebels are our countrymen again"?

3. **FORM AND SUPPORT OPINIONS** Explain whether you think the financial losses or personal losses of the war were greater, and support your opinion with information from the text.

3.5 ⊙ Ball's Bluff National Cemetery Leesburg, Virginia

The need to lay soldiers to rest respectfully after battle led to the creation of national cemeteries during the Civil War. These sites honor the bravery and sacrifice of the men and women who have served their country throughout its history.

In 1861, a Union raiding party crossed the Potomac River at Ball's Bluff in Leesburg, Virginia. They tangled with a Confederate patrol, and a skirmish began, moving down the steep slope of the bluff and into the river. Many soldiers drowned, dragged under the water by the weight of their heavy gear. Using their geographic advantage, Confederate troops shot down at Union soldiers from the top of the bluff, causing even more fatalities. To the horror of President Lincoln, the bodies of many Union soldiers washed up on the shores of the Potomac in Washington, D.C., after the battle. The embarrassing and devastating defeat prompted Congress to form a committee to investigate Union losses, the treatment of wounded soldiers, illegal trade with Confederate states, and military contracts.

More than 50 of the Union soldiers who fell at Ball's Bluff were buried near the battle site, at what would become a national cemetery. In what ways does a cemetery like Ball's Bluff serve as a shrine to the fallen?

CRITICAL VIEWING The Ball's Bluff National Cemetery is one of the nation's smallest military cemeteries. Established in 1865 as the burial place for Union soldiers killed at Ball's Bluff, only the name of one soldier is known: James Allen, a Union soldier and member of Company H, 15th Massachusetts Infantry. What does the unique perspective of this photo by National Geographic photographer Ken Garrett reveal about the cemetery?

4.1 Landmark Amendments and Terrible Loss

The end of slavery was a great moral victory for the nation. But it became a source of rage for some—rage that triggered violence and terrible loss.

MAIN IDEA Abraham Lincoln planned to rebuild the South and restore the Union, but others would have to follow through for him.

SLAVERY IS ABOLISHED

In January 1865, three months before Lee would surrender, Congress passed the **13th Amendment**, which prohibited slavery in the United States. As with all amendments, it was sent to the states for ratification. By December 1865, three-quarters of the states had approved it, and the 13th Amendment was added to the Constitution.

Slavery was over. Georgia, a former Confederate state, provided the final vote needed for ratification. The amendment states, "Neither slavery nor involuntary **servitude** [being enslaved] . . . shall exist within the United States, or any place subject to their **jurisdiction** [the authority to enforce laws within a given area]." The 13th Amendment abolished slavery, but African Americans were not guaranteed full equality under the law until 1868, with the ratification of the **14th Amendment**. African-American men received voting rights when the **15th Amendment** was ratified in 1870.

Outlawing the practice of slavery was a giant step toward equality and justice. However, discrimination and racism did not magically disappear with the passage of the 13th, 14th, and 15th Amendments. African Americans were frequent victims of violence at the hands of whites. With few options for employment, many southern African Americans went back to work on plantations, where they earned poverty-level wages. Further, African Americans could not depend on a legal system that still favored whites.

LINCOLN'S ASSASSINATION

After the Civil War ended, Lincoln's primary goal was, once again, reuniting the nation. He recognized that integrating newly freed African Americans into society and rebuilding the physical and social structures of the South would be a delicate operation. He planned to implement measures to remedy the injustices of slavery, bring the former Confederate states back into the Union, and rebuild the South.

These plans became known as **Reconstruction**. Lincoln knew he would have to act with careful diplomacy in order to carry out these measures without inflaming already volatile racial and sectional tensions. However, he realized some issues would cause an uproar, no matter the diplomacy used in proposing them. For example, on April 11, 1865, he suggested that some African-American men should have the right to vote. As you have read, that right would not be guaranteed for another five years.

Just three days later on April 14, 1865, **John Wilkes Booth**, an actor and Confederate sympathizer, fatally shot Lincoln at Ford's Theatre in Washington, D.C., as the president watched a play. Audience members rushed the president from Ford's Theatre to the Petersen House, a boarding house across the street. Lincoln never regained consciousness, and he died the next morning. For the first time in U.S. history, a sitting president had been **assassinated**, or murdered for political reasons.

On April 21, Lincoln's funeral train began a somber journey to Springfield, Illinois, where he had lived before becoming president. Thousands of Americans lined the train's route to mourn. Lincoln was buried on May 4, 1865.

Vice President **Andrew Johnson** succeeded Lincoln as president. Johnson favored Lincoln's Reconstruction policies, but he lacked Lincoln's leadership skills. Also, Republican congressmen distrusted him because he was a former Democrat and former slaveholder.

Johnson could not stop Congress from enacting harsh penalties on the southern states. In particular, the **Radical Republicans** believed the former Confederacy should be punished for secession and war. Their treatment of the South caused long-standing resentment and discontent among many southerners.

Lincoln's steady leadership had brought an end to the Civil War. Following his death, the nation struggled to regain a true sense of unity as it rebuilt without the leader who had saved it. The far-reaching consequences of his loss were yet to be realized. The morning he died, Lincoln's Secretary of War, Edwin M. Stanton, is reported to have said either, "Now he belongs to the ages" or "Now he belongs to the angels." For Americans in 1865, both statements rang true.

🏛 Chicago History Museum

After Lincoln was shot, he was taken to a small bedroom in the Petersen House and laid in this bed, diagonally, because he was so tall. Today, you can see Lincoln's death bed at the Chicago History Museum. *The Last Hours of Abraham Lincoln,* painted by Alonzo Chappel in 1868, hangs above the bed. It dramatizes Lincoln's last hours, features Mary Todd Lincoln weeping on his chest, and includes many of the people who visited Lincoln before he died.

HISTORICAL THINKING

1. **READING CHECK** How did Lincoln plan to reunite and heal the nation after the Civil War?

2. **ANALYZE LANGUAGE USE** What do you think is meant by the phrase "or any place subject to their jurisdiction" in the 13th Amendment?

3. **EVALUATE** In what ways did Lincoln's assassination affect Reconstruction and attitudes in the South?

4.2 The Legacy of the War

The Civil War was one of the most formative events in American history. Four years of battle and loss resulted in both positive and negative consequences.

MAIN IDEA The Civil War left a legacy of unresolved economic and political issues that would have long-lasting effects on the United States.

REBUILDING THE NATION

Conditions in the North and the South after the Civil War contrasted dramatically. The devastated South struggled to recover from the financial and physical destruction it suffered during the war. Its economy had been based on growing and exporting crops for cash. Invading armies had burned down farms and destroyed crops and fields, and, at least initially, few resources existed to rebuild them. The North's naval blockade of southern exports resulted in plantation owners' financial ruin. The biggest economic blow, however, was the abolition of slavery and the resulting loss of "free" labor. Southern plantation owners would have to find other ways to profit from agriculture as the South rebuilt.

Although the North had suffered some destruction and hundreds of thousands of **casualties**, or dead or injured men, it emerged from the war more prosperous than ever. The war effort had led to a rapid growth of the North's industrial economy. Manufacturing had expanded because of the need to build products necessary to fight the war, from guns to railroad cars to uniforms and shoes. Many northern business owners grew rich on wartime profits and the industrial boom that followed. Even northern agriculture prospered during and after the war, as the Union's farms began using more farm machinery to grow and harvest crops with fewer farmers in the fields. In fewer than 50 years after the Civil War, the expansion of primarily northern manufacturing, mining, and transportation made the United States the world's leading industrial nation.

LAND GRANTS AND HOMESTEADS

The Civil War achieved two significant goals: the preservation of the Union and the abolition of slavery. The United States banned slavery later than some other countries. Great Britain had outlawed slavery throughout its empire, including the British West Indies, with the 1833 **Slavery Abolition Act**. In the Western Hemisphere, many South American countries had already abolished slavery as well, though Brazil didn't outlaw the institution until 1888.

Another result of the war was the greatly expanded power and size of the federal government. The balance of power shifted from individual states and regions to Washington, D.C. The federal government was quick to use its power, and one of its goals was to encourage the settlement and development of the West. The government had already begun to put some of its planned programs in motion even before the end of the Civil War.

The **Morrill Act**, signed into law by President Lincoln on July 2, 1862, provided each state with 30,000 acres of federal land grants for each member of its congressional delegation. The land was then sold to the states, and the proceeds were used to fund public colleges that focused on agriculture and the mechanical arts. These land grants funded 69 colleges, including Cornell University, the Massachusetts Institute of Technology, and the University of Wisconsin at Madison.

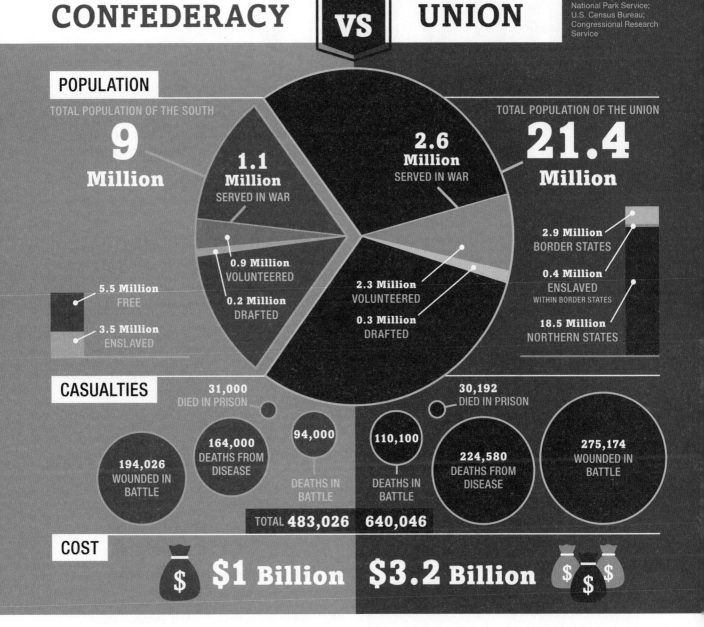

CIVIL WAR BY THE NUMBERS

CONFEDERACY VS UNION

Sources:
National Park Service;
U.S. Census Bureau;
Congressional Research
Service

POPULATION

TOTAL POPULATION OF THE SOUTH

9 Million

1.1 Million SERVED IN WAR

0.9 Million VOLUNTEERED

0.2 Million DRAFTED

5.5 Million FREE

3.5 Million ENSLAVED

2.6 Million SERVED IN WAR

2.3 Million VOLUNTEERED

0.3 Million DRAFTED

TOTAL POPULATION OF THE UNION

21.4 Million

2.9 Million BORDER STATES

0.4 Million ENSLAVED WITHIN BORDER STATES

18.5 Million NORTHERN STATES

CASUALTIES

31,000 DIED IN PRISON

194,026 WOUNDED IN BATTLE

164,000 DEATHS FROM DISEASE

94,000 DEATHS IN BATTLE

30,192 DIED IN PRISON

110,100 DEATHS IN BATTLE

224,580 DEATHS FROM DISEASE

275,174 WOUNDED IN BATTLE

TOTAL **483,026** **640,046**

COST

$ **$1 Billion** **$3.2 Billion** $ $ $

The **Homestead Act**, signed into law on May 20, 1862, set in motion a program of public land grants to small farmers. It provided that any adult citizen who headed a family could qualify for a grant of 160 acres of public land by paying a small registration fee and living on the land continuously for five years.

The main task of the country's political leaders, however, was, in Lincoln's words, "to bind up the nation's wounds." Many years would pass before the nation would recover politically, economically, and socially. This struggle would be especially difficult for the South.

HISTORICAL THINKING

1. **READING CHECK** What were the major economic and political impacts of the Civil War on American life?

2. **COMPARE AND CONTRAST** How did the aftermath of the Civil War affect the southern agricultural economy and northern industrial economy differently?

3. **ANALYZE CAUSE AND EFFECT** What effect did the land grants have on education and farming?

REVIEW

VOCABULARY

Use each of the following vocabulary words in a sentence that shows an understanding of the term's meaning.

1. stalemate
   Since they could not agree on a single point, their argument ended in a stalemate.

2. exemption

3. quarantine

4. conscription

5. scapegoat

6. bluff

7. Homestead Act

8. servitude

READING STRATEGY
ANALYZE LANGUAGE USE

If you haven't done so already, complete your graphic organizer to analyze how word choices throughout the text help convey the realities of war. Then answer the question.

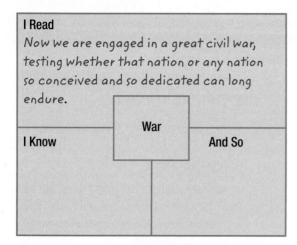

| I Read |
| Now we are engaged in a great civil war, testing whether that nation or any nation so conceived and so dedicated can long endure. |

War

| I Know | | And So |

9. How do the words used by President Lincoln in the Gettysburg Address help you understand the impact of the Civil War on the United States?

MAIN IDEAS

Answer the following questions. Support your answers with evidence from the chapter.

10. What major change in the war led to Lincoln's decision to issue the Emancipation Proclamation? **LESSON 1.1**

11. What challenges did the members of the 54th Massachusetts face as new members of the U.S. Army? **LESSON 1.3**

12. What provision of the 1863 Conscription Act was most responsible for sparking draft riots throughout the Northeast? **LESSON 2.1**

13. What measures did the North and the South take to pay for the war? **LESSON 2.2**

14. What problems did prison camps in the North and the South share? **LESSON 2.3**

15. Why are the Union victories at Vicksburg and Gettysburg considered turning points in the war? **LESSON 3.1**

16. What was the main military goal of Sherman's march through Georgia? **LESSON 3.2**

17. What were the main provisions of Grant's terms of surrender? **LESSON 3.4**

18. In what ways did Lincoln's assassination affect the treatment of the South during Reconstruction? **LESSON 4.1**

19. How did the federal government support its goal of expansion into western states after the war? **LESSON 4.2**

HISTORICAL THINKING

Answer the following questions. Support your answers with evidence from the chapter.

20. **MAKE CONNECTIONS** In what ways did having a strong central government help Lincoln wage war against the Confederacy?

21. **MAKE INFERENCES** How did the battles fought during Sherman's march through the South reflect broader struggles during the war?

22. **EVALUATE** How and why did the war become a war to end slavery?

23. **DRAW CONCLUSIONS** What is the main reason Lincoln chose Grant to lead the Union armies after the Battle of Vicksburg?

24. **SYNTHESIZE** How did the Civil War change the United States?

25. **FORM AND SUPPORT OPINIONS** What was the most important factor in the Union victory over the Confederacy? Support your opinion with evidence from the text.

26. **SEQUENCE EVENTS** What amendments followed the Civil War, and what meaning did they have? Create an annotated time line to illustrate your answer.

ANALYZE SOURCES

In his 1863 political cartoon, Thomas Nast imagines what impact emancipation would have on African Americans. Look closely at the cartoon and then answer the following questions.

27. How is slavery depicted in this cartoon?

28. How is emancipation depicted in this cartoon?

29. Why does Nast include Lincoln in this cartoon?

30. How might Americans in the North and the South have viewed this cartoon differently? Explain.

CONNECT TO YOUR LIFE

31. **NARRATIVE** Think about the events that became turning points in the Civil War. Connect your knowledge about this time in history to your own life. Have there been any turning points in your life? Do you expect there to be any turning points in your life in the future? Write a paragraph in which you compare turning points on a national scale like those in the Civil War to more personal turning points like those you've experienced or expect to experience in your life.

TIPS

- Make a time line of principal turning points in the Civil War. Then make a time line of possible turning points in your own life.

- Use two or three vocabulary terms from the chapter in your narrative.

- Conclude the narrative with a comment that ties Civil War turning points to your own life.

RECONSTRUCTION
AND THE NEW SOUTH

1865–1877

ESSENTIAL QUESTION

In what ways did Reconstruction both succeed and fail?

READING STRATEGY

DRAW CONCLUSIONS

When you draw conclusions, you make a judgment based on what you have read. You analyze the facts, make inferences, and use your own experiences to form your judgment. As you read the chapter, use a diagram like this one to draw conclusions about the impact of Reconstruction on American society.

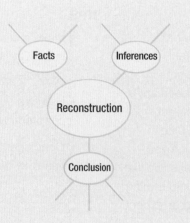

Facts   Inferences

Reconstruction

Conclusion

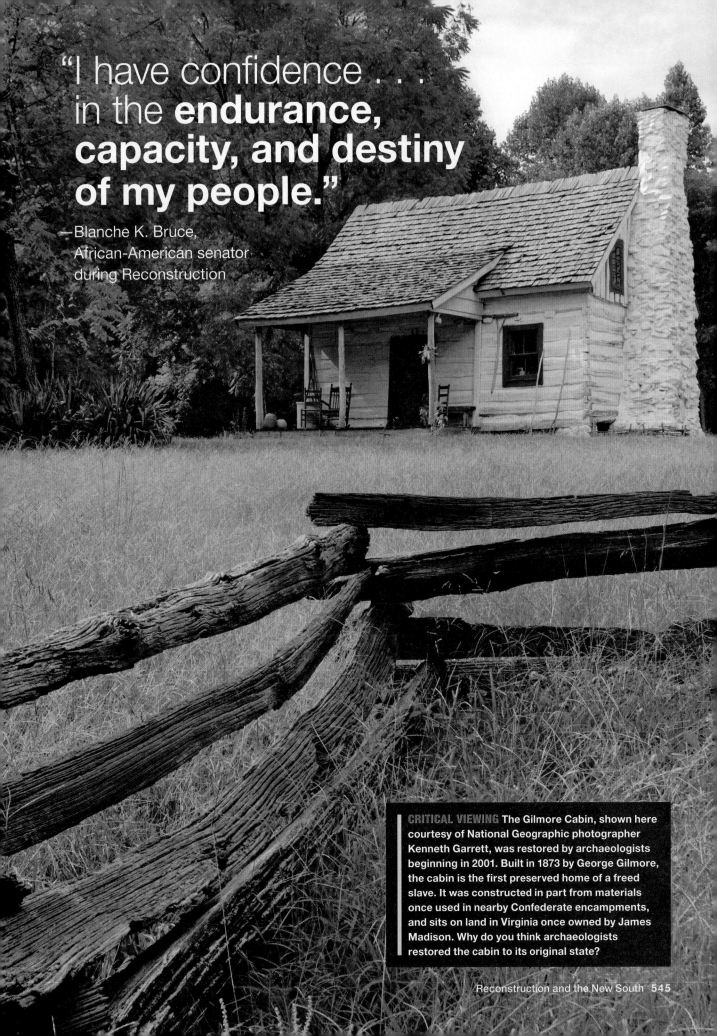

"I have confidence . . . in the **endurance, capacity, and destiny of my people.**"

—Blanche K. Bruce, African-American senator during Reconstruction

CRITICAL VIEWING The Gilmore Cabin, shown here courtesy of National Geographic photographer Kenneth Garrett, was restored by archaeologists beginning in 2001. Built in 1873 by George Gilmore, the cabin is the first preserved home of a freed slave. It was constructed in part from materials once used in nearby Confederate encampments, and sits on land in Virginia once owned by James Madison. Why do you think archaeologists restored the cabin to its original state?

CRITICAL VIEWING This mid-1800s photograph of enslaved women and children outside their southern cabin is unique in a significant way: it shows a young woman reading aloud to the group. How might the ability to read and write have affected the life of a slave before and after the Civil War?

FREEDOM READERS

BY FRAN DOWNEY

Vice President and Publisher,
National Geographic *Explorer* Magazine

African rebellion leaders Nat Turner, Gabriel Prosser,
Touissant L'Ouverture, and Denmark Vesey shared
one important power: literacy. Enslaved people
realized the value of reading, and many risked
everything—including their lives—to learn.
They were America's freedom readers.

When slavery first began in the colonies, slave owners often encouraged their slaves to read. In fact, literacy became a way for slave owners to assert control over them. Slave owners wanted to convert enslaved Africans to Christianity in order to "civilize" them, and believed that all Christians needed to be able to read the Bible. Helping his or her slaves learn to read was a critical part of a slave owner's "civilization" plan. Some slave owners also used scripture to justify the concept of slavery, believing the Bible implied it was acceptable to enslave people.

Many enslaved people had a very different goal in mind as they learned to read and write. They saw it as a way to resist bondage. Like breaking tools, working slowly, and pretending to be ill, learning to read and write was a passive way for the enslaved to revolt against the enslaver. Literate African Americans could learn about the larger world. They could read newspapers, plan escapes and rebellions, and send messages. A few, whose voices you have heard throughout this book, even wrote slave narratives, which exposed the evils of slavery. Instead of a lock that kept them shackled, enslaved people saw literacy as a way to unlock the chains of slavery.

Over time, slave owners began to fear the potential power of literate free and enslaved African Americans. States like North Carolina passed laws that severely punished African-American students and those who helped them. These laws forced African Americans to get inventive. Some slaves tricked their owners into teaching them. Others watched and listened as white children were taught to read, and practiced in secret.

Nat Turner's Rebellion in 1831, as represented by this illustration, panicked the South and prompted legislation that prevented the education, movement, and assembly of enslaved people.

EARLY LAWS AND LITERACY

Southern lawmakers began to outlaw African-American literacy as early as 1740. This date is no coincidence. A year earlier, 20 slaves in South Carolina tried to escape to Florida. This unsuccessful uprising, known as the Stono Rebellion, resulted in the deaths of 60 people. Believing that those who planned the rebellion had used reading and writing to communicate, lawmakers outlawed teaching slaves to write. This law did not impose a penalty on enslaved African Americans, who were considered property. Rather, it punished free people who taught slaves with a fine of 100 pounds.

In the New England Colonies, where slavery was less common, literacy rates among enslaved African Americans were higher. In the 1770s, literate slaves read that many colonists wanted to break from Britain. Believing these revolutionary leaders would be sympathetic to their cause, literate slaves in Massachusetts wrote to the legislature to request their freedom. Enslaved African Americans in Connecticut did the same about five years later. While neither legislature granted the slaves' request, one by one, northern states slowly began to end slavery in the 1780s.

After the American Revolution, African Americans continued to occupy the same social, economic, and political positions in the Northeast. But they began to create institutions to advance their rights and develop communities without racial discrimination. For example, Richard Allen, Absalom Jones, and others founded the African Methodist Episcopal Church in 1816. Additionally, some northern states passed laws to educate their newly emancipated fellow citizens. The state of New York did not abolish slavery until 1827. As a result, the New York African Free School, founded in 1787, became a haven for free African-American students and enslaved people whose owners allowed them to attend.

UNIVERSAL LITERACY?

One of the premises of the new republican government was that the nation's very existence depended on universal literacy—literacy for all. Even Thomas Jefferson, a slave owner himself, argued, "If a nation expects to be ignorant and free, in a state of civilization, it expects what never was and never will be."

Reinforcing the importance of education in the new nation, George Washington declared in his will that the enslaved children he owned who did not have parents should be taught a vocation, or trade, and educated. However, Washington's desire to teach enslaved children to read and write was not shared by most slave owners. In 1800, southern lawmakers passed a new law that restricted all "mental instruction" of both free and enslaved people of African descent, including teaching or simply talking about reading, writing, or mathematics.

The law also prohibited free and enslaved African Americans from gathering between sunset and sunrise. This restriction made it more difficult for African Americans to set up informal schools and gave authorities the right to barge in on anyone who they suspected of holding these "unlawful" meetings. This law punished both free and enslaved lawbreakers with a whipping, stating law officers, or justices of the peace, could "inflict corporal punishment on the offender or offenders . . . not exceeding twenty lashes."

Steel whips like this one from the 1800s were used to terrorize enslaved Africans during the Middle Passage and to punish plantation slaves and free African Americans for violating the rules and laws set forth by state legislatures.

FEARING THE LITERATE

Slave owners' worst fears about literate African Americans were realized in 1829, when David Walker, a free African-American abolitionist, published his *Appeal to the Colored Citizens of the World*. He wanted African Americans, especially slaves, to read his *Appeal*, in which he urged them to resist oppression violently, if necessary. He also argued for racial equality.

Born in North Carolina, Walker was considered free because his mother was free, but he had seen the impact of slavery. Walker became a radical voice against slavery. When authorities in the South discovered the first copies of the *Appeal*, they worried slaves had already been preparing a violent attack. African Americans in Charleston and New Orleans were promptly arrested for distributing Walker's *Appeal*, and a reward was offered for Walker: $10,000 alive, $1,000 dead.

Sunday Morning in Virginia, an oil painting by Winslow Homer, depicts children learning to read in their slave cabin.

LITERACY LAWS CONTINUE

By 1830, southern authorities had taken further steps to curb literacy among African Americans. They prohibited free African Americans, especially those from the North, from meeting with the enslaved, in an attempt to prevent slaves from gaining access to information.

Some northerners also grew concerned about educating free African Americans. You have read about the boarding school Prudence Crandall opened in Connecticut in 1832 for African-American girls. In 1833, the state passed a law requiring all African-American students be residents of the state. Authorities quickly arrested Crandall for violating this law. African Americans from Connecticut were still allowed to attend school, but those from out of state could not. Lawmakers feared migrating students would increase the state's African-American population, resulting in the "injury of the people." This way of thinking contributed to the characterization of free and educated African Americans as a separate and dangerous community.

AFTER THE CIVIL WAR

The Civil War was a watershed event that marked an important shift in American history and the end of slavery. Emancipation brought about many social changes, including the transformation of the

The Freedman's Village School in Arlington, Virginia, shown here around 1864, was established to educate enslaved people who escaped from the South during the Civil War.

RUNAWAY READING

As antiliteracy laws were passed and enforced, enslaved African Americans continued to disregard them. They learned to read and write, and then used these skills to escape slavery. Let's look at some of their remarkable stories.

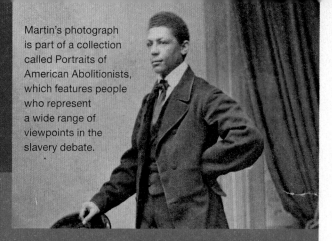

Martin's photograph is part of a collection called Portraits of American Abolitionists, which features people who represent a wide range of viewpoints in the slavery debate.

WILLIS

As valuable as reading was to slaves, writing was equally useful. An enslaved man called Willis used writing to escape slavery. What we know about him comes from a newspaper ad in which he is described as being 30 years old, stooped and downcast, and walking with a limp. On November 25, 1862, Willis ran away from his owner, W.H. Medlin, in South Carolina and headed north. Medlin placed the ad so people would look for Willis, but Willis had a special skill that helped him. To avoid capture, he wrote and signed a note that declared him free. He used his literacy skills to gain his freedom.

MATTIE JACKSON

Slavery crippled bodies and separated families, but it didn't stop people's quest for freedom. When Mattie Jackson was five years old, she and her mother tried to escape from Missouri to Chicago, but they were caught and sold back into slavery. Mattie decided to learn to read and demonstrated her literacy and resistance to slavery openly at times to her owner. When she finally managed to escape to Indiana, Mattie dictated, or spoke the story of her life so someone could record it, and sold the story. She used the money to pay for her education.

JOHN SELLA MARTIN

Runaway slave and abolitionist John Sella Martin (shown above) learned to read by listening. Working in a hotel in Georgia, he secretly listened to white co-workers as they played games and spelled words. By memorizing the sounds and spellings, Martin learned to spell even before he saw the shapes of the letters in the alphabet. He then applied this knowledge by trying to decode signs on the stores he walked by.

Other enslaved people saw Martin spelling words and assumed he could read. One day, three illiterate men gave him a newspaper and dared him to read it to them. Martin thought he might have to pretend he could read it. Instead he found he could read the headline and much of the article, which was about an abolitionist. Amazed and proud, Martin then knew there were abolitionists fighting slavery. And, perhaps even more important, he knew he could read.

Enslaved friends brought Martin newspapers and books they had stolen from their masters so he could practice reading, risking punishment for helping him. For Martin and other slaves, learning to read was one step on the road to freedom.

education system and a significant increase in the literacy rate among African Americans.

During the postwar Reconstruction era, the number of schools for African Americans rose substantially. Newly emancipated African Americans, or freedmen, recognized the value of literacy and education and set out to establish new schools and colleges. In 1865, Congress established an organization called the Freedmen's Bureau to provide support to the newly freed. The bureau aided the spread of African-American schools in the South, renting buildings for schools, providing books for teachers, and offering protection for students and teachers threatened by the opponents of black literacy. In the face of segregation, violence, and opposition, African Americans would continue to be challenged by the pursuit of equal education for many years.

THINK ABOUT IT

Why might access to public education have been one of the most important outcomes of the Civil War for African Americans?

1.1 Reconstruction Under Andrew Johnson

Imagine you've been fighting with your friend. You both said and did terrible things, but you know it's time to forgive. How do you become friends again? That was the dilemma President Andrew Johnson faced after the Civil War.

MAIN IDEA President Johnson and Congress clashed over different goals for Reconstruction.

LEADING THE WAY

1865 was a rough year. The war had torn the nation in two, and the war's end did not repair this division. Lincoln was dead, and citizens mourned the loss of his thoughtful guidance and strong leadership. The new president, Andrew Johnson, faced the monumental challenge of rebuilding the United States politically, socially, and economically. Many decisions had to be made. How should the Confederate states be readmitted to the Union? Should Confederate leaders be punished? What role should free African Americans play in the country?

Johnson had been an unusual choice as Lincoln's vice president. He was a southerner from Tennessee who had served in Congress as a Democrat. But he was definitely pro-Union, a stance fueled by his dislike for wealthy southern planters. When Tennessee seceded, he remained in the U.S. Senate. Lincoln later appointed Johnson as military governor of Tennessee. During the Civil War, military governors worked to re-establish the governments of southern states conquered by the Union Army.

When the 1864 election rolled around, the Republicans chose Johnson to run as Lincoln's vice president based on his loyalty to the Union. But Johnson didn't support equal rights for African Americans. Like most southern whites, he was deeply prejudiced, which offended many Republicans.

Among the first decisions Johnson made as president was to oversee Reconstruction himself, an approach called **Presidential Reconstruction**. Johnson's plan required Confederate states to ratify the 13th Amendment—which, as you may recall, abolished slavery—and create new governments with new constitutions before they could rejoin the Union.

Although he had repeatedly stated, "Treason is a crime, and crime must be punished," Johnson quickly pardoned, or legally forgave, most Confederates who took an oath of loyalty to the Union. The pardons restored their civil rights and protected their property from being seized. Only wealthy planters and high-ranking Confederate leaders had to apply individually for presidential pardons. Many in Congress felt Johnson's plans were too lenient, or forgiving. Congress wanted Confederates to pay for their actions.

THE FREEDMEN'S BUREAU

Johnson's perceived leniency toward the former rebels was not the only problem Republicans had with his plan. They were equally alarmed that Presidential Reconstruction did not provide a way for African-American men to vote, a right African Americans deeply desired. African Americans also wanted the right to own property. Without the protection of full citizenship and property rights, African Americans worried that white southerners would take away their newly won freedoms and economic opportunities.

AMERICAN PLACES

Arlington National Cemetery
Arlington, Virginia

Arlington National Cemetery was established in 1864 on land that had belonged to Robert E. Lee. Thousands of Union soldiers, including free African Americans, had already been buried there. Lee's home, which rises in the photo's background, now serves as a museum.

Republicans shared their concerns. In 1865, Congress created the Bureau of Refugees, Freedmen, and Abandoned Lands—more popularly known as the **Freedmen's Bureau**— to help the formerly enslaved, as well as impoverished white southerners. Congress appointed General Oliver Otis Howard to run the bureau. Army officers acting as bureau agents provided medicine, food, and clothing to newly freed African Americans and others displaced by the war. The officers also tried to settle former slaves on southern land that had been abandoned or seized during the war. Agents drew up labor contracts between landowners and African-American workers and created courts to settle conflicts between African Americans and whites.

Howard also saw education as a way to improve living conditions and economic opportunities for African Americans. The Freedmen's Bureau worked with northern aid groups to establish schools for the newly freed. By 1869, approximately 3,000 schools serving more than 150,000 students reported to the bureau. Yet in spite of this progress, neither President Johnson nor most whites were ready to grant full rights to African Americans. As a result, the Republicans in Congress decided to take control of Reconstruction.

HISTORICAL THINKING

1. **READING CHECK** What were the original aims of Reconstruction?

2. **MAKE INFERENCES** Why might Johnson have chosen to be lenient toward many Confederates?

3. **SUMMARIZE** How did the Freedmen's Bureau affect newly freed African Americans?

1.2 Radical Reconstruction

In a debate, you're pitted against a team that wants to make its case as badly as you do. In 1866, the president and Congress both wanted to win control of the South. The struggle deteriorated into name-calling and power grabs.

MAIN IDEA Unhappy with Johnson's Reconstruction plans, the Republican Congress took the responsibility away from him.

JOHNSON VERSUS CONGRESS

Made bold by the lenient terms of Presidential Reconstruction, some southern states refused to ratify the 13th Amendment. They even refused to admit that secession had been illegal. Southern states also passed **black codes**—laws for controlling African Americans and limiting their rights. The codes granted African Americans a few rights, such as the right to marry and pursue a lawsuit in court, but most of the codes dealt with what African Americans could not do. For example, they could not own land, work in certain industries, or serve on a jury.

Congress was furious over the black codes and the leniency of Johnson's Reconstruction plans. As a result, Republicans proposed the **Civil Rights Act of 1866**. The bill granted full equality and citizenship to "every race and color." Johnson vetoed the bill, but Republicans in Congress overrode the veto, and the bill became law. To solidify these rights, Radical Republicans also proposed the 14th Amendment. As you've read, this amendment guarantees citizenship and equal protection under the law to all American-born people. On President Johnson's urging, many southern states refused to ratify the new amendment. It took two years for two-thirds of the states to ratify it.

THE RECONSTRUCTION ACTS OF 1867

Shocked northerners watched as delegates at southern state conventions refused to accept the 14th Amendment. When Republicans won control of Congress in the 1866 elections, they decided it was time to take Reconstruction out of the president's hands. They put themselves in charge of the process by passing the **Reconstruction Acts of 1867**. Their plan of action came to be called **Radical Reconstruction**.

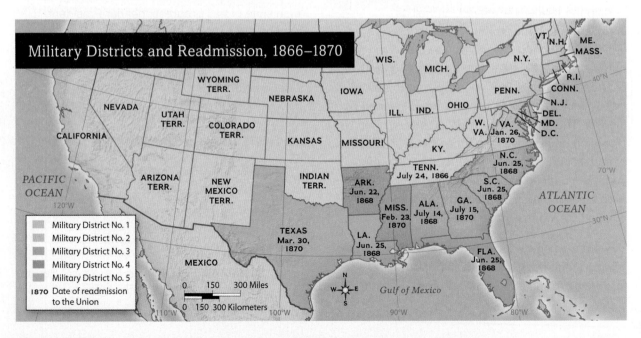

Military Districts and Readmission, 1866–1870

Military District No. 1
Military District No. 2
Military District No. 3
Military District No. 4
Military District No. 5
1870 Date of readmission to the Union

CRITICAL VIEWING Carl Schurz moved from Wisconsin to Missouri, where he was elected U.S. senator in 1868. In this political cartoon from 1872, he is shown as a carpetbagger. What details in the cartoon suggest what southerners thought of Schurz and other carpetbaggers?

Republicans had come to the South to get rich and called them "carpetbaggers," implying they had thrown everything they owned into a cheap suitcase, or carpetbag, and headed south. In reality, most of the Republicans from the North were Union veterans, preachers, teachers, or social workers. Free African Americans made up the rest of the delegates. Most were ministers or teachers.

To prevent Johnson from interfering with Radical Reconstruction, Congress passed the Tenure of Office Act, which prevented the president from removing government officials without Senate approval. The act clearly violated and ignored a Constitutional provision that granted the president the right to hire and fire Cabinet members. Johnson defied the act in August 1867, when he replaced his Secretary of War, Edwin M. Stanton, with Civil War hero Ulysses S. Grant. Stanton had been the only member of Johnson's Cabinet to support Radical Reconstruction. Congress responded by beginning the **impeachment** process, officially charging Johnson with "high crimes and misdemeanors," or extreme misconduct, while in office. They hoped to remove him from the presidency, and this was the first step. But the Senate tried Johnson and acquitted him, or found him not guilty, by one vote.

The Reconstruction Acts placed all of the former Confederate states except Tennessee, which had already officially been readmitted to the Union, into five districts under military rule. Once military leaders decided that order had been established, the states could draw up new constitutions. Each constitution had to accept the 14th Amendment. Then the majority of a state's citizens and the U.S. Congress had to approve the new constitution. Republican delegates were given the task of writing the new state constitutions. Many of the delegates were southern white Republicans who had opposed secession. Those in the South who hated Radical Reconstruction called the southern white Republicans "scalawags," or dishonorable people.

Northern white Republicans also made up a sizeable number of the delegates. Many southerners believed the northern white

HISTORICAL THINKING

1. **READING CHECK** What had to be done before a state could be readmitted to the Union?

2. **DRAW CONCLUSIONS** Why did many in Congress want to remove Johnson from the presidency?

3. **INTERPRET MAPS** Which southern state was the last to be readmitted to the Union?

2.1 Free African Americans Gain a Voice

Think of a time when you've stepped up to be a leader or you've done something hard and unfamiliar. You probably felt both nervous and proud. That may well have been how many African Americans felt as they took part in the political process for the first time.

MAIN IDEA During Radical Reconstruction, African Americans participated in government, established churches of their own, and tried to reestablish kinship structures.

TAKING PUBLIC OFFICE

After Congress passed the Reconstruction Acts, African Americans attained political freedom and wanted to exercise their new political power. As a result, many African-American citizens from the North, newly organized as Republicans, moved to the South hoping to fill appointed or elected government positions. African Americans from the South, some of whom had been free before the war, also sought leadership roles. These men became the backbone of the Republican Party in southern districts with large African-American populations.

African Americans everywhere wanted the ability to make their own choices. Many wanted to be involved in their states' readmission into the Union. Throughout the South, local African-American leaders, ministers, and Republicans encouraged newly freed men to register and vote. Their efforts helped Republican delegates dominate state constitutional conventions in every state except Georgia. African Americans also participated as delegates in all state conventions. Across the South, in fact, African Americans accounted for some 265 delegates out of a total of slightly more than 1,000. Between 1865 and 1877, African Americans influenced the direction of southern politics and elected 22 members of Congress. Republican-dominated legislatures established the first publicly financed education systems in the South, provided debt relief to the poor, and expanded women's rights.

About 600 African Americans also participated directly in the new state legislatures. Although no African Americans were elected governor, several served as lieutenant governors, secretaries of state, judges, or treasurers. **Pinckney Pinchback**, the lieutenant governor of Louisiana, became the acting governor when the state charged his boss with corruption.

African Americans became leaders at the national level when **Hiram Rhodes Revels** and **Blanche K. Bruce** served in the U.S. Senate. Revels, who was born a free man, served in Mississippi's state senate. He went on to fill a U.S. Senate seat left vacant when Mississippi seceded from the Union. He was the first African American to serve in the U.S. Senate. Bruce, who had been born into slavery, also represented Mississippi. He was the second African American to serve in the U.S. Senate and the first to be elected to a full term. In addition, 14 African Americans served in the U.S. House of Representatives during the Reconstruction era.

CHURCH AND FAMILY

Hiram Revels was already familiar in the African-American community in Mississippi through his work as a minister in the African Methodist Episcopal Church. Churches had long been at the center of African-American life. Because ministers were often the most educated members of the community, they became natural leaders—not only in religious matters but also in politics.

Following the Civil War, African Americans quickly established their own churches. The new churches were often Baptist because that denomination allowed each congregation to start a church independently and organize the services the way it wanted. By 1890, about 1.3 million African Americans were members of Baptist churches, mostly in the South. Churches were central to the African-American quest for **social justice**, or fair distribution of opportunities and privileges, including racial equality and rights. In addition to providing a place of worship, African-American churches often served as gathering places for social and political events and housed schools.

Like churches, family life had always been important to African Americans. But as you know, slavery had often split up families when members were sold to different owners. During Reconstruction, many African Americans tried to locate and reunite with their families. They were helped in this effort by the Freedmen's Bureau. In some cases, the bureau succeeded, particularly when the separated members of a family had gone to nearby plantations. Unfortunately, in other cases, family members had been sent far away. Some African Americans traveled hundreds of miles searching for their loved ones—often in vain.

First African Americans in U.S. Congress

The seven men in this print from 1872 are the first African Americans to serve in the U.S. Congress. Together, the seven represented five southern states. From left to right, the men are Senator Hiram Rhodes Revels of Mississippi (who filled the Senate seat that Jefferson Davis had held), Congressman Benjamin S. Turner of Alabama, Congressman Robert C. De Large of South Carolina, Congressman Josiah T. Walls of Florida, Congressman Jefferson F. Long of Georgia, Congressman Joseph Rainey of South Carolina, and Congressman Robert B. Elliot of South Carolina.

HISTORICAL THINKING

1. **READING CHECK** How did African-American political participation help strengthen the Republican Party in the South?

2. **MAKE INFERENCES** Why do you think it was important for African Americans to establish their own churches?

3. **DRAW CONCLUSIONS** Why were African Americans strongly motivated to influence and become leaders in government?

2.2 Education and Land

Like most Americans, you probably consider the education you receive as your right, rather than a privilege. But to African Americans during Reconstruction, school was an important sign of their new freedom.

MAIN IDEA The Freedmen's Bureau made education available to African Americans in the South, but other aspects of their lives changed very little.

AMERICAN PLACES
Howard University
Washington, D.C.

General Oliver Otis Howard's dedication to education is still visible today. Howard University in Washington, D.C., is named after the first commissioner of the Freedmen's Bureau and was the first American university dedicated to the education of African Americans. Howard himself served as the university's president when it occupied just one building. Today, more than 10,000 students are enrolled at the large campus, taking classes in subjects ranging from law to medicine and education.

AN OPPORTUNITY TO LEARN

African Americans appreciated the value of education. Slavery had denied many of them the opportunity to learn, so they saw education as a path to empowerment. **Literacy**, or the ability to read and write, and a solid working knowledge of mathematics gave African Americans the tools they needed to understand labor contracts. Education helped them advance in a **wage economy**, or an economy in which people are paid for their work. With a good education, they could fully participate in the political process and understand their civil rights.

The Freedmen's Bureau helped provide educational opportunities. The bureau and aid groups worked with individual communities to fund, build, and staff hundreds of Freedmen's Schools for African-American children and adults. These schools were often built on land owned by African Americans or housed in their churches. The schools were free, but since most African-American families counted on the labor or income their older children could provide, parents sacrificed a lot to send their children to school.

A shortage of teachers and space meant that schools often had to rotate students in three-hour groups. Typically, teachers worked all day teaching children and then held classes for adults at night. In some schools, however, young people worked and learned alongside adults in the classroom. In return, teachers experienced the satisfaction of teaching enthusiastic and motivated students. By the time the Freedmen's Bureau closed, about 150,000 students had attended classes.

BACK TO WORKING THE LAND

A good education was important to African Americans in the South because it offered their only chance for advancement. For the most part, uneducated African Americans worked the land of white landowners, but they faced discrimination in a southern economy on the edge of collapse. As a result, many former slaves wanted to obtain their own land to farm. Some freed African Americans had this wish fulfilled—at least for a short time.

In January 1865, General William T. Sherman issued Special Field Order No. 15, which set aside the Sea Islands for newly freed African Americans. The Sea Islands were located south of Charleston, South Carolina, and encompassed an area of approximately 400,000 acres. Each family would receive 40 acres to farm and a mule. News of the offer spread quickly, and about 40,000 African Americans rushed to settle on the land. But by the fall of 1865, President Andrew Johnson had overturned Sherman's order. The land was returned to the southern planters who had owned it before the Civil War.

With no land of their own, many African Americans went back to working for white landowners. At first, landowners insisted that the newly freed African Americans work in gangs, as they had under slavery. Over time, however, an agricultural system called **sharecropping** developed. In sharecropping, a farmer raised crops for a landowner in return for part of the money made from selling the crops. Some poor white families, devastated by the war, also took up sharecropping. But they did not face the discrimination that African Americans endured.

Sharecropping often left African-American families in debt to landowners. The sharecroppers needed supplies, such as tools and seeds, to work the land. Landowners would sell or rent the supplies to the sharecroppers on credit and at a high rate of interest. By the time the crops were harvested, sharecroppers had usually run up a large bill and, as a result, would receive very little of the profits from selling the crops. Sharecropping tied African Americans to a landowner's land and resulted in **black peonage**, a sort of economic slavery.

Unable to earn a living as sharecroppers or find other work, many African Americans began moving north or west. Some also fled to escape the terror generated by groups of white southerners.

HISTORICAL THINKING

1. **READING CHECK** How did the Freedmen's Bureau help educate former slaves?

2. **ANALYZE CAUSE AND EFFECT** What factors led to the development of sharecropping in the South?

3. **DRAW CONCLUSIONS** In what way did sharecropping replace slavery?

Resistance in the South

Terror is a powerful weapon. When combined with racism, its damage can last for generations. A reign of terror in the South set back African-American political gains and broke the Republican Party's hold in the region.

MAIN IDEA Afraid of losing political and economic power, some white southerners used terror tactics against African Americans and Republicans.

THE KU KLUX KLAN

Radical Reconstruction angered many white southerners and created a resistance movement based on racism and discrimination. Few white southerners accepted African Americans as their equals. Sometimes whites turned to violence in an attempt to keep African Americans from voting and exercising other rights. In 1866, white mobs attacked unarmed African-American men, women, and children and rioted in Memphis, Tennessee, and New Orleans, Louisiana. The mobs killed or injured many African Americans. In Memphis, the rioters, who included police officers, committed **arson** by purposefully burning homes, churches, and schools in African-American communities.

That same year, a group of young men in Tennessee founded the **Ku Klux Klan**. Originally intended as a social club, the group's purpose changed dramatically in 1867 when African Americans gained voting rights in the state under the Reconstruction Acts and began holding public office. Thereafter, the Ku Klux Klan, under the leadership of former Confederate officer Nathan Bedford Forrest, dedicated itself to maintaining the social and political power of white people.

To achieve its goals, members of the Klan terrorized and killed African Americans. They also attacked white people who associated with Republicans or supported African-American rights. To conceal their identities and maximize the terror, Klan members rode out at night dressed in hooded costumes. They whipped, tar-and-feathered, and even **lynched**, or hanged, their victims. They also committed arson. The Klan became the face of violent discrimination, carrying out punishments against people whom they felt had overstepped racial boundaries. Boosted by popular sentiment and federal acceptance, the Klan's popularity quickly spread across the South and even beyond.

CRITICAL VIEWING In 1874, this political cartoon by Thomas Nast appeared in *Harper's Weekly*. Why do you think the cartoonist included the words "worse than slavery" over the heads of the African-American family?

The Klan Through the Years

The Ku Klux Klan members in this photo traveled from New Jersey to take part in a Klan parade held in Washington, D.C., in 1926. The legal action brought against the Klan in 1871 drove its members into hiding, but it did not destroy the organization. Further actions by the government never succeeded in dissolving the group either. The Klan resurfaced in the 1920s, fueled by the arrival of immigrants whom they accused of taking jobs away from "real" Americans.

The Klan began to grab newspaper headlines once again as the civil rights movement gathered momentum in the 1950s and 1960s. After three civil rights volunteers were killed in Mississippi in 1964, FBI agents discovered the murderers were Klan members and police officers. Seven men were arrested for the murders. The Klan still exists today, although it is widely despised and wields very little political power. As of April 2014, official Klan groups were registered in 41 states with a total of as many as 8,000 members.

A POWER SHIFT

In response, the Republican-dominated Congress passed the Enforcement Acts in 1870 and 1871. The acts made it a crime to use violence or threats to interfere with a citizen's right to vote, hold office, or serve on a jury. The acts authorized the federal government to supervise congressional elections and gave the president the power to enforce the acts. The intent of the acts was to stop Klan activities and protect African-American rights.

Armed with the Enforcement Acts, the federal government took legal action against the Klan in 1871. In state after state, the government charged Klan leaders with crimes. The Klan became less visible, but their scare tactics had already damaged the Republican Party by preventing African Americans from voting. As a result, the Democratic Party began to gain back control in the South, and the number of African-American officeholders fell dramatically.

Meanwhile, many white voters in the North also thought the Radical Republicans had gone too far in promoting African-American rights. Even though the country would elect a Republican president in 1868, Reconstruction was starting to lose steam.

Members of the Ku Klux Klan often wore metal membership badges like these. The 1921 Klan badge on the right is shaped like the hood Klan members wore to scare and intimidate their victims.

HISTORICAL THINKING

1. **READING CHECK** What tactics did the Ku Klux Klan use to terrorize African Americans and white Republicans?

2. **MAKE INFERENCES** Why do you think the Klan's activities were allowed to continue in the South until 1870?

3. **SUMMARIZE** How did Klan activities change the balance of political power in the South?

Grant's Presidency

Think about how much has been at stake in recent presidential elections. The election of 1868 was similar, especially for Republicans and African Americans. A Democratic victory could deliver the end of Reconstruction.

MAIN IDEA After their party's victory in the 1868 presidential election, Republicans helped pass the 15th Amendment.

THE ELECTION OF GENERAL GRANT

In the 1868 presidential race, the Republicans nominated Ulysses S. Grant, the great Union hero of the Civil War. Although Grant had no experience in government, Republicans believed their candidate would be able to please members of both parties. When Grant accepted the nomination, he said, "Let us have peace." That phrase became a theme for the campaign. Republicans were aware that white voters had become less willing to help African Americans. As a result, the party did not promise to expand Reconstruction or to further promote the rights of African Americans.

The Democrats nominated **Horatio Seymour**, the former governor of New York, as their candidate. Seymour was part of a group of Democrats called the **Copperheads**. As you probably know, a copperhead is a poisonous snake. During the Civil War, this group, who called themselves "Peace Democrats," opposed emancipation and the draft. Republicans called the group "Copperheads" because they believed its members were Confederate sympathizers.

Seymour and the Copperheads relied on fear and racism to attract voters. Seymour criticized the Republicans for their aggressive handling of Reconstruction. He felt the government placed too much importance on African-American rights. His ideals appealed to many midwestern farmers who felt the Republicans did not understand their way of

1868 Campaign Buttons
Grant's running mate was Schuyler (SKY-ler) Colfax, a prominent Radical Republican. The candidates' campaign buttons feature ferrotypes, or photos printed on tin.

life. He also appealed to urban whites who believed free African Americans would move to the North and take their jobs.

Despite Seymour's rhetoric, or use of persuasive language, Grant led the Republicans to victory in the 1868 election. About 500,000 African Americans voted for Grant, helping him receive 53 percent of the ballots. In his inaugural speech, Grant declared, "I shall on all subjects have a policy to recommend, but none to enforce against the will of the people." He promised, unlike Andrew Johnson, to carry out the laws that Congress passed.

THE 15TH AMENDMENT

After the 1868 election, Republicans pushed for the adoption of the **15th Amendment** to the Constitution. Under the amendment's terms, the federal and state governments could not restrict the right to vote because of race, color, or

CRITICAL VIEWING Called *The 15th Amendment*, this 1870 print illustrates a parade celebrating the amendment's passage. The large image is surrounded by portraits of those who helped pass the amendment, including Abraham Lincoln, and scenes depicting African-American life. What do some of the scenes illustrate?

previous condition of servitude—in other words, slavery. The amendment would complete the political reforms sought by Reconstruction. Congress approved the amendment in February 1869 despite Democratic opposition, and it became part of the Constitution in 1870.

The intent of the amendment was to limit the southern states' ability to prevent African Americans from participating in the political process. But the new law did little for African Americans outside the former Confederacy. It also did not restrict or change any of the laws that states had placed on the rights of males to vote, such as charging **poll taxes**. A poll tax is a fee charged when people register to vote. Meanwhile, the Amnesty Act of 1872 removed voting restrictions on most of those who had belonged to the Confederacy.

The adoption of the 13th, 14th, and 15th amendments fundamentally changed the nation by establishing citizenship rights and full equality for anyone born in the United States. However, over the next couple of decades, courts and political interests would undermine the intent of the amendments.

Still, rights and equality were not on the minds of most people in the 1870s. They wanted their elected leaders to pay more attention to problems closer to home, including a severe economic depression. As an Illinois newspaper observed, "the negro is now a voter and a citizen. Let him hereafter take his chances in the battle of life."

HISTORICAL THINKING

1. **READING CHECK** What was the theme of Grant's presidential campaign?

2. **COMPARE AND CONTRAST** What differing views characterized the Republican and Democratic presidential candidates in the election of 1868?

3. **DRAW CONCLUSIONS** Why would a poll tax prevent African Americans from voting?

3.2 The Election of 1876

With our 24/7 online news feed, it can be hard to focus on one important problem when other issues arise. But this also happened in the 1870s, when scandals and economic woes distracted Americans from Reconstruction.

MAIN IDEA As scandals and a depression arose, a compromise reached over a contested election brought Reconstruction to an end.

SCANDAL AND PANIC

Ulysses S. Grant had been an effective general, but he proved to be a poor administrator. He often relied on Congress to make the types of decisions he should have made as the country's leader. He also was unable to keep his party from splintering into different factions, or groups, each promoting a different political viewpoint. The **Liberal Republicans** were among these factions. They believed the government had become too large and too powerful. They favored free trade and an end to Reconstruction. In American politics of the 1870s, the word *liberal* referred to someone who embraced these ideas.

Leading up to the election of 1872, the Liberal Republicans **defected**, or broke away, from the Republican Party and formed an alliance with Democrats. They nominated Horace Greeley, a newspaper editor from New York City, as the Democratic presidential candidate. Greeley's main goal was to end Reconstruction, but that was not enough to appeal to voters. Grant easily won re-election.

But accounts of dishonest behavior plagued Grant's second term. These scandals involved **bribery**, or offers of money or privileges in exchange for political favors. Financial wrongdoing among legislators and Cabinet members surfaced. For instance, Congress investigated Secretary of War William Belknap for **corruption**, another word for dishonesty. Congress accused Belknap of accepting cash gifts from army suppliers, which led to his resignation.

This painting by Howard Pyle called *The Rush from the New York Stock Exchange on September 18, 1873* conveys the fear and confusion sparked by the Panic of 1873.

The Election of 1876

Hayes (Republican)

Uncontested Electoral: 165 votes

Electoral Vote: 185 votes, 50.1%

Popular Vote: 4,034,311 votes, 48.5%

Tilden (Democrat)

Uncontested Electoral: 184 votes

Electoral Vote: 184 votes, 49.9%

Popular Vote: 4,288,546 votes, 51.5%

Territories, No Returns

Contested Electoral Votes

Twenty electoral votes from Florida, Louisiana, Oregon, and South Carolina were contested, or disputed, following charges of voter fraud. The controversial election was finally settled by the Compromise of 1877. All 20 votes went to Hayes, giving him the win by one electoral vote.

WASH. TERR.
MONTANA TERR.
OR 2 1
IDAHO TERR.
WYOMING TERR.
DAKOTA TERR.
MN 5
WI 10
MI 11
NH 5
VT 5
ME 7
NY 35
MA 13
NV 3
UTAH TERR.
NE 3
IA 11
IL 21
IN 15
OH 22
PA 29
RI 4
CT 6
NJ 9
CA 6
CO 3
KS 5
MO 15
KY 12
WV 5
VA 11
DE 3
MD 8
ARIZONA TERR.
NEW MEXICO TERR.
INDIAN TERR.
AR 6
TN 12
NC 10
SC 7
MS 8
AL 10
GA 11
TX 8
LA 8
FL 4

To make matters worse, economic disaster struck in 1873 when bank and railroad failures triggered an economic crisis called the **Panic of 1873**. Many people lost their money when banks closed and lost their jobs when businesses collapsed. As unemployment rose, the country slid into a depression that lasted six years.

END OF RECONSTRUCTION

As the depression wore on, economic concerns overshadowed the nation's interest in Reconstruction. In 1876, two court cases dealt a further blow to the cause of African Americans' civil rights. The U.S. Supreme Court ruled in *U.S.* v. *Cruikshank* that the civil rights amendments only allowed the federal government to prevent states from abusing African Americans' civil rights. The job of punishing individuals fell to the states. In *U.S.* v. *Reese,* the Court ruled that the 15th Amendment only made it illegal to deny a person the right to vote based on race. States could use other criteria, such as **literacy tests**, or tests of one's ability to read and write, to exclude voters.

By the 1876 presidential election, Democrats had regained control of several southern states and the U.S. House of Representatives. Democrats nominated Samuel J. Tilden as their candidate. The Republican nominee was **Rutherford B. Hayes**. The race was extremely close, with election results in several states disputed. Congress created an electoral commission to decide the election, but while it

met, Democrats and Republicans got together to negotiate a deal. In what came to be called the **Compromise of 1877**, Democrats agreed to award the victory to Hayes if Republicans agreed to end Reconstruction and pull federal troops out of the South. The deal was struck.

In the end, Reconstruction fell short of its goals. It had raised and then dashed hopes that African Americans would achieve equality. To some degree, African Americans made advances. But to help African Americans overcome the effects of hundreds of years of slavery and racism entirely would have required a great expansion of federal power. Still, although the promise of the 13th, 14th, and 15th amendments remained unfulfilled during Reconstruction, these amendments became the legal basis for the civil rights movement of the 1960s.

HISTORICAL THINKING

1. **READING CHECK** What views did Liberal Republicans promote?

2. **ANALYZE CAUSE AND EFFECT** What impact did the 1872 Amnesty Act, the 1876 election, and the withdrawal of federal troops from the South have on civil rights for African Americans?

3. **INTERPRET MAPS** How many contested electoral votes did Tilden need to win the election?

17 REVIEW

VOCABULARY

Use each of the following vocabulary words in a sentence that shows an understanding of the term's meaning.

1. **black codes**
   Southern states used black codes to restrict the rights of African Americans.

2. **corruption**

3. **Freedmen's Bureau**

4. **impeachment**

5. **Radical Reconstruction**

6. **sharecropping**

7. **15th Amendment**

8. **Panic of 1873**

READING STRATEGY
DRAW CONCLUSIONS

If you haven't done so already, complete your diagram to draw conclusions about the impact of Reconstruction on American society. Then answer the question.

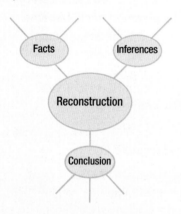

9. How did Reconstruction redefine what it meant to be an American?

MAIN IDEAS

Answer the following questions. Support your answers with evidence from the chapter.

10. Why was President Johnson at odds with many Republicans? **LESSON 1.1**

11. What did Presidential Reconstruction fail to do for African Americans? **LESSON 1.1**

12. What legislation did Congress propose to counteract Johnson's Reconstruction plans? **LESSON 1.2**

13. Why did African Americans often establish Baptist churches? **LESSON 2.1**

14. Why was education a symbol of their new freedom to African Americans in the South? **LESSON 2.2**

15. What was the goal of the Ku Klux Klan? **LESSON 2.3**

16. How did the 15th Amendment fail African Americans? **LESSON 3.1**

17. What was the Compromise of 1877? **LESSON 3.2**

HISTORICAL THINKING

Answer the following questions. Support your answers with evidence from the chapter.

18. **DRAW CONCLUSIONS** What did the outcome of Johnson's impeachment trial indicate about the power of Radical Republicans in the Senate?

19. **EVALUATE** What did the election of Blanche K. Bruce to the U.S. Senate probably mean to African Americans?

20. ANALYZE CAUSE AND EFFECT What impact did Reconstruction have on the political and social structures of the North and the South?

21. MAKE INFERENCES Why do you think some states charged poll taxes and made voters take literacy tests?

22. MAKE CONNECTIONS How were the 13th, 14th, and 15th amendments connected to Reconstruction?

INTERPRET PHOTOGRAPHS

The lives and work of sharecroppers remained largely unchanged for decades after the end of the Civil War. Look closely at the photograph of a sharecropper in Mississippi taken in the 1930s. Then answer the questions that follow.

23. How would you describe the work the woman is doing?

24. In what way is this work similar to that performed by enslaved persons?

ANALYZE SOURCES

In his second inaugural address delivered on March 4, 1873, Ulysses S. Grant discussed the problems African Americans still faced in the South. Read the following excerpt from the speech and answer the question.

> The effects of the late civil strife have been to free the slave and make him a citizen. Yet he is not possessed of the civil rights which citizenship should carry with it. This is wrong, and should be corrected. To this correction I stand committed, so far as Executive influence can avail [be of service or help].
>
> Social equality is not a subject to be legislated upon, nor shall I ask that anything be done to advance the social status of [an African American], except to give him a fair chance to develop what there is good in him, give him access to the schools, and when he travels let him feel assured that his conduct will regulate the treatment and fare [prices charged, food, material] he will receive.

25. Based on the excerpt, what is Grant's position on African-American civil rights?

CONNECT TO YOUR LIFE

26. EXPOSITORY Review the reasons many African Americans saw the opportunity for education as a way to improve their lives. Think about an activity you enjoy doing, for instance, reading comic books or playing basketball. Write a paragraph explaining how your education helps you better enjoy that activity.

TIPS

- Pick an activity you enjoy doing. Use an idea web to brainstorm what school subjects are involved in doing that activity.

- Conclude your paragraph with a comment about how your education has enabled you to enjoy the activity.

- Have you addressed the topic? Revise or rewrite your paragraph, as needed.

NATIONAL GEOGRAPHIC | CONNECTION

Lincoln's Funeral Train

by Adam Goodheart

Adapted from "How Abraham Lincoln's Funeral Train Made History,"
by Adam Goodheart, news.nationalgeographic.com, April 18, 2015

On the drizzly morning of April 19, 1865, when the train carrying the murdered president's coffin pulled out of Washington's central depot, it embarked on a journey that resonated deeply with many chapters of his life. As a 27-year-old novice state legislator in the 1830s, he was already advocating the construction of new train lines. He later served as an attorney for the Illinois Central and other companies.

In 1861, when Lincoln journeyed to Washington for his first inauguration, he traveled farther to reach the White House than any previous president-elect. As he made his way through midwestern and northern states, he reassured Americans that the nation would be saved. The trip itself was a powerful statement. It was a reminder of the 30,000 miles of steel that already bound the nation together, of the industrial economy that was vaulting the North ahead of the South, and of plans to build a transcontinental line joining Atlantic to Pacific.

Four years later, the funeral trip that carried Lincoln home for burial in Springfield, Illinois, was designed to recall the earlier journey. On the second day of travel, as it crossed the border between Maryland and Pennsylvania, the train rode over tracks that just a few years earlier had been used by slaves escaping to freedom. During the Civil War, trains laden with wounded soldiers often passed here as well, trundling their human burden from Virginia battlefields to the Union military hospitals in Pennsylvania.

On the 1865 trip, just two cars made the entire journey. One carried high-ranking military personnel and members of the Lincoln family. The other was the funeral car itself, named the United States. It had been completed in February 1865 as a lavish presidential office on wheels, a 19th-century version of Air Force One. It boasted gilded wood, etched glass, and wheels designed to accommodate tracks of varying gauges. For the funeral trip, it was draped inside and out in heavy black cloth fringed with silver.

The train's passage through towns and villages, usually in darkness, was an unparalleled event. "As we sped over the rails at night, the scene was the most pathetic ever witnessed," wrote one member of the entourage. "At every crossroads, the glare of innumerable torches illuminated the whole population from [old] age to infancy kneeling on the ground, and their clergymen leading in prayers and hymns."

Especially in the rural Midwest, ordinary Americans felt a connection with Lincoln that went beyond the tragedy of his assassination. Like him, they had suffered the agonies and triumphs of four years of war, and this emotional journey was bound up with memories of the railroad, too. It was at the local depots—the same ones where the funeral train now passed—that, long before, many had caught their last glimpses of sons and brothers who would never return. It was here that civilians brought the bandages, clothing, food, and flags that they contributed to the war effort. It was here that the first news of defeats and losses on distant battlefields arrived, carried by the telegraph lines that ran along the tracks.

For the 150th anniversary of the funeral journey, some people resurrected memories of when Lincoln's funeral car carried history through the midwestern heartland. It stopped in Springfield for a reenactment of the Lincoln funeral, two days shy of the actual anniversary.

A coffin—empty, of course—was unloaded onto a horse-drawn hearse and driven to the old Illinois State House for an all-night vigil. The next day, it was taken to Oak Ridge Cemetery. As in 1865, the last few miles of the homeward journey were powered by horses, not steam engines. But the ghostly presence of the railroad, like that of the murdered president himself, hovered somewhere close at hand.

For more from National Geographic, check out "Civil War Battlefields" online.

UNIT INQUIRY: Develop a Conflict Resolution Strategy

In this unit, you learned about the issues that fueled the Civil War and about the challenges that the United States faced after the war ended. Based on your understanding of the text, what unresolved conflicts eventually drove Americans to war? How did these conflicts get resolved? How did the Civil War and Reconstruction shape the American identity?

ASSIGNMENT

Develop a strategy that you think would have been successful in resolving one of the conflicts that Americans wrestled with before, during, and after the Civil War. Since you have knowledge about how events unfolded, your strategy should take into consideration the factors that led to conflict. Be prepared to present your strategy to the class and explain your reasoning.

Gather Evidence As you plan your strategy, gather evidence from this unit about the different ways in which conflicts and the way Americans did or didn't resolve them shaped the American identity. Also think about what Americans hoped to achieve through war and how the war affected ordinary citizens. Make a list of the causes and consequences of the war and address the most significant ones in your strategy. Use a graphic organizer like this one to help organize your thoughts.

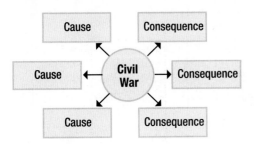

Produce Use your notes to produce descriptions of the causes and consequences of the Civil War. Write a short paragraph on each, using evidence from this unit to support your ideas.

Review Your Paragraphs Is the writing appropriate for your audience? Do you meet the purpose of the assignment? Revise or edit as needed.

Present Choose a creative and engaging way to present your conflict negotiation strategy to the class. Consider one of these options:

- Play the role of a diplomat and explain why a peaceful solution or compromise is preferable to a full-scale civil war.

- Write a dialogue between two people, one from the North and one from the South, that describes their perspectives on the causes and consequences of the Civil War.

- Create a multimedia presentation using paintings, photographs, and excerpts of documents to illustrate what caused the war, the realities of the war, and the consequences of the war.

NATIONAL GEOGRAPHIC | LEARNING FRAMEWORK ACTIVITIES

Create an Illustrated Time Line

SKILL Observation

KNOWLEDGE Our Human Story

Keeping track of events and their details can be a challenge, but understanding how events flow and relate to each other is how we make sense of them. Create an illustrated time line of the events surrounding the Civil War. You can organize events and details horizontally or vertically and illustrate the events you find most compelling. Include important dates and people. When you have completed your time line, share your work with the class.

Compose a Letter Home

ATTITUDE Empowerment

SKILLS Collaboration, Communication

In any war, letters from the front reveal the hard realities facing people on the front lines. Imagine that you are a soldier, medic, or reporter during the Civil War. Write a letter home that describes your experiences. Include specific details about time and place and observations about the people around you. Consider working with a partner who, as the recipient of your letter home, writes a letter back. When you have completed your letter or letters, present them to the class.

AMERICA ON THE MOVE

CRITICAL VIEWING People, cars, and horse-drawn carriages fill New York City's Lower Manhattan neighborhood in this photo taken around 1915. During the early 1900s, millions of mostly European immigrants flocked to American cities. What do you think life might have been like for the immigrants who lived or worked in Lower Manhattan?

AMERICA ON THE
MOVE

THE
UNITED
STATES

1876
Lakota and Cheyenne warriors defeat a cavalry division of the U.S. Army at the Battle of the Little Bighorn in Montana. (*photo of Major General George Armstrong Custer, who led the U.S. Army division at the battle*)

1886
Samuel Gompers founds the American Federation of Labor, a national organization of labor unions.

1869
The ceremonial last spike is driven in at Promontory Point in Utah Territory to join the tracks of the Central Pacific and Union Pacific railroads. (*replica of the original spike*)

1882
The Chinese Exclusion Act is passed, banning Chinese immigration for 10 years.

1862
The Homestead Act passes, encouraging western settlement by offering settlers free public land.

1875

1860

THE
WORLD

1884–1885 AFRICA
The Berlin Conference divides Africa among European powers and triggers a race for territory on the continent.

1871 EUROPE
A unified and self-ruling German Empire is proclaimed under Otto von Bismarck.

1896 EUROPE
The first modern Olympic Games are held in Athens, Greece. (*silver medal won by an American athlete at the 1896 Games*)

1892
Ellis Island opens and becomes the country's busiest immigration station. (*teddy bear belonging to an immigrant child who came through Ellis Island*)

HISTORICAL THINKING: DETERMINE CHRONOLOGY

What similar events occurred in the Americas and Asia in the late 1800s and early 1900s?

A WOMAN LIVING HERE HAS REGISTERED TO VOTE THEREBY ASSUMING RESPONSIBILITY OF CITIZENSHIP

1898
The Spanish-American War erupts after U.S. intervention in Cuba's war of independence against Spain.

1896
In *Plessy* v. *Ferguson*, the Supreme Court rules that facilities for African Americans can be "separate but equal."

1914
The United States finishes construction of the Panama Canal, which connects the Atlantic Ocean with the Pacific Ocean.

1919
The passage of the 19th Amendment grants women the right to vote. (*Women displayed signs like this one to show that they had exercised their right to vote.*)

1890
The U.S. Army kills nearly 200 Native Americans at Wounded Knee in South Dakota.

1905

1920

1890

1910 AMERICAS
The Mexican Revolution is fought to overthrow dictator Porfirio Díaz.

1912 ASIA
Two thousand years of imperial rule in China come to an end when revolutionary forces overthrow the Qing dynasty.

1917 EUROPE
The Russian Revolution begins. (*This Soviet poster of a man breaking his chains celebrates the revolution.*)

1914 EUROPE
Archduke Franz Ferdinand is assassinated, sparking the start of World War I. (*1914 illustration of the assassination*)

WESTWARD
MOVEMENT
1860–1900

ESSENTIAL QUESTION
How did westward migration affect the culture and way of life of Native American groups?

AMERICAN STORIES The Fall & Rise of the American Bison

SECTION 1 **Gold, Silver, and Cattle**

KEY VOCABULARY

cattle drive	hydraulic mining	posse
entrepreneur	lode	stockyard
ghost town	placer mining	

SECTION 2 **Farm Economics and Populism**

KEY VOCABULARY

bonanza farm	free silver movement	populist
cooperative	gold standard	prairie
creditor	Grange	recession
exoduster	industrialist	surplus
Farmers' Alliance	migrant worker	

SECTION 3 **Native Americans Fight to Survive**

KEY VOCABULARY

Americanization	Long Walk
Ghost Dance	reservation

AMERICAN GALLERY
ONLINE **Buffalo Soldiers**

READING STRATEGY

CATEGORIZE When you categorize, you sort people, places, things, situations, or ideas into groups. This can help you recognize patterns and trends. As you read, categorize details about the different groups of people who lived in the American West.

Rancher	Farmer
• Hired cowboys to lead cattle drives.	
Miner	**Native American**

"Don't fence me in."

—from the song "Don't Fence Me In," by Robert Fletcher and Cole Porter, 1934

AMERICAN STORIES | NATIONAL GEOGRAPHIC

THE FALL & RISE of the AMERICAN BISON

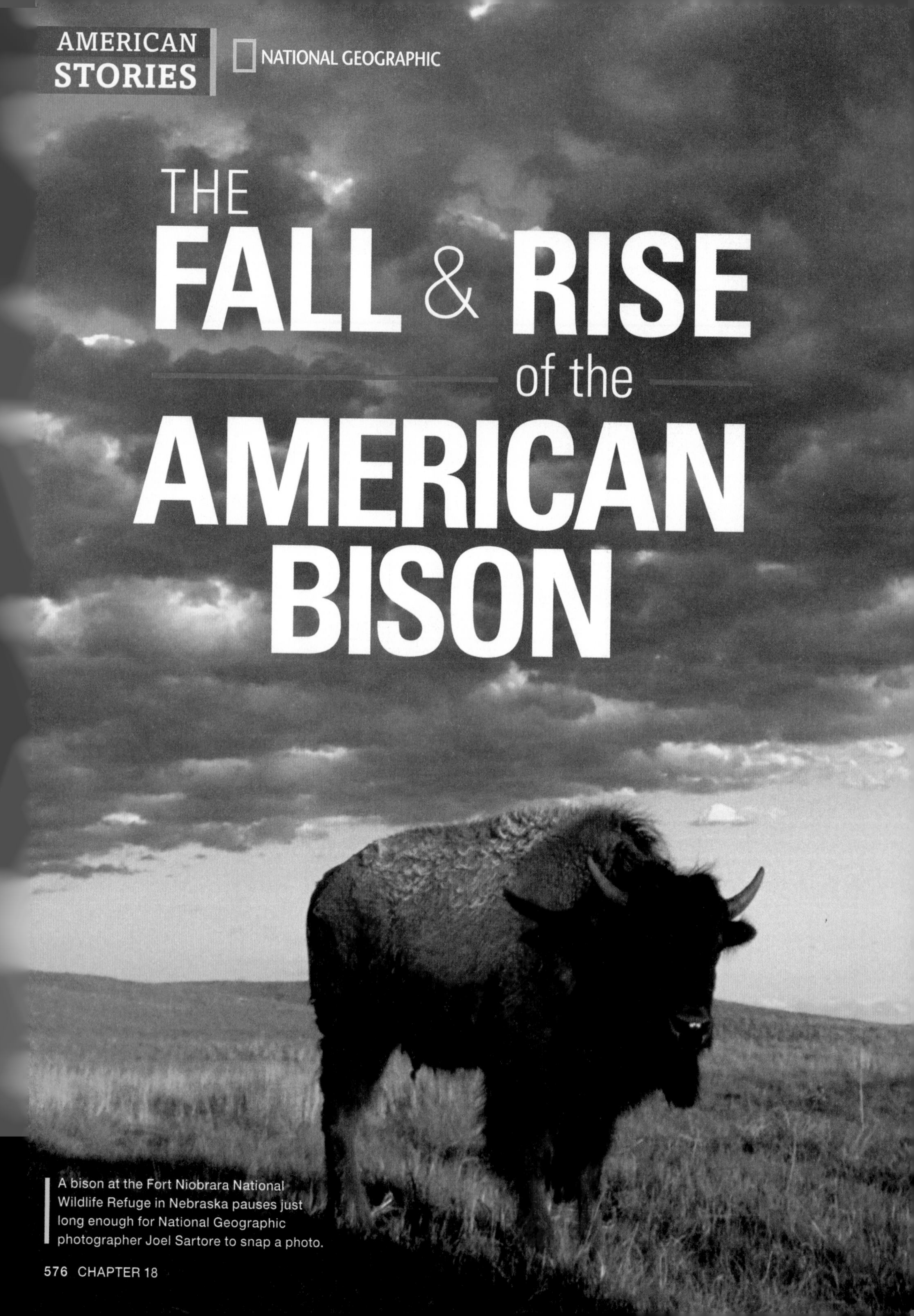

A bison at the Fort Niobrara National Wildlife Refuge in Nebraska pauses just long enough for National Geographic photographer Joel Sartore to snap a photo.

Everyone knows that the national animal of the United States is the bald eagle. But in 2016, President Barack Obama signed the National Bison Legacy Act, designating the American bison as the official national mammal.

Even if you've never seen one in person, you probably know what an American bison looks like. Commonly referred to as a buffalo, the American bison is portrayed on coins, company and sports team logos, and even the Wyoming state flag. What is the attraction to this unique North American mammal?

For one thing, the American bison is enormous. It can weigh more than 2,000 pounds and measure, at its shoulder, nearly 7 feet tall. It is also incredibly fast and strong. Because of its power, strength, and resilience, the American bison has become a national symbol for many Americans. It stands for both our past and our future, for damage done and the hope that arises when people unite to repair it.

Before 1500, tens of millions of bison roamed the North American plains. When horses and guns arrived on the continent, bison numbers declined drastically. By 1900, this iconic American mammal had become nearly extinct. How did this happen? To understand the decline and rise of the American bison, you have to go back to the beginning, thousands of years ago.

Bison Population in Millions
1500–1884

Sources: National Geographic,
U.S. Fish and Wildlife Service

FROM MILLIONS TO A FEW HUNDRED

For thousands of years, bison hunting was central to many Native American cultures, especially those living on the Great Plains. They relied on bison herds for survival, especially on the animals' meat for food and skins for shelter coverings. When Europeans arrived in the early 1500s, about 50 million bison ranged across most of the present-day United States. Spanish conquistadors brought horses with them, introducing a new species to the continent. Native Americans adopted the horse, specifically for hunting. Instead of following herds on foot, hunters pursued them on horseback, making the hunt more efficient. By 1750, bison numbers had fallen to 30 million.

When settlers arrived in the West, bison numbers declined rapidly for several reasons. Consumers in the East loved items made of bison skin or fur. Railroads wanted to eliminate the grazing herds that blocked trains for hours or even days. Ranchers wanted to use the land for grazing their cattle. Some army officers believed killing bison would starve out Native American groups in conflict with the U.S. government. In the 1860s and 1870s, hunters hired by the railroads and ranchers killed thousands of bison a day.

White hunters were not the sole threat. A severe drought in the mid-1880s and 1890s, diseases introduced by the settlers' cattle, and Native American hunters also contributed to the reduction in herd numbers. Whatever the precise causes, the result was devastating. By 1884, only 325 wild bison remained in the United States.

CRITICAL VIEWING Nineteenth-century artist George Catlin featured Native Americans in his paintings of the American West. In *The Buffalo Hunt,* painted in 1844, Catlin captures a bison hunt. Based on details you notice in the painting, what advantages would bison hunters on horseback have?

THE COMEBACK

At the height of the bison hunting and slaughter, many people expressed shock and worry. One observer in 1884 described it as "the ruthless, selfish destruction of what should have been protected as State property." Even so, the government voted down proposed measures to protect the bison.

In 1899, William Hornaday, the first director of the Bronx Zoo in New York City, took action. He acquired several bison and started a herd at the zoo. In 1905, Hornaday established the American Bison Society. President Theodore Roosevelt and several other influential men were members. In 1907, the Society persuaded Congress to set aside land in Oklahoma for bison from the Bronx Zoo herd to roam safely and freely. In the decades that followed, additional preserves were established. Soon, bison numbers climbed from the hundreds into the thousands.

BUFFALO BILL CODY

By the late 1800s, the sympathy of the American people had swung in favor of the bison, thanks in part to Buffalo Bill Cody. In the 1860s, the Kansas & Pacific Railroad had hired Cody to hunt bison to feed the railroad's workers. By his own report, he killed more than 4,000 bison in 18 months.

Cody popularized the bison, which eventually aided their preservation. In 1883, he launched a traveling show called Buffalo Bill's Wild West, featuring staged bison hunts using real animals. Other acts included skilled riders, sharpshooters, and Native Americans reenacting famous battles. People who saw the show emerged with an image of the American West as a place of thrills and adventure. Americans soon embraced the idea of the Wild West as part of the nation's identity. Front and center in this vision was the American bison.

More than 100 years after this bison left the Bronx Zoo for a new home in Oklahoma, the American Bison Society, in partnership with the Wildlife Conservation Society and many other conservation groups, continues to work toward the ecological restoration of the bison.

Bison Population in **Thousands,** 1884–2016

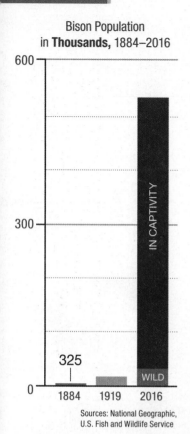

600
300
0

IN CAPTIVITY

325

WILD

1884   1919   2016

Sources: National Geographic,
U.S. Fish and Wildlife Service

PROTECTING AN AMERICAN ICON

Today, Native American groups are heading up one of the major efforts to save bison in the wild. The Intertribal Bison Cooperative has 51 member tribes and has successfully established herds on reservation lands. Other organizations, including the National Park Service and the Nature Conservancy, are reintroducing bison in preserves throughout their original range. The American Prairie Reserve in Montana focuses on increasing bison numbers, specifically on bison roaming freely on 1 million acres.

Thanks to the decades-long efforts of many concerned individuals and groups, American bison numbers have grown steadily. Estimates of the current population vary, but according to the National Geographic Society, the number on ranches in the United States stands at around 500,000. Who knows how bison numbers—protected and wild—might grow as citizens, scientists, and agencies work together to protect them? What's certain is that this symbolic and unique American species has a real hope for survival.

THINK ABOUT IT

What factors have changed over time that make both Native American and non-Native American groups want to restore the bison?

HOME, HOME ON THE RANGE

Perhaps you've heard the song "Home on the Range" on TV, in movies, or hummed by an older relative. To many, the song symbolizes the American West. The opening line inspires images of wide-open spaces and peacefully grazing bison herds. Brewster Higley wrote the song, originally as a poem, in the early 1870s. By 1934, "Home on the Range" was one of the most popular songs on the radio. In 1947, Kansas adopted it as its state song.

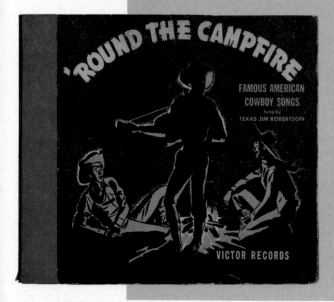

'ROUND THE CAMPFIRE

FAMOUS AMERICAN COWBOY SONGS

Sung by
TEXAS JIM ROBERTSON

VICTOR RECORDS

Home on the Range

Oh, give me a home where the buffalo roam,
Where the deer and the antelope play,
Where seldom is heard a discouraging word
And the skies are not cloudy all day.

Chorus

Home, home on the range,
Where the deer and the antelope play;
Where seldom is heard a discouraging word
And the skies are not cloudy all day.

Why do you think this song became so popular?

THE BISON OF YELLOWSTONE

Yellowstone National Park is the only place in the United States, outside of Alaska, where free-ranging bison have lived continuously for thousands of years. Established in 1872, the park sheltered some of the very few American bison to survive the slaughter of the 1800s.

In the early 1900s, the U.S. Army administered Yellowstone and protected the bison living there from illegal hunting. Today, the National Park Service runs the park and manages its bison herd, which numbers around 5,000.

Managing a free-ranging herd is a complex and delicate project. Ranchers and others who live or work near the park worry about the massive, sometimes dangerous animals wandering onto their land. Some bison carry a disease that can make cattle ill as well. The National Park Service works with government and tribal agencies that manage land around Yellowstone to balance the interests of both humans and bison.

What are the benefits and problems of having bison and people living near each other?

A frost-covered bison rests in Yellowstone National Park. The bison's thick fur offers impressive protection against winter. Its coat retains the animal's body heat incredibly well—even snow that falls on its back doesn't melt, keeping the animal dry.

1.1 Mining Boomtowns

Some opportunities sound too good to pass up, and everyone wants to be a part of them. In the 19th century, when people heard claims of gold and silver in the West, thousands traveled to find out if the claims were true.

MAIN IDEA The discovery of valuable metals in the American West caused a population explosion as people rushed to work in the mines or start businesses to support the miners.

MINING IN THE WEST

The Civil War delayed the dream of manifest destiny for many Americans, but once the war ended, people began to hit the westward trails again in record numbers, seeking new opportunities. The hot, arid climate of the West made farming a challenge, but the quest for land brought many farmers to the Great Plains. Opportunities in mining and cattle ranching also drew people west.

After the gold rush era ended in California in the late 1850s, it didn't take long for miners and merchants to move beyond California to seek mineral wealth. Prospectors began scouring the West for gold, silver, and other valuable metals and discovered gold and silver in Colorado, Nevada, and South Dakota. They also unearthed copper in Arizona and New Mexico. In 1859 in the mountains of Nevada, one of the largest deposits, or **lodes**,

Like Bodie, California, which you've already read about, Castle, Montana, shown here, sprang up after a mine opened nearby. Years later, Castle became a ghost town. At its peak around 1890, the town had 1,500 residents. By 1920, it had been completely abandoned.

of silver and gold in the West was found. The discovery of rich mineral lodes continued over the next few decades.

The mines provided resources essential to the nation's industrial development. Some miners set up operations near land that Native Americans had lived and hunted on for centuries. Eventually, the U.S. government forced the tribes off those lands, devastating tribal ways of life.

Early on, individual miners who panned for surface gold in riverbeds used a process called **placer mining**. This method works because gold is highly dense and sinks in water faster than other materials. As surface gold was depleted, individual miners went to work for mining companies that began to practice **hydraulic mining**. Workers shot pressurized water onto rocky mountainsides to remove topsoil and gravel, which they then processed with toxic chemicals, such as mercury, to draw out the precious metals. The mercury and mining waste was dumped into streams and rivers, affecting the usefulness of the water sources used by farmers, wildlife, and communities.

For years, farmers fought against mining companies to prevent this environmental damage. In 1884, hydraulic mining was outlawed in the West, but it continued to be used on a small scale. Still, the abandoned mines left ugly scars on the landscape, some of which remain to this day.

MINING CAMPS AND BOOMTOWNS

Populations in mining areas expanded quickly. Initially miners set up camps. Most camps quickly turned into bustling boomtowns, as **entrepreneurs**, such as merchants and business people, arrived to offer goods and services to the miners. People of all ethnicities came to the boomtowns to improve their lives. A few enslaved African-American women, who gained their freedom in the West, became successful business women and landowners.

Boomtowns throughout the West were similar in nature. No matter the state or territory, the pattern of quick growth was much the same. It was difficult to maintain order with a rapidly growing population, so boomtowns were often lawless places. Instead of a regular police force, residents formed **posses**, or groups selected by a sheriff to hunt down criminals.

Similar to the gold rush of 1848, after the mineral deposits were depleted, many boomtowns quickly faded into **ghost towns**, or abandoned towns that have fallen into ruin. Western states today list hundreds of ghost towns. In contrast, cities such as San Francisco and Sacramento, where businesses other than mining had taken hold, continued to flourish and grow.

HISTORICAL THINKING

1. **READING CHECK** How did the discovery of valuable mineral resources change the character of western North America?

2. **ANALYZE ENVIRONMENTAL CONCEPTS** What problem did hydraulic mining solve, and what problems did it cause for humans and the land?

3. **CATEGORIZE** List words from the text that describe life in a boomtown, then sort the words into two categories: *positive* and *negative*. What is one pattern or trend you see as you analyze the categories?

1.2 Cattle and the Long Drive

Moving to a new place and experiencing a change of scenery can be thrilling. After the Civil War, many people were eager to reach the West and the Great Plains. The territory was wide open, and there was plenty of work for those who could endure long, hard days.

MAIN IDEA The cattle industry relied upon a wide range of people doing vastly different kinds of work in different parts of the country.

THE CATTLE BOOM

Mining was only one of the industries pulling Americans west. Cattle ranching was another. Americans' taste for beef, as well as the ability of railroads to transport cattle quickly across the country to market, made ranching very profitable.

Across the Great Plains, from Texas to Montana, ranchers began raising herds of cattle that grazed across the open range. Ranchers depended on cowboys, who led **cattle drives** to move the herds across the plains to cow towns, railroad communities where cattle were loaded on trains to be taken to market. The earliest cow towns were in Kansas: Abilene, Wichita, and Dodge City. As the railroads pushed west, cow towns developed in Nebraska, Wyoming, and Montana.

The cattle were transported by train to **stockyards** at meat processing facilities. A stockyard is an enormous outdoor area where animals are penned until they can be slaughtered. Because it was a railroad hub and closer to the plains than eastern cities, Chicago, Illinois, boasted the nation's largest stockyards. The most successful meat processing companies of the day made innovations in butchering and processing, and were centered in Chicago. After 1878, advances in boxcar cooling and refrigeration allowed beef products to be processed and packaged at the meat company and then delivered to all corners of the United States.

THE LORE OF THE COWBOY

In folklore of the American West, cowboys were rugged, fearless, and self-sufficient heroes of the open range. In reality, cowboys' lives were difficult and dangerous. They worked 14-hour days, slept outside in all weather, spent hours riding and roping, and earned very modest pay. The average cowboy was young—only 24 years old—and just as likely to be a Mexican American, African American, or Native American as a European American. Cowboys worked together in teams to herd and manage the cattle.

Many of the tools western cowboys used originated with the Mexican *vaqueros*, or cattle

Fencing In the Open Range

Joseph Glidden received a patent for barbed wire in 1874. His invention forever changed the frontier and cattle grazing. Ranchers enclosed their land with barbed wire fences and kept their branded cattle within this boundary. Barbed wire fencing led to land disputes among ranchers. It also led to a decline in the need for cowboys. Prior to its use, many cowboys were needed to round up cattle from the open range. Then they had to separate and sort the animals by their brands, or identifying markings, to determine which cattle belonged to which ranch. With herds confined by barbed wire, ranchers no longer needed cowboys to perform this service.

CRITICAL VIEWING *The New Fence*, a 1946 painting by Thomas Hart Benton, shows two ranchers unrolling coils of barbed wire to make a fence. What does the windswept effect of the painting convey about life on the open range?

drivers. Mexican ranchers had a long-established tradition of working with cattle. Thus, many of the words associated with cattle ranching developed from Spanish. For example, cowboys wore leather leg coverings called *chaps* (from *chaparreras)* to protect against scrapes from sagebrush or thorny cacti that covered the landscape. They used a looped cord, which was made of braided strips of cowhide, called a *lariat* (from *la reata*) to rope a wayward cow or horse.

About 25 percent of cowboys were African Americans who migrated to the West after the Civil War. The war brought about poor economic conditions in the South and pushed African Americans to build new lives in a new land. They often performed the hardest and most dangerous work, such as taming wild horses, but only rarely became ranchers themselves. One exception was Daniel W. Wallace, who, as a cowboy, became known as "80 John" for the brand—the number "80"—he placed on his cattle. Wallace accepted cattle as payment for his work. He acquired 1,280 acres of land in Texas and became a successful rancher.

Cowboys still herd and manage cattle in the western United States today, but by the end of the 1880s, the era of the great cattle drives had ended. Much of the once-open range had been enclosed by barbed wire, and the railroads had expanded so much that long cattle drives were no longer necessary. The rails had come to the ranchers. Even so, the powerful image of the western cowboy continues to be part of the American identity.

HISTORICAL THINKING

1. **READING CHECK** Why was the West well suited for the cattle industry?

2. **ANALYZE CAUSE AND EFFECT** How did the expansion of the railroad impact cattle ranching and the work of cowboys?

3. **DISTINGUISH FACT AND OPINION** The American cowboy is an idealized figure today. What ideas about cowboys are merely opinions, and what facts does the text provide about cowboys' lives?

2.1 Farming in the West

Getting something for free sounds really great. How could people turn down 160 acres of land if they didn't have to pay for it? In truth, homesteaders quickly found out that their free land was more expensive than it seemed.

MAIN IDEA Many homesteaders rushed west to claim the free land in the West offered by the U.S. government.

HOMESTEADERS AND EXODUSTERS

As you have read, in 1862 the U.S. government's Homestead Act encouraged westward migration by offering 160 acres of land to every free American citizen or to those intending to become citizens. The offer was open to unmarried, widowed, or divorced women, as well as African Americans, eventually. If they claimed the land and lived there for five years, it became theirs.

By 1868, a steady stream of African Americans began to move to Kansas and farther west to claim land. Kansas had a strong pull factor. It had entered the Union as a free state, and the story of John Brown and his efforts to keep Kansas free were legendary. By 1879, a full-scale exodus, or mass migration, was underway, driven by racism in the South and encouraged by some northern legislators. The thousands of African Americans who headed to Kansas and a new life became known as the **exodusters**. Between 1870 and 1880, Kansas added about 27,000 African-American citizens who established farms, settled in cities, and founded communities such as the Nicodemus Town Company in 1877.

Although the Homestead Act offered a diverse group of people the opportunity to own land, the cost of livestock, seeds, and farm equipment often discouraged newcomers with no previous farming or ranching experience. Families who already had established farms elsewhere were more likely to claim the free land. Only 80 million acres of the 500 million dispersed by the General Land Office between 1862 and 1904 went to homesteaders. Between 1851 and 1871, approximately 130 million acres were given to railroads.

If a new farmer had the money to purchase cattle, the grasslands of the **prairie**, a vast area of flat land covered with tall plants, offered immediate grazing. Unlike in the East with its abundant rain, cultivating crops in the western United States and Great Plains proved challenging. Wheat grew well in this region, but the arid climate made irrigation both necessary and difficult. Farmers wanted to settle near rivers, but not everyone could. Farms farther away from water resources needed a way to transport water across other people's land, which required cooperation among the farmers. Homesteaders often fought over water rights. Discouraged, many farmers turned to ranching instead of growing crops until federal legislation led to irrigation projects at the beginning of the 20th century.

BONANZA!

You have also read that even before the Civil War, agricultural technology began to transform American farming with innovations such as the reaper, the thresher, and the plow. These machines allowed farmers to work larger areas of land with fewer people. In 1873 when the Northern Pacific Railroad needed money to cover its debts, it sold enormous tracts of land—some up to 100,000 acres—to investors who created **bonanza farms**. The name reflects the fact that the owners, who often did not live on the land, believed they would soon find a bonanza—a stroke of extreme good fortune. These farms made the American West and Great Plains major wheat-producing regions.

Bonanza farms specialized in one crop and used a farm manager and crews of **migrant workers**, or laborers who moved from one farm

Sod Houses

One big problem homesteaders faced on the prairie was that there were almost no trees—certainly not enough to provide wood to build a house or cabin. Families needed shelter in this treeless environment. Fortunately, there was plenty of grass that sent deep roots into the topsoil to form sod. Settlers used thick chunks of sod to build houses. Sod homes were practical: their thick walls kept out the cold in the winter and the heat in the summer. One type of sod home, called a dugout (shown above), was built by digging right into the side of a ridge. Dugouts were the fastest way to create a shelter, as not all sides of the home needed to be constructed using sod bricks.

to another as needed, to cultivate the land. For example, in California's Central Valley, Chinese, Japanese, Hindu, Turkish, Filipino, and Mexican migrant workers toiled on bonanza farms. The workers slept in bunkhouses and ate in dining halls built by the farm managers.

The success of bonanza farms was subject to wheat prices. When the farms produced a **surplus**, or excess, of wheat, the price of the grain dropped. Harvesting required thousands of migrant workers, but with lower wheat prices, there was little or no profit after paying the workers. Farming on a much smaller scale, homesteaders worked their own land. They were less affected by price changes, outlasting the bonanza farms for a time, but the homesteaders faced problems of their own.

HISTORICAL THINKING

1. **READING CHECK** What groups of people could take advantage of the Homestead Act?

2. **IDENTIFY PROBLEMS AND SOLUTIONS** How did homesteaders change the land to solve the problems they faced?

3. **ANALYZE ENVIRONMENTAL CONCEPTS** What effect did the sale of land by the Northern Pacific Railroad have on how the land was used?

2.2 Women and Children on the Prairie

Do you sew your own clothes? Bake your own bread? On the prairie, everything was made by hand. Daily tasks required demanding, time-consuming labor that was divided between men, women, and children.

MAIN IDEA On the prairie, a new American identity formed around community, religion, and hard work performed by all family members.

CHALLENGES FOR WOMEN

In 1870, the majority of Americans lived in small towns or on farms. Just as farm work on the American prairie was demanding, the responsibilities of rural housekeeping were extensive, and they were handled primarily by women. Women hauled water and kept a fire constantly burning in a stove. Just those two tasks took at least an hour each day. Women sewed by hand the clothing their family wore, washed the laundry in a tub, and used a heavy iron to press the clothes. In addition, the women had to watch and raise their children and keep a safe and clean home.

Prairie women fed the livestock, gathered chicken eggs, and tended the garden, which provided most of the family's food. They canned, or preserved, the ripened fruits and vegetables for use in the winter.

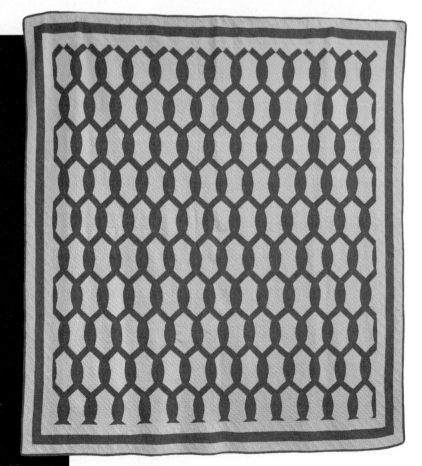

🏛 Iowa Quilt Museum
Winterset, Iowa

Made by machine and by hand in an unknown pattern, this quilt is from c. 1850–1900. Several U.S. museums, like this one in Iowa, are devoted to preserving the art and history of quilts. American quilts are their own art form, sewn from blocks of fabric. A quilt usually has a name related to its pattern, which can be an illustration or a geometric form, such as the quilt shown here.

Made like a sandwich, quilts usually have a decorated top, a back, and a warm filler in between. Quilts were needed to keep a family warm, but they were also a source of enjoyment. Women on the prairie helped each other at social "bees," where they did handwork together, such as quilting and sewing.

Prairie farms were miles apart, so a woman could go days without contact with anyone except her husband and children. During good weather, everyone looked forward to going to church on Sunday. It was a chance to see others and catch up on the community news. But during the winter, deep snow and dangerous winds kept most people confined to their homes, which contributed to a profound sense of isolation. Author Willa Cather describes the long prairie winters in her book *My Ántonia*: "Winter lies too long in country towns; hangs on until it is stale and shabby, old and sullen."

If a woman's husband died, she was often left alone on the land. Fortunately, she usually had the skills needed to manage the farm. Due to their contributions on the farm and in the home, prairie women gained great respect. It is no surprise that women in the West were the first to win the right to vote when the Wyoming Territory established women's suffrage in 1869.

THE LIVES OF PRAIRIE CHILDREN

In the first half of the 19th century, school was not mandatory in the United States, but most parents wanted their children to get at least a basic education. Many prairie communities built one-room schoolhouses in central locations. To attend, most children walked several miles each way. Early schools had dirt floors and were heated by a coal- or wood-fired stove. Children brought their lunches from home and used the same dipper to drink water from a community bucket. An outhouse stood behind the building; there was no indoor plumbing for bathrooms.

In a one-room schoolhouse, one teacher taught all of the grades. Some teachers managed classes as large as 48 students ranging in age from 6 to 18 years old. Students learned at their own pace. Among the common textbooks found in schools of that time were the **McGuffey Readers**, which were developed by William McGuffey in 1836. Children learned by reading stories that promoted

CRITICAL VIEWING Ada McColl was studying to be a photographer when she had her mother take this photo of her in 1893. The wheelbarrow is filled with cow chips (dried dung) for use as heating fuel. What does the photo convey about life on the prairie?

good character, a strong work ethic, and honesty. The books condemned lying, stealing, cheating, laziness, and alcohol use.

Even though education was important for prairie children, their work on the homestead was considered more valuable than schoolwork. Starting at about age four, children had many chores to do and little free time to play. Because families made or grew most of what they ate, children were expected to help milk cows, churn butter, and care for a vegetable garden to help their families survive.

When they finished their chores, the children played games, including many you might recognize, such as jump rope, hopscotch, checkers, and marbles. Prairie children also enjoyed getting together with friends at church socials, the Fourth of July celebration, and other gatherings.

HISTORICAL THINKING

1. **READING CHECK** In what ways did women and children play important roles on the American prairie?

2. **CATEGORIZE** How might you categorize details about the women who lived on the prairie? Explain your reasoning.

3. **COMPARE AND CONTRAST** How were the lives of children living on the prairie during the 19th century similar to and different from the lives of children today? Provide relevant details from the text.

2.3 Farmers and Populism

It's challenging—and risky—to start a small business, and most of them aren't instantly profitable. In the mid to late 1800s, new farmers struggled to earn a profit, and some lost their farms.

MAIN IDEA Farmers organized to promote political ideas they hoped would change the economy to be more favorable to agriculture.

FARMERS' ECONOMIC PROBLEMS

Farming is a difficult business. Seeds and equipment cost money, and it is especially hard for a new farmer to purchase them without any crops to sell. In the 1800s, many new farmers borrowed money to get started. When crop prices fell during an economic downturn, or **recession**, in the early 1870s, farmers in the South, Midwest, and West faced economic distress. Farmers who failed to pay their debts often lost their land to

their **creditors**, or the people from whom they had borrowed money. After the Civil War, Oliver Kelley, a clerk for the United States Bureau of Agriculture, toured the South to gather information about how best to help farmers during Reconstruction. He observed the struggles most farmers faced. In 1867, he started the **Grange**, an organization that brought farm families together, addressed farmers' economic issues, and encouraged advancements in agriculture.

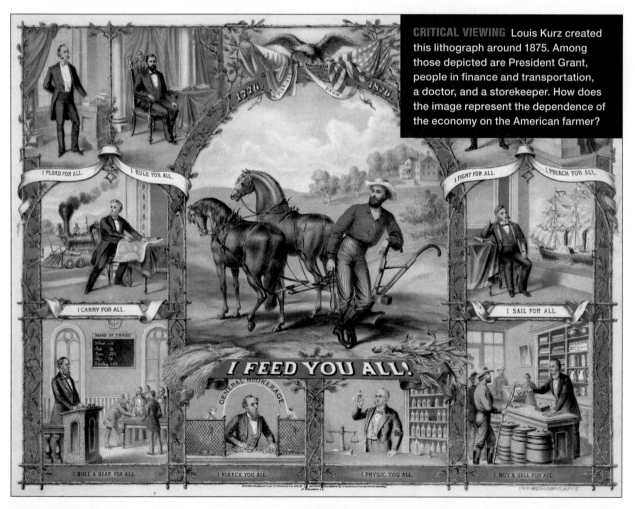

CRITICAL VIEWING Louis Kurz created this lithograph around 1875. Among those depicted are President Grant, people in finance and transportation, a doctor, and a storekeeper. How does the image represent the dependence of the economy on the American farmer?

As membership in the Grange grew, the organization began to promote farmer-owned **cooperatives**, or groups of farmers who pooled their money to buy the products and services they needed. By buying so many items or services at one time, a cooperative could negotiate better prices for machinery, seeds, and crop storage. This saved members money. The Grange also promoted the regulation of railroad and warehouse rates and operations in several states to control the shipping and storage of harvested crops.

THE POPULIST PARTY

When midwestern blizzards killed entire herds of livestock in the winter of 1887, many farmers and ranchers faced financial ruin. They needed help, and they wanted an alternative to the Republican and Democratic parties, which they believed had failed to support their interests. The **Farmers' Alliance**, an organization similar to the Grange but more political, emerged. The Farmers' Alliance started in the southern cotton belt and spread quickly into the Midwest and West.

The Farmers' Alliance pushed for a third political party, and in 1892, it helped form the **Populist Party**. A **populist** claims to represent the concerns of ordinary people. The Populist Party aimed to give farmers the equivalent political status of business people and **industrialists**, the people who own and run industries. It called on the government to reclaim the land held by railroads and wanted to put more currency, or paper money, into circulation. Doing so would mean farmers would get higher prices for their harvests, making it easier for them to pay their debts. Farmers began thinking of ways in which this could be accomplished.

You have read previously about the relationship between currency and gold and silver. In the 1890s, and continuing into the 1930s, American currency was held to the **gold standard**, a policy requiring that the government could only print an amount of money equal to the total value of its gold reserves. The only way to distribute more money was to obtain more gold. With a limited number of dollars, each dollar's value increased. The overall value of the currency shrank as the value of each dollar rose. As a result, prices of goods were low, and farmers worked harder to maintain the same level of income.

The Populist Party supported the **free silver movement**: Anyone holding silver could have it minted into U.S. silver dollar coins for a small fee, and these coins would be placed into circulation. Silver from American mines was plentiful, so introducing free silver would increase the money supply and inflate prices, as the farmers desired.

Currency was the main issue of the 1896 election. Republican nominee **William McKinley** supported the gold standard, while Democrat **William Jennings Bryan** was pro-silver. Bryan ran as the Democratic Party's presidential candidate in 1896. When the Populist Party chose to support Bryan, its members joined the Democratic Party. The Populist Party came to an end. McKinley won, and the gold standard remained in place until 1933.

The End of the Frontier

The 1890 U.S. census showed that with the arrival of farmers, ranchers, and miners to the West, there was no longer a "frontier," or a line beyond which population was so sparse that the land was considered to be uninhabited. In 1893, historian Frederick Jackson Turner used this fact to declare the American frontier "closed," meaning that there were no longer any wild and unsettled places in the West—only towns, cities, railroads, and lots of people. He wrote that the frontier had contributed to Americans' sense of optimism and rugged independence. It formed an American identity of ingenuity and self-reliance. Although Turner influenced many historians, his accounts left out the stories of women, African Americans, Latinos, Asians, and Native Americans.

HISTORICAL THINKING

1. **READING CHECK** Why did the Grange promote regulation of railroad and warehouse rates and operations?

2. **CATEGORIZE** What categories would you use to sort the interests of different groups of people you read about in this lesson?

3. **MAKE CONNECTIONS** Why did many farmers join the Democratic Party before the 1896 presidential election?

3.1 Native Americans of the Plains

Are you a peacemaker or a problem solver? Do you look for solutions that benefit people on both sides of an issue? In the 1860s, white settlers and the U.S. government stopped trying to solve problems and resorted to using force instead.

MAIN IDEA As more people moved onto the plains, Native Americans were forced to fight for their land and their culture.

CHANGING LIVES ON THE PLAINS

You may recall that in the 1830s, Andrew Jackson's Indian removal policies forced the Cherokee and other eastern tribes across the Mississippi River into Indian Territory on the southern plains. By the mid-1800s, Native Americans were once again being forced off their lands. Settlers laid claim to the land for farming and ranching, miners staked claims to areas with rich mineral resources, and railroad companies laid tracks across the entire country. In treaty after treaty with the U.S. government, land was allocated to tribes that were promised annual payments from the government, but one by one, those treaties were broken. Soon, Native Americans were clashing with settlers and the U.S. Army, attempting to defend their lands and their ways of life.

Although many settlers wanted the Native Americans completely removed from the Great Plains, President Grant authorized the U.S. government to set aside specific areas of land, called **reservations**. On the reservations, tribes could live apart from the settlers and, as some settlers believed, learn the "benefits" and values

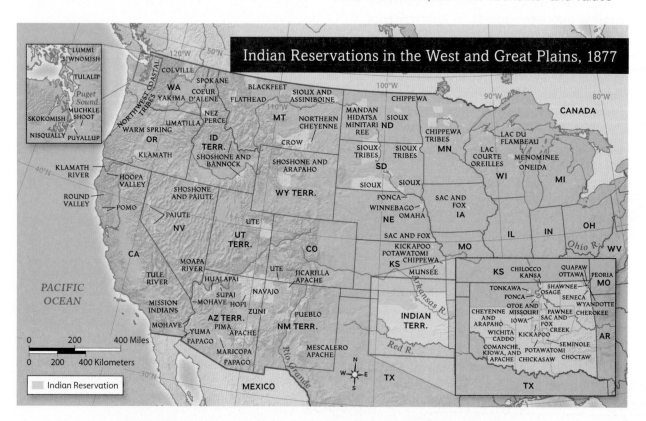

Indian Reservations in the West and Great Plains, 1877

of white society. They were encouraged to farm the land rather than hunt, in exchange for a small government income. The U.S. Army stood by to stop any resistance and to keep the tribes within the reservation boundaries.

THE NATIVE AMERICAN WARS

As settlers claimed land on the Great Plains, they also systematically hunted and killed off the vast bison herds on which Native Americans depended. In some instances, frustrated Native Americans attacked settlers.

The U.S. Army responded by building more forts and sending more troops. These troops included several African-American regiments, who built forts, mapped large areas of wilderness, strung telegraph lines, and protected railroad crews and settlers from Native American attacks on the Great Plains and in the Southwest. The Native Americans gave them the name "Buffalo Soldiers," possibly because of the soldiers' perseverance. In this way, the soldiers may have resembled the buffalo to the Native Americans.

Orlando Scott Goff photographed this Buffalo Soldier at Ft. Custer, Montana, sometime around 1885. The soldier stands in front of a painted background, one of several Goff carried with him in his wagon.

Still, the violence continued. In November 1864, Chief Black Kettle, his band of Cheyenne, and a group of Arapaho encamped near Sand Creek in what is now Colorado. Black Kettle flew both a white flag of peace and an American flag over the camp to show that his people did not seek war. At daybreak on November 29, the men went hunting, leaving the women, children, and elderly behind. Colonel John Chivington ignored the flags and led a volunteer militia into the camp. His troops slaughtered 200 unarmed Native Americans and mutilated the bodies. In response to this atrocity, now known as the **Sand Creek Massacre**, the Cheyenne, Lakota, and Arapaho attacked defenseless settlers.

One of the most well-known battles in the series of Native American wars took place in the **Black Hills** in present-day South Dakota. The Black Hills were part of the Lakota reservation in the 1870s when a government survey found gold there. To the Lakota, the region was, and still is today, sacred.

In 1875, the United States ordered the Lakota off the land, but a year later, **Colonel George A. Custer** and the 7th Calvary found Lakota and Cheyenne hunters camping there, along the Little Bighorn River. Although approximately 2,500 Native American warriors were in an advantageous position and Custer had only 210 men, the colonel ordered an attack. The warriors killed Custer and nearly all of his men in the **Battle of the Little Bighorn**. The victory was short-lived, however. More U.S. troops arrived the next day and forced the Lakota from the Black Hills. Although Native Americans won some battles, they ultimately lost the war.

HISTORICAL THINKING

1. **READING CHECK** What factors led Native Americans of the Great Plains to go to war against the U.S. Army?

2. **COMPARE AND CONTRAST** The Sand Creek Massacre and the Battle of Little Bighorn had different outcomes. How were they similar?

3. **INTERPRET MAPS** What does the map illustrate about the land set aside for Native American reservations?

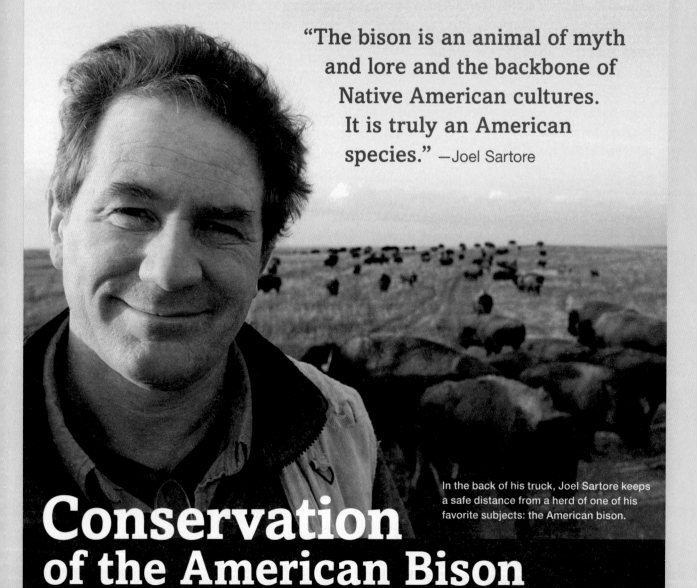

"The bison is an animal of myth and lore and the backbone of Native American cultures. It is truly an American species." —Joel Sartore

In the back of his truck, Joel Sartore keeps a safe distance from a herd of one of his favorite subjects: the American bison.

Conservation
of the American Bison

In his more than 25 years as a photographer, National Geographic Fellow and photographer Joel Sartore has encountered quite a few unusual situations. He's been chased by hungry animals, infected with flesh-eating parasites, and pinned underneath a truck by an American bison. Why does he do what he does? His mission is to introduce us to the amazing diversity of Earth's animal, bird, and insect life and to make us aware of their shrinking habitats.

A native of Lincoln, Nebraska, Sartore has been on location all over the world. The uniquely American animals he's photographed include bald eagles, gray wolves, grizzly bears, and the American bison. He is especially fond of the bison, which he argues is "the most iconic animal in the United States. The bison is more historically significant than the bald eagle because of human dependence on it."

Sartore is not only a champion of the American bison, but of the hundreds of other species facing habitat loss and threats of extinction. To save species, we have to save their habitats, which for bison means conserving the prairies. For Sartore, everything is connected. "When we save species," he says, "we save ourselves."

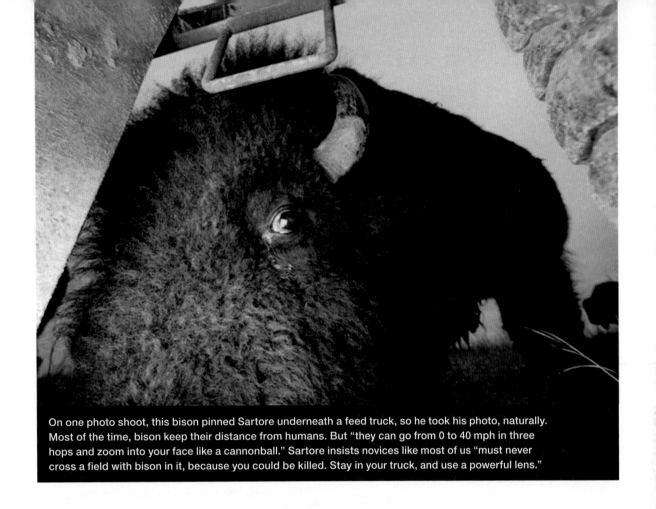

On one photo shoot, this bison pinned Sartore underneath a feed truck, so he took his photo, naturally. Most of the time, bison keep their distance from humans. But "they can go from 0 to 40 mph in three hops and zoom into your face like a cannonball." Sartore insists novices like most of us "must never cross a field with bison in it, because you could be killed. Stay in your truck, and use a powerful lens."

PHOTOGRAPHING BISON

Sartore admires bison for their self-sufficiency and their resilience. He remarks, "Bison are brutishly strong and hardier than cattle. They can handle any weather and they're very tough. Bison also herd together well, which helps herds do better. But even when they are confined to and raised on modern ranches for commercial consumption, bison remain wild animals." It is a wildness that he loves.

Sartore prefers photographing bison out in the open, not hidden in grasses, and "in the last 15 minutes of sunlight, so there is a nice glow, no harsh shadows." To capture how massive they are, Sartore photographs them from below. For Sartore, the goal is to be able to see the bison's eyes. And any day he gets to do that, he says, is a good day.

HISTORICAL THINKING

SUMMARIZE Why is Sartore drawn to the bison, and why does he believe it is an American symbol?

3.3 Native Americans of the Northwest and Southwest

It's bad enough when you're forced to live in one small place if you're used to traveling freely. It's devastating when you're forced to march hundreds of miles from your home to a place that lacks the resources you need to survive.

MAIN IDEA The U.S. government continued to push Native Americans off their ancestral lands and onto reservations throughout the West.

CONFLICT IN THE ROCKIES AND THE NORTHWEST

Native Americans in the Rocky Mountains and northwest regions of the United States faced the same pressures and problems as those on the Great Plains. For example, the Crow lived in the Yellowstone River Valley and northern plains of Montana and Wyoming. During U.S. Army campaigns against other tribes, the Crow actually fought alongside the United States because the Crow leader believed the U.S. government would treat them well after it won. His plan backfired; the Crow were treated just like other tribes and forced to move to a reservation.

In 1855, representatives from several tribes, including the Blackfoot, the Flathead, the Pend d'Oreille (pahn dor-AY), the Nez Perce, and the Cree, met with U.S. government officials. The tribes agreed to use common hunting grounds and stay within set boundaries on the northern plains of Montana. The Blackfoot believed their homeland was safe under this treaty. But by 1862, prospectors had found gold on their lands. Mining camps sprung up across the area, and, as with the Lakota, the U.S. government forced the Blackfoot to leave.

The Nez Perce, led by **Chief Joseph**, refused to move onto a reservation. In 1877, Chief Joseph led his band of about 700 people toward Canada to live free lives outside the reservation system. However, the U.S. Army apprehended them just before they crossed the border and sent them far south to Indian Territory. There, many died from disease. The surviving members of the group were eventually sent to reservations in the Pacific Northwest. Today, many Nez Perce live in eastern Washington.

CONFLICT IN THE SOUTHWEST

Similar events took place in the Southwest. In 1864, the U.S. government forced thousands of Navajo to walk 300 grueling miles from their homelands in Arizona to the Bosque Redondo (BOH-skeh reh-DOHN-doh) reservation in New Mexico. Hundreds died along the route, which became known as the **Long Walk**. Bosque Redondo was a desolate place with a poor water supply and terrible farming conditions. Nearly one-third of those who lived through the walk starved or died from disease at Bosque Redondo. The Navajo suffered there for four years before the army realized how badly this relocation had failed. The survivors were allowed to return to their traditional lands, where tribe members still live today.

Cochise (koh-CHEES) was an Apache (uh-PA-chee) chief. At first, his people got along so well with settlers that tribe members helped build the Apache Pass stagecoach station in Arizona. The relationship soured in 1861 when Cochise was wrongly accused of kidnapping a rancher's son. He escaped arrest and fled into Arizona's Dragoon Mountains with about 200 of his people. They evaded capture for nearly a decade, and survived by raiding ranches and settlements from their mountain stronghold. Eventually, the government,

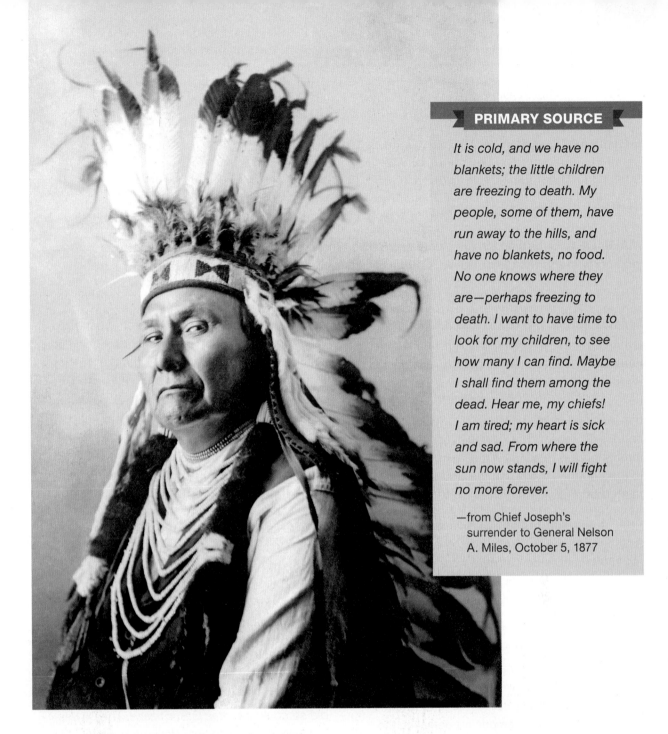

eager to end the hostilities, offered to make their homeland a huge reservation. Cochise agreed, and his people settled there.

Another Apache leader, **Geronimo,** was from New Mexico. The U.S. Army confined his people to a reservation in Arizona in the 1870s, but Geronimo refused to stay there. He left the reservation with a small group and raided settlements across the Southwest for two years. In September 1886, the army captured Geronimo, 16 men, 12 women, and 6 children and sent them and 300 others to prison. Released in 1887, Geronimo spent the rest of his life in present-day Oklahoma.

HISTORICAL THINKING

1. **READING CHECK** Why did Native Americans resist moving to reservations?

2. **CATEGORIZE** What categories can you use to describe the situations and actions of the Native Americans discussed in this lesson?

3. **DRAW CONCLUSIONS** What does Chief Joseph's surrender speech reveal about his character?

3.4 Wounded Knee

Does anyone benefit when a group is pressured to assimilate to a different culture? In the late 1800s, the U.S. government forced Native American youths to adopt the language, culture, and norms of American society.

MAIN IDEA Once the U.S. Army defeated Native Americans in the West, the government increased its efforts to force Native Americans to assimilate to American culture.

MASSACRE AT WOUNDED KNEE

By the late 1880s, most Native American tribes had moved to reservations, but they still offered resistance. Some Native Americans, including the Lakota, practiced the **Ghost Dance**, a religion that included rituals believed to make white settlers disappear. This new faith spread quickly throughout reservations in the West, giving hope to disheartened tribes that the land would be restored to Native Americans.

Every six weeks, tribes held a five-day ceremony that included meditation, prayer, chanting, and a nightly Ghost Dance. Dancers wore white shirts decorated with symbols, and they believed these "ghost shirts" could stop bullets.

The government feared the ghost dancers were planning a rebellion. The U.S. Army arrested their leaders, including Lakota Chief **Sitting Bull**, who was killed as he was taken into custody. A ghost dancer himself, Sitting Bull had long resisted government policies. Famous for defeating the U.S. Army at the Battle of the Little Big Horn, his death was a blow to his people, but even that did not stop their dancing.

On December 29, 1890, the army confronted a large group of Lakota ghost dancers at Wounded Knee Creek on the Pine Ridge Reservation in South Dakota and demanded the Lakota hand over their weapons. During the tense interaction, an unknown person fired a shot. U.S. troops opened fire immediately, killing between 200 and 300 Lakota. The **Wounded Knee Massacre** did not end the Ghost Dance, but from then on, the

ceremony was performed in secret. Wounded Knee marked the last major violent confrontation between Native Americans and the U.S. Army in the 19th century. As a result, many historians believe the capture of Geronimo and the Wounded Knee Massacre marked the end of the Native American wars.

MORE UNSUCCESSFUL POLICIES

When the wars ended, **Americanization** efforts began. The aim was to teach Native Americans the skills to assimilate into white, "civilized" society. In 1887, Congress passed the **Dawes General Allotment Act**, which divided reservations into parcels, or specific sections, of land for each Native American family. Land was allotted to the male as the head of the family, disregarding the status of females in tribal society. Recipients could not sell or lease their parcels for 25 years. The idea was that Native Americans would establish farms and adopt the "American" way of life. Those who did so could become U.S. citizens. The Dawes Act was intended to help Native Americans, but Congress refused to pass it until it was modified to allow the public sale of any unclaimed land. Few Native Americans participated.

The **Bureau of Indian Affairs**, established in the 1850s, was supposed to manage the reservations to benefit the tribes. However, the Bureau was corrupt, and the administration of the Dawes Act was mismanaged. White settlers quickly purchased the reservation land as "unclaimed," leaving Native Americans with the least desirable parcels. Additionally, Native Americans whose heritage did not include large-scale farming were

The Carlisle Indian Industrial School

The children shown in these two photos were among those captured in 1886 with Geronimo in Arizona. From Arizona, they were taken by train to Florida, and two months later, sent to the Carlisle Indian Industrial School of Pennsylvania. They arrived there on November 4, 1886, when the top photo was taken.

Richard Henry Pratt, former commander of a Buffalo Soldier unit, opened the school in 1879. He wanted the Native American students to speak only English and learn jobs he felt would help them fit into society. He thought the students would assimilate into white culture if they no longer practiced their traditional ideas and customs. Boys learned construction and farming; girls learned to clean, cook, and sew. All students learned geography, English, and arithmetic. Discipline was strict and enforced by physical punishment.

The children were desperately homesick, but after returning home, they found themselves lost in their own cultures and unable to use the skills they had learned at school. The school was a failure. Just 12 percent of the students graduated. Many ran away, and others died of disease or despair. The Carlisle School closed in 1918, but Native American children continued to be sent forcibly to boarding schools until the passage of the Indian Child Welfare Act in 1978.

accustomed to moving with the seasons and hunting. Their attempts to farm unsuitable land led to deteriorating community life on reservations and miserable poverty.

Another method of Americanization urged Native American children to reject their languages and customs. When this plan did not work, reformers decided that children couldn't assimilate if they were living with their own families. They sent Native American children to distant boarding schools where they were forced to speak English and forbidden to observe their own cultural practices.

HISTORICAL THINKING

1. **READING CHECK** What was the aim of U.S. government policies toward Native Americans in the late 1800s?

2. **DRAW CONCLUSIONS** Why do you think the U.S. Army arrested Sitting Bull and other leaders of the Ghost Dance religion?

3. **COMPARE AND CONTRAST** What effects did living at the Carlisle Indian Industrial School have on Native American children? Compare the photographs and use text evidence.

REVIEW

VOCABULARY

Use each of the following vocabulary words in a sentence that shows an understanding of the term's meaning.

1. cattle drive
   Cowboys moved herds of cattle to cow towns during cattle drives.

2. placer mining

3. stockyard

4. free silver movement

5. gold standard

6. Americanization

7. cooperative

8. reservation

9. Ghost Dance

READING STRATEGY
CATEGORIZE

If you haven't done so already, complete your graphic organizer by categorizing details about each group of people struggling for land in the American West. Then answer the question.

Rancher • Hired cowboys to lead cattle drives.	Farmer
Miner	Native American

10. Why did conflicts over land take place in the West in the last decades of the 1800s?

MAIN IDEAS

Answer the following questions. Support your answers with evidence from the chapter.

11. Why did boomtowns develop so quickly in the West? **LESSON 1.1**

12. Who played roles in the growing cattle industry in the United States? **LESSON 1.2**

13. What factors led the exodusters to migrate west? **LESSON 2.1**

14. What was the school experience like for children on the prairie? **LESSON 2.2**

15. How did the Grange help bring about populism? **LESSON 2.3**

16. Why did the U.S. government establish the reservation system? **LESSON 3.1**

17. What did the Crow do in the hopes that it would benefit them? **LESSON 3.3**

18. Why did reformers remove Native American children from their families living on the reservations? **LESSON 3.4**

HISTORICAL THINKING

Answer the following questions. Support your answers with evidence from the chapter.

19. **IDENTIFY PROBLEMS AND SOLUTIONS** Describe a technology that offered both solutions and problems in the West and Great Plains. Consider modes of transportation, tools and methods for farming and mining, and weapons in your response.

20. **CATEGORIZE** List and categorize the different reasons for western expansion in this period.

21. **DRAW CONCLUSIONS** Do you think it was wise to homestead on the Great Plains? Why or why not?

22. MAKE GENERALIZATIONS Why did the Populist Party appeal to many farmers?

23. DETERMINE CHRONOLOGY Choose a Native American tribe mentioned in the text. Describe the sequence of events that led to the tribe's relocation to a reservation.

24. DISTINGUISH FACT AND OPINION The U.S. government believed "Americanizing" Native Americans was essential for their welfare. What factors distinguish this idea as a fact or as an opinion? Use evidence from the text to support your response.

INTERPRET MAPS

Look closely at the map showing cities next to rivers flowing through the Great Plains in 1890. Then answer the questions that follow.

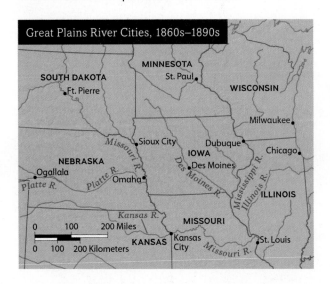

Great Plains River Cities, 1860s–1890s

25. From which cities and rivers could wheat farmers of South Dakota and Minnesota ship their grain south?

26. What is the most direct river route for shipping Kansas produce northward toward Chicago?

27. How many miles did passengers departing from St. Louis have to travel on a riverboat to get to Kansas City?

ANALYZE SOURCES

The Walker family homesteaded in Oklahoma in the late 1800s. As a married woman, Cudia Walker Ealum remembered her life in a sod house on the plains. Read the passage from an interview with Mrs. Ealum closely, and answer the question.

> We had a sod house [dugout], with dirt floor and dirt walls. . . . This was a hole about 12' x 16' and about 6' deep, dirt floors and walls. The top was made of heavy cottonwood logs laid across with grass, with dirt thrown on top. This made a nice snug house, but the bark on the logs was a good housing place for the centipedes. Often when lying awake we would see one crawl out and drop down on the bed, then how we would scramble to get out of bed.

28. What positive and negative memories does Cudia have about living in a sod house?

CONNECT TO YOUR LIFE

29. ARGUMENT Consider the inevitable clashes that occur among groups of people trying to claim the same land for themselves. Choose two groups of people who clashed over land in the American West, and ask yourself which group had the better claim to the land. Write a paragraph in which you describe the groups and the conflict, state your stance on it, and support your position with evidence from the text.

TIPS

- Before you write, list facts supporting both sides of the conflict. Decide which side you support and why.

- Note the evidence that best supports your position, and choose the two strongest reasons to include in your paragraph.

- State your argument clearly at the beginning of your paragraph.

- Have you addressed the topic? Revise or rewrite your paragraph, as needed.

National Geographic photographer Dan Westergren captured this photograph of 12-year-old Alex Lamont, a Native American of the Lakota Sioux. Alex performs traditional dances at gatherings called powwows.

NATIVE AMERICAN

CONFEDERACIES & NATIONS

BY DR. TERENCE CLARK

Director, Shíshálh Archaeological Research Project, University of Saskatchewan, Canada

You've read about how the Founding Fathers worked tirelessly to unite the colonies and create a form of government different from the hierarchies in Europe. But long before the United States was formed, many Native American tribes had determined they were stronger if they banded together. They already had democratic and inclusive governments in place. Some had even established voting rights for all, as well as basic law-making and amendment processes.

We don't know exactly how much the framers of the U.S. Constitution borrowed ideas from early Native American nations and confederacies. We do know that Thomas Jefferson, James Madison, James Monroe, and Benjamin Franklin were familiar with the governmental structure of Native American nations such as the League of the Iroquois. The framers even visited this group to learn from its strength and organization and observe its practices. Franklin in particular was so impressed by the organization of Native American governments, he felt it should be studied—and possibly imitated—by the colonies. And it was.

The Native American confederacy has persevered throughout history, through conflict, land loss, and relocation. Today, there are more than 550 of these federally recognized nations in the United States, including over 200 in Alaska alone. The nations are self-governing, which ensures they can retain and preserve their distinct cultural identities. As you read about two of the largest and most influential North American confederacies, the confederacies of the West and the Iroquois Confederacy, consider how these great nations formed and their impact on Americans and the U.S. government.

LIFE BEFORE CONFEDERACIES

As you have read, the Great Plains are the geographic heart of North America, stretching from the eastern slopes of the Rocky Mountains to the shores of the Mississippi River, from Texas well into Canada. Although they vary geographically, the Great Plains are primarily made up of open grasslands, wooded river valleys, and upland areas. This "sea of grass" has served as a habitat for huge numbers of bison, deer, pronghorn antelope, and other animals—resources relied upon by many Native American groups.

The Native American groups of the northern and western Great Plains, including the Blackfoot, Cheyenne, and Comanche, relied upon hunting large game, fishing, and gathering plants. Groups of the eastern Great Plains, such as the Hidatsa, Mandan, and Arikara, settled in villages and grew maize, beans, and squash, much like their Eastern Woodland neighbors.

Until the 1800s, the Native Americans of the Great Plains lived in small groups and made several short migrations each year. Camps were small but well connected. Trade and social gatherings brought people together into bigger groups to renew social ties and find marriage partners.

CONFEDERACIES OF THE WEST

As American settlers began moving into the Great Plains in the early and mid-1800s, independent Native American groups felt the need to create alliances to protect themselves from the settlers and from potentially hostile Native American neighbors. As you know, westward expansion drew miners, trappers, and traders to the region in search of their own fortunes, and the expansion of the railroad changed the trickle of newcomers to a torrent. As a result, Native American alliances grew and the great confederacies of the West were born.

Two of the most powerful western confederacies were the Sioux (SOO) Confederacy and the Blackfoot Confederacy. These were political and military powerhouses whose territories included large areas of the region. With neighboring communities competing for land and resources and threatening the culture and way of life of local peoples, confederacies gave Native Americans of the Great Plains strength and unity.

Bison and wildflowers fill the sweeping landscape of Wind Cave National Park in present-day South Dakota, traditional lands of the Sioux and Blackfoot Confederacies.

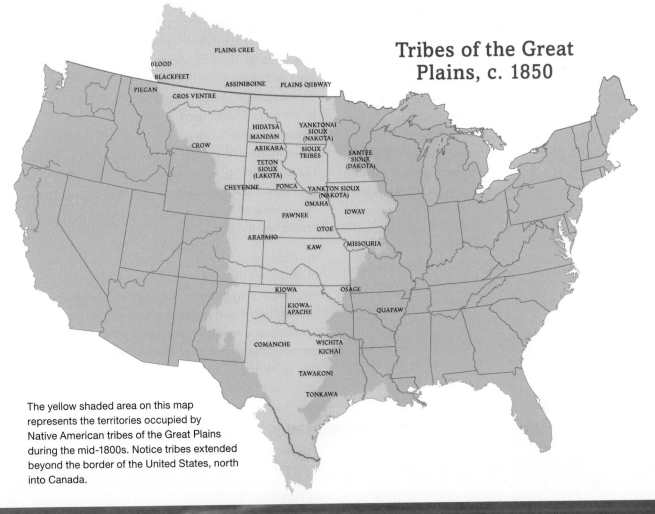

Tribes of the Great Plains, c. 1850

PLAINS CREE

BLOOD

BLACKFEET

PIEGAN

ASSINIBOINE   PLAINS OJIBWAY

GROS VENTRE

HIDATSA
MANDAN

YANKTONAI
SIOUX
(NAKOTA)

CROW

ARIKARA

SIOUX
TRIBES

SANTEE
SIOUX
(DAKOTA)

TETON
SIOUX
(LAKOTA)

CHEYENNE   PONCA

YANKTON SIOUX
(NAKOTA)

OMAHA

PAWNEE

IOWAY

ARAPAHO

OTOE

KAW

MISSOURIA

KIOWA

OSAGE

KIOWA-
APACHE

QUAPAW

COMANCHE

WICHITA
KICHAI

TAWAKONI

TONKAWA

The yellow shaded area on this map represents the territories occupied by Native American tribes of the Great Plains during the mid-1800s. Notice tribes extended beyond the border of the United States, north into Canada.

THE SIOUX AND THE BLACKFOOT

The Great Sioux Nation is a confederacy of groups that speak different dialects, or forms, of the Siouan language: Dakota, Nakota, and Lakota. You have probably seen the Sioux—especially the Lakota Sioux—in famous photographs, paintings, and movies as the proud and famous warriors on horseback from the northern Great Plains. Arguably the most iconic of all Native American groups, Lakota Sioux leaders include Crazy Horse, Sitting Bull, and Red Cloud. Lakota history contains some of the most recognizable Native American conflicts of all time, including the Battle of the Little Bighorn and the Wounded Knee Massacre. The people of the Great Sioux Nation have faced the challenges of relocation to reservations, assimilation, and poverty, and yet the nation has endured and remains strong in North and South Dakota to this day.

The Blackfoot Confederacy was once one of the largest Native American groups in the northern Great Plains. Its territory ran from the North Saskatchewan River in present-day Canada to the Yellowstone River, and from central Saskatchewan to the Rocky Mountains. By the 1750s, the Blackfoot were hunting on horses they got from other tribes with guns they got from British traders. Hunting, raiding, and trading helped the nation gain power and establish a thriving economy. However, a smallpox epidemic in 1837 significantly weakened the population.

In 1855, the U.S. government began the process of removing the confederacy from its native lands and dispersing groups onto reservations in the United States and Canada. Although the Blackfoot Confederacy was broken apart during the removal process, numerous Native American groups that were once part of the nation survived, and continue to thrive in the Great Plains and Canada.

This enormous mountain sculpture in the Black Hills—the Crazy Horse Memorial—has been in progress since 1948. When complete, this tribute to the Lakota Chief Crazy Horse will dwarf Mount Rushmore.

"INDIANS" IN HOLLYWOOD

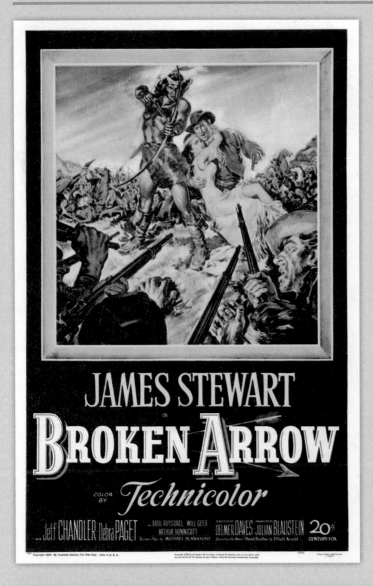

JAMES STEWART in **BROKEN ARROW** color by *Technicolor*

Jeff CHANDLER · Debra PAGET ... BASIL RUYSDAEL · WILL GEER · ARTHUR HUNNICUTT DIRECTED BY DELMER DAVES · PRODUCED BY JULIAN BLAUSTEIN   Screen Play by MICHAEL BLANKFORT Based on the Novel "Blood Brother" by Elliott Arnold   20th CENTURY-FOX

In the 1950s and 1960s, Westerns—fictional television series about the American West in the late 1800s—were on nearly every channel. Movie screens were filled with the same stories of scheming outlaws pursued by handsome lawmen, and noble cowboys protecting cattle from thieves and "civilized" white people from "uncivilized" Indians.

Some Native Americans played a legitimate role in Westerns that required skilled horse riders, but most Westerns represented Native American people as less than human. They were given few spoken lines, and were often shown being shot down or killed. Similarly, women in Westerns were often shown in need of rescue. Yet in reality, many women of the West were fiercely independent, taking on non-traditional roles and responsibilities. And contrary to their portrayal in movies, Native American women had great influence over their tribes and were sometimes warriors.

The 1950 Technicolor Western *Broken Arrow* featured several non-Native American actors playing the roles of Native American chiefs and being paid far more than Native-American actors.

DAVID BALD EAGLE

David Bald Eagle lived an extraordinary life. By the time of his 2016 death at the age of 97, he had been a Lakota tribal chief, a war hero, a champion dancer, a rodeo cowboy, a touring musician, an actor, a professional baseball player, and a race car driver. There was nothing he hadn't tried.

But most importantly, Bald Eagle was an advocate for Native people, a tribal leader, and an elder of the United Native Nations. His grandfathers entertained him with war stories to give him something to remember them by, making him a key connection between the past and present, the traditional and modern cultures.

Traditional Iroquois longhouses, like the one above in northern New York State, were made of tree bark.

The interior of this reconstructed 17th-century Seneca longhouse (left) represents how the people of the Iroquois Confederacy would have sheltered and lived.

THE IROQUOIS CONFEDERACY

Another example of a strong Native American nation is the Iroquois Confederacy, which you may remember reading about earlier in this book. This nation formed between 1570 and 1600. At first, this union of five tribes lived in present-day upstate New York and included the Mohawk, Oneida, Onondaga, Seneca, and Cayuga. The tribes were at one time enemies, but a Mohawk chief and an Onondaga speechmaker persuaded them they would be stronger if they united into a single confederacy, or nation. The tribes found security in this bond, forming what is known as the Great Law of Peace, which continues through today and is arguably the longest-lasting treaty in North America. In 1722, a sixth tribe, the Tuscarora, joined the League, and its territory expanded.

You might recall that together, the tribes in the Iroquois Confederacy became known as Haudenosaunee (hoe-dee-no-SHOW-nee)— People of the Longhouse—because of the types of dwellings they lived in. Their government revolved around a Council of Fifty, made up of representatives from the five tribes. This Council gathered to address issues and solve problems involving multiple tribes. All laws had to be passed unanimously, meaning a single person on the Council could block the law. That meant every man or woman—and there were women on the Council—had the same amount of power, regardless of how many members of his or her tribe sat on the Council. How does the structure of the Council of Fifty compare to the structure of today's U.S. government?

COMMON GROUND

The Iroquois Confederacy lasted through the 1780s, and at its height, reached from present-day Maine to North Carolina and from the Atlantic Ocean to the Mississippi River. It is possible many of our current U.S. government practices were influenced by those of the League. They include the use of discussion and debate before passing laws, removing leaders who were deemed ineffective, and making leaders accountable to the people. The Iroquois League also distinguished between its military and its civilians, as the United States does today.

It's not difficult to form connections between the tribes that united to form Native American confederacies and the colonies that came together to form the United States. Even the states that came together to form the Union and the Confederacy can be compared in a significant way to the formation of Native American nations: they saw strength in unity. Clearly the influence of Native American nations is evident in the government and social structure of the present-day United States.

Indian Nations have always been considered as distinct, independent political communities, retaining their original natural rights, as the undisputed possessors of the soil. The very term "nation" so generally applied to them, means "a people distinct from others."

—Chief Justice John Marshall, 1832

National Geographic photographer William Albert Allard captured this quiet moment as dancers check their makeup at a powwow on the Rocky Boy Indian Reservation in Montana.

INDUSTRIALIZATION AND IMMIGRATION
1860–1914

ESSENTIAL QUESTION
How did the Industrial Age transform America?

 AMERICAN STORIES A Country of Immigrants

AMERICAN GALLERY
ONLINE   The Skyscrapers of New York City

READING STRATEGY

IDENTIFY MAIN IDEAS AND DETAILS
When you identify a text's main idea and supporting details, you state the most important idea about a topic and determine which facts support that idea. Use a graphic organizer like this one to find main ideas and supporting details about the social and economic effects of the Industrial Age as you read the chapter.

Effects of the Industrial Age

Main Idea
Detail:
Detail:
Detail:

"Remember, remember always, that all of us . . . **are descended from immigrants."**

—Franklin D. Roosevelt

CRITICAL VIEWING People arriving from Europe to embark on new lives in the United States passed the welcoming Statue of Liberty just before reaching Ellis Island, above. What might the Statue of Liberty have symbolized for arriving immigrants?

A COUNTRY OF IMMIGRANTS

CRITICAL VIEWING Traveling to the United States was different for immigrants of different social classes. What do details in this photograph reveal about this family and their journey?

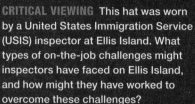

Teenager Annie Moore didn't know she'd be making history when she climbed aboard a boat in Ireland in 1891. On New Year's Day of 1892, she became the first immigrant to step ashore on Ellis Island in New York Harbor. There, a brand-new reception center had been built to receive the immigrants from Europe. Photographers were on hand to capture the moment the first immigrant landed at Ellis Island, making Annie special—but at the same time, she was just one of millions.

CROSSING THE ATLANTIC

Annie Moore was among the immigrants who came to the United States between 1870 and 1920. People seeking new lives arrived from all over the world. Millions of immigrants, many of whom were Jews fleeing persecution, landed on the East Coast from southern and eastern Europe. Others landed on the West Coast from different parts of Asia.

Those who could afford it traveled in comfortable first- or second-class cabins aboard the ships. Most, like Annie, made the journey in steerage—an open space below decks shared by all the poorer passengers. One immigrant described the conditions in steerage: "There must have been two to three hundred people in that huge, cavernous area. [There] was no such things as washing or bathing. The stench, the vermin, it was rat infested." It was a difficult journey, to say the least.

PRIMARY SOURCE

I'm smart enough to look out for myself. It's a new life now. In America, women don't need men to boss them. Thank God, I'm living in America! I'm going to make my own life. I'm going to live my own life. Nobody can stop me. I'm not from the old country. I'm an American!

—from *Bread Givers,* by Anzia Yezierska, 1925

ISLE OF TEARS, ISLE OF JOY

In 1907 alone, Ellis Island processed more than 1 million people. By the time the center closed in 1954, more than 12 million immigrants had passed through its halls. By one estimate, more than a third of present-day Americans have at least one ancestor who arrived at Ellis Island.

For many, Ellis Island was an overwhelming place. Few immigrants spoke English, but all had to go through an admission process. They were required to pass a health inspection and answer questions about their countries of origin and their finances.

They also had to reveal if they had relatives already in the United States. Many immigrants worried they would be denied admission to the country.

Some called Ellis Island the "Isle of Tears," but in reality, immigration officials made efforts to treat arriving immigrants decently. They were given meals, and the ill were cared for in an on-site hospital. In all, only about two percent of immigrants were refused entry into the country.

Memories of the Ellis Island experience vary wildly. One woman who arrived as a girl recounted, "[The] first meal we got—fish and milk, big pitchers

CRITICAL VIEWING New arrivals to Ellis Island lined up for health inspections and processing by Immigration Service officers in the Registry Room. On some days, more than 5,000 immigrants passed through this great hall. What do details from this 1900 photograph reveal about how immigrants might have felt while waiting in line in the Registry Room?

of milk and white bread. And I said, 'My God, we're going to have a good time here. We're going to have plenty to eat.'" But another immigrant recalled, "The people had such terrible sad faces. [There's] more tears in Ellis Island to ten people than, say, to a hundred people elsewhere."

An immigrant who arrived in 1921 summed up the experience in practical terms, "You had to wait in line to get the food. You had to get in line to get a blanket. And they weren't unkind, but . . . they had so many people to take care of."

LADY LIBERTY

For many immigrants entering Ellis Island, their first glimpse of the United States was the Statue of Liberty towering over New York Harbor. Completed in 1886, the statue was a gift from the French. Officially named "Liberty Enlightening the World," it stands an impressive 305 feet tall on Liberty Island, near Ellis Island. Every year, thousands of visitors climb up inside the hollow statue to enjoy the view through windows placed in its spiky crown.

Since its earliest days, the Statue of Liberty has served as a symbol of welcome to immigrants. In 1883, Emma Lazarus wrote a poem called "The New Colossus" to help raise funds to erect the statue. The poem's most famous lines depict Lady Liberty speaking to the countries of Europe, saying:

> *Give me your tired, your poor,*
> *Your huddled masses yearning to breathe free,*
> *The wretched refuse of your teeming shore.*
> *Send these, the homeless, tempest-tost to me,*
> *I lift my lamp beside the golden door!*

The poem was placed on a plaque at the base of the statue in 1903.

Why do you think Lazarus used a golden door as the image of a gateway to the United States?

Angel Island was more like a detention center than a welcome center. It was designed to control waves of Chinese coming into the country after the passage of the Chinese Exclusion Act of 1882. From 1910 to 1940, Angel Island processed Asian immigrants from China, Japan, Russia, and South Asia.

ANGEL ISLAND

While Ellis Island received European immigrants on the East Coast, a second reception center was built on the West Coast on Angel Island, just offshore from San Francisco. It was at Angel Island that many Hindu, Sikh, Chinese, Japanese, and Korean immigrants landed after journeying across the Pacific Ocean from Asia. While Angel Island is often compared to Ellis Island, the California center was built to exclude most Asian immigrants, not to welcome them.

At Angel Island, immigrants waited for days or weeks to find out whether they would be allowed to enter the United States. By contrast, the average time for processing at Ellis Island was less than a day. Some wrote poems on the walls, like the one shown on the right, to express their despair. One reads, "It's been seven weeks since my imprisonment / On this island—and I still do not know when I can land."

Angel Island closed in 1940. Precise numbers are not available, but it is estimated that officials there refused between 11 and 30 percent of immigrants.

These Chinese characters, which make up part of a poem, were carved into a wall in the Angel Island detention barracks. More than 200 poems written in Chinese have been transcribed from the walls of the immigration center. Hundreds more may have been buried by layers of paint.

Many of the poems at Angel Island express Chinese immigrants' frustration over their poor living conditions. Some even reveal their desire to seek revenge for their unfair treatment. This poet writes, "the American continent is the most difficult of difficulties."

PAPER SONS AND DAUGHTERS

Although the United States tried to keep out some Asian immigrants through Angel Island, they could not keep out Chinese immigrants who were already citizens because their fathers were U.S. citizens. According to immigration laws, Chinese immigrants who could prove their father's U.S. citizenship could not be denied entry into the United States. Immigration inspectors often suspected Chinese immigrants of avoiding Chinese exclusion laws by entering the country as "paper sons and daughters," a term used to describe immigrants who falsely claimed to be related to a U.S. citizen to gain citizenship for themselves.

Immigration inspectors subjected Chinese citizens to a much longer, more grueling admission process than those from Europe, Japan, or Korea. They spent hours interviewing Chinese immigrants with questions like these (right), designed to confirm their identities and call attention to paper sons and daughters. If an immigrant or his or her witnesses fumbled during the questioning process, the immigrant faced potential deportation back to China. Some of the questions were so abstract that even true children and wives occasionally failed the interrogation process.

What are the birth and death dates of your grandparents? Where are they buried?

Who lives in the third house in the fourth row of houses in your village?

How often did your father [or husband] write and how much money did he send home?

How many guests were at your wedding? What jewelry did your husband give you as wedding presents?

—from "Angel Island Immigration Station," by Judy Yung and Erika Lee, September 2015

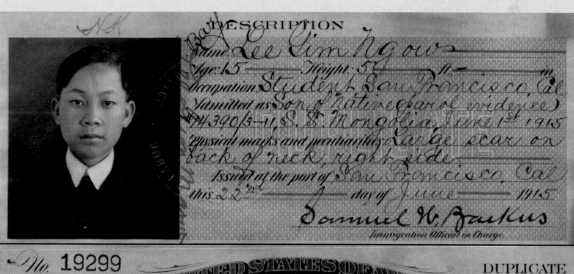

Gim Ngow Lee's immigration papers identify him as the child of Lee Yip Sing, a U.S. citizen, but Gim was a paper son. He arrived at Angel Island after a 35-day journey from China, passed the admission process, and moved to Chicago. Today, Gim Ngow Lee's son, Ben, is a docent on Angel Island, telling his father's story to the thousands of visitors who come to its shores.

ANNIE'S TALE

So what happened to Annie Moore after she stepped out of the headlines and into her new life in America? For nearly a century, it seemed she had disappeared without a trace, but in 1986, an elderly woman claimed Annie Moore was her mother. She said Annie had moved to the West, married, and opened the first hotel in Clovis, New Mexico.

It was a great story. The only problem was that the real Annie Moore had relatives who told a different tale. In 2006, Annie's true story came out. She had never been west or even traveled beyond New York City. Instead, she had lived the rest of her life in New York's Irish neighborhood, where she married and raised a large family. When a researcher gathered the real Annie's descendants, they were a diverse group including Dominicans, Chinese, Jews, and Italians. Annie's actual story may be less exciting than the colorful tales of her travels to the West, but it reflects the diverse and changing face of immigration.

Sculptor Jeanne Rynhart created two bronze sculptures of Annie Moore. One stands in Ireland, where Annie began her immigration journey. The other (shown here) is located at Ellis Island, where she landed.

THINK ABOUT IT

In what ways do Ellis Island and Angel Island reflect complex American attitudes toward immigration?

CRITICAL VIEWING Built in 1915 in Stockton, California, this Sikh temple, which Sikhs call a "Gurdwara" (gur-DWAR-ah) was the first permanent Indian religious building in the United States. What does this photograph reveal about the Sikh culture and traditions?

SIKH IMMIGRANTS

Sikhs (SEEKS or SIKZ) are followers of a religion called Sikhism, which was established in India around 1500. About 7,000 Hindu, Muslim, and Sikh immigrants came from India to the United States and Canada between 1899 and 1920. Angel Island records show that hundreds were processed in California.

Many Sikh immigrants had been skilled farmers in India. They sought agricultural jobs in California, and contributed to the state's development of farming. Many became migrant workers in the Sacramento Valley, eventually establishing permanent homes there. Inaccurately known as "Hindu crews," many faced discrimination and judgment in part because they dressed differently from other workers.

Other Sikhs found jobs in the railroad and lumber industries, oftentimes earning a lower wage than white workers doing the same tasks.

A NEIGHBORHOOD OF IMMIGRANTS

Many European immigrants settled in big industrial cities in the North, such as New York, Chicago, Detroit, and Philadelphia. They moved into neighborhoods with others from the same country or who had the same religion. There, they spoke their own languages and maintained their cultures. For example, in New York City, Jewish immigrants settled in the Tenth Ward, and Italians settled along Mott Street and Prince Street.

In the 1870s, a wave of Czech-speaking immigrants from Bohemia, an area of eastern Europe, was drawn to Chicago by the promise of jobs in lumber mills, garment factories, and railroad yards. Additionally, after Chicago's Great Fire in 1871, the city experienced an economic boom. More immigrants moved to Chicago to work to rebuild the city. The Bohemians settled into a neighborhood on the west side of the city. When one man opened a restaurant named after the Bohemian city of Plzen, the name stuck. Soon the whole neighborhood became known as Pilsen.

Like other immigrant groups, the Bohemians of Pilsen imprinted their culture on the neighborhood. They built buildings that reflected the architectural style of their homeland. They established stores, homes, and churches, creating a vibrant community within the larger city of Chicago.

Also like other groups, the Bohemians eventually left the neighborhood. The children and grandchildren of the original immigrants learned to speak English, and gradually moved away. In their place came immigrants from Mexico and other Spanish-speaking countries. Today, Pilsen is still notable for its Bohemian architecture, but now some buildings are decorated with bright, Mexican-themed murals. The language in the streets is Spanish, not Czech. The faces have changed, but Pilsen remains a lively, vital community within the city of Chicago. And so the immigrant story continues.

This 2006 mural is called *The Community*. It was commissioned by the Chicago Artist Coalition (CAC) in collaboration with Chicago's Pilsen community to celebrate the diversity of this neighborhood.

1.1 Industrial Revolution Gathers Steam

Imagine traveling to California by train in the 1860s. At one point after lunch, all the windows go dark—you are in a tunnel. When the train emerges, the beautiful peaks of the Sierra Nevada surround you.

MAIN IDEA In the late 1860s, railroads expanded across the Great Plains and the western mountain ranges to connect the East and West coasts.

RACING TO UTAH

Prior to the 1860s, the journey by land from the Midwest to the Pacific was difficult. To get to California, most settlers spent months traveling by wagon or stagecoach. To address the lack of efficient transportation west, the federal government passed the **Pacific Railway Acts** in 1862 and 1864, which put two companies in charge of building a **transcontinental railroad**, or a railroad that ran across the continent. The acts provided funds for the construction of rail lines by issuing government bonds and land grants. The **Central Pacific Company** would start building from Sacramento, California, and the **Union Pacific Company** from Omaha, Nebraska. They were to meet in the middle, and the federal government would pay for every mile of track the companies laid. The race was on.

The Central Pacific Company started off slowly. Equipment took several months to travel from the East Coast, where it was manufactured, to the West Coast because there were no reliable overland shipping routes through North America. Instead, ships had to carry the equipment all the way around the southern tip of South America and up its western coast in order to reach California.

The Central Pacific also had to figure out how to build a level track through the Sierra Nevada. Its solution was to blast tunnels through the rugged granite peaks. The railroad company had a hard time finding enough people for the difficult, dangerous job, but it eventually hired about 10,000 Chinese immigrants willing to take on the challenge. Even though the Nebraska prairie was smoother terrain than California's mountains, the Union Pacific faced difficulties, too. With few trees on the prairie, workers scrounged for adequate supplies of wood for constructing the ties that held the rails. Workers also faced the threat of attack by Native Americans, who saw the railroad as another invasion of their land.

Railroad laborers worked 12 to 16 hours a day, 7 days a week. They built bridges, blasted tunnels, and laid tracks through bitter winters and scorching summers. On May 10, 1869, the two lines met at Promontory, Utah. **Leland Stanford**, the president of the Central Pacific, hammered one last golden spike into the tracks to celebrate the achievement.

CHANGING TIMES

After the first transcontinental rail line opened, more railroad companies laid their own tracks. **Cornelius Vanderbilt**, who had dominated the steamship and ferry industries in the 1850s, turned his attention to railroads. He helped expand regional networks between Chicago and New York and make railroad transportation more efficient. By 1890, the United States boasted 185,000 miles of railroad track—more than in all of Europe. By 1895, four more railroads, the Northern Pacific, Southern Pacific, Great Northern, and Atlantic and Pacific, crisscrossed the country. People and goods could move across and around the nation in a relatively short time. Train passengers could travel from New

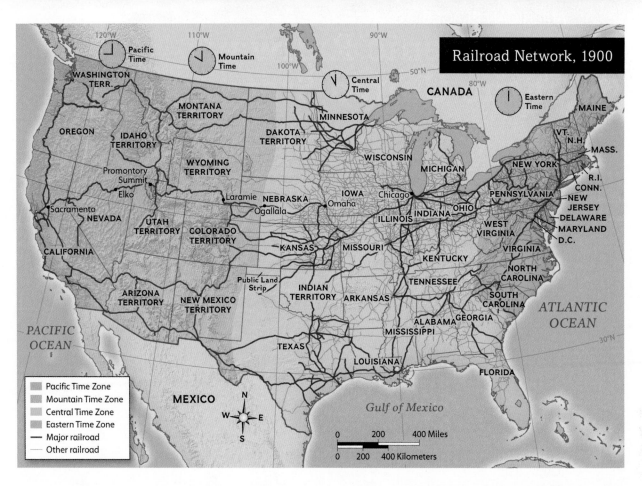

Railroad Network, 1900

York to California in one week instead of four to six months by stagecoach. Speedy rail transportation also opened up a national market. For instance, cattle ranchers in Nebraska could now transport their livestock to Chicago markets, and Chicago meatpackers could ship products to nationwide markets well before the meat spoiled.

The railroads did not benefit everyone, though. Train tracks cut through Native American land and hunting grounds. Small towns popped up quickly along the tracks. As a result, the government took more Native American land to satisfy the increasing desire for property. The natural environment suffered. Hunters came by train to kill buffalo for sport, even though Native Americans depended upon the animals for survival. The blasting of mountains and chopping down of trees required to lay the tracks changed the landscape forever.

The transcontinental railroad brought one unexpected change. Before trains, many towns ran on their own "local time" based on the sun's position in the sky. Railroad lines operated according to the local time of the town in which they originated. When passengers tried to make train connections, though, the differing times caused confusion. So in 1883, the railroads began operating according to four newly established time zones. The general public later adopted the time zones and standardized the time in each region. This concept is called **standard time**.

The transcontinental railroad had a huge impact on the country. But it was not the only major change the United States experienced in the late 1800s. Other important innovations soon followed.

HISTORICAL THINKING

1. **READING CHECK** Why was a transcontinental railroad important to the United States?

2. **ANALYZE ENVIRONMENTAL CONCEPTS** How did the railroads change the landscape, and what impact did they have on Native Americans?

3. **INTERPRET MAPS** What is the time change when traveling from Omaha to Laramie?

1.2 The Scenic Railways of the United States

As the nation continued to expand westward, the railways connected far-flung regions of the country. By the 1860s, tracks had extended westward into the gold- and silver-rich lands of Colorado. There, tracklayers met the towering peaks of the Rocky Mountains—not exactly easy ground for railway construction. But the Denver & Rio Grande Western Railroad Company met the challenge with the slogan "Through the Rockies, not around them." By 1881, the company's railroad had reached the town of Durango, Colorado, near the New Mexico border. A year later, it expanded to the mining town of Silverton, Colorado. There, trains began transporting precious metals down from the mountains. They also carried adventurous passengers who enjoyed both the gorgeous views from the train and the ability to visit parts of the country they would otherwise never have seen.

In recent decades, railway preservationists in Colorado have led a tourism effort beginning with the restoration of the "Painted Train," a gold and black sightseeing train on the Durango & Silverton Narrow Gauge line. A glass-topped car called the "Silver Vista" was also introduced to provide tourists with amazing views of the western scenery. Today, people still take this famous train route through the scenic San Juan range of the Rockies, as well as many other scenic railways throughout the United States.

CRITICAL VIEWING Based on what you have read and what you can tell from this image, what would tracklayers' biggest challenges have been when constructing railways like the Georgetown Loop Railroad in the Colorado Rockies?

GEORGETOWN LOOP RAILROAD

GEORGETOWN LOOP RAILROAD   C.L.R.X

705

1157

1.3 The Age of Invention

We use electric lights and telephones every day, so it is easy to take both inventions for granted. Thanks to the clever ideas of inventors of the late 1800s, we enjoy bright lights and speedy communication.

MAIN IDEA In the late 1800s, innovations in industries and technologies played important roles in the continued development of the Industrial Age.

NEW INDUSTRIES, NEW INVENTIONS

Railroads were the nation's first big business, but they weren't the only one. Other major industries emerged in the late 1800s that would change the ways Americans lived and worked.

Building railroads requires **steel**, a hard metal made from a mixture of iron and carbon. Railroad companies needed a lot of steel to make railroad tracks, locomotives, and train cars. And they needed it fast. Unfortunately, making steel was expensive and time-consuming. How could steel factories meet the demand? The answer came in the 1870s when improvements were made to a new technique, the **Bessemer process**. The process involved blowing air into molten iron to remove impurities. The result was a stronger metal that took only a half hour to produce. The Bessemer process made mass production of steel possible.

Another revolutionary development in the 1870s was made possible when **Thomas Alva Edison** invented the first reliable electric lights for home use. Within just five years of their debut, electric light bulbs lit 500 homes in New York City. When word about Edison's invention spread, many more people wanted electric lights installed in their homes. But that caused a problem. The lights relied on an electric current that lost power when it traveled from its source to people's homes. A former colleague of Edison's, Nikola Tesla, developed a system for delivering electric power using an alternating current. Alternating current, or AC, electric power could travel longer distances than the direct current, or DC, power Edison and his team had developed. Tesla sold his patent to industrialist George Westinghouse, who quickly embraced and marketed Tesla's new and improved method.

Reliable lights were not Edison's only electric invention. As a young man, Edison invented the electrographic vote recorder. The recorder allowed legislators in Congress to cast their votes electronically instead of voting by voice. Edison also invented the electric pen, which created a stencil as the person wrote. The writer could then use the stencil and ink to make copies of a document.

For his inventions, Edison received 1,093 U.S. **patents**, or exclusive rights granted to inventors. As an entrepreneur, he marketed his inventions to the public and started various manufacturing companies to make and sell devices based on his ideas.

RAPID COMMUNICATION

Other inventions also led to the development of new businesses and an expanding economy. The sewing machine, the refrigerated freight car, and inexpensive paper made from wood pulp were just a few of the inventions that grew into big businesses such as sewing machine manufacturers and paper goods companies. The rise of these businesses would make offices and factories common workplaces.

Edison's Filament Lamp
In 1879, Edison came up with a design for a light bulb that wouldn't burn out instantly. A longer-lasting bulb made lamps like this one more practical for daily use in American homes.

In 1868, **Christopher Sholes** invented the typewriter, a printing machine similar to a computer keyboard. The typewriter allowed people to produce written communication quickly. The need for easily readable notes and the ability to make copies became more important as other industries rapidly developed and expanded.

Eight years after the typewriter appeared, **Alexander Graham Bell** spoke the first words transmitted over a telephone to his assistant: "Mr. Watson—come here—I want to see you." Bell demonstrated his new invention that same year at the Centennial Exposition in Philadelphia. He then joined two investors, Gardiner C. Hubbard and Thomas Sanders, to form the Bell Telephone Company, which expanded rapidly because of Americans' high demand for telephones. Bell's invention has evolved into the cell phones and smartphones we use today. Alexander Graham Bell would become the first president of the National Geographic Society in 1898.

The First Flight

On December 17, 1903, after years of collecting data and building and testing their invention, the Wright brothers attempted the first powered airplane flight near Kitty Hawk, North Carolina. While Orville piloted, Wilbur ran alongside the plane to keep it steady. The first flight lasted just 12 seconds, but by the end of the day, another flight lasted almost a minute. Winter weather didn't allow more flights until the spring, but the Wright brothers knew they had built something that would change the world.

HISTORICAL THINKING

1. **READING CHECK** How did electric power transform American society?

2. **MAKE INFERENCES** In what ways do you think both telephones and typewriters helped make office work faster and more efficient?

3. **ANALYZE CAUSE AND EFFECT** What effect did the Bessemer process have on the steel industry?

1.4 Growth of Big Business

In some ways, success breeds more success. For shrewd businessmen in the late 1800s, successful companies relied upon and increased the industrial expansion of the United States.

MAIN IDEA American industries grew in size and complexity in the late 19th and early 20th centuries, and a few of their leaders became wealthy.

STEEL AND OIL

As the nation expanded, industries that enabled that expansion grew as well. In order to operate, industries such as railroads and steel mills needed access to large sums of money. Owners asked other wealthy businessmen to invest money in their companies in exchange for a share of future earnings. As a result, groups of people, rather than an individual or a family, owned the business. A business in which a group of people owns shares in a large company and that acts as one entity is called a **corporation**.

One of the industrial giants of the late 19th century was **Andrew Carnegie**, who bought his first steel plant in 1875. His expanding business eventually became the Carnegie Steel Company. Carnegie cut the cost of producing steel by more than half, which forced many of his competitors out of business. In the 1890s, Carnegie Steel shifted to the open-hearth method of steel production, in which workers added scrap metal to the molten iron ore. The new process surpassed the Bessemer process in efficiency. Steel production doubled between 1890 and 1900 because of the new technique. As production increased, the price of steel dropped even lower. In 1901, Carnegie became the richest man in the world when he sold his company, which became U.S. Steel Corporation.

Opened in 1909, the Manhattan Bridge spans the East River between Manhattan and Brooklyn, New York. It stands just upriver from the iconic Brooklyn Bridge, which opened 26 years earlier.

Andrew Carnegie (left) and John D. Rockefeller (right) both believed in the importance and value of higher education. Carnegie founded what would eventually be named Carnegie Mellon University in Pittsburgh, and Rockefeller helped establish the University of Chicago.

Oil was another high-growth industry in the late 1800s. Before electricity was in every home, Americans depended on oil for heat and light. Industries needed oil to keep machinery running smoothly. Transporting oil was big business for railroads and steamship companies. In 1870, **John D. Rockefeller** founded the Standard Oil Company in Ohio. By the end of the decade, Rockefeller controlled about 90 percent of the country's oil-refining capacity and had assumed control of most of his competitors. In fact, he nearly achieved a monopoly on the industry.

In 1882, Standard Oil became a **trust**, or a group of corporations managed, but not directly owned, by a board, or a group of people. This distinction allowed Standard Oil to bypass state laws and keep its business methods private. As a trust, Rockefeller's business could own stock in other oil companies and operate in multiple states.

POWER AND WEALTH

Corporations, trusts, and other businesses thrived in the United States because of **capitalism**. Capitalism is an economic system in which private individuals or groups, as opposed to the government, own and profit from factories and farms. In the late 1800s, federal and state governments rarely interfered with how businesses made money. This economic policy called **laissez-faire** (leh-say FAIR) capitalism, allowed

businesses to operate without much regulation. The phrase *laissez-faire* generally means "leave alone" in French. Leaving businesses alone might have been good for owners, but the lack of regulations and government oversight put workers at a disadvantage.

At the same time that companies and industries were growing larger and more powerful, the economy experienced several recessions, or periods of economic decline, and prolonged financial disruption. Intense **boom-and-bust cycles**, or periods of economic growth followed by sudden economic downturns, characterized the last decades of the 19th century. Boom-and-bust cycles had dramatic consequences on industries and individuals alike.

Though John D. Rockefeller and Andrew Carnegie were shrewd in business, they also believed in the Gospel of Wealth, or the idea that the very wealthy had a responsibility to share their wealth and help others. Both engaged in **philanthropy**, or the financial support of worthy causes.

During his lifetime, Rockefeller donated more than $500 million to various educational institutions, scientific and medical research, medical facilities, and international relief. Likewise, Carnegie established several philanthropic organizations and donated millions of dollars to education, scientific research, and international peace efforts. Carnegie also founded and funded more than 2,500 public libraries throughout the United States. By the end of his life, Carnegie had given away 90 percent of his wealth.

HISTORICAL THINKING

1. **READING CHECK** When and why did Andrew Carnegie and John Rockefeller become so powerful?

2. **DESCRIBE** How did the expansion of the nation depend on and encourage the growth of the steel and oil industries?

3. **IDENTIFY MAIN IDEAS AND DETAILS** What is laissez-faire capitalism, and why did it help industries grow in the late 19th century?

1.5 Mass Culture During the Gilded Age

Nowadays when people get bored, they can play games, read, or watch movies on their phones or computers. Turn-of-the-century Americans enjoyed reading, games, and shows, too—just not on electronic devices.

MAIN IDEA Americans enjoyed a variety of entertainments in the late 1800s, all of which helped to shape the American identity.

ALL THAT GLITTERS IS NOT GOLD

Big business in the United States expanded rapidly between 1870 and 1900, and those who profited from it became extremely rich. Some people believed these newly rich people were generous and moral in the public eye, but shrewd and greedy in private. Rockefeller donated millions of dollars to build schools and hospitals, but he earned that money by dominating his industry and avoiding business laws. Some people saw his philanthropy as a way to distract people from his immoral business tactics. Still, many people hoped to become similarly rich.

In 1873, authors **Mark Twain** and Charles Dudley Warner published *The Gilded Age*, a novel about the greed they believed was corrupting the country. "What is the chief end of man?—to get rich. In what way?—dishonestly if we can; honestly if we must," they lamented. Twain and Warner wrote about the underlying greed that was tarnishing the identity of the United States. They described the age as gilded because things that are gilded are covered in a thin layer of gold to make them appear more brilliant or luxurious. The name caught on, and the last three decades of the 19th century became known as the **Gilded Age**.

CULTURE AND ENTERTAINMENT

Twain and Warner's novel had the power to name a time period because of the development of **mass culture**, a culture that grows out of widespread access to media, music, art, and forms of entertainment. Americans were able to take advantage of this emerging mass culture because they were more literate. More American children were attending elementary school, and the number of students enrolled in high school rose every year from 1889 to 1900. Growing industry played a role, too. As production processes became more efficient and less expensive, books, magazines, and newspapers became more widely available and affordable. Even those who could not afford to buy books or magazines could visit one of the Carnegie-funded libraries and borrow books.

Urbanization also contributed to the development of mass culture. Working-class youth especially enjoyed the opportunities cities provided. Young men and women living in cities experienced a new independence, both socially and financially. The social convention of dating emerged. Young people met in public spaces such as movie houses, amusement parks, and dance halls. Young men, who on balance earned more than young women, paid their dates' way.

Souvenirs from the World's Columbian Exposition included decorative spoons and dishes, coin purses, and engraved matchboxes like this one featuring the Ferris wheel.

WORLD'S COLUMBIAN EXPOSITION CHICAGO 1893

E PLURIBUS UNUM

COLUMBUS 1492

Registered. Printed in Germany.

CRITICAL VIEWING The World's Columbian Exposition of 1893, sometimes called the Chicago World's Fair, occupied 630 acres of the city. More than 27 million people from all over the world visited the exposition between May and October. International fairs like this one were wildly popular with visitors. They were fascinating cultural events as well as opportunities for host cities to establish a national presence. How are the city of Chicago and the World's Fair portrayed through details in this poster?

Attending sporting events was another form of entertainment during the Gilded Age, and baseball was the most popular game of all. Cities responded to baseball's popularity by building large stadiums, including Fenway Park in Boston in 1912 and Ebbets Field in Brooklyn in 1913.

In 1893, the city of Chicago hosted the World's Columbian Exposition, to celebrate the 400-year anniversary of Columbus's arrival in the New World. Taking place within the context of rapid industrialization and an unpredictable economy— and only 28 years after the Civil War—this world's fair showcased the "progress of civilization," groundbreaking inventions, and the strength of American industry. One of the highlights for visitors was taking a ride on the world's first Ferris wheel. Purposely built taller than Paris's Eiffel Tower, the Ferris wheel rose 264 feet in the air and offered a spectacular view of the many buildings of the exposition and the city itself.

Electricity was presented to Americans for the first time at the Chicago World's Fair. Thousands gathered to watch President Grover Cleveland light the fairgrounds with a press of a button.

HISTORICAL THINKING

1. **READING CHECK** What was the Gilded Age?

2. **MAKE CONNECTIONS** How did rising literacy and more efficient production processes lead to the development of mass culture?

3. **IDENTIFY MAIN IDEAS AND DETAILS** What forms of entertainment did Americans enjoy during the Gilded Age?

2.1 The New Immigrants

Moving to a different country to start a new life can be exciting, but it can be scary, too. For the millions of immigrants who came to the United States beginning in the late 19th century, it was both.

> **MAIN IDEA** At the turn of the 19th century, millions of people from Europe and Asia moved to the United States.

ARRIVING IN A NEW LAND

Between 1870 and 1900, approximately 12 million people moved to the United States in search of new lives and better opportunities. Most came from countries in southern and eastern Europe and Asia, and from Mexico. In 1892, **Ellis Island** opened in New York, replacing Castle Garden as the main East Coast entry point to the United States. In 1907 alone, approximately 1.25 million immigrants entered through Ellis Island—more people than in any previous year.

The sheer number of people entering the United States strained the housing capacities of some cities. Quickly constructed apartment buildings called **tenements** were built to house immigrants and new city residents.

Southern and eastern European immigrants who came through Ellis Island were mainly Italian, Polish, Hungarian, Russian, and Czech. Many settled in New York City and worked in construction, building bridges and subway systems. Others worked in the shipping industry on the docks, or in the garment industry making clothes. Immigrants to midwestern cities such as Pittsburgh and Cleveland found work in steel mills. Coal mining in Pennsylvania and West Virginia drew many southern and eastern European immigrants.

Mining also drew immigrants to the West. People from Asia arrived on the West Coast, and they settled in California, Washington, and Oregon. Many Asian immigrants worked in agriculture and the logging, mining, railroad, and restaurant industries. People from China, Japan, Korea, India, and the Philippines arrived at different times and for different reasons. Some wanted to embrace new opportunities in the United States. Others wanted to escape poverty or break from oppressive social systems. Still others were **refugees**, or people who flee to another country to escape danger or persecution. Beginning in 1910, immigrants to the West Coast passed through **Angel Island,** located in the bay off the coast of San Francisco, California. Also in 1910, Mexican immigrants began to move to Texas, Arizona, and California where many worked in mining and agriculture.

BECOMING AMERICAN

Native-born Americans expected newly arrived immigrants to assimilate into American culture. Reformers in the late 19th century placed Native Americans in boarding schools and tried to force them to adopt new cultures and traditions. Similarly, some reformers believed that immigrants should "become American" by learning English and adopting American traditions.

Many immigrants wanted to Americanize. They learned English, adopted American holidays and culture, and prepared to become citizens. Others preferred to maintain ties with their home countries. Still others managed to incorporate facets of both worlds into their new American lives.

Immigrant children who entered public schools Americanized faster than their parents. At school, they socialized with native-born schoolmates and adopted American social customs. Most immigrants did not speak English, but children were placed in English-only classrooms. Some adjusted and learned the new language quickly, but others struggled with the language barrier.

Ukraine

India

Italy

Guadeloupe Islands

Russian Empire

Algeria

Whether immigrants settled in the East, Midwest, or West, they established communities, religious organizations, and **mutual aid societies**, or groups that helped other immigrants. At the same time they became American, they introduced their own cultures and traditions to the United States. Today, the legacy of millions of immigrants who ventured to a new country is evident in many cities and communities across the nation, from street signs and restaurants to places of worship.

HISTORICAL THINKING

1. **READING CHECK** What industries did immigrants work in once they arrived in the United States?

2. **IDENTIFY MAIN IDEAS AND DETAILS** In the years between 1870 and 1910, who immigrated to the United States, and why?

3. **DRAW CONCLUSIONS** What impact did Americanization efforts have on immigrants?

The Lower East Side Tenement Museum in Manhattan depicts life in the gritty housing available to the working poor in the late 1800s and early 1900s. The museum itself is housed inside a five-story brick tenement built in 1863 for the working class immigrants entering New York. Tenements were often overcrowded and unsanitary. This particular building had 20 apartments that housed anywhere from 77 to 111 people at any given time. The museum features apartments restored to show visitors how German, Irish, Italian, and eastern European immigrant families may have lived. What do the images below tell you about the lives of immigrants?

Levine Family Parlor

The Levine family emigrated from what is now Poland in 1890. Hundreds of thousands of Poles had moved into the United States seeking better employment opportunities and safety from political unrest. The Levines set up a dress shop in their parlor and sewed garments for a larger company. After paying their employees, the Levines were left to survive on 16 dollars a week.

Why do you think this sewing machine was placed next to the only window?

Confino Family Kitchen

The Confino family originally lived in the city of Kastoria in present-day Greece. In 1910, when they learned their teenage son Joseph could be drafted into the army, they chose to move to the United States. Ten Confinos lived in this small apartment for three years until they moved to East Harlem with other members of their Jewish community.

Rachel Confino and her daughters scrubbed their dirty laundry in a large sink using a wooden washboard.

Rogarshevsky Family Parlor

Members of the large Lithuanian Rogarshevsky family moved in and out of this tenement on Orchard Street for three decades. They were part of a group of some 250,000 Lithuanians who immigrated to the United States during the early 1900s.

After the death of her husband, Abraham, in 1918, Fannie Rogarshevsky supported her family by working as a janitor for the tenement. She was known for keeping her own apartment immaculately clean. Fannie remained in this apartment until 1941, six years after the building had officially been closed.

Challah is a type of bread made from braided dough. Jewish families like the Rogarshevskys eat challah on religious holidays.

Baldizzi Family Kitchen

Italians Adolpho and Rosaria Baldizzi raised their two children in this apartment. They had emigrated from Palermo, Sicily, in 1923 along with other southern Italians who came to America seeking jobs. Although they entered the country illegally, they later became citizens.

Rosaria spent a lot of time in this kitchen, caring for her family. With the radio blaring in the background, she cooked, cleaned, and joked with Adolpho and the kids. A popular figure in the neighborhood, Rosaria returned to the Lower East Side to socialize and shop even after the family was evicted from this tenement when the building closed in 1935.

Rosaria Baldizzi worked in a garment factory and likely used her sewing skills at home, too. Which items in this photograph might Rosaria have made herself?

2.3 Cities Grow Rapidly

What do you think of when you hear the word *city*? Crowds of people? Traffic jams? In the late 19th and early 20th centuries, American cities were just starting to grow into the bustling places we know today.

MAIN IDEA New methods of transportation and construction transformed American cities, and reformers addressed the challenges of urban poverty.

URBAN LIFE: PROS AND CONS

In the late 19th and early 20th centuries, the rapid and widespread growth of industries such as railroads and steel mills led to the growth of American cities. Economic, industrial, and population patterns shifted from rural areas to cities, a process known as **urbanization**. Rural migrants, including African Americans from the South, and immigrants moved to cities in search of new opportunities.

Beginning in the 1880s, **streetcars** became the main form of transportation in American cities. Streetcars could carry many passengers at once, and they ran on rails, like trains. Some ran directly on rails embedded in the streets. Others were elevated above street level or moved underground as subways. Many cities developed streetcar systems, including Boston, San Francisco, Chicago, and New York.

The shift from walking or riding in a horse-drawn carriage to other forms of transportation allowed **suburbs**, areas on the edges of cities made up mostly of residences, to develop. Suburbs developed along rail lines extending far past the growing city centers. Wealthy people moved away from the crowded cities to the nearby countryside where they could build more spacious homes. Railroad terminals in both cities and suburbs made transportation between them quick, easy, and convenient.

Cities were exciting places in which to live and work, but they were also filled with a range of problems. Corruption in big city governments was an accepted practice and **political machines**, or agreed-upon, exclusive power structures, were in charge. City officials bribed politicians, contractors, and voters, and these arrangements powered the machines. In cities such as Chicago and New York, political machines were efficient, if corrupt, ways by which mayors and political bosses managed their cities.

In New York City, William Magear Tweed, or "Boss Tweed," led a Democratic Party committee called **Tammany Hall.** Tweed secured city contracts for his supporters and associates to build New York's skyscrapers. In other words, if a person voted for one of Tweed's candidates, he would be more likely to get a well-paid job. Newspapers charged Tweed with corruption. Though the charges against Tweed eventually brought his political power to an end in 1873, political machines continued to operate.

Despite its corruption, Tammany Hall helped New York City's poor as well as immigrant populations. The contracts that Tweed awarded helped build roads and install sewers and gas lines. Impoverished parts of the city were overcrowded and had inadequate sanitation, and their residents were grateful for improvements.

CITIES AND REFORMERS

Help for people in need came from a variety of sources. Protestant ministers who had witnessed the suffering that accompanied poverty preached the gospel to promote social reforms as part of the **Social Gospel** movement. They advocated ending child labor, restricting work on Sundays, and providing disability insurance for workers injured on the job.

In 1889, **Jane Addams** and **Ellen Gates Starr** opened **Hull House** in a working-class Chicago neighborhood. It provided daycare, an art gallery, and libraries, among other services. Hull House was a **settlement house**, or a place that provided assistance to poor and immigrant residents. In its second year of operation, Hull House helped more than 2,000 people per week, including immigrants from Italy, Ireland, Germany, Russia, Poland, Bohemia, China, Sweden, and Norway. Because education was important to Addams and the other founders, Hull House offered arithmetic, sewing, job-hunting, drawing, and exercise classes. It also provided citizenship classes and language lessons in English, Italian, Latin, French, and German.

Addams, Starr, and others at Hull House also promoted laws that protected children and established social welfare programs. They persuaded Illinois leaders to pass child labor laws and to make public education mandatory for all children. Additionally, these committed reformers inspired the creation of the juvenile court system, so children did not have to be tried as adults.

▥ Jane Addams Hull-House Museum, Chicago

One of the first programs Jane Addams set up at Hull House was a nursery school, where she often read to and taught young children. The care of children was important to her vision of a diverse, democratic community. To support that view, Hull House also established a kindergarten and an early version of a formal playground, where instructors engaged children in games.

HISTORICAL THINKING

1. **READING CHECK** What structural changes did cities undergo in the late 1800s?

2. **MAKE GENERALIZATIONS** How did Tammany Hall demonstrate the pros and cons of political machines?

3. **IDENTIFY MAIN IDEAS AND DETAILS** What were some of the ways in which different groups tried to address urban poverty?

2.4 How Geology Defines Your Skyline

MAIN IDEA Skyscrapers transformed cities, and an understanding of geology made these buildings possible.

By Andrés Ruzo, **National Geographic Explorer**

When you think of **skyscrapers**, Chicago's Willis Tower or New York's Empire State Building probably come to mind. But the first modern skyscraper rose only 10 stories high—and it changed the way cities grew. This historic high-rise was the Home Insurance Building, built in Chicago in 1885. It towered over the wooden buildings of its day. It also looked vastly different. That's because it was supported by a steel frame.

In older buildings, the walls bore the weight of the structure. In this early skyscraper, the frame bore the weight of the walls. It was a revolutionary idea. And with its elevators and modern plumbing system, the Home Insurance Building set the standard for future skyscrapers.

It turned out the secret to building skyscrapers lay not in looking up, but in looking down. Way down. By the early 1900s, engineers had discovered that a skyscraper could be stabilized by anchoring its foundation deep into **bedrock**, the solid rock underlying loose soil. Builders set concrete pillars into the bedrock to support a skyscraper's steel frame and prevent the building from collapsing.

The skyscraper reached its height—literally—in 1931, when the Empire State Building rose 102 stories in the air. One of the reasons the building stands where it does is because the bedrock beneath it lies relatively close to the surface. This made it easier to lay the foundation. Although other factors may have been involved, including population distribution and the location of economic centers, most of New York's tallest buildings stand where the bedrock is shallow.

But sometimes a location's geology isn't so cooperative. In Chicago, a city that sits atop mostly swampy, shifting soil, the bedrock can be as much as 85 feet underground. In the late 1800s, engineers tried to float large buildings on a layer of clay, but this resulted in sinking, uneven floors.

Skyscrapers have come a long way since the Home Insurance Building, climbing from 10 stories to more than 100. We've soared into the sky thanks to improved technology and building methods and a solid understanding of what lies beneath our feet.

CRITICAL VIEWING People sit atop bedrock that rises high above the ground in New York City's Central Park. Do you think the area around the park is or is not suitable for skyscrapers? Why?

THINK LIKE A GEOLOGIST

1. **IDENTIFY MAIN IDEAS AND DETAILS** How does an area's geology have an impact on urban development?

2. **DRAW CONCLUSIONS** What geologic conclusions can you draw about an area of a city where there are no skyscrapers?

Basement

Column

Pillar cap

Pillar

Soft soil

Clay

Anchor bulb

Bedrock

Pillar

Anchor bulb

Bedrock

The Empire State Building's antenna spire sketches an exclamation point on New York's skyline. It was the tallest building in the world for 42 years. The diagram shows the concrete pillars anchored in bedrock to support the building's frame.

2.5 Urban Poverty

How do you get people to pay attention to an uncomfortable problem? In the late 19th and early 20th centuries, photographers, social reformers, and novelists used their talents to highlight the terrible conditions the poor endured in American cities.

Jacob Riis was a Danish immigrant who arrived in the United States at age 21. Often poor and homeless, he bounced from job to job until he landed work as a police reporter in New York City. He taught himself photography and began to capture in words and photos what he saw around him. In 1890, Riis published *How the Other Half Lives*, a pioneering work of photojournalism about the urban poor in late-19th

century New York City. An immediate success, the book included vital statistics as well as Riis's photographs.

CRITICAL VIEWING Riis photographed these children huddled together for warmth in a window well on New York's Lower East Side. What impact do you think this Jacob Riis photo might have had on people who saw it in *How the Other Half Lives*?

DOCUMENT ONE

Primary Source: Nonfiction Book
from *How the Other Half Lives*, by Jacob Riis, 1890

The tenements of New York City were unhealthy places to live. They were also the focus of many reformers who wanted to improve living conditions for their residents. In this excerpt, Riis describes conditions in the city's tenements.

CONSTRUCTED RESPONSE Why do you think tenements might have been a cause of "despair" for public health officials?

To-day three-fourths of its people live in the tenements, and the nineteenth century drift of the population to the cities is sending ever-increasing multitudes to crowd them. The fifteen thousand tenant houses that were the despair of the sanitarian [public health official] in the past generation have swelled into thirty-seven thousand. We know now that there is no way out; that the "system" that was the evil offspring of public neglect and private greed has come to stay.

DOCUMENT TWO

Primary Source: Novel
from *The Jungle*, by Upton Sinclair, 1906

In his novel *The Jungle*, Upton Sinclair explores the terrible working conditions of Chicago's stockyards and the labor abuses of immigrant workers. In this excerpt, Sinclair describes the dismal conditions of the city, as seen by immigrants who have arrived to work in the stockyards.

CONSTRUCTED RESPONSE How did Chicago appear to new immigrant workers in Sinclair's novel?

Down every side street they could see . . . ugly and dirty little wooden buildings. Here and there would be a bridge crossing a filthy creek, with hard-baked mud shores and dingy sheds and docks along it . . . here and there would be a great factory, a dingy building with . . . immense volumes of smoke pouring from the chimneys, darkening the air above and making filthy the earth beneath. But after each of these interruptions, the desolate procession would begin again—the procession of dreary little buildings.

DOCUMENT THREE

Primary Source: Autobiography
from *Twenty Years at Hull-House*, by Jane Addams, 1910

Jane Addams wrote *Twenty Years at Hull-House* about her work and experiences at Hull House, the settlement house she founded in Chicago. In it, she details many of the challenges poor immigrants faced in Chicago.

CONSTRUCTED RESPONSE What point do you think Addams is trying to make about the circumstances poor immigrants face?

This piteous dependence of the poor . . . was made clear to us in an early experience with a peasant woman straight from the fields of Germany, whom we met during our first six months at Hull-House. Her four years in America had been spent in patiently carrying water up and down two flights of stairs, and in washing the heavy flannel suits of iron foundry workers. For this her pay had averaged thirty-five cents a day.

SYNTHESIZE & WRITE

1. **REVIEW** Review what you have learned about these depictions of urban poverty by Riis, Sinclair, and Addams.

2. **RECALL** On your own paper, write down what the three passages and photograph tell you about urban poverty in the late 19th and early 20th centuries.

3. **CONSTRUCT** Construct a topic sentence that answers this question: What challenges did the urban poor encounter during the late 19th and early 20th centuries?

4. **WRITE** Write a paragraph that supports the statement in Step 3 by using evidence from the passages and photograph.

3.1 Racism and Segregation

Imagine what it might be like to be denied the right to do something that most others are allowed to do. What if you had been denied based on your birthplace or the color of your skin?

MAIN IDEA African Americans and other people of color encountered different forms of prejudice across the United States.

PREJUDICE AND EXCLUSION

The challenges of industrialization, urbanization, and immigration resulted in serious problems, including poverty and discrimination, or the unfair treatment of people based on their age, race, gender, or religious affiliation. Discrimination was not limited to cities or to certain parts of the country. It affected many people in many different ways.

In California, many native-born Americans blamed Chinese immigrants for high rates of unemployment during the economic downturns of the 1870s. As a result, the federal government passed the **Chinese Exclusion Act** in 1882. The act prohibited Chinese immigration for a 10-year period. Only people who could prove they were not coming to find work

could enter the country. Since proving this intention was difficult, very few Chinese immigrants entered the country after 1882.

Native-born Americans also discriminated against other Asian immigrants. On September 4, 1907, a mob of 500 white men in Bellingham, Washington, forced lumber mill workers from India—mostly Sikhs and Hindus—to leave town. Similar assaults against Indian immigrants occurred in Oregon and California.

Prejudice against Asian immigrants became law with the passage of the Immigration Act of 1917. This law banned broadly defined categories of people from entering the country, including "criminals and convicts," "political radicals," and "vagrants." It also introduced literacy tests for incoming immigrants and barred immigration from all Asian and Pacific Island countries, except for Japan and the Philippines.

Mexicans and Americans of Mexican descent also faced social and political barriers. The need for agricultural laborers brought thousands of Mexican immigrants to the West and Southwest. Though welcomed as workers, many became targets of violence.

HINDUS DRIVEN OUT.

Citizens at Marysville, Cal., Attack Them—British Consul Informed.

MARYSVILLE, Cal., Jan. 27.—Twenty citizens of Live Oak Saturday night attacked two houses occupied by seventy Hindus who had been discharged from the Southern Pacific Company and ordered the Hindus to leave town.

The Hindus were driven to the edge of the town and told to travel. One went to Yuba City and swore to complaints charging the members of the mob with stealing $1,950. They also took the case to the British Consul at San Francisco.

Hostility toward immigrants was often direct and violent, as demonstrated in this *New York Times* article from 1908. The term *Hindu* was often used in reference to any immigrant from India, whether Hindu, Sikh, or Muslim.

LEGALIZED DISCRIMINATION

The economy of the South still lagged behind that of other states in the late 1800s. Generally more rural, the South hadn't industrialized as quickly either. Although African Americans gained civil rights after the Civil War, southern politicians quickly stripped these rights away through black codes and laws.

LOOK!

LOOK At These Homes NOW!

An entire block ruined by negro invasion. Every house marked "X" now occupied by negroes. ACTUAL PHOTOGRAPH OF 4300 WEST BELLE PLACE.

SAVE YOUR HOME! VOTE FOR SEGREGATION!

In 1915, a group of white residents in St. Louis, Missouri, distributed this postcard supporting a "reform" ordinance. The legislation, which passed in 1916, prevented people of one race from buying homes in neighborhoods occupied by more than 75 percent of another race. St. Louis became the first northern city to impose racial segregation in housing, and other cities soon followed.

Some of these laws were called **Jim Crow laws**. "Jim Crow" was a derogatory name some whites used toward African-American men. Jim Crow laws varied from state to state. Many states prohibited African Americans and whites from marrying each other, as well as from using the same restrooms, telephone booths, libraries, hospitals, barbers, parks, classrooms, and even cemeteries. Whites used the legalized segregation enforced by Jim Crow laws to establish and maintain economic, social, and political power.

For decades, the Ku Klux Klan had threatened and terrorized African Americans throughout the South. In the 1890s, the Klan increased its activities, partly in response to a populist movement to unite African Americans and poor whites against large landowners, mill owners, and the conservative rulers of the South. Klan members burned large crosses in front of people's homes and lynched African Americans, usually without fear of arrest or conviction.

During the late 19th and early 20th centuries, many southern African Americans moved to northern cities such as New York, Chicago, and St. Louis. Discrimination, poverty, and segregation were the push factors that prompted many to move north. Job opportunities and the chance to start new lives were powerful pull factors.

However, leaving the South did not mean African Americans left discrimination and segregation behind. Northern, white real estate agents and landlords gave preference to whites and enforced racial divisions by refusing to sell or rent to African Americans in primarily white neighborhoods. The North, too, was a racially divided society.

HISTORICAL THINKING

1. **READING CHECK** How did state and federal governments discriminate against different groups of people during the late 19th century?

2. **IDENTIFY MAIN IDEAS AND DETAILS** How did Jim Crow laws protect the social, economic, and political power of whites?

3. **SYNTHESIZE** What push-pull factors contributed to African-American migration to northern cities?

3.2 "Separate but Equal"

One person's brave actions can change the course of history. When a man sat down in a train car in 1891, the cultural and legal reaction that followed would shape Americans' lives for more than a half century.

MAIN IDEA A Supreme Court ruling in 1896 led to even greater segregation throughout the United States.

A FATEFUL RIDE

Local Jim Crow laws had national consequences. In 1890, Louisiana passed the Separate Car Act. This act mandated "equal but separate accommodations" for white and African-American train passengers. The state government required that railroad companies have the same accommodations for whites and African Americans, but the two groups were not allowed to sit in the same rail cars.

A group of African-American activists in New Orleans formed the Citizens Committee to test the constitutionality of the new law. The Citizens Committee argued the act could not be applied consistently because it did not define what the terms used to describe the two races meant.

In 1891, the committee sent **Homer Plessy** to buy a train ticket in Louisiana. Plessy was one-eighth African American, which means one of his eight great-grandparents was of African descent, so he sat in the car reserved for whites. A train conductor told him to move out of the white car, but he refused. The police arrested him and he stood trial. The court upheld the state law but allowed that Plessy could take his case to a higher court.

Lawyers argued Plessy's case against the railroad company before the Supreme Court in 1896. The court ruled in **Plessy v. Ferguson** that the Separate Car Act did not violate the 14th Amendment, which guarantees "equal protection of the laws" to all citizens.

The Court reasoned that the accommodations on the train were the same for whites and African Americans, even if they were separate. Plessy lost the case, and the Supreme Court upheld the practice of segregation. The ruling allowed governments, businesses, and institutions to enact and enforce "separate but equal" policies for decades to follow.

SEPARATE, *NOT* EQUAL

Jim Crow laws required that African Americans and whites attend different schools as well. White communities received funding for their schools from local and state governments. Many African-American communities, however, had to build schools themselves without public funding.

Without proper funding, African-American schools could not maintain their facilities properly, nor could they improve students' education. Teachers

In response to the *Plessy* v. *Ferguson* decision, the *Richmond Planet*, an African-American newspaper founded in 1882 by 13 previously enslaved men, published this editorial.

PRIMARY SOURCE

We can be discriminated against, we can be robbed of our political rights, we can be persecuted and murdered and yet we cannot secure a legal redress [remedy] in the courts of the United States. Truly [have] evil days come upon us. But a reckoning day will come and all classes of citizens, sooner or later [will] realize that a government which will not protect cannot demand for itself protection.

—from "Another Decision," *Richmond Planet*, May 23, 1896

A Northern Critique of Jim Crow

In February 1913, the New York humor magazine *Puck* ran this cartoon. It represents the inequality that automatically results from requiring separate accommodations. In order for African Americans and whites to fly apart, the African-American passengers are crowded onto a platform held up by a balloon and towed by the plane. Though this cartoon was lampooning the idea of "separate but equal," the consequences of Jim Crow laws were far from humorous.

in African-American schools frequently used second-hand supplies and outdated textbooks handed down from white schools.

The invention and acceptance of segregation provided many southern whites with justification for denying African Americans the right to vote. For example, some communities forced eligible citizens to pay a fee called a poll tax before they could register to vote. In some places, even owning a certain amount of property was also considered a requirement for voting.

African-American voters were also required to take literacy tests. **Poll watchers**, or people appointed to guard against voting irregularities, were allowed to deny voting to any person they deemed illiterate, even if the test proved otherwise. In some states, white people who could not read or write were exempted from literacy tests if their fathers or grandfathers had voted.

Both poll taxes and literacy tests purposefully prevented people from voting, and they were specifically directed against African Americans.

Though voting requirements technically applied to all voters, they were mainly used to keep African-American men from voting.

In the late 19th and early 20th centuries, court rulings and state laws undermined the 14th and 15th amendments. This effectively kept many African-American males in the South from voting. African Americans responded by organizing and fighting back against injustices in the South and the rest of the nation.

HISTORICAL THINKING

1. **READING CHECK** How did *Plessy* v. *Ferguson* result in the expansion of segregation laws?

2. **IDENTIFY MAIN IDEAS AND DETAILS** In what ways did poll taxes and literacy tests keep poor people from voting?

3. **DESCRIBE** Why was the "separate but equal" policy never really equal for African Americans?

3.3 Fighting Against Segregation

Leaders faced with complicated problems often come up with different solutions. African-American leaders agreed that they should fight discrimination, but they didn't agree on how to go about it.

MAIN IDEA Prominent African-American leaders fought against segregation in American society using different strategies.

EMPOWERING THROUGH EDUCATION

As the effects of the *Plessy* v. *Ferguson* ruling rippled across the country, African-American leaders began to take action. The educator **Booker T. Washington** became the most influential African-American leader between 1890 and 1915. In 1881, he founded the **Tuskegee Institute** in Alabama to train African Americans to become teachers. Later, the school expanded its focus to include vocational education. Students could learn skilled trades, such as farming techniques and shoemaking, in addition to acquiring teaching techniques. Washington believed the work-related skills of a vocational education would help African-American students become economically independent.

Washington's strategy was to empower African Americans with practical skills and education, or **self-reliance**. By developing self-reliance, he argued, African Americans could "prove" their worthiness and value as functioning members of society. Washington's ideas attracted white philanthropists and helped him raise money for the institute. Andrew Carnegie was among the school's financial supporters. Even though Washington advocated self-reliance, he also funded and supported court challenges to segregation.

Despite Washington's success at drawing support from both whites and African Americans, a number of African-American leaders disagreed

CRITICAL VIEWING The accomplished scientist and inventor George Washington Carver (center) was a teacher at the Tuskegee Institute. What lab work might the class be doing?

with his approach. **W.E.B. Du Bois** (doo BOYS) was a sociologist, activist, and reformer who refused to accommodate the discriminations of society. He claimed that by trying to prove equality, Washington accepted discrimination and thus allowed it to continue. Du Bois believed that protest, not accommodation, would be the way fundamental change would take place.

PROTESTING RACISM

In 1909, Du Bois and **Ida B. Wells**, another activist, founded the **National Association for the Advancement of Colored People (NAACP)** to combat race-based discrimination. Like Du Bois, Wells believed protest was necessary for achieving justice. Du Bois and Wells led the NAACP in its fight against segregation and discrimination against African Americans.

Long before co-founding the NAACP, Wells taught school in Memphis, Tennessee. She then turned her attention to journalism, working as an editor for an African-American newspaper called the *Free Speech and Headlight.* Wells wrote editorials exposing discrimination against African Americans and eventually became a full-time journalist. After a group of white men lynched three of her friends, Wells began to write extensively about the horrors and violence of lynching. She even traveled to England to raise awareness about lynching in the United States. Many whites in the South became angry with her for speaking out.

When white protestors destroyed her newspaper office, Wells decided to move to Chicago. She married and began working for the *Chicago Conservator,* an African-American newspaper. Wells also wrote pamphlets on lynching and formed anti-lynching societies.

Together with social reformer Jane Addams, Wells worked to keep Chicago schools from becoming segregated. When a Chicago newspaper began campaigning in 1903 for segregating the integrated Chicago schools, Wells asked Addams to meet with the newspaper's editors. Addams did so, and the editors ceased printing more articles. Wells's writing about lynching and other racial injustices brought much-needed attention to the topic. The struggle for justice and equality in society would continue as workers in the late 19th century began to assert their rights.

W.E.B. Du Bois   Ida B. Wells

The Springfield Riots and the NAACP

In 1908, racial tensions turned violent in Springfield, Illinois. When an African-American prisoner accused of a crime against a white woman was transferred out of Springfield by police officers, white residents of the town lashed out. Thousands of white protestors burned houses, shot people, and lynched two men. At least seven people were killed. After the Springfield riots, 60 civil rights activists, including Du Bois and Wells, met in New York City to discuss how to prevent riots and mob violence. Together, those meeting in New York signed a mission statement that marked the beginning of the NAACP.

HISTORICAL THINKING

1. **READING CHECK** How did Booker T. Washington differ from W.E.B. Du Bois and Ida B. Wells on confronting discrimination?

2. **FORM AND SUPPORT OPINIONS** What are the pros and cons of self-reliance and protest as strategies to achieve equality?

3. **SUMMARIZE** What prompted Ida B. Wells to become a civil rights activist? Use details from the text to support your response.

4.1 The Lives of Workers

What are you doing after school today? Hanging out with friends? Relaxing? Many children in the late 1800s and early 1900s didn't have these options. They worked long hours in hard, dangerous jobs for little pay.

MAIN IDEA Work places at the turn of the century often involved dangerous conditions, long days, and low wages, with few labor laws to protect workers.

Child miners pause for a lunch break at the Woodward Coal Mine in Kingston, Pennsylvania, in 1900. Until 1916, mine operators hired boys as young as 8 years old to work 12-hour days, 6 days a week. These workers, called "breaker boys," broke chunks of coal into pieces and separated the coal from rocks, slate, and other debris. They sat on wooden benches and processed the coal with their bare hands. Injuries were common and sometimes deadly, and the breaker boys, like adult miners, had few protections.

WORKING CONDITIONS

Industrial progress brought prosperity to some, but for others, this progress was more problematic. As industrialization expanded in the late 19th century, companies looked for ways to increase profits—much like companies do today. In this regard, they benefited from laissez-faire business practices that allowed them to run their businesses with few restrictions. One way to increase profits was to lower **overhead**, or the cost of doing business. New machines replaced the work of individuals, and factory work became more common. Factory managers wanted the work done as quickly and cheaply as possible.

In the late 1800s and into the 1900s, it was not uncommon for workers in some factories to put in 10- to 12-hour days. Working conditions were often dangerous, and the rates of job-related injuries and deaths were very high. In addition to enduring long days and difficult conditions, workers also received low wages from employers. Because of the low wages, unsafe conditions, and long work hours, people started calling these factories **sweatshops**. Sweatshops were particularly common in the garment, shoe, and soap manufacturing industries.

Some industries had especially dangerous conditions. Coal mining, for example, was one of the most dangerous jobs of the late 19th century. Coal miners used dynamite to blast through underground rock, so they were constantly at risk of having mine tunnels collapse on them. Lethal gases such as methane collected in the tunnels. Such gases killed workers in seconds. When fires broke out, miners were trapped deep inside with no way out. After years of breathing in coal dust, miners often developed painful, debilitating, and deadly lung diseases.

Like coal miners, railroad workers performed life-threatening work, including setting off dangerous explosions as they blasted through rock to build tunnels. Operating the trains could also prove deadly. The brakemen, who were responsible for stopping trains, had to run on top of the train applying the brakes by hand on each car. Sometimes workers fell between the cars and were killed underneath the trains as they attempted this task.

WOMEN AND CHILDREN

In the late 19th century, native-born women typically entered the workforce as teachers and office workers. Immigrant women more often found work in manufacturing, such as in textile mills or shoe factories.

Working conditions for women were often even worse than they were for men. Not only did women have to work long hours in unhealthy surroundings, but they were paid much less than men. Even when performing the same work, whether as a teacher or factory worker, a woman was paid only about 60 percent of a man's wages.

Child labor continued to be a common practice during the late 19th and early 20th centuries, and few laws existed to protect children. As a result, companies were allowed to hire children to perform dangerous work in textile mills and glass factories. They even worked in the hazardous coal mines. Children often worked just as many hours as adults did. Employers preferred hiring them because they could get away with paying them even lower wages. Families living in poverty needed the wages earned by their children. Many children could not attend school because they were working in factories.

Labor practices and working conditions were far from ideal. As you have read, reformers responded by advocating and providing opportunities for people who were poor and vulnerable. Reformers helped many people get their basic needs met and somewhat improved their quality of life. But the efforts of reformers were not enough. Workers across industries had reached a breaking point and began to demand better conditions and pay.

HISTORICAL THINKING

1. **READING CHECK** What were working conditions like for factory workers in the late 19th and early 20th centuries?

2. **IDENTIFY MAIN IDEAS AND DETAILS** What industries were particularly dangerous, and why did workers enter them anyway?

3. **MAKE GENERALIZATIONS** Why were employers able to pay women and children less?

4.2 Rise of Labor Unions

Generally speaking, a group of people can be pushed around and taken for granted only so long before they fight back. When workers in the late 1800s had finally had enough of unfair demands from employers, they did just that.

MAIN IDEA American workers formed labor unions and staged strikes across the country as they advocated for better working conditions and fair wages.

ORIGINS OF LABOR UNIONS

By the late 1800s, long workdays, low wages, and dangerous work conditions began to take their toll. Ultimately, workers decided they needed more protection from employer abuses. Forming labor unions offered a way to achieve this.

In a labor union, people doing similar jobs unite as a group to demand improved working conditions. This is called **collective bargaining**. When an employer is unwilling to bargain for better wages or conditions, the union may call for a strike, refusing to work until its demands are met. The purpose of a strike is to persuade employers to grant the changes employees seek.

As you have read, workers had established craft and labor unions beginning in the 1840s. In the 1860s, unions formed in industries controlled by some of the worst violators of workers' rights, including coal mining, shoemaking, and cigar-making. These unions were often city- or even factory-specific, and they were not always able to assert power and protect workers. With the increase in size and scope of industry in the late 19th century, workers began to strategize on a national level.

In July 1877, railroad workers throughout the country participated in the **Great Railroad Strike**. When the Baltimore and Ohio (B&O) Railroad announced a 10 percent wage cut, the second cut that year, irate workers in Martinsburg, West Virginia, walked off the job. The strike then spread to other cities. When B&O managers tried to break the strike, or put an end to it by bringing in other workers to replace the strikers, rioting broke out in many cities, including Baltimore, Pittsburgh, and Chicago. Eventually, federal troops arrived to curb the violence. In the end, about 100,000 workers had participated in the strike, and about 100 people had been killed in the resulting riots.

THE KNIGHTS OF LABOR

One of the first significant national labor unions in the United States was the **Knights of Labor**, founded in 1869 as a union of Philadelphia tailors. **Terence V. Powderly** became the union's leader in 1879. Under his leadership the union became a national organization of many different types of workers, including farmers, shop owners, and laborers.

The union welcomed both skilled and unskilled workers. It also welcomed women and African

Knights of Labor Seal
A seal is a tool that stamps a design to guarantee an official statement or agreement or a document's authenticity. The inscription on this Knights of Labor seal reads, "That is the most perfect government in which an injury to one is the concern of all." The word *Prytaneum* at the center refers to the central hearth or fire in a village in ancient Greece.

Americans, a forward-thinking move for a 19th-century union. The Knights of Labor supported ideas considered radical by many: the abolition of child labor, reasonable working hours, and equal pay for men and women doing the same work.

After the Great Railroad Strike, membership in the Knights of Labor started to grow. Then in 1885, the Knights of Labor went on strike against the ruthless railroad owner **Jay Gould**. Gould had earned a reputation as a **robber baron**, or an industrial leader known for cutthroat tactics against workers and competitors. Within just one year of that first strike against Gould, the union added 500,000 members. Total membership peaked at 700,000 members in 1886.

That same year, in response to the firing of a union member in Texas, the Knights of Labor went on a second, much longer strike against Gould's railroad. This strike was known as the **Great Southwest Strike**, and it took place in several states and lasted for many months. Eventually, Gould called in the police to break it up.

The Great Southwest Strike was just one of thousands of strikes to take place in 1886. In fact, that year workers staged about 1,600 strikes as tensions between labor and management grew across industries.

HISTORICAL THINKING

1. **READING CHECK** Why did workers use collective bargaining as a strategy?

2. **EXPLAIN** What was Terence Powderly's goal in forming the Knights of Labor?

3. **MAKE INFERENCES** Why do you think membership in the Knights of Labor increased after 1877?

4.3 Labor Conflicts

When you arrive, a man is giving a speech about Congress ignoring the workingmen. Someone shouts "Police!" and you see a line of men walking toward the crowd. Then an explosion rattles the buildings around you, pistol shots fire, and everyone begins to run.

MAIN IDEA A series of violent strikes took place during the late 1800s as workers intensified their demands for better wages and working conditions.

THE HAYMARKET RIOT

As the Great Southwest Strike raged in the spring of 1886, another strike was brewing. In May of that year, workers protested at the McCormick Harvesting Machine Company in Chicago. The demonstration was part of a nationwide effort to establish an eight-hour workday.

On May 3, police officers killed one protestor and injured several others. In response, labor leaders called for a protest meeting the following day in Haymarket Square. Though the meeting on May 4 was initially peaceful, someone in the crowd threw a bomb, and police began shooting. Several police officers and members of the crowd were killed in the explosion and rioting that followed. Dozens more were injured. Afterward, police arrested eight people, claiming they were **anarchists**, or people who advocate lawlessness and the absence of all government. Four of the accused anarchists were hanged for the crime of throwing the bomb, and one was sentenced to 15 years in prison. Their guilt was never adequately proven, however, and the remaining defendants were eventually pardoned. The event became known as the **Haymarket Riot**.

CRITICAL VIEWING Evidence presented at the trial against the accused included these lead pipe bombs. Officers who had been on duty during the Haymarket Riot carried this banner in a parade honoring police veterans of the riot. What is the relationship of these two artifacts?

Many blamed the Knights of Labor for the events in Chicago, though there was no direct connection. As a result, membership in the Knights of Labor rapidly declined. Instead, workers who wanted to unionize joined the newly formed **American Federation of Labor**, which **Samuel L. Gompers** had formed that same year. Many considered that organization to be less radical than the Knights of Labor. Like the Knights of Labor, however, Gompers's organization supported demands for an eight-hour workday.

HOMESTEAD AND PULLMAN

Despite the violence that had overshadowed the Haymarket Riot and the Great Railroad Strike, labor unions grew in membership and strength in the late 1800s. But conflicts continued to flare up between labor and employers.

Pullman Strike

The Pullman Strike began as a "wildcat strike," meaning the workers at the factory walked out without the formal decision of a union. On July 3, 1894, federal troops arrived in Chicago to prevent interference with the operation of trains. In this photo, troops stand in formation outside the Pullman Arcade building, which housed shops and businesses serving the Pullman company town. Ultimately, as many as 250,000 railroad workers in 27 states went on strike or disrupted train traffic.

In 1892, workers at the Carnegie Steel Company in Homestead, Pennsylvania, went on strike. The manager had cut the workers' wages and refused to negotiate with them. He fired all 3,800 union workers and hired 300 private security guards to take over the plant. During the **Homestead Strike** that followed, clashes between the two groups led to the deaths of at least seven workers and three guards. The workers took control of the mill, but the company called in the National Guard to remove them. Then the company hired **scabs**, or people willing to cross union lines to work during a strike, to take the place of union workers.

Just two years later, in 1894, the **Pullman Strike** took place near Chicago. The head of the Pullman Palace Car Company, a railway car manufacturer, had refused to meet with workers to discuss wage cuts and long workdays. Instead, the owner fired them. The workers called a strike and walked off the job. **Eugene V. Debs,** the leader of the American Railway Union, coordinated a boycott of Pullman cars on rail lines. This meant rail workers refused to handle or service any Pullman cars. The boycott successfully brought midwestern rail traffic to a halt.

To get the trains moving again, President Grover Cleveland sent federal troops to Illinois. Violence erupted, and National Guard members shot and killed strikers. After the strike ended, Debs was arrested. The coming years would see more upheaval as reformers continued pressing for improvements in the lives of workers, immigrants, women, and children.

HISTORICAL THINKING

1. **READING CHECK** Why did labor unions strike in the late 1800s?

2. **IDENTIFY MAIN IDEAS AND DETAILS** How did the federal government respond to labor strikes in the 1890s?

3. **DETERMINE CHRONOLOGY** What events led to the rise of the American Federation of Labor?

VOCABULARY

For each pair of vocabulary words or terms, write one sentence that explains the connection between the two words or terms.

1. capitalism; laissez-faire

   Those who promote laissez-faire economics believe less government intervention in the economy is good for capitalism.

2. standard time; transcontinental railroad

3. overhead; sweatshop

4. Chinese Exclusion Act; Jim Crow laws

5. philanthropy; Social Gospel

6. Bessemer process; steel

7. mass culture; urbanization

8. Gilded Age; robber baron

9. Homestead Strike; scab

READING STRATEGY
IDENTIFY MAIN IDEAS AND DETAILS

If you haven't already, complete your Main Ideas and Details graphic organizer about the social and economic effects of the Industrial Age. Include at least three details. Then answer the question.

Social and Economic Effects of the Industrial Age

Main Idea: Workers were often treated unfairly.
Detail:
Detail:
Detail:

10. What were the main social problems of the Industrial Age?

MAIN IDEAS

Answer the following questions. Support your answers with evidence from the chapter.

11. How did construction of the first transcontinental railroad affect Native Americans? **LESSON 1.1**

12. What improvements did Andrew Carnegie make to the steel industry? **LESSON 1.4**

13. What did new immigrants experience after arriving in the United States? **LESSON 2.1**

14. What was the goal of the Social Gospel movement? **LESSON 2.3**

15. In what ways did the Ku Klux Klan intimidate African Americans? **LESSON 3.1**

16. What does the phrase "separate but equal" mean? **LESSON 3.2**

17. Why did Booker T. Washington promote self-reliance? **LESSON 3.3**

18. What effect did child labor have on children's education? **LESSON 4.1**

19. What purpose did strikes serve in workers' demands for change? **LESSON 4.2**

20. What event led to the Haymarket Riot in Chicago? **LESSON 4.3**

HISTORICAL THINKING

Answer the following questions. Support your answers with evidence from the chapter.

21. **DESCRIBE** Why were employers able to take advantage of immigrant workers, female workers, and child workers?

22. **SYNTHESIZE** What contributions did Ida B. Wells, Jane Addams, and Ellen Gates Starr make to social welfare programs?

23. EVALUATE How did new inventions and industries affect people both positively and negatively during the Industrial Age? Use examples from the chapter.

24. FORM AND SUPPORT OPINIONS Which reform movement during the late 19th and early 20th centuries had the biggest impact on people's lives? Use evidence from the chapter to support your answer.

25. ANALYZE CAUSE AND EFFECT What changes in transportation in the late 19th and early 20th centuries led to the development of suburbs?

26. MAKE INFERENCES Why did groups of American citizens support the Chinese Exclusion Act and other discriminatory practices against Asian Americans?

INTERPRET GRAPHS

Look closely at this graph showing population growth in the United States from 1880 to 1910. Then answer the questions that follow.

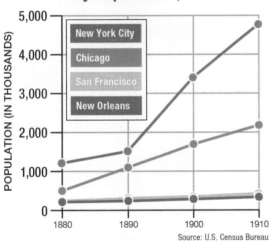

City Populations, 1880–1910

Legend: New York City, Chicago, San Francisco, New Orleans

POPULATION (IN THOUSANDS): 0, 1,000, 2,000, 3,000, 4,000, 5,000

Years: 1880, 1890, 1900, 1910

Source: U.S. Census Bureau

27. Which city had the most growth from 1880 to 1890?

28. In which city did the population grow the least during this 30-year time period?

ANALYZE SOURCES

On May 11, 1869, *The New York Times* published news of the transcontinental railroad's completion. The day before, workers had driven the last spike into the railroad, finally linking the coasts. Read the passage and answer the question.

> It was apparent everywhere throughout the City yesterday that an event of more than usual importance was taking place, and that there was an evident disposition among the people to be jubilant. Flags were displayed on the City Hall, on all the newspaper offices, and on the prominent hotels. Every countenance [face] seemed to bear a look of supreme satisfaction, and all were apparently awaiting with anticipations of delight the receipt of most welcome news . . . the last rail of the road connecting our opposite ocean-bound shores was laid; the last spike (a gold one, by the bye) was driven; and thereupon there was booming of cannon . . . and general rejoicing.

29. How did Americans react to the completion of the transcontinental railroad?

CONNECT TO YOUR LIFE

30. INFORMATIVE This chapter describes many different people who have had to fight for their own rights or those of others. Choose one of the people discussed in the chapter. Then write a paragraph in which you explain which traits you find admirable about the person. Tell how you try to mirror these same traits in your own life through actions you take.

TIPS

- Fill in a word web, listing the person's name in the middle and the person's admirable traits on the surrounding lines.

- Include in your informative paragraph textual evidence that supports your ideas about the person, along with two or three vocabulary terms from the chapter.

- Conclude the paragraph with a comment that explains how you try to mirror the same traits in your own life.

THE
PROGRESSIVE ERA
1890–1920

ESSENTIAL QUESTION
Why did the Progressive Era arise?

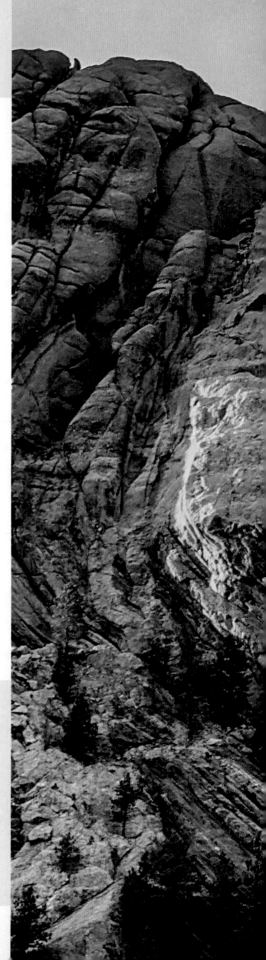

AMERICAN STORIES America's National Parks

SECTION 1 Teddy Roosevelt and Progressivism
KEY VOCABULARY

commissioner	Meat Inspection Act	referendum
conservation movement	populism	Sherman Antitrust Act of 1890
direct primary election	progressivism	
initiative	Pure Food and Drug Act	

SECTION 2 The Progressives
KEY VOCABULARY

assembly line	income tax	reserve bank
Clayton Antitrust Act	loophole	scientific management
Federal Reserve Act		

SECTION 3 Women Win New Rights
KEY VOCABULARY

lobbyist	social work	teetotaler
Prohibition	suffragist	

SECTION 4 America on the World Stage
KEY VOCABULARY

archipelago	isthmus	Rough Riders
autonomy	lock	sphere of influence
court-martial	Open Door Policy	spoil
imperialism	Platt Amendment	yellow journalism

AMERICAN GALLERY ONLINE Yosemite National Park

READING STRATEGY

SYNTHESIZE When you synthesize a text, you identify the most important information, look for evidence that connects the facts, and think about what you already know about the topic. Then you use the evidence, explanations, and your prior knowledge to form an overall understanding of what you have read. As you read the chapter, use a chart like this one to organize the evidence in each lesson and synthesize the information.

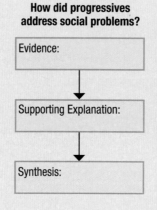

How did progressives address social problems?

Evidence:

↓

Supporting Explanation:

↓

Synthesis:

"Much has been given us, and much will rightfully be expected of us."

—Theodore Roosevelt

CRITICAL VIEWING Sculptor Gutzon Borglum carved these colossal heads of (from left to right) presidents Washington, Jefferson, Theodore Roosevelt, and Lincoln into the rock of Mount Rushmore in the Black Hills of South Dakota between 1927 and 1941. Borglum chose these presidents because he believed they led the country during its most important historical periods. Based on details in the photo, what types of challenges might the sculpting team have faced during the creation of this monument?

CRITICAL VIEWING Yellowstone National
Park contains many natural wonders,
including these travertine terraces. What
does this photo reveal about the type of
rock called travertine?

AMERICA'S
NATIONAL PARKS

In a book about the American West, writer and historian Wallace Stegner called the national parks "the best idea we ever had." He continued, "Absolutely American, absolutely democratic, they reflect us at our best rather than our worst."

Yellowstone, the first national park in the world, was created in 1872. The idea of setting aside and protecting wilderness areas, however, was not new. In 1832, artist George Catlin visited South Dakota and observed threats to both the buffalo herds and the Native American groups that relied on them. In his journal, he imagined a solution to the problem. It would be "some great protecting policy of the government preserved . . . in a *magnificent park . . . a nation's park,* containing man and beast, in all the wildness and freshness of their nature's beauty!"

AN EARLY VOICE FOR PARKS

One of the strongest voices in the early national parks movement was John Muir. Born in Scotland in 1838, Muir moved to the United States with his family when he was a boy. He was an inquisitive young man with a thirst for travel and a fascination with wild places. In 1868, Muir arrived in California. There, he found his spiritual home in the Yosemite Valley, part of the Sierra Nevada mountain range. Later, he described his first walk through the remote high country: "Then it seemed to me

the Sierra should be called not the Nevada, or Snowy Range, but the Range of Light . . . the most divinely beautiful of all the mountain chains I have ever seen."

Muir traveled widely and pursued several careers, but he never stopped writing about the wilderness he loved so passionately, and especially about Yosemite. Muir once wrote, "It is easier to feel than to realize, or in any way explain, Yosemite grandeur. The magnitudes [size and extent] of the rocks and trees and streams are so delicately harmonized, they are mostly hidden." His writings attracted the attention of many influential people. Along with others, Muir lobbied tirelessly for the protection of Yosemite from grazing by herds of sheep and cattle, until Congress created Yosemite National Park in 1890. Muir's continuing efforts also lent strong support to the creation of Sequoia, Mount Rainier, Petrified Forest, and Grand Canyon national parks.

In 1892, Muir and several associates founded the Sierra Club. In his own words, the club's mission was to "do something for wildness and make the mountains glad." Muir wanted to protect Yosemite

LEAVE IT AS IT IS

Theodore Roosevelt was both blunt and eloquent in his support for the protection of wilderness areas. During his 1903 tour of the western states, he spoke to a group near the rim of the Grand Canyon and made an important request.

PRIMARY SOURCE

I want to ask you to do one thing in connection with [the Grand Canyon] in your own interest and in the interest of our country—to keep this great wonder of nature as it now is.

Leave it as it is. You cannot improve it. The ages have been at work on it, and man can only mar it. What you can do is to keep it for your children, your children's children, and for all who come after you, as one of the great sights which every American, if he can travel at all, should see.

—President Theodore Roosevelt, 1903

How did the resources in the Grand Canyon influence Roosevelt's request to preserve the site?

Friends and early environmentalists Teddy Roosevelt and John Muir pose for this 1903 photo at Glacier Point in Yosemite Valley, California.

National Park from ranchers or others who would seek to turn the park's lands over for commercial use. Since then, the Sierra Club's mission has expanded greatly. Today, it is one of the world's oldest environmental organizations and works to protect wild spaces throughout the United States.

THE PARKS PRESIDENT

One fan of John Muir, President Theodore Roosevelt, did not need to be convinced that conservation was a good idea. An avid outdoorsman and hunter, Roosevelt had been involved for many years in efforts to create wilderness preserves and carefully manage natural resources such as forests, rivers, and streams.

Roosevelt became president in 1901. In 1903, he went on an extensive tour of the country, visiting

25 states in 8 weeks. He took advantage of his time in the West to explore the existing national parks. At Yosemite, local officials had planned a series of elaborate parties and dinners in the president's honor. Instead of attending any of these events, Roosevelt slipped away from the dignitaries and the journalists to spend three nights camping in the wilderness with John Muir.

Muir wasn't afraid to address the president directly. Of Roosevelt's hunting, he asked, "Mr. Roosevelt, when are you going to get beyond the boyishness of killing things?" Despite—or perhaps because of—Muir's lack of tact, the two men became firm friends. Muir later wrote of the encounter, "I had a perfectly glorious time. I never before had a more interesting . . . companion."

CRITICAL VIEWING A mountain goat mother and her kids cross the rocks above Hidden Lake in Glacier National Park in Montana. What does this photo reveal about the geography and wildlife of this park?

President Roosevelt emerged from Yosemite with a renewed commitment to conservation as well. After his outing with Muir, he told an audience at Stanford University in California, "There is nothing more practical than the preservation of beauty, than the preservation of anything that appeals to the higher emotions of mankind." Roosevelt turned out to be one of the national parks' most effective supporters. By the time he left office, he had created five new ones and added land to Yosemite. He also established 150 national forests, 51 federal bird reserves, 4 national game preserves, and 18 national monuments.

CONTINUED PROTECTION

In 1906, Congress established a new type of protected area. The Antiquities Act of that year made it possible for the president to create national monuments. These were pieces of public land that had "historic landmarks, historic and prehistoric structures, and other objects of historic and scientific interest."

The difficulty with the national parks and national monuments was that they were not managed by a single government agency. The national parks were part of the Department of the Interior. Some national monuments were on land owned by the War Department; others were controlled by the Department of Agriculture. Many national parks and monuments were poorly funded. "They were orphans," wrote Horace Albright, who later played an important role in creating the National Park Service. "They were anybody's business and therefore nobody's business."

MATHER AND ALBRIGHT

An unlikely hero stepped into the spotlight. Stephen Mather was not a government official. He was a businessman who had made millions of dollars selling a type of soap called Borax. In 1914, Mather sent a scathing letter to Secretary of the Interior Franklin Lane about the poor condition of roads and facilities in the national parks. Lane decided to try an unusual solution to the problem. He talked Mather into taking charge of the parks office in the Department of the Interior. To assist him, Mather brought along Horace Albright, a young law student. For both men, the job was supposed to be a one-year assignment.

CRITICAL VIEWING After a rigorous three-mile hike, visitors to Arches National Park in Moab, Utah, can see Delicate Arch, shown here, up close. What details from this photo by National Geographic photographer Paul Nicklen help explain the name of this famous geologic formation?

Mather knew the parks needed more money, and he decided the first step would be to attract more visitors. With increased tourism would come greater attention to the national parks and, he hoped, more funding from the government. To this end, he established a marketing plan. He recruited the help of the railroads and automobile associations to publicize the national parks. Mather's campaign worked. At Yosemite, the number of visitors grew from around 15,000 in 1914 to around 33,000 in 1915.

Mather took his campaign to the next step by inviting 15 influential American businessmen, journalists, congressmen, and politicians on a two-week tour through Sequoia National Park in California. At the end of the trip, he made his case for a single government agency to manage the national parks. "Just think of the vast areas of our land that should be preserved for the future," he told his guests. "Unless we can protect the areas currently held with a separate government agency, we may lose them to selfish interests."

PASSING THE ACT

Mather and his supporters succeeded in their goal. Congress passed the National Park Service Organic Act, which President Woodrow Wilson

NATIONAL GEOGRAPHIC AND THE NATIONAL PARKS

The National Geographic Society has had a close relationship with the National Park Service (NPS) since its earliest days. *National Geographic* editor Gilbert Grosvenor was one of the distinguished guests on Stephen Mather's guided tour through Sequoia National Park in 1915.

Upon his return, Grosvenor brought the Society's influence to bear in backing Mather's cause. The April 1916 issue of *National Geographic* was entirely devoted to the national parks, and copies were sent to every member of Congress. National Geographic Society members also lent their support, donating $80,000 (around $1.8 million today) to the effort in 1916. Grosvenor also helped write the wording for the bill that established the National Park Service later that year.

Since that time, National Geographic has sent scientists, explorers, journalists, and photographers to study the national parks and share their wonders with readers. Working in partnership with the National Park Service allows National Geographic to pursue its mission to use the "power of science, exploration, and storytelling" to inspire and teach. In 2016, National Geographic celebrated the National Park Service's 100th anniversary with television shows, feature articles online, and an issue of *National Geographic* devoted entirely to Yellowstone.

signed on August 25, 1916. The United States now had a single agency, the National Park Service, or NPS, in charge of its precious protected lands. Stephen Mather was chosen to be its director.

Mather's "one-year contract" ended with his retirement in 1929. During his time as director, he was tireless in his efforts to bring visitors into the national parks. He delighted in the idea that people from all income levels—not just the wealthy— enjoyed the parks. According to Albright, "There could never be too many tourists for Stephen Mather. He wanted as many as possible to enjoy his 'treasures.'" Horace Albright succeeded Mather as director of the National Park Service, continuing in the post until 1933. For his contributions to the national parks, Albright was awarded the Presidential Medal of Freedom in 1980.

Since Mather's and Albright's day, numerous national parks and monuments have been added to the list. Today, the system includes 413 national parks, monuments, battlefields, seashores, and recreation areas. Visitors can experience sites as diverse as the majestic six-million-acre Denali National Park in Alaska and Liberty Island in New York Harbor.

The creation of national parks has not always been popular with everyone. When Yellowstone became a national park, some Native American groups were displaced from their homes or lost the ability to hunt freely. In Yosemite, cattle and sheep ranchers bitterly resented the loss of grazing lands.

Sometimes, too, the goal of making the parks easy for visitors to explore conflicts with the need to protect wildlife from harm by humans. As in the past, today's National Park Service works to balance conservation with other human needs.

It's a difficult job, but worth every effort to keep the "best idea we ever had" safe for all generations.

THINK ABOUT IT

Do you agree with Wallace Stegner that the national parks are America's "best idea"? Explain your answer.

NATIONAL PARKS
IN THE UNITED STATES

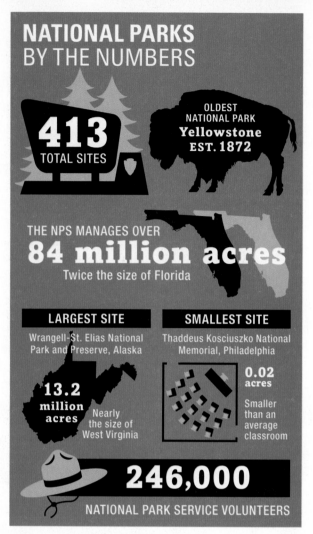

NATIONAL PARKS
BY THE NUMBERS

413
TOTAL SITES

OLDEST
NATIONAL PARK
Yellowstone
EST. 1872

THE NPS MANAGES OVER
84 million acres
Twice the size of Florida

LARGEST SITE	SMALLEST SITE
Wrangell-St. Elias National Park and Preserve, Alaska	Thaddeus Kosciuszko National Memorial, Philadelphia

13.2 million acres Nearly the size of West Virginia

0.02 acres Smaller than an average classroom

246,000
NATIONAL PARK SERVICE VOLUNTEERS

ANSEL ADAMS

In dramatic, crystal-sharp, black and white photographs, Ansel Adams captured the essence of some of America's wildest places. Born in California in 1902, Adams began to experiment with photography in 1916 after a trip to Yosemite. Before long, he was exhibiting and selling his photos at a studio called Best's, in Yosemite Valley. In 1928, he married the daughter of the studio owner, and Best's remained in the Adams family until 1971.

Although Adams traveled widely and photographed an impressive variety of subjects, Yosemite remained one of his inspirations and the scene of some of his most famous images. A strong believer in conservation, Adams sought to use his photos of Yosemite and the West to arouse people's interest in protecting wild spaces. His striking photos also helped photography gain acceptance as an art form, not just as a way to record information. Ansel Adams died in 1984.

How do you think photos like these affected people's opinions about the national parks?

Sand Dunes, Sunrise, Death Valley National Monument, California, 194[?] Photograph by Ansel Adams

These 1940s Ansel Adams photos reveal the striking geography of Sunrise Death Valley National Park (above) and Death Valley National Park (below) in California.

[?]rocks, Joshua Tree National Monument, California, 1942 Photograph by Ansel Adams

1.1 Progressives Attack Problems

Think of the changes you'd like to see in your school. Then consider how you might make them happen. In the 1890s, Americans had ideas that would change the country. All they needed was the right leader.

MAIN IDEA Americans grew angry at the lack of government control over business and began to call for reform.

CALL FOR CHANGE

The period after the Civil War saw a sharp rise in the growth of cities. Americans attracted by the promise of factory jobs and new immigrants swelled the cities. And there was work for most everyone who arrived. A largely laissez-faire economy led to the rapid growth of business. This meant, however, that the government paid little attention to business owners' financial dealings or their treatment of workers. Bosses forced many workers to toil long hours in dangerous factories for very low wages.

This economic prosperity was repeatedly disrupted, however, by a number of economic recessions during the intense boom and bust cycles at the end of the 19th century. The country experienced a deep depression beginning in 1893. The depression occurred when a major railroad collapsed, and banks and other businesses dependent on it failed as well. By the end of 1893, about 600 banks and 15,000 businesses had closed. Early the following year, about 2.5 million people were out of work. There were no safeguards in place for helping them through the tough times. And because leaders in both the Democratic and Republican parties believed that

For his re-election campaign in 1900, McKinley chose Theodore Roosevelt as his running mate. Photos of the two appear in this campaign poster.

FOR PRESIDENT · FOR VICE PRESIDENT

WM. McKINLEY. · THEO. ROOSEVELT.

a depression was part of the economic cycle, they did nothing to help restore the nation's economy.

Meanwhile, businesses unaffected by the depression continued to exploit, or take advantage of, their workforce. The inability—or unwillingness—of the government to change these practices sparked a rise in **populism,** the belief that common people, not the wealthy, should control their government. Remember that farmers formed the Populist Party, also called the People's Party, in 1892. The party focused on issues such as better pay and working conditions, workers' and immigrants' rights, better access to education, and an end to child labor.

In the election of 1892, the Populist Party nominated one of its members for president under the slogan "Equal rights to all; special privileges to none." The Populist candidate didn't win, but the party influenced the rise of another social movement called **progressivism**. Middle class and college-educated, progressives aligned themselves with the American workforce. They believed deeply in equality for all people and called for people and the government to work together to bring about social change.

A NEW ERA BEGINS

In 1896, Americans elected **William McKinley** as president. McKinley, who had served as governor of Ohio, undertook several progressive policies as president. For example, he worked to restore the economy, reform business practices, and open up trade with other countries. Much of his first term, however, was dominated by foreign policy and the Spanish-American War, which you'll learn about later in this chapter. A popular president, McKinley was elected to a second term in 1900. In 1901, however, while making a public appearance, McKinley was shot by an anarchist, a person who uses violence to overthrow authority. The shooter claimed he killed the president "because he was the enemy of . . . the working people."

Vice President **Theodore Roosevelt**, often called "Teddy" in the media, took over as president. Just 42 years old, he was much younger than any other president before him. He had grown up in a wealthy New York family but had spent years working on a ranch in the West. Energetic and outgoing, Roosevelt was an enthusiastic athlete, outdoorsman, and hunter. His bravery during the Spanish-American War had made him a war hero.

Roosevelt supported progressive ideas, and he looked forward to making changes as president. He especially hoped to expand U.S. power abroad and promote environmental causes. His enthusiasm spread throughout the country. Some of the most dramatic changes of the **Progressive Era** would occur during his presidency.

Following McKinley's death, President Roosevelt addressed Congress. He laid out a far-reaching progressive agenda that connected his own goals with McKinley's, including the relationships among big business, workers, and government.

PRIMARY SOURCE

The fundamental rule in our national life— the rule which underlies all others—is that, on the whole, and in the long run, we shall go up or down together. . . . Disaster to great business enterprises can never have its effects limited to the men at the top. It spreads throughout, and while it is bad for everybody, it is worst for those farthest down. The capitalist [business owner or investor] may be shorn [deprived] of his luxuries; but the wage-worker may be deprived of even bare necessities.

—from President Theodore Roosevelt's First Annual Address to Congress, December 3, 1901

HISTORICAL THINKING

1. **READING CHECK** What happened to many workers as a result of the depression that began in 1893?

2. **SUMMARIZE** What were some of the main beliefs and goals of populism in the 1890s?

3. **MAKE INFERENCES** How do you think both populists and progressives reacted when Theodore Roosevelt became president?

1.2 The Muckrakers

Early 1900s

"There is filth on the floor, and it must be scraped up with the muck-rake."—Theodore Roosevelt

When President Roosevelt made this statement in a 1906 speech, he coined the term "muckraker," referring to crusading journalists who exposed corruption and appalling social and working conditions. But Roosevelt didn't entirely support the journalists' work. Fearing that newspaper publishers would just use shocking headlines to increase their sales, he emphasized that muckrakers needed to know "when to stop raking the muck."

ABUSES OF POWER

As it turned out, though, there was a lot of muck to investigate. One of the first muckrakers was Ida Tarbell, who grew up near the oil derricks and refineries of northwestern Pennsylvania in the 1850s and 1860s. She experienced firsthand the practices of John D. Rockefeller, as his Standard Oil Company moved into the region and took over its small oil businesses. Many local workers lost their jobs, including Tarbell's father.

Tarbell never forgot the impact of Rockefeller's company on her family and home. As an adult, she researched and learned about Standard Oil and the secret deals and methods for crushing the competition its president had carried out to establish his monopoly.

CRITICAL VIEWING In this 1900 political cartoon called "What a Funny Little Government," John D. Rockefeller holds the White House and Treasury Department in his hand and peers at them through a magnifying glass. Illustrator Horace Taylor has turned the Capitol Building in the background into an oil refinery, with thick smoke pouring out of its smokestacks. What does the cartoon suggest about the relationship between industries like Rockefeller's and government?

Tarbell published her findings in *The History of the Standard Oil Company,* which appeared in monthly installments in *McClure's Magazine* between November 1902 and October 1904. She concluded her series with a character study of Rockefeller in which she claimed, "Our national life is on every side distinctly poorer, uglier, meaner, for the kind of influence he exercises."

Around the time Tarbell's articles came out, another muckraker named Lincoln Steffens took on corruption in government. Steffens had recently become managing editor at *McClure's,* which now published the work of many muckrakers. He launched a series of articles, which coincided with the publication of Tarbell's. In his series, Steffens focused on government corruption in cities such as Chicago, Minneapolis, New York, and St. Louis. The articles described the deals politicians in these places struck with greedy businessmen at the expense of citizens. Steffens's dramatic narratives were popular with readers but didn't bring about much change. Eventually he became disillusioned with muckraking and its ability to achieve lasting reform.

CONDITIONS IN THE MEATPACKING INDUSTRY

Unlike Steffens, muckraker Upton Sinclair did accomplish enduring change with his writing—it just wasn't the change he'd hoped for. Sinclair investigated the working conditions in the meatpacking industry and wrote about what he

THE JUNGLE
BY
UPTON SINCLAIR

DOUBLEDAY, PAGE & CO
NEW YORK

CRITICAL VIEWING This poster, printed in 1906, was used to advertise Upton Sinclair's novel and shows a lion standing on the head of a steer. Sinclair may have intended the title of his novel, *The Jungle*, to symbolize what he saw as the savage competition created by capitalism. With that in mind, what might the lion and steer in the poster represent?

found in his novel, *The Jungle,* published in 1906. He described the workers' long hours, low wages, and the dangerous machinery and chemicals they used, often resulting in lost fingers and limbs.

However, it was Sinclair's descriptions of the industry's unsanitary practices, sales of spoiled meat, and rats running everywhere that caught the readers' attention. They were sickened by his account of the way in which garbage and discarded animal parts were swept off the floor, ground up, and sold as "potted ham." As Sinclair said, "I aimed at the public's heart, and by accident I hit it in the stomach."

Roosevelt couldn't ignore the outcry that followed the publication of the novel. Within months, Congress passed both the Pure Food and Drug Act and the Meat Inspection Act. As Roosevelt once admitted, "The men with the muck-rakes are often indispensable to the well-being of society."

HISTORICAL THINKING

1. **READING CHECK** What was the focus of Ida Tarbell's articles?

2. **COMPARE AND CONTRAST** How were the muckraking efforts of Steffens and Sinclair similar and different?

3. **FORM AND SUPPORT OPINIONS** Do you agree with Roosevelt that muckrakers—today called investigative journalists—need to know when to stop? Explain your position.

1.3 Expanding Democracy and Reforming Government

You may have seen or heard about groups of people calling for change in government today. But that's not a new trend. It's exactly what reformers were doing during the late 1890s.

MAIN IDEA Progressives sought to strengthen government by reducing corruption at the state and local levels and giving voters a greater voice.

EMPOWERING THE PEOPLE

As the United States emerged from economic depression around 1897, Americans looked for ways to solve the deep-rooted problems facing the country. Most progressives believed government at all levels should promote a society that benefited everyone and provide a financial "safety net" for the most vulnerable Americans. They also believed government had a responsibility to try to solve the social and economic problems caused by industrialization, including health problems in cities, unfair and dangerous work practices, and the rise of monopolies and trusts.

A key idea for progressives was giving voters a more direct voice in government. They felt that if people had more say in how the government ran the country, the elite, or powerful and wealthy, political class would have less control. Several states introduced **direct primary elections** to give voters a role in selecting candidates for

The Great Galveston Hurricane
This 1900 photo shows some of the destruction caused by a hurricane after it slammed into Galveston. The disaster occurred on September 8 when the city was filled with vacationers. A local weather forecaster drove his horse-drawn cart to the beach and advised people to move to higher ground, but his warning came too late.

important offices. In these elections, members of each political party nominate candidates by a direct vote. By 1916, direct primaries had spread across most of the country.

Progressives also supported the processes of initiatives and referendums. In an **initiative**, citizens propose a new law and force a vote on it. If the initiative receives a majority vote, it becomes law. In a **referendum**, a direct vote allows voters to accept or reject a law. Progressives believed these practices could help reduce government control and keep corrupt leaders from remaining in office. In 1898, South Dakota became the first state to adopt a statewide process for initiatives and referendums. Other states soon followed.

REFORMING THE GOVERNMENT

As urban populations grew, political corruption became widespread at the local level. As you have read, Tammany Hall was one of the best-known examples of corruption in city government. Progressives worked to clean up and improve local governments. Reform-minded mayors in the cities of Detroit, Cleveland, and Toledo pushed for safer, cleaner cities and fought political corruption.

A powerful hurricane that hit Galveston, Texas, in 1900 sparked a progressive movement that changed the structure of that city's government. The hurricane was one of the worst natural disasters in the country's history. It killed about 6,000 people and devastated the coastal city.

Concerned that Galveston would never be rebuilt under its current leaders, residents placed their hopes in a new form of government called the commission form of government, or the "Galveston Plan." The citizens of Galveston elected five **commissioners**, or government representatives, to help the city recover from the disaster. The commissioners worked together to pass laws and collect taxes. In addition, each commissioner was in charge of a specific part of the government, such as public works and public safety. One of the commissioners served as mayor, but this position had little power. The commission form of city government is widespread throughout the United States today.

Many states also elected reform-minded governors. **Robert M. La Follette**, the governor of Wisconsin from 1900 to 1906 and then a U.S. Senator until

1925, became a symbol of the Progressive Era. He established a direct primary election for the state, regulated Wisconsin's railroads, and raised taxes on corporations. Leaders such as La Follette reflected the new policies President Roosevelt sought to pass on the national level.

The "Wisconsin Idea"
Today, the idea that politicians should consult with experts in fields such as economics and business before making policy decisions is routine. But that wasn't always the case. During his two terms as governor of Wisconsin, La Follette (shown here) forged relationships with professors at the University of Wisconsin to help him confront the state's economic and social problems. This relationship was called the "Wisconsin Idea."

HISTORICAL THINKING

1. **READING CHECK** According to many progressives, what were some of the responsibilities of government?

2. **ANALYZE CAUSE AND EFFECT** How did the 1900 Galveston hurricane lead to local government reform?

3. **SYNTHESIZE** How do direct primaries, initiatives, and referendums put more political power in the hands of everyday citizens?

Teddy Roosevelt and the Square Deal

When you eat a hamburger or drink a glass of milk, you probably don't think of Teddy Roosevelt. But maybe you should. As president of the United States, he pushed for laws that made foods purer and safer.

MAIN IDEA As president, Theodore Roosevelt worked to control corporations, protect consumers, and conserve the environment.

BUSINESS REFORM

The tremendous growth of business during the Industrial Revolution also brought an increase in inequality among some groups of people. The unfair treatment of poorly paid workers especially concerned progressives. Roosevelt wanted to find solutions that were fair to business owners, their workers, and the general public. He referred to his domestic policy as a "square deal." He meant that all sides would be treated fairly and would benefit equally. Like all progressives, Roosevelt wanted to promote the interests of those who did not share in the prosperity of the Industrial Revolution.

For decades, corporations had been allowed to grow and operate with very little government supervision. As a result, monopolies had arisen, and they were hurting the economy. Since a company with a monopoly has no competition, it can overcharge its customers, underpay its workers, produce inferior goods and services, and still be assured of a healthy profit because no other company supplies its product. To break up the monopolies, Roosevelt turned to an existing law—the **Sherman Antitrust Act of 1890**. You may remember that John D. Rockefeller transformed the Standard Oil Company into a trust so he could avoid following state laws and could buy up his competition. The Sherman Antitrust Act was the legislation that led to the end of Rockefeller's monopoly and others like it. For the most part, the end of the monopolies resulted in greater competition in prices and wages.

You have read about the journalists known as muckrakers and how one such journalist, Upton Sinclair, helped make the public aware of unsanitary practices in the meat-packing industry. Muckrakers also exposed

Booker T. Washington

Roosevelt, Washington, and Race Relations

Roosevelt was friends with African-American educator Booker T. Washington, but he did little to improve race relations. For example, in 1906, a group of African-American soldiers stationed near Brownsville, Texas, were accused of shooting a white bartender. Despite strong evidence of their innocence, Roosevelt ordered all of them to be discharged without honor. Washington pleaded with him to reconsider his decision, but Roosevelt refused.

Theodore Roosevelt National Park
To honor the time Roosevelt spent in the Dakota Territory, the Theodore Roosevelt National Park, shown here, was established in 1947. Roosevelt started a couple of cattle ranching operations in the badlands area of present-day North Dakota and built a home there in 1884. It was while spending time on this land that Roosevelt's conservation ideas first took root.

shocking problems relating to the quality and safety of other foods and of medicines. As you know, Roosevelt pushed Congress to pass the **Pure Food and Drug Act** and the **Meat Inspection Act** after these problems had been exposed. The laws empowered the federal government to protect the quality, purity, and safety of foods and drugs.

THE CONSERVATION MOVEMENT

Roosevelt deeply loved the outdoors, and his love only grew during the two years he spent on a cattle ranch in the Dakota Territory. Riding horses, tending to livestock, hunting, and fishing had given him a great respect for the values of individualism and self-reliance. He returned to his home state of New York committed to the **conservation movement**, the idea of conserving the country's lands and wildlife—especially in the West. The conservation movement was gaining strength at the time Roosevelt became president. Conservationists wanted laws in place to protect the country's environment from wasteful practices and exploitation by agricultural, industrial, and commercial development. They were fortunate to have a president who shared their principles.

As you've read, Roosevelt worked to preserve and protect areas of unspoiled land. He created the United States Forest Service and turned its leadership over to his close friend **Gifford Pinchot** (PIN-show). Under Pinchot, the Forest Service set aside 172 million acres of land for conservation. The protected areas allowed animal and plant species to thrive and guaranteed that future generations would be able to enjoy the country's beautiful natural resources.

HISTORICAL THINKING

1. **READING CHECK** What did Roosevelt mean by the phrase "a square deal"?

2. **ANALYZE ENVIRONMENTAL CONCEPTS** Why did Roosevelt believe the ecosystems in the protected areas set aside by the Forest Service were essential to human life and to the nation's economy and culture?

3. **IDENTIFY PROBLEMS AND SOLUTIONS** How did Roosevelt and Congress use government regulations to solve problems in the business world?

2.1 Progressivism Under Taft

Imagine working 12 hours a day, 6 days a week, at a factory job that pays very little. The work is exhausting, and the conditions are dangerous and unsanitary. In the early 1900s, many jobs were like this—even for children.

MAIN IDEA During William Taft's presidency, progressive gains included the growth of labor unions and the adoption of the 16th and 17th amendments to the Constitution.

THE TRIANGLE FACTORY FIRE

Despite his popularity, Teddy Roosevelt decided not to run for a second full term as president in 1908. Instead he supported his Secretary of War, **William Howard Taft,** to be his successor. Taft was a well-respected conservative judge, but he pursued progressive goals when he won the election and became president. He continued Roosevelt's work by putting into action antitrust laws and breaking up monopolies. In fact, Taft filed more antitrust suits against monopolies than Roosevelt had.

By this time, some progress had been made in improving conditions for workers, but many factories remained dangerous. In 1911, a terrible tragedy occurred at the Triangle Waist Company's factory in New York City, where shirtwaists, or women's blouses, were made. Triangle was a sweatshop—a clothing factory where workers labored for long hours with little pay. When a fire broke out on the eighth floor of the building and quickly spread to the ninth and tenth floors, the workers, mostly very young immigrant women, discovered they were trapped. Some doors had been locked to prevent the workers from taking unauthorized breaks. The weak fire escape quickly collapsed under the weight of the women trying to flee. Fire trucks arrived, but their ladders could only reach as high as the sixth floor. Some workers suffocated inside the building, and others jumped to their death. Newspaper photographs showed the lifeless bodies of some of the 146 dead.

The **Triangle Waist Company factory fire** outraged the public. Many people who had not been involved in the labor movement finally

The Triangle Waist Company was located in the Asch building, which, according to its owners, was fireproof. The fire, sparked by a cigarette or tossed match, started on the eighth floor and spread rapidly. The photo shows one of the fire escapes that collapsed when the women tried to flee the fire.

recognized the value of labor unions and their fight for higher wages, more benefits, and safer working conditions. Labor unions experienced an increase in membership and growth after the fire. Nevertheless, relations between workers and company owners remained strained. In 1914, for example, miners in Ludlow, Colorado, went on strike. In response, the mine's security force and the state militia fired on the strikers and killed a number of people, including many children. The **Ludlow Massacre** showed that workers' demands would sometimes be met with violence.

TWO PROGRESSIVE AMENDMENTS

Progressives had managed to convince government to make some of the reforms they sought. Government programs cost money, however. Adding social programs meant that the government would have to raise revenue.

At the start of the 20th century, Americans did not pay federal income taxes. An **income tax** is a tax paid by employed people to the government. The tax is usually a percentage of a person's income. The higher the income, the higher the percentage the person pays. The government can use income tax revenue for any of its expenses, including the funding of social programs. To gain that stream of money, Congress passed the **16th Amendment** to the Constitution in 1909, and it was ratified in 1913. This amendment gave Congress the power to collect taxes on money made as income.

Another amendment addressed the goal of progressives to expand democracy. The Constitution called for state legislatures to choose two people to represent the state in the U.S. Senate. The **17th Amendment**, which was ratified in 1913, changed the rules and allowed the people of each state to elect their senators by a direct vote. Taft had accomplished a great deal in his first term. He hoped to continue working for the country in a second term—but he ran up against an unexpected obstacle.

HISTORICAL THINKING

1. **READING CHECK** How did President Taft continue to build on Roosevelt's efforts?

2. **ANALYZE CAUSE AND EFFECT** In what ways did the Triangle Waist Company factory fire affect the labor movement?

3. **SYNTHESIZE** How did the 16th and 17th amendments further the aims of progressives?

2.2 Wilson Continues Reform

Teddy Roosevelt enjoyed being president. So watching William Taft govern for four years was probably hard for him to take. But when Roosevelt challenged Taft in 1912, they both lost to Woodrow Wilson.

MAIN IDEA During his presidency, Woodrow Wilson fought tariffs and trusts and established the Federal Reserve System.

WILSON'S ECONOMIC CHANGES

William Taft was up for re-election as president in 1912, but he got an unwelcome surprise: Theodore Roosevelt had decided to run as well. Though they had previously been allies, Taft and Roosevelt now disagreed about the direction the country should take. A few states held primary elections for the first time, and voters tended to prefer Roosevelt. Taft, however, was the choice of most of the Republican Party delegates. After Taft won the nomination, Roosevelt decided to run as the candidate for the newly created Progressive Party, also known as the Bull Moose Party.

With the Republican vote split between Taft and Roosevelt, the Democratic candidate, New Jersey governor **Woodrow Wilson** won the election. He used the slogan "The New Freedom" to describe his domestic policies. He hoped to focus on three things: tariffs, monopolies, and banks.

Wilson pushed for economic changes that would help average Americans. He persuaded Congress to reduce the tariffs on imported goods such as wool, sugar, and cotton. The 16th Amendment had recently passed, which, as you may recall, allowed Congress to collect taxes on people's income. Wilson believed the funds raised through these taxes would offset the loss from lower tariffs.

Roosevelt and Taft had been able to prevent monopolies from forming by applying laws such as the Sherman Antitrust Act of 1890. These laws were generally vague, however, and companies had discovered **loopholes**, or unclear language that allows people to get around laws and avoid obeying them. Wilson asked Congress to put clearer and stronger laws into place. As a result,

in 1914, the **Clayton Antitrust Act** spelled out, in detail, the illegality of trusts' unlawful business practices and closed the loopholes they used.

BANKING REFORMS

Next, Wilson turned his attention to banks. The many economic panics of the previous decades convinced him that the country needed a strong central bank. It took months of negotiation, but Congress and Wilson worked out terms for the **Federal Reserve Act**. Signed into law in 1913, the act established the Federal Reserve Board. Under the board's oversight, or supervision, 12 banks, called **reserve banks**, would control the nation's flow of money. They would determine the amount of money in circulation, expand or decrease credit, and make decisions about money flow in response to changes in the economy.

While Wilson reformed the economy and the banks, other progressives came up with new ways of making businesses more efficient and improving the working environment for employees. And roads were being filled with vehicles that would revolutionize transportation.

HISTORICAL THINKING

1. **READING CHECK** What were the goals of Woodrow Wilson's "New Freedom" program?

2. **ANALYZE CAUSE AND EFFECT** What happened as a result of Roosevelt's entry into the 1912 election?

3. **IDENTIFY MAIN IDEAS AND DETAILS** What was the purpose of the Federal Reserve Board, and what were its functions?

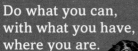
Do what you can, with what you have, where you are.

Presidents come and go, but the Supreme Court goes on forever.

If you want to make enemies, try to change something.

THE THREE PROGRESSIVES

There is something unique and unusual about each of the presidents you have read about in this chapter.

Theodore Roosevelt
26TH PRESIDENT

- He secured the territory and right for the United States to build and administer the Panama Canal.

- His children had quite a menagerie in the White House, including a small bear, a barn owl, a hyena, and a badger, in addition to dogs, birds, and guinea pigs.

- The teddy bear is named for him.

- The Progressive Party's nickname, "Bull Moose Party," was inspired by Roosevelt's image as an outdoorsman and a tough leader.

William Taft
27TH PRESIDENT

- He was the first U.S. president to have the use of an official automobile while in office.

- He established a Children's Bureau within the Labor Department, broadened civil service protection for thousands of government workers, and added thousands of acres to protected nature reserves.

- He was the only president to also serve as Chief Justice of the Supreme Court.

Woodrow Wilson
28TH PRESIDENT

- Highly educated, Wilson had served as the president of Princeton University.

- He was the first U.S. president to hold a press conference.

- He established the official national observance of Mother's Day.

- He was the first U.S. president to cross the Atlantic Ocean while in office.

2.3 Modern Technology and Mass Markets

Imagine that you're walking along a road in 1913 when suddenly several cars go chugging past you. You're fascinated. The cars are identical, and they're driven by regular working people, not the wealthy. Maybe you wouldn't mind taking a ride in one of them yourself.

MAIN IDEA New technologies and ideas that arose during the Progressive Era helped companies become more efficient and produce goods quickly.

THE MODEL T

Gasoline-powered automobiles had been around since the 1890s. But these cars were expensive to build, and their sale price was too high for most Americans. Then, in 1913, industrialist **Henry Ford** decided to use the **assembly line** system to build his cars. In this system, workers stand in place while the items to be put together move past them on a conveyor belt. The meat-packing industry had used an assembly line since the 1870s, and Ford adapted it to the production of automobiles. His Ford auto plant in Highland Park, Michigan, had conveyor belts that carried car parts ready to be assembled past workers. Each worker performed a single task and assembled the same parts over and over.

Ford chose the name "Model T" for the cars mass-produced, or manufactured in large quantities, in this manner. From the start, the time it took to build a single car was cut in half, from 12 hours to less than 6. But the repetitive nature of the work involved in assembling a Model T made many workers quit. So, in 1914, Ford raised his workers' salaries to five dollars a day, more than twice what it had been before. He also reduced their daily work

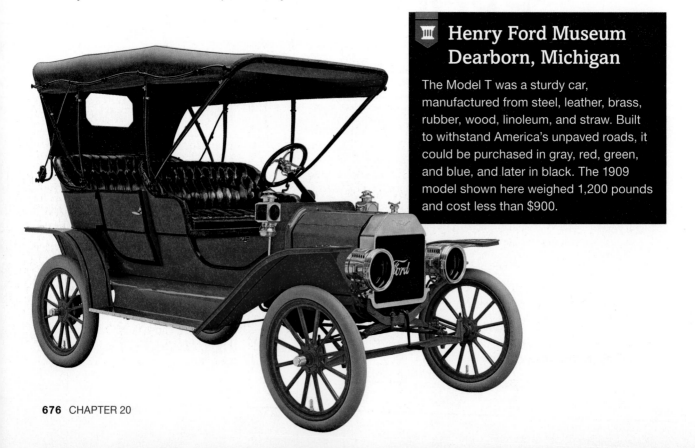

🏛 Henry Ford Museum Dearborn, Michigan

The Model T was a sturdy car, manufactured from steel, leather, brass, rubber, wood, linoleum, and straw. Built to withstand America's unpaved roads, it could be purchased in gray, red, green, and blue, and later in black. The 1909 model shown here weighed 1,200 pounds and cost less than $900.

hours from nine to eight. Not only did most of Ford's employees remain on the job after that, but many of them also purchased Model Ts. Because mechanization and factory production reduced labor costs and expanded production capacity, the price of the cars fell. In 1917, the Model T cost about $360, an affordable price for many people.

BUSINESS PRACTICES

Other factories and businesses also developed new practices during the Progressive Era. Some companies had tens of thousands of employees and manufacturing plants in several locations. With such large workforces, employers had to figure out new ways of managing how their employees carried out their work and making the workers more productive. Above all, employers wanted to increase industrial efficiency, or in other words, produce goods with the least amount of time and effort. Doing so would reduce production costs.

Many of the ideas for making the workplace more efficient came from an engineer named **Frederick Winslow Taylor**, who developed the idea of **scientific management**. He maintained that by carefully studying individual people at work, an employer could figure out the most effective way to do a job. Then other workers could be taught to complete the task in the same way.

Scientific management was popular with manufacturers. They discovered that, by using a strategically organized workforce, they could produce more goods for a lower price. But many workers resented it. Often the most efficient way to complete a job was through performing repetitive movements all day. Henry Ford had consulted with Taylor and used his methods when he set up the assembly lines in his Michigan auto plant.

It wasn't all about efficiency, however. Some employers tried to make the workday more pleasant for their workers. Lunchrooms, recreation areas, and bathroom facilities were put into many factories. Some employees received benefits such

The Sinking of the Titanic

The failure to put good business practices in place sometimes cost lives in the early 20th century. In 1912, the British-built ship Royal Mail Steamer (R.M.S.) *Titanic* set sail on its maiden, or first, voyage from Southampton, England, to New York City. Said to be unsinkable, the *Titanic* struck an iceberg and plunged into the North Atlantic Ocean. Because the ship's builders had neglected to provide enough lifeboats, and its crew had not conducted lifeboat drills to prepare passengers in case of an emergency, about 1,500 people died in the disaster. The watch above had belonged to John Starr March, one of five mail clerks who died while trying to save the heavy mail bags carried by the *Titanic*.

as a fund for retirement. Still, most Americans saw only small improvements in the workplace.

The development of electricity in the early 1900s also helped transform business and improve working conditions. The use of electric lights decreased the heat produced by gas lighting and reduced the risk of fire. By 1920, electricity powered more than half of the machines in American factories. Soon more than a third of American homes had electricity. Kerosene lamps, or lamps that burn oil for light, were quickly giving way to electric light bulbs. New electric appliances coming on the market would have a profound impact on daily life, especially for women.

HISTORICAL THINKING

1. **READING CHECK** How did Henry Ford revolutionize the production of automobiles?

2. **SYNTHESIZE** How did the idea of scientific management help businesses increase efficiency?

3. **MAKE INFERENCES** How do you think the availability of affordable cars changed people's lives in the early 20th century?

3.1 Women's Changing Roles

Today, more women than men attend college in the United States, and women work in every profession. Women vote in elections and hold political offices. Things were very different in the early 1900s, but change was already in the air.

MAIN IDEA The Progressive Era brought important changes to the roles of women in American society.

BREAKING MOLDS

Women began to find it easier to break from their traditional roles as mothers and homemakers during the Progressive Era for several reasons. For one thing, family size was starting to shrink. With fewer children to look after, women had more time for themselves. Thomas Edison's long-lasting light bulb brought electricity into the home. And household inventions such as the vacuum cleaner and washing machine made household chores less time-consuming. Electricity also allowed factories to produce clothing quickly and inexpensively. As a result, women could buy affordable clothes in stores rather than sew all their families' clothing themselves. These developments meant that women had more time to work outside the home.

An influential thinker and writer named **Charlotte Perkins Gilman** encouraged women to do just that and gain financial independence. If women had enough money to support themselves without relying on the income of men, she argued, they could pursue some of their own goals. Gilman published widely, sharing her ideas in several important women's publications of the day. She also spoke to women's clubs around the country.

This type of club was popular at the turn of the century. Initially, the clubs hosted cultural events and offered members a chance to socialize. But, just as groups of women had come together to discuss how they could aid the American Revolution, members of these women's clubs soon became involved in addressing the social and economic issues of their day. They opened libraries and free kindergartens for children. They worked to improve sanitation and public health services in overcrowded cities. They lobbied for better working conditions. The clubs became an important way for women to organize and carry out social reform.

The Singer Automatic

LATEST AND BEST

HAS MOST ROOM UNDER ARM

Absolutely the Simplest, Lightest-Running, Best-Constructed Strongest Chain-Stitch Sewing Machine ever invented. Has neither shuttle nor bobbin. No tensions to adjust. Always ready when needle is threaded.

SOLD ONLY BY **THE SINGER MANUFACTURING CO.**

OFFICES IN EVERY CITY IN THE WORLD.

Electric sewing machines, like the one in this advertisement, were among the household inventions that improved women's lives in the late 1800s. The machines allowed women to make clothing faster and more cheaply.

MAKING STRIDES

Many women in the Progressive Era took Gilman's advice. Actually, though, women had begun making strides in the workplace since the Civil War, when teaching and nursing became acceptable jobs for American women. The economic depression of 1893 brought an unexpected opportunity for other jobs. Greater numbers of women entered the workforce, taking on jobs men would not consider doing. Throughout the 1890s, women began to take on clerical work such as typing and other office tasks, and some also worked in factories. Women's wages kept many families afloat during the hard economic downturn. Even so, women made only about 60 percent of what men typically earned.

The beginning of the 20th century also witnessed more American women than ever attending and graduating from high school. Some even earned a college education but mostly in fields considered appropriate for women, such as elementary education. Women had few educational opportunities in fields such as law, medicine, and higher education, which were considered subjects only suitable for men. But a few pioneering women fought to overcome that way of thinking. Ellen Spencer Mussey and Emma Gillett had managed to become attorneys, but they knew how difficult it was for most women to study law and earn a degree in it. So, in 1898, after a woman approached Mussey about studying law with her, Mussey and Gillett decided to take action. They founded the Washington School of Law in Washington, D.C. Although the college also admitted men, its primary focus was educating women in the law. Today, it is part of American University.

Industrialization, economic growth, and urbanization increased women's chances for finding a job and securing an education. Women also asserted themselves more and more as leaders in the progressive movement.

HISTORICAL THINKING

1. **READING CHECK** Why did women begin to have more time to work outside the home during the Progressive Era?

2. **EVALUATE** In what way might Charlotte Perkins Gilman's ideas about women be considered modern?

3. **MAKE INFERENCES** Why do you think fields such as law, medicine, and higher education were not considered suitable for women around the turn of the 20th century?

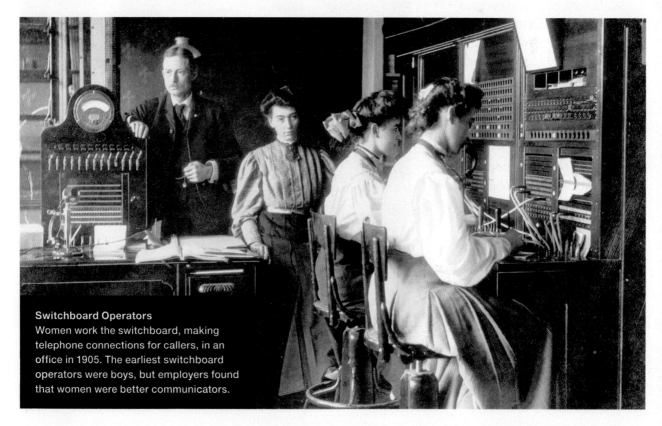

Switchboard Operators
Women work the switchboard, making telephone connections for callers, in an office in 1905. The earliest switchboard operators were boys, but employers found that women were better communicators.

3.2 Women as Leaders

When you help people in need, you show them they are not alone. Women who helped others at the beginning of the 20th century not only improved their communities but also gained political power.

MAIN IDEA In the early 20th century, women's roles became key to social reform movements in the United States.

SETTLEMENT HOUSES

Community organization was a key part of achieving reform during the Progressive Era, and many of the most important leaders among these organizers were women. You have read about Jane Addams and Ellen Gates Starr, who founded Hull House in Chicago. They were pioneers in the field of **social work**, or work aimed at improving the lives of others. Hull House was a settlement house that sheltered and fed struggling immigrants and helped them settle into their new lives in the United States. Hull House also helped the working poor. Settlement houses played an important role because the populations of Chicago and other major U.S. cities had surged. The cities' mostly immigrant working-class populations suffered from poverty, overcrowding, and poor sanitation conditions.

Henry Street Settlement in New York City was founded to help ease health issues that arose as a result of these conditions. Lillian Wald, a nurse and social worker, established the settlement in 1893 to offer a free nursing service to immigrants in the city's Lower East Side neighborhood. She coined the term *public health* to refer to nursing care provided in such poor communities. As the settlement grew, Wald organized clubs, lectures, and activities there. She also set up a playground in the settlement's backyard—one of the first in the city.

On Her Rounds
A nurse from the Henry Street Settlement visits an immigrant mother and her children in the early 1900s. By 1914, a team of more than 100 nurses worked at the settlement. Wald insisted the nurses treat not only their patients' illnesses but also their social and economic problems.

By 1910, there were more than 400 settlement houses across the country, offering free services including childcare and job training. Some of the women who provided these services became influential in local government. Wald, for example, persuaded New York City's Board of Education to provide free lunches for all public school children and hire the first nurse to work at a public school. Some of the women even had an impact on the national government, working as lobbyists to pass industrial-era reforms. A **lobbyist** is someone who meets with lawmakers and tries to persuade them to support particular laws and political ideas.

Carry Nation
During her temperance rallies, Carry Nation, shown here, used a small hatchet to smash containers of alcohol. Nation and her hatchet became a symbol of the temperance movement.

TEMPERANCE WINS

As you may remember, women were the primary supporters of temperance, a movement calling for the consumption of little or no alcohol, when it first became a social issue in the early 1800s. Women continued to lead and support the movement during the rest of that century and into the next.

A reformer of the Progressive Era named **Carry A. Nation** was instrumental in the passage of an amendment to the U.S. Constitution that prohibited the sale of alcohol. Nation was a **teetotaler**, someone who does not drink alcoholic beverages. She believed alcohol was a social problem that harmed the health and well-being of Americans. Nation had witnessed the effect of excessive drinking on families, with husbands losing their jobs, beating their wives, or spending much of their wages on drink. As a result, she became a leader in the temperance movement, campaigning to ban the sale of alcoholic drinks completely. An imposing figure at almost six feet tall, Nation inspired respect.

In 1919, due in large part to the efforts of activists like Nation, the United States ratified the **18th Amendment** to the Constitution, popularly known as **Prohibition**. This legislation banned the production, sale, importation, and transportation of liquor in the United States. Household consumption of alcoholic beverages was still legal, but unless people made their own, they couldn't obtain a drink. The amendment's ratification showed that women could have a profound influence on national policy. This influence would be critical in the struggle for a woman's right to vote, which women had been demanding for many years.

HISTORICAL THINKING

1. **READING CHECK** What purpose did the settlement houses play during the Progressive Era in the United States?

2. **FORM AND SUPPORT OPINIONS** Do you think Carry Nation's methods were an effective way to combat social problems? Why or why not?

3. **SYNTHESIZE** What similar goals motivated the women of Henry Street Settlement and Carry Nation?

3.3 The Nineteenth Amendment

Think of the outcry if your principal denied half of the student body the right to vote in a school election. American women had been protesting and calling for the right to vote since before the Civil War. Many in the Progressive Era hoped that perhaps now their time had come.

MAIN IDEA Strong leadership and the organization of woman suffrage groups finally helped women gain the right to vote.

EARLY STRUGGLES

In 1869, the government granted women in the Wyoming Territory the right to participate in all elections. The victory was a small but important one. When Wyoming became a state in 1890, an amendment to the state constitution officially granted women voting rights. Other western states, such as Colorado, Utah, and Idaho, followed suit in 1896. Despite these gains, women understood that only an amendment to the U.S. Constitution establishing women's right to vote would guarantee their rights and protections. They continued to fight.

Do you remember reading about Susan B. Anthony and Elizabeth Cady Stanton? They were both influential suffragists. A **suffragist** (SUH-frih-jist) is someone who fights for the right to vote, particularly a woman's right to vote. Anthony's and Stanton's women's rights newspaper called *The Revolution* was small in comparison to other publications of its time, but it had a huge influence. Begun in 1868, it became the official voice of the National Woman Suffrage Association (NWSA), which Anthony and Stanton had founded in 1869. In 1890, the NWSA merged with the American Woman Suffrage Association, to form the **National American Woman Suffrage Association (NAWSA)**.

In this photo, women in 1913 take part in the first suffrage parade in Washington, D.C. About 8,000 participants marched to the White House to call for a constitutional amendment granting women the right to vote. Along the way, some spectators heckled, tripped, and threw things at the suffragists.

WOMEN VOTE

WE DEMAND AN AMENDMENT TO THE CONSTITUTION OF THE UNITED STATES ENFRANCHISING THE WOMEN OF THIS COUNTRY

The group formed after other suffrage groups split up due to differing views over voting rights for African-American women.

Anthony became president of the NAWSA in 1892. Under her leadership, it gained the support of every women's suffrage society in the United States. State by state, the NAWSA worked to achieve women's suffrage, and the group had some success. But the suffragists wanted more.

VICTORY FOR WOMEN

In 1900, **Carrie Chapman Catt** succeeded Anthony as president of the NAWSA and continued to fight for women's suffrage at the state level. In time, though, Catt led the organization's first national campaign. Its goal was to amend the Constitution to finally guarantee suffrage for all women.

From 1905 to 1915, Catt recruited and trained political campaigners. Then, in 1917, after the United States entered World War I, the NAWSA's membership grew as a result of Catt's shrewd strategy of linking women's voting rights to the war effort. Because so many men were away fighting in the war, the government had asked women to step into jobs necessary to support the war effort. Catt and other NAWSA members argued that women's patriotism and war work should be rewarded with equal rights, including the right

to vote. The plan worked. Woodrow Wilson, the president at that time, had initially opposed voting rights for women. But the war and Catt's argument changed his mind. Calling its passage "vital to the winning of the war," President Wilson supported the **19th Amendment**, the bill that would make woman suffrage the law of the land.

Still, the road to ratification was somewhat rocky. The House of Representatives and Senate voted on the 19th Amendment in January 1918. The House approved the bill, but the Senate voted against it. Suffragists in the National Women's Party, an extension of the NAWSA, responded by campaigning to vote senators who had opposed the bill out of office. Their efforts proved successful. On August 18, 1920, the 19th Amendment was finally ratified, guaranteeing all women the right to vote under the Constitution.

In 1917, Catt wrote an essay answering objections to guaranteeing women's suffrage by federal amendment. In this excerpt from her essay, Catt points out why not allowing women to vote is unreasonable.

PRIMARY SOURCE

The system which admits the unworthy to the vote provided they are men, and shuts out the worthy provided they are women, is so unjust and illogical that its perpetuation [continuation] is a sad reflection upon American thinking.

—from "Objections to the Federal Amendment," by Carrie Chapman Catt, 1917

HISTORICAL THINKING

1. **READING CHECK** What did the NAWSA seek to accomplish?

2. **SYNTHESIZE** How did the NAWSA combine some of the goals of both women's rights activists and abolitionists?

3. **ANALYZE CAUSE AND EFFECT** What led President Wilson to change his mind about women's suffrage?

The United States Expands

Ever since the establishment of the 13 colonies, Americans had been on the lookout for new land to settle. Up until the late 1800s, the United States had confined its expansion within North America. But that was about to change, as Americans started to eye territory in other countries.

MAIN IDEA In the second half of the 19th century, the United States gained new territories and began to take on a larger role in world affairs.

ENTERING THE WORLD STAGE

The Founders of the United States were wary of getting involved in the affairs of other countries. You may remember that, during his presidency, George Washington had advised having "as little political connection as possible" with foreign nations. And as president, Thomas Jefferson warned against engaging in "entangling alliances" with any country. Having suffered oppression under the British Empire, the Founders were suspicious of **imperialism**, a system in which a stronger nation controls weaker nations or territories.

During the Progressive Era, some American leaders agreed with the Founders. They argued that the United States should only use military force abroad to protect the freedom of its own citizens. Many progressives, on the other hand, argued that the United States was obligated to promote democracy and progress around the world.

And the nation's military was ready to carry out that mission. The U.S. Navy, in particular, grew very powerful during the Progressive Era, building the Pacific Fleet in 1907. A key figure behind the development of the navy was **Alfred Thayer Mahan**, a retired naval officer who wrote an influential book about the importance of sea power and control over sea trade. Technological advances, meanwhile, were revolutionizing warships.

As Americans watched European nations building empires in Africa and Asia, many believed the United States should also begin to expand its territory and power beyond its borders. Three main reasons lay behind American imperialism. The first reason was economic. Industrialization had greatly increased the quantity and quality of the country's manufactured goods. Many industrialists—and farmers—were eager for new markets in which to sell their goods. They also desired the natural resources that colonies abroad might provide. The second was the desire to expand American military power. The United States wanted to establish a military presence in other parts of the world to demonstrate its strength and protect its economic interests. The third reason was ideological. Many Americans believed they should spread not only democracy but also Christianity to

CRITICAL VIEWING Queen Liliuokalani, the last queen of Hawaii, was a well-educated woman who met with European royalty and dined at the White House. She was also proud of her Hawaiian culture and loyal to her kingdom. What details in the photograph reveal her royal status?

The natural wonders of Alaska are dramatic. Wildlife like this brown bear and cub thrive among its snow-capped mountains and many lakes. Alaska also has abundant supplies of natural gas and oil. Buying Alaska was a wise purchase.

other people. Underlying this belief was the racist assumption of the superiority of Western society and white culture.

EXPANDING THE NATION

Of course, the United States had been expanding westward for most of its history. Then in 1867, Secretary of State **William Henry Seward** arranged for the United States to purchase Alaska from Russia. At the time, Russia was struggling with war debt and eager to sell. Some Americans supported the purchase of this enormous territory. They also wanted to annex, or take possession of, Canada and considered acquiring Alaska a necessary step toward that goal. Many more Americans were critical of the purchase, however. Alaska, they claimed, was too far from the rest of the country. It was an "icebox" and, at a cost of $7.2 million, too expensive. These critics called the purchase "Seward's Folly." As Americans would discover, Alaska had abundant natural resources. The United States made a good deal.

Around this time, American economic interests were growing in the Hawaiian Islands, an **archipelago** (ahr-kuh-PEL-uh-goh), or chain of islands, that lies in the middle of the Pacific Ocean. Wealthy Americans who owned sugar plantations on the islands were gaining financial and political power there at the expense of the Hawaiian monarchy. These planters helped secure a treaty

in 1875 that established free trade between Hawaii and the United States. Then, in 1887, the United States gained the right to build a naval base at Pearl Harbor in Hawaii.

Queen Liliuokalani (lee-lee-oo-oh-kah-LAH-nee), who became Hawaii's queen in 1891, hoped to restore the power of the monarchy and maintain the islands' independence. Concerned that the queen's actions would threaten their interests, American and foreign businessmen, supported by U.S. Marines, rebelled against the queen and forced her from power. Recognizing the strategic naval importance of the Hawaiian Islands and the value of their rich agricultural lands, the U.S. government annexed the islands in 1898. Meanwhile, events in another part of the world would lead to the acquisition of yet more territory.

HISTORICAL THINKING

1. **READING CHECK** How did progressives feel about U.S. involvement in the affairs of other countries?

2. **MAKE INFERENCES** Why do you think some Americans thought that acquiring Alaska might help lead to the acquisition of Canada?

3. **SYNTHESIZE** How does the U.S. annexation of Hawaii illustrate the three main reasons behind American imperialism?

4.2 The Spanish-American War

Do you believe everything you read on the Internet? You've probably learned to be skeptical of claims made on many sites. The public wasn't always so critical of the press, though. The tales told by some journalists in the 1890s might even have persuaded the United States to go to war with Spain.

MAIN IDEA Due in part to exaggerated claims reported in the press, the United States waged the Spanish-American War, which resulted in new territorial acquisitions.

"REMEMBER THE *MAINE*!"

Spain had been a major imperialist power since the late 1400s. By the end of the 1800s, Spain's colonial holdings included the Caribbean islands of Puerto Rico and Cuba, the Philippines in Southeast Asia, and several Pacific islands, including Guam.

People in the Caribbean began to call for independence toward the end of the 19th century. Around 1890, a journalist named **Luis Muñoz Rivera** became a leading voice in a movement to gain **autonomy**, or self-rule, for Puerto Rico. Success came in 1897 when Spain granted the island its autonomy. Although Spain still maintained a governor in Puerto Rico, the island's citizens were allowed to set up their own government and manage local affairs.

Cuba was not as fortunate in its goals as Puerto Rico. In 1895, **José Martí** led Cuba in a rebellion to break from Spain. Instead of granting Cuba its independence, however, Spanish troops repressed the rebels with brutal force in its early battles and killed Martí. Cuban guerrillas continued the fight.

Though the United States had not been involved in the rebellion, the American press wrote sensationalized, or exaggerated, stories about it. Publisher **William Randolph Hearst** decided to frame the story in a dramatic way designed to sell his newspapers. His reporters wrote about the

On February 17, 1898, the front page of William Randolph Hearst's newspaper, the *New York Journal and Advertiser*, announced the destruction of the U.S.S. *Maine*.

PRIMARY SOURCE

George Eugene Bryson, the Journal's *special correspondent at Havana, cables* [telegraphs] *that it is the secret opinion of many Spaniards in the Cuban capital, that the* Maine *was destroyed and 258 men killed by means of marine mine or fixed torpedo. This is the opinion of several American naval authorities. The Spaniards, it is believed, arranged to have the* Maine *anchored over one of the harbor mines. Wires connected the mines with a . . . magazine* [supply of ammunition], *and it is thought the explosion was caused by sending an electric current through the wire. If this can be proven, the brutal nature of the Spaniards will be shown by the fact that they waited to spring the mine after all the men had retired for the night.*

—*New York Journal and Advertiser,*
   February 17, 1898

A five-foot nameplate from the wreck of the U.S.S. *Maine*

bravery of Cuban soldiers and the suffering of women and children—much of it made up. The publisher also sent American artists, including Frederic Remington, to Cuba to draw pictures of the violence occurring there. When Remington reported that the violence had been overstated, Hearst replied, "You furnish the pictures, and I'll furnish the war." Purposely exaggerating and dramatizing these events, a practice that came to be called yellow journalism, raked in big profits for Hearst, but it left readers with a distorted view of the truth. The term was coined as a result of a battle between Hearst and rival newspaper publisher Joseph Pulitzer over a comic strip featuring a character called "the yellow kid."

Through his coverage of the rebellion, Hearst built wide public support for Cuba. He got his biggest story in 1898, when the U.S.S. *Maine*, a naval battleship, sailed to the Cuban harbor of Havana to protect American interests there. On February 15, a mysterious explosion sank the ship, and more than 250 American sailors died. The cause of the disaster was never determined, but Hearst blamed Spain. Much like the slogan "Remember the Alamo" earlier in the century, "Remember the *Maine*!" became a rallying cry for those demanding war against Spain.

A WORLD POWER

The public outcry led the U.S. government to take action. Congress declared that Cuba should be independent and that President William McKinley should send military forces to make sure Spain obeyed. In response, Spain declared war against the United States on April 24, 1898.

The Spanish-American War was fought on several fronts. It started in the Philippines with the Battle of Manila Bay on May 1. Under Commodore **George Dewey**, the U.S. Navy easily destroyed the Spanish fleet. The war was also fought in Cuba. Future president Theodore Roosevelt played a leadership role in these battles. He was an effective recruiter and persuaded an untrained but tough group of cowboys, miners, police officers, and Native Americans to volunteer. Nicknamed the **Rough Riders**, these soldiers helped capture key locations in Cuba , including Kettle Hill. The Rough Riders also played a supporting role in the **Battle of San Juan Hill** on July 1, which led to a critical victory. Spanish troops left Cuba shortly thereafter.

Completely unprepared for an expanded war with the powerful U.S. military, Spain surrendered on July 17. Through the treaty that ended the war, the United States gained control of Puerto Rico, the Philippines, and the Pacific island of Guam. In 1901, under an agreement with Cuba known as the **Platt Amendment**, the United States agreed to withdraw from Cuba but retained the right to intervene in Cuban affairs. The United States had become a world power.

CRITICAL VIEWING In this painting, W. G. Read's *Rough Riders*, Roosevelt leads his forces in the charge on San Juan Hill. In the actual battle, Roosevelt and his men ascended the hill on foot. And although the African-American troops, the Buffalo Soldiers, did the bulk of the fighting, Roosevelt got most of the credit for the victory. What details in the painting depict Roosevelt as a heroic figure?

HISTORICAL THINKING

1. **READING CHECK** What is yellow journalism?

2. **EVALUATE** How does the newspaper article use facts and opinions to make readers conclude that Spain destroyed the *Maine*?

3. **DRAW CONCLUSIONS** Why do some people consider the Spanish-American War a "newspaper war"?

4.3 The Filipino-American War

The people of the Philippines had longed to be free of Spanish rule, and now they were. But they had merely exchanged one ruler for another. And they were more than disappointed—they were angry.

MAIN IDEA The people of the Philippines fought for independence from American rule in the Filipino-American War.

RESISTANCE IN THE PHILIPPINES

After more than 300 years of Spanish rule, the people of the Philippines, called Filipinos, didn't want to be controlled by another colonial power. They wanted their independence. The island nation's independence movement had grown strong during the long struggle against Spanish rule, and it now turned its full force against the United States.

Resistance leader **Emilio Aguinaldo** did not waste any time rallying his forces after the Spanish-American treaty was signed. On the night of February 4, 1899, Filipino insurrectionists, or rebels, and American troops clashed outside the capital city of Manila. The **Filipino-American War** had begun. Fierce fighting continued through the night, but by morning, the Americans had defeated the outnumbered Filipinos. Aguinaldo and his troops retreated northward into the mountains to regroup and rethink their strategy.

GUERRILLA WARFARE

Since conventional warfare against the American military had ended in defeat, the Filipinos turned to guerrilla warfare. This military tactic, which involves quick, unexpected attacks by small groups, is often effective for those fighting on their own land. The geography of the Philippines was well suited for guerrilla warfare. The country consists of thousands of islands, most with heavily forested mountains and, at that time, also with dense tropical rain forests.

The Filipino soldiers' tactics proved successful and resulted in the deaths of many American soldiers. In retaliation, the U.S. Army resorted to killing and torturing some Filipino prisoners of war. After an incident in which Filipino guerrillas massacred American troops, American general Jacob F. Smith engaged in a campaign of revenge. The violence committed by soldiers under his command was so extreme that the U.S. Army **court-martialed** Smith, or tried him in a military court, for his conduct and forced him to retire.

The brutality of the war strengthened an American movement against imperialist expansion. The American Anti-Imperialist League had been formed in 1898 to protest the expansion of the United States and its treatment of the Filipino people. Politicians, businesspeople, and writers joined the league to speak out against U.S. imperialism.

Mark Twain and the Filipino-American War
The famous U.S. novelist Mark Twain (shown here in a painting by Frank Larson) paid close attention to the Filipino-American War. At first he supported the war, but Twain grew dismayed by the imperialist aspirations of his government and joined the American Anti-Imperialist League.

During the Filipino-American War, entire villages, like this one, were damaged or completely destroyed. Residents were often driven from their homes or imprisoned.

Despite this opposition, the United States was determined to maintain its hold on the Philippines and eventually defeated the insurrectionists. The war officially came to an end in 1902, though guerrillas continued to battle American troops for a few more years. The fighting had resulted in a tremendous loss of life in the Philippines. Around 20,000 Filipino troops had been killed, and more than 200,000 civilians had died from combat wounds, disease, and starvation. On the American side, about 1,500 troops had been killed, and disease had claimed some 2,800 additional lives. The Philippines remained a U.S. territory until 1946 when the United States granted the country its independence. For a time, Filipinos were allowed to migrate freely to the United States because of their U.S. national status. As a result, many Filipinos immigrated to Hawaii around 1910 to work on its sugar plantations.

In the early 1900s, the United States continued to exert its influence in the world. But rather than acquire more territory, the nation focused on protecting its interests in Latin America and Asia.

In 1899, the Anti-Imperialist League issued its platform, or statement of beliefs, on U.S. imperialist policy. In this excerpt, the league explains why it condemns that policy.

PRIMARY SOURCE

We earnestly condemn the policy of the present National Administration in the Philippines. It seeks to extinguish the spirit of 1776 in those islands. We deplore the sacrifice of our soldiers and sailors, whose bravery deserves admiration even in an unjust war. We denounce the slaughter of the Filipinos as a needless horror. We protest against the extension of American sovereignty by Spanish methods.

—from "Platform of the American Anti-Imperialist League," 1899

HISTORICAL THINKING

1. **READING CHECK** How did the people of the Philippines react to American rule following the Spanish-American War?

2. **DRAW CONCLUSIONS** What does the Anti-Imperialist League mean when it claims that U.S. policy "seeks to extinguish the spirit of 1776" in the Philippines?

3. **MAKE INFERENCES** Why do you think the United States was so determined to hold onto the Philippines?

4.4 Involvement in Latin America and Asia

Do you know the saying, "Actions speak louder than words"? It means that people should be judged by what they do rather than what they say. As a man of action, Theodore Roosevelt practically embodied the saying. But he used another one to describe his foreign policy.

MAIN IDEA During the Progressive Era, the United States became increasingly involved in the affairs of Latin American and Asian countries.

BIG STICK POLICY

President Theodore Roosevelt favored American involvement in foreign affairs. He characterized his foreign policy with the saying, "Speak softly and carry a big stick." That meant that he would "speak softly," or negotiate with a country in a calm, assured manner. But if the country did not cooperate, he might use his "big stick"—U.S. military power.

Since 1823, the United States had followed the principles of the Monroe Doctrine. According to this policy, Europe would not acquire new colonies in the Western Hemisphere. In exchange, the United States would not get involved in political affairs in Europe and would respect existing European colonies in the Western Hemisphere.

Roosevelt decided to take this policy a step further by adding the **Roosevelt Corollary** to the Monroe Doctrine. This addition asserted that, under certain circumstances, the United States had the right to intervene in the affairs of Latin American countries.

Several presidents after Roosevelt followed his lead in policing the Western Hemisphere. A revolution in the Central American country of Nicaragua in 1909 resulted in a government that the United States viewed as a threat to its economic interests. President William Taft sent in troops to dismantle this government and set up a new one—one that would be friendly to American businesses.

President Woodrow Wilson got involved in Mexico's political affairs after General Victoriano Huerta overthrew the country's elected president in 1913. Mexico had been engaged in an on-going revolution since 1899. Calling Mexico's new leaders "a government of butchers," Wilson took steps to weaken Huerta's control and overthrow him. His measures worked, but the United States became involved in Mexico's revolution until 1917, when Wilson withdrew all U.S. forces from the country.

OPEN DOOR POLICY

Meanwhile, the United States had been exerting its influence in East Asia since the mid-1800s. For centuries, Japan had adopted a policy of isolation and greatly limited trade with other countries. On July 8, 1853, four American ships under the command of Commodore **Matthew Perry** sailed into Japan's Tokyo Bay. Perry had been sent to negotiate diplomatic relations and trade between Japan and the United States. As a result, Japan opened its ports to American ships for the first time in more than 200 years.

Like Japan, China tried to resist involvement with other countries. But the 19th century was an unsettled period for China. Following a series of wars with Britain, China had been forced to remove its barriers to foreign trade in 1842. Then around 1899, several countries—primarily Britain, France, Germany, and Russia—sought to establish spheres of influence in China. A **sphere of influence** is a

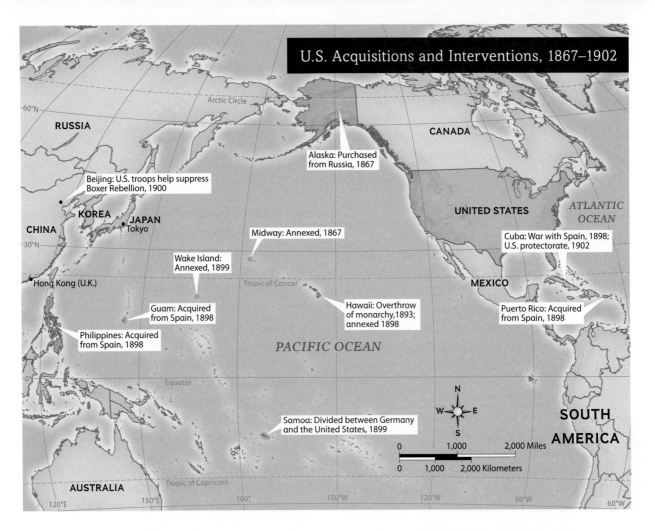

U.S. Acquisitions and Interventions, 1867–1902

Alaska: Purchased from Russia, 1867

Beijing: U.S. troops help suppress Boxer Rebellion, 1900

Midway: Annexed, 1867

Cuba: War with Spain, 1898; U.S. protectorate, 1902

Wake Island: Annexed, 1899

Hong Kong (U.K.)

Guam: Acquired from Spain, 1898

Hawaii: Overthrow of monarchy,1893; annexed 1898

Puerto Rico: Acquired from Spain, 1898

Philippines: Acquired from Spain, 1898

Samoa: Divided between Germany and the United States, 1899

claim a country makes to be the exclusive influence on another country's political or economic activities. Within China, each European power carved out a sphere of influence and controlled investment within that area.

The United States opposed these claims, fearing that the countries controlling their spheres of influence would monopolize all trade in China. As a result, the United States proposed the **Open Door Policy**. This policy called for equal trading privileges for all nations with economic interests in China. Although the nations that had carved out spheres of influence in China were not enthusiastic about this plan, they didn't openly oppose it either. So the U.S. government claimed that the powers had accepted the policy's terms and called their responses "final and definitive."

Many people in China were not happy with the flow of foreigners coming to their country. In 1900, a Chinese secret society known as the Society of the Righteous and Harmonious Fists rebelled against

the spread of Western and Japanese influence and sought to drive all foreigners out of China. Westerners called the society "Boxers" because its members carried out ritual boxing exercises. The Boxers killed foreigners and missionaries and destroyed property. An international coalition, which included American troops, was finally brought in and suppressed what would become known as the **Boxer Rebellion**. But the violent episode had exposed the unpredictable nature of increased contact with countries around the globe.

HISTORICAL THINKING

1. **READING CHECK** What was Theodore Roosevelt's big stick policy?

2. **SYNTHESIZE** How did presidents Taft and Wilson implement the Roosevelt Corollary?

3. **INTERPRET MAPS** How would you describe the location of most of the lands acquired by the United States?

4.5 Building the Panama Canal

MAIN IDEA In the early 1900s, the United States overcame geographic challenges and built the Panama Canal to connect the Atlantic and Pacific oceans.

THE DREAM OF A CANAL

For decades, people dreamed of building a shortcut between the Atlantic and Pacific oceans: a canal across the **isthmus** of Panama, a narrow strip of land connecting North and South America. Before the Panama Canal, ships had to sail around the southern tip of South America to get from America's East Coast to the West Coast. A canal would shorten this voyage by nearly 8,000 miles.

The French had tried to build a canal, but they failed because of the geographic challenges. The canal had to be about 50 miles long, and had to cut through rugged mountains. Additionally, a nearby river caused frequent flooding in the region, landslides were common, and mosquitoes infected construction workers with diseases.

But President Theodore Roosevelt was determined to have a canal built. First, he had to acquire the land. This was a big problem, because the isthmus belonged to the country of Colombia. Colombia and other Latin American countries did not trust the United States because of the Spanish-American War. Roosevelt didn't care. In 1903, he engineered a rebellion in which Panama broke away from Colombia and established its own country. Then the United States negotiated a treaty to create the Canal Zone, a ten-mile-wide strip of land the United States could lease from Panama. That was where the canal would be built.

Once they had the land, the Americans had to overcome the same geographic obstacles that had defeated the French, but the Americans succeeded. The Panama Canal opened in 1914 and has operated continuously since. Read about these challenges and the technology Americans used to overcome each one.

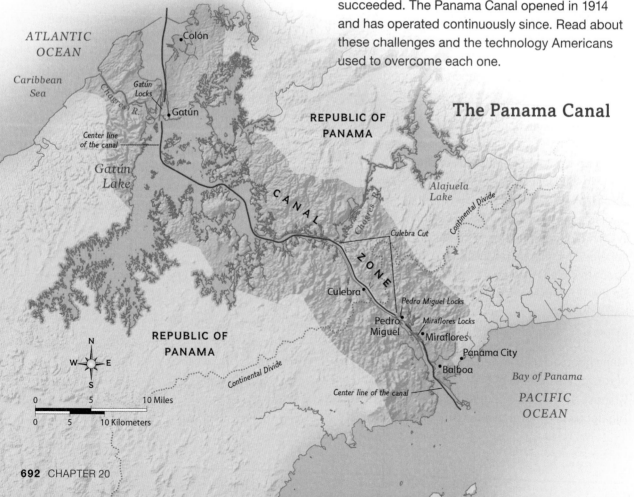

The Panama Canal

GEOGRAPHIC CHALLENGE	TECHNOLOGICAL SOLUTION

MALARIA AND YELLOW FEVER

Two dangerous diseases were widespread in Central America: malaria and yellow fever. The illnesses killed one in five workers, and no one knew what caused them.

When the chief medical officer for the project discovered mosquitoes could pass both diseases to humans, he insisted on placing screens on every building's windows. He had all standing water treated to prevent mosquito breeding. Then workers agreed to come to Panama.

DIGGING THE LOCKS

Panama is an extremely mountainous country. The engineers decided to build the canal at the level of the mountains rather than at sea level. To do so, they needed to build **locks**. A lock is a confined section of water used to raise or lower ships.

To build the locks, workers used steam shovels, which had only recently been developed, to dig enormous holes where the locks would be. They then poured more than four million barrels of cement to form the locks.

DIGGING THE CULEBRA CUT

The most difficult part of the canal was a 9-mile section called the Culebra Cut. It was a human-made ditch 45 feet deep and 9 miles long that would carry ships past the highest mountains.

First engineers blasted the rock loose with dynamite. Then they used huge steam shovels to lift the **spoil**, or excess dirt and rock, into waiting railroad cars. Each shovel could lift eight tons of spoil at a time. Railroad cars would carry the spoil away from the worksite.

DAMMING THE CHAGRES RIVER

Another major geographic challenge was the Chagres River, which fed into the Canal Zone. This river was wild, and during the rainy season, it flooded the entire region.

Engineers built an earthen dam in a valley about four miles east of the Atlantic Ocean. The dam controlled the river and prevented flooding by backing up the waters of the Chagres to form Gatun Lake. Ships sailed across the lake on their way to the locks at the canal's ends.

From New York to San Francisco:

BEFORE THE CANAL
13,000 Miles

AFTER THE CANAL
5,200 Miles

THINK LIKE A GEOGRAPHER

1. **IDENTIFY MAIN IDEAS AND DETAILS** How was the mountainous terrain of Panama a problem, and how did the engineers solve it?

2. **ANALYZE ENVIRONMENTAL CONCEPTS** How did the Chagres River benefit from being dammed during the building of the Panama Canal?

3. **MAKE INFERENCES** In 1977, President Jimmy Carter signed a treaty promising to return control of the Canal Zone to the country of Panama by the year 2000. Why do you think he might have signed this treaty?

VOCABULARY

Match the following vocabulary terms with their definitions.

1. referendum
2. autonomy
3. suffragist
4. sphere of influence
5. imperialism
6. loophole
7. initiative
8. conservation movement

a. unclear language that allows people to avoid obeying laws

b. a group of people working together to protect plants, animals, and the natural environment

c. a proposed law that citizens vote on to accept or reject

d. a law that citizens propose

e. an area of a country where another country has a great deal of power

f. a person who actively supports the right to vote, particularly a woman's right to vote

g. self-rule or independence

h. the use of power to gain control over other areas of the world

READING STRATEGY
SYNTHESIZE

If you haven't already, complete your chart by organizing the evidence in each lesson and synthesizing the information. Then answer the question.

9. What measures and strategies did progressives use to address social problems?

How did progressives address social problems?

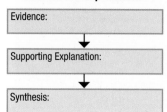

MAIN IDEAS

Answer the following questions. Support your answers with evidence from the chapter.

10. What 19th-century movement promoted equality for people of all races, genders, and sexual orientations? **LESSON 1.1**

11. Why did progressives promote primary elections, referendums, and initiatives? **LESSON 1.3**

12. How did Theodore Roosevelt help protect the environment? **LESSON 1.4**

13. How did Woodrow Wilson encourage business expansion through the Clayton Antitrust Act? **LESSON 2.2**

14. What was different about how Henry Ford ran his factories? **LESSON 2.3**

15. How did Jane Addams and Ellen Gates Star help the immigrant population of Chicago? **LESSON 3.2**

16. Who was Carrie Chapman Catt? **LESSON 3.3**

17. Why did many Americans oppose the purchase of Alaska? **LESSON 4.1**

18. How did newspaper accounts of the sinking of the U.S.S. *Maine* affect public opinion? **LESSON 4.2**

19. Why did the United States propose the Open Door Policy for China? **LESSON 4.4**

Answer the following questions. Support your answers with evidence from the chapter.

20. COMPARE AND CONTRAST What similar ideas about business practices did Roosevelt, Taft, and Wilson share?

21. DRAW CONCLUSIONS Why was the passage of the 19th Amendment so significant?

22. SYNTHESIZE How did increased mechanization lead to phenomenal growth in industrial efficiency?

23. FORM AND SUPPORT OPINIONS Do you think the pursuit of imperialist goals during the Progressive Era helped or hurt the United States? Explain your answer.

ANALYZE VISUALS

Look closely at the photograph on the right taken in 1913 at the Ford plant in Highland Park, Michigan. Then answer the questions that follow.

24. What are the workers in the plant doing?

25. What is the purpose of the tracks on the floor?

26. What issues might the workers have had as they completed this task and worked in this way all day, every day?

ANALYZE SOURCES

Jane Addams strongly believed women should have the right to vote. In the following excerpt from her 1915 pamphlet, "Why Women Should Vote," Addams offers one reason.

> To turn the administration of our civic affairs wholly [only] over to men may mean that the American city will continue to push forward in its commercial and industrial development, and continue to lag behind in those things which make a city healthful and beautiful. . . . If women have in any sense been responsible for the gentler side of life which softens and blurs some of its harsher conditions, may they not have a duty to perform in our American cities?

27. How does Addams use information about the traditional roles of men and women as an argument for granting women's suffrage?

CONNECT TO YOUR LIFE

28. EXPOSITORY News coverage of events and ideas during the Progressive Era shaped people's opinions. Think about how news is covered today. Then write a paragraph comparing the two.

TIPS

- Review the influence of newspaper coverage of the Spanish-American War and how the NAWSA used media to spread its message.

- Consider how people learn about the news today. Think about the role of the Internet and social media in spreading news.

- Write a paragraph comparing and contrasting the media of the Progressive Era with today's media. Include observations about how the speed at which news spreads affects people's opinions today.

This Land Is Your Land

BY DAVID QUAMMEN

Adapted from "This Land Is Your Land," by David Quammen, in *National Geographic*, January 2016

The year 2016 marked the 100th anniversary of one of the brightest moments in American history. In 1916, President Woodrow Wilson signed a law creating the National Park Service. Setting aside land for national parks might be the best idea America ever had. With the creation of the National Park Service, America took the preservation of our most precious resource to a higher level. There would now be a system dedicated to doing this work.

A half century before the National Park Service was born, the United States took its first step toward preserving its scenic treasures. In 1864, President Abraham Lincoln signed the Yosemite Valley Grant Act. This law placed California's Yosemite Valley and a nearby grove of giant Sequoia trees under protection. The president and Congress were persuaded to act by the efforts of private citizens. And it didn't hurt that stunning photographs of Yosemite's grandeur were presented as part of their effort.

A few years later, a 29-year-old John Muir stopped a passerby in San Francisco to ask for directions out of town. The man asked where Muir wanted to go. He answered, "Anywhere that is wild." Muir's love for the great outdoors led him to the Yosemite Valley. Later, it became the center of his conservation movement.

By 1916, only 14 parks had been created, and many were difficult for visitors to reach. Yellowstone had been set aside by federal law in 1872, making it the first national park not only in the United States, but in the world. The other U.S. parks, like Yellowstone, lay west of the Mississippi. There were also 21 national monuments. The Antiquities Act of 1906 gave the president the power to protect land not only for its natural beauty, but also for its cultural or scientific value. President Theodore Roosevelt took full advantage of this law. In his last three years in office, he created eight monuments, including the Grand Canyon in Arizona and Devils Tower in Wyoming.

Since Roosevelt's time, the list of both parks and monuments has grown dramatically. Today the NPS manages 390 areas located in 49 states, the District of Columbia, and islands in the Pacific and Caribbean. The NPS has grown to 20,000 full-time employees, and the number of yearly visits has risen from 350,000 to nearly 300 million. But this good news is also the bad news. During the busy season, bumper-to-bumper traffic causes visitor frustration and pumps damaging levels of pollution into delicate ecosystems. Today, one of the great challenges is managing crowds of eager tourists who are "loving the parks to death."

Yet it was precisely citizens' love that played a role in even the earliest stages of forming the National Park Service. The early parks in the American West had been established to protect scenic wonders. In other words, they had little economic value. Some foresaw the flood of tourists and the restaurants and hotels they would need. But few others saw any chance of making money from national parks. Not many complained when new areas were added to the national park system. Early on, the NPS found it far easier to get approval for creating new parks than it would later.

National parks were a good idea that has gotten better—and bigger. The system now includes national parks, monuments, battlefields, forts, seashores, scenic rivers, grave sites, historic landmarks, and noteworthy paths through landscape and history. It may take but one act of Congress and a presidential signature to put a park on the map, but that's just a formality. From the very beginning, private citizens have done much of the work to make it possible. The responsibility of preserving these places and their stories falls to us now, as citizens, as owners. And the work is never done.

For more from National Geographic, check out "The Native American Photography of Edward Sheriff Curtis" online.

UNIT INQUIRY: Innovate a New Solution

In this unit, you learned about a number of economic, social, and political problems Americans confronted in the late 19th and early 20th centuries. You also learned how Americans tried to solve those problems. Based on your understanding of the text, in what ways did different individuals, groups, and governments serve as problem-solvers? How did these solutions shape American identity?

ASSIGNMENT

Innovate a solution to a problem you read about in this unit. Your solution should demonstrate an understanding of the historical context of the problem and illustrate how your approach is similar to or different from the solution that was actually proposed. Be prepared to present your solution to the class.

Gather Evidence As you plan your solution, gather evidence from this unit about the cultures that came into contact with each other during this time period and about how some groups sought to achieve or maintain power over others. Also consider the ways in which some solutions led to unexpected consequences. Take notes on problems, cultures, unexpected consequences, and solutions. Use a graphic organizer like this one to help organize your thoughts.

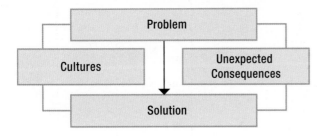

Produce Use your notes to produce an explanation of your new solution. Write a paragraph that identifies your problem within its historical context. Then write a paragraph proposing your solution.

Review Your Paragraphs Is your writing appropriate for your audience? Do you meet the purpose of the assignment? Revise or edit as needed.

Present Choose a creative way to present your new solution to the class. Consider one of these options:

- Design a colorful brochure for a target audience advertising your new solution.

- Illustrate a poster that shows the different parts of the problem you selected and describes how your new solution would address them.

- Draw and annotate a political cartoon about the problem you select and the new solution you propose. Your cartoons might be humorous, serious, or both.

NATIONAL GEOGRAPHIC | LEARNING FRAMEWORK ACTIVITIES

Research American Species

ATTITUDE Curiosity

KNOWLEDGE Critical Species

As the United States expanded, it increased the number of unique animal and plant species within its borders. At the same time, the processes of industrialization and urbanization had a tremendous impact on many species. Research an American species and learn about its characteristics, its location, its habitat, and the ways in which it has thrived or diminished since the late 19th century. Prepare a species report that includes photos or illustrations of your species and present it to the class.

Write a Journal Entry

ATTITUDE Empowerment

SKILLS Communication, Problem-Solving

Immigrants traveling to and settling in the United States encountered a number of difficult situations. Write a journal entry in the voice of an immigrant. Include where you are emigrating from, why you have chosen to immigrate to the United States, where you are settling, what difficulties you encounter, and how you solve those problems. You might consider writing one long entry or a series of shorter entries. When you have completed your journaling, present your entry or entries to the class.

TWENTIETH-CENTURY
CRISES

The bombing of Pearl Harbor during World War II inspired two government-sponsored art exhibitions in 1942. For one exhibit, artist William H. Johnson painted scenes of African Americans involved in the war effort. *Soldiers Training* depicts an African-American unit at an army base.

CRITICAL VIEWING Some believe this painting contrasts the U.S. military's segregation policies with the patriotism of African-American soldiers. What details in the painting convey the soldiers' patriotism?

THE UNITED STATES

I WANT YOU
for the **U.S. ARMY**
ENLIST NOW

1921
Italian immigrants Nicola Sacco and Bartolomeo Vanzetti are convicted of robbery and murder.

1927
Charles Lindbergh becomes the first person to fly solo nonstop across the Atlantic Ocean.
(Lindbergh's plane, the Spirit of St. Louis*)*

1919–1920
Government officials conduct the Palmer Raids to root out suspected communists and other radicals.

1929
The stock market crashes and ushers in the Great Depression.

1917
The United States declares war on Germany and enters World War I.
(an Uncle Sam poster used to recruit soldiers during World War I)

1920

1910

1928 AMERICAS
President Álvaro Obregón of Mexico is assassinated.

THE WORLD

1914 EUROPE
War spreads throughout Europe, giving rise to World War I.

1919 EUROPE
The Treaty of Versailles, signed in France, ends World War I and imposes harsh terms on Germany.
(an original booklet from the signing of the treaty)

1942
President Roosevelt signs an order that forces thousands of Japanese Americans to relocate to internment camps. *(1942 painting by artist Henry Sugimoto showing a Japanese American family reacting to the news about Pearl Harbor)*

HISTORICAL THINKING: DETERMINE CHRONOLOGY

Which event occurred in response to the crisis of the Great Depression?

1941
Japan bombs Pearl Harbor in Hawaii, which causes the United States to enter World War II.

1945
The United Nations is established. *(United Nations flag showing a map of the world)*

1933
The Roosevelt administration enacts the New Deal, a series of federal programs intended to bring economic relief to Americans.

1932
Franklin Delano Roosevelt wins his first term as president.

1940

1945

1945 ASIA
Japan surrenders after the United States bombs Hiroshima and Nagasaki, and World War II comes to an end.

1930

1939 EUROPE
World War II begins after Germany invades Poland. *(jacket worn by an inmate of a German concentration camp during World War II)*

1933 EUROPE
Adolf Hitler becomes chancellor of Germany.

1943 AFRICA
British and American forces defeat the German Army in Tunisia in North Africa. *(photo of British soldiers during the advance on Tunisia's capital, Tunis, on May 6, 1943)*

Twentieth-Century Crises **701**

THE GREAT WAR
1914–1920

ESSENTIAL QUESTION

What did the United States gain and lose by going to war?

 AMERICAN STORIES The Great War's Killer Technology

SECTION 1 **War Breaks Out in Europe**

KEY VOCABULARY

antiaircraft gun	militarism	tank
front	poison gas	U-boat

SECTION 2 **Pushing the Germans Back**

KEY VOCABULARY

armistice	conscientious objector	morale
civil liberty	dissent	propaganda
communism	Liberty Bond	sabotage

SECTION 3 **The Legacy of World War I**

KEY VOCABULARY

Great Migration	reparations
influenza	self-determination
League of Nations	Treaty of Versailles
moral diplomacy	

AMERICAN GALLERY
ONLINE The Great War: A Photo Essay

READING STRATEGY

MAKE INFERENCES

Inferences are conclusions or interpretations a reader makes from information that a writer does not state directly. When you make inferences, you "read between the lines" to figure out what the writer means. As you read the chapter, use a two-column chart like this one to list facts about the Great War and the inferences you draw from them.

Facts	Inferences
Many European nations formed alliances.	

"The world must be made safe for democracy."

—Woodrow Wilson

CRITICAL VIEWING American soldiers "go over the top" as they charge out of a trench to fight the Germans in 1918. What does this photo convey about battle conditions during World War I?

THE GREAT WAR'S
KILLER
TECHNOLOGY

CRITICAL VIEWING An American soldier walks ahead of a British-made tank in this photograph, taken around 1918. What can you observe about tank technology from this photo, and what might it suggest about the usefulness of tanks during World War I?

The word *modern* has many positive meanings. Modern things are often new, up-to-date, and better than the older things they are replacing. However, when historians say the Great War— or World War I, as it would come to be known—was the first modern war, there's nothing positive about that. The Allies and the Germans used advances in technology to fight a more deadly war at sea, on land, and in the skies.

ON LAND: TANKS

In 1915, British navy secretary Winston Churchill wrote a letter to Prime Minister H. H. Asquith on the subject of the land war. "The question to be solved," he wrote, "is the actual getting across of 100 or 200 yards of open space and wire entanglements." In clinical terms, Churchill summed up the life-or-death problem that soldiers faced on the war's merciless battlefields. Men were dying by the thousands in charges against enemy trenches protected by machine guns and artillery.

Tanks, invented by the British, were designed to solve this problem. The first British tank, called the Mark I, fought at the Battle of the Somme in France in 1916. The Mark I proved to be unreliable—49 of the tanks were present at the battle but only 18 were able to fight. Later tank models, however, were much more effective, including the massive German 36-ton A7V tank.

Tanks were powerful weapons, but they had some weaknesses. Early tanks had a range of only 25 miles and were difficult to maneuver. They suffered frequent mechanical failures and broken tracks. Later models were more reliable, although they remained vulnerable to some types of mechanical problems. The Mark V, introduced in 1918, had a sophisticated steering system, two six-pounder guns, and four machine guns.

For the men serving inside them, tanks and submarines had many awful similarities. Both were hot, cramped, enclosed spaces. The air inside an unventilated tank was sometimes so bad that crews became sick or fainted. Tank crews could be killed by their own equipment. A light tank could become hot enough to explode its ammunition.

Armies continued to use and improve tanks well after the close of World War I. Today, the U.S. military employs several models of tanks as well as armored personnel carriers and specialized armored vehicles designed to protect against dangers such as land mines.

Mark IV Tank

Materials: 0.5-inch thick steel armor

Length: 26 feet, 5 inches

Weight: 62,600 pounds, loaded

Top speed: 4 miles per hour

Range: 35 miles

Crew: up to 8 people

Armaments: 2 QF (quick firing) 6-pounder, and three 0.303-inch machine guns

TOP VIEW

crew shown in red

exhaust silencer

engine

driver

rear gunner

gas tank

side gunners

armored tread

GUNS

Machine guns were invented in the late 1800s, but they first saw extensive use during World War I, which has been called the "machine gun war." Early hand-cranked machine guns, such as the Gatling gun, were used in the Civil War. In the 1880s, American inventor Hiram Maxim was the first to create the modern form of the machine gun. Maxim guns used ammunition that was fed into the weapon on a belt. Both Germany and the Allied nations used Maxim-style machine guns, to lethal effect. The guns could fire up to 600 bullets per minute.

Stationed at intervals along a trench, machine guns could mow down waves of attacking foot soldiers. According to one estimate, during one day of battle in France, German machine guns killed or injured two British soldiers for each yard of a 16-mile battlefield.

World War I also saw the development of antiaircraft guns. As the war took to the skies, land-based troops needed artillery that could aim sharply upward at airplanes. Antiaircraft guns were mounted on bases that could swivel to point in any direction and at any angle.

In addition to more nimble weapons, the Germans put their resources into building the largest guns ever seen at the time. Guns nicknamed Big Berthas could fire explosive projectiles weighing 1,785 pounds nearly 6 miles. Big Berthas weighed around 47 tons and required a crew of 240 men. They had to be shipped on special wagons or railroad cars. While terrifying, Big Berthas were huge and heavy and required a lot of effort to move. In the first two years of the war, however, they were instrumental in conquering cities in both Belgium and Russia.

GAS

The most terrifying weapon of World War I arrived not with an explosion but in chilling silence. The first major release of poison gas was made by

Nurses driving their ambulance in Pervyse, Belgium, c. 1917

HEALING TECHNOLOGIES

New weapons caused the number of casualties to skyrocket, and medical technology scrambled to catch up. The use of x-rays in medicine was still a new science in 1914, but it was quickly put to use in treating the wounded of World War I. Ambulances equipped with x-ray machines brought diagnosis and treatment to the battle zones. Marie Curie, a pioneer in x-ray science and winner of two Nobel Prizes, helped install the x-ray machines. She trained ambulance drivers, many of whom were women, to use the machines and also drove an ambulance herself.

Advancements in blood transfusions also benefited wounded soldiers. It was during this war that doctors first discovered a way to store blood successfully. As a result, soldiers could receive transfusions at hospitals near the battlefields, and many lives were saved.

the Germans in Belgium at the Second Battle of Ypres in 1915, but it was later used by both sides. Different types of gases provoked different symptoms. Some caused blindness or burned and blistered the skin. Others choked soldiers and burned their throats. All were deadly if inhaled. Some killed instantly, while others caused painful, lingering deaths. Around 1,200,000 soldiers were gassed. Of that number, more than 91,000 died.

At first there was no protection from attack by poison gas, but within a short time, both the Germans and Allies developed gas masks. These masks, which covered the entire face to protect eyes, nose, and throat, became standard equipment for soldiers on the battlefield. After the war, recognizing the horrors inflicted by the weapon, many countries signed a treaty banning the use of poison gas.

IN THE SKIES: AIRPLANES

By 1914, airplanes had come a long way from the Wright brothers' first flying machine, built only 11 years earlier. But they were still flimsy compared with today's high-tech jets. World War I fighter planes were made of canvas stretched over light wooden frames, and pilots sat exposed in open cockpits. In the hands of their daring pilots, these delicate birds were highly effective war machines.

At first, planes were used for observing and reporting enemy positions and occasionally dropping bombs. Pilots also engaged with enemy fliers in spectacular aerial fights called dogfights. In the earliest dogfights, pilots would shoot at each other with pistols. It was impossible to use a machine gun because such a weapon would have to be mounted in front of the pilot and fired forward, thus shooting into the plane's own propeller. The Germans solved this problem in 1915, when airplane designer Anthony Fokker invented a machine gun that could be synchronized with the propeller, firing bullets between the propeller's blades as it spun.

Pilots were glamorous figures, admired for their daring and bravery. But the price of this celebrity was high. In battlefield conditions, a new pilot survived between three and six weeks, on average.

AIRSHIPS

Planes, of course, remain a key part of the modern battle arsenal today. Airships, on the other hand, have largely disappeared from the skies. An airship was basically a huge balloon filled with hydrogen gas. The captain and crew controlled the ship from a cockpit suspended beneath the balloon. Airships were slow and hard to steer, but they could stay in the air for hours, allowing the crew to observe troop movements or conduct bombing raids. German airships bombed London several times.

As airplanes and other technology improved, airships quickly lost their usefulness. Hydrogen gas is very flammable, so they were vulnerable to weapon fire from ground guns or planes. Overall, airships did a better job of terrifying people on the ground with their ominous bulk than by causing real damage.

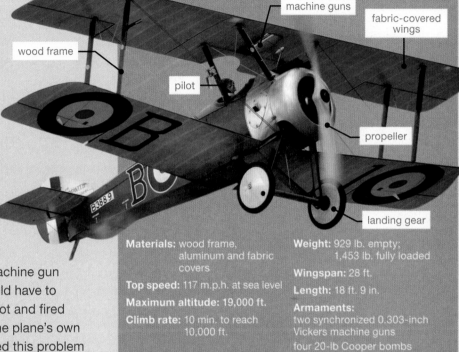

F.1 Sopwith Camel Biplane

machine guns

fabric-covered wings

wood frame

pilot

propeller

landing gear

Materials: wood frame, aluminum and fabric covers

Top speed: 117 m.p.h. at sea level

Maximum altitude: 19,000 ft.

Climb rate: 10 min. to reach 10,000 ft.

Weight: 929 lb. empty; 1,453 lb. fully loaded

Wingspan: 28 ft.

Length: 18 ft. 9 in.

Armaments: two synchronized 0.303-inch Vickers machine guns four 20-lb Cooper bombs

THE GREAT INDESTRUCTIBLE

The most successful World War I pilots—those who had shot down at least 10 enemy planes—were called "aces." American pilot Eddie Rickenbacker was one of the most dashing American aces. By the end of World War I, he had flown 300 combat hours, been in 134 air battles, and shot down 26 enemy planes. He had survived plane crashes and dogfights that left his plane riddled with bullet holes.

During World War II, Rickenbacker acted as a nonmilitary advisor and once narrowly escaped death when the plane he was riding in crashed in the Pacific Ocean. After he drifted in a lifeboat for 22 days before being rescued, the *Boston Globe* newspaper dubbed Rickenbacker "the Great Indestructible."

American Air Medal awarded for heroic action

AT SEA: U-BOATS

Even though Britain had a much larger navy, better technology allowed Germany to dominate the war beneath the waves. German submarines were nicknamed U-boats because the German word for "submarine" is *unterseeboot*.

In February 1917, German leader Wilhelm II told his submarine commanders, "We will frighten the British flag off the face of the waters." U-boats were so effective at attacking Allied ships that Wilhelm's threat may have seemed quite believable. During one 4-month period in 1916, U-boats sank nearly 500 ships. By the end of the war, German subs had sunk more than 5,000 ships—that is, around one-quarter of the world's shipping tonnage.

Diesel engines allowed the U-boats to travel great distances. The subs carried torpedoes to fire underwater and had guns mounted on their decks for fighting when the boats were attacked at the surface. As the war progressed, the German Navy rushed to build U-boats with longer ranges and increased torpedo capacities. At the start of the fighting, Germany had 38 functioning subs. By the end of the war, it had 170 new U-boats at sea and 226 more under construction. In between, 203 U-boats were lost to Allied defenses, accidents, or unknown causes.

HOW TO SINK A U-BOAT

The Allies developed various technologies for countering the U-boat threat. Two of these were mines and depth charges. It is believed that during World War I, 30 U-boats were sunk by depth charges, while at least 48 were lost to mines.

A depth charge was a bomb that could be dropped into the water and rigged to detonate at a certain depth. It was shaped like a barrel, filled with high explosives, and triggered by a device that could sense the water pressure surrounding the bomb. The first effective depth

THE ULTIMATE WWI U-BOAT

In 1916, Germany started building the UA class of U-boats. Only nine of these subs entered service before the end of the war, but they were formidable fighting ships.

UA Class U-Boat

Length: 230 feet

Weight: about 1,500 tons

Speed: 15.3 knots on the surface

Range: 12,630 miles at 8 knots

Crew: 56, with room for 20 additional crewmembers

The battery engines generated explosive hydrogen gas.

Armaments:
two 5.9-inch deck guns with 1,000 rounds of ammunition

19 torpedoes

charge, produced by the British Navy in 1916, could be triggered to explode as deep as 300 feet and carried nearly 300 pounds of explosives. By the end of the war, the Allies had 600-pound depth charges.

A U-boat could shrug off the shock of an individual depth charge exploding nearby because the subs' hulls were designed to survive the intense strain of water pressure at great depths. However, when an Allied ship detected a submarine, it would attack with multiple depth charges. A surface ship could send a U-boat to the bottom of the ocean if it succeeded in battering the sub with several well-placed explosions.

Mines were also explosive devices, but instead of being dropped from ships, they floated in the ocean, anchored at different depths across a certain span of water. When a submarine bumped into a mine, it triggered an explosion. Near the end of the war, the United States and Britain laid the North Sea Mine Barrage, a gigantic grid of mines to block the passage of U-boats between Scotland and Norway. The barrage used a new type of mine with long antennas that would set off the explosives when brushed by a U-boat. When completed, this deadly curtain of explosives had more than 70,000 mines, and it blocked one of the Germans' main routes to the North Atlantic.

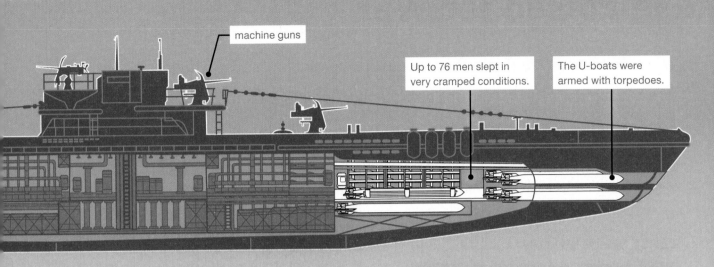

machine guns

Up to 76 men slept in very cramped conditions.

The U-boats were armed with torpedoes.

CRITICAL VIEWING The photo above shows a German U-boat stranded on the English coast after the German surrender. The photo on the right shows the engine room of a German submarine. What do these photos reveal about wartime technology?

THE WORST PLACE TO LIVE

Living conditions aboard a U-boat were often unbearable. During World War I, submarines did not have the technology to recirculate air. Instead, during the hours that a sub cruised underwater, the air became hot, stale, smelly, and occasionally scarce. Fresh air would be restored only when the U-boat surfaced and hatches could be opened. Because the U-boats carried a limited supply of fresh water, bathing and shaving were not options. In addition, the men were at constant risk not only from enemy ships, but also from their own equipment. The battery cells that ran the U-boat's electrical systems could explode if the ventilation failed. Also, if the batteries were touched by sea water, they would create poisonous chlorine gas.

One officer who served on a World War I U-boat later recalled life aboard the vessel. He explained that space was so tight inside the sub that whenever a torpedo had to be loaded into a forward tube, the commanding officers' cabins had to be cleared out to make room for the men and equipment coming through. Describing the crew's situation, he wrote, "The crew space had bunks for only a few of the crew—the rest slept in hammocks. . . . Since the temperature inside the boat was considerably greater than the sea outside, moisture in the air condensed on the steel hull-plates; the condensation had a very disconcerting way of dropping on a sleeping face, with every movement of the vessel. It was in reality like a damp cellar."

THINK ABOUT IT

What do you think was the most significant technological advancement of World War I? Explain your answer.

1.1 Poised for War

When conditions are dry in the woods, one spark can set the whole forest blazing. By 1914, tensions had reached a high point in Europe. A single act would trigger war.

MAIN IDEA Alliances, nationalism, imperialism, and militarism all contributed to the outbreak of World War I.

TENSIONS IN EUROPE

In 1914, Europe was divided by hostilities, some of which had deep roots. After losing the Franco-Prussian War to Germany in 1870, France made an alliance, or an agreement of mutual support, with Russia and Great Britain. The three countries pledged to come to each other's defense if attacked. Germany, Austria-Hungary, and the Ottoman Empire had formed a similar alliance.

Nationalism, a strong belief in one's country and in its superiority to others, and imperialism fueled tensions in Europe. In the early 1900s, Austria-Hungary and Serbia competed for the **Balkan Peninsula** in southeastern Europe. Serbia, a Slavic nation, wanted to unite with other Slavs in the Balkans to form a large state. When Austria-Hungary annexed, or seized, the Slavic territories of Bosnia (BAHZ-nee-uh) and Herzegovina (HURT-zih-goh-VEE-nuh) in 1908, the Serbians were outraged. Other powers, including Germany, Great Britain, and France, competed for natural resources and colonies in Africa and Asia.

To achieve their nationalist and imperialist goals, many European countries embraced **militarism**, the belief that a government must build a strong military force and be ready to use it to defend its interests. In 1914, Germany was a major military power. Other countries scrambled to catch up. All of these factors brought Europe to the brink of war.

ASSASSINATION TRIGGERS WAR

The continent tipped over the edge on June 28, 1914, when **Archduke Franz Ferdinand** of Austria-Hungary and his wife were visiting Sarajevo (sair-uh-YAY-voh), the capital of Bosnia. As the couple toured the city in an open car, a Bosnian Serb nationalist named Gavrilo Princip (GA-vrih-loh PRIHN-sihp) shot and killed the archduke and his wife. The assassination set the alliances in motion. Germany supported Austria-Hungary when the latter blamed Serbia for the assassination. As Serbia's ally, Russia came to that country's defense, and France pledged to support Russia. In August, Germany declared war on Russia and France. Soon Britain declared war on Germany.

Within months, war spread throughout Europe. Countries joined one of two alliances. The Central Powers were primarily made up of Germany, Austria-Hungary, and the Ottoman Empire. The principal nations belonging to the Allies were Great Britain, France, and Russia. The United States declined to take part in the war. Many Americans believed in the principles of the Progressive Era, with its faith in progress and the betterment of humanity. War was unthinkable.

Those who lived at the time of the conflict called it "the Great War" because so many nations took part in it and so many soldiers died or were wounded fighting it. When war once again arose in Europe in the 1930s, the conflict that began in 1914 would also be known as "World War I."

HISTORICAL THINKING

1. **READING CHECK** What is militarism?

2. **INTERPRET MAPS** What geographic advantages did the Allies have in the war?

3. **ANALYZE CAUSE AND EFFECT** Why did the assassination of Archduke Ferdinand trigger the war in Europe?

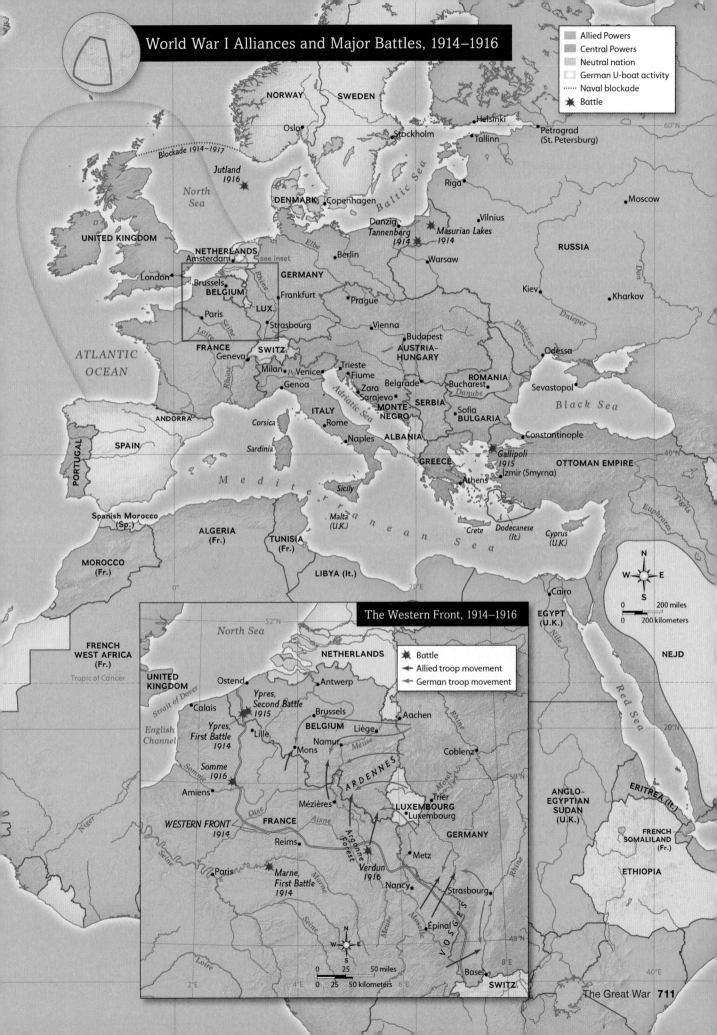

World War I Alliances and Major Battles, 1914–1916

Allied Powers
Central Powers
Neutral nation
German U-boat activity
Naval blockade
Battle

NORWAY
SWEDEN
Oslo
Stockholm
Helsinki
Petrograd (St. Petersburg)
Tallinn
Blockade 1914–1917
Jutland 1916
North Sea
Riga
Moscow
DENMARK
Copenhagen
Danzig
Tannenberg 1914
Masurian Lakes 1914
RUSSIA
UNITED KINGDOM
NETHERLANDS
Amsterdam
see inset
Elbe
Berlin
Warsaw
GERMANY
London
Brussels
BELGIUM
Frankfurt
Prague
Kiev
Kharkov
Paris
LUX.
Strasbourg
Rhine
Dnieper
Don
Dniester
FRANCE
SWITZ.
Geneva
Vienna
Budapest
Odessa
ATLANTIC OCEAN
Loire
Seine
Rhone
Milan
Po
Venice
Trieste
Fiume
AUSTRIA-HUNGARY
ROMANIA
Bucharest
Sevastopol
Genoa
Zara
Sarajevo
Belgrade
Danube
Black Sea
ANDORRA
ITALY
Rome
Adriatic Sea
MONTE-NEGRO
SERBIA
Sofia
BULGARIA
SPAIN
Corsica
Naples
ALBANIA
Constantinople
PORTUGAL
Sardinia
GREECE
Gallipoli 1915
Izmir (Smyrna)
OTTOMAN EMPIRE
Athens
Mediterranean Sea
Sicily
Malta (U.K.)
Crete
Dodecanese (It.)
Cyprus (U.K.)
Euphrates
Tigris
Spanish Morocco (Sp.)
ALGERIA (Fr.)
TUNISIA (Fr.)
LIBYA (It.)
MOROCCO (Fr.)
Cairo
N W E S
0   200 miles
0   200 kilometers
EGYPT (U.K.)
NEJD
Nile
FRENCH WEST AFRICA (Fr.)
Tropic of Cancer

The Western Front, 1914–1916

Battle
Allied troop movement
German troop movement

North Sea
NETHERLANDS
UNITED KINGDOM
Ostend
Antwerp
Calais
Ypres, Second Battle 1915
Brussels
Aachen
Strait of Dover
Ypres, First Battle 1914
BELGIUM
Liège
Namur
Coblenz
English Channel
Lille
Mons
Meuse
Rhine
Somme 1916
ARDENNES
Amiens
Mézières
Moselle
Trier
Oise
WESTERN FRONT 1914
FRANCE
Aisne
LUXEMBOURG
Luxembourg
GERMANY
Argonne Forest
Reims
Verdun 1916
Metz
Paris
Marne, First Battle 1914
Nancy
Strasbourg
Seine
Marne
Épinal
VOSGES
Rhine
Meuse
Moselle
Basel
SWITZ.
N W E S
0   25   50 miles
0   25   50 kilometers

ANGLO-EGYPTIAN SUDAN (U.K.)
ERITREA (It.)
FRENCH SOMALILAND (Fr.)
ETHIOPIA
Red Sea

1.2 A New Kind of War

The Germans had come up with a war plan and intended to end the conflict quickly. But plans don't always work out. Everyone fighting in World War I was in for a long, brutal war.

MAIN IDEA Soldiers in World War I fought on two fronts and used deadly new weaponry.

WAR ON TWO FRONTS

Germany had been preparing for war against France and Russia for years. General Alfred von Schlieffen, a German officer, had come up with a plan for such a war in 1906. According to his strategy, the German Army would attack and conquer France quickly and then march on to Russia. Germany put the strategy in motion at the outset of the war by sending its troops to capture Paris, the French capital. German troops swept through Belgium and invaded France from the north.

A gas mask worn during World War I offered soldiers some protection from toxic gases. Made of rubber and fabric, the mask had a hose connected to a filter that blocked poisonous particles from entering the nose or mouth.

At first, things went according to plan for the German Army. But in September 1914, when their troops reached the Marne River—just 30 miles from Paris—the French and British armies launched a successful counterattack. The Germans were forced to retreat in what would be called the First Battle of the Marne. Schlieffen's plan had not taken into account the support of the British Army. By the end of 1914, Germany found itself fighting the war on two **fronts**, or battle lines. On the **Western Front**, Germany and the Central Powers faced off against France, Britain, and other Allies. On the **Eastern Front**, Germany and the Central Powers battled Russia along an area that would eventually stretch from the Baltic Sea to the Black Sea.

On both fronts, armies employed trench warfare, a battle strategy you might recall from the Civil War. Troops from the two alliances dug long, deep ditches into the ground that were large enough for them to hunker down in. Trenches were often lined with boards so that the soldiers could use them as passageways. The boards also helped troops avoid potential diseases caused by sitting or standing in mud and dirty water. Soldiers could fight from the trenches and shelter there from enemy fire.

Trench warfare often resulted in staggering death tolls, as opposing armies struggled to take an enemy trench. In the July 1916 battle along the Somme River in France, fierce fighting went on for four months. During the First Battle of the Somme, the Allies managed to push the Germans back only six miles. More than a million soldiers from both sides were killed or wounded during the battle.

DEADLY TECHNOLOGY

Weapons technology made World War I deadlier than any previous war. The new and improved machine guns mounted on top of the trenches resulted in high death tolls on both sides. You

The British soldiers in this photo were temporarily blinded by a poison gas attack during a World War I battle. What details in the photo help convey their condition?

may recall that the British invented the **tank**, an armored, heavily armed vehicle with treads instead of wheels, to counter machine gun fire. Originally known as "landships," tanks could be driven right into enemy trenches.

Airplanes filled the sky for the first time in any war. Piloting a war plane was a dangerous assignment. In addition to attacks in the air, firepower from the ground could take down the planes. The **antiaircraft gun** was a heavy weapon that could be pointed to the sky to fire missiles from a metal tube or barrel. Weaponry even filled the seas when Germany used submarines, also called **U-boats**, to shoot torpedoes and sink enemy warships.

On the ground, chemical weapons terrorized soldiers. Cylinders filled with chlorine, mustard, or other types of **poison gas** were tossed and released into enemy trenches. The Germans also developed the flamethrower, which shot a stream of fire about 20 or 30 feet long through a length of pipe. Flamethrowers could only be used at short

range, but they caused panic when they were turned on soldiers in a trench. These weapons were first used by the German Army in Belgium at the 1915 Battle of Hooge. A British soldier who took part in the battle said the flamethrowers were "like a line of powerful fire hoses spraying fire instead of water across my [trench]." Just sheltering in the trenches posed a danger to troops. Many soldiers perished from exposure to cold and from illnesses contracted in the crowded, filthy, rat- and lice-infested ditches.

HISTORICAL THINKING

1. **READING CHECK** Why did Germany's plan to wage a quick, efficient war fail?

2. **MAKE INFERENCES** What can you infer about the effectiveness of trench warfare in World War I?

3. **DRAW CONCLUSIONS** What impact did new weapons technology have on the numbers of casualties suffered in the war?

1.3 America Enters the War

To Americans, the war in Europe seemed far away. Most didn't want to have anything to do with it. But soon the war would come a little closer and be harder to ignore.

MAIN IDEA After events led the United States to enter World War I on the side of the Allies, the nation prepared for the conflict.

MOVING TOWARD WAR

Most Americans didn't want to get involved in World War I and neither did their president, Woodrow Wilson. When the war began, Wilson made an official declaration of neutrality, urging Americans to act in "the spirit of impartiality," which meant to avoid taking sides. However, a series of events made it impossible for the United States to remain on the sidelines. The first was the sinking of the British passenger ship *Lusitania* (loos-ih-TAY-nee-uh) by a German submarine on May 7, 1915. At least 129 Americans were among the nearly 1,200 people who drowned that day. The attack outraged Americans, and President Wilson demanded an apology from the German government. But he still refused to enter the war.

Two years later, other developments arose that finally changed Wilson's mind. British intelligence

In this U.S. government factory, women wrap rockets that will be sent to the front lines. Some of the war work women performed was repetitious, but it could also be difficult and dangerous.

The Sinking of the *Lusitania*

When the *Lusitania* set sail from New York City for England on May 1, 1915, it carried almost 2,000 passengers and ammunition for the British war effort. German submarines had begun attacking any ship suspected of carrying war supplies. On May 7, off the coast of Ireland, a German submarine torpedoed the ocean liner. Terrified passengers tried to board the ship's lifeboats, but only six were successfully launched. Within 18 minutes of the attack, the ship sank. The cork life ring shown here was recovered from the wreckage.

agents intercepted a telegram sent by the German foreign minister, Arthur Zimmermann, to Germany's ambassador in Mexico. Zimmermann proposed that Mexico join the war on the German side. In return, Zimmermann said, Mexico could regain Texas, New Mexico, and Arizona. Wilson released the **Zimmermann Telegram**, as it came to be known, through the newspapers to the American public on March 1, 1917.

On March 18, German submarines sank three U.S. ships, resulting in many deaths. Americans were infuriated, and this was the last straw for the president. On April 2, Wilson asked Congress to declare war on Germany, pledging the United States would fight for "the ultimate peace of the world and for the liberation of its peoples, the German peoples included." Congress declared war on Germany on April 6, 1917.

GEARING UP FOR WAR

Once the United States joined the Allies, the government took immediate steps to build up its military. In 1917, U.S. Army and National Guard troops numbered only about 309,000. To increase these numbers, Congress passed the Selective Service Act in May, requiring all men between the ages of 21 and 30 to register for the draft. By the end of the war, 3.7 million American men had taken part in World War I.

The soldiers sent to fight in Europe belonged to the **American Expeditionary Forces (AEF)**. They fought under the command of General John J. Pershing, who had led troops in Cuba, Mexico, and the American West. The battle-weary Allies enthusiastically welcomed the Americans' help. Intense fighting and high casualties on both sides were taking their toll. In 1915, more than 1.4 million French soldiers had been killed or wounded fighting on the Western Front. A single battle in the French town of Verdun in 1916 claimed more than 300,000 men on both sides of the combat.

To take part in the conflict, the United States had to manufacture the machinery of war, including airplanes, guns, and ammunition. Wilson established the **War Industries Board (WIB)** to produce these supplies. Factories that had manufactured items such as cars and bicycles in peacetime converted to wartime production. The WIB oversaw manufacturing and came up with ways to make the factories more efficient.

As men left for the war, women filled many of the jobs in these factories and other workplaces. Some labor unions threw their support behind the war effort. They promised not to strike for the duration of the war or to insist that the war production factories hire only union members. Armed for battle, the United States soon sent troops to Europe.

HISTORICAL THINKING

1. **READING CHECK** What events led President Wilson to ask Congress to declare war on Germany?

2. **MAKE INFERENCES** How do you think Americans reacted when they heard about the Zimmermann Telegram?

3. **ANALYZE CAUSE AND EFFECT** How did entering World War I affect many American businesses and workers?

Americans on the Western Front

The Allies had looked forward to this day for almost three years. American entry into the war came later than the Allies had hoped, but they greatly welcomed the help.

MAIN IDEA The arrival of U.S. troops brought a much-needed boost to the Allied effort in the war.

BATTLING IN FRANCE

In late June 1917, the first 14,000 American troops landed in France. For several months, the soldiers of the American Expeditionary Forces (AEF) trained for combat and set up communication and supply networks. They began to take part in the fighting in October. The buildup of the AEF continued, and by 1918, millions of American troops had poured into France.

In contrast with the other Allied troops, the Americans were fresh and well fed. The U.S. soldiers brought a renewed sense of optimism to the war effort. The Americans were especially needed after Russia pulled out of the war. In March 1917, a revolution in Russia overturned its monarchy. A second revolution erupted in November, and the Bolsheviks, a party of communist extremists, took power. The

CRITICAL VIEWING American gunners of the Coastal Artillery fire a 1,400-pound shell from a U.S. Navy gun mounted on a railcar during a battle in France in September 1918. Shells shot from this large-caliber gun had a range of about 24 miles. What details in the photo convey the size and power of the gun?

Russian Revolution would usher in **communism**, a form of government in which all means of production and transportation are owned and controlled by the state. The new government declared an end to Russia's part in the war.

With the Russian withdrawal, the Germans hoped to win the war before the arrival of more American troops could reinforce the Allies. Germany quickly transferred huge numbers of its troops from the Eastern Front to the Western Front. Then, on March 21, 1918, the Germans launched an offensive attack. Over the next two months, the German Army gained ground in Belgium and France.

By May, however, millions of well-supplied American troops had arrived in France. The U.S. First Infantry Division attacked German positions in and around Cantigny (KAHN-tee-nyee) in northern France. After a brief battle, the Americans captured the town. The Germans launched a counterattack, but the Americans refused to yield. The Battle of Cantigny was the first sustained offensive the United States fought. Germany's bid for victory in the war had failed. In June, the AEF fought in battles at Belleau (BEHL-oh) Wood and Chateau-Thierry (shah-TOH TEE-uh-ree). They suffered tremendous losses but succeeded in blocking German forces that had advanced dangerously close to Paris. These victories greatly boosted the Allies' **morale**, or confidence.

ROLE OF MINORITIES AND WOMEN

American soldiers belonging to minority groups contributed to the victories on the Western Front. Thousands of African Americans volunteered to fight in World War I and served in segregated army units. Most of these soldiers provided support and were not assigned combat duties. However, several units fought alongside white soldiers in France and served with distinction. Asian Americans also chose to serve in the war

and were granted U.S. citizenship as a reward. Some Hispanic Americans from Texas and New Mexico refused to register for the draft to protest the discrimination they faced in the United States. Others, however, enlisted and fought bravely in the war in Europe.

During World War I—and for the first time in U.S. history—women were allowed to officially join the armed forces. Most of these servicewomen performed clerical work. Several hundred accompanied the AEF to France to serve as telephone operators. Women of the Army Nurse Corps treated the injured at the front, and some drove ambulances filled with wounded soldiers to hospitals behind the lines. One American nurse, **Julia C. Stimson**, arrived in France shortly after the United States entered the war. She later became head of the nursing services of the AEF.

While Americans fought overseas, men and women at home also supported the war effort. They, too, played a significant role in World War I.

Croix de Guerre

The African-American soldiers of the 369th Regiment from New York City, nicknamed the "Harlem Hellfighters," fought with the French. These soldiers were the first Americans to be awarded the French medal shown here, known as the Croix de Guerre (krwah dih GAIR), or War Cross, for gallantry.

HISTORICAL THINKING

1. **READING CHECK** Why did the Allies welcome the arrival of U.S. troops on the Western Front?

2. **DRAW CONCLUSIONS** Why did the Germans believe they could win the war after Russia pulled out?

3. **MAKE INFERENCES** Why might it have been important to African Americans and other minorities to fight in World War I?

2.2 On the Home Front

Would you be willing to make sacrifices to support a war? Many Americans during World War I were. They helped out financially and made changes in their daily lives. Some were even willing to give up a few of their liberties.

MAIN IDEA On the American home front, World War I was a time of sacrifice, patriotism, and suppressed liberties.

SUPPORTING THE WAR

As you know, the U.S. government had factories produce goods for the war after the country entered the conflict. The government also called on civilians to support the war by buying **Liberty Bonds**. Millions of Americans loaned the government money by buying these bonds. The government promised to repay the cost of a bond in 30 years. In the meantime, the buyer received annual interest on each bond at a rate of 3.5 percent.

The Allies needed food as well as financial support, so Americans were also asked to help the war effort by changing their eating habits. The Food Administration was established to oversee the country's agricultural resources. President Wilson named **Herbert Hoover** to head the agency.

Hoover urged Americans to do without meat and wheat sometimes because "wheatless days in America make sleepless nights in Germany." Many families also grew their own fruits and vegetables in what became known as "victory gardens."

To heighten support for the war and inspire patriotism, the government established the **Committee on Public Information (CPI)** to launch an extensive propaganda campaign. **Propaganda** is information used to promote a particular point of view. The committee created posters, pamphlets, billboards, and movies to influence public opinion about World War I. The posters designed by the committee used colorful graphics and thought-provoking messages to fuel hostility toward the enemy and, indeed, everything German. Hamburgers, named after a city in Germany,

The woman in this 1918 photo is Mrs. Drewry, a well-known figure in Cincinnati, Ohio, during World War I. She encouraged other women in Cincinnati to take part in the war effort and was even called their "commander in chief." Here, Mrs. Drewry uses a tractor to plow a victory garden.

Spies Are Listening

A U.S. propaganda poster presents German ruler Kaiser, or emperor, Wilhelm II as a spider weaving a web to snare information that could be used to harm the American war effort. Posters like this inspired distrust of German Americans or anyone else who might be considered a spy.

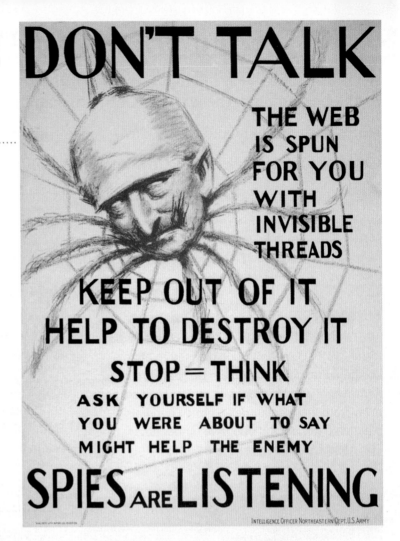

DON'T TALK

THE WEB IS SPUN FOR YOU WITH INVISIBLE THREADS

KEEP OUT OF IT HELP TO DESTROY IT

STOP = THINK

ASK YOURSELF IF WHAT YOU WERE ABOUT TO SAY MIGHT HELP THE ENEMY

SPIES ARE LISTENING

INTELLIGENCE OFFICER NORTHEASTERN DEPT. U.S. ARMY

came to be called "Salisbury steaks" or "liberty steaks." Schools stopped offering instruction in the German language. Unfortunately, some of this hostility was turned on German Americans. Many experienced prejudice and became the targets of suspicion, threats, and even violence.

SUPPRESSING OPPOSITION

Not all Americans supported the war. Some men expressed their **dissent**, or disagreement, with the government's decision to go to war by refusing to go themselves. These men, known as **conscientious objectors**, often cited religious reasons for not fighting. Others simply failed to register for the draft. Many German Americans and Irish Americans also opposed the war.

To ensure patriotic behavior, President Wilson and Congress enacted the **Espionage Act of 1917**. The act was designed to prevent espionage, or spying, and sabotage. **Sabotage** is action carried out to harm a nation's war effort. The government had sound reasons to be concerned about German espionage. While maintaining neutrality, the United States had supplied the Allies with ammunition and other goods in the early years of the war. In 1916, German agents had caused the explosion of a munitions depot in New Jersey. These were serious crimes, but Americans could be arrested for simply speaking out against the war.

The **Sedition Act of 1918** took these restrictions even further. The act prohibited Americans from "uttering, printing, writing, or publishing any disloyal, profane, scurrilous [insulting], or abusive language" about the government or the armed forces. Any public criticism could be considered sedition, the crime of inciting others to rebel against or overthrow government. Many Americans

felt the act limited their **civil liberties**—individual rights, such as freedom of speech, that are protected by law. Even criticizing President Wilson could land the speaker in jail.

While life changed for everyone at home, the war continued. But the American troops were making a difference. Soon the long war would finally come to an end.

HISTORICAL THINKING

1. **READING CHECK** How did Americans at home support the war?

2. **MAKE INFERENCES** Why do you think propaganda is particularly effective during times of war?

3. **FORM AND SUPPORT OPINIONS** Do you think the U.S. government was right to restrict civil liberties during the war? Explain your answer using evidence from the text.

2.3 Victory for the Allies

At the beginning of the war, the Germans had believed they would win it fairly quickly and easily. Now, more than four years later, a German victory was looking less and less likely. The American armed forces had tipped the balance.

MAIN IDEA In the summer and fall of 1918, the Allies gained the upper hand in World War I and forced Germany to surrender.

FINAL BATTLES

The German Army made one more offensive push in July 1918. German troops planned to attack northern France and southern Belgium, an area known as Flanders. However, to draw Allied troops away from their real target, German generals planned a misleading offensive farther south. On July 15, the push began.

However, the French Army launched a surprise counter-offensive of its own. When the Germans advanced, they ran into thousands of French and American soldiers ready to attack. The German forces soon found themselves surrounded. The confrontation that followed is called the **Second Battle of the Marne**, and it turned the tide of the war in the Allies' favor.

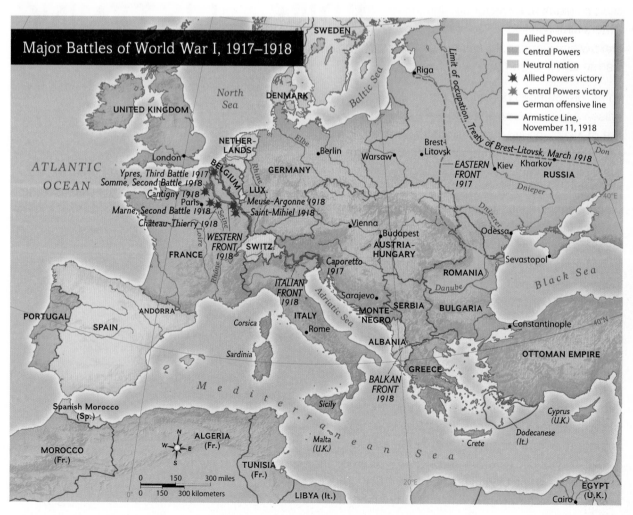

Major Battles of World War I, 1917–1918

After that, the Allies attacked the German forces and pushed them back. Then, in a final drive to end the war, the Allies began an operation called the **Meuse-Argonne offensive** in September. American divisions disabled the railroad tracks that brought supplies to the German Army. In October, General Pershing, now the commander of the Allied forces, led his troops to force the German Army out of the Argonne Forest in northeastern France. The bloody **Battle of Argonne Forest** took a terrible toll on both sides. German casualties rose to 100,000. French casualties totaled 70,000. In the deadliest campaign in U.S. history, American casualties reached 117,000, with 26,000 killed. But the American troops distinguished themselves in the offensive. Three African-American regiments took part, fighting alongside the French, and earned the respect of their French counterparts.

Pilots also displayed great bravery. As you have learned, American ace fighter pilot Eddie Rickenbacker was the most famous flier on the Allied side. In September 1918, at the start of the Meuse-Argonne offensive, he engaged in a fierce aerial battle with 7 German warplanes. Outmaneuvering the aircraft, he shot down 2 of them. By the end of the war, Rickenbacker was known as "the Ace of Aces."

THE WAR ENDS

After the Meuse-Argonne offensive, the war ground down to its end. Germany's hopes for victory had been replaced by fear of an Allied invasion that would force a humiliating surrender. In addition, an Allied blockade of German ports caused severe food shortages in Germany.

In early October, German leaders had asked President Wilson to arrange an **armistice**, or an end to the fighting. Following weeks of negotiation, Germany surrendered and reached a peace agreement with the Allies. The war came to an end on November 11, 1918, at 11:00 a.m.—the 11th hour of the 11th day of the 11th month. The day would come to be known as Armistice Day, or Veterans Day. Relief that day was evident. Britain's prime minister, David Lloyd George, said, "This is no time for words. Our hearts are too full of gratitude to which no tongue can give adequate expression."

The devastation of the war was overwhelming. As many as 9 million soldiers died, and another

In 2014, artists Paul Cummins and Tom Piper observed the 100th anniversary of Britain's entry into World War I with an art installation of 888,246 ceramic poppies, one for each British soldier killed in the war. Poppies grew in the battlefields of Flanders and came to represent the blood spilled in the war. Here, British prince William, his wife, Kate Middleton, and Lord Richard Dannatt visit the installation, called *Blood Swept Lands and Seas of Red*.

21 million were wounded. Millions of civilians perished from starvation and disease. The death toll, the numbers of countries involved, and the cost of the Great War exceeded that of any previous war in history. Because the bloodshed and destruction were so extreme, people called World War I "the war to end all wars." The French and the British blamed Germany for the war, and they were determined to make the country pay.

HISTORICAL THINKING

1. **READING CHECK** What happened at the Second Battle of the Marne?

2. **INTERPRET MAPS** Where were most of the battles fought between 1917 and 1918?

3. **IDENTIFY MAIN IDEAS AND DETAILS** Why did people call World War I "the war to end all wars"?

3.1 Wilson's Goals

Woodrow Wilson dreamed of a world with no more war and an organization of nations dedicated to keeping the peace. But the rest of the Allied leaders had other ideas.

MAIN IDEA After the war, President Wilson met with other Allied leaders to negotiate a peace treaty and present his proposal for the world.

THE FOURTEEN POINTS

In 1918, before the war ended, President Wilson had outlined his vision for world peace in the **Fourteen Points**. The Fourteen Points consisted of principles that promoted fairness, openness, and democracy. Recognizing that secret treaties had played a major role in the outbreak of World War I, Wilson called for all future diplomacy to be carried out "frankly and in the public view." Recalling Germany's attacks against merchant ships and passenger vessels, such as the *Lusitania*, Wilson called for free navigation of the seas.

He also proposed national arms reduction, free trade among countries, and national **self-determination**. This is the idea that countries should form their own governments and borders to reflect the national origins of the people who live there. In his last point, Wilson called for the formation of a "general association of nations." This organization would provide a place for all countries to settle arguments through discussion and diplomacy rather than war.

Wilson wanted his principles to be used as the basis for peace negotiations. However, Britain and France objected to the Fourteen Points. They didn't like Wilson's interference with European policies, and his proposal didn't call for heavy penalties against Germany. The two European nations wanted to punish Germany and prevent it from waging any more wars in the future.

> ### ◥ PRIMARY SOURCE ◤
>
> President Wilson delivered his Fourteen Points to Congress on January 8, 1918. Points 1–5 deal with diplomatic issues that he believed were essential to prevent further war. Point 14 calls for a peacekeeping organization.
>
> *1. Open covenants [agreements] of peace, openly arrived at, . . . [and] diplomacy shall proceed always frankly and in the public view.*
>
> *2. Absolute freedom of navigation upon the seas, outside territorial waters, alike in peace and in war. . . .*
>
> *3. The removal, so far as possible, of all economic barriers and the establishment of an equality of trade conditions among all the nations consenting to the peace. . . .*
>
> *4. Adequate guarantees given and taken that national armaments [weaponry] will be reduced to the lowest point consistent with domestic safety.*
>
> *5. A free, open-minded, and absolutely impartial adjustment of all colonial claims, based upon a strict observance of the principle that in determining all such questions of sovereignty, the interests of the populations concerned must have equal weight with the equitable [fair] claims of the government. . . .*
>
> *14. A general association of nations must be formed under specific covenants for the purpose of affording mutual guarantees of political independence and territorial integrity to great and small states alike.*

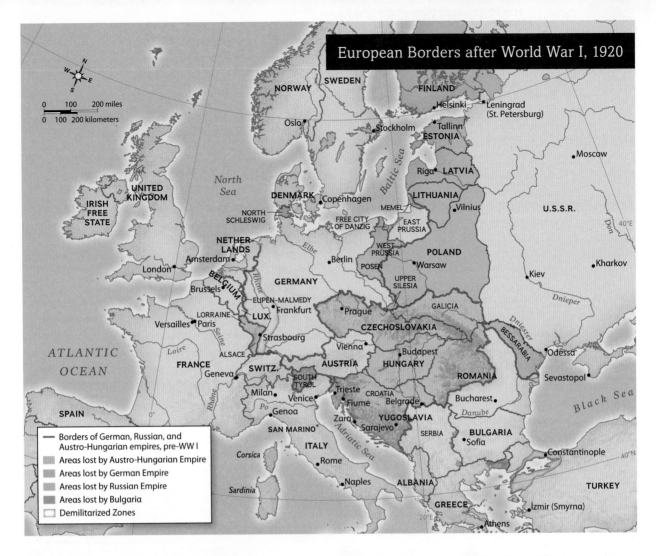

European Borders after World War I, 1920

Borders of German, Russian, and Austro-Hungarian empires, pre-WW I
Areas lost by Austro-Hungarian Empire
Areas lost by German Empire
Areas lost by Russian Empire
Areas lost by Bulgaria
Demilitarized Zones

THE TREATY OF VERSAILLES

German leaders hoped Wilson's proposals would shape the postwar peace settlement, but they were bitterly disappointed. The terms were worked out at the Paris Peace Conference, which began in January 1919 in Versailles (vur-SY), France.

On June 28, 1919, negotiations among the Allies produced the **Treaty of Versailles**, which formally ended the war. In spite of Wilson's objections, the treaty blamed Germany for starting the war. It also called for Germany to make **reparations**, or payments, of about $33 billion to the Allies for the damages and casualties caused by the war. These terms fueled resentment in Germany that deepened in the following decades. However, Wilson achieved his main goal: the creation of an international peacekeeping organization, which would be called the **League of Nations**.

When Wilson returned to the United States, he tried to persuade the Senate to ratify the treaty. Most Republicans opposed the League of Nations, believing it would force the United States to give up too much of its sovereignty. Wilson set off on a tour in September 1919 to promote the treaty but suffered a stroke that left him partially paralyzed. He could no longer govern effectively or speak in favor of the Treaty of Versailles. The treaty came up for a vote in the Senate twice and was defeated both times. The United States would not be part of the League of Nations. Wilson died in 1924.

HISTORICAL THINKING

1. **READING CHECK** What were the Fourteen Points?

2. **MAKE INFERENCES** Why might Germany have struggled to pay the reparations demanded by the Treaty of Versailles?

3. **INTERPRET MAPS** Which nations formed in northeastern Europe on land that was part of the Russian Empire before the war?

3.2 Woodrow Wilson and World Peace

President Woodrow Wilson dreamed of a peaceful world in which countries would settle their differences diplomatically. Admirers considered him an ambassador of peace, while detractors mocked his ideas. In time, World War I forced Wilson to adjust his thinking about how peace could best be achieved.

When Woodrow Wilson ran for re-election in 1916, his campaign featured the slogan "He kept us out of war." Wilson believed deeply in the importance of peace. He supported a policy called **moral diplomacy**, which called for reduced interference in the affairs of other countries. He also thought the United States should be an example of democracy to the world. In 1917 and 1918, Wilson delivered several speeches in which he discussed his ideals.

CRITICAL VIEWING When Woodrow Wilson first ran for president in 1912, he focused largely on domestic issues. Here, candidate Wilson delivers a campaign speech in September to supporters in New York City's Union Square, pledging to lower tariffs. He made good on this promise in his first term as president. The focus of his second term, of course, would be the war and foreign affairs. What details in the photo suggest Wilson was a forceful speaker?

DOCUMENT ONE

Primary Source: Speech
from Wilson's "Peace Without Victory" speech,
January 22, 1917

In Wilson's "Peace Without Victory" speech to the U.S. Senate, the president appealed to nations on both sides of World War I to stop the fighting and negotiate a peace. In this excerpt from the speech, Wilson describes the price of victory.

CONSTRUCTED RESPONSE According to Wilson, why would peace be temporary if one side achieved victory in the war?

Victory would mean peace forced upon the loser, a victor's terms imposed upon the vanquished [defeated]. It would be accepted in humiliation, . . . at an intolerable sacrifice, and would leave a sting, a resentment, a bitter memory upon which terms of peace would rest, not permanently but only as upon quicksand. Only a peace between equals can last. Only a peace the very principle of which is equality and a common participation in a common benefit.

DOCUMENT TWO

Primary Source: Speech
from Wilson's declaration of war message to Congress,
April 2, 1917

Once he determined that American involvement in the Great War was inevitable, Wilson delivered his "war message" to a special session of Congress to ask for a declaration of war against Germany. Here, he explains why he has decided to take such a serious step.

CONSTRUCTED RESPONSE What ideas and values did Wilson claim the United States would fight for in the war?

It is a fearful thing to lead this great peaceful people into war, into the most terrible and disastrous of all wars, civilization itself seeming to be in the balance. But the right is more precious than peace, and we shall fight for the things which we have always carried nearest our hearts—for democracy, for the right of those who submit to authority to have a voice in their own governments, for the rights and liberties of small nations, for a universal dominion of right . . . as shall bring peace and safety to all nations and make the world itself at last free.

DOCUMENT THREE

Primary Source: Speech
from Wilson's Fourteen Points speech, January 8, 1918

The president presented his Fourteen Points to Congress nine months after the United States entered the war. Before discussing the individual points, Wilson made the demands of the United States clear and explained what he expected to result from the war.

CONSTRUCTED RESPONSE How did Wilson envision the world after the war, and why did he characterize his view as "nothing peculiar to ourselves"?

What we demand in this war, therefore, is nothing peculiar to ourselves. It is that the world be made fit and safe to live in; and particularly that it be made safe for every peace-loving nation which, like our own, wishes to live its own life, determine its own institutions, be assured of justice and fair dealing by the other peoples of the world, as against force and selfish aggression. All the peoples of the world are in effect partners in this interest, and for our own part we see very clearly that unless justice be done to others it will not be done to us.

SYNTHESIZE & WRITE

1. **REVIEW** Review what you have learned about President Woodrow Wilson and his ideas about world peace.

2. **RECALL** On your own paper, write the main idea that Wilson expressed in each excerpt from his speeches.

3. **CONSTRUCT** Construct a topic sentence that answers this question: How did President Wilson adjust his ideas about world peace after the United States entered World War I?

4. **WRITE** Using evidence from this chapter and the documents, write an informative paragraph that supports your topic sentence in Step 3.

3.3 Aftermath of the War

World War I launched the United States onto the world stage, and the country became a major global power. But the end of the war also brought social and economic challenges to the nation.

MAIN IDEA The United States became a world leader after World War I but struggled with disease, economic woes, and racial discrimination.

A WORLD POWER

In many ways, the war changed how the rest of the world regarded the United States. American forces had played a key role in defeating Germany and ending the war. And President Wilson had been a major leader in hammering out the terms of the Treaty of Versailles. His idea that the United States should engage diplomatically with other nations and promote democracy and national self-determination would influence U.S. foreign policy for the rest of the 20th century—and into the 21st.

Since the war hadn't been fought on American soil, the United States hadn't suffered as many casualties as the other Allies or the Central Powers. American dead and wounded totaled about 320,000, while those of countries such as Great Britain and France numbered in the millions. However, the United States was not spared from an epidemic, or widespread outbreak of disease, that affected much of the world. A powerful strain of **influenza**, the virus we now call "the flu," swept the country at the end of 1918. Scientists had not

yet developed an effective vaccine that could treat or prevent the spread of the disease, which killed about 600,000 Americans in 1918 and 1919. By the time the influenza had run its course in 1920, it had caused about 50 million deaths worldwide.

ECONOMIC AND SOCIAL UPHEAVAL

The war's aftermath also brought economic turmoil to the United States. Many industries had to convert back to peacetime production, and inflation greatly raised prices. Soldiers returning from war discovered that jobs were few, and unemployment soared to nearly 12 percent in 1921. Wages also fell. In early 1919, labor unions staged major strikes calling for higher wages at shipyards across the country. The largest industrial strike of the year, the Great Steel Strike of 1919, involved steelworkers in the Midwest and lasted for months. Strikers called for an end to the 7-day workweek and the 12-hour workday. As many as

350,000 workers took part in the strike, but they couldn't hold out under the financial strain of being without a paycheck. In early 1920, the strike ended, having failed to achieve its goals.

Although they served their country honorably in the war, African-American soldiers returned home to face widespread segregation and discrimination. Racial tensions flared in the years following the war. There were frequent lynchings in the South. Great numbers of southern African Americans came to cities in the North in a mass movement known as the **Great Migration**. The movement began in 1910, but the stream of African Americans swelled during the war, when thousands of jobs opened up in northern industrial centers. About 500,000 African Americans moved north between 1914 and 1920.

As jobs became scarce after the war, the flood of African Americans led to confrontations with angry urban whites who feared the newcomers would compete with them for jobs. Race riots broke out in Chicago, Washington, D.C., and other U.S. cities during the summer of 1919, a period of violence and bloodshed known as "the red summer." The riot in Chicago was triggered when an African-American teenager swimming in Lake Michigan drowned after being stoned by whites. The incident touched off 5 days of violent chaos that left 38 people dead, more than 500 injured, and roughly 1,000 families homeless.

As a result of all this unrest, Americans were too focused on problems at home to embrace the country's new role as a world leader. Many wanted little to do with the outside world. In particular, they feared that foreign influences could result in the spread of communism to the United States.

This mural, located at a youth center in Chicago, is called *The Great Migration* and was completed in 1995 by artist Marcus Akinlana. It represents the continuing migration of African Americans to Chicago and other northern cities in the 1940s. The mural contrasts the farm labor of African Americans in the South (on the right) with the job opportunities in industry and entertainment available to them in the North (on the left).

HISTORICAL THINKING

1. **READING CHECK** Why did the United States emerge as a major power after World War I?

2. **SUMMARIZE** What postwar economic problems did the United States face?

3. **MAKE INFERENCES** How do you think African Americans who fought in the war reacted to the racism they encountered when they returned home?

VOCABULARY

Use each of the following terms in a sentence that shows an understanding of the term's meaning.

1. militarism

   A country practicing militarism builds up its armed forces and is prepared to use them.

2. front

3. morale

4. conscientious objector

5. propaganda

6. reparations

7. sabotage

8. armistice

9. Liberty Bond

READING STRATEGY
MAKE INFERENCES

If you haven't already, complete your chart by listing facts from the chapter about the Great War and then writing the inferences you draw from each one. Then answer the question

Facts	Inferences
Many European nations formed alliances.	

10. Why do you think Americans on the home front were willing to make so many sacrifices to support the war?

MAIN IDEAS

Answer the following questions. Support your answers with evidence from the chapter.

11. Why did hostility begin to arise between Austria-Hungary and Serbia before 1914? **LESSON 1.1**

12. Describe some of the deadly new weapons used in World War I. **LESSON 1.2**

13. What position did President Woodrow Wilson take when World War I broke out? **LESSON 1.3**

14. Why did Russia withdraw from the war? **LESSON 2.1**

15. During the war, what new legislation was passed in the United States to suppress opposition? **LESSON 2.2**

16. What role did Americans play in the Meuse-Argonne offensive? **LESSON 2.3**

17. Why did Wilson want to create an international peacekeeping organization? **LESSON 3.1**

18. What event in 1918 and 1919 caused more American deaths than World War I? **LESSON 3.3**

HISTORICAL THINKING

Answer the following questions. Support your answers with evidence from the chapter.

19. **SEQUENCE EVENTS** List some of the key events that led up to the outbreak of World War I.

20. **DRAW CONCLUSIONS** What was life probably like for soldiers who fought in the trenches in World War I?

21. **MAKE PREDICTIONS** What might have happened if the United States had not entered the war?

22. **ANALYZE CAUSE AND EFFECT** Why did race riots take place in the United States after the war?

23. **FORM AND SUPPORT OPINIONS** Do you think the United States was right to take part in World War I? Explain your answer.

24. **MAKE INFERENCES** How do you think the war changed the roles of women in the United States?

INTERPRET VISUALS

Much of the propaganda created in the United States during World War I was designed to inspire patriotism and stir Americans to action. The poster below calls on men to "enlist," or join the armed forces; "plow," or provide food for the troops and the country; and "buy bonds," or help pay down the cost of the war. Study the poster, and then answer the questions that follow.

25. Whom or what does each figure in the poster represent?

26. What elements in the poster were probably meant to inspire patriotism?

ANALYZE SOURCES

When the Senate debated the Treaty of Versailles, the most divisive issue was U.S. involvement in the League of Nations. On the last day of the debate, Idaho senator William Borah delivered a long, passionate speech against the League of Nations. Read the following excerpt from his address. Then answer the question that follows.

> It imperils [endangers] . . . the very first principles of this Republic. It is in conflict with the right of our people to govern themselves free from all restraint, legal or moral, of foreign powers. I will not, I can not, give up my belief that America must, not alone for the happiness of her own people, but for the moral guidance and greater contentment of the world, be permitted to live her own life.

27. According to Borah, what American freedoms would the League of Nations imperil?

CONNECT TO YOUR LIFE

28. **EXPOSITORY** Imagine you are an American soldier or nurse who has just returned home from the war. Write a letter to a friend pointing out the social, political, and economic changes you see in the country. Discuss how these changes affect you.

TIPS

• Consider the political changes that took place during the war.

• Review the social and economic challenges that developed after the war.

• Identify who you are as the letter writer and what you did during the war. You can include your gender, race, or ethnic origin if it helps explain your experiences.

• Tell how the country has changed and how the changes have—or haven't—affected you.

• Use two or three vocabulary terms from the chapter in your letter.

• Conclude the letter with a brief summary about the direction the country has taken.

THE
ROARING TWENTIES
1919–1929

ESSENTIAL QUESTION
What economic, political, and social changes
occurred in the United States after World War I?

READING STRATEGY

DRAW CONCLUSIONS
Drawing conclusions can help
you make judgments about what
you read. You analyze the facts,
make inferences and consider
your own experiences to decide
what those facts mean. Use a
graphic organizer to help you draw
conclusions about how the events
of the 1920s changed American
life and identity.

I Read	
	Changes
I Know	And So

"Here was a new generation."

—F. Scott Fitzgerald, from *This Side of Paradise*

CRITICAL VIEWING Marquees and billboards flash as automobiles and streetcars drive through Times Square in New York City circa 1926. What details in this photo might indicate changes in the American identity?

1.1 Challenges After the War

After a tough day, you probably feel like retreating to your room and enjoying a little peace and quiet. After the suffering and hardships of World War I, most Americans wanted a return to "normalcy" and peace.

MAIN IDEA Exhausted by war, most Americans looked back with longing at the life they lived prior to World War I and hoped to return to that way of life.

THE RED SCARE

As you have read, during World War I, many Americans became increasingly suspicious of foreigners and radicals, or those who hold extreme political beliefs. These feelings were fueled largely by the federal government's propaganda campaigns promoting national pride during the war and by the Russian Revolution. After communists came to power in Russia, they were able to win a civil war within Russia, and they changed the country's name to the Union of Soviet Socialist Republics (U.S.S.R.), or the **Soviet Union**. In the United States, the end of World War I failed to disperse, or dissolve, the cloud of fear and resentment that had settled over the country.

In April 1919, a package exploded inside the home of a Georgia senator. In the following months, anarchists, people who advocate the absence of all government, mailed more bombs to prominent Americans around the country. Some bombs reached their destinations and blew windows out of houses. Some were discovered at post offices before they were detonated. Many Americans feared the bombings were part of a communist takeover plot. The incidents helped to trigger what came to be known as the **Red Scare**. Communists were called "reds" after the Soviet Red Army. The Red Scare characterized a period of near hysteria in the United States over the perceived threat from **dissidents**, people who strongly disagree politically, such as communists and anarchists.

The Election of 1920

Warren G. Harding (Republican)

Electoral Vote: 404 votes, 76%
Popular Vote: 16,151,916 votes, 60.3%

James M. Cox (Democrat)

Electoral Vote: 127 votes, 24%
Popular Vote: 9,134,074 votes, 34.1%

Eugene Debs and other candidates

Popular Vote: 1,482,467 votes, 5.6%

Socialist Eugene Debs and Parley Christensen, a Farm-Labor party candidate, won significant popular votes in Wisconsin, Minnesota, South Dakota, and Washington.

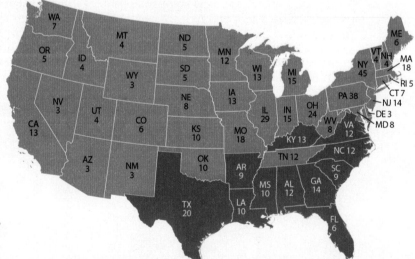

270 ELECTORAL VOTES NEEDED TO WIN

404		127
Electoral Vote: 404 votes, 76%		127 votes, 24%

60.3%	5.6%	34.1%
Popular Vote: 16,151,916 votes		9,134,074 votes

The Red Scare came to a climax in the **Palmer Raids** of late 1919 and early 1920. Under the direction of U.S. Attorney General **A. Mitchell Palmer**, federal, state, and local authorities conducted raids on numerous organizations to root out suspected communists, anarchists, and other radicals. Police officers arrested thousands of immigrants, some of whom were then deported. Many of the arrests were carried out without warrants and with little or no evidence that the individuals were traitors or that they had violent intentions.

HARDING'S ELECTION

Feelings of suspicion and alarm fostered by the Red Scare were part of a larger, more general fear felt by many Americans. Their familiar world had been torn apart by the war, and they feared it would be impossible to put it back together. The horrific accounts soldiers brought home from the war and the fear that such a conflict could happen again caused many Americans to worry that the world would never return to normal. Politicians strongly disagreed with each other, arguing over the League of Nations, the Russian Revolution, the unpopularity of President Wilson, and the collapse of the economy.

Building confidence that the United States would return to what it had been before the war became one of the biggest issues of the 1920 presidential campaign, which pitted Republican **Warren G. Harding** against Democrat James M. Cox. Harding's emphasis on a return to normality, or as he put it, "normalcy," struck a chord with Americans weary of fear, confusion, and disorder. Harding won the election by a landslide. But *normalcy* would be hard to define. The world was changing, and there would need to be a "new normal" going forward.

CRITICAL VIEWING This sheet music cover promoted Warren G. Harding's 1920 run for president during the first national election after World War I. What are the many patriotic symbols on the cover, and why do you think they were used in 1920?

HISTORICAL THINKING

1. **READING CHECK** Why were Americans so suspicious of foreigners and radicals after World War I?

2. **INTERPRET MAPS** What conclusions can you draw about political party loyalty in the United States by studying the electoral map of 1920?

3. **FORM AND SUPPORT OPINIONS** Do you think authorities who carried out the Palmer Raids went too far in their efforts to arrest suspected radicals? Support your response with evidence from the text.

1.2 Prohibition

When someone tells you not to do something, do you then feel the urge to do it? That's what happened for many Americans during Prohibition. After being told they could not drink alcohol, they ignored the law and turned illegal drinking into a multimillion-dollar business.

MAIN IDEA After World War I, alcohol consumption became illegal, but anti-alcohol laws were difficult to enforce and came with unintended consequences.

THE 18TH AMENDMENT

You'll recall that anti-alcohol, or temperance, movements had been growing in the United States since the early 1800s. Women had led temperance efforts in an attempt to reduce domestic violence and abuse. Some states had banned the sale of alcohol, but members of the temperance movement sought to extend prohibition to a national level. In January 1919, they succeeded with the passage of the 18th Amendment.

The amendment prohibited the "manufacture, sale, or transportation of intoxicating liquors . . . for beverage purposes" throughout the United States. To enforce the amendment, Congress passed the **Volstead Act**, which created a new division within the Treasury Department to focus on executing the laws and gave federal agents the power to arrest violators. But enforcing Prohibition proved to be much more difficult than its advocates expected.

ENFORCING THE LAW

Although alcohol consumption decreased during Prohibition, many Americans still wanted to drink. Enforcement was spotty. In small towns and rural areas, where citizens supported the law, there was greater enforcement and obedience. But most of the people who lived in urban areas, especially the nation's largest cities, were opposed to Prohibition. As a result, urban enforcement of the law was weak, and people found creative ways to get around the Volstead Act.

Prohibition agents often wore plain clothes while searching for illegal alcohol. When they found it, they removed and disposed of the beverages. In this 1925 photo, agents empty bottles of whiskey into a sewer.

In many cities, **speakeasies**, or secret saloons and drinking halls, provided access to illegal alcohol. To enter a speakeasy, a patron had to know a special password and tell it to the guard at the door. Some speakeasies were hidden underground in basements or in tunnels, while others were concealed in hard-to-reach sections of shops and other legal businesses. Frequent police raids forced owners to change the locations of these speakeasies often.

In addition to selling alcoholic beverages, some speakeasies offered jazz music and dancing. These establishments were very popular. In one block on West 58th Street in New York City, for instance, a person could drink liquor in any of 39 clubs and speakeasies during Prohibition.

The reign of gangster Al Capone (left) came to its official end upon his conviction of tax evasion in 1931. U.S. Marshall Henry C. W. Laubenheimer (right) escorted Capone on the train that would take him to prison for his 11-year sentence.

The illegal manufacture and sale of alcohol, or **bootlegging**, was widespread. In coastal areas, rumrunners in small, fast boats dodged law enforcement to deliver alcohol from Canada or the Caribbean. Other bootleggers made their own alcohol and sold it on the **black market**, a system through which prohibited items are bought and sold illegally. Chief among these bootleggers was the crime boss of Chicago, **Al Capone**, whose income from illegal alcohol reached an estimated $60 million a year.

Capone had joined a New York gang in his youth. He followed another crime boss to Chicago, where he took charge of the operations for manufacturing and selling alcohol. Rumors claim he murdered anyone who challenged him. Capone ruled the world of Chicago gangsters from 1925 until 1931, when he was convicted on charges of income tax evasion and sentenced to prison. He was never charged with the other crimes he committed.

Prohibition did not create **organized crime**, planned illegal activities carried out by powerful leaders, but it did help strengthen it. During Prohibition, gangsters in one city frequently sought partners in other cities and states. However, the 1920s was not a decade of rising crime rates. Rather, awareness of crime as a social problem increased during Prohibition, due largely to the well-publicized activities of gangsters. One positive outcome of Prohibition was its influence in advancing recognition of alcoholism, the excessive consumption of alcoholic drinks, as a health issue. In addition, the rate of alcohol-induced diseases dropped during Prohibition and the years that followed. However, Americans realized that Prohibition was nearly impossible to enforce effectively. As the 1920s progressed, support for the 18th Amendment began to weaken.

HISTORICAL THINKING

1. **READING CHECK** What was Prohibition, and why did so many people support it?

2. **DRAW CONCLUSIONS** What specific factors made Prohibition so difficult to enforce?

3. **MAKE INFERENCES** Why do you think the U.S. government charged Al Capone with tax evasion rather than other crimes?

1.3 Social Conflicts

If you work hard and contribute to society, you expect to receive respect and equal treatment in return. During the 1920s, African Americans and immigrants did not receive such treatment.

MAIN IDEA In the 1920s, conflicts arose between Americans who embraced new ideas of society and those who held more traditional beliefs.

RACIAL TENSIONS

Earlier, you learned that the Great Migration brought millions of African Americans from the rural South to northern cities seeking greater equality and job opportunities. They did not face the same types of Jim Crow laws as they did in the South, but they still faced discrimination. Many had served the country during World War I. Now these African-American veterans did not have equal access to good jobs and homes. The riots of the summer of 1919 set the tone for continuing racial tensions throughout the 1920s.

In response to continued discrimination, **Marcus Garvey** formed the Universal Negro Improvement Association (UNIA), which promoted the establishment of a separate African-American society apart from the white-dominated mainstream. Born in Jamaica, Garvey immigrated to the United States in 1916. He formed the UNIA soon afterward, hoping to organize African Americans to return to Africa and settle a great nation there. He urged African Americans to be proud of their history and race.

By the middle of the 1920s, the UNIA had 700 branches in large northern cities and in the rural South, a newspaper, restaurants, factories, and grocery stores. Garvey never achieved his dreams of a separate society or an African homeland, but his efforts showed what African Americans could do if they worked together to build economic and political power.

As racial tensions rose, so did membership in the white supremacist Ku Klux Klan. The organization spread northward, particularly into the Midwest. By the early 1920s, about 4 million people had joined the organization and local chapters had been established throughout the United States. The 20th-century Klan did not target only African Americans, however. They also opposed and threatened immigrants, Catholics, Jews, and women.

IMMIGRATION RESTRICTIONS

The Klan's stance against immigrants mirrored a growing national sentiment. In 1921, Congress enacted **immigration quotas**, or limits, that capped the number of people arriving from Europe at 600,000 per year. Three years later, in 1924, the **National Origins Act** reduced annual legal immigration from Europe to about 150,000.

Religion vs. Science

In addition to contributing to the increasing distrust of immigrants, religious **fundamentalism**, or the strict belief in the literal truth of the Bible, rose in the 1920s in opposition to new scientific ideas. In the **Scopes trial**, science teacher John Scopes was accused of violating Tennessee law by teaching about the theory of evolution. The theory states that species, or types of living things, change over time.

The judge refused to let defense attorney Clarence Darrow bring scientists as witnesses. So Darrow questioned prosecutor William Jennings Bryan as a Bible expert. During the trial, Bryan became uncertain as he tried to explain his interpretation of the Bible. But the judge ordered Bryan's testimony to be struck from the record, and the jury convicted Scopes. The judge fined him $100. Although Scopes lost the trial, many Americans believed traditional religious values had lost to modern science. The decision has impacted the subjects students are allowed to learn in school.

The laws gave preference to northern Europeans and reduced quotas for southern and eastern Europeans, who were seen as "lacking the qualities" of successful American citizens. Many Americans feared the U.S. culture would be negatively impacted if too many foreigners were allowed into the country. Without basis, immigrants were viewed as likely to express radical views. All Asians, including the previously unrestricted Japanese, were denied entry. This damaged the relationship between the United States and Japan.

The **Sacco-Vanzetti case** illustrates the anti-immigrant attitude of the time. **Nicola Sacco** and **Bartolomeo Vanzetti** were Italian immigrants who had come to the United States in 1908. They were also anarchists. In 1921, they were arrested and accused of stealing the payroll at a Massachusetts shoe factory, killing a guard and a clerk in the process. Even though another man confessed to the crimes, a jury found Sacco and Vanzetti guilty. They were executed on August 23, 1927. Many believed the men had not received a fair trial because of their political beliefs and because they were immigrants.

A GLOBAL PERSPECTIVE On January 27, 2017, President Donald Trump ordered that people from seven specified countries could not enter the United States. Hundreds of people were already in mid-flight from those countries to their U.S. destinations. Many were detained on arrival, causing confusion at airports. Lawyers went to airports to offer their services for free, hoping to help release people to go to their families and friends. What type of views do the lawyers shown above appear to have toward Trump's order?

HISTORICAL THINKING

1. **READING CHECK** What challenges did African Americans and immigrants face in the early 1920s?

2. **COMPARE AND CONTRAST** How were Marcus Garvey's solutions for the problem of racial discrimination different from those of other African Americans?

3. **DRAW CONCLUSIONS** Based on the evidence provided in the text, what conclusion can you draw about the verdict in the Sacco-Vanzetti case?

2.1 The Consumer Economy

You probably don't give much thought to the colorful images on TV or on the Internet that tempt you to buy things. But in the 1920s, such messages, conveyed through print and the radio, were new to Americans.

MAIN IDEA In the 1920s, consumer spending and new technologies helped build a prosperous economy.

NEW TECHNOLOGIES

The technological advances of the 1920s changed people's lives. Americans could purchase an increasing variety of household appliances and labor-saving gadgets, such as washing machines and vacuum cleaners. Before these appliances were available, people had to hand wash dishes, scrub floors and rugs on their hands and knees, and have blocks of ice delivered regularly to their homes to keep their food cold inside ice boxes.

To make sure people knew about and wanted to buy these products, a booming advertising industry arose in the 1920s. **Advertising** is the act of presenting products and ideas to the public. Advertising is an important part of **marketing**, which is the process of promoting products or services. Companies hired marketers to determine the best way to reach specific groups of **consumers**, or those who might buy their products. They then used advertising to attract consumers and persuade them to buy. For example, Ford marketed the Model T automobile to the middle class by placing targeted advertisements in the mass media that middle-class people listened to and read. **Mass media** refers to sources of information and entertainment, such as publications, radio, and movies, meant to reach a large group of people at once.

The result of the combination of available goods, consumers, and advertising was a new **consumer economy**, an economy in which people have many choices about what to buy and in which they make purchases often. Soon consumers faced more purchasing decisions than ever before. And since the newest appliance or automobile was expensive, average consumers needed a way to afford these items. In response, companies offered consumers the option to buy on credit, or to put a little money down and pay the rest over time.

One result of the consumer economy was that by 1927, there were more than 20 million cars on the roads. Additionally, there were more than 3 million trucks and buses. The Federal Highway Act of 1921 left road construction to the states, but it set national standards for concrete road surfaces and smaller roads to access the highways. The size of the American road network grew from 7,000 miles at the end of World War I to 50,000 miles in 1927. Gasoline taxes brought in revenues for the states, enabling them to build more roads. This led to the continued development of areas outside of the old city centers and to the greater need for consumers to buy cars to travel those distances.

SELLING A DREAM

Soon companies weren't just selling cars and household products. They were selling the idea of the American dream. At a 1923 advertising convention, speaker Helen Landon Cass advised, "Sell them their dreams. Sell them what they longed for and hoped for and almost despaired of having. After all, people . . . buy *hope*—hope of what your merchandise will do for them. Sell them this hope and you won't have to worry about selling them goods."

Women were recognized as critical members of the new consumer society. Typical advertisements for household products presented the ideal American housewife: a stylishly dressed manager of the home with plenty of leisure time and a spotless house. Brightly colored graphics caught the consumer's eye, while photographs

Use Old Dutch Cleanser
and you are protecting your family
with Healthful Cleanliness

Old Dutch cleans perfectly. It gets rid of all the dirt at once—hidden uncleanliness and impurities at the same time the visible dirt is removed. In the bathroom, which is devoted to personal cleanliness, this distinctive Old Dutch feature is reassuring. It means that the tub, bowl and fixtures, when Old Dutch is used, are sanitary and hygienic. Healthful Cleanliness prevails.

Old Dutch cleans quickly. You'll marvel at the ease and quickness with which the tiny, flat-shaped Old Dutch particles work. One smooth sweep and the dirt is gone. Old Dutch is a natural cleanser—cleans quicker than anything else you can use. Saves you time and effort.

Old Dutch cleans safely, too. You'll be surprised with the sparkle of the porcelain, tile and enamel. Old Dutch is kind to lovely surfaces. It doesn't scratch—contains no harsh, scratchy grit or other abrasives. Old Dutch preserves and protects original lustre.

Old Dutch has modernized cleaning completely. Use it throughout the house; keep a can in the bathroom, kitchen and laundry. Old Dutch is the one and only thing to use for bathrooms, floors, walls, woodwork, kitchen utensils, refrigerators, metal work, in fact on any surface on which water may be used for cleaning. And it's economical to use because a little goes a long way.

Old Dutch homes are Healthful Homes

CLEANS QUICKER

A full-page magazine ad boasts of the many benefits of Old Dutch cleanser. The ad appeals to the female consumer who wants to protect her family's health and save time: Old Dutch "cleans quicker" for a beautifully polished bathtub and washstand. Products like the soap Boraxine (below) came wrapped in eye-catching designs.

defined the modern, affluent American family and home. Such strategies reinforced the idea that a truly modern consumer would buy whatever the advertisement was selling, at any cost.

Advertising had another message. To stay ahead of the crowd, consumers had to replace some of the things they owned with the latest versions. This idea, which would later come to be called **planned obsolescence**, aimed at convincing consumers not to wait until an item was broken or worn out to purchase a new one. They needed to replace it when it was out of style. Buying on credit made it possible to replace previous purchases—up to a point. But advertising conveyed the message that if consumers could not afford to replace an item with cash on hand, they not only could, but should, purchase it on credit.

HISTORICAL THINKING

1. **READING CHECK** How did advertising change American culture in the 1920s?

2. **DRAW CONCLUSIONS** Why did advertisers try to persuade consumers to replace items even if they weren't broken or worn out?

3. **IDENTIFY MAIN IDEAS AND DETAILS** What factors drove the 1920s consumer economy?

2.2 Mass Culture

In the 1920s, the idea of a "celebrity" arose. Technology had made it possible for an actor, an athlete, a novelist, a pilot, or a wealthy businessperson, to be known by almost everyone in a very short time.

MAIN IDEA In the 1920s, radio and the movies changed the way that people got their information and entertainment.

"The One and Only"

Charlie Chaplin
His Signature

In his First Million Dollar Picture
"A DOG'S LIFE"
A "First National" Attraction

CRITICAL VIEWING Charlie Chaplin didn't only star in films. He also wrote, directed, and produced them. He obtained the industry's first million-dollar contract. In *A Dog's Life* (1918), the first film he made under that contract, Chaplin plays a homeless man who rescues a dog, finds a wallet of money that some shady characters have gotten dishonestly and buried, and begins a romance with a lonely singer. What does this poster convey about the film?

UNIFYING AMERICAN CULTURE

One of the most influential new technologies of the 1920s was the radio, which became a fixture in almost every American home. By 1922, there were more than 500 radio stations in the United States. Radio played an important role in the development of mass media and advertising, as many radio programs were sponsored, or paid for, by companies that aired commercials to sell goods and services during broadcasts.

Technology also had a great impact on the movie industry. Motion picture projectors were originally developed in the early 1890s, and at first, all movies were silent. Musicians in the theater played as the film rolled, providing background music and sound effects. The film's dialogue appeared on title cards inserted between action scenes. Actors conveyed emotions with facial expressions and exaggerated movements.

Throughout the 1920s, filmmakers experimented with aligning film and sound so they occurred at the same time. At first, the technology was crude and unreliable, but in 1927, Warner Brothers studio released *The Jazz Singer*, a feature film with scenes that contained synchronized sound, or sound that aligned with the words and action in the film. Now audiences could hear the actors speak and sing.

Once the movie industry developed synchronized sound, movie fans packed the theaters to see these new "talkies." By the end of the decade, more than 80 million people

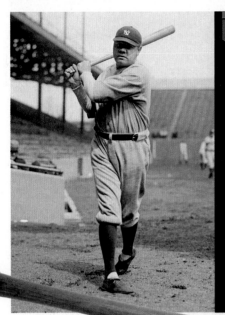

Before halls of fame for other sports began opening in the 1950s, the Baseball Hall of Fame was known simply as the "Hall of Fame," recognizing the sport as the one national pastime. New York Yankee outfielder George Herman "Babe" Ruth was one of the first five players inducted into the museum when it opened in 1936. "The Bambino," as Ruth was called—Italian for "baby"—was more than his overwhelming batting statistics. Sportswriters said that to understand Babe's effect on his fans, you had to see him play. His home runs went higher and farther than anyone else's, and he swung with a unique kind of drama. This photo from the 1930s, along with Ruth's Louisville Slugger bat, shown below, are on display at the Baseball Hall of Fame.

people went to the movies each week—more than double the number in 1922. As Americans started listening to the same popular radio programs and watching the same hit movies, a mass culture, or similar worldview based on shared experience, began to emerge.

AN ERA OF CELEBRITIES

Mass culture made it possible for athletes, entertainers, and other people of note to become celebrities. Movie actors such as **Charlie Chaplin**, Gloria Swanson, Louise Brooks, and Buster Keaton became world famous, as did the characters they played in the movies. Chaplin, **Mary Pickford**—one of the biggest stars of the 1920s—her husband, actor Douglas Fairbanks, and director D. W. Griffith started their own film company, United Artists. They sought to give actors and directors more artistic control than did the studio system, where actors were simply assigned to their films by studio bosses.

Mass culture also spread through short news and sports films that played before feature films. Called **newsreels**, they helped make heroes out of athletes such as Babe Ruth, the New York Yankee who is considered by many to be the greatest baseball player of that era, and Olympic swimming star Gertrude Ederle, who became the first woman to swim across the English Channel. Johnny Weissmuller, who won five gold medals at the 1924 and 1928 Olympics, was such a popular sports hero that he was offered the lead role as Tarzan in a Hollywood film, even though he had very little acting experience.

Aviation was also a new and exciting pursuit, and newsreels and other mass media promoted the adventures of daredevil pilots such as **Charles Lindbergh** and **Amelia Earhart**. Lindbergh was the first person to fly solo nonstop across the Atlantic Ocean. Earhart was the first person to fly across both the Atlantic and Pacific oceans, before she disappeared while attempting to circumnavigate, or travel completely around, the world.

HISTORICAL THINKING

1. **READING CHECK** How did mass culture shape American identity in the 1920s?

2. **MAKE INFERENCES** Why do you think movie attendance increased so much by the end of the 1920s?

3. **ANALYZE CAUSE AND EFFECT** How did newsreels make celebrities out of people like Babe Ruth and Amelia Earhart?

2.3 All That Jazz

Do you listen to the music your parents listened to at your age? Probably not! As times change, music, literature, and art change as well. An exciting new form of music emerged in the 1920s, shaping the culture of that decade.

MAIN IDEA In the 1920s, a unique form of African-American music grew in popularity in the United States and Europe.

A NEW KIND OF MUSIC

The music that came to be called **jazz** began with African-American musicians in New Orleans. Jazz grew out of a number of musical styles and has fast-paced, interacting rhythms. Jazz musicians use a variety of instruments to create the sound unique to this form of music. They also **improvise**, or create and play music without rehearsing, often inventing musical lines as they play.

From its beginnings, jazz brought together black and white musicians. Though very few jazz bands of the time allowed musicians of different races to play together in public, in private they improvised together and shared techniques as they learned

this new form of music. Jazz spread northward from New Orleans to St. Louis, Kansas City, Chicago, and New York. Thanks to record players and radio, jazz quickly spread from coast to coast in the United States and to parts of Europe, especially Britain and France. With its lively rhythms and innovative sounds, jazz appealed to a younger, modern audience. It also defined the 1920s as the Jazz Age.

One of the leading early jazz musicians was **Louis** (LOO-ee) **Armstrong**. A jazz trumpeter and singer from New Orleans, Armstrong influenced and played with many musicians. One such musician was a native of Washington, D.C., **Duke Ellington.**

Singer Ma Rainey toured with her Georgia Jazz Band and recorded with Louis Armstrong, playing trumpet in this photo.

Ellington started out as a piano player at age 17. He went on to pioneer the "big-band" jazz sound that became extremely popular in the 1940s.

The popularity of jazz also helped increase the appeal of the **blues**, another African-American genre, or form, of music. Unlike upbeat jazz music, blues songs are usually about hard times. Jazz and blues singer **Gertrude "Ma" Rainey** often drew upon heartache in her own life when she sang and in lyrics she created. In tracing the history of the blues, music historians cite her as a bridge from early African-American folk music and vaudeville to the blues. Hailed as the "Mother of the Blues," Rainey and her Georgia Jazz Band performed blues and jazz music to sellout crowds in the 1920s. Rainey discovered **Bessie Smith**, a young blues artist who sang with Rainey and one of her bands. Smith became known as "Empress of the Blues" and was the highest paid African-American performer by the end of the 1920s.

LITERATURE OF THE JAZZ AGE

The Jazz Age was also a time of experimentation and achievement in literature. Two of the most popular authors in the 1920s were **F. Scott Fitzgerald** and **Ernest Hemingway**. Fitzgerald published his most famous novel, *The Great Gatsby*, in 1925. It's the story of Jay Gatsby, a troubled young man whose wealth came from bootlegging. The novel gives readers a glimpse into the lives of people caught up in the Jazz Age, including the music, parties, and excesses of the time.

Ernest Hemingway served as an ambulance driver in World War I, which greatly influenced his work. In his bestselling novels *The Sun Also Rises* (1926) and *A Farewell to Arms* (1929), Hemingway wrote about how the war affected Americans and others who had fought in it. Hemingway wrote in short, plain sentences—an innovative writing technique for which he became famous.

Women authors also gained popularity during the 1920s. **Willa Cather** grew up in Nebraska. Her frontier childhood on the Nebraska prairies influenced many of her novels, including *O Pioneers!* (1913) and *My Ántonia* (1918). **Edith Wharton** began her writing career as a poet, but she also wrote short stories, plays, and novels. In 1921, Wharton became the first woman to win the Pulitzer Prize for her novel *The Age of Innocence.*

A New Kind of Woman

American women gained more rights and freedoms in the 1920s, including the right to vote. Many young women also embraced new social freedoms. Called **flappers** by the media, they expressed the same spontaneity that jazz did, but through fashion and dance. They wore bobbed hair and a freer, shorter style of dress. The flapper in this photo is dancing to music played by the jazz band in the background.

HISTORICAL THINKING

1. **READING CHECK** What kinds of music and literature became popular in the 1920s?

2. **COMPARE AND CONTRAST** How did women's lives change in the 1920s from what they were before World War I?

3. **DRAW CONCLUSIONS** Why do you think the 1920s became known as the Jazz Age? Support your response with text evidence.

The National Jazz Museum in Harlem, New York City

nal Jazz Museum in Harlem is a place
ulates hearts and minds through music.
in 1997, its mission is "to preserve,
and present jazz by inspiring knowledge,
ion, and the celebration of jazz music
ationally, and internationally."

The museum achieves its mission by reaching o
to diverse audiences. Its staff organizes free mu
education programs, hosts live performances, a
presents exhibitions of musical recordings and
instruments so people around the world can enj
this uniquely American music.

---

lie Parker with Strings" Album
e "Yardbird" Parker was one of the most
tant and influential saxophonists and jazz
s of the 1940s. His impressive career as a
ian revolved around jazz-infused cities such
nsas City, Chicago, and New York.

bum "Charlie Parker with Strings" includes
dings from the late 1940s and early 1950s.
ngs feature Parker with a small group of
ed instruments and a jazz rhythm section
d of the bebop quintet with whom he typically
med and recorded.

What other instruments
are commonly used by jazz
musicians? Conduct online
research and explore the
museum's website to find out.

Charlie Parker's Saxophone
Saxophones come in many sizes. Charlie Parke
played an alto sax, which is smaller than its
cousin, the tenor sax. Musicians can play the
same music with both instruments, but the size
difference makes the voice of an alto sax natur
higher than the voice of a tenor sax. Parker
used this alto sax (left) to record such hits as
"Ornithology" (1946) and "Out of Nowhere" (194

"Jelly Roll's Jazz" Album

Born in 1890 in New Orleans, Jelly Roll Morton was an African-American jazz pianist and composer. Morton helped the New Orleans music scene move from the earliest forms of jazz to jazz played with an orchestra. In the 1920s and early 1930s, Morton recorded many national hits with his band, Morton's Red Hot Peppers.

In 1951, 10 years after Morton's death, the Lawson-Haggart Band paid tribute to Morton by recording some of his most famous original compositions, such as "King Porter Stomp," "Dead Man Blues," and "Kansas City Stomp," on an album called "Jelly Roll's Jazz."

Duke Ellington's Baby Grand

African-American pianist Duke Ellington is considered to be the greatest jazz composer and bandleader. After beginning his musical career at the age of 17, Ellington went on to compose thousands of musical scores and lead a jazz orchestra for over 50 years.

During his long career, Ellington also wrote music for movies and composed pieces for the ballet and theatre. At the height of the civil rights movement, Ellington composed the score for the 1964 show *My People*, a celebration of African-American life.

Ellington's distinctive white baby grand piano was on exhibit in the National Jazz Museum in Harlem. In 2016, several of Ellington's personal artifacts, including the piano and sheet music, were put up for auction at the museum. Photos of the collection still remain on-site.

WANN Radio Station Microphone

In 1948, WDIA in Memphis, Tennessee, became the first radio station to feature only African-American announcers. Soon, more radio stations dedicated to African-American listeners began to emerge, including WANN in Baltimore, Maryland. These stations reached the growing black, middle-class population with music and advertising.

Legendary disc jockey Hoppy Adams joined WANN founder Morris Blum in 1953 and together, they used the station's airwaves for more than just music. For example, after the assassination of Dr. Martin Luther King, Jr., Blum gave airtime to a group of teenagers who wanted to express their concerns. He frequently gave civil rights activists a voice on the station.

3.1 The Great Migration

MAIN IDEA A number of factors led to millions of African Americans moving from the South to cities in the North during the Great Migration.

THE PULL OF THE NORTH

As you know, the Great Migration involved the movement of about 6 million African Americans from the rural South to the urban North between 1910 and 1970. The numbers of African Americans on the move increased during World War I and World War II and significantly decreased during the Great Depression of the 1930s. During the first wave of the Great Migration, between 1910 and 1930, the African-American population in cities such as New York, Chicago, Detroit, and Cleveland grew by about 40 percent.

African Americans traveled north by bus, train, boat, and even horse-drawn carts. The arrival of these migrants transformed the culture of northern cities. It also created a new African-American urban culture. As you'll learn in this chapter, the migration resulted in a great flowering of the arts in New York City.

So what led African Americans to move north? Like all migrations, the Great Migration was the result of push-pull factors. As you may remember, push factors are the reasons that make people want to leave one place. Pull factors are the reasons that make people want to settle in a new one. During the first wave of the Great Migration, push factors included the discrimination, poverty, and fear African Americans endured in the South. Pull factors included the dream of greater equality, opportunities, and safety in the North.

PUSH FACTORS

DISCRIMINATION

African Americans in the South faced racial discrimination. Jim Crow laws enforced the segregation of schools, transportation, restaurants, and drinking fountains. The facilities for African Americans were inferior to those for white people. Living as second-class citizens, African Americans in the South were also regularly denied their constitutional right to vote.

POVERTY

Few employment opportunities were available to African Americans in the rural South. The best jobs were reserved for whites, and so unemployment rates among African Americans were high. Many of those who had jobs worked as sharecroppers in a system that kept them in poverty. As a result, many African Americans lived in extremely poor conditions.

FEAR

African Americans in southern society were expected to regard white people as their superiors. On the other hand, whites showed African Americans little courtesy. Whites could beat and kill African Americans with little fear of punishment. All-white juries would acquit them of the crimes—even lynching.

PULL FACTORS

EQUALITY

African Americans had more freedom in northern cities. Segregation in the North was not widespread. African Americans could exercise their right to vote more easily. In addition, northern states passed laws guaranteeing all students an education, regardless of race. However, schools and cities in the North were often segregated, with African Americans forced to live in ghettos, or slums.

OPPORTUNITY

Immigration from Europe and men leaving to fight in World War I had caused labor shortages in northern factories. African-American newspapers encouraged people to move north with promises of plentiful jobs, good wages, and better living conditions. While many African Americans did find work, the higher cost of living in the North largely erased the benefit of earning a higher wage.

SAFETY

The threat of violence against African Americans was lower in the North. Lynching was rare. Yet the threat of violence did not go away completely. As you know, in 1919, an African-American teenager was killed for swimming in the white section of a segregated beach in Chicago, which caused race riots to sweep through the country.

The Great Migration, 1916–1940

Percent change in African-American population between 1910 and 1940

Increase
- 10.0 or more
- 5.0 to 9.9
- 2.5 to 4.9
- 0.0 to 2.4

Decrease
- −0.1 to −2.4
- −2.5 to −4.9
- −5.0 to −9.9
- −10.0 or less

City population, 1940
- 1,000,000 or more
- 500,000 to 999,999
- 150,000 to 499,999
- 50,000 to 149,999
- Less than 50,000

Migration Corridors
- Southwest to Midwest
- South Central to Midwest
- Southeast to Northeast

THINK LIKE A GEOGRAPHER

1. **IDENTIFY MAIN IDEAS AND DETAILS** In the first wave of the Great Migration, why did many African Americans relocate to northern cities?

2. **FORM AND SUPPORT OPINIONS** Do you think the African Americans who migrated in the first wave of the Great Migration had better lives in the North? Explain why or why not.

3. **INTERPRET MAPS** From which states did most of those who relocated to Chicago come?

3.2 The Harlem Renaissance

Sometimes a community can be so inspiring that it ignites creativity and new ideas. That's just what happened in a New York City neighborhood called Harlem in the 1920s.

MAIN IDEA During the Great Migration, large numbers of African Americans settled in the North, where they led a rebirth in culture and the arts.

A DIVERSITY OF TALENT

The neighborhood of Harlem, located north of Central Park in New York City, was one of the vibrant communities that emerged from the Great Migration. By the 1920s, Harlem was the thriving center for a movement of African-American arts and culture, known as the **Harlem Renaissance**. A **renaissance** is a rebirth, and the Harlem Renaissance marked a revival of African-American pride and creativity that spread across the country.

The magazine of the National Association for the Advancement of Colored People (NAACP), *The Crisis,* became a leading voice of the Harlem Renaissance. It was launched by W.E.B. DuBois in 1910. With a circulation of 100,000, *The Crisis* provided African-American authors a platform for expressing their ideas.

At an important dinner party in 1924, African-American writers and scholars met some of New York's influential white editors and critics. Before the evening ended, publications were being planned, including a special edition of the magazine *Survey Graphic* that focused on "Harlem: Mecca of the New Negro." That issue included an essay by **Alain Locke**, a Howard University professor, who urged his African-American readers to take pride in their culture.

CELEBRATING A CULTURE

The Harlem Renaissance gave African-American authors, poets, playwrights, musicians, performers, and visual artists a new stage upon which to express their creativity and identity. They sought not just acceptance, but a celebration of their achievements and what it meant to live the African-American experience.

Among the most famous of the Harlem Renaissance authors was **Langston Hughes**. He wrote plays and novels, but he is best remembered for his poetry. Hughes used the rhythms of jazz and blues in his poems to speak to African Americans throughout the country.

Many authors, including **Zora Neale Hurston**, wrote in a variety of genres. An **anthropologist**, or person who studies cultures, as well as an author, Hurston collected folktales from the Caribbean, Latin America, and the South. The novel *Their Eyes Were Watching God* (1937) is considered her masterpiece. Other major literary figures in the Harlem Renaissance included poets **Countee Cullen** and **Claude McKay**. While in his twenties, Cullen won prizes in many of America's leading literary journals for his racially themed poetry. McKay was born in Jamaica but later became an American citizen. He wrote about life in Harlem in one of his poetry collections, *Harlem Shadows.*

Music, art, and performance were also part of the Harlem Renaissance. **James Weldon Johnson** was a leading figure in the United States even before the Harlem Renaissance. He composed "Lift Every Voice and Sing," a well-known song in the genre of **gospel music**, blending biblical subjects with melodic themes similar to those of jazz. Artist **Jacob Lawrence** became known for a series of paintings, *The Migration of the Negro*, depicting African-American life during the early 20th century. **Paul Robeson** was an attorney, but racism at his firm led him to quit law and turn to acting and singing. Given respect in other nations that he did not receive at home, Robeson became an outspoken supporter of civil rights.

The Harlem Renaissance occurred in part because of the diversity of those who migrated to Harlem. In the words of Alain Locke, "their greatest experience has been the finding of one another."

1 **Strivers' Row** was the home of W. C. Handy, writer of the iconic "St. Louis Blues."

2 **Smalls Paradise** featured jazz and was a haunt of Harlem Renaissance writers.

3 **Liberty Hall** hosted Marcus Garvey's UNIA meetings every Sunday.

5 **James Weldon Johnson** lived on 135th Street from 1925–1938, publishing his own and others' poetry.

4 **Langston Hughes** spent the last 20 years of his life in a home on 127th Street.

6 **Apollo Theater** Ella Fitzgerald first performed at amateur night at the Apollo.

145th St

Strivers' Row
1

James Weldon Johnson's home **5**

Garvey's
3 Liberty Hall

Harlem River

135th St

Harlem Branch of N.Y. Public Library

2
Smalls Paradise

Langston Hughes's home **4**

Apollo Theater
6 125th St

Lennox

Fifth Avenue

110th St

N
W   E
S

HISTORICAL THINKING

1. **READING CHECK** What was the Harlem Renaissance?

2. **DRAW CONCLUSIONS** How did writers and artists of the Harlem Renaissance help change perceptions of American identity?

3. **INTERPRET VISUALS** What aspects of the Harlem Renaissance are represented in the illustrated map?

3.3 Writers and Artists of the Harlem Renaissance

Artists express themselves in music, words, and images. They show where people have been and where they are going, acknowledging the past and expressing hope for the future. Alain Locke, Zora Neale Hurston, Langston Hughes, and William H. Johnson were among the great creative influences of the Harlem Renaissance.

The term "Harlem Renaissance" did not come into use until the 1940s, but in his 1925 essay "Harlem," Alain Locke (right) called Harlem "the sign and center of the renaissance of a people." Also in 1925—a busy year for Locke—he published an anthology entitled *The New Negro,* consisting of over 40 works by African-American authors, many of them young. The anthology included writings by Locke and the two writers on the next page, Zora Neale Hurston and Langston Hughes.

CRITICAL VIEWING Locke helped to define the Harlem Renaissance by describing the Harlem neighborhood and calling attention to its best writers and artists. What does Winold Reiss's portrait convey about Locke?

🏛 National Portrait Gallery Washington, D.C.

African-American writer and philosopher Alain Locke is pictured here in a 1925 drawing by artist Winold Reiss. Reiss contributed this portrait and similar drawings of many other Harlem Renaissance figures to an illustrated edition of Locke's *The New Negro.*

DOCUMENT ONE

Primary Source: Essay
from "How It Feels to Be Colored Me"
by Zora Neale Hurston, 1928

Zora Neale Hurston was one of the most productive writers of the Harlem Renaissance. Though largely forgotten by the time she died, Hurston was reintroduced to a younger generation by later African-American authors such as Alice Walker.

CONSTRUCTED RESPONSE What does Hurston mean when she writes that being discriminated against doesn't anger her so much as astonish her?

At certain times I have no race, I am me. When I set my hat at a certain angle and saunter down Seventh Avenue, Harlem City, feeling as snooty as the lions in front of the Forty-Second Street Library, for instance. . . . The cosmic Zora emerges. I belong to no race nor time. . . . I have no separate feeling about being an American citizen and colored. I am merely a fragment of the Great Soul that surges within the boundaries. My country, right or wrong. Sometimes, I feel discriminated against, but it does not make me angry. It merely astonishes me. How can any deny themselves the pleasure of my company?

DOCUMENT TWO

Primary Source: Painting
Soldiers Dancing by William H. Johnson, 1942-1943

Artist William H. Johnson studied in New York City in the 1920s during the height of the Harlem Renaissance. However, the movement influenced Johnson's art for the rest of his life. Characteristics of the movement in his paintings included using simple shapes and bright colors to depict scenes of racial pride.

CONSTRUCTED RESPONSE In what other ways does this painting convey racial pride?

DOCUMENT THREE

Primary Source: Essay
from "The Negro Artist and the Racial Mountain"
by Langston Hughes, 1926

Langston Hughes was one of the most important figures in the Harlem Renaissance. A playwright, novelist, and poet, he was one of the first writers to incorporate jazz rhythms into his writing.

CONSTRUCTED RESPONSE What do you think Hughes is saying about art and the African-American experience when he says, "If white people are pleased we are glad. If they are not, it doesn't matter"?

We younger Negro artists who create now intend to express our individual dark-skinned selves without fear or shame. If white people are pleased we are glad. If they are not, it doesn't matter. We know we are beautiful. And ugly too. The tom-tom cries and the tom-tom laughs. If colored people are pleased we are glad. If they are not, their displeasure doesn't matter either. We will build our temples for tomorrow, strong as we know how, and we will stand on top of the mountain, free within ourselves.

SYNTHESIZE & WRITE

1. **REVIEW** Review what you have learned about the Harlem Renaissance.

2. **RECALL** On your own paper, write the main ideas from the excerpts from Zora Neale Hurston's and Langston Hughes's essays and the painting from William H. Johnson.

3. **CONSTRUCT** Construct a topic sentence that answers this question: What cultural changes came about because of the Harlem Renaissance?

4. **WRITE** Using evidence from this chapter and the documents, write an informative paragraph that supports your topic sentence in Step 3.

3.4 Zora Neale Hurston 1891–1960

"I do not weep at the world—I am too busy sharpening my oyster knife."—Zora Neale Hurston

Zora Neale Hurston brushed aside any limitations society might have placed on an African-American woman in the early 20th century. As far as she was concerned, the world was her oyster. In other words, Hurston felt that life was full of possibilities, and she could do whatever she wanted. Outgoing and charming, Hurston used her intellectual talents, sense of humor, and "gift of walking into hearts," as one friend put it, to pursue her many interests and achieve her goals.

GETTING OFF THE GROUND

Hurston very likely formed her optimistic view of the world as a child. She grew up in Eatonville, Florida, the country's first incorporated township run entirely by African Americans. Hurston's father, a former slave, served as the town's mayor several times, and her mother had a prominent teaching position in the community's two churches. Surrounded by positive African-American role models, Hurston developed into a confident young girl.

It probably helped that, as a child, Hurston rarely encountered a white person and so was never made to feel inferior. Hurston's mother encouraged her children's high spirits and urged them to "jump at de sun." Hurston later said, "We might not land on the sun, but at least we would get off the ground."

When she was 13, Hurston's happy childhood came abruptly to an end with the death of her mother. Her father remarried but then showed little interest in his daughter. Hurston spent the next few years being passed around among various family members. According to Hurston, she learned she was just "a little colored girl" while staying with her sister and brother in Jacksonville, Florida.

Zora Neale Hurston is known for her fiction writings, but she was also a published scientist. In 1928, she received a degree in Anthropology from Barnard College in New York City. After college, she researched the folklore of Haiti and Jamaica and published her findings in a book called *Mules and Men* in 1935.

in 1931 and published her first novel, *Jonah's Gourd Vine*, in 1934. After studying anthropology at Barnard College and Columbia University in New York City, she researched and published a collection of African-American folktales called *Mules and Men* in 1935. Hurston's most famous work, *Their Eyes Were Watching God*, followed two years later.

Her autobiography, *Dust Tracks on a Road*, came out in 1942. In this, as in most of her writing, Hurston didn't discuss the segregation, or separation of races, that was widespread at the time. Although Hurston certainly encountered discrimination in her life, she laughed it off. "How can any deny themselves the pleasure of my company?" she once said. "It's beyond me."

Most of Hurston's works were well-received but earned little money. For the rest of her life, Hurston struggled with her finances. When she died in Florida in 1960, her friends paid for her funeral but could not afford a gravestone. Hurston and her works were nearly forgotten. Then in 1973, Alice Walker, an African-American writer who had been inspired by Hurston, located the unmarked grave. Walker introduced Hurston's work to a whole new audience. She also had a gravestone erected over the burial site with the inscription "Zora Neale Hurston: A Genius of the South."

When she struck out on her own, Hurston had to neglect her education and work in several low-paying jobs instead. She wasn't able to return to finish high school until she was 26. To take advantage of free public schooling, the youthful-looking Hurston convinced school officials she was 16. After graduating, she spent two years at Howard University in Washington, D.C.

LANDING ON THE SUN

In 1925, Hurston moved to Harlem where she met some of the leading figures of the Harlem Renaissance, including Langston Hughes and Countee Cullen. Some of Hurston's short stories had been published in literary journals and had come to their attention. She soon became an important part of the Harlem Renaissance and often hosted parties for the movement's writers and artists. Still, Hurston sometimes stole away to her bedroom to write while a party continued in her living room.

Her hard work paid off. Over the next 10 years or so, Hurston enjoyed considerable success. In addition to writing short stories and articles, she collaborated with Hughes on the play *Mule Bone*

HISTORICAL THINKING

1. **READING CHECK** Why were Hurston's early years in Eatonville so happy?

2. **MAKE INFERENCES** Why do you think Hurston was not upset by the racial discrimination she encountered?

3. **EVALUATE** Based on what you have read, what words would you use to describe Hurston's personality?

VOCABULARY

Use each of the following vocabulary words in a sentence that shows an understanding of the term's meaning.

1. **jazz**
   Jazz was a unique form of American music that came to define the 1920s.

2. immigration quota

3. advertising

4. renaissance

5. consumer

6. dissident

7. fundamentalism

8. mass media

READING STRATEGY
DRAW CONCLUSIONS

If you haven't done so already, complete your diagram about how changes that occurred in the United States during the 1920s transformed American life and identity.

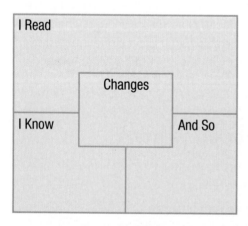

I Read

Changes

I Know

And So

9. Identify one change that occurred during the 1920s that has had a long-lasting impact on American life, and explain why you think it has.

MAIN IDEAS

Answer the following questions. Support your answers with evidence from the chapter.

10. What was the Red Scare? **LESSON 1.1**

11. What was the Volstead Act? **LESSON 1.2**

12. How did U.S. laws reflect the prejudice many Americans had against immigrants in the early 1920s? **LESSON 1.3**

13. Why did the advertising industry grow so quickly in the 1920s? **LESSON 2.1**

14. How did new forms of entertainment help create a mass culture? **LESSON 2.2**

15. In what way was jazz a unifying factor in 1920s America? **LESSON 2.3**

16. What was one effect of the Harlem Renaissance? **LESSON 3.2**

HISTORICAL THINKING

Answer the following questions. Support your answers with evidence from the chapter.

17. **DRAW CONCLUSIONS** Why do you think Sacco and Vanzetti were accused, tried, and executed?

18. **SYNTHESIZE** How do you think the Red Scare affected the election of 1920?

19. **COMPARE AND CONTRAST** In what way did the enforcement of Prohibition in cities differ from enforcement in rural areas?

20. **MAKE INFERENCES** What conflicts might have arisen in a home where the parents, who had been raised in the late 1800s, were adjusting to life with a "flapper" daughter?

21. **FORM AND SUPPORT OPINIONS** Do you think the development of a consumer economy was positive or negative for the United States? Explain why or why not.

22. ANALYZE CAUSE AND EFFECT Describe how racial and ethnic tensions arose as a result of social changes in the 1920s.

23. FORM AND SUPPORT OPINIONS How do you think American identity changed in the 1920s? Include evidence from the chapter to support your answer.

INTERPRET VISUALS

Following World War I, fear of the communist Bolsheviks led to a period of mass hysteria in the United States. Cartoonist Sidney Joseph Greene responded to this Red Scare with a political cartoon focusing on a character, "Labor," descending a staircase. His cartoon, entitled "Step by Step," appeared in the *New York Evening Telegram* newspaper in 1919.

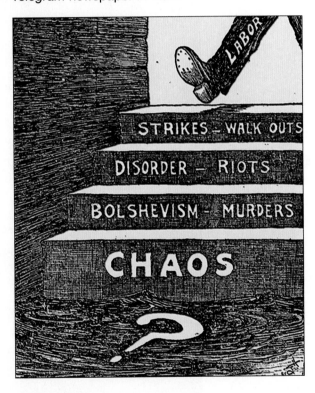

24. What does the cartoon imply will happen "step by step"?

25. Do you think the cartoonist has presented his genuine belief, or is he viewing it as an absurd idea? Support your answer with evidence from the cartoon and what you have learned about labor unions.

ANALYZE SOURCES

Few people portrayed the free and loose spirit of the 1920s as well as author F. Scott Fitzgerald. In his essay "My Lost City," Fitzgerald looks back at the glamour and the excesses of the time period. Read the excerpt from Fitzgerald's essay, and then answer the question.

> The uncertainties of 1920 were drowned in a steady golden roar and many of our friends had grown wealthy. But the restlessness of New York in 1927 approached hysteria. The parties were bigger . . . the pace was faster . . . the shows were broader, the buildings were higher, the morals were looser and the liquor was cheaper; but all these benefits did not really minister to much delight [make people happy].

26. What is the key point Fitzgerald is making in this quotation about the 1920s?

CONNECT TO YOUR LIFE

27. NARRATIVE The 1920s were a decade of great change in the United States. How has U.S. life changed in the last year or two? What change affected you the most? Identify connections you can make between this change and one that occurred in the 1920s. Write a paragraph describing these connections.

TIPS

• In a two-column chart, describe life in the 1920s on one side and your life on the other. Think about things like advertising, the consumer economy, and human rights.

• How is the information similar? Cite evidence from the text to support your ideas.

• Use two or three vocabulary terms from the chapter in your narrative.

• Conclude the narrative with a sentence that connects how the 1920s changed American life to how current events changed your life.

THE
GREAT DEPRESSION

1929–1940

ESSENTIAL QUESTION
Were President Franklin Roosevelt's attempts to resolve the nation's economic problems successful? Explain.

AMERICAN STORIES Surviving the Great Depression

SECTION 1 **Economic Collapse**

KEY VOCABULARY

bank run	Hooverville	speculate
buying on margin	installment plan	supply and demand
consumer debt	investor	

SECTION 2 **Franklin Roosevelt and the New Deal**

KEY VOCABULARY

bank holiday	Dust Bowl	pension fund
court-packing plan	fireside chat	socialism
drought	hydroelectric power	

SECTION 3 **Impact of the New Deal**

KEY VOCABULARY

deficit spending	repatriation

AMERICAN GALLERY
ONLINE Franklin and Eleanor Roosevelt

READING STRATEGY

IDENTIFY MAIN IDEAS AND DETAILS
When you identify a text's main idea and supporting details, you state the most important idea and determine which facts support it. As you read the chapter, use an organizer like this one to record details supporting the main idea that President Franklin Roosevelt introduced new programs to aid unemployed Americans during the 1930s.

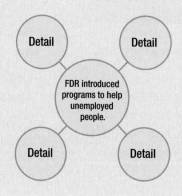

Detail

Detail

FDR introduced programs to help unemployed people.

Detail

Detail

During the 1930s, thousands of New Yorkers lined up outside this emergency food station for men operated by the Salvation Army on 17th Street. Long lines for food and jobs were common sights across the United States throughout the decade.

Edward F. Hutton
EMERGENCY
FOOD STATION
OPERATED BY
THE SALVATION ARMY

CUTEX MANICURE SPECIALTIES

"The only thing we have to fear is fear itself."
—Franklin D. Roosevelt

SURVIVING THE GREAT DEPRESSION

CRITICAL VIEWING In this 1938 photograph, a Depression-era child stands in a downtrodden neighborhood of New York City. What does this photograph convey about economic conditions in the United States during the Great Depression?

The 1920s were nicknamed the "Roaring Twenties" for a reason: The economy was booming, and many Americans were sharing in the wealth. Millions of people had the luxury of wondering how to spend their larger incomes—perhaps on a few more trips to the movies, a radio for the house, or even a car. Then in 1929, stock prices fell suddenly and dramatically, contributing to a sharp decline in the economy. Many Americans lost their jobs—and their optimism. Between 1929 and 1933, unemployment rose from 3 percent to 25 percent of the labor force. Now people were asking a new question: How will we survive?

HEADING WEST

With little work at home, millions of people took to the roads in search of jobs during the economic downturn that became known as the Great Depression. Most headed west because they thought they had a better chance of finding a job in California. Unable to pay for a bus or train ticket, some decided to "ride the rails." That is, they illegally jumped onto freight trains to travel. Many survived by finding temporary jobs, begging, and occasionally stealing.

According to some estimates, about 2 million men, 8,000 women, and 250,000 children rode the rails during the Great Depression. Eric Sevareid, a well-known American journalist, rode the rails as a teen during the 1930s. He later described this temporary community as "a great underground world, peopled by tens of thousands of American men, women, and children, white, black, brown, and yellow."

Life on the rails was difficult and extremely dangerous. Thousands died in the act of trying to jump onto a moving train, and most suffered from injuries, hunger, and thirst. Despite the harsh conditions, however, some rail riders went on to have successful careers after the Depression.

CALIFORNIA, HERE I COME!

For farmers living in the Great Plains, an environmental disaster added to the economic problems of the 1930s. Poor farming practices and a long period with little rainfall caused the soil in the region to dry out. The drought was especially severe in Texas, Oklahoma, Colorado, Kansas, and New Mexico. The dried-out soil could not support crops or livestock. Even worse, it was often swept up into the air by strong prairie winds, causing dangerous dust storms called black blizzards. In 1935, a journalist coined the term "Dust Bowl" to describe the region, and the nickname stuck.

Most farmers in the Dust Bowl remained on their land and endured the years of heat, hunger, and choking dust. About one-quarter of them, however, were forced to move in order to survive. Between 1930 and 1940, about 2.5 million people left the Great Plains. Some 300,000 of them headed for California because they believed they could find work in the fertile fields of the Golden State. This group was known as the Okies, even though most were not from Oklahoma.

Unlike the rail riders, most people who left the Dust Bowl drove, piling their possessions into cars or trucks and heading west on Route 66. American novelist John Steinbeck wrote about a fictional journey by an Okie family to California in his 1939 novel *The Grapes of Wrath*.

The trip was a days-long trial. Often short of money, the travelers would camp out by the roadside at night. To reach California, they had to cross the desert in their hot, overstuffed, and often run-down cars. By the time these migrants arrived, California looked like paradise to them.

For most, the joy of arrival did not last long, since Californians were not happy to see thousands of new farm workers in search of jobs. Some towns tried to set up blockades to prevent newcomers from crossing into the state. Okies who did make it to California found that the competition for jobs was fierce and wages were low.

Many Dust Bowl refugees found themselves living in "ditch camps," clusters of shacks set up near drainage or irrigation ditches. The camps were crowded and dirty, and families struggled to maintain their dignity and patterns of life. One social worker described a family living in the shell of an old car: "The mother . . . was trying to carry on a home life as best she could, using cupboards and tables made of old boxes, a rusty tin can as her stewpot, wash water taken out of an irrigation ditch." Eventually, the federal government stepped in to improve conditions and build better camps. For most migrants, however, true relief would come only when the Great Depression ended in the 1940s.

CRITICAL VIEWING Two men trudge down a deserted highway on their way to California, passing by a Southern Pacific railroad advertisement, in this 1937 photograph. How do the men and the billboard convey the story of the Great Depression?

BUILDING AND REBUILDING

In 1932, Franklin Roosevelt was elected president based on his promises to take strong action to end the Great Depression. One of his ideas was to put unemployed workers back on the job—working for the government. To this end, he created the Civilian Conservation Corps (CCC) in 1933 and the Works Progress Administration (WPA) in 1935. Both agencies hired workers for projects to benefit the country. CCC employees worked mainly in the nation's parks, building lodges, planting trees, maintaining roads and trails, and fighting fires. The WPA put people to work building bridges, schools, and airports; running nursery schools; and serving school lunches.

Neither agency paid well, and most of the jobs were temporary, but even a low-paying job could mean the difference between survival and starvation. One WPA laborer in North Carolina earned $18.50 every two weeks working at a printing plant. It was barely enough money to support a family with eight children, but his wife later remarked, "If it hadn't been for the WPA, I don't know what we would have done."

WPA employees lived at home and worked in their communities. Working for the CCC, in contrast, was like a combination of military boot camp and school. The CCC hired young men and brought them to camps in national parks and other federal lands. By day, the men maintained and improved natural areas, and by night many of them attended school or job training programs. Over 9 years, 57,000 men learned to read and write in CCC classes.

The WPA oversaw some job programs that targeted specific groups. The National Youth Administration (NYA), for example, employed students and helped young people find job training programs.

Two other specialized programs were the Federal Writers' Project and the Federal Arts Project. The Federal Writers' Project employed writers to create travel guides for the United States. Well-known writers who worked on the guides included Ralph Ellison, John Cheever, and Saul Bellow.

The Federal Arts Project and other government agencies hired artists to create paintings, sculptures, and other forms of art to adorn public

THE GRAPES OF WRATH

Published in 1939, John Steinbeck's novel, *The Grapes of Wrath*, introduces the Joads, a family of Dust Bowl refugees. The book is a sympathetic portrayal of a family determined to rise above desperate conditions and build a better life. One of its major themes is the power of love and generosity shared by strangers. To write the book, Steinbeck researched the real lives of Dust Bowl migrants and visited a migrant camp in California.

PRIMARY SOURCE

And here's a story you can hardly believe, but it's true, and it's funny and it's beautiful. There was a family of twelve and they were forced off the land. They had no car. They built a trailer out of junk and loaded it with their possessions. They pulled it to the side of 66 and waited. And pretty soon a sedan picked them up. Five of them rode in the sedan and seven on the trailer, and a dog on the trailer. They got to California in two jumps. The man who pulled them fed them. And that's true. But how can such courage be, and such faith in their own species? Very few things would teach such faith.

The people in flight from the terror behind—strange things happen to them, some bitterly cruel and some so beautiful that the faith is refired forever.

places. They commissioned many artists to create large wall paintings called murals for public buildings. These colorful works of art decorated post offices across the United States. The murals were generally patriotic and optimistic, portraying scenes of industry or agriculture. Many influential artists of the 20th century were WPA muralists early in their careers.

Some people objected to the government spending taxpayers' money to support struggling writers and artists. Harry Hopkins, the head of the WPA, replied, "They've got to eat, just like other people."

THE HOOVER DAM

Plans to dam the Colorado River had been in the works for decades before the Great Depression began. But the timing of the dam's construction could not have been better. By the time work began in 1931, thousands of unemployed workers had arrived in nearby Las Vegas hoping for a job.

🏛 Renwick Gallery, Washington, D.C.

This oil painting, entitled *Apple Vendor*, was created by American artist Barbara Stevenson around 1933 as part of a New Deal program that supported American artists during the Depression. Artists were encouraged to paint "the American Scene" and capture the look and feel of the country. How do you think the subject matter reflects the Depression?

Work on the Hoover Dam was hard—and sometimes terrifying. Laborers had to dig tunnels through solid rock, enduring temperatures of 140 degrees and high levels of carbon monoxide. Other workers, called "high scalers," dangled 800 feet above the ground while using heavy jackhammers to carve canyon walls. Still, many men were grateful even for dangerous, low-paying work.

Near the construction site, the government built a town called Boulder City with dormitories for single men and cottages for married men who had come with their families. A worker could pay $1.60 a day for a room and three hearty meals. The town had strict rules that sometimes frustrated the workers, but it provided a welcome shelter from even worse

conditions in many parts of the country. African-American, Native American, and Hispanic workers, however, had to find housing elsewhere because they were not permitted in Boulder City.

When the Hoover Dam was completed in 1935, it was the tallest dam in the world. Its construction required about 5 million barrels of cement, 45 million pounds of reinforcement steel, and 6.6 million tons of concrete. More important for the people concerned, it had employed about 21,000 workers, helping them survive some of the hardest years of the Great Depression.

THINK ABOUT IT

Why do you think it's important to remember how people survived the Great Depression?

DOCUMENTING THE DEPRESSION: WALKER EVANS

In 1935, President Franklin Roosevelt created the Resettlement Administration (RA) to help address the problems of farmers during the Great Depression. The agency was later renamed the Farm Security Administration. The RA hired American economist and photographer Roy Stryker to head up a team of photographers called the Historical Section. Their mission was to document conditions in rural areas and show Americans why the work of the RA was necessary. In Stryker's words, the group "introduced Americans to America."

One of Stryker's photographers—Walker Evans— proved to be a genius at making the introduction. His photos revealed the lives of Depression survivors in sharply defined black and white. He later became one of the most influential American photographers of the century.

Evans, born in 1903, once wanted to become a writer. By the late 1920s, however, he had turned to photography to express himself. In 1935, Roy Stryker hired Evans to photograph a community of unemployed coal miners in West Virginia. Next, Evans traveled throughout the southeastern states with his camera. He had a special interest not only in people but also in places. He photographed buildings and objects that represented people's lives and concerns, and he also captured many striking images of individuals and families.

In 1936, Evans took a break from his work for the Historical Section and traveled to Alabama with a friend, American writer James Agee. There, they documented the lives of three cotton sharecropper families struggling to make a living. Evans's photos and Agee's text appeared in a 1941 book called *Let Us Now Praise Famous Men*, which has been described as a "stunningly honest" portrayal of families confronting the challenges of the Depression. Some of the individuals featured in the book, however, were upset over how they were represented, in spite of the dignity and honesty of the photos.

After the Depression, Evans continued working as a photographer, expanding his interests to such subjects as people on the New York City subway. He died on April 10, 1975. Many prominent photographers today credit him as an inspiration for their own work.

CRITICAL VIEWING (top) Evans captured this everyday street scene in Selma, Alabama, in 1936. (bottom) Sharecropper Floyd Burroughs rests on a porch in Hale County, Alabama, in 1936, surrounded by the children of a neighboring family. Why might the people in these photographs have objected to the way they were portrayed?

Weaknesses in the Economy

Imagine that you're a midwestern farmer in the 1920s. You keep hearing stories about how great the country is doing. But on your farm, it sure doesn't seem that way. You've lost money for five years in a row, in spite of great harvests. What has gone wrong?

MAIN IDEA The 1920s were prosperous years for many Americans, but the economy had significant weaknesses.

AN UNEVEN PROSPERITY

The "Roaring Twenties" are remembered as years of progress and plenty, but not all Americans prospered. Some people were wealthy, and the middle class lived comfortably, but many people just scraped by. While the average person's income rose, the distribution of income became more unequal. By 1929, the top 0.1 percent of Americans had a combined yearly income equal to that of the bottom 42 percent.

American farmers in particular struggled financially. Their troubles began soon after World War I ended. During the war, demand for agricultural products increased, especially overseas. Prices rose too, following the economic principle of **supply and demand**, which states that the price of a product depends on how much is available (the supply) and how much is wanted (the demand). To increase their production of crops, many farmers borrowed money to buy more land and new or better machinery. But after the war ended, the demand for U.S. agricultural products dropped

CRITICAL VIEWING This automobile showroom of the late 1920s reflects the prosperity that some Americans enjoyed during the decade. At the time, advertisements and installment plans made the purchase of expensive cars seem possible to a broad range of buyers. What types of customers do you think this showroom attracted?

as Europeans returned to farming. Prices also decreased, but production did not, resulting in surpluses throughout the 1920s. American farmers found themselves caught in a web of deep debt, low prices, and overproduction.

Other struggling industries included textiles and coal mining. Like agriculture, the textile industry had boomed during World War I. But a postwar drop in demand for textiles reduced prices by 60 percent, forcing the industry to reduce production. Textile mills closed, and many people lost their jobs. The coal industry also suffered as the nation began to use more oil, natural gas, and electrical energy. Production of bituminous coal, the most common type of coal, dropped from 144 million tons in 1929 to 75 million in 1932. Between 1920 and 1930, the price of coal dropped by more than a third.

Another disturbing trend was the high level of **consumer debt**, which is the amount of money that people have borrowed to purchase goods. During the 1920s, many Americans bought cars, appliances, and other goods on credit using an **installment plan**, which meant they made a series of partial payments over time. By 1929, according to one estimate, 75 percent of the radios and washing machines and 80 to 90 percent of the furniture sold in the United States was financed through an installment plan.

INVESTING IN THE STOCK MARKET

Despite these troubling signs, the U.S. economy boomed during the 1920s. So did the stock market, in which people called **investors** buy shares in companies in the hope of making money when they sell the shares. Investors commonly track the performance of the stock market using a stock market index, such as the **Dow Jones Industrial Average (DJIA)**, often simply referred to as "the Dow." The Dow charts the daily prices of a select number of stocks on the New York Stock Exchange, the largest market where stocks are bought and sold, and since 1971, on NASDAQ, the second-largest market. As the value of the selected stocks rises, the Dow rises too.

During the 1920s, many ordinary people began to **speculate**, or invest in stocks, hoping to make a quick profit. Some people depended on **buying on margin**, or buying a stock for a percentage of

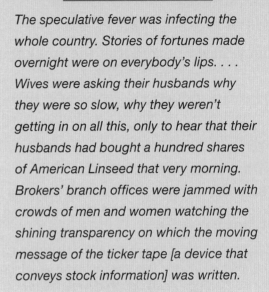

American journalist and social historian Frederick Lewis Allen remarked on the spread of stock speculation in the late 1920s.

PRIMARY SOURCE

The speculative fever was infecting the whole country. Stories of fortunes made overnight were on everybody's lips. . . . Wives were asking their husbands why they were so slow, why they weren't getting in on all this, only to hear that their husbands had bought a hundred shares of American Linseed that very morning. Brokers' branch offices were jammed with crowds of men and women watching the shining transparency on which the moving message of the ticker tape [a device that conveys stock information] was written.

—from *Only Yesterday: An Informal History of the 1920s*, by Frederick Lewis Allen, 1931

its price and borrowing to pay for the rest. If the stock's price rises, the borrower repays the lender after selling the stock for a profit. But if the price declines, the borrower owes the lender the balance, plus interest. Between September 1922 and December 1927, the value of the Dow doubled from 100 to 200 points. Investors believed the market was on a permanent upward trend. Thousands of small business owners invested their company's working capital, the money that is typically used to cover short-term expenses, in the stock market.

HISTORICAL THINKING

1. **READING CHECK** How did the end of World War I affect American farmers?

2. **COMPARE AND CONTRAST** How are the installment plan and buying on margin similar and different? Explain your answer with evidence from the text.

3. **DRAW CONCLUSIONS** What problems might a high level of consumer debt create for a nation's economy, especially when unemployment is rising?

1.2 Stock Market Crash

Investors celebrated as the value of stocks rose to new heights in September 1929. More people rushed to buy stocks with borrowed money. Few realized that the stock market was about to crash.

MAIN IDEA After years of often reckless speculation, the stock market experienced a rapid and steep drop in stock prices on October 29, 1929, throwing the economy into a deep decline.

STOCK PRICES DRIFT LOWER

On September 3, 1929, the Dow Jones Industrial Average reached its peak of 381.17 points, having doubled in only 18 months. During the same period, the value of stocks bought on margin, or with borrowed money, had also doubled, reaching about $6.2 billion. Mostly ignored were the few experts who questioned how this rapid growth, fueled by borrowed money, could continue.

Through the rest of September and early October, stock prices varied, but they generally declined. By the last week in October, fearful investors were ready to cut their losses and sell their stock for whatever price they could get. On October 24, which became known as Black Thursday, investors traded nearly 13 million shares of stock, setting a record. In early trading, the market fell 11 percent. To help stabilize the market, several major banks and investment companies made large stock purchases, which served to raise prices. As a result, the Dow Jones Industrial Average lost only six points that day.

PANIC ON WALL STREET

Investors breathed a sigh of relief, but the worst was yet to come. By the following Monday, the market fell another 13 percent. Panic set in again, and many investors tried to sell all their shares of stock. A stock market crash—a rapid, steep decline in stock prices—occurred on **Black Tuesday**, October 29, 1929. Over the two days, the Dow dropped by 25 percent, and eventually, the stock market lost an estimated $30 billion. Thousands of investors were wiped out and had no way to repay the money they had borrowed to buy stocks. An article in the October 30, 1929, edition of the *New York Times* described the reaction of people learning the bad news:

> The crowds [gathered] about the ticker tape, like friends about the bedside of a stricken friend. There were no smiles. There were no tears either. Just the camaraderie [companionship] of fellow-sufferers. Everybody wanted to tell his neighbor how much he had lost. Nobody wanted to listen. It was too repetitious a tale.

Black Tuesday began a long, miserable period for **Wall Street**, the home of the New York Stock Exchange. Stock prices fell even lower. The Dow hit a low of 41.22 on July 8, 1932, which was a stunning 89 percent below its high of 381.17 in 1929. It would take a little more than 25 years for the Dow to rise above 381.17 once again.

The stock market crash led to the most severe depression, or period of low economic activity, in U.S. history. But the crash wasn't the only cause of the depression. Other causes included declining demand in such industries as agriculture, coal, and textiles; high levels of consumer debt; and unequal distribution of income and wealth.

HISTORICAL THINKING

1. **READING CHECK** Why is October 29, 1929, called Black Tuesday?

2. **ANALYZE CAUSE AND EFFECT** What effect did the 1929 stock market crash have on the economy of the United States?

3. **IDENTIFY PROBLEMS AND SOLUTIONS** What problems resulted from the practice of buying stocks on margin?

Wall Street, Manhattan, New York City

Only about seven city blocks long, Wall Street doesn't occupy much space, but the business conducted there reaches into every corner of the world. Recognized as the financial center of the United States for more than 150 years, Wall Street has come to symbolize both financial opportunity and financial ruin. It has been a magnet, drawing immigrants to the United States, as well as a symbol of greed, arousing anger and disgust. The bronze statue *Charging Bull*, a symbol of Wall Street, was installed in front of the New York Stock Exchange in 1989 without permission. The city soon moved the statue to a nearby park. To some, the statue represents the unpredictable and sometimes dangerous nature of the stock market. Installed in 2017, the statue *Fearless Girl* faces off against the raging bull, symbolizing the power of strong women in the workplace and the nation.

1.3 Hard Times

The entire nation experienced a roller-coaster ride when the stock market crashed in 1929. One year people were prosperous, and the next they were destitute. It was a ride no one would want to take twice.

MAIN IDEA The severe depression that followed the stock market crash of 1929 spread from the United States to the rest of the world.

THE DEPRESSION SPREADS

After the stock market crashed, many banks failed. The slumping farm economy had already weakened rural banks. Now the vast sums of money lost in the stock market crash made the financial condition of urban banks even worse. Some banks ran short of money and closed. One bank failure often led to another as large numbers of depositors panicked and caused **bank runs** by trying to withdraw all their money. In 1930, banks failed at an alarming rate: 1,350 in that year alone.

In that same year, Congress passed the **Smoot-Hawley Tariff Act**. The act raised the import tax, or tariff, that the United States placed on a wide range of agricultural and manufactured goods.

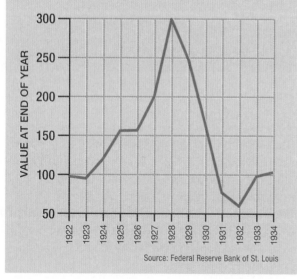

Dow Jones Industrial Average, 1922–1934

This chart shows the steady climb and abrupt fall of the Dow from 1922 to 1932. Following the crash in October 1929 and through 1932, the Dow lost 89 percent of its value.

VALUE AT END OF YEAR

300
250
200
150
100
50

1922 1923 1924 1925 1926 1927 1928 1929 1930 1931 1932 1933 1934

Source: Federal Reserve Bank of St. Louis

Many countries responded by passing high tariffs of their own, and worldwide trade declined markedly. The Smoot-Hawley Tariff Act's greatest export was, unfortunately, economic distress.

With the bad signs in the economy, businesses of all sizes cut back. They produced fewer goods, stopped hiring, and laid off workers. By 1932, industrial production in the United States had declined nearly by half. Ordinary people stopped spending money and cut their consumption, which in turn reduced manufacturing even more. Additional wage cuts and layoffs followed. The growing ranks of the unemployed had no money to spend, so the cycle continued to worsen. Two years into the depression, the rate of unemployment topped 20 percent. Many of the unemployed became homeless and could not even afford to buy food.

This economic downturn, called the **Great Depression**, lasted from 1929 to about 1939. From the United States, the depression spread worldwide, though its severity varied. In Canada, the depression was about as long and severe as it was in the United States. In Germany, it was slightly longer and nearly as harsh. In the United Kingdom, Sweden, and Japan, however, it was shorter and less difficult. The international economic instability also caused political instability, especially in Europe, which was still recovering from World War I.

HOOVER'S ACTIONS

Herbert Hoover, elected president in 1928, was a self-made millionaire—a mining engineer with a knack for business. But he grew up poor and was orphaned at the age of nine. His rise from poverty

shaped his views on the nature of American character and the role of government in people's lives. A strong believer in self-reliance, Hoover felt that Americans would thrive if they simply applied their own creativity and work ethic. He thought that federal aid would make Americans dependent on the government. At first, he championed the efforts of local governments, civic and religious groups, and voluntary organizations to provide help to the hungry and homeless.

But the crisis was too great for local charities to handle. Hoover eventually saw that federal action was needed. He began to provide limited financial relief to banks and other lenders, insurance companies, and railroads. Hoover also endorsed efforts to finance public works projects that were aimed at creating jobs. However, the president stuck by his belief that direct financial aid to needy people would make them permanently reliant on government handouts.

For everyday Americans, Hoover's measures were too little, too late. Joblessness and homelessness kept growing. Shantytowns, or communities of makeshift shacks, sprang up across the United States. As an insult to the president, people began to call the shantytowns **Hoovervilles**.

The Bonus Army

In 1924, Congress voted to give World War I veterans a bonus, to be paid in 1945. But with the arrival of the Great Depression, many men needed the money right away. Calling themselves the **Bonus Army**, about 15,000 veterans gathered in Washington, D.C., in 1932 to pressure Congress to pay them immediately. They set up a Hooverville near the U.S. Capitol. After a bill to allow immediate bonus payments failed in Congress, most of the veterans went home. On President Hoover's orders, federal troops, using tanks and tear gas, cleared out the remaining 2,000 to 5,000 protesters. To many Americans, this action was evidence of Hoover's uncaring treatment of needy citizens.

HISTORICAL THINKING

1. **READING CHECK** How did the depression deepen and spread after the stock market crash of 1929?

2. **IDENTIFY MAIN IDEAS AND DETAILS** How did President Hoover respond to the Great Depression?

3. **MAKE CONNECTIONS** If you were president, how would you have handled the protest of the Bonus Army, and why?

2.1 Franklin Roosevelt Takes Office

Who among your friends and family is the best at solving difficult problems? In the election of 1932, voters chose a new president to solve problems that many Americans believed had no solutions.

MAIN IDEA Franklin D. Roosevelt promised strong action to address the problems of the Great Depression.

ROOSEVELT'S ELECTION

The 1932 presidential election pitted President Hoover against the Democratic governor of New York, **Franklin Delano Roosevelt (FDR)**, who would become one of the most important leaders of the 20th century.

Franklin Roosevelt was born into a wealthy New York family and was the fifth cousin of President Theodore Roosevelt, whom he greatly admired. Franklin Roosevelt attended an exclusive prep school, graduated from Harvard College, and became a lawyer. But he was never a highly committed student or lawyer. It wasn't until Roosevelt entered politics that he found his real calling in life.

After winning election to the New York State Senate in 1910, Roosevelt became known as a progressive reformer. His innate, or natural, charm and confidence as a public speaker helped spark his rapidly advancing political career. In late summer 1921, however, Roosevelt contracted poliomyelitis, a disease commonly called polio. The illness left his legs permanently paralyzed. His recovery—both personally and politically—was due partly to the hard work of his wife, Eleanor.

Franklin Roosevelt throws out the first pitch to start Game 3 of the 1932 World Series at Wrigley Field in Chicago. The Cubs-Yankees baseball game was a Midwest campaign stop for FDR, who caught the action with his son James (right) and Chicago mayor Anton Cermak (left).

The Election of 1932

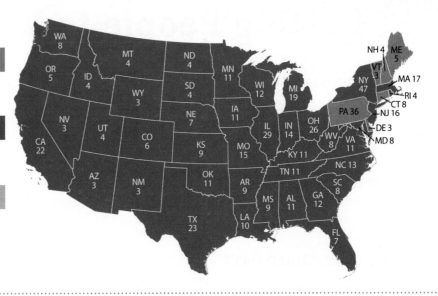

Herbert Hoover (Republican)

Electoral Vote: 59 votes, 11.1%

Popular Vote: 15,760,425 votes, 39.6%

Franklin Roosevelt (Democrat)

Electoral Vote: 472 votes, 88.9%

Popular Vote: 22,818,740 votes, 57.4%

Socialist and Other Parties

Electoral Vote: 0

Popular Vote: 1,169,367 votes, 3%

Like her husband, **Eleanor Roosevelt** came from a wealthy family. A distant cousin of Franklin's, she became a lifelong champion of equal rights for women and minorities and an advocate for the underprivileged. Eleanor Roosevelt advised her husband on a wide range of social and political issues. She helped him campaign for and win the governorship of New York in 1928.

A successful governor, Franklin Roosevelt developed a national reputation for leadership. During his 1932 presidential campaign, Roosevelt offered few specific plans to address the nation's economic problems. He told voters he would expand the government's role to help those in need and to regulate the excesses of big business. Overall, he promised the people action.

American voters apparently did not require specific details. They were fed up with Hoover and the Republicans. Roosevelt won the presidential election by a large margin, and Democrats gained majorities in both the U.S. House and Senate.

THE NEW DEAL

In his inaugural speech on March 4, 1933, Roosevelt sought to boost the confidence and hope of the American people. He reassured them with these words: "This great Nation will endure as it has endured, will revive and will prosper." Roosevelt promised to experiment with new ideas to fight the Depression. His plan of action was to establish programs that would provide what became known as the "three Rs": relief, recovery, and reform. To develop his plan, called

the **New Deal**, Roosevelt depended on a group of academic advisors known as his "brain trust." This group of university professors helped the president-elect prepare his strategy for immediate action after Inauguration Day.

Roosevelt's first move as president was to declare a **bank holiday** on March 6. This measure closed the country's banks for four days to avoid another bank run. It would keep people from withdrawing so much money that the banks might be forced into failure. After four days, only those banks judged able to succeed in the long run would reopen. Roosevelt's plan seemed to work. By March 15, the banks that reopened controlled 90 percent of U.S. banking resources. Inspired by Roosevelt's assured leadership, more people were putting money into the banks than were taking money out.

HISTORICAL THINKING

1. **READING CHECK** Why did President Roosevelt declare a bank holiday two days after taking office?

2. **IDENTIFY MAIN IDEAS AND DETAILS** During his campaign, how did Franklin Roosevelt persuade American voters to support him in the 1932 presidential election?

3. **INTERPRET MAPS** How many states did Herbert Hoover win in the presidential election of 1932, and in what region were they located?

2.2 Putting People to Work

If you couldn't afford food because you didn't have a job, what would you want the government to do? During the Depression, President Roosevelt believed the government should provide both food and jobs.

MAIN IDEA President Roosevelt acted boldly and swiftly in establishing New Deal programs and agencies to resolve the country's economic problems.

THE FIRST HUNDRED DAYS

Unlike Hoover, Roosevelt approached the nation's financial crisis by looking for ways to provide direct relief to Americans in need. Within his first few months in office, the president and his brain trust initiated 15 laws to provide money and jobs for Americans and to strengthen the economy. These laws established government programs that focused on the three Rs. Relief programs helped the jobless and hungry directly. Recovery programs were aimed at returning agriculture and industry to profitability. Reform programs sought to correct banking and investment practices that had contributed to the Depression.

New Deal legislation was based on the ideas of **John Maynard Keynes**, a British economist. Keynes proposed a new approach to government spending during an economic downturn. He argued that the government should spend money to help people rather than cut spending to limit debt. Roosevelt's New Deal proposals applied this approach. With little debate, Congress passed the New Deal legislation. This period of intense lawmaking was later named the **First Hundred Days**.

THE TENNESSEE VALLEY AUTHORITY

The Great Depression hit almost everyone hard, whether they lived in large cities or rural areas. But among the most impoverished regions in the nation was the Tennessee Valley, located in Tennessee and several surrounding states. The 4 million people who lived in the region included some of the country's poorest farmers. Many lived in isolated communities that lacked doctors, good schools, paved roads, and electricity.

Geography played a role in the problems that farmers in the region faced. The Tennessee Valley forms the watershed, or drainage area, of the Tennessee River, which flows through parts of seven southern states. The river and its tributaries, which are smaller streams that flow into a larger body of water, periodically experienced severe flooding. Deforestation, the cutting down of trees, added to the problem of soil erosion in the valley. In the river itself, a series of shallow areas along its middle course made navigation difficult.

Key Programs of the New Deal	
Program	**Description**
Federal Emergency Relief Administration (FERA)	Established as a temporary measure to provide money and work to unemployed citizens through grants given to state and local agencies
Civilian Conservation Corps (CCC)	Provided conservation jobs, mostly to young single men
Public Works Administration (PWA)	Provided jobs by funding such large construction projects as roads, dams, bridges, and public buildings
Agricultural Adjustment Administration (AAA)	Designed to make agriculture profitable by paying subsidies to farmers who agreed to reduce production
National Recovery Administration (NRA)	Designed to help industries recover by establishing fair business practices that would reduce labor strikes
Federal Deposit Insurance Corporation (FDIC)	Created to insure depositors' bank accounts up to a certain amount
Tennessee Valley Authority (TVA)	Established to control flooding and provide electricity to impoverished areas along the Tennessee River and its tributaries

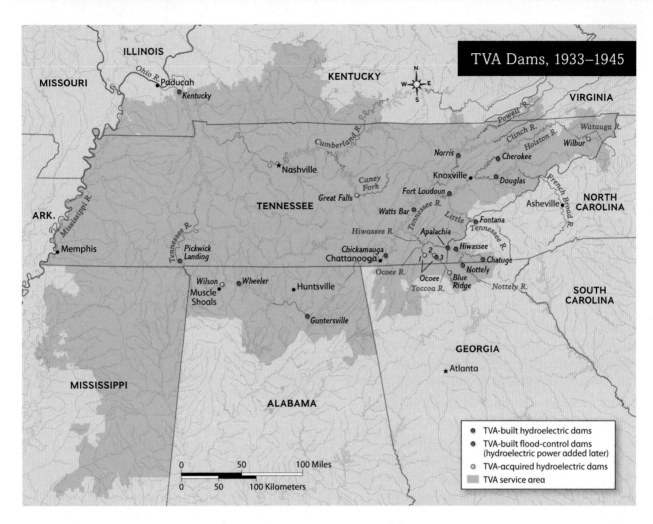

TVA Dams, 1933–1945

To aid struggling farmers and others living in the Tennessee Valley, President Roosevelt established a federal agency called the **Tennessee Valley Authority (TVA)** in May 1933. Roosevelt envisioned the TVA as an agency that would combine the power of government with the initiative of private business. The TVA aimed to reduce flooding, improve river navigation, and provide electricity to the region. The agency built dams to control flooding and produce inexpensive **hydroelectric power**, or electricity generated by the energy of flowing water. Over the next decade, the TVA constructed 16 dams and hydroelectric plants along the river, providing thousands of jobs. In addition, the TVA deepened the river's channel, which helped boost shipping along the river. It replanted trees and promoted better farming methods.

The TVA brought dramatic changes to the Tennessee Valley. Its inexpensive electricity stimulated industrial development and improved standards of living in the region. Its flood control efforts were so effective that no major flood

damage occurred in the Tennessee Valley until 2010, when flooding occurred along the Cumberland River, especially in the Nashville area.

The TVA is still active today. It currently provides electricity for 9 million people in parts of Alabama, Georgia, Kentucky, Mississippi, North Carolina, Tennessee, and Virginia. In addition, the artificial lakes that were created by the dams have become popular recreation areas.

HISTORICAL THINKING

1. **READING CHECK** What were the goals of the New Deal agencies and programs?

2. **IDENTIFY MAIN IDEAS AND DETAILS** How did Roosevelt and his brain trust apply the ideas of John Maynard Keynes in the first hundred days of FDR's presidency?

3. **INTERPRET MAPS** In which states did the TVA build hydroelectric dams between 1933 and 1945?

2.3 The Dust Bowl

You've probably experienced a rainstorm or snowstorm that was so heavy you couldn't see very far. But can you imagine being in a storm of dust so thick you can't see your own hands?

MAIN IDEA At the height of the Great Depression, an environmental disaster in the Great Plains caused a massive migration out of the region.

ENVIRONMENTAL DISASTER

As you know, most American farmers were struggling financially even before the Great Depression, and the economic downturn caused many to lose their farms. For those living in the Great Plains, a serious environmental crisis brought disaster. For almost 20 years, the Great Plains farmers had been plowing up grasslands and planting wheat. They did not realize that the prairie's natural, deep-rooted grasses anchored the rich topsoil. Without the grasses, the soil became vulnerable to wind erosion, especially during a **drought**, or a long period with little rainfall.

In 1931, a lengthy drought hit the region. With little grass left to hold the dry soil in place, the wind carried it off. In parts of Oklahoma, Colorado, Kansas, New Mexico, and Texas, high winds picked up the dry soil and whipped it into massive dust clouds. "Black blizzards," dust storms that blocked the sunlight, engulfed whole towns. The dust destroyed crops and sickened and killed people and livestock. Following a dust storm, farmers often found their horses and cattle buried alive. The devastated region became known as the **Dust Bowl**.

MIGRATING WEST

Unable to grow crops, many Dust Bowl farmers could not pay their mortgages, and so they lost their farms. Hundreds of thousands of farmers and their families fled the region. Some remained because of pride, determination, or hope. Others stayed because they were too poor to leave.

Many Dust Bowl farmers migrated to California, where they were called "Okies," though only some were from Oklahoma. In California, most Okies experienced extreme poverty. The fortunate ones found steady but low-wage work picking fruit, boxing vegetables, and baling hay.

In response to the Dust Bowl crisis, the **Civilian Conservation Corps (CCC)** planted shelter belts, or rows of trees that serve as windbreaks and so reduce soil erosion. The federal government also educated farmers about soil conservation techniques and promoted their use.

To help farmers throughout the country, Roosevelt instituted programs to make farming more profitable. The **Agricultural Adjustment Administration (AAA)**, for example, paid farmers who agreed not to grow crops on some of their land. The AAA also established price supports, in which the government guaranteed farmers certain prices for their crops.

The drought that helped produce the Dust Bowl ended in the fall of 1939, and the region recovered in the early 1940s. But by then, an estimated 2.5 million people, both farmers and nonfarmers, had left the region.

HISTORICAL THINKING

1. **READING CHECK** What caused the environmental disaster called the Dust Bowl?

2. **IDENTIFY PROBLEMS AND SOLUTIONS** How did the CCC help solve one problem of the Dust Bowl?

3. **MAKE INFERENCES** Under what conditions could the Great Plains again become a Dust Bowl?

Documenting the Dust Bowl

A man and his son in rural Cimarron County, Oklahoma, work to raise their fence above the drifting sand of the Dust Bowl (top photograph). This photo was taken in 1936 by Arthur Rothstein, the first photographer hired by the **Farm Security Administration (FSA)** to document the lives of America's rural poor, including the Great Plains farmers. The agency wanted to use photographs to show who the New Deal programs were helping and to convey how misuse of the land led to the region's dust storms.

While some farmers battled for survival in the Dust Bowl, one-quarter of the region's population left. Many migrants hoped to find work in California, where the climate was mild and the growing season long. In 1936, FSA photographer Dorothea Lange took the photo at right of a family who left Abilene, Texas, for California, looking for farm work.

2.4 Social Security

Even before the Great Depression, most older Americans had only their savings and relatives to rely on for support when they could no longer work. But what if they lost their savings to a bank closure? Or their farm failed? Or they had no relatives? Whom or what could they depend on?

MAIN IDEA The New Deal introduced a pension system for elderly Americans that still exists today.

HELPING THE ELDERLY

The Great Depression focused more attention on the problem of poverty among older Americans. Surveys conducted in New York in 1929 and in Connecticut in 1932 showed that half of Americans 65 years of age and older lived on less than $300 per year. Even at a time when the average annual income had dropped from $2,500 per year to about $1,100 per year, this amount was alarmingly low. Clearly, something needed to be done.

President Roosevelt and his advisors proposed the **Social Security Act**, which would provide not only a pension fund for the elderly but also unemployment insurance and aid for the disabled and others in need. A **pension fund** is a pool of money used to pay retirees a certain income. To support the program, both workers and employers would pay a federal tax.

When the Social Security Act was presented to Congress, some legislators criticized it as being a step toward **socialism**, a system in which the government controls the economy. One critic of the plan, Oklahoma senator Thomas Gore, stated, "Isn't this plan . . . in effect to take private property for public use?" In response, supporters pointed out that every tax takes citizens' money and uses it for the public good, including tax dollars that pay for roads, schools, police and fire protection, and national defense.

Despite the criticism from opponents, Congress readily passed the Social Security Act, and President Roosevelt signed it into law on August 14, 1935. The Social Security Act is one of the New Deal programs that still benefit Americans today.

A monthly check to you—

FOR THE REST OF YOUR LIFE ·· BEGINNING WHEN YOU ARE 65

GET YOUR SOCIAL SECURITY ACCOUNT NUMBER promptly

APPLICATIONS ARE BEING DISTRIBUTED AT ALL WORK PLACES

Your monthly Social Security check

WHO IS ELIGIBLE·· ··EVERYBODY WORKING FOR SALARY OR WAGES (WITH ONLY A FEW EXCEPTIONS, SUCH AS AGRICULTURE, DOMESTIC SERVICE, AND GOVERNMENT WORK). APPLICATIONS FOR SOCIAL SECURITY ACCOUNTS ARE AVAILABLE THROUGH EMPLOYERS. IF YOU DO NOT GET ONE FROM YOUR EMPLOYER, ASK FOR ONE AT THE POST OFFICE.

HOW TO RETURN APPLICATION
1. HAND IT BACK TO YOUR EMPLOYER, or
2. HAND IT TO ANY LABOR ORGANIZATION OF WHICH YOU ARE A MEMBER, or
3. HAND IT TO YOUR LETTER CARRIER, or
4. DELIVER IT TO LOCAL POST OFFICE, or
5. MAIL IT IN A SEALED ENVELOPE ADDRESSED: POSTMASTER, LOCAL
DO IT NOW. NO POSTAGE NEEDED.

—Social Security Board

INFORMATION MAY BE OBTAINED AT ANY POST OFFICE

CRITICAL VIEWING The federal government's Social Security Board distributed posters to inform citizens about the 1935 Social Security Act. How does the poster grab the viewer's attention and make Social Security appear appealing?

President Franklin Roosevelt is about to deliver a **fireside chat** in this photo from the mid-1930s. Roosevelt's **fireside chats** were informal radio broadcasts in which he **spoke directly to the** American people. He used these addresses **to reassure people and** inspire hope and to introduce, explain, and **defend his New Deal** programs. Tens of millions of Americans listened to each chat.

ROOSEVELT'S RE-ELECTION

Although Roosevelt was a popular president, he also had critics in the run-up to the 1936 election. One vocal critic was Father Charles Coughlin, a Catholic priest who hosted a radio program that had 40 million listeners. Coughlin thought the president's reforms did not go far enough. He proposed that the government take control of the banking and energy industries. But Coughlin was removed from his radio show for expressing anti-ethnic views. Huey Long, a former governor of Louisiana who had been elected a U.S. Senator in 1932, also attacked FDR for not doing enough. He called for heavily taxing the wealthy to support programs that helped the needy. Many leaders in business, though, attacked FDR and the New Deal because they opposed increasing taxes to pay for expanding government programs.

Roosevelt's position as the front-runner in the 1936 presidential election was never really challenged, however. The Democratic Party consisted of a broad coalition, or alliance, of diverse voters, including African Americans, women, union workers, intellectuals, and southern Democrats.

The Republican Party nominated Kansas governor Alf Landon as its candidate. Landon campaigned against Roosevelt by attacking the New Deal for wasting money and by accusing the president of exercising more executive power than the Constitution allowed.

The 1936 election showed that the majority of voters approved of the president's leadership and activism. As in 1932, Roosevelt won easily; in fact, Landon got only eight electoral votes.

HISTORICAL THINKING

1. **READING CHECK** How did the Social Security Act of 1935 affect Americans' lives, and how was it funded?

2. **FORM AND SUPPORT OPINIONS** You've read the opinions of opponents and supporters of the Social Security Act. What is your opinion of the act? Give reasons for your opinion.

3. **MAKE CONNECTIONS** How do you think Americans today would respond to fireside chats given by their president?

2.5 The Second New Deal

Sometimes, instead of fighting your critics, it's smart to follow their direction. Some critics thought the New Deal didn't go far enough, so Roosevelt reached farther.

MAIN IDEA Roosevelt expanded the New Deal by introducing additional programs as he contended with the Supreme Court over his legislation.

NEW PROGRAMS

By the mid-1930s, the U.S. economy had begun to recover, but many Americans were still out of work. To boost employment and help those still in need, Roosevelt initiated a second wave of relief legislation, which formed the **Second New Deal**. The Social Security Act of 1935 was a major component of the Second New Deal. The chart on this page summarizes the Social Security Act and other key components of this new progressive legislation.

In the same year that he signed the Social Security Act, the president launched the **Works Progress Administration (WPA)**, which became one of the most famous and far-reaching pieces of New Deal legislation. During its eight-year run, the WPA employed workers who completed thousands of construction projects throughout the nation. These projects included 950 airports, 651,000 miles of highways, 124,000 bridges, 18,000 playgrounds and athletic fields, and 125,000 public buildings.

In addition to hiring workers for construction projects, the WPA also provided jobs to unemployed artists and writers through the Federal Art Project (FAP) and the Federal Writers' Project (FWP). The FAP employed as many as 10,000 artists over the course of 8 years. Artists in the FAP created nearly 2,600 murals and 18,000 sculptures, many of which still adorn public buildings throughout the nation today. FWP writers produced such works as regional guidebooks and folklore studies. Some great American authors worked for the FWP, including Richard Wright and Saul Bellow.

EXPANDING THE SUPREME COURT

Some of Roosevelt's critics believed the president had overstepped his executive power in establishing the New Deal. These critics took their complaints to the courts. In 1935, the Supreme Court declared the law that created the **National Recovery Administration (NRA)** unconstitutional, ruling that lawmaking powers assigned to the NRA belonged to Congress. The Court also ruled the Agricultural Adjustment Act (AAA) to be unconstitutional because it infringed on the regulatory authority of the state governments. These decisions angered Roosevelt and led him to make one of the biggest mistakes of his presidency.

Roosevelt worried that conservative justices on the Supreme Court might strike down other New Deal legislation,

Key Programs of the Second New Deal	
Program	Description
Social Security Act	Provided income to elderly, unemployment insurance, and aid to the disabled and needy
Works Progress Administration (WPA)	Provided construction jobs and funded projects that employed artists, photographers, writers, and musicians
Wagner Act	Established the right of employees to form and join labor unions and to bargain collectively with employers
National Labor Relations Board (NLRB)	Created to resolve disputes between labor and management
National Youth Administration (NYA)	Provided educational grants, job training, and jobs to young Americans
Rural Electrification Administration	Expanded electrical service to rural homes

such as the Social Security Act. He felt such action would endanger his agenda and the country's recovery. But his plan to protect the New Deal from court interference met with opposition from his friends and enemies alike.

In February 1937, FDR announced a plan to reorganize the federal court system. The plan would allow up to six additional justices on the Supreme Court. Critics viewed the plan as an attempt by Roosevelt to fill the Supreme Court with his allies.

Even Roosevelt's supporters felt this scheme would weaken the judicial branch of government. Hiram Johnson, a progressive Republican and New Deal supporter, summed up the beliefs of many: "Down that road lies dictatorship." Roosevelt's **court-packing plan** failed. It turned out to be unnecessary anyway, because the Court did not oppose any other New Deal legislation.

HISTORICAL THINKING

1. **READING CHECK** Why did Roosevelt introduce his court-packing plan in 1937?

2. **INTERPRET CHARTS** Review the two charts in this chapter, which summarize New Deal programs and Second New Deal programs. How did the Second New Deal expand on the original New Deal?

3. **MAKE CONNECTIONS** What products of the WPA do Americans still enjoy today?

The New Deal's Effects on Women and Minorities

Eleanor Roosevelt was an outspoken and assertive woman at a time when women were expected to take a back seat to men. She asserted the right of women—and minorities—to take a front seat.

MAIN IDEA Women and minorities benefited from the New Deal but not as much as white men did.

WOMEN AND THE NEW DEAL

As you have read, Eleanor Roosevelt championed equal rights for women, and she strongly influenced her husband's policies. At her urging, women were appointed to important positions in the federal government for the first time.

Frances Perkins, a New York labor rights activist, became the first woman in American history to serve as a cabinet secretary after President Roosevelt appointed her as secretary of labor. She helped develop the Civilian Conservation Corps, the Federal Emergency Relief Administration, the Social Security Act, and the Fair Labor Standards Act. Roosevelt implemented so many of Perkins's ideas in his New Deal programs that she was later called "the architect of the New Deal." **Ellen Woodward**, a Mississippi legislator, served as director of the Women's Division of FERA. She greatly improved FERA's formerly dismal record in finding jobs for women. She also served in the WPA and on the Social Security Board.

Although women played important roles in Roosevelt's administration, the New Deal programs mostly focused on helping men find jobs. In 1938, for example, women held only 13.5 percent of the jobs in the Works Progress Administration (WPA), and they were often placed in lower-paying jobs.

In 1935, Frances Perkins (center), U.S. secretary of labor, toured the construction site of the Golden Gate Bridge in San Francisco, California. Perkins strongly promoted workplace safety and workers' rights.

MINORITIES AND THE NEW DEAL

African Americans also played more significant roles in the Roosevelt administration than they had in any previous one. FDR gathered a group of esteemed African-American leaders, known informally as the "black cabinet," to advise him on minority issues. The chair of the black cabinet was **Mary McLeod Bethune**, the founder of Bethune-Cookman College in Florida and a friend of Eleanor Roosevelt's. In 1936, FDR put her in charge of African-American affairs for the National Youth Administration. The black cabinet also included Dr. Robert Weaver, a Harvard-educated economist, and William Hastie, who became the first African-American federal judge in 1937.

The Great Depression hit African Americans especially hard. By 1932, the unemployment rate of African Americans in cities had climbed to nearly 50 percent. The WPA employed about 350,000 African-American workers per year, and the National Youth Administration helped to educate and employ more than 300,000 young African Americans.

Although many African Americans were employed through the New Deal, the Roosevelt administration failed to support important civil rights legislation. For decades, African Americans in the South had lived under the threat of lynching. In 1935, the NAACP pushed Congress to pass federal anti-lynching legislation. Roosevelt declined to back the bill, fearing he would lose the crucial support of white southern Democrats for New Deal legislation.

Mexican Americans and Mexican immigrants confronted a different threat during the Great Depression. Many Mexican immigrants had arrived in the United States during the 1920s. Most came to work on farms. They faced competition from white workers, including Dust Bowl migrants, during the Great Depression. In 1929, the federal government began a repatriation program, which deported hundreds of thousands of people of Mexican descent, including American citizens. **Repatriation** is the act of sending immigrants back to their home countries.

CRITICAL VIEWING During the 1940s, noted African-American photographer Gordon Parks took this photo of students attending a popular radio technology class at Bethune-Cookman College. What details are emphasized by the angle from which this photograph was taken?

Native Americans benefited from the appointment of John Collier, a social worker, as commissioner of Indian affairs in 1933. Collier pushed Congress to pass the **Indian Reorganization Act (IRA)** of 1934, which reduced federal control of Native American affairs and promoted self-government. The act helped Native Americans regain control of their communities, improve their schools and health services, and buy millions of acres of land for tribal use.

HISTORICAL THINKING

1. **READING CHECK** In what ways did the Roosevelt administration both help and fail women and minorities?

2. **EVALUATE** What is your assessment of President Roosevelt's reason for not supporting anti-lynching legislation?

3. **MAKE INFERENCES** Why do you think the Great Depression was especially devastating for minorities, such as African Americans and Mexican Americans?

3.2 Legacy of the New Deal

A historian called it "the only light in the darkness." A political writer described it as "one of the greatest acts of wreckage in world history." Both people were describing the New Deal.

MAIN IDEA The New Deal affected American government and society in ways that are still evident today.

EXPANDING GOVERNMENT

By the end of the 1930s, the New Deal had lost support in Congress, and most of the programs came to an end due to a lack of funding. The New Deal was not a complete success; it had not restored the country to the prosperity of the 1920s. However, the New Deal had provided hope and relief to millions of Americans when they desperately needed it. It restored the public's confidence in the nation's future.

Grand Coulee Dam in Washington State was a federal relief project of the New Deal. It was designed to benefit the country in the long term as well as to help people recover from the Depression in the short term. The dam provides hydroelectric power, irrigation, and flood control and generates enough hydroelectric power to supply two cities the size of Seattle.

The New Deal also changed the nature of the federal government by expanding its power and size. The president developed legislation that Congress simply approved. The federal government became more involved in the economy by creating jobs; supporting agriculture; and regulating banking, investment, and business activities. The administration of New Deal programs required a much larger executive staff, which resulted in the hiring of many additional federal employees. Besides concentrating power in the executive branch, the New Deal made the federal government far more of a presence in the daily lives and business of Americans.

LASTING IMPACT

A number of New Deal programs continue to play a significant role in American life, though they have undergone changes over the years. For example,

most Americans count on Social Security payments for at least partial financial support after retirement. Social Security also provides benefits to disabled Americans who are unable to work, to children who have lost a parent, and to husbands or wives who have lost their spouses. The federal government continues to provide farmers with price supports for crops.

Several New Deal regulatory agencies continue to operate today. The National Labor Relations Board, created by the Wagner Act, still regulates relations between unions and employers. The Federal Deposit Insurance Corporation (FDIC) guarantees bank deposits against loss. The Securities and Exchange Commission (SEC), created in 1934, still protects investors from illegal and deceptive practices.

Every day, Americans use roads, bridges, airports, and other infrastructure originally built by New Deal workers. They hike park trails and view artwork created by New Deal employees.

To this day, Americans disagree on whether the changes brought about by the New Deal have been positive or negative. As they did in the 1930s, conservatives generally object to the increased size and power of the federal government. They also oppose **deficit spending**, or spending more money than the government receives from taxes. Liberals generally believe the government should take more responsibility for citizens' welfare, business regulation, and environmental protection. The gap between the two points of view has not lessened. Rather, it has widened in recent years.

HISTORICAL THINKING

1. **READING CHECK** How did FDR's presidency affect the power and size of the executive branch of government?

2. **IDENTIFY MAIN IDEAS AND DETAILS** What were some successes and failures of the New Deal?

3. **FORM AND SUPPORT OPINIONS** How involved do you think the federal government should be in helping citizens, regulating business, and protecting the environment? Give reasons for your opinion.

VOCABULARY

Match the following vocabulary terms with their definitions.

1. supply and demand
2. consumer debt
3. bank run
4. speculate
5. pension fund
6. bank holiday
7. buying on margin
8. repatriation

a. a situation in which a large number of depositors withdraw their money from a bank because they fear the bank will close

b. buying stock for a small percentage of its price and borrowing to pay the rest

c. to buy and sell stocks in the hope of making a quick profit

d. a pool of money used to pay retirees a certain income

e. the act of sending immigrants back to their home country

f. a day or period of time during which banks are closed by law

g. the amount of a good or service that is available compared to the amount that people want to buy

h. the amount of money that people have borrowed to purchase goods

READING STRATEGY
IDENTIFY MAIN IDEAS AND DETAILS

If you haven't done so already, complete your graphic organizer by recording details that support the identified main idea. Then answer the question below.

9. How did President Roosevelt's New Deal help unemployed people?

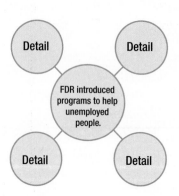

MAIN IDEAS

Answer the following questions. Support your answers with evidence from the chapter.

10. What difficulties did American farmers encounter after World War I? **LESSON 1.1**

11. What happened to the stock market on Black Tuesday? **LESSON 1.2**

12. How did many business owners respond to the economic troubles at the beginning of the Great Depression? **LESSON 1.3**

13. What did Franklin Roosevelt promise voters in his 1932 campaign for president? **LESSON 2.1**

14. How long did it take FDR to push his first 15 New Deal laws through Congress? **LESSON 2.2**

15. Why did many farmers leave the Dust Bowl region and migrate westward? **LESSON 2.3**

16. What was the purpose of the Social Security Act? **LESSON 2.4**

17. Why did FDR try to increase the number of justices on the Supreme Court? **LESSON 2.5**

18. Who was Frances Perkins, and what was her role in the New Deal? **LESSON 3.1**

19. How did FDR change the office of the presidency? **LESSON 3.2**

Answer the following questions. Support your answers with evidence from the chapter.

20. **COMPARE AND CONTRAST** How did Herbert Hoover and Franklin Roosevelt differ in their ideas for dealing with the Great Depression?

21. **ANALYZE CAUSE AND EFFECT** Summarize the causes and effects of the Dust Bowl.

22. **SYNTHESIZE** How was the Roosevelt administration more inclusive—that is, open to everyone—than previous presidential administrations?

23. **FORM AND SUPPORT OPINIONS** What do you think is the most important legacy of the New Deal, and why?

INTERPRET VISUALS

This graph shows the unemployment rate from the early years of the Depression through the partial recovery achieved by 1940. Study the graph and answer the questions that follow.

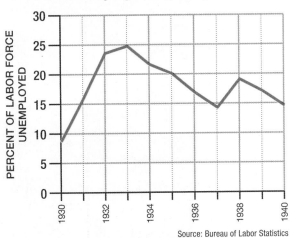

U.S. Unemployment Rate, 1930–1940

Source: Bureau of Labor Statistics

24. During which years was the unemployment rate higher than 20 percent?

25. In which year was the unemployment rate highest, and how high was it?

26. About what percentage of the labor force was unemployed in 1937?

ANALYZE SOURCES

In a fireside chat on September 30, 1934, President Roosevelt responded to opponents' criticisms of the New Deal.

> To those people who say that our expenditures [costs] for public works and for other means for recovery are a waste that we cannot afford, I answer that no country, however rich, can afford the waste of its human resources. Demoralization [discouragement] caused by vast unemployment is our greatest extravagance. Morally, it is the greatest menace to our social order.

27. What effects of unemployment does the president focus on in this passage?

CONNECT TO YOUR LIFE

28. **EXPLANATORY** The Great Depression was one of the most difficult domestic struggles Americans faced in the 20th century. The government programs designed to help people were controversial. Some thought they didn't do enough, and others thought of them as "handouts" that threatened American identity. Yet some of those programs still exist and affect the lives of many Americans. Choose a New Deal program, agency, or project that exists now and write a paragraph explaining how it is important today in the lives of people you know.

TIPS

- Review the lesson on the New Deal's legacy and research the subject. Identify a New Deal program, project, or agency you think is significant in the lives of people you know.

- In a topic sentence, clearly state why the program, project, or agency matters to people you know.

- Provide supporting details that further explain the effects on people today.

- Write a concluding sentence that sums up your thoughts.

CHAPTER 24

WORLD WAR II

1931–1945

ESSENTIAL QUESTION
How did World War II impact Americans?

 Japanese Internment

SECTION 1 Steps to War
KEY VOCABULARY

Allied Powers	chancellor	Munich Agreement
appeasement	dictator	Nazi Party
Atlantic Charter	fascism	Rome-Berlin Axis
Axis Powers	ideology	prisoner of war
blitzkrieg	isolationism	puppet government

SECTION 2 Americans at War
KEY VOCABULARY

barracks	executive order	munition
battalion	internment camp	ration
deploy		

SECTION 3 War in Africa and Europe
KEY VOCABULARY

amphibious landing craft	D-Day	ghetto
anti-Semitism	death camp	Holocaust
concentration camp	exposure	panzer
crematorium	genocide	partition

SECTION 4 Victory in Asia
KEY VOCABULARY

atoll	island hopping	Marshall Plan
atomic bomb	kamikaze pilot	nuclear fission
incendiary bomb	Manhattan Project	

AMERICAN GALLERY
ONLINE **The Holocaust**

READING STRATEGY

ANALYZE CAUSE AND EFFECT
When you analyze cause and effect, you note the consequences of an event, an action, or a condition. As you read the chapter, use a graphic organizer like this one to identify the causes and effects of the United States becoming an Allied Power during World War II.

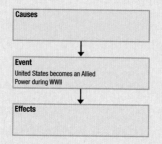

Causes

Event
United States becomes an Allied
Power during WWII

Effects

"They fight not for the lust of conquest.
They fight to end conquest.
They fight to liberate."
—President Franklin D. Roosevelt

CRITICAL VIEWING U.S. soldiers plunge into the
English Channel from their small barge and head to a
Normandy beach on D-Day, June 6, 1944. What do you
think the soldiers felt as they waded toward the shore?

1.1 New Dictators Arise

During times of trouble, governments often question whether their priority should be protecting citizens' freedoms or making the nation secure. Historically, security usually wins the debate. That is what happened in Europe in the 1930s.

MAIN IDEA In the 1930s, dictators and military leaders rose to power in Italy, Germany, the Soviet Union, and Japan.

At a 1933 rally in Erfurt, Germany, members of Nazi youth organizations, including Hitler Youth, salute dictator Adolf Hitler. Hitler Youth was formed in 1926 to teach young people Nazi ideas.

DICTATORS COME TO POWER

During the Great Depression, Americans focused on their own hardships, but in Europe and Asia, economic turmoil was making countries vulnerable to the rise of **dictators**. A dictator is an absolute ruler, not subject to controls within his or her government. Dictatorships would lead to an international catastrophe that has continued to affect world politics to this day.

As you know, World War I ended with the defeat of the Central Powers. The Treaty of Versailles forced Germany to accept blame for the war, give up large amounts of territory, and pay billions of dollars in reparations to the Allies. Austria-Hungary signed a similarly harsh treaty. The treaties bankrupted these nations. The Central Powers felt their punishments were unfair.

Italy and Japan had sided with the Allies and faced disappointments following the victory. Italy did not receive the territory it had been promised in return for supporting the Allies. Both countries suffered from the post-war economic turmoil that occurred worldwide. In Italy, widespread strikes and fighting split political parties. Political power in Japan began to shift to the military.

The Great Depression came as an additional blow. Across Europe, unemployment rose, and food prices skyrocketed. People grew angry, blaming their governments for these problems. The growing civil unrest and lack of strong democratic conditions gave cunning politicians an opportunity to seize power.

In Italy, a war veteran named **Benito Mussolini** used economic and social discontent to take control of the government, eventually banning all political parties but his own. Mussolini declared himself dictator in 1925. Meanwhile, the emperor of Japan, **Hirohito**, was allowing military leaders to take over the government. In Germany, a young politician named **Adolf Hitler** promised to restore the country to its pre-war greatness. In 1933, Hitler was appointed **chancellor**, a leader whose role is similar to that of a U.S. president. Soon Hitler was a dictator as well. In the Soviet Union, a high-ranking politician named **Joseph Stalin** secretly began to appoint his friends to key government positions beginning in 1922. By 1924, Stalin was dictator of the Soviet Union.

TENSIONS RISE IN EUROPE

Both Mussolini and Hitler practiced **fascism**, a political system that depends on nationalism, militarism, and racism to control a nation's population. Hitler's **ideology**, or set of beliefs, included the idea that the world was divided into superior and inferior races. With the help of his political party, the **Nazi Party**, Hitler began to blame members of ethnic groups and religions he deemed inferior, specifically Jewish people, for Germany's problems. The Nazis won public support by using propaganda, including posters and films that promoted the party's ideas for fixing the country.

Both Mussolini and Hitler desired conquest. On March 7, 1936, Hitler sent 22,000 German troops into the Rhineland, an area in western Germany that the Treaty of Versailles had placed under Allied control. The treaty stated that Germany could not keep military forces in the Rhineland, but neither Great Britain nor France took action. The invasion marked the beginning of Hitler's aggressive strategy in Europe.

Similarly, Mussolini sought to conquer more land for Italy, hoping to restore the glory of the ancient Roman Empire. On May 9, 1936, Italian forces took over the African nation of Abyssinia (now Ethiopia). Sharing a common goal, Hitler and Mussolini signed a pact of friendship in October 1936 known as the **Rome-Berlin Axis**, the alliance that established the two countries as the **Axis Powers**. The nations that would eventually band together to fight the Axis would once again be known as the **Allied Powers**.

HISTORICAL THINKING

1. **READING CHECK** What factors allowed dictators to take power in Europe?

2. **COMPARE AND CONTRAST** How were German, Italian, and Japanese objections over the treaties ending World War I similar, and how were they different?

3. **ASK AND ANSWER QUESTIONS** What questions do you have about the European dictators mentioned in this lesson, and where can you find the answers?

1.2 Germany on the Attack

It is never easy dealing with bullies. Do you ignore them or confront them? In the 1930s, many European countries and the United States had to decide how to deal with Adolf Hitler, whom they considered a mere bully at first. But Hitler was on his way to setting a new standard for brutal tyranny.

MAIN IDEA Hitler's capture of areas that were previously part of Germany led to the start of World War II.

Hitler's Advance, 1938–1940

Legend:
- Allied territory
- Axis powers
- Axis satellite
- Axis-controlled by 1940
- Soviet territory
- Neutral nation
- German troop movements

HITLER STAYS ON THE ATTACK

Encouraged by his military success in the Rhineland, Adolf Hitler decided to unite all German-speaking countries under his authority. He tried to bully the Austrian president into appointing Nazis to government positions. When that plan failed, Hitler ordered German troops to invade Austria on March 12, 1938. The Austrian government quickly accepted Hitler's demands.

Austria became a part of Germany that same day without any shots being fired.

Sudetenland (soo-DAY-tuhn-land), the name for a region in Czechoslovakia where many Germans lived, was next. In May 1938, Hitler ordered German troops into position along the Czechoslovakian border. His aim was to intimidate the Czech government into surrendering the region.

In response, the Czechs sent their troops to meet the German army. A fear of war spread throughout Europe.

As tensions rose in Europe, the United States enacted isolationism, a policy of staying out of the disputes of foreign nations. The country passed laws called Neutrality Acts, which banned the United States from making loans with or transporting goods to hostile countries in an effort to avoid war.

In September 1938, British Prime Minister Neville Chamberlain and French Premier Édouard Daladier (EHD-wahr duh-lah-dee-AY) flew to Munich, Germany, to compromise with Hitler. The meeting resulted in the Munich Agreement, which gave Sudetenland to Germany in return for Hitler's promise to stop invading countries. Chamberlain and Daladier's decision to sign the agreement was an act of appeasement, or a policy of agreeing to demands of a powerful opponent in order to avoid conflict. The Allies continued to appease Hitler to avoid another war. The men did not expect Hitler to break his promise.

In August 1939, the world was shocked to learn that sworn enemies Nazi Germany and the Soviet Union had signed an agreement. Under the German-Soviet Nonaggression Pact, the two countries vowed to take no military action against each other for 10 years. A secret part of the pact set the stage for a joint invasion of Poland by both countries, which occurred the following month.

EUROPE AT WAR AGAIN

The pact allowed Hitler to attack other countries without fear of retaliation from the Soviet Union. On September 1, 1939, he sent the German army, called the Wehrmacht (VAIR-mahkt), into Poland, where his troops introduced a new type of warfare, blitzkrieg (BLIHTS-kreeg) or "lightning war." This strategy involved bombarding important targets from the air and taking out railroads, landing strips, and communication lines before sending in a massive land invasion. The speed of these assaults confused enemy armies and allowed the Germans to launch more surprise attacks. As planned, Stalin's army invaded Poland

Winston Churchill addresses sailors in London in 1940, shortly before becoming Prime Minister. The sailors had just survived the destruction of their ship by German warships in Norway.

in October. The two countries quickly conquered and divided Poland. This violation of the Treaty of Versailles forced Britain and France to declare war on Germany, and World War II began.

In April 1940, the Wehrmacht blitzkrieg overran Denmark and Norway. Next it attacked Belgium, Holland, and Luxembourg. As a new British prime minister named Winston Churchill took office in May, the Wehrmacht invaded France. Hitler's army trapped British and French forces in the French port of Dunkirk, on the English Channel. The British were able to evacuate thousands of troops by sea while the Wehrmacht turned toward Paris. The French capital fell on June 14, 1940, and France surrendered on June 17. The terms of the surrender divided France. Only an area in southeastern France known as Vichy (VISH-ee) was left unoccupied by German troops. A free government was established there, but it quickly fell under Nazi influence. Britain now stood alone.

HISTORICAL THINKING

1. **READING CHECK** How did Great Britain become the only major Allied Power left to fight against the Axis?

2. **DETERMINE CHRONOLOGY** What German and Soviet actions led to the start of World War II?

3. **INTERPRET MAPS** On which continents had the Axis conquered countries by 1940?

1.3 Hitler Attacks West and East

As the war continued, the United States found it increasingly difficult to remain neutral. Dozens of American merchant ships delivering cargo around the world were detained or sunk by both the Allies and the Axis.

MAIN IDEA Major German campaigns against Great Britain and the Soviet Union ended Hitler's string of victories.

THE BATTLE OF BRITAIN

On June 18, the day after France fell to the Nazis, Winston Churchill declared, "The Battle of France is over. The **Battle of Britain** is about to begin." Great Britain was the only Allied country left to fight Nazi Germany. The British people prepared for an invasion. The Battle of Britain mostly took place in the air. Between June and September 1940, the Luftwaffe (LOOFT-vahf-uh)—the German air force—and Britain's Royal Air Force (RAF) battled in the skies over Great Britain. Sticking to the blitzkrieg strategy, the Germans bombed strategic British cities relentlessly. Their goal was to force Britain's surrender.

British civilians suffered greatly. Hoping to keep their children safe, urban parents sent them to stay in homes in the countryside. Many children never saw their parents again. Whole neighborhoods in

CRITICAL VIEWING Stations along London's Underground, or subway system, provided shelter for many British citizens during the German bombing raids of 1940. What does the photo convey about life for Londoners during the war?

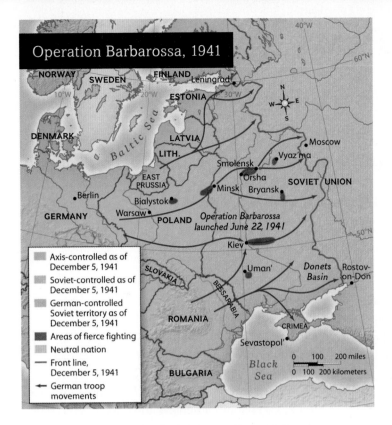

Operation Barbarossa, 1941

Map legend:
- Axis-controlled as of December 5, 1941
- Soviet-controlled as of December 5, 1941
- German-controlled Soviet territory as of December 5, 1941
- Areas of fierce fighting
- Neutral nation
- Front line, December 5, 1941
- German troop movements

Map labels: NORWAY, SWEDEN, FINLAND, Leningrad, ESTONIA, DENMARK, LATVIA, LITH., Moscow, Baltic Sea, EAST PRUSSIA, Smolensk, Vyaz'ma, Berlin, Orsha, Minsk, Bryansk, SOVIET UNION, Bialystok, Warsaw, POLAND, *Operation Barbarossa launched June 22, 1941*, GERMANY, Kiev, SLOVAKIA, Uman', Donets Basin, Rostov-on-Don, BESSARABIA, ROMANIA, CRIMEA, Sevastopol', Black Sea, BULGARIA

0 100 200 miles
0 100 200 kilometers

London and other cities were destroyed. Residents took cover in underground bunkers, bomb shelters, and subway stations. One of the deadlier attacks killed 1,500 Londoners in one night.

The Germans had conquered most of western Europe in fewer than two months, but they were no match for the RAF. The Royal Air Force drove the Luftwaffe into retreat before Nazi land troops could arrive. Hitler decided to turn his attention to the Soviet Union.

OPERATION BARBAROSSA

On June 21, 1941, in violation of his nonaggression pact with Stalin, Hitler ordered more than 3 million German soldiers, 3,000 tanks, and 2,500 airplanes to attack the Soviet Union. It was the largest invasion the world had ever seen. Hitler named it **Operation Barbarossa** after a medieval emperor of German-speaking people who also conquered countries in Europe. Hitler did not trust Stalin and wanted to take the Soviet Union out of the picture. He also wanted to secure oil supplies in Romania.

The Germans started off strong. The Wehrmacht captured more than 1 million **prisoners of war**, or soldiers captured by an enemy force, as they invaded the Soviet Union. But the Germans miscalculated three key factors: the number of Soviet soldiers, the weather, and the unity of

the Allies. The Soviets quickly raised approximately 200,000 more soldiers to join the fight. The Germans found themselves unprepared for the bitterly cold Soviet winters. The Soviets, however, were well clad and trained for battle in extremely cold conditions. As the war raged on, Soviet supplies dwindled, but help was on the way.

In response to Germany's aggression, President Roosevelt pushed Congress to pass the **Lend-Lease Act** in 1941. The legislation authorized the United States to sell, lease, or lend military equipment to any country whose defense was vital to American security. The act boosted Great Britain and other allies efforts to defeat Germany. Many Americans had no desire to engage in another foreign war. They believed fighting in World War I was a mistake that should not be repeated. But Roosevelt believed Hitler must be stopped at any cost. Therefore, the United States helped arm the Soviets.

Even though the United States had not entered the war, President Roosevelt and Winston Churchill met to outline their goals for defeating Hitler. The document that resulted was called the **Atlantic Charter**. In it, they agreed not to wage any war to expand their territories and committed to help improve living conditions worldwide. They encouraged other countries to do the same. By late 1941, 26 nations had agreed to these terms. Meanwhile, Operation Barbarossa began to fail as the Soviet Union held off the German advance.

HISTORICAL THINKING

1. **READING CHECK** Why did Germany end its effort to conquer Great Britain?

2. **MAKE INFERENCES** Think about the wars Americans had fought in the past. Why do you think many Americans had no desire to engage in a war in Europe?

3. **INTERPRET MAPS** Why do you think the routes that German troops took toward Moscow and Leningrad diverge, or split?

1.4 Attack on Pearl Harbor

Focused on the war in Europe, Americans were shocked by an early morning bombing of their homeland. Everyone was in disbelief and felt fear on December 7, 1941.

MAIN IDEA Japan's sudden attack on the U.S. Pacific fleet at Pearl Harbor, Hawaii, brought the United States into World War II.

JAPAN ON THE ATTACK

Like Germany, Japan looked beyond its borders for ways to improve its economy in the 1930s. The Chinese region of **Manchuria** was rich in resources, including oil, rubber, and lumber. Controlling this region could boost Japan's resource-hungry industries and expand the market for Japanese goods. On September 18, 1931, Japanese armed forces invaded Manchuria and installed a **puppet government**, or a set of political leaders who would follow Japan's orders. The Japanese moved into China itself and captured Beijing, Shanghai, and Nanjing. By 1937, the situation had developed into an all-out war.

In 1940, Japan announced a plan to conquer Southeast Asia and the Western Pacific by overpowering the European colonies there. Realizing their common goals of expansion, Japanese leaders met with German and Italian officials on September 27, 1940. The three countries signed the **Tripartite Pact**, an agreement to help one another achieve their goals. With the signature of its representative, Japan became part of the Axis.

By April 1941, Japan had invaded and occupied French Indochina (now Vietnam, Laos, and Cambodia). This aggression finally persuaded President Roosevelt to act. He banned the sale of

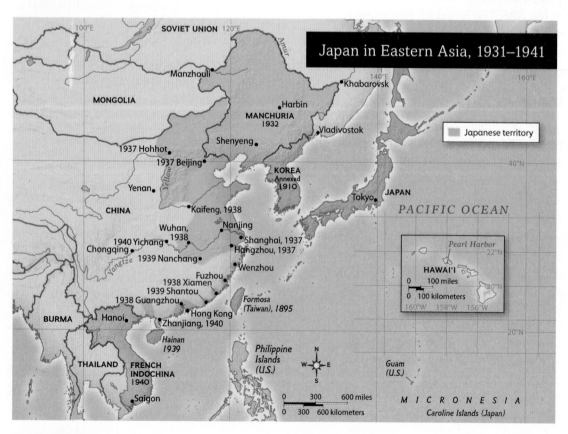

Japan in Eastern Asia, 1931–1941

U.S.S. *Arizona* Memorial, Honolulu, Hawaii

Built crosswise over the sunken remains of the U.S.S. *Arizona*, the museum provides portals from which visitors can view the ship. The *Arizona* is the resting place of most of the 1,177 sailors killed during the Pearl Harbor attack.

scrap metal and halted U.S. oil exports to Japan. He increased the size of the U.S. Navy, and moved the Navy's Pacific fleet from San Diego to **Pearl Harbor**, in Hawaii, hoping to deter Japan from moving against other nations in the region.

TARGET: PEARL HARBOR

In 1941, **Hideki Tojo** (hee-DAY-kee TOH-joh) became Prime Minister of Japan. He was an army officer who had risen through the military and political ranks. Tojo and U.S. officials tried to solve their differences diplomatically, but neither side would budge. After several months, peaceful efforts failed. Tojo was ready to act.

American politicians believed a war with Japan was likely, but they did not believe Japan would dare to attack the United States. Japan and Hawaii are separated by 4,000 miles of open ocean, and Hawaii is more than 2,000 miles from the American mainland. The distance alone made staging any attack very difficult. But the Japanese wanted to annihilate, or utterly destroy, the U.S. Pacific fleet before it could be used against them. Japan moved a fleet of aircraft carriers toward Hawaii under strict radio silence, meaning they were not to communicate with each other while steaming toward their target. Detectable radio signals could give away a ship's location.

On Sunday morning, December 7, 1941, Japanese warplanes headed for Pearl Harbor to bomb the U.S. naval base there. The battleships U.S.S. *Oklahoma* and U.S.S. *Arizona* were hit before the sailors on board could respond, and both ships quickly sank. The *Arizona* went under with more than 1,000 men trapped below decks. The surprise attack destroyed 18 American ships and more than 180 airplanes. In a famous speech he gave on December 8, 1941, President Roosevelt referred to December 7 as "a date which will live in infamy," and asked Congress for a declaration of war against Japan. The request was granted. Bound by the Tripartite Pact, both Italy and Germany declared war on the United States on December 11. The United States was now involved in World War II as an Allied Power.

HISTORICAL THINKING

1. **READING CHECK** Why did Japan invade Manchuria?

2. **INTERPRET MAPS** Geographically, what was the military strategy of the Japanese in their efforts to occupy China?

3. **IDENTIFY MAIN IDEAS AND DETAILS** Why did Japan decide to attack Pearl Harbor?

1.5 National Air and Space Museum Washington, D.C.

III

Devoted to the subject of flight, the National Air and Space Museum features the world's largest collection of historic aircraft and spacecraft. Among its famous artifacts are the first plane to achieve flight and the first aircraft to carry a human to the moon.

More than 60,000 artifacts are housed in two separate locations. The museum on the National Mall in Washington, D.C., features an observatory and planetarium. A facility in Chantilly, Virginia, displays such artifacts as the space shuttle *Discovery*.

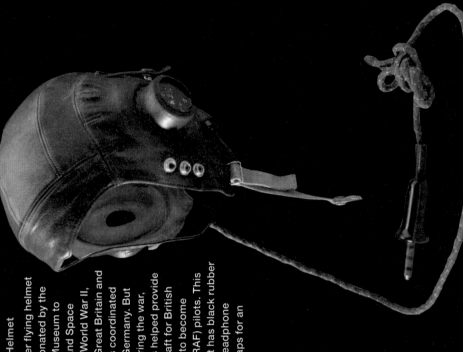

Royal Air Force Helmet

This brown leather flying helmet from 1941 was donated by the Royal Air Force Museum to the National Air and Space Museum. During World War II, the air forces of Great Britain and the United States coordinated their attacks on Germany. But even before entering the war, the United States helped provide training and aircraft for British soldiers learning to become Royal Air Force (RAF) pilots. This RAF flying helmet has black rubber receptacles for headphone receivers and snaps for an oxygen mask.

Aircraft Recognition Dial

During World War II, military personnel had to quickly distinguish between friendly and enemy aircraft. American soldiers studied pictorial manuals to help build their aircraft recognition skills. Some civilians in both the United States and Great Britain also received training in aircraft recognition to help spot enemy aircraft. This aircraft recognition dial from 1942 is a wheel chart that rotates to allow pictures of different aircraft to appear in the triangular window at the top. The blocks of text around the outer edge provide basic information about each type of aircraft.

Why do you think the military trained civilians to recognize enemy aircraft?

KNOW YOUR AIRPLANES

UNITED STATES ARMY FIGHTERS, LIGHT AND HEAVY BOMBERS, TRANSPORTS

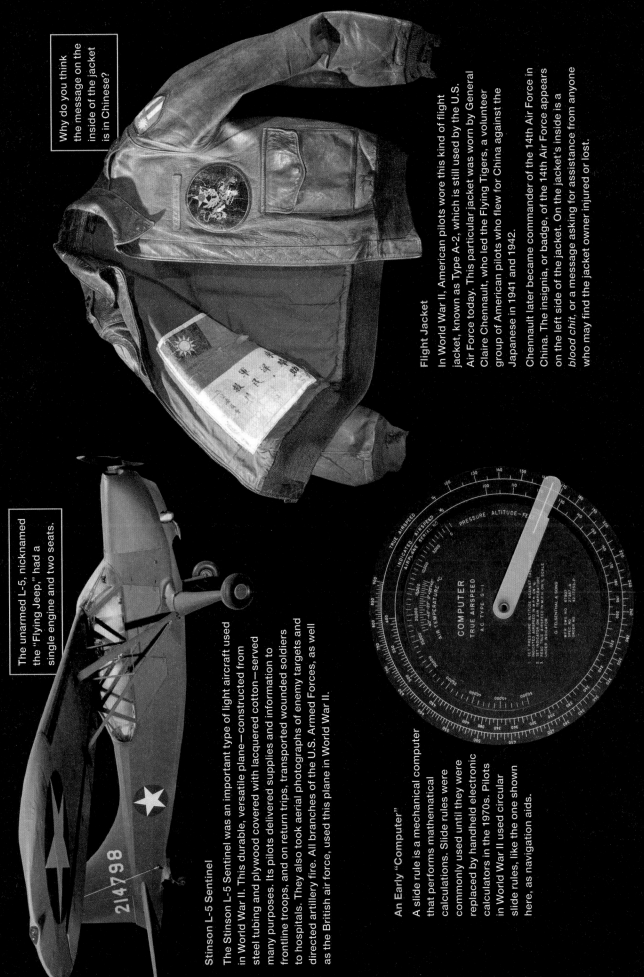

Why do you think the message on the inside of the jacket is in Chinese?

The unarmed L-5, nicknamed the "Flying Jeep," had a single engine and two seats.

Stinson L-5 Sentinel

The Stinson L-5 Sentinel was an important type of light aircraft used in World War II. This durable, versatile plane—constructed from steel tubing and plywood covered with lacquered cotton—served many purposes. Its pilots delivered supplies and information to frontline troops, and on return trips, transported wounded soldiers to hospitals. They also took aerial photographs of enemy targets and directed artillery fire. All branches of the U.S. Armed Forces, as well as the British air force, used this plane in World War II.

An Early "Computer"

A slide rule is a mechanical computer that performs mathematical calculations. Slide rules were commonly used until they were replaced by handheld electronic calculators in the 1970s. Pilots in World War II used circular slide rules, like the one shown here, as navigation aids.

Flight Jacket

In World War II, American pilots wore this kind of flight jacket, known as Type A-2, which is still used by the U.S. Air Force today. This particular jacket was worn by General Claire Chennault, who led the Flying Tigers, a volunteer group of American pilots who flew for China against the Japanese in 1941 and 1942.

Chennault later became commander of the 14th Air Force in China. The insignia, or badge, of the 14th Air Force appears on the left side of the jacket. On the jacket's inside is a *blood chit*, or a message asking for assistance from anyone who may find the jacket owner injured or lost.

2.1 Pulling Together

The Axis was a powerful enemy. After the surprise attack on Pearl Harbor, the United States knew it would require a unified, far-reaching effort to prepare quickly for war.

MAIN IDEA The United States built up its armed forces rapidly and found ways to get the entire country behind the war effort.

BUILDING AN ARMY AND A NAVY

In a presidential address in January 1942, Franklin Roosevelt said of the war, "Powerful enemies must be out-fought and out-produced." That was the goal the United States set as it moved into 1942 determined to defeat the Axis.

The first efforts involved rebuilding the U.S. Pacific fleet and boosting the U.S. military. Some of the ships that sank in the attack on Pearl Harbor were salvaged and repaired. They sailed again to fight the Axis. The government also built new ships and expanded shipyards on both coasts.

Army Chief of Staff General **George C. Marshall** led the mobilization effort, or the act of gathering and preparing troops for war. When he took the position in 1939, the United States had only

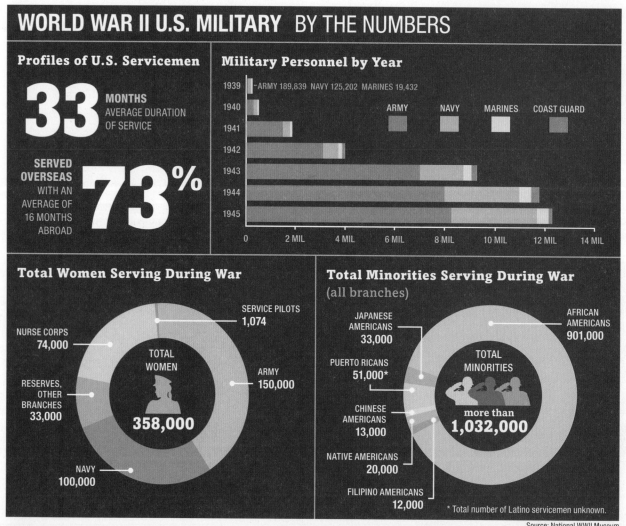

WORLD WAR II U.S. MILITARY BY THE NUMBERS

Profiles of U.S. Servicemen

33 MONTHS
AVERAGE DURATION OF SERVICE

SERVED OVERSEAS WITH AN AVERAGE OF 16 MONTHS ABROAD **73**%

Military Personnel by Year

1939 — ARMY 189,839 NAVY 125,202 MARINES 19,432
1940
1941
1942
1943
1944
1945

ARMY   NAVY   MARINES   COAST GUARD

0   2 MIL   4 MIL   6 MIL   8 MIL   10 MIL   12 MIL   14 MIL

Total Women Serving During War

NURSE CORPS 74,000
SERVICE PILOTS 1,074
RESERVES, OTHER BRANCHES 33,000
ARMY 150,000
NAVY 100,000

TOTAL WOMEN 358,000

Total Minorities Serving During War
(all branches)

JAPANESE AMERICANS 33,000
PUERTO RICANS 51,000*
CHINESE AMERICANS 13,000
NATIVE AMERICANS 20,000
FILIPINO AMERICANS 12,000
AFRICAN AMERICANS 901,000

TOTAL MINORITIES more than 1,032,000

* Total number of Latino servicemen unknown.

Source: National WWII Museum

around 180,000 soldiers serving to protect 130 million citizens. When war broke out in Europe, Marshall pushed the president to supply more men. In September 1940, President Roosevelt signed the Selective Service and Training Act into law, requiring men aged 21 to 35 to register for the draft. Once war was declared, many men did not wait to be drafted. Instead, the attack on Pearl Harbor inspired them to enlist on their own. Marshall also utilized the National Guard, smaller military units charged with defending their home states, for war duty. The number of soldiers in the army increased to more than 3 million by 1942. By 1945, the total number of men serving in all military branches was more than 12 million.

Roosevelt established the **War Production Board** in January 1942 to transform U.S. factories into producers of war supplies. Automobile manufacturers began to make airplanes, ships, tanks, and weapons. War supply factories expanded. As a result, employment grew, boosting the economy and pulling the United States out of the Great Depression.

EVERYONE JOINS THE WAR EFFORT

With the War Production Board creating so many new civilian jobs, African Americans, Latinos, and women entered the workforce as never before. They filled numerous defense jobs, joining together to help defeat the Axis and bring the troops home. The government continually reminded civilians of their important roles in assisting the troops overseas. One such reminder is shown in the poster at the right.

Knowing that war required numerous resources, the government realized American citizens would need to consume less food and fewer supplies. The War Production Board implemented **rationing**, or the controlled distribution of important foods and supplies, to reserve limited resources for the war effort. Though it caused some inconvenience, rationing such items as butter and gasoline allowed American civilians to help the war effort. Price limits set by the government ensured rationed items remained affordable for everyone. Americans also contributed by planting victory gardens, as they had done during World War I. Growing vegetables, fruits, and herbs at home prevented food shortages.

When you ride ALONE you ride with Hitler!

Join a Car-Sharing Club TODAY!

CRITICAL VIEWING One of the U.S. government's poster campaigns stressed the need to conserve resources at home so more would be available for the war effort. Why might this poster have been effective in reducing the amount of gasoline used by U.S. civilians?

Fighting a war is expensive. The United States spent about $300 billion in its efforts to stop Germany and Japan. That's more than $4 trillion in today's economy. To help raise the funds, the U.S. Treasury issued war bonds. People bought a bond for $18.75, for example, with the understanding that the government would pay them back $25 in 10 years. Some Americans bought war bonds of higher denominations. Children and people from lower incomes bought war stamps for a dime. After buying a certain number of stamps, they could trade them in for a war bond.

HISTORICAL THINKING

1. **READING CHECK** How did the United States prepare for war?

2. **ANALYZE GRAPHS** According to the graph, between which years did the number of military personnel grow the most?

3. **ANALYZE CAUSE AND EFFECT** What was the effect of the war on the U.S. economy?

2.2 Women in the War

When you feel strongly about a cause, you don't hesitate to volunteer your support. In desperate times, women answered the call and took on leadership roles at home and abroad to help win the war.

MAIN IDEA The roles and expectations of American women changed drastically during World War II.

WOMEN IN THE MILITARY

As the United States waged war, every citizen became involved. Women, especially, were needed to help keep the country war-ready. As was the case in every war in which the United States was engaged, many women joined the war effort as nurses, taking care of wounded soldiers. Early in the United States' involvement in the war, the government expanded official wartime opportunities for women.

In May 1942, Congress established the Women's Auxiliary Army Corps, later called the **Women's Army Corps (WAC)**. Volunteers who enlisted in the WACs program worked in more than 200 noncombat jobs in the United States and worldwide where U.S. soldiers were stationed.

In this 1945 photograph, WACs climb down nets in a simulation designed to mimic the escape from a damaged transport ship into lifeboats. As the war came to a close, women in non-combat military roles helped establish order in areas in Europe and the Pacific where life had been disrupted by war.

A female welder works on an escape hatch of the Bream (SS-243) submarine in a Connecticut shipyard. This photo was part of a 1943 *Life* magazine color photo essay that documented the building of submarines. Other photos featured women painting and tightening bolts.

March 10, 2010, about 200 WASPs were awarded the Congressional Gold Medal for their service in World War II.

WOMEN IN THE WORKFORCE

With so many men serving in the armed forces, who was left to keep up war production in U.S. factories? The answer was women. War industries actively sought female workers to build tanks, ships, guns, and airplanes. Before the war, it was rare to find women working in factories that made weapons. In 1943, more than 310,000 women worked in the U.S. aircraft industry alone, making up 65 percent of the aircraft industry's total workforce. Industries that produced **munitions**, or military weapons, also employed large numbers of female workers.

The government honored these women in its **"Rosie the Riveter"** campaign. Rosie was an illustrated character based on a metal presser named Geraldine Doyle. Rosie's image appeared on posters everywhere during the war. She became a symbol of the power of women war workers and inspired more women to join the war effort. Women responded in large numbers. The social impact of so many women entering the workforce was strong. Many women felt they had proven that they could do any job a man could do. When the war ended, many of them hoped a wider range of career options would still be available to them.

At first, they worked tracking aircraft, in clerical jobs, or as motor pool drivers. As the war continued, they learned to break enemy codes, operate and repair radios, rig parachutes, and maintain special equipment, among many other responsibilities. By the end of the war, more than 150,000 WACs had served in the military, and more than 6,000 of them had been promoted as officers.

The U.S. Navy, too, benefited from women volunteers. Members of **Women Accepted for Volunteer Emergency Service (WAVES)** supported worldwide Navy efforts from bases in the United States. In the U.S. Air Force, women pilots served in the **Women's Airforce Service Pilots (WASP)**. These women piloted planes to deliver cargo from factories to bases, which freed thousands of male pilots to fly planes into combat.

In all, about 350,000 women enlisted in the U.S. Armed Forces during World War II. Their contributions continue to be celebrated today. On

HISTORICAL THINKING

1. **READING CHECK** Why was there an increase in the number of women working in factories during the war?

2. **EVALUATE** What evidence in the text suggests that there were still limitations to women's roles in the military?

3. **IDENTIFY MAIN IDEAS AND DETAILS** What impact did World War II have on women's expectations in the U.S. workforce?

2.3 A Diverse War Effort

If you need help, you don't care about the race, gender, or ethnicity of the person who comes forward. American leaders found that to succeed during World War II, they had to include everyone in the effort.

MAIN IDEA African Americans, Asian Americans, Latinos, and Native Americans all played important roles in fighting World War II.

MINORITIES IN THE MILITARY

During World War II, many African Americans were conflicted about the war. They were eager to fight for democracy and freedom abroad, but they were too often denied equal rights at home. One African American named James Thompson expressed his feelings in a letter to the editor of the *Philadelphia Courier* newspaper in January 1942. He suggested that African Americans fight two battles at the same time. They could fight the Axis Powers abroad and fight for equality at home. Thompson called his idea the **Double V campaign**, as in "double victory."

In response, the editors of the newspaper had "Double V" lapel pins and stickers made to distribute to the African-American community.

The campaign took off, lifting the spirits of African Americans and encouraging them to enlist.

About 1.1 million African Americans served in separate units in all branches of the armed forces during World War II. The 92nd Infantry Division, an African-American army unit, **deployed**, or was sent, to Italy in August 1944 and captured more than 20,000 German prisoners there. The **Tuskegee Airmen** were one of the most famous World War II African-American units. Trained at Tuskegee Institute in Alabama, these 450 pilots were the first African Americans to fly missions for the Army Air Corps overseas. They defended larger bomber planes traveling to and from their missions. They lost 25 bombers during the war, far fewer bombers than other units in the air force.

The Tuskegee Airmen

In the photo at left from 1942, five Tuskegee airmen pose in front of their fighter planes at the training center in Alabama. A bronze replica of the Congressional Gold Medal is shown below. The medals were given to the soldiers at a White House ceremony in 2007 to honor their military contributions.

Asian Americans, Latinos, and Native Americans also made major contributions to the war. About 58,000 Japanese-, Chinese-, and Filipino-Americans fought for their country. Around 500,000 Mexican Americans and around 51,000 Puerto Ricans served. More precise numbers aren't known, because Latinos were counted as white people on enlistment papers.

Of the estimated 350,000 Native Americans living in the United States in 1941, as many as 44,000 saw military service during the war. Native American soldiers were involved in all areas of the conflict.

OPPORTUNITIES AT HOME

As it did for women, the war created numerous job opportunities for all minorities. More than 40,000 Native Americans left their reservations for the very first time to work in the defense industry. Many African Americans also migrated to northern cities and to California to find jobs in the defense industry. There, both groups faced discrimination. Some factories refused to hire Native Americans and African Americans, while others segregated the workers.

Witnessing this discrimination and segregation, some civil rights leaders decided to act. One activist, **A. Philip Randolph**, started planning a large march on Washington, D.C., for the summer of 1941, to protest discrimination in the workplace. Randolph put increased pressure on the government to address the issue, and it worked. President Roosevelt introduced an executive order that ended racial discrimination in the defense industry. He signed the bill on June 25, 1941, and Randolph canceled the protest.

Farms also needed more workers. Congress passed the **Bracero Program**, a plan for replacing farmers who had left to fight in the war. The word braceros means "strong armed ones" in Spanish. It included a series of agreements that opened the U.S. border to Mexican farm and transportation workers. Forty thousand workers came from Mexico to the United States in 1942. The program continued until 1964.

The Navajo Code Talkers

U.S. forces in the Asia-Pacific region sent and received messages in the Navajo language. In this 1943 photo, U.S. Marine Preston Toledo (above) dictates a message while his cousin and fellow Marine Frank Toledo writes down a message he is receiving. The cousins were Navajos. The Japanese had broken all the codes used by the American military, but in 1942, the Marine Corps began using an unbreakable code based on the Navajo language.

Navajo was a difficult language to learn, and the Japanese had no knowledge of its existence. The U.S. Marines enlisted 29 Navajo soldiers, who came to be known as "Code Talkers," to transmit messages in their language. By the end of the war, more than 375 Navajo soldiers had served their country as Code Talkers. The Japanese never broke this code.

HISTORICAL THINKING

1. **READING CHECK** What series of events led to the Double V campaign?

2. **MAKE INFERENCES** How do you think the experiences of minority groups during World War II influenced the country after the war?

3. **COMPARE AND CONTRAST** What difference do you notice between the treatment of African-American and Latino soldiers during the war?

Soaring
to New Heights

"I want to use aviation to excite and empower a new generation to become scientists, engineers, and explorers." —Barrington Irving, Jr.

Barrington Irving, Jr., became the youngest person—and first African American—to fly solo around the world at the age of 23. He accomplished the feat in 2007 in a single-engine plane without weather radar or a de-icing system. Irving piloted the plane, fittingly named *Inspiration*, through snowstorms, monsoons, and sandstorms. Without question, he's a remarkable pilot, but he's also an innovative and ambitious educator. While planning his record-breaking flight, he founded a nonprofit educational organization to attract inner-city youth to aviation and other science- and math-related careers.

ᴧ
Barrington Irving, Jr., lands safely in Opa-Locka, Florida, on June 27, 2007, after becoming the youngest person and first African-American pilot to circumnavigate the globe in a solo flight.

MAIN IDEA National Geographic Explorer, pilot, and educator Barrington Irving, Jr., uses his aviation expertise to inspire young people to pursue careers in math and science.

Irving flew his single-engine Columbia 400 aircraft named *Inspiration* for three months to accomplish his goal. Based on details in this photograph, what types of physical challenges do you think Irving likely faced during his flight?

A YOUNG PILOT

The path for Irving's entry into aviation was paved by other remarkable African-American pilots—the Tuskegee Airmen. As a young pilot, Irving met some Tuskegee Airmen who had served in World War II. "These men had fought two wars—one for their country and another for equality and respect when they got back home," says Irving. "They are my heroes."

Raised in Miami's inner city, surrounded by crime, poverty, and failing schools, Irving became interested in aviation at age 15 when a pilot asked Irving if he'd like to become a pilot. "I told him I didn't think I was smart enough," explains Irving. "But he gave me the chance to sit in the cockpit of the commercial airplane he flew, and just like that I was hooked." Irving began spending his free time at a local airport, washing planes and talking to pilots. He also practiced flying using flight simulator software at home.

Irving turned down a full football scholarship to the University of Florida and majored in aeronautical science at a community college. He also began speaking to groups of inner-city youth in Miami, sharing his passion for aviation. In 2003, his volunteer work earned him a scholarship to Florida Memorial University. While excelling academically, he earned several piloting licenses—and set a new goal.

FLYING SOLO

At the age of 20, Irving wanted to fly around the world. Although he couldn't find an aircraft company that would donate a plane, Irving persuaded companies to donate aircraft parts. Then the aircraft manufacturer Columbia began building him a plane using these donated parts.

While his plane was being built, Irving established a nonprofit educational organization in 2005 called Experience Aviation. Funded by donations and grants, Irving and his staff set up a learning center at a Miami airport where students could operate flight simulators, chart flights, and do other projects.

Irving's historic flight began in Florida on March 23, 2007. The trip in his newly-built plane took 97 days, and he made 26 stops. He piloted through a blinding sandstorm over Saudi Arabia and an ice storm that forced him to land on an Alaskan island with only 12 minutes of fuel left. On June 27, 2007, Irving landed before a youthful crowd in Miami.

That reception made a strong impression on Irving. "Stepping from the plane, it wasn't all the fanfare that changed my life. It was seeing so many young people watching and listening. I had no money, but I was determined to give back with my time, knowledge, and experience."

In Irving's Build and Soar program, 60 students from failing schools built an airplane from scratch in 10 weeks and watched Irving pilot the aircraft into the clouds. For his Flying Classroom initiative, Irving transformed the jet into an "exploration vehicle" and shared live data involving science, technology, engineering, math, geography, culture, and history with students in classrooms. Taking the jet on a "Journey for Knowledge" across the globe, Irving flew the plane to visit all seven continents and teach science to children around the world.

HISTORICAL THINKING

1. **READING CHECK** In what ways is Barrington Irving, Jr., a remarkable pilot and educator?

2. **MAKE CONNECTIONS** How did the Tuskegee Airmen pave the way for Irving's future?

2.5 Japanese American Internment

Fear makes people do things they normally wouldn't think of doing. When a country is engaged in war, its citizens begin to imagine enemies all around them.

MAIN IDEA During World War II, the U.S. government imprisoned thousands of Japanese Americans because they shared ancestry with an enemy.

TARGETING JAPANESE AMERICANS

The bombing of Pearl Harbor caused panic and outrage among Americans. They feared Japan would strike the United States again. Rumors spread questioning the loyalty of Japanese Americans living in the country and implying they might interfere with the American war effort. Newspapers fed into the hysteria by printing dramatic headlines accusing Japanese Americans of being threats to national security. Some Italian Americans and German Americans were also targeted as "enemy aliens."

Japanese immigrants and their American-born children, who were called **Nisei** (NEE-say), were a small minority in the United States. Only about 125,000 people of Japanese ancestry lived in the states along the West Coast. More lived in Hawaii, which was a U.S. territory, not yet a state. Japanese Americans had little political power and historically had been required to live and work within their own culture. They were not in a position to fight the damaging rumors about their loyalty to their country.

As the fear of Japanese Americans grew, the U.S. government felt it must take action. In early 1942, President Roosevelt passed an **executive order**, a law issued by the president. **Executive Order 9066** forced most Japanese Americans to leave their homes on the West Coast. The government relocated them to ten **internment camps**, or detention centers, around the country. Congress and the Supreme Court quickly approved the bill, but some Americans questioned whether forced relocation violated Japanese Americans' constitutional rights.

THE INTERNMENT CAMPS

Before they were relocated in 1942, Japanese Americans were forced to report to government processing centers. They lived there until soldiers packed them into trains and sent them to their assigned camps. The families arrived at the camps with the few belongings they could carry with them. They were housed in large **barracks**, simple buildings meant to shelter many people without much privacy. Most of the barracks had no running water. Bathing facilities and toilets were located in separate buildings. Walls topped with barbed wire surrounded the camps, and armed soldiers guarded detainees from watchtowers day and night. Escape wasn't an option.

Some Nisei men in the camps volunteered to fight in the war. They were given a test to determine their loyalty to the United States. If they passed, they trained to become members of the 442nd Regimental Combat Team. As the 92nd Infantry was restricted to African Americans, the 442nd was restricted to Nisei. About 1,200 Nisei from the camps volunteered, but only 800 were accepted into the army. Those men joined the Hawaiian Nisei, who had not been sent to internment camps. Nearly 10,000 Hawaiian men volunteered for the 442nd, and 2,600 were accepted.

The 442nd fought heroically, liberating several Italian and French towns in 1944. In October 1944, a U.S. **battalion**, a large group of soldiers on a single mission, had become cut off and surrounded by the Germans in the mountains of eastern France. Called upon to rescue the soldiers, the 442nd broke through German defenses and freed 230 soldiers while losing half of their own. The unit suffered the highest casualty rate in the

Japanese American National Museum, Los Angeles

Hisako Hibi, whose painting *Laundry Room* is shown here, taught at an art school formed at the Topaz Internment Camp in Utah. Hibi painted scenes of daily life in the camp, expressing both the drabness of the camp confines and the spirit of the internees in overcoming it. Laundry facilities, like many other aspects of the camp, were communal or shared. Here, women use laundry tubs to bathe their children. Through the doorway, a row of barracks is visible. The small, dull living quarters contrasts with the liveliness and activity in the laundry room.

war. The 442nd's record in battle answered the question of Japanese Americans' loyalty to the United States.

In 1980, a congressional commission looked into the treatment of Japanese Americans during World War II. The result was the 1988 Civil Liberties Act. The act required victims of the internment camps to be paid reparations for the violation of their civil rights. Congress issued a formal apology and awarded $20,000 to each camp survivor. The investigation arose out of a resolution at the 1978 convention of the Japanese American Citizens League.

HISTORICAL THINKING

1. **READING CHECK** What was the purpose of Executive Order 9066?

2. **ANALYZE CAUSE AND EFFECT** Why did the attack on Pearl Harbor spark suspicion of Japanese Americans living on the West Coast?

3. **MAKE GENERALIZATIONS** Why do you think many Japanese American men enlisted in the armed forces after they had been sent to internment camps?

3.1 Fighting in Africa and Italy

Assessing a situation before jumping in can be the difference between success and failure. That is why the Allies sent reconnaissance teams to find out the size and organization of the German army in France. With this new information, the Allies decided not to invade France quite yet.

MAIN IDEA As the United States joined the war in Europe, the Allies fought the Axis armies in North Africa and Italy.

CHASING THE DESERT FOX

With the United States finally involved in the war, the Allies needed to set new strategies in place. Rather than send forces immediately against German forces in Europe, Churchill and Roosevelt planned **Operation Torch**, an invasion of areas in North Africa controlled by Nazi Germany, such as Morocco, Algeria, and Tunisia. The German presence there was small and spread out over a large distance. Overtaking them seemed like a good first task for the fresh American forces.

A German commander, Field Marshall **Erwin Rommel**, and his troops had moved into North Africa early in 1941. Rommel's ability to strike quickly, outmaneuver the enemy in the arid region, and win battles against larger Allied forces earned

The War in Europe and Africa, 1942–1943

In 1942, Lieutenant General Dwight D. Eisenhower was named supreme commander of the Allied forces in North Africa and of Operation Torch. Eisenhower won the respect of the British, French, and Canadian officers and soldiers. In this photo from January 1943, Eisenhower (second from right) inspects British troops in Tunisia.

him the nickname "the Desert Fox." His mission was to capture the **Suez Canal**, a waterway in Egypt that connects the Mediterranean and Red seas. The Allies used the canal to receive necessary oil shipments from the Middle East. They could not let Rommel have his way.

On October 23, 1942, Rommel's troops and British Allied forces collided in eastern North Africa at El Alamein (ehl ah-luh-MAYN), Egypt. Rommel had 500 tanks and about 100,000 men. **Bernard Law "Monty" Montgomery**, a British military leader and nobleman, had more than twice the number of men and tanks, as well as warplanes. After 10 days of furious combat, the Allies eventually forced Rommel to withdraw his army to Tunisia.

On November 8, 1942, American General **Dwight D. Eisenhower** and his Allied troops landed in western North Africa and successfully surrounded Rommel's troops. The Germans had no way to receive reinforcements or supplies. They surrendered on May 13, 1943. With the Nazis defeated in North Africa, the Allies planned to invade Sicily, a Mediterranean island off the

southern coast of Italy. From there, they intended to sweep up the Italian peninsula into the heart of Europe.

ALLIES ADVANCE INTO ITALY

The victory in North Africa made it much safer for the Allies to ship supplies and troops in the Mediterranean. Led by General **George S. Patton**, more than 150,000 troops, 3,000 ships, and 4,000 aircraft traveled north from Tunisia to Sicily in July 1943. Sicily's volcanoes and mountainous terrain made for difficult and fierce fighting, but by August 17, the Allies controlled the island. The British 8th Army then crossed the narrow strait between the island and mainland Italy on September 3, 1943.

Many opposing forces were at work in Italy while the Allies were fighting in Africa. Mussolini's hold on the Italian government had weakened and new, anti-fascist leaders were positioning themselves to grab power. In response to the instability, Hitler moved his troops into Italy.

On July 25, 1943, Italians successfully overthrew and arrested Mussolini. But the Allies still had to battle German troops as they made their way up the Italian peninsula. By June 1944, the Allies had reached Rome, but then they were called to fight on another front: a massive invasion of northern France. You will read about that turning point in the war in the next lesson. In April 1945, the Allies resumed battling the Nazis in Italy, but this time they had the advantage. German forces surrendered Italy on May 2.

HISTORICAL THINKING

1. **READING CHECK** What was Operation Torch?

2. **ANALYZE CAUSE AND EFFECT** What factors aided the defeat of Rommel's troops in Egypt and Tunisia?

3. **INTERPRET MAPS** Why did Allied control of North Africa make it safer to move troops and supplies on the Mediterranean Sea?

3.2 The Allies Advance

Joggers talk of getting their "second wind," feeling energized about halfway through a run. During World War II, a similar feeling spread among the Allied troops between 1943 and 1944. Despite brutal combat, the Allies sensed they were winning.

MAIN IDEA Two key victories changed the course of the war in favor of the Allies.

THE BATTLE OF STALINGRAD

Though the Soviets had managed to slow Operation Barbarossa, by the end of 1941, German armies had penetrated deep into the Soviet Union. When the United States joined the war, Stalin hoped the Allies would attack the Germans in France, taking the heat off of his troops. But the Allies invaded North Africa instead. The Soviet and German armies continued battling fiercely on a front that spanned more than 2,000 miles.

The Nazis soon learned that invading such a large country was not easy. The winter of 1942 was one of the worst in history. Deep snow and blizzard conditions slowed the German advance. **Exposure**—having no shelter or protection from severe weather—killed many soldiers. The vast expanse of the front greatly delayed the delivery of supplies. These conditions wore down the German troops as they fought to take the city of Stalingrad (now called Volgograd).

The **Battle of Stalingrad** was horrific. Early on, Stalin decided that losing the city that bore his name would look terrible for him as a leader. He ordered his troops to hold it at all costs. Hitler was just as determined. He forbade his forces to retreat, even after they ran out of fuel and food. Civilians also suffered from hunger and were trapped in the ruined city. Surrounded by Soviet troops and overwhelmed by starvation and low morale, the Germans finally surrendered on February 2, 1943. Around 2 million soldiers and civilians had lost their lives in total. Despite the casualties, the Soviets had successfully defended the city and won a victory.

THE D-DAY INVASION

After the victories in Italy and the Soviet Union, the United States and Great Britain felt the war had swung to their advantage. They commanded the skies above western Europe and sailed the oceans with little fear of German submarines. Their replenished armies were strong and well-equipped. They were finally ready to invade Europe from the west.

In January 1944, General Dwight Eisenhower was appointed commander of the invasion called **Operation Overlord**. Eisenhower and other military leaders planned for thousands of American, Canadian, and British troops to land on and overwhelm the Atlantic shore of northern France. Eisenhower chose June 5, 1944, for the invasion. He assigned General **Omar Bradley** to lead the ground fighting. As Eisenhower built up his troops in southwestern England, the Allies mounted a massive deception campaign to fool the Germans into believing the Allies would strike farther north at Calais, France. The campaign involved a fictitious force headed by General Patton, spies, impersonation, fake radio transmissions, inflatable replicas of tanks and landing craft, and dummies with sound equipment parachuting into France. When the dummies landed, a mechanism triggered sounds of gunfire and grenades.

Bad weather and rough seas on June 5 delayed the operation. However, on June 6, 1944, also known as **D-Day**, approximately 160,000 Allied soldiers mainly from the United States, Great Britain, and Canada stormed beaches in northern France. The troops arrived by airplane, cargo boat,

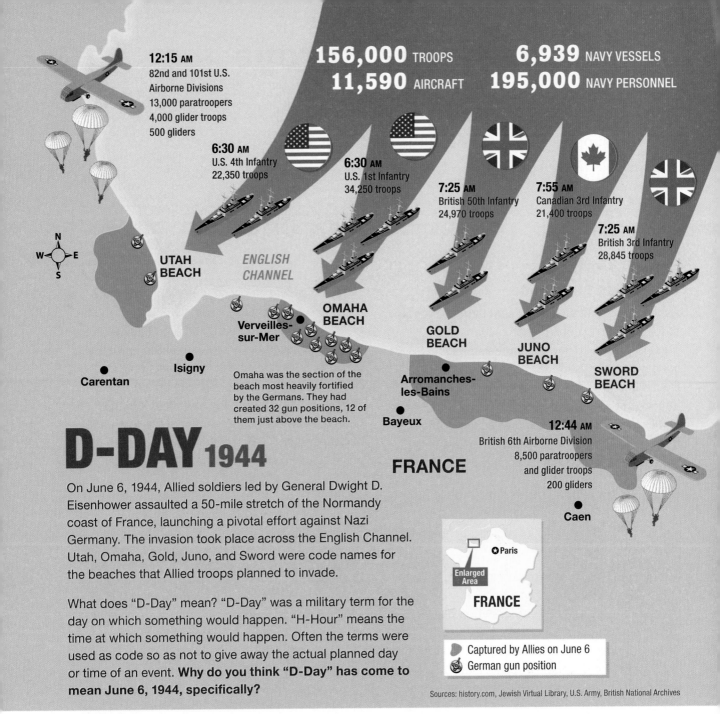

12:15 AM
82nd and 101st U.S.
Airborne Divisions
13,000 paratroopers
4,000 glider troops
500 gliders

156,000 TROOPS **6,939** NAVY VESSELS
11,590 AIRCRAFT **195,000** NAVY PERSONNEL

6:30 AM
U.S. 4th Infantry
22,350 troops

6:30 AM
U.S. 1st Infantry
34,250 troops

7:25 AM
British 50th Infantry
24,970 troops

7:55 AM
Canadian 3rd Infantry
21,400 troops

7:25 AM
British 3rd Infantry
28,845 troops

N W E S

UTAH BEACH

ENGLISH CHANNEL

OMAHA BEACH

Verveilles-sur-Mer

GOLD BEACH

JUNO BEACH

SWORD BEACH

Isigny

Carentan

Omaha was the section of the beach most heavily fortified by the Germans. They had created 32 gun positions, 12 of them just above the beach.

Arromanches-les-Bains

Bayeux

D-DAY 1944

FRANCE

12:44 AM
British 6th Airborne Division
8,500 paratroopers
and glider troops
200 gliders

Caen

On June 6, 1944, Allied soldiers led by General Dwight D. Eisenhower assaulted a 50-mile stretch of the Normandy coast of France, launching a pivotal effort against Nazi Germany. The invasion took place across the English Channel. Utah, Omaha, Gold, Juno, and Sword were code names for the beaches that Allied troops planned to invade.

What does "D-Day" mean? "D-Day" was a military term for the day on which something would happen. "H-Hour" means the time at which something would happen. Often the terms were used as code so as not to give away the actual planned day or time of an event. **Why do you think "D-Day" has come to mean June 6, 1944, specifically?**

⊕ Paris

Enlarged Area

FRANCE

Captured by Allies on June 6
German gun position

Sources: history.com, Jewish Virtual Library, U.S. Army, British National Archives

or **amphibious landing craft**, boats that could be used as trucks when they hit shore. During the previous night, paratroopers and gliders had landed behind German lines. The surprised Germans recovered quickly. The Allied soldiers encountered land mines and persistent gunfire. Many died that day, but they drove the Nazi army into retreat. Eisenhower's deception had worked.

More than 800,000 Allied soldiers flowed into France within two months of D-Day. By late August, Paris was free. By September, the Germans were pushed back into their own country, but they still had some fight left in them.

HISTORICAL THINKING

1. **READING CHECK** How did the Battle of Stalingrad and the D-Day invasion help turn the tide of the war to the Allies' advantage?

2. **DESCRIBE** What barriers did the Allied forces overcome as they invaded the French coast?

3. **ANALYZE CAUSE AND EFFECT** What was the effect of Eisenhower's deception campaign to fool the Germans?

3.3 End of War in Europe

How do you know when you are beat? Surrounded by the enemy with few supplies, the Nazis had little trouble in answering this question in 1944 and 1945.

MAIN IDEA Allied forces ended the war in Europe by defeating the Germans on two fronts, and Allied leaders decided the future of Germany and the world.

BATTLE OF THE BULGE

As the Allies made their way east through France to the German border, French civilians often greeted them with flowers and celebrations. Spirits were high, but this mood wouldn't last long. In December 1944, the Germans reorganized and attacked at the German border shared with France and Belgium. The battle, known as the **Battle of the Bulge**, was the last German offensive of the war, but it surprised American and British troops.

Hitler's plan was to divide the Allied forces and capture Antwerp, a city in Belgium. He put most of his army on the operation. Some 200,000 soldiers guarded by swift German tanks called **panzers** (PAN-zurz) thundered into the forests of the Ardennes (ahr-DEHN) Mountains in northeastern France. With help from the mountain fog, the Germans forced the Allies into retreat. In an act of desperation, General George Patton, who had played a key role in driving the Germans from

CRITICAL VIEWING In December 1944, U.S. soldiers line up for food while on their way to break up the line of German tanks surrounding Bastogne, Belgium. How would the conditions shown have affected the troops?

northern Africa, broke through the German lines and rescued Bastogne (bah-STAWN), a town in Belgium that was vital to Allied supply and defense lines. The Germans ceased their attack. Both sides suffered tremendous losses. Germany alone lost 100,000 men.

Meanwhile, the Soviet army was sweeping west through Nazi territory, retaking the land they had controlled before the war. They recaptured Ukraine, Poland, and Lithuania. They were advancing on Germany's eastern border by August 1944. The Soviet Union's march through Eastern Europe had a resounding impact on the future of Europe. With Allied troops making their way into Germany from both sides, the war was swiftly coming to an end.

VICTORY IN EUROPE

Knowing that Hitler's chances of winning the war were dwindling, the Allied leaders decided to meet face-to-face in February 1945. President Franklin D. Roosevelt, British prime minister Winston Churchill, and Soviet premier Joseph Stalin gathered at Yalta, a small city in the south of the Soviet Union. During the **Yalta Conference**, the men discussed the future of Europe and the world. Together they planned to force Germany's surrender and to **partition**, or separate, Germany into four regions controlled by their nations and France. Their plan became known as the **Yalta Accords**. They discussed the need for an international peace-keeping organization, which would become the **United Nations (UN)**. Roosevelt and Churchill urged Stalin to allow democracy in Eastern Europe and help the Allies defeat Japan.

Franklin Roosevelt did not live to see the Allied victory, however. On April 12, 1945, he died suddenly while visiting Warm Springs, Georgia. Vice President **Harry S. Truman** became president and took charge of the U.S. role in the last stage of the war. By the end of April, Soviet troops were fighting the Nazis in the streets of Berlin, the German capital.

In February 1945, the Allied leaders known as the "Big Three" met at Yalta, a town in the Soviet Union along the Black Sea. Left to right, the leaders, seated, are Winston Churchill, Franklin Roosevelt, and Joseph Stalin. Their advisors stand at attention behind them.

Hitler knew he had lost the war. He committed suicide on April 30, 1945. The Nazis surrendered to Allied forces on May 7 and to the Soviets on May 9. In the nations that made up the Allied Powers, citizens celebrated in the streets. The war in Europe was finally over, and the Allies were victorious. Allied attention shifted to the horrifying reality of Hitler's death camps. Meanwhile, the war between the Allies and Japan continued.

HISTORICAL THINKING

1. **READING CHECK** On what two fronts did the Allies finally defeat the Nazi army?

2. **DETERMINE CHRONOLOGY** Describe the events that led to the Yalta Conference and the need for the meeting.

3. **ASK AND ANSWER QUESTIONS** What other questions do you have about the end of fighting in Europe, and how might you find the answers?

3.4 The Holocaust

Hitler's hatred of Jews was not a secret. But it wasn't until the end of the war that the extent of his violence became widely known. The world would never be the same.

MAIN IDEA The Nazis killed millions of Jews and others they deemed "undesirable" during World War II.

PERSECUTION OF THE JEWS

As the Allied army marched east and the Soviet army marched west through Eastern Europe, they came upon places of unspeakable horror. They found huge compounds filled with starving people and piles of dead bodies. The Nazis had attempted to commit genocide, or wipe out a particular group of people through mass killing. Hitler's genocide became known as the Holocaust.

As you read earlier, before Adolf Hitler rose to power, he traveled through Germany making political speeches blaming the problems of the country on the Jewish people. This hatred of Jews is called anti-Semitism. After Hitler became Germany's chancellor, his Nazi Party began instituting national laws restricting Jewish rights. Regional and local politicians also passed anti-Semitic laws. Most of the early laws limited Jews' social lives and their ability to work. They were no longer allowed to be members of certain organizations and could no longer work in certain professions, including in the government.

In September 1935, the Nazi Party released new policies called the Nuremberg Laws, which stripped Jews of their German citizenship and voting rights. They were not permitted to marry non-Jewish people. Businesses fired their Jewish workers and no longer let Jewish doctors and lawyers help German people. Jewish children could no longer attend school. Then Nazi soldiers moved Jewish families to ghettoes, forced housing for a particular race or ethnicity, far away from their homes.

On November 7, 1938, the situation became dire for German Jews. A 17-year-old Polish Jew shot and killed a German diplomat in France. Joseph Goebbels (GEH-buhlz), the Nazi propaganda minister, immediately used the assassination to whip up anti-Semitic sentiments, or feelings. On November 9, Nazis burned down synagogues and damaged Jewish homes, schools, and businesses in Germany. Around 100 people were killed that night. The incident was called Kristallnacht (krees-TAHL-nahkt), which means "Night of Broken Glass" in German.

Soon, many German Jews were forced to wear an armband or badge that identified their heritage and religion. The badge made it easier for Nazis and racists to humiliate and segregate the Jews. Eventually, all Jews had to wear some form of identification in Germany and in some of the countries controlled by Germany.

NAZI CONCENTRATION CAMPS

In the months following Kristallnacht, tens of thousands of Jewish men were arrested. They were transported to work camps known as concentration camps, where they were forced to perform hard labor. Many people died on the journey and in the camps due to starvation and disease. Eventually, entire Jewish families were sent there, as well as the Roma people, also known as gypsies; homosexuals; people with disabilities; and people who opposed the Nazis.

Some of the concentration camps had gas chambers where prisoners who could not work, pregnant women, children, and the elderly, were killed with poisonous gas. Their bodies were burned in rooms equipped with large ovens called crematoria. These places were called death camps, and they were part of a Nazi plan to kill all of Europe's Jewish people, called the

CRITICAL VIEWING In this June 1944 photograph, a group of Hungarian Jews arrive in the Auschwitz-Birkenau concentration camp in Poland. They wore yellow stars identifying them as Jews, as required by the Nazis. The stars were similar to the one at right, which was worn by a Jew in the Netherlands. *Jood* is the Dutch word for *Jew*. What details of the photo indicate the treatment the people were receiving?

Final Solution. The plan resulted in the genocide of 6 million Jews and from 4 to 6 million others. In all, the Nazis killed or imprisoned a total of up to 20 million people in their camps and ghettoes.

While Allied leaders knew about the death camps, they failed to investigate them or address them during the war. Allied warplanes flew within 35 miles of Auschwitz-Birkenau in Poland, but they didn't bomb the railroad lines the Nazis used to transport their prisoners. In the United States, immigration boards allowed few Jewish refugees entrance. The U.S. State Department claimed some of the refugees could be spies, and could pose a security risk.

HISTORICAL THINKING

1. **READING CHECK** Why did the Nazis force Jews to wear badges and armbands?

2. **MAKE CONNECTIONS** How did Joseph Goebbels exploit the death of the German diplomat in France?

3. **DESCRIBE** What did witnesses to the Kristallnacht riots see?

4.1 War in the Pacific

Even if you are on the right side of a conflict, you may not win every battle. The first year of the war in the Pacific was a great challenge for the Allies, particularly for the United States.

MAIN IDEA After the United States entered the war, Japan continued to expand its power in the Pacific through a string of victories.

EARLY JAPANESE VICTORIES

After its successful attack on Pearl Harbor, Japanese forces moved swiftly through southeastern Asia, capturing American territories and other Allied colonies in the region. For the United States, an early defeat took place within hours of the attack on Pearl Harbor. Japanese forces struck the Philippines, which had been designated a commonwealth, or territory, of the United States in 1935.

General Douglas MacArthur arrives in Melbourne, Australia, from the Philippines on March 21, 1942.

American troops, including many Filipino soldiers, were headquartered there under the command of American general **Douglas MacArthur**, but they were not yet fully prepared for battle. The Japanese air force bombed airfields, bases, harbors, and shipyards. More than 40,000 Japanese soldiers came ashore at Luzon, the largest island of the Philippines. By January 2, 1942, Japanese troops had taken Manila, the capital of the Philippines. American troops retreated to the jungles of the Bataan Peninsula, which they defended for 99 days.

In March 1942, Roosevelt ordered MacArthur to leave the Philippines. MacArthur was too valuable an officer for the United States to lose, so to avoid capture by the Japanese, he was brought to safety in Australia. He vowed to one day return to the Philippines. Still, the Filipino and American troops continued to fight, even though they suffered from starvation and disease. Meanwhile in Australia, MacArthur became supreme commander of Allied forces in the southwestern Pacific.

Finally, on April 9, 1942, the remaining 75,000 Filipino and American troops surrendered. The Japanese forced them to march without food, water, or shelter, for 60 miles to a prison camp. Those who collapsed during the ordeal were beaten, bayoneted, shot, and even beheaded by their Japanese captors. Thousands died in what became known as the **Bataan Death March**, and thousands more died in the prison camp at their destination. Many American prisoners were later transported to the Japanese main island. There, they mainly worked as slave laborers in mines. Thousands more died while traveling, crowded into the coal holds of the ships or while enslaved.

This photo, taken on June 4, 1942, shows the U.S.S. *Yorktown* moments after it was bombed by the Japanese during the Battle of Midway. It took four torpedoes and two air raids over the course of three days for the Japanese to finally capsize the boat.

AMERICAN STRATEGIES PAY OFF

Even though the news from the Pacific was not good, the United States fought on. Under the command of **Lieutenant Colonel James H. Doolittle**, American B-25 bombers attacked the Japanese mainland on April 18, 1942. Although the attack did not do much damage to the Japanese infrastructure, it was a great embarrassment to the Japanese government. Within a month, the U.S. Navy began to win some important battles.

In early May 1942, the Japanese attempted to attack air bases in the South Pacific. Instead, U.S. naval forces turned them back at the **Battle of the Coral Sea**. Between June 3 and June 6, the United States defeated Japan in the **Battle of Midway**, sinking 4 Japanese aircraft carriers, destroying about 300 enemy aircraft, and killing more than 3,000 enemy sailors. Though the Americans lost about 145 aircraft and more than 300 sailors, the Battle of Midway was a major Allied victory.

Midway Islands consist of an **atoll**, a ring-shaped coral reef that forms a series of islands. The strategic location of the atoll gave the United States and the Allies a much-needed advantage. By retaining control of Midway, the United States was in a stronger position to defend Hawaii and launch attacks on Japanese territories.

HISTORICAL THINKING

1. **READING CHECK** How successful was the war in the Pacific for the Allies immediately following the attack on Pearl Harbor?

2. **MAKE INFERENCES** Why was the attack by American bombers on April 18, 1942, a great embarrassment to the Japanese government?

3. **ANALYZE CAUSE AND EFFECT** What was the strategic effect of the U.S. victory at Midway?

4.2 Island Hopping

How do you fight a war against an enemy positioned on islands scattered thousands of miles across the ocean? This was a question the U.S. military needed to answer.

MAIN IDEA The United States targeted Japanese islands in the Pacific one after the other, attacking the easiest to secure first.

ONE ISLAND AT A TIME

Island hopping was the strategy employed by the United States to gain military bases and secure many of the small islands in the Pacific. At first, U.S. troops targeted islands that were not as strongly defended by the Japanese. The U.S. military swept in and built landing strips and bases on those islands, inching U.S. military power closer and closer to Japan itself. Island hopping was made possible partly by the U.S. victory at Midway, which limited Japan's reach in the Pacific.

The **Battle of Guadalcanal** in the Solomon Islands was an early Allied victory. U.S. Marines launched the attack in August 1942, two months after the Battle of Midway. They quickly seized a Japanese air base that was under construction, but the battle itself raged for another six months. By the battle's end, only about a third of the Japanese troops who had been on the island at the peak of fighting survived. American forces lost fewer than 2,000 of the 60,000 troops deployed. After its defeat on Guadalcanal, Japan questioned its

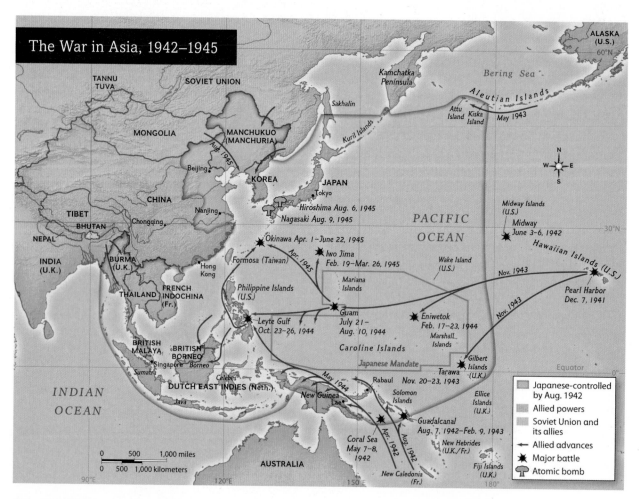

The War in Asia, 1942–1945

ALASKA (U.S.)

TANNU TUVA

SOVIET UNION

Kamchatka Peninsula

Bering Sea

Aleutian Islands

Sakhalin

Attu Island Kiska Island May 1943

MONGOLIA MANCHUKUO (MANCHURIA)

Kuril Islands

Beijing

KOREA

JAPAN
Tokyo

CHINA

Nanjing

Hiroshima Aug. 6, 1945
Nagasaki Aug. 9, 1945

Chongqing

TIBET
BHUTAN

NEPAL

Okinawa Apr. 1–June 22, 1945

Midway Islands (U.S.)

Midway
June 3–6, 1942

PACIFIC OCEAN

30°N

Hawaiian Islands (U.S.)

Iwo Jima
Feb. 19–Mar. 26, 1945

INDIA (U.K.)

BURMA (U.K.)

Hong Kong

Formosa (Taiwan)

Wake Island (U.S.)

Nov. 1943

THAILAND FRENCH INDOCHINA (Fr.)

Philippine Islands (U.S.)

Mariana Islands

Nov. 1943

Pearl Harbor Dec. 7, 1941

Leyte Gulf
Oct. 23–26, 1944

Guam
July 21– Aug. 10, 1944

Eniwetok
Feb. 17–23, 1944

Marshall Islands

BRITISH MALAYA BRITISH BORNEO

Singapore Borneo

Sumatra

Caroline Islands

Celebes

DUTCH EAST INDIES (Neth.)

Japanese Mandate

Gilbert Islands

Tarawa (U.K.)
Nov. 20–23, 1943

Rabaul

Equator 0°

Java

May 1944

New Guinea

Lae

Solomon Islands

Ellice Islands (U.K.)

INDIAN OCEAN

Guadalcanal
Aug. 7, 1942–Feb. 9, 1943

Coral Sea
May 7–8, 1942

New Hebrides (U.K./Fr.)

AUSTRALIA

New Caledonia (Fr.)

Fiji Islands (U.K.)

	Japanese-controlled by Aug. 1942
	Allied powers
	Soviet Union and its allies
←	Allied advances
✳	Major battle
☁	Atomic bomb

0   500   1,000 miles
0   500   1,000 kilometers

90°E   120°E   150°E   180°

Photographer Joe Rosenthal captured one of the most famous images of the 20th century—U.S. Marines raising the American flag over Mount Suribachi on Iwo Jima. The image has been used for a wide variety of purposes, appearing on postage stamps and on the memorial statue at the entrance to Arlington National Cemetery.

MOVING TOWARD JAPAN

On February 19, 1945, the U.S. Marines invaded the island of Iwo Jima, around 760 miles from Tokyo, Japan. Roughly 22,000 Japanese troops defended the island. They had dug miles of tunnels connecting man-made caves in which to hide. This made it difficult for the Marines to find them and resulted in fierce fighting over most of the island. By the time fighting ended in late March, the entire Japanese force had been wiped out except for around 1,000 prisoners of war. American losses were estimated at 6,000 dead and 21,000 wounded.

On March 9, 1945, the Allies brought the war to the Japanese mainland as U.S. warplanes released 2,000 tons of **incendiary bombs**, or fire bombs, on Tokyo. Fifteen square miles were set ablaze, and between 80,000 and 130,000 Japanese lives were lost. Some say it was the deadliest firestorm in recorded history.

Then, from April 1 to June 22, 1945, U.S. troops battled to capture Okinawa, a large island only 340 miles from mainland Japan. The final battle of the island-hopping campaign was also the largest. As a result of their victory there, the Allies could now use Okinawa as a base for the planned ground invasion of the Japanese home islands.

ability to defeat the United States. Over the next few years, the Allies continued island hopping as Japan fought back, with mixed success.

In October 1944, American forces focused on recapturing the Philippines. The Japanese sent almost all of their remaining naval forces to the Philippines to fight against the Allies. As in the case of Midway, U.S. commanders were ready for the Japanese strategy. Some historians say the resulting clash, the **Battle of Leyte Gulf,** was not just the largest naval battle in the war but the largest naval battle ever. The U.S. 7th Fleet annihilated, or destroyed, one of the Japanese forces and drove a second into retreat. In desperation to keep the Philippines, the Japanese deployed **kamikaze pilots**. These pilots crashed their planes into Allied ships, taking their own lives as they took the lives of many Allied sailors.

The stage was set for the Allies to retake the Philippines. U.S. General Douglas MacArthur declared his triumphant return to the nation he was forced to flee more than two years earlier. By March 1945, the United States again controlled the Philippines, but at great cost. Two-thirds of the Allied soldiers MacArthur left behind in March 1942 had perished by the time he returned.

HISTORICAL THINKING

1. **READING CHECK** What was the significance of the U.S. capture of Okinawa?

2. **DETERMINE WORD MEANING** Think about how incendiary bombs affected the Japanese. What does that reveal about the meaning of the word *incendiary*?

3. **MAKE INFERENCES** What does the image of the Marines raising the flag on Iwo Jima symbolize?

4.3 Final Victory

Is it acceptable to sacrifice the few to save the many? No doubt it is a difficult decision to make, but it is one sometimes required of doctors, police officers, and world leaders during conflicts.

> **MAIN IDEA** President Truman was forced to make a decision between ordering an atomic strike on Japan or risking an invasion that might cost more than a million American lives.

THE ATOMIC BOMB

The planned U.S. invasion of Japan was referred to as "Operation Downfall." It was to be the largest amphibious operation in history, using all available combined resources of the Army, Navy, Marines, and Air Force, attacking from the sea. Massive fatalities on both sides were almost a certainty, and the lives of millions of Japanese civilians would be at risk. Battle planners estimated that hundreds of thousands of American troops could die in the invasion, even though they were almost certain to win in the long run. But President Truman had another option.

On August 9, 1945, the second atomic bomb exploded over Nagasaki, Japan. This photo shows the resulting mushroom cloud and blast wave moving out from it.

Truman and some of his advisors believed that attacking Japan with a terrible new weapon might prevent the casualties of a full-scale invasion. That weapon was the **atomic bomb**, a type of nuclear weapon whose violent explosion is triggered by **nuclear fission**, or splitting atoms. Nuclear fission releases intense heat and radioactivity. In 1940, the U.S. government had begun funding an atomic weapons program code-named the **Manhattan Project**. Over the next four years, the program's scientists worked on extracting the key materials for nuclear fission—uranium 235 and plutonium. At Los Alamos, New Mexico, **J. Robert Oppenheimer** and his team of physicists used these materials to develop the first atomic bomb.

By the time the bomb was successfully tested at Alamogordo, New Mexico, the Allied powers had already defeated Germany. In late July 1945, Japan's government rejected the Allies' demand for surrender, which threatened Japan with "prompt and utter destruction" if it refused. In the wake of Japan's refusal, Truman hoped to bring the war to a decisive end by dropping atomic bombs on one or more Japanese cities.

HIROSHIMA AND NAGASAKI

On the morning of August 6, 1945, the United States sent out the *Enola Gay,* a modified B-29 bomber that carried an atomic bomb. The target was **Hiroshima**, a military center with a population of 350,000. At 8:15 in the morning, the plane dropped the bomb, and within seconds five square miles of the city had been reduced to rubble. Some 90,000 to 166,000 people were instantly killed or died within four months from burns and radiation sickness.

Three days later, another B-29 plane dropped an atomic bomb on the city of **Nagasaki**. Again, tens of thousands of Japanese civilians died in an instant, and Nagasaki lay in ruins. On August 15, Emperor Hirohito announced that Japan would surrender to the Allied Powers. The news spread quickly and "Victory in Japan" or "V-J Day" celebrations broke out across the United States and in other Allied nations. With General MacArthur presiding over negotiations, Japan formally surrendered aboard the U.S.S. *Missouri,* anchored in Tokyo Bay, on September 2, 1945.

Ari Beser, Fulbright-National Geographic Fellow

Ari Beser's grandfather (below) flew as the radar specialist on the planes that dropped atomic bombs on Hiroshima and Nagasaki in 1945. In 2015, Beser (right) traveled to Japan to interview survivors of the bombings. Many survivors were eager to talk. They hoped that their stories would end the possibility of nuclear warfare forever. The survivors recalled the blinding flash of the bomb detonating, the heat, and the strong wind. They also recounted the physical effects of the attack, such as chronic pain, they still experience today.

HISTORICAL THINKING

1. **READING CHECK** What was the result of the Manhattan Project?

2. **FORM AND SUPPORT OPINIONS** Do you agree with President Truman's justification for dropping atomic bombs on Japan? Support your opinion with evidence from the text.

3. **IDENTIFY MAIN IDEAS AND DETAILS** Why didn't the United States use atomic weapons on Germany to end the war in Europe?

4.4 Legacy of World War II

How does a region recover from a devastating war? How can we rebuild and prevent war in the future? The Allies together sought answers to these questions as World War II ended.

MAIN IDEA After the war, the Allies put German leaders on trial for war crimes and attempted to rebuild Europe from the devastation of World War II.

THE NUREMBERG TRIALS

World War II was history's most destructive war. Total war deaths—both civilian and military—are estimated to have numbered at least 60 million people. The Soviet Union lost approximately 24 million soldiers and civilians, and China lost at least 20 million, although some estimates reach as high as 50 million. Germany lost between 6 and 8 million. American deaths totaled 418,500, of which more than 99 percent (416,800) were soldiers, airmen, and sailors.

After the war was over, the Allies decided to try Nazi leaders for war crimes. The trials were held in the German city of Nuremberg between 1945 and 1946. The charges against the defendants included crimes against peace, war crimes, and crimes against humanity.

The Holocaust was a major factor in establishing the trials. In December 1942, the Allies had issued a joint declaration that called out Germany for the mass murder of Europe's Jews. Once the war ended and the horrific brutality of Germany's work and death camps was exposed, the Allies became even more determined to see justice done. They vowed to prosecute anyone responsible for violence against civilian populations. The Trial of Major War Criminals, best-known as the **Nuremberg trials**, lasted from November 20, 1945, to October 1, 1946. All but three of the defendants received a guilty verdict. Twelve were sentenced to death, and the rest were given prison terms ranging from 10 years to life behind bars.

In later trials, 183 defendants that included Nazi government officials, military leaders, industrialists, physicians, and judges, were convicted on the same charges. Between 1946 and 1948, Japanese leaders were also charged for the Bataan Death March and other war crimes.

REBUILDING THE WORLD

The United States emerged from the war as the world's most powerful nation. In June 1947, U.S. Secretary of State George C. Marshall asked Congress to give the war-ravaged European countries billions of dollars in aid for the countries to spend as they saw fit. The resulting **Marshall Plan** was a $13 billion aid plan to ensure the recovery of Western Europe from the economic devastation caused by the war there. The United States provided most of the money by pledging

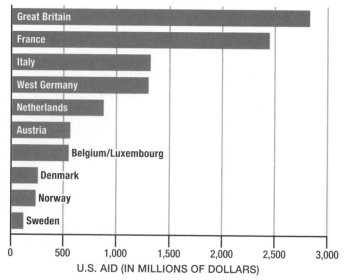

The Marshall Plan

Great Britain
France
Italy
West Germany
Netherlands
Austria
Belgium/Luxembourg
Denmark
Norway
Sweden

0   500   1,000   1,500   2,000   2,500   3,000
U.S. AID (IN MILLIONS OF DOLLARS)

Source: "The Marshall Plan: A Reality Check," by Nicholas Crafts, 2011

GLI AIUTI D'AMERICA
GRANO·CARBONE·VIVERI·MEDICINALI
CI AIUTANO AD AIUTARCI DA NOI

Italian citizens read a poster (also shown at right) that roughly translates to "American aid—wheat, coal, food, medicine— helps Italians to help themselves." The photograph was taken in 1948 at a time when Europe relied heavily on foreign aid for basic necessities.

more than 10 percent of its entire federal budget. The Marshall Plan was an important part of American and Western European policy to halt the spread of communism from the Soviet Union into the countries of Eastern Europe.

Several weeks later, 17 European nations met in Paris, France, to assess their needs under the Marshall Plan. The Soviets declined their invitation to the meeting. They did not like the idea of giving critical economic information to outsiders. They also felt that taking aid from capitalist countries might undermine the communist Soviet system. Even without Soviet participation, the Marshall Plan successfully restored economic confidence throughout Western Europe.

At the end of World War I, President Woodrow Wilson proposed an international organization to help avoid war by dealing with conflicts among members diplomatically rather than with force. The U.S. Congress failed to ratify the treaty that established this organization. After World War II ended in Europe, the nations of the world tried this idea again. On April 25, 1945, representatives of 50 nations attended a conference in San Francisco, California, where they formed the United Nations (UN). There they agreed upon the principles of the United Nations Charter: to prevent another war through open communications and to work to guarantee basic human rights for everyone in the world.

HISTORICAL THINKING

1. **READING CHECK** What was the purpose of the Nuremberg trials?

2. **ANALYZE CAUSE AND EFFECT** How were the Marshall Plan and the creation of the UN expected to affect Europe and the rest of the world?

3. **ANALYZE GRAPHS** In total, how much money did the Marshall Plan give to former Axis powers, West Germany and Italy?

VOCABULARY

For each pair of vocabulary words, write one sentence that establishes a connection between the words.

1. ideology; fascism

   The ideology of fascism is to put nation and race before the needs of individual citizens.

2. panzer; blitzkrieg

3. anti-Semitism; genocide

4. Allied Powers; deploy

5. barracks; internment camp

6. atoll; island hopping

7. D-Day; amphibious landing craft

8. incendiary bomb; atomic bomb

READING STRATEGY
ANALYZE CAUSE AND EFFECT

If you haven't done so already, complete your chart showing the causes and effects of the United States becoming an Allied Power during World War II. List causes of the event in the top box and the effects of the event in the bottom box.

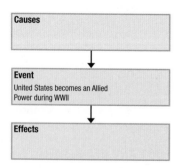

Causes

↓

Event
United States becomes an Allied Power during WWII

↓

Effects

9. How did United States involvement in World War II impact average Americans at home?

MAIN IDEAS

Answer the following questions. Support your answers with evidence from the chapter.

10. What was the significance of the Rome-Berlin Axis? **LESSON 1.1**

11. What did Winston Churchill mean when he said "The Battle of France is over. The Battle of Britain is about to begin."? **LESSON 1.3**

12. What was the Selective Service and Training Act of 1940? **LESSON 2.1**

13. How did the activities of the War Production Board help the country prepare for war? **LESSON 2.1**

14. What was the "Double V" campaign? **LESSON 2.3**

15. How did the Final Solution connect to Hitler's political ideologies? **LESSON 3.4**

16. Why did U.S. military leaders choose the strategy of island hopping to fight the Japanese? **LESSON 4.2**

17. What war strategy was replaced by the deployment of atomic weapons on Japanese cities? **LESSON 4.3**

18. What steps did the Allies take to help keep peace and rebuild after World War II? **LESSON 4.4**

HISTORICAL THINKING

Answer the following questions. Support your answers with evidence from the chapter.

19. **DETERMINE CHRONOLOGY** What military events in 1940 led to the Battle of Britain?

20. **MAKE INFERENCES** What was the appeal of the fascist movement to citizens in Italy, Germany, and Spain?

21. **SYNTHESIZE** What events and attitudes led to the establishment of internment camps for Japanese Americans during the war?

22. ANALYZE CAUSE AND EFFECT How did events of World War I influence the start of World War II?

23. MAKE CONNECTIONS How did technology affect the way World War II was fought?

24. FORM AND SUPPORT OPINIONS What was the most important factor in President Truman's decision to drop atomic bombs on Hiroshima and Nagasaki?

INTERPRET VISUALS

In this 1941 political cartoon by Daniel Bishop, Uncle Sam carries a cannon to the shores of England. In the background, Adolf Hitler offers a warning. Think about what you have learned about the Lend-Lease Act. Then answer the questions that follow.

Uncle: 'It Would Be Dynamite if I Didn't'   By Bishop

YOU'RE PLAYING WITH DYNAMITE!

PLAN TO LEND BRITAIN ARMS

25. Based on the title at the top of the cartoon, what is the illustrator's view of the act?

26. Based on the cartoon and text evidence from the chapter, what was the significance of the United States offering assistance to Great Britain and other countries fighting against Nazi Germany?

ANALYZE SOURCES

Elie Wiesel was a survivor of the Auschwitz concentration camp and an author. He wrote a book about his experiences there called *Night* (1960). In this excerpt, Wiesel explains why he felt it was important to share his story with the world.

> For the survivor who chooses to testify, it is clear: his duty is to bear witness for the dead and for the living. He has no right to deprive [rob] future generations of a past that belongs to our collective memory. To forget would be not only dangerous but offensive; to forget the dead would be akin to killing them a second time.

27. Why would forgetting the victims of the Holocaust be like "killing them a second time"?

CONNECT TO YOUR LIFE

28. NARRATIVE In 1945, representatives of the United Nations signed a statement called a preamble that declared the new organization's purpose. In the statement, they expressed that they would like to prevent future wars, support human rights, and promote better standards of living. If you were writing a preamble for your own life, what goals would you list? Think about the kinds of personality traits you would want your friends to say you possessed. Then write four or five points that would help you demonstrate those traits.

TIPS

- Make sure your points reflect your image of yourself in terms of how you choose to act and not the outcomes you seek. A statement like "I promise to get rich" reflects outcomes. A statement like "I will fight for equality" reflects action.

- Use precise words and phrases to convey a vivid description of your traits.

- Conclude the narrative with a summary of the kind of person you would like to be.

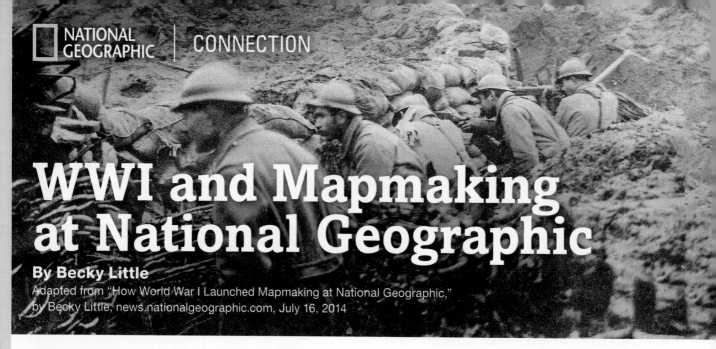

NATIONAL GEOGRAPHIC | CONNECTION

WWI and Mapmaking at National Geographic

By Becky Little

Adapted from "How World War I Launched Mapmaking at National Geographic," by Becky Little, news.nationalgeographic.com, July 16, 2014

In the summer of 1914, Americans began reading news accounts of a conflict that would be called the Great War. The conflict would draw in the United States three years later and eventually also become known as World War I. According to Robert Poole, a former executive editor of *National Geographic*, people followed the war by reading newspapers, "and maps were a very important way to make sense of these faraway places [and] strange names."

World War I broke out in Europe on July 28, 1914. The August 1914 issue of *National Geographic* was changed to include a map of "New Balkan States and Central Europe." The map featured the names of the places where fighting was most severe. The popular map boosted the organization's visibility. By year's end, membership in the National Geographic Society had grown 50 percent, to more than 336,000.

The Balkans map was ready to print on short notice because the magazine's editor, Gilbert H. Grosvenor, had commissioned it in the summer of 1913. He had anticipated heightened conflict in Europe after visiting Great Britain, France, and Russia that summer.

"He could tell that something important was happening in Europe," Poole says. "[He knew] that people needed this sort of information that they weren't getting anywhere else. There was this niche that National Geographic could fit that no one else was fitting. He began to get favorable responses not only from the public, but [also] from the White House, the Navy."

National Geographic is well known today for its maps and atlases. But the magazine did not actually create its own maps during the first 27 years of its existence. Grosvenor had commissioned outside companies to produce both the Balkans map and a 1915 follow-up map of the expanding war front. However, Grosvenor was disappointed with the quality of the initial drafts of the war-front map. Mapmaking at the outside companies also took longer than Grosvenor wanted.

To produce the maps he wanted, Grosvenor established National Geographic's map department in 1915 with a single cartographer, Albert Bumstead. The department's first map supplement was the 1918 "Map of the Western Theatre of War." It provided readers with the name and location of every town or small village that they would likely encounter in reports from the front. The secretary of the Geographic Society of France called it the most complete map of the Western Front. The map launched National Geographic's reputation for detailed mapping.

Those war years marked a turning point for the National Geographic Society—and for the cartography field. "The mapmaking became much more professional during and as a result of World War I," Poole says. "People began to associate Nat Geo with cartographic authenticity. They knew that they could go to National Geographic for reliable info."

The development of mapmaking expertise during World War I laid the foundation for the role that National Geographic would play in World War II. During the Second World War, the *New York Times* wrote that the Society's maps were "to be found at the front, in the air, in our embassies and consulates."

"National Geographic supplied the White House with maps for the White House map room," Poole says. "[President Roosevelt] would go over the maps with his chief advisers, keep track of the action, what was happening in the war, by following those maps." Later, according to Poole, the leaders of the United States, Great Britain, and the Soviet Union "were actually using a National Geographic map to decide what postwar Europe would look like."

For more from National Geographic, check out "Untold Stories of D-Day" online.

UNIT INQUIRY: Respond to a Crisis

In this unit, you learned about major crises that Americans faced in the first half of the 20th century. They confronted not only two world wars but also the worst economic depression the country had ever known. Based on your understanding of the text, in what ways did government leaders, businesses, organizations, and individual Americans respond to these crises? How did leaders, groups, and individuals work together to survive and prevail through the troubled times?

ASSIGNMENT

Choose one of the crises that you've read about in this unit, such as America's entry into World War I, the stock market crash of 1929, the Dust Bowl, or the bombing of Pearl Harbor. Consider what the ideal response of your community's government, schools, businesses, and individual citizens would be to the crisis. Outline an action plan for the various groups. Be prepared to present your action plan to the class and explain the reasons for the actions you suggest.

Gather Evidence As you consider your action plan, gather evidence from this unit about the ways Americans actually responded to the crisis you have chosen. Note the challenges that the crisis posed and how those challenges were addressed. Think about the benefits and drawbacks of the various reactions to the crisis. Use a graphic organizer like this one to help organize your evidence.

CRISIS	
CHALLENGES	RESPONSES

Produce Use your notes to create an action plan for the following groups in your community: the government, schools, businesses, and individual citizens. For each group, outline a list of actions they might take to help address the challenges posed by the crisis.

Present Choose a creative way to present your action plan to the class. Consider one of these options:

- Create an illustrated poster that shows the challenges you've identified and the actions that you propose each group take.

- Stage a debate with a classmate in which each of you present your ideas and debate the best actions to take.

- Organize teams based on the particular crisis that students chose. Hold team discussions on ways to respond to the crisis.

NATIONAL GEOGRAPHIC | LEARNING FRAMEWORK ACTIVITIES

Research War Damage

SKILLS Communication

KNOWLEDGE Our Living Planet

Besides taking the lives of many people, warfare also kills other living organisms and scars the natural environment. Environmental damage results not only from the warfare itself but also from the need to exploit natural resources to manufacture weapons and supplies. Research the environmental damage caused by World War I or World War II. You might focus on the damage in a specific area or region, such as Europe or Hiroshima, or investigate the overall environmental damage. Use your findings to prepare a multimedia presentation for the class.

Share the Arts of the 1920s

ATTITUDE Empowerment

SKILLS Collaboration, Observation

At the end of World War I, drastic changes in attitude and expression occurred in the United States. Young Americans sought something different and exciting. New developments in art, architecture, fashion, music, and literature occurred. Work in pairs or as a small group to investigate one of these forms of expression. Share examples of the art, fashion, or music of the 1920s with the class through a presentation or demonstration. Explain how the form of expression differs from those of previous generations.

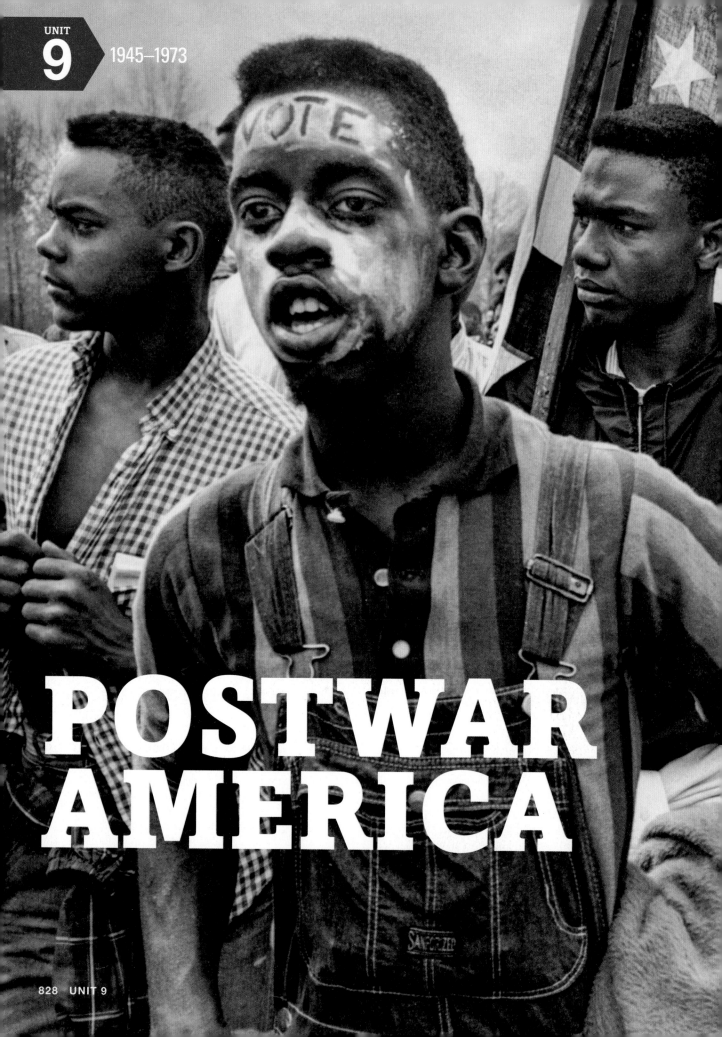

POSTWAR AMERICA

CRITICAL VIEWING In 1965, Selma, Alabama, was arguably the hub of civil rights activism. This photo shows protesters led by Martin Luther King, Jr., marching from Selma to Montgomery to demand voting rights for African Americans. Months later, Congress would pass the Voting Rights Act of 1965, outlawing literacy tests and other discriminatory practices used to deny minorities the right to vote. What does this photo reveal about the mood of the Selma-to-Montgomery marches and the sentiments of the marchers?

POSTWAR AMERICA

THE UNITED STATES

1955
Rosa Parks is arrested for refusing to give up her seat on a bus to a white man in Montgomery, Alabama. *(bus Rosa Parks was riding when she refused to give up her seat)*

1957
Angry mobs confront nine African-American students trying to attend an all-white high school in Little Rock, Arkansas. *(The National Guard escorts the Little Rock Nine students as they leave the school.)*

1950
Senator Joseph McCarthy begins his hunt for communists in the U.S. government.

1954
In *Brown* v. *Board of Education*, the Supreme Court rules that schools segregated by race are unconstitutional.

1948
President Harry S. Truman signs an executive order abolishing racial discrimination in the U.S. military.

1950

1945

1948 EUROPE
Western powers conduct the Berlin Airlift to drop supplies into West Berlin after the Soviet Union blocks access to the city.

1949 ASIA
Mao Zedong establishes the communist-controlled People's Republic of China. *(statue of Mao)*

1954 ASIA
The Geneva Accords divide Vietnam into communist North Vietnam and anticommunist South Vietnam.

1950 ASIA
Communist North Korea invades South Korea, and the Korean War begins.

THE WORLD

HISTORICAL THINKING: DETERMINE CHRONOLOGY

What earlier occurrence in Asia is probably related to events that took place in the United States in 1964 and in Asia in 1968?

1962
Astronaut John Glenn becomes the first American to orbit Earth. *(helmet Glenn wore when he orbited Earth)*

1964
The Gulf of Tonkin Resolution gives President Lyndon Johnson the power to expand the U.S. presence in the Vietnam War. *(carrier U.S.S. Constellation involved in the Gulf of Tonkin incident)*

1968
Martin Luther King, Jr., and Robert Kennedy are assassinated.

1973
Members of the American Indian Movement occupy Wounded Knee, South Dakota, to protest the conditions on reservations.

1963
President Kennedy is assassinated.

1970

1961
President John F. Kennedy establishes the Peace Corps.

1960

1975

1962 AMERICAS
The United States and the Soviet Union face off after the Soviets begin building missile sites in Cuba.

1961 EUROPE
Communists construct a wall between East Berlin and West Berlin to prevent people from leaving East Germany.

1960 AFRICA
Seventeen African nations gain their independence.
(flag of Mauritania)

1968 ASIA
North Vietnam launches the Tet Offensive against South Vietnamese cities and military bases.
(a battle in Saigon following the Tet Offensive)

CHAPTER 25

THE COLD WAR AND THE AMERICAN DREAM

1945–1959

ESSENTIAL QUESTION
How did the United States change after World War II?

 AMERICAN STORIES TV Nation

SECTION 1 **Peacetime Adjustments**
KEY VOCABULARY
demobilization   national health insurance
low-cost housing

SECTION 2 **The Cold War, Korea, and McCarthyism**
KEY VOCABULARY
blacklist   containment   occupation zone
bloc   McCarthyism   reunify
brinkmanship

SECTION 3 **The Fifties**
KEY VOCABULARY
baby boom   situation comedy
Frostbelt   Sunbelt

AMERICAN GALLERY
ONLINE **Rock and Roll**

READING STRATEGY

SUMMARIZE

When you summarize, you restate text in your own words and shorten it by including only the most important main ideas and details. As you read this chapter, use a graphic organizer like this one to help you summarize important information about topics in the text. In the three columns, note key details. Then use your notes to write your summary about one of the topics in this chapter.

Supporting Detail	Supporting Detail	Supporting Detail
Many service members came home all at once after World War II.		
Summary		

"Anything you want we got right here in the U.S.A."

—Chuck Berry, "Back in the U.S.A."

TVNATION

CRITICAL VIEWING New Yorkers watch the 1953 live coronation of Queen Elizabeth on a display television in a store window. What does this photograph suggest about the availability of televisions in the early 1950s and the impact television had on society?

Today, our viewing options are almost staggering in number. We can watch content on a smartphone, tablet, laptop, or desktop computer. We can choose from cable networks, Internet streaming services, and videos posted by friends and strangers. Or we can relax in front of a flat-screen TV at home, watching a program produced by an old-fashioned broadcast network.

In the 1950s, the entertainment scene was much simpler. Sitting in front of your family's one TV set to watch one show at a time was the only option. Television had three national networks—NBC, ABC, and CBS—and color TVs were not common until the mid-1960s. Even so, families were hurrying to buy their first TVs, and the United States was becoming a TV nation.

THE 1950s: HAPPY FAMILIES

While the number of networks was small, the variety of programming was broad enough to satisfy even the pickiest viewer. You could watch comedies, dramas, Westerns, variety shows, and news programs. The situation comedy, or "sitcom," originated in the earliest days of television and remains popular today. A sitcom is a half-hour comedy show with a cast of characters that appears every week. In the 1950s, like today, many sitcoms revolved around the lives and adventures of a single family.

The sitcoms of the 1950s generally reflected both the stereotypes and dreams of some Americans. Popular shows such as *Father Knows Best, Ozzie*

The Cold War and the American Dream **835**

CRITICAL VIEWING The Beatles (from left: Paul McCartney, George Harrison, John Lennon, and Ringo Starr) rehearse before performing on *The Ed Sullivan Show* in 1964. What might be challenging about playing in front of a live studio audience and a TV audience simultaneously?

and Harriet, and *Leave It to Beaver* portrayed the charmed lives (and minor problems) of middle- to upper-class white families in the suburbs. Mother was a housewife. Dad was a businessman who left for work every day wearing a suit and carrying a briefcase. The kids were well adjusted and witty, money was never a problem, and nobody stayed angry for long. "You know, Mom," says the young son in *Leave It to Beaver*, "when we're in a mess, you kind of make things seem not so messy." "Well," his mother replies cheerfully, "isn't that sort of what mothers are for?"

Dialogue like that is almost painfully cute to today's audiences. However, it reflects the optimistic mind-set and idealized vision of the American family common in the 1950s. Still, family sitcoms did portray some realities of life in the 1950s. Millions of people were moving to newly built suburbs, and the number of women working outside the home was much lower than it had been during World War II. On the other hand, even though people of color formed a large percentage of the U.S. population, they rarely appeared on TV. Few sitcoms featured a minority family or a single-parent household.

VARIETY SHOWS AND NEWS

Like sitcoms, variety shows were a 1950s favorite. The reigning king of the genre was Ed Sullivan, whose program debuted in 1948. *The Ed Sullivan Show* featured acts from every realm of entertainment, including opera singers, ballet dancers, acrobats, magicians, comedians, jugglers, jazz musicians, and rock stars. Elvis Presley, the Beatles, and the Rolling Stones all appeared on the *The Ed Sullivan Show*, which ran until 1971.

In the 1950s, TV was also becoming Americans' favorite way to get the news. Many journalists who had previously worked in radio made the transition to TV, including Edward R. Murrow. Murrow was much admired for the reports he had broadcast from London during World War II. He began hosting a news program on CBS called *See It Now* in 1951. In 1956, NBC launched *The Huntley-Brinkley Report*, anchored by Chet Huntley in New York City and David Brinkley in Washington, D.C. It was the first news program broadcast from two locations at the same time. News anchors such as Murrow, Huntley, and Brinkley became familiar and trusted faces night after night.

THE CALL OF THE WEST

Possibly the most popular TV genre of the 1950s and 1960s was the Western. Heroic sheriffs and brave cowboys chased after bad guys night after night during prime time. Westerns for children, such as *The Roy Rogers Show*, dominated Saturday TV. By the end of the 1950s, 31 prime-time Westerns were appearing each week—on just three networks.

Some of the most beloved Westerns enjoyed long runs. *The Lone Ranger* aired from 1949 to 1957. Even more extraordinary, *Gunsmoke* ran for 20 years, from 1955 to 1975. Short-run Westerns also could be wildly successful. One children's five-part series about Davy Crockett, which first aired in 1954, started a regular craze. Millions of children begged for Davy Crockett shirts, blankets, toothbrushes, and lunch boxes. Backyards and playgrounds were filled with boys wearing coonskin caps just like the one Crockett wore on TV.

Westerns may have been popular because they supported the upbeat American outlook of the 1950s. In a Western, it was always easy to tell the good guys from the bad guys, and the good guys always won. Very few characters were seriously harmed or killed, even in gunfights. Justice and the law always prevailed.

TV Westerns and other programs led to a boom in television-related merchandise, like this lunch box featuring Roy Rogers.

It was a Western series that brought the first Latino characters to television. In *The Cisco Kid,* Duncan Renaldo and Leo Carrillo portrayed Cisco and Pancho, two Mexican adventurers traveling around the Southwest. The show's tone was light hearted, and much of its humor came from Pancho making mistakes with the English language. Still, the pair were portrayed as admirable characters. They regularly helped the innocent and sent villains packing. Running from 1950 to 1956, *The Cisco Kid* was also the first TV series filmed in color.

THE 1960s: AN EXPANDING WORLD

The 1960s ushered in many cultural changes in the United States. The civil rights movement was gaining strength. Women, Latinos, and other minorities joined African Americans in seeking equal treatment in schools, workplaces, and society in general. Many young people began to rebel against the comfortable suburban lifestyle their parents had built. TV, as it always does, responded to the trends of the time.

African Americans had rarely appeared on-screen in the 1950s. The one notable exception was a comedy called *Amos 'n' Andy*, which, according to the NAACP, portrayed African Americans as either "clowns" or "crooks." Gradually this began to change in the 1960s. *Julia*, a comedy starring African-American actress Diahann Carroll as a widow raising her son on her own, was a hit with viewers. But the show was also criticized for skipping too lightly over real challenges faced by African Americans.

The face of television comedy also changed in 1968 when comedians Dan Rowan and Dick Martin launched a sketch comedy show called *Laugh-In*. The look of the show was a true departure from *Leave It to Beaver*'s calm suburban living room. The sets were painted in the wild colors and patterns fashionable among youth and teens in the late 1960s. The comedy was fast paced, featured a mixed-gender cast, and often poked fun at people in the news.

CRITICAL VIEWING On the TV show *Julia*, actress Diahann Carroll played a nurse and single mother raising a son. Why might *Julia* have been considered a revolutionary program in the late 1960s and early 1970s?

NBC pushed for increased cast diversity in the original *Star Trek* series by including characters from different cultures and giving an African-American female character, Lieutenant Uhura, a rare position of authority at the time.

Many people fondly remember the 1960s program *Star Trek*. Set in the 23rd century, the science fiction series revealed a future of harmony and equality among races, genders, and even species. The officers of the starship *Enterprise* included Lieutenant Uhura, played by African-American actress Nichelle Nichols, and Lieutenant Sulu, played by Japanese American actor George Takei.

THE MOST TRUSTED MAN IN AMERICA

News anchor Walter Cronkite was not glamorous or flashy. He had a deep, steady voice and a way of addressing viewers as if they were sitting across the table from him. His comforting presence and reputation for honesty earned him the nickname "most trusted man in America."

Cronkite served as the anchor of the *CBS Evening News* from 1962, when he helped launch the program, until 1981. From the anchor desk, he informed viewers of the most important stories of the 1960s—the highs and lows of the decade. He told the country about the assassinations of President Kennedy and Dr. Martin Luther King, Jr., and about the first moon landing.

Walter Cronkite also showed that news reporting can influence as well as inform. In 1968, according to his biographer, "Cronkite got up from his anchor desk, and flew to Vietnam, and put on a helmet and flak jacket, and interviewed anybody and everybody he could." Because Americans trusted Walter Cronkite, his "embedded reporting" from the battlefield was especially effective in bringing home the realities of war, and many were convinced by his conclusion that the war could not be won. Later, his coverage of the environment and the first Earth Day gave the environmental movement a boost.

After retiring from the *CBS Evening News*, Cronkite hosted numerous TV programs and short series for different channels and wrote several books. He died in 2009 at the age of 92.

CRITICAL VIEWING These images show Cronkite in one of his most difficult television moments: delivering the news, live, that President Kennedy had been assassinated on November 22, 1963. What do the photos reveal about Cronkite's emotional state?

Dr. Martin Luther King, Jr., a *Star Trek* fan, once told Nichols to stay with the show because Uhura was a symbol of promise for African Americans.

In the realm of current events, TV continued to be both a news reporter and a news maker. The Vietnam War became the first war to be extensively viewed on live television. Reporters filmed battles and their gory aftermath. They interviewed politicians at home and exhausted soldiers in Vietnam coping with the miseries of war. As commentator Marshall McLuhan remarked, "Television brought the brutality of war into the comfort of the living room." The shocking footage inspired many Americans to support the antiwar movement.

Another landmark moment for television news was the assassination of President John F. Kennedy in 1963. Within an hour of the president's shooting, both CBS and NBC had interrupted their programming to announce that the president had been shot. Soon after, CBS anchor Walter Cronkite, visibly upset, told the country that the president was dead. For the next four days, the networks covered the events that followed as millions of grieving viewers remained glued to their TV sets. Cameras were present when Lee Harvey Oswald, the man who killed Kennedy, was transferred from one jail building to another. Among the reporters, a man named Jack Ruby slipped close to Oswald and shot him to death on live TV.

AND ALWAYS, THE COMMERCIALS

Where there is TV, there is advertising. This was as true at the dawn of the television age as it is today. When sales of TV sets took off in the 1950s, advertisers followed. By the end of the decade, advertising took up 15 percent of airtime. More money was spent making commercials than producing the shows themselves. Like the sitcoms of the 1950s, many commercials portrayed a wealthy, happy, suburban America. Families were shown enjoying the many consumer goods that went on sale after the end of World War II.

Some advertising trends that exist today were set in those early days. Advertisers quickly recognized that children and teens were a growing and receptive audience. As a result, companies began targeting certain ads toward the youth market. Many brands also began using celebrities as on-screen spokespeople, and a few fictional "spokespeople," such as Tony the Tiger, also got their start in the 1950s.

TV advertising also made its presence known in the presidential elections in the 1950s. In the 1952 race, General Dwight D. Eisenhower's campaign produced a series of ads called "Eisenhower Answers America." Each spot showed the candidate appearing to answer questions from a variety of citizens. After the election, some people criticized these ads. They thought that selling a candidate as if he were a product hurt the dignity of the office. These criticisms were largely ignored, and campaign advertising became a mainstay on American TV.

In the 1960s, commercials once again moved with the times. In the middle of the decade, almost 50 percent of the U.S. population was younger than 25 years old. Advertisers continued their strong focus on the youth market. They noticed that many young people were rebelling against the consumer society of the 1950s, so they got creative with their approach and used humor and irony instead of images of traditional families to sell their products.

Advertising was slow to begin featuring people of color. Throughout the 1960s, most commercials featured only white actors. By the end of the decade, however, they were becoming more diverse. This movement reached a landmark moment in 1971, when Coca-Cola's "I'd Like to Buy the World a Coke" ad debuted. The spot showed young people of many races and nationalities singing a catchy jingle about living in harmony—and, of course, buying Coke. It has been called the world's most famous ad.

In many ways, the world of television and video we know today simply continues in the patterns that were first set in the 1950s. News programs are live

GIVE A HOOT! DON'T POLLUTE

Thanks for giving a hoot! Woodsy

Introduced by the U.S. Forest Service in the 1970s, Woodsy Owl became the face of conservation efforts through posters, like the one shown above, and TV commercials (right) during the 1980s.

THE MAGIC OF A MOUSE

Every weekday evening from 1955 to 1959, kids across the United States took a break from their homework to tune in the family TV set to *The Mickey Mouse Club*. Considered revolutionary, this brainchild of Walt Disney himself was the first children's TV show that featured mostly child actors.

The young performers danced, sang, and entertained on the hour-long show, which also included a newsreel, a Mickey Mouse cartoon, and an ongoing drama series. Viewers were hooked. The wholesome Mouseketeers reached their audience in positive ways through songs and skits about such topics as the importance of drinking milk and bicycle safety. The show's iconic theme song emphasized its appeal to all children with lyrics that included, "Hey there, hi there, ho there, you're as welcome as can be. M-I-C-K-E-Y M-O-U-S-E." New versions of *The Mickey Mouse Club* aired in the 1970s and 1990s.

With their signature ears and labeled sweaters, the talented Mouseketeers, shown in this 1956 photo, charmed audiences from coast to coast.

CRITICAL VIEWING Compare the photograph of the original *Addams Family* TV cast with the modern movie poster. How are they similar and different?

FROM CLASSIC TV TO THE MOVIES

The appeal of many TV series from the 1950s and 1960s has lasted into the 21st century. In recent decades, movie producers have often looked back to old hit shows for inspiration. This is a short list of classic TV shows that have been made into movies:

— *Star Trek* (numerous movies, beginning in 1979 and ongoing)
— *The Addams Family* (1991)
— *The Fugitive* (1993)
— *Maverick* (1994)
— *Leave It to Beaver* (1997)
— *The Mod Squad* (1999)
— *Get Smart* (2008)
— *The Lone Ranger* (2013)
— *The Man from U.N.C.L.E.* (2015)

and utterly up-to-date, sitcoms and dramas still draw viewers during the evenings, and the three major networks still exist. On the other hand, much has changed. Many more comedies and dramas now feature a diverse cast of characters, including gay and transgender people. Major networks face powerful competition from cable channels, streaming services, and newer broadcast networks. Variety shows have largely vanished, and reality shows now entrance viewers. Many people act as their own series creators and news reporters, posting their footage on different social media platforms. But one thing remains the same: TV and video provide a mirror that reflects who Americans are and who we want to be.

THINK ABOUT IT

How did the United States become a "TV Nation," and what influence has television had on American culture?

1.1 A Postwar Economic Boom

As World War II came to an end, Americans looked cautiously to the future. Would good times finally return, or would the country sink back into the joblessness, poverty, and despair of the Great Depression?

MAIN IDEA In the years after World War II, the United States enjoyed an economic boom and the civil rights movement gained momentum.

THE PEACETIME ECONOMY

As you have learned, World War II revitalized U.S. industry and brought an end to the Great Depression. The country enjoyed prosperity in the postwar years, but the transition from war to peace brought many challenges.

The **demobilization** of the U.S. Armed Forces following the war meant that millions of service members were discharged from the military. This huge wave of veterans returned home over a period of months, and most of them set out to find jobs. At the same time, the federal government began to cancel military contracts, which led to massive layoffs in defense-related industries. Too many applicants for too few jobs caused many Americans to fear that the Great Depression might return.

The wartime Congress had anticipated these developments, and in 1944 it had passed the Servicemen's Readjustment Act, which became known as the

GI Bill of Rights. This popular bill had a profound impact on American society and on the country's economy. It fueled a nationwide construction boom by encouraging veterans to buy homes. The government provided long-term, low-interest home loans to returning GIs, including loan guarantees of up to $2,000. Further, by providing grants for college tuition, it allowed former soldiers to fulfill

VETERANS— prepare for your future thru **EDUCATIONAL TRAINING**

CONSULT YOUR NEAREST OFFICE OF THE

VETERANS ADMINISTRATION

While the fighting still raged, the federal government was concerned about the veterans who were already returning from active duty and the millions who would be demobilized at the war's end. In 1943, the Office for Emergency Management created this poster advising veterans that education and training were available to them.

the dream of earning a college degree. Determined to make up for lost time, veterans formed the core of the United States' growing white-collar, or professional, workforce in the prosperous years ahead.

At the same time, many women were leaving the workforce. The war had given American women new opportunities in both military and civilian jobs. After the war, however, these gains largely disappeared, at least temporarily. Returning servicemen reclaimed jobs in offices and industries. Women were pressured to return to traditionally female roles, such as teaching, nursing, and homemaking.

At home, Americans enthusiastically embraced newly affordable consumer goods after the sacrifices of the Great Depression and World War II. Mass advertising encouraged this trend. Sales of new homes and cars soared. So did sales of home appliances such as refrigerators, washing machines, and clothes dryers. These purchases were made possible by the savings that many Americans had accumulated during the war and by the availability of easy credit.

PRESSURE FOR CIVIL RIGHTS

African Americans had played a major role in the U.S. war effort, both in the armed services and on the home front. After the war, however, they found that the country they had served faithfully still treated them as second-class citizens. Throughout the nation, African Americans faced job and housing discrimination. In the South in particular, laws mandated that blacks and whites use segregated, or separate, public services. Many felt a renewed determination to fight for their civil rights. This term refers to the fundamental rights and liberties promised to all Americans by the U.S. Constitution and its amendments.

In 1941, President Franklin Roosevelt had signed an executive order prohibiting racial discrimination in the U.S. defense industry. The armed forces, meanwhile, had remained racially segregated throughout World War II. Civil rights groups such as the NAACP and leaders like A. Philip Randolph pressured President Harry Truman to take action. Ultimately, he did so. In 1948, Truman signed **Executive Order 9981**, which abolished racial segregation in the U.S. military.

The Transistor Revolution

Measuring just three by five inches, the Zephyr 9 transistor radio sported a curved design that fit comfortably in a person's hand. The small radio and its "big" sound were made possible by the invention of the transistor, a very tiny electronic device. Radio had been losing its stars and audiences to the new medium of television throughout the 1950s, but it rebounded when the lightweight, portable transistor radios hit the market. Over the following two decades, transistor radios sold in the billions.

HISTORICAL THINKING

1. **READING CHECK** How did American consumer behavior after the war reflect the return to prosperity?

2. **MAKE INFERENCES** Why do you think President Truman decided to end segregation in the U.S. Armed Forces? Support your response with evidence from the text.

3. **SUMMARIZE** What impact did the GI Bill of Rights have on returning veterans?

1.2 Truman's Fair Deal

You've seen it happen in sports. Everyone knows which team is going to win, but then the underdog pulls off an upset. In the 1948 presidential election, Harry Truman looked like a candidate on a losing team, but he aimed confidently for a major upset at the polls.

MAIN IDEA Following a period of tensions between labor and government, Harry Truman renewed his efforts to bring about liberal domestic reforms.

LABOR TENSIONS

One of the biggest problems the United States faced after World War II was inflation—that is, rising prices and a decrease in the value of money. During the war, the federal government had set price controls on many goods and services. When most of the controls were lifted in June 1946, prices shot up.

Higher prices meant a drop in workers' real income because basic purchases took up more of their paychecks. In late 1945, the United Auto Workers (UAW), a large automotive industry union, had already tackled the issue of low wages. It demanded an average pay increase of 33 cents an hour from General Motors. When the corporation refused to meet the demand, the union began a strike that

Striking auto supply workers walk a picket line at the Kelsey-Hayes Wheel Company in September 1945. That year, union auto workers went on strike without the union's consent and caused the Ford Motor Company to shut down production.

NO RAISE SINCE THE WAR WE WANT 30% INCREASE

WE CAN'T AFFORD TO LOSE *Now!*

After winning the 1948 election, a laughing and triumphant President Harry S. Truman holds up the *Chicago Daily Tribune* to show off the newspaper's error in declaring his Republican rival, Thomas Dewey, the winner. Other newspapers, radio broadcasters, and even some Democrats had expected Truman to lose the election.

lasted 113 days. Soon, a wave of strikes hit the country. By 1946, more than 4.5 million U.S. workers had walked off their jobs, crippling entire industries.

These labor actions provoked a strong backlash against unions. In 1947, the Republican-controlled Congress passed the **Taft-Hartley Act**, which curbed the power of organized labor. It gave the president authority to impose a "cooling off" period to prevent strikes that threatened the national interest. More important, the bill made it illegal to require workers to join a union. It also encouraged states to pass "right-to-work" laws that made union organizing more difficult.

Despite the Taft-Hartley Act, union membership remained high, and the ability of unions to bargain on behalf of employees was largely unaffected. Workers in manufacturing industries enjoyed much higher wages and better benefits than they had during the Great Depression.

THE FAIR DEAL

As the presidential election of 1948 approached, few people thought Truman stood a chance of winning. His popularity was low, and he faced a strong Republican challenger, Governor Thomas Dewey of New York. Undaunted, Truman pursued a vigorous campaign of personal appearances and fiery speeches in which he laid out his policy ideas before the voters. His popularity began to climb, and on Election Day he pulled off one of the greatest upsets in American political history.

In his second term, Truman pursued an agenda of domestic reforms that he called the **Fair Deal**. The reforms included expansion of Social Security, an increase in education spending, and the creation of more **low-cost housing**—that is, housing affordable to people with lower incomes. As in his first term, Truman pushed for **national health insurance**, an insurance plan run by the government and open to any American who chose to join, but it failed to pass Congress. So did many other parts of the Fair Deal.

Truman did achieve wins in a few areas, however, including low-cost housing and an expansion of Social Security that greatly increased the number of people covered as well as the benefits they would receive. Truman also pushed for the federal minimum wage to be raised from 40 cents to 75 cents per hour, and Congress complied.

HISTORICAL THINKING

1. **READING CHECK** What events led up to the passing of the Taft-Hartley Act?

2. **DRAW CONCLUSIONS** Why do you think Fair Deal reforms might have appealed to struggling Americans? Cite evidence from the text to support your response.

3. **ANALYZE LANGUAGE USE** Why do you think Truman named his reform agenda the Fair Deal?

2.1 The Cold War Starts

What do you call a war that is fought with words instead of bombs and with political strategy instead of battlefield maneuvers?

MAIN IDEA After World War II, the United States and the Soviet Union plunged into a political and diplomatic rivalry that threatened to spark a war between the two countries.

THE IRON CURTAIN

The United States and the Soviet Union had been uneasy allies in World War II. After the war, anger and suspicion grew on both sides. Soviet leaders felt that the United States cared little about the security needs of the Soviet people. American leaders increasingly viewed the Soviet Union as a warmongering force focused on expanding its communist empire.

In the summer of 1945, the United States, Great Britain, France, and the Soviet Union divided Germany into four **occupation zones**. The Soviets controlled the eastern part of Germany. The United States, Great Britain, and France each controlled an occupation zone in the west. Berlin, Germany's capital, was entirely within the Soviet occupation zone, but it was governed by a joint agency of all four nations. The Soviets controlled

the eastern section of the city, or East Berlin, and the Western Allies controlled the rest, or West Berlin.

In addition to the zone it controlled in eastern Germany, the Soviet Union had gained dominance over many countries in Eastern and central Europe, including Bulgaria, Romania, Poland, and Hungary. Together with the Soviet Union, these nations came to be known as the Soviet **bloc**, or alliance. The expansion of the Soviet bloc and the resulting spread of communism worried the United States and its Western European allies.

In March 1946, former British prime minister Winston Churchill told an audience at Westminster College in Missouri that an **Iron Curtain** had descended across Europe. He was referring to the political and military barrier the Soviet Union

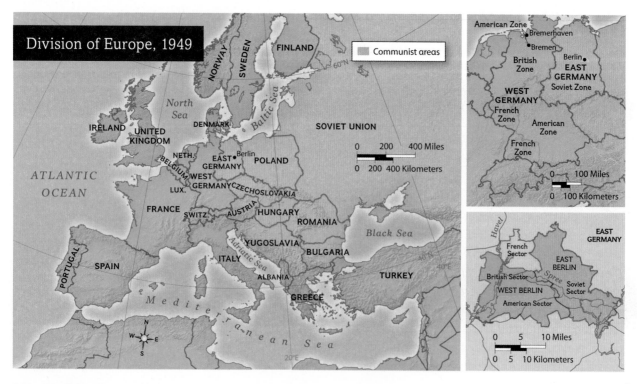

Division of Europe, 1949

In 1948, German children scrambled up a pile of rubble left from World War II to wave excitedly at a U.S. cargo plane participating in the Berlin Airlift. The United States and its allies airlifted food and other supplies to the city after the Soviets had cut off the West Berliners' access to the outside world.

had put in place to discourage contact between the communist Soviet bloc and the democratic countries to the west.

Amid the growing tensions, the **Cold War** began. It was a political conflict that simmered for decades, but it never heated up into full-blown warfare. It was also global: The Soviet Union sought to bring other countries under Soviet influence. In response, the United States adopted a policy of **containment**, using diplomatic and military strategies to halt the spread of communism.

To help contain communism in Europe, the United States and 11 Western European countries founded the **North Atlantic Treaty Organization (NATO)** in 1949. NATO members pledged to come to one another's aid in the event of an attack by the Soviet Union.

THE BERLIN AIRLIFT

You have read about the Marshall Plan and the role it played in rebuilding Europe after the war. It also was instrumental in the United States' containment efforts. By restoring economic confidence throughout Western Europe, it curbed the influence of local communist parties in Italy and France. The plan also increased American trade and investment in Europe, opening new markets for American goods and political ideas.

The **Berlin Airlift** was another notable postwar aid effort. In June 1948, the Soviet Union blockaded West Berlin, cutting off land access to the city. The Western Allies responded by delivering supplies such as food and fuel by air. At one point, Allied planes were landing every 45 seconds at Berlin's airport. Recognizing that the blockade had failed, the Soviets lifted it in May 1949.

HISTORICAL THINKING

1. **READING CHECK** What was the Soviet bloc?

2. **INTERPRET MAPS** What do you see on the map that helps you understand why West Berlin was a source of tension between the Soviet Union and the Western Allies?

3. **IDENTIFY MAIN IDEAS AND DETAILS** How did the Marshall Plan help the United States' containment efforts?

2.2 Communism in Asia

Sometimes what works in one situation won't work in another. The U.S. policy of containment seemed to be doing a good job controlling the spread of communism in Europe. Asia, however, was a different story.

MAIN IDEA The Cold War intensified at the end of the 1940s as communism began to spread in Asia.

In Shanghai, China, a young girl glances at a huge picture of the late Chinese leader Mao Zedong, who died in 1976. To the left of the image is written "In memory of Chairman Mao's 110th birthday," which was commemorated in 2003. During his lifetime, the government produced millions of images promoting Mao's leadership.

COMMUNIST CHINA

In the late 1940s, the Cold War turned into a "hot war" in Asia. Developments in China and Korea had profound implications for the political battle that the United States and its democratic allies were waging against communist expansion.

A civil war had been raging in China since before World War II. On one side was the Nationalist Party, headed by **Chiang Kai-shek** (jee-AHNG ky-SHEHK), which relied heavily on U.S. support. On the other side was the Chinese Communist Party, whose leader was **Mao Zedong** (MOW dzuh-DUNG). When the Nationalists came to power in the 1920s, Mao recruited farmers and other rural residents to revolt against the government. Under his leadership, they joined the fighting force called the Red Army. When Chiang's forces drove the communists into a lengthy retreat, called the Long March, Mao's military strategies kept the Red Army together. Once Japan began its invasion of China during the 1930s, both Mao and Chiang turned their attention to defending the nation, putting the internal fighting on hold.

When the world war ended, the civil war began again in earnest. At first, the Nationalists seemed to have the upper hand. But in 1948, the course of the war changed. Mao's communist army, now called the People's Liberation Army (PLA), handed Chiang's forces one defeat after another. The United States sent weapons and funds to Chiang to help defeat Mao's forces, but much of this American weaponry ended up in the hands of the communists as the Nationalists retreated. By late 1949, the PLA had gained control of the entire country except for Taiwan—an island off China's southeast coast—and a few other islands. On October 1, Mao proclaimed the establishment of the **People's Republic of China**. He also declared his solidarity with the Soviet Union.

The communist takeover of China shocked many Americans. How well did the containment policy really work, they wondered, when more than 600 million people had just been "lost" to communism?

Chiang Kai-shek and other Nationalist leaders retreated to Taiwan, along with Nationalist troops and about 2 million refugees. The leaders did not admit defeat. Rather, they claimed they were still the rightful government of China.

TWO KOREAS

China wasn't the only communist threat in Asia. Communism also arose in Indochina and in Korea. Japan had annexed Korea in 1910 and had ruled it oppressively for more than three decades. With Japan's defeat in World War II, Koreans looked forward to regaining their independence. Their hopes were not met.

Two days after the bombing of Hiroshima, the Soviet Union declared war on Japan. Within days, the Soviets landed troops in the northern part of Korea. U.S. and Soviet officials arranged for Korea to be split into two occupation zones. The Soviet Union controlled the zone that lay north of the **38th parallel**—that is, the imaginary line representing 38 degrees north latitude. The United States occupied the zone south of the line.

U.S. leaders expected the division to be temporary, since both the United States and the Soviet Union had pledged to support Korea's independence. But soon the two zones began to move in different directions politically. They established separate identities as **North Korea** and **South Korea**.

In 1947, the United States handed responsibility for South Korea and Korean independence over to the United Nations. The following year, South Korea declared its independence as the Republic of Korea. The new country adopted a presidential system of government and an anticommunist stance. North Korea declared itself the Democratic People's Republic of Korea, a communist regime backed by the Soviet Union. Tensions grew between the two Koreas as their leaders made daily threats to "liberate" each other's land.

HISTORICAL THINKING

1. **READING CHECK** How did China become a communist country?

2. **SUMMARIZE** Why did Americans become disillusioned with the containment policy?

3. **MAKE PREDICTIONS** What do you think might happen in Korea after the establishment of two separate republics in 1948? Explain your response.

2.3 The Korean War

It is said that war teaches geography. Until the conflict began in Korea in 1950, most Americans knew little about that distant country. Suddenly, they were reading about Korea every day in the newspapers and about the American soldiers who were risking their lives there.

MAIN IDEA U.S. forces helped repel North Korea's invasion of South Korea, but they were forced to retreat after China entered the war.

NORTH KOREA INVADES SOUTH KOREA

On June 25, 1950, troops from communist North Korea launched a massive invasion into South Korea. The North Koreans, with Soviet support, sought to forcibly **reunify**, or reunite, the two Koreas and establish communist rule over the entire Korean peninsula.

The attack put great pressure on President Truman. His administration had withdrawn American combat troops from Korea and implied that the country was not vital to the free world's security. That did not keep Truman from viewing the invasion as a clear-cut act of aggression. He also believed failure to take action might make him appear "soft" on communism.

Truman moved quickly, proposing a United Nations resolution that offered assistance to South Korea to repel the attack. A week later, without consulting Congress, Truman sent U.S. ground troops to South Korea as part of a UN military effort. In addition to American troops, soldiers and medical personnel from Australia, New Zealand, Great Britain, France, Turkey, Thailand, and 14 other countries took part.

For two months, North Korean forces pushed the UN forces back. By September, North Korea controlled all of South Korea except the southeastern corner. Then UN forces under the command of U.S. general Douglas MacArthur took the offensive. In a stroke of brilliance, MacArthur

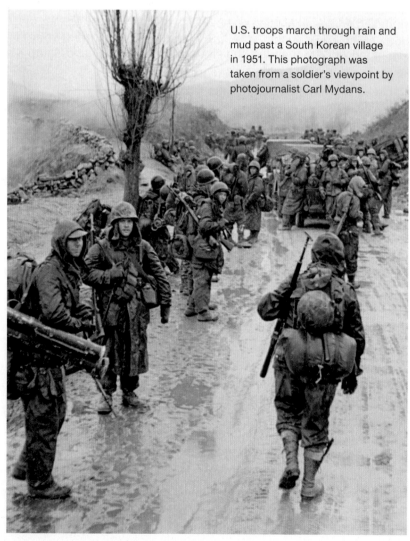

U.S. troops march through rain and mud past a South Korean village in 1951. This photograph was taken from a soldier's viewpoint by photojournalist Carl Mydans.

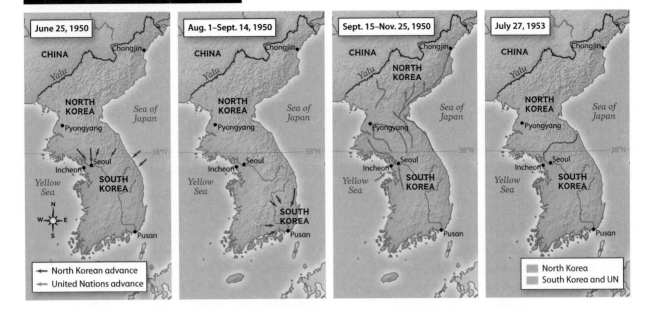

The Korean War, 1950–1954

June 25, 1950
CHINA · Chongjin · NORTH KOREA · Pyongyang · Yalu · Sea of Japan · 38°N · Incheon · Seoul · SOUTH KOREA · Yellow Sea · Pusan
→ North Korean advance
← United Nations advance

Aug. 1–Sept. 14, 1950
CHINA · Chongjin · NORTH KOREA · Pyongyang · Yalu · Sea of Japan · 38°N · Incheon · Seoul · Yellow Sea · SOUTH KOREA · Pusan

Sept. 15–Nov. 25, 1950
CHINA · Chongjin · NORTH KOREA · Pyongyang · Yalu · Sea of Japan · 38°N · Incheon · Seoul · SOUTH KOREA · Yellow Sea · Pusan

July 27, 1953
CHINA · Chongjin · NORTH KOREA · Pyongyang · Yalu · Sea of Japan · 38°N · Incheon · Seoul · SOUTH KOREA · Yellow Sea · Pusan
■ North Korea
■ South Korea and UN

landed troops at **Incheon** on South Korea's west coast, deep behind enemy lines. His strategy forced the North Korean army into a hasty retreat. Within weeks, UN forces had chased the North Koreans back to the 38th parallel.

CHINA CROSSES THE YALU RIVER

Sweeping into North Korea, UN forces soon captured **Pyongyang** (pee-UHNG-YAHNG), the capital city. Ignoring warnings from China, they continued their swift northward advance. By late October, some regiments had reached the **Yalu River** on North Korea's border with China.

China responded quickly and forcefully. A large Chinese force attacked MacArthur's army and pushed it southward. After weeks of fierce fighting, American army and marine units managed to halt the Chinese advance just south of the 38th parallel. Although disaster had been avoided, Americans were shocked by what *Time* magazine described as "the worst military setback the United States has ever suffered."

Meanwhile, MacArthur and President Truman were increasingly at odds with one another. MacArthur chafed at fighting a limited war. He recommended a naval blockade of China's coast, massive bombing of its factories and power plants, and an invasion of the Chinese mainland to be led by the forces of Chiang Kai-shek. MacArthur even suggested using nuclear weapons against

North Korea. Truman worried that expanding the war would alarm the other members of the UN coalition and could even draw the Soviet Union into the conflict. In April 1951, after MacArthur had repeatedly challenged his authority, an infuriated Truman relieved the general of his command.

By June, the war had reached a stalemate. Neither side could achieve victory. Peace negotiations began in July and dragged on for two years. During this period, fighting continued along the front, and U.S. voters elected a new president: Dwight D. Eisenhower, who had commanded the Allied forces in Europe during World War II. In July 1953, North and South Korea signed an armistice that ended the hostilities but left Korea divided.

HISTORICAL THINKING

1. **READING CHECK** How did China's entry into the Korean conflict change the war for UN forces?

2. **INTERPRET MAPS** What challenges do you think Korea's terrain posed to the marines and soldiers on the ground in the Korean War?

3. **MAKE INFERENCES** Why do you think President Truman did not ask for Congress's approval before sending troops to Korea?

2.4 Fear of Communism

At first glance the senator from Wisconsin didn't look very intimidating. But for a short time in the 1950s, Joseph McCarthy held the country in fearful suspense with his very public search for communists in the United States.

MAIN IDEA In the late 1940s and early 1950s, fear of communism gripped citizens and government officials in the United States, leading to prosecutions of both suspected and avowed communists.

THE COMMUNIST THREAT

As the Soviet Union grew more powerful and communist regimes gained control in Eastern Europe and Asia, Americans became increasingly worried about the spread of communism. Their fears multiplied in 1949 when President Truman announced that the Soviet Union had exploded an atomic bomb. The end of the U.S. monopoly on atomic weapons raised the horrifying prospect of an all-out nuclear war.

The Soviet Union was supposedly years behind the United States in nuclear technology. How, then, had it managed to develop an atomic weapon so quickly? Some officials believed the only possible answer was espionage. Authorities soon suspected that **Julius and Ethel Rosenberg**, a husband-and-wife spy team, had provided the Soviet Union with top-secret information from the Manhattan Project. The Rosenbergs were tried, convicted, and executed. But they weren't the only Americans suspected of being communist agents.

In the late 1930s, the U.S. House of Representatives had established the **House Un-American Activities Committee (HUAC)** to investigate Nazi propaganda in the United States. After World War II, the committee was revived as a watchdog against communist activities. In 1947, HUAC launched an investigation of the motion picture industry. The Hollywood Ten, a group of pro-communist writers and directors, refused to answer HUAC's questions about their political associations. They were sent to prison for contempt of Congress. Hollywood studio heads, caught up in the anticommunist whirlwind, put the names of those ten people and many others on a **blacklist**. Studios would not hire writers, directors, or performers who had been blacklisted.

Another person caught up in HUAC's investigation was **Alger Hiss**, a former federal government official who had served as an advisor to President Franklin Roosevelt. He was accused of stealing classified State Department documents and passing them on to a Soviet agent. Hiss was convicted and jailed for perjury, or lying under oath, sending shock waves through the nation.

During this period, the United States and the Soviet Union became locked in an arms race, a deadly serious contest to develop the most powerful weapons. It led to the development of the hydrogen bomb and to the production of rockets capable of delivering nuclear weapons to targets

The only two Americans executed for spying during the Cold War, Ethel and Julius Rosenberg were photographed during their trial in 1951. Later, the couple's sons worked to prove their parents' innocence. In 2016, new evidence proved their father's guilt but cast doubt on their mother's.

COMMUNIST PARTY ORGANIZAT

thousands of miles away. Each side sought to gain advantage through **brinkmanship**, the practice of pushing interactions to the brink, or edge, of dangerous confrontation.

THE RISE AND FALL OF McCARTHY

In 1950, **Senator Joseph McCarthy** of Wisconsin began making sensational claims about communists in the federal government. In 1952, McCarthy became chairman of the Senate's Committee on Government Operations and its subcommittee on investigations. In this powerful position, he looked for "communist influence" in the State Department and other government agencies. His hearings did not uncover many communists. They did, however, ruin many careers, undermine worker morale, and make the United States look fearful in the eyes of the world. This phenomenon became known as **McCarthyism**.

One of McCarthy's biggest targets was the U.S. Army. In the spring of 1954, the Senate held nationally televised hearings on charges that a communist spy ring was operating at an Army base in New Jersey. For 36 days, the nation watched McCarthy's frightening outbursts and crude personal attacks. His popularity plummeted, and a few months later the Senate censured him for acting "contrary to senatorial ethics." McCarthyism finally came to an end.

During McCarthy's televised hearings against the U.S. Army, the senator accused one of the attorneys working with the Army's lawyer, Joseph Welch, of associating with communists. Welch uttered the now famous words that effectively ended McCarthy's career:

PRIMARY SOURCE

Until this moment, Senator, I think I never really gauged your cruelty or your recklessness. . . . Let us not assassinate this lad further, Senator. You have done enough. Have you no sense of decency?

—Attorney Joseph Welch, June 9, 1954

HISTORICAL THINKING

1. **READING CHECK** What events led to the execution of Julius and Ethel Rosenberg?

2. **SUMMARIZE** How was the rise of Joseph McCarthy related to the dominant mood of Americans at the time?

3. **FORM AND SUPPORT OPINIONS** Do you think it was right for the motion picture industry to blacklist people because of their political beliefs? Support your opinion with evidence from the text.

The Cold War and the American Dream **853**

3.1 The American Dream?

What is your idea of the American dream? Millions of Americans in the 1950s dreamed of earning a good wage, providing for their families, and owning a nice home and car. For some, the dream was possible.

MAIN IDEA The 1950s were a time of population shifts, social change, and—for some but not all Americans—rising prosperity and living standards.

THE AMERICAN FAMILY

During the 1950s, many different forces were at work shaping American life. These included economic prosperity, new consumer products, and shifting population patterns.

Shortly after World War II, marriage rates had spiraled upward. Birthrates had risen sharply, too, and they remained high through the 1950s and into the 1960s. This prolonged period of high birthrates came to be known as the **baby boom**.

In addition to population growth, the decade saw two significant population shifts. Seeking more space and greener, safer environments for their families, large numbers of mostly white middle-class Americans moved from cities to suburbs. Explosive suburban growth fueled booms in the housing, automobile, and construction industries. For many large cities, though, it led to declines in population, political power, and quality of life.

The other population shift was from the **Frostbelt**—the Northeast and upper Midwest regions known for their harsh winters—to the **Sunbelt**, a 15-state region stretching from coast to coast across the southern United States. The Sunbelt's low taxes, inexpensive land, and warm climate attracted businesses, especially the growing military defense, electronics, and aerospace industries. At the same time, improvements in air conditioning made hot summers more bearable. Millions migrated from the Frostbelt to the Sunbelt for the new jobs or to retire.

Not everyone was content with the trends in family life. During the war, as you have learned, many women entered the U.S. workforce for the first time. After the war ended, they were encouraged to return to the more traditional roles of wife and mother. By the end of the 1950s, however, many women were questioning the notion that their place was in the home.

THE OTHER AMERICA

Not all Americans shared in the prosperity and rising living standards of the 1950s. Despite progress due to the growing civil rights movement, African Americans continued to face widespread discrimination and segregation. Doors to advancement that were open to other Americans were closed to them.

Those doors were often closed to Americans of Mexican descent, too. The Mexican American population had soared since 1942, the year the federal government had launched the Bracero Program. As you have read, this program aimed to address a labor shortage during World War II by

Reaching 50 States

In 1959, the U.S. territories of Alaska and Hawaii were admitted to statehood, rounding out the 50 United States we celebrate today. During World War II, the United States had expanded its army and navy bases in both territories as they became important to military strategy. That importance carried over into the Cold War era. Citizens of the two territories began their statehood efforts right after the end of World War II, but it took many years for Congress to pass measures admitting Alaska and Hawaii to the Union. Alaska became the 49th state on January 3, 1959. Hawaii followed suit as the 50th state on August 21, 1959. On July 4, 1960, the 50th star was officially added to the American flag.

bringing several hundred thousand *braceros*, or manual laborers, from Mexico to the United States to plant and harvest crops. Some of the braceros chose to stay in the country illegally, prompting anger and resentment among Americans. Unfortunately, this resentment extended to Mexican Americans and legal immigrants as well.

Although President Eisenhower worked to trim government spending, he kept in place popular New Deal programs aimed at struggling Americans. These programs included Social Security and unemployment insurance. "In all those things which deal with people, be liberal, he stated. "In all those things which deal with people's money . . . be conservative."

In a groundbreaking 1962 book titled *The Other America*, author Michael Harrington challenged the widely held belief that the New Deal had almost eliminated poverty. He claimed that 40 to 50 million Americans remained poor but that they were nearly invisible to more affluent, or wealthy, Americans. Harrington called for a "comprehensive assault on poverty" through federal legislation addressing education, medical care, housing, and jobs.

HISTORICAL THINKING

1. **READING CHECK** Why might people have been tempted to leave the Frostbelt for the Sunbelt?

2. **MAKE INFERENCES** What do you think Michael Harrington meant when he stated that the poor were "invisible" to other Americans?

3. **SUMMARIZE** What are some ways in which the United States changed during the 1950s?

3.2 The Suburbanization of America

MAIN IDEA After World War II, millions of Americans moved to the suburbs, which had a significant impact on the country's economy, society, and culture.

LIVING THE AMERICAN DREAM

As you know, Congress passed the GI Bill in 1944 to help World War II veterans readjust to civilian life. The bill helped cover education costs and provided low-interest home loans to veterans. Many of the men and women who returned from the war were starting families and wanted to buy a house. Home ownership is a big part of the American dream. However, most cities couldn't keep up with the demand for housing.

As a result, veterans paid contractors to build affordable single-family houses in the suburbs. By 1950, more than 18 million people, or 1 of every 8 Americans, had moved from the cities to the suburbs. This population shift is called **suburbanization**. In addition to offering space for larger houses, suburbs often had better schools and a lower crime rate than cities. You've learned that many Americans began buying more consumer goods in the 1950s, and automobiles were at the top of the list. Cars allowed workers to travel from the suburbs to jobs in the city. Access to the suburbs became easier when President Dwight Eisenhower signed the **Federal-Aid Highway Act of 1956**. The act included the **Interstate Highway System**, which linked towns, cities, and suburbs nationwide.

In 1947, William Levitt purchased several thousand acres of farmland on New York's Long Island for the mass production of homes. Using the assembly-line system developed by Henry Ford at his automobile plants, Levitt manufactured precut building materials in his factories. Then, on the building site, each construction worker performed a single task to complete each house. Builders made as many as 180 houses in a week. Once the homes were finished, schools, parks, churches, and shopping centers were added to the neighborhoods. The Long Island Levittown, as it was called, was

completed in 1951. Levitt would go on to build several other Levittowns in the Northeast.

Suburbanization transformed the American landscape and changed American life. The mass movement had an impact on the country economically, socially, and culturally. Many of these effects continue to influence American life today.

ECONOMIC IMPACT

Suburbanization contributed to the economic boom of the 1950s. It provided jobs in several sectors, including the construction and automobile industries. However, many businesses and factories also moved from the cities to the suburbs. With fewer people and businesses remaining in cities, local governments began to have trouble funding schools, transportation, and other city services.

SOCIAL IMPACT

The suburbs provided a generally safe and clean but ultimately segregated environment. Most African Americans couldn't afford to buy a car and move to the suburbs, and those who could were often prevented from moving. Many suburban neighborhoods, including the Long Island Levittown, refused to sell to African Americans. As a result, African Americans, other minorities, and the less wealthy remained in the cities. Suburbanization forced some farmers to sell their farms. It also disrupted wildlife habitats.

CULTURAL IMPACT

Suburban residents enjoyed many conveniences they hadn't had before, including modern kitchens. But some people criticized suburban life for its homogeneity, or sameness. The houses tended to look alike, and the people living in them did many of the same things. While the men went to work in their offices, the women stayed home to cook, clean, and look after the children.

THINK LIKE A GEOGRAPHER

1. **ANALYZE CAUSE AND EFFECT** What led many people to move to the suburbs after World War II?

2. **COMPARE AND CONTRAST** How did cities and suburbs differ following suburbanization?

3. **ANALYZE ENVIRONMENTAL CONCEPTS** How did suburbanization affect rural communities?

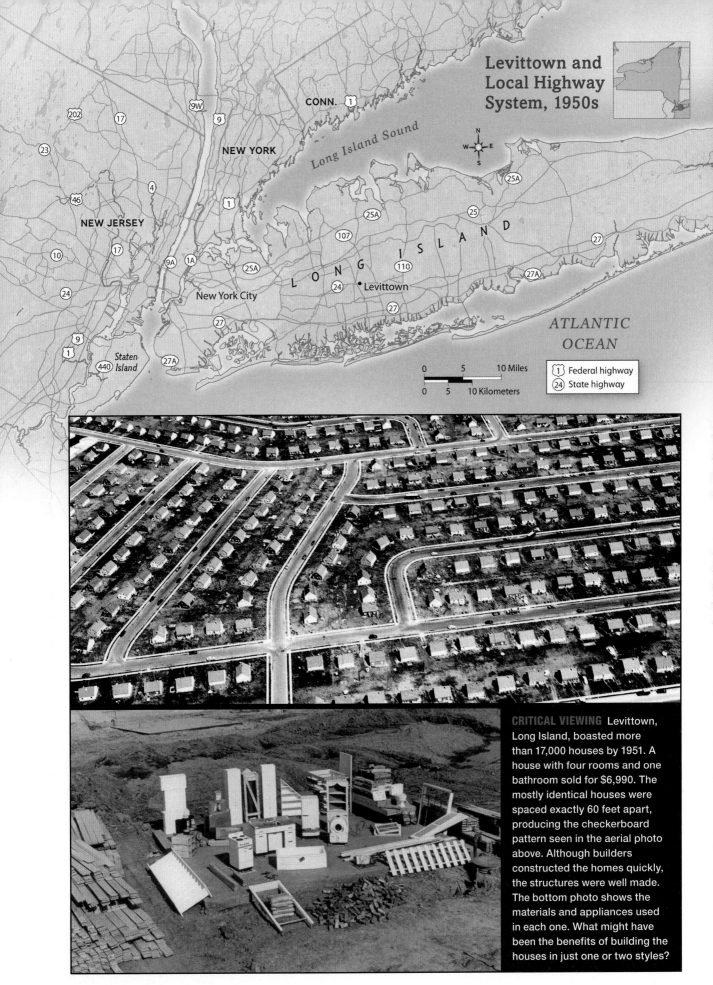

Levittown and Local Highway System, 1950s

Long Island Sound

CONN.

NEW YORK

NEW JERSEY

New York City

LONG ISLAND

• Levittown

ATLANTIC OCEAN

Staten Island

| 0 | 5 | 10 Miles |
| 0 | 5 | 10 Kilometers |

① Federal highway
㉔ State highway

CRITICAL VIEWING Levittown, Long Island, boasted more than 17,000 houses by 1951. A house with four rooms and one bathroom sold for $6,990. The mostly identical houses were spaced exactly 60 feet apart, producing the checkerboard pattern seen in the aerial photo above. Although builders constructed the homes quickly, the structures were well made. The bottom photo shows the materials and appliances used in each one. What might have been the benefits of building the houses in just one or two styles?

3.3 Television and Rock and Roll

Today, the average TV receives more crystal-clear channels than you can count. In the 1950s, the television experience featured a handful of channels, a sometimes wavy picture, and an antenna you had to adjust by hand. To the baby boomers and their families, it was the best entertainment ever.

MAIN IDEA In the 1950s, television emerged as a powerful medium of mass communication, and a youth culture centered on rock and roll music began to develop.

TELEVISION AND MASS CULTURE

As you have read, a mass culture arose in the United States in the 1920s. It was shaped and spread by radio and movies as well as by advertising, newspapers, and magazines. In the 1950s, television dominated American entertainment and helped transform mass culture.

In the early 1950s, television was still new. At the end of World War II, about 7,000 television sets existed in the United States. But by 1950, Americans were buying 20,000 televisions a day.

Early programming emphasized entertainment, with variety shows, quiz shows, Westerns, and **situation comedies**, such as *I Love Lucy*, in which a set cast of characters amused viewers with a funny adventure each week. The networks also aired quality dramas written by well-known authors and performed by famous stage and film actors. These programs were usually sponsored by name-brand products. Some critics have called this era the "golden age" of television.

The King of Rock and Roll
Teenage girls surround singer **Elvis Presley**, clamoring for an autograph. It was 1956—the year 21-year-old Elvis skyrocketed from a regional sensation to a national one. Girls flocked to his concerts and joined fan clubs; boys took guitar lessons and adopted his hairstyle. Admirers still call Elvis "the King."

Advertisers soon recognized television's enormous potential, and by the end of the decade advertising consumed 15 percent of television airtime. In this way, television, like radio before it, promoted the consumer society. Many economists believed that advertising contributed to prosperity by encouraging Americans to buy more goods.

The direction in which American society was heading did not sit well with all Americans. A youth rebellion that came to be known as the Beat movement took root in places such as New York City and San Francisco. Novelist **Jack Kerouac**, poet **Allen Ginsburg**, and other Beat writers criticized mass culture and the way it encouraged people to act and think alike. The Beat movement emphasized individuality and freedom of expression.

YOUTH CULTURE

Another major development in the 1950s was the rise of rock and roll music. It was deeply rooted in African-American rhythm and blues, but its influences also included country, gospel, and bluegrass music. It was characterized by a strong beat and loud singing and playing.

African-American performers such as **Chuck Berry** and **Little Richard** played leading roles in the development of rock and roll. Little Richard, in fact, proclaimed himself "the architect of rock and roll." His songs "Tutti Frutti" and "Long Tall Sally" and Berry's "Maybellene" and "Johnny B. Goode" were among the early hits that helped the genre gain broad appeal.

Rock and roll's popularity exploded with performers such as **Bill Haley**, **Elvis Presley**, and **Jerry Lee Lewis**. In 1953, Haley's "Crazy Man, Crazy" became the first rock and roll song to appear on *Billboard* magazine's pop music charts. Presley burst onto the popular music scene in 1955, and by 1956, he was a national sensation. Between 1956 and 1957, ten of his songs went to number one on the pop music chart.

Rock and roll became an important part of the youth culture emerging in the United States. This culture was rooted in the enormous prosperity and population growth that followed World War II. Unlike their parents, who had lived through desperate economic times and war, Americans

of the baby boom era were raised in relative comfort and wealth. Freed from the obligation to help support their families, many teens had money in their pockets. They bought records and listened with their friends. Nothing defined these young baby boomers more clearly than the music they shared.

In 2011, rocker Chuck Berry donated the guitar he played in his early days of touring and recording to the Smithsonian National Museum of African American History and Culture. Berry named this guitar and all his guitars for his first hit song, "Maybellene."

Chuck Berry's 1959 Gibson electric guitar

HISTORICAL THINKING

1. **READING CHECK** What kinds of programs were popular during television's "golden age"?

2. **COMPARE AND CONTRAST** What was one important difference between the youth of the 1950s and their parents?

3. **MAKE INFERENCES** Why do you think young people in the 1950s embraced rock and roll instead of the music their parents listened to?

THE COLD WAR AND THE AMERICAN DREAM

25 REVIEW

VOCABULARY

Match the following vocabulary terms with their definitions.

1. Sunbelt
2. brinkmanship
3. demobilization
4. occupation zone
5. blacklist
6. baby boom
7. bloc
8. McCarthyism
9. containment
10. national health insurance

a. removing all or part of a nation's military from active service

b. a campaign against alleged communists in the government and other U.S. institutions

c. an extended period of elevated birthrates

d. an insurance program established by a national government to ensure that all or most citizens have access to health care

e. an alliance of countries

f. a warm, sunny region that stretches across the southern United States

g. a list of people who are forbidden to work in an industry

h. the U.S. policy of using strategic force to block the expansion of communism

i. the practice of pushing interactions to the edge of a dangerous confrontation

j. one of the four zones into which the United States, Great Britain, France, and the Soviet Union split Germany

READING STRATEGY
SUMMARIZE

If you haven't already done so, complete your graphic organizer by identifying the important information discussed in this chapter and summarize the supporting details you have collected. Then answer the question.

Supporting Detail	Supporting Detail	Supporting Detail
Many service members came home all at once after World War II.		
Summary		

11. How were returning war veterans and many American families able to achieve a kind of American dream?

MAIN IDEAS

Answer the following questions. Support your answers with evidence from the chapter.

12. What action did President Truman take in 1948 that showed his support for the civil rights of African Americans? **LESSON 1.1**

13. How did labor unions respond to inflation in the postwar years? **LESSON 1.2**

14. What was the Berlin Airlift? **LESSON 2.1**

15. Why did the 38th parallel become significant in Korea after World War II? **LESSON 2.2**

16. Why was General MacArthur's move to land U.S. troops at Incheon daring? **LESSON 2.3**

17. What were Julius and Ethel Rosenberg convicted of and executed for? **LESSON 2.4**

18. What two major population shifts occurred in the United States in the 1950s? **LESSON 3.1**

19. How did television influence mass culture during the 1950s? **LESSON 3.3**

Answer the following questions. Support your answers with evidence from the chapter.

20. COMPARE AND CONTRAST How did the relationship between the United States and the Soviet Union change after World War II?

21. MAKE CONNECTIONS What connection can you make between the Great Depression and the consumerism of the postwar period?

22. DISTINGUISH FACT FROM OPINION Was Senator Joseph McCarthy's claim that the U.S. government was overrun with communist spies a fact or an opinion? Use evidence from the text to support your response.

INTERPRET MAPS

This U.S. map uses colors to show population change between 1950 and 1960. Study the map and then answer the questions that follow.

23. Which Sunbelt states grew in population by more than 50 percent between 1950 and 1960?

24. Name the Sunbelt states that have coasts on either the Pacific Ocean or the Atlantic Ocean (including the Gulf of Mexico).

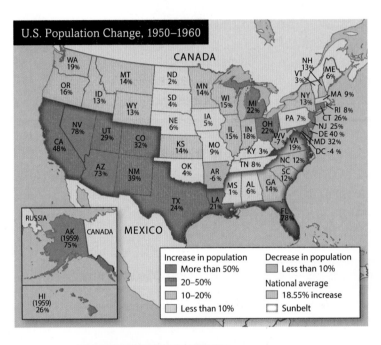

U.S. Population Change, 1950–1960

ANALYZE SOURCES

On July 26, 1948, President Truman issued Executive Order 9981, which barred segregation and discrimination in the U.S. military. Read the excerpt from the order and answer the question.

> NOW THEREFORE, by virtue of the authority vested in me as President of the United States, by the Constitution and the statutes of the United States, and as Commander in Chief of the armed services, it is hereby ordered as follows:
>
> 1. It is hereby declared to be the policy of the President that there shall be equality of treatment and opportunity for all persons in the armed services without regard to race, color, religion or national origin.

25. Why do you think the introductory section cites the president's "authority" and roles as a leader?

CONNECT TO YOUR LIFE

26. EXPOSITORY What are some ways in which society and popular culture in the United States have changed since the 1950s? Write a paragraph comparing the United States then and now.

TIPS

• Review the chapter and make notes about developments relating to society and popular culture.

• Use textual evidence and two or three vocabulary words from the chapter in your paragraph.

• Conclude the paragraph with a statement summarizing your ideas about changes in society and culture.

CHAPTER

26

THE **CIVIL RIGHTS MOVEMENT**
1945–1963

ESSENTIAL QUESTION

How did the civil rights movement impact American society?

AMERICAN STORIES

Civil Rights: People Who Made a Difference

SECTION 1 **The Struggle Begins**

KEY VOCABULARY

civil disobedience	integration
dehumanize	Montgomery Bus Boycott
desegregate	nonviolent resistance
grassroots	

SECTION 2 **The Struggle Broadens**

KEY VOCABULARY

Freedom Riders	solitary confinement
oration	voter registration drive
sit-in	

AMERICAN GALLERY
ONLINE

The Protest Movement

READING STRATEGY

DETERMINE CHRONOLOGY

When you determine chronology, you place events in the order in which they occurred to understand the relationship between them. As you read the chapter, use a time line like this one to order key events from the civil rights movement during the 1950s and early 1960s.

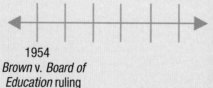

1954
Brown v. *Board of Education* ruling

"Freedom is never given;
it is won."

—A. Philip Randolph

CRITICAL VIEWING On August 28, 1963, more than 200,000 Americans took part in the March on Washington for Jobs and Freedom in Washington, D.C., calling for Congress to pass a new civil rights act. Union leader and activist A. Philip Randolph had planned a similar march in 1941, but the event was canceled. Based on the photo of these young men, what do you think was the general mood of those who participated in the march?

CIVIL RIGHTS
PEOPLE WHO MADE A DIFFERENCE

When faced with injustice, what can a single person do? Senator Robert F. Kennedy had an answer to that question. In a 1966 speech, he told a group of young people, "Few will have the greatness to bend history itself, but each of us can work to change a small portion of events." The acts of individuals, he said, would add up to write the "history of this generation." Kennedy was in a position to witness the many individuals acting to fight injustice in the 1950s and 1960s. During that time, people from all walks of life joined together to fight for civil rights. This American Story profiles a few of the people whose actions helped write the history of their generation and form the world we live in today.

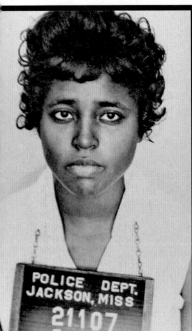

CRITICAL VIEWING On May 4, 1961, African-American civil rights activist and CORE leader James Farmer led 13 Freedom Riders—7 African Americans and 6 whites—from Washington, D.C., into the South on Greyhound and Trailways buses. These are the mug shots of Freedom Riders arrested in Jackson, Mississippi, that summer, including Farmer (above). They were charged for "breach of peace" and refusal to obey a police officer after attempting to use restrooms and lunch counters designated "whites only." Do you think nonviolent actions, like those of the Freedom Riders, expose injustice? Explain your reasoning.

THE FREEDOM RIDERS

Most passengers would probably find a cross-country bus trip tiring or dull. For African Americans in the South in the 1960s, it was downright dangerous. According to one witness, "Travel in the segregated South for black people was humiliating." In theory, segregation was illegal in bus stations and other facilities involved with travel between states. In practice, however, several states in the South enforced rules that separated African Americans from whites and forced them to use poorly maintained facilities.

The Congress of Racial Equality (CORE) believed the federal government was not doing enough to ensure anti-segregation laws were being followed. The group announced plans to test travel facilities in the South. CORE's national director said the goal was "to provoke the southern authorities into arresting us and thereby prod the Justice Department into enforcing the law of the land."

In May 1961, 13 "Freedom Riders" left Washington, D.C., on two buses bound for New Orleans, Louisiana. During their trip, they ignored the "white" and "colored" signs that hung by restrooms and lunch counters. Trouble erupted in Anniston, Alabama, when a white mob firebombed one of the buses. As the Freedom Riders escaped, they were attacked by the mob.

CRITICAL VIEWING Freedom Riders make the dangerous trip from Montgomery, Alabama, to Jackson, Mississippi, in 1961, accompanied by armed National Guard soldiers. Based on the expressions of the passengers in this photo, what do you think they may have been observing out the bus window?

In Montgomery, Alabama, a mob attacked a church where the riders and their supporters were attending a service led by Martin Luther King, Jr. Federal troops had to be sent in to restore order.

The original CORE riders were forced to complete their trip to New Orleans by plane, but another group, the Nashville Student Movement, decided to complete the ride by bus. After more intense violence, the riders were arrested and jailed in Jackson, Mississippi. The freedom rides were far from over, though. Throughout the summer, riders continued to pour into the southern states. The media flooded the country with images of Freedom Riders being attacked and beaten by angry segregationists. Forced to act, the federal government banned interstate bus lines from using segregated bus stations.

Who were the Freedom Riders? Most were young people and many were college students. They knew they were risking arrest, beatings, and even death when they signed up to board the buses. Diane Nash, the leader of the Nashville Student Movement, was not on the bus. She was coordinating the ride from Nashville and working

to recruit more riders. John Siegenthaler, who was an assistant to U.S. Attorney General Robert Kennedy, remembered trying to talk Nash out of supporting the freedom rides. "She, in a very quiet but strong way, gave me a lecture," he said. In 1962, Nash was arrested for civil rights work in Jackson, Mississippi. She continued to participate in major civil rights campaigns during the 1960s and later worked to support fairness in housing.

John Lewis was a 19-year-old member of the Nashville Student Movement, and being a Freedom Rider was not his first confrontation with segregationist law. In fact, he had already been arrested five times for protests. The son of poor farmers from Alabama, he was well acquainted with hardship and prejudice. He was arrested during the first CORE ride and spent time in prison. Lewis later took leadership roles in the civil rights movement and spoke at the March on Washington in 1963. He was elected to the U.S. House of Representatives in 1986 and continues to serve as a representative for the state of Georgia.

THE LITTLE ROCK NINE

They were called the Little Rock Nine—teenagers preparing to become the first African-American students to attend Central High School in Little Rock, Arkansas. The year was 1957, and Arkansas had been ordered by the federal government to desegregate its schools. The state, led by Governor Orval Faubus, refused. No African-American student had ever attended a white school in Arkansas.

A year earlier, it is likely that none of the students knew they would soon find themselves in the headlines. Then, sometime before the 1957 school year began, they were chosen by Arkansas civil rights leaders looking for students who had shown determination and strength of character. During the summer, they received training and counseling to help them prepare for the challenges they would encounter when they tried to attend Central High.

On the second day of school, the Little Rock Nine arrived to find troops from the Arkansas National Guard blocking the entrance. Eight of the students arrived together, driven by one of the civil rights workers, and left quickly. Elizabeth Eckford arrived on her own. For her, the day was a nightmare. She had come by bus and approached the school on foot. As she was turned away from the entrance, a mob of some 250 angry white protesters and students followed her, yelling curses and threats.

After further protests and refusals, President Eisenhower sent federal troops to take charge of the National Guardsmen and escort the teens into the school. The students' troubles were far from over, however. Every day they encountered regular harassment from a core group of segregationist students. Other students who might have been more sympathetic stayed away for fear of running into trouble themselves. Elizabeth Eckford recalled having objects thrown at her. Carlotta Walls remembered strategizing to avoid some of the abuse in the lunchroom.

After the 1957–1958 school year, Governor Faubus chose to close Arkansas high schools rather than integrate them. The schools remained closed until August 1959. That year, Carlotta Walls returned to Central High for her senior year. "I really did want that diploma," she later said, "to validate all of the [things] that I had gone through."

That year had a profound effect on the country and on the lives of the Little Rock Nine. Several followed careers in public service and continued to work for the civil rights cause. Today, Carlotta Walls LaNier is the president of the Little Rock Nine Foundation, which advocates for equal access to education. Minnijean Brown served in the Department of Work Force Diversity in the Department of the Interior during Bill Clinton's presidency. Ernest Green served as assistant secretary of the Federal Department of Labor. In 1999, all nine received the Congressional Gold Medal.

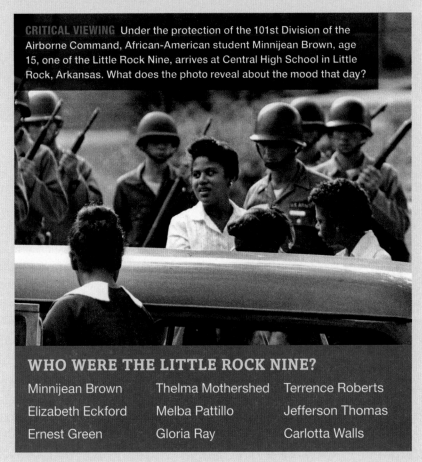

CRITICAL VIEWING Under the protection of the 101st Division of the Airborne Command, African-American student Minnijean Brown, age 15, one of the Little Rock Nine, arrives at Central High School in Little Rock, Arkansas. What does the photo reveal about the mood that day?

WHO WERE THE LITTLE ROCK NINE?

Minnijean Brown	Thelma Mothershed	Terrence Roberts
Elizabeth Eckford	Melba Pattillo	Jefferson Thomas
Ernest Green	Gloria Ray	Carlotta Walls

THE EAST L.A. WALKOUTS

The Mexican American students who participated in the East Los Angeles Walkouts of 1968 had much in common with the Little Rock Nine. California did not have an official policy of school segregation, like the one that had existed in Arkansas. Even so, several of the city's high schools were attended primarily by Mexican Americans. Conditions in those schools were poor, and dropout rates were high. In addition, the school system discouraged Mexican American youths from seeking to go to college.

In protest, leaders from the school community organized a series of events they called "blowouts." Between March 1 and March 8, around 15,000 students walked out of 5 East Los Angeles high schools to demand a higher quality education. Several college groups also supported the blowouts. Within a week, 20,000 students in East L.A. and other parts of the city had walked out of class to support the protesters.

Eventually, the Los Angeles School Board agreed to meet most of the students' demands. The blowout organizers themselves, however, still had a struggle on their hands. On March 31, 13 of the leaders were arrested on charges of conspiracy to disturb schools and the peace. After further public protest, the 13 were released. In the end, the Los Angeles School Board, for the most part, did not follow through on its promises, claiming it did not have enough money to improve the schools. However, the East L.A. Walkouts remain an important civil rights milestone because they helped unite and focus the Mexican American community in California and the Southwest. Some of the leaders, too, made ongoing contributions to the cause of civil rights for Hispanic Americans.

THE SHOWMAN

Russell Means was a complicated figure. Many admired the Lakota Sioux for his years of activism on behalf of Native Americans. Others, including some Native Americans, disagreed with his tactics or thought he was mainly out to call attention to himself. One thing everyone agreed on: Russell Means knew how to make people notice him.

Means was born in 1939. He was an unsuccessful student and spent much of his youth wandering in the West and getting into trouble. In 1969, he found direction when he was hired by the Rosebud Sioux Tribal Council in North Dakota. In 1970, he became the national director of the American Indian Movement (AIM), an organization promoting the rights of Native Americans.

Means proceeded to lead a series of highly visible protests. In 1970, he and a group of fellow protesters took control of the Mayflower replica at Plymouth, Massachusetts, confronting several re-enactors dressed as Pilgrims. He also led a prayer vigil on the top of the presidential faces carved into Mount Rushmore, which is sacred to Native Americans. At the Little Bighorn battlefield site, Means and his group did a victory dance in honor of Custer's defeat.

In AIM's most famous protest, Means led the occupation of Wounded Knee, South Dakota. In 1890, around 350 Lakota people had been killed there by U.S. troops. In 1973, hundreds of Native Americans and white activists took over the site for 71 days, demanding the government honor treaties it

THE FEMALE PRIEST

In 1960, the dean of a medical school explained, "We do keep women out, when we can. We don't want them here." Only 6 percent of American doctors were women in the 1960s. The numbers were similarly low in other professions. Many women faced daily workplace discrimination and earned lower salaries than men, leaving them feeling powerless at home and at work.

During the 1960s, leaders emerged in a new movement to break down these barriers and establish women's rights. Women like Betty Friedan and Gloria Steinem are most often linked with the women's movement, but many others played key roles. Pauli Murray was one of them.

As an African American, Murray stood at the intersection of two civil rights movements: those of race and gender. In 1938, she tried unsuccessfully to enter the all-white University of North Carolina. In the 1940s, Murray studied law, joined CORE, and wrote poems, articles, and essays about the situation of African Americans. In the 1960s, she remained active in civil rights, working closely with Martin Luther King, Jr., and A. Philip Randolph. But she was troubled by the lack of female leadership. In 1963, she sent Randolph a letter expressing her concern about the "minor role of leadership" that women had been given.

In 1966, Murray joined with Betty Friedan and others to found the National Organization for Women to advocate for the rights of all women. At the time of her death in 1985, the woman who had once been refused admission to the University of North Carolina held honorary degrees from Yale and Dartmouth and had become the first African-American priest in the Episcopal church.

CRITICAL VIEWING In 1977, Murray extended her extraordinary career by becoming an Episcopal priest. What types of challenges do you think female members of the clergy face today? Explain.

had made with Native American tribes. The event turned violent: two Native Americans were killed and a federal agent was paralyzed. Means was charged with assault, larceny, and conspiracy as a result of the Wounded Knee siege, but the case was dismissed.

In 1988, Russell Means retired from AIM after years of arguing with the movement's other leaders, who had lost trust in him. He then launched a new career that was just as visible as his previous one. In 1992, he made his debut as an actor by starring in a major Hollywood movie, *The Last of the Mohicans*. He went on to appear in more than 30 movies and TV shows and recorded music with Native American themes. He died in 2012.

AIM patch commemorating the 1973 Wounded Knee occupation

Senator Robert Kennedy sits with César Chávez during a rally in Delano, California, for the United Farm Workers union. Weak and tired in this 1968 photo, Chávez had endured a 25-day hunger strike to draw attention to the farmworkers' movement.

THE PRESIDENT'S BROTHER

To some, Robert F. Kennedy may have seemed like an unlikely champion of civil rights. Born to a wealthy family, he was raised with comfort, privilege, and access to education. While he did encounter occasional discrimination because he was Catholic, his family's status shielded him from the worst effects. However, during his years of government service, Kennedy became a strong advocate for many people and groups.

In 1961, when Robert Kennedy was appointed attorney general by his brother, President John F. Kennedy, he was cautious in his support of civil rights. He asked activists not to engage in loud public protests, hoping they would accept more gradual progress toward their goals. However, he was willing to take action when necessary. He sent federal troops to protect the Freedom Riders and other protesters from violent opponents.

Over time, Kennedy abandoned his soft approach and became increasingly forceful in his support of civil rights. He helped his brother write important legislation that made racial discrimination illegal in voting and hiring. After John Kennedy was assassinated in 1963, Robert helped President Lyndon Johnson convince Congress to pass the bill into law. It became the Civil Rights Act of 1964.

Kennedy was elected to the U.S. Senate in 1964 and continued his civil rights advocacy. In 1966, he met César Chávez, founder of the United Farm Workers union, at a Senate hearing on farm labor in Delano, California. Shocked by the way the police were treating peaceful protesters, Kennedy ordered the sheriff to read the U.S. Constitution during his lunch break. His appearance drew national attention to the farmworkers' movement and energized striking workers. Kennedy returned to Delano again in 1968 to show his continued support of Chávez and the UFW movement.

THE CITY COUNCILMAN

Harvey Milk was one of the country's first openly gay elected officials. Born in New York in 1930, Milk knew he was gay before he started high school. Because the national attitude toward lesbian, gay, bisexual, and transgender, or LGBT, people at the time was mostly hostile, he kept quiet about his identity. As a young man, he probably never imagined he would someday live as an openly gay man and prominent activist for gay rights. His early career took him in many directions. He served in the U.S. Navy, taught in a public school, helped produce several Broadway shows, and worked as an investment banker. Sometime during the 1960s, he also became friends with gay activists living in the Greenwich Village neighborhood of New York City.

In 1972, Harvey Milk moved to San Francisco, California. He opened a camera shop on Castro Street, right at the center of the city's vibrant gay neighborhood. At the time, San Francisco was more tolerant of openly LGBT people than most American cities. Milk was no longer keeping his identity a secret but rather was becoming increasingly vocal about supporting gay rights. He organized Castro area businesses, which were largely LGBT-owned, into an association and coordinated events to bring more customers into the neighborhood. It did not take long for Harvey Milk to gain the nickname, the "Mayor of Castro Street."

After running unsuccessfully for city and state offices, Milk was elected to San Francisco's city council. Once in office, he advocated for many causes in addition to the protection of gay rights. He supported childcare for working mothers, community policing, and housing for low-income families, among other reforms. At a time when discrimination against the LGBT community was common, Milk was able to gather support to defeat proposed antigay laws in California.

On November 27, 1978, a former city official shot and killed Milk and San Francisco mayor, George Moscone. That night, thousands of people marched from Castro Street to City Hall. There, they held a silent candlelight vigil to honor the man who had earned the respect of people both inside and outside the gay community. As the gay rights movement continued to grow after his death, many remembered Milk's challenge to supporters: "Gay people, we will not win our rights by staying quietly in our closets. We are coming out to fight the lies, the myths, the distortions. We are coming out to tell the truths about gays, for I am tired of the conspiracy of silence, so I'm going to talk about it. And I want you to talk about it."

Harvey Milk sits outside of his camera shop in 1977. How does antidiscrimination legislation help members of the LGBT community enjoy the same rights as others? Do additional research on this topic, including Milk's involvement, and explain.

THINK ABOUT IT

What common goals did these "people who made a difference" share? How did their work and challenges differ?

1.1 Foundations of the Movement

When ordinary people join together to support a cause, they can make a difference. After World War II, African Americans demonstrated this fact as they tried to secure their rights guaranteed by the Constitution.

MAIN IDEA The NAACP and the Truman administration helped lay the foundation for the postwar struggle for African-American civil rights.

GRASSROOTS MOVEMENTS

Even though African Americans had made sacrifices and served the nation courageously in World War II, few shared in the postwar prosperity. As you have learned, the Jim Crow laws and black codes enforced throughout the South **dehumanized** African Americans, or treated them as though they were less than human. The laws denied them full equality and economic progress. But after fighting in a war described as a battle against the racist empires of Germany and Japan, African Americans were determined to claim their rights at home.

As a result, many African Americans worked to form equal rights movements at the **grassroots**, or community, level. Churches played an important

In 1946, lynchings in Georgia triggered protests and a call for a federal anti-lynching law. These demonstrators standing in front of the White House took their appeal to President Truman. Some of the signs refer to John Rankin and Theodore Bilbo, Mississippi legislators who opposed the law.

role in these movements. Church leaders stressed community support and inspired their members to work for racial justice. The NAACP, which you have read about, began as a grassroots movement. When the organization was established in 1909, it had 60 members. But by 1946, it had 600,000 members and was working to persuade Congress to pass federal anti-lynching laws. In addition, NAACP leaders, including **Walter White**, **Thurgood Marshall**, and **James Weldon Johnson**, tried lawsuits in the courts against people accused of civil rights violations.

TRUMAN AND CIVIL RIGHTS

The struggle for civil rights also received strong support at the federal level from President Harry Truman. Truman grew up in a segregated town in Missouri, and his grandparents had been slave owners. However, Truman came to recognize that everyone should be treated fairly under the law. He established the **President's Committee on Civil Rights (PCCR)** in 1946 to protect the rights of all Americans. The PCCR report, "To Secure These Rights," detailed widespread instances of discrimination and recommended what should be done to end this injustice.

In 1948, Truman also sent Congress a plan for stronger civil rights laws, the enforcement of voting rights, and federal protection against lynching. Some Republicans and many southern Democrats blocked the plan. Even many moderate Democrats, including some of the president's own aides, thought the plan went too far. They feared its passage would cost Truman votes in the South.

Liberal Democrats, on the other hand, wanted to adopt Truman's plan as the official party platform. At the 1948 Democratic Convention, **Hubert Humphrey** of Minnesota, a candidate for the Senate, urged his fellow Democrats to vote for this platform. Humphrey stated, "The time is now arrived in America for the Democratic Party to get out of the shadow of states' rights and walk forthrightly [directly] into the bright sunshine of human rights." His speech helped the liberals win a close vote. That same year, as you know, Truman abolished segregation in the U.S. military. He also banned discrimination in the hiring practices of the federal civil service. When Truman ran for president in 1948, he won the election, thanks in part to the support of African-American voters.

Jackie Robinson

From the beginning, Major League Baseball had been reserved for white players. African-American athletes played in separate leagues. All that changed when Branch Rickey, the Brooklyn Dodgers' general manager, offered Negro League player Jackie Robinson the chance to break the color barrier. Robinson was a gifted athlete who had served in World War II.

Rickey set one condition: The African-American player could not respond to the abuse he would certainly face. Robinson agreed. In April 1947, he joined the Dodgers and endured racial slurs and insults—even from his own teammates. But Robinson proved himself on the field by helping the Dodgers win six pennants and a World Series over the course of his career with the team. In time, other teams began to recruit players from minority groups.

HISTORICAL THINKING

1. **READING CHECK** How did World War II inspire African Americans to fight for their civil rights?

2. **MAKE INFERENCES** Why do you think it was important for the NAACP to fight civil rights violations in the courts?

3. **DRAW CONCLUSIONS** What did Humphrey mean when he said it was time to "get out of the shadow of states' rights"?

School Segregation

Think about the factors you and your parents might consider when deciding what school you will attend. These probably include the quality of the school and the courses it offers. Until the 1950s, the key factor in deciding what public school a student attended was his or her race.

MAIN IDEA In the 1950s, civil rights activists successfully challenged segregation in public education.

OPPOSING "SEPARATE BUT EQUAL"

As the NAACP handled civil rights lawsuits, the organization sought to overturn the doctrine of "separate but equal" established by the 1896 case *Plessy* v. *Ferguson*. Attorney Thurgood Marshall headed the NAACP's Legal Defense and Educational Fund. The fund fought inequality and segregation in educational institutions.

Marshall and his team achieved a major victory in the 1946 case *Mendez* v. *Westminster*. The court decided in favor of five Mexican American families whose children were being forced to attend schools for Mexican Americans only. With the judge's declaration that such segregation was unconstitutional, the case provided a basis for further challenges to the "separate but equal" doctrine.

In 1946, Marshall also took on the case of Heman Marion Sweatt, an African American who had applied for admission to the University of Texas School of Law. The university

CRITICAL VIEWING In 1953, as *Brown* v. *Board of Education* was being argued in the Supreme Court, Linda Brown continued to attend her segregated school. In this photo taken by *Life* magazine photographer Carl Iwasaki, Linda (left) and her sister Terry Lynn walk along railroad tracks on their way to the bus that would take them to their school. What possible dangers did the girls face on their walk?

Linda Brown's Activism

The young girl who became the face of the *Brown* v. *Board of Education* decision, Linda Brown, went on to become a teacher and civil rights activist. She reopened the *Brown* case in 1979, arguing that the Topeka schools remained segregated. In 1993, the court finally agreed, and three new schools were built to help integrate the city's schools.

denied Sweatt's application but established a new law school for African Americans to satisfy the "separate but equal" doctrine. Marshall argued the case for years. Finally, in 1950, the Supreme Court ruled in *Sweatt* v. *Painter* that the university had to admit Sweatt to the all-white law school under the terms of the 14th Amendment. As you may recall, the 14th Amendment guarantees African Americans citizenship and all its rights and privileges. The ruling in this case and others like it meant that colleges across the country were to be integrated. **Integration** is the act of allowing people of all races to participate equally in society and have equal access to the same facilities.

BROWN v. BOARD OF EDUCATION

Soon, "separate but equal" was being challenged in schools throughout the nation. By 1953, five civil rights lawsuits from different parts of the country had reached the Supreme Court. The lawsuits were combined in one case under the name *Brown* v. *Board of Education of Topeka*. The case challenged the constitutionality of segregation and inequality in public schools. Once again, NAACP lawyers took on the civil rights case. One person the lawyers represented was Reverend Oliver Brown, who was suing the Topeka, Kansas, school board. When the suit was first filed in 1950, Reverend Brown's daughter, Linda, was eight years old. His lawyers argued that Linda should not have to walk several miles to attend a segregated African-American school when an all-white school was much closer.

On May 17, 1954, the Supreme Court ruled 9–0 in favor of *Brown* v. *Board of Education*. At this time, the Chief Justice of the Supreme Court was **Earl Warren**, whom President Dwight Eisenhower had appointed the year before. Warren held more liberal views than the president. In his decision, Warren wrote, "Separate educational facilities are inherently [by their nature] unequal."

The court ordered the integration of the country's public schools "with all deliberate speed." Eisenhower kept quiet on the issue of school integration. When journalists asked for his opinion on the *Brown* decision, he replied, "The Supreme Court has spoken . . . and I will obey." Many Americans and members of Congress, however, actively opposed the decision. They would fight it for years to come.

HISTORICAL THINKING

1. **READING CHECK** What doctrine did the NAACP work to overturn?

2. **DETERMINE CHRONOLOGY** How did the Supreme Court ruling in 1950 affect the *Brown* ruling in 1954?

3. **DRAW CONCLUSIONS** Why do you think educational institutions in the early 1950s designed solely for minority groups might have been inferior to those for whites?

1.3 Resistance to School Integration

It's hard to change a law, but it can be even harder to change people's minds. Segregation had been practiced for so long in some places that many people could not imagine an integrated school, much less an integrated world.

MAIN IDEA Southerners and government leaders tried to prevent the integration of public schools and colleges.

Escorted by soldiers and the National Guard, nine African-American students finally attend their first full day of class at Central High School in Little Rock, Arkansas, on September 25, 1957. Troops remained at the school throughout the year.

THE LITTLE ROCK NINE

By 1956, only a few schools in the South had **desegregated**, or put an end to the separation of races. That year, about 100 southern members of Congress claimed the decision in *Brown* v. *Board of Education* was a misinterpretation of the 14th Amendment. They vowed to use "all lawful means" to resist court-ordered integration. The conflict between federal authority and states' rights erupted in 1957 in Little Rock, Arkansas, when nine African Americans were admitted to a local high school. Shortly before school began, Arkansas governor Orval Faubus announced he would use the state's National Guard to prevent the African-American students from entering the building. He claimed the measure was for the students' own safety.

On their first day of school, the students, who came to be known as the **Little Rock Nine**, were confronted by an angry mob. The students were spat on and threatened as they walked to the school before being turned away by the Arkansas National Guard. They tried to attend classes several more times in the following weeks. On September 23, President Eisenhower finally sent federal troops to escort the students to their classes and restore order. That month Eisenhower signed the **Civil Rights Act of 1957** to protect the voting rights of African Americans. The president also later signed the **Civil Rights Act of 1960**. However, both acts proved to be ineffective.

AN ONGOING BATTLE

Other states also challenged desegregation. In 1956, the Virginia legislature passed a law that would close any school that attempted to integrate. In 1958, several schools and an entire school district in Virginia were shut down to avoid integration. Parents who could afford the fees sent their children to private schools. Poor students, including many whites and African Americans, were denied any public education at all.

In 1960, officials developed a purposefully difficult test for African-American students who wished to attend white schools in New Orleans. However, a six-year-old girl named **Ruby Bridges** was one of the few students who passed the test. She gained admission to an elementary school just five blocks from her home. The Louisiana state government found a number of ways to stall and put off the school's integration but finally had to give in. Federal marshals escorted Ruby and her mother to the school in November. The child walked past a screaming crowd of angry white parents and was led directly to the principal's office, where she spent her first day of school. Only one teacher at the school agreed to instruct Ruby. The two of them worked alone in a classroom for the entire school year. Ruby Bridges became the youngest African-American student to integrate a school in the South.

The battle over integration also continued on college campuses. In 1962, a federal court ordered the all-white University of Mississippi to admit **James Meredith**, an African-American Air Force veteran. However, when Meredith arrived on campus to register, the governor of Mississippi, Ross Barnett, blocked the entrance to the office. About a week later, U.S. marshals escorted Meredith to the registrar's office, setting off riots that ended in the deaths of two students and injured many others. Once the violence died down, Meredith was finally able to attend classes.

George Wallace had vowed to block school integration during his successful campaign for governor of Alabama in 1962. In his inaugural address, he exclaimed, "Segregation now, segregation tomorrow, segregation forever!" On June 11, 1963, Wallace kept his promise and stood in a doorway at the University of Alabama to prevent two African-American students from enrolling. In response, the U.S. government sent in National Guard troops, who forced Wallace to step aside. While schools and colleges were being desegregated, civil rights leaders also fought for equality in other public places—including buses.

HISTORICAL THINKING

1. **READING CHECK** Who were the Little Rock Nine?

2. **SUMMARIZE** How did Barnett and Wallace try to block integration on college campuses?

3. **DESCRIBE** What words would you use to describe the character of the African-American students who desegregated schools in the 1950s and 1960s?

1.4 Women in the Movement

Do you think unjust laws should be broken? During the civil rights movement, many people did. In 1955, one woman took a stand against an unfair law by sitting down and refusing to get up.

MAIN IDEA A yearlong boycott of the bus system in Montgomery, Alabama, led to a Supreme Court decision that ordered the desegregation of the city's buses.

THE ARREST OF ROSA PARKS

On December 1, 1955, an African-American woman named **Rosa Parks** boarded a public bus in Montgomery, Alabama, prepared to break a city law. At that time, buses in Montgomery were segregated. According to a city ordinance, the first four rows were reserved for white passengers. African Americans had to pay the driver at the front of the bus and then get off to reboard at the rear. When Parks got on the bus that day, she sat in the first row behind the white section. She knew she would be asked to give up her seat to a white person if the front seats filled up.

That's just what happened. When the white section was full and more white passengers stepped aboard the bus, the driver told Parks and three other African Americans in her row to move to the back of the bus. The others gave up their seats, but Parks refused. The bus driver called the police, who arrested Parks for disobeying the ordinance. Parks worked as a seamstress, but she was also a civil rights activist and secretary of the Montgomery chapter of the NAACP. She knew that the NAACP wanted to challenge Montgomery's segregated bus law and chose to be the plaintiff in their case. As Parks said later, "The only tired I was, was tired of giving in."

MONTGOMERY BUS BOYCOTT

Parks's **civil disobedience**, or refusal to obey a law as a form of protest, energized and united Montgomery's African-American community. **Jo Ann Robinson**, the president of the city's Women's Political Council, organized a one-day boycott of Montgomery's buses. Robinson and the council had been working for at least two years to achieve bus reform, including the desegregation of Montgomery's buses.

In February 1956, two months after her arrest for refusing to give up her bus seat, Parks was again arrested in Alabama for violating a state law against organized boycotting. She had volunteered as a dispatcher, arranging carpool rides for bus boycotters.

Not all of the women involved in the civil rights movement were activists. Some, such as Mamie Till-Mobley, shown here, took personal stands against racism that commanded the nation's attention. In August 1955, Mrs. Till-Mobley's son Emmett Till was murdered by two white men in Mississippi. The men believed that the 14-year-old, who was visiting from Chicago, had flirted with a white woman. When the men were tried for the crime, an all-white jury found them not guilty.

Mrs. Till-Mobley brought Emmett's body back to Chicago. Although her son's body was horribly mutilated, Mrs. Till-Mobley insisted on having Emmett's coffin open during his funeral. "Let the people see what I've seen," she said. Photos of the funeral were published, forcing the American public to witness the impact of racism.

The **Montgomery Bus Boycott**, as it came to be called, was held on December 5, four days after Rosa Parks's arrest. The protest was such a success that Robinson, members of the NAACP, and other civil rights activists decided to continue the boycott and make it a long-term campaign. These activists joined with a group of local ministers to form the Montgomery Improvement Association (MIA). They chose **Martin Luther King, Jr.**, a 26-year-old Baptist minister and leading member of the NAACP, to be the association's president and coordinate the boycott.

Organizers believed the boycott would be successful because about 75 percent of Montgomery's bus riders were African Americans. Still, because few African Americans owned cars, they had to make some sacrifices during the boycott. Protesters walked, biked, or carpooled rather than take the bus. They also endured threats, violence, and even arrest. Boycott leaders held regular meetings to keep the participants' spirits up.

On June 5, 1956, citing the *Brown* v. *Board of Education* decision, a federal court finally declared segregation on buses unconstitutional. The U.S. Supreme Court upheld that decision on November 13, and soon after, a court order was delivered to Montgomery City Hall requiring the integration of the city's buses. The boycott ended on December 21. It had lasted 381 days. The boycott proved that collective action and peaceful protest could bring about social change.

HISTORICAL THINKING

1. **READING CHECK** Why was Rosa Parks arrested on December 1, 1955?

2. **DETERMINE CHRONOLOGY** What happened after Parks's first arrest?

3. **DRAW CONCLUSIONS** How did the *Brown* decision set a precedent for the federal court's ruling on the Montgomery bus ordinance?

1.5 Dr. King and Peaceful Protest

Many men and women played crucial roles in the civil rights movement.
But one person came to symbolize the cause and emerged as its leader.
That person was Dr. Martin Luther King, Jr.

MAIN IDEA Martin Luther King, Jr., with his principles of peaceful protest, became the leader of the civil rights movement.

MAN OF PEACE

Martin Luther King, Jr., grew up in Atlanta, Georgia, in a close-knit, middle-class family. His father was a minister at the Ebenezer Baptist Church. King's grandfather had also served as a pastor at the church. King entered Morehouse College in 1944 to study law and medicine. However, he eventually decided to follow in his father's and grandfather's footsteps and become a minister. His decision was influenced by Morehouse president Benjamin Mays, who also strongly supported racial equality. King went on to study at Crozer Theological Seminary in Pennsylvania and earned a doctoral degree in theology from Boston University. In Boston, King met Coretta Scott, and the pair married in 1953.

In 1954, while completing his doctoral studies, Dr. King accepted a position as pastor at Dexter Avenue Baptist Church in Montgomery, Alabama. As you know, he led Montgomery's successful bus boycott the following year. In the wake of that achievement, King, other African-American ministers, and civil rights activists formed the **Southern Christian Leadership Conference (SCLC)**. The organization pledged to fight for racial equality using peaceful protest, or **nonviolent resistance**, and encouraged other protesters to adopt the same strategy.

Dr. King was deeply influenced by **Mohandas Gandhi**, a civil rights leader who had used nonviolent protest to help India gain independence from Great Britain in 1947. The African-American minister and his wife traveled to India in 1959 to visit political and social leaders in the country and further their understanding of Gandhi's methods. (Gandhi himself had been assassinated in 1948.)

After his trip, King became more convinced than ever in the power of nonviolent resistance. He believed the method would be an effective weapon in the fight for achieving racial equality and human dignity for all Americans.

SIX PRINCIPLES OF NONVIOLENCE

While others in the civil rights movement called for change using any means necessary—including violence—Dr. King insisted on using only peaceful methods. He knew that not responding to the insults, taunts, and violence would be hard. So King developed six principles of nonviolence to guide protesters and strengthen their resolve.

The first principle emphasizes that nonviolence requires courage. While seeming to be passive, a protester is actually being assertive spiritually, mentally, and emotionally. The second principle states that the goal of nonviolent resistance is to create understanding and community, not to

SIX PRINCIPLES OF NONVIOLENCE
1 Nonviolent resistance is assertive, not passive.
2 Its goal is to create understanding.
3 Nonviolence is directed at the evil itself, not at people.
4 Suffering for a cause can be liberating.
5 Hate is not an effective weapon against hate.
6 Justice will triumph.

On March 22, 1956, supporters cheer as Dr. Martin Luther King, Jr., emerges from the Montgomery, Alabama, courthouse with his wife, Coretta, at his side. King had been found guilty of organizing the Montgomery Bus Boycott. The maximum penalty for the crime was $1,000 and 6 months in prison. However, because King had advocated nonviolence throughout the boycott, the judge decided to be lenient and only fine the civil rights leader $500.

humiliate opponents. According to the third principle, nonviolence seeks to defeat injustice and evil, not those who commit evil acts. The fourth principle encourages nonviolent resisters by asserting that their suffering can be liberating. The fifth principle insists that protesters must be unselfish and refuse to hate their opponents. Finally, the sixth principle teaches that nonviolent resisters should believe that justice will eventually triumph.

King called on fellow activist **James Lawson** to use these principles to conduct nonviolence training workshops for members of the SCLC. While in college in Tennessee, Lawson had organized similar workshops. Soon, protesters both inside and outside the SCLC would use nonviolent resistance to achieve their goals.

HISTORICAL THINKING

1. **READING CHECK** How was King influenced by Mohandas Gandhi?

2. **MAKE INFERENCES** Why do you think workshops in nonviolent resistance were necessary to train protesters?

3. **FORM AND SUPPORT OPINIONS** Do you think nonviolent resistance can achieve better results than violent protest? Why or why not?

2.1 A Growing Movement

What would you do if a server at a fast-food restaurant refused to take your meal order but served other people? A group of students chose to wait politely for their lunch—no matter how long it took.

MAIN IDEA In the early 1960s, the call for civil rights expanded as more and more activists tried to desegregate public places.

STUDENT POWER

A few years after the Montgomery Bus Boycott, civil rights activism began to transform into a mass movement. Inspired by Dr. King's principles of nonviolent resistance, four African-American college students entered a Woolworth's store in Greensboro, North Carolina, on February 1, 1960, and sat at the lunch counter designated "For Whites Only." In the 1950s, the Supreme Court had ruled that such segregation was unconstitutional. Nevertheless, when the students ordered lunch, they were asked to leave. The students remained in their seats until the store closed, however, and came back the next day with 25 more protesters.

Reports of the protest appeared in newspapers and on television, and soon people staged sit-ins in other cities. A **sit-in** is a form of protest in which people occupy seats or floor space and refuse to leave. Besides lunch counters, activists occupied segregated churches in "pray-ins" and public swimming pools in "wade-ins." Many protesters endured abuse and were arrested, but others quickly came to take their places. By the summer of 1960, many dining establishments across the South had become desegregated—including the Greensboro lunch counter.

Encouraged by the success of the sit-ins, a group of African-American students formed the **Student Nonviolent Coordinating Committee (SNCC)**. Many of its members were frustrated with the cautious approach of the SCLC. Another organization called the **Congress of Racial Equality (CORE)**, which was founded in 1942 by **James Farmer**, had pledged to fight discrimination through nonviolent protest. The two organizations would soon work together.

FREEDOM RIDERS

In 1960, the U.S. Supreme Court had ruled in *Boynton* v. *Virginia* that the segregation of public facilities serving travelers, such as bus terminals and restrooms, was illegal. The following year, CORE decided to test that decision. In May 1961, seven African-American and six white **Freedom Riders** left Washington, D.C., on two buses bound for New Orleans, Louisiana. As they traveled from one terminal to another along the way, they ignored "white" and "colored" signs posted by restrooms, lunch counters, and waiting rooms and used whatever facilities they chose.

CORE had announced the bus rides to the press, so white segregationists were waiting at some stops to ambush and attack the riders. At this time, **John F. Kennedy** was president of the United States. In the wake of the violence, he sent U.S. marshals to protect the riders. With assistance from SNCC, CORE continued to organize freedom rides. As a result of their efforts, in September 1961, the federal government banned buses and trains traveling across state lines from using any terminal that segregated people by race.

REVIEW & ASSESS

1. **READING CHECK** How did African-American students try to desegregate a lunch counter in Greensboro, North Carolina?

2. **ANALYZE CAUSE AND EFFECT** What resulted from the Greensboro protest?

3. **MAKE INFERENCES** Why do you think CORE announced the freedom rides to the press?

Two Civil Rights Tactics

Students added two new tactics to the nonviolent struggle for civil rights: the sit-in, shown in the top photo; and the freedom ride, shown in the bottom photo. The tactics captured the attention of the American public and helped spread the civil rights movement.

Students fill the seats at this lunch counter during the Greensboro sit-in. By the sit-in's fifth day, the number of protesters exceeded 300.

Freedom Riders in Anniston, Alabama, sit beside their bus, which had been firebombed by segregationists. As the passengers fled the burning bus, the mob beat them with their fists and baseball bats.

2.2 Confrontation in Birmingham

In the early 1960s, Dr. Martin Luther King, Jr., claimed that "a virtual reign of terror" existed in Birmingham, Alabama. White segregationists bombed African-American homes and churches so frequently that some residents called it "Bombingham."

MAIN IDEA In 1963, peaceful protests against segregation in Birmingham, Alabama, were met with brutality by the city's police force.

THE BIRMINGHAM CAMPAIGN

Dr. Martin Luther King, Jr., had observed the successful desegregation efforts of the students who staged sit-ins and freedom rides. Using some of their tactics, King soon turned his attention to Birmingham, Alabama. In 1962, he declared that Birmingham was "by far the worst big city in race relations in the United States." For years, white segregationists in the city had committed acts of violence against African Americans, including attacks on the Freedom Riders. The segregationists had also repeatedly bombed an African-American church in Birmingham and were not punished for the crimes. Segregation laws were strictly enforced under police commissioner **Eugene "Bull" Connor**, who had ties to the Ku Klux Klan.

In April 1963, King and the SCLC began a campaign to end segregation in Birmingham. They staged sit-ins at whites-only lunch counters, organized boycotts of local businesses, and held

CRITICAL VIEWING Members of the Birmingham Fire Department use powerful hoses against African Americans during a protest in May 1963. How are the protesters trying to withstand the spray?

PRIMARY SOURCES

[W]e are now confronted by a series of demonstrations by some of our Negro citizens, directed and led in part by outsiders.

—from a letter by Alabama clergy for the *Birmingham News* and *Post-Herald* newspapers, April 12, 1963

I cannot sit idly by in Atlanta and not be concerned about what happens in Birmingham. Injustice anywhere is a threat to justice everywhere.

—from "Letter from Birmingham City Jail," by Dr. Martin Luther King, Jr., April 16, 1963

marches throughout the city. As the protests continued, more and more people took part. The police arrested and jailed many of the protesters, including Dr. King.

In response to the protests, eight white ministers from Alabama wrote a letter to the editor of the *Birmingham News* on April 12, 1963. They blamed King and other civil rights leaders for causing the chaos in their city and urged African Americans to stop supporting the demonstrations. The ministers called the protests "unwise and untimely." After King's arrest, he had been placed in a jail cell. He wrote an answer to the clergymen from his cell in what came to be known as his "**Letter from Birmingham City Jail**." In the letter, he explained the need for nonviolent resistance and defended the justice of his cause. He pointed out that those who had endured segregation had waited long enough for equal treatment in American society.

VIOLENCE IN THE CITY

King was released from jail after eight days in **solitary confinement**, or being locked in a cell alone. Meanwhile, support for the protests had decreased. Perhaps recalling the progress young people had made in the last couple of years, King recruited local students to re-energize the Birmingham campaign. On May 2, students of all ages marched through the city. Many of the protesters were arrested, but Connor also resorted to violence against them. The police and other city officials beat the demonstrators and used dogs and high-pressure fire hoses to break up the protest. However, news agencies had sent reporters to Birmingham to cover the demonstrations. The reporters captured images

of children being attacked by police dogs and peaceful protesters getting knocked off their feet by the water hoses. Finally, on May 10, the campaign ended when Birmingham city leaders agreed to some of the protesters' demands. The two groups established a timetable for the desegregation of the city's public facilities.

Other events in Alabama soon took center stage. As you may recall, the state's governor, George Wallace, tried to prevent the desegregation of the University of Alabama on June 11, 1963. The governor's actions and the protests in Birmingham prompted President Kennedy to respond that evening. The president delivered a televised speech on civil rights and declared "the cries for equality" could no longer be ignored. The following week, he sent a proposal to Congress for a civil rights bill that was far stronger than those passed in 1957 and 1960. As a result of Kennedy's speech and the violent images from Birmingham, more people began to support the civil rights movement.

HISTORICAL THINKING

1. **READING CHECK** Why did King consider Birmingham the worst big city in America on race relations?

2. **DETERMINE CHRONOLOGY** What events in Birmingham led the eight white ministers to write a letter to the local newspaper?

3. **ANALYZE CAUSE AND EFFECT** What happened as a result of Birmingham's brutal treatment of the civil rights demonstrators?

2.3 The March on Washington

There was no social media as we know it in 1963. Still, word got out about the march in Washington, D.C. Reporters had estimated that only about 25,000 people would come, but the crowds kept arriving in buses and on trains. Apparently, the message had gone viral.

MAIN IDEA In 1963, hundreds of thousands of people took part in the March on Washington, and Dr. Martin Luther King, Jr., electrified the crowd with his speech.

MARCH FOR FREEDOM

As you know, President Kennedy sent a proposal for a new civil rights bill to Congress in June 1963. The bill faced strong opposition from many legislators there, however, and wasn't making much progress. To increase support for the bill and to call attention to the high unemployment rate among African Americans, civil rights leaders planned a major rally in Washington, D.C. The demonstration was called the **March on Washington for Jobs and Freedom** and took place on August 28, 1963.

The main organizer of the event was long-time civil rights activist **Bayard Rustin**. He and A. Phillip Randolph brought together civil rights, labor, and religious organizations to support and promote the demonstration. They printed and distributed flyers and posters and coordinated buses to bring as many people as they could to the march.

Their efforts paid off. Rustin expected 100,000 people to attend the March on Washington, but more than 200,000 took part. People came from all over the country. Most were African-American, but about one-fourth of the crowd was white. Demonstrators assembled by the Washington Monument and then marched along the National Mall to the Lincoln Memorial.

As they walked, participants sang "We Shall Overcome," a gospel song that had become an anthem of the civil rights movement. Once the marchers arrived at the Lincoln Memorial, the day's program began. It featured a welcoming speech by Rustin and speeches from several civil rights leaders. Gospel singer Mahalia Jackson performed, as did folk singers Bob Dylan, Joan Baez, and the group Peter, Paul, and Mary.

"I HAVE A DREAM"

The most highly anticipated speaker of the day was Dr. Martin Luther King, Jr. Known for his eloquence, or articulate and powerful speaking, King did not disappoint. He began by referring to the march as "the greatest demonstration for freedom in the history of our nation." Then he launched into a prepared speech, pointing out that almost 100 years had passed since President Abraham Lincoln had freed enslaved people.

But as Dr. King neared the end of the speech, Mahalia Jackson called out, "Tell them about the dream, Martin!" King had spoken often about his dream of an integrated American society. During a recent speech delivered in Detroit, King had repeated the phrase, "I have a dream." Inspired by Jackson's request, he stopped reading from his notes and drew on his earlier speeches from memory. He used "I have a dream" as a constant refrain while he described his vision of a brighter future. Dr. King's "I Have a Dream" speech is considered one of the greatest **orations**, or speeches, in American history.

The March on Washington showed how strong and unified the civil rights movement had become. However, on September 15, 1963, the Ku Klux Klan detonated a bomb at the 16th Street Baptist Church in Birmingham that killed four African-American girls. The church was a center for organizing civil rights activities.

The National Mall is one of the country's most visited national parks. The site of monuments, memorials, and museums, it stretches from the U.S. Capitol Building to the Potomac River. This photo shows the large crowds that gathered in the mall for the 1963 March on Washington. Behind them rises the Washington Monument. The people are positioned in front of the Lincoln Memorial to listen to the day's speakers.

In 1964, SNCC and CORE launched **Freedom Summer**, a voter registration drive to sign up as many African-American voters in Mississippi as possible. More than 700 student volunteers from the North, many of them white, worked with civil rights groups in Mississippi to register new voters. In June, though, three of the students—two white and one black—disappeared. Their bodies were found six weeks later. They had been murdered, probably by a mob of Ku Klux Klansmen. These events demonstrated how far the country was from realizing King's dream.

HISTORICAL THINKING

1. **READING CHECK** What was the purpose of the March on Washington?

2. **DETERMINE CHRONOLOGY** What previous events might have helped swell the crowds at the March on Washington?

3. **DRAW CONCLUSIONS** What message did the people who murdered the student volunteers in Mississippi want to send?

DOCUMENT-BASED QUESTION
2.4 Voices of Equality

During the civil rights movement in the 1950s and early 1960s, many African-American leaders spoke out against segregation and inequality. Through their deeds, they fought for equality. Through their words, they articulated what they envisioned for themselves, the movement, and the country. Their voices helped African Americans believe that change really was possible.

In this photo, Dr. Martin Luther King, Jr., delivers his "I Have a Dream" speech at the 1963 March on Washington from the steps of the Lincoln Memorial. The photo captures the end of his speech when he dramatically raised his arm and echoed some of the words of an old African-American spiritual, exclaiming: "Free at last! Free at last! Thank God Almighty, we are free at last!"

CRITICAL VIEWING Why do you think the organizers of the March wanted to have speeches delivered from the Lincoln Memorial?

DOCUMENT ONE

Primary Source: Interview
from a radio interview with Rosa Parks, 1992

In 1992, 37 years after Rosa Parks refused to give up her seat on a public bus in Montgomery, Alabama, she spoke to a National Public Radio interviewer about her decision. In this excerpt, Parks discusses why she kept her seat and what happened after her arrest.

CONSTRUCTED RESPONSE What took Parks by surprise after she was arrested?

[T]he more we gave in and the more we complied with that kind of treatment, the more oppressive it became. My main reason for keeping my seat was that I did not want to be mistreated. I did not have any idea at all what would be the result of my . . . arrest. I was totally surprised to know that so many others were concerned enough to stay off the buses and let it be known that we would no longer financially support the unjust treatment that we were receiving.

DOCUMENT TWO

Primary Source: Speech
from "I Have a Dream," by Dr. Martin Luther King, Jr., August 28, 1963

In this excerpt from King's speech, he describes how he believes the United States will be transformed when the country achieves racial equality.

CONSTRUCTED RESPONSE In his speech, why does King quote the line from the Declaration of Independence that begins, "We hold these truths to be self-evident"?

I have a dream that one day this nation will rise up and live out the true meaning of its creed: "We hold these truths to be self-evident, that all men are created equal."

I have a dream that my four little children will one day live in a nation where they will not be judged by the color of their skin but by the content of their character.

DOCUMENT THREE

Primary Source: Interview
from an interview with Bayard Rustin conducted for *Eyes on the Prize*, a PBS television series on the civil rights movement, 1979

Bayard Rustin, the chief organizer of the 1963 March on Washington, wanted the march to be a message that would convince Congress to support pending civil rights legislation. In this interview, Rustin explains how he thinks the members of Congress who attended the march were affected.

CONSTRUCTED RESPONSE Why did Rustin insist that the congressmen attending the march simply listen and not say a word?

There were about three hundred congressmen there, but none of them said a word. We had told them to come, but we wanted to talk with them, they were not to talk to us. And after they came and saw that it was very orderly, that there was fantastic determination, that there were all kinds of people there other than black people, they knew there was a consensus [agreement] in this country for the civil rights bill. After the March on Washington, when Kennedy called into the White House the leaders who had been resistant before the march, he made it very clear to them now he was prepared to put his weight behind the bill.

SYNTHESIZE & WRITE

1. **REVIEW** Review what you have learned about the civil rights movement of the 1950s and early 1960s and its leaders.

2. **RECALL** On your own paper, write the main idea expressed in the excerpt from King's speech and those from the interviews of Parks and Rustin.

3. **CONSTRUCT** Construct a topic sentence that answers this question: How did the leaders of the civil rights movement use their voices to help advance African-American equality?

4. **WRITE** Using evidence from this chapter and the documents, write an informative paragraph that supports your topic sentence in Step 3.

2.5 National Museum of African American History and Culture, Washington, D.C.

Open to the public in September 2016, the National Museum of African American History and Culture (NMAAHC) is the only national museum devoted exclusively to the documentation of African-American life, history, and culture. It was established by an act of Congress in 2003, following decades of efforts to promote and highlight the contributions of African Americans.

The museum has collected more than 36,000 artifacts, many of which are displayed in exhibits carefully curated around such themes as slavery, war, civil rights, photography, sports, and music. The NMAAHC is a Smithsonian museum.

Stained Glass from 16th Street Baptist Church

On September 15, 1963, a bomb exploded at the predominantly African-American 16th Street Baptist Church in Birmingham, Alabama, as the congregation gathered for services. Four young girls—Addie Mae Collins, Denise McNair, Carole Robertson, and Cynthia Wesley—were killed by the blast. This stained glass rosette was part of the rubble.

Birmingham was plagued by violence in the 1960s. In fact, the tragedy at the church was the third bombing in the city in 11 days.

Why do you think those who violently opposed racial equality targeted African-American churches? Explain.

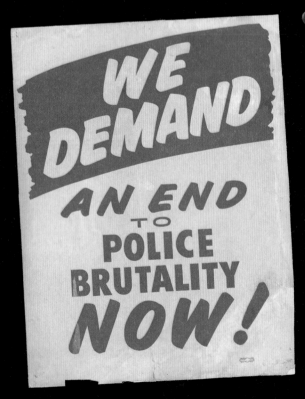

March on Washington Poster

A white high school teacher named Samuel Y. Edgerton carried this poster when he attended the 1963 March on Washington to demonstrate public support for the civil rights bill proposed by President Kennedy. Edgerton had joined the NAACP in July of that year and spoken out against the segregation at a nearby school. Edgerton would become an art historian and professor at Boston University and Williams College.

Through the Lens of James Karales

From 1962 to 1964, civil rights photographer James Karales was granted remarkable access to Dr. Martin Luther King, Jr. Portraits like this one, featuring King with Rosa Parks, are some of Karales's most famous works. They tell the story of King's involvement in civil rights events, protests, and rallies, and reveal intimate family moments.

Karales took this photo at a rally at the 16th Street Baptist Church prior to its bombing on September 15, 1963. The NMAAHC has several of Karales's civil rights movement prints in its collection.

NAACP Hat

Roy Wilkins, an African-American civil rights activist from the 1930s to the 1970s, served as the executive secretary and director of the NAACP from 1955 to 1977. He wore this cloth hat during the 1963 March on Washington for Jobs and Freedom.

The NAACP was established in 1909 by W.E.B. Du Bois and other African-American and white leaders, including Jane Addams. The goal of the organization was to be a force for change in ending segregation and discrimination against African Americans.

Freedom Rider's Button

In 1961, many Freedom Riders who boarded buses to the South wore a button like this one as they tried to call attention to segregated public travel facilities along their journey.

Segregated Bus Station Sign

The plywood sign above hung in a segregated bus station in Birmingham, Alabama, in the 1950s. African Americans living and traveling in the South faced segregated, unpleasant, and dangerous conditions on trains and buses. Forced to sit in the backs of buses, they also suffered the humiliation of using separate restrooms, water fountains, and waiting rooms. And the threat of violence was a constant concern.

How and where else have African Americans encountered segregation throughout history? Provide examples.

VOCABULARY

Use each of the following vocabulary terms in a sentence that shows an understanding of its meaning.

1. integration

    After the Supreme Court ruling, schools began the process of integration, allowing students of all races to attend.

2. desegregate

3. grassroots

4. sit-in

5. civil disobedience

6. Freedom Riders

7. oration

8. nonviolent resistance

READING STRATEGY
DETERMINE CHRONOLOGY

If you haven't done so already, complete your time line to order key events from the civil rights movement during the 1950s and early 1960s. Then answer the question.

1954
Brown v. *Board of Education* ruling

9. What subsequent events were made possible by the ruling in *Brown* v. *Board of Education?*

MAIN IDEAS

Answer the following questions. Support your answers with evidence from the chapter.

10. How did President Truman support the civil rights of African Americans? **LESSON 1.1**

11. How did the decision in *Brown* v. *Board of Education* affect schools? **LESSON 1.2**

12. What happened when James Meredith tried to register at the University of Mississippi in 1962? **LESSON 1.3**

13. What did the Montgomery Bus Boycott achieve? **LESSON 1.4**

14. What strategy did Martin Luther King, Jr., use to fight for racial equality? **LESSON 1.5**

15. Who were the Freedom Riders? **LESSON 2.1**

16. How did King try to end segregation in Birmingham in 1963? **LESSON 2.2**

17. Who made up the crowd at the 1963 March on Washington? **LESSON 2.3**

HISTORICAL THINKING

Answer the following questions. Support your answers with evidence from the chapter.

18. **COMPARE AND CONTRAST** How were the actions taken by presidents Eisenhower and Kennedy during the civil rights movement alike and different?

19. **EVALUATE** What qualities did King possess that helped him become the leader of the civil rights movement?

20. **SYNTHESIZE** How did the civil rights movement gain momentum during the 1950s and early 1960s?

21. **FORM AND SUPPORT OPINIONS** Which major event of the movement do you think had the greatest impact on helping to advance equality for African Americans? Explain your answer.

22. **MAKE INFERENCES** Why do you think the sit-ins and freedom rides energized the civil rights movement?

23. **DRAW CONCLUSIONS** What role did news outlets and reporters play in spreading the civil rights movement?

Elizabeth Eckford, the young African-American woman in the foreground of this photo taken by Will Counts, was one of the Little Rock Nine. The nine African-American students determined to integrate Central High School in Little Rock, Arkansas, on September 4, 1957, were supposed to meet that day and enter the school together. But the other students were not able to contact Eckford to let her know the plan. As a result, she endured the hostility of the white students at the school on her own.

24. How would you describe Eckford's behavior as the crowd heckles her?

25. How would you describe the face of Hazel Bryan, who is directly behind Eckford in the photo?

ANALYZE SOURCES

John Lewis has been a Georgia congressman since 1987. He was also a prominent activist during the civil rights movement. Lewis took part in lunch counter sit-ins and in the freedom rides. In the 1963 March on Washington, he delivered a forceful speech, calling on all Americans to be part of the movement.

> I appeal to all of you to get into this great revolution that is sweeping this nation. Get in and stay in the streets of every city, every village and hamlet of this nation until true freedom comes, until the revolution of 1776 is complete. We must get in this revolution and complete the revolution. For in the Delta in Mississippi, in southwest Georgia, in the Black Belt of Alabama, in Harlem, in Chicago, Detroit, Philadelphia, and all over this nation, the black masses are on the march for jobs and freedom.

26. What does Lewis mean by suggesting that the revolution of 1776 is not "complete"?

CONNECT TO YOUR LIFE

27. EXPOSITORY Imagine the year is 1963, and you have just taken part in the March on Washington. Write a letter to a friend describing the event and explaining how the experience has affected you.

TIPS

- Review what you have read about the march and consider what it might have been like to attend the event.

- Describe the crowds at the march and the speakers you heard, particularly Dr. Martin Luther King, Jr.

- Use two or three vocabulary words from the chapter in your letter.

- End the letter with a brief summary statement about how the march has affected you.

THE FIRST
CONSERVATIONISTS

CRITICAL VIEWING Opponents of the Dakota Access Pipeline demonstrate on a tributary of the Missouri River in 2016. What do their signs reveal about their mission?

In 1971, an organization called Keep America Beautiful launched one of the most effective campaigns in advertising history. Billboards, magazine ads, and television commercials featured a solemn-faced man in traditional Native American clothing. As he regarded a landscape littered with garbage, a single tear trickled down his weathered cheek. The "Crying Indian" image, accompanied by such slogans as "Pollution hurts all of us," became widely recognized. The ad campaign was hugely successful in enlisting Americans to help reduce litter and fight pollution.

CRITICAL VIEWING What emotions do you think advertisers hoped to evoke when they chose the "Crying Indian" image for this 1970s ad campaign?

IRON EYES CODY

The story of the "Crying Indian" from the Keep America Beautiful ad campaign contains some curious twists. The craggy-faced man featured in the ads was an actor named Iron Eyes Cody. He had played Native Americans in movies since the 1920s. Sometime after the famous ad campaign, however, it was revealed that Iron Eyes Cody was not of Cherokee and Cree ancestry, as he claimed. In fact, he was a Sicilian American, born in Louisiana with the name Espera Oscar de Corti.

It would be easy to dismiss Cody as a cheap fake, but he took his pseudo-Native American identity very seriously. He married a Native American woman and adopted two Native American sons. He followed Native American practices and beliefs during his entire adult life. He also vigorously supported numerous Native American causes. In 1995, the Hollywood Native American community honored him for his work. However, some Native Americans were angered by Cody's false ancestry claims.

The "Crying Indian" image also illustrates a long-held stereotype of Native Americans as simple hunters or farmers living in harmony with nature. A common idea is that they left no trace on the environment— they were the original conservationists. While some may consider this portrayal as flattering, it may also be overly simplified. Native Americans have been using natural resources in a variety of sophisticated ways since long before the first Europeans arrived. Native American groups are as diverse as the nationalities found on any continent, and their relationships with nature reflect that diversity.

Defiance House is a well-preserved Ancestral Puebloan cliff dwelling located in the Glen Canyon area of Utah. Used as a residence from about A.D. 1250 to 1285, it was most likely abandoned because of drought, lack of food, enemies, or land overuse.

BEFORE EUROPEAN CONTACT

The term *pre-contact* is sometimes used to refer to Native Americans before their first encounters with European explorers and settlers. Scholars believe that most pre-contact groups shared a broadly similar worldview. According to this worldview, animals, plants, and the earth itself harbored sacred spirits, and humans could ask these spirits to influence the weather, harvests, or the outcome of an upcoming battle. However, the numerous groups had widely different ways of life that varied to fit the diverse North American geography. Some groups did indeed leave little trace on the land, while others took an active role in molding the ecosystems in which they lived. Historian Louis S. Warren wrote, "To claim that Indians lived without affecting nature is akin to saying that they lived without touching anything, that they were a people without a history."

Different groups manipulated their environments in different ways to suit their needs. The Choctaw, Iroquois, and Pawnee, for example, cleared forests to create fields for farming. When those fields were no longer fertile, the tribes would abandon them and clear new land. When land was abundant, this practice could continue for a long time. But it led to deforestation and stress on local species. Certain tribes may have even caused their own downfall by overusing local resources. Some researchers believe the Ancestral Puebloans of southeastern Utah disappeared from their villages in the 13th century because they had depleted the wood in the region by burning it for fuel.

Fire was a powerful tool used by Native Americans to shape an ecosystem to their advantage. For example, some groups used fire to help create open prairies where large game animals such as bison, deer, elk, and antelope could graze. Fires were sometimes used to force animals into narrow canyons, lakes, or small areas where they could be easily hunted. Burning was also used to clear land for crops or drive out pests.

But many pre-contact groups actively practiced conservation techniques to protect game species. The Algonquian lived along the Atlantic Coast and divided hunting territories among families. Each family followed hunting practices that helped maintain the game supply. In the Pacific Northwest, some Native American tribes trapped salmon swimming up rivers to spawn. They were careful to let enough fish escape and lay their eggs so that the supply would be maintained from year to year.

AFTER EUROPEAN CONTACT

For years after European settlers arrived in North America, Native Americans continued their traditional ways of life. However, as groups were pushed onto reservations in the 19th century, these ways of life were disrupted. In the centuries since the first European contact, Native Americans have faced the challenge of adapting to new environments and maintaining their cultures in an ever-changing world. Today, climate change may pose one of the most severe threats to some groups, particularly in Alaska. The melting of ice and permafrost there is greatly affecting such game species as polar bear and caribou.

Native American groups remain at the forefront of conservation efforts. Many tribes are uniquely positioned to protect the wild lands they inhabit. According to one study, "many tribal lands still represent some of the largest intact habitats . . . in North America." Native American tribes control more than 81,236 square miles of land in the lower 48 states and 62,500 square miles of land in Alaska. "Much of this land is relatively undisturbed, providing a significant amount of rare and important fish and wildlife habitat," the authors of the study claim.

Examples abound of Native American tribes working to restore habitats and species. Perhaps the best-known example is the fight to restore the American bison. Historically, the bison provided a living for many Great Plains tribes and played an important role in their cultures. By 1884, as a result of overhunting, only 325 wild bison remained in the United States. Today, organizations such as the Intertribal Buffalo Council (ITBC) work to reintroduce American bison to tribal lands in South Dakota, Montana, Oklahoma, and New Mexico. As of 2017, the ITBC has 63 member tribes spread across 20 states. Those tribes, including the Lakota, Crow, Blackfeet, Ho Chunk, and Choctaw, manage a collective herd of more than 15,000 bison. Emphasizing the cultural importance of bison, the ITBC asserts, "To re-establish healthy buffalo populations on tribal lands is to re-establish hope for Indian people."

Still, like all Americans, Native Americans must balance conservation with the use of natural resources. Members of the Hoopa Valley Tribe in California, for example, have a strong belief in conservation and powerful cultural ties to the species that populate their land. At the same time, cutting and selling trees for timber is necessary for the tribe's economy. Thus, the Hoopa have developed ways to maintain a sustainable logging industry while protecting the forest habitat. Similarly, on the Great Plains, some groups harvest and sell bison meat as a healthier alternative to beef while also working to preserve the wild herds.

Occasionally, traditional practices bring tribes into conflict with environmental organizations. The Makah in Washington State had been whaling for thousands of years when they stopped in 1929, in the face of a declining whale population. In 1999, they resumed hunting, having been authorized by the International Whaling Commission to take up to four whales a year. The Makah argue that whaling is central to their culture. They also point to the Treaty of Neah Bay, signed in 1855, which granted whaling rights to the Makah in exchange for tribal

THE GREAT LAW OF PEACE

The Iroquois Confederacy was bound by a constitution that had existed for centuries before the first Europeans arrived. In pre-contact times, the constitution was passed on orally. Today, it has several names, including the Great Law of Peace.

One passage in the constitution forms the basis of an idea called seven-generation sustainability, or the seventh-generation principle. The concept is that humans should base decisions on the way they will affect the future seven generations. Today's decisions, in other words, should lead to healthy, sustainable ecosystems for many generations to come.

PRIMARY SOURCE

In all of your deliberations in the Confederate Council, in your efforts at lawmaking, in all your official acts, self-interest shall be cast into oblivion. Cast not over your shoulder behind you the warnings of the nephews and nieces should they chide you for any error or wrong you may do, but return to the way of the Great Law which is just and right. Look and listen for the welfare of the whole people and have always in view not only the present but also the coming generations, even those whose faces are yet beneath the surface of the ground—the unborn of the future Nation.

—from the Constitution of the Iroquois Nations

lands. Environmentalists argue that certain gray whale groups are nearly depleted, and whaling by the Makah could threaten their dwindling numbers. Some also criticize the Makah for using modern technology, in addition to traditional tools, to kill whales.

In 2000, former Tribal Council chairman Ben Johnson summed up the frustration many Native Americans feel about stereotypes that simplify Native American culture and freeze it in time. "Times change and we have to change with the times," he said. "[People] want us to be back in the primitive times. We just want to practice our culture."

THE DAKOTA ACCESS PIPELINE

From April 2016 through February 2017, an environmental protest placed the Standing Rock Sioux tribe in headlines across the country. The Sioux were fighting the construction of the last segment of the Dakota Access Pipeline (DAPL) beneath the Missouri River on land that is adjacent to the Standing Rock Reservation in North Dakota. The DAPL is a 1,170-mile-long underground pipeline built to transport oil from fields in North Dakota to southern Illinois, where it can be shipped to refineries.

The Standing Rock Sioux objected to the pipeline on both cultural and environmental grounds. They claimed its construction would disrupt sacred tribal burial sites. They also feared an oil spill would contaminate the Missouri River, the reservation's principal source of water. Protesters claimed the land through which the pipeline runs is in fact Sioux land, deeded to them in the Treaties of Fort Laramie in 1851 and 1868. Since 1851, the government has taken much of the land, but the treaties were never canceled.

In spring 2016, tribe members set up a camp on the reservation in North Dakota and publicized their mission statement: "Our goal is to peacefully and prayerfully defend our rights, and rise up as one to sustain Mother Earth and her inhabitants." Protests staged from the camp were largely peaceful, although some clashes with police did occur. Environmentalists, celebrities, and others joined the Standing Rock Sioux in their protests. Many others used donations or social media to express their

Protesters march on the Standing Rock Indian Reservation in North Dakota in 2016, attempting to halt the construction of a pipeline along the northern edge of the reservation.

support. For example, in November 2016, the rumor circulated that police officers were using Facebook check-ins to track the locations of protesters. More than 1 million people across the United States "checked in" at the Standing Rock Reservation.

On the other side of the issue, many Americans favored construction of the DAPL, which some claimed had created thousands of jobs. Several labor unions supported the pipeline for that reason. Some supporters believed transporting oil through the pipeline would be much safer than using trucks, tankers, and trains. However, experts debate the relative safety of moving oil through pipelines. A major leak discovered in 2016 in an older North Dakota pipeline added to safety concerns about the new one.

In January 2017, President Donald Trump signed an executive order to speed up the approval process for construction of the remaining section of the pipeline. In late February, police cleared demonstrators from the main protest camp. Construction was completed and oil had begun flowing through the pipeline by June 1, 2017. The Standing Rock Sioux vowed to continue their fight in the courts.

THINK ABOUT IT

In what ways have Native Americans had a positive influence on the environment?

NATIONAL GEOGRAPHIC

RESTORING THE RIO GRANDE

In September 2016, National Geographic Freshwater Fellow Sandra Postel reported that Native American tribes and Audubon New Mexico, a conservation society, were working together to restore flow to the Rio Grande. The Rio Grande is the second largest river in the Southwest. But parts of it dry up in the summer as water is diverted for irrigation and other purposes. This situation alarms water conservations like Postel. Numerous native fish and birds, including some that are threatened or endangered, depend on the Rio Grande.

Audubon New Mexico developed a plan to restore some of the river's flow. The various communities along the Rio Grande are allocated a certain amount of water from the river each year. Audubon asked Native American groups in the Middle Rio Grande Valley to transfer to Audubon a portion of the water they receive. In exchange, Audubon committed to use the water for the river's benefit and to seek funding to restore river habitats on tribal lands. The Sandia, Isleta, Santa Ana, and Cochiti Pueblos agreed, transferring over 130 million gallons of water to Audubon New Mexico. With contributions from another user, the total water donation came to more than 260 million gallons.

National Geographic Freshwater Fellow (2009–2015) Sandra Postel

The water was stored in a reservoir and released at strategic locations during the summer of 2016. At the same time, the Pueblos and Audubon New Mexico worked to plant trees and restore habitats along the river's banks. Postel praised the partnership. "River by river," she wrote, "the movement of water stewardship and restoration we are working to build is growing."

CRITICAL VIEWING Why is cooperation among tribes and outside agencies important in restoring the Rio Grande, shown below?

CHAPTER

27

CONFLICT AND EXPANDING RIGHTS

1960–1968

ESSENTIAL QUESTION

How did American identity change in the 1960s?

 **AMERICAN STORIES**
ONLINE · **Protesting the Vietnam War**

SECTION 1 **Kennedy and the Cold War**

KEY VOCABULARY

astronaut	Cuban Missile Crisis	satellite
ballistic missile	exile	space race
Berlin Wall	naval quarantine	status quo
conspiracy		

SECTION 2 **Progress and Unrest**

KEY VOCABULARY

affirmative action	landmark legislation	Medicare
black separatism	Medicaid	

SECTION 3 **The Civil Rights Movement Expands**

KEY VOCABULARY

feminist	termination policy
gender bias	wage gap
hunger strike	

SECTION 4 **Conflict at Home and Abroad**

KEY VOCABULARY

Agent Orange	dove	napalm
cease-fire	draft exemption	search-and-destroy mission
counterculture	escalation	silent majority
domino theory	hawk	

AMERICAN GALLERY
ONLINE · **President John F. Kennedy**

READING STRATEGY

COMPARE AND CONTRAST

To compare and contrast, note similarities and differences between people, places, events, or things. As you read, use a Venn diagram like this one to compare and contrast the nation's concepts of American identity at the beginning of the 1960s to those nearer the end of the decade.

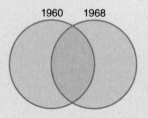

1960   1968

In 1965, early in the Vietnam War, U.S. Marines of the 163rd Helicopter Squadron airlifted South Vietnamese troops to an assault against the Viet Cong. Photojournalist Larry Burrows documented what instead became a trap. The Viet Cong, hidden behind the distant tree line, ambushed the troops and the marines immediately after this photo was taken.

"The guns and the bombs, the rockets and the warships, **are all symbols of human failure.**"

—President Lyndon B. Johnson

1.1 The New Frontier

Sometimes, maturity and experience seem to be the most important qualities a leader can possess. At other times, a leader's youthful confidence and optimism can inspire a nation to move forward.

MAIN IDEA The 1960 presidential election was a tough, close race, but Americans looked to a new generation of leadership in John F. Kennedy.

THE 1960 ELECTION

As the November 1960 presidential election approached, Republicans nominated Eisenhower's vice president **Richard M. Nixon**, and Democrats nominated Senator John F. Kennedy of Massachusetts. Nixon campaigned on the **status quo**, or the way things were at the moment. He reminded Americans that the nation was prosperous and at peace. Kennedy took a different approach.

In his acceptance speech at the Democratic National Convention, Kennedy referred to a wealth of new opportunities awaiting the nation in the new decade, which he described as a **New Frontier**. Those opportunities included innovations in science and technology that positioned the United States for achievements in space only imagined previously. Challenges included re-energizing a sluggish economy and getting more people back to work. This New Frontier required creative

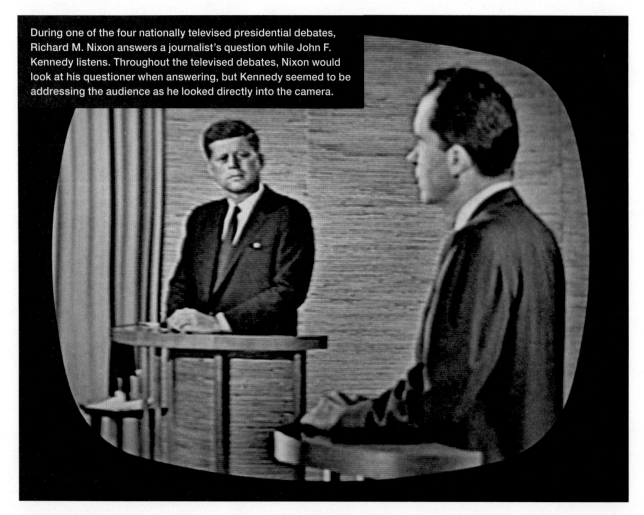

During one of the four nationally televised presidential debates, Richard M. Nixon answers a journalist's question while John F. Kennedy listens. Throughout the televised debates, Nixon would look at his questioner when answering, but Kennedy seemed to be addressing the audience as he looked directly into the camera.

problem solving and a new and forward-thinking leader. It also required an administration that shared the president's vision and confidence.

Although Kennedy did not make civil rights a campaign issue, his actions supported the civil rights movement. On October 19, 1960, Dr. Martin Luther King, Jr., was jailed for participating in a sit-in at a department store lunch counter in Atlanta. With journalists present, Kennedy phoned Dr. King's wife and offered his sympathy. His action likely won him votes, especially among African Americans.

The race between Kennedy and Nixon was extremely tight. However, Kennedy gained an advantage over Nixon when—for the first time in a presidential election—a series of debates were televised. The first debate had the greatest impact, as about 74 million Americans followed it on television or radio. On screen, Kennedy radiated confidence and charm. In contrast, Nixon appeared sweaty and nervous. The differences in their appearance had an effect on television viewers. Most of those listening on the radio thought the debate was a tie. Most who saw it on television, however, agreed that Kennedy had won. The election's popular vote was extremely close, with Kennedy defeating Nixon by fewer than 120,000 votes. But Kennedy did better in the electoral college vote, winning 303 electoral votes to Nixon's 219. As you've read, the person with the most electoral votes wins the election.

A NEW GENERATION TAKES CHARGE

As the first U.S. president born in the 20th century, Kennedy displayed optimism and confidence about the United States' future. In his inauguration speech, he declared, "the torch has been passed to a new generation of Americans—born in this century, tempered by war, disciplined by a hard and bitter peace." Kennedy's words encouraged those of his generation, who, like him, were raising young families. His words also inspired many

In 1972, the U.S. Post Office issued this 8-cent stamp to commemorate the 10th anniversary of the Peace Corps. The artist drew the stars morphing into flying birds to represent daring ideas like the Peace Corps becoming real.

young people who were taking part in U.S. politics for the first time.

Because Kennedy's victory had been so narrow, he needed to be cautious about pressing Congress with his proposed social reforms. Even so, Kennedy successfully persuaded Congress to support the **Alliance for Progress**, an agreement between the United States and 22 Latin American countries. The alliance was intended to win and strengthen allies in Latin America by providing foreign aid to those countries. The aid would help modernize industry and agriculture, improve the health and education of citizens, and help promote and maintain democratic governments.

On March 1, 1961, Kennedy issued an executive order establishing one of his great triumphs—the **Peace Corps**, which is still active today. A program of volunteers who work in developing countries to aid in the advancement of health, agriculture, and education, the Peace Corps showcases American idealism and know-how throughout the world. The early Peace Corps volunteers were mostly young people energized by Kennedy's call for patriotic selflessness. Kennedy's most visionary goal, however, involved a new frontier that would not be found on Earth, but in space.

HISTORICAL THINKING

1. **READING CHECK** What important role did appearances have in the first debate between Kennedy and Nixon?

2. **COMPARE AND CONTRAST** How did Nixon's and Kennedy's visions for the future of the United States differ?

3. **MAKE INFERENCES** Why do you think Kennedy emphasized the need for his generation to take up the responsibilities of governing the country?

1.2 The Space Race

What if you were given the opportunity of a lifetime—to try to become the first person to travel into outer space? The dangers are great and unknown. Should you risk it?

MAIN IDEA Cold War competition between the United States and the Soviet Union led both nations to expand space exploration and technology.

A NEW CHALLENGE

Three years before Kennedy's election in 1960, the United States and the Soviet Union became engaged in a new type of Cold War rivalry—one that relied more on science and less on military weapons and conflicts. Known as the **space race**, it was a competition to see which nation could make the greatest advances in space travel and technology. It started in October 1957, when the Soviets surprised the Americans by launching *Sputnik 1.* This was the world's first artificial **satellite** to orbit Earth. Any object that orbits a larger object is a satellite. For example, the moon is a satellite of Earth. Artificial satellites such as *Sputnik* were the world's first successful spacecraft.

Fearing that the Soviets might use such technology to spy on or attack the United States, Americans rushed to catch up. President Eisenhower supported increased funding for space exploration as well as for math and science education. The government created what would become the **National Aeronautics and Space Administration (NASA)** to lead this effort.

The United States launched *Explorer 1,* the first American satellite, in January 1958. This satellite carried equipment to test the level of cosmic rays hitting Earth from space. Several more *Explorer* satellites followed. In 1959, NASA chose seven men to become the first American **astronauts**, or space travelers. It would take several more years of training and experiments before the men and equipment would be ready for travel into space.

🏛 National Air and Space Museum Washington, D.C.

John H. Glenn, Jr., was the first American to fully orbit Earth when he flew the Mercury *Friendship 7* (above) around the globe three times. During the first orbit, the automatic control system developed a problem, but Glenn switched to a manual electric system and kept the flight going. Traveling sometimes at more than 17,000 miles per hour, he completed the orbits in just 4 hours, 55 minutes, and 23 seconds. The successful mission brought millions of people into the U.S. space industry to plan future human space flights. It also proved that the United States could compete with the Soviet Union in the space race.

Before venturing into space, astronauts John W. Young (left) and Gus Grissom trained at an indoor swimming pool on how to exit the *Gemini* capsule. Upon returning to Earth, the capsule would splash down in the ocean, where the astronauts would need to exit quickly and inflate their rafts.

THE SPACE PROGRAM

As part of his vision for the New Frontier, President Kennedy proposed a bold expansion of the U.S. space program. In April 1961, shortly after Kennedy took office, Soviet **Yuri Gagarin** (YOO-ree guh-GAHR-ihn) became the first human in space. He orbited Earth in less than two hours. One month later, **Alan Shepard** became the first American in space. He was not able to make a full orbit around Earth, but he was able to control his spacecraft. His entire suborbital flight—a flight that doesn't complete a full orbit of Earth—lasted only 15 minutes and 22 seconds. Still, Shepard was the first American to see our entire planet from space. "What a beautiful view," he noted. That same month, on May 25, President Kennedy addressed a joint session of Congress and announced, "I believe that this nation should commit itself to achieving the goal, before this decade is out, of landing a man on the moon and returning him safely to the earth."

That July, **Gus Grissom** became the second American in space. At the end of Grissom's 15-minute suborbital flight, his capsule splashed down in the Atlantic Ocean and accidentally filled with water and sank. Grissom had to tread water and wait to be rescued. In February 1962, **John Glenn** became the first American to orbit Earth. For the rest of the 1960s, the United States and the Soviet Union continued to compete with each other in the space race. Each side hoped to "win" the contest by being the first to land a human on the moon. This competition produced many great advances in science and technology. Inventions from the space race often became part of daily life, improving everyday items such as light bulbs. It also led to new developments, such as the global positioning system (GPS).

HISTORICAL THINKING

1. **READING CHECK** Why did the United States create NASA?

2. **MAKE INFERENCES** What kind of training would be helpful to the astronauts, and why?

3. **IDENTIFY MAIN IDEAS AND DETAILS** Against which country did Americans hope to win the space race, and how?

1.3 Cold War Concerns

The year is 1959. Thousands of people have fled the island nation of Cuba following a violent revolution. Settling close by in southern Florida, many of these Cubans wonder if they will ever be able to return to their native land.

MAIN IDEA Soon after taking office, President Kennedy faced Cold War challenges in Cuba and Germany.

TROUBLE IN CUBA

In 1959, a year before Kennedy's election, rebels led by Fidel Castro had taken power in Cuba, a U.S. ally located in the Caribbean Sea only 90 miles south of Florida. Castro, a communist, helped overthrow the brutal dictator Fulgencio Batista, who had encouraged both lawful U.S. investors and criminal gangsters to finance Cuban businesses. Batista and his followers had profited from the millions of American dollars that poured into Cuba, while many working Cubans lived in poverty.

Castro was popular while he supported reforms to the corrupt government, but when he seized private and American-owned property and businesses in Cuba, thousands of Cubans fled the country. Many became **exiles**, or political outcasts, in Florida. Castro then established strong economic and political ties with the Soviet Union. Now the Soviets had an ally right in America's backyard. This foreign policy crisis was the first challenge Kennedy faced as president.

As tensions between the United States and Cuba grew, President Kennedy decided to put a secret plan into action. Developed by the Eisenhower administration, the plan called for the United States to train and equip anti-Castro exiles who would then invade Cuba and inspire Cubans to launch an anticommunist revolution. The plan's goals were to remove Castro from power and drive Soviet influence from the Western Hemisphere.

On April 17, 1961, about 1,500 exiles waded ashore at the **Bay of Pigs** on Cuba's southern coast. They hoped to land in secret and launch a surprise attack. Unfortunately, Castro's forces were waiting for them. Cuban intelligence agents in Florida had learned about the plan from gossip among Cuban exiles in Miami. Castro's troops quickly overtook the invaders. Nearly 1,200 of the attackers were captured and held prisoner for 20 months while the United States negotiated for their release.

The failed Bay of Pigs mission was a humiliating defeat for the United States. Some critics worried that the young president lacked the foreign policy experience to handle the Cold War. Kennedy reacted by approving more secret operations to undermine, or weaken, Castro's government.

TENSIONS IN BERLIN

The Soviet Union's support for Cuba increased after the Bay of Pigs invasion. Sensing weakness in the United States government's response to the Cuban crisis, Soviet leader **Nikita Khrushchev** (nih-KEE-tuh KROOSH-chehf) began to challenge Kennedy in other areas.

As you have read, when the Allies divided control of Germany after World War II, West Berlin remained part of democratic West Germany, even though it was surrounded by communist East Germany. Each day, people from communist East Berlin poured into West Berlin, seeking jobs and greater freedom. Khrushchev complained that a capitalist city in the middle of communist-controlled East Germany "stuck like a bone in the Soviet throat."

In June 1961, Kennedy met with Khrushchev. The Soviet leader threatened to limit access to West Berlin. Kennedy declared that Western military forces would defend the city at all costs. He followed up by tripling draft calls, mobilizing U.S. reserve units, and requesting more defense funding from Congress.

In August 1961, workers in East Berlin began building a wall of barbed wire and concrete along the western border of the city. Armed troops were stationed at the crossing points that divided the city. The wall stopped the flow of people leaving East Germany, and those who were caught trying to cross over the wall or tunnel under it were arrested or even shot as they fled. For many years the **Berlin Wall** stood as a symbol of the Cold War. The increasing tension between the United States and the Soviet Union soon threatened to erupt into full-blown war.

HISTORICAL THINKING

1. **READING CHECK** What was the goal of the Bay of Pigs invasion?

2. **ANALYZE CAUSE AND EFFECT** Why was the Berlin Wall constructed?

3. **COMPARE AND CONTRAST** In what way was the situation between the United States and communist Cuba different from the situation the United States faced in Berlin?

In 1961, East German soldiers stand guard as the concrete and barbed-wire Berlin Wall is constructed. The East German government built the wall to surround West Berlin and slow the steady exit of East Berliners to the West.

1.4 Cuban Missile Crisis

If you pay attention to the news, you may find yourself worrying about your future or that of your family or community. But what if the news is so alarming that you begin to fear that the world as we know it might be coming to an end?

MAIN IDEA President Kennedy successfully faced a tense standoff with the Soviets that brought the world to the brink of nuclear war.

SOVIET MISSILES IN CUBA

In October 1962, the world faced the most dangerous moment of the entire Cold War. It began when American spy planes discovered that the Soviets were placing ballistic missiles with nuclear warheads in Cuba. **Ballistic missiles** are rocket-powered missiles that can travel from about 620 to 3,400 miles and are guided on their ascent but fall freely on their descent. Kennedy's advisors believed that the missiles would be in place and ready to fire in a few weeks. With Cuba so close to the American mainland, such missiles could endanger the United States.

Since the Bay of Pigs invasion, Cuba had come to rely heavily on its alliance with the Soviet Union. An economic boycott of Cuba, led by the United States, was hurting the island's economy. Fearing further threats, Castro asked the Soviets for military help. At first, this aid included only defensive missiles. Then the Soviets began equipping Cuba with the offensive missiles detected by the United States— missiles capable of striking Washington, D.C., or even Chicago, Illinois. To the United States, the threat was clear.

The conflict that followed became known as the **Cuban Missile Crisis**. Kennedy met with his advisors and then ordered a **naval quarantine**, or blockade, of Cuba. The blockade prevented any ships from entering or leaving Cuba. As U.S. naval forces surrounded Cuba, the Soviets prepared to challenge them, sending their own armed ships toward the blockade.

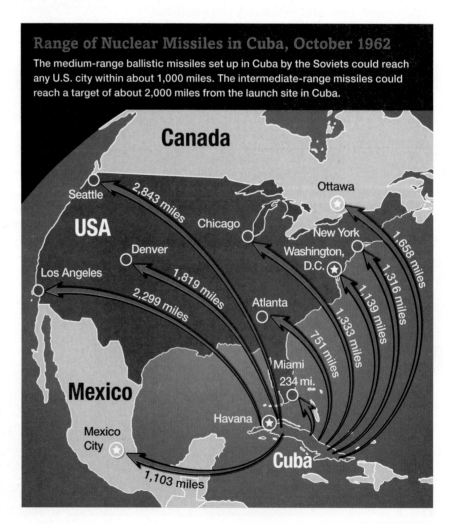

Range of Nuclear Missiles in Cuba, October 1962

The medium-range ballistic missiles set up in Cuba by the Soviets could reach any U.S. city within about 1,000 miles. The intermediate-range missiles could reach a target of about 2,000 miles from the launch site in Cuba.

President Kennedy discusses strategy with General Curtis LeMay and reconnaissance, or survey, pilots who flew over Cuba to get information during the Cuban Missile Crisis. LeMay recommended a more aggressive approach than Kennedy's idea to place a naval blockade around Cuba.

RESOLVING THE CRISIS

On October 22, 1962, Kennedy addressed the nation on television. He reported what he told the Soviets: Take away the missiles in Cuba and destroy the sites. He also warned that any missile fired from Cuba would be considered an attack on the United States by the Soviet Union and would require a military response. American forces went on full alert.

While the world watched and waited, the Soviet ships inched closer to the U.S. warships surrounding the island nation. On October 26, Khrushchev wrote to Kennedy. The Soviets would remove the missiles from Cuba, he said, if the United States guaranteed that it would never invade Cuba. Khrushchev then sent a second message in which he demanded that the United States remove the missiles it had installed in Turkey near the Soviet border. On October 27, Kennedy formally agreed to the Soviets' first offer, and Khrushchev accepted the deal. In return, the United States later quietly removed some of its old missiles from Turkey.

Khrushchev had badly misjudged how strongly the Americans would respond to the placement of missiles so close to the U.S. mainland. However, his willingness to compromise helped lead to a peaceful solution.

After a tense 13 days in October, the world avoided the threat of a nuclear war when the two countries chose to be cautious rather than reckless. That fact alone seemed to shake the leaders of both sides. In July 1963, officials installed a direct telephone link, known as the "hot line," between the White House and the Kremlin, which was the center of the Soviet government. Shortly after that, the United States and the Soviet Union joined other nations in agreeing to a **Nuclear Test-Ban Treaty**, which banned the testing of nuclear weapons in the atmosphere, in space, and under water and limited the future development of nuclear weapons.

HISTORICAL THINKING

1. **READING CHECK** What was so dangerous about the missiles U.S. spy planes discovered in Cuba in October 1962?

2. **IDENTIFY MAIN IDEAS AND DETAILS** How was the Cuban Missile Crisis resolved?

3. **INTERPRET MAPS** Examine the map in this lesson. Which cities were within striking distance of the medium-range missiles?

1.5 Kennedy's Assassination

It was a beautiful late fall day in Dallas, Texas. President Kennedy was visiting the city. As the president's motorcade passed by, the crowds strained to catch a glimpse of him. Suddenly, shots rang out. The country would never be the same.

MAIN IDEA President Kennedy's violent death shocked the nation and the world.

A FATEFUL DAY IN DALLAS

After the peaceful resolution of the Cuban Missile Crisis, President Kennedy gained Americans' confidence and his popularity soared. Members of the press now treated his youth as a positive trait, calling the Kennedy administration "Camelot," a reference to the legendary kingdom where King Arthur presided over his knights of the Round Table.

In late November 1963, the president and his wife, Jacqueline, traveled to Texas on a political tour to win southern support in his upcoming re-election campaign. On November 22, the Kennedys rode in a motorcade with Governor John Connally and his wife, Nellie, through Dallas. Along the route, people waved from office buildings and cheered from the sidewalks. Even Kennedy supporters were surprised by the size of the welcoming crowds.

As the car reached Dealey Plaza, a park in downtown Dallas, gunfire came from the window of a nearby textbook warehouse. The president suddenly slumped in his seat. He had been shot in the head. President Kennedy was rushed to Parkland Hospital and pronounced dead. His assassination stunned the world.

Less than two hours after President Kennedy's assassination, **Lyndon Johnson** took the presidential oath of office aboard Air Force One before it flew back to Washington, D.C. Johnson's wife, Lady

Bird, and Jacqueline Kennedy stood by his side. As the nation mourned its fallen leader, Johnson vowed to continue the programs and policies of the Kennedy administration.

That same day, local police arrested a suspect named **Lee Harvey Oswald** after he shot and killed a Dallas police officer. Officials initially charged

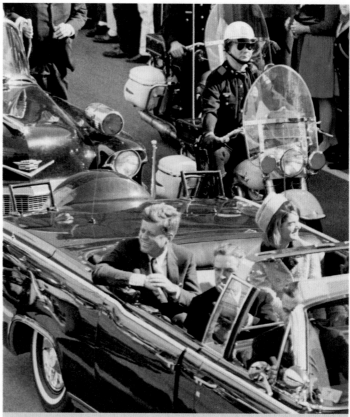

On November 22, 1963, people lined the streets of Dallas, Texas, to greet President and Mrs. John F. Kennedy as they rode by in their motorcade. The Kennedys, joined by Texas Governor and Mrs. John Connally, smiled and waved at the crowds just minutes before a gunman murdered the president and wounded Connally.

Aboard Air Force One shortly after President Kennedy's assassination, Vice President Lyndon Baines Johnson takes the oath of office with a grieving Jacqueline Kennedy beside him. U.S. District Judge Sarah T. Hughes (with her back to the camera) administers the oath.

Oswald only with the death of the police officer, but they considered him the prime suspect in Kennedy's assassination. On November 24, as law enforcement officers were attempting to move Oswald to a different jail location, Dallas nightclub owner Jack Ruby shot and killed him, as shown on live television. Ruby claimed he killed Oswald out of a sense of patriotism. Ruby died in prison four years later.

A NATION GRIEVES

On November 25, 1963, thousands of people gathered in Washington, D.C., for President Kennedy's funeral. Millions of others watched his funeral on television. For many of his supporters, it felt as if they were mourning the death of the hope, innocence, and idealism that Kennedy had inspired.

Some people suspected the events surrounding Kennedy's assassination were part of a larger **conspiracy**, or a plot organized by several people. President Johnson tried to reassure Americans who doubted Oswald had acted alone. The federal government immediately put together a special group led by Chief Justice of the United States Earl

Warren to investigate. The **Warren Commission** concluded that both Oswald and Ruby had acted alone. Despite this conclusion, there were still people who continued to suspect a cover-up.

Such doubts reflected the depth of shock over Kennedy's assassination. Few other events in the nation's history have produced so much shared public grief. Charming and handsome, a war hero with a glamorous wife, Kennedy represented youth and optimism. When he died, so did the dreams of many of his supporters.

HISTORICAL THINKING

1. **READING CHECK** Why were the President and First Lady traveling in Texas?

2. **COMPARE AND CONTRAST** How did the Warren Commission's conclusion about the Kennedy assassination differ from that of many Americans?

3. **MAKE GENERALIZATIONS** Why did the assassination of Kennedy cause so much grief and shock among his supporters?

2.1 Johnson Acts on Civil Rights

Voting is one of the fundamental rights and responsibilities of adult citizens in the United States. At least, it's supposed to be. But in many parts of the South, whites made it impossible for African Americans to exercise that right.

MAIN IDEA The new president supported the civil rights movement, but each step toward equality was a struggle.

THE CIVIL RIGHTS ACT OF 1964

President Johnson vowed to continue Kennedy's policies, including the late president's support of civil rights. During his short term in office, Kennedy had used federal marshals and state National Guard units to enforce existing civil rights laws. The violence against demonstrators in Birmingham had inspired Kennedy to draft a comprehensive civil rights bill, which was already in congressional committees when he was assassinated.

Johnson, who was first elected to Congress in 1937, had been a Texas senator since 1949. He was a southern Democrat, but he championed civil rights at a time when many southern Democrats supported segregation and other Jim Crow laws. As Senate majority leader, Johnson had worked with Republicans and compromised with fellow southern Democrats to help pass the Civil Rights Act of 1957. He was determined to repeat his success with Kennedy's civil rights legislation. Johnson brought together congressional leaders with opposing interests to make sure the Civil Rights Act of 1964 passed.

The bill passed in June after Senate revisions, and President Johnson signed it into law on July 2. The act withholds funds from segregated public programs and outlaws segregation and discrimination in public places. In addition, it created the **Equal Employment Opportunity Commission (EEOC)**, an agency that monitors and protects workplace rights. The law prohibits workplace discrimination based not only on race but also on religious beliefs, national origin, and gender. As a result of the Civil Rights Act, women and minorities now have legal protection against employment discrimination.

CRITICAL VIEWING Upon signing the Civil Rights Act of 1964, President Lyndon B. Johnson (seated) turns to shake hands with Dr. Martin Luther King, Jr., and give Dr. King the pen Johnson had used to sign the bill. Dr. King was instrumental in lobbying for passage of the bill, which was debated in the Senate for months. Others in the room include Republican and Democratic representatives who voted for the bill. How would you describe the mood captured by this photo?

Following the March 7, 1965, Bloody Sunday march, Dr. Martin Luther King, Jr., led a second voting rights march, which became known as Turnaround Tuesday. On March 9, Dr. King and more than 2,000 people marched across the Edmund Pettus Bridge in Selma, Alabama. Blocked by state police officers from continuing to Montgomery, the marchers knelt in prayer and then turned around, going back over the bridge.

THE VOTING RIGHTS ACT OF 1965

Even with federal law backing them, African Americans still found voter registration, or the process of signing up to vote, nearly impossible in the South. Southern states had found ways to keep African-American citizens from voting, including poll taxes, literacy tests, and even threats of physical violence. In 1965, determined African-American citizens in Selma, Alabama, began marching daily to the courthouse to register to vote. But the white sheriff repeatedly turned them away. Many were arrested and beaten.

On March 7, 1965, a day now remembered as Bloody Sunday, protesters began a 50-mile march from Selma to the state capitol building in Montgomery. Dr. Martin Luther King, Jr., and the Southern Christian Leadership Conference (SCLC) joined the protesters. They hadn't walked very far when police attacked them, sending more than 50 marchers to the hospital. They tried again and again to complete their march. People from all over the country traveled to join in the Selma-to-Montgomery marches. On March 25, protected by federal officials, Dr. King and 25,000 marchers arrived safely in the capital.

Spurred by President Johnson and events in Selma, Congress passed the **Voting Rights Act of 1965** on August 6. The act outlawed all obstacles that prevented African Americans from voting. This landmark legislation, or important and historic law, soon had an impact. By the end of 1965, as many as 250,000 African-American citizens had successfully registered to vote. Within three years, the registration rate of African Americans in the South had climbed to more than 60 percent. Even so, many activists felt the struggle for civil rights was progressing too slowly. Some were thinking of changing their strategy.

HISTORICAL THINKING

1. **READING CHECK** What was the purpose of the Selma-to-Montgomery marches?

2. **COMPARE AND CONTRAST** How were the Civil Rights Act of 1964 and the Voting Rights Act of 1965 alike and different in the ways they promoted civil rights in the United States?

3. **SYNTHESIZE** How did the Civil Rights Act of 1964 provide benefits not just to African Americans, but to other citizens as well?

2.2 Rising Discontent

Waiting for something to change can be hard, especially if it affects your life. You might grow impatient or feel like giving up. Or you might decide to try a different strategy.

MAIN IDEA Not all civil rights leaders agreed with Dr. King's peaceful methods, and patience began to turn into tension and violence.

URBAN VIOLENCE

Racial discrimination was a problem not only in the South. In the urban centers of the North and West, many African-American families lived in high-crime neighborhoods with failing schools and limited public services. In some cities, banks refused home loans to African Americans who sought to buy property outside their traditional neighborhoods. Although there were no laws prohibiting African Americans and other minorities from living wherever they wanted, such practices kept many from moving into certain areas. In addition, many people chose to stay in their neighborhoods to avoid conflicts. Yet as the civil rights movement gained strength, both supporters and opponents felt threatened, and conflicts arose anyway. Riots erupted in Los Angeles, Chicago, Detroit, and other major American cities.

While older activists believed in Dr. King's nonviolent approach, some younger African Americans believed that these methods weren't working fast enough. The **Black Power movement** arose out of their frustration. Members of this movement proclaimed pride in their African-American heritage, rejecting the importance of integration. Instead, they advocated for **black separatism**, the political and cultural division of blacks and whites.

The Nation of Islam, a religious black nationalist organization that preaches self-help, moral discipline, and black separatism, was founded in 1930 in Detroit, Michigan. The group's influence increased as the civil rights movement grew. By the late 1950s, **Malcolm X** had become one of its most forceful speakers. He preached self-defense rather than nonviolence, stating that African

Americans should protect themselves "by any means necessary." Angry members of the Nation of Islam assassinated Malcolm X after he left the group over disputes with its leader.

Malcolm X

Malcolm Little was the son of a murdered civil rights activist. When he was a boy, white supremacists burned down the family home. A wild and wayward youth, he was arrested and sentenced to prison on a burglary charge. While in prison, he learned about the Nation of Islam. After prison, he joined the Nation of Islam and changed his name to Malcolm X, dismissing the name "Little" as his slave name. His intelligence, drive, and charismatic speaking style made him the most well-known member of the Nation of Islam, eclipsing the fame of the organization's leader, Elijah Muhammad.

Three female members of the Black Panthers solemnly hold Panther flags in a photograph taken around 1968 in California. While the mainstream press mostly portrayed the Black Panthers as criminals, photographers Pirkle Jones and Ruth Marion Baruch revealed the members' humanity, concerns for family, commitment to ideals, and hope for the future.

Members of another group, the **Black Panther Party**, saw themselves as the armed enemies of a racist "police state." Organized in Oakland, California, in 1966, the Black Panthers openly carried weapons and studied the law, strategies meant to protect themselves and their neighbors from police harassment and brutality. The Black Panthers also established many community service programs, such as health clinics, after-school enrichment classes, and free breakfasts for public school students.

THE COURTS DECIDE

Even as unrest increased, President Johnson took more steps to promote civil rights. In 1965, he signed an executive order instituting **affirmative action**, a government policy establishing racial quotas to favor groups that face discrimination. The goal of affirmative action was to improve educational and employment opportunities for all Americans. Affirmative action proved to be controversial, and it was challenged in court. In 1978, the U.S. Supreme Court ruled that affirmative action programs were constitutional but basing quotas solely on race was not.

In 1967, yet another form of racial discrimination was struck down: state bans on interracial marriage. All but nine states had enacted such bans at some time. But most northern and western states had repealed those laws by the mid-1960s and allowed couples of different races to marry. The southern states did not. When the Lovings, an interracial couple legally married in Washington, D.C., were arrested for living together in marriage in Virginia, they appealed their case to the U.S. Supreme Court. In the matter of *Loving* v. *Virginia*, the Court agreed with the Lovings, declaring all laws against interracial marriage unconstitutional.

President Johnson's progressive plans for the nation did not end with civil rights. He also hoped to end poverty in the United States.

HISTORICAL THINKING

1. **READING CHECK** Why did some younger African Americans turn away from Dr. King's nonviolent movement?

2. **COMPARE AND CONTRAST** How was discrimination similar and different in the North and the South?

3. **IDENTIFY MAIN IDEAS AND DETAILS** How did the U.S. Supreme Court's decisions discussed in this lesson affect the civil rights of Americans?

2.3 The Great Society

Teddy Roosevelt introduced the Square Deal in 1902. Franklin Roosevelt proposed the New Deal in 1933, and Harry Truman promoted the Fair Deal in 1949. It was only a matter of time before the United States required another government program to bring about sweeping change.

MAIN IDEA In 1964, President Lyndon Johnson unveiled a new plan to address the nation's problems with poverty, health care, and education.

ATTACKING POVERTY

On May 22, 1964, President Johnson announced his sweeping new plan to improve the lives of the American people. He called it the **Great Society**, and its aim was to tackle the country's social problems: racial inequality, poverty, and lack of health care and educational opportunities.

Between the time of his announcement and the 1964 presidential election, Johnson built the foundation of his Great Society by working with Congress to pass the Civil Rights Act of 1964 and the **Economic Opportunity Act of 1964**, which established organizations that provided jobs for people living at or near the poverty level. These groups helped young people from impoverished neighborhoods gain work experience. He also created the **Office of Economic Opportunity**, a government agency that would oversee Great Society programs.

Johnson won the 1964 election in a landslide. During his State of the Union address on January 4, 1965, Johnson declared the central component of the Great Society would be the **War on Poverty**, which he had introduced in 1964.

During the 1960s, about 20 percent of the nation was living in poverty, and the rates among African Americans, Native

Americans, and Hispanics were two to three times higher than those of whites. But poverty affected white families as well, especially in rural areas of the country, such as Appalachia. **Appalachia** is a region of the Appalachian Mountains, stretching from southern New York State to northern Alabama, and it included remote and economically disadvantaged areas. Johnson's plan was to mobilize entire communities to his cause. Organizations such as the **Neighborhood Youth Corps** and the **Volunteers in Service to America (VISTA)** employed citizens in jobs that benefited their communities.

Ted Lovato mills a tool holder in a 1972 Neighborhood Youth Corps equipment-making program in Denver, Colorado. The Youth Corps was one of many Great Society programs funded by federal, state, and local governments.

Fred Montgomery reads to a Head Start preschool class in Clarksdale, Mississippi, in 1966. The local community had convinced the governor not to veto funds for Head Start.

PRIMARY SOURCE

Your imagination, your initiative, and your indignation will determine whether we build a society where progress is the servant of our needs, or a society where old values and new visions are buried under unbridled [uncontrolled] growth. In your time we have the opportunity to move . . . upward to the Great Society. The Great Society rests on abundance and liberty for all. It demands an end to poverty and racial injustice, to which we are totally committed.

—from President Lyndon B. Johnson's Great Society speech, May 22, 1964

HUNDREDS OF NEW LAWS

Over the course of his presidency, Johnson's skill as a legislator helped him encourage Congress to pass more than 200 new Great Society bills. In addition to his efforts to fight poverty, Johnson sought to improve the nation's health care.

In 1965, Congress passed Social Security amendments that created Medicare and Medicaid. **Medicare** gave much needed government-subsidized health insurance to older Americans. More than 33 percent of Americans 65 years of age or older lived in poverty in 1960—double the percentage for the rest of the population. And of those seniors, almost half could not afford health insurance. Medicare gave them affordable access to medical care. The other program, **Medicaid**, provided health care for the poor.

Johnson also addressed the low rates of literacy, or the ability to read, and the low rates of high school graduations. In 1965, Congress passed the **Elementary and Secondary Education Act**. The law funded elementary schools and high schools in low-income areas to improve education and lower school dropout rates. One program, **Head Start**, prepared preschool-aged children for elementary school by providing learning activities, balanced meals, medical and dental care, and supervised field trips.

HISTORICAL THINKING

1. **READING CHECK** How would you summarize President Johnson's Great Society agenda?

2. **MAKE INFERENCES** What do you think President Johnson meant when he said Americans should build a society in which "progress is the servant of our needs"?

3. **SUMMARIZE** How did the Great Society programs seek to reduce poverty in the United States?

3.1 Latinos Organize

Momentum and motivation often build over time, especially when they are leading to successes. Latinos had been working to combat discrimination since the 1920s, and they continued their fight in the decades that followed.

> **MAIN IDEA** Latinos and Hispanics in the United States remained committed to their quest for civil rights and against discrimination and poor wages during the 1960s.

MEXICAN AMERICANS CONTINUE THEIR FIGHT

As early as the 1920s, Mexican Americans had organized to address discrimination. Formed in 1929, the **League of United Latin American Citizens (LULAC)** was one such organization. In 1945, LULAC sued a segregated California school system for discriminating against Latino children. LULAC also protested the 1948 **Longoria incident**, in which Felix Longoria, a Mexican American soldier killed in action during World War II, was denied a wake by a funeral home owner because Longoria was a Latino. In 1947, postwar events like these helped launch another Mexican American organization called the **Unity League**, which campaigned against discrimination in housing, education, and employment.

In the 1950s, most Mexicans and Mexican Americans, or **Chicanos**, in the United States lived in California and states in the Southwest. Many were employed as migrant workers on huge farms owned by large corporations, and they labored for low pay and no benefits. An entire family might make 20 cents for 2 hours of backbreaking work. The makeshift housing for migrant workers was crowded and often lacked electricity or running water. The companies that owned the farms prohibited unions, so the workers had no collective voice to demand higher wages and better conditions.

In 1962, two political activists, **César Chávez** and **Dolores Huerta**, formed the National Farm Workers Association, which later became a full-fledged union, the **United Farm Workers (UFW)**. Influenced by the nonviolent methods of

Dr. Martin Luther King, Jr., Chávez and Huerta led peaceful strikes, marches, boycotts, and **hunger strikes**, in which they protested by refusing to eat, in order to win rights and better wages for migrant workers. In 1965, they joined forces with Filipino American grape laborers to start a boycott to protest conditions in California's Central Valley vineyards. The effort was particularly effective.

I Am Somebody

Together We Are Strong

CRITICAL VIEWING The farmworker portrayed in this poster represents one of the many migrant workers who joined Huerta and Chávez in laying the groundwork for the current union, United Farm Workers of America. What do you think is the main message of this poster, and why?

UFW workers crisscrossed the country urging consumers not to buy California grapes. Soon millions of Americans supported the boycott. The boycott ended in 1970, when public pressure forced California's large farming companies to agree to higher wages for migrant workers and to acknowledge that farmworkers had the right to unionize.

CHALLENGES FOR OTHER HISPANIC GROUPS

Hispanic groups from the Caribbean also faced challenges in the United States. Inhabitants of Puerto Rico, for example, sometimes experienced severe poverty. Puerto Ricans had become American citizens beginning in 1917 after being residents of a U.S. territory for almost 20 years. The lure of jobs and the open immigration policies between Puerto Rico and the United States encouraged thousands to migrate to the mainland.

By the mid-1960s, about 1 million Puerto Ricans lived on the mainland. Most lived in big cities, such as New York, Philadelphia, and Chicago. Even in their new homes, many Puerto Ricans still dealt with poverty, unemployment, unsafe neighborhoods, and discrimination. They formed political groups to fight for their civil rights. They pressed for equal access to jobs and education as well as greater federal economic aid to Puerto Rico.

As you have read, the communist takeover of Cuba in 1959 caused many Cubans to immigrate to the United States. About 500,000 of them flew to the United States before Castro ceased all flights there in 1973. Most Cuban immigrants in the United States settled in Florida, mainly in Miami. Many started successful businesses, though some still faced discrimination. Cuban Americans are known for their political activism, fighting for political change both in the United States and in Cuba.

In 1973, Dolores Huerta and César Chávez shared the podium at the founding convention of the United Farm Workers union. By this time, the UFW had 50,000 dues-paying members, for whom it negotiated union contracts with grape growers, established a hiring hall, and furnished a health clinic.

Latino or Hispanic?

Though the two words are often used interchangeably, *Latino* and *Hispanic* have different meanings. *Hispanic* describes people who are from Spanish-speaking cultures or have Spanish-speaking ancestry. *Latino* (or *Latina*) describes someone exclusively of Latin American origin, including Brazilians, who speak Portuguese, not Spanish. So, while Brazilians are considered Latinos, it would be inaccurate to refer to them as Hispanics. And while people from Spain are Hispanics, they are not Latinos.

HISTORICAL THINKING

1. **READING CHECK** Why are César Chávez and Dolores Huerta significant figures in American history?

2. **IDENTIFY MAIN IDEAS AND DETAILS** Why did so many Cubans immigrate to the United States starting in 1959?

3. **ANALYZE CAUSE AND EFFECT** How might the Latino and African-American civil rights movements have influenced each other?

Preserving Objects
Left Behind by Migrants

"Migrants are some of the most optimistic, resilient,
inspirational people I've ever met." —Jason De León

Why pick up trash in the desert? Anthropologist Jason De León
searches parched lands along the U.S.-Mexico border for things
people have thrown away. But the tattered backpacks, old shoes, and
other dropped items aren't trash. They're traces of human lives. Using
science and storytelling, De León is shining a spotlight on Mexican
migrants and their struggles and giving them a voice.

^
De León collaborated with
artist Amanda Krugliak on
State of Exception, a wall of
discarded backpacks left by
Mexican migrants trying to
cross into the United States
through the Sonoran Desert.

MAIN IDEA Anthropologist Jason De León studies and preserves the objects left behind by people crossing the U.S.-Mexico border.

ANTHROPOLOGY AND IMMIGRATION

Some anthropologists study cultures in remote locations or in the distant past. Jason De León, a National Geographic Explorer and professor of anthropology at the University of Michigan, focuses on people. He studies the lives of undocumented migrants crossing the border from Mexico into the United States—people at the center of a major debate today.

De León's interest in the topic of immigration goes back to his childhood. Growing up in the United States near the Mexican border, he could watch migrants swimming across the Rio Grande from Mexico. De León's own grandparents were born in Mexico, and his mother came from the Philippines. "Being raised on the border in a bicultural household with a long immigration history makes me very attuned to issues of cultural identity and discrimination," he says.

CROSSING THE BORDER

To learn more about Mexican migrants, De León founded the Undocumented Migration Project (UMP). The UMP team works toward a deeper understanding of immigration by studying the lives of those who cross the border. In the desert, the team gathers artifacts. "We inventory survival-based items, like water bottles, food wrappers, and first-aid supplies, as well as very personal belongings, such as letters, baby photos, Bibles, and rosaries," De León explains.

The team also conducts personal interviews with undocumented migrants and the people whose lives they affect, such as law enforcement officers, human traffickers who smuggle migrants into the country, and U.S. citizens living near the border. Together, the objects and the stories help De León and the UMP team create a picture of the complex migrant experience.

One of De León's goals is to challenge the stereotypes tied to immigrants from Latin America. He believes everyone should have the opportunity to view undocumented migrants as individuals, each with his or her own story. De León also

Jason De León, shown here in front of a section of the U.S.-Mexico border wall, is a 2017 MacArthur Fellow and "genius" grant recipient for his work with migrants.

feels it is important for Americans to understand immigration from multiple perspectives. In 2015, De León published the book *Land of Open Graves*, in which he illustrated the lives of migrants in vivid, often heartbreaking detail. Additionally, he helped create an exhibit called *State of Exception/Estado de excepción* (see photo, left) featuring some of the objects he and his team have found, along with photos and stories. The exhibit has been shown at universities throughout the country.

De León's work places today's undocumented migrants in the larger context of American history. He compares people's present-day trek from Mexico into the United States to the journey pioneers made on the Oregon Trail. Surely, as they pushed westward, they left cast-off objects behind on the trail. Considering how people have moved from location to location throughout history in search of a better life, De León poses an important question: "If you only had a backpack to carry, what would you bring with you?"

HISTORICAL THINKING

1. **READING CHECK** What does the Undocumented Migration Project do?

2. **FORM AND SUPPORT OPINIONS** Do you agree with De León that learning about undocumented migrants helps us understand American history as a whole? Explain.

3.3 Native American Activism

Native Americans living on reservations in the United States in 1970 had to be tough. Many families lived in shacks with no running water or electricity. Outbreaks of disease, such as pneumonia and strep throat, were common in the communities. But there was hope to turn things around.

MAIN IDEA Native American activists fought to improve conditions for their people in the 1960s and 1970s.

CHALLENGES FACING NATIVE AMERICANS

While other minority groups slowly gained rights in the mid-20th century, Native Americans remained one of the most impoverished minorities in the United States. In 1970, 40 percent of Native Americans lived in poverty, and their unemployment rate was 10 times higher than the national average.

Most reservations were recognized as independent governments within the United States, with their own court systems, school districts, and tax laws. But since the reservations depended on U.S. resources, many government policies still applied. This system did not allow tribal governments to fully control their own affairs.

The Indian Reorganization Act (IRA)—Roosevelt's New Deal policy enacted in 1934—gave Native Americans more power to govern themselves and their lands. But in 1953, President Eisenhower reversed IRA policies and promoted an "Indian Termination and Relocation Policy," also known as the **termination policy**.

In 1953, Congress also passed Public Law 280, which transferred federal and tribal oversight of civil and criminal justice to five state governments. The Indian Relocation Act of 1956 encouraged Native Americans to leave their reservations and sell off the land. This plan was presented to Native Americans as a way to improve their lives by becoming integrated into the larger American society and having better access to jobs. As a result, 109 tribes voted in favor of the policy.

In reality, the policy was a way for the government to persuade Native Americans to forfeit, or give up, federal recognition, aid, services, and protection, as well as their reservation land. Most tribes remained impoverished after the policy took effect. Many hundreds of thousands of people left the reservations and moved to cities through a federal relocation program that promised to help them find jobs and affordable housing. About 33 percent of them returned to their reservations, though, as the government's promises fell through.

In 1961, the **National Congress of American Indians (NCAI)** held a conference in Chicago. More than 60 tribes came together to write the **Declaration of Indian Purpose**. The document proposed how to preserve Native American cultures and demanded greater tribal sovereignty, or self-government. It also called for a greater tribal voice in federal Native American programs.

THE AMERICAN INDIAN MOVEMENT

Native American activism increased during the 1960s. In the spirit of the civil rights movement, tribes and nations pressed their demands with demonstrations and lawsuits. In 1968, a group of Ojibwe (oh-JIHB-way) in Minnesota, led by **Dennis Banks** and George Mitchell, founded the **American Indian Movement (AIM)**. The group's purpose was to help impoverished Native Americans in cities. Soon the focus expanded to include the return of tribal lands, the protection of legal rights, and the elimination of poverty on reservations.

AIM organized and participated in a number of protests. In 1973, AIM joined the armed takeover

The Occupation of Alcatraz Island

In 1969, young people were photographed as they explored the abandoned prison on Alcatraz Island in San Francisco Bay. They were part of a group of Native Americans who had organized an occupation of the island, where they hoped the government would let them establish a Native American education and cultural center. Although the government denied their request, the occupation grew. It lasted 18 months and drew support and extensive publicity for the Native American rights movement.

of **Wounded Knee**, South Dakota, on the site of a massacre of Native American women and children by the U.S. Army in 1890. The occupation was a protest against conditions on reservations and government policies toward Native Americans.

Several lawsuits filed in the 1970s attempted to take back Native American rights that had been promised by the federal government in past treaties. Tribes filed other lawsuits to regain (or be paid for) lands that had been taken from them. They also fought to keep guaranteed hunting and fishing rights on land they had been forced to give up as well as on their reservations.

HISTORICAL THINKING

1. **READING CHECK** How did the goals of the American Indian Movement change over time?

2. **IDENTIFY MAIN IDEAS AND DETAILS** What major issues did Native American organizations address during the 1960s, and what actions did they take?

3. **COMPARE AND CONTRAST** How did the termination policy enacted in the 1950s contrast with the Indian Reorganization Act of 1934?

3.4 The Women's Rights Movement

People have often been kept from pursuing a dream career just because it wasn't a job that a man or a woman was expected to do. Until recently in some states, women, especially married women, couldn't own property or take out a loan, simply because of their gender.

MAIN IDEA In the 1960s, American women fought to change attitudes and laws that denied them their full range of rights.

ORGANIZING FOR CHANGE

By the 1960s, women still made less money than men who were working the same job, and laws still limited women from selling property and signing certain contracts. Even though more women than ever were attending college and planning careers in the 1950s, American society presumed most women would abandon their ambitions once they married. They were expected to take on traditional roles as homemakers and stay-at-home mothers, roles many found to be unfulfilling. Increasingly, women began to speak out for equal rights.

In 1966, **Betty Friedan**, an author who wrote about the growing frustration of American women, and 48 other women and men founded the **National Organization for Women (NOW)** to fight for women's rights. NOW focused mainly on job equality and eliminating the **wage gap**, or the difference in pay between women and men in similar jobs. Members pressured Congress to pass laws that would allow more women to buy and sell property. Other organizations soon formed to address the issues of minority women. Women and men who supported this movement were (and still are) called **feminists**.

In 1971, Friedan joined feminists **Gloria Steinem**, **Bella Abzug**, and **Shirley Chisholm** in founding the **National Women's Political Caucus**. The organization's main purpose has been to increase women's participation in the political process. Steinem became the founder of *Ms.*, a feminist magazine. Abzug and Chisholm served in Congress, representing districts in New York State.

At a news conference in 1971, members of the National Women's Political Caucus, Congresswoman Bella Abzug (standing), and from left, Gloria Steinem, Congresswoman Shirley Chisholm, and Betty Friedan, announced their goal to have women make up half of the delegates to the 1972 presidential conventions.

Shirley Chisholm

This modern, stylized oil portrait is a tribute to Shirley Chisholm. Painted by Kadir Nelson, it is exhibited in the U.S. Capitol Building, where Chisholm served seven terms in the House of Representatives. As a woman, as an African American, and as a feminist, Shirley Chisholm was a pioneer. In 1968, she became the first African-American woman elected to the U.S. Congress, where she worked on the House Committee on Veterans' Affairs and the powerful Rules Committee and was a founding member of the Congressional Black Caucus. In 1972, Chisholm became the first African-American politician from a major party to run for president. After her political career, she taught at Mount Holyoke College. When she died in 2005 at the age of 80, a local NAACP official said, "She was our Moses that opened the Red Sea for us."

BATTLES FOR WOMEN'S RIGHTS

Feminists promoted the **Equal Rights Amendment (ERA)**, which demanded that equal treatment under the law, regardless of gender, be written into the U.S. Constitution. The amendment was originally proposed in 1923, only three years after American women won the right to vote, but it had been stalled for decades. In the late 1960s, feminists brought it back to Congress.

After the Senate passed the bill in 1972, the amendment needed 38 states to ratify it. Within a year, 30 states had done so. But opposition arose, led by antifeminist **Phyllis Schlafly**, who believed the ERA would overturn protections women already had. Male-dominated state legislatures began voting against the bill. In the end, the ERA missed ratification by only three states.

Knowing that most Americans supported the amendment, feminists continued their battle. They fought for a woman's right to serve in the military, and they set up shelters for women experiencing abuse at home. They won the passage of an education law in 1972 that established **Title IX**, which prohibited gender bias, or the preference of one gender over the other, in federally funded schools. Thanks to Title IX, public schools began promoting female sports teams in addition to male athletics. Women and girls became eligible for academic and athletic scholarships that had once only been available to men. NOW and other organizations successfully lobbied Congress to get legislation passed and changed American attitudes toward women's rights.

In 1973, feminists won another battle for women's rights. In the landmark Supreme Court case **Roe v. Wade**, the court ruled that women have the right to choose to end a pregnancy—a ruling that remains controversial today. This decision supported a woman's right to make personal choices in her life, including to choose when and if to have children.

HISTORICAL THINKING

1. **READING CHECK** What change to the U.S. Constitution did the ERA propose?

2. **COMPARE AND CONTRAST** In what ways did the high hopes that educated women had in the early 1960s contrast with the expectations American society had for women?

3. **FORM AND SUPPORT OPINIONS** Beginning in the late 1960s, feminists brought about a number of changes in women's rights. Which change discussed in this lesson do you think is most important today, and why?

4.1 U.S. Involvement in Vietnam

In the summer of 1964, American news outlets reported that U.S. ships had been fired on off the coast of North Vietnam. At the time, most Americans were unaware of how much this event on the other side of the world would affect the United States and hundreds of thousands of lives.

MAIN IDEA The United States' military involvement in Vietnam increased dramatically after a crisis in the Gulf of Tonkin.

EARLY U.S. INVOLVEMENT

In the 1800s, Vietnam was a Southeast Asian country rich in fertile land. France had colonized Vietnam as part of French Indochina and profited from its rice and rubber plantations. Many Vietnamese yearned for their country to be independent again. In the 1930s, communist activist **Ho Chi Minh** began to organize an independence movement within Vietnam.

During World War II, Japanese forces occupied Vietnam. Ho Chi Minh and his followers assisted the Allied Powers in undermining the Japanese

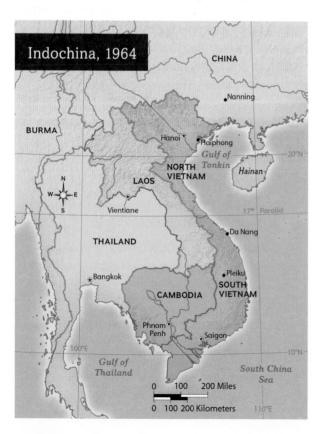

Indochina, 1964

efforts. After the war, Ho Chi Minh thought the Western nations would reward their efforts by recognizing an independent Vietnam. Instead, fearing Ho Chi Minh would establish a communist government, the Allies backed French efforts to reclaim colonial control over Vietnam. This sparked a revolution for independence, led by Ho Chi Minh.

Even with U.S. backing, the French could not defeat the Vietnamese fighters. After losing a decisive battle to Ho's forces in 1954, France seemed ready to give up the colony. But by this time, the **domino theory** was driving U.S. policy in Asia. This was the belief that if one Asian country fell to communism, the rest would soon follow, like dominoes falling in line. China and North Korea had already fallen to communism. American officials were determined not to let Vietnam follow suit.

After Ho defeated the French, a peace agreement negotiated in Geneva, Switzerland, temporarily divided Vietnam in half at the 17th parallel. Called the **Geneva Accords**, the plan established that Ho and the communists would govern the northern part of the country while the U.S.-backed **Ngo Dinh Diem** (ungh-oh dihn zih-EHM), led the new Republic of Vietnam in the southern part. Corruption was common in Diem's government, and, though he claimed to embrace democracy, he was a dictatorial leader. Many South Vietnamese opposed him. Soon a civil war erupted in the south between Diem's government and rebel fighters the Americans called **Viet Cong**. The Viet Cong, or VC, received funding and support from Ho Chi Minh. Throughout the presidencies of Eisenhower

Marines of the Seventh Regiment march past U.S. tanks while heading to their outpost in South Vietnam. They were among the first 3,500 U.S. forces to arrive in Vietnam in 1965. By the end of that year, 200,000 American service members were stationed there.

and Kennedy, the United States gradually increased its financial and military support for Diem, who was murdered just a few weeks before Kennedy's assassination.

THE GULF OF TONKIN INCIDENT

Like President Kennedy before him, President Johnson also believed in the domino theory. Rather than taking the chance that Vietnam might reunify under communist Ho Chi Minh, Johnson continued U.S. support for the unstable nation of South Vietnam and the string of new leaders who came into and fell out of power after Diem's death. This support included increasing the presence of the U.S. military in the region.

On August 4, 1964, reports emerged that North Vietnamese forces had attacked American ships in the Gulf of Tonkin. Although these reports later proved flawed and inaccurate, they spurred Congress into hasty action. The **Gulf of Tonkin Resolution** granted President Johnson the power

to respond to the assault with whatever force he deemed necessary. In other words, it gave Johnson the power to wage war. Johnson began a gradual military **escalation**, or increase, in South Vietnam. General **William Westmoreland** led U.S. forces in the region. As the need for troops rose, so did the number of young men drafted into the military.

HISTORICAL THINKING

1. **READING CHECK** Why did the United States refuse to support Ho Chi Minh's fight for an independent Vietnam?

2. **COMPARE AND CONTRAST** How did the newly formed countries of North Vietnam and South Vietnam differ politically?

3. **INTERPRET MAPS** What two countries were part of Indochina other than Vietnam?

4.2 War Strategies in Vietnam

As the war heated up, more and more young American men were drafted and sent halfway across the world to fight in the rice paddies and jungles of Vietnam. The letters they sent home painted a grim picture for the young men still waiting to be drafted.

MAIN IDEA Fighting an unpopular war on unfamiliar terrain proved difficult for U.S. troops in Vietnam.

FIGHTING A GUERRILLA WAR

American forces faced many obstacles in carrying out their mission. Fighting in Vietnam was very different from most World War II battles. The Viet Cong engaged in guerrilla warfare much as the Continental Army did during the American Revolution. They fought in small groups, hid in the dense vegetation, and carried out sneak attacks to catch their enemies off guard. Most U.S. soldiers had not been trained for such fighting.

The landscape of Vietnam was well suited to the tactics of guerrilla warfare. There were few cities or paved roads. American soldiers often had to march through miles of thick jungles and wade through waist-deep swamps. It was easy for the enemy to set traps for them. The Viet Cong dug miles of underground tunnels to move men and supplies undetected. They also used a long trail, called the **Ho Chi Minh Trail**, that ran from North Vietnam to Saigon, the capital of South Vietnam.

American GIs hurriedly transport a wounded soldier in a makeshift stretcher made from a shirt. The men had been engaged in heavy fighting in South Vietnam, near the Cambodian border, during a large military operation involving all military branches.

It ran along the western border of both nations and even extended into the neighboring countries of Laos and Cambodia.

The unstable and still corrupt government of South Vietnam complicated American efforts. Many South Vietnamese disliked their government. They wanted to determine their own future and resented U.S. interference. That's why many South Vietnamese aided the rebels. U.S. troops often found it difficult to tell whether civilians were friends or foes.

ESCALATING MISSIONS

Knowing the United States did not have the full support of the South Vietnamese people, the American military adopted a strategy to "win the hearts and minds" of the population. They hoped that convincing the South Vietnamese of the United States' good intentions would persuade them to join the fight against North Vietnamese communists. Winning hearts and minds was easier to discuss than to achieve, however, especially when U.S. military actions often spoke much louder than words.

Resentment against American forces grew as the United States expanded the use of **search-and-destroy missions**. This tactic cleared out entire villages suspected of aiding the enemy, destroying all the homes and crops as people fled. Many civilians were injured or killed in such operations, increasing the distrust and outright rage of the South Vietnamese.

Some of the weapons used in search-and-destroy missions caused long-lasting damage to the environment. **Napalm**, a type of gelled gasoline, burned thousands of homes and miles of jungle. Other weapons, such as the chemical **Agent Orange**, were used to kill off vegetation. The

United States military hoped that by destroying miles of forestland, they could end the Viet Cong's ability to hide in the dense jungles and ambush U.S. troops.

Agent Orange left the environment unusable for years. It poisoned water supplies, killing off livestock and leading to long-lasting health problems in humans. It has even been shown to cause high rates of unusual birth defects in the children of people exposed to it. Many American soldiers who handled Agent Orange suffered from severe health problems after the war. Given all of these conditions, it is not hard to understand why Americans found winning the hearts and minds of the South Vietnamese to be a difficult mission.

HISTORICAL THINKING

1. **READING CHECK** What was the main fighting tactic of the Viet Cong?

2. **DRAW CONCLUSIONS** What was the purpose of search-and-destroy missions?

3. **ANALYZE CAUSE AND EFFECT** Why did the U.S. military use Agent Orange, and what were the long-term effects of that strategy?

4.3 The Tet Offensive

Often in wartime, enemy forces cease fighting during major holidays. As people throughout both North and South Vietnam prepared to celebrate the Lunar New Year, or Tet, in January 1968, one side saw the holiday as a perfect opportunity to catch its enemy off guard.

MAIN IDEA After a surprise attack by enemy forces, many Americans began to question the U.S. mission in Vietnam.

COMMUNIST ATTACKS ON THE TET HOLIDAY

Tet, or the Lunar New Year, is the biggest holiday of the year in Vietnam. In 1968, the holiday fell on January 30. Hoping to catch the American and South Vietnamese forces off guard, Ho Chi Minh and the North Vietnamese planned a coordinated attack on a large number of key sites throughout South Vietnam. They would launch the **Tet Offensive** against South Vietnamese cities and military bases just as everyone was expecting a traditional **cease-fire**, or the brief suspension of hostilities. They prepared for the attack by smuggling weapons deep into the south as they distracted U.S. forces by staging some attacks closer to the border between the two nations.

The North Vietnamese hoped that a successful attack might slow U.S. military efforts and possibly even force American leaders into peace talks to end the conflict. The attack did, indeed, catch the Americans and their allies off guard. The North Vietnamese seized several towns and even threatened the U.S. embassy in Saigon for a short time.

Soon, however, the American and South Vietnamese forces rallied. After several weeks of fighting, they had reclaimed almost all the areas that had fallen in the initial attack. From a military standpoint, the Tet Offensive did not meet North Vietnam's goals. However, the attack clearly showed that the communist forces were not as close to surrender as many American leaders had thought. The conflict promised to drag on for a long time.

TURNING AGAINST THE WAR

From the time President Johnson escalated U.S. military involvement, teams of television reporters had been stationed, or embedded, with the troops. They filed stories from the very midst of the fighting, bringing the war's blood and violence right into American homes, usually at the dinner hour. Many Americans were horrified by what they saw. In late 1967 and early 1968, they had been

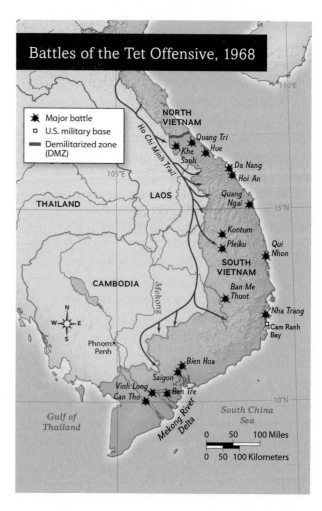

Battles of the Tet Offensive, 1968

assured by U.S. military and political leaders that the communists were nearly defeated and the war would be over soon. The sheer scale of the Tet Offensive made that promise seem like a lie. After the Tet Offensive, many more Americans began to turn against the war. They began to doubt if the United States should be involved or questioned the way in which the United States was fighting the war.

Not long after the Tet Offensive, an incident occurred that reinforced many people's worst fears about war. In March 1968, a group of U.S. soldiers murdered more than 500 innocent men, women, and children in the village of My Lai (MEE LY). The troops involved claimed it had been a search-and-destroy mission gone horribly wrong. When the shocking details of the **My Lai massacre** became known, even more people questioned the purpose of the war. They feared it was turning young American soldiers into cold-blooded killers.

Even President Johnson decided the U.S. strategy was not working as planned. In February, as the offensive ended, General Westmoreland asked for more than 200,000 additional soldiers. He compared the offensive to the Battle of the Bulge in World War II, which you have read about. Johnson refused and sent only 13,500 troops. He then announced that he would not run for a second full term as president.

HISTORICAL THINKING

1. **READING CHECK** Why did the North Vietnamese choose to attack on the Tet holiday?

2. **INTERPRET MAPS** What was the most likely route used by the North Vietnamese to supply weapons necessary to fight in and around Saigon?

3. **DISTINGUISH FACT AND OPINION** U.S. military leaders saw the Tet Offensive as a failure for the communists, while many American civilians saw it as a victory for the communists. Which opinion is supported by the facts?

American troops of the Ninth Division sit atop their tank as it rides through a Saigon street destroyed during the May, or Mini-Tet, Offensive in 1968.

4.4 The Counterculture

As President Johnson sits in the White House, he can hear protesters shouting outside: "Hey, hey, LBJ! How many kids did you kill today?" More and more people are angry about the Vietnam War and blame the president. How could everything have gone so wrong?

MAIN IDEA As the conflict in Vietnam dragged on, many young Americans became politically active and joined the antiwar movement.

CRITICAL VIEWING In 1968, this large group of young people took to the streets in New York City to protest the Vietnam War. The antiwar movement began gaining public support in 1965 on college campuses and by 1968 had spread throughout the United States. What can you infer about the feelings and ideas of these young people from this photograph?

THE ANTIWAR MOVEMENT

By the time of the Tet Offensive, many groups had begun protesting the U.S. role in Vietnam. A diverse group of people opposed the war, but the most vocal tended to be students, civil rights leaders, writers, teachers, the clergy, and mothers.

Many protesters focused on the military draft. They argued it was unfair to force young men to fight in an unjust war. Others raised questions about the fairness of the draft system. The government allowed **draft exemptions**, or being excluded from military service, for various reasons. The system favored those wealthy enough to afford to go to college or to pay lawyers to find loopholes in the system. This meant that a higher percentage of poor and powerless men were drafted. Some young men left the United States and went to countries that allowed them to stay and avoid being returned to the United States to be drafted.

War protests were part of broader trends in youth culture. Throughout the 1960s, younger Americans had been embracing what some adults viewed as ever more radical hairstyles, fashion, and behavior. For example, men began to wear their hair long and grow facial hair, a big change from the clean-cut styles of the 1950s. Women dressed up less often and wore blue jeans more.

Some youthful behavior could be quite dangerous, such as the increased use of illegal drugs. By the late 1960s, a **counterculture** had emerged. Young people began to reject the consumerism and social expectations of their parents, focusing instead on "turning on" (taking drugs), "tuning in" (to new ideas about the individual and society), and "dropping out" (ignoring or not participating in the mainstream culture).

Music had become one of the biggest influences on youth culture, and baby boomers dominated the market for record sales. Noting this trend, record companies produced more youth-oriented music. Originally, rock and roll lyrics were mostly about cars, falling in and out of love, and other teenage concerns. But as the 1960s progressed, the lyrics grew more serious and controversial, even contributing to the growing war protest movement. Rock bands now sang about antiwar sentiments, social justice, or, in many cases, drug use.

A COUNTRY DIVIDED

By 1967, the country was divided politically between **doves**, or those who opposed the war, and **hawks**, or those who supported it. Hawks accused doves of being unpatriotic. Many doves countered that the United States weakened its own values by fighting an unjust war. Prior to the Tet Offensive, hawks outnumbered doves by a large percentage.

However, the doves had gained a valuable ally in April 1967 when Dr. Martin Luther King, Jr., gave a speech opposing the war. Dr. King said that the war was unjust, and its high cost was taking funding from programs that could help Americans here at home. He urged American leaders to stop the bombings, declare a cease-fire, and work toward a peaceful resolution to the conflict.

Then, in the months after the Tet Offensive, polls showed that a majority of Americans considered the war to have been a mistake. As you have read, before the offensive, Americans had been told that the war would soon come to a successful conclusion. The images of the Tet Offensive they saw on TV told them otherwise. From that point on, the percentage of Americans who opposed the war continued to increase as the conflict dragged on.

As support for the war decreased, many soldiers returning from Vietnam found the nation's anger and distrust directed at them. Most Vietnam veterans served honorably and to the best of their ability under difficult circumstances. Yet, unlike in World War II, when returning soldiers received a hero's welcome, some Vietnam veterans experienced poor treatment from civilians opposed to the war. Many returning veterans joined the antiwar movement.

HISTORICAL THINKING

1. **READING CHECK** Why was the military draft a focus of antiwar protests?

2. **DRAW CONCLUSIONS** Why do you think so many of the members of the counterculture were against the war in Vietnam?

3. **COMPARE AND CONTRAST** What is the difference between a hawk and a dove?

The Year 1968

In 1968, U.S. achievements were often overshadowed by painful events. While some Americans experienced those events, others learned of them through vivid news reports and images. Americans often wondered if the country could survive such a terrible year.

MAIN IDEA During 1968, the United States was marked by many crises—over civil rights, war, poverty, and politics—that reshaped the nation and its future.

THE DEATH OF DR. KING

The year 1968 was one of the most eventful and chaotic of the 20th century. It started with the Tet Offensive in Vietnam and only seemed to worsen from there. The struggles dividing the United States all seemed to collide at once, some in tragic fashion.

In addition to speaking out in support of civil rights and against the war, Dr. Martin Luther King, Jr., increasingly focused his attention on helping poor Americans of all races from all regions. He traveled to northern cities to organize for change where people faced poverty and housing discrimination, obstacles to living healthy and successful lives.

Taken just seconds after **Martin Luther King, Jr.**, was assassinated, this photograph shows **Andrew Young** and other civil rights leaders on the balcony of the **Lorraine Motel** in Memphis, Tennessee. They are standing near Dr. King's body and pointing toward the assailant as he runs away.

On June 6, 1968, Americans awoke to the grim news of Senator Robert F. Kennedy's death on the front pages of the country's newspapers, including the *San Francisco Chronicle*. Kennedy's assassin, Sirhan Sirhan, is believed to have been motivated by his resentment of some of Kennedy's foreign policy views.

King also spoke out for the rights of workers who were underpaid and mistreated. In early April, he traveled to Memphis, Tennessee, to support a garbage workers' strike. On the evening of April 4, as Dr. King stood on his hotel balcony, a sniper's bullet took his life. It would be months before law enforcement caught his murderer. Rage over Dr. King's assassination sparked violent rioting in some cities.

A CHAOTIC DEMOCRATIC CONVENTION

Shortly before Dr. King's murder, on March 31, President Johnson announced he would not run for re-election. Evidence of the strengthening antiwar movement had come on March 12, when antiwar candidate Senator **Eugene McCarthy** won the New Hampshire Democratic primary election, winning 20 out of the 24 delegates to the upcoming National Democratic Convention. Many people thought this threatened Johnson's chances of winning the general election in November. Johnson said he wanted to focus the remainder of his time in office on ending the war. This move left open the opportunity for new leadership over a deeply divided country.

Even with McCarthy's early primary win, many people hoped that **Robert Kennedy**, President Kennedy's brother, would win the Democratic nomination. Kennedy was a progressive candidate who supported civil rights and social justice, and many voters hoped he would continue the legacy of his fallen brother. However, only two months after Dr. King's death, the nation was shocked once again when Robert Kennedy was shot by a gunman on June 5, 1968, just after winning the California primary. He died a day later.

The Democratic Party was deeply divided when it gathered in Chicago to hold its national convention in August. Outside, antiwar protesters clashed with police. As the Democrats selected Vice President **Hubert Humphrey** as their presidential nominee, news crews were showing live images of chaos and shocking police brutality outside. To many television viewers, the convention reflected how out of control the country had become under Democratic Party leadership. To the counterculture, the doves, and civil rights' supporters, it represented a defeat.

These events provided an opportunity for the Republicans. They nominated former vice president Richard M. Nixon, who claimed to have a secret plan for ending the war that would result in "peace with honor." Nixon won the election with a narrow majority of the popular vote but a wide majority of the electoral college. He promised to stand up for the "**silent majority**" of Americans— those who quietly supported the government and who didn't protest.

HISTORICAL THINKING

1. **READING CHECK** Why was Dr. King in Memphis in April 1968?

2. **MAKE INFERENCES** Why do you think President Johnson decided not to run for re-election in 1968?

3. **ANALYZE CAUSE AND EFFECT** How did the events of the 1968 Democratic Convention help the Republicans?

VOCABULARY

Use each of the following terms in a sentence that shows an understanding of the term's meaning.

1. satellite

   Explorer 1 was the first satellite successfully launched into space by the United States.

2. gender bias
3. naval quarantine
4. domino theory
5. escalation

6. hawk
7. counterculture
8. Medicare
9. feminist

READING STRATEGY
COMPARE AND CONTRAST

If you haven't already, complete your graphic organizer by noting similarities and differences in the United States between 1960 and 1968. Then answer the question.

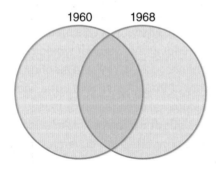

10. How did our concept of the American identity change during the 1960s, and how did it remain the same?

MAIN IDEAS

Answer the following questions. Support your answers with evidence from the chapter.

11. What impact did the first presidential debate have on the 1960 election? **LESSON 1.1**

12. What structure became a symbol of the Cold War? **LESSON 1.3**

13. What crisis brought the United States and the Soviet Union to the brink of nuclear war in 1962? **LESSON 1.4**

14. In what ways did President Johnson show his commitment to civil rights? **LESSON 2.1**

15. How were the goals of the Black Power movement different from those of earlier civil rights activists? **LESSON 2.2**

16. In what ways was President Johnson's Great Society program successful? **LESSON 2.3**

17. What issues did politically active Latino groups confront during the civil rights era? **LESSON 3.1**

18. How did the Indian Relocation Act of 1956 affect Native Americans? **LESSON 3.3**

19. What inequalities between men and women did women want to change in the 1960s and 1970s? **LESSON 3.4**

20. What power did the Gulf of Tonkin Resolution give to the U.S. president? **LESSON 4.1**

21. What was the significance of the 1968 Tet Offensive in Vietnam? **LESSON 4.3**

HISTORICAL THINKING

Answer the following questions. Support your answers with evidence from the chapter.

22. **MAKE CONNECTIONS** How did the Cold War competition affect the expansion of technology in daily life?

23. **ANALYZE CAUSE AND EFFECT** How did the domino theory affect President Johnson's foreign policy in Asia?

24. **DESCRIBE** What event at the 1968 Democratic Convention helped Nixon's campaign?

25. **FORM AND SUPPORT OPINIONS** Some historians claim 1968 was the most pivotal year in 20th-century U.S. history. Do you agree with this assessment? Explain your answer.

In a 1965 political cartoon, Paul Conrad contrasted two ongoing conflicts being fought in very different locations. Although those two struggles had little in common, one purpose they shared was to enable a group of people to experience free and equal representation. Look closely at the political cartoon featuring a U.S. soldier who holds a letter. Then answer the questions that follow.

26. Where is the soldier in this cartoon, and why is he there?

27. Why do you think the soldier in this cartoon looks so upset?

28. What is the significance of the cartoon's title, "A Letter from the Front"?

A Letter From the Front

On March 31, 1968, President Johnson addressed the nation to announce that he would not seek re-election. Read the following excerpt from the speech and then answer the question.

> Tonight I want to speak to you of peace in Vietnam and Southeast Asia.
>
> No other question so preoccupies our people. No other dream so absorbs the 250 million human beings who live in that part of the world. With America's sons in the fields far away, with America's future under challenge right here at home . . . I do not believe that I should devote an hour or a day of my time to any personal partisan causes or to any duties other than the awesome duties of this office—the Presidency of your country. Accordingly, I shall not seek, and I will not accept, the nomination of my party for another term as your President.

29. According to this speech, what was Johnson's main reason for not running for re-election?

30. EXPOSITORY Events of the 1960s challenged Americans as they confronted a war that seemed, to many, both immoral and unwinnable. In addition, a counterculture emerged that defied many basic ideas about what made the United States a great nation. Of the challenges that face our nation today, which one do you think is most difficult to solve? Write a paragraph about it in which you explain your answer.

TIPS

• Review the chapter and write down the similarities you notice between life then and life now.

• List five challenges that face our nation today, and rank them in order of importance. Choose the challenge you ranked highest to share and explain.

• Use at least two vocabulary words from the chapter in your response.

• Conclude your paragraph by summarizing your thoughts in one final statement.

50 Years of Wilderness

By Elizabeth Kolbert

Adapted from "50 Years of Wilderness," by Elizabeth Kolbert, in *National Geographic*, September 2014

Fred Lavigne is looking for a tree. It's a beautifully clear day with a deep blue sky. Though the calendar says early spring, several feet of snow still cover the ground in the Sandwich Range Wilderness in New Hampshire.

We're surrounded by trees: towering spruces, scraggly beeches, maples, oaks, and birches. But Lavigne, a logger and outdoorsman, is looking for one tree in particular. We've left the trail behind, and he's navigating the steep terrain by memory, on snowshoes. Finally, he finds what he's been searching for: a red pine with a wide gash right at eye level. Plucking a coarse black hair from the frozen sap, Lavigne says that the gash was made by bears as a form of communication. (Though what they're telling each other no one's quite sure.) We spend several more hours snowshoeing through the forest and do not come across any other human footprints.

The Sandwich Range Wilderness isn't big—just 55 square miles—and it's not remote. Some 70 million people, including my own family, live within a day's drive. But for precisely these reasons, it's a good place to reflect on the legacy of the Wilderness Act. As I follow Lavigne through the woods, I wonder what explains our enduring attachment to wilderness and what that term even means today.

The Wilderness Act was signed into law by President Lyndon Johnson on September 3, 1964. But to understand the origin of the act, you have to go back to the 1930s. During the Great Depression, the federal government put tens of thousands of Americans to work in national parks and forests, clearing trails, erecting shelters, and building roads. The new highways opened up the parks to millions more visitors.

But the very success of these efforts troubled many conservationists, who worried that the country's most majestic landscapes were being turned into roadside attractions. A group of them formed the Wilderness Society to defend the national parks and forests against overuse, and their first mission statement condemned the roadbuilding "craze." They worked to persuade Congress to specify tracts of land as roadless wilderness.

The resulting Wilderness Act created a new category of federal lands, off-limits to commercial ventures like logging and new mines. Humans could explore, but not with mechanized vehicles. The statute, or law, defined wilderness as "an area where the earth and its community of life are untrammeled [unrestricted] by man, where man himself is a visitor who does not remain." The 1964 act set aside 54 wilderness areas, a number that has increased to more than 750. Few of these areas are wild in any rigorous [strict] sense, however. Nearly all have at some point been logged, grazed, farmed, or otherwise altered by humans.

Today, global warming is altering even the most remote wilderness areas. In Alaska, sea ice is disappearing, permafrost [frozen soil] is thawing, and woody plants are invading the tundra. With widespread climate changes, the Wilderness Act has become even more important. Many species are on the move, following the changing climate. Plants and animals that find their routes blocked by cities or highways are likely to be in trouble. Wilderness areas, which allow for freer movement, may provide the best hope for new plant and animal communities to form.

Ecologist Peter Landres explains, "These big pieces [of land] are needed to let ecological and evolutionary processes play out. So if I'm an animal and I don't like it here, I can move over there. Yes, wilderness is affected by climate change, but it's exactly because our world is now so dominated by people that it's so important to have places where we let nature be."

For more from National Geographic, check out "Slipping the Bonds" online.

UNIT INQUIRY: Protest an Injustice

In this unit, you learned about the social, political, and economic injustices that African Americans, Latinos, Native Americans, and women faced in the postwar period. You also learned how they protested these injustices. Based on your understanding of the text, what kinds of methods did protesters use to bring attention to their causes and gain support for reforms? Which protest methods, or combination of methods, proved effective in bringing about change?

ASSIGNMENT

Identify a social, political, or economic injustice that you learned about in this unit. Devise a plan to protest the injustice, and prepare support materials designed to inspire and persuade people to remedy the injustice. Be prepared to present your plan and support materials to the class.

Gather Evidence As you plan your protest, gather evidence from this unit about the methods that African Americans, Latinos, Native Americans, and women used to draw attention to the problems they faced and to promote the reforms they sought. Think about how these protests were organized and carried out. Use a graphic organizer like this one to help develop your plan.

Protest Plan

Who is protesting, and **who** is the intended audience?
What is the issue, and **what** reforms are sought?
What form will the protest take?
Where will the protest occur?
When will it occur?
Why is this issue important?
How will you publicize and promote the protest?

Produce Use your notes to write a detailed description of your protest plan. Then prepare support materials, such as a flyer, protest sign, poster, video, press release, chant, or online post, to publicize and promote your protest.

Present Choose a creative way to present your protest plan and support materials to the class. Consider one of these options:

- Create a video that publicizes your planned protest. In the video, explain the injustice you are protesting and present your demands. Provide information that will encourage others to join your protest.

- Design a flyer and protest sign that convey your message. Give your group a name and create a catchy slogan that might appear on a bumper sticker. Display the materials in your classroom.

- Work with a partner to stage a TV interview in which a "reporter" stops you as you carry a protest sign in a demonstration. Give detailed answers to the reporter's questions.

NATIONAL GEOGRAPHIC | LEARNING FRAMEWORK ACTIVITIES

Compile a Song Medley

ATTITUDE Responsibility

SKILLS Communication

Protest songs performed and recorded by such American musicians as Bob Dylan, Joan Baez, and Sam Cooke became popular during the 1960s and 1970s. Research the protest songs of the period and compile a medley of songs to share with the class. Write and present an introduction to the medley, identifying the song titles, the recording artists, and the issues presented in each of the songs. As an alternative, you might compose and perform an original protest song of your own.

Build Models

SKILLS Observation, Collaboration

KNOWLEDGE New Frontiers

The space race began in the late 1950s with the launching of crewless satellites by the Soviet Union and United States. *Sputnik 1* was the Soviets' first successful Earth satellite, and *Explorer 1* was the Americans' satellite. Using simple materials, work with a partner to build models of these two satellites. Prepare a placard that provides identifying information and compares the two spacecraft, focusing on their design, purpose, and results. Display the models and placard in your classroom.

AMERICA IN A
CHANGING
WORLD

Ellis Island National Museum of Immigration, New York City

The American Flag of Faces, an interactive digital exhibit in the reception center of the museum on historic Ellis Island, features portraits of immigrants to the United States. This exhibit celebrates the diversity of the United States and the role immigration has played in this country. The museum invites all Americans to submit photos of themselves, their families, and their relatives to become a part of the animated red, white, and blue flag—artwork the museum calls a "living, ever-changing American mosaic."

CRITICAL VIEWING In what ways is The American Flag of Faces a symbol of the United States and the world today?

AMERICA IN A CHANGING WORLD

THE UNITED STATES

1969
Astronauts Neil Armstrong and Buzz Aldrin are the first human beings to land and walk on the moon. *(photo taken by Armstrong of Aldrin walking on the surface of the moon)*

1980
Ronald Reagan is elected president and ushers in a new era of conservative politics. *(1980 campaign button showing Reagan and his vice presidential running mate, George H.W. Bush)*

1973
The United States withdraws its troops from Vietnam, ending its involvement in the Vietnam War.

1974
President Richard Nixon resigns from office following the Watergate scandal.

1990
The United States and a coalition of allies launch the Persian Gulf War after Iraq invades Kuwait.

1960

1975

1990

1975 ASIA
The Vietnam War ends when North Vietnam seizes control of South Vietnam, and the countries unite as one communist nation.

1979 ASIA
Islamic fundamentalists hold 52 Americans hostage in the U.S. embassy in Tehran, Iran.

1989 EUROPE
German citizens tear down the Berlin Wall.

1991 EUROPE
The Soviet Union breaks up, bringing an end to the Cold War. *(photo of the Great Kremlin Palace, official home of the Russian president)*

THE WORLD

HISTORICAL THINKING:
DETERMINE CHRONOLOGY

Choose an event on this time line and explain how it impacted the world.

2001

On September 11, al Qaeda terrorists carry out attacks that result in the deaths of more than 3,000 people in New York City, Washington, D.C., and Pennsylvania. *(Alan Wallace, a firefighter from nearby Fort Myer, was on duty at the Pentagon fire station on 9/11 and wore this coat as he helped Pentagon workers escape after a plane hit the building.)*

2016

Republican candidate Donald Trump defeats Democratic candidate Hillary Clinton in the 2016 presidential election. *(campaign posters of both candidates)*

2017

President Trump pulls the United States out of the Paris Agreement, an international pact to slow global warming.

2008

Voters elect Barack Obama as the nation's first African-American president.

2007

The Great Recession begins, which leads to widespread unemployment and a collapse in housing prices.

2000

2020

2015 EUROPE

The Islamic State in Iraq and Syria (ISIS) takes responsibility for a series of attacks in Paris, France, that kills about 130 people.

2008 AMERICAS

Fidel Castro resigns after leading Cuba for 49 years, and his brother Raúl succeeds him.

1994 AFRICA

South Africa holds its first democratic elections, and Nelson Mandela becomes the country's first black president. *(Mandela featured on South African paper money)*

2011 AFRICA

An uprising against the government in Egypt forces the country's president, Hosni Mubarak, from power. *(Egyptians celebrating the president's overthrow in Cairo's Tahrir Square)*

NEW AMERICAN
POLITICS
1969–1990

ESSENTIAL QUESTION

How did new ideas in American politics in the 1980s impact the country and the world?

AMERICAN STORIES **The Fall of the Berlin Wall**

SECTION 1 Nixon, Watergate, and Years of Doubt
KEY VOCABULARY

catalytic converter	post-traumatic stress disorder (PTSD)	special prosecutor
command module		Vietnamization
cover-up	revenue sharing	Watergate scandal
lunar module	smog	wiretapping

SECTION 2 A Time of Crisis
KEY VOCABULARY

fundamentalist   human rights   pardon   stagflation

SECTION 3 A New Conservative Era
KEY VOCABULARY

acquired immunodeficiency syndrome (AIDS)	deregulation	Moral Majority
	human immunodeficiency virus (HIV)	supply-side economics
continental shelf		televangelist

SECTION 4 From Cold War to Gulf War
KEY VOCABULARY

coalition   coup   glasnost   perestroika

AMERICAN GALLERY ONLINE   **The Gulf Wars**

READING STRATEGY

IDENTIFY PROBLEMS AND SOLUTIONS

By identifying problems and solutions, you can better understand the decisions leaders make. As you read this chapter, use a graphic organizer like this one to analyze the energy crisis of the 1970s.

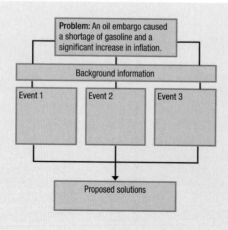

Problem: An oil embargo caused a shortage of gasoline and a significant increase in inflation.

Background information

Event 1   Event 2   Event 3

Proposed solutions

"It's morning again in America."

—President Ronald Reagan

CRITICAL VIEWING On November 10, 1989, people were once again permitted to move between East and West Berlin. Berliners flocked to the Berlin Wall, celebrating and chanting, "Tor auf!" (Open the gate!) What does this photo reveal about the feelings of Berliners during the fall of the wall?

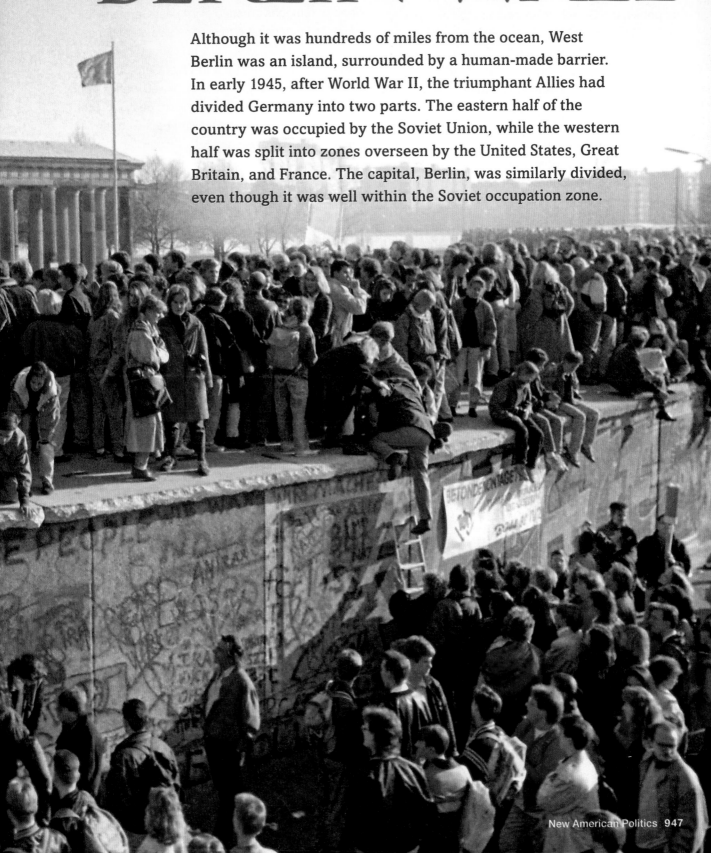

THE FALL OF THE BERLIN WALL

Although it was hundreds of miles from the ocean, West Berlin was an island, surrounded by a human-made barrier. In early 1945, after World War II, the triumphant Allies had divided Germany into two parts. The eastern half of the country was occupied by the Soviet Union, while the western half was split into zones overseen by the United States, Great Britain, and France. The capital, Berlin, was similarly divided, even though it was well within the Soviet occupation zone.

BUILDING THE WALL

In 1949, the United States, Great Britain, and France merged their occupation zones to create the Federal Republic of Germany, which was commonly known as West Germany. In response, the Soviet Union decreed the eastern half of Germany to be an independent entity as well. Its official name was the German Democratic Republic, but it was popularly called East Germany. Although hopes for a national reunification lingered, Germany was now partitioned into two countries. West Berlin remained a capitalist, western European city deep within the Soviet realm of influence. As Soviet leader Nikita Khrushchev described it, the city was "stuck like a bone in the Soviet throat."

At first, residents of East and West Berlin could travel freely between the halves of the city for jobs, shopping, and entertainment, or to visit with friends and family. To the growing embarrassment of Soviet and East German authorities, a steady flood of refugees crossed from East Germany to West Berlin to escape the repressive conditions in the communist East. By 1961, about 3 million people had fled from East to West Germany. Many of them were young, educated, skilled workers and professionals. In 1961, the numbers peaked, with more than 18,000 people leaving East Germany in the first 12 days of August.

AN IMPASSABLE WALL

The Berlin Wall was a system of concrete walls and other fencing that separated West Berlin from East Berlin and adjacent parts of East Germany. A restricted zone prevented most East Berliners from getting near the wall that marked West Berlin's border. Guards with orders to shoot on sight staffed watchtowers and patrolled the zone at all hours. Despite these obstacles, more than 5,000 East Germans managed to cross the barrier and escape into West Berlin from 1961 to 1989, including about 600 border guards. Some escapees found a way to climb over the barrier. More dramatic escape plans included crawling through tunnels and sewers, smashing through weaker parts of the barrier with vehicles, and flying over the border in a hot air balloon.

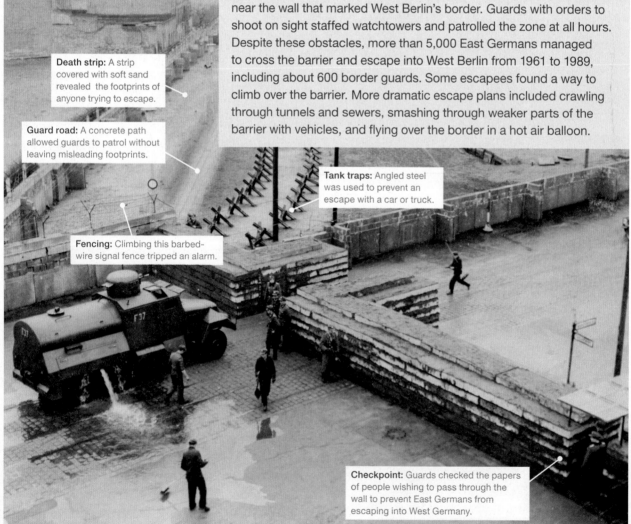

Death strip: A strip covered with soft sand revealed the footprints of anyone trying to escape.

Guard road: A concrete path allowed guards to patrol without leaving misleading footprints.

Fencing: Climbing this barbed-wire signal fence tripped an alarm.

Tank traps: Angled steel was used to prevent an escape with a car or truck.

Checkpoint: Guards checked the papers of people wishing to pass through the wall to prevent East Germans from escaping into West Germany.

TUNNEL 57

A wall, an abandoned bakery, and students with shovels. That's what it took to dig a tunnel under the Berlin Wall in 1964, through which 57 people escaped. Tunneling was only one of many plans used to secretly move from East to West Germany, and frankly, it wasn't that successful. Over 30 years, only about 300 people escaped through tunnels, which were hard to dig and were oftentimes discovered before they could be used.

But civil engineering student Joachim Neumann, who had himself escaped to West Germany using a borrowed passport, spearheaded a tunneling success. His first attempt to tunnel under the wall failed when the East German secret police, the Stasi, learned of his tunnel and arrested many of those attempting to escape. But Neumann wasn't ready to give up. He found an old bakery in West Germany and started tunneling from the bakery to the East German side of the wall. Neumann and several other students spent 5 months digging under a city street, the Berlin Wall, an alarm-equipped signal fence, and the "death strip," a no-man's-land area complete with guard towers, floodlights, and steel spikes. Their tunnel came up on the East German side in an outhouse behind an apartment building.

CRITICAL VIEWING A woman scrambles through Tunnel 57 to reach West Berlin in October 1964. What inferences can you make about her life in East Berlin based on what you observe in this photo?

On October 3, 1964, the tunnel was finally ready. Friends and family members of the tunnel diggers gathered at the East German apartment building and whispered the code word "Tokyo" to gain access to the escape route. Fifty-seven people crawled and slithered underground more than the length of a football field to the freedom of West Germany. Neumann's tunnel was discovered by East German police and closed on October 4. However, in the two days it was open, Tunnel 57 became the most successful escape path in the history of the Berlin Wall.

For Khrushchev, enough was enough. He gave the East German government permission to build a barrier that would stop the outpouring. Within two weeks, the Berlin Wall was constructed. The initial barrier consisted of barbed wire fencing. It gradually developed into a series of intimidating concrete walls and electric fencing in a border zone patrolled by armed guards and attack dogs.

In the United States, reaction to the building of the wall was mixed. Some felt the United States and its allies should destroy the wall immediately. President Kennedy did not like the wall, but he recognized that it solved a problem. The flow of people defecting—or permanently leaving—from East Germany caused tension between the Soviet Union and the United States. "It's not a very nice solution," he privately told his aides, "but a wall is a . . . lot better than a war."

For the United States, the Berlin Wall was a public relations advantage during the Cold War. It served as evidence to the world that citizens had to be forced to stay in a Soviet-dominated country. At the same time, it made West Berlin a symbol of the personal freedoms denied to individuals under communism. For many Berliner families, the construction of the wall had tragic results. With travel between the halves of the city completely shut down for citizens, some families had members trapped on the wrong side of the wall. Parents were separated from children and husbands from wives for nearly 30 years. One former East Berliner later recalled how he felt when the wall was built: "I was 14 when the Wall went up. So for me, it meant that I was stranded behind the wall and that I couldn't get out anymore. I couldn't move. I couldn't make my own decisions."

THE FALL OF THE WALL

By 1989, the political situation had changed enormously. Soviet leader Mikhail Gorbachev had instituted several reforms in an effort to improve the country's failing economy. He allowed elections for many political offices within the Soviet Union and loosened control over countries that the Soviet Union had previously dominated. Several countries, such as Poland and Hungary, replaced their old, Soviet-dominated governments. East Germany would not be far behind.

In October 1989, Gorbachev visited East Berlin and was greeted by crowds who were restless for a change in their government. Wanting his support, they cried out, "[Gorbachev], help us!" In the month following his visit, East Germans expressed their anger in demonstrations throughout the country. At the same time, a new portal for freedom had opened for East Germans. They could pose as tourists in Hungary, where they were allowed to travel, and then cross the border into Austria.

On November 9, 1989, the East Berlin authorities announced that at midnight they would open the gates in the Berlin Wall. Citizens on both sides would be free to cross the borders between East and West Germany at will. By the time midnight arrived, the streets near the wall were filled with Berliners celebrating and shouting, "Open the gate!" What followed has been described by one witness as "the greatest street party in the history of the world." More than 2 million people from East Berlin flooded into West Berlin. Young people explored a city they had never seen before, while their elders rediscovered places that were once familiar to them. All generations shared in the joy of the moment. Amid

"TEAR DOWN THIS WALL"

On June 12, 1987, President Ronald Reagan was scheduled to give a speech in West Berlin as part of a celebration marking the founding of Berlin 750 years earlier. The speech would be delivered in front of the Brandenburg Gate, a monument built in the late 1700s by the Prussian king Frederick William II. The gate was an important symbol of both Berlin's history and its division. It was located in East Berlin inside the restricted zone of the Berlin Wall, so that it could not be reached from either side.

In April, a young speechwriter named Peter Robinson had been assigned to write the president's speech for the occasion. Using strong language, Robinson crafted a speech that bluntly implored Gorbachev to get rid of the Berlin Wall. Some members of the State Department worried that the lines about tearing down the wall might offend the Soviet leader Mikhail Gorbachev. Reagan himself, however, liked the lines. As he was being driven to the Berlin Wall to make the speech, Reagan confided to an aide, "The boys at State are going to kill me, but it's the right thing to do." It was another two years before the Berlin Wall actually came down, but Reagan's speech is remembered as a landmark moment in the progress toward reunifying Germany.

PRIMARY SOURCE

We welcome change and openness; for we believe that freedom and security go together, that the advance of human liberty can only strengthen the cause of world peace. There is one sign the Soviets can make that would be unmistakable, that would advance dramatically the cause of freedom and peace. General Secretary Gorbachev, if you seek peace, if you seek prosperity for the Soviet Union and Eastern Europe, if you seek liberalization, come here to this gate. Mr. Gorbachev, open this gate. Mr. Gorbachev, tear down this wall!

the celebrations, a young woman named Angela Merkel crossed over into West Berlin and called her aunt in Hamburg, West Germany. After that night, she would become active in politics, and in 2005 she took office as chancellor, the highest government post in the reunified Germany.

Once the gates were open, elated Berliners determined the entire wall must come down. Unwilling to wait for official demolition crews, people began chipping away at it with hammers, picks, and whatever tools they could gather.

These "wall woodpeckers" continued to remove chunks of cement even as heavy construction equipment moved in to tear down the Berlin Wall. In 1990, East Germany, West Germany, the United States, Great Britain, France, and the Soviet Union signed the Treaty on the Final Settlement with Respect to Germany. When the treaty went into effect on March 15, 1991, the reunion of Germany was complete and official.

Today, the Berlin Wall is memorialized in various places throughout the city. The official memorial has been installed in a section of the former "death strip," where many people were killed while attempting to escape. The site features original sections of the wall that were left standing and informational displays about the wall's history. A few other Berlin Wall sections remain in different parts of the city. One section was transformed after the wall fell. It became a gallery that features about 100 large paintings created directly on the wall by various artists. The murals were painted on the side of the wall that had

been protected by soldiers and was therefore, understandably, untouched. The west side of the wall had been covered with graffiti and political slogans by the West Berliners who hated the separation it symbolized.

In the United States, Americans eagerly viewed scenes of joyous Berliners celebrating and tearing into the wall with sledgehammers. Many sympathized with the Berliners' desire for reunification and freedom. The event quickly came to symbolize the end of the Cold War and of the nuclear threat that had hovered in the background during those decades. The United States had first opened diplomatic relations with West Germany in 1955. In 1991, it allied itself with the reunified Germany. Today, the two countries maintain close ties as allies and strong trading partners.

THINK ABOUT IT

Why do important events abroad, such as the building and removal of the Berlin Wall, matter to the United States?

1.1 Nixon and Vietnam

How would you feel about being drafted to fight in a war you didn't believe in? That's the situation many 18-year-old American males faced during most of the Vietnam War years.

MAIN IDEA President Nixon expanded the war in Vietnam before finally withdrawing American troops in 1973, but the war continued until North Vietnam took control of South Vietnam in 1975.

VIETNAMIZATION

During his presidential campaign, Richard Nixon declared that he had a "secret plan" to end the Vietnam War. After taking office in 1969, he announced a military strategy he called **Vietnamization**. It involved slowly withdrawing U.S. troops as the South Vietnamese took over more of the fighting. However, Nixon's plan actually began an escalation of the war. For example, he began bombing communist supply lines in the neutral country of Cambodia. These supply lines ran through thick jungles just over South Vietnam's western border. Nixon tried to hide the attacks from the American public because he knew the escalation of the war would incite more protests.

The F-4 Vietnam patch (left) was given to war pilots who had flown 200 missions. The U.S. Air Force Aviator patch (below) shows an eagle holding a missile.

On April 30, 1970, Nixon publicly announced another plan. This time he wanted to send U.S. ground troops to Cambodia to finish destroying military supply lines there. Nixon's announcement provoked massive anti-war protests on college campuses across the nation.

During a large protest at **Kent State University** in Ohio, students set fire to an army training building on campus. The governor of Ohio sent National Guard troops to maintain order. On May 4, 1970, guardsmen and protesters clashed. Several guardsmen shot their rifles directly into the crowd, killing four students and wounding nine others. Some of the students shot were not even involved in the protest. They had merely been walking across campus, headed to their next class.

Post-Traumatic Stress Disorder

A number of veterans returning from service in Vietnam were suffering from **post-traumatic stress disorder (PTSD)**, a condition that had been called "shell-shock" in World War I and "battle fatigue" in World War II. Marked by flashbacks—sudden, vivid memories of terrifying events—anger-management problems, and sleeping disorders, PTSD is long-lasting and difficult to treat. Veterans who were not adequately treated for the condition often self-medicated with drugs or alcohol. Some even took their own lives. For them, the war never really ended.

A 14-year-old girl reacts to the shooting of a student by National Guard troops at Kent State University on May 4, 1970, during an anti-war protest. This photograph became a powerful symbol of Americans' pain over the Vietnam War.

The Kent State shootings horrified Americans and weakened the public's faith in the government. Public trust suffered another blow when the media published portions of the Pentagon Papers in 1971. The papers were a secret Department of Defense study of U.S. military involvement in Vietnam. A researcher who worked on the study leaked the documents to the press. The Pentagon Papers proved that government officials had lied to the public about the progress of the war.

WITHDRAWAL FROM VIETNAM

As the Vietnam War became increasingly unpopular, Nixon increased efforts to negotiate a peace settlement. In January 1973, representatives from the United States, North and South Vietnam, and the Vietcong reached an agreement to end all combat. The terms of the agreement included the complete withdrawal of U.S. troops by March. In exchange, the North Vietnamese would release American prisoners of war (POWs), and North and South Vietnam would cease combat.

These terms were not kept, however. After the bulk of U.S. troops withdrew, the North Vietnamese invaded South Vietnam, taking complete control by April 30, 1975. In the last days before South Vietnam's capital city of Saigon fell, thousands of remaining Americans and U.S. allies fled the country. North and South Vietnam then reunited as one communist nation.

The long war to prevent the spread of communism had failed. In the end, some 58,000 Americans and more than 2 million Vietnamese died in the conflict. The war influenced the ratification of the **26th Amendment**, which lowered the voting age to 18. It also led to passage of the **War Powers Act**, which limited the president's ability to wage a war without Congressional approval. In January 1973, two months before the last U.S. troops left Vietnam, the U.S. military discontinued the draft and moved to an all-volunteer army.

HISTORICAL THINKING

1. **READING CHECK** What was Vietnamization?

2. **ANALYZE CAUSE AND EFFECT** Why did the Vietnam War incite so much public opposition?

3. **DRAW CONCLUSIONS** Why do you think the Vietnam War helped promote the ratification of the 26th Amendment?

1.2 Governing a Divided Nation

For years, American officials had refused to even recognize China's communist government. So President Nixon's visit to the country in 1972 made quite a statement. As he toured the Great Wall of China with communist guides, he hoped other nations were watching closely.

MAIN IDEA President Nixon generally took a moderate approach to domestic policy and a flexible, realistic approach to foreign policy.

STRIKING A BALANCE AT HOME

On domestic issues, President Nixon tried to find a political balance. He knew that the Democrats, who controlled both houses of Congress, would oppose a conservative course of action. The Senate, for example, rejected two of his conservative choices for Supreme Court justices. As a result, Nixon appointed four moderate judges to the Supreme Court.

Nixon supported certain programs promoted by the Democrats that provided government aid to needy families. But he took a conservative approach to implementing the programs. He believed it would be better for state governments, not the federal government, to control the programs' funds. To accomplish this, he promoted **revenue sharing**, which involves distributing a portion of federal tax money directly to state and local governments. The state or local governments then decide which programs to support and how much money to allocate.

In his first years in office, Nixon faced a series of economic problems. The United States had experienced an economic boom during the 1960s. But government debt from the Vietnam War and rising energy prices took their toll. By 1970, the unemployment rate had risen to 6 percent, and the economy had slowed down. Nixon's administration also struggled to halt or slow rapid inflation, or the rising prices of goods and services. To address these problems, Nixon put in place tax cuts and limits on increases in wages and prices.

FOREIGN POLICY

Nixon adopted a flexible, realistic approach in dealing with foreign countries. To help guide foreign policy, he relied on his national security advisor, later his secretary of state, **Henry Kissinger**.

Both Nixon and Kissinger saw an opportunity to improve the U.S. economy by establishing a diplomatic and trade relationship with the People's Republic of China. On February 21, 1972, Nixon became the first American president to visit the communist country. He left with a promise from China's leaders for more open trade and cultural

In his campaign for the presidency, Richard Nixon expressed a conservative outlook on the high crime rates and civic unrest in the United States. He promised to restore law and order to the nation. In his presidential nomination speech, he described a nation torn apart.

PRIMARY SOURCE

As we look at America, we see cities enveloped in smoke and flame. We hear sirens in the night. We see Americans dying on distant battlefields abroad. We see Americans hating each other; fighting each other; killing each other at home. And as we see and hear these things, millions of Americans cry out in anguish. Did we come all this way for this?

—from Richard Nixon's presidential nomination speech, August 8, 1968

During his historic visit to China in February 1972, President Nixon inspects an honor guard of Chinese soldiers along with Chinese Premier Zhou Enlai (left). The establishment of relations with China was a major foreign policy achievement.

exchanges. Nixon used China's promise to bargain with the Soviet Union. China and the Soviet Union had a tense relationship, and Nixon knew the Soviets feared an alliance between China and the United States. The U.S. agreement with China made the Soviet Union more eager to negotiate with the United States. Three months after his trip to China, Nixon visited Moscow. Soviet leaders agreed to work with the United States to slow the arms race and open up trade. The two countries signed the first **Strategic Arms Limitation Treaty (SALT I)**, which limited each nation's number of nuclear missiles. Nixon also agreed to a trade deal, selling farming equipment and grain to the Soviet Union. The Moscow meetings eased tensions between the Soviet Union and the United States.

In October 1973, the powerful **Organization of Petroleum Exporting Countries (OPEC)** instituted an embargo on oil exports to the United States. Still in existence today, OPEC is a multinational organization that influences global policies and prices for gasoline and oil. In the early 1970s,

OPEC wanted to punish the United States for backing Israel in a short war between Israel and a few OPEC member nations in the Middle East. Because the United States relied heavily on foreign oil imports, the embargo added to the nation's already high inflation. Americans had to reduce their energy use and wait in long lines to buy gasoline for their cars. The embargo ended in April 1974, but oil prices continued to rise.

HISTORICAL THINKING

1. **READING CHECK** How did revenue sharing give power back to states?

2. **IDENTIFY PROBLEMS AND SOLUTIONS** How did Nixon use foreign policy to help solve domestic economic problems?

3. **ANALYZE CAUSE AND EFFECT** What effect did Nixon's visit to China have on U.S. relations with the Soviet Union?

1.3 Earth and Space

As technological advances carried humans farther into space, American astronauts saw Earth from a different perspective. Their reports and photos helped many Americans see the extraordinary beauty of our world—and made them want to protect it.

MAIN IDEA In the late 1960s and early 1970s, the United States explored space and took steps to solve environmental problems on Earth.

CRITICAL VIEWING On July 20, 1969, Apollo 11 mission commander Neil Armstrong took this photograph of astronaut Buzz Aldrin on the surface of the moon. You can see Armstrong's reflection in the visor of Aldrin's helmet. What does this photo convey about what it is like to walk on the moon?

MEN ON THE MOON

As you've read, President John F. Kennedy set the goal of sending American astronauts to the moon in a speech he made in 1961. On July 16, 1969, during Nixon's presidency, Kennedy's dream was realized when the **Apollo 11** mission landed the first two humans on the moon. Apollo 11 included a **lunar module**, the part of the spacecraft that landed on the moon, and a **command module**, the part that housed the crew and returned to Earth. Astronauts **Neil Armstrong** and **Buzz Aldrin** landed the lunar module, called the *Eagle*, while **Michael Collins** remained in orbit around the moon in the command module, called *Columbia*. Television and radio stations broadcast Armstrong's words as he stepped onto the moon: "That's one small step for [a] man, one giant leap for mankind."

Five more Apollo missions sent astronauts to Earth's moon between 1969 and 1972. Scientists collected rocks and soil samples and determined no life existed on the moon. NASA later shifted its focus and began working with other nations on space projects. One result was the International Space Station, a large spacecraft that has been orbiting Earth since it was launched in 1998. Scientists live on the station for months at a time and conduct experiments on a variety of topics. Besides maintaining the space station, NASA also has launched small, unmanned spacecraft equipped with cameras to explore Mars, Jupiter, and other places in the solar system.

CARING FOR EARTH

Photos of Earth from space inspired many Americans to support the environmental movement, which developed during the 1960s and 1970s. American marine biologist **Rachel Carson** drew public attention to environmental pollution with her book *Silent Spring*, published in 1962. Carson described how DDT, a commonly used pesticide, poisoned birds and contaminated human food sources. Then in 1969, a massive oil spill off the coast of Santa Barbara, California, opened many people's eyes to the potentially harmful effects of underwater oil drilling. The oil spill inspired U.S. Senator Gaylord Nelson of Wisconsin to organize the first **Earth Day**, a nationwide celebration focusing attention on environmental issues. Held on April 22, 1970, the

Rachel Carson takes a break from writing her book *Silent Spring* in July 1961 to examine a coastal specimen.

event drew about 20 million Americans, who rallied in the streets, attended teach-ins, and cleaned up parks. Earth Day became an annual event, held each year on April 22.

As Americans demanded action on environmental problems, Congress and the president responded with new laws—and a new agency. The **Clean Air Act** of 1970 focused on reducing the air pollution caused by vehicles and factories. The **Clean Water Act,** passed in 1972, set aside federal money to clean up polluted rivers and lakes. The 1973 **Endangered Species Act** provided protection for rare plants and animals. In 1970, President Nixon created a new agency, the **Environmental Protection Agency (EPA),** dedicated to enforcing environmental laws. In the next lesson, you'll read about some effects of these laws.

HISTORICAL THINKING

1. **READING CHECK** What actions did the federal government take in the 1970s to address environmental concerns?

2. **DETERMINE WORD MEANINGS** In your own words, explain the meaning of Armstrong's quote: "That's one small step for [a] man, one giant leap for mankind."

3. **MAKE CONNECTIONS** What environmental issues would you want to receive attention on the next Earth Day? Explain why.

1.4 Cleaner Air and Water

Perhaps you've seen recent photos of people in Beijing, China, wearing masks to protect their lungs from the city's polluted air. Environmental laws passed during the 1970s are helping the United States avoid a similar situation.

MAIN IDEA In the 1970s, federal, state, and local governments took steps to reduce air and water pollution in the United States.

A CLEANER LOS ANGELES

Los Angeles, California, is a prime example of the air pollution problems that have plagued the United States. By the 1970s, the city had some of the worst air quality in the country. The air reached unhealthy pollution levels more than 200 days per year, contributing to breathing problems, heart disease, and other illnesses—and sometimes causing death.

Los Angeles became famous for a type of air pollution called **smog**, which can develop when sunlight reacts with chemicals in the air. The chemicals may come from a number of sources, including car exhaust and emissions from factories, power plants, and oil refineries. Car exhaust was a major contributor to Los Angeles's air pollution. As the population grew, the city and its suburbs spread over a great distance. Most residents relied on cars, rather than mass transit, to get around. The geography of the Los Angeles area also contributed to the problem. Mountains partly surround the area, creating a basin that traps smog over the city.

A GLOBAL PERSPECTIVE A woman and her daughter hold a sign that says "Today I do not breathe" to protest air pollution in Mexico City in January 2017. Like Los Angeles, Mexico City is surrounded by mountains that trap air pollution.

Although smog remains a problem in Los Angeles, air quality in the city has improved dramatically due to actions taken in the 1970s. The Clean Air Act of 1970 and the creation of the EPA were key factors in the reduction of air pollution in Los Angeles and other cities. A state agency, the California Air Resources Board, helped implement the Clean Air Act.

Federal and California legislators also passed laws requiring gas stations to seal hoses and storage tanks to prevent harmful chemicals from leaking. In addition, scientists developed the **catalytic converter**, a device installed on the underside of automobiles to scrub pollutants from car exhaust before it is released into the air.

Three Mile Island

In 1979, an accident at the nuclear power station at Three Mile Island in Pennsylvania posed a temporary threat to air quality in the region. A partial meltdown of the reactor's core resulted in the release of a small amount of radioactive gases into the atmosphere. Although no one was harmed, the accident increased public opposition to nuclear power.

A CLEANER LAKE ERIE

Just as the Clean Air Act improved the nation's air quality, the Clean Water Act of 1972 had a major impact on U.S. water quality. Besides funding the cleanup of polluted rivers and lakes, the Clean Water Act set federal standards for water quality and made it illegal to dump pollutants into waterways. The **Safe Drinking Water Act** of 1974 established additional standards for drinking water drawn from reservoirs and wells.

The severe pollution of Lake Erie, one of the Great Lakes, helped inspire the passage of the Clean Water Act of 1972. For many years, industrial waste, urban sewage, and fertilizers and pesticides from farms had flowed into the lake. These pollutants stimulated the growth of algae, a water plant. The algae reduced the oxygen content in the water, killing off fish and other aquatic life. By the late 1960s, Lake Erie was so polluted that scientists described it as a "dead lake."

In 1969, the Cuyahoga River, which flows through Cleveland, Ohio, into Lake Erie, caught fire. Industrial pollutants floating on its surface ignited and burned. The river had caught fire many times before, but this time it became the subject of a national news magazine article. The Cuyahoga river fire became a dramatic symbol of the nation's mounting environmental problems.

The "dead" lake and the burning river motivated the federal government and local officials to take action. Cleveland's mayor, Carl Stokes, sought federal aid to improve the city's sewer system and to clean up its waterways. Agencies from the U.S. and Canadian governments worked to clean up Lake Erie. Within decades, the lake was again safe for fishing and swimming. However, algae growth in the lake must be continually monitored.

HISTORICAL THINKING

1. **READING CHECK** How did geography contribute to Los Angeles's smog problem?

2. **IDENTIFY PROBLEMS AND SOLUTIONS** What steps were taken to combat air and water pollution in the 1970s?

3. **MAKE CONNECTIONS** How does population growth contribute to environmental problems such as polluted water and air?

1.5 The Watergate Scandal

On June 17, 1972, the night security guard on duty at the Watergate complex in Washington, D.C., was making his rounds when he noticed a piece of tape that prevented a door from locking. His discovery would bring down the President of the United States.

MAIN IDEA President Nixon's extreme efforts to get re-elected led to his resignation from office.

WATERGATE BREAK-IN

Near the end of his first term in office, President Nixon seemed to be in an excellent position to win re-election. Yet he was worried about the election. Though he was leading in the polls, he wanted to ensure a landslide victory. To achieve this goal, some of his supporters formed a group in 1971 called the **Committee to Re-Elect the President (CRP)**, later mockingly nicknamed CREEP. Over the next year, CRP members leaked unflattering and sometimes false information about potential Democratic candidates to the press.

On June 17, 1972, police arrested five men for breaking into the Democratic National Headquarters at the Watergate complex in Washington, D.C.

One of the men was the security director for CRP. The men were trying to install listening devices on telephones so they could spy on Democratic Party leaders. Hiding a device on a telephone in order to secretly listen to conversations is called **wiretapping**. President Nixon was quick to claim that he and his administration had nothing to do with the Watergate break-in. Few people paid attention to the crime after his statement.

In July 1972, the Democrats chose South Dakota Senator **George McGovern** as their presidential candidate. McGovern was not as well known or experienced as Nixon, and he staunchly opposed the Vietnam War. Nixon won the election with the landslide he desired.

Washington Post journalists Carl Bernstein (left) and Bob Woodward prepare for a radio interview on June 17, 1974, the second anniversary of the Watergate break-in. The discoveries of the two journalists kept the Watergate story alive.

NIXON'S RESIGNATION

In his second term, Nixon faced the crisis that became known as the **Watergate scandal**. In April 1973, the Watergate burglars tried to plead guilty to minor charges of theft and wiretapping in order to avoid a public trial. The judge refused to accept their pleas because he suspected a **cover-up**, or an attempt to hide the truth. In the trial that followed, some of the burglars admitted that White House officials were involved in planning the break-in. These confessions, combined with explosive articles published in the *Washington Post* by reporters **Bob Woodward** and **Carl Bernstein**, turned the story of a small break-in into front-page news.

To handle the case, the U.S. Attorney General named a **special prosecutor**, or a private lawyer appointed to investigate and perhaps prosecute a legal case when there is a conflict of interest for the usual prosecuting attorney. The Senate also held investigative hearings. The prosecutor and the Senate hearings uncovered 69 people who had either helped to plan the break-in or tried to cover up its true purpose. Most of the people were close to the president. But Nixon denied involvement.

When evidence emerged that Nixon had secretly recorded his White House conversations, investigators demanded the tapes. At first Nixon provided transcripts, or typed versions of the conversations, which had been edited. When the tapes were finally turned over, they confirmed that Nixon had tried to cover up the burglary and block the investigation into it. The House Judiciary Committee presented the House of Representatives with charges of obstruction of justice and abuse of power. However, before the House could impeach, or formally charge, Nixon, he resigned. On August 8, 1974, he became the first president to do so.

HISTORICAL THINKING

1. **READING CHECK** What events led to President Nixon's resignation?

2. **MAKE INFERENCES** What do you think would have happened to Nixon had he not resigned?

3. **DRAW CONCLUSIONS** Why did it take officials so long to uncover Nixon's involvement in the Watergate scandal?

2.1 Ford and Carter

You know the age-old advice that the best way to deal with someone who has wronged you is to forgive and forget. But would Americans be able to take that approach to the president who gave them the Watergate scandal?

MAIN IDEA Presidents Ford and Carter both struggled to improve the nation's ailing economy.

FORD BECOMES PRESIDENT

One day after President Nixon resigned on August 8, 1974, Vice President **Gerald R. Ford** became president. Ford was an experienced politician who had been a Congressional representative from Michigan for 25 years before serving in the White House. Over that time, he had gained the reputation of being honest and fair.

Ford was the first vice president who had not been elected to that office. Nixon's first vice president, Spiro Agnew, resigned in 1973 after pleading guilty to charges of income tax evasion. The **25th Amendment** allowed the president to name a replacement. Adopted in 1967 in the aftermath of the Kennedy assassination, this amendment clarified the process for replacing a vice president who dies, resigns, or is removed from office. It also provides a way for the vice president and Congress to remove a president they deem unfit to serve.

In September 1974, about a month after taking office, President Ford formally forgave Nixon of all crimes he "may have committed" during the Watergate scandal. The **pardon** was controversial. Ford had previously promised the American people that Nixon would pay for any wrongdoing for which he was convicted. But Ford changed his mind, hoping that forgiveness would allow the country to move forward and forget the Watergate scandal. Instead, many Americans criticized his decision, and he lost their support.

As president, Ford inherited a weak and worsening economy. Years of high unemployment and slow growth had caused the economy to stagnate, or come to a standstill. At the same time, the cost of goods and services remained high. This combination of stagnation and high inflation was named **stagflation**. Ford proposed increasing taxes and limiting government spending, but Congress refused to support this plan.

Pardoning the Turkey

Who started the Thanksgiving Day tradition of the president pardoning a turkey so that it would not be killed for dinner? In 1863, Abraham Lincoln saved a turkey that was intended for his family's Thanksgiving dinner because his son had grown fond of the bird, but modern mythology names Harry Truman as the first president to start the yearly tradition. As it turns out, there is no evidence to support this claim, although Truman and other presidents, including Gerald Ford (shown above), posed with birds sent for the White House festivities. The official annual tradition began with George H.W. Bush. Since 1989, every sitting president has annually and publicly pardoned a gobbler.

Traditionally, the sitting president invites the incoming president to the White House to discuss the transition. In this photo, President-elect Jimmy Carter, left, meets with President Ford in November 1976.

CARTER IS ELECTED

In the presidential election of 1976, President Ford ran against Democrat **Jimmy Carter**, a former governor of Georgia. Carter promised to bring honesty back to the White House and called for an end to secrecy in government. "I'll never tell you a lie," he told voters. On November 2, 1976, Carter narrowly defeated Ford by a margin of 57 electoral votes. As the nation's 39th president, Carter inherited the nation's economic woes from Nixon and Ford. He also inherited an energy crisis.

As you've read, members of OPEC placed an embargo on oil shipments to the United States in 1973. The embargo caused gasoline shortages and long lines at gas stations. When Carter took office four years later, the United States was still dependent on OPEC for its oil. The situation grew worse in December 1979, when OPEC nations doubled the price of their oil from 1976 rates. Inflation in the United States continued to climb, in part because of the price hike. Consumers had less money to spend on other goods and services.

Carter proposed a new U.S. energy program to reduce the country's dependence on foreign oil. The program combined energy conservation, investment in oil production in the United States, and research into other forms of energy, such as nuclear, solar, and wind power. But Congress failed to pass Carter's energy program. In fact, Carter had so much difficulty working with Congress that little progress was made on either the economy or the energy crisis during his presidency.

HISTORICAL THINKING

1. **READING CHECK** What economic problems did President Ford inherit?

2. **ANALYZE CAUSE AND EFFECT** How did the OPEC oil embargo affect the U.S. economy in the 1970s?

3. **MAKE INFERENCES** Why did Jimmy Carter make honesty a highlight of his 1976 presidential campaign?

2.2 Carter's Foreign Policy

When you think about the rights you enjoy in a democracy, which right is most important to you? Perhaps it's your right to express your own ideas, or wear the kind of clothes you like. For many people around the world, more basic rights might be most important—like the right to have food and water.

MAIN IDEA President Carter focused his foreign policy on promoting human rights and peace.

HUMAN RIGHTS AND PEACE

As a deeply religious man, President Carter strongly believed in the importance of **human rights**, which are rights that most nations recognize as belonging to all humans. They include the rights to food, housing, and education as well as political rights. One of Carter's main goals as president was to promote human rights—and peace—throughout the world.

To protest human rights violations, Carter cut off federal aid to dictatorships in Chile and Nicaragua. He encouraged the governments of Argentina and Brazil to make democratic reforms. Carter's critics pointed out, however, that he allowed continued U.S. support for **Ferdinand Marcos**, the president of the Philippines. Although he had originally been elected by a majority, Marcos ruled as a dictator from 1972 to 1981.

On November 4, 1979, Iranian militants captured 52 Americans, blindfolded them, and paraded them in front of television cameras.

To improve relations with Central America, Carter began the process of returning the Panama Canal Zone to Panama in 1977. The United States had controlled the area since the canal opened in 1914. Panamanians had staged many protests over the years, demanding that the United States give the land back. Carter believed returning the land would help promote peace in the region.

Carter also negotiated an extension of the SALT I Treaty with the Soviet Union. Called **SALT II**, the agreement set limits on the number of nuclear weapons each country could own. However, Carter himself withdrew SALT II from Senate consideration after the Soviet Union invaded Afghanistan in December 1979.

CRITICAL VIEWING In 1978, Egyptian President Anwar Sadat (left), President Carter (center), and Israeli Prime Minister Menachem Begin (right) celebrate the signing of a treaty that ended 31 years of war between Egypt and Israel. What does the photo convey about the feelings of the three leaders?

TRIUMPH AND TRAGEDY IN THE MIDDLE EAST

Carter's greatest peacemaking efforts focused on Israel's relationship with its Arab neighbors. Since its founding in 1948, Israel had fought four wars with Egypt and Syria. The most recent war had ended in 1973, and Carter hoped to prevent another one.

In August 1978, Carter invited Egyptian President **Anwar Sadat** (AHN-war suh-DAHT) and Israeli Prime Minister **Menachem Begin** (muh-NAH-kuhm BAY-gihn) to meet for peace talks in the United States at Camp David, the presidential retreat in Maryland. As a result, Egypt agreed to recognize Israel as a country, and Israel agreed to return land taken from Egypt in a war. Begin and Sadat formally signed the **Camp David Accords** at the White House on September 17, 1978. They were jointly awarded the 1978 Nobel Peace Prize for their efforts.

President Carter had little time to celebrate. In January 1979, Islamic **fundamentalists** overthrew the shah, or king, of Iran. A fundamentalist believes in the strict, literal interpretation of religious documents and doctrine. When the shah, a strong American ally, developed cancer, Carter allowed him to come to the United States for medical treatment. Angry fundamentalists took over the U.S. embassy in Tehran, Iran's capital. In what became known as the **Iran hostage crisis**, they held 52 Americans hostage there for more than a year, demanding that the shah be returned to Iran for trial. Carter refused.

Diplomats from around the world tried to persuade the fundamentalists to release the hostages. President Carter tried, unsuccessfully, to negotiate with Iran through the United Nations. Finally, in April 1980, Carter ordered a secret military mission to rescue the American hostages. The mission was a disastrous failure, resulting in the deaths of eight American soldiers. Carter faced the 1980 presidential election with a tarnished reputation as a leader.

HISTORICAL THINKING

1. **READING CHECK** How did President Carter promote human rights around the world?

2. **FORM AND SUPPORT OPINIONS** Do you think human rights should be a focus of American foreign policy? Why or why not?

3. **EVALUATE** How would you evaluate President Carter's leadership in the Iran hostage crisis?

3.1 Reagan's Victory in 1980

It's often said that Americans vote with their pocketbooks. In the 1980 presidential election, they chose Ronald Reagan to improve the nation's economy.

MAIN IDEA The election of Ronald Reagan marked the beginning of a new era of conservative politics in the United States.

THE 1980 ELECTION

The presidential campaign of 1980 took place during the Iran hostage crisis. Carter's outlook for re-election was not promising. Many Americans viewed him as a weak leader because of his handling of the crisis. In addition, Americans were upset that inflation was still high.

Carter's Republican opponent was **Ronald Reagan**, a former movie actor and a popular two-term governor of California. Reagan was a conservative and believed in low taxes, limited government regulation, a strong military, and traditional social values. Known as the "Great Communicator," Reagan had a knack for connecting with an audience. When cameras were aimed at him, he spoke directly to the viewers and won them over with his charm. During the presidential debates, he asked Americans, "Are you better off than you were four years ago?" He suggested they vote for Carter if they were better off and vote for him if they were not.

Reagan won the election with 51 percent of the popular vote. Because his support

was distributed throughout the nation, he won more than 90 percent of the electoral vote. On January 20, 1981, the day of Reagan's inauguration, Iran released the American hostages in Tehran.

REAGAN'S FIRST TERM

Reagan's first actions as president were aimed at improving the economy. He based his economic policy on a theory called **supply-side economics**, which holds that increased production (the "supply") of goods and services creates economic growth. According to the theory, tax cuts and **deregulation**, or loosening

Presidential candidate Ronald Reagan campaigns in Columbia, South Carolina, in October 1989 with his wife, Nancy, and Senator Strom Thurmond (right) of South Carolina. In his campaign, Reagan reassured voters with his view that America's best days were still to come.

Striking air traffic controllers picket outside a terminal at La Guardia Airport in New York City on August 5, 1981. This photo shows the strikers shortly before President Reagan fired them.

government restrictions, help businesses expand and increase production. This economic policy became known as "Reaganomics."

Reagan's presidency was soon interrupted by violence. On March 30, 1981, a mentally ill citizen named John Hinckley, Jr., attempted to assassinate Reagan. Hinckley fired several shots as the president was leaving a Washington, D.C., hotel, hitting Reagan's press secretary James Brady, a police officer, and a Secret Service agent. The last bullet bounced off the president's car and hit Reagan in the chest. Everyone survived the attack, though Brady was seriously injured. Hinckley was placed in a psychiatric institution.

On August 3, 1981, nearly 13,000 members of the Professional Air Traffic Controllers Organization (PATCO) went on strike for higher wages. Air traffic controllers are federal employees who direct airplanes as they take off and land. Federal law, however, prohibited such employees from striking. Reagan ordered the strikers to return to work or be fired. Most of the controllers maintained their strike, and they lost their jobs. Commercial air travel was cut back until new controllers could be hired and trained. Despite the transportation disruption, Reagan's response was seen by many as a show of strength. In the long-term, his actions weakened the power of organized labor.

Before the end of Reagan's first year in office, the country sank into a recession. This economic slowdown deepened in 1982. As huge military-spending increases raised the national debt, the unemployment rate hit almost 11 percent. To address the problem, Reagan approved a tax increase. The economy picked up by early 1983 and continued to grow.

In November 1984, Reagan won re-election in a landslide victory over former vice president **Walter Mondale** and his running mate, **Geraldine Ferraro**. A U.S. representative from New York, Ferraro was the first female vice-presidential candidate of a major political party.

HISTORICAL THINKING

1. **READING CHECK** What was Ronald Reagan's political philosophy?

2. **EVALUATE** Why was Reagan's decision to fire striking PATCO union members significant for his presidency?

3. **ASK AND ANSWER QUESTIONS** What questions could you ask to better understand supply-side economics, and where might you find the answers?

3.2 Ronald Wilson Reagan 1911–2004

"My philosophy of life is that if we make up our mind what we are going to make of our lives, then work hard toward that goal, we never lose."—Ronald Reagan

Ronald Reagan didn't always believe he could achieve his goals. He admitted to lacking confidence and suffering feelings of inferiority when he was a child. To bolster his self-image, Reagan's mother encouraged him to recite a passage for a dramatic society she belonged to. The enthusiastic applause that followed his performance "was music," Reagan recalled. It was a life-changing experience. Soon he would tackle his goals with the optimism for which he would become famous.

FROM DIXON TO HOLLYWOOD

Reagan's early insecurity may have stemmed from an unsettled early childhood. His father frequently moved his family from place to place. As a result, it was hard for the young Reagan to make friends. Finally, in 1920, the family settled in Dixon, Illinois. During high school, Reagan played football, acted in the drama club, and served as student body president. In many ways, these activities foreshadowed the course his life would take.

After graduating from college in 1932, Reagan worked as a sports announcer on the radio. Five years later, he took a screen test for Warner Brothers and subsequently signed a contract with the movie studio. Over the next 20 years, Reagan appeared in more than 50 films. One of his best-known movies is the 1940 film *Knute Rockne, All American*, in which he played University of Notre Dame football player George Gipp. Reagan married actress Jane Wyman that same year. The couple divorced in 1948, and Reagan married another actress, Nancy Davis, in 1952.

CRITICAL VIEWING Reagan strikes a pose on a football field as George Gipp in *Knute Rockne, All American*. The film tells the true story of Rockne, the University of Notre Dame's football coach in the early 1900s, and Gipp, the team's first star player. Gipp developed pneumonia in 1920 and died at the age of 25. In the film, Reagan delivers his most famous on-screen line, "win one for the Gipper," as his character lies on his deathbed. After the movie became a hit, Reagan was often called "the Gipper." How might Reagan's experience as an actor have helped him as a politician?

In this photo, Reagan delivers a speech in Florida during his first successful bid for the presidency in 1980. Reagan used the slogan, "Let's Make America Great Again," during the campaign. When he ran for re-election in 1984, he developed an effective television ad using the phrase "It's morning again in America," which promised a bright future for the country.

ONTO THE POLITICAL STAGE

As an actor, Reagan closely followed the investigations into communist activities in the entertainment industry during the 1940s and 1950s and became a firm anticommunist. Once a supporter of Franklin Roosevelt's New Deal, Reagan's political views became increasingly conservative. He began to speak publicly in favor of business and lashed out against the wastefulness and excessive regulations of government. Reagan emerged as a national political figure in 1964 when he delivered a well-received speech in support of Republican presidential candidate Barry Goldwater. The speech helped Reagan secure the first of his two terms as governor of California in 1966.

After two failed bids to become the Republican presidential nominee, Reagan won the nomination and the presidency in 1980. A popular president, he was known for his sense of humor. As the oldest person at that time ever elected to the presidency, for instance, Reagan joked: "Thomas Jefferson once said, 'We should never judge a president by his age, only by his works.' And ever since he told me that, I stopped worrying."

After they left the White House, Ronald and Nancy Reagan returned to California. In 1994, the former president revealed that he had Alzheimer's disease, which causes progressive mental deterioration. With characteristic optimism he wrote, "I now begin the journey that will lead me into the sunset of my life. I know that for America there will always be a bright dawn ahead." Reagan died 10 years later.

HISTORICAL THINKING

1. **READING CHECK** How did Reagan's early interests reflect the course of his career?

2. **IDENTIFY MAIN IDEAS AND DETAILS** How had Reagan's political views changed by the 1950s?

3. **MAKE INFERENCES** What did Reagan mean when he wrote that "there will always be a bright dawn ahead" for America?

3.3 A Changing Nation

In the 1980s, the conservative movement gained power as Ronald Reagan—a true believer in smaller government, lower taxes, and traditional values—took over the White House. But the values of conservatives often clashed with those of other groups.

MAIN IDEA Both the conservative movement and the gay rights movement became vocal forces in American society in the 1980s.

THE CONSERVATIVE MOVEMENT

As you've read, millions of Americans moved from the Frostbelt to the Sunbelt in the 1950s. The Sunbelt states had long been more conservative than the Frostbelt states, and many of these migrants were attracted to the region's conservatism, or conservative political philosophy. They were drawn to the Republican Party because of its positions on taxes and national security.

California, however, was more politically diverse than most Sunbelt states. While its major coastal cities were politically liberal, California's rural and suburban regions, such as Orange County, became strongholds of conservatism. Both Ronald Reagan and Richard Nixon were California politicians before becoming president. Outside the Sunbelt, many states experienced a similar urban versus rural and suburban split in political orientation.

The social changes taking place in American society since the 1960s alarmed many conservatives. The number of single-parent households rose as divorce became more common. Drug abuse became more widespread. Conservatives claimed that American society was losing its moral compass.

The conservative movement included Christian fundamentalists, people who believed in strict adherence to the Bible. **Televangelists**, preachers who use television shows to spread their beliefs, encouraged their viewers to uphold what they believed to be traditional family values. Some televangelists, such as **Reverend Jerry Falwell** and **Reverend Billy Graham**, became deeply involved in politics. In 1979, Falwell formed a political group called the **Moral Majority**. The group supported prayer and religious teachings in public schools. It helped elect religious conservatives to local, state, and national offices.

Reverend Billy Graham addresses a crowd at Pilot Field in Buffalo, New York, in August 1988. Members of more than 600 churches gathered at Pilot Field, now known as Coca-Cola Field, to hear the televangelist speak.

By 1983, the gay rights movement had gained significant momentum. This gay pride march in Des Moines, Iowa, was one of many that took place around the world that year.

THE GAY RIGHTS MOVEMENT

Though it often faced conservative opposition, the gay rights movement became more prominent during the 1970s and 1980s. The movement began in earnest in the late 1960s, when gay people began to fight back publicly against social discrimination and harassment. In many places, it was not only socially unacceptable but also illegal to be gay. As the gay rights movement grew, more gay people "came out," or openly acknowledged their orientation. They staged protests calling for an end to discrimination in employment, housing, and other areas of life. In 1977, San Francisco city supervisor **Harvey Milk** became the first openly gay person to be elected to public office in the United States. In the 1990s, the term **LGBT**, an acronym for "lesbian, gay, bisexual, and transgender," emerged as an alternate name covering distinct groups within the gay community.

During the 1980s, a public health crisis struck the world. An alarming number of people began dying of an unidentified disease that made their bodies unable to fight infections. In the United States, most of the first victims were gay men. Scientists learned the disease is caused by a virus, which they named the **human immunodeficiency virus (HIV)**. This is also the name of the first stage of the disease. The last stage is called **acquired immunodeficiency syndrome (AIDS)**, but not all people with HIV advance to the AIDS stage. HIV/AIDS quickly spread beyond the gay community to affect other groups of people. The initial lack of information about HIV/AIDS caused panic in the country.

Once scientists discovered that HIV was transmitted through bodily fluids, programs arose worldwide to educate people on prevention methods. Unfortunately, millions of people have died from HIV/AIDS. No cure exists, but scientists have developed medicines to help infected people manage the disease.

HISTORICAL THINKING

1. **READING CHECK** What parts of the country were conservative strongholds in the 1980s?

2. **MAKE GENERALIZATIONS** Why might many conservatives oppose the gay rights movement?

3. **IDENTIFY PROBLEMS AND SOLUTIONS** What action was taken to prevent the spread of HIV/AIDS?

3.4 Deregulation and Defense

Do you ever feel that your school has too many rules? President Reagan felt that way about government regulations—and so he began getting rid of them.

MAIN IDEA President Reagan loosened regulations on businesses and increased spending on defense.

DEREGULATION

President Reagan strongly believed that too many government regulations, including environmental regulations, hurt businesses by increasing costs. He thought these costs were stifling the economy.

Reagan appointed Colorado legislator Anne Gorsuch from Colorado to head the Environmental Protection Agency (EPA) and James G. Watt, a former assistant to the Secretary of the Interior, to lead the Department of the Interior. Gorsuch slashed the EPA's budget by 25 percent and abolished many EPA regulations. Watt handed over huge areas of federal land to coal mining companies. He also opened up the U.S. **continental shelf** —the submerged, relatively shallow land surrounding a continent and extending into the ocean—to oil drilling. Environmentalists strongly opposed the actions of both officials. Gorsuch and Watt were forced to resign in 1983, and in the following years, Congress renewed and strengthened various environmental laws.

Reagan also eased rules on the savings and loan industry. Experts argue that this action led to a crisis in the late 1980s and 1990s after savings and loan associations lent money to people who could not pay it back. Many of the companies failed. Taxpayers ended up paying billions of dollars as the government reimbursed depositors at the failed companies.

Reagan cut funding for such social programs as food stamps and school lunches but kept popular programs that benefited the middle class, such as Medicare and Social Security. When experts announced Social Security funds were running low in 1983, Reagan gathered economists to solve the funding problem.

BUILDING UP DEFENSE

While Reagan reduced the size and power of the federal government through deregulation, he increased it by building up the military. A strong anticommunist, Reagan wanted to bolster the nation's defense to challenge the Soviet Union, which he called "the Evil Empire." Between 1980 and 1985, he doubled the military's budget. As you have read, Reagan approved a tax increase to pay for the increased military spending.

In 1983, the Reagan administration proposed development of a defense system called the **Strategic Defense Initiative (SDI)**, which the press dubbed "Star Wars." SDI was a system of satellites that would be launched into space to defend the United States by intercepting attacking missiles in flight. Once operational, SDI would give the United States a military advantage over the Soviet Union. Critics argued that the system was too expensive, required too much energy, and depended on technology not yet invented. The initiative was abandoned after experts determined the system would raise tensions between the United States and the Soviet Union.

In 1986, midway through his second term, Reagan faced a major political scandal called the **Iran-Contra Affair**. Because of concerns about the possible spread of communism in Central America, the Reagan administration provided military aid to a militia group called the Contras, who were fighting the leftist government in Nicaragua. In 1984, Congress passed a law banning aid to the Contras. However, the White House secretly continued to fund the group, in violation of the law.

The scandal also involved Iran because the Reagan administration was secretly selling weapons to Iran in the hopes of securing the

AMERICAN PLACES
Lake Michigan
Chicago, Illinois

Like other Great Lakes, Lake Michigan benefits from a variety of federal and state environmental laws. Most of these laws either safeguard the quality of the water or provide protection from invasive species, which are non-native plants and animals that are introduced into an ecosystem and cause damage. To protect Lake Michigan from an invasive species of fish called Asian carp, for example, a series of electronic barriers have been installed in the waterways that flow into the lake.

release of American hostages in Lebanon. Besides being illegal, these sales contradicted the U.S. government's stated policy of refusing to negotiate with terrorists. A portion of the money gained from these arms sales was given to the Contras.

After several investigations of the scandal, a number of members of Reagan's administration were charged and convicted of crimes. Reagan himself was never charged, but his reputation was temporarily tarnished.

HISTORICAL THINKING

1. **READING CHECK** Why did President Reagan abolish many government regulations?

2. **DRAW CONCLUSIONS** How did Reagan's anticommunism influence his foreign policy?

3. **EVALUATE** What were the pros and cons of the Strategic Defense Initiative?

The End of the Cold War

For more than 45 years, the Cold War cast a dark cloud over the lives of Americans. It led Americans to build bomb shelters in backyards and practice nuclear attack drills in schools. No one imagined the war would end quickly once Soviets got a taste of democracy.

MAIN IDEA The Cold War ended with the breakup of the Soviet Union and the collapse of communist regimes in Eastern Europe between 1989 and 1991.

CHANGES IN THE SOVIET UNION

During Reagan's second term in office, in 1985, **Mikhail Gorbachev** (mih-KAY-uhl GOHR-buh-chawf) became leader of the Soviet Union. Gorbachev inherited serious domestic problems, including a stagnant economy and an inefficient government. He proposed a political program called **perestroika** (pair-ih-STROY-kuh), which means "restructuring." Perestroika called for

reducing government control of the economy and taking steps toward democracy. At the same time, Gorbachev introduced a policy called **glasnost** (GLAS-nawst), which means "openness." Under glasnost, freedom of the press was expanded and criticism of the Soviet government was allowed.

Gorbachev also promoted better relations with the United States. In 1987, Reagan and Gorbachev signed the Intermediate-Range Nuclear Forces

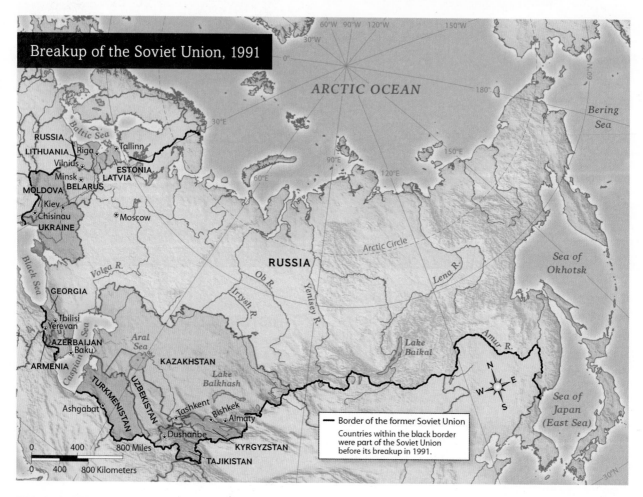

Breakup of the Soviet Union, 1991

— Border of the former Soviet Union

Countries within the black border were part of the Soviet Union before its breakup in 1991.

Treaty (INF), which called for both nations to eliminate their intermediate-range and medium-range nuclear missiles. The agreement eased tension between the two countries, but Reagan still spoke out against communism. During a visit to West Germany in 1987, the president stood in front of the Berlin Wall and challenged Gorbachev to "tear down this wall."

In November 1988, Reagan's vice president **George H.W. Bush** was elected president. As a former ambassador to the United Nations and director of the CIA, Bush had experience in foreign affairs. He continued the work of improving relations with the Soviet Union.

Pro-democracy protesters ride in a truck through Tiananmen Square in Beijing, China, in May 1989. Similar demonstrations occurred in other Chinese cities at the time.

GLOBAL CHANGES

Gorbachev not only introduced democratic reforms in the Soviet Union, he also encouraged reforms in the communist nations of Eastern Europe. Throughout the summer of 1989, citizens in these countries staged peaceful protests demanding democracy. In Poland, voters elected a democratic government in August. The communist governments in Hungary and Czechoslovakia fell in early fall. In November came East Germany, where journalists photographed crowds of people tearing down the Berlin Wall. In 1990, East Germany and West Germany reunited.

Gorbachev's democratic reforms had some unintended consequences. The republics that made up the Soviet Union, except for Russia, pushed to become independent nations. Then in August 1991, a group of loyal communists staged a **coup** (KOO), or government overthrow, and arrested Gorbachev. After three days of protests by Soviet citizens, the coup leaders surrendered. Even though the coup had failed, Gorbachev had lost power. On December 25, 1991, he resigned and was replaced by **Boris Yeltsin**. The next day, a joint declaration by the leaders of the Soviet republics announced the breakup of the Soviet Union. Each of the 15 former Soviet republics became an independent nation. In February 1992, President Bush and President Yeltsin of the Soviet Union announced the end of the Cold War.

Meanwhile, in China, a push for democratic reform did not succeed. In May 1989, nearly a million protesters gathered in a huge public space in Beijing called **Tiananmen Square**. For three weeks, they called for communist leaders to resign and for a new democratic government. By June 4, the Chinese government had sent troops and tanks into the square to end the protests. At least 300 people were killed that day and thousands were injured. The Bush administration denounced, or spoke out against, the attack and started an arms embargo against China.

HISTORICAL THINKING

1. **READING CHECK** What were glasnost and perestroika?

2. **MAKE GENERALIZATIONS** What does the rapid breakup of the Soviet Union indicate about life under Soviet control?

3. **ANALYZE CAUSE AND EFFECT** Why did citizens in so many Eastern European countries decide to revolt against communism in 1989?

4.2 War in the Middle East

Handling foreign relations can be like fighting forest fires. As soon as one fire is put out, another one starts somewhere else. After declaring the end of the Cold War, President George H.W. Bush had to fight another fire.

MAIN IDEA President Bush faced the challenges of rising national debt and major conflict in the Middle East.

BUSH'S DOMESTIC POLICIES

As you have read, George H.W. Bush won the 1988 presidential election. His bid for the office was bolstered by President Reagan's popularity and the lessening of tensions in the world. His campaign promise that he would not raise taxes also swayed voters to his side. This pledge turned out to be a problem, however, after Bush became president. The national debt continued to increase in the first two years of his presidency. In 1990, Bush had no choice but to introduce new taxes and cut government spending to keep the deficit under control.

With little money to spend on domestic programs, Bush promoted education reform and volunteerism. One significant law he signed was the **Americans with Disabilities Act (ADA)**. Bush said, "I am going to do whatever it takes to make sure the disabled are included in the mainstream." The new law made it illegal for employers to discriminate against disabled people. It also ensured that people with disabilities would have access to places of business, public facilities, and transportation. Although some conservatives opposed

the law, claiming it was too expensive and yet another example of government overregulation, it gained widespread public support. Under Bush, the federal government also began to fund AIDS research with the goal of finding a cure.

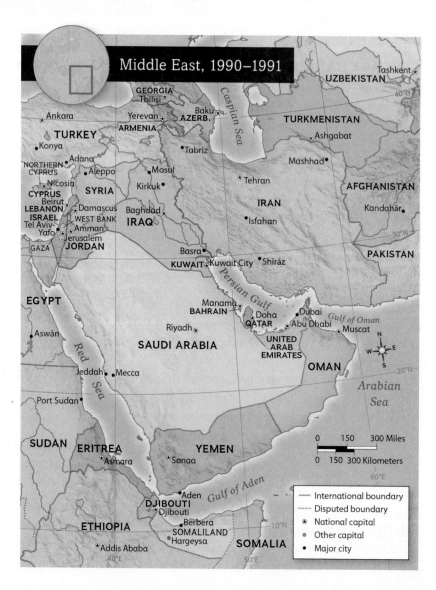

Middle East, 1990–1991

U.S. Marines wearing desert camouflage patrol Kuwait in 1991 as oil fires burn on the horizon. The vehicle on the right is spray-painted with the slogan "Free Kuwait," a reference to the Allied intervention in the country after it was taken over by Iraq.

THE PERSIAN GULF WAR

As the Cold War ended, tensions increased between two dictatorships in the Middle East, Iran and Iraq. Religious leader **Ruhollah Khomeini** (roo-HOH-luh koh-MAY-nee) headed Iran's Islamic government, and the brutal dictator **Saddam Hussein** (sah-DAHM hoo-SAYN) ruled Iraq. Hussein invaded Iran in 1980, beginning a war that would last until 1988. The war ended with neither country gaining any territory.

In August 1990, Hussein declared peace with Iran and then invaded the neighboring country of **Kuwait**. He claimed that oil companies from Kuwait had taken oil that belonged to Iraq. But experts believe he invaded the country to gain its oil reserves, since he needed money to pay off his expensive war with Iran. The invasion posed a major threat to Kuwait's neighbor and U.S. ally, Saudi Arabia, which was also the world's largest oil producer. In response to the invasion, the United Nations threatened military action unless Hussein left Kuwait. Hussein refused.

With help from the United Nations, President Bush put together a **coalition**, or a group of nations that join together for a common purpose. The coalition contributed 700,000 troops, with Americans

numbering 540,000. The coalition's goal was to drive the Iraqis out of Kuwait. The short war that followed is officially known as the **Persian Gulf War**. It began on January 16, 1991, with a U.S.-led air campaign called **Operation Desert Storm**. The war lasted 42 days, thanks, in part, to modern military technology. This war saw the first use of weaponry controlled by microcomputers and enhanced by digital guidance systems and laser technology. Saddam's forces were driven from Kuwait in defeat. Bush decided not to pursue Saddam or remove him from office, believing that the coalition would not support an occupation of Baghdad, Iraq's capital.

HISTORICAL THINKING

1. **READING CHECK** What was the cause and the result of the Persian Gulf War?

2. **IDENTIFY PROBLEMS AND SOLUTIONS** How did President Bush respond to the growing national deficit?

3. **FORM AND SUPPORT OPINIONS** What is your opinion of conservatives' objections to the Americans with Disabilities Act?

VOCABULARY

For each pair of vocabulary terms, write one sentence that explains the connection between the two terms.

1. command module; lunar module

   In 1969, Apollo 11's command module remained in orbit around the moon as its lunar module landed on the moon.

2. Watergate scandal; cover-up

3. catalytic converter; smog

4. HIV; AIDS

5. deregulation; continental shelf

6. stagflation; supply-side economics

7. Moral Majority; televangelist

8. perestroika; glasnost

READING STRATEGY
IDENTIFY PROBLEMS AND SOLUTIONS

If you haven't already done so, complete your chart by identifying events and proposed solutions in the energy crisis of the 1970s. Then answer the question below.

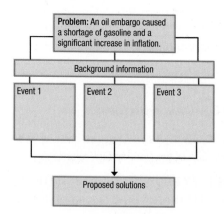

9. How did the energy crisis shape American politics during the 1970s?

MAIN IDEAS

Answer the following questions. Support your answers with evidence from the chapter.

10. How did the Nixon administration respond to environmental problems in the 1970s? **LESSON 1.3**

11. What role did newspaper reporters Bob Woodward and Carl Bernstein play in the Watergate scandal? **LESSON 1.5**

12. What is the purpose of the 25th Amendment? **LESSON 2.1**

13. How did President Carter promote peace in the Middle East? **LESSON 2.2**

14. What conservative policies did President Reagan enact? **LESSON 3.1**

15. What effect did the Moral Majority have on American government in the 1980s? **LESSON 3.3**

16. What was the Iran-Contra Affair? **LESSON 3.4**

17. How did the Cold War end? **LESSON 4.1**

18. What were the provisions of the Americans with Disabilities Act that improved the lives of the disabled? **LESSON 4.2**

HISTORICAL THINKING

Answer the following questions. Support your answers with evidence from the chapter.

19. **DETERMINE CHRONOLOGY** What events led to the collapse of the Soviet Union in 1991?

20. **COMPARE AND CONTRAST** How did the policies of Republican presidents Richard Nixon and Ronald Reagan differ?

21. **ANALYZE CAUSE AND EFFECT** Why did Reagan's increased military spending lead to a tax increase?

22. **DRAW CONCLUSIONS** How do you think Americans reacted to the Watergate scandal?

23. IDENTIFY PROBLEMS AND SOLUTIONS What problems did the Vietnam War cause in the United States?

24. FORM AND SUPPORT OPINIONS What was the more serious problem facing the United States in the 1970s: stagflation or pollution? Explain your answer.

INTERPRET GRAPHS

As you have read in Lesson 2.1, stagflation arose in the mid-1970s, caused by rising inflation paired with a slow, stagnant economy and a decrease in employment. Study the graph at right. Then answer the following questions.

25. What happened to the unemployment rate a year after inflation began to rise in 1972?

26. What happened to the unemployment rate a year after inflation began to decrease in 1974?

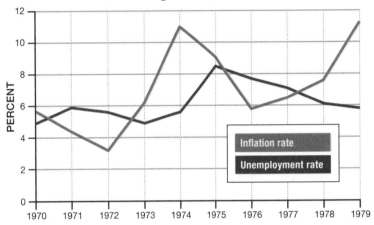

U.S. Stagflation, 1970–1979

Source: U.S. Bureau of Labor Statistics

ANALYZE SOURCES

Ronald Reagan easily won the 1980 presidential election, bringing a wave of conservatism to the Oval Office and the nation. This excerpt from his inaugural speech highlights the economic problems he planned to address.

> Idle industries have cast workers into unemployment, human misery, and personal indignity. Those who do work are denied a fair return for their labor by a tax system which penalizes successful achievement and keeps us from maintaining full productivity.
>
> The economic ills we suffer . . . will not go away in days, weeks, or months, but they will go away . . . because we as Americans have the capacity now, as we've had in the past, to do whatever needs to be done to preserve this last and greatest bastion [stronghold] of freedom.
>
> — from Ronald Reagan's First Inaugural Address, January 20, 1981

27. How does this excerpt reflect Reagan's conservative philosophy?

CONNECT TO YOUR LIFE

28. ARGUMENT Reread the excerpt from President Reagan's first inaugural address at left. If you were writing your own inaugural address today, what problem would you focus on, and what solution would you offer? Prepare a short persuasive speech on the subject.

TIPS

• Choose one major problem in the United States today. Research the problem and solutions that have been proposed, using appropriate sources.

• Begin your speech by introducing the problem and the solution you've chosen.

• Elaborate on your solution and explain why you chose it.

• Conclude your speech with a promise or an inspirational thought.

CHAPTER 29

BRIDGE TO THE
21st CENTURY
1992–Present

ESSENTIAL QUESTION
How has the United States responded to crises in
the early years of the 21st century?

 The Refugee Crisis

SECTION 1 **Challenges in the 1990s**

KEY VOCABULARY

centrist   neoconservative
government shutdown

SECTION 2 **Crises and Responses**

KEY VOCABULARY

first responder   levee   weapon of mass destruction (WMD)
insurgent   storm surge

SECTION 3 **A Historic Election**

KEY VOCABULARY

economic stimulus   loan default   subprime

SECTION 4 **Rapid Changes in the 21st Century**

KEY VOCABULARY

alternative energy   globalization   social media
browser   greenhouse effect   swing state
climate change   Internet   World Wide Web
free trade

AMERICAN GALLERY
ONLINE **The Attacks of September 11, 2001**

READING STRATEGY

FORM AND SUPPORT OPINIONS
You often form opinions while reading,
and thinking through these opinions
can help you understand historical
events. As you read this chapter,
decide what you think is the greatest
challenge the United States has
faced so far in the 21st century. Use a
graphic organizer like this one to write
your opinion and record your reasons
to support it.

Opinion
Supporting Statement:
Supporting Statement:
Supporting Statement:
Supporting Statement:
Supporting Statement:

"If someone wants to **accomplish great things,** there is no better place than the United States."

—Elon Musk, American entrepreneur

CRITICAL VIEWING Skyscrapers rise above Chicago's multi-use, environmentally friendly Millennium Park. Inside the park, native plants growing in the Lurie Garden reduce stormwater runoff and attract wildlife, including bees and birds. Four glass pavilions convert solar energy into electricity. The curving structure in the photograph arches over a 4,000-seat, open-air auditorium and a huge grass lawn. And underneath it all are parking garages and a rail line. What makes the park unique to the 21st century?

1.1 Reform Under Clinton

The Republicans and Democrats have dominated American elections for so long it's easy to forget that other parties can mount a presidential run. What happens when a third-party candidate presents a real challenge at the polls?

MAIN IDEA President Bill Clinton enacted measures to lower the budget deficit and faced diplomatic challenges abroad.

CLINTON'S DOMESTIC AGENDA

At first, President George H.W. Bush seemed poised to win a second term. He had an 83 percent job approval rating in March 1991. But as the 1992 election approached, he grew vulnerable. He had broken his promise of "no new taxes." The federal budget deficit was high, and the nation was in another recession, a period of declining economic activity. A third-party candidate, businessman **H. Ross Perot**, entered the race. Because his views were conservative, Perot had the potential to draw Republican voters.

The Democrats nominated Arkansas governor **Bill Clinton**, who considered himself a "new Democrat." Clinton was a **centrist**, which means his positions often represented compromises between liberal and conservative ideas. This proved to be a successful strategy. Clinton won the presidential election with 43 percent of the popular vote to Bush's 37.4 percent. Perot received 18.9 percent. Clinton dominated in the electoral college, winning 370 votes to Bush's 168. Perot did not win any electoral votes.

Presidential candidate Bill Clinton (left) and his running mate, Al Gore, exit a bus during their 1992 "buscapade" campaign tour of the Great Lakes area.

During his campaign, Clinton promised to end the recession. In August 1993, he persuaded Congress to pass tax increases and spending cuts in order to lower the federal budget deficit. In 1993, Clinton signed the controversial **North American Free Trade Agreement (NAFTA)** with Canada and Mexico, which reduced trade barriers among the three countries. Supporters claimed NAFTA would improve the economy by boosting trade. Critics believed it favored corporations over most citizens, family farms, and local governments.

Clinton met with less success in his efforts to institute a universal health care system. He named his wife, **Hillary Clinton**, to lead a health care reform group. Mrs. Clinton was a respected lawyer and an advocate for children and education. Conservatives, insurance companies, and the American Medical Association opposed the plan for universal coverage—a single health care system that would cover all Americans. The proposal failed to pass Congress.

CLINTON AND THE WORLD

Internationally, Clinton faced several challenges. The breakup of the Soviet Union and the Soviet bloc caused unrest in parts of Eastern Europe. War broke out in the Balkans, a region that was once part of Yugoslavia. Three ethnic groups—the Serbs, Croats, and Bosnians—each sought independence and control of the area. Clinton tried military means to end the violence, but he limited the U.S. commitment. Both the UN and Congress resisted requests for more military action. Critics complained that Clinton "muddled through" the crisis.

In September 1993, Clinton invited Israeli prime minister **Yitzhak Rabin** (yiht-SAHK rah-BEEN) and **Palestine Liberation Organization (PLO)** leader **Yassir Arafat** (YAH-sur AIR-uh-faht) to meet in Washington in hopes of easing high tensions between the Israelis and Palestinians. While there, Israeli and Palestinian representatives signed the Oslo Accord, granting limited self-rule for Palestinians in Gaza and the West Bank while promising withdrawal of Israeli troops from those areas.

On the domestic front, Clinton faced energized Republican opposition during the 1994 midterm elections, led by Representative **Newt Gingrich**. Gingrich's "Contract with America" promised tax cuts, welfare reform, and other typically Republican policies. Republicans won control of both houses of Congress in what one journalist called "the most consequential nonpresidential election of the 20th century."

HISTORICAL THINKING

1. **READING CHECK** What effect did H. Ross Perot's candidacy have on the outcome of the 1992 election?

2. **IDENTIFY PROBLEMS AND SOLUTIONS** What was one domestic problem President Clinton faced, and how did he try to solve it?

3. **MAKE INFERENCES** Why might the 1994 elections have been the "most consequential nonpresidential election of the 20th century"?

1.2 Crises and Responses

What happens when the federal government shuts down? National parks close their gates, important medical research halts, and individuals have nowhere to turn for help with Social Security. Voters become very angry at those they hold responsible.

MAIN IDEA Re-elected in 1996, Clinton oversaw a healthy economy, helped resolve conflict in the Balkans, and remained president despite being impeached.

CHALLENGES AT HOME AND ABROAD

On April 19, 1995, the United States was shaken by a deadly terrorist attack. A former U.S. soldier, Timothy McVeigh, set off a car bomb next to the **Alfred P. Murrah Federal Building** in Oklahoma City, Oklahoma. The blast nearly destroyed the building, killing 168 people and injuring more than 500. McVeigh and his accomplice, Terry Nichols, were right-wing radicals who justified the attack as an act of self-defense against an oppressive government. After arrest and trial, Nichols was sentenced to life in prison. McVeigh was executed.

In that same year, Clinton again turned his attention to Europe and the international crisis in the Balkans. The conflict had escalated, but the Bosnian and Croat forces won their first victory over the Serbs in years. Clinton, who was previously accused of weak leadership in this crisis, sent representatives to the region to discuss peace. In November 1995, leaders of Bosnia, Serbia, and Croatia met with American and European representatives outside Dayton, Ohio. There, they worked out a peace plan. To enforce it, the United States and 25 other nations would send troops to the Balkans. In a speech, Clinton outlined the political and humanitarian reasons to send 20,000 troops. Congress agreed, and polls showed that Americans had greater confidence in Clinton.

During the dedication of the Oklahoma City National Memorial, an honor guard faces the field of memorial chairs that represent the 168 people who lost their lives in the bombing of the federal building.

Clinton's approval ratings also grew after Republicans forced a **government shutdown** that closed federal facilities. The country had a divided government. That is, one party controlled the presidency and the other controlled Congress. In November 1995, budget negotiations between Clinton and the Republican-controlled Congress failed. Clinton vetoed the budget Congress had passed. With no budget, the government could not pay its employees or its bills, so federal offices and agencies had to close. After five days, both sides agreed to end the shutdown and continue negotiations. Clinton was willing to compromise, but many Americans saw the Republicans as stubbornly demanding their budget, which included tax cuts and limits to Medicare growth.

A National Park Service employee posts a sign in front of the Lincoln Memorial in Washington, D.C., during a government shutdown in 2013. As during the 1995 shutdown, many federal facilities, including national parks, were closed because Congress failed to pass a funding bill.

A second government shutdown lasted 21 days, during which most federal employees stopped receiving paychecks. Republicans in Congress finally gave in, accepting a budget similar to the one they had originally rejected. Voters were angry and frustrated.

RE-ELECTION AND IMPEACHMENT

In the 1996 election, Senator Bob Dole ran as the Republican candidate. Clinton won the election with 49 percent of the vote to Dole's 41 percent. H. Ross Perot ran again, receiving 8 percent of the vote. Republicans kept control of Congress, so Clinton again faced a divided government. Still, he entered his second term with a strong economy, which would produce budget surpluses from 1998 to 2001.

But scandal plagued Clinton's second term. Questions were raised about some financial deals Clinton and his wife had made. In 1998, independent counsel Kenneth Starr began investigating these deals but found no evidence they were illegal. Then he began pursuing tips that Clinton had had a romantic relationship with a young White House intern. Clinton denied the relationship. Eventually, investigators found solid evidence. Clinton apologized to the nation and his family. Based on Starr's report, the House approved impeachment against Clinton for perjury and obstruction of justice. In 1999, the Senate acquitted him, and his approval ratings remained high.

In 1999, Clinton again faced challenges in the Balkans. Serbian forces were conducting mass killings of ethnic Albanians in the Serbian province of Kosovo. Clinton and other world leaders worked with NATO to authorize a bombing campaign against Serbia that led to UN intervention in Kosovo's government. In 2008, Kosovo became independent. Clinton's leadership in dealing with Kosovo enhanced his reputation in foreign affairs.

HISTORICAL THINKING

1. **READING CHECK** What two events in 1995 helped improve President Clinton's approval ratings?

2. **ANALYZE CAUSE AND EFFECT** What was the main cause of the government shutdowns?

3. **FORM AND SUPPORT OPINIONS** Do you think Clinton's decision to participate in a bombing campaign against Serbia was necessary? Support your opinion.

The Contested Election of 2000

You run for class president and lose by one vote out of hundreds.

Then you learn that some of your supporters had problems voting.

What's your next move?

MAIN IDEA The election of 2000 was so close that it had to be settled by a controversial Supreme Court decision, leading to an even more divided nation.

BUSH v. GORE

As the 2000 election approached, the economy was booming and the federal budget had a surplus. Running on Clinton's economic and foreign policy successes, Vice President **Albert (Al) Gore** won the Democratic nomination. The Republicans ran Texas governor **George W. Bush**, son of former president George H.W. Bush, as their candidate.

Bush promised tax cuts, saying he could make up the resulting lost revenue with more efficient government. Gore argued that only the wealthiest Americans would benefit from Bush's tax cuts. On foreign policy, Bush favored the views of the **neoconservatives**, who believed the United States should assert its military power to promote its interests and overthrow anti-American

governments. Gore claimed these were Cold War ideas and no longer relevant. He advocated a foreign policy that focused more on diplomacy.

The close election ultimately hinged on who would win Florida's 25 electoral votes. In the final popular vote count, Bush led by only about 600 votes out of about 6 million. With such a close tally, Florida law required a recount, which showed Bush's lead as 327 votes.

During that first recount, officials discovered that some punch card ballots were incorrectly punched. A small fragment of paper, called a "chad," was still attached where many of the holes were meant to be. Voting machines may have failed to count votes with these "hanging chads." So the Florida Supreme Court ordered a recount

The Election of 2000

Albert (Al) Gore (Democrat)

Electoral Vote: 266 votes, 49.4%
Popular Vote: 50,992,335 votes, 48.4%

George W. Bush (Republican)

Electoral Vote: 271 votes, 50.4%
Popular Vote: 50,455,156 votes, 47.9%

Ralph Nader (Green)

Popular Vote: 2,882,738 votes, 2.7%

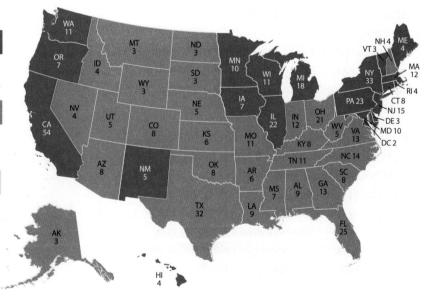

by hand of ballots from several counties. Officials had to examine each card by hand and assign it a vote, if possible. Bush appealed to the U.S. Supreme Court, asking that the recount be halted. In *Bush* v. *Gore*, the Court reversed the Florida recount order, awarding Bush the presidency.

Many people believe that **Ralph Nader**, the Green Party candidate in 2000, played a part in Gore's loss. He received only 2.74 percent of the popular vote, but his votes in New Hampshire and Florida suggest that had he not run, Gore would have won those states and, presumably, the election. Nader's supporters argued that if Nader hadn't run, they might not have voted for Gore anyway.

A DIVIDED NATION

Bush v. *Gore* divided the nation even more. The justices who made the decision to stop the recount had all been appointed by Republican presidents. Bush had lost the national popular vote, so he came into office without widespread support. Many hoped he would try to bring the nation together, but instead, he issued a divisive executive order creating the Office of Faith-Based and Community Initiatives. The order provided funds for church-affiliated schools, an action that many Americans felt violated the Constitution's First Amendment. This move represented the beginning of Bush's plan to increase the power of the presidency through executive action.

After the hard-fought 2000 election, divisions among Americans were symbolized by the "red state–blue state" pattern on electoral maps. Before 2000, mapmakers had used various colors to show which way the states voted. But after 2000, states with Democratic majorities were colored blue, and states with Republican majorities were colored red. The red-blue symbolism has become part of American politics, though many people think it creates an oversimplified view.

Bush kept his promise to cut taxes, successfully pushing $1.35 trillion in cuts through Congress in 2001 and $350 billion more in 2003. These tax cuts reduced government revenue, erased the budget surpluses, and created deficits, all of which contributed to recessions in 2002 and 2008. However, disagreements over taxes and policies were overshadowed in 2001 by an event that horrified and briefly unified the nation.

On November 8, the day after the 2000 election, Texas governor and presidential candidate George W. Bush walked out of the governor's mansion to meet with reporters for a news conference in Austin, Texas. The U.S. Supreme Court upheld Bush's election to the presidency on December 12.

HISTORICAL THINKING

1. **READING CHECK** What were the two main issues on which the candidates differed during the 2000 presidential election?

2. **INTERPRET MAPS** Examine the 2000 election map. Why would Gore have won the election if he had won Florida?

3. **MAKE INFERENCES** Why did the Florida Supreme Court rule that the problem ballots had to be recounted by hand?

2.1 September 11, 2001

Most of us feel relaxed, even happy, when we spend time in parks, theaters, and restaurants. When terrorists strike, their goal is to make people feel afraid and tense in everyday places such as these, often through violent acts.

MAIN IDEA On September 11, 2001, terrorists staged a massive attack on New York City and Washington, D.C., leading President Bush to initiate a "war on terror."

ATTACKS ON NEW YORK AND WASHINGTON

On September 11, 2001, terrorists crashed two hijacked airplanes into the two 110-story buildings known as the twin towers of New York City's World Trade Center. Others from the same group crashed another plane into the Pentagon in Washington, D.C. Hijackers had captured a fourth plane and diverted it toward Washington, D.C., but the passengers fought back, causing the plane to crash in a Pennsylvania field instead of into its intended target. The terrorist group **al Qaeda** and its leader, **Osama bin Laden**, had planned the attacks.

Terrorism is the use of threats and violence against civilians as a way of achieving political goals. Terrorists commonly stage attacks in crowded public locations, hoping to spread fear and force political change. Many terrorist groups that follow a radical fundamentalist form of Islam profess hatred toward the United States and other Western countries. Al Qaeda is one of these groups.

September 11 (9/11) was not the first attack on the World Trade Center. On February 26, 1993, terrorists detonated a car bomb in the center's underground garage, killing six and injuring more than a thousand. In the deadlier 9/11 attacks, the

Almost two weeks after the collapse of the World Trade Center, rescue workers confronted the enormity of their task as they sifted through the rubble, looking for the thousands of people still missing.

The Pentagon, Washington, D.C.

The Pentagon is the headquarters of the Department of Defense and houses the offices of the U.S. Army, Navy, Air Force, and Marines. It was built after President Franklin D. Roosevelt asked for a central headquarters for the War Department following Germany's invasion of the Soviet Union in 1941. The five-sided shape echoes the design of various U.S. forts, including Fort Sumter. On September 11, 2001, a hijacked passenger jet crashed into one of its walls at more than 500 miles per hour. Next to the Pentagon is the National 9/11 Pentagon Memorial, which consists of a steel bench for each of the 184 people killed in the attack.

twin towers collapsed with many people trapped inside. Clouds of debris billowed through the streets as frightened people fled. Many **first responders**, the people such as firefighters and police officers who are first on the scene in an emergency, died when the buildings fell. Others contracted fatal illnesses from the resulting toxic dust. The death toll was more than 2,750 people in New York City, more than 180 at the Pentagon, and 40 in the Pennsylvania plane crash.

RESPONDING TO TERRORISM

The attacks of 9/11 brought Americans together in sorrow and anger, and at first, President Bush maintained that unity. Some of his actions re-established the rift, however. In October 2001, he signed the **Patriot Act** into law. The act gave the government broad powers to fight terrorism, including expanded abilities to search people's phone, email, and financial records without a court order. Many Americans feared these powers came at the price of civil liberties. A year later, Congress established the **Department of Homeland Security (DHS)**.

Sparked by 9/11, Bush's war on terror began by unleashing air strikes and troops on Afghanistan, where the extremist Islamic **Taliban** government harbored al Qaeda and Osama bin Laden. The Taliban fell, but American forces remained in the country to support the Afghan government and counter antigovernment forces. Some Afghans resented the presence of Americans, especially when innocent Afghan civilians were killed as different factions within the country attacked the U.S. troops.

Bush next targeted Iraq, insisting it had ties to al Qaeda and possessed **weapons of mass destruction (WMD)**. Iraqi president Saddam Hussein accepted UN demands for inspections, which revealed no WMD, but Bush continued to press for war despite opposition from the international community and many Americans. In 2003, the United States and Great Britain launched an offensive against Iraq, and in three weeks they controlled the country. U.S. leaders had no detailed plans for the occupation, however, and Iraqi **insurgents**, or rebels, attacked U.S. forces. By 2008, almost 4,000 U.S. troops had been killed and many more wounded. No WMD were found.

In 2004, Bush narrowly won re-election against Democrat John Kerry. But the Iraq war dragged on, and revelations that Iraqi prisoners were being tortured created a scandal. Bush's poll numbers declined steeply. Then, in 2005, a massive hurricane struck the Gulf Coast.

HISTORICAL THINKING

1. **READING CHECK** Why did President Bush send U.S. forces to Afghanistan and Iraq?

2. **ANALYZE CAUSE AND EFFECT** What events contributed to President Bush's falling popularity in the years after the 9/11 attacks?

3. **FORM AND SUPPORT OPINIONS** What alternatives to invading Iraq might President Bush have chosen? Support your opinion.

2.2 How Geology Affects Flooding

MAIN IDEA The geology of New Orleans made the city especially vulnerable to Hurricane Katrina.

By Andrés Ruzo, **National Geographic Explorer**

A BRUTAL STORM

The storm that came to be known as Hurricane Katrina battered the Gulf Coast on August 29, 2005, and was one of the deadliest hurricanes in U.S. history. It resulted in nearly 2,000 deaths and displaced hundreds of thousands of people from their homes. Katrina also caused an estimated $100 billion in damage, making it the nation's costliest natural disaster. The slow response of President Bush and government agencies to come to the aid of those affected by the storm in New Orleans, Louisiana, compounded Katrina's impact. Stranded in their homes and in shelters, many people in the city waited desperately for help. The president's failure to deal efficiently with the emergency greatly hurt his reputation.

As it happened, New Orleans was spared a direct hit by the storm. The city didn't experience the extreme winds and heavy rain that other places in the region endured. Nevertheless, New Orleans sustained more deaths and damage than any other location in Katrina's path. This destruction was caused by floodwaters. On August 29, 20 percent of the city had flooded. By the next day, about 80 percent was underwater.

IMPACT ON NEW ORLEANS

So what caused the terrible flooding in New Orleans? The answer lies, in part, with the city's geology. New Orleans is situated between Lake Pontchartrain (PAHN-shuh-trayn) and the Mississippi River. Over thousands of years,

CRITICAL VIEWING On August 31, the high waters that resulted from Hurricane Katrina broke through this artificial levee in New Orleans, causing the structure to give way. In many parts of the city, the floodwaters did not recede for weeks. What details in the photo help convey the devastation the storm inflicted on New Orleans?

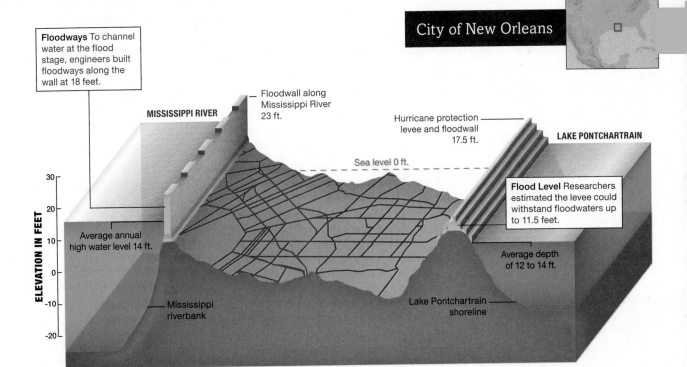

Floodways To channel water at the flood stage, engineers built floodways along the wall at 18 feet.

Floodwall along Mississippi River 23 ft.

MISSISSIPPI RIVER

Hurricane protection levee and floodwall 17.5 ft.

LAKE PONTCHARTRAIN

Sea level 0 ft.

Flood Level Researchers estimated the levee could withstand floodwaters up to 11.5 feet.

Average annual high water level 14 ft.

Average depth of 12 to 14 ft.

ELEVATION IN FEET

30 — 20 — 10 — 0 — -10 — -20

Mississippi riverbank

Lake Pontchartrain shoreline

Source: Tulane University

natural **levees**, or ridges of earth that run along the sides of a stream or river, had built up around the area as the Mississippi overflowed and deposited soil along its edges. In time, this process created higher ground on the riverbank. In 1718, New Orleans was founded on this natural high ground to protect the city from being flooded by the Mississippi.

As New Orleans grew, however, some of the surrounding swamps and wetlands were drained to provide more land. But while the original city lies about 17 feet above sea level, the newer areas are about 6 feet below sea level. Floodwaters can easily flow into the low-lying areas of New Orleans. To help prevent floods, engineers developed a system of pumps to remove the water and canals to channel it out. In the 20th century, they also built artificial levees to hold back the waters of Lake Pontchartrain and the Mississippi. As a result, roughly half of New Orleans sits below sea level in a sort of bowl, surrounded by these levees. Any water entering the bowl would be hard to drain.

That's just what happened when Hurricane Katrina struck. The storm dumped 10 inches of rain on New Orleans and created a **storm surge**, or an abnormal rise of the water level, in Lake Pontchartrain. This surge caused the lake to rise 30 feet in some places. The sheer volume of water overwhelmed many of the lake's levees.

Floodwaters breached, or broke through, the levees and spilled over them. Water also seeped into the soil beneath some of the levees, washing sections of them away. Most of the original city experienced relatively little flooding. However, other parts flooded so badly that people tried to escape the high waters by climbing onto the roofs of their homes.

It is likely that another major hurricane will hit New Orleans in the future. Since Katrina, engineers have repaired the levees and improved the structures' ability to hold back floodwaters. For example, engineers have increased the height of some of the levees and topped them with rock or concrete to prevent erosion by waves. But protecting New Orleans from the next big hurricane needs to be an ongoing process. Experts warn that the city is going to keep sinking below sea level. In some ways, geology is working against keeping New Orleans dry.

THINK LIKE A GEOLOGIST

1. **IDENTIFY MAIN IDEAS AND DETAILS** What steps did engineers take to try to prevent New Orleans from flooding before Hurricane Katrina?

2. **ANALYZE CAUSE AND EFFECT** Why did the geology of New Orleans lead to flooding in some parts of the city and not others?

Preserving New Orleans Through Oral Histories

"I dedicate my life to cultural preservation because I want to pass on history and traditions to future generations." —Caroline Gerdes

As a National Geographic Explorer, Caroline Gerdes journeys through her hometown of New Orleans, Louisiana, to understand what life was like for 20th-century immigrants. But the clock is ticking. Many of the immigrants who helped make New Orleans a cultural "hot spot" are now elderly. Additionally, Hurricane Katrina's destruction reduced a neighborhood called the Ninth Ward to rubble. Gerdes's mission is to document the beauty of the Ninth Ward, before it is lost forever.

^
While much of the Ninth Ward in New Orleans has been rebuilt since Hurricane Katrina struck in 2005, ruined and abandoned houses like this one are still a common sight.

MAIN IDEA National Geographic Explorer Caroline Gerdes captures the oral histories of a generation of New Orleans residents.

Journalist and oral historian Caroline Gerdes was born and raised in the greater New Orleans area. In 2005, Hurricane Katrina struck the city. Gerdes was just 15 years old. Her family evacuated their home, which was miraculously left standing. But most other residents were not so lucky, including her grandmother, who was able to salvage little after the disaster. In all, more than 1,400 people in Louisiana were killed in Hurricane Katrina. Most of them were elderly, and many of them drowned.

Hurricane Katrina did more than take lives. It destroyed homes, businesses, restaurants, and schools—whole communities. The place it hit the hardest was the Lower Ninth Ward. That's where Gerdes's father and paternal grandparents had grown up. As a child, Gerdes listened to her grandmother's stories about the Italian market, her uncle's jazz club, and other incredible places in her community. Those places are no longer standing—they exist only in memories now.

Living through Hurricane Katrina helped shape Caroline Gerdes as a person. "I am a writer and an explorer, in many ways because of Katrina. At a young age, I learned that we are shaped by our experiences, and we don't always have a choice in what we can take with us. But, upon closer inspection, we can find something in the bleakest of places and make it beautiful again."

That's just what Gerdes set out to do. In a partnership with National Geographic, she conducted an oral history project in the Ninth Ward to capture the feel of the area. She couldn't take photographs to show what the area once was—that time had come and gone. But many of the immigrants who had created the Lower Ninth Ward, shaping its history, culture, and communities, still lived there.

The Lower Ninth Ward was the subject of many news reports during and after Hurricane Katrina, so it is best known for the destruction it endured. However, this area was culturally rich for decades before Katrina, and Gerdes set out to explore that richness. She spoke with many people who shared stories about the community's history—both the

Caroline Gerdes discusses her book, *An Oral History of the New Orleans Ninth Ward,* at the National Geographic Society in Washington, D.C., in 2017.

bad events and the good. She learned about immigrant settlements, jazz music, food, faith, the Great Depression, Prohibition, desegregation, and, of course, hurricanes.

The Ninth Ward was made up of immigrant populations—French, Sicilian, African-American, Hispanic, Jewish, German, Irish, and many others. Overflowing with culture, it was a community full of life. After Katrina, it became lifeless and desolate. "The Lower Ninth Ward . . . has never regained its pre-Katrina population," Gerdes explains. "In addition to fractured streets, many homes remain abandoned. Nature has taken over. Trees envelop flood-worn homes." But the people of New Orleans are resilient. And while the Ninth Ward may no longer be the thriving cultural hub it was before Katrina, life is returning to New Orleans.

Gerdes's book, *An Oral History of the New Orleans Ninth Ward*, was published in April 2017.

HISTORICAL THINKING

1. **READING CHECK** Why is Gerdes concerned about capturing the oral history of the Ninth Ward?

2. **MAKE INFERENCES** How can a natural event impact the culture of a region?

3. **SYNTHESIZE** If you could take an oral history from anyone, who would it be? Explain your choice and what you would hope to learn.

3.1 The Election of Barack Obama

American children are often told that anyone can grow up to be president. All of the first 43 U.S. presidents, however, were white males. That trend was broken in 2008.

MAIN IDEA In the eventful year 2008, the United States slipped deeper into recession, and Barack Obama was elected as the country's first African-American president.

President Barack Obama and First Lady Michelle Obama smile and wave at the people lining the route of the traditional Inaugural Parade in Washington, D.C. Held on January 20, 2009, the inauguration of the 44th president of the United States was attended by about 1.8 million people.

A HISTORIC CAMPAIGN

The year 2008 opened on a pessimistic note in the United States. The unpopular war in Iraq was dragging into its sixth year, and a recession was pulling down the economy. These factors gave Democrats an advantage in the approaching presidential election.

A two-way race for the Democratic nomination developed between former First Lady and New York senator Hillary Clinton and Illinois senator **Barack Obama**. Clinton, the wife of former president Bill Clinton, was the early favorite. She faced many obstacles, however, including anger over her vote in the Senate in favor of the U.S. invasion of Iraq.

Obama was relatively unknown at the start of the campaign, but he soon won a large and enthusiastic following. An inspiring speaker, he offered a message of hope and change that struck a chord with many voters. Unlike Clinton, he had opposed the war in Iraq from the beginning. And unlike any major presidential candidate before him, he was biracial. His mother was white, and his father was African, born in Kenya. The race was very close, but Obama emerged as the Democratic nominee. He chose Delaware senator Joe Biden as his running mate.

In the Republican primary elections, Senator John McCain, a former prisoner of war during the Vietnam War, pulled away from seven other candidates to win his party's nomination. For his running mate, McCain selected the governor of Alaska, Sarah Palin.

THE GREAT RECESSION

As Obama and McCain squared off, the recession that had begun in late 2007 worsened dramatically. The **Great Recession**, as it came to be known, developed into the nation's worst economic downturn since the Great Depression. In large part, the recession was rooted in the housing market. In the years immediately leading up to the crisis, more people wanted to buy houses, which caused home prices to rise sharply. The belief that they would keep rising had fueled speculation, or risky investing in the hope of making big profits. Banks had put themselves in danger by making large numbers of **subprime** home loans—that is, loans to borrowers with poor credit ratings.

Other economic issues, some of which had been developing for decades, contributed to the Great Recession. Lenders had been making increasing use of certain risky financial practices, for example. In addition, consumers were taking on greater debt, but their wages had failed to increase for several years.

By 2007, large numbers of homeowners discovered that they could not afford their mortgage payments. To make matters worse, the market had cooled and home prices were dropping. People were forced to sell their houses for less than what they had paid in the first place. As **loan defaults**, or failures to repay mortgages, increased, the economy fell into chaos. Many small banks failed, and other industries took severe hits. Shrinking revenues pushed some states to the brink of bankruptcy. Millions of Americans lost their jobs, their homes, and their savings.

To prevent the country's biggest banks from failing, Congress passed the Emergency Economic Stabilization Act (EESA) in 2008. This legislation provided the U.S. Secretary of the Treasury up to $700 billion to buy risky mortgages and other potentially poor investments from banks and other financial institutions, saving them from collapse.

On the campaign trail, Barack Obama impressed many voters with his focused, confident response to the economic crisis. At the same time, many blamed the Republicans for the Great Recession because they were the party in power during the buildup and the crash. Obama won the election with 53% of the popular vote and 365 electoral votes, becoming the first African-American president in the country's history.

HISTORICAL THINKING

1. **READING CHECK** How did Hillary Clinton and Barack Obama differ in their positions on the war in Iraq?

2. **IDENTIFY PROBLEMS AND SOLUTIONS** What problem did the Emergency Economic Stabilization Act address, and how?

3. **ANALYZE LANGUAGE USE** What are the root and prefix of the word *subprime*, and what do they mean?

3.2 Recovery and Reform

The president is sometimes called "the captain of the ship of state." President Barack Obama became captain at a time when the ship seemed in danger of sinking.

MAIN IDEA After taking office as president, Barack Obama focused on pulling the country out of a recession and reforming the health care system.

RECOVERING FROM THE RECESSION

Barack Obama inherited the worst economy since Franklin D. Roosevelt took office in 1933. Obama's priority was to lead the country out of the crippling recession that had begun more than a year earlier. As the Democratic president, Obama could expect cooperation from Congress because his party had gained firm control of both the House of Representatives and the Senate.

Just days after Obama's inauguration, House Democrats introduced a major bill aimed at stimulating the economy. Although every House Republican voted against it, the bill passed easily. Two weeks later, the bill made it through the Senate. Three Republicans and two independents joined all the Democratic senators in voting yes. On February 17, 2009, Obama signed the bill into law as the **American Recovery and Reinvestment Act (ARRA)**.

Totaling $787 billion, this **economic stimulus** package was the largest in U.S. history. It sought to save existing jobs, create new ones, and encourage long-term economic growth. In addition to authorizing tax cuts, it included payments to states and localities to help fund community programs, an increase in infrastructure projects such as the construction of roads and schools, and funds to enhance energy independence.

By summer 2009, the recession had officially ended. Recovery, however, was slow. Millions of Americans remained unemployed or under-employed. In fact, the unemployment level climbed for several more months to 10 percent before slowly beginning to drop in early 2010. By late 2015, unemployment had reached its pre-recession level of 5 percent.

HEALTH CARE REFORM

Another of President Obama's priorities was health care reform. In a speech to Congress in September 2009, he pointed out that more than 30 million Americans lacked health insurance. He spoke of the devastating cost of health care and the waste within the medical system and accused insurance companies of unethical practices.

In November, a sweeping health care reform bill squeaked through the House of Representatives. Then, on December 24, the Senate approved a significantly different version of the bill. Congressional Republicans fiercely opposed it, but the determined efforts of House Speaker Nancy Pelosi and President Obama kept it alive.

Finally, in March 2010, the House passed the Senate version of the bill, and Obama signed the **Patient Protection and Affordable Care Act (ACA)** into law. It came to be known as **Obamacare**. Its aim was to broaden health insurance coverage by making it more affordable and easier to obtain through online exchanges, or marketplaces. The government also provided subsidies, or money to help people pay for insurance. The ACA sought to end discriminatory insurance practices such as denial of coverage for preexisting conditions and limits on how much a policy would pay in a lifetime. To help low-income citizens, states were given the option to apply for federal grants to expand Medicaid.

Early in Obama's presidency, a conservative populist movement arose to oppose the new president and his progressive agenda. It was known as the **Tea Party**, a connection with the patriots of the Revolutionary era. Its members were united in their belief that the American

The American Recovery and Reinvestment Act (ARRA)

Infrastructure projects funded by the ARRA included bridge repairs and expansions, like the one shown below. Signs erected alongside these projects identified the ARRA as their financial source. A primary goal of the ARRA was to jump-start the economy and save or create 3.5 million jobs. Toward that goal, about 65 percent of the act's appropriations were spent investing in activities that would stimulate the economy. The remaining amount went to tax cuts. The pie chart at right shows the major categories Congress chose to fund.

Major Categories Funded by the ARRA

Education and Training
$105.9 billion

Infrastructure and Science
$120.0 billion

Law enforcement, oversight, and other programs
$7.8 billion

Health
$14.2 billion

Helping Americans most severely hit by the economic crisis
$24.3 billion

Energy
$37.5 billion

An infrastructure project near Warsaw, Kentucky, 2009

PUTTING AMERICA TO WORK

PROJECT FUNDED BY THE American Recovery and Reinvestment Act

USDOT TIGER

people were victims of excessive taxation and too much government intervention. The Tea Party objected to the amount of money the government was spending to fight the recession. It supported stronger controls over immigration and objected to reforms to the health care system. Most Tea Party members were Republicans.

Energized by the fast-growing movement, Republicans made historic gains in the 2010 midterm elections. They gained 6 seats in the Senate and took control of the House by gaining 63 seats there. The federal government was once again divided.

HISTORICAL THINKING

1. **READING CHECK** What was the biggest challenge facing Barack Obama when he took office as president?

2. **IDENTIFY PROBLEMS AND SOLUTIONS** What were some of the problems that President Obama hoped to solve through the reform of health care?

3. **ANALYZE DATA** Which two categories in the pie chart received the most funding, and why do you think they were given that much?

3.3 Serving Others

We often look to our leaders to bring about positive change. In turn, leaders sometimes remind us that every citizen can make a difference through public service. In his 1961 inaugural address, President John F. Kennedy famously made this request to Americans: "Ask not what your country can do for you—ask what you can do for your country."

In different words but with the same intention, American leaders have reminded citizens of the rewards that come with helping others. President Barack Obama was one of the many government and civilian leaders who continued this tradition of encouraging Americans to become involved in community service.

CRITICAL VIEWING A Houston, Texas, SWAT officer carries a mother and her baby to safety after rescuing them from their flooded home. In 2017, civilians and officers took to the streets to help people caught by the drenching rains and high winds of Hurricane Harvey. Describe the dangers visible in this photograph.

DOCUMENT ONE

Primary Source: Speech
from President Barack Obama's inaugural address,
January 20, 2009

In his inaugural address, Obama spoke of Americans who embody "the spirit of service" through their "willingness to find meaning in something greater than themselves." This spirit, he continued, "must inhabit us all."

CONSTRUCTED RESPONSE

What does President Obama suggest about the types of people who can perform public service?

For as much as government can do, and must do, it is ultimately the faith and determination of the American people upon which this nation relies. It is the kindness to take in a stranger when the levees break, the selflessness of workers who would rather cut their hours than see a friend lose their job which sees us through our darkest hours. It is the firefighter's courage to storm a stairway filled with smoke, but also a parent's willingness to nurture a child that finally decides our fate.

DOCUMENT TWO

Primary Source: Speech
from First Lady Laura Bush's address to the Global Literacy
Conference in New York, September 18, 2006

Laura Bush was a teacher and school librarian before she met and married George W. Bush. As First Lady, she strongly supported literacy programs not only within the United States but also throughout the world. She also established the Laura Bush Foundation for America's Libraries to help the neediest school libraries.

CONSTRUCTED RESPONSE

Why does Laura Bush encourage her audience to teach by example?

Investing in literacy and education helps governments meet their fundamental obligations, by improving opportunities for children and families, by strengthening their economies, and by keeping their citizens in good health. . . . Today, as we discuss how to improve educational opportunities around the world, it's important to remember that we're all teachers. A person who's never stood by a blackboard still teaches by example. By demonstrating our commitment to literacy, we can let millions of people know that reading and writing are important, and we can help build a healthier, more prosperous, and more hopeful world.

DOCUMENT THREE

Primary Source: Interview
from The Gathering's interview with former NBA star
David Robinson, May 19, 2005

After a stellar career with the San Antonio Spurs, David Robinson retired from basketball in 2003. He and his wife then founded the Carver Academy, a K–12 school serving a poor inner-city area of San Antonio, Texas.

CONSTRUCTED RESPONSE

Why does Robinson think that children should be taught to use their talents to serve other people?

Why can't we teach [children] that the most important thing they can ever do with their lives is to use their talents to serve other people? There are plenty of role models out there who have done just that. George Washington Carver, the African-American botanist whom we named the academy after, helped farmers produce a wide range of crops through his inventions, thereby promoting better health and sound nutrition for all Americans.

SYNTHESIZE & WRITE

1. **REVIEW** Review what you have learned about volunteerism and serving others.

2. **RECALL** On your own paper, write down the main idea presented in each document and in the photograph.

3. **CONSTRUCT** Construct a topic sentence that answers this question: Why is it important to serve others?

4. **WRITE** Write a paragraph that supports the statement in step 3. Use evidence from the documents to support your statement.

4.1 From Computers to Social Media

Website, search engine, blog, social media, unfriend. You won't find any of these terms in a dictionary published before 1990. The explosion of new tech terms since that year reflects the tremendous speed at which the world has been changing.

MAIN IDEA The invention of the computer, the creation of the Internet, and the birth of social media led to major changes in American work and society.

DEVELOPMENT OF THE COMPUTER

Along with radio and television, the computer ranks as one of the most significant electronic inventions of the 20th century. Computers have transformed the way people learn, work, shop, interact with one another, and spend their free time.

One of the earliest general-purpose electronic digital computers was built during World War II by a team at the University of Pennsylvania. This enormous and enormously complex machine was known as ENIAC, or Electronic Numerical Integrator and Computer. It measured about 130 feet in length and used 18,000 vacuum tubes to control its electric current. Its main function was to calculate the paths that bombs would follow after they were launched.

The 1947 invention of the transistor, a little device that regulates and switches electrical current, allowed for the production of computers that were smaller, faster, more accurate, and more energy efficient. Another key development was the invention of the integrated circuit (IC), or computer chip, in the late 1950s. An IC packed numerous transistors onto a small surface.

By the late 1970s, several companies, including Apple, Inc., had begun selling computers for home use. These devices came to be known as personal computers (PCs). International Business Machines (IBM), the world's largest computer manufacturer, entered the PC market in 1981. As people learned how useful PCs could be, sales began to skyrocket and prices dropped, making the machines more affordable for the average family.

THE INTERNET AND SOCIAL MEDIA

In the late 1950s and early 1960s, some government agencies and large companies began to create networks of computers that could share information with one another. One of the first general-purpose networks was the U.S. Department of Defense's ARPANET, which was first used in 1969. Within a few years, computer engineers had worked out ways to connect networks to one another. The expanding "network of networks" came to be known as the **Internet**.

In the late 1980s and early 1990s, a British computer scientist named Tim Berners-Lee led the development of a system that allowed sites or documents to be identified by individual addresses. That made it possible to link sites to one another in the way we are used to seeing today. The result was the **World Wide Web**. Usage of the web expanded rapidly after the introduction of Mosaic, a free, user-friendly browser developed at the University of Illinois. A **browser** is a computer program that helps users navigate the Internet.

After becoming available to the general public in 1991, the Internet exploded in popularity. People eagerly took to email and online shopping. Computer programs called search engines provided easy and instant access to a world of

information. The Internet's impact on society increased dramatically in the early 2000s with the birth of **social media** . This term refers to services, such as Twitter, Facebook, and Instagram, that enable people to interact on electronic devices.

Groups and individuals use social media to express their opinions as well as to share personal news. As a result, issues of privacy and free speech have arisen. Social media companies and the government are grappling with questions about what types of speech on the Internet are protected when they cause personal offense or even harm. The framers of the First Amendment could never have imagined the conflicts between allowing free speech and defending against online bullying, for example.

Like computer technology, mobile telephone technology advanced rapidly after World War II. The introduction of cell phones—handheld mobile phones that use cellular network technology—in the mid-1980s meant that people could make and receive phone calls from any location. The communication revolution took another leap forward in the early 1990s with the emergence of smartphones. These devices combine the features of a cell phone with those of a handheld computer. By 2017, more than three-quarters of Americans owned a smartphone.

🏛 Smithsonian American Art Museum, Washington, D.C.

Nam June Paik, a Korean American video artist, created the work above, titled *Electronic Superhighway*, in 1995. It consists of 336 television monitors displaying scenes from across the United States and from famous films that took place in specific states. Paik has taken the centuries-old idea of a map and presented it in a new way for an audience that lives in a tightly networked world. His creation is a virtual experience of driving across the country on its superhighways.

HISTORICAL THINKING

1. **READING CHECK** Why is the Internet described as a "network of networks"?

2. **ANALYZE CAUSE AND EFFECT** How did changes in electronic technology affect American society?

3. **FORM AND SUPPORT OPINIONS** Do you think the effects of social media on society are mostly positive or mostly negative? Support your opinion with evidence from the text and from your own experiences.

Computer History Museum
Mountain View, California

outer History Museum is aptly located
nia's Silicon Valley—the home of Apple,
nd other major technology corporations.
timedia exhibitions, the museum tells the
the companies, people, and equipment
e up computer history.

Museum visitors can play computer game
experiment with coding, and view demons
The museum also offers extensive online e
How does the equipment shown on these
compare with the digital devices you use ir
home and classroom today?

Apple I

Electronics engineer and Apple Computer co-founder Steve Wozniak, or "Woz," showed
the first Apple I prototype to the Homebrew Computer Club in 1976. Interested members
got a blank printed circuit board, some parts, and a 16-page assembly manual. Wozniak
showed them how to assemble the computers and add a keyboard, display screen, and
power supply. When a store in Mountain View, California, ordered
00 assembled Apple I computers, Wozniak and his friend Steve
Jobs sold some personal possessions to pay for parts and began
small-scale production to fill the order. The early computers were
sold for $666.66—and that was the start of Apple Computer.

> Research the functionality of the
> Apple I (shown here) and compare
> it to today's computers. How has
> computer technology evolved?

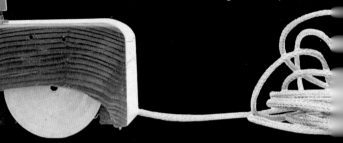

In 1961, American engineer and inventor Doug Engelbart came [up with a]
new idea for a tool to move a cursor on a computer screen. He e[nvisioned a]
simple, handheld mechanical device with a pair of small wheels [—one turning]
horizontally and one vertically when moved across a tabletop. B[ill English,]
the lead engineer of Engelbart's research team at Stanford Rese[arch]
Institute, built the first prototype of a mouse, shown here, in 196[4. It]
wasn't until the 1980s that the mouse came into general use. To[day, it is]
considered an essential tool for interacting with computers.

Inventor Doug Engelbart
cannot recall who named
the mouse. He says,
"It just looked like a
mouse with a tail, and
we all called it that."

Kenbak-1

In 1986, the Computer Museum in Boston held a contest
to answer the question "What was the first PC?" Judges
decided that the first personal computer was the Kenbak-1,
which was introduced in 1971. Working in his garage,
American computer engineer John Blankenbaker designed
and built the machine.

The Kenbak-1 had switches for
entering input and lights to
display output. Blankenbaker
intended his invention to
be educational, introducing
the user to computer
programming. But at a cost
of $750 each, only 40 of the
computers were sold.

The Kenbak-1 offered 256 bytes of
memory—or about 1,000 words.
How does that compare with the
memory of today's computers?

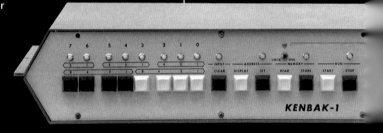

The Lisa

Along with some [other products,]
Apple has had a f[ew flops. In 1983,]
the company rele[ased the Lisa, the]
first commercial [personal computer]
featuring a graphi[cal user interface.]
Instead of typing [commands to]
operate the Lisa, [a user employed a]
mouse to direct a [cursor to click]
on windows, icon[s, and menus. Slow]
and expensive, th[e Lisa failed.]
Apple introduced [the Lisa]
2, shown here, in [1984. It faced]
stiff competition f[rom a computer]
called the Macint[osh, also released]
by Apple that yea[r.]

4.3 Challenges of Globalization

Despite its massive continents, vast oceans, and billions of people, our planet sometimes feels like a small world. Rapid shipping and instant communication make distant countries seem like they're just next door. But is this always a good thing?

MAIN IDEA Globalization has brought profound changes and ignited fierce debate about its pros and cons for the United States.

THE IMPACT OF GLOBALIZATION

One of the most powerful forces affecting the United States in the 21st century is **globalization**. This term refers to the fast and free flow of people, resources, goods, services, information, technology, and ideas across national borders.

Globalization is not a new trend. It was at work in the 15th century when the urge to colonize and explore swept Europe. But the pace of globalization has greatly increased in recent decades, due to several factors. One is the revolution in communication. Computers, the Internet, and cell phones make it far easier for people around the world to share information rapidly.

Another factor is the revolution in transportation. Transportation technology has advanced quickly since the mid-20th century, transforming the movement of people and goods around the world. High-speed rail lines now crisscross Japan, China, and Western Europe. Between 1970 and 2015, annual global air travel grew from 310 million passengers to 3.44 billion. With advances in shipping technology, goods, too, travel more cheaply, efficiently, and in higher volumes. Huge container ships and barges have increased the oceangoing commercial traffic.

A third factor is the growth of **free trade**, or the reduction or elimination of trade barriers, such as tariffs. This expansion has occurred through the creation of free trade zones such as the **European Union**, which facilitates trade among European member nations, and the North American Free Trade Agreement (NAFTA) zone that spans Mexico, Canada, and the United States. The **World Trade Organization** has also worked toward freer trade among its member countries, which account for roughly 90 percent of all world trade.

Most economists agree that free trade's benefits outweigh its drawbacks. NAFTA, for example, has increased trade between the United States and Mexico, enabling Americans to buy inexpensive goods and American businesses to invest in Mexican businesses. But not all Americans have benefited. Under NAFTA, some manufacturing jobs have moved from the United States and Canada to Mexico, where labor costs are lower.

The most challenging aspect of globalization, however, may be that it has enabled groups like al Qaeda to spread terrorism on a larger scale. As a result, the pursuit of terrorists has also become global. For example, during President Obama's administration, the search continued for Osama bin Laden, who planned the 9/11 terrorist bombings. In 2011, the U.S. military found the al Qaeda leader in Pakistan and killed him.

THE IMMIGRATION DEBATE

Migration and immigration are important aspects of globalization. Migration is the movement of people from one place to another. Immigration is the movement of people from one country to another. As you know, push-pull factors drive such movement. Push factors such as war, persecution, unstable governments, natural disasters, lack of jobs, and poverty cause people to leave their homes. Pull factors, which attract people to a country, include plentiful jobs, a good education, freedom, and the chance to build a better life.

In recent decades, immigration has again become the subject of heated debate in the United States. The number of unauthorized immigrants entering the country rose sharply toward the end of the 20th century. Many came from Mexico and Central America, including children sent by their parents to escape dangerous conditions in their homelands.

Critics argued that these immigrants took jobs away from Americans, increased crime rates, and burdened social services. Some studies suggest that these arguments have little basis in fact. Immigrants are often employed in low-paying service jobs and farm work, which are jobs that employers have trouble filling. Nevertheless, some people called for greater border security and government efforts to deport unauthorized immigrants. On the other hand, some Americans advocated offering these immigrants a legal path to earning citizenship.

During the 2010s, immigration growth leveled off. According to 2013 figures, of about 41 million immigrants living in the United States, 24.2 million were employed. Thirty percent of those people worked in management, professional, and related occupations, while the remaining 70 percent worked in service jobs, sales, office support, production, transportation, outdoor jobs, and maintenance. In 2012, unauthorized immigrants in the United States were estimated to be about 11.4 million, a small drop from the previous year.

Throughout the 2010s, the intense debates over immigration continued, and no single response was supported by a majority of people. In 2016, one candidate mobilized voters over concerns about unauthorized immigrants and won the Republican presidential nomination.

HISTORICAL THINKING

1. **READING CHECK** What are three main causes of the acceleration of globalization?

2. **MAKE PREDICTIONS** Do you think the trend toward globalization will continue? Support your prediction with facts from the text and your own knowledge or experience.

3. **MAKE CONNECTIONS** Immigration from Mexico dropped during the Great Recession. What do you think explains this drop?

CRITICAL VIEWING National Geographic photographer Kirsten Luce framed the moment a group of women and children from Central America were apprehended just after crossing the Rio Grande into Texas. Each year, thousands of women and children ask for entry to the United States. What do the details in this photo suggest about their journey?

4.4 The Election of 2016

Two historic candidates ran for president in 2016. One had no political experience and had never run for any elected office. The other was a woman. The election and its outcome exposed a severely divided nation.

MAIN IDEA Presidential candidate Donald Trump's campaign promise to "Make America Great Again" attracted enough voters to secure him the electoral vote and the presidency.

A POPULIST PREVAILS

Recall that a populist is someone who claims to represent the concerns of ordinary people. You have read about such populists as William Jennings Bryan and H. Ross Perot, who both staged unsuccessful presidential campaigns. **Donald Trump**, the controversial Republican candidate, ran a populist campaign in which he promised to use his business expertise to solve the nation's problems. But unlike previous populists, he won the 2016 presidential election, defeating Democrat Hillary Clinton.

Clinton was a former U.S. senator from New York who had also served as President Obama's secretary of state. She was the wife of former president Bill Clinton. Trump was a wealthy real estate developer and host of a popular television reality show. He had no political experience but had long been extremely outspoken in his views. As his running mate, Trump chose **Mike Pence**, the conservative governor of Indiana. Clinton's running mate was Tim Kaine, a senator from Virginia.

Trump's populist campaign rallies won the support of traditional Republicans and a number of independent voters. His ultra-nationalistic message, which strongly emphasized the superiority of the United States over all other nations, included promises to build a wall along the entire length of the border with Mexico, deport

CRITICAL VIEWING Donald Trump and Hillary Clinton take the stage for their second of three 2016 presidential debates. The debate was held at Washington University in St. Louis, Missouri, on October 9. The backdrop shows part of the Declaration of Independence. What do the candidates' expressions and body language convey in this photo?

undocumented immigrants, and ban foreign Muslims from entering the United States. He pledged to repeal the Affordable Care Act, put an end to NAFTA, and withdraw from a nuclear treaty with Iran. Trump also promised a swift end to international terrorism.

In the election, Trump won a narrow majority of voters in a number of **swing states**, or states where the election might go to either party. In the end, even though 3 million more Americans cast their votes for Clinton, Trump won the electoral vote 306 to 232.

In 2017, the March for Science took place on Earth Day, April 22, in cities throughout the United States. The march was organized in response to President Trump's promise that the United States would withdraw from international climate accords. In this photo, **Bill Nye**, the host of a children's television show about science, leads marchers.

THE EARLY TRUMP PRESIDENCY

Trump began his presidency by issuing a number of executive orders, including a controversial directive banning people from seven specified, primarily Muslim, nations from entering the United States. The order was issued and began to be enforced as many travelers were already on their way to the United States, causing massive confusion at airports. Federal courts initially blocked this order, stating it was unconstitutional. Parts of the ban were reinstated, and the government issued new versions of the ban in 2017. These were contested in federal courts.

Building on his campaign promises, Trump ordered the construction of a border wall with Mexico. But Congress approved only a small fraction of the funds needed. He also ordered a sharp increase in the number of **Immigration and Customs Enforcement (ICE)** agents, thus raising the deportation rate of undocumented immigrants. As of September 2017, his promised repeal of the Affordable Care Act had failed in Congress.

On the international front, Trump ended the **Trans-Pacific Partnership (TPP)**, a trade agreement with Asia. Although Trump had threatened to leave NAFTA, he decided it was better to try renegotiating it. Perhaps his most controversial claim was that he would withdraw the United States from international agreements on climate. This, along with his pledge to promote the use of coal and other fossil fuels, as opposed to the Obama administration's support of increased wind and solar power, put the United States at odds with many of its allies. Trump argued that NAFTA and climate accords cost U.S. jobs, but many experts believed that these agreements actually created new employment.

HISTORICAL THINKING

1. **READING CHECK** What role did swing states play in the election of 2016?

2. **MAKE INFERENCES** Why do you think Donald Trump appealed to so many independent voters?

3. **SUMMARIZE** How would you summarize Trump's presidency through the first part of 2017?

Climate Change and Energy Choices

For decades, scientists made predictions about the effects of rising global temperatures. Many of these predictions are now coming true. Climate change is a reality, and it is having a major impact on our planet.

MAIN IDEA Two of the biggest issues facing the United States in the 21st century are how to address climate change and how to achieve greater energy independence.

WARMING TEMPERATURES

In the 19th century, scientists began to study what we now call the **greenhouse effect**. It works like this: Carbon dioxide, methane, ozone, and other greenhouse gases in Earth's atmosphere allow sunlight to pass through, but they trap heat radiated back from Earth's surface. This trapping warms the lower atmosphere. Scientists established that burning carbon-based fossil fuels, such as coal, oil, and natural gas, intensifies the greenhouse effect.

Scientific monitoring that began in the mid-20th century shows that the concentration of carbon dioxide in the atmosphere has increased dramatically. Ocean and air temperatures are rising. The vast ice sheets that cover Antarctica and Greenland are shrinking, and the sea ice in the Arctic Ocean is melting, causing sea levels to rise.

The great majority of climate scientists agree that human activity is driving **climate change**. Some in the minority argue that this warming is part of a natural cycle and is not caused by humans. Others have expressed doubt as to whether warming is occurring at all.

In 1988, as concern about global warming grew, the United Nations and the World Meteorological Organization created the **Intergovernmental Panel on Climate Change (IPCC)**. The panel's mission was to assess and report on climate science findings to help world leaders set climate policies.

Muir Glacier, 1980

Muir Glacier, 2003

These photos show the melting of Muir Glacier in Alaska over the course of two decades. Because of climate change, the glacier has retreated more than a mile, revealing the once hidden mountaintop behind it.

In California, the Sacramento Municipal Utility District deactivated the poorly performing Rancho Seco nuclear power plant (shown in the background) in 1989. In its place, the district built a solar power facility that delivers clean energy to several buildings in downtown Sacramento.

In 2015, President Obama and the U.S. Environmental Protection Agency unveiled the **Clean Power Plan**. It established nationwide standards aimed at greatly reducing carbon dioxide emissions from power plants. The following year, the United States joined nearly 200 other countries in signing an ambitious climate treaty called the Paris Agreement. In doing so, the United States committed itself to substantially reducing greenhouse gas emissions. In 2017, however, President Trump stated his intention to pull the United States out of the Paris Agreement. Even so, many American companies, states, and cities claimed that they would continue to pursue the goal of reducing harmful emissions.

ENERGY CHOICES FOR THE FUTURE

How will the United States meet its huge energy demands in the future? This question has been hotly debated as worries about climate change and U.S. dependence on oil from foreign countries have grown. In recent decades, use of **alternative energy** sources such as solar and wind power has grown significantly. Nevertheless, the country is still primarily powered by oil, coal, and natural gas.

A controversial technology called hydraulic fracturing, or fracking, has greatly increased U.S. natural gas output since the late 1990s. It uses tremendous amounts of water, can contaminate

groundwater with toxic chemicals, and can cause earthquakes. Nuclear energy is controversial, too, because accidents and natural disasters can lead to the release of harmful radiation.

Improving energy efficiency is another strategy for reducing energy dependence and combating climate change. Energy-efficient cars, buildings, and factories help reduce the amount of carbon dioxide released into the atmosphere.

Climate change poses one of the greatest threats humanity has ever faced. As evidence and awareness of the danger has increased, governments and private companies have stepped up their efforts to solve the problem. The eventual solution may come through cooperation not only among businesses and governments, but also among individual citizens.

HISTORICAL THINKING

1. **READING CHECK** What is the connection between fossil fuels and climate change?

2. **ANALYZE LANGUAGE USE** Why are greenhouse gases called by that name?

3. **MAKE INFERENCES** Why are rising sea levels a cause for concern?

29 REVIEW

VOCABULARY

Use each of the following vocabulary words in a sentence that shows an understanding of its meaning.

1. centrist

   President Bill Clinton ran as a centrist who adopted both liberal and conservative ideas.

2. government shutdown

3. neoconservative

4. first responder

5. insurgent

6. economic stimulus

7. free trade

8. globalization

9. Internet

10. alternative energy

READING STRATEGY
FORM AND SUPPORT OPINIONS

If you haven't already done so, complete your graphic organizer by writing an opinion and listing your reasons. Then answer the question.

Opinion
Supporting Statement:
Supporting Statement:
Supporting Statement:
Supporting Statement:
Supporting Statement:

11. What is the greatest challenge the United States has faced during the period from 1992 to the present? Summarize your reasons.

MAIN IDEAS

Answer the following questions. Support your answers with evidence from the chapter.

12. What was one major challenge facing President Bill Clinton during his first term, and how did he confront that challenge? **LESSON 1.1**

13. How did President Clinton's responses to the government shutdown and the crisis in Kosovo affect his reputation and popularity? **LESSON 1.2**

14. What events led to the U.S. Supreme Court deciding the 2000 presidential election? **LESSON 1.3**

15. How did President George W. Bush respond to the September 11 terrorist attacks? **LESSON 2.1**

16. What was the outcome of the 2008 presidential election, and why was it historic? **LESSON 3.1**

17. What action did President Obama and Congress take to try to end the recession shortly after Obama took office? **LESSON 3.2**

18. What key developments in the 1940s and 1950s led to computers that were much smaller, faster, and more accurate than ENIAC? **LESSON 4.1**

19. How have advances in technology contributed to globalization? **LESSON 4.3**

20. What changes in the late 20th and early 21st centuries increased the controversy about immigration to the United States? **LESSON 4.3**

21. What changes did Donald Trump promise to make to U.S. policies? **LESSON 4.4**

22. What is the Paris Agreement, and why is it important? **LESSON 4.5**

Answer the following questions. Support your answers with evidence from the chapter.

23. **IDENTIFY PROBLEMS AND SOLUTIONS** Choose one major problem a president has faced in the 21st century. What solutions did the president attempt, and how successful were they?

24. **COMPARE AND CONTRAST** In what ways are the Clinton and Bush tax policies—and their results—similar and different?

25. **DRAW CONCLUSIONS** What are some ways in which globalization has brought about changes to the United States?

26. **FORM AND SUPPORT OPINIONS** Do you think the United States should be taking stronger action to promote the use of renewable energy? Why or why not?

Study the graph below, which shows how the percentage of people without health insurance in the United States changed between 1990 and 2015. Then answer the questions that follow.

Health Insurance in the United States
(Full population uninsurance rate estimates)

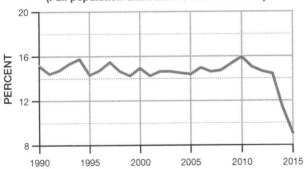

Source: Council of Economic Advisors and National Center for Health Statistics

27. According to the graph, approximately what percentage of people in the United States did not have health insurance in 2010?

28. How did the percentage of uninsured people change after 2010, the year that the Affordable Care Act became law?

Barack Obama delivered his farewell speech as president on January 10, 2017. While handing the nation's leadership over to Donald Trump, Obama summed up the American identity in these words.

> For 240 years, our nation's call to citizenship has given work and purpose to each new generation. It's what led patriots to choose republic over tyranny, pioneers to trek west, slaves to brave that makeshift railroad to freedom. It's what pulled immigrants and refugees across oceans and the Rio Grande. It's what pushed women to reach for the ballot. It's what powered workers to organize. It's why GIs gave their lives at Omaha Beach and Iwo Jima; Iraq and Afghanistan— and why men and women from Selma to Stonewall were prepared to give theirs as well. So that's what we mean when we say America is exceptional. Not that our nation has been flawless from the start, but that we have shown the capacity to change, and make life better for those who follow.

29. According to President Obama, what qualities make the United States exceptional?

30. **EXPOSITORY** Review what you learned about the 21st century in this chapter. Think about how you would define the American identity today. Write a paragraph connecting what you have learned to your own experiences.

TIPS

- Review the chapter and make notes about how American society has changed in the 21st century as a result of globalization, technology, and other forces.

- Use textual evidence and two or three vocabulary words from the chapter in your paragraph.

- Conclude the paragraph with a summary of your definition of the American identity.

Changing Faces

By Lise Funderburg

Adapted from "Changing Faces," by Lise Funderburg, in *National Geographic*, October 2013

What is it about the faces on this page that we find so intriguing? Is it simply that their features disrupt our expectations? We're not used to seeing those eyes with that hair, that nose above those lips. Out in the world, the more curious (or less polite) among us might approach, asking, "Where are you from?" or "What are you?" We wonder because what we see says a lot about our country's past, present, and future.

The U.S. Census Bureau has collected detailed data on multiracial people only since 2000. In that year, it first allowed respondents to check more than one race, and 6.8 million people chose to do so. Ten years later, the number jumped by 32 percent. The multiple-race option is a step toward fixing a categorization system that is both wrong and essential. It is wrong because geneticists have demonstrated that race has no biological basis. However, it is essential because the tracking of race is used both to enforce antidiscrimination laws and to identify health issues specific to certain populations.

The Census Bureau is aware that its racial categorization system is flawed. Indeed, for most multiple-race Americans, identity is influenced by politics, religion, history, and geography, as well as by how the person believes the answer will be used. "I just say I'm brown," McKenzi McPherson, 9, says. "And I think, why do you want to know?" Maximillian Sugiura, 29, says he responds with whatever ethnicity provides a situational advantage. Loyalties figure in, too. Yudah Holman, 29, self-identifies as half Thai and half black, but marks Asian on forms and puts Thai first "because my mother raised me, so I'm really proud of being Thai."

Sandra Williams, 46, grew up at a time when the nation still turned on a black-white axis. The 1960 census depicted a country that was 99 percent black or white. When Williams was born 6 years later to parents of mixed black and white ancestry, 17 states still had laws against interracial marriage. To link her own fair skin and hair to her white ancestry, Williams says, would have been seen by blacks as a rejection. And so she checks black on the census.

Tracey Williams Bautista says her seven-year-old son identifies himself as black when he's with her, his African-American parent. When he's with his father, he'll say Mexican. "We call him a Blaxican," she jokes. Black relatives warn Williams about the one-drop rule, the long-standing practice of seeing anyone with a trace of black "blood" as black.

Certainly, race still matters in this country, despite claims that the election of Barack Obama heralded a post-racial world. We may be a pluralist nation by 2060, when the Census Bureau predicts that non-Hispanic whites will no longer be the majority. But head counts don't guarantee opportunity or wipe out the legacy of past discrimination. Whites, on average, have twice the income and six times the wealth of blacks and Hispanics.

When people ask Celeste Seda, 26, what she is, she lets them guess before she explains her Dominican-Korean background. The attention she gets for her unusual looks can be both flattering and exhausting. "It's a gift and a curse," Seda says.

It's also, for the rest of us, an opportunity. If we can't slot people into familiar categories, perhaps we'll be forced to reconsider who is us and who is them. Perhaps we'll be less stingy about who we feel connected to as we increasingly come across people whose faces seem to speak the line from Walt Whitman's poem "Song of Myself":

"I am large, I contain multitudes."

For more from National Geographic, check out "The Drones Come Home" online.

UNIT INQUIRY: Negotiate a Political Compromise

In this unit, you learned about the ongoing and growing divisions between conservatives and liberals, Republicans and Democrats. You also learned about leaders who attempted to bridge the divisions and negotiate agreements on important issues. Based on your understanding of the text, what are the issues that the Republican Party and Democratic Party disagree on? Do they agree on *any* points?

ASSIGNMENT

Identify three political issues that divide the Democratic Party from the Republican Party. You could choose from such issues as government spending, government regulations on businesses and other organizations, energy policy, immigration, and health care. Examine the positions of both sides on the three issues. Develop a political compromise, or agreement, by writing position statements on these issues that you think both sides could agree to.

Gather Evidence As you plan your position statements, gather evidence from this unit about the opposing ideas of the two sides. State each side's point of view on the three issues you've identified. If necessary, conduct additional research. Use a graphic organizer like this one to organize your notes.

Political Positions		
Issue	Democratic Party	Republican Party

Produce Use your notes to develop a political compromise that the two sides might accept. For each issue, create a position statement in which both sides give up something their party could bear to let go.

Present Choose a creative way to present your political compromise to the class. Consider one of these options:

- Play the role of an independent political candidate who can bridge the divide between the two sides. Give a campaign speech in which you present your positions.

- Work with a partner to stage a dialogue between a Democrat and a Republican in which they reach the compromise you've developed.

- Write a letter to your state representative or senator outlining your ideas for political compromise. Share your letter with the class.

NATIONAL GEOGRAPHIC | LEARNING FRAMEWORK ACTIVITIES

Create a Comic Strip

SKILLS Problem-Solving, Communication

KNOWLEDGE Our Human Story

Imagine a natural event or a power outage that makes it impossible to use cell phones, tablets, and computers for a week. Team up with a partner or a small group and create a comic strip in which you portray how the loss of cell phones, tablets, and computers affects you, your friends, and your family. Think about the positive as well as the negative effects. Portray in the comic strip how you would overcome any challenges or how you would make the most out of any benefits presented by the disruption. Share your comic strip with the class, and discuss whether people have become overly dependent on electronic devices in the 21st century.

Debate the Effects of Environmental Regulations

ATTITUDE Responsibility

KNOWLEDGE Our Living Planet

Prepare an argument in response to the following question: Does helping the environment harm or benefit the U.S. economy? Review what you've learned about environmental regulations and how businesses and governments have tried to minimize climate change. Then conduct online research about the Clean Power Plan of 2015 and the Paris Agreement of 2016 and how these acts have affected the U.S. and global economies. Present your argument to the class and hold a debate about the positive and negative effects of regulations on the economy.

Looking Ahead

Now that you've explored centuries of American history, you might wonder: How does it all add up? Take a look at the graphics on these pages—they'll give you a good idea of the United States today and how you fit into the larger picture of your country.

Fred Hiebert
Archaeologist-in-Residence,
National Geographic Society

MOVING TO CITIES RURAL AND URBAN POPULATION

1800 RURAL
93.9%

2010 RURAL
19.3%

URBAN
80.7%

Source: U.S. Census Bureau

MOVING TO THE UNITED STATES TOTAL FOREIGN-BORN POPULATION

1870 5.6 million

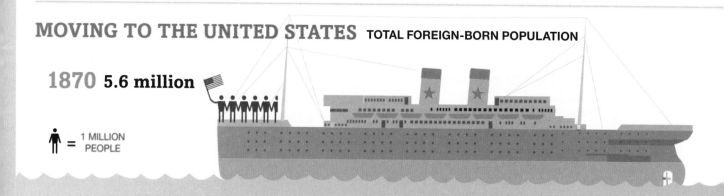

👤 = 1 MILLION PEOPLE

2016 40 million

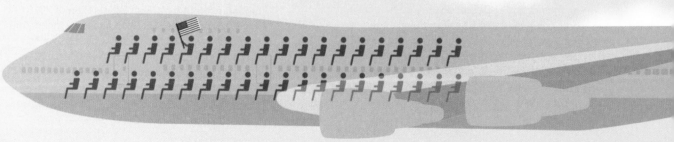

RISING EDUCATION LEVELS

Check out how education expectations have changed over the last century.

HIGH SCHOOL COMPLETION
All persons ages 25 and older

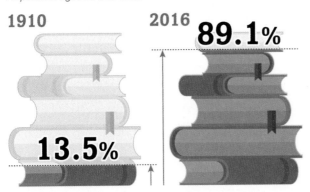

1910

13.5%

2016

89.1%

Source: National Center for Education Statistics

BACHELOR'S DEGREE OR HIGHER
All persons ages 25 and older

1910

2.7%

2016

33.4%

URBAN
6.1%

WORKING WOMEN
EMPLOYED POPULATION
All persons ages 25 to 34

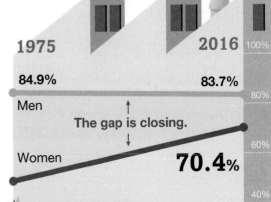

1975   **2016**

84.9%   83.7%

Men

The gap is closing.

Women   **70.4%**

100%
80%
60%
40%
20%
0%

Source:
U.S. Census Bureau

FOREIGN-BORN POPULATION

1870
← **14.4%**
of the population

2016
← **12.9%**
of the population

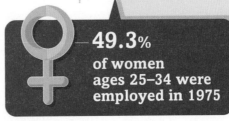

49.3% of women ages 25–34 were employed in 1975

Think About It

1. Which major historical events or trends that you've studied were likely to have impacted the data represented in the Moving to Cities graph? Explain why.

2. Identify a data set in this lesson that has affected you or your relatives. What connections can you make between the information on these pages and your American identity?

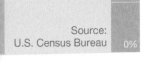

Source: U.S. Census Bureau

STUDENT REFERENCES

This famous Civil War battlefield in Gettysburg, Pennsylvania is a peaceful place today.

CITIZENSHIP
HANDBOOK

This Citizenship Handbook will help you take a detailed look at our two most important documents: the Declaration of Independence and the U.S. Constitution, which contains the Bill of Rights. The handbook includes notes to help you understand the formal language and difficult concepts contained in the more than 225-year-old documents. At the end of the handbook, you will learn about citizenship and the rights and responsibilities that come along with it. You will also find out how you can build and practice citizenship skills.

The Charters of Freedom, as the Declaration of Independence, U.S. Constitution, and Bill of Rights are collectively known, are housed in the National Archives Museum in Washington, D.C.

DECLARATION OF INDEPENDENCE

Introduction

The American colonists wrote the Declaration of Independence in 1776 to call for their separation and independence from Britain. During the first half of the 1700s, the colonists had lived in relative isolation from British authority and largely governed themselves. They modeled their colonial governments on Parliament, Britain's legislative body, by forming elected assemblies similar to the House of Commons. Unlike the British legislature, however, elected officials in the assemblies lived in the areas they represented. The colonists believed that representatives who lived among the people who elected them would better understand local interests and needs. They had no representatives in Parliament and sometimes resented what they felt to be unfair treatment by Britain.

GROWING RESENTMENT

The colonists' resentment grew after they fought alongside the British in the French and Indian War. The Americans had joined the fight so that they could expand their settlements westward into Native American territory. After Britain won the war against the French in 1763, however, the British government issued a proclamation stating that colonists could not settle west of the Appalachian Mountains. To make matters worse, British king George III charged a series of taxes against the colonists to help pay for the war. The king believed that the role of a colony was to support the mother country—in this case, Britain.

Crying "No taxation without representation," the colonists protested against the British legislation. As tensions rose, violence erupted in 1770 with the Boston Massacre, resulting in the deaths of five colonists at the hands of British soldiers. Three years later, colonists demonstrated their anger over a law on the sale of tea by staging the Boston Tea Party in Boston Harbor. A group of colonists boarded British ships and threw more than 300 crates of tea overboard.

Finally, in 1775, feelings on both sides reached the boiling point. After British troops learned that the colonists had stored weapons in Concord, Massachusetts, the troops marched to the town. Colonial militiamen rushed to face down the British soldiers in nearby Lexington. Shots rang out at what would later be called the first battle of the American Revolution.

DECLARING INDEPENDENCE

Colonial delegates to the two Continental Congresses met in Philadelphia in 1774 and 1775. Some delegates called for the colonies to separate completely from Britain. While the 1775 Congress debated the issue, a committee was formed to write an official document to declare independence from Britain. The committee included Thomas Jefferson, John Adams, and Benjamin Franklin, three of America's Founding Fathers.

Jefferson became the principal author of the Declaration of Independence. Like many American colonists, Jefferson had been deeply influenced by the Enlightenment, a movement that spread from Britain to the colonies in the 1700s. Enlightenment thinkers, such as John Locke, claimed that humans were born free and equal and that a leader could rule only with the consent of the people.

Inspired by the Enlightenment philosophy of unalienable, or natural, rights, Jefferson called for "Life, Liberty, and the Pursuit of Happiness" in the Declaration. These unalienable rights, he insisted, could not be taken away. Jefferson also drew on the principles of freedom contained in the Magna Carta as he wrote the document. On July 4, 1776, the delegates to the Continental Congress adopted the Declaration of Independence. In 1782, more than six years after the first shots were fired, the American Revolution officially ended. The American colonists had fought for and won their freedom and independence from Britain.

THE DECLARATION OF INDEPENDENCE

IN CONGRESS, JULY 4, 1776

The Declaration begins by explaining why the colonists want to break away from Britain and become independent. The Founding Fathers believed it was important to explain why they wanted to take this step.

The unanimous Declaration of the thirteen united States of America, When in the Course of human events, it becomes necessary for one people to dissolve the political bands which have connected them with another, and to assume among the powers of the earth, the separate and equal station to which the Laws of Nature and of Nature's God entitle them, a decent respect to the opinions of mankind requires that they should declare the causes which impel them to the separation.

The American colonists believed people are born equal and have rights that should be kept safe by the government. The Declaration explains that government is necessary to make sure people keep their natural rights; for example, the right to life, liberty, and the pursuit of happiness.

Once a government takes such rights away, the people must work to change or overthrow the government.

Such action is taken very seriously but is necessary because of King George's treatment of the colonies.

We hold these truths to be self-evident, that all men are created equal, that they are endowed by their Creator with certain unalienable Rights, that among these are Life, Liberty and the pursuit of Happiness.—That to secure these rights, Governments are instituted among Men, deriving their just powers from the consent of the governed, —That whenever any Form of Government becomes destructive of these ends, it is the Right of the People to alter or to abolish it, and to institute new Government, laying its foundation on such principles and organizing its powers in such form, as to them shall seem most likely to effect their Safety and Happiness. Prudence, indeed, will dictate that Governments long established should not be changed for light and transient causes; and accordingly all experience hath shown, that mankind are more disposed to suffer, while evils are sufferable, than to right themselves by abolishing the forms to which they are accustomed. But when a long train of abuses and usurpations, pursuing invariably the same Object evinces a design to reduce them under absolute Despotism, it is their right, it is their duty, to throw off such Government, and to provide new Guards for their future security.—Such has been the patient sufferance of these Colonies; and such is now the necessity which constrains them to alter their former Systems of Government. The history of the present King of Great Britain is a history of repeated injuries and usurpations, all having in direct object the establishment of an absolute Tyranny over these States. To prove this, let Facts be submitted to a candid world.

The Declaration goes on to explain exactly what King George has done. This section is commonly referred to as the list of grievances.

The king has refused to approve laws that people need.

He has refused his Assent to Laws, the most wholesome and necessary for the public good.

He has forbidden his Governors to pass Laws of immediate and pressing importance, unless suspended in their operation till his Assent should be obtained; and when so suspended, he has utterly neglected to attend to them. He has refused to pass other Laws for the accommodation of large districts of people, unless those people would relinquish the right of Representation in the Legislature, a right inestimable to them and formidable to tyrants only.

Laws are needed, but the king has failed to approve or disapprove them, so no new laws can be put into effect. He has claimed that unless people in the colonies give up the right to have representatives in their own government in America, he will not pass laws those people need.

He has called together legislative bodies at places unusual, uncomfortable, and distant from the depository of their public Records, for the sole purpose of fatiguing them into compliance with his measures.

He has dissolved Representative Houses repeatedly, for opposing with manly firmness his invasions on the rights of the people.

The king has put an end to lawmaking bodies that opposed laws representatives believed were harmful to people's rights.

He has refused for a long time, after such dissolutions, to cause others to be elected; whereby the Legislative powers, incapable of Annihilation, have returned to the People at large for their exercise; the State remaining in the mean time exposed to all the dangers of invasion from without, and convulsions within.

After the legislatures were dismissed, some colonies had no laws to protect them.

He has endeavored to prevent the population of these States; for that purpose obstructing the Laws for Naturalization of Foreigners; refusing to pass others to encourage their migrations hither, and raising the conditions of new Appropriations of Lands.

He has obstructed the Administration of Justice, by refusing his Assent to Laws for establishing Judiciary powers.

Judges have been appointed who favor the king's interests.

He has made Judges dependent on his Will alone, for the tenure of their offices, and the amount and payment of their salaries.

He has erected a multitude of New Offices, and sent hither swarms of Officers to harass our people, and eat out their substance.

He has kept among us, in times of peace, Standing Armies without the Consent of our legislatures.

The king has sent soldiers to America, without the agreement of its lawmakers. He has made his soldiers more powerful than the colonists.

He has affected to render the Military independent of and superior to the Civil power.

DECLARATION OF INDEPENDENCE

The king has allowed others to pass and enforce new laws in the colonies.

He has combined with others to subject us to a jurisdiction foreign to our constitution, and unacknowledged by our laws; giving his Assent to their Acts of pretended Legislation:

For example:

- making sure that soldiers who kill colonists are given a fake trial and not held accountable for murder;
- stopping American trade with other countries;
- taxing without permission;
- often refusing the right of trial by jury;
- sending colonists far away to be tried in courts for things they have not done;
- abolishing laws made by the colonies;
- stopping lawmaking groups in America and declaring that only the British government can make laws for people in America.

For Quartering large bodies of armed troops among us:

For protecting them, by a mock Trial, from punishment for any Murders which they should commit on the Inhabitants of these States:

For cutting off our Trade with all parts of the world:

For imposing Taxes on us without our Consent:

For depriving us in many cases, of the benefits of Trial by Jury:

For transporting us beyond Seas to be tried for pretended offences

For abolishing the free System of English Laws in a neighboring Province, establishing therein an Arbitrary government, and enlarging its Boundaries so as to render it at once an example and fit instrument for introducing the same absolute rule into these Colonies:

For taking away our Charters, abolishing our most valuable Laws, and altering fundamentally the Forms of our Governments:

For suspending our own Legislatures, and declaring themselves invested with power to legislate for us in all cases whatsoever.

The colonists claim that the king has essentially given up ("abdicated") his power to govern in America—because he refuses to protect America and has started a war against the colonies.

He has abdicated Government here, by declaring us out of his Protection and waging War against us.

He has plundered our seas, ravaged our Coasts, burnt our towns, and destroyed the lives of our people.

In a way that has almost never been seen before, the king is now sending soldiers from other countries to harm and kill Americans.

He is at this time transporting large Armies of foreign Mercenaries to complete the works of death, desolation and tyranny, already begun with circumstances of Cruelty & perfidy scarcely paralleled in the most barbarous ages, and totally unworthy the Head of a civilized nation.

He has constrained our fellow Citizens taken Captive on the high Seas to bear Arms against their Country, to become the executioners of their friends and Brethren, or to fall themselves by their Hands.

He has excited domestic insurrections amongst us, and has endeavored to bring on the inhabitants of our frontiers, the merciless Indian Savages, whose known rule of warfare, is an undistinguished destruction of all ages, sexes and conditions.

He has encouraged conflict among Americans and incited Native Americans to attack the colonists.

In every stage of these Oppressions We have Petitioned for Redress in the most humble terms: Our repeated Petitions have been answered only by repeated injury. A Prince whose character is thus marked by every act which may define a Tyrant, is unfit to be the ruler of a free people.

We have repeatedly and unsuccessfully made formal requests for this behavior to stop. The king has become cruel and oppressive.

Nor have We been wanting in attentions to our British brethren. We have warned them from time to time of attempts by their legislature to extend an unwarrantable jurisdiction over us. We have reminded them of the circumstances of our emigration and settlement here. We have appealed to their native justice and magnanimity, and we have conjured them by the ties of our common kindred to disavow these usurpations, which, would inevitably interrupt our connections and correspondence. They too have been deaf to the voice of justice and of consanguinity. We must, therefore, acquiesce in the necessity, which denounces our Separation, and hold them, as we hold the rest of mankind, Enemies in War, in Peace Friends.

We have appealed to the British people, pointing out the injustice of our treatment and our close ties to them ("consanguinity"), but they have ignored us. So we have no choice but to consider them our enemies.

We, therefore, the Representatives of the united States of America, in General Congress, Assembled, appealing to the Supreme Judge of the world for the rectitude of our intentions, do, in the Name, and by Authority of the good People of these Colonies, solemnly publish and declare, That these United Colonies are, and of Right ought to be Free and Independent States; that they are Absolved from all Allegiance to the British Crown, and that all political connection between them and the State of Great Britain, is and ought to be totally dissolved; and that as Free and Independent States, they have full Power to levy War, conclude Peace, contract Alliances, establish Commerce, and to do all other Acts and Things which Independent States may of right do. And for the support of this Declaration, with a firm reliance on the protection of divine Providence, we mutually pledge to each other our Lives, our Fortunes and our sacred Honor.

For all of these reasons, we declare that the United Colonies are free and independent states with no further allegiance to Britain. Because we are free, we can declare war, declare peace, make agreements to work with other countries, establish commerce, and participate in all other activities allowed by independent states.

CONSTITUTION OF THE UNITED STATES

Introduction

In 1787, after much debate, delegates at the Constitutional Convention in Philadelphia, known as the Framers, signed the U.S. Constitution, which became the supreme law of the land in the United States. Considering the size and complexity of the United States today and its position as a world power, the U.S. Constitution is relatively simple. It consists of a Preamble, 7 articles, and currently 27 amendments, based on the 7 key principles discussed below. About the simplicity of the Constitution, John Adams wrote, "Our Constitution was made only for a moral and religious People. It is wholly inadequate to the government of any other."

1. Popular Sovereignty This principle addresses the idea that people together create a social contract in which they agree to be governed.

2. Republicanism In a republic, citizens have the power and authority to make decisions as to how they are governed. The citizens elect representatives, and the representatives then have the power to make and enforce laws.

3. Federalism A government operating under federalism features a strong central government, but states do not lose all rights and power. The federal government holds some powers, which are enumerated, or listed, powers. The states have other powers, which are reserved, or unwritten, powers. And some powers are concurrent powers, which means that they may be practiced by both the federal government and the state governments.

4. Separation of Powers To reduce the potential for abuse of power, the government was divided into three branches: the legislative branch (made up of the Senate and the House of Representatives), which makes the laws; the executive branch (led by the president), which enforces the laws; and the judicial branch (made up of the U.S. Supreme Court and additional federal courts), which interprets the laws.

5. Checks and Balances Each branch of the government provides a check for the others, which means that it can limit the power of those branches. Such checks provide a balance among the three branches. For example, while the legislative branch can make laws, the judicial branch interprets them and decides if those laws are constitutional. And while the president can veto a law made by Congress, Congress can override a presidential veto.

6. Limited Government A strong central power was important to those who developed the Constitution. Still, the Framers believed the strong central government should not be allowed to abuse its power by providing particular rights to some groups or taking away rights from others. This principle of government seeks to protect rights by limiting the power of the central government.

7. Individual Rights Amendments, or articles added to the Constitution, have become part of the U.S. Constitution over the years. The first 10 amendments, known as the Bill of Rights, were added in 1791. These amendments address many individual rights, such as freedom of religion, freedom of speech, and the right to trial by jury. The Bill of Rights was added to the Constitution to ensure that all states would accept and ratify this new plan for government.

THE CONSTITUTION

Preamble **We the People** of the United States, in Order to form a more perfect Union, establish Justice, insure domestic Tranquility, provide for the common defense, promote the general Welfare, and secure the Blessings of Liberty to ourselves and our Posterity, do ordain and establish this Constitution for the United States of America.

Article I Legislative Branch

SECTION 1: CONGRESS

All legislative Powers herein granted shall be vested in a Congress of the United States, which shall consist of a Senate and House of Representatives.

SECTION 2: THE HOUSE OF REPRESENTATIVES

1 The House of Representatives shall be composed of Members chosen every second Year by the People of the several States, and the Electors in each State shall have the Qualifications requisite for Electors of the most numerous Branch of the State Legislature.

2 No Person shall be a Representative who shall not have attained to the Age of twenty five Years, and been seven Years a Citizen of the United States, and who shall not, when elected, be an Inhabitant of that State in which he shall be chosen.

3 *Representatives and direct Taxes shall be apportioned among the several States which may be included within this Union, according to their respective Numbers, which shall be determined by adding to the whole Number of free Persons, including those bound to Service for a Term of Years, and excluding Indians not taxed, three fifths of all other Persons.* The actual Enumeration shall be made within three Years after the first Meeting of the Congress of the United States, and within every subsequent Term of ten Years, in such Manner as they shall by Law direct. The Number of Representatives shall not exceed one for every thirty Thousand, but each State shall have at Least one Representative; and until such enumeration shall be made, the State of New Hampshire shall be entitled to choose three, Massachusetts eight, Rhode-Island and Providence Plantations one, Connecticut five, New-York six, New Jersey four, Pennsylvania eight, Delaware one, Maryland six, Virginia ten, North Carolina five, South Carolina five, and Georgia three.

4 When vacancies happen in the Representation from any State, the Executive Authority thereof shall issue Writs of Election to fill such Vacancies.

5 The House of Representatives shall choose their Speaker and other Officers; and shall have the sole Power of Impeachment.

PREAMBLE
UNDERSTANDING THE CONSTITUTION The phrase "We the People" begins the Preamble to the Constitution. The Preamble states the "why" and the "how" of Americans' agreement to be governed. The Preamble also states that the Constitution will define the government and that the document will be a social contract.

ARTICLE I
UNDERSTANDING THE CONSTITUTION Section 2
The House of Representatives provides one of the most direct ways in which citizens can participate in the political process. People can communicate with representatives by mail, email, and phone, and by visiting the lawmakers' offices.

UNDERSTANDING THE CONSTITUTION 2.3 Each state can have one representative for every 30,000 people in the state. The phrase "their respective Numbers" refers to the states' populations. Today every state has a population greater than 30,000, but the Constitution made sure that states with fewer people had a representative. The Constitution indicates the initial numbers of representatives for each of the original 13 states.

HISTORICAL THINKING In 2.3, the italicized phrase "three fifths of all other persons" refers to enslaved people. Why do you think slaves were not counted in the same way as free persons?

UNDERSTANDING THE CONSTITUTION 2.5 The Speaker presides over sessions of Congress, but the Constitution says nothing about what the Speaker or other officers will do.

UNDERSTANDING THE CONSTITUTION 3.1 The Constitution originally provided for the election of senators by the state legislatures, but the 17th Amendment changed that in 1913 with the election of senators by voters.

UNDERSTANDING THE CONSTITUTION 3.2 The terms of senators are staggered. One class of senators begins their term in an even-numbered year, the next class begins two years later, and the third class begins two years after that.

HISTORICAL THINKING In the previous section, the Constitution states the House has the power of impeachment, and in 3.6, it says the Senate tries impeachments. Why do you think the Constitution separates these powers?

HISTORICAL THINKING Only two U.S. presidents have been impeached: Andrew Johnson in 1868 and William Clinton in 1998, but neither was convicted by the Senate. Why do you think impeachment is part of the Constitution?

Visitors with tickets could observe President Andrew Johnson's impeachment trial from the gallery of the Senate. Each ticket was valid for one day in March through May 1868, indicated by the ticket's color.

UNDERSTANDING THE CONSTITUTION 4.2 In 1933, the 20th Amendment changed the starting date for meetings of Congress to January 3.

SECTION 3: THE SENATE

1 The Senate of the United States shall be composed of two Senators from each State, chosen by the Legislature thereof, for six Years; and each Senator shall have one Vote.

2 Immediately after they shall be assembled in Consequence of the first Election, they shall be divided as equally as may be into three Classes. The Seats of the Senators of the first Class shall be vacated at the Expiration of the second Year, of the second Class at the Expiration of the fourth Year, and of the third Class at the Expiration of the sixth Year, so that one third may be chosen every second Year; and if Vacancies happen by Resignation, or otherwise, during the Recess of the Legislature of any State, the Executive thereof may make temporary Appointments until the next Meeting of the Legislature, which shall then fill such Vacancies.

3 No Person shall be a Senator who shall not have attained to the Age of thirty Years, and been nine Years a Citizen of the United States, and who shall not, when elected, be an Inhabitant of that State for which he shall be chosen.

4 The Vice President of the United States shall be President of the Senate, but shall have no Vote, unless they be equally divided.

5 The Senate shall choose their other Officers, and also a President pro tempore, in the Absence of the Vice President, or when he shall exercise the Office of President of the United States.

6 The Senate shall have the sole Power to try all Impeachments. When sitting for that Purpose, they shall be on Oath or Affirmation. When the President of the United States is tried, the Chief Justice shall preside: And no Person shall be convicted without the Concurrence of two thirds of the Members present.

7 Judgment in Cases of Impeachment shall not extend further than to removal from Office, and disqualification to hold and enjoy any Office of honor, Trust or Profit under the United States: but the Party convicted shall nevertheless be liable and subject to Indictment, Trial, Judgment and Punishment, according to Law.

SECTION 4: CONGRESSIONAL ELECTIONS

1 The Times, Places and Manner of holding Elections for Senators and Representatives, shall be prescribed in each State by the Legislature thereof; but the Congress may at any time by Law make or alter such Regulations, except as to the Places of choosing Senators.

2 *The Congress shall assemble at least once in every Year, and such Meeting shall be on the first Monday in December, unless they shall by Law appoint a different Day.*

SECTION 5: RULES

1 Each House shall be the Judge of the Elections, Returns and Qualifications of its own Members, and a Majority of each shall constitute a Quorum to do Business; but a smaller Number may adjourn from day to day, and may be authorized to compel the Attendance of absent Members, in such Manner, and under such Penalties as each House may provide.

2 Each House may determine the Rules of its Proceedings, punish its Members for disorderly Behavior, and, with the Concurrence of two thirds, expel a Member.

3 Each House shall keep a Journal of its Proceedings, and from time to time publish the same, excepting such Parts as may in their Judgment require Secrecy; and the Yeas and Nays of the Members of either House on any question shall, at the Desire of one fifth of those Present, be entered on the Journal.

4 Neither House, during the Session of Congress, shall, without the Consent of the other, adjourn for more than three days, nor to any other Place than that in which the two Houses shall be sitting.

SECTION 6: PAY AND EXPENSES

1 The Senators and Representatives shall receive a Compensation for their Services, to be ascertained by Law, and paid out of the Treasury of the United States. They shall in all Cases, except Treason, Felony and Breach of the Peace, be privileged from Arrest during their Attendance at the Session of their respective Houses, and in going to and returning from the same; and for any Speech or Debate in either House, they shall not be questioned in any other Place.

2 No Senator or Representative shall, during the Time for which he was elected, be appointed to any civil Office under the Authority of the United States, which shall have been created, or the Emoluments whereof shall have been increased during such time; and no Person holding any Office under the United States, shall be a Member of either House during his Continuance in Office.

SECTION 7: PASSING LAWS

1 All Bills for raising Revenue shall originate in the House of Representatives; but the Senate may propose or concur with Amendments as on other Bills.

2 Every Bill which shall have passed the House of Representatives and the Senate, shall, before it become a Law, be presented to the President of the United States; If he approve he shall sign it, but if not he shall return it, with his Objections to that House in which it shall have originated, who shall enter the Objections at large on their Journal, and proceed to reconsider it. If after such Reconsideration two thirds of that House shall agree to pass the Bill, it shall be sent, together with

---

UNDERSTANDING THE CONSTITUTION Section 5

This section calls for a "journal" of each house's proceedings. These proceedings include debates, bills introduced, laws passed, and a record of how each member voted on each bill introduced. Debates were recorded in writing in the House and Senate *Journals* until 1873. Since then, debates have been recorded in the *Congressional Record*.

UNDERSTANDING THE CONSTITUTION 7.2

How a Bill Becomes a Law in Congress

A A representative in either the House or Senate introduces a bill. A citizen may bring the idea for a bill to the attention of a representative.

B The bill is debated, and revisions may be made.

C A committee irons out any differences if the House and Senate pass different versions of the bill.

D If both houses accept the compromises, Congress sends the bill to the president.

E The president either signs the bill—and it becomes law—or vetoes the bill. Congress can override the veto with a vote of two-thirds of the members present in each house, making the bill become a law.

the Objections, to the other House, by which it shall likewise be reconsidered, and if approved by two thirds of that House, it shall become a Law. But in all such Cases the Votes of both Houses shall be determined by yeas and Nays, and the Names of the Persons voting for and against the Bill shall be entered on the Journal of each House respectively. If any Bill shall not be returned by the President within ten Days (Sundays excepted) after it shall have been presented to him, the Same shall be a Law, in like Manner as if he had signed it, unless the Congress by their Adjournment prevent its Return, in which Case it shall not be a Law.

3 Every Order, Resolution, or Vote to which the Concurrence of the Senate and House of Representatives may be necessary (except on a question of Adjournment) shall be presented to the President of the United States; and before the Same shall take Effect, shall be approved by him, or being disapproved by him, shall be re-passed by two thirds of the Senate and House of Representatives, according to the Rules and Limitations prescribed in the Case of a Bill.

SECTION 8: POWERS OF CONGRESS

1 The Congress shall have Power To lay and collect Taxes, Duties, Imposts and Excises, to pay the Debts and provide for the common Defense and general Welfare of the United States; but all Duties, Imposts and Excises shall be uniform throughout the United States;

2 To borrow Money on the credit of the United States;

3 To regulate Commerce with foreign Nations, and among the several States, and with the Indian Tribes;

4 To establish an uniform Rule of Naturalization, and uniform Laws on the subject of Bankruptcies throughout the United States;

5 To coin Money, regulate the Value thereof, and of foreign Coin, and fix the Standard of Weights and Measures;

6 To provide for the Punishment of counterfeiting the Securities and current Coin of the United States;

7 To establish Post Offices and post Roads;

8 To promote the Progress of Science and useful Arts, by securing for limited Times to Authors and Inventors the exclusive Right to their respective Writings and Discoveries;

9 To constitute Tribunals inferior to the supreme Court;

10 To define and punish Piracies and Felonies committed on the high Seas, and Offences against the Law of Nations;

11 To declare War, grant Letters of Marque and Reprisal, and make Rules concerning Captures on Land and Water;

UNDERSTANDING THE CONSTITUTION Section 8
Section 8 provides a list of 17 specific powers given to Congress and empowers it "to make all laws" necessary to support those functions. Additionally, the first paragraph of the section empowers Congress to provide for the "general welfare" of the nation. However, the Constitution includes little detail on how some of these powers should be carried out.

HISTORICAL THINKING How does the Constitution balance the power of Congress to raise and support armies?

UNDERSTANDING THE CONSTITUTION 8.3 Regulating commerce with foreign nations means controlling imports and exports to provide maximum benefit for U.S. businesses and consumers. Regulating commerce between states means maintaining a common market among the states, with no restrictions. Remember that at the time the Constitution was written, Native Americans traded fur and other items with U.S. citizens.

HISTORICAL THINKING What problems might arise if the United States did not have a common coinage?

12 To raise and support Armies, but no Appropriation of Money to that Use shall be for a longer Term than two Years;

13 To provide and maintain a Navy;

14 To make Rules for the Government and Regulation of the land and naval Forces;

15 To provide for calling forth the Militia to execute the Laws of the Union, suppress Insurrections and repel Invasions;

16 To provide for organizing, arming, and disciplining, the Militia, and for governing such Part of them as may be employed in the Service of the United States, reserving to the States respectively, the Appointment of the Officers, and the Authority of training the Militia according to the discipline prescribed by Congress;

17 To exercise exclusive Legislation in all Cases whatsoever, over such District (not exceeding ten Miles square) as may, by Cession of particular States, and the Acceptance of Congress, become the Seat of the Government of the United States, and to exercise like Authority over all Places purchased by the Consent of the Legislature of the State in which the Same shall be, for the Erection of Forts, Magazines, Arsenals, dock-Yards, and other needful Buildings;—And

18 To make all Laws which shall be necessary and proper for carrying into Execution the foregoing Powers, and all other Powers vested by this Constitution in the Government of the United States, or in any Department or Officer thereof.

SECTION 9: RESTRICTIONS ON CONGRESS

1 *The Migration or Importation of such Persons as any of the States now existing shall think proper to admit, shall not be prohibited by the Congress prior to the Year one thousand eight hundred and eight, but a Tax or duty may be imposed on such Importation, not exceeding ten dollars for each Person.*

2 The Privilege of the Writ of Habeas Corpus shall not be suspended, unless when in Cases of Rebellion or Invasion the public Safety may require it.

3 No Bill of Attainder or ex post facto Law shall be passed.

4 *No Capitation, or other direct, Tax shall be laid, unless in Proportion to the Census or Enumeration herein before directed to be taken.*

5 No Tax or Duty shall be laid on Articles exported from any State.

6 No Preference shall be given by any Regulation of Commerce or Revenue to the Ports of one State over those of another: nor shall Vessels bound to, or from, one State, be obliged to enter, clear, or pay Duties in another.

UNDERSTANDING THE CONSTITUTION Section 9 Section 9 lists specific areas in which Congress may not legislate. These include laws governing the importation of slaves—a provision made obsolete with the abolition of slavery (9.1); holding a person without charging him or her with a crime (9.2); passing an act that declares a specific person guilty of a crime ("bill of attainder") (9.3); and making an action illegal after it has been committed ("ex post facto") (9.3).

UNDERSTANDING THE CONSTITUTION 9.4 A "capitation tax" is a tax charged on an individual.

UNDERSTANDING THE CONSTITUTION 9.6 Congress cannot pass laws that favor commerce in one state over that of another. For example, Congress cannot pass a law requiring shipping to go through a particular state's port.

7 No Money shall be drawn from the Treasury, but in Consequence of Appropriations made by Law; and a regular Statement and Account of the Receipts and Expenditures of all public Money shall be published from time to time.

8 No Title of Nobility shall be granted by the United States: And no Person holding any Office of Profit or Trust under them, shall, without the Consent of the Congress, accept of any present, Emolument, Office, or Title, of any kind whatever, from any King, Prince, or foreign State.

SECTION 10: LIMITING THE AUTHORITY OF STATES

1 No State shall enter into any Treaty, Alliance, or Confederation; grant Letters of Marque and Reprisal; coin Money; emit Bills of Credit; make any Thing but gold and silver Coin a Tender in Payment of Debts; pass any Bill of Attainder, ex post facto Law, or Law impairing the Obligation of Contracts, or grant any Title of Nobility.

2 No State shall, without the Consent of the Congress, lay any Imposts or Duties on Imports or Exports, except what may be absolutely necessary for executing its inspection Laws: and the net Produce of all Duties and Imposts, laid by any State on Imports or Exports, shall be for the Use of the Treasury of the United States; and all such Laws shall be subject to the Revision and Control of the Congress.

3 No State shall, without the Consent of Congress, lay any Duty of Tonnage, keep Troops, or Ships of War in time of Peace, enter into any Agreement or Compact with another State, or with a foreign Power, or engage in War, unless actually invaded, or in such imminent Danger as will not admit of delay.

Article II The Executive Branch
SECTION 1: ELECTING THE PRESIDENT

1 The executive Power shall be vested in a President of the United States of America. He shall hold his Office during the Term of four Years, and, together with the Vice President, chosen for the same Term, be elected, as follows

2 Each State shall appoint, in such Manner as the Legislature thereof may direct, a Number of Electors, equal to the whole Number of Senators and Representatives to which the State may be entitled in the Congress: but no Senator or Representative, or Person holding an Office of Trust or Profit under the United States, shall be appointed an Elector.

UNDERSTANDING THE CONSTITUTION Section 10
Section 10 sets out actions that the states are not permitted to take on their own: for example, entering into a treaty, coining money, or passing laws that interfere with contracts.

HISTORICAL THINKING How can Section 10 be used to prove that the secession of the southern states was unconstitutional?

ARTICLE II
UNDERSTANDING THE CONSTITUTION Section 1
Section 1 describes a detailed process for choosing the president. This process was replaced in 1804 by another detailed in the 12th Amendment.

UNDERSTANDING THE CONSTITUTION 1.2 Each state determines how its electors are chosen, but all follow the same principle. Voters cast their ballots for a ticket consisting of a president and a vice president. In most states, whoever wins the most votes in the state wins all that state's electoral votes.

HISTORICAL THINKING Some Americans believe voters should directly elect the president. Do you agree or disagree? Explain.

3 *The Electors shall meet in their respective States, and vote by Ballot for two Persons, of whom one at least shall not be an Inhabitant of the same State with themselves. And they shall make a List of all the Persons voted for, and of the Number of Votes for each; which List they shall sign and certify, and transmit sealed to the Seat of the Government of the United States, directed to the President of the Senate. The President of the Senate shall, in the Presence of the Senate and House of Representatives, open all the Certificates, and the Votes shall then be counted. The Person having the greatest Number of Votes shall be the President, if such Number be a Majority of the whole Number of Electors appointed; and if there be more than one who have such Majority, and have an equal Number of Votes, then the House of Representatives shall immediately choose by Ballot one of them for President; and if no Person have a Majority, then from the five highest on the List the said House shall in like Manner choose the President. But in choosing the President, the Votes shall be taken by States, the Representation from each State having one Vote; A quorum for this Purpose shall consist of a Member or Members from two thirds of the States, and a Majority of all the States shall be necessary to a Choice. In every Case, after the Choice of the President, the Person having the greatest Number of Votes of the Electors shall be the Vice President. But if there should remain two or more who have equal Votes, the Senate shall choose from them by Ballot the Vice President.*

4 The Congress may determine the Time of choosing the Electors, and the Day on which they shall give their Votes; which Day shall be the same throughout the United States.

5 No Person except a natural born Citizen, or a Citizen of the United States, at the time of the Adoption of this Constitution, shall be eligible to the Office of President; neither shall any Person be eligible to that Office who shall not have attained to the Age of thirty five Years, and been fourteen Years a Resident within the United States.

6 *In Case of the Removal of the President from Office, or of his Death, Resignation, or Inability to discharge the Powers and Duties of the said Office, the Same shall devolve on the Vice President, and the Congress may by Law provide for the Case of Removal, Death, Resignation or Inability, both of the President and Vice President, declaring what Officer shall then act as President, and such Officer shall act accordingly, until the Disability be removed, or a President shall be elected.*

7 The President shall, at stated Times, receive for his Services, a Compensation, which shall neither be increased nor diminished during the Period for which he shall have been elected, and he shall not receive within that Period any other Emolument from the United States, or any of them.

UNDERSTANDING THE CONSTITUTION 1.3 The italicized text refers to how vice presidents were originally elected. Voters cast ballots for presidential candidates, and the one who came in second became vice president. Today, a presidential candidate selects a running mate, and voters cast a single vote for the entire ticket.

Both houses of Congress convene each year in the House chamber to hear the president's State of the Union address. In this photo, Congress listens as President Barack Obama delivers his 2016 address.

CONSTITUTION OF THE UNITED STATES

UNDERSTANDING THE CONSTITUTION 1.8 Every president has taken the same oath of office, saying these exact words at the inauguration.

8 Before he enter on the Execution of his Office, he shall take the following Oath or Affirmation:—"I do solemnly swear (or affirm) that I will faithfully execute the Office of President of the United States, and will to the best of my Ability, preserve, protect and defend the Constitution of the United States."

SECTION 2: EXECUTIVE POWERS

UNDERSTANDING THE CONSTITUTION Section 2 Section 2 outlines the president's authority. Among other duties, the president is commander in chief of the armed forces, has the power to make treaties, and can appoint ambassadors and Supreme Court justices. However, the treaties and appointments are subject to approval by the Senate.

1 The President shall be Commander in Chief of the Army and Navy of the United States, and of the Militia of the several States, when called into the actual Service of the United States; he may require the Opinion, in writing, of the principal Officer in each of the executive Departments, upon any Subject relating to the Duties of their respective Offices, and he shall have Power to grant Reprieves and Pardons for Offences against the United States, except in Cases of Impeachment.

2 He shall have Power, by and with the Advice and Consent of the Senate, to make Treaties, provided two thirds of the Senators present concur; and he shall nominate, and by and with the Advice and Consent of the Senate, shall appoint Ambassadors, other public Ministers and Consuls, Judges of the supreme Court, and all other Officers of the United States, whose Appointments are not herein otherwise provided for, and which shall be established by Law: but the Congress may by Law vest the Appointment of such inferior Officers, as they think proper, in the President alone, in the Courts of Law, or in the Heads of Departments.

3 The President shall have Power to fill up all Vacancies that may happen during the Recess of the Senate, by granting Commissions which shall expire at the End of their next Session.

SECTION 3: THE PRESIDENT AND CONGRESS

HISTORICAL THINKING On what "extraordinary occasions" might a president wish to address both houses of Congress?

He shall from time to time give to the Congress Information of the State of the Union, and recommend to their Consideration such Measures as he shall judge necessary and expedient; he may, on extraordinary Occasions, convene both Houses, or either of them, and in Case of Disagreement between them, with Respect to the Time of Adjournment, he may adjourn them to such Time as he shall think proper; he shall receive Ambassadors and other public Ministers; he shall take Care that the Laws be faithfully executed, and shall Commission all the Officers of the United States.

SECTION 4: IMPEACHMENT

UNDERSTANDING THE CONSTITUTION Section 4 In the phrase "high crimes and misdemeanors," the word *high* does not mean "more serious" but rather refers to highly placed public officials.

The President, Vice President and all civil Officers of the United States, shall be removed from Office on Impeachment for, and Conviction of, Treason, Bribery, or other high Crimes and Misdemeanors.

Article III The Judiciary Branch

SECTION 1: SUPREME COURT AND LOWER COURTS

The judicial Power of the United States, shall be vested in one supreme Court, and in such inferior Courts as the Congress may from time to time ordain and establish. The Judges, both of the supreme and inferior Courts, shall hold their Offices during good Behavior, and shall, at stated Times, receive for their Services, a Compensation, which shall not be diminished during their Continuance in Office.

The Supreme Court justices posed for this photo in 2017. In the top row, from left to right, are Elena Kagan, Samuel Alito, Jr., Sonia Sotomayor, and Neil Gorsuch. In the bottom row, from left to right, are Ruth Bader Ginsburg, Anthony Kennedy, John Roberts, Jr. (chief justice), Clarence Thomas, and Stephen Breyer.

SECTION 2: AUTHORITY OF THE SUPREME COURT

1 The judicial Power shall extend to all Cases, in Law and Equity, arising under this Constitution, the Laws of the United States, and Treaties made, or which shall be made, under their Authority;—to all Cases affecting Ambassadors, other public Ministers and Consuls;—to all Cases of admiralty and maritime Jurisdiction;—to Controversies to which the United States shall be a Party;—*to Controversies between two or more States;—between a State and Citizens of another State;—between Citizens of different States;—between Citizens of the same State claiming Lands under Grants of different States, and between a State, or the Citizens thereof, and foreign States, Citizens or Subjects.*

2 In all Cases affecting Ambassadors, other public Ministers and Consuls, and those in which a State shall be Party, the supreme Court shall have original Jurisdiction. In all the other Cases before mentioned, the supreme Court shall have appellate Jurisdiction, both as to Law and Fact, with such Exceptions, and under such Regulations as the Congress shall make.

3 The Trial of all Crimes, except in Cases of Impeachment, shall be by Jury; and such Trial shall be held in the State where the said Crimes shall have been committed; but when not committed within any State, the Trial shall be at such Place or Places as the Congress may by Law have directed.

SECTION 3: TREASON

1 Treason against the United States, shall consist only in levying War against them, or in adhering to their Enemies, giving them Aid and Comfort. No Person shall be convicted of Treason unless on the Testimony of two Witnesses to the same overt Act, or on Confession in open Court.

2 The Congress shall have Power to declare the Punishment of Treason, but no Attainder of Treason shall work Corruption of Blood, or Forfeiture except during the Life of the Person attainted.

ARTICLE III
UNDERSTANDING THE CONSTITUTION 2.1 The italicized portion of this section was changed in 1795 by the 11th Amendment, which states that the Judicial Department does not have jurisdiction in matters between states or between a foreign country and a U.S. state.

UNDERSTANDING THE CONSTITUTION 2.2 When the Supreme Court serves as an appeals court, it reviews decisions made by lower courts.

UNDERSTANDING THE CONSTITUTION Section 3 Treason is the only crime specifically defined in the Constitution. Between 1954 and 2016, one person was charged with treason for collaborating in the production of propaganda videos for the terrorist group al-Qaeda.

Article IV States and Citizens

SECTION 1: MUTUAL RESPECT AMONG STATES

Full Faith and Credit shall be given in each State to the public Acts, Records, and judicial Proceedings of every other State. And the Congress may by general Laws prescribe the Manner in which such Acts, Records and Proceedings shall be proved, and the Effect thereof.

SECTION 2: CITIZENS OF STATES AND OF THE UNITED STATES

1 The Citizens of each State shall be entitled to all Privileges and Immunities of Citizens in the several States.

2 A Person charged in any State with Treason, Felony, or other Crime, who shall flee from Justice, and be found in another State, shall on Demand of the executive Authority of the State from which he fled, be delivered up, to be removed to the State having Jurisdiction of the Crime.

3 *No Person held to Service or Labor in one State, under the Laws thereof, escaping into another, shall, in Consequence of any Law or Regulation therein, be discharged from such Service or Labor, but shall be delivered up on Claim of the Party to whom such Service or Labor may be due.*

SECTION 3: NEW STATES

1 New States may be admitted by the Congress into this Union; but no new State shall be formed or erected within the Jurisdiction of any other State; nor any State be formed by the Junction of two or more States, or Parts of States, without the Consent of the Legislatures of the States concerned as well as of the Congress.

2 The Congress shall have Power to dispose of and make all needful Rules and Regulations respecting the Territory or other Property belonging to the United States; and nothing in this Constitution shall be so construed as to Prejudice any Claims of the United States, or of any particular State.

SECTION 4: PROTECTION OF STATES BY THE UNITED STATES

The United States shall guarantee to every State in this Union a Republican Form of Government, and shall protect each of them against Invasion; and on Application of the Legislature, or of the Executive (when the Legislature cannot be convened), against domestic Violence.

ARTICLE IV
UNDERSTANDING THE CONSTITUTION Section 1 "Full faith and credit" means that states agree to respect and honor each other's laws and documents.

UNDERSTANDING THE CONSTITUTION 2.3 The text in italics is known as the fugitive slave clause, which barred people who had escaped slavery in the South from living as free people in northern states. It became obsolete with the abolition of slavery.

HISTORICAL THINKING Why do you think the Framers felt the Constitution needed to place limits on the formation of a state within an existing one?

UNDERSTANDING THE CONSTITUTION Section 4 Here the Constitution commits the U.S. government to protecting the people of a state from attack by a foreign government, but also from violence originating within the United States, or "domestic violence."

Article V Amending the Constitution

1 The Congress, whenever two thirds of both Houses shall deem it necessary, shall propose Amendments to this Constitution, or, on the Application of the Legislatures of two thirds of the several States, shall call a Convention for proposing Amendments, which, in either Case, shall be valid to all Intents and Purposes, as Part of this Constitution, when ratified by the Legislatures of three fourths of the several States, or by Conventions in three fourths thereof, as the one or the other Mode of Ratification may be proposed by the Congress; **2** Provided that no Amendment which may be made prior to the Year One thousand eight hundred and eight shall in any Manner affect the first and fourth Clauses in the Ninth Section of the first Article; and that no State, without its Consent, shall be deprived of its equal Suffrage in the Senate.

Article VI The Supreme Law of the Land

1 All Debts contracted and Engagements entered into, before the Adoption of this Constitution, shall be as valid against the United States under this Constitution, as under the Confederation.

2 This Constitution, and the Laws of the United States which shall be made in Pursuance thereof; and all Treaties made, or which shall be made, under the Authority of the United States, shall be the supreme Law of the Land; and the Judges in every State shall be bound thereby, any Thing in the Constitution or Laws of any State to the Contrary notwithstanding.

3 The Senators and Representatives before mentioned, and the Members of the several State Legislatures, and all executive and judicial Officers, both of the United States and of the several States, shall be bound by Oath or Affirmation, to support this Constitution; but no religious Test shall ever be required as a Qualification to any Office or public Trust under the United States.

ARTICLE V
UNDERSTANDING THE CONSTITUTION Article 5
This article describes the process for amending the Constitution but states that the first and fourth clauses in Article 1's ninth section cannot be amended before 1808. Remember that these clauses refer to the importation of slaves and to a tax charged on an individual.

ARTICLE VI
UNDERSTANDING THE CONSTITUTION Article 6
This article states that all judges and legislators must uphold and be bound by the Constitution, the supreme law of the land. When any state law or part of a law conflicts with the Constitution or federal laws and treaties, the federal law is the one that must be followed. This concept was important to keep the states of the new nation united in their dealings with each other, with foreign powers, and with the federal government.

HISTORICAL THINKING What might happen if a state established laws that contradicted those in the Constitution?

Today, "the people" referred to in the Constitution includes all adult U.S. citizens.

Article VII
UNDERSTANDING THE CONSTITUTION Article 7

On June 21, 1788, New Hampshire became the 9th state to ratify the Constitution and make it the law of the United States. The Framers clearly stated in Article 7 that the Constitution required the approval of only 9 states, not the 13 then in existence. However, the Framers wanted each state to ratify the Constitution through a state convention. They knew the new nation's survival depended on the populous and wealthy states of Virginia and New York, which were slow to ratify. After lengthy debates, first Virginia and then New York gave approval, becoming the 11th and 12th states to ratify the Constitution. But Rhode Island was the main roadblock to unanimous approval. It officially joined the United States only after being told the state would be treated like a foreign government if it did not.

HISTORICAL THINKING Do you think your state would ratify the Constitution today? Why or why not?

Article VII Ratification

The Ratification of the Conventions of nine States, shall be sufficient for the Establishment of this Constitution between the States so ratifying the Same.

[Here appears some text noting corrections that were made on the original copy of the document.]

Done in Convention by the Unanimous Consent of the States present the Seventeenth Day of September in the Year of our Lord one thousand seven hundred and Eighty seven and of the Independence of the United States of America the Twelfth In witness whereof We have hereunto subscribed our Names,

G°. Washington
President and deputy from Virginia

Massachusetts
Nathaniel Gorham
Rufus King

New York
Alexander Hamilton

Delaware
George Read
Gunning Bedford, Jr.
John Dickinson
Richard Bassett
Jacob Broom

Virginia
John Blair
James Madison, Jr.

Pennsylvania
Benjamin Franklin
Thomas Mifflin
Robert Morris
George Clymer
Thomas Fitzsimons
Jared Ingersoll
James Wilson
Gouverneur Morris

New Hampshire
John Langdon
Nicholas Gilman

New Jersey
William Livingston
David Brearley
William Paterson
Jonathan Dayton

Connecticut
William Samuel Johnson
Roger Sherman

North Carolina
William Blount
Richard Dobbs Spaight
Hugh Williamson

South Carolina
John Rutledge
Charles Cotesworth Pinckney
Charles Pinckney
Pierce Butler

Maryland
James McHenry
Daniel of St. Thomas Jenifer
Daniel Carroll

Georgia
William Few
Abraham Baldwin

Introduction

Individual rights are fundamental to liberty. As you've read, the Magna Carta influenced the Declaration of Independence, but it also helped inspire the Bill of Rights. The people who came to America from Britain had enjoyed the freedoms granted to them under both the Magna Carta and the English Bill of Rights. They believed they were entitled to these rights when they settled their colonies. After the American Revolution, the new country's leaders wanted citizens' individual freedoms to become law. In 1787, Thomas Jefferson wrote to James Madison, "[A] bill of rights is what the people are entitled to against every government on earth, general or particular, and what no just government should refuse."

As a result, a list of basic citizenship rights became a permanent part of the Constitution. The following is a transcription of the first 10 amendments to the Constitution in their original form: the Bill of Rights. As you'll see, over time, more amendments were added to the Constitution to address issues that arose as the nation grew and changed.

The Preamble to the Bill of Rights

Congress of the United States begun and held at the City of New York, on Wednesday the fourth of March, one thousand seven hundred and eighty nine.

THE Conventions of a number of the States, having at the time of their adopting the Constitution, expressed a desire, in order to prevent misconstruction or abuse of its powers, that further declaratory and restrictive clauses should be added: And as extending the ground of public confidence in the Government, will best ensure the beneficient ends of its institution.

RESOLVED by the Senate and House of Representatives of the United States of America, in Congress assembled, two thirds of both Houses concurring, that the following Articles be proposed to the Legislatures of the several States, as amendments to the Constitution of the United States, all, or any of which Articles, when ratified by three fourths of the said Legislatures, to be valid to all intents and purposes, as part of the said Constitution; viz.

UNDERSTANDING THE PREAMBLE *Viz* is Latin for "that is to say" or "namely."

ARTICLES in addition to, and Amendment of the Constitution of the United States of America, proposed by Congress, and ratified by the Legislatures of the several States, pursuant to the fifth Article of the original Constitution.

Amendment 1 (1791)

Congress shall make no law respecting an establishment of religion, or prohibiting the free exercise thereof; or abridging the freedom of speech, or of the press; or the right of the people peaceably to assemble, and to petition the Government for a redress of grievances.

Amendment 2 (1791)

A well regulated Militia, being necessary to the security of a free State, the right of the people to keep and bear Arms, shall not be infringed.

Amendment 3 (1791)

No Soldier shall, in time of peace be quartered in any house, without the consent of the Owner, nor in time of war, but in a manner to be prescribed by law.

Amendment 4 (1791)

The right of the people to be secure in their persons, houses, papers, and effects, against unreasonable searches and seizures, shall not be violated, and no Warrants shall issue, but upon probable cause, supported by Oath or affirmation, and particularly describing the place to be searched, and the persons or things to be seized.

UNDERSTANDING AMENDMENT 1 The determination to protect religious freedom arose in part from Thomas Jefferson's 1786 Statute for Religious Freedom, which he composed for Virginia's legislature. In his statute, Jefferson called for religious liberty and the separation of church and state.

HISTORICAL THINKING Why do you think the Framers insisted there should be "no law respecting an establishment of religion"?

UNDERSTANDING AMENDMENT 2 This amendment has been hotly debated for decades. Many Americans believe the amendment grants them the right to possess guns. Others think gun ownership should be controlled.

HISTORICAL THINKING Do you think the Framers intended to grant all Americans the right to own guns or just those in militias? Explain your ideas.

UNDERSTANDING AMENDMENT 3 This amendment stemmed from the colonists' experience during the American Revolution. Back then, British soldiers could come into colonists' homes and demand food and shelter. This isn't an issue anymore.

Amendment 5 (1791)

No person shall be held to answer for a capital, or otherwise infamous crime, unless on a presentment or indictment of a Grand Jury, except in cases arising in the land or naval forces, or in the Militia, when in actual service in time of War or public danger; nor shall any person be subject for the same offence to be twice put in jeopardy of life or limb; nor shall be compelled in any criminal case to be a witness against himself, nor be deprived of life, liberty, or property, without due process of law; nor shall private property be taken for public use, without just compensation.

Amendment 6 (1791)

In all criminal prosecutions, the accused shall enjoy the right to a speedy and public trial, by an impartial jury of the State and district wherein the crime shall have been committed, which district shall have been previously ascertained by law, and to be informed of the nature and cause of the accusation; to be confronted with the witnesses against him; to have compulsory process for obtaining witnesses in his favor, and to have the Assistance of Counsel for his defence.

Amendment 7 (1791)

In Suits at common law, where the value in controversy shall exceed twenty dollars, the right of trial by jury shall be preserved, and no fact tried by a jury, shall be otherwise re-examined in any Court of the United States, than according to the rules of the common law.

Amendment 8 (1791)

Excessive bail shall not be required, nor excessive fines imposed, nor cruel and unusual punishments inflicted.

Amendment 9 (1791)

The enumeration in the Constitution, of certain rights, shall not be construed to deny or disparage others retained by the people.

Amendment 10 (1791)

The powers not delegated to the United States by the Constitution, nor prohibited by it to the States, are reserved to the States respectively, or to the people.

UNDERSTANDING AMENDMENTS 4–6 These three amendments protect people who are suspected of a crime or being tried for one.

- Amendment 4 says that police must have a good reason ("probable cause") before they can seize, or take someone's possessions.
- Amendment 5 means that a person has the right to remain silent when charged with a crime. The amendment is the basis for the Miranda rights warning, which requires police to tell those they arrest their rights.
- Amendment 6 guarantees those accused of a crime to a speedy and public trial.

UNDERSTANDING AMENDMENT 7 This amendment provides the right to a trial by jury. Common law is unwritten law created by judges that apply to all people.

UNDERSTANDING AMENDMENT 8 This amendment proclaims that no punishment should be "excessive" or "cruel and unusual." In other words, the harshness of the punishment should match the seriousness of the crime.

HISTORICAL THINKING How might this amendment be used to either justify or oppose the death penalty as punishment for a crime?

UNDERSTANDING AMENDMENTS 9 and 10 Amendment 9 promises that other rights not stated in the Bill of Rights, such as the right to travel freely, are still covered. Amendment 10 says each state has the power to make laws that are not covered by the Constitution, including laws about starting a business.

UNDERSTANDING AMENDMENT 11
According to this amendment, the United States has no power in lawsuits against individual states.

UNDERSTANDING AMENDMENT 11
According to this amendment, the United States has no power in lawsuits against individual states.

UNDERSTANDING AMENDMENT 12
This amendment established the electoral college, which decides who the president and vice president will be. The electoral college was challenged in 2000 and 2016, when the candidates who won the popular vote (Al Gore in 2000 and Hillary Clinton in 2016) lost the elections to George W. Bush and Donald Trump, respectively.

HISTORICAL THINKING Do you think presidential elections should be decided by the electoral college? Explain why or why not.

Amendment 11 (1798)

[**Note:** Article 3, Section 2, of the Constitution was modified by the 11th Amendment.]

The Judicial power of the United States shall not be construed to extend to any suit in law or equity, commenced or prosecuted against one of the United States by Citizens of another State, or by Citizens or Subjects of any Foreign State.

Amendment 12 (1804)

[**Note:** Part of Article 2, Section 1, of the Constitution was replaced by the 12th Amendment.]

The Electors shall meet in their respective states and vote by ballot for President and Vice-President, one of whom, at least, shall not be an inhabitant of the same state with themselves; they shall name in their ballots the person voted for as President, and in distinct ballots the person voted for as Vice-President, and they shall make distinct lists of all persons voted for as President, and of all persons voted for as Vice-President, and of the number of votes for each, which lists they shall sign and certify, and transmit sealed to the seat of the government of the United States, directed to the President of the Senate; —the President of the Senate shall, in the presence of the Senate and House of Representatives, open all the certificates and the votes shall then be counted; —The person having the greatest number of votes for President, shall be the President, if such number be a majority of the whole number of Electors appointed; and if no person have such majority, then from the persons having the highest numbers not exceeding three on the list of those voted for as President, the House of Representatives shall choose immediately, by ballot, the President. But in choosing the President, the votes shall be taken by states, the representation from each state having one vote; a quorum for this purpose shall consist of a member or members from two-thirds of the states, and a majority of all the states shall be necessary to a choice. *And if the House of Representatives shall not choose a President whenever the right of choice shall devolve upon them, before the fourth day of March next following, then the Vice-President shall act as President, as in case of the death or other constitutional disability of the President.* The person having the greatest number of votes as Vice-President, shall be the Vice-President, if such number be a majority of the whole number of Electors appointed, and if no person have a majority, then from the two highest numbers on the list, the Senate shall choose the Vice-President; a quorum for the purpose shall consist of two-thirds of the whole number of Senators, and a majority of the whole number shall be necessary to a choice. But no person constitutionally ineligible to the office of President shall be eligible to that of Vice-President of the United States.

Amendment 13 (1865)

[**Note:** A portion of Article 4, Section 2, of the Constitution was superseded by the 13th Amendment.]

SECTION 1: Neither slavery nor involuntary servitude, except as a punishment for crime whereof the party shall have been duly convicted, shall exist within the United States, or any place subject to their jurisdiction.

SECTION 2: Congress shall have power to enforce this article by appropriate legislation.

Amendment 14 (1868)

[**Note:** Article 1, Section 2, of the Constitution was modified by Section 2 of the 14th Amendment.]

SECTION 1: All persons born or naturalized in the United States, and subject to the jurisdiction thereof, are citizens of the United States and of the State wherein they reside. No State shall make or enforce any law which shall abridge the privileges or immunities of citizens of the United States; nor shall any State deprive any person of life, liberty, or property, without due process of law; nor deny to any person within its jurisdiction the equal protection of the laws.

SECTION 2: Representatives shall be apportioned among the several States according to their respective numbers, counting the whole number of persons in each State, excluding Indians not taxed. But when the right to vote at any election for the choice of electors for President and Vice-President of the United States, Representatives in Congress, the Executive and Judicial officers of a State, or the members of the *Legislature thereof, is denied to any of the male inhabitants of such State, being twenty-one years of age, and citizens of the United States,* or in any way abridged, except for participation in rebellion, or other crime, the basis of representation therein shall be reduced in the proportion which the number of such male citizens shall bear to the whole number of male citizens twenty-one years of age in such State.

SECTION 3: No person shall be a Senator or Representative in Congress, or elector of President and Vice-President, or hold any office, civil or military, under the United States, or under any State, who, having previously taken an oath, as a member of Congress, or as an officer of the United States, or as a member of any State legislature, or as an executive or judicial officer of any State, to support the Constitution of the United States, shall have engaged in insurrection or rebellion against the same, or given aid or comfort to the enemies thereof. But Congress may by a vote of two-thirds of each House, remove such disability.

UNDERSTANDING AMENDMENT 14 Section 1 This section defines citizenship and ensures that all citizens enjoy the same rights and the same protections by the law.

UNDERSTANDING AMENDMENT 14 Section 2 This section overrides the Three-Fifths Compromise in Article I. As a result of this amendment, each citizen is counted as a whole person—except Native Americans.

UNDERSTANDING AMENDMENT 14 Sections 3 and 4 These sections of the amendment refer to those who supported or fought for the Confederacy.

UNDERSTANDING AMENDMENT 15 As a result of this amendment, African-American men were granted voting rights. No woman of any race or color could vote. Unfortunately, even after this amendment was passed, some states passed laws that required taxes, tests, and other unfair requirements for people to be permitted to vote.

HISTORICAL THINKING Why do you think the 13th, 14th, and 15th amendments are sometimes referred to as the "Reconstruction amendments"?

SECTION 4: The validity of the public debt of the United States, authorized by law, including debts incurred for payment of pensions and bounties for services in suppressing insurrection or rebellion, shall not be questioned. But neither the United States nor any State shall assume or pay any debt or obligation incurred in aid of insurrection or rebellion against the United States, or any claim for the loss or emancipation of any slave; but all such debts, obligations and claims shall be held illegal and void.

SECTION 5: The Congress shall have the power to enforce, by appropriate legislation, the provisions of this article.

Amendment 15 (1870)

SECTION 1: The right of citizens of the United States to vote shall not be denied or abridged by the United States or by any State on account of race, color, or previous condition of servitude—

SECTION 2: The Congress shall have the power to enforce this article by appropriate legislation.

Amendment 16 (1913)

[**Note:** Article 1, Section 9, of the Constitution was modified by the 16th Amendment.]

The Congress shall have power to lay and collect taxes on incomes, from whatever source derived, without apportionment among the several States, and without regard to any census or enumeration.

In this illustration, a group of men who helped bring about the 15th Amendment, including Abraham Lincoln, Hiram Revels, and Frederick Douglass, watch as President Ulysses S. Grant signs the amendment.

Amendment 17 (1913)

[Note: Article 1, Section 3, of the Constitution was modified by the 17th Amendment.]

The Senate of the United States shall be composed of two Senators from each State, elected by the people thereof, for six years; and each Senator shall have one vote. The electors in each State shall have the qualifications requisite for electors of the most numerous branch of the State legislatures.

When vacancies happen in the representation of any State in the Senate, the executive authority of such State shall issue writs of election to fill such vacancies: Provided, That the legislature of any State may empower the executive thereof to make temporary appointments until the people fill the vacancies by election as the legislature may direct.

This amendment shall not be so construed as to affect the election or term of any Senator chosen before it becomes valid as part of the Constitution.

Amendment 18 (1919)

Repealed by the 21st Amendment.

SECTION 1: *After one year from the ratification of this article the manufacture, sale, or transportation of intoxicating liquors within, the importation thereof into, or the exportation thereof from the United States and all territory subject to the jurisdiction thereof for beverage purposes is hereby prohibited.*

SECTION 2: *The Congress and the several States shall have concurrent power to enforce this article by appropriate legislation.*

SECTION 3: *This article shall be inoperative unless it shall have been ratified as an amendment to the Constitution by the legislatures of the several States, as provided in the Constitution, within seven years from the date of the submission hereof to the States by the Congress.*

Amendment 19 (1920)

The right of citizens of the United States to vote shall not be denied or abridged by the United States or by any State on account of sex.

Congress shall have power to enforce this article by appropriate legislation.

UNDERSTANDING AMENDMENT 18 Known as the Prohibition Amendment, the 18th Amendment was repealed only 14 years later, in 1933, by the 21st Amendment. Alcohol was associated with social problems including abuse of women and children.

HISTORICAL THINKING Why do you think the 18th Amendment was repealed?

Federal agents pour a barrel filled with beer down a sewer during Prohibition.

UNDERSTANDING AMENDMENT 19 With the passage of the 19th Amendment, all women received the right to vote in all states. Prior to ratification of this amendment, a number of states already permitted women to vote.

HISTORICAL THINKING Why was it important to add an amendment to the Constitution granting women voting rights and not just leave the matter to individual states?

UNDERSTANDING AMENDMENT 20 This amendment is often called the "Lame Duck Amendment." In government, a lame duck is an elected official whose term in office is about to end. So, for instance, a president who has already served two terms is a lame duck. Officials who have not won re-election are also considered lame ducks.

HISTORICAL THINKING Why do you think it is more difficult for so-called lame-duck officials to enact legislation?

Amendment 20 (1933)

[**Note:** Article 1, Section 4, of the Constitution was modified by Section 2 of the 20th Amendment. In addition, a portion of the 12th Amendment was superseded by Section 3.]

SECTION 1: The terms of the President and the Vice President shall end at noon on the 20th day of January, and the terms of Senators and Representatives at noon on the 3d day of January, of the years in which such terms would have ended if this article had not been ratified; and the terms of their successors shall then begin.

SECTION 2: The Congress shall assemble at least once in every year, and such meeting shall begin at noon on the 3d day of January, unless they shall by law appoint a different day.

SECTION 3: If, at the time fixed for the beginning of the term of the President, the President elect shall have died, the Vice President elect shall become President. If a President shall not have been chosen before the time fixed for the beginning of his term, or if the President elect shall have failed to qualify, then the Vice President elect shall act as President until a President shall have qualified; and the Congress may by law provide for the case wherein neither a President elect nor a Vice President elect shall have qualified, declaring who shall then act as President, or the manner in which one who is to act shall be selected, and such person shall act accordingly until a President or Vice President shall have qualified.

SECTION 4: The Congress may by law provide for the case of the death of any of the persons from whom the House of Representatives may choose a President whenever the right of choice shall have devolved upon them, and for the case of the death of any of the persons from whom the Senate may choose a Vice President whenever the right of choice shall have devolved upon them.

SECTION 5: Sections 1 and 2 shall take effect on the 15th day of October following the ratification of this article.

SECTION 6: This article shall be inoperative unless it shall have been ratified as an amendment to the Constitution by the legislatures of three-fourths of the several States within seven years from the date of its submission.

Amendment 21 (1933)

SECTION 1: The eighteenth article of amendment to the Constitution of the United States is hereby repealed.

SECTION 2: The transportation or importation into any State, Territory, or possession of the United States for delivery or use therein of intoxicating liquors, in violation of the laws thereof, is hereby prohibited.

SECTION 3: This article shall be inoperative unless it shall have been ratified as an amendment to the Constitution by conventions in the several States, as provided in the Constitution, within seven years from the date of the submission hereof to the States by the Congress.

Amendment 22 (1951)

SECTION 1: No person shall be elected to the office of the President more than twice, and no person who has held the office of President, or acted as President, for more than two years of a term to which some other person was elected President shall be elected to the office of the President more than once. But this Article shall not apply to any person holding the office of President when this Article was proposed by the Congress, and shall not prevent any person who may be holding the office of President, or acting as President, during the term within which this Article becomes operative from holding the office of President or acting as President during the remainder of such term.

SECTION 2: This article shall be inoperative unless it shall have been ratified as an amendment to the Constitution by the legislatures of three-fourths of the several States within seven years from the date of its submission to the States by the Congress.

UNDERSTANDING AMENDMENT 21 This amendment repealed the 18th Amendment and ended Prohibition.

UNDERSTANDING AMENDMENT 22 Franklin D. Roosevelt served three terms as president of the United States and was elected to a fourth term shortly before he died in 1945. All presidents before Roosevelt served two terms. Within months of Roosevelt's death, Republicans in Congress presented the 22nd Amendment for consideration.

HISTORICAL THINKING Do you think the U.S. president should be limited to serving two terms? Why or why not?

UNDERSTANDING AMENDMENT 23 Although the District of Columbia is the official seat of the U.S. government, it is a federal territory, not a state, and has only a nonvoting representative in Congress. Washington, D.C., began as a very small community. However, by 1960, more than 760,000 people who paid federal taxes and could be drafted to serve in the military lived in the District. The states ratified Amendment 23 in 1961 to give the residents of the District the right to have their votes counted in the presidential elections.

UNDERSTANDING AMENDMENT 24 This amendment abolished poll taxes, election fees charged by states to keep low-income and mostly African-American citizens from voting. The amendment was passed in response to the demands of the civil rights movement of the 1960s, which condemned the poll tax.

HISTORICAL THINKING What impact did the poll tax probably have on election results?

Amendment 23 (1961)

SECTION 1: The District constituting the seat of Government of the United States shall appoint in such manner as the Congress may direct:

A number of electors of President and Vice President equal to the whole number of Senators and Representatives in Congress to which the District would be entitled if it were a State, but in no event more than the least populous State; they shall be in addition to those appointed by the States, but they shall be considered, for the purposes of the election of President and Vice President, to be electors appointed by a State; and they shall meet in the District and perform such duties as provided by the twelfth article of amendment.

SECTION 2: The Congress shall have power to enforce this article by appropriate legislation.

Amendment 24 (1964)

SECTION 1: The right of citizens of the United States to vote in any primary or other election for President or Vice President, for electors for President or Vice President, or for Senator or Representative in Congress, shall not be denied or abridged by the United States or any State by reason of failure to pay any poll tax or other tax.

SECTION 2: The Congress shall have power to enforce this article by appropriate legislation.

Amendment 25 (1967)

[**Note:** Article 2, Section 1, of the Constitution was affected by the 25th Amendment.]

SECTION 1: In case of the removal of the President from office or of his death or resignation, the Vice President shall become President.

SECTION 2: Whenever there is a vacancy in the office of the Vice President, the President shall nominate a Vice President who shall take office upon confirmation by a majority vote of both Houses of Congress.

SECTION 3: Whenever the President transmits to the President pro tempore of the Senate and the Speaker of the House of Representatives his written declaration that he is unable to discharge the powers and duties of his office, and until he transmits to them a written declaration to the contrary, such powers and duties shall be discharged by the Vice President as Acting President.

SECTION 4: Whenever the Vice President and a majority of either the principal officers of the executive departments or of such other body as Congress may by law provide, transmit to the President pro tempore of the Senate and the Speaker of the House of Representatives their written declaration that the President is unable to discharge the powers and duties of his office, the Vice President shall immediately assume the powers and duties of the office as Acting President.

Thereafter, when the President transmits to the President pro tempore of the Senate and the Speaker of the House of Representatives his written declaration that no inability exists, he shall resume the powers and duties of his office unless the Vice President and a majority of either the principal officers of the executive department or of such other body as Congress may by law provide, transmit within four days to the President pro tempore of the Senate and the Speaker of the House of Representatives their written declaration that the President is unable to discharge the powers and duties of his office. Thereupon Congress shall decide the issue, assembling within forty-eight hours for that purpose if not in session. If the Congress, within twenty-one days after receipt of the latter written declaration, or, if Congress is not in session, within twenty-one days after Congress is required to assemble, determines by two-thirds vote of both Houses that the President is unable to discharge the powers and duties of his office, the Vice President shall continue to discharge the same as Acting President; otherwise, the President shall resume the powers and duties of his office.

UNDERSTANDING AMENDMENT 25 The 25th Amendment was ratified in 1967 to set up procedures to follow if a president becomes disabled while in office. It was proposed after the assassination of President John F. Kennedy in 1963. Following his death, some people began to wonder what would have happened if he'd survived the shooting but been unable to govern. This amendment provides for an orderly transfer of power.

HISTORICAL THINKING Why is there a plan of succession for the presidency?

AMENDMENTS

President Richard Nixon signs the 26th Amendment in 1971. Looking on are members of the youth choir Young Americans.

UNDERSTANDING AMENDMENT 26 The voting age had been 21 since 1868. However, while the United States fought the Vietnam War in the 1960s and 1970s, people began to question why 18-year-old men could be drafted to serve in the military but could not vote. As a result, the 26th Amendment was passed by Congress and ratified by the states on July 1, 1971.

Through the progressive expansion of voting rights, the Constitution has provided ever-increasing opportunities for citizens to participate in the political process.

HISTORICAL THINKING Why do you think many Americans questioned the fairness of denying voting rights to 18-year-olds, especially to those who could be drafted to go to war?

Amendment 26 (1971)

[**Note:** Amendment 14, Section 2, of the Constitution was modified by Section 1 of the 26th Amendment.]

SECTION 1: The right of citizens of the United States, who are eighteen years of age or older, to vote shall not be denied or abridged by the United States or by any State on account of age.

SECTION 2: The Congress shall have power to enforce this article by appropriate legislation.

Amendment 27 (1992)

No law, varying the compensation for the services of the Senators and Representatives, shall take effect, until an election of Representatives shall have intervened.

Citizenship and You

Imagine your parents have given you the right to play a computer game during your free time. To keep enjoying this right, you have some responsibilities. You're responsible for having your homework and chores done before you play the game. You're responsible for using the computer according to your family's or school's rules. Similarly, our responsibilities as citizens balance the rights we receive as citizens. Let's take a closer look at the whats, whys, and hows of **citizenship**—being a full member of a country in exchange for certain responsibilities.

AS DEFINED BY THE FRAMERS

As you have observed by studying the U.S. Constitution and Bill of Rights, privileges and rights like citizenship and voting have been contested, reshaped, and amended over time. We started with the freedoms outlined by the Framers, but many contributions have been made throughout history by Americans who have worked to expand our rights. These include the civil rights of individuals and minorities, the right to participate in government, the right to speak freely, the right to a fair trial, and many others. The efforts of those activists have helped us move forward in our continuing struggle to become a more perfect union—a struggle that continues today.

A COUNTRY WITHOUT RULES?

Picture this: You arrive at school on the first day of classes, but no schedules are available for the students. Nobody knows the school rules. Teachers and office workers can't answer any questions, and no one has been assigned a locker. Everything is completely disorganized and confusing.

This is similar to what would happen in a government without clear rules—or laws—that define the rights and responsibilities of its citizens. Order, organization, equality, and safety would all suffer without these laws. Is it fair that a government makes the laws that define the rights and responsibilities of a nation? In essence, a democratic government IS the people of its nation. The people who serve in the government and make its laws are elected by people across the country. So, these lawmakers represent the people of that country.

In the United States, we work to be *good citizens* by obeying laws, *participatory citizens* by voting and serving on juries, and *socially-just citizens* by standing up for the rights of others. Read on to learn more about the rights and responsibilities of citizenship.

While you might not be old enough to vote in the United States, you have many other rights, and as you'll see, those rights come with responsibilities.

THINK ABOUT IT

SUMMARIZE How have the rights and responsibilities of U.S. citizens been defined and changed over time?

The Rights and Responsibilities of Citizens

In the United States, citizens have many rights, regardless of whether they were born here or came here from another country. Knowing their rights helps citizens understand the responsibilities they have to balance and support their rights. Rights are simple: they are established in the U.S. Constitution and Bill of Rights. Responsibilities are pretty simple, too. Mostly they consist of simply doing what is right and showing good character. As you read, think about specific actions you might take to be a good, participatory, and socially-just citizen.

BECOMING A CITIZEN

Some residents of the United States are citizens because they were born in the country. Others came from foreign countries to legally enter and live in the United States. They worked to become citizens through an immigration process called **naturalization**. People becoming naturalized citizens work hard to learn the laws, rights, and responsibilities of American citizenship. They take a citizenship test and are sworn in as citizens during a naturalization ceremony. Immigrants enhance the diversity of the United States and have contributed greatly throughout history. It is a proud day when they become U.S. citizens who can enjoy the rights of citizens listed below.

Rights of Citizens
Right to freedom of religion
Right to freedom of speech
Right to freedom of the press
Right to assemble
Right to trial by jury (in specific types of cases)
Right to vote
Right to buy and sell property
Right to freely travel across the country and to leave and return to the country

LIMITS ON RIGHTS

By now, you're probably pretty familiar with the basic rights of citizens as guaranteed in the Constitution. It's worth noting there are limitations that apply to some of these rights. Some of these restrictions were built into the laws that established the rights. Others have come into being because of cases that have come before the Supreme Court and tested various rights. For example, it's true that as stated in the First Amendment to the U.S. Constitution, people have the right to free speech—to say what they are thinking without fear of the government punishing them for expressing their thoughts or ideas. But this freedom of speech is not absolute. For example, suppose someone shouted "Fire!" in a movie theater or crowded shopping mall when there actually was no fire. That person would not be protected by the right to free speech, as his or her clearly intentional "speech" could cause harm to others.

CIVIC RESPONSIBILITIES

U.S. citizens have two different types of responsibilities: civic and personal. **Civic responsibilities** include voting, paying taxes, and serving on juries. **Personal responsibilities** include respecting others, helping in the community, standing up for others, and staying informed about issues.

If people didn't exercise their civic responsibilities, rights would not exist. In the United States, for example, many people take for granted their right to vote and don't bother to vote at all. Perhaps they don't consider the fact that the right to vote is a privilege that doesn't exist in all countries. People in many countries do not have the opportunity to elect officials who will represent them and make decisions that determine how everyone will be governed.

A six-year old stands in proud support as her mother receives her citizenship. This naturalization ceremony took place in 2014 in the Metropolitan Museum of Art in New York City.

Because people in the United States have the right to vote, they have a corresponding responsibility to exercise that right. They are also responsible for being informed voters. Voters have an obligation to use reliable sources to learn about candidates who are running for office. Voters must determine the similarities and differences between the candidates' positions on issues and use evidence to analyze the credibility of their claims. Similarly, voters have the same obligation to inform themselves about new laws before casting votes in favor of or against them.

How can a young person exercise civic responsibilities related to voting if he or she is not old enough to vote? You can participate in mock elections or student government elections in your school. You can create posters and pamphlets to encourage adults to vote, or volunteer to help with a candidate's campaign. Remember, the decisions of voters impact people of every age.

PERSONAL RESPONSIBILITIES

When you think of your personal responsibilities as a citizen, consider the choices you make in terms of your actions. Being a responsible citizen means behaving in ways that are right, moral, and just, and acting in a way that benefits you and those around you. Considering the rights of all people, not just the rights of a select few, will help you be a personally responsible citizen.

Citizens have many personal responsibilities, such as being open-minded, respecting the opinions of others, and showing respect for the beliefs and individuality of people with different backgrounds. People of any age can take on personal responsibilities by doing community service projects, standing up for the rights of others, and respecting all people regardless of ethnicity, nationality, gender identity, sexual orientation, or beliefs. Living up to these personal responsibilities helps citizens contribute to an environment of respect and caring.

THINK ABOUT IT

EXPLAIN How does a democracy depend on people fulfilling their civic and personal responsibilities?

Building and Practicing Citizenship Skills

Building citizenship skills is like building muscle. It takes hard work and repetition, but the rewards pay off for everyone. Some citizenship skills, such as helping raise voter participation, will require you to seek out specific opportunities. Others, such as refusing to tolerate bullying, can be exercised whenever appropriate situations arise. Citizenship affords many rights and requires many responsibilities. Enjoying these rights and responsibilities is the reward of being a good citizen.

The following chart includes ways you can build and apply citizenship skills and become an active participant in our democracy. Study the chart and check out the Active Citizenship for the Environment Activities in this program's online resources. Then brainstorm more ways you can be a good, participatory, socially-just citizen.

THINK ABOUT IT

DESCRIBE What citizenship project would you be interested in undertaking, and how would you carry it out?

Citizenship in Action

Responsibilities	Citizenship Projects: Ways to Take Action
Become informed.	• Read books and articles from reliable sources. • Attend, watch, or read transcripts of debates and speeches. • Watch broadcast journalists on reliable cable and digital sources. • Ask questions of others who are well informed.
Make decisions based on facts.	• Think about whether you are acting on emotion or fact. • Use reliable sources to evaluate statements you hear and read. • Check reliable sources to see if others' statements are accurate.
Listen to the opinions of others. Discuss differences of opinion in a kind and civil manner.	• When friends or acquaintances express opinions that differ from yours, explain why you disagree, if you do. • Use appropriate language and remain calm as you discuss opinions. If the other person refuses to be calm or civil, end the conversation and walk away.
Respect the value of individuals. Respect differences among people.	• Enjoy the differences among people. • Make friends with people who are different from you. • Volunteer in your community to interact with and help others.
Stand up for rights of others. Work to stop bullying.	• Do not stand by silently when someone is being bullied. Speak up. If you do not feel safe, immediately seek the help of an adult. • Write articles and blog posts about the importance of stopping the act of bullying. Develop or participate in an antibullying program.
Volunteer in your community.	• Determine how your skills and interests could help someone else. • Talk with your parents, teachers, and friends to learn what types of volunteer services your community needs. • Make volunteering a regular part of your life. You could consider serving food to the homeless, collecting clothing or canned goods to help a local shelter, cleaning or restoring a local park or playground, or tutoring students who are struggling with their school work.

Responsibilities	Citizenship Projects: Ways to Take Action
Express political opinions.	• Write a letter or an email to a newspaper editor about an issue that concerns you. • Use clear and concise language. Edit your letter carefully.
Obey the law.	• Become familiar with the laws in your state, city, and town that apply to people your age.
Pay taxes.	• Read more about your local and state taxes, and what the revenue is used for. • Recognize that you are already paying sales taxes when you purchase many items.
Lobby for change.	• Form a lobbying committee with other students to influence legislation or public policy. • Establish a goal for your lobbying campaign. • Identify whom to lobby. (Who are the people who can help you accomplish your goal?) • Find information and statistics to support your goal. • Get public support for your cause. You might consider gathering signatures on a petition or creating flyers to publicize your campaign. • Present your case to the appropriate individuals.
Accept responsibility for your actions.	• If someone asks about a mistake you have made, tell the truth. • Ask what you might do to make up for the mistake.
Participate in the democratic process.	• Ask a teacher to organize a trip to a local courtroom to see the law in action. • Contact a local political candidate whose ideas you support to see how you might help with his or her campaign. • Plan and/or participate in mock elections, student government elections, and student government meetings. • With the help of a parent or teacher, seek opportunities to participate in a naturalization ceremony. • Research how you and your classmates can participate in National History Day at a state or national level.

One way of practicing citizenship is by volunteering.

GLOSSARY

A

abolition *n.* (a-buh-LIH-shuhn) the act of putting an end to something, such as slavery (page 349)

abolitionist *n.* (a-buh-LIH-shuhn-ihst) a person who wants to end slavery (page 446)

acquired immunodeficiency syndrome (AIDS) *n.* (uh-KWYRD ih-MYOO-noh-dih-FIH-shun-see SIHN-drohm) the final stage of a disease caused by a virus that attacks the system in the human body that fights off illnesses (page 971)

advertising *n.* (AD-vuhr-ty-zhing) the act of presenting products and ideas to the public (page 738)

affirmative action *n.* (uh-FUR-muh-tihv AK-shuhn) a government policy that institutes racial quotas to favor groups that suffer from discrimination (page 915)

African diaspora *n.* (A-frih-kuhn DY-as-poh-rah) the removal of Africans from their homelands to the Americas (page 74)

Agent Orange *n.* (AY-juhnt OR-ihnj) a potent herbicide used to kill vegetation (page 929)

agrarian *adj.* (ah-GRAR-ee-ehn) related to agriculture or farming (page 366)

Agricultural Revolution *n.* (AHG-rih-kuhl-chuhr-uhl REV-oh-luh-shuhn) the transition in human history from hunting and gathering food to planting crops and raising animals (page 9)

Alien and Sedition Acts *n.* (AY-lee-uhn AND sih-DIH-shun AKTS) a series of four laws passed to keep certain groups from immigrating to the United States; the laws gave the government power to expel aliens living in the United States and targeted U.S. citizens who criticized the U.S. government (page 293)

alliance *n.* (ah-LY-ans) an agreement between nations to fight each other's enemies or otherwise collaborate; a partnership (page 111)

Allied Powers *n.* (AHL-ayhd POHW-uhrs) Several countries, including France and Great Britain, working together to oppose the Axis Powers of Germany, Italy, and Japan during World War II (page 789)

alternative energy *n.* (awl-TUR-nuh-tihv EH-nur-jee) electricity or power that is created from a source that will not run out, such as wind or solar power (page 1009)

amendment *n.* (uh-MEND-muhnt) a formal change to a law, usually referring to a formal change to the U.S. Constitution (page 263)

American System *n.* (uh-MAIR-uh-kuhn SIHS-tuhm) a policy of promoting the U.S. industrial system through the use of tariffs, federal subsidies to build roads and other public works, and a national bank to control currency (page 342)

Americanization *n.* (uh-mair-uh-kan-ih-ZAY-shuhn) the act of teaching immigrants and Native Americans the mainstream culture and language of the United States with the expectation that they will adapt to and embrace it (page 598)

amphibious landing craft *n.* (am-FIH-bee-uhs LAN-ding KRAFT) boats used to convey soldiers and equipment from the sea to the shore during military attacks (page 811)

Anaconda Plan *n.* (a-nuh-KAHN-duh PLAN) a military strategy during the Civil War in which the North planned to set up a blockade around the southern coast to ruin the South's economy and secure ports on the Mississippi River; much as a huge snake, like an anaconda, crushes its prey (page 504)

anarchist *n.* (AHN-ark-ist) a person who advocates lawlessness and the absence of all government (page 650)

annex *v.* (a-NEX) to add (page 391)

antebellum *adj.* (an-tih-BEH-luhm) before the American Civil War (page 340)

anthropologist *n.* (an-thruh-PAH-luh-jist) a person who studies cultures (page 748)

antiaircraft gun *n.* (AN-ty-AIR-kraft GUHN) a piece of heavy artillery modified so that it can be pointed skyward at enemy planes (page 713)

antifederalist *n.* (an-tee-FEH-duh-ruh-list) a person who opposed the U.S. Constitution of 1787 because of its emphasis on a strong national government (page 262)

anti-Semitism *n.* (AN-tee SEHM-ih-tih-zuhm) discrimination, prejudice, and hostility against the Jewish people (page 814)

appeasement *n.* (uh-PEEZ-muhnt) a policy of making political compromises in order to avoid conflict (page 791)

apprentice *n.* (ah-PREHN-tis) a person who learns a craft or trade by working with a skilled member of that craft or trade (page 129)

arable *adj.* (AIR-ah-bl) able to grow crops; fertile (page 140)

archipelago *n.* (ahr-kuh-PEL-uh-goh) a chain of islands (page 685)

armistice *n.* (AHR-muh-stuhss) an agreement between opposing sides in a conflict to stop fighting (page 721)

arson *n.* (AR-son) the purposeful burning of buildings illegally (page 560)

Articles of Confederation *n.* (AHR-TIH-kuhls UHV kuhn-feh-duh-RAY-shuhn) a set of laws adopted by the United States in 1777 that established each state in the union as a republic, replaced by the Constitution in 1789 (page 222)

artillery *n.* (ahr-TIH-luh-ree) large guns that can fire over a long distance (page 203)

artisan *n.* (AR-tih-san) a person skilled at making things by hand (page 136)

assassinate *v.* (uh-SA-suh-nayt) to murder for political reasons (page 538)

assembly line *n.* (uh-SEHM-blee LYN) a system in which workers stand in place as work passes from operation to operation in a direct line until a product is assembled (page 676)

assimilate *v.* (ah-SIM-ih-late) to adopt the culture or way of life of the nation in which one currently lives; to become absorbed in a culture or country (pages 368, 433)

astronaut *n.* (AS-truh-nawt) a person who is trained to travel in space (page 904)

asylum *n.* (uh-SY-luhm) a hospital dedicated to treating the mentally ill (page 441)

Atlantic Charter *n.* (aht-LAHN-tick CHAHR-tuhr) a charter that lists eight principles for a better world, composed during a meeting between President Franklin Roosevelt and British Prime Minister Winston Churchill in 1941 (page 793)

atoll *n.* (A-tawl) a ring-shaped reef, island, or series of islands formed from coral (page 817)

atomic bomb *n.* (uh-TAH-mihk BAHM) a type of nuclear bomb whose violent explosion is triggered by splitting atoms, which releases intense heat and radioactivity (page 821)

attorney general *n.* (uh-TUR-NEE JEN-ruhl) a member of the president's Cabinet, whose primary role is to represent the United States before the Supreme Court (page 281)

autonomy *n.* (aw-TAH-nuh-mee) self-rule (page 686)

Axis Powers *n.* (ACK-sihs POHW-uhrs) Germany, Italy, and Japan, which formed an alliance together at the start of World War II (page 789)

B

baby boom *n.* (BAY-bee BOOM) a significant increase in the birthrate (page 854)

backcountry *n.* (BAK-kuhn-tree) the western part of the Southern Colonies just east of the Appalachian Mountains (page 134)

ballistic missile *n.* (buh-LIHS-tihk MIH-suhl) a nuclear weapon that is propelled by a rocket and guided using a GPS system (page 908)

banish *v.* (BA-nish) to send away as punishment, usually without hope of return (page 101)

bank holiday *n.* (BANGK HAH-luh-day) a day or period of time when banks are closed by government order (page 771)

bank run *n.* (BANGK RUHN) an event in which many customers panic and rush to withdraw their money from a bank at the same time (page 768)

barrack *n.* (BAIR-uhk) a building or group of buildings used to house large numbers of people (page 806)

battalion *n.* (buh-TAL-yuhn) a large group of military troops (page 806)

bayonet *n.* (BAY-uh-nuht) a sharp blade attached to the end of a rifle (page 228)

bedrock *n.* (BEHD-rahk) solid rock that lies under loose soil (page 636)

GLOSSARY

Bering Land Bridge *n.* (BARE-ingh LAND BRIJ) a piece of land between Alaska and Siberia that was above sea level 13,000 years ago and allowed early humans to cross into North America (page 6)

Berlin Wall *n.* (buhr-LIHN WAWL) a concrete and barbed wire wall that surrounded the democratic West Berlin, built by the communist East Berlin to prevent citizens of East Berlin from moving to the democratic city (page 907)

Bessemer process *n.* (BEH-seh-mur PRAH-sehs) a steel manufacturing process that involves blowing air into molten iron to remove impurities, which results in a stronger metal (page 624)

Bill of Rights *n.* (BIHL UHV RITES) the first 10 amendments to the U.S. Constitution; a list of guarantees to which every person in a country is entitled (page 263)

black codes *n.* (BLAK KOHDZ) laws passed by southern states immediately after the Civil War for controlling African Americans and limiting their rights; repealed by Reconstruction in 1866 (page 554)

black market *n.* (BLAK MAHR-khut) a system through which prohibited goods are bought and sold illegally (page 735)

black peonage *n.* (BLAK PE-eh-nij) economic slavery that tied African Americans to sharecropping landlords' lands (page 559)

black separatism *n.* (BLAK SEH-puh-ruh-ti-zuhm) the political and cultural division of blacks and whites within a society (page 914)

blacklist *v.* (BLAK-lihst) to put one or more people on a list indicating they are to be shunned or punished (page 852)

blight *n.* (BLYT) a fungus or an insect that causes plants to dry up and die (page 432)

blitzkrieg *n.* (BLIHTS-kreeg) a war strategy performed swiftly that involves bombarding transportation and communication targets from the air before starting a land invasion (page 791)

bloc *n.* (BLOK) a group that is formed to support a common interest or purpose (page 846)

blockade *v.* (blah-KAYD) to block ships from entering or leaving a harbor (page 228)

blues *n.* (BLOOZ) a style of music originating among African-American musicians that tells stories about hard times and heartache (page 743)

bluff *n.* (BLUHF) a cliff (page 528)

bonanza farm *n.* (buh-NAN-zuh FAHRM) an enormous farm established by an investor who runs it for profit (page 586)

bond *n.* (BAHND) a certificate offered for sale to the public with the promise that the government will pay the money back at a later date (page 524)

boom-and-bust cycle *n.* (BOOM AND BUHST SY-kuhl) a series of periods of economic growth followed by sudden economic downturns (page 627)

boomtown *n.* (BOOM-town) a town that experiences a great population increase in only a short time period (page 418)

bootlegging *n.* (BOOT-lehg-ihng) illegally making, transporting, or supplying alcohol (page 735)

border state *n.* (BOR-dur STAYT) at the time of the Civil War, a state that bordered both Union and Confederate states, namely Maryland, Kentucky, Delaware, Missouri, and West Virginia (page 489)

Boston Massacre *n.* (BAWS-tuhn MA-sih-kur) the 1779 incident in which British soldiers fired on locals who had been taunting them (page 188)

Boston Tea Party *n.* (BAWS-tuhn TEE PAR-tee) the 1773 incident in which the Sons of Liberty boarded British ships and dumped their cargo in protest of British taxes on the colonists (page 191)

boycott *n.* (BOY-kaht) a form of protest that involves refusing to purchase goods or services (page 183)

bribery *n.* (BRY-buh-ree) offers of money or privileges to those in power in exchange for political favors (page 564)

brinkmanship *n.* (BRIHNGK-muhn-ship) the practice of pushing a conflict to the edge of violence without getting into a war, usually as a tactic to gain a favorable outcome (page 853)

browser *n.* (BROW-zur) a computer application that is used to view websites (page 1000)

burgeon *v.* (BUR-jehn) to grow quickly (page 146)

buying on margin *n.* (BY-ihng AWN MAHR-juhn) buying a stock by paying a small amount of what it is worth and borrowing the rest of the money to pay for it (page 765)

C

Cabinet *n.* (KAB-niht) the heads of the departments that assist the U.S. president (page 279)

Californio *n.* (kal-uh-FOWR-nee-oh) a resident of California who was of Spanish or Mexican descent and lived there before the gold rush (page 417)

capitalism *n.* (KAP-ih-tuh-lih-zuhm) an economic system in which private individuals, as opposed to the government, own and profit from businesses (page 627)

caravan *n.* (KARE-uh-van) a group of people and animals traveling together, usually for trade (page 42)

caravel *n.* (KEHR-ah-vehl) a small, fast ship used by Spanish and Portuguese explorers (page 40)

cash crop *n.* (KASH KRAHP) a crop grown for sale rather than for use by farmers (page 132)

casualty *n.* (KA-zhuhl-tee) a dead or injured person (page 540)

catalytic converter *n.* (ka-tuh-LIH-tihk kuhn-VUR-tur) a part of a vehicle's exhaust system that changes harmful gases from the vehicle into less harmful or harmless gases (page 959)

cattle drive *n.* (KA-tuhl DRYV) the process of moving a herd of cows and steers from one place to another, usually from ranch to railroad hub (page 584)

cavalry *n.* (KA-vuhl-ree) army troops who fight on horseback (page 491)

cease-fire *n.* (SEEHS FY-ur) a military order to end fighting (page 930)

cede *v.* (SEED) to give up (page 288)

centrist *n.* (SEHN-trihst) a person who holds politically moderate views (page 982)

chancellor *n.* (CHAN-suh-lur) a leader in some European countries whose role is similar to that of the U.S. president (page 789)

charter *n.* (CHAHR-tuhr) a written grant establishing an institution and detailing members' rights and privileges (page 92)

chattel slavery *n.* (CHA-tuhl SLAY-veh-ree) a system in which enslaved people have no human rights and are classified as goods (page 72)

checks and balances *n.* (CHEKS AND BAH-luhn-suhz) the system established by the U.S. Constitution that gives each of the branches of government the power to limit the power of the other two (page 258)

Chief Justice *n.* (CHEEF JUH-stuhs) the head of the judicial branch of the government; presides over the Supreme Court (page 281)

chiefdom *n.* (CHEEF-duhm) a large community of people ruled by a chief (page 9)

child labor *n.* (CHYLD LAY-bur) the practice of hiring children to perform paid work, often in dangerous conditions and for low wages (page 647)

Chinese Exclusion Act *n.* (chy-NEEZ ihk-SKLOO-zhuhn AKT) an 1882 law prohibiting Chinese workers from immigrating to the United States for a 10-year period (page 640)

circumnavigate *v.* (sur-cuhm-NAV-ih-gayt) to travel completely around Earth (page 62)

citizenship *n.* (SIH-tuh-zuhn-ship) the condition of having the opportunities and duties of citizens (page R32)

civic responsibility *n.* (SIH-vihk rih-spawn-suh-BIHL-uh-tee) responsibility that is either required or essential that people perform, such as voting, paying taxes, and serving on juries (page R34)

civil disobedience *n.* (SIH-vuhl dihs-uh-BEE-dee-uhnts) the nonviolent disobeying of laws as a form of protest (page 878)

civil liberty *n.* (SIH-vuhl LIH-bur-tee) individual rights protected by law from government interference (page 719)

Civil Rights Act of 1866 *n.* (SIH-vuhl RITES AKT UHV 1866) a bill granting full equality and citizenship to "every race and color" (page 554)

civilian *n.* (suh-VIHL-yuhn) a person who is not in the military (page 497)

civilization *n.* (sih-vuhl-ih-ZAY-shun) a society with a highly developed culture and technology (page 24)

Clayton Antitrust Act *n.* (KLAY-tuhn an-tee-TRUHST AKT) a 1914 law that described the illegality of trusts' unlawful business practices and closed the loopholes they used (page 674)

climate change *n.* (KLY-muht CHAYNJ) changes in Earth's weather patterns (page 1008)

coalition *n.* (koh-uh-LIH-shuhn) an alliance of people, parties, or states focused on a common goal (page 977)

collective bargaining *n.* (kuh-LEHK-tihv BAHR-guhn-ihng) a negotiation carried out by a labor union with an employer to try to improve wages, working conditions, and hours (page 648)

Columbian Exchange *n.* (kuh-LUM-bee-uhn ehks-CHAYNJ) the exchange of plants, animals, microbes, people, and ideas between Europe and the Americas following Columbus's first voyage to the Western Hemisphere (page 70)

command module *n.* (kuh-MAND MAH-jool) the main part of a space vehicle that carries the crew, main supplies, and equipment to return to Earth (page 957)

commerce clause *n.* (KAH-murs KLAWZ) a provision in Article 1 of the U.S. Constitution granting Congress the power to make laws concerning foreign trade as well as trade among the states and with Native American nations (page 261)

commissioner *n.* (kuh-MIH-shuh-nur) a government representative (page 669)

committee of correspondence *n.* (kuh-MIH-tee UHV KAWR-uh-spahn-dunts) in the Revolutionary era, a group of colonists whose duty it was to spread news about protests against the British (page 191)

commodity *n.* (kuh-MAH-duh-tee) a trade good (page 142)

common market *n.* (KAH-muhn MAHR-kuht) a group of countries or states that allows the members to trade freely among themselves (page 261)

common school *n.* (KAH-muhn SKOOL) a colonial elementary school (page 129)

common school movement *n.* (KAH-muhn SKOOL MOOV-muhnt) an educational reform movement in the 1830s that promoted free public schools funded by property taxes and managed by local governments (page 441)

communism *n.* (KAHM-yuh-nih-zuhm) a form of government in which all the means of production and transportation are owned by the state (page 717)

Compromise of 1877 *n.* (KAHM-pruh-myz UHV 1877) a deal in which Democrats agreed to make Rutherford B. Hayes president if Republicans ended Reconstruction and pulled federal troops out of the South (page 565)

concentration camp *n.* (kahnt-suhn-TRAY-shuhn KAMP) a place where prisoners of war or members of persecuted minorities are confined; in World War II, the camps where Jews and others were held and murdered by the Nazis (page 814)

Conestoga wagon *n.* (kah-nuh-STOH-guh WA-guhn) a kind of wagon, made by German settlers in North America, that could carry heavy loads (page 143)

confederacy *n.* (kon-FED-ur-uh-see) an agreement among several groups, states, or governments to protect and support one another in battle or other endeavors (page 111)

Confederacy *n.* (kon-FED-ur-uh-see) the 11 southern states that seceded from the Union to form their own nation, the Confederate States of America (page 474)

conformity *n.* (kuhn-FAWR-mih-tee) an obedience to a set of beliefs (page 144)

conquistador *n.* (kon-KEE-stuh-dohr) a Spanish conqueror who sought gold and other riches in the Americas (page 56)

conscientious objector *n.* (KAHN-shee-ehnt-shuhs ahb-JEHK-tur) a person who refuses to fight in a war, often for religious reasons (page 719)

Conscription Act *n.* (kuhn-SKRIHP-shuhn AKT) a law instituted by the Union in 1863 stating that men between the ages of 20 and 45 years of age were liable to be drafted into the military but they could pay $300 to avoid service (page 522)

conservation movement *n.* (kahn-sur-VAY-shuhn MOOV-muhnt) a movement to promote the protection of natural resources and wildlife (page 671)

conspiracy *n.* (kuhn-SPIHR-uh-see) a secret plan to harm or commit an illegal act (page 911)

constitution *n.* (kahn-stuh-TOO-shuhn) a document that organizes a government and states its powers (page 250)

constitutionalism *n.* (kahn-stuh-TOO-shuh-nuh-lih-zuhm) the concept of governing based on a constitution (page 251)

consumer *n.* (kuhn-SOO-mur) a person who buys a product or service (page 738)

consumer debt *n.* (kuhn-SOO-mur DEHT) the amount of money people have borrowed to purchase goods (page 765)

consumer economy *n.* (kuhn-SOO-mur ih-KAH-nuh-mee) an economy in which people make purchases often and have many choices about what products to buy (page 738)

containment *n.* (kuhn-TAYN-muhnt) a U.S. security policy during the Cold War in which diplomatic and military action was used to stop the Soviet Union from spreading communism (page 847)

contiguous *adj.* (kuhn-TIH-gyuh-wuhs) connected (page 413)

Continental Army *n.* (kahn-tuh-NEHN-tuhl AHR-mee) the American army formed in 1775 by the Second Continental Congress and led by General George Washington (page 203)

Continental Divide *n.* (kahn-tuh-NEHN-tuhl duh-VYD) the high point in the Rocky Mountains that divides the watersheds of the Atlantic and Pacific oceans (page 395)

continental shelf *n.* (kahn-tuh-NEHN-tuhl SHELF) a relatively shallow area of land under the ocean water that extends outward from a continent before a steep drop-off into the open ocean (page 972)

convert *v.* (kuhn-VERT) to persuade to change one's beliefs; often refers to a change in religion (page 43)

cooperative *n.* (koh-AH-pruh-tihv) a group of farmers or others who combine their money to purchase needed products and services (page 591)

Copperhead *n.* (KAH-pur-hed) a negative nickname for Democrats who opposed emancipation of enslaved people and the draft (page 562)

corporation *n.* (kor-puh-RAY-shuhn) a company or group that acts legally as a single unit to run a business (page 626)

corruption *n.* (kuh-RUHP-shuhn) dishonesty, unlawfulness (page 564)

cotton gin *n.* (KAH-tuhn JIHN) a machine that separates the cotton seeds and hulls from the cotton boll (tuft of cotton) (page 338)

counterattack *n.* (KOWN-tur uh-TAK) an attack made in response to a previous attack (page 227)

counterculture *n.* (KOWN-tur-KUHL-chur) a movement in the 1960s that promoted a way of life that was in opposition to American society's established rules and behavior (page 933)

coup *n.* (KOO) an illegal overthrow of the government (page 975)

court-martial *v.* (KORT-mahr-shuhl) to try a member of the armed services accused of offenses against military law (page 688)

court-packing plan *n.* (KORT PA-king PLAN) President Franklin Roosevelt's controversial plan to increase the number of justices on the Supreme Court from nine to fifteen and to add six justices who shared his progressive views (page 779)

cover-up *n.* (KUH-vur UHP) an attempt to hide the truth from the public (page 961)

craft union *n.* (KRAFT YOON-yuhn) a labor union that advocates for workers' rights and protections, whose members are specialized skilled workers or craftsmen (page 443)

credit *n.* (KREH-diht) the privilege of purchasing something or borrowing money and paying the money back over time (page 254)

creditor *n.* (KREH-dih-tur) a person to whom a debt is owed (page 590)

crematorium *n.* (kree-muh-TOR-ee-uhm) a furnace or oven used to burn human or animal remains; in World War II, the ovens used by Nazis to burn their victims' bodies (page 814)

Crittenden Plan *n.* (KRIHT-uhn-duhn PLAN) a proposal that stated the federal government would have no power to abolish slavery in the states where it already existed; it reestablished and extended the Missouri Compromise line to the Pacific Ocean (page 476)

Cuban Missile Crisis *n.* (KYOO-buhn MIH-suhl CRY-suhs) a political showdown in 1962 between the United States and the Soviet Union caused by the presence of nuclear weapons in Cuba (page 908)

Currency Act *n.* (KUR-uhn-see AKT) the British law that regulated paper money in the American colonies (page 181)

customs *n.* (KUH-stuhmz) the taxes placed on imported and exported goods (page 319)

D

D-Day *n.* (DEE DAY) the day, June 6, 1944, in World War II when Allied forces invaded northern France by landing on beaches at Normandy (page 810)

death camp *n.* (DEHTH KAMP) a camp where Jews and others were held and murdered by the Nazis during World War II (page 814)

Declaration of Independence *n.* (deh-kluh-RAY-shun UHV ihn-duh-PEHN-duhns) the document declaring U.S. independence from Great Britain, adopted July 4, 1776 (page 208)

defect *v.* (dih-FEKT) to break away (page 564)

defensive war *n.* (dih-FEHN-sihv WOR) a war to protect one's own land, on familiar ground, from outside attackers (page 222)

deficit spending *n.* (DEH-fuh-suht SPEHND-ihng) a practice in which the government spends more money than it receives from taxes (page 783)

dehumanize *v.* (dee-HYOO-mahn-ize) to treat people as if they are not human beings (page 872)

delegate *n.* (DEH-lih-guht) a person chosen or elected to represent a group of people (page 256)

demobilization *n.* (dih-moh-buh-ly-ZAY-shuhn) the release of soldiers from military duty (page 842)

democratic republic *n.* (deh-muh-KRA-tihk RE-puhb-lik) an independent country ruled by its citizens through elections and other forms of voting (page R32)

deploy *v.* (dih-PLOY) to send into military action (page 802)

depression *n.* (dee-PREH-shuhn) a period of slow economic activity when many people are without work (page 375)

deregulation *n.* (dee-reh-gyuh-LAY-shun) the removal of laws or regulations governing a particular industry (page 966)

desegregate *v.* (dee-SEH-grih-GAYT) to end a policy that forces the separation of groups of people in public spaces (page 877)

desert *v.* (dih-ZURT) to run away from the army or another branch of the military to avoid military service (page 231)

dictator *n.* (DIHK-tay-tur) a leader who rules with absolute power (page 789)

diplomat *n.* (DIH-pluh-mat) a person sent to another nation to represent his or her country's interests (page 409)

direct primary election *n.* (duh-REKT PRY-mair-ee ih-LEK-shuhn) an election in which members of a political party nominate candidates by a direct vote (page 668)

dissent *n.* (dih-SEHNT) a disagreement with the government's official opinion (page 719)

dissenter *n.* (dih-SEHN-tur) a person who disagrees with a majority belief or position (page 100)

dissident *n.* (DIH-suh-duhnt) a person who strongly disagrees with official policy (page 732)

diversity *n.* (duh-VUR-suh-tee) a wide variety (page 143)

doctrine *n.* (DAHK-truhn) a principle or set of beliefs accepted by a group (page 109)

doctrine of nullification *n.* (DAHK-truhn UHV nuh-luh-fuh-KAY-shun) a doctrine that said a state could nullify, or reject, a federal law they felt was unconstitutional, held by some southern politicians before the Civil War (page 366)

domestic service *n.* (duh-MEHS-tihk SUR-vuhs) housework in another person's home, performed as a job (page 433)

domesticate *v.* (duh-MEHS-tih-kayt) to raise plants and animals for human benefit and consumption (page 27)

domestication *n.* (duh-mehs-TIH-kay-shuhn) the practice of raising animals and growing plants for human benefit (page 9)

domino theory *n.* (DAH-muh-noh THEER-ee) an idea during the Cold War that countries that neighbor communist countries are more likely to fall to communism (page 926)

dove *n.* (DUHV) a person who opposes war (page 933)

draft *n.* (DRAFT) a mandatory term of military service (page 522)

draft exemption *n.* (DRAFT ihg-ZEHM-shuhn) a reason to exclude a citizen from performing involuntary military service (page 933)

Dred Scott decision *n.* (DRED SKAHT dih-SIH-zhuhn) a Supreme Court decision that African Americans held no rights as citizens and that the Missouri Compromise of 1820 was unconstitutional; Dred Scott, the escaped slave at the center of the case, was returned to slavery (page 468)

drought *n.* (DROWT) a prolonged period with little or no rainfall (page 774)

drumlin *n.* (DRUHM-luhn) a smooth-sloped hill made of glacial sediments (page 204)

dual sovereignty *n.* (DOO-uhl SAH-vuh-ruhn-tee) the concept that state governments have certain powers the federal government cannot overrule (page 257)

Dust Bowl *n.* (DUHST BOHL) a region of the Great Plains, including parts of Oklahoma, Colorado, Kansas, New Mexico, and Texas, that suffered from severe drought, soil erosion, and dust storms during the 1930s (page 774)

duty *n.* (DOO-tee) a tax on imports (page 181)

E

earthworks *n.* (URTH-wurks) human-made land modifications (page 204)

economic activity *n.* (eh-kuh-NAH-mihk ak-TIH-vuh-tee) actions that involve the production, distribution, and consumption of goods and services (page 114)

economic stimulus *n.* (eh-kuh-NAH-mihk STIHM-yuh-luhs) a measure aimed at promoting and enabling financial recovery and growth (page 996)

Electoral College *n.* (ee-lehk-TAWR-uhl KAH-lihj) the group that elects the U.S. president; each state receives as many electors as it has congressional representatives and senators combined (page 258)

emancipation *n.* (ih-man-suh-PAY-shuhn) the ending of slavery (page 446)

Emancipation Proclamation *n.* (ih-man-suh-PAY-shuhn prah-kluh-MAY-shuhn) an 1863 document issued by Abraham Lincoln that freed all slaves living in Confederate-held territory during the American Civil War (page 517)

embargo *n.* (ihm-BAHR-goh) a law that restricts commerce with one or more nations (page 319)

Embargo Act of 1807 *n.* (ihm-BAHR-goh AKT UHV 1807) a federal legislation that stopped all foreign imports from entering American harbors (page 319)

emigrate *v.* (EH-muh-grayt) to move away from a country in order to live in another (page 430)

encomienda *n.* (en-coe-mee-AYN-dah) a system in Spain's American colonies in which wealthy settlers were given plots of land and allowed to enslave the people who lived there (page 66)

Enlightenment *n.* (ihn-LY-tuhn-muhnt) an intellectual movement that emphasized the use of reason to examine previously accepted beliefs (page 149)

enlist *v.* (ehn-LIST) to join (page 520)

entrepreneur *n.* (ehn-treh-preh-NEUR) a person who starts, manages, and is responsible for a business (page 583)

envoy *n.* (AHN-voy) an ambassador (page 292)

escalation *n.* (ehs-kuh-LAY-shuhn) an increase of intensity, as during war (page 927)

espionage *n.* (EH-spee-uh-nahj) the practice of spying to obtain information (page 232)

evacuate *v.* (ih-VA-kyoo-wayt) to leave a location, usually for one's own protection (page 488)

evangelize *v.* (ih-VAN-juh-lyz) to spread one's religious beliefs through public speaking and personal witness (page 438)

executive branch *n.* (ihg-ZEH-kyuh-tihv BRANCH) the section of the U.S. government headed by the president; responsible for enforcing the law (page 258)

executive order *n.* (ihg-ZEH-kyuh-tihv OR-dur) a directive, or command, issued by a president, that has the force of law (page 806)

exemption *n.* (ihg-ZEHMP-shuhn) a release from obligations (page 522)

exile *n.* (EHG-zyl) a person who is a political outcast (page 906)

exodus *n.* (EHK-suh-duhs) a mass departure (page 395)

exoduster *n.* (EHK-suh-duhs-tur) one of the thousands of African Americans who migrated to the midwestern plains from the post-Civil-War South to start a new life (page 586)

expertise *n.* (ehk-spur-TEEZ) an expert knowledge or skill (page 241)

GLOSSARY

exposure *n.* (ihk-SPOH-zhur) having no shelter or protection from severe weather or cold temperatures (page 810)

F

factory system *n.* (FAK-tuh-ree SIHS-tuhm) a method of production in which large crews of people perform work in one location (page 328)

famine *n.* (FA-muhn) an extreme lack of crops or food causing widespread hunger (page 432)

Farmers' Alliance *n.* (FAHR-murz ah-LY-ans) one of several organizations founded in the 1880s to advance political and economic concerns of farmers; similar to the Grange but more political (page 591)

fascism *n.* (FA-shih-zuhm) a political movement based on extreme nationalism, militarism, and racism promoting the superiority of a particular people over all others (page 789)

federal *adj.* (FEH-duh-ruhl) relating to a government where power is shared between the central, national government and that of states or provinces (page 250)

federal marshal *n.* (FEH-duh-ruhl MAHR-shuhl) a law enforcement officer who works for the United States government (page 463)

Federal Reserve Act *n.* (FEH-duh-ruhl rih-ZURV AKT) the 1913 law that established the Federal Reserve Board that oversaw 12 reserve banks; the banks would control the nation's flow of money (page 674)

federalism *n.* (FEH-duh-ruh-lih-zuhm) the support of a government where power is shared between the central, national government and that of states or provinces (page 257)

federalist *n.* (FEH-duh-ruh-lihst) a person who supported the U.S. Constitution of 1787 as it was written during the process of ratification (page 262)

feminist *n.* (FEH-muh-nihst) people who practice the idea that women are equal to men socially and politically (page 924)

feudalism *n.* (FEW-dahl-izm) a political and social system in which a vassal receives protection from a lord in exchange for obedience and service (page 36)

15th Amendment *n.* (15th uh-MEND-muhnt) an amendment to the Constitution that says that federal and state governments cannot restrict the right to vote because of race, color, or previous condition of servitude (page 562)

financier *n.* (fih-nuhn-SIHR) a person who lends or manages money for a business or undertaking (page 229)

fireside chat *n.* (FY-ur-syd CHAT) one of a series of radio broadcasts that President Franklin Roosevelt made to the nation throughout his presidency (page 777)

First Continental Congress *n.* (FURST kahn-tuh-NEHN-tuhl KAHN-gruhs) the 1774 meeting of representatives from all American colonies to decide on a response to the Intolerable Acts (page 195)

first responder *n.* (FURST rih-SPAHND-ur) a person such as an emergency medical worker or police officer who provides rapid assistance at the scene of an accident or crime (page 989)

flapper *n.* (FLA-pur) a young woman in the 1920s who embraced a freer style of dress and the use of cosmetics (page 743)

flotilla *n.* (flo-TIHL-ah) a small fleet (page 528)

fortification *n.* (fawr-tuh-fuh-KAY-shuhn) a structure built to protect a place from attack (page 227)

forty-niner *n.* (for-tee-NY-nur) one of the thousands of prospective miners who traveled to California seeking gold in 1849 (page 417)

framers *n.* (FRAYM-urz) delegates to the 1787 Constitutional Convention who helped shape the content and structure of the U.S. Constitution (page 257)

free silver movement *n.* (FREE SIHL-vur MOOV-mehnt) a late-19th-century economic movement that promoted a monetary system based on silver in addition to gold (page 591)

free trade *n.* (FREE TRAYD) a form of international trade that has few or no restrictions (page 1004)

Freedmen's Bureau *n.* (FREED-muhns BYOOR-oh) the Bureau of Refugees, Freedmen, and Abandoned Lands, created by Congress in 1865 to help former slaves, as well as poor white southerners (page 553)

Freedom Riders *n.* (FREE-duhm RY-durz) interracial groups who participated in bus trips through the South to protest and call attention to segregation (page 882)

French Revolution *n.* (FRENCH re-vuh-LOO-shuhn) the 1789 rebellion against the French monarchy that sought to put an end to upper-class privilege and demanded equality for the lower classes (page 289)

front *n.* (FRUHNT) a battle line between armies (page 712)

Frostbelt *n.* (FRAHST-behlt) the north-central and northeastern regions of the United States, which have cold winters (page 854)

fugitive slave clause *n.* (FYOO-juh-tihv SLAYV KLAWZ) a provision in Article 4 of the U.S. Constitution that prevented free states from emancipating enslaved workers who had escaped from their masters in other states (page 260)

Fundamental Orders of Connecticut *n.* (fuhn-duh-MEHN-tahl AWR-duhr UHV kuh-NEH-tih-kuht) a founding document of the Connecticut colony that listed 11 laws and stood as the framework for governing the colony (page 101)

fundamentalism *n.* (fuhn-duh-MEHN-tah-lih-zuhm) a movement that promoted the idea that every word of the Bible was the literal truth (page 736)

fundamentalist *n.* (fuhn-duh-MEHN-tuh-lihst) a person who believes in strict or literal adherance to a belief system (page 965)

G

Gadsden Purchase *n.* (GADZ-duhn PUHR-chuhs) a sale of land in 1853 from Mexico to the United States that established the current U.S. southwestern border (page 413)

galleon *n.* (GAL-eeahn) a large sailing ship used especially by the Spanish in the 16th and 17th centuries (page 62)

garrison *n.* (GAIR-uh-suhn) a defense force of soldiers (page 477)

gender bias *n.* (JEHN-dur BY-uhs) the preference for one gender over another (page 925)

genocide *n.* (JEH-nuh-syd) the deliberate murder of a large number of people belonging to a specific racial, cultural, or political group (page 814)

geographic perspective *n.* (jee-uh-GRA-fihk pur-SPEHK-tihv) the examination of how geography affects people and culture (page 34)

geology *n.* (jee-AH-luh-jee) the study of the processes that shape Earth's rocks and landforms (page 204)

Gettysburg Address *n* (GEH-teez-burg uh-DREHS) an 1863 speech delivered by President Lincoln to commemorate the loss of life at the Battle of Gettysburg and to dedicate a military cemetery (page 529)

ghetto *n.* (GEH-toh) forced housing for a particular race or ethnicity (page 814)

Ghost Dance *n.* (GOHST DANTS) a Native-American religious movement based on a dance ritual meant to communicate with the dead and bring an end to white control of the West; began in the 1870s (page 598)

ghost town *n.* (GOHST TOWN) an abandoned town that has fallen into ruin (page 583)

Gilded Age *n.* (GIHL-duhd AJ) the last three decades of the 19th century, characterized by greed and corruption (page 628)

glacial period *n.* (GLAY-shuhl PEER-ee-uhd) a period of time in history during which huge sheets of ice covered much of Earth (page 5)

glasnost *n.* (GLAS-nawst) a government policy of open communication in the former Soviet Union (page 974)

globalization *n.* (gloh-buh-luh-ZAY-shuhn) the faster and freer flow of people, resources, goods, and ideas across national borders (page 1004)

gold standard *n.* (GOLD STAN-durd) a monetary policy requiring that the government can print only an amount of money equal to the total value of its gold reserves (page 591)

gospel music *n.* (GAH-spuhl MYOO-zik) music that combines biblical subject matter and melodic themes similar to jazz songs (page 748)

government shutdown *n.* (GUH-vur-muhnt SHUHT-down) a time when the executive branch of the government has to close federal government offices and federal government services because of a failure to pass funding legislation for these offices or services (page 985)

Grange *n.* (GRAYNJ) a U.S. farmers' organization founded in 1867 to provide social and economic support to agricultural families (page 590)

grassroots *adj.* (GRAS-roots) organized by ordinary people, who do not have money or power, to bring about change (page 872)

Great Awakening *n.* (GRAYT uh-WAY-kuhn-ing) a series of Protestant religious revivals that swept across the American colonies (page 148)

Great Migration *n.* (GRAYT my-GRAY-shuhn) the mass movement of African Americans who left the South for cities in the North, beginning in 1910 (page 727)

greenhouse effect *n.* (GREEN-hows uh-FEHKT) the warming of Earth's surface caused when greenhouse gas emissions trap the sun's heat (page 1008)

grievance *n.* (GREE-vuhnts) an objection or reason to complain (page 181)

gristmill *n.* (GRIHST-mihl) a building that houses machinery for grinding grain (page 140)

guerrilla *adj.* (guh-RIH-luh) relating to an independent military group that uses methods such as sneak attacks and sabotage (page 237)

gunboat *n.* (GUHN-boht) a small, fast ship carrying mounted guns (page 508)

H

habeas corpus *n.* (HA-be-as COR-pus) the right of an arrested person to be brought before a judge before going to jail (page 523)

hacienda *n.* (hah-see-EHN-dah) a large plantation in a Spanish-speaking colony (page 66)

hawk *n.* (HAWK) a person who supports war (page 933)

heretic *n.* (HAIR-uh-tihk) a person who holds beliefs different from the teachings of the Catholic Church (page 61)

Hessians *n.* (HEH-shuhnz) German soldiers hired by the British to fight during the American Revolution (page 206)

hierarchy *n.* (HY-uh-rahr-kee) the classification of a group of people according to ability or to economic, social, or professional standing (page 36)

Holocaust *n.* (HOH-luh-cawst) the mass slaughter by the Nazis of six million Jews and others during World War II (page 814)

Homestead Act *n.* (HOHM-stehd AKT) an act that started a program of public land grants to small farmers (page 541)

Hooverville *n.* (HOO-vur-vil) a makeshift village for homeless Americans with shelters made of cardboard, scrap metal, or other cheap and available materials, built during the Great Depression and named after President Herbert Hoover (page 769)

human geography *n.* (HYOO-muhn jee-AH-gruh-fee) the study of how people and their cultures are affected by physical geography and how human activities affect the environment (page 34)

human immunodeficiency virus (HIV) *n.* (HYOO-muhn ih-MYOO-noh-dih-FIH-shun-see VY-ruhs) a virus that attacks the system in the human body that fights off illnesses (page 971)

human right *n.* (HYOO-muhn RYT) a basic right that most societies believe should be given to all people (page 964)

humanism *n.* (HYOO-muh-nih-zhum) a movement that focuses on the importance of the individual (page 39)

hunger strike *n.* (HUNG-gur STRYK) the act of refusing to eat as a protest to show disapproval or disagreement (page 918)

hunter-gatherer *n.* (HUHN-tuhr GAHTH-ur-ur) a human who hunts animals and gathers wild plants to eat (page 7)

hydraulic mining *n.* (hy-DRAW-lik MY-nihng) a system of mining in which pressurized water is used to remove topsoil and gravel, which are then processed to draw out precious metals (page 583)

hydroelectric power *n.* (hy-droh-ih-LEHK-trihk POHW-uhr) a source of electricity created by flowing water that turns turbines, which generate power (page 773)

I

ice age *n.* (AISS AJ) a period of time in history during which huge sheets of ice covered much of Earth (page 5)

ideology *n.* (I-dee-AH-luh-jee) a belief system that guides a political or social plan (page 789)

immigrate *v.* (IH-muh-grayt) to permanently move to another country (page 430)

immigration quota *n.* (ih-muh-GRAY-shuhn KWOH-tuh) a limit on the number of people that are allowed to emigrate from certain countries (page 736)

immunity *n.* (ih-MYOO-nih-tee) a protection against disease, either natural or induced by vaccination (page 70)

impeachment *n.* (ihm-PEECH-muhnt) the official charge of a president with misconduct while in office (page 555)

imperialism *n.* (ihm-PIHR-ee-uh-lih-zhm) a governmental system in which a stronger nation controls weaker nations or territories (page 684)

implied power *n.* (ihm-PLYD POW-ur) a power not explicitly stated in the Constitution (page 343)

impressment *n.* (ihm-PRESS-muhnt) the act of forcing men into military or naval service (page 319)

improvise *v.* (IHM-pruh-vyz) to create and play music without rehearsing it, often making up the musical lines on the spot (page 742)

inauguration *n.* (uh-NAW-gyuh-ray-shun) the ceremony that marks the beginning of a presidency (page 279)

incendiary bomb *n.* (ihn-SEHN-dee-ehr-ee BAHM) a bomb that is designed to start fires (page 819)

income tax *n.* (IHN-kuhm TAKS) a tax on the income of an individual (page 673)

incumbent *n.* (ihn-KUHM-buhnt) the person currently in office; the incumbent president is the current president (page 306)

indentured servant *n.* (ihn-DEHN-churd SUR-vuhnt) a person under contract to work, usually without pay, in exchange for free passage to the colonies (page 93)

Indian Removal Act *n.* (IHN-dee-uhn rih-MOO-vuhl AKT) a law that ended the U.S. government's earlier policy of respecting the rights of Native Americans to remain on their land (page 368)

Indian Territory *n.* (IHN-dee-uhn TAIR-uh-tawr-ee) the area of land in present-day Oklahoma and parts of Kansas and Nebraska to which Native Americans were forced to migrate (page 368)

indigo *n.* (IHN-dih-goh) a plant that produces a blue dye for cloth (page 132)

individualism *n.* (ihn-duh-VIHJ-wuh-lih-zuhm) self-reliant independence (page 390)

Industrial Revolution *n.* (ihn-DUH-stree-uhl rev-oh-LUH-shuhn) an era in which widespread production by machinery replaced goods made by hand (page 328)

industrialist *n.* (ihn-DUH-stree-uh-lihst) a person who owns and runs an industry (page 591)

infantry *n.* (IHN-fuhn-tree) foot soldiers (page 491)

inflation *n.* (ihn-FLAY-shuhn) a decrease in the value of money that causes an increase in the price of goods and services (page 374)

influenza *n.* (ihn-floo-EHN-zuh) an acute and highly contagious illness commonly called "the flu" (page 726)

initiative *n.* (ih-NIH-shuh-tihv) a process by which regular citizens propose a law and require that fellow citizens vote on it (page 669)

installment plan *n.* (ihn-STAWL-muhnt PLAN) a plan for purchasing goods by making a series of partial payments over a set time period (page 765)

institution *n.* (ihn-stuh-TOO-shuhn) an established and accepted practice in a society or culture (page 74)

insurgent *n.* (ihn-SUR-juhnt) a rebel or revolutionary (page 989)

insurrection *n.* (ihn-suh-REK-shun) a rebellion (page 410)

integration *n.* (ihn-tuh-GRAY-shuhn) the act of allowing the free association of people of different races or ethnicities (page 875)

interchangeable part *n.* (ihn-tur-CHAYN-juh-buhl PAHRT) parts of a mechanism that can be substituted one for another (page 330)

Internet *n.* (IHN-tur-neht) the electronic network that allows computers to communicate (page 1000)

internment camp *n.* (ihn-TURN-muhnt KAMP) a prison camp to hold enemy aliens and other prisoners of war during wartime (page 806)

interstate slave trade *n.* (IHN-tur-stayt SLAYV TRAYD) the buying and selling of slaves within the United States (page 339)

Intolerable Acts *n.* (ihn-TAHL-ruh-buhl AKTS) the British laws passed to punish the people of Boston after the Boston Tea Party; also called the Coercive Acts (page 194)

GLOSSARY

investor *n.* (ihn-VEH-stuhr) a person who buys shares of a company with the intent of making a profit when he or she sells the stock shares (page 765)

ironclad ship *n.* (I-urn-klahd SHIP) a ship armored with iron plates to protect it from cannon fire (page 495)

Iroquois League *n.* (IHR-uh-kwoy leeg) the confederation of five Iroquois-speaking nations: the Mohawk, Oneida, Onondaga, Cayuga, and Seneca; later joined by the Tuscarora (page 29)

irrigation *n.* (eer-uh-GAY-shun) the supply of water to fields using human-made systems (page 24)

island hopping *n.* (I-luhnd HAH-pihng) a strategy that involves capturing and setting up military bases on island groups one island at a time (page 818)

isolationism *n.* (I-soh-LAY-shuh-nih-zuhm) a policy in which a nation stays out of the affairs of other nations (page 791)

isthmus *n.* (IHS-muhs) a narrow strip of land that connects two larger landmasses and separates two bodies of water (page 692)

J

Jacksonian democracy *n.* (jak-SOH-nee-uhn dih-MAH-kruh-see) a political movement that celebrated the common man and defended the will of the people, named for President Andrew Jackson (page 362)

jazz *n.* (JAZ) a style of music originating among African-American musicians that contains lively rhythms, sounds from a variety of instruments, and improvisation (page 742)

Jim Crow laws *n.* (JIHM KROH LAWZ) laws created in the 1880s by southern politicians to take away the rights of African Americans (page 640)

joint-stock company *n.* (JOYNT STAHK KUHM-puh-nee) a company whose shareholders own stock in the company (page 92)

judicial branch *n.* (joo-DIH-shehl BRANCH) the section of the U.S. government that includes the courts and legal system, led by the Supreme Court; responsible for interpreting the law (page 258)

judicial review *n.* (joo-DIH-shuhl rih-VYOO) the power to invalidate any law the Supreme Court deems unconstitutional, even if it has been passed by Congress and signed into law by the president (page 310)

Judiciary Act of 1801 *n.* (joo-DIH-shee-air-ee AKT UHV 1801) the federal legislation that reduced the number of justices on the Supreme Court from 6 to 5 (page 310)

jurisdiction *n.* (jur-uhs-DIHK-shuhn) the authority to enforce laws within a given area (page 538)

K

kamikaze pilot *n.* (kah-mih-KAH-zee PI-luht) one of a group of Japanese suicide bomber pilots who crashed their planes, loaded with explosives, into American ships during World War II (page 819)

kayak *n.* (KAI-yak) a canoe with a light frame and a small opening on top in which to sit (page 26)

King Philip's War *n.* (KING FIH-luhps WOR) a violent conflict between Native Americans and English colonists from New England, who were aided by Native American allies (page 106)

Know-Nothing Party *n.* (NOH NUH-thing PAHR-tee) a political party formed in the 1850s to oppose immigration, also called the American Party (page 436)

Ku Klux Klan *n.* (KOO KLUHKS KLAN) the group whose purpose was to maintain the social and political power of white people (page 560)

L

labor union *n.* (LAY-bur YOON-yuhn) a voluntary association of workers that uses its power to negotiate better working conditions (page 442)

laissez faire *n.* (leh-say FAIR) an economic policy in which a government lets businesses operate without much regulation; laissez-faire means "allow to" in French (page 627)

landmark legislation *n.* (lahnd-MARK lehj-iss-LAY-shun) an important and historic law (page 913)

League of Nations *n.* (LEEG UHV NAY-shuhnz) an international peacekeeping organization proposed by President Woodrow Wilson after World War I (page 723)

Legal Tender Act *n.* (LEE-guhl TEHN-dur AKT) an act that replaced the notes of individual banks with a unified national currency (page 524)

legislative branch *n.* (LEH-jeh-slay-tihv BRANCH) the section of the U.S. government led by Congress; responsible for making the law (page 258)

levee *n.* (LEH-vee) a ridge of earth that runs along the sides of a stream or river (page 991)

levy *v.* (LEH-vee) to require the payment of a tax (page 105)

libel *n.* (LY-buhl) the publishing of lies (page 152)

Liberal Republicans *n.* (LIH-buh-ruhl rih-PUH-blih-kuhnz) a group during the 1870s that believed the government had become too large and too powerful (page 564)

Liberty Bond *n.* (LIH-bur-tee BAHND) a government bond sold to individuals to help support U.S. involvement in World War I (page 718)

literacy *n.* (LIH-tur-uh-see) the ability to read and write (page 559)

literacy test *n.* (LIH-tur-uh-see TEST) test of one's ability to read and write (page 565)

loan default *n.* (LOHN dih-FAWLT) a failure to repay a loan (page 995)

lobbyist *n.* (LAH-bee-ihst) a person who tries to persuade lawmakers to support particular laws and political ideas (page 681)

lock *n.* (LAHK) a confined section of water used to raise or lower ships (page 693)

lode *n.* (LOHD) a large deposit of ore, such as silver or gold (page 582)

Long Walk *n.* (LONG WAWK) the 300-mile forced walk of the Navajo from their homeland to a reservation at Bosque Redondo, New Mexico; imposed by the U.S. government in 1864 (page 596)

loophole *n.* (LOOP-hohl) unclear language that allows people to get around laws and avoid obeying them (page 674)

loose interpretation *n.* (LOOS ihn-tur-pruh-TAY-shuhn) an understanding of the Constitution as one that gives Congress and the president broad powers (page 286)

Louisiana Purchase *n.* (lu-ee-zee-A-nuh PUR-chuhs) a treaty between France and the United States in which a large area of land between the Mississippi River and the Rocky Mountains was purchased (page 313)

low-cost housing *n.* (LOH KAWST HOW-zingh) housing that is affordable to people with low incomes (page 845)

Loyalist *n.* (LOY-uh-lihst) an American colonist who supported Britain during the American Revolution (page 198)

lunar module *n.* (LOO-nuhr MAH-jool) a part of a space vehicle meant to carry astronauts from the command module to the surface of the moon and back to the command module (page 957)

lynch *v.* (LINCH) to hang someone illegally by mob action (page 560)

M

Manhattan Project *n.* (man-HA-tuhn PRAH-jehkt) the code name for the U.S. government-funded atomic weapons program during the 1940s (page 821)

manifest destiny *n.* (MAN-uh-fehst DEHS-tuh-nee) the idea that the United States had the right and the obligation to expand its territory across North America to the Pacific Ocean (page 391)

manor system *n.* (MA-nur SIHS-tuhm) an economic system in which peasants are bound to a lord and work his land, or manor, in exchange for food and shelter (page 37)

margin *n.* (MAHR-juhn) the amount by which something is won or lost (page 403)

market revolution *n.* (MAHR-kuht rev-uh-LOO-shuhn) the transition from a pre-industrial economy to a market-oriented, capitalist economy (page 328)

marketing *n.* (MAHR-kuh-ting) the process of promoting products or services (page 738)

Marshall Plan *n.* (MAHR-shuhl PLAN) an aid plan to help European countries rebuild and recover economically after World War II (page 822)

mass culture *n.* (MAS KUHL-chur) the set of popular values and ideas that arise from widespread access to media, music, art, and other entertainment (page 628)

GLOSSARY

mass media *n.* (MAS MEE-dee-uh) the sources of information and entertainment that reach large groups of people at the same time (page 738)

matrilineal *adj.* (ma-truh-LIN-ee-uhl) relating to descendants traced through the mother (page 29)

Mayflower Compact *n.* (MAY-flow-uhr KAHM-pakt) a shipboard contract signed by the Pilgrims on the *Mayflower* before they landed in North America, binding them to abide by their own laws and establish a civil society (page 100)

McCarthyism *n.* (muh-KAHR-thee-ih-zuhm) the practice of accusing people of being traitors to their country without offering proof (page 853)

Meat Inspection Act *n.* (MEET ihn-SPEHK-shuhn AKT) a 1906 law that sought to ensure the purity and safety of meat (page 671)

Medicaid *n.* (MEH-dih-kayd) a U.S. government program started in 1965 that gives medical insurance to impoverished people (page 917)

Medicare *n.* (MEH-dih-kair) a U.S. government program started in 1965 that gives medical insurance to older people (page 917)

megafauna *n.* (MEH-guh-faw-nuh) the large animals of a particular area in the world or a particular time in history (page 6)

mercantilism *n.* (MUHR-kuhn-teel-ih-zuhm) an economic policy that gives a country sole ownership of the trade occurring in its colonies (page 52)

mercenary *n.* (MUR-suh-nair-ee) a soldier who is paid to fight for a country other than his or her own (page 222)

mestizo *n.* (mes-TEE-zoh) a person who has mixed Spanish and Native American ancestry (page 66)

Middle Passage *n.* (MIH-duhl PA-sihj) the long trip across the Atlantic Ocean by which enslaved Africans were brought to the Americas; the second leg of the triangular trade route (page 73)

midwife *n.* (MIHD-wyf) a person who is trained to help deliver babies (page 146)

migrant worker *n.* (MY-gruhnt WUR-kur) a laborer who moves from one job to another as needed; usually a farm laborer (page 586)

migrate *v.* (MY-grayt) to move from one place to another (page 27)

militarism *n.* (MIH-luh-tuh-rih-zuhm) the belief that a government must create a strong military and be prepared to use it to achieve the country's goals (page 710)

militia *n.* (muh-LIH-shuh) military force made up of local citizens to help protect their town, land, or nation (page 178)

minuteman *n.* (MIH-nuht-man) an American colonial militia member who was ready to join in combat at a moment's notice (page 196)

mission *n.* (MIH-shuhn) a Christian church settlement established to convert native peoples (page 66)

missionary *n.* (MIH-shuh-nair-ee) a person who tries to spread Christianity to others (page 53)

Missouri Compromise *n.* (mih-ZUR-ee KAHM-pruh-myz) an agreement that stated the people of Missouri could own slaves and be admitted to the Union along with Maine, a free state (page 344)

mobilize *v.* (MOH-buh-lyz) to organize and prepare troops for war (page 490)

monopoly *n.* (muh-NAH-puh-lee) the complete and exclusive control of an industry by one company (page 343)

Monroe Doctrine *n.* (muhn-ROH DAHK-truhn) an approach to foreign policy that stated the American continents were no longer under European influence (page 345)

Montgomery Bus Boycott *n.* (mahnt-GUH-muh-ree BUHS BOY-kaht) a mass protest, sparked by the arrest of Rosa Parks, against the racial segregation practices of the public bus system in Montgomery, Alabama (page 879)

moral diplomacy *n.* (MOR-uhl duh-PLOH-muh-see) the concept that the United States should drastically reduce its intervention in the affairs of other countries (page 724)

Moral Majority *n.* (MOR-uhl muh-JOR-uh-tee) a politically conservative group formed by the Reverend Jerry Falwell, a televangelist, in 1979 (page 970)

morale *n.* (muh-RAL) the amount of confidence or enthusiasm felt by a group of people (page 717)

morphine *n.* (MOR-feen) a powerful painkiller (page 534)

mortality *n.* (mor-TAH-luh-tee) the death rate (page 495)

mountain men *n.* (MOWN-tuhn MEHN) the American fur trappers and explorers who began to explore and move west (page 390)

Munich Agreement *n.* (MYOO-nihk uh-GREE-muhnt) an agreement Hitler made with the rulers of Great Britain, France, and Italy, declaring that Germany had the right to seize the Sudetenland, a portion of Czechoslovakia (page 791)

munitions *n.* (myoo-NIH-shuhns) military weapons (page 801)

mutual aid society *n.* (MYOO-chuh-wuhl AYD suh-SY-uh-tee) an organization formed by members of a particular group to provide economic and other assistance to each other (page 631)

N

napalm *n.* (NAY-pahlm) a thick flammable, jellylike substance used in bombs to cause and spread fires (page 929)

national debt *n.* (NA-shuh-nuhl DEHT) the amount of money a government owes to all its creditors, including to other nations and to companies from which it purchases goods and services (page 282)

national health insurance *n.* (NA-shuh-nuhl HELTH ihn-SHUR-uhns) an insurance plan run by the government and open to anyone to join (page 845)

nationalism *n.* (NA-shuh-nuh-lih-zuhm) the concept of loyalty and devotion to one's nation (page 342)

nativist *n.* (NAY-tih-vihst) a person who believes native-born people should be favored more than immigrants (page 436)

natural resource *n.* (NACH-uh-ruhl REE-sawrs) a material or substance found in nature that can be used to sustain a society or exploited for economic gain, such as minerals, water, or living things (page 114)

natural rights *n.* (NACH-uh-ruhl RYTS) rights such as life or liberty that a person is born with (page 149)

naturalization *n.* (NACH-uh-ruh-lih-ZAY-shuhn) the process of becoming a U.S. citizen for people who are not native-born citizens (page R32)

naval quarantine *n.* (NAY-vuhl KWAWR-uhn-teen) a blockade imposed on the ports of another country (page 908)

navigation *n.* (nav-ih-GAY-shuhn) the science of finding position and planning routes, often used in relation to seafaring (page 40)

Navigation Acts *n.* (nav-ih-GAY-shuhn AKTS) a series of laws passed by the English Parliament to protect English shipping by restricting the transport of goods to and from the English colonies (page 125)

Nazi Party *n.* (NAHT-see PAHR-tee) a political party led by Adolf Hitler that used force to exert complete control over Germany from 1933 to 1945 (page 789)

neoconservative *n.* (nee-oh-kuhn-SUR-vuh-tihv) a person who strongly supports a free-market economy and believes the United States should actively promote its ideals around the world (page 986)

neutrality *n.* (noo-TRA-luh-tee) the refusal to take sides or become involved (page 111)

newsreel *n.* (NOOZ-reel) a short news or sports film that plays before a feature film (page 741)

nonviolent resistance *n.* (nahn-VI-uh-luhnt rih-ZIHS-tuhns) a practice of using civil disobedience, noncooperation, and other means of peaceful protest to achieve social change (page 880)

Northwest Ordinance of 1787 *n.* (nawrth-WEHST AWR-duh-nuhns UHV 1787) a legislation adopted by Congress to establish stricter control over the government of the Northwest Territory (page 252)

Northwest Passage *n.* (nawrth-WEHST PA-sihj) a passage by water between the Atlantic and Pacific oceans along the northern coast of North America (page 60)

nuclear fission *n.* (NOO-klee-ur FIH-shuhn) the splitting of atoms that causes a release of energy (page 821)

O

oasis *n.* (oh-AY-sihs) a fertile place with water in a desert (page 42)

occupation zone *n.* (AH-kyoo-pay-shuhn ZOHN) an area of a country in which a foreign military takes control (page 846)

Open Door Policy *n.* (OH-puhn DOHR PAH-luh-see) the late 19th century and early 20th century policy calling for equal trading privileges for all nations with economic interests in China (page 691)

oration *n.* (uh-RAY-shuhn) a formal speech (page 886)

ordinance *n.* (AWR-duh-nuhns) an official law, decree, or directive (page 252)

Ordinance of 1785 *n.* (AWR-duh-nuhns UHV 1785) a federal law that set up a system to allow settlers to purchase land in the undeveloped West (page 252)

organized crime *n.* (AWR-guh-nyzd KRYM) planned illegal activities that are carried out by powerful criminals (page 735)

overhead *n.* (oh-vur-HEHD) the cost of doing business (page 647)

overseer *n.* (OH-vur-see-ur) a supervisor (page 134)

P

Pacific Railway Acts *n.* (puh-SIH-fihk RAYL-way AKTS) two acts passed in the 1860s that gave two companies the contracts to construct a transcontinental railroad (page 620)

pacifist *n.* (PA-suh-fihst) a person who stands against war and violence (page 239)

Panic of 1837 *n.* (PA-nihk UHV 1837) the widespread fear of a failing economy that caused the beginning of a U.S. economic recession that lasted until 1840 (page 375)

Panic of 1873 *n.* (PA-nihk UHV 1873) an economic crisis triggered by bank and railroad failures (page 565)

panzer *n.* (PAN-zur) a thickly armored German tank with impressive firepower used during World War II (page 812)

parallel *n.* (PAIR-uh-lehl) a line of latitude (page 413)

pardon *n.* (PAHR-duhn) a release from legal punishment (page 962)

Parliament *n.* (PAHR-luh-muhnt) the legislative body of England, and, later, Great Britain (page 150)

partition *v.* (pahr-TIH-shuhn) to divide a whole into parts (page 813)

passive resistance *n.* (PA-sihv rih-ZIHS-tuhns) a nonviolent refusal to obey authority and laws (page 341)

patent *n.* (PA-tuhnt) a document that gives the bearer exclusive rights to make and sell an invention (page 624)

Patriot *n.* (PAY-tree-uht) an American colonist who supported the right of the American colonies to govern themselves (page 198)

pension fund *n.* (PEHN-shuhn FUHND) a pool of money used to pay people a small, established income after they retire (page 776)

perestroika *n.* (pair-ih-STROY-kuh) a government policy of economic and political reform in the former Soviet Union (page 974)

persecute *v.* (PUR-seh-kyoot) to punish, particularly because of beliefs or background (page 61)

personal responsibility *n.* (PURS-uh-nuhl rih-SPAWN-suh-BIHL-uh-tee) responsibility that is not required but that contributes to a more civil society, such as respecting and standing up for others' rights, helping in the community, and staying informed (page R34)

philanthropist *n.* (fuh-LAN-thruh-pihst) someone who actively promotes human welfare (page 496)

philanthropy *n.* (fuh-LAN-thruh-pee) the financial support of a worthy or charitable cause (page 627)

physical geography *n.* (FIH-zih-kuhl jee-AH-gruh-fee) the study of Earth's exterior physical features (page 34)

Piedmont *n.* (PEED-mont) a relatively flat area between the Appalachian Mountains and the coastal plain (page 134)

pilgrimage *n.* (PILL-gruhm-ij) a religious journey (page 45)

pioneer *n.* (py-uh-NIHR) a settler moving to a new and unfamiliar land (page 392)

placer mining *n.* (PLAH-sur MY-nihng) a system of mining in which individual miners find gold nuggets in riverbeds, usually by panning (page 583)

planned obsolescence *n.* (PLAND abh-suh-LES-uhns) the idea that people should plan to replace an item before it is broken or worn out (page 739)

plantation *n.* (plan-TAY-shuhn) a large farm; on southern plantations, slaves worked to grow and harvest crops (page 66)

Platt Amendment *n.* (PLAHT uh-MEND-muhnt) a 1901 amendment to military legislation establishing the conditions by which the United States would withdraw from Cuba after the Spanish-American War but retain the right to intervene in Cuban affairs (page 687)

Pleistocene epoch *n.* (PLEIS-toh-seen EH-puhk) a period in the history of Earth in which large animals and plants existed and glaciers covered Earth (page 5)

poison gas *n.* (POY-zuhn GAS) a chemical released into the air that causes harm or death (page 713)

political machine *n.* (poh-LIH-tih-kuhl muh-SHEEN) a party organization that ran big cities, ruled by strong and often corrupt leaders who offered favors to members in exchange for votes and other support (page 634)

poll tax *n.* (POHL TAKS) a fee charged when people register to vote (page 563)

poll watcher *n.* (POHL WAH-chur) a person assigned to a polling place to guard against voting irregularities (page 643)

pontoon *n.* (pahn-TOON) a portable, cylindrical float used to build a temporary bridge (page 511)

popular sovereignty *n.* (PAH-pyuh-lur SAHV-run-tee) the idea that the residents of a region or nation decide an issue by voting (page 466)

populism *n.* (PAH-pyuh-lih-zuhm) the belief that common people, not the wealthy, should control their government (page 665)

populist *n.* (PAH-pyuh-lihst) a politician who claims to represent the concerns of ordinary people (page 591)

posse *n.* (PAH-see) a group organized by a sheriff to hunt down criminals or fugitives (page 583)

post-traumatic stress disorder (PTSD) *n.* (POHST truh-MAH-tihk STREHS dihs-AWR-dur) a condition brought on by injury or psychological trauma (page 952)

potlatch *n.* (PAHT-lach) a gift-giving ceremony practiced by the Kwakiutl and Haida Native American tribes (page 26)

power base *n.* (POW-ur BAYS) an area or group of people providing the biggest influence over a political candidate (page 286)

prairie *n.* (PRAIR-ee) a vast area of flat land covered with tall plants (page 586)

precedent *n.* (PREH-suh-duhnt) a prior event or decision that serves as an example for events or decisions that follow (page 278)

prejudice *n.* (PREH-juh-duhs) a broad judgment about a group of people not based on reason or fact (page 436)

Presidential Reconstruction *n.* (preh-zuh-DEN-shuhl ree-kuhn-STRUHK-shuhn) a policy that stated Confederate states must ratify the 13th Amendment and create new governments with new constitutions before they could rejoin the Union (page 552)

presidio *n.* (prih-SIH-dee-oh) a military post or settlement (page 398)

printing press *n.* (PRIHN-ting PREHS) an invention that used movable metal type to print pages (page 39)

prisoner of war *n.* (PRIH-zuhn-ur UHV WOR) a soldier captured by an enemy force (page 793)

privateer *n.* (PRY-vah-teer) an armed but privately owned ship that acts under the authority of a government to participate in warfare; or a sailor on such a ship (page 62)

Proclamation of 1763 *n.* (prah-kluh-MAY-shuhn UHV 1763) a law requiring colonists to stay east of a line drawn on a map along the crest of the Appalachian Mountains (page 178)

profit *n.* (PRAH-fuht) the amount of money left for a business after expenses are deducted (page 40)

progressivism *n.* (pruh-GREH-sih-vih-zuhm) a social movement that believes in equality for all people and calls for people and the government to work together to bring about social change (page 665)

Prohibition *n.* (proh-uh-BIH-shuhn) the 18th Amendment to the Constitution banning the production, sale, importation, and transportation of liquor in the United States (page 681)

propaganda *n.* (prah-puh-GAN-duh) information spread to influence people's opinions or advance an organization's or party's ideas (page 718)

prophet *n.* (PRAH-fuht) someone who is believed to deliver messages from God or some other divine source (page 321)

proprietor *n.* (pruh-PRY-uh-tuhr) a person with ownership of a colony, including the right to manage and distribute land and to establish government (page 112)

prospector *n.* (PRAH-spek-tur) a person who searches in the earth for valuable resources, such as gems or precious metals (page 416)

Protestant *n.* (PRAH-teh-stant) a follower of the Reformation in Christianity (page 39)

provision *n.* (pruh-VIH-zhuhn) a legal condition that anticipates future needs (page 244)

provisions *n.* (pruh-VIH-zhuhnz) the supplies of food, water, and other items needed for a journey (page 124)

proviso *n.* (pruh-VY-zoh) a condition attached to a legal document or legislation (page 413)

puppet government *n.* (PUH-puht GUH-vur-muhnt) a government that appears to have authority but is controlled by another power (page 794)

Pure Food and Drug Act *n.* (PYOOR FOOD AND DRUHG AKT) a 1906 law that empowered the federal government to protect the quality, purity, and safety of foods and drugs (page 671)

push-pull factor *n.* (PUSH PUL FAK-tur) a reason why people immigrate, such as lack of economic opportunity or freedom in one country and the promise of a better life in another (page 430)

Q

quarantine *v.* (KWAWR-uhn-teen) to keep infected people away from those who have not yet contracted a disease (page 527)

Quartering Act *n.* (KWAWR-tuh-ring AKT) one of several British laws that required American colonists to provide housing and food for British soldiers stationed in North America (page 178)

quinine *n.* (KWHY-nyn) a substance made from the bark of a tree that is an effective remedy for malaria (page 71)

R

racism *n.* (RAY-sih-zuhm) the belief that one race is better than others (page 464)

radical *n.* (RA-dih-kuhl) a person who supports complete social or political change (page 289)

Radical Reconstruction *n.* (RA-dih-kuhl ree-kuhn-STRUHK-shuhn) the name given to the Republicans' plan in passing the Reconstruction Acts of 1867 (page 554)

rancho *n.* (RAN-choh) land granted by Mexico to settlers in the form of large estates in what is now California (page 415)

ratify *v.* (RA-tuh-fy) to approve formally, by vote (page 250)

rationing *v.* (RA-shuh-nihng) the controlled distribution of important food or supplies (page 799)

rations *n.* (RA-shuhnz) supplied food (page 527)

raw material *n.* (RAW muh-TIHR-ee-uhl) the basic substances and elements used to make products (page 114)

reaper *n.* (REE-pur) a machine that cuts stalks of wheat or oats (page 331)

recession *n.* (rih-SEH-shuhn) an economic downturn (page 590)

Reconstruction *n.* (ree-kuhn-STRUHK-shuhn) the effort to rebuild and reunite the United States following the Civil War (page 538)

Reconstruction Acts of 1867 *n.* (ree-kuhn-STRUHK-shuhn AKTS UHV 1867) acts that put the Republican Congress in charge of Reconstruction instead of the president (page 554)

referendum *n.* (reh-fuh-REN-duhm) the practice of submitting a law directly to voters to accept or reject the law (page 669)

refugee *n.* (REH-fyoo-jee) a person who flees to another country to escape danger or persecution (page 630)

reinforcements *n.* (ree-uhn-FAWRS-muhnts) more soldiers and supplies sent to help military troops engage in warfare (page 224)

religious freedom *n.* (rih-LIH-juhs FREE-duhm) the right to practice the religion of one's choosing without government interference (page 126)

renaissance *n.* (reh-nuh-SAHNTS) a rebirth or revival of interest in the arts or academics (page 748)

rendezvous *n.* (RAHN-deh-voo) a temporary market where trappers met to trade and socialize (page 390)

reparations *n.* (reh-puh-RAY-shunz) the money paid to compensate for damages in war (page 723)

repatriation *n.* (ree-PAY-tree-ay-shuhn) the act of returning or being returned to the country of one's origin or citizenship (page 781)

repeal *v.* (rih-PEEL) to cancel or nullify, especially a law (page 183)

republic *n.* (RE-puhb-lik) a form of government in which the people elect representatives to speak for them and enact laws based on their needs (page 222)

republican motherhood *n.* (rih-PUH-blih-kuhn MUH-thur-hud) the idea that women should raise their children to be good citizens who participate in the government (page 348)

Republican Party *n.* (rih-PUH-blih-kuhn PAHR-tee) a political party founded in 1854 by antislavery leaders (page 468)

republicanism *n.* (rih-PUH-blih-kuh-nih-zuhm) a government in which people choose representatives to make their laws (page 244)

reservation *n.* (reh-zur-VAY-shuhn) an area of land in the United States that is kept specifically for Native Americans to live on (page 592)

reserve bank *n.* (rih-ZURV BAYNK) a bank that, under the Federal Reserve Board's supervision, controls the nation's flow of money (page 674)

reunify *v.* (ree-YOO-nuh-fy) to bring something that split apart back together again (page 850)

revenue *n.* (REH-vuh-noo) income; money that is received (page 180)

revenue sharing *n.* (REH-vuh-noo SHAIR-ing) a method of distributing federal tax revenue to state and local governments (page 954)

revival meeting *n.* (rih-VY-vuhl MEE-ting) an informal religious gathering meant to inspire people to join the faith, often held outdoors or in tents (page 438)

robber baron *n.* (RAHB-ur BA-ruhn) an industrial leader known for cutthroat tactics against workers and competitors (page 649)

Rome-Berlin Axis *n.* (ROHM burh-LIHN ACK-sihs) an agreement formed between Germany and Italy in 1936 (page 789)

Rough Riders *n.* (RUHF RY-durz) the untrained but tough group of cowboys, miners, police officers, and Native Americans who volunteered to be soldiers under the command of Theodore Roosevelt in the Spanish-American War (page 687)

royal colony *n.* (ROY-uhl KAH-luh-nee) a colony ruled by a monarch through an appointed governor (page 112)

S

sabotage *n.* (SA-buh-tahzh) the action of harming, interfering with, or destroying something (page 719)

salutary neglect *n.* (SAL-yuh-tair-ee nih-GLEKT) the policy of the British government to not strictly enforce its colonial policies (page 151)

salvation *n.* (sal-VAY-shuhn) the act of being forgiven for wrongdoings or sins (page 148)

satellite *n.* (SA-tuh-lyt) an object that moves around a larger object (page 904)

scab *n.* (SKAB) a person willing to cross union lines to work during a strike (page 651)

scapegoat *n.* (SKAYP-goht) an individual or group blamed for the mistakes or faults of others (page 523)

scientific management *n.* (sy-uhn-TIH-fihk MA-nihj-muhnt) the process of studying individual people at work to determine the most efficient, most cost-effective way to do a job (page 677)

scurvy *n.* (SCUR-vee) a disease linked to malnutrition and a diet lacking in fruits and vegetables (page 527)

search-and-destroy mission *n.* (SUHRCH AND dih-STROY MIH-shuhn) a method used by the U.S. military to empty and wreck entire villages that may have provided help to the enemy (page 929)

secede *v.* (seh-SEED) to formally withdraw from a nation or organization in order to become independent (page 474)

secession *n.* (seh-SEHSH-ehn) the act of formally withdrawing from an organization, a nation, or any other group in order to be independent (page 367)

Second Continental Congress *n.* (SEHK-und kahn-tuh-NEHN-tuhl KAHN-gruhs) a group of leaders of the American colonies who met to address the problem of British tyranny, declared independence in 1776, and led the United States through the American Revolution (page 203)

Second Great Awakening *n.* (SEHK-und GRAYT uh-WAYK-ning) an American Protestant movement based on revival meetings and a direct and emotional relationship with God (page 438)

sectionalism *n.* (SEHK-shnuh-lih-zuhm) a loyalty to whichever section or region of the country one was from, rather than to the nation as a whole (page 344)

sedition *n.* (sih-DIH-shuhn) the act of provoking rebellion (page 293)

segregation *n.* (seh-grih-GAY-shuhn) the separation of people based on race (page 465)

self-determination *n.* (SELF dih-tur-muh-NAY-shuhn) the idea that countries should form their own governments and borders to reflect the national origins of the people who live there (page 722)

self-governance *n.* (SELF GUH-vur-nuhnts) the control of one's own affairs; the control of community affairs and laws by those who live there rather than by an outside ruler or monarch (page 105)

self-reliance *n.* (SELF rih-LY-uhns) individual independence developed through practical skills and education (page 644)

Seneca Falls Convention *n.* (SEH-nih-kuh FAWLS kuhn-VEHN-shuhn) an 1848 women's rights convention organized by Elizabeth Cady Stanton and Lucretia Mott in Seneca Falls, New York (page 450)

separation of powers *n.* (seh-puh-RAY-shuhn UHV POW-urs) the division of governmental power among the three branches of U.S. government: the executive branch, the judicial branch, and the legislative branch (page 258)

separatist *n.* (SEH-prah-tihst) a person in the 16th and 17th centuries who wished to leave the Church of England (page 100)

serf *n.* (SURF) a person who lived and worked on the private land of a landowner such as a noble or medieval lord (page 37)

servitude *n.* (SUR-vuh-tood) the state of being enslaved (page 538)

settlement house *n.* (SEH-tuhl-muhnt HOWS) a place that provides assistance to poor and immigrant residents of a community (page 635)

sharecropping *n.* (SHAIR-krahp-ing) an agricultural system in which a farmer raises crops for a landowner in return for part of the money made from selling the crops (page 559)

Shays's Rebellion *n.* (SHAYZ rih-BEL-yuhn) the 1786–1787 uprising of Massachusetts farmers in protest of high taxes (page 255)

Sherman Antitrust Act of 1890 *n.* (SHUR-muhn an-tee-TRUHST AKT UHV 1890) a federal statute passed to prohibit monopolies (page 670)

siege *n.* (SEEJ) a tactic in which a military force surrounds a city in an attempt to take control of it (page 401)

silent majority *n.* (SY-luhnt muh-JOR-uh-tee) a term used by Richard Nixon in the late 1960s to describe a large group of moderate voters who did not publicly express their political opinions (page 935)

sit-in *n.* (SIT IN) an organized protest where people sit down and refuse to leave (page 882)

situation comedy *n.* (sih-chuh-WAY-shuhn KAH-muh-dee) a weekly series that features a familiar setting and a group of characters who face amusing problems (page 858)

skirmish *n.* (SKUR-mish) a small, short-lasting battle (page 231)

skyscraper *n.* (SKY-skray-pur) a very tall building (page 636)

slash-and-burn agriculture *n.* (SLASH AND BURN A-grih-kuhl-chur) a method of clearing fields for planting that involves cutting and setting fire to existing trees and plants (page 29)

slave importation clause *n.* (SLAYVE ihm-pohr-TAY-shuhn KLAWZ) a provision in Article 1 of the U.S. Constitution that established that the United States would not consider prohibiting the international slave trade in the United States until 1808 (page 260)

slavery *n.* (SLAY-veh-ree) a social system in which human beings take complete control of others (page 72)

slogan *n.* (SLOH-guhn) a catchy phrase meant to attract and keep attention (page 362)

smallpox *n.* (SMAWL-poks) a deadly virus that causes a high fever and small blisters on the skin (page 56)

smog *n.* (SMAHG) a type of air pollution that develops when sunlight reacts with chemicals from such sources as car exhaust and factory emissions (page 958)

smuggle *v.* (SMUH-guhl) to import or export goods illegally (page 125)

Social Gospel *n.* (SOH-shuhl GAH-spuhl) a Protestant religious movement that stressed the importance of churches to become involved with social issues and reform (page 634)

social justice *n.* (SOH-shuhl JUH-stuhs) the fair distribution of opportunities and privileges, including racial equality (page 557)

social media *n.* (SOH-shuhl MEE-dee-uh) electronic media that allow people to communicate and form online communities (page 1001)

social work *n.* (SOH-shuhl WURK) work aimed at improving the lives of others (page 680)

socialism *n.* (SOH-shuh-lih-zuhm) an economic system in which the government controls economic resources, which are publicly owned (page 776)

solitary confinement *n.* (SAHL-it-tar-ee cuhn-FINE-ment) a form of punishment, isolating a prisoner from contact with other people (page 885)

Sons of Liberty *n.* (SUHNS UHV LIH-bur-tee) the groups of merchants, shopkeepers, and craftsmen who successfully opposed the Stamp Act by establishing networks to boycott British goods (page 183)

sovereign *adj.* (SAH-vuh-ruhn) having the right to self-rule or independent government (page 250)

space race *n.* (SPAYSS RAYSS) the competition between the United States and the Soviet Union to be the first to travel outside Earth's atmosphere (page 904)

speakeasy *n.* (SPEEK-ee-zee) an illegal drinking club where people secretly gathered in the evenings during Prohibition (page 735)

special prosecutor *n.* (SPEH-shuhl PRAH-sih-kyoo-tur) a private attorney or official appointed by the court to investigate or bring legal action against a party when the regular prosecutor is unable or has a conflict of interest with the accused (page 961)

speculate *v.* (SPEH-kyuh-layt) the act of buying stocks with the hope of selling and making a profit, while taking the risk of a loss (page 765)

sphere of influence *n.* (SFEER UHV IHN-floo-ents) a claim a country makes to be the exclusive influence on another country's political or economic activities (page 690)

spiritual *n.* (SPIHR-ih-chuh-wuhl) a religious song based on scripture and biblical figures in the Bible, first sung by enslaved people in the South (page 341)

spoil *n.* (SPOY-uhl) excess dirt and rock from a construction site (page 693)

spoils system *n.* (SPOY-uhlz SIHS-tuhm) the practice of rewarding political backers with government jobs (page 365)

stagflation *n.* (stag-FLAY-shuhn) an economic condition in which stagnation, or slow economic growth, is accompanied by inflation, or rising prices (page 962)

stalemate *n.* (STAYL-mayt) a situation in which neither side in a conflict is able to win (page 516)

Stamp Act *n.* (STAMP AKT) the British law requiring colonists to purchase a stamp for official documents and published papers (page 182)

standard time *n.* (STAN-durd TYM) the uniform division of time among locations that lie roughly on the same line of longitude, establishing time zones (page 621)

states' rights *n.* (STAYTS RITES) the concept that individual states have rights that the federal government cannot violate (page 293)

status quo *n.* (STA-tuhs KWOH) the existing state of a situation (page 902)

statute *n.* (STA-choot) a formal, written law (page 267)

steamboat *n.* (STEEM-boht) a boat outfitted with steam boiler engines to power the paddle wheels that propel it forward (page 331)

steel *n.* (STEEL) a hard metal made from a mixture of iron and carbon (page 624)

steerage *n.* (STEER-ehg) the inferior section of a ship housing passengers who pay the lowest fare for the journey (page 430)

steppe *n.* (STEP) a vast, grassy plain (page 42)

stockyard *n.* (STAHK-yard) an enormous outdoor corral in which animals are penned until they can be slaughtered (page 584)

Stono Rebellion *n.* (STOH-noh rih-BEL-yuhn) a 1739 revolt by enslaved Africans against their owners (page 137)

storm surge *n.* (STAWRM SUHRJ) an abnormal rise of water generated by a storm, over and above the predicted tides, and pushed toward the shore by storm winds (page 991)

streetcar *n.* (STREET-kahr) a vehicle on rails set in city streets that can transport many passengers at once, like a train (page 634)

strict interpretation *n.* (STRIHKT ihn-tur-pruh-TAY-shuhn) an understanding of the Constitution as one in which the Constitution is strictly followed as it was written (page 286)

strike *n.* (STRYK) a work stoppage in order to force an employer to comply with demands (page 328)

subprime *adj.* (SUHB-prym) describes a type of home loan issued to buyers with poor credit history (page 995)

subsidy *n.* (SUHB-suh-dee) government funds for improvements or support of commerce (page 342)

subsistence farming *n.* (suhb-SIHS-tuhnts FAHR-ming) the practice of producing enough food for a farmer and his family but not enough to sell for profit (page 123)

suburb *n.* (SUH-burb) a residential area on the edge of a city or town (page 634)

suburbanization *n.* (suh-bur-buh-nuh-ZAY-shuhn) a population shift from cities to outlying communities (page 856)

suffrage *n.* (SUH-frihj) the right to vote (page 451)

suffragist *n.* (SUHF-rih-jihst) a person who supports and fights for the right to vote, particularly a woman's right to vote (page 682)

Sugar Act *n.* (SHU-gur AKT) the British law that lowered the duty on molasses to cut out smuggling so that the British would get the revenue (page 181)

Sunbelt *n.* (SUHN-behlt) the southern and southwestern regions of the United States, which have mild winters (page 854)

supply and demand *n.* (suh-PLY AND dih-MAND) an economic principle that states that the price of something depends on how much is available, the supply, and how much is wanted, the demand (page 764)

supply-side economics *n.* (suh-PLY SYD eh-kuh-NAH-mihks) a financial theory that promotes lowering tax rates for businesses and investors in the hope of boosting production and trade (page 966)

Supreme Court *n.* (soo-PREEM KORT) the highest court in the United States (page 258)

surplus *n.* (SUR-plus) the amount left over; an excess (page 587)

sweatshop *n.* (SWEHT-shahp) a factory that pays low wages, provides crowded, unsafe conditions, and requires long work hours (page 647)

swing state *n.* (SWIHNG STAYT) a state in which voters are evenly divided between parties, making it difficult to predict which candidate will gain the state's electoral votes (page 1006)

T

tank *n.* (TANGK) an armored, heavily armed vehicle that uses treads instead of wheels (page 713)

tariff *n.* (TAIR-uhf) a tax on imports and exports (page 282)

Tariff of Abominations *n.* (TAIR-uhf UHV uh-bah-muh-NAY-shuhns) the term used by southerners to refer to the Tariff of 1828 because it stirred feelings of disgust and hatred (page 366)

Tea Act *n.* (TEE AKT) the British law stating that only the East India Company was allowed to sell tea to the American colonists (page 191)

teetotaler *n.* (TEE-toh-tuh-lur) a person who does not drink alcoholic beverages (page 681)

telegraph *n.* (TEHL-uh-graf) a machine that sends messages long distances by sending electrical pulses in code over electrical wires (page 331)

televangelist *n.* (teh-lih-VAN-juh-lihst) a religious leader who shares Christian teachings on a regularly scheduled television broadcast (page 970)

temperance movement *n.* (TEHM-pur-uhns MOOV-mehnt) a 19th-century reform movement that encouraged the reduction or elimination of alcoholic beverage consumption (page 438)

tenement *n.* (TEH-nuh-muhnt) a quickly constructed apartment building; usually refers to a crowded urban dwelling for immigrants and the poor (page 630)

tepee *n.* (TEE-pee) a cone-shaped tent made of bison hides (page 27)

termination policy *n.* (tur-muh-NAY-shuhn PAH-luh-see) a policy enacted under President Eisenhower that removed Native Americans from reservations, while the government ended the limited sovereignty of individual tribes and nations (page 922)

terrain *n.* (tuh-RAYN) the physical features of the land (page 204)

textile *n.* (TEHKS-ty-uhl) the cloth and clothing made from cotton and other raw materials (page 328)

Three-Fifths Compromise *n.* (THREE FIFTHS KAHM-pruh-myz) the agreement that determined that only three-fifths of the total population of enslaved persons in a state would be counted for purposes of taxation and representation (page 260)

tolerance *n.* (TAH-luh-runts) the acceptance of others (page 144)

total war *n.* (TOH-tuhl WOR) a war in which all rules and laws of war are ignored and all resources are used for defeating the enemy (page 530)

Townshend Acts *n.* (TOWN-sehnd AKTS) a set of British laws that placed duties on tea, glass, paper, lead, and paint; required colonists to purchase from Britain (page 186)

trading post *n.* (TRAYD-ing POHST) a small settlement established for the purpose of exchanging goods (page 155)

Trail of Tears *n.* (TRAYL UHV TEHRS) the route the Cherokees and other Native Americans took during their forced migration from the southeast United States to Oklahoma (page 373)

traitor *n.* (TRAY-tohr) a person who betrays his or her own people, nation, or cause (page 99)

trans-Saharan *adj.* (tran-suh-HAHR-uhn) across the Sahara (page 42)

transcendentalism *n.* (tran-sehn-DEHN-tuh-li-zuhm) an intellectual and social movement of the 1830s and 1840s that called for rising above society's expectations (page 444)

transcontinental railroad *n.* (tranz-kahn-tuh-NEHN-tuhl RAYL-rohd) a railroad that runs across a continent (page 620)

treason *n.* (TREE-zuhn) the crime of aiding the enemy of one's nation or plotting to overthrow one's nation; the act of being disloyal to one's nation (page 367)

treaty *n.* (TREE-tee) a peace agreement (page 158)

Treaty of Greenville *n.* (TREE-tee UHV GREEN-vihl) a treaty between the United States and a number of Native American nations in which the Native American nations gave up their lands in present-day Ohio and Indiana to the United Sates (page 288)

Treaty of Paris of 1783 *n.* (TREE-tee UHV PAIR-uhs UHV 1783) the binding agreement between Britain and the United States in which Britain acknowledged American independence, and the initial borders of the United States were determined (page 244)

Treaty of Versailles *n.* (TREE-tee UHV vur-SY) the treaty that officially brought World War I to a close (page 723)

trench warfare *n.* (TREHNCH WOR-fair) a battle strategy that uses a system of ditches to give soldiers a protected place from which to fire during battle (page 495)

triangular trade *n.* (try-ANG-gyuh-lur TRAYD) a transatlantic trade network formed by Europe, West Africa, and the Americas (page 73)

tributary *n.* (TRIH-byoo-tair-ee) a creek, stream, or river that flows into a larger river or other body of water (page 112)

truce *n.* (TROOS) an agreement to stop fighting (page 371)

trust *n.* (TRUHST) a group of corporations managed, but not directly owned, by a board (page 627)

tundra *n.* (TUHN-druh) the flat treeless land found in arctic and subarctic regions (page 26)

tyranny *n.* (TEER-uh-nee) unjust rule by an absolute ruler (page 181)

U

U-boat *n.* (YOO BOHT) a German submarine (page 713)

unalienable right *n.* (uhn-AY-lee-uhn-ah-buhl RITE) a right that cannot be taken away (page 208)

unconstitutional *adj.* (uhn-KAHNT-stuh-too-shnuhl) an idea or law that goes against the principles of the U.S. Constitution (page 310)

Underground Railroad *n.* (uhn-dur-GROWND RAYL-rohd) a network of people who worked together to help African Americans escape from slavery from the southern United States to the northern states or to Canada before the Civil War (page 447)

Unionist *n.* (YOON-yuh-nihst) a member of the Constitutional Union Party (page 472)

unorganized territory *n.* (uhn-AWR-guh-nyzd TAIR-uh-tawr-ee) lands governed by the federal government but not belonging to any state (page 345)

urbanization *n.* (ur-buh-nuh-ZAY-shuhn) a process in which economic, industrial, and population patterns shifted from rural areas to cities (page 634)

V

vassal *n.* (VA-suhl) in the medieval European feudal system, a person, usually a lesser nobleman, who received land and protection from a feudal lord in exchange for obedience and service (page 36)

veteran *n.* (VEH-tuh-ruhn) a person who has served in the military (page 534)

veto *v.* (VEE-toh) to formally reject a decision or proposal made by a legislature (page 375)

viceroy *n.* (VYSE-roy) a governor of Spain's colonies in the Americas who represented the Spanish king and queen (page 58)

viceroyalty *n.* (vyse-ROHY-uhl-tee) a territory governed by a viceroy (page 58)

Vietnamization *n.* (vee-eht-nuh-muh-ZAY-shun) a military strategy that allowed for the gradual replacement of U.S. troops with South Vietnamese troops during the Vietnam War (page 952)

voter registration drive *n.* (VOH-tur reh-juh-STRAY-shuhn DRYV) an effort by groups or government to sign up as many eligible voters in a targeted area as possible (page 887)

voting rights *n.* (VOHT-ing RITES) the laws that tell who can vote and when; the civil right to vote (page 362)

W

wage economy *n.* (WAYJ ih-KAH-nuh-mee) an economy in which people are paid for their work (page 559)

wage gap *n.* (WAYJ GAP) the difference in pay between men and women who perform similar jobs; men usually earn more than women (page 924)

wagon train *n.* (WA-guhn TRAYN) a large group of covered wagons that traveled together across the North American continent as American pioneers moved westward (page 396)

War Hawk *n.* (WOR HAWK) a person who approved of and encouraged war; an American who favored war with Great Britain in 1812 (page 321)

War of 1812 *n.* (WOR UHV 1812) the war against Great Britain that James Madison declared (page 322)

Watergate scandal *n.* (WAH-tur-gayt SKAN-duhl) a break-in at the Democratic National Headquarters in the Watergate complex in Washington, D.C., in 1972 by burglars associated with President Richard Nixon's re-election committee (page 961)

watershed *n.* (WAH-tuhr-shed) an area of land that includes a particular river or lake and all the bodies of water that flow into it (page 64)

weapon of mass destruction (WMD) *n.* (WEH-puhn UHV MAS dih-STRUHK-shuhn) weapons that use nuclear, chemical, or biological substances to harm large numbers of people (page 989)

Whig Party *n.* (WIHG PAHR-tee) a political party formed to oppose the policies of Andrew Jackson, who the party believed had exceeded his power as president (page 376)

Whiskey Rebellion *n.* (HWIH-skee rih-BEL-yuhn) a series of violent protests among farmers in western Pennsylvania against a tax on whiskey (page 289)

wiretapping *n.* (WY-urh-tap-ihng) the act of placing a device on a telephone in order to secretly listen to conversations (page 960)

World Wide Web *n.* (WURLD WYD WEHB) the system that allows Internet sites to be identified by addresses, linked to each other, and located by search engines (page 1000)

writ *n.* (RIHT) a legal document (page 310)

writ of assistance *n.* (RIHT UHV uh-SIHS-tuhns) a legal document giving authorities the right to enter and search a home or business (page 186)

X

XYZ Affair *n.* (X Y Z uh-FAIR) the meeting with French agents after France began seizing American ships in the late 18th century in an effort to prevent U.S. trade with Britain (page 293)

Y

yellow fever *n.* (YEH-loh FEE-vur) an often fatal disease carried by mosquitoes in tropical climates (page 312)

yellow journalism *n.* (YEH-loh JUR-nuh-lih-zuhm) a type of news reporting that exaggerates and dramatizes events, presenting readers with distorted views of the truth, in order to sell newspapers (page 687)

Z

Zimmermann Telegram *n.* (ZIH-mur-muhn TEH-luh-gram) secret German telegram sent to the German ambassador in Mexico, proposing that Mexico join World War I on the German side (page 715)

abomination *n.* (uh-bah-muh-NAY-shuhn) a thing worthy of hatred or disgust (page 366)

acclaim *n.* (uh-KLAYM) enthusiastic praise (page 285)

acquisition *n.* (a-kwuh-ZIH-shuhn) the act of obtaining something as one's own; an item obtained (page 37)

affluent *adj.* (A-floo-uhnt) wealthy, prosperous (page 855)

allegory *n.* (A-luh-gor-ee) a story told through symbols, in which the characters and other story elements represent human actions and emotions (page 444)

allocate *v.* (A-luh-kayt) to divide and give out for a specific purpose (page 954)

annihilate *v.* (uh-NY-uh-layt) to destroy totally (page 795)

ardent *adj.* (AHR-duhnt) very eager; passionate (page 282)

arduous *adj.* (AHR-juh-wuhs) difficult; requiring great effort to achieve (page 395)

arid *adj.* (AIR-uhd) extremely dry (as a desert) (page 24)

atrocity *n.* (uh-TRAH-suh-tee) an extremely brutal, cruel act (page 593)

consensus *n.* (kuhn-SEHNT-suhs) general agreement, harmony (page 889)

covenant *n.* (KUH-vuh-nuhnt) an agreement or promise between two parties (page 179)

debilitating *adj.* (di-BIH-luh-tayt-ing) harming the strength or power of someone or something; making effective action impossible (page 647)

derogatory *adj.* (dih-RAH-guh-tor-ee) degrading or unflattering; meant to cast someone or something in a negative light (page 641)

destitute *adj.* (DEHS-tuh-toot) lacking wealth or resources; impoverished (page 768)

disperse *v.* (dih-SPURS) to scatter and spread widely (page 586)

divisive *adj.* (duh-VY-sihv) causing angry dissent and disunity (page 462)

dumbfounded *adj.* (DUHM-fownd-uhd) at a loss for words (page 58)

elite *n.* (ih-LEET) a person or group that is superior in wealth, intellect, education, or athletic ability (page 668)

eloquence *n.* (EH-luh-kwuhnts) an elegant, articulate speaking ability (page 886)

encompass *v.* (ihn-KUHM-puhs) to form a circle around; to surround; to include (page 559)

evade *v.* (ih-VAYD) to avoid capture or to avoid giving a straight, truthful answer (page 596)

evasion *n.* (ih-VAY-zhuhn) the act of avoiding discovery or punishment, usually by stealth (page 735)

exploit *v.* (EHK-sployt) to make use of, often for one's own gain at the expense of another person or of a resource (page 665)

fertile *adj.* (FUR-tuhl) capable of growing plants (page 24)

fervor *n.* (FUR-vur) an intense feeling (page 439)

forfeit *v.* (FOR-fuht) to give up, often as a result of a loss or the imposition of a fine (page 922)

formidable *adj.* (FOR-mih-duh-buhl) awe inspiring, usually in a menacing way (page 223)

forthrightly *adv.* (FORTH-ryt-lee) directly, honestly (page 873)

iconography *n.* (ai-kuh-NAH-gruh-fee) the representative objects or symbols of a culture or religion (page 131)

impartiality *n.* (ihm-PAR-shee-al-ih-tee) neutrality; fairness (page 714)

indispensable *adj.* (ihn-dih-SPENT-suh-buhl) necessary; cannot be done without (page 103)

inherently *adv.* (ihn-HAIR-uhnt-lee) essentially, naturally (page 875)

intervene *v.* (ihn-tur-VEEN) to interfere, usually to force or prevent an action (page 397)

intimidate *v.* (ihn-TIH-muh-dayt) to use threats, usually to make someone do one's bidding (page 371)

knack *n.* (NAK) a person's natural talent or skill (page 768)

legacy *n.* (LEH-guh-see) a body of knowledge or accomplishment from the past (page 250)

lenient *adj.* (LEE-nee-uhnt) tolerant; easygoing (page 552)

lethal *adj.* (LEE-thuhl) deadly (page 647)

manor *n.* (MA-nur) an estate, or the central house on an estate (page 64)

martyr *n.* (MAHR-tur) a person who sacrifices his or her life or something of great value for the good of a cause (page 469)

mechanized *adj.* (MEH-kuh-nyzd) carried out entirely or in part with machines (page 328)

militant *adj.* (MIHL-uh-tuhnt) combative and aggressive; acting as one fighting a war (page 467)

monetary *adj.* (MAH-nuh-tair-ee) taking the form of money (page 303)

nullify *v.* (NUH-luh-fy) to negate, especially in legal terms (page 366)

offensive *n.* (uh-FENT-sihv) the fighting initiated by one side in a war (page 231)

orthodox *adj.* (OR-thuh-dahks) following a strict religious doctrine (page 101)

parcel *n.* (PAHR-suhl) a plot or designated area of land (page 598)

pardon *v.* (PAHR-duhn) to forgive or excuse (page 552)

philosophy *n.* (fuh-LAH-suh-fee) the basic beliefs of a person or group (page 39)

poised *adj.* (POYZD) ready for something to happen (page 982)

prestigious *adj.* (preh-STIH-juhs) having a reputation of quality, esteem, and respect (page 362)

prominent *adj.* (PRAH-muh-nuhnt) widely known (page 971)

prosperous *adj.* (PRAHS-pur-uhs) economically successful (page 842)

prosthetic *n.* (prahs-THEH-tihk) an artificial limb or body part (page 494)

rehabilitate *v.* (ree-uh-BIH-luh-tayt) to restore to previous health or reputation (page 441)

replenish *v.* (rih-PLEH-nish) to fill up again (page 495)

retaliation *n.* (rih-ta-lee-AY-shuhn) the act of getting revenge or working against someone because he or she has harmed you (page 791)

rhetoric *n.* (REH-tuh-rihk) the way words are used to express an idea, usually to persuade (page 562)

sentiment *n.* (SEHN-tuh-muhnt) an attitude based on feelings (page 815)

shrapnel *n.* (SHRAP-nuhl) the sharp pieces of an exploded shell or cannonball (page 172)

specimen *n.* (SPE-suh-muhn) one example of something from nature, such as a certain plant, animal, or mineral (page 300)

sphere *n.* (SFEER) an area defining one's function or authority (page 328)

suborbital *adj.* (suhb-OR-buh-tuhl) less than one complete circling of an object or body around another; less than a complete circular path (page 905)

survey *n.* (sur-VAY) a measurement to establish land boundaries (page 252)

susceptible *adj.* (suh-SEHP-tuh-buhl) open to being affected or influenced by something (page 527)

synchronize *v.* (SING-kruh-nyz) to cause to occur at the same time (page 740)

tenure *n.* (TEHN-yur) the act of holding something of value, such as land or an important position, or the term during which such a thing is held (page 555)

turmoil *n.* (TUR-moyl) confusion; upheaval (page 727)

undermine *v.* (UHN-dur-myn) to weaken (page 906)

unethical *adj.* (uhn-EH-thih-kuhl) morally wrong (page 996)

usher *v.* (UH-shur) to bring in something new (page 717)

valor *n.* (VA-lur) the quality of great courage or bravery (page 520)

vigorous *adj.* (VIH-guh-ruhs) done with energy or with force (page 845)

GLOSARIO

A

abolición *s.* acto de poner fin a algo, como la esclavitud (página 349)

abolicionista *s.* persona que quería que la esclavitud terminara (página 446)

abolir la segregación *v.* terminar con una política que obliga a la separación de las personas en espacios públicos (página 877)

abstemio *s.* persona que no consume bebidas alcohólicas (página 681)

acatamiento *s.* obediencia a un conjunto de creencias (página 144)

acción afirmativa *s.* política gubernamental que estableces cuotas raciales para favorecer a los grupos que han sufrido discriminación (página 915)

acero *s.* metal muy resistente hecho a partir de una mezcla de hierro y carbono (página 624)

acreedor *s.* persona a quien se le adeuda un préstamo (página 590)

actividad económica *s.* operaciones de producción, distribución y consumo de bienes y servicios (página 114)

Acuerdos de Múnich *s.* un acuerdo que Hitler hizo con los líderes de Gran Bretaña, Francia e Italia, declarando que Alemania tenía derecho a anexarse los Sudetes, una parte de Checoslovaquia (página 791)

afluente *s.* arroyo, riachuelo o río que desemboca en un río más grande o en otra masa de agua (página 112)

agente federal (marshal) *s.* agente federal (marshal) *s.* agente del orden público que trabaja para el gobierno de los Estados Unidos (página 463)

Agente Naranja *s.* un potente herbicida, usado para exterminar la vegetación (página 929)

agrario(a) *adj.* relativo al campo o la agricultura (página 366)

agricultura de subsistencia *s.* modo de producir suficientes alimentos para el granjero y su familia, pero no para la venta (página 123)

agricultura de tala y quema *s.* método de despejar los campos para sembrar cultivos que consiste en cortar y quemar los árboles y las plantas existentes (página 29)

aislacionismo *s.* política en la que una nación se mantiene lejos de los asuntos de otras naciones (página 791)

alfabetizar *s.* enseñar a leer y escribir (página 559)

alianza *s.* acuerdo entre naciones para luchar en contra de los enemigos de cada una o para colaborar entre ellas; pacto (página 111)

Alianza de Agricultores *s.* una de las muchas organizaciones fundadas en la década de 1880 para promover los intereses políticos y económicos de los agricultores; similar a La Granja, pero con un perfil más político (página 591)

alistarse *v.* unirse a la milicia (página 520)

alocución *s.* discurso formal (página 886)

americanización *s.* proceso de inducción dirigido a los inmigrantes e indígenas norteamericanos para que aprendan la cultura y lengua convencionales de los Estados Unidos con el objetivo de que se adapten y acojan a este país (página 598)

anarquista *s.* persona que defiende la anarquía y, por lo tanto, la ausencia de todo gobierno (página 650)

anexar *v.* agregar (página 391)

antifederalista *s.* persona que se oponía a la Constitución de EE. UU. de 1787 porque el énfasis de esta era un gobierno nacional poderoso (página 262)

antisemitismo *s.* discriminación, prejuicio y hostilidad contra el pueblo judío (página 814)

antropólogo *s.* persona que estudia las culturas (página 748)

apaciguamiento *s.* política de hacer concesiones políticas para evitar los conflictos (página 791)

aparcería *s.* sistema agrícola en donde los jornaleros levantan la cosecha de un terrateniente a cambio de recibir una parte de la venta de dichas cosechas (página 559)

aprendiz *s.* persona que aprende un arte u oficio manual trabajando junto a un experto en ese arte u oficio (página 129)

arancel *s.* impuesto a las importaciones y exportaciones (página 282)

arancel de aduana *s.* impuesto a las importaciones (página 181)

arancel de las abominaciones *s.* término usado por los sureños para referirse al arancel de 1828 porque lo consideraban odioso y opresivo (página 366)

archipiélago *s.* conjunto de islas en una misma zona marina (página 685)

armas de destrucción masiva *s.* armas que usan sustancias nucleares, químicas o biológicas para dañar a un gran número de personas (página 989)

armisticio *s.* un acuerdo entre los lados opuestos de un conflicto para dejar de pelear (página 721)

arreo *s.* proceso de conducir el ganado de un lugar a otro, comúnmente der un rancho a una estación ferroviaria (página 584)

artesano *s.* persona que realiza a mano objetos con gran destreza (página 136)

Artículos de la Confederación *s.* conjunto de leyes adoptado por los Estados Unidos en 1777, que establecía cada estado de la Unión como una república, reemplazado por la Constitución en 1789 (página 222)

artillería *s.* cañones y armas largas que disparan a gran distancia (página 203)

asimilar *v.* adoptar la cultura o forma de vida de la nación donde se vive; integrarse por completo a una cultura o a un país (páginas 368, 433)

astronauta *s.* persona entrenada para viajar al espacio (página 904)

Asunto XYZ *s.* reunión con agentes franceses luego de que Francia comenzara a capturar barcos estadounidenses para prevenir el comercio entre EE. UU. y Gran Bretaña (página 293)

atolón *s.* arrecife o conjunto de islas coralinas en forma de anillo (página 817)

autodeterminación *s.* la idea de que cada país debe tener sus propios gobiernos y fronteras para reflejar los orígenes nacionales del pueblo que allí vive (página 722)

autonomía *s.* control de sus propios asuntos por parte de uno mismo; control de los asuntos y leyes de una comunidad por parte de aquellos que viven en ella y no por parte de un monarca o gobernante ajeno (página 105)

autónomo *s.* gobernado por sí mismo (página 686)

autosuficiencia *s.* independencia individual obtenida a través de destrezas prácticas con base en la educación (página 644)

B

baby boom *s.* un incremento significativo en la tasa de natalidad (página 854)

baja *s.* persona muerta o herida en combate (página 540)

banco de la reserva *s.* uno de los bancos que supervisa la Junta de la Reserva Federal, y controla el flujo de dinero en los Estados Unidos (página 674)

bar clandestino *s.* un local ilegal donde las personas se reunían en secreto para consumir alcohol durante la Prohibición (página 735)

barco de vapor *s.* barco equipado con calderas de vapor que impulsaban ruedas giratorias para hacerlo navegar (página 331)

barraca *s.* construcción usada para albergar a un gran número de personas (página 806)

base de poder *s.* zona o grupo de personas que provee la mayor influencia sobre un candidato político (página 286)

batallón *s.* amplio grupo de tropas militares (página 806)

bayoneta *s.* cuchillo afilado que se une a la boca de un fusil (página 228)

Bimetalismo *s.* movimiento económico que surgió a finales del siglo XIX para promover un sistema monetario basado en la plata además del oro (página 591)

Blitzkrieg *s.* estrategia de guerra ejecutada de forma rápida que implica bombardear desde el aire objetivos de comunicaciones y transporte, antes de comenzar la invasión por tierra (página 791)

bloque *s.* un grupo que se forma para apoyar un interés o propósito común (página 846)

bloquear *v.* cortar la entrada o salida de barcos de una bahía (página 228)

blues *s.* un estilo musical que se originó entre los músicos afroamericanos, que cuenta historias sobre tiempos difíciles y penas (página 743)

GLOSARIO

boicot *s.* forma de protesta que rechaza la compra de bienes o servicios (página 183)

boicot de autobuses de Montgomery *s.* una protesta masiva contra las prácticas de segregación racial en el sistema de autobuses públicos en Montgomery, Alabama, que estalló con el arresto de Rosa Parks (página 879)

bomba atómica *s.* un tipo de bomba cuya violenta explosión es provocada por la división de los átomos, lo cual libera un intenso calor y radioactividad (página 821)

bomba incendiaria *s.* una bomba diseñada para iniciar incendios (página 819)

bono *s.* bono s. certificado puesto a la venta al público por el gobierno con la promesa de pagar esa cantidad en una fecha posterior (página 524)

Bonos de la Libertad *s.* bonos del gobierno que fueron vendidos a individuos para apoyar la participación de los Estados Unidos en la Primera Guerra Mundial (página 718)

C

caballería *s.* tropas de un ejército que luchan montadas a caballo (página 491)

Cabeza de Cobre *s.* apodo peyorativo para designar a los miembros del Partido Demócrata que en los estados de la Unión se oponían a la emancipación de los esclavos y al reclutamiento (página 562)

cabildero *s.* persona que intenta persuadir a los legisladores para que apoyen ciertas leyes y proyectos políticos (página 681)

cacicazgo *s.* comunidad de personas regida por un cacique o jefe (página 9)

californio *s.* residente de California de descendencia española o mexicana y que vivía allí antes de la fiebre del oro (página 417)

cambio climático *s.* un cambio en los patrones climáticos de la Tierra (página 1008)

Camino de Lágrimas *s.* ruta que los cheroquis y otras tribus norteamericanas tomaron durante su migración forzada desde el sureste de los Estados Unidos hacia Oklahoma (página 373)

campaña de registro de votantes *s.* esfuerzo de grupos o del gobierno por inscribir a todos los votantes posibles en un área determinada (página 887)

campo de concentración *s* un lugar donde se confinar a los prisioneros de guerra o miembros de minorías perseguidas; durante la Segunda Guerra Mundial, fueron los campos en que judíos y otros prisioneros fueron recluidos y asesinados por los nazis (página 814)

campo de exterminio *s.* un campo donde judíos y otros fueron recluidos y asesinados por los nazis durante la Segunda Guerra Mundial (página 814)

campo de internamiento *s.* campo de prisioneros para mantener a los soldados enemigos u otros prisioneros de guerra durante la contienda (página 806)

canciller *s.* un líder que en algunos países europeos juega un papel similar al del presidente en los Estados Unidos (página 789)

cañón antiaéreo *s.* una pieza de artillería pesada, modificada para apuntar a los aviones enemigos (página 713)

cañonero *s.* embarcación rápida y pequeña que llevaba cañones (página 508)

capataz *s.* supervisor (página 134)

capitalismo *s.* sistema económico donde las entidades privadas, por oposición al gobierno, son propietarias de negocios que administran con fines de lucro (página 627)

carabela *s.* barco pequeño y rápido usado por los exploradores españoles y portugueses (página 40)

caravana *s.* grupo de personas y animales que viajan juntos, usualmente para comerciar (página 42)

caravana *s.* grupo grande de carretas cubiertas, una detrás de otra, donde viajaban los pioneros a través de Norteamérica hacia el Oeste (página 396)

carrera espacial *s.* la competencia entre los Estados Unidos y la Unión Soviética para ser los primeros en viajar al espacio fuera de la atmósfera terrestre (página 904)

carreta Conestoga *s.* tipo de carreta diseñada por colonos alemanes en Norteamérica para llevar cargas pesadas (página 143)

Carta del Atlántico *s.* un documento que enlista ocho principios para un mundo mejor, redactado durante la reunión entre el presidente Franklin Roosevelt y el primer ministro británico Winston Churchill en 1941 (página 793)

casa de asistencia *s.* lugar donde se proporciona ayuda a los inmigrates y a las personas más necesitadas de una comunidad (página 635)

caso Dred Scott *s.* decisión de la Corte Suprema que dictaminó que los afroamericanos no tenían derechos como ciudadanos y que invalidó el Compromiso de Missouri de 1820; Dred Scott, el esclavo en cuestión, fue devuelto a la esclavitud (página 468)

cateador *s.* persona que busca en la tierra recursos minerales valiosos, especialmente piedras y metales preciosos (página 416)

cazador-recolector *s.* ser humano que cazaba animales y recolectaba plantas silvestres para su alimentación (página 7)

ceder *v.* renunciar (página 288)

cédula real *s.* título por escrito que concede el establecimiento de una institución y que detalla derechos y privilegios de los miembros (página 92)

centrista *s.* una persona que profesa visiones políticas moderadas (página 982)

cese al fuego *s.* la orden militar de terminar la lucha (página 930)

charlainformal *s.* una de las transmisiones radiales que el presidente Roosevelt hizo para dirigirse a la nación durante su presidencia (página 777)

chivo expiatorio *s.* individuo o grupo culpado por los errores o las faltas de otros (página 523)

ciclo de auge y depresión *s.* serie de periodos de crecimiento económico seguidos de repentinas crisis económicas (página 627)

cierre de la Administración *s.* cuando la rama ejecutiva del gobierno tiene que cerrar las oficinas y los servicios del gobierno federal debido a que la legislatura no ha aprobado la financiación para estas oficinas o servicios (página 985)

circunnavegar *v.* viajar por completo alrededor de la Tierra (página 62)

ciudad en auge *s.* ciudad cuya población aumenta repetinamente y en grandes cantidas (página 418)

ciudadanía *s.* la condición de tener los derechos y deberes de los ciudadanos (página R32)

civil *s.* persona que no es militar (página 497)

civilización *s.* sociedad con una cultura y una tecnología muy desarrolladas (página 24)

cláusula *s.* condición adjunta a un documento legal o ley (página 413)

cláusula de comercio *s.* disposición del Artículo 1 de la Constitución de EE. UU., que otorga al Congreso el poder de hacer leyes con respecto al comercio internacional, entre estados y con las naciones indígenas (página 261)

cláusula de esclavo fugitivo *s.* disposición del Artículo 4 de la Constitución de EE. UU., que prohíbe a los estados libres la liberación de trabajadores esclavos que se hayan escapado de sus amos en otros estados (página 260)

cláusula de importación de esclavos *s.* disposición del Artículo 1 de la Constitución de EE. UU., que establece que los Estados Unidos no considerará prohibir el comercio internacional de esclavos en el país hasta 1808 (página 260)

clientelismo *s.* práctica que recompensa a los partidarios políticos con puestos en el gobierno (página 365)

coalición *s.* una alianza de personas, partidos o estados dedicados a un objetivo común (página 977)

códigos negros *s.* leyes aprobadas por los estados sureños inmediatamente después de la Guerra Civil para controlar y limitar los derechos de los afroamericanos; fueron revocadas durante la Reconstrucción en 1866 (página 554)

Colegio electoral *s.* grupo que elige al presidente de los EE. UU.; cada estado tiene un número de electores igual al número de sus representantes y senadores en el Congreso (página 258)

colonia real *s.* colonia gobernada por un monarca a través de un gobernador designado (página 112)

comedia costumbrista *s.* programa semanal que muestra a una familia o a un grupo de personajes que enfrenta problemas divertidos (página 858)

comercio de esclavos interestatal *s.* la compra y venta de esclavos dentro de los Estados Unidos (página 339)

comercio triangular *s.* red transatlántica de comercio formada por Europa, África Occidental y las Américas (página 73)

comisionado *s.* representante de un gobierno (página 669)

comité de correspondencia *s.* en la época de la independencia, grupo de colonos cuyo deber era hacer correr la voz para la organización de protestas contra los británicos (página 191)

comité de vigilancia *n.* grupo armado y comandado por un alguacil para capturar criminales o fugitivos (página 583)

Compra de Gadsden *s.* venta de tierras de México a los Estados Unidos en 1853, que estableció la frontera suroeste actual de los EE. UU. (página 413)

Compra de Louisiana *s.* tratado entre Francia y los Estados Unidos, por el cual fue comprada una gran extensión de tierras entre el río Mississippi y las montañas Rocosas (página 313)

comprar a préstamo *v.* comprar algo pagando una pequeña cantidad de lo que vale y pedir prestado el resto del dinero para irlo pagando (página 765)

Compromiso de 1877 *s.* acuerdo mediante el cual el Partido Demócrata se comprometió a reconocer a Rutherford B. Hayes como presidente a cambio de que los Republicanos concluyeran la Reconstrucción y retiraran a las tropas federales del Sur (página 565)

Compromiso de las tres quintas partes *s.* acuerdo en el cual se determinó que solo tres quintas partes de la población total de esclavos en un estado se tomarían en cuenta para objetivos de impuestos y representación (3/5) (página 260)

Compromiso de Missouri *s.* acuerdo que estableció que Missouri podía tener esclavos y a su vez ser admitido a la Unión junto con Maine, un estado libre (página 344)

comunismo *s.* una forma de gobierno en la que todos los medios de producción y transporte son del estado (página 717)

comunitario *a.* esfuerzo organizativo de la gente común, de base, que no tiene dinero ni poder, pero son capaces de lograr un cambio (página 872)

confederación *s.* acuerdo entre varios grupos, estados o gobiernos para protegerse y apoyarse unos a otros en batallas u otros emprendimientos (página 111)

Confederación *s.* los 11 estados que se separaron de la Unión para formar su propia nación: los Estados Confederados de América (página 474)

confinamiento en solitario *s.* una forma de castigo que consiste en aislar al preso del contacto con otras personas (página 885)

conquista de isla-en-isla *s.* una estrategia que implicó capturar y establecer campamentos militares en las islas, una por una (página 818)

conquistador *s.* explorador español que buscaba oro y otras riquezas en las Américas (página 56)

conspiración *s.* un plan secreto para dañar o cometer un acto ilegal (página 911)

constitución *s.* documento que organiza los poderes de un gobierno y los estados (página 250)

constitucionalismo *s.* sistema de gobernar basándose en una constitución (página 251)

consumidor *s.* persona que compra un producto o servicio (página 738)

contención *s.* política de seguridad norteamericana durante la Guerra Fría, en la que la acción diplomática y militar se usaba para impedir que la Unión Soviética difundiera el comunismo (página 847)

contiguo *adj.* junto a algo (página 413)

contraataque *s.* ataque en respuesta a un ataque previo (página 227)

contrabandear *v.* importar y exportar productos de manera ilegal (página 125)

contrabando *s.* fabricación, transporte o suministro ilegal (página 735)

contracultura *s.* un movimiento que en los 60 promovió un modo de vida que era lo opuesto a las reglas y conductas establecidas en la sociedad norteamericana (página 933)

contrato colectivo *s.* negociación llevada a cabo entre un sindicato y un empleador y que tiene por finalidad elevar los salarios y mejorar las condiciones laborales (página 648)

Convención de Seneca Falls *s.* convención por los derechos de la mujer, organizada por Elizabeth Cady Stanton y Lucretia Mott en Seneca Falls, Nueva York, en 1848 (página 450)

conventillo *s.* edificio de apartamentos construido de prisa; comúnmente se refiere a una vivienda urbana en donde los inmigrantes y los más necesitados viven temporalmente en condiciones de hacinamiento (página 630)

convertidor catalítico *s.* una parte del sistema de escape de un vehículo que cambia los gases nocivos en gases menos dañinos o inofensivos (página 959)

convertir *v.* persuadir a alguien para que cambie sus creencias; generalmente se refiere a un cambio de religión (página 43)

cooperativa *s.* grupo de agricultores o de otros trabajadores que se forma para adquirir productos y servicios mediante la contribución económica de cada miembro (página 591)

corporación *s.* compañía o grupo empresarial que opera legalmente como una sola entidad para administrar un negocio (página 626)

corral *s.* área protegida de gran tamaño en donde se encierra el ganado hasta que esté listo para su sacrificio (página 584)

corrupción *s.* deshonestidad, ilegalidad (página 564)

corsario *s.* buque mercante privado autorizado por un gobierno para perseguir a las embarcaciones enemigas siguiendo las leyes de guerra, o un marinero a bordo ese tipo de barco (página 62)

Corte Suprema *s.* la corte o tribunal más alto de justicia en EE. UU. (página 258)

crédito *s.* privilegio para comprar algo o pedir prestado dinero, devolviendo el dinero con el tiempo (página 254)

crematorio *s.* un horno usado para quemar restos humanos o animales; durante la Segunda Guerra Mundial, los Nazis los usaron para quemar los cuerpos de sus víctimas (página 814)

crimen organizado *s.* actividades ilegales planeadas y llevadas a cabo por criminales poderosos (página 735)

Crisis de los Misiles *s.* una confrontación política que tuvo lugar en 1962 entre los Estados Unidos y la Unión Soviética, causada por la presencia de armas nucleares en Cuba (página 908)

cuarentena *v.* acción de mantener aislados a quienes han contraído alguna enfermedad de aquellas personas que aún no han sido infectadas (página 527)

cuarentena naval *s.* un bloqueo impuesto a los puertos de otro país (página 908)

cuenca *s.* área de tierra que incluye un río o lago en particular y todos los cuerpos de agua que afluyen al mismo (página 64)

cultivable *adj.* apto para cultivos; fértil (página 140)

cultivo comercial *s.* cultivo plantado para la venta y no para el consumo del granjero (página 132)

cultura de masas *s.* conjunto de valores e ideas populares que surge a partir del amplio acceso a los medios de comunicación, a la música, al arte y a otras formas de entretenimiento (página 628)

cuota de refugiados *s.* un límite en el número de personas a las que se le permite emigrar desde ciertos países (página 736)

D

Danza de los Espíritus *s.* movimiento religioso impulsado por los nativos amerindios y basado en una danza ritual cuyo fin era comunicarse con los muertos y lograr el fin del dominio blanco en el Oeste; comenzó en la década de 1870 (página 598)

de alto riesgo (préstamos hipotecarios) *a.* un tipo de préstamo hipotecario concedido a compradores con un pobre historial crediticio (página 995)

Decimoquinta Enmienda *s.* una enmienda efectuada a la Constitución de los Estados Unidos de América, que establece que los gobiernos federal y estatal no pueden limitar el derecho al voto en virtud de la raza, el color de la piel o por una condición previa de esclavitud (página 562)

Declaración de Derechos *s.* las diez primeras enmiendas a la Constitución de EE. UU.; lista de garantías a las que tienen derecho todas las personas del país (página 263)

GLOSARIO

Declaración de Independencia *s.* documento que declara la independencia de los Estados Unidos de Gran Bretaña, emitido el 4 de julio de 1776 (página 208)

déficit presupuestario *s.* una práctica en que el gobierno gasta más dinero del que recibe por los impuestos (página 783)

delegado *s.* persona elegida para representar a un grupo de personas (página 256)

democracia jacksoniana *s.* movimiento político que honraba al hombre común y defendía la voluntad del pueblo; su nombre deriva de Andrew Jackson (página 362)

depresión *s.* período de baja actividad económica, cuando muchas personas se quedan sin trabajo (página 375)

derecho al voto *s.* ley que establece quién puede votar y cuándo; derecho civil a votar (página 362)

derecho estatal *s.* concepto de que los estados individuales tienen derechos que el gobierno federal no puede violar (página 293)

derecho humano *s.* derecho básico que la mayoría de las sociedades cree que debe garantizarse a todas las personas (página 964)

derecho inalienable *s.* derecho que no se puede quitar (página 208)

derechos civiles *s.* derechos individuales, que la ley protege de la interferencia gubernamental (página 719)

derechos naturales *s.* derechos de una persona desde su nacimiento, como a la vida o a la libertad (página 149)

derogar *v.* cancelar o revocar, especialmente una ley (página 183)

desertar *v.* abandonar una obligación o causa (página 564)

desertar *v.* huir del ejército o de otra fuerza armada para evitar el servicio militar (página 231)

deshumanizar *v.* tratar a las personas como si no fueran seres humanos (página 872)

desmotadora de algodón *s.* máquina que separa las fibras de algodón de sus semillas y vainas (página 338)

desmovilización *s.* la liberación de los soldados de su deber militar (página 842)

desobediencia civil *s.* desobediencia no violenta de las leyes como una forma de protesta (página 878)

desplegar *v.* enviar en misión militar (página 802)

desregulación *s.* la eliminación de leyes o reglamentos que rigen una industria en particular (página 966)

desterrar *v.* expulsar a alguien de un territorio como castigo, generalmente sin la esperanza de regresar (página 101)

destino manifiesto *s.* idea de que los Estados Unidos tenían el derecho y la obligación de expandir su territorio a través de Norteamérica hacia el océano Pacífico (página 391)

deuda del consumidor *s.* la cantidad de dinero que se ha pedido prestada para comprar bienes (página 765)

deuda nacional *s.* cantidad de dinero que un país debe a todos sus acreedores, que incluyen otros países y compañías a las que compra bienes y servicios (página 282)

Día D *s.* el día 6 de junio de 1944, cuando las fuerzas aliadas invadieron el norte de Francia y desembarcaron en las playas de Normandía (página 810)

diáspora africana *s.* el traslado de africanos de su lugar natal a las Américas (página 74)

dictador *s.* un líder que gobierna con el poder absoluto (página 789)

difamación *s.* publicación con la intención de desacreditar (página 152)

diferencia salarial *s.* la diferencia de salario entre hombres y mujeres que realizan trabajos similares; los hombres usualmente ganan más que las mujeres (página 924)

diplomacia moral *s.* el concepto de que los Estados Unidos debían reducir drásticamente su intervención en los asuntos de otros países (página 724)

diplomático *s.* persona enviada a otro país para representar los intereses del suyo propio (página 409)

dique *s.* cresta de tierra que corre a lo largo de los dos lados de un arroyo o río (página 991)

Discurso de Gettysburg *s.* discurso pronunciado en 1863 por el presidente Lincoln para conmemorar a los caídos en la Batalla de Gettysburg, y para instaurar un cementerio militar en ese sitio (página 529)

disenso *s.* desacuerdo con la opinión oficial del gobierno (página 719)

disidente *s.* persona que se separa de la creencia u opinión de la mayoría (página 100)

disidente *s.* persona que se opone firmemente a la política oficial (página 732)

disposición *s.* condición legal que anticipa necesidades futuras, o para evitar un mal (página 244)

diversidad *s.* amplia variedad (página 143)

dividir/división *v./ s.* dividir un conjunto en varias partes (página 813)

divisoria continental *s.* punto alto en las montañas Rocosas que marca la divisoria de aguas, o vertientes hidrográficas, que van a los océanos Atlántico y Pacífico (página 395)

doble soberanía *s.* sistema en el cual los gobiernos de los estados tienen ciertos poderes que el gobierno federal no puede desautorizar (página 257)

doctrina *s.* conjunto de ideas o creencias aceptadas por un grupo (página 109)

doctrina de anulación *s.* doctrina que decía que un estado podía anular o rechazar una ley federal si creía que era inconstitucional, apoyada por un político sureño antes de la Guerra Civil (página 366)

Doctrina Monroe *s.* enfoque de política exterior que expresaba que las Américas ya no estaban bajo el influjo europeo (página 345)

domesticación *s.* práctica de criar animales y cultivar plantas para el beneficio humano (página 9)

domesticar *v.* cultivar plantas y criar animales para que sean útiles a los seres humanos (página 27)

drumlin *s.* montículo pequeño de laderas lisas formado por sedimientos glaciares; también llamado "cresta de una colina" (página 204)

Dust Bowl *s.* una región de las Grandes Llanuras, que incluye partes de Oklahoma, Colorado, Kansas, Nuevo México y Texas, y que sufrió una severa sequía, erosión del suelo y tormentas de polvo durante los años 30 (página 774)

E

economía asalariada *s.* economía donde se remunera a los trabajadores (página 559)

economía de consumo *s.* una economía en que la gente compra frecuentemente y tienen muchas opciones de productos para comprar (página 738)

economía de la oferta *s.* una teoría financiera que promueve la reducción de impuestos para las empresas y los inversores con la esperanza de impulsar la producción y el comercio (página 966)

efecto invernadero *s.* el calentamiento de la superficie de la Tierra causado cuando las emisiones de gases de efecto invernadero atrapan el calor del sol (página 1008)

Eje Roma-Berlín *s.* un acuerdo entre Alemania e Italia, firmado en 1936 (página 789)

Ejército Continental *s.* ejército norteamericano formado en 1775 en el Segundo Congreso Continental y liderado por el general George Washington (página 203)

el Eje *s.* Alianza de Alemania, Italia y Japón durante la Segunda Guerra Mundial (página 789)

elección primaria directa *s.* elección donde los militantes de un partido político nominan a sus candidatos por medio del voto directo (página 668)

emancipación *s.* fin de la esclavitud (página 446)

embarcaciones de desembarco anfibio *s.* botes o barcazas usadas para transportar soldados y equipamiento militar desde el mar a la costa durante ataques militares (página 811)

embargo *s.* ley que limita o prohíbe el comercio con una o más naciones (página 319)

emigrar *v.* irse de un país para vivir en otro (página 430)

empleados de emergencia *s.* una persona (por ejemplo, un trabajador médico de emergencia o un oficial de policía) que proporciona asistencia urgente en caso de accidente o delito (página 989)

emprendedor *s.* persona que inicia, administra y es responsable de un negocio (página 583)

en ejercicio *adj.* persona que ocupa el cargo en el presente; el presidente en ejercicio es el presidente actual (página 306)

encomienda *s.* sistema de España en sus colonias en América, en el cual colonos ricos recibían terrenos y se les permitía esclavizar a las personas que allí vivían (página 66)

encubrimiento *s.* un intento de esconder la verdad al público (página 961)

energía alternativa *s.* electricidad o energía que se crea a partir de una fuente que no se agotará, como la energía eólica o solar (página 1009)

energía hidroeléctrica *s.* una fuente de electricidad creada por el flujo del agua que mueve turbinas generadoras (página 773)

enmienda *s.* cambio oficial a una ley, generalmente con respecto a un cambio oficial a la Constitución de EE. UU. (página 263)

Enmienda Platt *s.* enmienda hecha en 1901 a la legislación militar y en donde se establecían las condiciones para que los Estados Unidos se retirara de Cuba al cabo de la Guerra Hispanoamericana, pero sin que por ello perdiera su derecho a seguir interviniendo en los asuntos de ese país caribeño (página 687)

enviado *n.* embajador (página 292)

Era Dorada *s.* época que abarca las últimas tres décadas del siglo XIX, caracterizada por la codicia y la corrupción (página 628)

escalada *s.* un incremento de intensidad, como en la guerra (página 927)

escándalo de Watergate *s.* una intrusión en la Sede Nacional Demócrata del complejo Watergate en Washington, D.C., en 1972 por ladrones asociados con el comité de reelección del presidente Richard Nixon (página 961)

escaramuza *s.* lucha de corta duración (página 231)

esclavitud *s.* sistema social en el cual unas personas toman control total sobre otras (página 72)

esclavitud como propiedad personal *s.* sistema según el cual las personas esclavizadas no tienen ningún derecho humano y se clasifican como bienes (página 72)

esclusas *s.* sección reducida de agua que se usa para subir o bajar barcos. (página 693)

escombros *s.* exceso de tierra y rocas (página 693)

escorbuto *s.* enfermedad vinculada a la malnutrición y a una dieta carente de frutas y verduras (página 527)

escuela común (common school) *s.* nombre que se le daba a la escuela primaria en las colonias (página 129)

eslogan *s.* frase breve y fácil de recordar hecha para atraer y llamar la atención (página 362)

especular *v.* acto de comprar acciones con la esperanza de venderlas y obtener beneficios, mientras se corre el riesgo de una pérdida (página 765)

espionaje *s.* práctica de espiar para obtener información (página 232)

espiritual *s.* canto religioso basado en figuras bíblicas y de las escrituras de la Biblia cristiana, cantado por primera vez por los esclavos del Sur (página 341)

esquirol *s.* persona dispuesta a ignorar las disposiciones sindicales para trabajar durante una huelga (página 651)

estado decisivo *s.* un estado en el cual los votantes están divididos equitativamente entre los partidos, lo que hace difícil predecir qué candidato ganará los votos electorales del estado (página 1006)

estado fronterizo *s.* estado, durante la Guerra Civil, que limitaba tanto con los estados de la Unión como con los estados Confederados, específicamente Maryland, Kentucky, Delaware, Missouri y Virginia Occidental (página 489)

estancamiento *s.* situación en la que ninguna de las partes de un conflicto tiene posibilidad de ganar (página 516)

estanflación *s.* una condición económica en la que el estancamiento o el lento crecimiento económico va acompañado de inflación o aumento de los precios (página 962)

estatuto *s.* ley oficial escrita (página 267)

estepa *s.* planicie amplia y cubierta de hierbas (página 42)

estímulo económico *s.* una medida destinada a promover y permitir la recuperación financiera y el crecimiento (página 996)

evacuar *v.* dejar un lugar, generalmente para evitar el peligro (página 488)

Evangelio social *s.* movimiento religioso protestante que hizo hincapié en la importancia de que las iglesias se involucraran más en los asuntos sociales y en la reforma (página 634)

evangelizar *v.* predicar las creencias de una religión mediante charlas públicas y testimonios personales (página 438)

examen de lectoescritura *s.* prueba aplicada para evaluar la capacidad de alguien para leer y escribir (página 565)

excedente *s.* cantidad sobrante, exceso de algo (página 587)

exención *s.* librar de obligaciones a alguien (página 522)

exención de servicio *s.* una razón para excluir a un ciudadano de realizar un servicio militar en contra de su voluntad (página 933)

exiliado *s.* una persona que es un marginado político (página 906)

éxodo *s.* salida masiva de personas (página 395)

exoduster *s.* uno de los miles de afroamericanos sureños que migraron hacia las planicies del Medio Oeste al término de la Guerra de Secesión en la esperanza de comenzar una nueva vida (página 586)

expandirse *v.* extenderse; aumentar de manera rápida (página 146)

expuestos a congelación *s.* permanecer en temperaturas muy frías o clima severo sin protección (página 810)

F

factor de expulsión o atracción *s.* razón por la cual las personas migran, por ejemplo, por falta de oportunidades económicas o de libertad en un país y la promesa de una vida mejor en otro país (página 430)

fascismo *s.* movimiento político, basado en el nacionalismo extremo, el militarismo y el racismo, que promueve la superioridad de cierto pueblo sobre los otros (página 789)

federal *adj.* gobierno en el cual el poder es compartido entre el gobierno nacional central y el de los estados o provincias (página 250)

federalismo *s.* apoyo al gobierno en el cual el poder es compartido entre el gobierno nacional central y los estados o provincias (página 257)

federalista *s.* persona que apoyaba la Constitución de EE. UU. de 1787 según se redactó durante el proceso de ratificación (página 262)

feminista *s.* persona que practica la idea de que las mujeres son política y socialmente iguales a los hombres (página 924)

feriado bancario *s.* un día o periodo de tiempo en que los bancos cierran por disposición gubernamental (página 771)

ferrocarril transcontinental *s.* ferrocarril que opera a lo largo de un continente (página 620)

feudalismo *s.* sistema político y social en el que un vasallo recibe protección de un señor feudal a cambio de prestarle obediencia y servicio (página 36)

fiebre amarilla *s.* enfermedad, con frecuencia mortal, transmitida por mosquitos en climas tropicales (página 312)

filantropía *s.* apoyo financiero a favor de una causa noble y caritativa (página 627)

filántropo(a) *s.* persona que promueve activamente el bienestar de los demás (página 496)

financista *s.* persona que presta o maneja dinero para un negocio u emprendimiento (página 229)

fiscal especial *s.* un abogado privado o funcionario designado por el tribunal para investigar o entablar acciones legales contra una parte cuando el fiscal ordinario no puede o tiene un conflicto de intereses con la parte acusada de un delito (página 961)

fiscal general *s.* miembro del Gabinete del presidente, cuyo papel principal es representar a los EE. UU. ante la Corte Suprema (página 281)

fisión nuclear *s.* la separación de los átomos, que provoca una liberación de energía (página 821)

flapper *s.* mujer joven que en los años 20 asumía un estilo más libre de vestir y maquillarse (página 743)

flotilla *s.* flota pequeña o compuesta de buques de menor calado (página 528)

fondo de pensiones *s.* un fondo monetario usado para pagar a las personas un ingreso pequeño y estable luego que se retiren (página 776)

fortificación *s.* estructura construida para proteger un lugar de un ataque (página 227)

forty-niner (buscador de oro) *s.* uno de los miles de futuros mineros que viajaron a California a buscar oro en 1849 (página 417)

***Framers* (autores de la Constitución)** *s.* término histórico para los delegados en la Convención Constitucional de 1787, quienes ayudaron a crear y redactar la Constitución de los Estados Unidos (página 256)

frente *s.* una línea de batalla entre ejércitos (página 712)

Frostbelt *s.* regiones del norte y noreste de Estados Unidos que tienen inviernos muy fríos (página 854)

fuga de depósitos *s.* momento en el que muchos clientes se asustan y corren a retirar su dinero de un banco al mismo tiempo (página 768)

fundamentalismo *s.* un movimiento que promueve la idea de que cada palabra de la Biblia es una verdad literal (página 736)

fundamentalista *s.* Una persona que cree en la adhesión estricta o literal a un sistema de creencias (página 965)

G

Gabinete *s.* los jefes de los departamentos que asisten al presidente de los EE. UU. (página 279)

galeón *s.* buque de vela grande usado especialmente por los españoles en los siglos XVI y XVII (página 62)

ganancia *s.* cantidad de dinero que sobra en un negocio después de descontar los gastos (página 40)

gas venenoso *s* un producto químico dispersado en el aire, que causa daño o muerte (página 713)

gastos corrientes *s.* el costo de operar un negocio (página 647)

genocidio *s.* asesinato deliberado de un gran número de personas que pertenecen a una raza específica o a un determinado grupo cultural o político (página 814)

geografía física *s.* estudio de las características físicas externas de la Tierra (página 34)

geografía humana *s.* estudio de la influencia que tiene la geografía física sobre las personas y su cultura, así como de los efectos que producen las actividades humanas sobre el medio ambiente (página 34)

geología *s.* estudio de los cambios que formaron las rocas y los accidentes geográficos de la Tierra (página 204)

gestión científica *s.* proceso que busca estudiar a los trabajadores para determinar la manera más eficiente y rentable de hacer un trabajo (página 677)

Glaciación *s.* período en la historia durante el cual inmensas capas de hielo cubrían gran parte de la superficie terrestre (página 5)

glásnost *s.* una política gubernamental de transparencia comunicativa en la antigua Unión Soviética (página 974)

globalización *s.* el flujo más rápido y más libre de personas, recursos, bienes e ideas a través de las fronteras nacionales (página 1004)

gobierno títere *s.* gobierno que parece tener autoridad pero en realidad es controlado por otro poder (página 794)

golpe *s.* el derrocamiento ilegal de un gobierno (página 975)

Gran Despertar *s.* serie de avivamientos religiosos protestantes que se extendieron por las colonias en Norteamérica (página 148)

Gran Migración Negra *s.* movimiento masivo de afroamericanos que abandonaron el Sur y emigraron a las ciudades del norte a principios de 1910 (página 727)

granja de bonanza *s.* granja de gran tamaño propiedad de un inversionista, quien la administra para obtener ganancias (página 586)

guarnición *s.* tropa de defensa (página 477)

Guerra de 1812 *s.* guerra contra Gran Bretaña declarada por James Madison (página 322)

guerra de trincheras *s.* estrategia de guerra que usa un sistema de zanjas de protección desde donde los soldados disparan durante la batalla (página 495)

guerra defensiva *s.* guerra para proteger su propio país de ataques extranjeros, luchada en tierras conocidas (página 222)

Guerra del rey Philip *s.* conflicto violento entre indígenas americanos y colonos ingleses de Nueva Inglaterra, ayudados estos últimos por indígenas aliados (página 106)

guerra sin cuartel *s.* guerra en la cual se ignoran todos los convenios bélicos y se usan todos los recursos para vencer al enemigo (página 530)

guerrillero(a) *adj.* que usa tácticas de ataque encubiertas y sabotajes (página 237)

gueto *s.* alojamiento obligatorio para una determinada raza o etnia (página 814)

H

hábeas corpus *s.* derecho de una persona arrestada para comparecer ante un juez antes de ser encarcelada (página 523)

hacienda *s.* plantación grande en una colonia española (página 66)

halcón *s.* una persona que apoya la guerra (página 933)

Halcón de Guerra *s.* persona partidaria de la guerra; estadounidense que estaba a favor de la guerra contra Gran Bretaña en 1812 (página 321)

hambruna *s.* escasez extrema de cultivos o alimentos, que causa hambre generalizada (página 432)

hereje *s.* persona que tiene creencias diferentes a las enseñanzas de la Iglesia Católica (página 61)

***Hessians* (hesianos)** *s.* soldados alemanes contratados por los británicos para luchar durante la Guerra de Independencia (página 206)

Hijos de la Libertad *s.* grupos de mercaderes, comerciantes y artesanos que se organizaron con éxito para rechazar la Ley del Timbre mediante el boicot a los productos británicos (página 183)

historia oral *s.* entrevista grabada con una persona cuyas experiencias y recuerdos tienen un significado histórico (página R38)

Holocausto *s.* la matanza masiva por parte de los nazis de seis millones de judíos y otros durante la Segunda Guerra Mundial (página 814)

hombres de montaña *s.* cazadores y comerciantes de pielesconocidos como tramperos que contribuyeron con la exploración del Oeste (página 390)

Hooverville *s.* grupo de viviendas improvisadas para dar albergue a gente sin techo, hechas con restos de cartón, placas metálicas u otros materiales baratos, que se construyeron durante la Gran Depresión y fueron bautizadas con el nombre del presidente Herbert Hoover (página 769)

horario estándar *s.* división uniforme del tiempo entre lugares que se encuentran aproximadamente en la misma línea de longitud, estableciendo así zonas horarias (página 621)

huelga *s.* huelga s. interrupción del trabajo para forzar a un empleador a cumplir con ciertas demandas (página 328)

huelga de hambre *s.* el acto de negarse a comer como protesta para mostrar desaprobación o desacuerdo (página 918)

humanismo *s.* movimiento basado en la importancia del individuo (página 39)

I

ideología *s.* sistema de creencias que guía un plan social o político (página 789)

Ilustración *s.* movimiento intelectual caracterizado por el uso de la razón para revisar creencias aceptadas anteriormente (página 149)

imperialismo *s.* sistema político mediante el cual un país más poderoso controla a países o territorios más débiles (página 684)

imponer *v.* requerir el pago de un impuesto (página 105)

imprenta *s.* invención que usaba letras móviles de metal para imprimir páginas (página 39)

improvisar *v.* crear o ejecutar música sin ensayarla previamente, a menudo inventándola en el acto (página 742)

impuesto electoral *s.* cuota impuesta a los ciudadanos al registrarse en el padrón electoral (página 563)

impuesto sobre la renta *s.* impuesto que grava los ingresos de cada contribuyente (página 673)

incendio intencional *s.* incendio ilegal provocado de manera deliberada en contra de propiedades y edificios (página 560)

GLOSARIO

inconstitucional *adj.* idea o ley que va en contra de los principios de la Constitución de los EE. UU. (página 310)

incumplimientos de pago *s.* una falla en el pago de un préstamo (página 995)

independizarse *v.* separarse oficialmente de una nación u organización para hacerse independiente (página 474)

indiferencia saludable *s.* política del gobierno británico que evitaba que sus leyes en las colonias se cumplieran estrictamente (página 151)

índigo *s.* planta que produce un tinte azul para teñir telas (página 132)

individualismo *s.* independencia autosuficiente (página 390)

industrial *s.* propietario que administra una compañía industrial (página 591)

infantería *s.* tropas de soldados a pie (página 491)

inflación *s.* disminución en el valor de una moneda que causa el aumento en el precio de bienes y servicios (página 374)

influenza *s.* una grave enfermedad, altamente contagiosa, comúnmente llamada "gripe" (página 726)

ingreso *s.* recaudación de dinero; dinero que se recibe (página 180)

iniciativa *s.* proceso por medio del cual los ciudadanos proponen una ley y es necesario que los demás ciudadanos emitan su voto al respecto (página 669)

inmigrar *v.* llegar a vivir a un país de manera permanente (página 430)

inmunidad *s.* protección contra una enfermedad, ya sea natural o provocada por vacunación (página 70)

institución *s.* práctica establecida y aceptada en una sociedad o una cultura (página 74)

insurgente *s.* un rebelde o revolucionario (página 989)

insurrección *s.* rebelión (página 410)

integración *s.* el acto de permitir la asociación libre de personas de diferentes razas o etnias (página 875)

intercambio colombino *s.* intercambio de plantas, animales, microbios, personas e ideas entre Europa y las Américas después del primer viaje de Colón al Hemisferio Occidental (página 70)

Internet *s.* la red electrónica que permite comunicarse a los ordenadores (página 1000)

interpretación estricta *s.* un entendimiento de la Constitución en el cual la Constitución debe ser seguida estrictamente como fue redactada (página 286)

interpretación flexible *s.* un entendimiento de la Constitución que le da al Congreso y al presidente amplios poderes (página 286)

inversor *s.* persona que compra parte de una compañía con la intención de obtener beneficios al vender su parte de acciones (página 765)

ironclad (barco blindado) *s.* barco revestido con planchas de hierro para protegerlo del fuego de los cañones (página 495)

irrigación *s.* suministro de agua a los campos mediante el uso de sistemas hechos por el hombre (página 24)

istmo *s.* franja estrecha de tierra que conecta dos masas de tierra más grandes y separa dos cuerpos de agua (página 692)

J

jazz *s.* un estilo musical que se originó entre los músicos afroamericanos, que contiene ritmos animados, sonidos de una variedad de instrumentos e improvisaciones (página 742)

jerarquía *s.* clasificación de un grupo de personas de acuerdo con su capacidad o con su posición económica, social o profesional (página 36)

Jinetes Duros *s.* grupo de vaqueros, mineros, oficiales de policía e indígenas norteamericanos que, aunque no contaban con entrenamiento militar, eran considerados muy rudos, y participaron de manera voluntaria en la guerra hispanoamericana bajo el mando de Theodore Roosevelt (página 687)

Juicio Político *s.* acusación formal para destituir a un presidente en funciones a causa de malos manejos en su administración (página 555)

jurisdicción *s.* poder o autoridad concedida a alguien para aplicar la ley en determinado territorio (página 538)

justicia social *s.* régimen caracterizado por una justa distribución de las oportunidades y los privilegios, incluyendo la igualdad racial (página 557)

juzgar ante una corte marcial *v.* juzgar a un miembro de las fuerzas armadas que ha sido acusado de haber violado la ley militar (página 688)

K

kayak *s.* canoa con un armazón liviano y con una pequeña abertura superior para sentarse (página 26)

Ku Klux Klan *s.* grupo clandestino cuyo propósito era mantener el poder social y político de la comunidad blanca en los Estados Unidos (página 560)

L

La Granja *s.* organización fundada en 1867 por agricultores estadounidenses para proporcionar apoyo social y económico a las familias dedicadas a la agricultura (página 590)

laissez faire *s.* política económica aplicada por el gobierno para permitirles a las empresas operar sin muchas regulaciones; laissez-fairesignifica "dejar hacer" en francés (página 627)

La Larga Marcha *s.* marcha forzosa que los navajos debieron emprender desde su lugar de origen hasta una reservación en Bosque Redondo, Nuevo México, a 300 millas (482.8 km) de distancia; fue impuesta por el gobierno de los Estados Unidos en 1864 (página 596)

leal a Gran Bretaña *s.* colono que apoyaba a Gran Bretaña en la Guerra de Independencia (página 198)

lecho de roca *s.* roca sólida que se localiza debajo del suelo (página 636)

legislación histórica *s.* ley importante e histórica (página 913)

Ley Clayton Antimonopolio *s.* ley de 1914 que describía la ilegalidad de las prácticas comerciales de los monopolios, y buscaba llenar los vacíos legales de que solían aprovecharse esos monopolios (página 674)

Ley de Alimentos y Fármacos No Adulterados *s.* ley de 1906 que le otorgaba mayor poder al gobierno federal para que protegiera la calidad, pureza y sanidad de los alimentos y los fármacos (página 671)

Ley de Alojamiento *s.* una de varias leyes británicas que exigía a los colonos proporcionar vivienda y comida a los soldados británicos en Norteamérica (página 178)

Ley de Asentamientos Rurales (Ley de Homstead) *s.* ley que impulsó un programa para otorgar tierras públicas a pequeños agricultores (página 541)

Ley de Conscripción *s.* ley promulgada en 1863 por la Unión mediante la cual se estipulaba que todos los hombres de entre 20 y 45 años de edad podrían ser reclutados en el ejército, pero también podían pagar $300 dólares para evitar el servicio militar (página 522)

Ley de Derechos Civiles de 1866 *s.* proyecto de ley que les otorgaba plena igualdad y ciudadanía a los estadounidenses de "cualquier color y raza" (página 554)

Ley de Desalojo de los Indígenas *s.* ley que terminó con una ley anterior de los EE. UU. que respetaba los derechos de los indígenas norteamericanos a permanecer en sus tierras (página 368)

Ley de Embargo de 1807 *s.* legislación federal que prohibió la entrada de todas las importaciones extranjeras a los puertos estadounidenses (página 319)

Ley de Exclusión China *s.* ley que, en 1882, prohibía la inmigración de trabajadores chinos a los Estados Unidos durante un periodo de diez años (página 640)

Ley de Inspección de Productos Cárnicos *s.* ley de 1906 que pretendía asegurar la pureza y sanidad de la carne (página 671)

Ley de Judicatura de 1801 *s.* legislación federal que redujo de 6 a 5 la cantidad de jueces de la Corte Suprema (página 310)

Ley de la Moneda *s.* ley británica que regulaba el papel moneda en las colonias de Norteamérica (página 181)

Ley de la Reserva Federal *s.* ley de 1913 mediante la cual se creó la Junta de la Reserva Federal, que supervisaría las operaciones de otros doce bancos de reserva; todos ellos controlarían el flujo de dinero en los Estados Unidos (página 674)

Ley del Azúcar *s.* ley británica que rebajaba el arancel de aduana a la melaza importada para disminuir su contrabando, y así los británicos recibían las ganancias (página 181)

Ley del Té *s.* ley británica que otorgaba a la Compañía Británica de las Indias Orientales el monopolio de la venta del té en las colonias (página 191)

Ley del Timbre *s.* ley británica que exigía a los colonos la compra de un timbre para documentos oficiales y materiales impresos (página 182)

Ley Seca *s.* decimoctava enmienda hecha a la Constitución de Estados Unidos para prohibir la producción, venta, importación y transportación de bebidas alcohólicas dentro del territorio nacional (página 681)

Ley Sherman Antimonopolio de 1890 *s.* estatuto federal aprobado para prohibir la formación de monopolios (página 670)

Ley sobre Moneda de Curso Legal *s.* ley que reemplazó los billetes emitidos por los bancos privados con una moneda unificada a nivel nacional (página 524)

Leyes de Extranjería y Sedición *s.* serie de cuatro leyes aprobadas para prevenir que ciertos grupos inmigraran a los Estados Unidos; las leyes dieron al gobierno el poder para expulsar extranjeros que vivían en el país y perseguir a ciudadados estadounidenses críticos del gobierno (página 293)

Leyes de Jim Crow *s.* leyes promovidas en la década de 1880 por políticos sureños con la intención de privar de sus derechos a los ciudadanos afroamericanos (página 640)

Leyes de Navegación *s.* leyes aprobadas por el Parlamento inglés para proteger las compañías navieras inglesas al restringir el transporte de bienes desde y hacia las colonias inglesas (página 125)

Leyes de Townshend *s.* grupo de leyes británicas que imponían aranceles de aduana a las importaciones de té, vidrio, papel, plomo y pintura; los colonos tenían que comprar estos productos a Gran Bretaña (página 186)

Leyes del Tren del Pacífico *s.* dos leyes promulgadas en la década de 1860 por medio de las cuales se le otorgaron a dos compañías los contratos para la construcción de una vía ferroviaria transcontinental (página 620)

Leyes Intolerables *s.* leyes británicas aprobadas para castigar a la gente de Boston después del Motín del Té; llamadas también Leyes Coercitivas (página 194)

Leyes para la Reconstrucción de 1867 *s.* leyes que le otorgaban al Congreso Republicano el poder necesario para llevar a cabo la Reconstrucción, por encima del Presidente (página 554)

libertad de religión *s.* derecho a practicar la religión que uno desee sin intervención del gobierno (página 126)

libre comercio *s.* una forma de comercio internacional que tiene pocas o ninguna restricción (página 1004)

Liga de las Naciones *s.* organización internacional pacificadora, propuesta por el presidente Woodrow Wilson después de la Primera Guerra Mundial (página 723)

Liga Iroquesa *s.* confederación compuesta por cinco naciones de habla iroquesa: los mohawk, los oneida, los onondaga, los cayuga y los seneca; más tarde se sumaron los tuscarora (página 29)

linchar *v.* ejecución ilegal por parte de una turba (página 560)

línea de ensamblaje *s.* sistema en el cual cada trabajador se coloca en determinado lugar, y el proceso de producción pasa de una función a otra, en línea recta, hasta que un producto se ensambla por completo (página 676)

los Aliados *s.* grupo de países, incluyendo a Francia y Gran Bretaña, que colaboraron para oponerse a los países del llamado Eje (Alemania, Italia y Japón) durante la Segunda Guerra Mundial (página 789)

M

macartismo *s.* la práctica de acusar a personas de ser traidores a su país sin ofrecer pruebas (página 853)

madres republicanas (Republican Motherhood) *s.* término histórico que describía la idea de que las mujeres debían educar a sus hijos como buenos ciudadanos participantes del gobierno (página 348)

magnate ladrón *s.* líder industrial conocido por sus tácticas despiadadas en contra de los trabajadores y sus competidores (página 649)

magnicidio *v.* el asesinato de una persona muy importante por su cargo o poder (página 538)

maquinaria política *s.* organización partidista que gobernaba grandes ciudades, y era dirigida por líderes fuertes, y a menudo corruptos, que ofrecían favores a los miembros de dicha organización a cambio de votos y otros apoyos (página 634)

marejada *s.* un aumento anormal del nivel del mar generado por una tormenta, por encima de las mareas pronosticadas, y empujada hacia la costa por los vientos de la tormenta (página 991)

margen *s.* la cantidad de diferencia por la que se gana o se pierde algo (página 403)

Masacre de Boston *s.* incidente en 1779, en el cual soldados británicos dispararon contra personas locales que los estaban insultando (página 188)

materia prima *s.* materia o sustancia básica necesaria para la fabricación de un producto (página 114)

matrilineal *adj.* relacionado con los descendientes que provienen de la madre (página 29)

Mayoría Moral *s.* un grupo político conservador formado por el reverendo Jerry Falwell, un tele-evangelista, en 1979 (página 970)

mayoría silenciosa *s.* un término usado por Richard Nixon a finales de los 60 para describir a un amplio grupo de votantes moderados que no expresaban públicamente sus opiniones (página 935)

Medicaid *s.* programa gubernamental norteamericano iniciado en 1965 para proporcionar un seguro médico a las personas de bajos ingresos (página 917)

Medicare *s.* programa gubernamental norteamericano iniciado en 1965, que proporciona un seguro médico a las personas mayores (página 917)

medios de comunicación masiva *s.* fuentes de información o entretenimiento que llegan a una gran cantidad de personas al mismo tiempo (página 738)

megafauna *s.* animales gigantescos, o muy grandes, que habitan un área particular o que vivieron en un período histórico determinado (página 6)

mercado común *s.* grupo de países o estados que permite que sus miembros comercien libremente entre ellos (página 261)

mercado negro *s.* un sistema a través del cual mercancías prohibidas se venden y compran ilegalmente (página 735)

mercadotecnia *s.* proceso de promover productos o servicios (página 738)

mercancía *s.* bien comerciable (página 142)

mercantilismo *s.* política económica que le da a un país la propiedad exclusiva del comercio en sus colonias (página 52)

mercenario *s.* soldado al que se le paga para luchar por un país que no es el suyo (página 222)

mestizo *s.* persona que tiene ascendencia mixta española e indígena americana (página 66)

migrar *v.* mudarse de un lugar a otro (página 27)

milicia *s.* fuerza militar compuesta por ciudadanos civiles locales con el fin de proteger su pueblo, tierra o nación (página 178)

miliciano *s.* miembro de la milicia colonial que estaba dispuesto a luchar en cualquier momento (página 196)

militarismo *s.* creencia en que un gobierno debe crear un ejército fuerte y estar preparado para usarlo para alcanzar los objetivos nacionales (página 710)

minería aluvial *s.* sistema minero en donde gambusinos o buscadores de oro intentan encontrar pepitas de oro en el lecho de los ríos, comúnmente mediante cribas (página 583)

minería hidráulica *s.* sistema minero en donde se usa agua a presión para remover la parte superior del suelo y la grava, los cuales se procesan después para extraer metales preciosos (página 583)

misil balístico *s.* un arma nuclear que es propulsada por un cohete y guiada con un sistema de GPS (página 908)

misión *s.* asentamiento de una iglesia cristiana establecida para convertir a las personas indígenas (página 66)

misionero *s.* persona que se esfuerza por divulgar el cristianismo a los demás (página 53)

GLOSARIO

módulo de mando *s.* la parte principal de un vehículo espacial que lleva a la tripulación, los suministros principales y el equipo de regreso a la Tierra (página 957)

módulo lunar *s.* la parte de un vehículo espacial que debe transportar a los astronautas del módulo de mando a la superficie lunar, y de regreso al módulo de mando (página 957)

molino harinero *s.* pieza donde estaba la maquinaria que molía los granos (página 140)

monopolio *s.* el control total y exclusivo de una industria por parte de una sola compañía (página 343)

moral *s.* el nivel de confianza o entusiasmo que siente un grupo de personas (página 717)

morfina *s.* potente analgésico (página 534)

mortalidad *s.* tasa de muertes (página 495)

Motín del Té *s.* incidente en 1773, en el cual los Hijos de la Libertad subieron a bordo de barcos británicos y botaron al mar los cargamentos de té en protesta por los impuestos británicos a los colonos (página 191)

movilizar *v.* organizar y preparar tropas para la guerra (página 490)

movimiento conservacionista *s.* movimiento que promueve la protección de los recursos naturales y de la fauna salvaje (página 671)

movimiento de escuelas comunes (common schools) *s.* movimiento de reforma a la educación en la década de 1830 para promover escuelas públicas gratuitas financiadas por la recolección de impuestos a la propiedad y manejadas por los gobiernos locales (página 441)

movimiento por la moderación *s.* movimiento de reforma del siglo XIX que buscaba reducir o eliminar el consumo de bebidas alcohólicas (página 438)

municiones *s.* proyectiles militares (página 801)

Muro de Berlín *s.* un muro de concreto y alambre de espino que rodeaba la democrática Berlín oeste, y que fue construido por los comunistas de Berlín Este, para prevenir que sus ciudadanos se fugaran a la parte democrática de la ciudad (página 907)

música gospel *s.* música que combina los temas bíblicos y un estilo musical semejante a las canciones de jazz (página 748)

N

nacionalismo *s.* concepto de lealtad y devoción al país de uno (página 342)

napalm *s.* una sustancia gelatinosa, altamente inflamable, usada en las bombas para provocar y propagar incendios (página 929)

nativist (antiinmigrante) *s.* término histórico para aquella persona que creía que los nacidos en un lugar debían tener más privilegios que los inmigrantes (página 436)

naturalización *s.* el proceso de convertirse en ciudadano estadounidense para quienes no son ciudadanos nativos (página R32)

navegación *s.* ciencia que consiste en determinar la ubicación de un barco y en planificar rutas, a menudo usado para referirse a los viajes por mar (página 40)

navegador *s.* un programa de ordenador que se usa para ver sitios web (página 1000)

neoconservador *s.* una persona que apoya firmemente una economía de libre mercado y cree que Estados Unidos debería promover activamente sus ideales en todo el mundo (página 986)

neutralidad *s.* negativa a tomar parte en un conflicto entre otros (página 111)

noticiero cinematográfico *s.* corto noticioso o deportivo que se proyecta antes de una película (página 741)

O

oasis *s.* lugar fértil con agua en un desierto (página 42)

objetor de conciencia *s.* una persona que se niega a pelear en una guerra, a menudo por razones religiosas (página 719)

observador electoral *s.* persona asignada a una casilla electoral con el fin de detectar cualquier irregularidad en el proceso electoral (página 643)

obsolescencia programada *s.* la idea de que las personas deben planear reemplazar un objeto antes de que éste se rompa o se gaste (página 739)

oferta y demanda *s.* un principio económico que establece que el precio de algo depende de cuánto haya disponible (la oferta) y cuán deseado sea (la demanda) (página 764)

Oficina de Libertos *s.* Oficina para Refugiados, Hombres Libres y Tierras Abandonadas, creada por el Congreso en 1865 para brindar ayuda a los afroamericanos que habían sido esclavos, así como a los sureños blancos más pobres (página 553)

orden de asistencia *s.* documento legal que daba a las autoridades el derecho de entrar y registrar una casa o negocio (página 186)

orden ejecutiva *s.* directiva o mandato de un presidente que tiene la fuerza legal (página 806)

orden judicial *s.* documento legal (página 310)

ordenanza *s.* mandato, decreto o ley oficial (página 252)

Ordenanza de 1785 *s.* Ordenanza de 1785 *s.* ley federal que creó un sistema que permitía a los colonos comprar tierras en el oeste (página 252)

Ordenanza del Noroeste de 1787 *s.* legislación adoptada por el Congreso para establecer un control más estricto sobre el gobierno del Territorio del Noroeste (página 252)

Órdenes Fundamentales de Connecticut *s.* acta de fundación de la colonia de Connecticut que establecía 11 leyes y fue el marco de gobierno de la colonia (página 101)

P

pacifista *s.* una persona que se opone a la guerra (página 933)

pacifista *s.* persona que se resiste a la guerra y a la violencia (página 239)

Pacto del *Mayflower* *s.* documento que firmaron los peregrinos a bordo del Mayflower antes de llegar a Norteamérica, que los vinculaba a obedecer sus propias leyes y establecer una sociedad civil (página 100)

Pánico de 1837 *s.* episodio de temor por una caída de la economía, que causó el comienzo de una recesión económica en los EE. UU. hasta 1840 (página 375)

Pánico de 1873 *s.* crisis económica desencadenada por la quiebra de algunos bancos y empresas ferroviarias (página 565)

panzer *s.* tanque alemán fuertemente armado con un impresionante poder de fuego, usado durante la Segunda Guerra Mundial (página 812)

paralelo *s.* línea de latitud (página 413)

Parlamento *s.* cámara legislativa de Inglaterra, y después de Gran Bretaña (página 150)

partera *s.* persona entrenada para atender partos (página 146)

partes intercambiables *s.* partes de un mecanismo que pueden ser sustituidas unas por otras (página 342)

Partido de los Know-Nothing *s.* partido político que se formó alrededor de 1850 para oponerse a la inmigración, y cuyos miembros secretos contestaban "no sé nada" (know nothing) a cualquier pregunta; también se llamó American Party (página 436)

Partido de los Whigs *s.* partido político que se opuso a las políticas de Andrew Jackson, de quien consideraban que tenía demasiado poder (página 376)

Partido Nazi *s.* partido político comandado por Adolf Hitler, que usó la fuerza para ejercer un control absoluto sobre Alemania de 1933 a 1945 (página 789)

Partido Republicano *s.* partido político fundado en 1845 por líderes antiesclavistas (página 468)

pasaje medio *s.* el largo viaje a través del océano Atlántico durante el cual los africanos esclavizados eran llevados a las Américas; segunda etapa de la ruta del comercio triangular (página 73)

Pasajeros de la Libertad *s.* grupos interraciales que participaron en las caravanas de autobuses por todo el Sur para protestar contra la segregación (página 882)

paso del noroeste *s.* canal entre los océanos Atlántico y Pacífico a lo largo de la costa norte de América del Norte (página 60)

patente *s.* documento que le concede a su poseedor el derecho exclusivo de fabricar y vender un invento (página 624)

patriota *s.* colono que apoyaba el derecho de las colonias en Norteamérica a gobernarse a sí mismas (página 198)

patrón oro *s.* política monetaria que le exige al gobierno emitir exclusivamente una cantidad de dinero equivalente al valor total de sus reservas en oro (página 591)

perdón *s.* una liberación del castigo legal (página 962)

peregrinación *s.* viaje religioso (página 45)

perestroika *s.* una política gubernamental de reforma política y económica en la antigua Unión Soviética (página 974)

pericia *s.* conocimiento de una ciencia o habilidad (página 241)

periodismo amarillista *s.* forma de reportar las noticias que exagera y dramatiza los eventos, ofreciéndoles a los lectores una perspectiva distorsionada de la realidad, con el ánimo de vender más ejemplares (página 687)

perseguir *v.* castigar, en particular debido a creencias o antecedentes (página 61)

perspectiva geográfica *s.* examen de la influencia que tiene la geografía sobre las personas y su cultura (página 34)

pesos y contrapesos *n.* sistema establecido en la Constitución de EE. UU. que da a cada una de las ramas del gobierno el poder para controlar a las otras dos (página 258)

Piedmont *s.* región relativamente plana entre los montes Apalaches y la llanura costera (página 134)

piloto kamikaze *s.* pilotos suicida de los bombarderos japoneses que estrellaban su avión cargado con explosivos contra los barcos norteamericanos durante la Segunda Guerra Mundial (página 819)

pinchar las líneas telefónicas *v.* colocar un aparato en un teléfono para escuchar en secreto las conversaciones (página 960)

pionero *s.* colono que va a una tierra nueva y desconocida (página 392)

plaga *s.* hongos o insectos que causan que las plantas se sequen y mueran (página 432)

Plan Anaconda *s.* estrategia militar durante la Guerra Civil, en la cual el Norte planeó un bloqueo alrededor de las costas sureñas para arruinar la economía del Sur y tomar los puertos en el Mississippi; al igual que una enorme serpiente, como la anaconda, estrangula a su presa (página 504)

plan de "empaquetamiento de la Corte" *s.* un controversial plan del presidente Franklin Roosevelt para incrementar el número de jueces de la Suprema Corte de 9 a 15, añadiendo seis jueces que compartieran sus visiones progresistas (página 779)

Plan de Crittenden *s.* propuesta que establecía que el gobierno federal no tuviera poderes para abolir la esclavitud en los estados donde ya existía; reestablecía y extendía el límite del Compromiso de Missouri hasta el océano Pacífico (página 476)

plan de pagos *s.* un plan para comprar algo haciendo una serie de pagos parciales durante un periodo determinado (página 765)

Plan Marshall *s.* un plan para ayudar a los países europeos a reconstruir y recuperarse económicamente después de la Segunda Guerra Mundial (página 822)

plantación *s.* granja grande; en las plantaciones del Sur, los esclavos trabajaban plantando y cosechando cultivos (página 66)

plataforma continental *s.* un área de tierra relativamente poco profunda bajo el océano que se extiende hacia afuera desde un continente antes de una caída abrupta en el océano abierto (página 972)

Pleistoceno *s.* período en la historia de la Tierra durante el cual existieron animales y plantas gigantescos, y grandes extensiones de tierra se cubrieron de hielo (página 5)

poder ejecutivo *s.* rama del gobierno de EE. UU. presidida por el presidente; responsable de que se cumpla la ley (página 258)

poder implícito *s.* poder que no está explícito en la Constitución (página 343)

poder judicial *s.* rama del gobierno de EE. UU., que incluye las cortes o tribunales y el sistema legal, presidida por la Corte Suprema; responsable de interpretar las leyes (página 258)

poder legislativo *s.* rama del gobierno de EE. UU. presidida por el Congreso; responsable de hacer las leyes (página 258)

Política de Puertas Abiertas *s.* política impulsada a finales del siglo XIX y principios del XX para exigir igualdad de privilegios comerciales para todos los países que tuvieran intereses económicos con China (página 691)

política de riesgo calculado *s.* la práctica de llevar un conflicto hasta el borde de la violencia sin caer en una guerra, usualmente una táctica para obtener un resultado favorable (página 853)

política de terminación *s.* una política promulgada por el presidente Eisenhower que sacaba a los indígenas americanos de las reservas, al mismo tiempo que el gobierno terminaba con la soberanía de las naciones y tribus individuales (página 922)

política de tierra arrasada *s.* un método usado por el ejército norteamericano para vaciar y destruir pueblos completos que podrían haber proporcionado ayuda al enemigo (página 929)

poner en la lista negra *v.* poner una o más personas en una lista indicando que deben ser rechazadas o castigadas (página 852)

pontón *s.* flotador cilíndrico portable, que se usaba para construir un puente temporal (página 511)

populismo *s.* posición política que afirma que el control del gobierno debe recaer en la gente común y corriente, y no en los miembros de la élite (página 665)

populista *s.* político que asegura representar los intereses de los ciudadanos comunes y corrientes (página 591)

potlatch *s.* ceremonia de entrega de obsequios practicada por las tribus indígenas norteamericanas kwakiutl y haida (página 26)

pradera *s.* extensa área territorial cubierta de plantas altas (página 586)

prebélico *adj.* anterior a la Guerra Civil de los Estados Unidos (página 340)

precedente *s.* suceso anterior o resolución que sirve de ejemplo para sucesos o resoluciones futuras (página 278)

preferencia de género *s* preferencia por un género sobre otro (página 925)

prejuicio *s.* juicio generalizado acerca de un grupo de personas que no está basado en razones o hechos (página 436)

presidente de la Corte Suprema *s.* jefe máximo del poder judicial del gobierno; preside la Corte Suprema (página 281)

presidio *s.* puesto o asentamiento militar (página 398)

Primer Congreso Continental *s.* reunión en 1774 de los representantes de todas las colonias norteamericanas para dar una respuesta a las Leyes Intolerables (página 195)

prisionero de guerra *s.* soldado capturado por una fuerza enemiga (página 793)

Procedimiento Bessemer *s.* proceso de fabricación de acero que implica soplar aire en hierro fundido para eliminar impurezas, gracias a lo cual es posible producir un metal más fuerte (página 624)

Proclamación de 1763 *s.* ley que establecía que los colonos debían mantenerse al este de una línea dibujada en un mapa, a lo largo de la cima de los montes Apalaches (página 178)

Proclamación de Emancipación *s.* documento de 1863, emitido por Abraham Lincoln, que abolió la esclavitud en los estados gobernados por la Confederación durante la Guerra Civil de los Estados Unidos (página 513)

profeta *s.* alguien de quien se cree que trae mensajes de Dios o de cualquier otra fuente divina (página 321)

progresismo *s.* movimiento social que cree en la igualdad para todas las personas, e invita a los ciudadanos y al gobierno a trabajar todos juntos para lograr un cambio social (página 665)

propaganda *s.* información difundida para influenciar las opiniones de las personas o promover la ideas de un partido o una organización (página 718)

propietario *s.* dueño de una colonia, que tenía el derecho a manejar y distribuir tierras y a establecer un gobierno (página 112)

protestante *s.* seguidor de la Reforma en el cristianismo (página 39)

provisiones *s.* conjunto de alimentos, agua y otras cosas reservadas para un viaje (página 124)

Proyecto Manhattan *s.* el nombre en clave del programa atómico financiado por el gobierno norteamericano durante los años 40 (página 821)

psiquiátrico *s.* hospital o clínica donde se trata a los enfermos mentales (página 441)

publicidad *s.* el acto de presentar productos e ideas al público (página 738)

pueblo fantasma *s.* pueblo abandonado que ha quedado en ruinas (página 583)

puente de Beringia *s.* territorio entre Alaska y Siberia que se encontraba por encima del nivel del mar hace unos 13,000 años, lo que permitió el paso a grupos humanos que migraban hacia Norteamérica (página 6)

puesto comercial *s.* pequeño asentamiento establecido con el propósito de intercambiar bienes (página 155)

Q

quinina *s.* sustancia hecha de la corteza de un árbol que es un remedio eficaz contra la malaria (página 71)

R

ración *s.* porción de comida suministrada (página 527)

racionamiento *s.* distribución controlada de la comida u otros suministros (página 799)

racismo *s.* creencia de que una raza es mejor que otras (página 464)

radical *n.* persona partidaria de cambios sociales o políticos extremos (página 289)

rancho *s.* terreno cedido por México a los colonos, en forma de grandes fincas, en lo que hoy es California (página 415)

rascacielos *s.* edificio muy alto (página 636)

ratificar *v.* aprobar formalmente mediante el voto (página 250)

Rebelión de Shays *s.* revuelta de los granjeros de Massachusetts en protesta por los altos impuestos, ocurrida entre 1786 y 1787 (página 255)

rebelión del Stono *s.* revuelta de esclavos africanos en contra de sus dueños ocurrida en 1793 (página 137)

Rebelión del Whiskey *s.* serie de protestas violentas de los granjeros del oeste de Pennsylvania contra un impuesto al whiskey (página 289)

recesión *s.* grave desaceleración económica (página 590)

reclamación *s.* objeción o motivo para quejarse (página 181)

reclutamiento forzoso *s.* acto que obliga a los hombres a prestar el servicio militar o naval (página 522)

reclutamiento forzoso *s.* acto que obliga a los hombres a prestar el servicio militar o naval (página 319)

Reconstrucción *s.* etapa posterior a la Guerra de Secesión caracterizada por el anhelo de reunificar a los Estados Unidos de América (página 538)

Reconstrucción Presidencial *s.* política impulsada para obligar a los estados confederados a ratificar la Decimotercera Enmienda y a formar nuevos gobiernos, regidos por nuevas constituciones, como condición para poder reintegrarse a la Unión (página 552)

Reconstrucción Radical *s.* nombre dado al plan del Partido Republicano que buscaba aprobar las Leyes de Reconstrucción de 1867 (página 554)

recurso natural *s.* material o sustancia que se encuentra en la naturaleza que se usa para mantener una sociedad o para ser explotado con fines económicos, como minerales, agua o seres vivos (página 114)

redes sociales *s.* medios electrónicos que permiten a las personas comunicarse y formar comunidades online (página 1001)

redistribución de ingresos *s.* un método para distribuir los ingresos de los impuestos federales a los estados y gobiernos locales (página 954)

referendo *s.* práctica democrática que consiste en someter una ley directamente a los votantes para que la aprueben o rechacen (página 669)

refuerzos *s.* más soldados y suministros que se envían para ayudar a las tropas en batalla (página 224)

refugiado *s.* persona que huye a otro país para escapar de un peligro o una persecución (página 630)

regionalismo *s.* lealtad a cualquier sección o región del país de donde una persona es, en vez de a la nación como tal (página 344)

renacimiento *s.* acción de renacer o despertar un interés renovado por las artes o temas académicos (página 748)

rendezvous *s.* mercado temporal donde los tramperos y cazadores se encontraban para comerciar y socializar (página 390)

reparaciones de guerra *s.* el dinero que se paga para compensar los daños de guerra (página 723)

repatriación *s.* regreso o retorno al país de origen o ciudadanía (página 781)

república *s.* forma de gobierno en la cual la gente elige a sus representantes para hablar por ellos y aprobar leyes según sus necesidades (página 222)

república democrática *s.* un país independiente gobernado por sus ciudadanos a través de elecciones y otras formas de votación (página R32)

republicanismo *s.* gobierno en el que la gente elige a sus representantes para crear las leyes (página 244)

Republicanos liberales *s.* grupo durante la década de 1870 que pretendía contrarrestar el creciente tamaño y poderío del gobierno (página 564)

reserva *s.* área territorial dentro de los Estados Unidos destinada específicamente para que los indígenas norteamericanos vivan allí (página 592)

resistencia no violenta *s.* el uso de la desobediencia civil, la no cooperación y otras formas de protesta pacífica para conseguir el cambio social (página 880)

resistencia pasiva *s.* negativa no violenta a obedecer a la autoridad y las leyes (página 341)

responsabilidad cívica *s.* responsabilidad que es obligatoria o esencial para las personas, como votar, pagar impuestos y servir en jurados (página R34)

responsabilidad personal *s.* responsabilidad que no es obligatoria pero que contribuye a una sociedad más civilizada, como respetar y defender los derechos de los demás, ayudar a la comunidad y mantenerse informado (página R34)

reunificar *v.* juntar de nuevo algo que había sido separado (página 850)

reunión de reavivamiento *s.* reunión religiosa informal que buscaba avivar la fe en la religión del grupo, y que generalmente se hacía en carpas o al aire libre (página 438)

revisión judicial *s.* poder de la Corte Suprema para invalidar cualquier ley que considere inconstitucional, incluso si fue aprobada por el Congreso o firmada por el presidente (página 310)

revolución del mercado *s.* transición de una economía preindustrial a una economía capitalista, o sea orientada hacia el mercado (página 328)

Revolución francesa *s.* rebelión de 1789 contra la monarquía francesa que buscó poner fin al privilegio de las clases altas y demandó igualdad para las clases más bajas (página 289)

Revolución industrial *n.* época en que la producción de bienes hechos con máquinas reemplazó de manera generalizada a los productos hechos a mano (página 328)

Revolución neolítica *s.* transición, en la historia de la humanidad, de una forma de vida basada en la caza y recolección a una forma productora agrícola y ganadera (página 9)

risco *s.* peñasco (página 528)

S

sabotaje *s.* acción de dañar, interferir con o destruir algo (página 719)

salvación *s.* acto de ser perdonado por pecados o faltas cometidas (página 148)

satélite *s.* un objeto que se mueve alrededor de otro mayor (página 904)

secesión *s.* acto de separación formal de una nación o de un territorio para ser independiente (página 367)

sedición *s.* alzamiento contra la autoridad (página 293)

segadora *s.* máquina que corta las plantas de trigo y avena (página 331)

segregación *s.* separación de las personas de acuerdo a su raza (página 465)

Segundo Congreso Continental *s.* grupo de líderes de las colonias norteamericanas que se reunieron para tratar el tema de la tiranía británica, declarar la independencia en 1776 y conducir la Guerra de Independencia hasta formar los Estados Unidos (página 203)

Segundo Gran Despertar *s.* movimiento protestante estadounidense basado en las reuniones de reavivamiento y en una relación directa y emocional con Dios (página 438)

seguro nacional de salud *s.* un plan de seguro médico dirigido por el gobierno y abierto a cualquiera que desee sumarse (página 845)

sentada *s.* una protesta organizada donde la gente se sienta en el suelo y se niega a abandonar el sitio (página 882)

separación de poderes *s.* división de poderes gubernamentales entre las tres ramas del gobierno de los EE. UU.: el poder ejecutivo, el poder judicial y el poder legislativo (página 258)

separatismo negro *s.* la división política y cultural de los negros y blancos dentro de una sociedad (página 914)

separatista *s.* persona que quería dejar la Iglesia de Inglaterra (página 100)

sequía *s.* periodo prolongado con poca o ninguna lluvia (página 774)

servicio doméstico *s.* trabajo o tareas del hogar que hace una o varias personas en la casa de otro (página 433)

servidumbre *s.* estado o condición de siervo o esclavo (página 538)

servidumbre negra *s.* esclavitud de tipo económico que condenaba a los trabajadores afroamericanos a permanecer como aparceros de los terratenientes (página 559)

siervo *s.* persona que vivía y trabajaba en la tierra perteneciente a un noble o a un señor feudal (página 37)

sindicato de oficio *s.* sindicato que defiende los derechos y protecciones de los trabajadores, cuyos miembros se especializan en el mismo oficio de quienes defienden (página 443)

sindicato de trabajadores *s.* asociación voluntaria de trabajadores que usa su poder para negociar condiciones mejores de trabajo (página 442)

Síndrome de Inmunodeficiencia Adquirida (SIDA) *s.* la etapa final de una enfermedad causada por un virus que ataca el sistema del cuerpo humano que combate las enfermedades (página 971)

sirviente ligado por contrato *s.* persona obligada por contrato a trabajar, generalmente sin paga, a cambio de un boleto gratis a las colonias (página 93)

Sistema americano (American System) *s.* política para promover el sistema industrial de los EE. UU. mediante aranceles, subsidios federales para construir carreteras y otras obras públicas y un banco nacional para controlar la moneda (página 342)

sistema de fábrica *n.* método de producción en el que grandes grupos de operarios trabajaban en un solo lugar (página 328)

sistema de señorío *s.* sistema económico en el cual los campesinos están vinculados a un señor feudal y trabajan su tierra, o señorío, a cambio de comida y vivienda (página 37)

sitio *s.* táctica militar durante la cual las tropas de soldados rodean una ciudad para intentar apoderarse de ella (página 401)

smog *s.* un tipo de contaminación atmosférica que se desarrolla cuando la luz solar reacciona con los productos químicos de fuentes tales como los escapes de los automóviles y las emisiones de las fábricas (página 958)

soberanía popular *s.* idea de que los residentes de una región o país deciden sobre un tema mediante el voto (página 466)

soberano *adj.* que posee la autoridad para gobernarse o que es un gobierno independiente (página 250)

soborno *s.* dádiva en dinero o en privilegios que se da subrepticiamente a funcionarios a cambio de favores políticos (página 564)

socialismo *s.* sistema económico en que el gobierno controla los recursos económicos, que son de propiedad colectiva (página 776)

sociedad de ayuda mutua *s.* organización formada por miembros de un determinado grupo para apoyarse mutuamente con recursos económicos u otro tipo de asistencia (página 631)

sociedad fiduciaria *s.* grupo de corporaciones administrado por un consejo, sin que éste sea el propietario directo (página 627)

sociedad por acciones *s.* compañía cuyos accionistas poseen acciones en la propia compañía (página 92)

status quo *s.* el estado existente de una situación (página 902)

subsidio *s.* fondo del gobierno para mejoras y apoyo al comercio (página 342)

suburbanización *s.* asentamiento de la población de las ciudades en comunidades de la periferia (página 856)

suburbio *s.* área residencial que se localiza en los límites de una ciudad o de un pueblo (página 634)

sufragio *s.* derecho al voto (página 451)

sufragista *s.* persona que apoya la lucha por el derecho a votar y ser votado, especialmente en beneficio del derecho de las mujeres a participar en los procesos electorales (página 682)

sumergible *s.* un submarino alemán (página 713)

Sunbelt *s.* regiones del sur o suroeste de Estados unidos que tienen invierno cálidos (página 854)

sweatshop *s.* tipo de fábrica en donde se pagan salarios muy bajos, en condiciones de hacinamiento e inseguridad, y donde las jornadas laborales son extenuantes (página 647)

T

tanque *s.* un vehículo blindado y fuertemente armado, que usa bandas de rodaje en vez de ruedas (página 713)

tasa de aduana *s.* impuesto sobre bienes importados y exportados (página 319)

tele-evangelista *s.* líder religioso que comparte enseñanzas cristianas en una emisión televisiva con horario regular (página 970)

telégrafo *s.* máquina que envía mensajes a grandes distancias mediante señales eléctricas en código a través de cables eléctricos (página 331)

telegrama Zimmermann *s.* telegrama secreto que los alemanes enviaron al embajador alemán en México, proponiéndole que México se sumara a la Primera Guerra Mundial del lado alemán (página 715)

teoría del dominó *s.* una idea de la Guerra Fría que sostenía que los países cercanos a un vecino comunista son más propensos a adoptar ese régimen (página 926)

tercera clase *s.* término histórico para la sección inferior de un barco en la que viajaban los que pagaban el boleto más barato (página 430)

terraplén *s.* movimiento de tierra hecho por el hombre, que se levanta como defensa (página 204)

terreno *s.* características físicas de la tierra (página 204)

Territorio Indígena *s.* área de tierra, en lo que hoy es Oklahoma y parte de Kansas y Nebraska, a la cual fueron obligados a migrar los indígenas norteamericanos (página 368)

territorio no organizado *s.* tierras bajo el gobierno federal pero que no le pertenecían a ningún estado (página 345)

textil *s.* tela o tejido hecho de algodón u otras materias primas (página 328)

tierras fronterizas (backcountry) *s.* la zona oeste de las Colonias del Sur justo al este de los montes Apalaches (página 134)

tipi *s.* tienda de campaña que tiene forma de cono y que está hecha con pieles de búfalo (página 27)

tiranía *s.* abuso de poder injusto por parte de un gobernante absoluto (página 181)

tolerancia *s.* aceptación de otros (página 144)

toma de posesión *s.* ceremonia que marca el comienzo de una presidencia (página 279)

trabajador migratorio *s.* trabajador que se desplaza de un empleo a otro según sea necesario; por lo general, se trata de trabajadores agrícolas (página 586)

trabajo infantil *s.* contratación de niños para realizar algún tipo de trabajo, a menudo en condiciones peligrosas y con salarios muy bajos (página 647)

trabajo social *s.* trabajo cuyo propósito es mejorar las condiciones de vida de otras personas (página 680)

traición *s.* delito cometido por ayudar al enemigo o planear un derrocamiento; la falta de lealtad a su propia nación (página 367)

traidor *s.* persona que traiciona a su propia gente, nación o causa (página 99)

transahariano *adj.* que cruza el Sahara (página 42)

tranvía *s.* vehículo sobre rieles que recorre las avenidas de una ciudad y puede transportar a muchos pasajeros en un solo viaje, como un tren (página 634)

trascendentalismo *s.* movimiento intelectual y social en las décadas de 1830 y 1840 que pedía ir más allá de lo que la sociedad esperaba de cada uno (página 444)

Trastorno de Estrés Postraumático *s.* un síndrome provocado por una herida o trauma psicológico (página 952)

tratado *s.* acuerdo de paz (página 158)

Tratado de Greenville *s.* tratado entre los Estados Unidos y varias naciones indígenas en el cual las naciones indígenas cedieron sus tierras a los Estados Unidos, en lo que hoy es Ohio e Indiana (página 288)

Tratado de París de 1783 *s.* Tratado de París de 1783 acuerdo entre Gran Bretaña y los Estados Unidos, en el cual Gran Bretaña reconoce la independencia de sus colonias en Norteamérica y se determinan los límites iniciales de los Estados Unidos (página 244)

Tratado de Versailles *s.* el tratado que acabó oficialmente con la Primera Guerra Mundial (página 723)

tregua *s.* acuerdo para dejar de luchar (página 371)

Tren Clandestino *s.* red de personas que trabajaron juntas para ayudar a los afroamericanos a escapar de la esclavitud en los estados sureños de los EE. UU. hacia los estados del Norte y Canadá antes de la Guerra Civil (página 447)

tundra *s.* terreno plano y sin árboles de las regiones ártica y subártica (página 26)

U

unionista *s.* miembro del Partido de la Unión Constitucional (página 472)

urbanización *s.* proceso mediante el cual los patrones de tipo económico, industrial y social pasaron de las zonas rurales a las ciudades (página 634)

V

vacío legal *s.* lenguaje poco claro que les permite a ciertas personas burlar las leyes y no obedecerlas (página 674)

vasallo *s.* en el sistema feudal medieval europeo, era una persona, usualmente un noble de menor rango, que recibía tierras y protección de un señor feudal a cambio de prestarle obediencia y servicio (página 36)

veta *s.* rico depósito de minerales, como plata u oro (página 582)

vetar *v.* rechazar oficialmente una decisión o propuesta dictada por el poder legislativo (página 375)

veterano *s.* persona que sirvió al ejército (página 534)

vietnamización *s.* estrategia militar que permitió el reemplazo gradual de las tropas estadounidenses con tropas sudvietnamitas durante la Guerra de Vietnam (página 952)

virreinato *s.* territorio gobernado por un virrey (página 58)

virrey *s.* gobernador de las colonias españolas en las Américas que representaba al Rey y la Reina de España (página 58)

viruela *s.* virus mortal que causa fiebre alta y pequeñas ampollas en la piel (página 56)

virus de la inmunodeficiencia humana (VIH) *s.* un virus que ataca el sistema del cuerpo humano que combate las enfermedades (página 971)

vivienda de bajo costo *s.* viviendas que pueden ser pagadas por personas con bajos ingresos (página 845)

W

World Wide Web *s.* el sistema que permite que los sitios de Internet sean identificados por direcciones, vinculados entre sí y localizados mediante búsquedasel sistema (página 1000)

Z

zona de influencia *s.* declaración hecha por un país para tener influencia exclusiva en las actividades políticas o económicas de otro país (página 690)

zona de ocupación *s.* área de un país en la que un ejército extranjero tiene el control (página 846)

a punto de *a.* listo para que algo suceda (página 982)

abarcar *v.* formar un círculo en torno a algo; redondear; incluir (página 559)

abominable *a.* digno de odio o malestar (página 366)

aclamación *s.* elogio entusiasta (página 285)

activista *a.* combativo y determinado; que actúa como si combatiera en una guerra (página 467)

adquisición *s.* acción de obtener algo en calidad de propiedad; artículo obtenido por alguien (página 37)

agitación *s.* confusión, turbulencia (página 727)

alegoría *s.* historia contada a través de símbolos, en la cual los personajes y otros elementos narrativos representan acciones y emociones humanas (página 444)

aniquilar *v.* destruir totalmente (página 795)

ardiente *a.* quien se muestra muy ansioso o apasionado en el objetivo de realizar su deseo (página 282)

arduo *a.* difícil; que requiere de un gran esfuerzo para poder lograrse (página 395)

árido *a.* extremadamente seco (como un desierto) (página 24)

asignar *v.* dividir y repartir con un fin específico (página 954)

atrocidad *s.* acto extremadamente brutal o cruel (página 593)

consenso *s.* acuerdo general, armonía (página 889)

dar lugar *v.* traer algo nuevo (página 717)

delimitación *s.* acción mediante la cual se miden y establecen los límites entre dos o más áreas territoriales (página 252)

despectivo *a.* degradar o despreciar algo o a alguien; siempre con la intención de rebajar a alguien o a algo (página 641)

directamente *adv.* francamente, honestamente (página 873)

dispersar *v.* esparcir y desplegar a todo lo largo y ancho (página 586)

divisivo *a.* que causa disenso y desunión con ánimo de discordia (página 462)

élite *s.* persona o grupo que se considera superior en términos de riqueza, intelecto, educación o, incluso, en capacidades atléticas (página 668)

elocuencia *s.* capacidad de hablar de manera elegante y articulada (página 886)

espécimen *s.* muestra de alguna criatura o parte de la naturaleza, tal como una planta, un animal o un mineral (página 300)

evadir *v.* evitar ser capturado o eludir la obligación de dar una respuesta directa y verdadera (página 596)

evasión *s.* el acto de evitar ser descubierto o castigado, usualmente con sigilo (página 735)

explotar *v.* aprovecharse de personas o recursos, por lo general con fines de lucro (página 665)

fértil *a.* capaz de dar vida, como parir crías o hacer crecer plantas (página 24)

fervor *s.* sentimiento o celo muy intenso hacia algo, generalmente espiritual (página 439)

filosofía *s.* conjunto de creencias argumentadas por una persona o por un grupo (página 39)

formidable *a.* asombroso, generalmente de manera temible (página 223)

habilidad *s.* talento natural o destreza que tiene una persona (página 768)

iconografía *s.* objetos o símbolos representativos de una cultura o religión (página 131)

imparcialidad *s.* neutralidad, equidad (página 714)

indigente *a.* carente de riqueza o recursos; empobrecido (página 768)

indispensable *a.* necesario; algo de lo que no se puede prescindir (página 103)

indulgente *a.* tolerante; comprensible (página 552)

inherentemente *adv.* esencialmente, naturalmente (página 875)

inhibidor *a.* capaz de aminorar la fuerza o el poder de alguien o de algo; que cuenta con una acción efectiva en términos negativos (página 647)

inmoral *a.* moralmente equivocado (página 996)

intervenir *v.* interferir, generalmente para provocar o prevenir una acción (página 397)

intimidar *v.* servirse de amenazas, por lo general para obligar a alguien a hacer lo que se le exige (página 371)

legado *s.* conjunto de conocimientos o realizaciones transmitido de una generación a otra (página 250)

letal *a.* mortal (página 647)

mártir *s.* persona que sacrifica su vida o algo de gran valor en beneficio de una causa superior (página 469)

mecanizado *a.* que ha sido realizado íntegra o parcialmente por máquinas (página 328)

metralla *s.* conjunto de pedazos filosos lanzados por un proyectil, una granada o, incluso, por una bala de cañón (página 172)

monetario *a.* que tiene, representa o asume la forma del dinero (página 303)

nulificar *v.* eliminar o negar, especialmente en términos legales anular algo (página 366)

ofensiva *s.* lucha iniciada por uno de los bandos que participan en una guerra o disputa (bélica, política, personal e, incluso, deportiva) (página 231)

ortodoxo *a.* que sigue una doctrina religiosa de manera estricta (página 101)

pacto *s.* acuerdo o promesa que negocian dos o más partes en conflicto (página 179)

parcela *s.* terreno o cierta área delimitada de tierra (página 598)

perdonar *v.* eximir, excusar a otra persona de alguna culpa por voluntad propia (página 552)

perplejo *a.* quien se queda de pronto sin palabras para expresar sus ideas o emociones (página 58)

prestigioso *a.* que cuenta con una reputación de calidad, estima y respeto (página 362)

prominente *s.* ampliamente conocido (página 971)

próspero *a.* que tiene éxito económico (página 842)

prótesis *s.* miembro, extremidad o parte artificial del cuerpo humano (página 494)

pudiente *a.* rico, próspero (página 855)

quinta *s.* finca o casa principal de una hacienda (página 64)

rehabilitar *v.* restaurar la salud o la reputación original (página 441)

rellenar *v.* volver a poner todo el contenido que originalmente tenía algo (página 495)

renunciar *v.* rendirse, a menudo como resultado de una derrota o la imposición de una multa (página 922)

represalia *s.* el acto de vengarse o de actuar en contra de alguien porque te ha perjudicado (página 791)

retórica *s.* manera de usar las palabras para expresar una idea, comúnmente para persuadir (página 562)

sentimiento *s.* una actitud basada en emociones (página 815)

sincronizar *v.* hacer que ocurran al mismo tiempo (página 740)

soberanía *s.* área donde se puede ejercer a plenitud la función o la autoridad de una entidad (página 328)

socavar *v.* debilitar (página 906)

suborbital *a.* menos de un círculo completo de un objeto o cuerpo alrededor de otro; menos que un recorrido circular completo (página 905)

susceptible *a.* capaz de percibir la acción o intención de otra persona (página 527)

tenencia *s.* acción de ostentar algo valioso, como un terreno o una posición relevante, o el período durante el cual dicho cargo u objeto es ostentado (página 555)

valentía *s.* tener gran valor, coraje o voluntad para enfrentar cualquier obstáculo (página 520)

vigoroso *a.* hecho con energía o con fuerza (página 845)

INDEX

H

NATIONAL GEOGRAPHIC LEARNING | CENGAGE

National Geographic Learning gratefully acknowledges the contributions of the following National Geographic Explorers and affiliates to our program:

Jason De León, National Geographic Explorer
Ken Garrett, National Geographic Photographer
Caroline Gerdes, National Geographic Explorer
Fredrik Hiebert, National Geographic Archaeologist-in-Residence
Barrington Irving, Jr., National Geographic Explorer
Kathryn Keane, Vice President, National Geographic Exhibitions
John Kelly, National Geographic Explorer
William Kelso, National Geographic Explorer
William Parkinson, National Geographic Explorer
Robert Reid, National Geographic Digital Nomad
Andrés Ruzo, National Geographic Explorer
Pardis Sabeti, National Geographic Explorer
Joel Sartore, National Geographic Photographer
Donald Slater, National Geographic Explorer

Photographic Credits

Gianni DagliOrti/Corbis. **168–169** (spread) Kenneth Garrett. **170** Richard Freeda/Aurora Photos. **171** Richard Freeda/Aurora Photos. **172–173** (spread) AP Images/Ric Tapia. **174** National Postal Museum, Smithsonian. **174** KevorkDjansezian/Getty Images News/Getty Images. **175** (cl) Ken Cedeno/ Corbis. (bl) HALSTEAD; DIRCK/Corbis. (cr) Tim Sloan/AFP/Getty Images. (br) Apollo 11 Commander Neil Armstrong/NASA Kennedy Space Center (NASA-KSC)/National Aeronautics and Space Administration (NASA). **176–177** (spread) ©National Musuem of American History. **177** ©National Musuem of American History. **178** North Wind Picture Archives/The Image Works. **179** Library of Congress Geography and Map Division Washington, D. C. 20540-4650 USA dcu. **180** Alfredo DagliOrti/Art Resource, NY. **181** (tl) North Wind Picture Archives/The Image Works. (cr) The Colonial Williamsburg Foundation. Gift of the Lasser family. **182** The New York Public Library/Art Resource, NY. **183** (tr) Sons of Liberty Bowl, from Boston, 1768 (silver)/Revere, Paul (1735–1818)/MUSEUM OF FINE ARTS, BOSTON/ Museum of Fine Arts, Boston, Massachusetts, USA. (cr) ACME Imagery/ ACME Imagery. **184** National Portrait Gallery, Smithsonian Institution/Art Resource, NY. **185** John Paul Bonanno. **186** Art Resource. **187** Private Collection/Art Resource, NY. **189** (tl) Art Resource, NY. (b) Death of Crispus Attucks at the Boston Massacre, 5th March, 1770, 1856 (chromolitho)/ Champney, James Wells (1843–1903)/AMERICAN ANTIQUARIAN SOCIETY/American Antiquarian Society, Worcester, Massachusetts, USA/ Bridgeman Images. **190** REUTERS/Eric Gaillard. **192** ©Museum of the American Revolution. **193** ©Museum of the American Revolution. **194** SuperStock/SuperStock. **195** James McWilliams/Alamy Stock Photo. **196** Concord Musuem. **197** John Burke/Getty Images. **199** Marcelo Baez/ National Geographic Learning. **200–201** (spread) Brian Jannsen/Alamy Stock Photo. **202** Richard Timberlake/TimberlakePhotos LLC. **203** Niday Picture Library/Alamy Stock Photo. **206** Division of Military History and Diplomacy, National Museum of American History. **208** SuperStock/ SuperStock. **209** Hisham Ibrahim/Exactostock-1598. **210** SuperStock/ SuperStock. **214–215** (spread) ©Crossroads of the American Revolution NHA. **216–217** (spread) aimintang/Getty Images. **218** National Park Service. **220** Courtesy National Park Service, Museum Management Program and The George C. Neumann Collection, Valley Forge National Historical Park. **221** (bl) Courtesy National Park Service, Museum Management Program and The George C. Neumann Collection, Valley Forge National Historical Park. (br) Courtesy National Park Service, Museum Management Program and Valley Forge National Historical Park. **223** (t) ©Glenn Cantor. (c) Library of Congress, Rare Book and Special Collections Division. **225** (tl) George Romney/Getty Images. (cr) ©Joseph Brant Museum/Museums of Burlington. **226** shyflygirl/Getty Images. **227** ©Early American. **229** Franklin at the court of France, 1778, receiving the homage of his genius and the recognition of his country's advent among the nations, 1853 (hand-coloured mezzotint)/Jolly, Baron (18th-19th century) (after)/BOSTON ATHENAEUM/© Boston Athenaeum, USA/Bridgeman Images. **230–231** (spread) SuperStock/Getty Images. **233** (tr) Abigail Smith Adams, c. 1766 (pastel on paper)/Blyth, Benjamin (c. 1746–c. 1786)/MASSACHUSETTS HISTORICAL SOCIETY/Massachusetts Historical Society, Boston, MA, USA/Bridgeman Images. (bl) Culver Pictures/The Art Archive at Art Resource, NY. **234** ©Beverly Historical Society & Museum. **235** Trim the Sails illustration © SEPS licensed by Curtis Licensing Indianapolis, IN. All rights reserved. **236–237** (spread) ©Swamp Fox Murals Trail Society, Manning, Clarendon County, SC, www. swampfoxtrail.com. **240** Architect of the Capitol. **241** raclro/Getty Images. **242** Paul Grossmann/Tetra Images/ Getty Images. **245** National Archives, Washington, D. C. **248–249** (spread) Rick Wilking/REUTERS. **250** Everett Collection Inc/Alamy Stock Photo. **251** RGB Ventures/SuperStock/Alamy Stock Photo. **253** Prisma/Prisma/ Superstock. **254** Photograph courtesy of the Pocumtuck Valley Memorial Association, Memorial Hall Museum, Deerfield, Massachusetts. **255** IllustratedHistory/Alamy Stock Photo. **256** National Geographic Learning. **256** National Archives. **257** Joseph Sohm/Getty Images. **259** (tl) Library of Congress, Prints & Photographs Division, Reproduction number LC-DIG-det-4a26389. (tr) Everett Collection Historical/Alamy Stock Photo. (c) Classic Image/Alamy Stock Photo. **261** Life of George Washington—The Farmer, pub. 1853 (colourlitho)/Stearns, Junius Brutus (1810–85)/ STAPLETON COLLECTION/Private Collection/Bridgeman Images. **263** The Signing of the Constitution of the United States in 1787, 1940 (oil on canvas)/Christy, Howard Chandler (1873–1952)/Hall of Representatives, Washington D. C. , USA/Bridgeman Images. **264** Mrs James Warren (Mercy Otis) c. 1763 (oil on canvas)/Copley, John Singleton (1738–1815)/MUSEUM OF FINE ARTS, BOSTON/Museum of Fine Arts, Boston, Massachusetts, USA/Bridgeman Images. **267** JAMES P. BLAIR/National Geographic Creative. **269** Mark Summerfield/Alamy Stock Photo. **270** LOUIS S. GLANZMAN/National Geographic Creative. **272–273** (spread) KENNETH GARRETT/National Geographic Creative). **274** (tr) Lyn Alweis/The Denver Post/Getty Images. (b) STEPHANE GAUTIER/AGE Fotostock. **275** (tl) United States, Eagle Motif Painted Wooden Infantry Drum Circa 1810–20/Private Collection/Photo. Don Troiani/Bridgeman Images. (tr) Larasoul/Getty Images. (b) HaraldSund/Getty Images. **276–277** (spread) Pat & Chuck Blackley/Alamy Stock Photo. **278** George Washington, 1796–1803 (oil on canvas)/Stuart, Gilbert (1755–1828)/CLARK ART INSTITUTE/Sterling and Francine Clark Art Institute, Williamstown, Massachusetts, USA/ Bridgeman Images. **279** ©Mark Finkenstaedt/Mount Vernon Museum. **280** Photographs in the Carol M. Highsmith Archive, Library of Congress, Prints and Photographs Division. **282** akova/Getty Images. **283** Getty Images/Getty Images. **284–285** (spread) Theo Wargo/Getty Images. **287** Richard Levine/ Alamy Stock Photo. **289** AKG Images. **290** ©Cameron Davidson. **292–293** (spread) AFP/Getty Images. **296–297** (spread) ©Chris Gibson/500px. **298–299** (spread) Sam Abell/National Geographic Creative. **299** Everett Collection Inc/Alamy Stock photo. **300** ©Missouri History Museum, St. Louis. **301** Sam Abell/National Geographic Creative. **300–303** (spread) Marc Moritsch/Getty Images. **303** (tr) Greg Vaughn/Alamy Stock photo. (bl) Division of Political History, National Museum of American History, Smithsonian Institution. **304** IRA BLOCK/National Geographic Creative. **305** (tl) ©American Philosophical Society. (cl) (bl) (br)©Missouri History Museum, St. Louis. **306** ©Gift of Mr. and Mrs. Gherardi Davis and Ellen King/The New-York Historical Society. All Rights Reserved. **308** Collection of the New-York Historical Society/Bridgeman Images. **309** Edwin Remsberg/Newscom/Dreams of the Blue Communications (Visual&Written)/Charlottesville/Virginia/USA. **311** L. Toshio Kishiyama/ Getty Images. **313** Johnny Stockshooter/age fotostock/Superstock. **316** Sam Abell/National Geographic Creative. **317** Robert Reid/National Geographic Creative. **318** Don Mason/AGE Fotostock. **320** ©National Museum of the American Indian. **321** Bettmann/Getty Images. **322** Richard T. Nowitz/ Science Source. **323** © 2004 White House Historical Association. **326–327** (spread) Jody Dole. **330** ©1996–2011 Deere & Company. **331** Blaine Harrington III/Getty Images. **334–335** (spread) Erik Sampers/Getty Images. **336** (cl) StudioSmart/Shutterstock. (br) ©From the Collections of The Henry Ford/Henry Ford Museum. **337** (tl) ©From the Collections of The Henry Ford/Henry Ford Museum. (tr) ©From the Collections of The Henry Ford/ Henry Ford Museum. (bl) ©From the Collections of The Henry Ford/Henry Ford Museum. (br) ©From the Collections of The Henry Ford/Henry Ford Museum. **338** The Athenaeum. **339** ©Slave Dwelling Project. **340** (tr) Chicago History Museum, ICHi-052442. (br) ©Chicago Historical Society. **341** ©A slave family in a Georgia cotton field, c. 1860 (b/w photo), American Photographer, (19th century)/Private Collection/Peter Newark American Pictures/Bridgeman Images. **343** (tl) Fotosearch/Getty Images. (tr) Peter Steiner/Alamy Stock Photo. **345** ©Bruce White for the White House Historical Association/Collection of the James Monroe Museum and Memorial Library. **346** Bettmann/Getty Images. **348** Christie's Images/ Bridgeman Images. **349** The Beecher Family, c. 1860 (b/w photo), American Photographer, (19th century)/Schlesinger Library, Radcliffe Institute, Harvard University/The Bridgeman Art Library. **352** Russell, Charles Marion (1865–1926)/Private Collection/Peter Newark American Pictures/ The Bridgeman Art Library. **354** Mark Thiessen/National Geographic Creative. (b) ©2007 Delaware County (PA) History, haverford_000. **355** ©Wilbur Hall/Haverford Township Historical Society. **356–357** (spread) Barney Burstein/Getty Images. **358** (tl) Everett Collection/age fotostock. (tr) The Last Stand at the Alamo, 6th March 1836 (colourlitho), Wyeth, Newell Convers (1882–1945)/Private Collection/The Bridgeman Art Library. (b) chrisbrignell/Getty Images. **359** (tl) World History Archive/Alamy Stock Photo. (tr) Library of Congress, Prints and Photographs Division, LC-DIG-ppmsca-07531. (br) Steve Allen Travel Photography/Alamy Stock Photo. **360–361** (spread) WimWiskerke/Alamy Stock Photo. **363** (t) Peter Turnley/Getty Images. (cl) Azad Lashkari/REUTERS. (c) Omar Sobhani/©REUTERS. (cr) RIZWAN TABASSUM/Getty Images. **364** ©Armed Forces History Division, National Museum of American History, Smithsonian Institution. **365** (tr) National Portrait Gallery, Smithsonian Institution; transfer from the National Gallery of Art; gift of the A. W. Mellon Educational and Charitable Trust, 1942; Frame conserved with funds from the Smithsonian Women's Committee. (cr) National Archives and Records Administration. **367**ClassicStock/Alamy Stock Photo. **369** (tr) ©National Museum of the American Indian. (bl) National Museum of the American Indian. (br) ©National Museum of the American Indian. **370** Gary Cameron/REUTERS. **371** Portrait of Black Hawk (1767–1838) by Homer Henderson c. 1870 (oil on canvas)/King, Charles Bird (1785–1862) (after)/ CHICAGO HISTORY MUSEUM/Chicago History Museum, USA/Bridgeman Images. **373** ©David Fitzgerald/Cherokee Heritage Center. **374** (cr) ©Courtesy of the Federal Reserve Bank of San Francisco. (br) Library of Congress Prints and Photographs Division[LC-USZ62-89594]. **376** (br) ©Jeff R. Bridgman Antiques, Inc. **377** (tr) Album/Prisma/Album/Superstock. (cr) ©Jeff R. Bridgman Antiques, Inc. (br) Fine Art/Getty Images. **379–380** (spread) JAMES L. AMOS/National Geographic Creative. **382–383** (spread) PiriyaPhotography/Getty Images. **384** ©Division of Work & Industry, National Museum of American History, Smithsonian Institution. **385** Courtesy of the California History Room, California State Library, Sacramento, California. **386** Garden Photo World/David C Phillips/Getty Images. **388** (c) Superstock. (b)Photo Tan Yilmaz/Getty Images. **389** Citizen of the Planet/Alamy Stock Photo. **390** Universal History Archive/Getty Images. **391** Across the Continent: 'Westward the Course of Empire Takes it's Way', pub. by Currier and Ives, New York, 1868 (colourlitho), Palmer, Frances Flora Bond (Fanny) (c. 1812–76) (after)/Museum of the City of New York, USA/Bridgeman Images. **392** American Progress, 1872 (oil on canvas)/ Gast, John (1842–1896)/CHRISTIES IMAGES/Private Collection/Bridgeman Images. **393** RuslanSemichev/Shutterstock.com. **395** ©Smithsonian Institution, National Museum of American History, Division of Home and Community Life. **397** Oregon Trail (oil on canvas tacked over board), Bierstadt, Albert (1830–1902)/Private Collection/Photo Christie's Images/ Bridgeman Images. **399** ©HerronStock.com. **400** Robin Jerstad/Alamy Stock Photo. **402** ©Star of the Republic Museum. **403** Kevin Coombs/REUTERS. **404** (tl) Sam Houston, c. 1851 (oil on canvas)/Flintoff, Thomas (1809–92)/ MUSEUM OF FINE ARTS, HOUSTON/Museum of Fine Arts, Houston, Texas, USA/Bridgeman Images. (tr) UniversalImagesGroup/Getty Images. **405** ©State Preservation Board, Austin, Texas. **406** ©San Jacinto Museum of History. (tl) ©San Jacinto Museum of History. (br) ©San Jacinto Museum of History. **407** ©San Jacinto Museum of History. **408** IngeJohnsson/Alamy Stock Photo. **409** Playing card: King of Diamonds (colourlitho), American School, (19th century)/Dallas Historical Society, Texas, USA/Bridgeman Image. **410** The Art Archive/The Picture Desk, Inc. **411** The New York Public Library/Art Resource, NY. **414** Jim Wilson/The New York Times/ Redux. **416** Gold Rush prospector, 1849 (b/w photo)/American Photographer, (19th century)/PETER NEWARK'S PICTURES/Private Collection/Bridgeman Images. **417** Pictorial Press Ltd/Alamy Stock Photo. **419** (t) Print Collector/Getty Images. (b) Archive Images/Alamy Stock Photo. **422–423** (spread) Tetra Images/Getty Images. **424–425** (spread) ARS, NY, Photo: The Jacob and Gwendolyn Lawrence Foundation/Art Resource, NY. **426** Library of Congress Prints and Photographs Division [LC-USZ62-7816]. **428** George Eastman House/Getty Images. **429** Library of Congress. **431** Outward Bound, The Quay of Dublin, engraved by T. H. Maguire, 1854 colourlitho) (see 189921), Nicol, J (19th century) (after)/Collection of the New York Historical Society, USA/Bridgeman Images. **432** An Irish Eviction (oil on panel)/Goodall, Frederick (1822–1904)/LEICESTER ARTS AND MUSEUMS SERVICE/New Walk Museum & Art Gallery, Leicester, UK/ Bridgeman Images. **433** ©National Museum of American History. **434–435** (spread) ©Robert Pettus/500px. **437** (t) American 'Know-Nothing' Party Cartoon, 1854 (engraving), American School, (19th century)/Private Collection/Peter Newark American Pictures/Bridgeman Images. (b) Everett Collection Historical/Alamy Stock Photo. **439** ©Old Dartmouth Historical Society-New Bedford Whaling Museum. **440** Primer (printed textile), American School, (19th century)/Private Collection/Photo Civil War Archive/Bridgeman Images. **442** Library of Congress. **443** ©The Metropolitan Museum of Art. Image source: Art Resource, NY. **445** Tomas Abad/Alamy Stock Photo. **446** Esclave/Photo Gerald Bloncourt/Bridgeman Images. **447** MPI/Getty Images. **448** Fotosearch/Getty Images. **450** Library of Congress/Getty Images. **451** Library of Congress/Getty Images. **454** JIM RICHARDSON/National Geographic. **456–457** (spread) Jennifer Counter/ Moment/Getty Images. **458** (tl) Schomburg Center, NYPL/Art Resource, NY. (tr) ©National Museum of American History, Political History. (bc) Pictorial Press Ltd/Alamy Stock Photo. **459** (tr) ©National Museum of American History Smithsonian. (cl) ©Chicago History Museum. (bc) John Stevenson/ Getty Images. **460–461** (spread) DamirFrkovic/Masterfile. **464** (bl) National Portrait Gallery, Smithsonian Institution/Art Resource, NY. (br) Schomburg Center, NYPL/Art Resource, NY. **465** Iberfoto/Superstock. **467** John Brown, 1859 (colourlitho), Balling, Ole Peter Hansen (1823–1906)/Private Collection/Peter Newark American Pictures/Bridgeman Images. **468** Pictorial Press Ltd/Alamy Stock Photo. **469** ©Kenneth Garret Photography. **470** Abraham Lincoln and Stephen A. Douglas debating at Charleston, Illinois on 18th September 1858, 1918 (oil on canvas), Root, Robert Marshall (1863–1937)/Private Collection/Bridgeman Images. **471** Niday Picture Library/Alamy Stock Photo. **472** Niday Picture Library/Alamy Stock Photo. **474** Everett Collection Inc/Alamy Stock Photo. **475** Abraham Lincoln (1809–65) 1860 (b/w photo), Hesler, Alexander (1823–95)/Private Collection/ Peter Newark American Pictures/Bridgeman Images. **477** Charles Phelps Cushing/ClassicStock/Getty Images. **480–481** (spread) ©Kenneth Garrett Photography. **482** The Library of Congress. **483** ©Armed Forces History Division, National Museum of American History, Smithsonian Institution. **484** The Library of Congress. **484** (b) ©Armed Forces History Division, National Museum of American History, Smithsonian Institution. **485** (tl) Smithsonian American Art Museum, Washington, DC/Art Resource, NY. (tr) ©Historical Society of Carroll County. **487** ©The Library of Congress. **489** ©Jason Demek/500px. **490** Library of Congress, Prints & Photographs Division, Reproduction number LC-DIG-cwpb-04402 (digital file from original neg.)LC-B8172-0001 (b&w film neg.). **491** (tl) ©Chicago Historical Society. (tr) ©Confederate Memorial Hall Museum, New Orleans. **492** (bl) ©Confederate Memorial Hall Museum. (br) ©Confederate Memorial Hall Museum. **493** (t) ©Confederate Memorial Hall Museum. (b) ©Confederate Memeorial Hall Museum. **494** Wellcome Images/Science Source. **495** Science & Society Picture Library/Getty Images. **496** ©Clara Barton National Historic Site/National Parks Service. **497** Fotosearch/Getty Images. **498** ©George Ohrstrom II. **499** ©Kenneth Garrett Photography. **500** ©Kenneth Garrett Photography. **501** ©Kenneth Garrett Photography. **502** ©Kenneth Garrett Photography. **503** ©Kenneth Garrett Photography. **505** National Geographic Learning. **508** Library of Congress, Prints & Photographs Division, LC-DIG-cwpb-07310. **509** Library of Congress, Prints & Photographs Division, LC-DIG-ppmsca-31277. **513** Library of Congress, Prints & Photographs Division, LC-DIG-stereo-1s02987. **514–515** (spread) ©Kenneth Garrett Photography. **516** Library of Congress, Prints & Photographs Division, LC-DIG-cwpb-04351. **518** The Art Institute of Chicago, IL, USA/Major Acquisitions Centennial Endowment/Bridgeman Images. **519** Smithsonian American Art Museum, Washington, DC/Art Resource, NY. **521** B Christopher/Alamy Stock Photo. **523** The Everett Collection. **525** LynseyAddario/Getty Reportage. **526** Library of Congress, Prints & Photographs Division, LC-DIG-ppmsca-33993. **529** Library of Congress, Prints & Photographs Division, LC-B8184-7964-A. **531** Ian Dagnall/Alamy Stock Photo. **532** Library of Congress, Prints & Photographs Division, LC-DIG-ds-03106. **535** TOM LOVELL/National Geographic Creative. **536–537** (spread) ©Kenneth Garrett Photography. **539** Chicago History Museum, USA/Bridgeman Images. **543** Library of Congress, Prints & Photographs Division, LC-DIG-pga-03898. **544–545** (spread) Kenneth Garrett Photography. **546** Hulton Archive/Staff/Getty Images. **548** Library of Congress. **549** (tr) SSPL/Science Museum/Art Resource, NY. (br) Library of Congress. **550** (t) Sunday morning in Virginia, 1877 (oil on canvas)/Homer, Winslow (1836–1910)/CINCINNATI ART MUSEUM/Cincinnati Art Museum, Ohio, USA/Bridgeman Images. (b) National Archives Washington DC/The Art Archive at Art Resource, NY. **551** ©Collection of the Massachusettes Historical Society. **553** Victor Cardoner/Moment Open/ Getty Images. **555** Bettmann/Getty Images. **557** Library of Congress Prints and Photographs Division Washington, D. C. **558** Angus Osborn/Getty Images. **560** MPI/Getty Images. **561** (tl) Everett Collection Historical/Alamy Stock photo. (cr) Universal Images Group/Art Resource, NY. **562** ©National Parks Service. **563** Library of Congress Prints and Photographs Division Washington, D. C. **564** The Rush from the New York Stock Exchange on September 18, 1873, from 'A History of the Last Quarter Century' by E. Benjamin Andrews, published in Scribner's Magazine, July 1895 (oil on canvas), Pyle, Howard (1853–1911)/Delaware Art Museum, Wilmington, USA/The Bridgeman Art Library. **567** MPI/Getty Images. **568** Library of Congress, Prints and Photographs Division, LC-DIG-ppmsca-23855. **570–571** (spread) PhotoQuest/Archive Photos/Getty Images. **572** (cl) George H. H. Huey/Alamy Stock Photo. (cl) Atlaspix/Alamy Stock Photo. (br) AP Images/ JOEL PAGE. **573** (tl) National Park Service, Statue of Liberty National Monument and Ellis Island. (tr) ©National Museum of American History, Political History. (bl) DEA/A. DAGLI ORTI/Getty Images. (br) Michael Nicholson/Getty Images. **574–575** (spread) CHRIS JOHNS/National Geographic Creative. **576–577** (spread) JOEL SARTORE/National Geographic Creative. **578** The Buffalo Hunt (colourlitho)/Catlin, George (1796–1872)/Private Collection/Bridgeman Images. **579** (tr) Hulton Archive/ Getty Images. (b) William Hornaday and Bison c. 1905. **579** (b) ©Wildlife Conservation Society. Reproduced by permission of the WCS Archives. **580** ©Division of Culture & the Arts, National Museum of American History, Behring Center, Smithsonian Institution. **581** ©Sean Beckett/500px. **582–583** (spread) Pete Ryan/Getty Images. **584** Tar_Design/Shutterstock. com. **585** Christie's Images/Bridgeman Images; Art © T. H. Benton and R. P. Benton Testamentary Trusts/UMB Bank Trustee/Licensed by VAGA, New York, NY. **587** PhotoQuest/Getty Images. **588** National Geographic Learning. **589** Bettmann/Getty Images. **590** Library of Congress Prints and Photographs Division Washington, D. C. **593** Library of Congress Prints and Photographs Division Washington, D. C. **594** Canton, Kansas/National Geographic. **595** (t) Joel Sartore/National Geographic Creative. (b)JOEL SARTORE/National Geographic Creative. **597** Photo Researchers, Inc/ Alamy Stock photo. **599** (t) ©National Museum of the American Indian/ Smithsonian Institution. (b) ©National Museum of the American Indian/ Smithsonian Institution. **602** Dan Westergren/National Geographic. **604–605** (spread) Richard T. Nowitz/Corbis Documentary/Getty Images. **606** Christian Heeb/Prisma/SuperStock. **607** (tl) Christian Heeb/Prisma/ SuperStock. (br) ©Chad Coppess/South Dakota Department of Tourism. **608** (t) Philip Scalia/Alamy Stock Photo. (cl) Stillman Rogers/Alamy Stock Photo. **609** WILLIAM ALBERT ALLARD/National Geographic Creative. **610–611** (spread) iofoto,2009/Used under license from Shutterstock.com. **612–613** (spread) The Library of Congress. **613** ©NPS. **614–615** (spread) Fotosearch/Getty Images. **615** Photo by Scott Dunn/Getty Images. **616** Time Life Pictures/Getty Images. **616** Justin Sullivan/Getty Images. **617** ©Ben Lee. **618** (tr) Statue of Liberty National Monument, National Park Service. (bl) ©Holt-Atherton Special Collections, University of the Pacific Library. **619** ©Holt-Atherton Special Collections, University of the Pacific Library. **622–623** (spread) Danita Delimont/Getty Images. **624** SSPL/Getty Images. **625** The Wright Brothers testing an early plane at Kitty Hawk, North Carolina (sepia photo), American Photographer, (20th century)/Private Collection/The Stapleton Collection/Bridgeman Images. **626** ©Ana Gómez/500px. **627** (tl) Underwood Archives/Getty Images. (tr) Hulton Archive/Getty Images. **628** ©Chicago Historical Society. **629** ©Chicago Historical Society. **631** ©Jordan J. Lloyd/Dynamichrome. **632** (tl) ©Lower East Side Tenement Museum. (c) National Geographic Learning. (br) ©Lower East Side Tenement Museum. **633** (tl) ©Lower East Side Tenement Museum. (cr) National Geographic Learning. **633** ©Lower East Side Tenement Museum. **635** Fotosearch/Getty Images. **636** Patti McConville/ Alamy Stock Photo. **637** johnkellerman/iStock/Getty Images. **638** Jacob A. Riis/Getty Images. **640** ©New York Times Archive. **641** ©Missouri History Museum. **643** Library of Congress, Prints and Photographs Division [LC-USZC2-1058]. **644** Bettmann/Getty Images. **645** (tl) Bettmann/Getty Images. (tr) Chicago History Museum/Getty Images. **646** Library of Congress Prints and Photographs Division Washington[LC-D401-11590]. **648** ©ACUA—Archives of The Catholic University of America. **649** Everett Collection Inc/Alamy Stock Photo. **650** ©Chicago Historical Society. **651** ©Chicago Historical Society. **644–645** (spread) ©Johnnie Welborn,Jr./500px. **656** Jim Brandenburg/Minden Pictures. **658** The Library of Congress. **659** Danita Delimont/Getty Images. **660–661** (spread) PAUL NICKLEN/National Geographic Creative. **663** (tr) ©The Ansel Adams Publishing Rights Trust. 76. 577. 40. (b) ©The Ansel Adams Publishing Rights Trust. 84. 92. 156. **664** Photo Researchers, Inc/Alamy Stock Photo. **666** Photo 12/Getty Images. **667** Everett Collection Historical/Alamy Stock Photo. **668** Library of Congress Prints and photographic Division[LC-USZ62-56439]. **669** Library of Congress/Getty Images. **670** Archive Pics/Alamy Stock Photo. **671** DOMINIQUE BRAUD/ANIMALS ANIMALS/ EARTH SCENES/National Geographic Creative. **672** National Archives. **673** AP Images/Casillas/REX Shutterstock.com. **675** Marcelo Baez/Shannon Associates/National Geographic Learning. **676** From the Collections of The Henry Ford. **677** AP Images/J. SCOTT APPLEWHITE. **678** North Wind Picture Archives/Alamy Stock Photo. **679** FPG/Getty Images. **680** Bettmann/Getty Images. **681** American Stock Archive/Getty Images. **682–683** (spread) American Stock Archive/Getty Images. **684** Haeckel collection/ullsteinbild/Premium Archive/Getty Images. **685** ©David Silverman/500px. **686** Armed Forces History, Division of History of Technology, National Museum of American History. **687** Theodore Roosevelt leading the 'Rough Riders' during the Spanish-American War, detail of a painting by W. G. Road, 1898 (colourlitho)/American School, (19th century)/PETER NEWARK'S PICTURES/Private Collection/Bridgeman Images. **688** National Portrait Gallery, Smithsonian Institution/Art Resource, NY. **689** Library of Congress/Getty Images. **693** FransLanting/National Geographic Creative. **695** From the Collections of The Henry Ford. Gift of Ford Motor Company. **696** Archive Photos/Getty Images. **698–699** (spread) Smithsonian American Art Museum, Washington, DC/Art Resource, NY. **700** (cl) The Library of Congress. (tr) National Air and Space Museum, Smithsonian Institution. (b) Popperfoto/Getty Images. **701** (tl) ©Japanese American National Museum. (cr) Leonard Zhukovsky/Shutterstock.com. (bl) ©United States Holocaust Memorial Museum. (br) IWM/Getty Images/Getty Images. **702–703** (spread) American infantry in WWI leaving their trench to advance against the Germans, 1918 (b/w photo)/American Photographer, (20th century)/PETER NEWARK'S PICTURES/Private Collection/Bridgeman Images. **704** Hulton Archive/Getty Images. **706** IWM/Getty Images/Getty Images. **707** (tr) Jim Tannick/Getty Images. (br) National Air and Space Museum. **709** (cl) Library of Congress, Prints & Photographs Division, LC-USZ62-93699. (cr) Everett Collection/AGE Fotostock. **712** Science & Society Picture Library/ Getty Images. **713** UniversalImagesGroup/Getty Images. **714** Library of Congress/Getty Images. **715** National Geographic Learning. **716** US Army Signal Corps/Getty Images. **717** Collection of the Smithsonian National Museum of African American History and Culture, Gift of Gina R. McVey, grand daughter. **718** Cincinnati Museum Center/Getty Images. **719** Library of Congress, Prints & Photographs Division, LC-USZC4-2793. **721** WPA Pool/ Getty Images. **724** Library of Congress/Getty Images. **726–727** (spread)

©Marcus Akinlana. **729** Library of Congress/Prints & Photographs Division, LC-USZC4-7817. **730–731** (spread) Edwin Levick/Getty Images. **733** Sheridan Libraries/Levy/Gado/Getty Images. **734** Niday Picture Library/Alamy Stock Photo. **735** SUETONE Emilio/AGE Fotostock. **737** REUTERS/Mike Theiler. **739** The Advertising Archives/Alamy Stock Photo. **740** SilverScreen/Alamy Stock Photo. **741** (t) Glasshouse Images/Alamy Stock Photo. (c) ©Milo Stewart Jr./National Baseball Hall of Fame and Museum. **742** Pictorial Press Ltd/Alamy Stock Photo. **743** Sueddeutsche Zeitung Photo/Alamy Stock Photo. **744** National Geographic Learning. **745** (tl) (bl) ©Smithsonian National Museum of American History. (cr) Jemal Countess/Getty Images. **750** National Portrait Gallery, Smithsonian Institution/Art Resource, NY. **751** ©Smithsonian American Art Museum, Washington, DC/Art Resource, NY. **752** The Everett Collection. **753** INTERFOTO/Alamy Stock Photo. **755** ©Sidney Joseph Greene/Newman Libary, CUNY. **756–757** (spread) Bettmann/Getty Images. **758–759** (spread) AKG Images. **760** Library of Congress, Prints & Photographs Division [LC-USZC4-8174]. **762** Smithsonian American Art Museum, Washington, DC/Art Resource, NY. **763** (c) AKG Images. (b) Library of Congress, Prints & Photographs Division, LC-DIG-fsa-8a44522. **761** SilverScreen/Alamy Stock Photo. **764** ClassicStock/Alamy Stock Photo. **767** quietbits/Shutterstock.com. **769** The Library of Congress—Prints & Photographs Division, LC-USZ62-31111. **770** Bettmann/Getty Images. **775** (t) Library of Congress, Prints & Photographs Division, Reproduction number LC-DIG-ppmsca-31916. (br) Dorothea Lange/Getty Images. **776** GraphicaArtis/Getty Images. **777** MPI/Getty Images. **779** Smithsonian American Art Museum, Washington, DC/Art Resource, NY. **780** AP Images. **781** Everett Collection Inc/Alamy Stock Photo. **782–783** (spread) Spring Images/Alamy Stock Photo. **786–787** (spread) Education Images/UIG/Getty Images. **788** Chronicle/Alamy Stock Photo. **791** Popperfoto/Getty Images. **792** Hulton Deutsch/Getty Images. **795** Danita Delimont/Getty Images. **796** (t) ©Smithsonian National Air and Space Museum. (b) Image by Plane Facts, Inc., National Air and Space Museum, Smithsonian Institution. **797** ©Smithsonian National Air and Space Museum. **799** Hulton Archive/Getty Images. **800** Bettmann/Getty Images. **801** Bernard Hoffman/Getty Images. **802** (bl) Afro Newspaper/Gado/Getty Images. (br) ©National Museum of the US Airforce. **803** Everett Collection Inc/Alamy Stock Photo. **804** Robert Sullivan/AFP/Getty Images. **805** AP Images/Alan Diaz. **807** ©Japanese American National Museum. **809** Keystone-France/Getty Images. **812** Photo 12/Getty Images. **813** U.S. GOV'T GSA : ROOSEVELT, FRANKLIN D. LIBRARY/National Geographic Stock. **814** (t) Galerie Bilderwelt/Getty Images. (cr) ©United States Holocaust Memorial Museum Collection, Gift of Evelyn Levy Paswell. **816** AP Images. **817** Official U.S. Navy Photograph, now in the collections of the U.S. National Archives. **819** AP Images/JOE ROSENTHAL. **820** Galerie Bilderwelt/Getty Images. **821** (tr) ©Courtesy of the Beser family. (cr) ©Courtesy of the Beser family. **823** (tr) De Agostini Picture Library/Getty Images. (tc) Keystone-France/Getty Images. **826** adoc-photos/Getty Images. **828–829** (spread) Bruce Davidson/Magnum Photos. **830** (tl) Ian Dagnall/Alamy Stock Photo. (tr) ©Bettmann/Getty Images. (b) wanderworldimages/Alamy Stock Photo. **831** (tl) ©National Air and Space Museum. (tr) Bettmann/Getty Images. (bl) Aleksandar Milosavljevic/Alamy Stock Photo. (br) Bettmann/Getty Images. **832–833** (spread) Bettmann/Getty Images. **834–835** (spread) Bettmann/Getty Images. **836** Mirrorpix/Courtesy The Everett Collection. **837** (t) ClassicStock/Alamy Stock Photo. (cr) ©Smithsonian National Museum of American History. **838** (tr) 20thCentFox/Courtesy The Everett Collection. (br) CBS Photo Archive/Getty Images. **839** (tr) CBS Photo Archive/Getty Images. (tcr) CBS Photo Archive/Getty Images. (cr) CBS Photo Archive/Getty Images. (br) CBS Photo Archive/Getty Images. **840** (tr) Nature and Science/Alamy Stock Photo. (br) National Archives. **841** (tr) (cl) The Everett Collection. (c) Paramount/Courtesy The Everett Collection. **842** war posters/Alamy Stock Photo. **843** (tr) Skim New Media Limited/Alamy Stock Photo. **844** William C. Shrout/Getty Images. **845** Bettmann/Getty Images. **847** Bettmann/Getty Images. **848** Claro Cortes/Reuters. **850** Carl Mydans/Getty Images. **852** NYPL/Science Source/Getty Images. **853** Bettmann/Contributer/Getty Images. **855** AP Images/Nap. **857** (c) Ewing Galloway/Alamy Stock Photo. (bl) Tony Linck/Getty Images. **858** Bettmann/Getty Images. **859** ©Collection of the Smithsonian National Museum of African American History and Culture, Donation of Charles E. Berry; ©Gibson Brands, LLC. **862–863** (spread) Bruce Davidson/Magnum Photos. **864–865** (spread) The Washington Post/Getty Images. **866** Bruce Davidson/Magnum Photos. **867** A. Y. Owen/Getty Images. **868** ©Los Angeles Public Library. **869** (cr) AP Images. (br) ©Minnesota Historical Society. **870** Michael Rougier/Getty Images. **871** Bettmann/Getty Images. **872** Bettmann/Getty Images. **873** JOHN LENT/AP Images. **874** Carl Iwasaki/Getty Images. **875** AP Images/TOM LEININGER. **876** Burt Glinn/Magnum Photos. **878** Underwood Archives/Getty Images. **879** AP Images/Anonymous. **881** AP Images/GENE HERRICK. **883** (t) Bruce Roberts/Getty Images. (b) Bettmann/Getty Images. **884** AP Images/BILL HUDSON. **887** Bruce Davidson/Magnum Photos. **888** ©Bob Adelman. **890** (bl) Collection of the Smithsonian National Museum of African American History and Culture, Gift of Samuel Y. Edgerton, 2013.187.4. (cr) Collection of the Smithsonian National Museum of African American History and Culture, Gift of the Family of Rev. Norman C. "Jim" Jimerson and Melva Brooks Jimerson, 2013.138a–c. **891** (tl) Collection of the Smithsonian National Museum of African American History and Culture, 2012.107.10. (cr) Collection of the Smithsonian National Museum of African American History and Culture, Gift from Dawn Simon Spears and Alvin Spears, Sr., 2011.159.3.25. (cl) Collection of the Smithsonian National Museum of African American History and Culture, 2012.107.10. (b) Collection of the Smithsonian National Museum of African American History and Culture, Gift of University of Mary Washington, Fredericksburg, VA in honor of Dr. James Farmer, 2011.130. **893** Bettmann/Getty Images. **894–895** (spread) Terray Sylvester/Redux Photo. **895** Everett Collection Inc/Alamy Stock Photo. **896** MICHAEL MELFORD/National Geographic Creative. **898** Alyssa Schukar/The New York Times/Redux. **899** Mark Thiessen/National Geographic Creative. **899** Robert Alexander/Getty Images. **900–901** (spread) Larry Burrows/Getty Images. **902** Paul Schutzer/Getty Images. **903** ©Smithsonian National Postal Museum. **904** ©National Air and Space Museum. **905** Bettmann/Getty Images. **906–907** (spread) Keystone-France/Getty Images. **909** Charles Phelps Cushing/ClassicStock/Getty Images. **910** Bettmann/Getty Images. **911** UniversalImagesGroup/Getty Images. **912** Bettmann/Getty Images. **913** Bettmann/Getty Images. **914** AP Images/Anonymous. **915** ©Pirkle Jones/UC Santa Cruz. **916** ©Denver Post/Getty Images. **917** AP Images/Charles Kelly. **918** ©Graphic Arts Group, San Francisco/Center for the Study of Political Graphics; "Yo Soy Alguien" poster image is the intellectual property of the UFW and is used with permission of the United Farm Workers of America. **919** Bob Fitch photography archive, © Stanford University Libraries. **920** ©Richard Barnes. **921** ©Michael Wells. **923** Bettmann/Getty Images. **924** AP Images/Charles Gorry. **925** ©Collection of the U.S. House of Representatives. **927** Paul Schutzer/Getty Images. **928** Bettmann/Getty Images. **929** Thomas White/REUTERS. **931** tim page/Getty Images. **932** Harvey Silver/Getty Images. **934** Joseph Louw/Getty Images. **936** (tr) ©San Francisco Chronicle/Polaris. **937** Conrad cartoons are used with permission of the Conrad Estate. **938** MICHAEL MELFORD/National Geographic Creative. **940–941** (spread) Library of Congress, Prints & Photographs Division, LC-DIG-highsm-12456. **942** (tl) Courtesy of NASA. (tc) ©Smithsonian National Museum of American History. (b) Evgeniya Anikienko/Shutterstock.com. **943** (tl) EQRoy/Shutterstock.com. (tr) Leonard Zhukovsky/Shutterstock.com. (cl) ©2014 The Washington Post/Getty Images. (bl) Jonny White/Alamy Stock Photo. (cr) ©Ron Haviv/VII. **944–945** (spread) David Hume Kennerly/Getty Images. **946–947** (spread) Agencja Fotograficzna Caro/Alamy Stock Photo. **948** Keystone/Getty Images. **949** AKG Images. **951** (l) mauritius images GmbH/Alamy Stock Photo. (r) Rolf Adlercreutz/Alamy Stock Photo. **952** (c) PJF Military Collection/Alamy Stock Photo. (br) Stuart Lutz/Gado/Getty Images. **953** John Filo/Getty Images. **955** Historical/Getty Images. **957** Alfred Eisenstaedt/Getty Images. **958** Edgard Garrido/Reuters. **959** Bloomberg/Getty Images. **960** Waring Abbott/Getty Images. **961** Bettmann/Getty Images. **962** Smith Collection/Gado/Getty Images. **963** AP Images/Benjamin E. "gene" Forte. **964** Bettmann/Getty Images. **965** ©Tel Or Beni/GPO/Getty Images. Getty Images/Getty Images. **966** MPI/Getty Images. **967** Yvonne Hemsey/Getty Images. **968** Entertainment Pictures/Alamy Stock Photo. **969** Robert R. McElroy/Getty Images. **970** Joe Traver/Getty Images. **971** Bettmann/Getty Images. **973** Panoramic Images/Getty Images. **975** Bobby Yip/Reuters. **977** Wally McNamee/Corbis Premium Historical/Getty Images. **980–981** (spread) Richard Ellis/AGE Fotostock. **982** Visions of America/Getty Images. **983** AP Images/J. Scott Aplewhite. **984** JM/BM/AA/REUTERS. **985** AP Images/Carolyn Kaster. **986** Robert King/Getty Images. **987** AP Images/ERIC DRAPER. **988** POOL Old/REUTERS. **989** Universal Images Group North America LLC/DeAgostini/Alamy Stock Photo. **990** REUTERS/Marc Serota. **992** REUTERS/Carlos Barria. **993** ©Taylor Mickal. **994** Pool/Getty Images. **997** AP Images/ Ed Reinke. **998** AP Images/David J. Phillip. **1001** The Smithsonian American Art Msueum, Gift of the artist ©Nam June Paik Estate. **1003** ©Mark Richards, Computer History Museum. (br) ©Mark Richards/Zuma Press/Alamy. **1005** ©Kirsten Luce. **1006** MANDEL NGAN/Getty Images. **1007** Aaron Bernstein/Reuters. **1008** Bruce Molnia/U.S. Geological Survey. **1009** Roger Ressmeyer/Corbis/VCG/Getty Images. **1012** Martin Schoeller/National Geographic Creative. **1014** Mark Thiessen/National Geographic Creative. **R0–R1** (spread) GREG DALE/National Geographic Creative. **R2** Bettmann/Getty Images. **R10** Bygone Collection/Alamy Stock Photo. **R15** SAUL LOEB/Getty Images. **R17** ©REUTERS/Jonathan Ernst **R19** National Archives. **R26** Library of Congress, Prints & Photographs Division, LC-DIG-pga-03453. **R27** Library of Congress, Prints & Photographs Division, LC-USZ62-123257. **R32** Bettmann/Getty Images. **R33** Tetra Images/Shutterstock.com. **R35** Spencer Platt/Getty Images. **R37** Hill Street Studios/Eric Raptosh/Getty Images.

Text Credits

Pg. 885 "Letter from Birmingham City Jail," by Dr. Martin Luther King Jr. April 16, 1963. Reprinted by arrangement with The Heirs to the Estate of Martin Luther King Jr., c/o Writers House as agent for the proprietor New Nork, NY. ©1963 Dr. Martin Luther King Jr. ©Renewed 1991 Loretta Scott King.

Pg. 886, 889 "I Have a Dream," by Dr. Martin Luther King Jr. Reprinted by arrangement with The Heirs to the Estate of Martin Luther King Jr., c/o Writers House as agent for the proprietor New Nork, NY. ©1963 Martin Luther King Jr. ©Renewed 1991 Coretta Scott King.

Illustration Credits

Unless otherwise indicated, all illustrations are created by Lachina and all maps are created by Mapping Specialists.